D0128209

FileMaker Pro 14

the missing manual®

The book that should have been in the box®

Susan Prosser and Stuart Gripman

O'REILLY®

Beijing | Cambridge | Farnham | Köln | Sebastopol | Tokyo

FileMaker Pro: The Missing Manual

by Susan Prosser and Stuart Gripman

Published by O'Reilly Media, Inc.,
1005 Gravenstein Highway North, Sebastopol, CA 95472.

O'Reilly books may be purchased for educational, business, or sales promotional use. Online editions are also available for most titles (*http://safaribooksonline.com*). For more information, contact our corporate/institutional sales department: (800) 998-9938 or *corporate@oreilly.com*.

May 2015:   First Edition.

Revision History for the First Edition:
   2015-04-29   First release
   2015-07-24   Second release
See *http://oreilly.com/catalog/errata.csp?isbn=9781491917480* for release details.

ISBN-13: 978-1-491-91748-0

[LSI]

Contents

Part Six: **Appendixes**

The Missing Credits

ABOUT THE AUTHORS

Susan Prosser (coauthor) discovered FileMaker Pro in the early nineties, while working as a newspaper reporter. It took her two years to realize that most people don't want more information; they need to know what to do with the stuff they've already got. As the founder and technical lead at DBHQ, a FileMaker Pro consulting company, Susan sees fresh proof of this lesson every day. She has a knack for asking the questions that help clients figure out what business intelligence they've got and how to organize it so everybody's job gets a little easier. DBHQ works with Wells Fargo, NIH, Banner Health Systems and other companies to tame the mountains of data and business processes that affect thousands of users. Susan is a certified FileMaker Developer, the author of three white papers for FileMaker, Inc., and a repeat speaker at the annual FileMaker Developer's Convention on subjects like web publishing, charting, building dashboards, document management, and creating good user experience. This is her seventh book on FileMaker Pro.

Susan has three work rules: The simplest solution is usually the best; commenting code helps organize your thoughts; and using nerd words is a surefire way to make people doze off. As a child, Susan would carry Sherpa-worthy loads of groceries or bagged leaves or pig slop to avoid making two trips. She has recently learned to enjoy walking with a lighter load and now spends weekends making art quilts. Send photos of your second trips to *susanprosser@gmail.com*. Follow *@prosserDBHQ* on Twitter and visit DBHQ at *www.dbhq.net*.

Stuart Gripman (coauthor) is a native of Akron, Ohio who grew up in suburban Orange County, California before migrating to San Francisco to get out of the sun. After a two-year stint at FileMaker Inc., he went on to found Crooked Arm Consulting, providing custom FileMaker databases for a wide variety of clientele. His databases have since benefited the U.S. space program, fine art patrons, oenophiles, aspiring mixologists, architects, advertising firms, and a Grammy award-winning ensemble.

Now a senior developer for FullCity Consulting, he continues helping clients tame their data. Check out his FileMaker Function of the Week at *www.fullcityconsulting. com/blog*. Email: *stuart@crookedarm.com*.

ABOUT THE CREATIVE TEAM

Nan Barber (editor) is associate editor for the Missing Manual series. She lives in Massachusetts with her husband and various electronic devices. Email: *nanbarber@ gmail.com*.

Melanie Yarbrough (production editor and compositor) lives, works, and plays in Cambridge, MA. In her free time, she knits and bakes, and moonlights as an ice cream maker and scooper. Email: *myarbrough@oreilly.com*.

Ilene Hoffman (technical reviewer) Macintosh Consultant Ilene Hoffman is an Apple product specialist and a photographer. She has been involved in the Macintosh user community and forums support through the Boston Computer Society, Apple on AOL, eWorld, MacFixIt, and My Apple Space. Ilene's articles and blog posts can be found in The Unofficial Apple Weblog, MacNN.com, MyMac.com, TechRepublic, MacTech, MacFixit, TidBITs, NetGuide, and IDG Online. She has also written parts of and tech edited a number of Macintosh OS books. You can find her photography and product reviews on her blog at *www.ilenesmachine.net*.

Koji Takeuchi (technical reviewer) works as an independent FileMaker developer, doing custom databases, server development, training, and consulting. He is a File-Maker 7-13 Certified Developer and has worked as a FileMaker Authorized Trainer and Apple Certified Trainer. He heads the FileMaker Tokyo User Group and has spoken at every FileMaker Conference Japan since 2009. He won the FileMaker Excellence Award in 2006 and has led over 100 monthly FileMaker events at Apple Store Ginza, Tokyo. Email: *takeuchi@nemoux.com*.

Molly Ives Brower (proofreader) has a husband, a small boy, and two cats. She likes hiking and going on long road trips with the husband and the boy, but the cats are ter-rible travelers and hikers, so with them she just sits and reads. She spends far too much time on Twitter, where she goes by *@vintagereader*. Email: *molly@mjibrower.com*.

Ron Strauss (indexer) specializes in the indexing of information technology publica-tions of all kinds. Ron is also an accomplished classical violist and lives in Northern California with his wife and fellow indexer, Annie, and his miniature pinscher, Kanga. Email: *rstrauss@mchsi.com*.

ACKNOWLEDGMENTS

Technical reviewing is thankless work, figuratively speaking. Literally, I am more grateful than I can express for the keen eyes and gentle corrections that Ilene Hoff-man and Koji Takeuchi provided. Our fearless editor Nan is an author's best friend. We couldn't do this work without her guidance. George, thanks for keeping the production ship aright so I could focus. Stuart, each edition has its challenges ,and I might have been one of them this time around. Thanks for listening while I stewed. Looking forward to epic evenings at DevCon with you as our reward. What with Paul being in grad school, and me writing a book, not everything that needed doing got done this spring. Here's hoping the summer lets us catch up and keep on moving.

— *Susan Prosser*

My sincere thanks to our editor Nan, our production editor Melanie, and all the good folks at O'Reilly who brought this book to fruition. Thanks to Ilene and Koji who, despite having done this tedious job before, agreed to be our technical reviewers again. A heaping bucket of appreciation goes to George Ziemann whose assistance was abundant and timely. If we were antelopes on the savannah, George would be bounding majestically and I would be lunch. And, of course, my friend and coauthor Susan. It's always a pleasure to be in your orbit and I look forward to our upcoming appointment/bender at M&M World.

Unlimited love and affection to Jen and our son Ben who again put up with my absence on so many nights and weekends. You guys are the best! I'm ready to go outside now.

— *Stuart Gripman*

THE MISSING MANUAL SERIES

Missing Manuals are witty, superbly written guides to computer products that don't come with printed manuals (which is just about all of them). Each book features a handcrafted index and cross-references to specific pages (not just chapters). Recent and upcoming titles include:

- *Access 2013: The Missing Manual* by Matthew MacDonald
- *Adobe Edge Animate: The Missing Manual* by Chris Grover
- *Buying a Home: The Missing Manual* by Nancy Conner
- *Creating a Website: The Missing Manual, Third Edition* by Matthew MacDonald
- *CSS3: The Missing Manual, Third Edition* by David Sawyer McFarland
- *Dreamweaver CS6: The Missing Manual* by David Sawyer McFarland
- *Dreamweaver CC: The Missing Manual, Second Edition* by David Sawyer McFarland and Chris Grover
- *Excel 2013: The Missing Manual* by Matthew MacDonald
- *FileMaker Pro 13: The Missing Manual* by Susan Prosser and Stuart Gripman
- *Fire Phone: The Missing Manual* by Preston Gralla
- *Flash CS6: The Missing Manual* by Chris Grover
- *Galaxy Tab: The Missing Manual* by Preston Gralla
- *Galaxy S5: The Missing Manual* by Preston Gralla
- *Google+: The Missing Manual* by Kevin Purdy
- *HTML5: The Missing Manual, Second Edition* by Matthew MacDonald
- *iMovie: The Missing Manual* by David Pogue and Aaron Miller
- *iPad: The Missing Manual, Seventh Edition* by J.D. Biersdorfer

- *iPhone: The Missing Manual, Eighth Edition* by David Pogue
- *iPhone App Development: The Missing Manual* by Craig Hockenberry
- *iPhoto: The Missing Manual* by David Pogue and Lesa Snider
- *iPod: The Missing Manual, Eleventh Edition* by J.D. Biersdorfer and David Pogue
- *iWork: The Missing Manual* by Jessica Thornsby and Josh Clark
- *JavaScript & jQuery: The Missing Manual, Third Edition* by David Sawyer McFarland
- *Kindle Fire HD: The Missing Manual* by Peter Meyers
- *Living Green: The Missing Manual* by Nancy Conner
- *Microsoft Project 2013: The Missing Manual* by Bonnie Biafore
- *Motorola Xoom: The Missing Manual* by Preston Gralla
- *NOOK HD: The Missing Manual* by Preston Gralla
- *Office 2011 for Macintosh: The Missing Manual* by Chris Grover
- *Office 2013: The Missing Manual* by Nancy Conner and Matthew MacDonald
- *OS X Mavericks: The Missing Manual* by David Pogue
- *OS X Yosemite: The Missing Manual* by David Pogue
- *Personal Investing: The Missing Manual* by Bonnie Biafore
- *Photoshop CS6: The Missing Manual* by Lesa Snider
- *Photoshop CC: The Missing Manual, Second Edition* by Lesa Snider
- *Photoshop Elements 13: The Missing Manual* by Barbara Brundage
- *PHP & MySQL: The Missing Manual, Second Edition* by Brett McLaughlin
- *QuickBooks 2015: The Missing Manual* by Bonnie Biafore
- *Switching to the Mac: The Missing Manual, Mavericks Edition* by David Pogue
- *Windows 7: The Missing Manual* by David Pogue
- *Windows 8: The Missing Manual* by David Pogue
- *WordPress: The Missing Manual, Second Edition* by Matthew MacDonald
- *Your Body: The Missing Manual* by Matthew MacDonald
- *Your Brain: The Missing Manual* by Matthew MacDonald
- *Your Money: The Missing Manual* by J.D. Roth

For a full list of all Missing Manuals in print, go to *www.missingmanuals.com/library.html.*

Introduction

The word "database" can be alarming. It calls to mind images of software engi-neering degrees and pocket protectors. But databases have been around much longer than computers—a phone book, a cookbook, and an encyclopedia are all databases. In fact, if you look up the word "database" in a dictionary (which is a database, too), you'll find that a database is just a collection of information, or *data*.

The purpose of any database is to organize information so you can find what you're looking for quickly and easily. Image a business card file (yep, that's also a database) that organizes information about people alphabetically by name. You can find any person's card because you know where in the alphabet to look, even though there may be *thousands* of cards to look through. Such physical databases have major limitations compared with their digital cousins. What if you want to get a list of all your associates in California? Your card file isn't organized by state, so you have to flip through every card, one by one, to create a list. Digital databases help you avoid that kind of tedium.

FileMaker Pro helps you build a database so you can store information and then see that information the way you need to see it. At heart, a digital database isn't much different from one collected on business cards. It contains lots of information, like addresses, Zip codes, and phone numbers, and it organizes that info in useful ways (see Figure I-1 for an example). The program lets you organize the same informa-tion in numerous ways with ease—say, by name *or* by state. That list of associates in California you took hours to generate from a card file? FileMaker Pro can do in less than a second what it would take hours to do on physical cards.

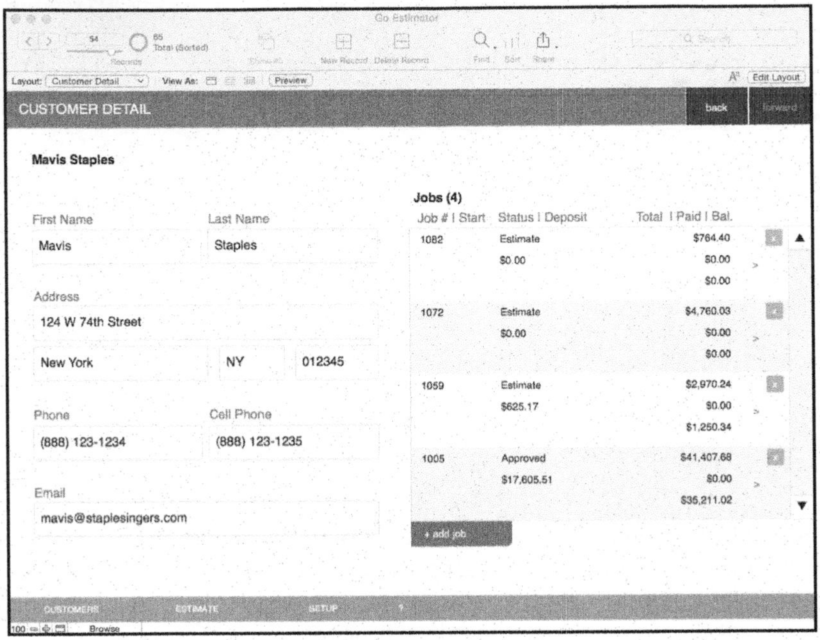

FIGURE I-1

FileMaker Pro lets you do just about anything with the information you give it. You can use it like a business card file to store and retrieve customer information, or run your entire business with one program. FileMaker's built-in number crunching and word processing tools let you track people, processes, and things, creating all your reports, correspondence, and collateral documents along the way.

This book shows you how FileMaker Pro stores your information and how you can rearrange that information to get the answers to meaningful questions—like which employees are due for performance reviews, who's coming to the company picnic, and which amusement park has the best deal on laser tag so you can throw a party for your top 50 performers. You don't have to learn to think like a programmer (or know the arcane terms they use), but you will learn how to bend FileMaker Pro's hidden power to your will, and make it tell you everything it knows about your company, the photographs you're selling on the Web, or how long it typically takes each member of your staff to get through his workload.

What About the Big Guys?

The word *database* is a little abused in the computer world. Both FileMaker Pro and MySQL—an open-source database that you can use for free, if you have the manpower, hardware, and know-how—are considered database programs, but they're about as similar as chocolate cake and dry flour. There are two basic kinds of database programs you can use. One kind is very powerful (as in run-the-federal-government powerful) and very complicated. This type of database program just holds data, and computer programmers use sophisticated (and expensive) tools to structure and put a user interface on that data. SQL and Oracle are examples of that type of database.

The other kind of database program—sometimes called a *desktop database*—is less powerful and a lot easier, but it actually has more features. In addition to holding lots of data,

these programs provide an interface to access, organize, and search the data. This interface includes the menus, graphics, and text that let you work with the data, much like any other computer program. In other words, you don't need a computer science degree to create a powerful database with a desktop program like FileMaker Pro.

And with FileMaker Pro 14's powerful External SQL Source (ESS) connection feature, you can have the best of both worlds. You (or even better, an IT person who's a database nerd) can create and administer a SQL database and then use FileMaker to create a snazzy display for the SQL data. Your nerd colleague would say you're using FileMaker as a "front end" to the SQL database. You can just call it common sense.

Why FileMaker Pro?

Choosing a database program from the many options on the market is overwhelming. Some are enormously powerful but take years to learn how to use. Others let you easily get started but don't offer much help when you're ready to incorporate some more advanced features. Here are a few reasons why FileMaker Pro may be your choice:

- **FileMaker Pro is the ease-of-use champion.** While other programs use jargon words like *query, join,* and *alias*, FileMaker Pro uses simple concepts like *find, sort,* and *connect*. FileMaker Pro is designed from the ground up for nontechnical people who have a *real* job to do. It's designed to let you get in, build your database, and get back to work.

- **FileMaker Pro can do almost anything.** FileMaker Pro, despite its focus on ease of use, is very powerful. It can handle large amounts of data. It lets lots of people in locations around the office or around the world share information in real-time. It even meets the needs of bigger companies, like integrating with high-end systems. And it's adaptable enough to solve most problems. For example, if your home-based crafting business is taking off and you need to figure out how much it costs you to create your top-selling items, FileMaker can do that. But if you're a large school district tracking dozens of test scores for more than 50,000 students in grades K–12, and you have to make sure those scores are tied to federal standards, FileMaker can handle that, too.

- **FileMaker Pro works on Macs and PCs.** If you use both types of computers, FileMaker Pro makes the connection seamless. You can use the exact same databases on any computer, or better still, share them over the network simultaneously without a hitch (Chapter 20).

- **FileMaker Pro lets you take your data with you.** FileMaker Pro understands that people work on the road these days. Road warriors can access FileMaker databases from remote cities with an iPhone, iPad, or iPod Touch using FileMaker Go. If you don't have an iOS device, you can still communicate with your database using a web browser (Chapter 21).

- **FileMaker Pro is fun!** It may sound corny, but it's exciting (and a little addictive) to have such a powerful tool at your fingertips. If you get the bug, you'll find yourself solving all kinds of problems you never knew you had. You might not think that getting married is an occasion for breaking out a new database, but you'd be amazed at how helpful it is. You can make a mailing list for your invitations, track RSVPs, note which favorite aunt sent you a whole set of bone china (and which cousin cheaped out by signing his name on his brother's gift card), and you can even record what date you mailed the thank-you notes.

- **You have plenty of company.** Perhaps best of all, FileMaker Pro is very popular—there are more than 20 million copies of FileMaker Pro running around the globe. And the program's fans love it so much they're actually willing to help you if *you* get stuck. You can find user groups, websites, discussion boards, chat rooms, mailing lists, and professional consultants all devoted to FileMaker Pro. This is one case where there's good reason to follow the crowd.

About This Book

FileMaker Pro comes with an impressive online help system, containing links to PDF user's guides. These resources are helpful—if you're a programmer, that is, or if you've been working with FileMaker for a while. Between the user's guides and the help system, you can figure out how FileMaker works. But you have to jump back and forth to get the complete picture. And neither resource does a great job of guiding you toward the features that apply to the problem you're trying to solve.

This book is designed to serve as the FileMaker Pro manual, the book that should have been in the box. It explores each feature in depth, offers shortcuts and work-arounds, and explains the ramifications of options that the help system and user's guides don't even mention. Plus, it lets you know which features are really useful and which ones you should worry about only in very limited circumstances. And you can bookmark or highlight the most helpful passages!

FileMaker comes in several flavors, and this book addresses them all. FileMaker Pro, the base program, takes up most of the book's focus. FileMaker Go is the free app that lets you run FileMaker databases on your iPhone or iPad. The iPad's remarkable acceptance in boardrooms, factory floors, medical settings, and even the restaurant and retail realms has given FileMaker Pro a whole other life as an app-creation program. See Chapter 3 for an introduction to FileMaker Go.

FileMaker Pro Advanced contains advanced tools and utilities aimed at making development and maintenance of your databases easier. It's a must-have for people who spend most of their time making databases for others. Its features are covered in Part 4. FileMaker Server lets you share your databases more safely and quickly than FileMaker Pro's peer-to-peer sharing.

This book was written for advanced-beginner or intermediate computer users. But if you're a first-timer, special sidebar articles called Up to Speed provide the introductory information you need to understand the topic at hand. Advanced users should watch for similar boxes called Power Users' Clinic. They offer more technical tips, tricks, and shortcuts for the experienced FileMaker user.

About the Figures

The hundreds of figures in the book are snapshots of the FileMaker Pro screen, chosen to illustrate the objects and concepts covered in these pages. They were created using FileMaker Pro Advanced. If you're using the standard version of FileMaker Pro, a handful of these images may differ from what you see on your own screen.

Except for the sections that cover the developer tools available only in FileMaker Pro Advanced—which includes most of Chapter 14—the examples and exercises in this book aren't affected by any minor differences in what you see onscreen. As you learn to create more complex and powerful databases, or if you plan to become a professional FileMaker developer, you'll eventually want to invest in FileMaker Pro Advanced. The additional cost is worth the programming efficiencies you'll reap.

■ Macintosh and Windows

FileMaker Pro works almost the same in its Macintosh and Windows versions. For the most part, dialog boxes have exactly the same choices and the software behaves exactly the same way. When that's not true, you'll learn how and why there is a difference. In this book, the illustrations get even-handed treatment, rotating between Windows and Mac OS X by chapter.

One of the biggest differences between the Mac and Windows versions is the keystrokes, because the Ctrl key in Windows is the equivalent of the Macintosh ⌘ (command) key.

Whenever this book refers to a key combination, you'll see the Windows keystroke listed first (with + symbols, as is customary in Windows documentation); the Macintosh keystroke follows in parentheses (with - symbols, in time-honored Mac fashion). In other words, you may read, "The keyboard shortcut for closing a window is Ctrl+W (⌘-W)."

▣ About the Outline

FileMaker Pro 14: The Missing Manual is divided into six parts:

- **Part One, Getting Started with FileMaker Pro.** Here, you'll learn about File-Maker Pro's interface and how to perform basic tasks, like entering data and then sorting through it again. You'll also find out how FileMaker Pro stores your data inside fields and then organizes those fields into units called *records.* You'll learn how to filter the records you're looking at with *finds* and how to snazz up your data with basic formatting. You'll also learn how to manage a database in FileMaker Go.

- **Part Two, Building Your First Database.** It's time to put theory into practice and build a new database from scratch. You'll see how to *define* fields and make them do some of the data entry work for you. Just as your actual data is organized into fields and records, a database's appearance is organized into *layouts;* you'll learn how to use them to make your data easier to interpret and use. You'll learn the ingredients that go into a functional database, and then spice it up with calculations that do some thinking for you and scripts that do some grunt work for you. You'll take your flat database, which is two-dimensional, like a spreadsheet or table, and make it *relational,* so different tables of information can work together in powerful ways.

- **Part Three, Thinking Like a Developer.** You've kicked the tires and driven around town with FileMaker. Now, do you want to see what this baby can really do? You'll learn some theory behind relational database design and how to create a variety of relationship types. The world of fields will open up with *auto-enter data* and *validation* to keep your information consistent and accurate. You'll dig into the vast capabilities offered in Layouts—like using colors and images for an attractive look, making clickable *buttons,* and building *reports.* And you'll get a handle on the remarkable power of *calculations* and *scripts.*

- **Part Four, Becoming a Power Developer.** Now that you're a living, breathing database creation machine, it's time to trade up to FileMaker Pro Advanced, the FileMaker version created expressly for power developers. You'll learn how to reuse database components, step through a running script with the Script Debugger, and even bend FileMaker's menus to your will. You'll literally tunnel deeply into relationships, make layouts pop with conditional formatting and charts, and even put a real live web browser *inside* your database. You'll learn enough about calculations to derive the answer to life, the universe, and everything (well, almost)!

- **Part Five, Security and Integration.** FileMaker knows your data is important enough to keep it safe from prying eyes. In this section, you'll learn how to protect your database with passwords and how to use privileges to determine what folks can do once they get into your database. This part also teaches you how to move data into and out of your database, and how to share that data with other people, and even with other databases.

- **Part Six, Appendixes.** No book can include all the information you'll need for the rest of your FileMaker Pro career. Well, it could, but you wouldn't be able to lift it. Eventually, you'll need to seek extra troubleshooting help or consult the program's online documentation. So, at the end of the book, Appendix A explains how to find your way around FileMaker's built-in help files and website. It also covers the vast online community of fans and experts—people are the best resource for fresh ideas and creative solutions. Appendix B will come in handy when you're learning how to lay out your databases: It lists all of the badges that identify different types of layout objects. Geared toward developers, Appendix C demystifies using Insert commands with FileMaker Pro 14's enhanced container fields. Appendix D is a list of all the error codes you may encounter when scripting FileMaker.

What's New in FileMaker Pro 14

FileMaker Pro 14 is a single software package that serves two fundamentally different types of people: users and developers. Users are the folks who need a database to help them organize and manage the data they work with in order to do their jobs. Developers create the databases that users use. No matter which category you're in (and lots of people fall into both categories, sometimes popping back and forth dozens of times a day), you'll find that FileMaker doesn't play favorites. The features you need for both roles are equally accessible.

FileMaker Pro 14 introduces a boatload of new features to make database creation more powerful and efficient. Here are the most notable:

- **The Script Workspace** is a fundamentally new way to create scripts. The endless clicking and scrolling has been replaced with quick and efficient composing and editing from the keyboard. You can now work on multiple scripts in the Script Workspace's tabs, and the script steps are color-coded for better readability.

- **Calculation editing** also has a new look and feel. Extensive use of predictive type suggests functions as you start to type them. Better still, it offers to fill in the names of your fields as you start to type them, too.

- **Buttons** can now have embedded icons along with, or instead of, text. You can also create **Button Bars**—single layout objects comprised of several independently clickable areas.

- **Navigation parts** are ideal spots for those Button Bars. These non-printing parts remain anchored to the top and bottom of the FileMaker window regardless of how much scrolling takes place in between.

- **Placeholder text** offers a new way to label your fields. The text appears when the field is empty, but disappears as soon as some information has been entered.

- **Security** gets a streamlined interface with easy access to the most frequently used options and all the more complicated stuff just a step away.

- The improved **color palette** gives a leg up to the chromatically challenged with a wider range of colors, collections of hues that work well together, and the ability to paste hexadecimal color values right into the palette.

- **Twelve new or improved script steps** including Refresh Portal to update related data in a portal without having to update the whole screen, and Set Allowed Orientations to protect your finely crafted iOS solutions from undesired screen rotations.

- **Twelve new or improved functions** bring more control over touchscreen keyboard and information about the state of the improved Audio/Visual player.

- **New script triggers** aimed at improving the user experience on iOS.

- **Gesture support** comes to Windows 8 touchscreen users.

Even users who never get beyond Browse mode will benefit from enhancements like:

- The **Launch Center,** where you see your favorite, recent, and network-hosted files are all in one friendly place. And to prevent it from becoming a sea of identical icons, the Launch Center lets you apply **custom solution icons** to files so they're easier to spot.

- **Audio and video playback** provides a new set of controls that make playing, pausing, scrubbing, and going fullscreen more intuitive.

- Windows users now benefit from **saved passwords**, bringing the formerly Mac-only feature to everyone.

- **Signature screens** in FileMaker Go can now be more than just "Sign Here." Users can see just what they're agreeing to right above the signature.

- **WebDirect** now officially supports well-equipped mobile devices on Google Android and Microsoft Surface operating systems, with faster performance for all WebDirect users.

If you're planning to host your own databases, here are two new FileMaker Server capabilities worth noting:

- **Reconnect** attempts to gracefully re-establish dropped user connections to hosted databases putting you back in where you left off so you don't have to reopen your databases from scratch.

- **Standby Server** is like an insurance policy. The feature lets you have a second FileMaker Server in constant readiness. Should your primary server crash, you can cut over to the standby server in minutes.

Meanwhile, three features present in earlier versions do not appear in FileMaker Pro 14:

- **Bento import** has been discontinued in the wake of that product's demise.

- The **Quick Start screen** no longer appears when you open FileMaker, as it's been supplanted by the new Launch Center.

- **Insert QuickTime** has become Insert Audio/Video in support of improved media handling and playback.

MOBILE MOMENT

Stay Connected with FileMaker Go

Your iPad is so convenient that you've already stopped carrying your laptop when you're away from the office. That's where FileMaker Go comes in. If your company shares a FileMaker database using FileMaker Server, you can connect to it via your device's data plan or its wireless connection. Or you can go rogue and use a standalone file while you're in the field and then sync it up with the server version when you're back from your roaming. Either way, you now get to interact with your FileMaker databases by using ubercool gestures like the two-finger swipe and the pinch zoom.

But FileMaker Go isn't just for road warriors or early-adopting tech geeks. Some doctors already leave an iPad in each exam room and then take notes for their FileMaker database, using FileMaker Go. Waiters have been seen handing iPads to customers so they can make a choice by using pictures from the restaurant's wine cellar. High-tech lab companies send iPads with their techs so they can make real-time observations about the equipment they're testing. In fact, with more than 50 million iPads and iPhones sold in just the last two years, FileMaker has a major new market to dominate.

Don't worry, though. This upstart isn't going to make the desktop version of FileMaker Pro obsolete. FileMaker Go doesn't handle any file creation or modification tasks (Chapter 4). You'll still use FileMaker Pro and FileMaker Pro Advanced to create databases, use plug-ins, and import data from other sources.

And you'll need to add some new skills to your arsenal because with the iPad and iPhone's very different screen height-to-width ratio and their ability to switch seamlessly from landscape to portrait layout, you'll be creating special layouts that are meant just for your iPhone or iPad.

■ The Very Basics

Throughout this book, you'll run into a few terms and concepts that you'll encounter frequently in your computing life:

- **Clicking.** This book includes instructions that require you to use your computer's mouse or track pad. To *click* means to point your cursor (the arrow pointer) at something on the screen and then—without moving the cursor at all—press and release the left button on the mouse (or laptop track pad). To *right-click* means the same thing, but pressing the *right* mouse button instead (or, if you have a Mac with a one-button mouse, press ⌘ as you click). Usually, clicking selects an onscreen element or presses an onscreen button, whereas right-clicking typically reveals a *shortcut menu*, which lists some common tasks specific to whatever you're right-clicking. To *double-click*, of course, means to click twice in rapid succession, again without moving the pointer at all. And to *drag* means to move the cursor while holding down the (left) mouse button the entire time. To *right-drag* means to do the same thing but holding down the right mouse button.

  When you're told to *Shift-click* something, you click while pressing the Shift key. Related procedures, like *Ctrl-clicking*, work the same way—just click while pressing the corresponding key.

- **Tapping.** If you're using a mobile device you won't have a mouse, but you can still interact with your database. You just use your finger instead of a mouse or trackpad. Whenever you read the word "click," just point to the item and *tap* lightly with the pad of your finger. Most of the variations above work the same way: you can *double-tap* an item, or keep your finger pressed to the screen while you drag an item. But since you don't have buttons on your fingers (well, most people don't), there's no such thing as a *right-drag* on a mobile device.

- **Keyboard shortcuts.** Nothing is faster than keeping your fingers on your keyboard to enter data, choose names, trigger commands, and so on. That's why many experienced FileMaker users prefer to trigger commands by pressing combinations of keys on the keyboard. For example, in most word processors, you can press Ctrl+B to produce a boldface word. In this book, when you read an instruction like "Press Ctrl+A to open the Chart of Accounts window," start by pressing the Ctrl key; while it's down, type the letter A; and then release both keys.

About→These→Arrows

Throughout this book, and throughout the Missing Manual series, you'll find sentences like this one: "Open your Documents→eBooks→Downloads folder." That's shorthand for a much longer instruction that directs you to open three nested folders in sequence, like this: "Choose Open→Documents. In your Documents folder, you'll find a folder called eBooks. Open that. Inside the eBooks window is a folder called Downloads. Click or tap to open it, too."

Similarly, this kind of arrow shorthand helps to simplify the business of choosing commands in menus, as shown in Figure I-2.

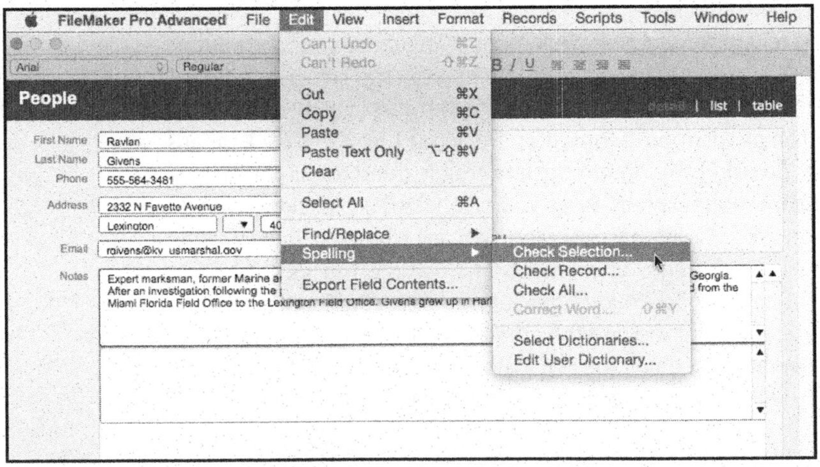

FIGURE I-2

When you read "Edit→ Spelling→Check Selection," that means: "Click the Edit menu to open it, in that menu, click Spelling and then, in the resulting submenu, choose Check Selection."

■ About the Online Resources

As the owner of a Missing Manual, you've got more than just a book to read. Online, you'll find sample databases so you can get some hands-on experience, as well as tips, articles, and maybe even a video or two. You can also communicate with the Missing Manual team and tell us what you love (or hate) about the book. Head over to *www.missingmanuals.com*, or go directly to one of the following sections.

The Missing CD

Each chapter contains *living examples*—step-by-step tutorials that help you learn how to build a database by actually doing it. If you take the time to work through these examples at the computer, you'll discover that these tutorials give you invaluable insight into the way professional developers create databases. To help you along, online database files provide sample data and completed examples against which to check your work.

You can get these files any time from the Missing CD page. Go to *www.missingmanuals.com/cds/fmp14mm*. To download, simply click this book's title and then click the link for the relevant chapter.

Feedback

Got questions? Need more information? Fancy yourself a book reviewer? On our Feedback page, you can get expert answers to questions that come to you while reading, share your thoughts on this Missing Manual, and find groups of folks who share your interest in FileMaker. To have your say, go to *www.missingmanuals.com/feedback*.

Errata

In an effort to keep this book as up to date and accurate as possible, each time we print more copies, we'll make any confirmed corrections you've suggested. We also note such changes on the book's website, so you can mark important corrections into your own copy of the book, if you like. Go to *http://tinyurl.com/fmp14-mm* to report an error and to view existing corrections.

Register Your Book

If you register this book at oreilly.com, you'll be eligible for special offers—like discounts on future editions of *FileMaker Pro 14: The Missing Manual*. Registering takes only a few clicks. To get started, type *http://oreilly.com/register* into your browser to hop directly to the Registration page.

■ Safari® Books Online

Safari Books Online is an on-demand digital library that delivers expert *content* in both book and video form from the world's leading authors in technology and business.

Technology professionals, software developers, web designers, and business and creative professionals use Safari Books Online as their primary resource for research, problem solving, learning, and certification training.

Safari Books Online offers a range of *plans and pricing* for *enterprise, government, education,* and individuals.

Members have access to thousands of books, training videos, and prepublication manuscripts in one fully searchable database from publishers like O'Reilly Media, Prentice Hall Professional, Addison-Wesley Professional, Microsoft Press, Sams, Que, Peachpit Press, Focal Press, Cisco Press, John Wiley & Sons, Syngress, Morgan Kaufmann, IBM Redbooks, Packt, Adobe Press, FT Press, Apress, Manning, New Riders, McGraw-Hill, Jones & Bartlett, Course Technology, and hundreds *more*. For more information about Safari Books Online, please visit us *online*.

Getting Started with FileMaker Pro

Working with Your Database

FileMaker Pro databases can be as simple as a list of things you need to pack for a camping trip (complete with pictures) or as complex as a company-wide system for purchasing, sales, inventory, invoicing, shipping, and customer tracking. But all of them essentially *work* the same way. This chapter gives you a tour of FileMaker's major features and gets you ready to use your very first database.

FileMaker's vast assortment of tools and options can make the program's window as intimidating as an Airbus cockpit. But the program's menu commands, dialog boxes, keyboard shortcuts, and other options stay largely consistent across all databases, so everything you learn in the next few pages will apply to almost every database you'll ever use.

TIP Because a database usually solves a problem of some kind, some FileMaker experts call a database a *solution*, as in, "I can create an inventory solution for your bakery, but it's going to cost you some dough." Usually, *database* and *solution* mean the same thing, although the term *solution* sometimes implies a system of several connected databases.

A Very Quick Database Tour

Every FileMaker Pro database has two major parts. First, there's the information (data) you're storing. And second are the tools that help you view and manage this data. Since data changes from file to file, you'll start this tour focusing on the tools you find in nearly every FileMaker database. These buttons, pop-up menus, and other controls help you put information into your database or manage the information that's already there.

Every database window has the same basic structure. The *content area* in the middle is where the data goes, and as you can see in Figure 1-1, a handful of special items appear at the top and bottom.

NOTE To follow along in this chapter, you'll find it helpful to download the sample databases from this book's Missing CD page at *www.missingmanuals.com/cds/fmp14mm.*

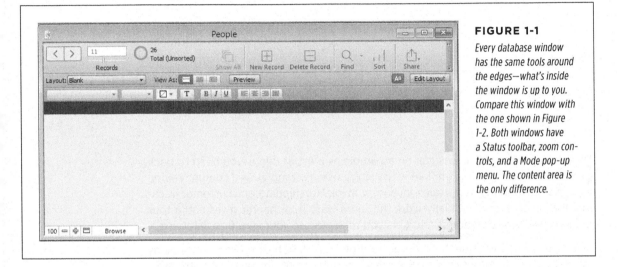

FIGURE 1-1

Every database window has the same tools around the edges—what's inside the window is up to you. Compare this window with the one shown in Figure 1-2. Both windows have a Status toolbar, zoom controls, and a Mode pop-up menu. The content area is the only difference.

NOTE The figures in this chapter were all created in the desktop version of FileMaker Pro Advanced. If you have the non-Advanced version, your window may look a little different. You'll also see a different rendition of the window in the mobile versions of FileMaker 14 (page 82), or if you're viewing the database in a web browser (page 832).

Content Area

The content area is where you put the information that makes your database work for you. When you create a new FileMaker database, the standard view looks like Figure 1-2. It's plain, with just a few boxes for storing data and some buttons and stuff at the top and bottom. That's because you haven't added any content yet, and you haven't started arranging your data in a way that mirrors your needs. In Figure 1-3, you can see that data has been entered, and the fields are arranged so that they look more like information the way it's normally used. For example, the address fields look like addresses on envelopes. (In Chapter 4, you'll learn more about changing the way your data looks.)

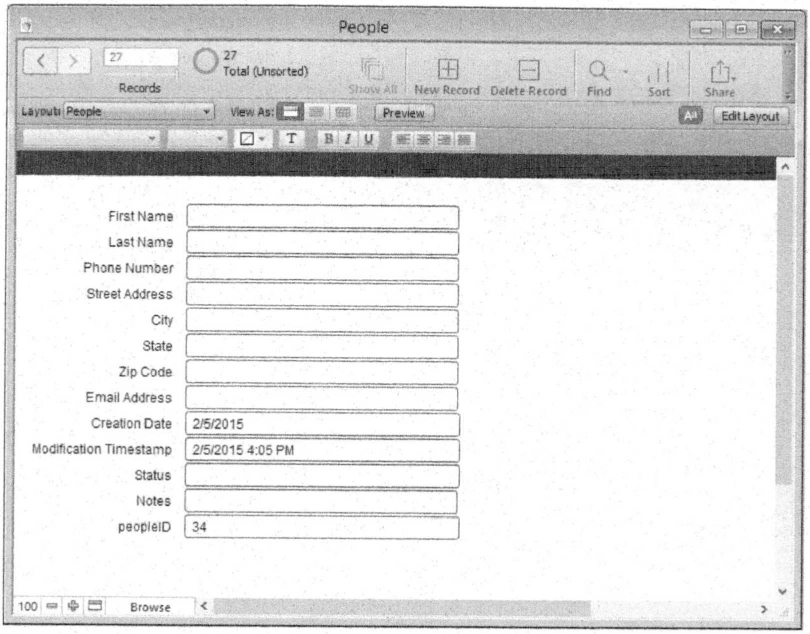

FIGURE 1-2

Unlike the stark emptiness shown in Figure 1-1, this view of the database has fields for entering information, and some fields even have something in them before you start to type (see page 245 for more information on auto-enter fields). The fields are arranged in a column, the way FileMaker throws them on the screen when you first create them. Compare this screen with Figure 1-3, where the fields are resized and rearranged to create a more pleasing interface to showcase your data.

Scroll Bars

As with most windows on your computer, you can resize FileMaker's windows. And if you make your window too small to display all the data in the content area, scroll bars appear so you can see the stuff outside the current window size.

Drag the scroll bars to reveal any areas of the screen that aren't visible. Use the Page Up and Page Down keys to scroll by keyboard.

If your mouse has a scroll wheel or similar feature, it scrolls differently based on where you put your mouse cursor. That's FileMaker's *contextual* scrolling. The scroll wheel:

- Scrolls through the window when the cursor is inside the window's content area.

- Scrolls through the records in your database when you run the cursor over the arrow buttons in the Status toolbar.

- Scrolls through the text in the field when you put your cursor over a field that has a scroll bar (like the Notes field in your sample database).

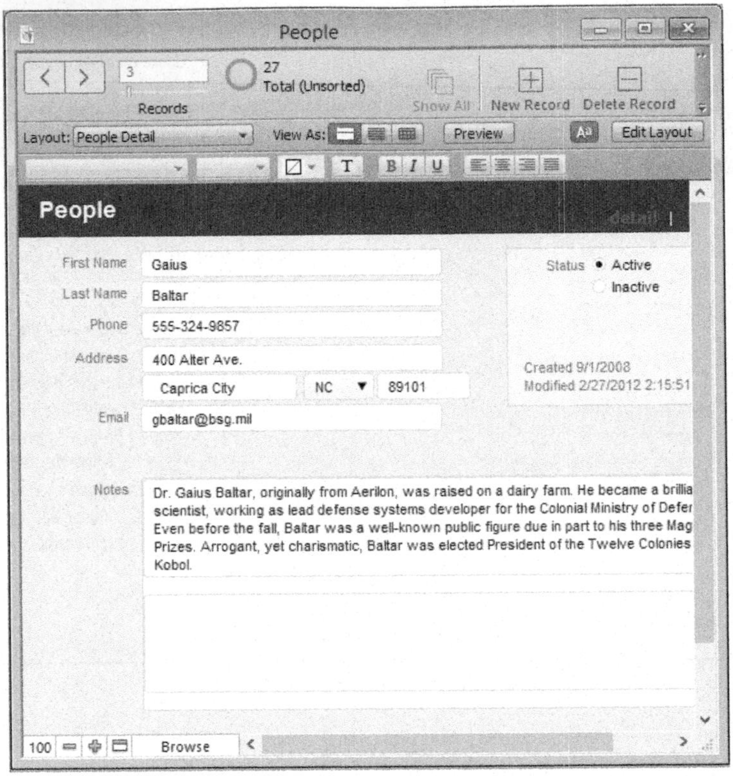

FIGURE 1-3

You can't see everything in this window, as evidenced by the thin, light-gray scroll bar along the bottom edge. You've got three options for viewing more information. You can reduce the zoom level so everything fits in the window, make the window larger (if your display is big enough), or drag the scroll bar to scan across the screen.

Zoom Controls

For when resizing the window isn't enough, FileMaker gives you a *zoom control* to magnify or shrink what you're seeing onscreen. Click the Zoom In and Zoom Out buttons to make everything bigger and smaller incrementally, from 400 percent all the way down to 25 percent. The Zoom Level shows your current level, and clicking it takes you back to 100 percent. Clicking Zoom Level a second time returns you to the last zoom level you were viewing.

> **NOTE** Since you probably don't need to examine the words and numbers in your database on a microscopic level, you'll probably use the zoom control mostly in Preview mode to fit the whole page on the screen, or to adjust the contents of your FileMaker window to the most easily readable size (depending on your screen's resolution). You may notice, though, that some fonts don't enlarge well, so they're actually most legible at 100 percent.

Understanding Modes

Each of FileMaker's four *modes* is a work environment specially designed to help you view, edit, organize, or present your information in a specific way.

- **Browse mode** is the one you see when you first open a database, since it's the one you use most often. In this mode, you add, change, and view your data. Browse mode is the view shown in all the figures so far, and it's where you'll spend most of this chapter.

- When you have a lot of data, looking through it all for a particular bit of information can be tedious. Use **Find mode** to let FileMaker do the looking for you. You tell FileMaker what you're looking for; when it's done looking, FileMaker returns you to Browse mode and shows what it found. (For more details on finding specific records, see page 20.)

- In addition to using databases (viewing, finding, sorting, adding, and changing data), you can use FileMaker to *build* databases (in fact, that's what most of this book is about). **Layout mode** is where you design the screens (called *layouts* in FileMaker parlance) that present your database information to best advantage. Part Two of this book is all about Layout mode.

- Once you've put all that information into your database, eventually you'll want to print something out, like a set of mailing labels or a batch of invoices. If you're ever curious about how something will look when printed, switch to **Preview mode**. It shows a one-page-at-a-time view of your data exactly as it'll appear when printed. Get more info on page 71.

The Mode pop-up menu is the easiest way to change modes. It appears near the bottom-left corner of Figure 1-1, displaying Browse mode. Click it and choose one of the four modes. Your FileMaker window instantly switches to the new mode. You can also glance at the Mode pop-up menu to see which mode you're currently in. (The Mode pop-up menu is the most popular way to mode-hop, but you have plenty more options; see the box on page 8.)

NOTE Don't be alarmed when the menus across the top of your screen change a bit when you switch modes. That's just FileMaker being smart. Some commands aren't useful in some modes, so the program doesn't clutter up your screen—or your brain space—with menus when you don't need them. For example, the Arrange menu appears only when you're in Layout mode, and the Records menu changes to Requests in Find mode and to Layouts in Layout mode.

Changing Modes

Switching between modes is so common that FileMaker gives you a few ways to do it. The Mode pop-up menu (near the bottom-left corner of Figure 1-1) is the primary mouse-driven way. The Status toolbar, along the top of your screen, offers buttons to move among modes, though they vary based on your current mode and don't appear in one place (as shown in Figure 1-4). Or, from FileMaker's View menu, you can pick a mode.

The keyboard shortcuts are speediest of all:

• Press Ctrl+B (⌘-B) to switch to Browse mode.

• Press Ctrl+F (⌘-F) to switch to Find mode.

• Press Ctrl+L (⌘-L) to switch to Layout mode.

• Press Ctrl+U (⌘-U) to switch to Preview mode.

If you forget these shortcuts, check the View menu to refresh your memory. FileMaker also gives you a couple of ways to find out which mode you're in. The Mode pop-up menu at the bottom of the window displays the current mode, and the View menu indicates the current mode with a checkmark.

TIP Get in the habit of glancing at the Mode pop-up menu before you type. If you enter information in Find mode, thinking you're in Browse mode, FileMaker doesn't save that information, and you have to start over.

Status Toolbar

Changing modes may be confusing when you're getting started, but the Status toolbar gives you constant feedback about the features available in your current mode. So as you switch modes, you see the tools in the Status toolbar changing, too. In fact, the Status toolbar changes so much, you'll soon find that you barely have to glance at the Mode pop-up menu anymore, because you can see the tools you need for the job at hand.

Figure 1-4 shows the Status toolbar in each of its four modes. If your sample database isn't showing all the tools you expect, try widening the window: Some buttons and commands disappear when the window is too narrow.

◼ Opening and Closing Database Files

Each database you create with FileMaker Pro is stored as a *file* on your hard drive—just like your documents and spreadsheets. This file contains all the information about how the database is structured, plus all the information stored inside it, which means you can open, close, copy, or back up a database as you would any other file. This section explains those tasks in detail, along with some quirks that are particular to FileMaker files.

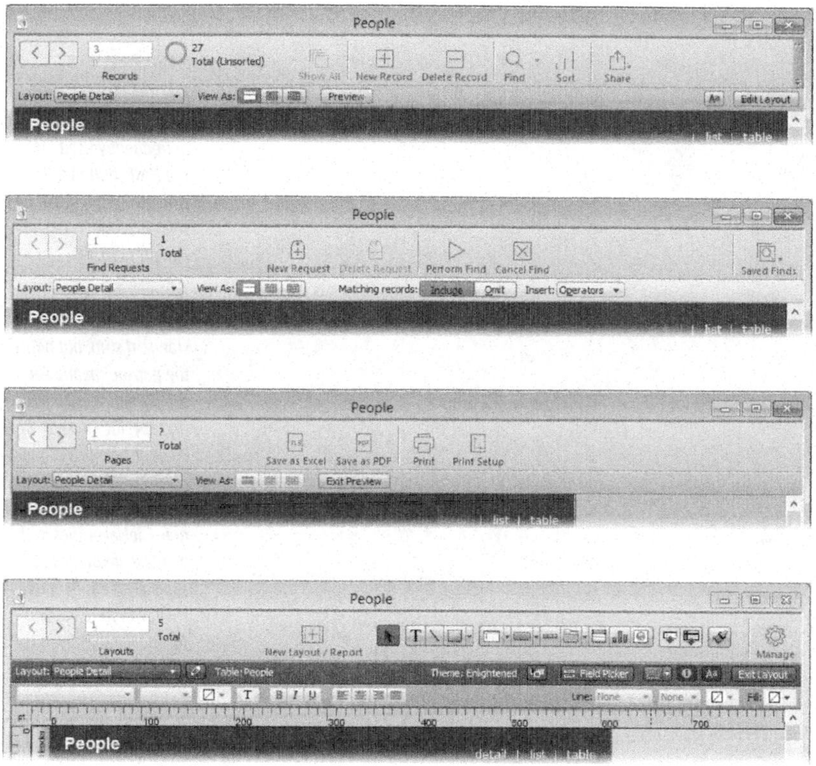

FIGURE 1-4

In Browse mode (top), you can click the New Record button and then start entering information. Find mode (second from top) lets you look for records with all the tools you need to create new Find requests or to select a recent or Saved Find. And if you inspect a report by clicking the Preview button before you print it (third from top), you get tools for saving the report as a PDF, exporting the data to Excel, and plain old printing. Layout mode lets you change the appearance of your database with tools for text, field, and object formatting (bottom).

Opening a Database

To open a database, open FileMaker Pro and then choose File→Open. The Launch Center opens (Figure 1-5), displaying recently opened files or those you've marked as favorites. If you don't see what you're looking for, click the Browse button in the lower left to pull up the Open File dialog box. Select the file you want to work with and then click Open. If you prefer, you can find the file by using Windows Explorer (Windows) or the Finder (Mac) and then double-clicking its icon.

When you open a database, you see one or more windows on your screen. If you open the People database that you downloaded at the beginning of this chapter, you see one database window.

Closing a Database

To close a database, choose File→Close or press Ctrl+W (⌘-W). If your database has only one open window, the Close Window command closes the whole database. But you can open more than one window into a single database (page 31), and if you do, you need to close each window individually to close the file. To complicate things further, when you have more than one database open, you can't always easily tell which windows go with which database.

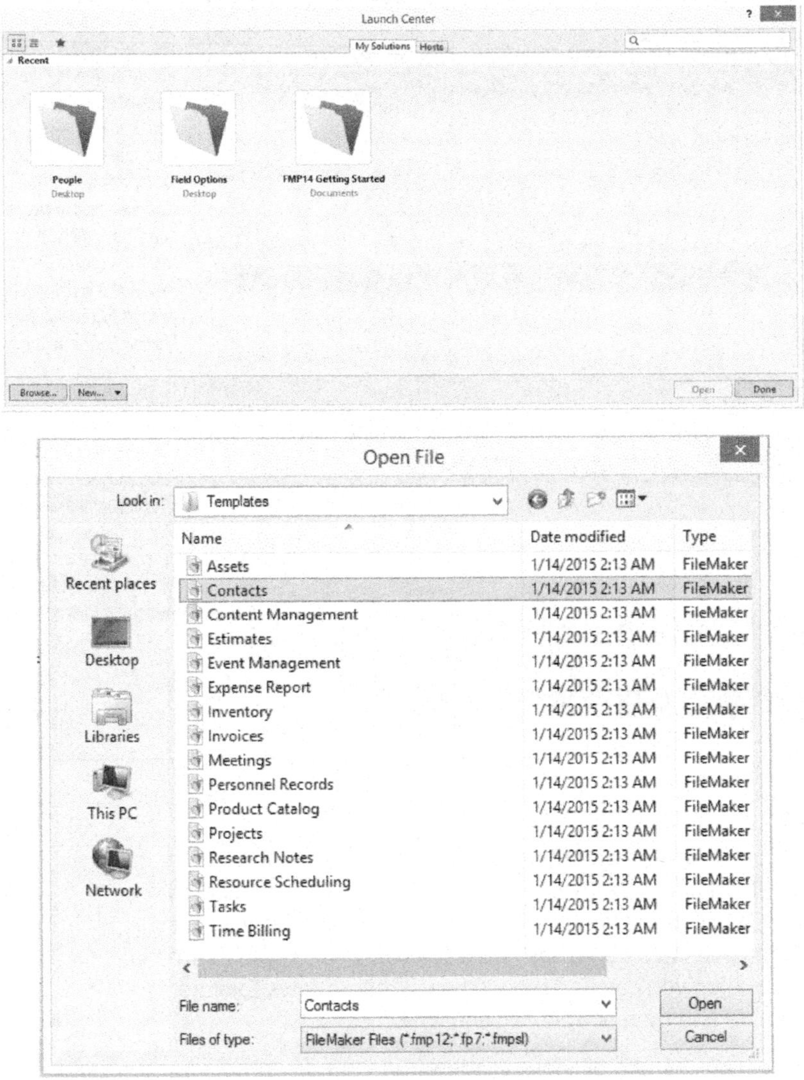

FIGURE 1-5

Top: The Launch Center gives you quick access to frequently used files. The Hosts button at top is where you find databases shared by FileMaker Server (Chapter 20).

Bottom: FileMaker's Open File dialog box is pretty standard stuff, but notice the pop-up menu near the bottom that helps you find specific kinds of files on your hard drive. If you choose FileMaker Files as shown here, then all non-FileMaker files in the window are grayed out, so you can easily ignore them as you're looking for the database you want to open.

To close all the windows in *all* the databases you currently have open, simply press Alt (Windows) or Option (Mac) and then click the File menu. In Windows, the menu command doesn't look any different, but as long as you're holding down Alt when you choose Close, you close all open FileMaker windows. On a Mac, the Close command is replaced by Close All. Choose it, and FileMaker closes all its windows, which also saves and closes all your open databases.

■ Adding Data to Your Database

Now that you understand the basic components of a FileMaker database, it's time to start adding your own information. Whether your database contains information about individual people, eBay auctions, products you sell, student grades, or whatever, FileMaker always thinks of that information in individual chunks called *records*. Each record contains everything the database knows about that person, auction, product, or student.

Since you store many smaller pieces of information in each record (like a person's phone number, address, birthday, and so on), FileMaker lets you give each record an almost infinite number of *fields*—the specific bits of data that define each record.

For example, each person in a database of magazine subscribers gets her own record. First name, last name, phone number, street address, city, state, Zip code, and her subscription's expiration date are all examples of fields each record can include.

The techniques in this section work the same way whether you're creating a new database or adding to an existing one.

> **NOTE** All records in a database have to have the same fields, but that doesn't mean you have to fill them all in. For instance, in your saltshaker collection database, you may not know the year a particular shaker was manufactured, so you can leave that field blank.

Creating a Record

Adding a new record is simple: Choose Records→New Record or press Ctrl+N (⌘-N). (Since you'll be creating lots of records in your FileMaker career, memorize this keyboard shortcut.)

> **NOTE** When you're adding new records, you have to be in Browse mode. If you're in Find mode and use the Ctrl+N (⌘-N) keyboard shortcut, you'll make new find requests instead of new records, and if you're in Layout mode, you'll create new layouts.

Entering Information

Once you create a new record, you can enter information about the person you want to keep track of—that's where those fields come in handy. To enter information in any field in a record, just click it and then type. What to type? As Figure 1-6 shows, most fields in this database have a label at left indicating the type of information the field contains. Field borders have turned to dotted lines—a confirmation that you're doing data entry.

> **NOTE** A label is just a bit of text that appears near a field. It's meant to help you figure out what kind of data belongs in the field. See the box on page 12 for more on recognizing fields and labels.

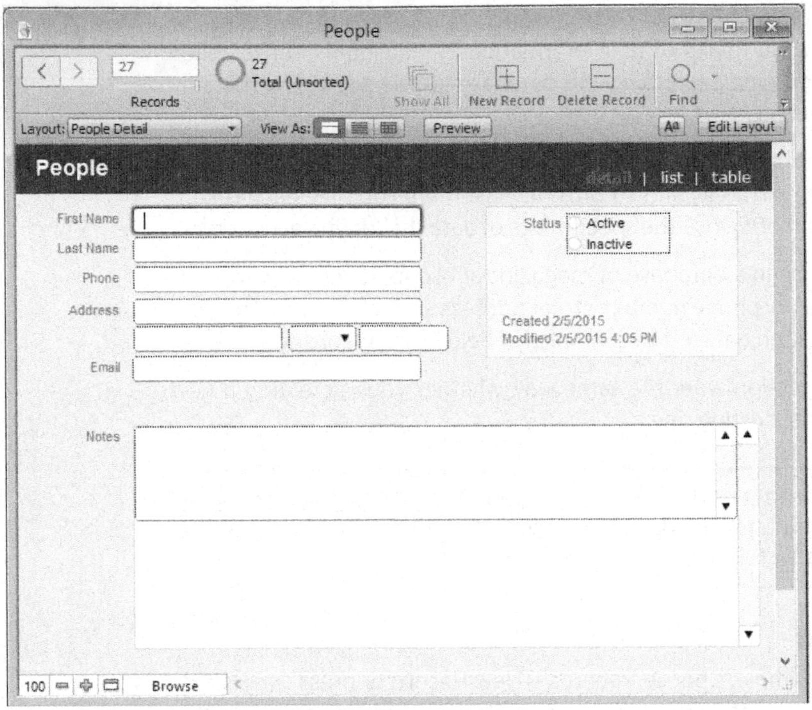

FIGURE 1-6

Fields can look like just about anything, but in the People database, they're pretty simple. When you click in a field, dotted borders indicate the fields you can edit. The field you're currently editing gets a solid border. With the miracle of In Focus formatting, the fields in the People database are shaded as you type in them, which helps keep you oriented when you're entering information in a screen full of fields.

The Many Faces of a Field

Fields always appear inside the content area, but other than that, they can have amazing variety. You can let your creative urges go wild. A field can have a label next to, below, above—even inside—where you enter data, or no label at all.

You can color in a field with a solid color, a gradient, or a picture. You can make borders thick or thin. You can even give them rounded corners, so rounded that they look like little pills. In fact, if mystery is your thing, then you can make your field invisible—no label, no border, and no color. (But here's a tip:

If you want happy database users, make sure they can tell where the fields are and what goes in them.)

When you're editing a record, the fields usually appear with the dotted outline shown in Figure 1-6, but you can turn this feature on and off, as described on page 289. So don't expect every field to look the same.

See Chapter 4 for more detail on customizing and beautifying the fields in your database.

MOVING BETWEEN FIELDS

Efficient data entry means typing something in a field and then moving right along to the next field. You can use the mouse to click the next field, but using the Tab key is faster:

- Press the Tab key to move to the next field. If you're not in any field, the Tab key puts you in the first field.

- Press Shift-Tab to move to the previous field. This time, if you're not in any field, FileMaker puts you in the *last* field.

NOTE Who decides which field is *next* or *previous*? You do. When you design a database, you get to set the *tab order*. That's the order FileMaker follows when you press Tab or Shift-Tab to move among fields (page 321).

EDITING A RECORD

You're not stuck with the data you enter in a record if something changes. For example, when people move, you can change their address data. Just click in the field to be updated, select the data, and start typing the new information.

NOTE If you try this on the sample People file provided on the Missing CD page, you'll notice that a field called "Modified" changes when you click out of the record. You'll learn what that field is used for on page 249.

REVERTING A RECORD

As you edit a record, you may decide you've made a mistake and wish you could put things back the way they were before. That's no problem for the Revert Record command: When you choose Records→Revert Record, FileMaker throws away any changes you made since you began editing the record. This trick comes in handy when you accidentally modify a field by bumping into the keyboard, or realize you accidentally entered Kathy Griffin's address in Carol Burnett's record. Just revert the record, and you can be confident that whatever you did has been forgotten.

The Revert Record command is available only when you're in a record (see the box on page 14) *and* you've made changes. If you don't have the record open, or you haven't made any changes since you last committed the record, then the Revert Record command is grayed out.

NOTE One of the easiest ways to commit a record is to simply click some empty space (not in a field) in the content area. FileMaker dutifully saves the record for you. Once you've committed a record, you can no longer choose the Revert Record command. (How's that for commitment?) If you want a little more control, visit page 289 to learn how you can set FileMaker to ask for confirmation before committing a record.

Commitment, or On the Record

To get *out* of all fields, so you're not in any field at all, click a blank spot in the content area. Pressing Enter on your numeric keypad usually has the same effect, although you can alter that behavior, as you'll see in Chapter 8. This process is called *committing* the record. In other words, you're telling FileMaker you're ready to save the changes you've made and move on. If you don't want to commit to the changes you've made, choose Records→Revert Record to get out of all fields and discard those changes.

When you first click into a field, you've *opened* the record. In that respect, a FileMaker record is like a cardboard file folder—you have to open it before you can change something inside it.

As long as you have a record open, you're *in* the record. You can be in only one record at any given moment, and that record is said to be *active*. Rounding out this technobabble, when you've committed the record, you're *on* the record but you're not *in* the record. Believe it or not, getting this terminology straight will make things easier later on.

■ DUPLICATING A RECORD

While no two people are alike, it may not always seem that way from their contact information. For instance, if you want to include three people from the same household in your database, the data in the Address, City, State, Zip, and probably Last Name fields will all be the same for each person.

The Email and Phone fields probably won't be the same, but they might be close. It's time for a little organized laziness: Instead of making new blank records and retyping all that stuff, just choose Records→Duplicate Record or press Ctrl+D (⌘-D). FileMaker copies everything from the first record into a new one for you. Now you can edit just the information that needs to be changed—just be sure you don't accidentally leave in the first person's email address or phone number, lest a message or phone call get misdirected later.

■ DELETING RECORDS

Getting rid of a record you don't need is a breeze. FileMaker Pro gives you three commands that let you delete one record, a group of records, or even *all* the records in your database.

NOTE You can't undo deleting a record, because FileMaker saves changes automatically. So when you delete a record (or all the records in a database), make sure you're ready to part with the information. Consider saving a backup copy of your file first (page 34).

- **One record.** Choose Records→Delete Record or press Ctrl+E (⌘-E) to delete the record you're currently on. FileMaker shows you a message box with a handy Cancel button that asks if you're sure you want to delete the record. That way, you won't accidentally send, say, your best client's address to the trash bin. But if you've indeed written him out of your life, then click Delete to complete the purge.

- **Multiple records.** FileMaker has a helpful command that trashes any group of records of your choosing. Before you use this command, you have to tell File-Maker which records to delete. You do that with the Find command (page 20). Once you have the found set of records to be deleted, choose Records→Delete Found Records. Again, FileMaker gives you a chance to change your mind with a message box that tells you how many records you have in your found set and asks you to click either the Delete All or the Cancel button.

- **All records.** In some cases, you may want to delete all the records in a database. Maybe a colleague wants an empty copy of your database for his own use. Or perhaps your database holds data you just don't need anymore, like test results you're about to reproduce. You can easily accomplish complete record elimination with two menu commands: Just choose Records→Show All Records and then choose Records→Delete All Records. (But if you just want an empty copy of your database, cloning is easier; see page 35.)

> **NOTE** In reality, the Delete Found Records and Delete All Records commands are one and the same. But FileMaker knows whether you're in a subset of your database or looking at all the records, and changes the wording of the menu command accordingly. It's just another bit of smart feedback.

Once you get used to deleting records, you may get tired of FileMaker nagging you about being sure you want to delete. You can bypass the dialog box, and the chance to click the Cancel button, by holding down the Shift (Windows) or Option (Mac) key when you choose Records→Delete Record. Or, if you're a fan of keyboard shortcuts, you can type Shift+Ctrl+E (Option-⌘-E) to get the same results.

Fields for Lots of Text

FileMaker fields can hold *a lot* of text. Technically, each field is limited to 2 GB of data *per record*, which is a technical way of saying, "Way more than you'll ever need."

To see for yourself, in the People database, click in the Notes field. When you do, a scroll bar appears at the right side of the field. If you type lots of notes, then you can scroll through them. (When you design a database, you get to decide which fields have scroll bars, as discussed on page 5.) Even if a field doesn't have scroll bars, you can still add lots of text. As you type, FileMaker just makes the field grow to hold whatever you type. When you leave the field, it shrinks back to its normal size, hiding anything that goes outside the edges. Don't worry, though; the text reappears when you click back into the field.

You can enter text into a field in all the usual ways, like typing on your keyboard or pasting text you copied from another field or another program.

> **NOTE** That second scroll bar you see right next to the Notes field lets you see if there are lots of notes for a record. That scroll bar controls a portal, and you'll learn what it's for on page 154.

Adding a New Button to the Toolbar

If you've been looking at the Status toolbar during the last few sections, you may have noticed that it contains some handy buttons, like New Record and Delete Record. If you're a mouse fan, you can use those buttons instead of the menu or keyboard shortcuts. But what about Duplicate Record? That sounds pretty handy, but there's no sign of a Duplicate Record button (Figure 1-7, top).

Fortunately, you can add the Duplicate button to your toolbar. Choose View→Customize Status Toolbar. You'll see the dialog box that lets you make the Toolbar your own (Figure 1-7, bottom). You can add buttons for other commonly used commands, or delete buttons that you'll never use. The top section of the dialog box shows all the buttons you can add to the toolbar. Don't worry about messing up: To undo your customization, in Windows, choose Toolbars, then highlight Status Toolbar, and then click Reset. On a Mac, the middle section gives you a pristine copy of the default toolbar that you can drag into place to put things back to normal.

The toolbar's default is to show buttons and a bit of helpful text below them. (On a Mac, you can make a selection from the Show pop-up menu to show Icon Only or Text Only instead.)

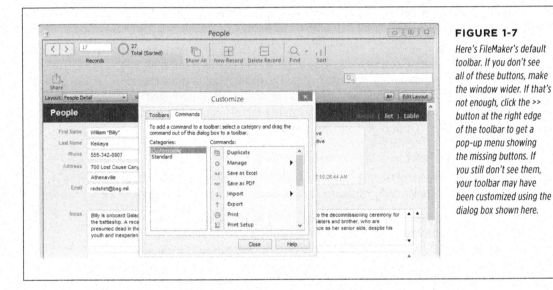

FIGURE 1-7

Here's FileMaker's default toolbar. If you don't see all of these buttons, make the window wider. If that's not enough, click the >> button at the right edge of the toolbar to get a pop-up menu showing the missing buttons. If you still don't see them, your toolbar may have been customized using the dialog box shown here.

Understanding Browse Mode Error Messages

As you just learned in the section on deleting records, FileMaker gives you frequent feedback about what you're doing. The program isn't being a control freak (although after the umpteenth dialog box it's understandable if you feel that way). FileMaker is just trying to keep you informed so you can make good choices. So you sometimes see dialog boxes that FileMaker calls *error messages*. Unlike the Delete warning, you only get once choice: to click OK. That's not a real choice, but you usually have to take some kind of action after you've dismissed the error message.

■ TYPING IN VAIN

If you try typing something *before* you've clicked in a field, FileMaker warns you with the box shown in Figure 1-8. You'll see this same message if you try to type into a database with no records in the found set, or indeed no records at all. It may seem overly protective to warn you that you're not actually entering data, but in this day of multitasking and distractions, it's helpful to know that FileMaker doesn't let your information vanish as you type it.

You'll have to dismiss an error message every time you accidentally bump a key, and you can't get rid of the error message for good. Just remember that you must be viewing an actual record and have your cursor *in* a field before you can start typing. (And take that book off your keyboard, eh?)

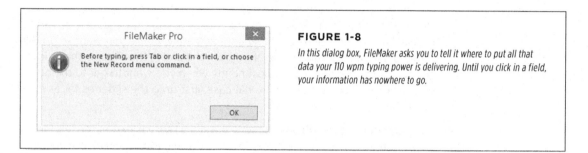

FIGURE 1-8

In this dialog box, FileMaker asks you to tell it where to put all that data your 110 wpm typing power is delivering. Until you click in a field, your information has nowhere to go.

■ Navigating Your Database

Once you've entered a few dozen—or a few hundred—records into your database, the next challenge is to get back to a specific record. But first, you need to learn how to *navigate* through the records in the database. Hint: It's not called Browse mode for nothing, you know. The Status toolbar gives you several tools that help you get where you need to go.

> **NOTE**   As you go through this section on navigating, it helps to have a database open in front of you so you can follow along and try some of these techniques. You can download a sample on this book's Missing CD page at *www.missingmanuals.com/cds/fmp14mm—CH01 People.fmp12*.

Navigating Record by Record

In the People database, or indeed any FileMaker database, you can add as many records as you want. To tell FileMaker which record you want to look at, you have three options:

- The **arrow buttons** let you flip from record to record one at a time. Pretend your database is a number line, and each record is numbered. To get to the next record, click the right arrow. To go back, click the left arrow. If you can't go any further in one direction, the appearance of the button changes, as shown in Figure 1-9.

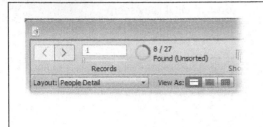

FIGURE 1-9

In addition to displaying the controls for switching records, the Status toolbar indicates where you are in the database. You're looking at the first record in the found set of records. And the pie chart tool tells you that your current found set is showing 8 of the 27 total records in the database. If you click the pie chart, the found set switches to show you the 19 records that aren't in the current found set.

- The **slider** is kind of a turbocharged version of the arrow buttons. Instead of clicking once for each record, you can advance through a bunch of records by dragging the slider. If you know approximately where you want to go (like "around halfway" or "about one-third from the end"), the slider is the quickest way to get there. The slider is most handy when you want to get to the beginning or the end of a database. In that case, just drag the slider as far as it will go in either direction.

- The **Current Record indicator** (above the slider) serves two purposes. First, it shows you which record you're on. Second, if you know which record you *want* to be on, then you can simply type the record number to jump to it. Beside the Current Record, the Found Set display shows you how many records you have in your database.

NOTE All navigation methods let you move within what FileMaker calls a *found set,* which lets you look at a specific set of records at one time. Learn more about finds and found sets on page 44.

Navigating with Keyboard Shortcuts

FileMaker also has a few keyboard shortcuts to make record navigation painless. If you haven't used a database program before, you'll notice that some keys act in ways you may not expect—like the Enter key. Spending a little time getting used to using these keystrokes saves you hours of time down the road:

- To go to the next record, press Ctrl+down arrow.

- To move to the previous record, press Ctrl+up arrow.

NOTE If the up and down arrow keys don't work, check your operating system for custom keystrokes (PC and Mac) or disable the OS X Mission Control arrow keystrokes (Mac only). Both of these settings will override FileMaker's behavior.

Numbers Sometimes Lie

As you create the records in your database, FileMaker numbers each new record as you add it—the record number that appears next to the arrow buttons (see Figure 1-9). You may think that this number is a great way to locate a particular record later: "I need to give Daniel over at Graystone Industries a call to reorder supplies. I put his contact information in record #87. I'll just go to that number." Alas, record numbers are ephemeral and change when you perform a find, add records, delete records, or sort them.

For instance, if you delete the first record in a database, every record below it moves up one slot. Now, what used to be record #2 becomes record #1, what used to be #3 is now #2, and so on. Daniel may have his business sold out from under him before you find his record that way. If you want to assign every record its own number, and have that number stay with the record forever, then you want *serial numbers*. You'll learn all about serial numbers on page 146.

- To activate the Current Record indicator without using the mouse, press Esc. Now type a record number and then press Enter to go to that record. (This shortcut works only when you're not *in* the record; see the box on page 14.)

- Pressing Enter on your keyboard's numeric keypad automatically *commits* the record, rather than inserting a new line in a field, as you may expect based on what the Enter key does in other programs. To insert a new line in FileMaker, press Return.

> **NOTE** Some keyboards don't have a Return key—instead, two keys are labeled Enter. In this case, the Enter key that's near the number keypad commits the record, while the other (normal) Enter key enters a blank line in the field. If you don't have a numeric keyboard—if you're on a laptop or mini keyboard—look for a Function key (labeled "func" or "fn"). Press and hold it while you press the Enter key to commit the record. Apple laptops and compact keyboards have a single Return key. On these devices, hold the fn key while pressing Return.

- Pressing Tab moves you from one field to another. (To indent a line, you have to *type* a tab character into a field, by pressing Ctrl+Tab [Option-Tab].)

Finally, bear in mind that you can change which key moves the cursor on a field-by-field basis, as you'll learn in Chapter 8. For instance, FileMaker lets you decide if Enter—not Tab—should move from field to field. If you make that choice, then Tab types a *tab* into a field, and Enter doesn't commit the record. Unfortunately, you can't tell which key does what by looking at a field; you just have to try some of these keys to find out.

■ Finding Records

When your database really gains some size, you realize that even keyboard shortcuts aren't the fastest way to get to the record you want. You need to *tell* FileMaker to pull up the record for you. For example, you have a season ticket holder whose last name is Adama, who just renewed his subscription for a year. You need to find his record and make the update, and you don't have all day.

If you have hundreds of records in your People database, it could take ages to find the one you want by clicking the arrow buttons. Instead, switch to Find mode, tell FileMaker what you're looking for, and the program finds it for you. This section explains how to use Find mode to search for a record or group of records, and how to edit your search if you don't get the results you anticipated. (If you downloaded the example file discussed on page 4, you can open it and try out Find mode now.)

You can get to Find mode in four ways:

- From the Mode pop-up menu, choose Find.

- Choose View→Find Mode.

- In the Status toolbar, click Find.

- Press Ctrl+F (⌘-F).

The Mode pop-up menu and View menu indicate which mode you're currently in. Once you're in Find mode, your window should look like Figure 1-10. In Find mode, even though it may look like you're editing records, you're actually not—you're editing *requests* instead. Requests are descriptions of data you're looking for, so FileMaker can find them for you.

To make a request, enter enough information to tell FileMaker what you want. It will show you records that have the same information you entered, much like searches you conduct using other programs, like a Google or Bing search.

Performing a Find

To find every person in your People database whose last name is Adama, do the following:

1. **In the sample database** *CH01 People.fmp12,* **choose View→Find Mode (or use any of the other methods described above to get to Find mode).**

   Magnifying glass icons show up in all the fields you can use for searching, indicating that you're in Find mode.

2. **In the Last Name field, type** *Adama.*

   This part works just as in Browse mode: Click the field and then type. (Remember, you aren't editing a record—you're editing a *request.*)

3. **In the Status toolbar, click Perform Find. (Or choose Requests→Perform Find, or press the Enter key.)**

FileMaker finds all records that have "Adama" in the Last Name field and then puts you back in Browse mode so you can scroll through the found set.

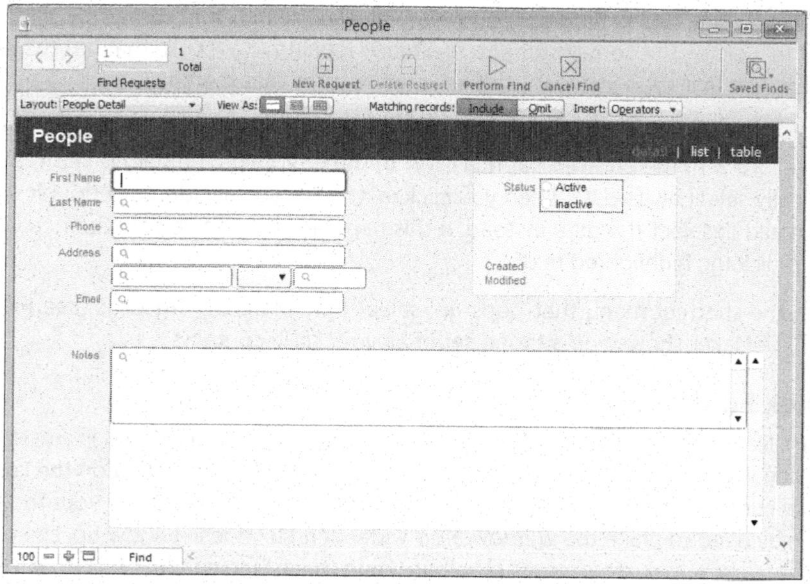

FIGURE 1-10

Because Find mode looks so much like Browse mode, FileMaker gives you lots of feedback about the mode change. Instead of data, the fields show magnifying glass icons to remind you that you're typing search criteria, not new informa-tion. The Status toolbar now has a Perform Find button, and even better, a Saved Finds tool that lets you store frequently used find criteria. That way, you don't have to recreate complicated finds.

You can see how many records you found by looking at the count in the Status toolbar, as shown in Figure 1-11.

FIGURE 1-11

After a find, the Status toolbar shows how many records match your request. Here, FileMaker found two records with the last name Adama. You can flip between these two records to your heart's content, but you can't see any records not in your found set. To see the other records, click the blue ring or choose Records→Show Omitted Only. FileMaker swaps your found set and shows you the other records in your database. Then, when you're ready to look at all your records again, click the Show All button.

TIP If your find didn't come out exactly the way you wanted, don't go right back to Find mode. If you do, then you get an empty request and you have to start all over again. Instead, choose Records→Modify Last Find, which takes you to Find mode and then displays your most recent request. Now you can make any necessary modifications and perform the find again.

Fast Match

In the previous find examples, you had FileMaker search for records by telling it what to look for. But sometimes you're already looking at a record that has the right information in it—you just want to find more records that match.

Say you need a list of everybody in the People file who lives in Caprica City. Flip to any record with the phrase "Caprica City" in the City field. The field is set to automatically select all its data when you click in it, but if you accidentally double-click you could deselect the data instead. If this happens, drag to select "Caprica City." Right-click the highlighted text.

From the shortcut menu that pops up, select Find Matching Records (see Figure 1-12). FileMaker shows you a found set of all your sci-fi contacts.

Quick Find

If Fast Match isn't flexible enough for you, try Quick Find. Quick Find is a text box residing in the Status toolbar that automatically searches every field on the layout you're currently browsing. If you don't see it on the right-hand side of your toolbar, you may need to make the window a bit wider. If it still doesn't show up, see page 16 to learn how to customize your toolbar. Using Quick Find couldn't be easier—click in the box, type a word or phrase, and then press Enter (Return). FileMaker displays a found set of records that contain your search term in any visible field. Click the magnifying glass in the Quick Find box for a list of recent finds. Choose one to perform that find again.

Viewing All Records

After you've performed a find, your found set stays intact until you take some action that changes the found set, like performing another find, or using one of the techniques for omitting records (page 46). To view all your records, choose Records→Show All or click the Show All button in the Status toolbar.

NOTE Each time you perform a Find, FileMaker searches all your records. So there's no need to choose Show All before you do a new find. But you can change FileMaker's native behavior and search *within* a found set. See page 47 to learn how.

Understanding Find Mode Error Messages

Just as it does in Browse mode, FileMaker warns you if something goes wrong when you're trying to find specific records. There are three main types of errors. Read on to see why each one occurs and what you need to do to correct the error.

NO RECORDS MATCH

If FileMaker can't find any records that match your request, you see the message pictured in Figure 1-13. You might see this error if you're looking for a record that doesn't exist in your database, or maybe you've misspelled the search criteria. Click the Cancel button to return to Browse mode, or Modify Find to try again. If you click Modify Find, you end up back in Find mode, with your original search terms showing so you can check your typing or enter new search terms.

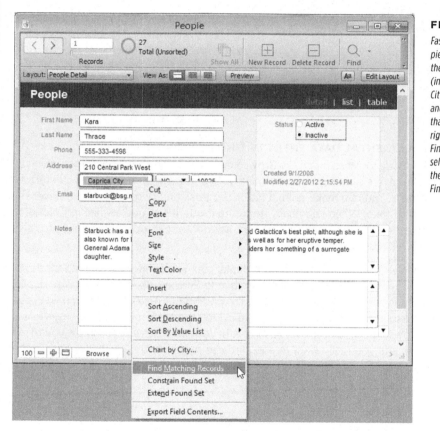

FIGURE 1-12

Fast Match lets you select a piece of information from the record you're viewing (in this case, it's "Caprica City" from the City field) and find all other records that match it without the rigamarole of switching to Find mode. Right-click the selection and then, from the shortcut menu, choose Find Matching Records.

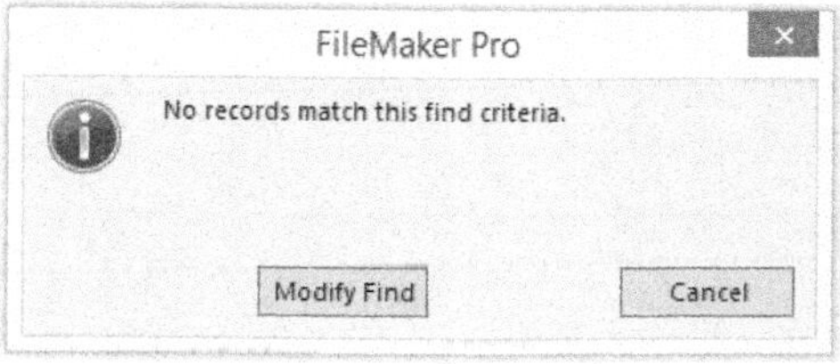

FIGURE 1-13

If FileMaker can't find any records that match what you're looking for, then you see this message. If that's all you needed to know, just click Cancel, and you wind up back in Browse mode as though you'd never performed a find.

■ NO VALID CRITERIA

If you don't type anything into any of the fields before you click Perform Find, File-Maker doesn't try to find records with all empty fields. Instead, it warns you that you didn't enter any search terms. You'll see the message shown in Figure 1-14. Just as with the No Records Match error, you can click Cancel to return to Browse mode, or you can click Modify Find to try again.

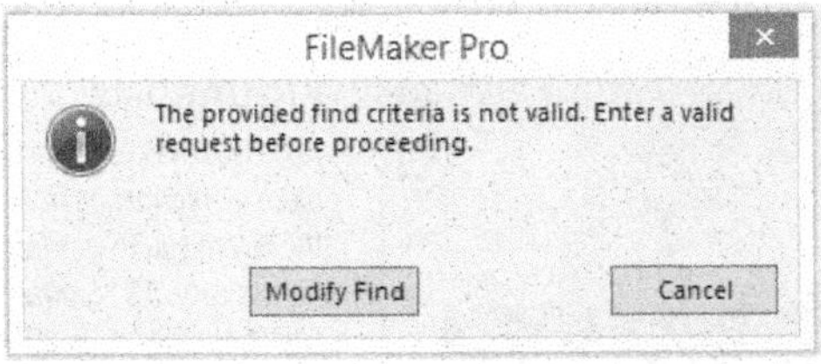

FIGURE 1-14

You see this message if you don't enter search terms in at least one field before you click the Perform Find button. Sometimes, though, you may really want to find records that don't have data in them. In that case, you can enter = in a field. FileMaker finds blank fields, and now you can start entering the missing data in those records. Chapter 2 gives you lots more detail on special search symbols and other tricky finds.

■ ACCIDENTAL DATA ENTRY IN FIND MODE

Find mode looks so much like Browse mode that you can easily forget which mode you're in. It's a real drag if you *think* you're in Browse mode and you start entering data. You can make quite a bit of progress entering records and never realize your mistake. When you finally do figure it out, it's a rude awakening: None of the requests you've just entered can be turned into real records; you have to re-enter them all in Browse mode.

FileMaker gives you a warning if it thinks you're entering data in Find mode. If you create more than 10 find requests while in Find mode, then FileMaker shows the message in Figure 1-15. (At least you're finding out now, not after you've typed for 3 hours.) If you've been entering data in Find mode by mistake, just click No, switch to Browse mode, and then start over with your data entry. If you know you're in Find mode, and you really want to add all these requests, then just click Yes. FileMaker doesn't bother you again.

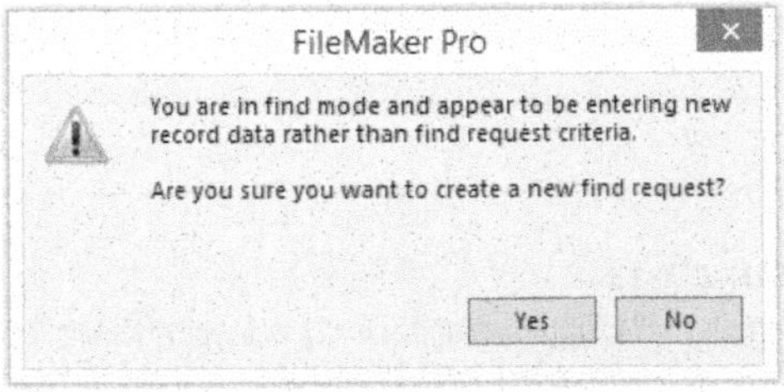

FIGURE 1-15

If you create more than 10 requests in Find Mode, then FileMaker wonders if you're actually trying to enter data. If you're setting up a magnificently complex find, you may be annoyed. Just click Yes and keep up the good work. But if you just forgot to switch back to Browse mode, this warning can save you more lost keystrokes.

Refining Your Finds

When FileMaker looks for records, it expects them to match your find request *exactly*. For example, if you put "William" in the First Name field, and "Adama" in the Last Name field, FileMaker finds only William Adama. William Keikeya doesn't cut it, and neither does Lee Adama. FileMaker ignores any fields that are empty in your request, so it doesn't matter what William's title is, because you didn't type anything into the Title field when setting up your find request.

Finding the right records can be a real balancing act. Be too specific and you may not find anything at all; be too vague and you find more than you can handle. When determining whether or not a given record matches your Find request, FileMaker may be more liberal than you'd expect. The next chapter explains how FileMaker decides when a match is good enough, and how you can change its decision-making process.

Here are some rules of thumb for creating find requests:

- Since FileMaker matches field values flexibly, you can often save typing and improve accuracy by being brief. For example, if you're looking for someone named "Rufus Xavier Sarsaparilla," just type *ruf* in the First Name field and *sar* in the Last Name field. Chances are you'll find the right guy, and you don't have to worry about spelling out the whole name.

- Enter data only in fields you're sure you need. For example, even if you know Rufus lives in Montana, you don't have to put Montana in the State field in your find request.

- If you find more records than you wanted, choose Records→Modify Last Find and enter more specific data in more fields to narrow the search. Better yet, read Chapter 2, where you'll learn about the many powers of Find mode.

■ Sorting Records

Alphabetical order is probably the most common way to sort things, but FileMaker is by no means limited to the good ol' ABCs. You can sort the records in any order you want, as often as you want. You can even do a sort within a sort, as you'll see later in this section.

Understanding Sorting

Don't confuse sorting with finding. When you sort, FileMaker doesn't change the records included in your found set. Instead, it rearranges the records you're viewing into a new order. For example, if you need a short-term loan, you might sort your contacts by annual income. FileMaker still shows the same found set of contacts, but with Uncle Moneybags at the very top of the list.

The process always begins the same way: First, choose Records→Sort Records or click the Sort button in the Status toolbar. You see the Sort Records dialog box shown in Figure 1-16, with all available fields listed on the left. You tell FileMaker how to sort by moving a field to the list on the right.

FileMaker starts out by listing the fields shown on the Current Layout. If the field you want to sort by isn't in the list, then from the pop-up menu above the list, choose the second option. Instead of Current Layout, that option starts with Current Table. (Learn more about tables in Chapter 6.)

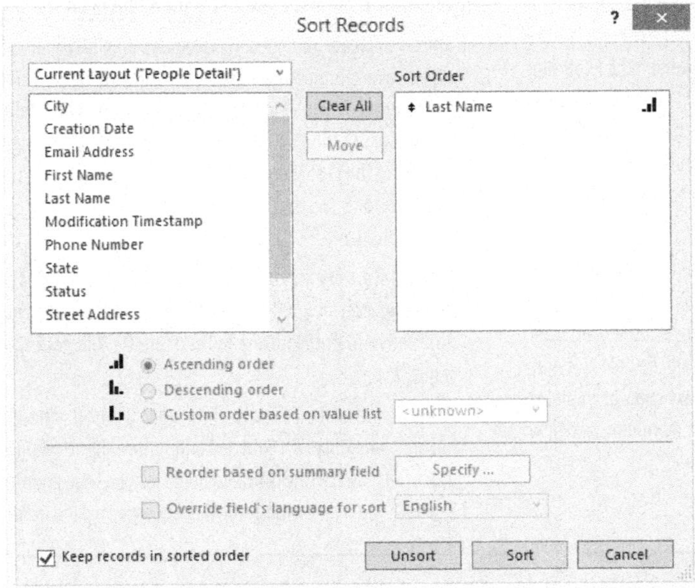

FIGURE 1-16

The Sort Records dialog box has a lot of options, but the two lists on top and the first two radio buttons are critical to every sort you'll ever do in FileMaker. You pick the fields you want to sort by and the order in which they should be sorted and then click Sort. That's the essence of any sort, from the simplest to the most complex.

Here's how to sort your found set of records by Last Name:

1. **In the Status toolbar, click Sort. Or choose Records→Sort Records, or press Ctrl+S (⌘-S).**

   The Sort Records dialog box (Figure 1-16) appears.

2. **From the list on the left, select the Last Name field and then click Move. (Or double-click the field name.)**

   The field name appears in the Sort Order list on the right.

3. **Click Sort.**

   FileMaker sorts the records in the traditional alphabetical-by-last-name order.

You can browse the sorted found set by using any of your favorite navigation methods.

Sort Order

FileMaker figures that if you've sorted your data once, you'll probably want to sort it the same way again, so once you've done a sort, the dialog box retains the last sort order you set up. That's a nice shortcut if you want to repeat the last sort or refine it by adding more fields. But if you want something new, just click Clear All and then start with a clean slate.

FREQUENTLY ASKED QUESTIONS

Feeling Out of Sorts?

When I haven't sorted my records, the Status toolbar says "Unsorted." What order is that, exactly? Is it completely random?

Remain calm. When the records are unsorted, they're in creation order. So the first record you ever created (but haven't deleted yet) comes first, followed by the next one you created, and so on. Creation order is FileMaker's natural order for the records. Once you sort the records, they stay in that order until you sort again or explicitly unsort them. (In the Sort dialog box, use the Unsort button.)

Whew, that's a relief. But if I create a new record while I'm viewing a list that's sorted, I can't always tell where the new record will appear.

Yes, that can be disorienting. The record lands in a different place in the list depending on how your data is sorted. If it's sorted by Last Name only and you duplicate a record with "Adama" in the Last Name field, the new record appears at the end of all the Adama records. But if you have a multisort by Last Name and then by First Name, then the duplicate record appears right after the original. In other words, FileMaker creates the new record *within* the sort order you've chosen. You can avoid this confusion by unsorting your list before you create new records. In that case, they'll appear at the end of the found set, just as you expect.

I've just sorted a found set of records and everything looked fine until I edited the data. My record was number 20 in the sort order, but as soon as I finished editing it, the record jumped to record number 1. What the heck just happened?

If you tell FileMaker to sort the records by Last Name and then edit the last name data in one of your records, FileMaker dutifully puts the edited record into its new position in the sort order when you commit the new record. You'll probably notice a flash as the current record number is updated just above the slider. It's important to remember that you won't get the re-sorting behavior unless you edit the data in one of the fields you've just sorted by.

Alarming as this is when you're looking at one record, it's even more alarming if you're viewing a found set of records in List view. In that case, it may even look like your newly edited record has disappeared because it's changed order so much that it's no longer visible on your screen.

But you're in control. At the bottom of the Sort dialog box (Figure 1-16), there's an option that gives you a break from all the automatic sorting. At the bottom left of the dialog box, turn off the "Keep records in sorted order" checkbox. Now FileMaker won't re-sort your edited records until you ask it to.

Each sort field has an *order* associated with it. Most of the time, you'll choose either "Ascending order" or "Descending order." For numbers, Ascending means from smallest to largest and for text, that's A to Z. The Descending option is the reverse (largest to smallest or Z to A). Once you've selected a field on the left, you can turn on one of these radio buttons *before* you click Move, and the field has the setting by the time it makes it to the Sort Order list. It's OK, though, if you move the field over before you think about the order. In this case, from the Sort Order list, just click to select the field and then pick the order. Each field in the Sort Order list shows a bar chart icon representing the order assigned to it, which matches the icons next to each radio button.

If you change your mind and don't want to sort after all, click Cancel, and FileMaker forgets everything you've done in this window.

The Status toolbar lets you know if your records are sorted (no surprise there). Below the Record Count, it says Sorted if you've done a sort, and Unsorted otherwise.

> **TIP** Once you've done a sort, the Sort dialog box remembers the sort order, so if you forget how the records are sorted, just press Ctrl+S (⌘-S) to check.

Multiple Sort Fields

FileMaker lets you pick more than one field to sort by, which comes in handy when you have lots of records with the same data in some fields. For example, you might often have several people in your database with the same last name. If you just sort by last name, there's no telling in which order the like-named people will fall. In this case, it would be ideal to sort by last name first and then, when the last names are the same, break the tie using the first name.

To set up this scheme, open the Sort dialog box using Records→Sort Records or Ctrl+S (⌘-S) and then add the First Name field to the Sort Order list after the Last Name field. The order in which you list the fields is important: The first field you want to sort by (called the *primary* sort field) has to be at the top of the list, followed by each subsort field in order. In this example, the Last Name field is the primary sort field, followed by First Name. You can see the results of this multiple sort in Figure 1-17. If your sort fields don't appear in the desired order in the Sort dialog box, fret not. FileMaker provides a convenient way to shuffle them around. Drag the double arrow immediately to the left of any field in the sort list to rearrange it as needed.

> **NOTE** If you change your mind about one of the fields in the Sort Order list, click it. The Move button changes to Clear, and a click removes the selected field from the list.

Multifield sorts can get as complicated as you like. Sometimes, they're a little tricky to get right, particularly if you're sorting by more than two or three fields (Figure 1-17 shows a report that uses multiple sorts).

> **NOTE** Sorting records when you're creating a report can change the way FileMaker tallies data. See page 277 for info on creating layout parts that use sorted data to make sophisticated reports.

If you do a multifield sort and then discover you didn't get quite what you expected (because you had the fields in the wrong order), just choose Records→Sort Records again, move the fields in the Sort Order list to the right places, and then click Sort.

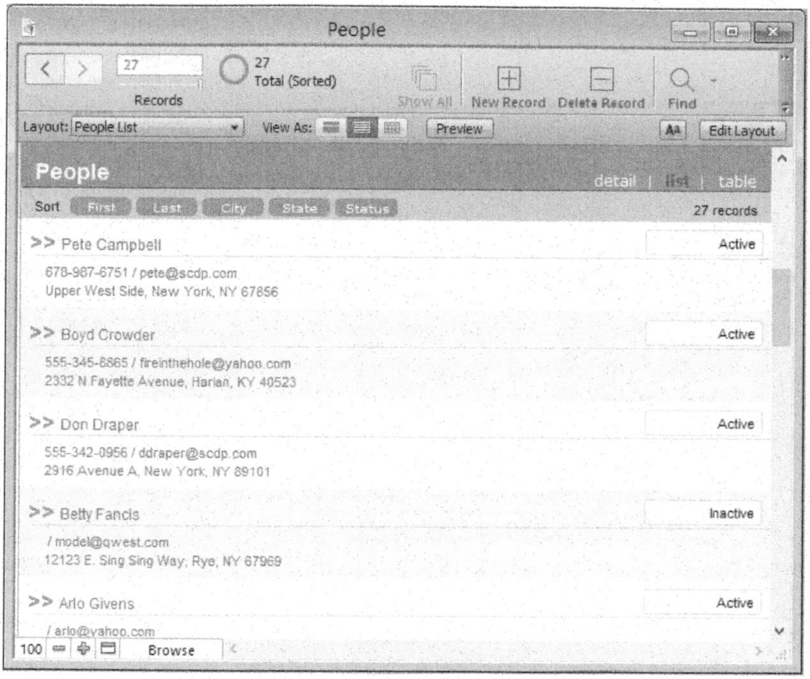

FIGURE 1-17

The records in this window are sorted by Last Name and then First Name. The last names are in alphabetical order, and when several people have the same last name, they appear together, alphabetized by First Name. Check out the first two records, Pete Campbell and Boyd Crowder. The Status toolbar shows you're viewing Sorted (as opposed to Unsorted) records. And a series of custom buttons, labeled First, Last, City, State, and Status, perform two functions. They're a quick way to re-sort your found set, and their display shows you which sort is in effect.

Same Database, Different Views

So far, you've spent all your time in one People window, where you can see either a single record or a list, but not both at the same time. With only one window, you can't compare two records or found sets side by side. This section will show you how to open and manage multiple windows.

Viewing a List

In the People file, you've probably noticed the word "list" near the content area's upper right. Turns out, that's giving you feedback about the data you're currently viewing. If you click the word "detail" (it's written in lowercase letters, because the database developers like it that way), then the scene switches to a detail view of the current record shown in Figure 1-18.

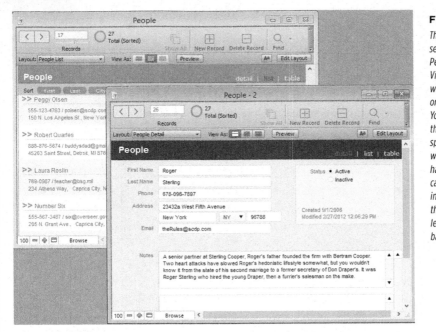

FIGURE 1-18

The back window shows several records in the People database's List View layout. But the window in the front shows one record in detail view. You can also tell that the front window was spawned from the back window because its name has a "-2" added to it. You can flip through records in the front window in their detailed glory and leave your list intact in the background.

Lost in the Wilderness of Sorts

Most databases have *buttons* in their content area (like the Sort buttons in Figure 1-17). These buttons can look like tabs, text links, or just about anything else (a few even look like buttons). Clicking one of these may show you things you're not familiar with—maybe even make you feel like you've lost your place.

To avoid an accidental left turn when you try to commit the record, try not to click a button. Instead click somewhere in the empty white area around the fields.

If you've already clicked a button, and now you're lost in the wilderness, finding your way back doesn't require a trail of breadcrumbs.

Just follow these steps, in order:

- If you see a button in the Status toolbar called Continue, click it. (If you don't see that button, don't worry—just skip to the next step.)

- If the Mode pop-up menu doesn't say Browse, click it and go back to Browse mode.

- In the Status toolbar, beside Layout and under the arrow buttons, you should see a pop-up menu. Use it to return to the database's main layout (People Detail in this case).

You should now be back in your comfort zone. Phew!

NOTE The word you're clicking is called a "button," which is just a tool that you can configure yourself. See page 177 to learn how you can create custom buttons for your database. You can also see the View menu for the menu commands that switch views of your data.

Viewing a Table

Since it's a database, FileMaker has lots of power that spreadsheets don't have. But lots of people prefer to see their data in columns and rows that look like a spreadsheet. That's what the "table" button does. Click the button to view your found set in FileMaker's Table view—and see page 41 for more information on how you can customize this view of your data.

Creating a New Window

You can make another window by choosing Window→New Window. A second window doesn't mean you have a second database—you just have a new view into the one you're already looking at. Your new window is the same size and shape as the original, just offset a little down and to the right. It has the exact same set of records you were browsing, along with the same current record. Now you can switch to another record or do something completely different in the new window, without affecting what's displayed in the first one.

NOTE If your original window is maximized, the new window lands right on top of it, not to the lower right.

Multiple windows are useful when you're working with one set of found records and you need to do another search. You can perform a find in a new window without losing your found set in the original window. Say you've been working with a list of all your contacts who don't have email addresses and then suddenly get the paperwork you need to edit the detail on another record. Although you can enter data on the list layout, all the fields you need may not be on that layout. Just create a new window, switch to the detail layout, and then look up the record you want to edit (see Figure 1-18). Your missing email group is safe and sound in the first window. (See the box on page 32 to see what problems can happen when you edit the same record in multiple windows.)

NOTE If you have two windows open, both of them *are* connected in one way. If you edit the data in one window and the record is visible in another window, the changes show up in the second window (and every other window you have open that shows that same record).

Hiding Windows

If you have a window just the way you want it (for example, showing a list of ad campaigns copywriter Paul Kinsey was assigned to), but it's in your way onscreen, then you can *hide* it instead of closing it. When you *close* a window after using the Find command, your results disappear. Hiding a window makes it disappear from your screen, but FileMaker remembers everything about the window and can pop it back into view instantly. It's a great timesaver when your screen is crowded—or when you want to keep prying eyes away from your information.

To hide the current window (that's the one displayed at the front of your screen), choose Window→Hide Window. To bring it back again, choose Window→Show Window and then, from the list, pick the window you want. If you have several windows open, you'll need to remember the *name* of the window you hid (its name appears in the title bar, across the top of the window).

UP TO SPEED

Record Locking

If you try editing a record in one window while it's showing in another window, then your changes don't appear in the second window as you type. In order for the changes to appear, you have to first commit the record (see the box on page 14). Once you do, the changes appear everywhere else.

Here's a hypothetical example. Suppose you start making changes to Peggy Olsen's contact information in one window, but you're interrupted by a phone call before you finish. To help the caller, you need to look something up in the database. Since you're a savvy FileMaker guru, you make a new window and look it up there so you don't have to lose track of the changes you're making to Peggy's record. (She's taking over all of Paul's campaigns.)

Unfortunately, by the time you finish the phone call, you've forgotten that you already started editing Peggy's record. So you go to Peggy's record *in the new window* to make the changes. Remember that the record is already half-changed but uncommitted in the first window. Which set of changes wins?

To avoid the problem, FileMaker automatically performs *record locking* for you. If you try to edit a record that's already being edited in another window, you see an error message that reads, "This record cannot be modified in this window because it is already being modified in a different window." Yes, it's frustrating to get this message, but just remember that automatic record locking really is your protection against major problems. (This is especially true when you have multiple users accessing your database at the same time—see Chapter 19.) This message is your friend.

NOTE Take care if you use your operating system's built-in features for dealing with windows, like minimizing them to the OS X Dock. These techniques work just fine in FileMaker, but they can play havoc when a FileMaker *script* needs to control the same window. If you're using FileMaker Scripts to automate tasks, as you'll learn about in Chapter 12, it's best to stick to FileMaker's own window commands.

■ CLOSING HIDDEN WINDOWS

You learned earlier in this chapter to close a database by closing all its windows. As with most rules, there's an exception: Even if you close all visible windows, the database itself may still be open—in a hidden window.

The easiest way to close all of FileMaker's open windows, hidden ones included, is to press Alt (Option) and then choose File→Close (File→Close All on Mac). The ordinary Close command closes every window, hidden or not, when you press this key.

Automatically Arranging Windows

Since FileMaker lets you create dozens of windows on your screen at one time, it also provides some commands to help you manage them. From the Window menu, you can choose one of four commands: Tile Horizontally, Tile Vertically, Cascade Windows, or Bring All To Front (Mac only). Each of these commands works on all visible windows (hidden or minimized ones are not affected). You get a lot of action from these commands, but they may not save you a lot of time, as discussed in Figure 1-19.

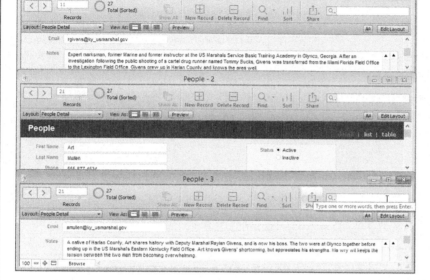

FIGURE 1-19

Each of FileMaker's automatic window arrangements has its limitations. Each uses all available space to decide how to arrange your visible windows. For example, horizontally tiled windows aren't the best use of space, but they can be useful if you have so many windows (shown here) open that you can't remember which one is which (those numbers at the end of the window name tell you what order you created them in).

Auto-arranging is a blunt tool, however, and will move and resize your windows without any regard for a window's content. So use these commands with the understanding that you'll *still* have to do some rearranging yourself. Manually resize your windows or use the square Maximize button (Windows) or the green Zoom button (Mac) to return your windows to their proper size once you've found the one you need.

■ Saving Your Database

Everybody knows it's important to save files early and often. So you're working along in FileMaker entering information about your office birthday roster, and as good habit dictates, you type the keyboard shortcut that saves in practically every program in the known universe (Ctrl+S in Windows and ⌘-S on the Mac). Up pops the wrong dialog box. This one's asking you how you want to sort your data! What's going on?

What's going on is FileMaker doesn't need a keyboard shortcut to save your changes, because every time you commit a record, the program automatically saves all your work in a *cache,* which is part of your computer's RAM (random access memory). Then, periodically, FileMaker transfers the information from the cache to your hard drive, where it's less likely to be lost in case of a crash.

You can control how much work is held in cache before it's saved to your hard drive, as described in Figure 1-20. In Windows, choose Edit→Preferences and then click the Memory tab. On the Mac, choose FileMaker Pro→FileMaker Pro Preferences and then click the Memory tab.

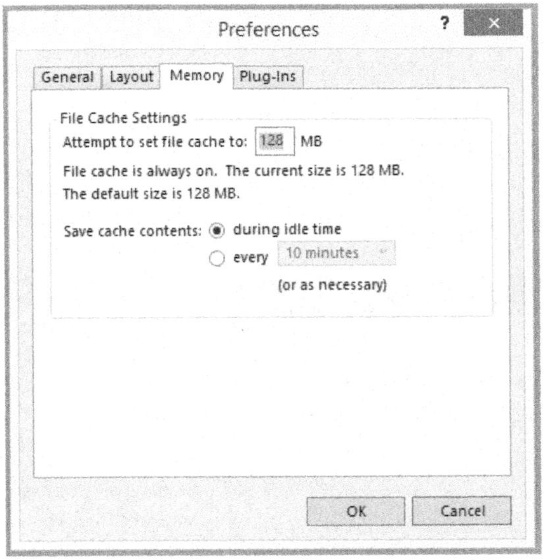

FIGURE 1-20

Specify the size of FileMaker's cache and how often your work is moved from the cache to your hard drive. (Nerds call that "flushing the cache.") A larger cache yields better performance but leaves more data in RAM. If you're working on a laptop, you can conserve battery power by saving cache contents less frequently. But infrequent cache saving comes with some risk: In case of a power outage or other catastrophe, the work that's in the cache is lost for good.

Saving a Copy of Your Database

Although FileMaker automatically saves your work as you go, what if the database file itself gets lost or suffers some digital harm? It's in your best interest to *back up* your database periodically. You can perform a backup by closing all your database's windows and then simply copying the database file. For example, you can copy it to cloud storage, email it to a friend, or duplicate it and tuck the copy away in another folder. When your database is open, the easiest way to make a backup is to choose File→Save a Copy As. In the dialog box that appears, make sure that "copy of current file" is selected as the Type option. When you click Save, FileMaker makes your copy in the background, and you can continue working in the original file.

But if you want to start working in the copy you've just made, select the "Automatically open file" option before you click Save. FileMaker makes the copy of your file and then opens it for you. FileMaker *doesn't* close the original file, so if you're finished with the original, choose it from the Window menu and then close it to avoid confusion. Now only your new copy of the file is open.

If you want to make a copy of your database to email to an associate, choose the "Create email with file as attachment" option. FileMaker copies your file, launches your email program, creates a new email, and then attaches your newly minted file copy to it. All you have to do is provide an email address, type your message, and then click Send. See page 844 to see how you can use similar options if you want to send data to your associate in another format, like a PDF file.

> **NOTE** *Always* make sure a database is *closed* before you copy its file by using any of the desktop methods (like Edit→Copy in Windows Explorer or the Mac's Finder). If you copy a database file while it's open in FileMaker, both the original and the copy may be damaged, lose information, or in the most serious cases, be rendered totally unusable! If you have any doubt about whether your file is still open, check your Window menu for hidden files, or for the ultimate in safety choose Exit (PC) or Quit (Mac) FileMaker.

Saving a Clone of Your Database

Clones are clean copies of your database, but without the data. Clones are really useful, like when you've designed a killer database for running sales in your dart and billiards supply shop, and you want to send the files to all your franchisees without giving away your store's sales data. Just make clones of your files and then give them to your proud new owners. To make a clone, choose File→Save a Copy As, and then make sure "clone (no records)" is selected as the Type option.

■ Using FileMaker's Help Menu

As helpful as this introduction to databases has been, you may want to use FileMaker's onboard help to get more information (Figure 1-21). There you'll find commands for FileMaker's Help application and for online help at FileMaker's website. See Appendix D for more information from those sources, plus help from third parties.

The quickest way to get help, outside of sitting beside a willing guru, is to use the handy search field at the top of the Help menu. To get help, just start typing the subject you need help with. As you type each letter, the Help application changes its menu items to display topics it thinks you may need. When you see the item you need, select it from the menu, and Help appears, showing the page for the term or topic you chose.

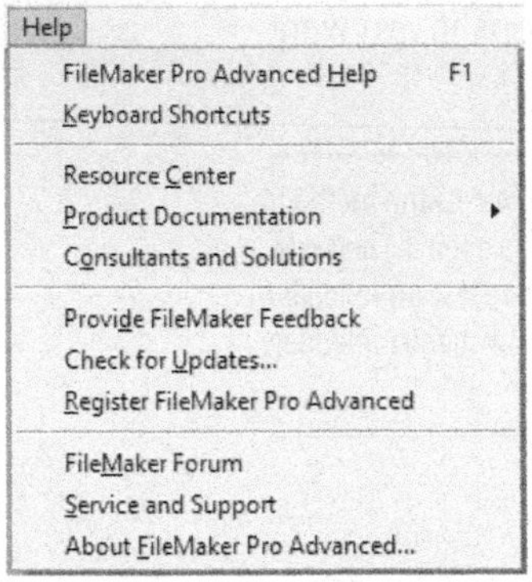

Help	
FileMaker Pro Advanced Help	F1
Keyboard Shortcuts	
Resource Center	
Product Documentation	▶
Consultants and Solutions	
Provide FileMaker Feedback	
Check for Updates...	
Register FileMaker Pro Advanced	
FileMaker Forum	
Service and Support	
About FileMaker Pro Advanced...	

FIGURE 1-21

Here's the Help menu on a Mac in its pristine state, and showing its initial menu items. As you type a search term, FileMaker searches its Help application to create a list of choices that may relate to your search terms.

TIP Printed instruction manuals have gone the way of software that came in boxes. Instead, there's a lengthy PDF document that gets installed along with FileMaker. To check out the instructions that come with the program, choose Help→Product Documentation→User's Guide.

Organizing and Editing Records

So far, you've learned how to use FileMaker's basic tools and get around your database. But you've just begun to scratch the surface of FileMaker's power. Now it's time to learn how to see, sort, move, and shape your information in different ways. For example, you may want to print a list of names and addresses for all the folks in your database who live in the western U.S. In an invoicing database, you may want to find everybody who's ordered 16-pound offset widgets in the last month so you can email them a special offer for widget accessories. In a student database, you may need to print a report of all third-grade students who were involved in lunchroom disciplinary actions during the first semester.

Whatever your needs, you can build on basic techniques to view your data in ever more sophisticated ways. After all, slicing, dicing, and analyzing your data is the whole point of storing the information in a database.

Views

In Chapter 1, you saw a few different ways you can view your data. Now it's time to learn more about these views. The most common way to view and edit records is called *Form view*. In Form view, you work with just one record at a time. In *List view*, you see the same arrangement of your records in, well, a list. If the records don't all fit in the window, you can use the vertical scroll bar to roll through them. *Table view* looks a lot like a spreadsheet, with one row for each record, and one column for each field.

To switch among views in any FileMaker database, use the View menu. Choose View→"View as Form," View→"View as List," or View→"View as Table." You'll see what each view looks like on the following pages.

NOTE The Chapter 1 version of the People database had custom buttons that let you switch views of your data, but that's not the only way to customize the views of your database. You can even turn *off* certain views if you want. For example, if your database holds mostly digital photographs, it wouldn't make sense to look at it in Table view, so you can make sure no one ever sees it that way. (You'll learn how in Chapter 8.) If you can't choose View→"View as List" in the People file you have open, then download the Chapter 2 version of the file from this book's Missing CD page at *www.missingmanuals.com/cds/fmp14mm.*

Form View

In Form view, you see only one record at a time. To see the next record, click the pages of the arrow buttons, press Ctrl+down arrow, or use some other method of switching records (page 17). Most of the database work you did in the first chapter was in Form view, so it should be very familiar by now. You can use Form view when you have a lot of information to see about one record, or when you want to focus on just one record without being distracted by all the others.

TIP The Status toolbar has handy buttons for switching between views. The tools are well designed so you can easily guess which is which, but if you're not sure, just point your mouse to any button to see a tooltip that explains what the tool is for.

List View

List view works *almost* the same as Form view. All the fields are arranged exactly as on a form, but if you stretch or scroll your window, then you see that your records appear one on top of the other, like a long list of forms. You can sort or find data in List view, but since you have more than one record onscreen at once, you need to know which record you're in. You can tell by the thin black line along the left edge of the window at the edge of the active record.

Some people don't like seeing that thin black line because it shifts everything a few pixels to the right to make room. You can turn off the line (it's called the *Current Record Indicator*) by using the Layout Setup dialog box (page 159). But you still need to know which record is active. In that case, you can use a less visually intrusive bit of feedback called *active row state*. You can see it in Figure 2-1. Read about it on page 158.

When you're working with a *group* of records—updating one field in several records or browsing through all your records in search of something—List view comes in handy.

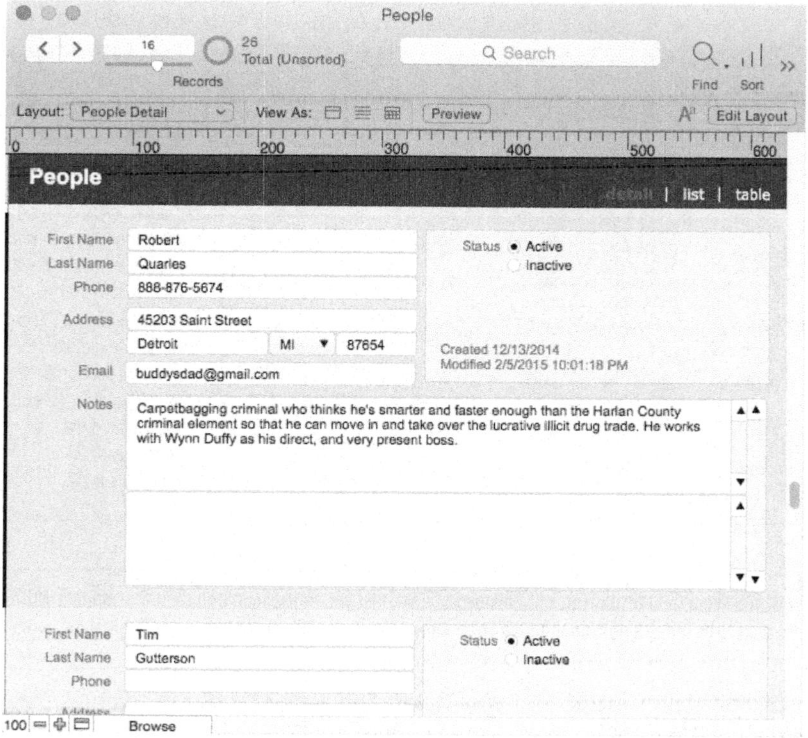

FIGURE 2-1

When you switch to List view, your records look just as they do in Form view, but you can scroll down through them with the scroll bar. The active record (the one your cursor is clicked into) appears in a different color. Just as in Form view, you can click a record's fields to edit information if you need to. Also as in Form view, fields change color when you hover over them or click into them. Though you can see part of the next record here, the People Detail layout doesn't lend itself very well to scrolling vertically. So most databases have special layouts that are designed to show a condensed view of your records in a List view.

Table View

If List view doesn't show enough information, try Table view (Figure 2-2). Like a spreadsheet, it offers a consistent rows-and-columns design, the ability to sort with the click of a button, and the freedom to rearrange columns by dragging them around. You can add, edit, delete, and find records in Table view, just as in the other two views.

When you put your layout into Table view, most of your graphical embellishments disappear from the content area. A few options, like a field's fill color and its attached pop-up value list (page 127), carry over to the new view.

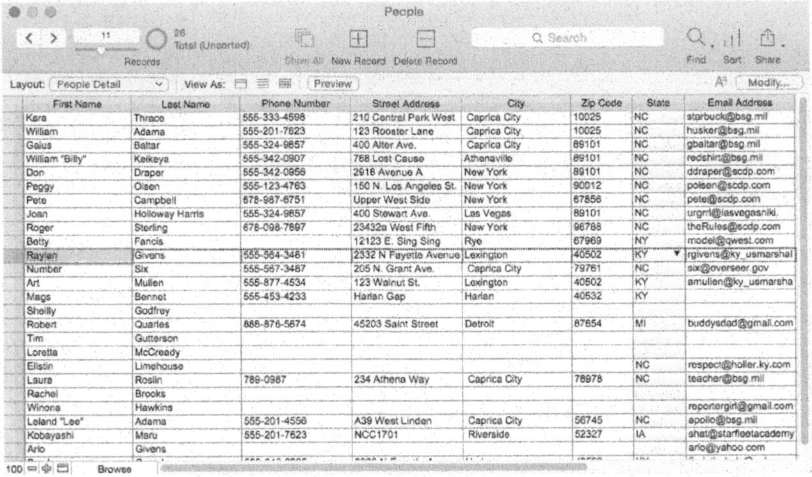

FIGURE 2-2

This database is the same one shown in Figure 2-1, showing the same active record, but this time the layout is in Table view. The field labels are now column heads, showing a small triangle when you hover over them. Click the triangle to see a pop-up menu of commands you can use to sort and summarize your records. Much as with a spreadsheet, you can drag the right edge of each field to change its width.

TIP If you see a field displaying a "?" instead of data, just widen the field and the data appears. Notice that the State field, which has a pop-up menu in Form view, also shows the pop-up menu in Table view.

Each column represents one of your fields, and the order of the columns matches the order you go through the fields when tabbing. For example, the first column is the field you wind up in when you press Tab for the first time. Another Tab takes you to the second column.

REARRANGING COLUMNS IN TABLE VIEW

In Table view, you can move columns around by dragging them. In the following steps, you'll switch the First Name and Last Name columns. For this example, and for the steps in the rest of this chapter, use the sample database *CH02 People Start. fmp12*. The *CH02 People End.fmp12* file shows you how the database will look when you're done.

1. **Point to the words Last Name and then press the mouse button.**

   FileMaker darkens the column header to show you it's selected.

2. **Drag the column to the left of the First Name column.**

   You see a blue line extending from the top of the window to the bottom. This line shows you where the column lands when you let go. All the other columns shift around to make room. In this case, you want the blue line to appear to the left of the First Name column.

3. **Let go of the mouse button.**

FileMaker moves the Last Name column to its new home, shifting the other columns to the right to make room.

The column headings also make it easy to sort your data, but if you use the column headings to sort by Last Name, that doesn't automatically sort the First Name field, too. You can do a multifield sort, but it's a bit tricky. Here's how to do a multifield sort by Last Name and then First Name:

1. **Click the Last Name column head and then Ctrl+click (Windows) or ⌘-click (Mac) on the First Name column head.**

Both columns are selected.

2. **Click the triangle to the right of either column head to display the menu. Then choose Sort Ascending.**

The records are sorted by Last Name, and then, where last names are the same, they're subsorted by First Name.

If you prefer, you can choose the Sort Records dialog box (page 26) instead.

▉ MODIFYING TABLE VIEW

Table view is handy for scanning through a lot of data quickly. It's the only view where the Status toolbar shows a Modify button that lets you customize the view. Out of the box, Table view shows every field you see in Form view, but you may prefer to see less information when you're scanning tables, and you can do that with the Modify button. For example, the Created and Modified fields may not be useful to you in Table view, so you can turn off their display; the fields still show up in Form view, though. Here's how to change the fields you see in Table view:

1. **In the Status toolbar, click Modify.**

The Modify Table View dialog box appears with all the fields from your Form view listed and checked.

2. **Click the checkbox to the left of the fields you don't want to see, like Creation Date and Modification Timestamp, as shown in Figure 2-3.**

In the background, you can see the fields disappear from Table view as you click each one.

3. **Drag the double arrow to the left of a field name to rearrange the columns.**

The columns behind the dialog box move as you rearrange the list.

4. **Click OK when you're done.**

The dialog box disappears, and you're back to an unobstructed Table view.

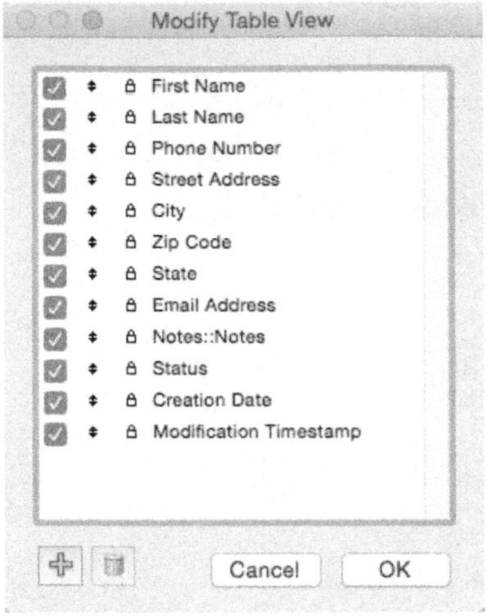

FIGURE 2-3

Modify Table View lets you change the order of your columns. Deselect a field name to keep it from appearing in Table view. There's a Plus button on the lower left that lets you add fields from your table that aren't displayed in Form view. Although it looks like a regular field in Form view, you can see that the Notes::Notes field has an odd-looking name. That's because it comes from a related table. You'll learn about related tables and fields in Chapter 6.

■ MODIFYING TABLE VIEW IN LAYOUT MODE

The Modify Table View dialog box seems powerful, but you can make only a limited set of changes to a layout with it. To see all the changes you can make, you need to tap into Layout Mode. Use the same sample database *CH02 People Start.fmp12* that you've been working in. Here's how:

1. **Choose View→Layout Mode, or press Ctrl+L (⌘-L).**

   FileMaker switches to Layout mode, showing you the structure of your Form view. Although this window is where you usually go to change the way Form view looks, you can also change Table view in this mode.

2. **Choose Layouts→Layout Setup.**

   The Layout Setup dialog box appears. You can ignore all these settings for now, but see page 281 if you want to know what these options do.

3. **Click the Views tab.**

   The Views options appear. If you want to, you can turn off the options for Form and List view so this layout is available only in Table view. But that's not what you're after right now.

4. **Beside the Table view option, click Properties.**

   The Table View Properties dialog box appears (Figure 2-4). Options in this dialog box let you turn off the ability to move or resize columns.

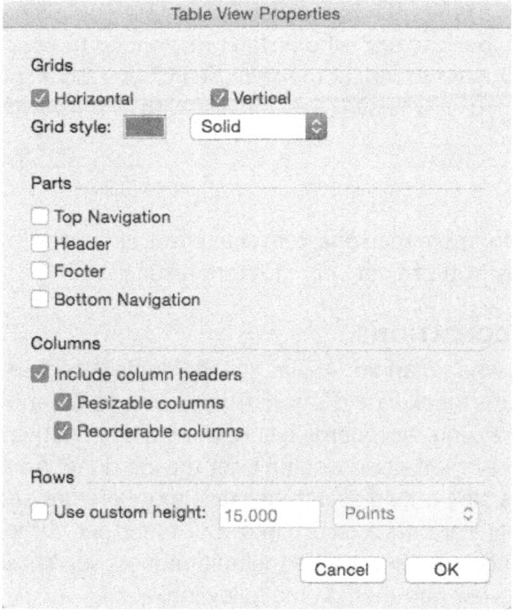

FIGURE 2-4

The Table View Properties dialog box gives you control over how the view looks while you're in Browse mode. Of course, those changes also affect how the screen prints. Switch to Preview Mode to see how the layout will print. You probably need to make changes to the layout to make it print-worthy, so check out the section beginning on page 324 to see how to design a layout for printing.

5. **Turn off the Vertical checkbox.**

   This option removes the lines between each column.

6. **Turn on the "Use custom height" checkbox, and then, in the measurement field, type *25*. If necessary, from the increment pop-up menu, choose Points.**

   This setting makes each table row a little taller.

7. **Click OK to close each dialog box until you're back in Layout mode and then switch to Browse mode.**

   If your layout isn't set to save changes automatically, FileMaker will ask if you want to save the changes you've just made. Confirm that you want to save the changes and you'll see all the changes you made to the table layout.

By controlling the appearance of your different views, you can start to see how much customization power FileMaker gives you over your data in Browse mode. And now that you've gotten your feet wet in Layout mode, be sure to read Chapter 8 to learn how to control the look and behavior of the Form layout itself. Now, though, it's time to learn some sophisticated ways to find specific records.

■ Advanced Find Techniques

In Chapter 1, you learned about using Find mode for simple searches, like finding all the people who live in a certain city (page 22). But often searching in a single field isn't specific enough to give you the records you need. For example, you may want to find people who live outside your city and who haven't responded to your last email campaign. Or you may just need to repeat the same search you did a couple of hours ago. To get what you need, you'll have to be familiar with all the ways you can search your data.

Multiple Requests

You can tell FileMaker to search for more than one item at a time. But depending on how you enter your search terms, you can get very different results.

■ SEARCHING WITH "AND" CONDITIONS

If you want to find every person who's marked "Active" in the People database and who lives in Kentucky, a computer geek would say that you need to do an *AND search*. This term means you're asking for records where the status is Active *and* the State field is KY. Either Active or KY alone wouldn't get the job done. An AND search is more restrictive than a single-field search because more of your search terms have to match before FileMaker puts a record into your found set. Although it's complex to think about, you can easily set up a multiple request search. Start by switching the layout to Form view and then do the following:

1. **Choose View→Find Mode or, in the Status toolbar, click Find.**

   FileMaker opens a new find request.

2. **From the State field pop-up menu, choose KY.**

   You're telling FileMaker to find all records for people who live in the state of Kentucky. That's your first search term.

3. **In the Status field, click to the left of the word *Active* to select it.**

   This second search term narrows the range of matching records. FileMaker knows that it has to show only those records that match *both* search terms you've entered.

4. **In the Status toolbar, click Perform Find.**

   FileMaker shows you the three records that match both your search terms. Click the arrow buttons to flip through the three records. Or switch to Table view to see them all at once.

■ SEARCHING WITH "OR" CONDITIONS

If an AND search is more restrictive than a single criteria search, an OR search is less restrictive. That is, you almost always find more records with an OR search, since a record has to match only *one* of the many search terms you set up in order to get into the found set. To convert the previous example to an OR condition, think of it like this: "I need to find everybody who *either* lives in Kentucky *or* is marked as Active." So your active people who live in Nebraska (or anywhere, for that matter) show up in your found set, as do inactive Kentuckians.

To create an OR condition, you add one small step to the process you just learned. Before you type the second search term, create a new find request by choosing Requests→Add New Request. Notice that the New Request command is the same one that creates a new record when you're in Browse mode. Different modes, different menus, same keyboard shortcut—Ctrl+N (⌘-N). Once you've typed the info for your second request, you can use the arrow buttons to flip back and review or edit the first one. When you're done, click Perform Find.

TIP You can make your search criteria as complicated as you like, with dozens of requests, even mixing AND and OR terms within the same search. Just remember that you put a new term in the same request for an AND condition, and you create a new request for an OR condition.

GEM IN THE ROUGH

Finding Duplicate Records

Every database user eventually makes the mistake of entering the same data twice. Maybe you assume a person isn't in your database and add him, only to discover months later that he was there all along. If you think you've added Joan Holloway to your database twice, you could type *Holloway* in the Last Name field to find out. But if you type *!* there (which finds all duplicate records) instead, you'll find both Joan Holloway records as well as the two Ken Cosgrove records you didn't remember typing. Take care to compare the records carefully, though. The ! operator might also find the record for Claudia Cosgrove, but unless it finds two records for her, she's not duplicated in your database.

If you want to find *whole records* that are exact duplicates, then you have to put *!* in every field when you're in Find mode. But

it isn't at all uncommon for "duplicate" records to be slightly different. Maybe you updated the phone number in one but not the other, for instance.

Maybe you misspelled the street name the first time you entered this person and spelled it right the second time. Finding exact duplicate records doesn't catch these kinds of duplicate records.

If you're looking for duplicate records, it's better to put the ! operator in as few fields as possible. Try to pick fields that tend to be entered the same every time, and stand a good chance of identifying an individual person. You can use just First Name and Last Name, for instance.

Finding by Omitting

FileMaker's normal search behavior is to *include* everything you type in search fields in the found set. You can confirm this fact in Find mode by looking at the Include and Omit buttons in the Status toolbar (Figure 2-5). Every time you start a search, the Include button is automatically selected.

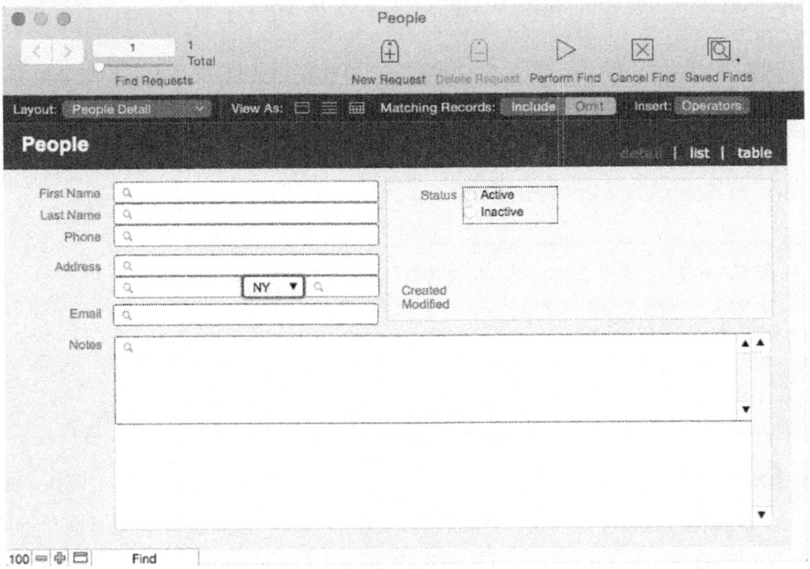

FIGURE 2-5

The Omit button tells File-Maker to do an "unfind." You can see the Omit button near the center of the Status toolbar. And, of course, it appears only when you're in Find mode. In this example, the Omit button tells FileMaker to show you all the records for people who don't live in New York. Once you get used to this inverted logic, you see that it's often easier to create an Omit search than the complicated Include search you may have to come up with if you use FileMaker's normal Include behavior.

The Omit button comes in handy when the records you're looking for can best be described by what they aren't. For example, "Every person who isn't from New York" is a lot easier to say (and to search for) than "Everyone from Alabama, Alaska, Arizona, Arkansas, Colorado...." In this case, you can get what you want by creating one find request, with NY in the State field. Then, before you perform the find, just click the Omit button, which you can see in Figure 2-5. That's all there is to it. When you click Perform Find, FileMaker starts with every record in the table and then omits all the records with NY in the State field, so you're left with everything else.

Refining a Found Set with Omit Commands

FileMaker gives you a few menu commands to help you fine-tune your found set. Sometimes, after you've done the best find request you can, you still end up with a couple of records in the found set that you don't really want to see. FileMaker offers three commands that make tossing out misfit records as easy as pie:

- **Omit Record.** Go to the record you don't want (using the arrow buttons, for example), and then choose Records→Omit Record or use the shortcut Ctrl+T (⌘-T). This one-off command tosses the record out of the found set, reducing your found count by one. Don't confuse it with the Omit button that shows up in the Status toolbar when you're in Find mode, which tells FileMaker to omit all the records that match your find request. The Records→Omit Record command omits just the single record you're sitting on.

- **Omit Multiple.** If you have a whole stretch of records you don't want, then use Records→Omit Multiple. It omits a contiguous group of records from the found set, starting with the current record. For instance, if you want to omit 10 records in a row, then navigate to the *first* record of the 10. Choose Records→Omit Multiple and then, in the dialog box that appears, type *10*. Click Omit, and the job is done. See the box below to learn how to use this option like the pros do.

- **Show Omitted Only.** You can use this option when you're printing two separate lists—one of the New York customers, and one of everyone else, for example. Once you've printed the New York records, your found set happens to be exactly what you *don't* need. Choose Records→Show Omitted Only or click on the blue and gray circle in the status toolbar. This command effectively puts every record that's *not* in the found set into the new found set, and takes every currently found record out. That is, it swaps sets.

TIP You can also use Show Omitted Only if you forgot to use the Omit option in your find request. Instead of going back to Find mode to fix your request, just choose Records→Show Omitted Only, and you get the same effect.

POWER USERS' CLINIC

Over-Omitted

If you're using the Omit Multiple command, and you try to omit more records than possible (for example, you're on the third-to-last record, and you ask FileMaker to omit 12 records), FileMaker complains. But don't take offense: It's also nice enough to fix the problem for you. When you click OK, FileMaker returns you to the Omit dialog box and changes the number you entered to the maximum number possible. You need only to click Omit again to get what you probably wanted in the first place.

Use this feature to your advantage. If you know you're looking at the last record that should be in your found set, you could try

to do the math the dialog box needs. But that's more trouble than it's worth. Just choose Records→Omit Multiple and then enter something really big, like "999," or "9999999." When you click Omit, FileMaker complains, does the math for you, and then enters the right value.

This routine may sound contrived, but it's fairly common among FileMaker pros. Imagine you're doing a direct-mail campaign and you can afford to send only 1,200 postcards. Your find request, however, produces 1,931 potential recipients. Rather than do the math, just go to record 1201 and then use this Omit Multiple trick.

Constraining and Extending the Found Set

When you perform a regular find, FileMaker doesn't start with your current found set. It always searches through all the records in the database and then produces a *new* found set. But you can also tell FileMaker to *constrain* the found set (that is, search within your last find results) or *extend* it (add matching records to the current found set).

■ CONSTRAINING THE FOUND SET

Suppose you've just created a great product, and you want to send out some free samples to see how people like it. You can't afford the shipping charges to send everyone in your database a sample, so you decide to start with a smaller sampling—just people who live in North Carolina.

Problem is, a simple find reveals that your database has too many North Carolinians listed. Some quick math in your head reveals that postage is still too expensive. How about sending samples to just the North Carolinians who are Active? You could go back to Find mode and construct a request to find based on both criteria (by putting NC in the State field and Active in the Status field), but FileMaker gives you an easier way. After all, you've already got all the North Carolinians in your found set. You really want to search *inside* this found set for all the records with Active in the Status field.

Here's how the whole procedure goes:

1. **First, you find all the North Carolinians. Switch to Find mode and, in the State field, choose NC from the pop-up menu, and then click Perform Find.**

   FileMaker shows you a found set of all your North Carolina residents.

2. **Switch back to Find mode (using the Mode menu, for example).**

   Be careful *not* to choose Records→Show All Records, and don't do anything to tamper with the current found set, or else the Constrain search won't work. You're now in Find mode again, ready to enter a request.

NOTE In Find mode, you can't see your current found set. You just have to remember that you last searched for NC in the State field. If you need to see the found set, just switch back to Browse mode and then flip through the records.

3. **In the Status field, select Active.**

   Since the found set already has only North Carolinians in it, you don't need to repeat that information.

4. **Choose Requests→Constrain Found Set.**

   FileMaker searches, but this time it looks only *within* the current found set of North Carolina residents.

At this point, you're probably thinking that Constrain Found Set is just like doing an AND search. In fact, an AND search is usually easier. But sometimes, you don't know all the conditions you need until you do a search and scan through the list of found records. And if you've just done a complex search with seven conditions and tricky spellings, and then you omitted some records manually, you don't want to have to redo all that stuff, so Constrain Found Set saves the day.

NOTE Once you're in Find mode, FileMaker is just itching for you to perform a find. If you press Enter, it assumes you want to abandon your last found set and make a new one. Fortunately, FileMaker remembers more than just your last find request. In Browse mode, click the triangle on the Find button in the status toolbar (on a Mac you can also click and hold the Find button itself) to see a list of your saved and recent finds, and then choose the appropriate item listed under Recent Finds. Faster than you can say "flux capacitor," your old found set is restored and you can try again. See page 53 for a complete description of the Find pop-up menu.

■ EXTENDING THE FOUND SET

Extending the found set works a lot like constraining it. This time, though, you're asking FileMaker to perform a new find (through all records in the database) and then *add* the records it finds into your found set. You end up with all the records you already had, plus any new ones found. Suppose you've already found your North Carolinian folks, and you want all the Kentuckians as well:

1. **In Find mode, in the State field, select KY.**

   So far, you're doing exactly what you'd do in every other find.

2. **Choose Requests→Extend Found Set.**

   This time, FileMaker looks through every record in the database for any Kentucky residents. Each time it finds one, it adds it to your existing found set. When it's done, you have all the North Carolinians *and* Kentuckians in one found set.

Refining Searches with Find Operators

Normally, FileMaker uses a pretty simple rule to decide whether a field's value matches the search term (the *criteria*) you entered: If every search term appears at the *beginning* (matching the first characters) of any word in the field, then FileMaker considers it a match. Techies call this kind of search a *leading-edge search*.

For example, if you put *for* in the Note field in a find request, any of these notes match:

- All for one and one for all.
- We will forever remember.
- Back and forth it went.

On the other hand, neither of these matches:

- Wherefore art thou Romeo?
- Before there was art, there was an artist.

NOTE This match-the-beginning mode of operation may seem odd, but it's surprisingly useful. Imagine you're looking for someone named Giovanni Pierluigi de Palestrina in your database. Of course, you could find the record by typing the full name, but chances are you'll get the same results if you search for *Gio Pal* instead. Since Giovanni starts with Gio and Palestrina starts with Pal, FileMaker finds him with this abbreviated request, saving you from all that typing—and from remembering how to spell the full name.

How do you tell FileMaker that you're seeking the term "for" *wherever* it appears in a word, not just at the beginning? You can use a special *operator*—a character that has special meaning in a Find request—to stand for part of a word.

The Insert Operators pop-up menu, which appears in the Status toolbar when you're in Find mode, lets you add these special characters to your searches, thus gaining more control over FileMaker's decision-making process when it's looking for records (Figure 2-6).

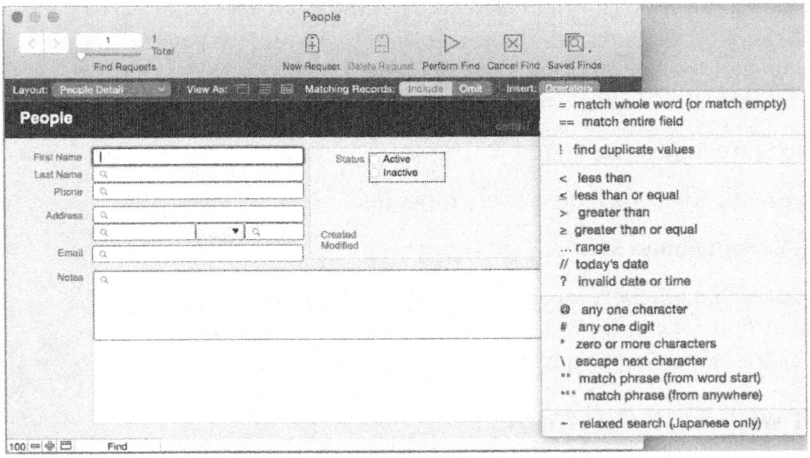

FIGURE 2-6

Sometimes a simple search won't get the job done, so FileMaker gives you special operators for dialing in your search. Enter Find mode, then click the Operators pop-up menu on the right end of the toolbar (widen the window if you don't see it). To use an operator, click in the field you want to search, choose the proper operator, and finish adding your criteria by typing it into the field after the operator.

▓ MATCH WHOLE WORD (=), MATCH PHRASE (""), AND MATCH ENTIRE FIELD (= =)

The rule FileMaker uses automatically for determining a match is pretty loose. But sometimes you want exactly what you say: "Smith," not "Smithers" or "Smithey" or "Smithsonian." In this case, use the Match Whole Word operator (=). In this example, type *=Smith* in the Last Name field and then perform your find.

If you want to exactly match *more* than one word, put the words in quotes. This Match Phrase capability is also good for criteria that contain punctuation, like "Mr. Smith."

NOTE Like French fries, quote marks come in two varieties: curly and straight. The curly type are usually used for typesetting, and they're preferred for printed material like letters or electronic communications like email. But for measurements (feet/inches or minutes/seconds) straight quotes are preferred. Unless you're exporting FileMaker data to be used as code (as for some types of web programming), the type of quote usually doesn't matter. But FileMaker lets you turn on *smart quotes*, which are the curly kind that know whether they should be right- or left-facing. Choose File→Options and then click the Text tab to find the smart quotes option.

For the ultimate in specificity, use the Match Entire Field operator (==) instead. Match Whole Word requires that each *word* in your criteria match one or more words in the field. Match Phrase seeks to match only what's in the quotes *anywhere* in the field. Match Entire Field insists that the entire field matches the criteria text exactly. For example, *=Smith* matches "Smith," "Mr. Smith," and "Smith-Johnson." However, *==Smith* matches only "Smith" in the field and nothing else.

> **NOTE** Match Phrase doesn't actually match text *anywhere* in the field. The criteria text has to match starting at the beginning of a word. For instance, a search for "Mr. Smith" matches "Mr. Smith" and "Mr. Smithers," but if you search for *"r. Smith"* (no M) instead, then you get the "no matches found" error. To match a phrase anywhere in the field, use the * operator.

Use the "=" operator to find records that don't have data in them. If you need to find all the records with missing email addresses, just type = in the Email field.

▨ FIND DUPLICATE VALUES (!)

When you put *!* in a field in Find mode, FileMaker finds records with *duplicate data* in that field. In other words, it shows only the records that match at least one other record. If you have only *one* person in your database with the Zip code 90012, and you perform a find with *!* in the Zip Code field, then the 90012 person won't appear. That's because "90012" doesn't match any other record in the database. On the other hand, if you have two people with Zip code 10025 and four with Zip code 89101, they'll *all* be found because they all have duplicates (each record has at least one other like it). To figure out what's going on, sort your database by the Zip Code field and then switch to List view. Then you can more easily compare the duplicates with one another.

Unlike most other operators, the ! operator is always used alone in a field in Find mode. You never put *! Smith* in the Last Name field. Instead, you just put *!* all by itself. See the box on page 53 for more on finding duplicate records.

▨ LESS THAN (<), LESS THAN OR EQUAL (≤), GREATER THAN (>), AND GREATER THAN OR EQUAL (≥)

These operators tell FileMaker to use your criteria as a maximum or minimum rather than a direct match. For example, the criteria *<David* finds every person whose name comes before David alphabetically. *≤David* is just about the same, but it includes anyone named David as well.

People use these operators more frequently to find numeric or date information rather than text. For example, *<10* in a number field finds real numbers less than 10 (like 9). FileMaker performs the correct function with dates and times as well, in which case Less Than means *before* and Greater Than means *after*.

▨ RANGE (...)

The Range operator is like the "Greater Than or Equal To" and "Less Than or Equal To" operators combined. The criteria "5/22/2016...12/22/2016" matches those two dates and everything in between. Just like the other operators, the Range operator is smart enough to understand numbers, dates, and times, as long as the field contains that kind of data.

■ TODAY'S DATE (//) AND INVALID DATE OR TIME (?)

Like the ! operator, these operators can go in a field in Find mode all by themselves. The double slash is convenient shorthand for the current date. If you're looking for all the payments due today, you can type // in the Due field more quickly than "July 15, 2016" or even 7/15/2016.

The Invalid Date or Time operator (?) helps when it comes time to clean house. It's possible to end up with the wrong kind of data in fields that are supposed to hold dates or times (like "N/A," "Never," or "Next Week"). Put ? in the Due field, and FileMaker finds every payment whose due date isn't valid, giving you an opportunity to fix them.

> **NOTE** You can mix and match these operators in combination, as long as they make sense. For example, to find everything after today's date, just search for >// instead of >11/7/2016.

■ ZERO OR MORE CHARACTERS (*)

The * operator—popularly called the *wildcard*—stands for "anything." It tells FileMaker that you don't mind whether there's something *right before or right after* the search term. If you type *for*, FileMaker finds records that contain "therefore," "before," "George Foreman," and so on.

■ ANY ONE CHARACTER (@) AND ANY ONE DIGIT (#)

If the wildcard operator is too loose for your needs, you can instead permit just one character (letter, number, or punctuation) with the Any One Character (@) operator. When matching numbers, you can be even more specific, permitting just one numerical digit with the Any One Digit (#) operator. Here are a few examples:

- *smith* matches "Smith," "blacksmith," "Smithsonian," and "blacksmiths"

- *smith matches "Smith" and "blacksmith," but not "blacksmiths" or "Smithsonian"

- smith@ matches "smithy" but not "Smith" or "smithers"

- @*smith matches "blacksmith" but not "Smith" or "blacksmiths"

- smith# matches "smith1" but not "smithy"

Finding Special Characters

How do I find ddraper@scdp.com when "@" means something special?

The @ symbol is one of 17 special *operators* in FileMaker. The operators change the character of a search term to make your find more or less precise. If what you're actually looking for includes one of these special operators, you need to take extra precautions. When searching for *ddraper@scdp.com*, the @ operator matches any letter, number, or punctuation

mark. But the @ in the email address is none of these, so the search doesn't work.

To prevent FileMaker from interpreting the @ as a special character, use the Match Phrase operators described on page 50. In other words, putting the search text in quotes ("*ddraper@scdp. com*") does the trick. You could also search for *ddraper scdp*, since FileMaker sees these as two separate words.

NOTE As discussed at the start of this section, when you do a Find, FileMaker matches the *beginning* of a word in the field. Adding wildcard operators to your search changes the behavior to allow a search anywhere in any word. But pay attention: You might expect **smith* to match "blacksmiths." But it doesn't, because FileMaker excludes words that have characters after your search term.

■ RELAXED SEARCH (~)

The last operator, called Relaxed Search (~) applies only to searching Japanese language text. It instructs FileMaker to consider characters to match if they make the same sound, even if they aren't exactly the same character. Alas, in English, spelling always counts (you can't expect "~phat" to match "fat").

Modify Last Find

FileMaker always keeps track of your most recent find criteria, even If it's been a while since you did the search. So if you have to run another copy of your last report, or you just need to see if any new records match since the last time you did the find, all you have to do is choose Records→Modify Last Find. FileMaker does the equivalent of entering Find mode and typing in your find criteria. You can edit the criteria if you want, or just click Perform Find, and you're done.

Modify Last Find (Ctrl+R or ⌘-R) isn't just a speedy way to recreate a find, though. You may have a found set of records, but you can't remember the search criteria. Choose Modify Last Find and you'll be looking at them. Then you can click the Cancel Find and you're right back in your found set.

Using the Find Pop-Up Menu

Once you've figured out how to create the complex find to get that end-of-month report showing, say, all females in a 10–Zip code range who've emailed you, but who haven't made a purchase in the last quarter, you can use the Find pop-up menu (Figure 2-7) to recreate that find if you need it again. If you've done the find recently (within your last 10 finds), then it appears in this menu. Plus, you see another way to access the Modify Last Find command. Best of all, Save Current Find lets you save as many frequently used finds as you need.

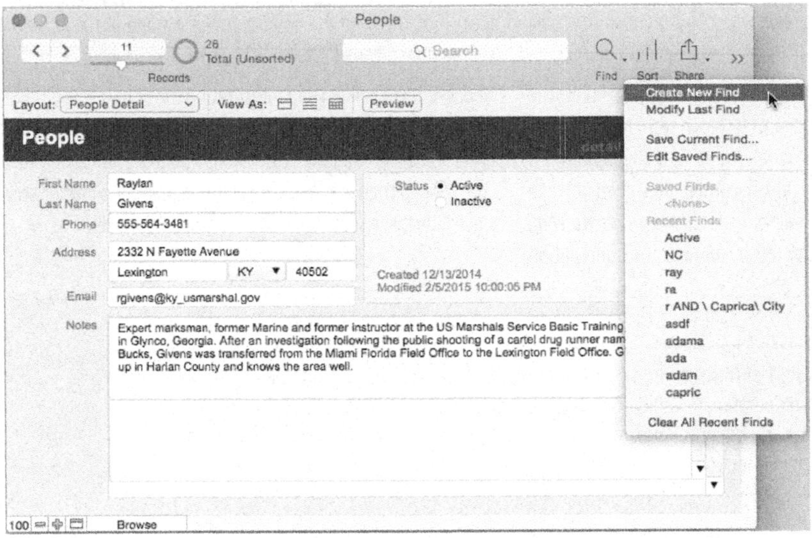

FIGURE 2-7

The Find pop-up menu appears when you click and hold on the Find icon. The menu gives you an easy way to manage finds that you have to perform repeatedly. The Recent Finds section shows the search criteria used, but not the fields into which they were entered. You have to rely on your memory for the fields the search refers to. If you can't recall, the Clear All Recent Finds command lets you start from scratch.

SAVING FINDS

When you perform a find, FileMaker remembers the criteria you set. To get started, search for all Zip codes that start with either "10" or "89" (see page 44 for help creating an OR condition search). Then follow these steps:

1. **In the Status toolbar, click the Find icon, and keep the mouse button pressed.**

   A pop-up menu appears, with the Find you just performed at the top of the menu's Recent Finds section.

2. **Choose Save Current Find.**

   The Specify Options for the Saved Find dialog box appears. FileMaker suggests a name for your saved find.

3. **In the Name field, type *Target Zip Codes.***

   Type a name to help you remember what the find does. Consider putting the field you're searching somewhere in the name. You have 100 characters to work with, but a lengthy name can make the menu unwieldy.

4. **Click Save.**

   Open the Find pop-up menu again, and you see the saved find.

Now you can test the new find by choosing it from the pop-up menu. FileMaker does all the work: It enters Find mode, enters the search criteria, and then performs the find. You can also enter Find mode and then, from the Saved Finds pop-up menu, choose a saved find. In that case, though, FileMaker enters your criteria, but you have to click Perform Find. Using this method, you can create a find that's slightly different from the saved version—just edit the request any way you like before clicking Perform Find.

NOTE Saved Finds are specific to a database, and to a single user account in each file. To see your saved finds, log in with the account under which you created the finds. Chapter 19 tells you about accounts and privileges.

■ EDITING SAVED FINDS

If you have a saved find that needs tweaking—maybe the end of the month report needs to include a new set of Zip codes from now on, or maybe you just made a mistake when you set it up—use Edit Saved Finds. You can choose the command from the Find pop-up menu or by choosing Records→Saved Finds→Edit Saved Finds (Figure 2-8). Either way, you see a dialog box that shows you all your saved finds and lets you create a new find without performing it first. You can also delete or edit finds.

To edit a saved find:

1. **From the Saved Finds pop-up menu, choose Edit Saved Finds.**

   The Edit Saved Finds dialog box appears (Figure 2-8).

2. **Click the Target Zip Codes find.**

   The selected find appears highlighted, and the Edit button becomes active.

3. **Click Edit. Or you can double-click the Zip Code find or press Enter.**

   Whichever method you use, the Specify Options for the Saved Find dialog box appears. If you're changing the action of the find, it makes sense to change its name. In this case, though, you're just adding a new Zip code to an existing find, so leave the name the same.

4. **Click the Advanced button.**

   The Specify Find Requests dialog box appears. The actions that create the find requests are in a list.

5. **Click the New button.**

   The Edit Find Request dialog box appears.

6. **Scroll through the list of fields near the bottom left of the window until you see the Zip Code field. Or click in the list and type z to automatically scroll the list. Click the Zip Code field to select it.**

   You're telling FileMaker to search the Zip Code field.

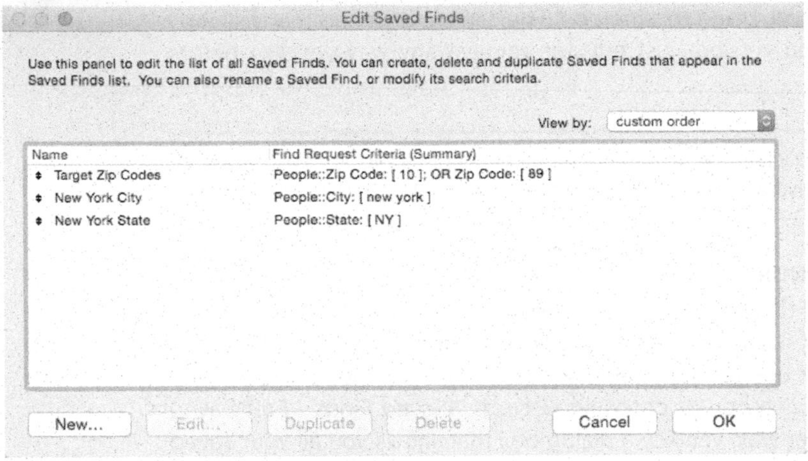

FIGURE 2-8

The Edit Saved Finds dialog box shows all your saved finds. You can sort the list with the "View by" pop-up menu. You can sort alphabetically by name, by creation order, or in a custom order, by dragging the arrow to the left of each find's name. Use the Duplicate button as a starting point for creating a new find that's similar to one you've already saved. The Delete button cleans up finds you won't be using anymore.

7. **Click into the box on the right marked Criteria and then type *40*.**

   You've entered the second part of the new request, which is to search the field for the Zip codes beginning with "40." See Figure 2-9 for the settings.

8. **Click Add and then click OK or Save in all the dialog boxes until you're back on your People Detail layout.**

   If you click Cancel on the last dialog box, then FileMaker warns you that all your changes will be discarded. Use this option when you're not sure if your settings are correct. Since the Delete button doesn't warn you before it deletes a find request or a saved find, you can use this technique as a fail-safe. When you click Cancel, FileMaker discards all the changes you made while the dialog box was open.

   Try out the edited search by choosing it from the Find pop-up menu or by choosing Records→Saved Finds→Target Zip Codes. This process involves a lot of steps, but once you understand the Edit Find Request dialog box, the process is easy. You can use a slight variation to create a new saved find without performing it first. Just choose Edit Saved Finds and then click New instead of selecting an existing find and editing it.

   TIP Practicing creating finds from scratch comes in handy when you start scripting static finds (page 516). Several find script steps use the Specify Find Requests and Edit Find Request dialog boxes you've just seen.

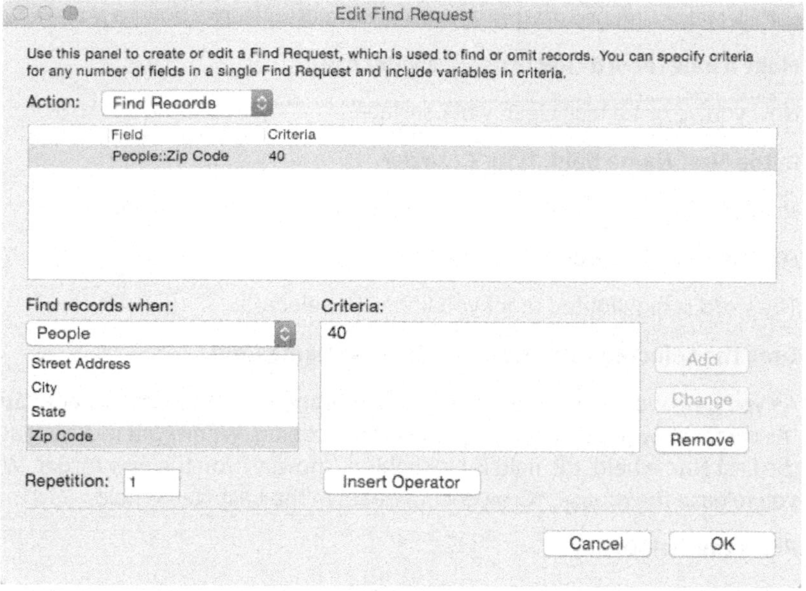

FIGURE 2-9

This dialog box lets you specify which field to search and what to look for. This request will search for "40" in the Zip Code field. The Action pop-up menu lets you choose between Find Records and Omit Records. In a single request, you can search more than one field, which is like setting up an AND condition in Find mode. Multiple requests within a single find are the same as an OR condition in Find mode.

■ Editing the Contents of Your Fields

Once you've found the records you want to work on, it's time to learn time-saving and creative ways to revise and format your record text. Each field is actually like a mini word processor, with features that you're familiar with if you've ever written a letter on a computer. You can do basic things like select text and cut, copy, and paste. You even have a Find and Replace feature, and flexible text-formatting powers.

Drag-and-Drop Editing

In addition to copying and pasting, you can drag text from one place to another. But first, you have to turn that feature on in FileMaker's preferences, like so:

1. **In Windows, choose Edit→Preferences. On a Mac, choose FileMaker Pro→Preferences.**

   The Preferences dialog box appears.

2. **From the General tab, select "Allow drag and drop text selection."**

   If you find that drag-and-drop doesn't suit you, just come back here and turn it off.

3. **Click OK.**

The dialog box disappears.

This setting changes the way FileMaker behaves. Any database you open in your copy of FileMaker can use drag-and-drop editing now. Here's how to make it work:

1. **Make a new record (Records→New Record).**

Now you've got a nice clean work surface.

2. **In the First Name field, type *Crowder*.**

Next you'll drag the text to the Last Name field, where it belongs.

3. **Double-click the word "Crowder."**

The word is highlighted to let you know it's selected.

4. **Drag the selected word down to the Last Name field.**

As you drag, you won't see the text you're dragging, but a + badge appears on the cursor showing that you have something copied. When your mouse reaches the Last Name field, the field is highlighted, showing you the new target. When you release the mouse, "Crowder" appears in the Last Name field.

5. **Press the Delete key.**

The text in the First Name field is still highlighted when you release the mouse, and that's what disappears.

You can also drag and drop text within the same field, say if you want to rearrange the words you've typed into your Notes field. In that case, though, the text isn't copied, it's moved, so there's no need to delete the original text. If your whole layout doesn't fit in your window, it will scroll as you drag. Just make sure you don't release the mouse until you see the place you want to drag your text to.

TIP If you want to copy your text when dragging *within* a field, then hold down the Ctrl (Option) key while you drag. You'll see the "+" that indicates your text is being copied and not moved.

Using the Replace Command

Sometimes the whole reason you performed a find is to change something in several records. Maybe you just noticed that your data entry person put a few spaces before "Caprica City" on all the records she entered. The first step to fixing them is to *find* them. Once your found set includes the proper records, you could change the City field one record at a time (especially if you're billing by the hour). But you use your time better if you use the Replace Field Contents command. Here's how it works:

1. **Click the City field (it doesn't matter which record), and delete the extra spaces in the city's name.**

You've just fixed one of the records. All the others in the found set need the same fix. (Make sure your cursor is still in the City field, or the next step won't work.)

2. **Choose Records→Replace Field Contents.**

The Replace Field Contents dialog box appears (Figure 2-10). It has a handful of options that may not make sense to you yet. That's OK; just choose the first one: "Replace with." The corrected data is listed beside this option.

3. **Click Replace.**

FileMaker now updates the City field in *every record in the found set*. When it's done, you're still sitting on the same record, but if you use the arrow buttons to click through the records, then you see that they've all been changed.

WARNING   The Replace Field Contents command can be very dangerous. It really does change every record in the found set, even if that wasn't your intent. Make *sure* you have the right found set before clicking Replace, because you can't use the Undo command afterward. Saving a backup copy of your database just *before* using Replace Field Contents is advisable.

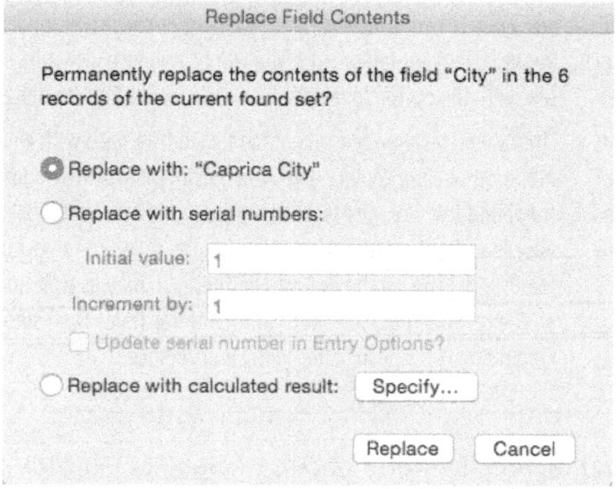

FIGURE 2-10

The Replace Field Contents dialog box has three options: "Replace with," "Replace with serial numbers," and "Replace with calculated result." You're concerned only with the first option right now. It replaces the contents of the current field in every record in the found set with whatever is in the current record when you click Replace. So, in the current record, type what you want to be in every record before you call up this dialog box. (You'll learn about serial numbers in Chapter 5 and calculations in Chapter 10.)

Find and Replace

FileMaker fields can hold a lot of information, and people often put things like letters, email messages, product descriptions, and other potentially long documents into fields. In cases like this, the Find/Replace command (Edit→Find/Replace) is just as useful as it is in your word processing program.

Suppose one of your clients is called MegaBank. For one reason or another, they decide to change their name to Bay Lout Bank. Unfortunately, you have 27 folks in your database with the old name, and the name is sprinkled in Company Name fields, Notes fields, and so on. You could look through your records one by one and fix them yourself, but you're never going to become a database maestro that way. Instead, do a Find/Replace operation.

Find with Replace vs. Find/Replace

You may be wondering how Find mode combined with Replace Field Contents is different from Find/Replace. In fact, they're very different, but deciding which to use can be confusing. Here are some guidelines:

- Find mode is significantly faster at finding things than Find/Replace. In Find mode, FileMaker uses the field's *index* (page 260), which lets it find the matching records quickly. Find/Replace, on the other hand, looks through the fields the same way you would: one by one. It's faster than you, but it still takes time.

- Replace Field Contents always operates on one field across the entire found set. Find/Replace, on the other hand, also lets you replace across all fields in just the current record, as well as all fields in all records of the found set.

- Replace Field Contents always replaces the *entire* contents of the field. You can't replace every occurrence of "teh" with "the," for example, without using a carefully crafted and tested calculation (page 383). You can only give a new value that replaces everything in the field.

- Most important, Replace Field Contents assumes you've already found the records you want, and always modifies every record in the found set. Find/Replace adds a second layer of searching, as it scours the record or the found set looking for matches.

So why would you ever use Replace Field Contents? Sometimes you really do want to replace everything in the field, just like in the City example on page 58. Also, Replace Field Contents is *significantly* faster at changing lots of records than Find/Replace. It takes just a few seconds to accomplish what Find/Replace would spend several minutes doing.

In general, if you want to find records, use Find mode, but if you want to find certain bits of text, use Find/Replace. Likewise, if you want to replace everything in a field in *every* record, use Replace Field Contents, but if you want to replace little bits of text with the option to review each change, use Find/Replace.

Finally, you have no reason not to mix Find/Replace with Find mode. Since Find/Replace gives you the option to search in just the found set, you can establish a good found set *first* to make your Find/Replace go faster. For example, if you're replacing "teh" with "the" in the Notes field, then you may as well find all the records that have "teh" in their Notes fields first, since Find mode is so much faster than Find/Replace.

Since FileMaker has fields and records to worry about, though, its Find/Replace dialog box is a little more complicated than what you may be familiar with. Luckily, the concepts are simple, as shown in Figure 2-11. The Find/Replace dialog box lets you search for a snippet of text in one field or all fields of one record or all found records. It can also replace every occurrence of that text with something new—either one at a time, or all at once.

NOTE Don't confuse Find/Replace with Find mode. Find/Replace is for finding *specific characters* in one or more fields and one or more records. Find mode is for finding *records*. You'll probably use Find mode much more often than Find/Replace. For the full story, see the box above.

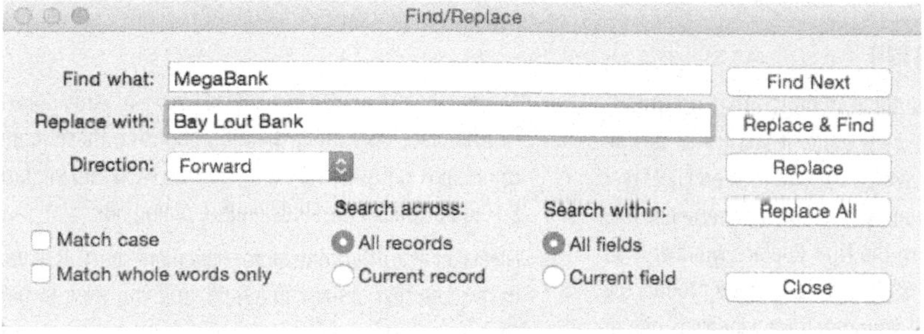

FIGURE 2-11

If you wish to find without replacing anything, just don't click any of the Replace buttons. The text you're looking for goes in the "Find what" text box. If you're replacing it with something new, type that text in the "Replace with" text box. (If you want to clear the text, leave the "Replace with" box empty.)

Here's FileMaker's version of Find and Replace:

1. **Choose Edit→Find/Replace→Find/Replace.**

   The Find/Replace dialog box opens, as shown in Figure 2-11.

TIP Turning on "Match case" ensures that FileMaker looks for an exact uppercase and lowercase match. For example, when "Match case" is turned on, "Kite" and "kite" don't come up as a match. If you turn on "Match whole words only," FileMaker eliminates partial word matches. For example, "Drag" matches "Drag" but not "Dragon."

---

2. **Under "Search across," select "All records."**

   You've just told FileMaker you want it to look through all the records in the found set.

3. **Under "Search within," select "Current field."**

   "Current field" refers to the field you were editing when you opened the Find/Replace dialog box. If you weren't clicked into a field when you opened the dialog box, FileMaker still lets you select the "Current field" option, but it complains when you start the find, so if you want to search a specific field, close the dialog box, click in your intended field, and then reopen the dialog box. You can select any combination of "Search across" and "Search within." Here's how that shakes out:

UP TO SPEED

Find and Find Again

Unlike the Find/Replace window in most other programs, FileMaker's doesn't politely step aside. If you try to click in your database window to switch back to it, then FileMaker just beeps at you. In fact, you can't do *anything else* but find and replace unless you close the Find/Replace window first. You can always move the Find/Replace window around the screen by dragging it, but if your database window is big, or your screen is small, the Find/Replace window can really get in the way, keeping the very results it's finding hidden behind it. Here are a few pointers to help you cope:

- Make sure the Find/Replace window is as small as possible by dragging the resize handle in the lower-right corner. Like most windows, it's resizable, but its smallest size is almost always big enough.

- If you close the Find/Replace window (click Close or press Esc), then FileMaker keeps the last-found item highlighted. Since FileMaker remembers all your settings, you can always open the Find/Replace window again and then continue searching where you left off.

- Wouldn't it be great if you could click the buttons in the Find/Replace window without having it open onscreen? Fact is, you can. In the Edit→Find/Replace menu, you see two handy commands: Find Again and Replace & Find

Again. (They're grayed out unless you've already done a Find/Replace operation, though.) Choosing these menu commands is just like clicking the Find Next and Replace & Find buttons in the Find/Replace dialog box.

- FileMaker also offers one more convenient shortcut. If you have some text already in a field, and you want to find *the next* occurrence of the same text, then you can choose Edit→Find/Replace→Find Selected. This one command does the same thing as copying the text, opening the Find/Replace window, pasting into the "Find what" box, clicking Find Next, and then clicking Close. All the other options in the Find/Replace window stay just as when you last used them.

These handy commands all have keyboard shortcuts that, somewhat confusingly, work only when the Find/Replace dialog box is *closed*:

- To find the next occurrence (Find Again), just press Ctrl+G (⌘-G).

- To replace the currently selected text, and find the next occurrence (Replace & Find Again), press Ctrl+Alt+G (Option-⌘-G).

- To find other occurrences of the selected text, press Ctrl+Alt+H (Option-⌘-I).

- **All records and All fields.** FileMaker looks through every field on the layout for a match, and repeats the process for each record in the found set.

- **Current record and All fields.** FileMaker looks through every field on the layout in the current record only.

- **Current record and Current field.** FileMaker looks only in the current field. When it reaches the end of the text in that field, it stops.

- **All records and Current field.** FileMaker looks through the current field, and then moves to the next record. It keeps looking through records for more matches, but it pays attention only to the current field.

4. **From the Direction pop-up menu, choose All.**

The Direction pop-up menu controls which way FileMaker goes when it starts its search:

- **Forward.** The search starts wherever your cursor is and moves through each field in every record until it gets to the last record in the database, where it will stop.

- **Backward.** The opposite: the search starts from the cursor location and goes to the first record in your database.

- **All.** FileMaker starts off just like a Forward search. The search will then circle around until it gets back to the starting point.

5. **Click Find Next.**

Find Next starts FileMaker looking. When it finds a match, it highlights the match right in the field. The Find/Replace window stays put, so you can click Find Next as many times as necessary to find what you're looking for and then click Replace to change it to your replacement text. Click Find Next again to go to the next match.

If you feel the need to work more quickly—say you've done Find Next and Replace a couple of times, and everything looks in order—click Replace & Find instead. It replaces the current match and then finds the next one all in one step. Repeat as many times as necessary.

If you're sure you want *every* match replaced, then click Replace All, and File-Maker does the entire find-replace-find-replace dance for you. FileMaker always asks you if you're sure about Replace All first, just in case. For instance, if you have some clients whose last name is Anderson and others whose company name is Anderson, you may not want to use the Replace All option. You need to check each occurrence Individually to make sure you don't accidentally change someone's last name.

6. **When you're done with the Find/Replace window, click Close.**

WARNING Find/Replace has no undo, and since you can replace across all records and fields, it can be dangerous. Be careful with this command. Also, it can take a long time because it looks through the individual words in each field. If you're searching across all records, and you have lots of records, be prepared to wait a while as FileMaker does its magic.

■ Changing Text Appearance

Much like a word processor, FileMaker has commands to set the font, size, style, and alignment of the text in a field. When a field is active, or you've selected some text in a field, you can choose from any command in the Format menu. Also like a word processor, you can apply formats to paragraphs of text, and you can even create tab stops within a field.

Text Formatting

You can use all the usual commands (font, size, style, alignment, line spacing, and text color) individually, by selecting them from the Format menu or using the handy Formatting bar (View→Formatting Bar).

Each of these text-formatting commands lets you override the original formatting for selected text on a record-by-record basis. That is, changing a word to bold on one record doesn't affect any words in any other record in the database. So while it can be handy to make the occasional note stand out (as you see in Figure 2-12), professional database designers rarely use these commands to format individual chunks of text. Instead, they change the formatting of a given field in Layout mode. Formatting performed in Layout mode will apply to every record in the database. You'll learn how to do that in Part Two of this book.

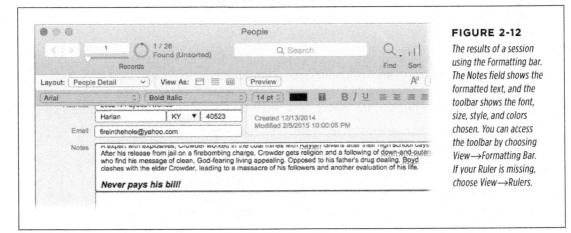

FIGURE 2-12

The results of a session using the Formatting bar. The Notes field shows the formatted text, and the toolbar shows the font, size, style, and colors chosen. You can access the toolbar by choosing View→Formatting Bar. If your Ruler is missing, choose View→Rulers.

TIP If you change your mind about formatting and want to put the text back to its normal state, here's a trick that lets you do it with four quick keystrokes: Select all the text (Ctrl+A or ⌘-A), cut the selection (Ctrl+X or ⌘-X), paste it right back in the field (Ctrl+V or ⌘-V), and finally Undo (Ctrl+Z or ⌘-Z). The pasted text comes back with its ugly formatting at first, but the undo doesn't remove the *text*, it removes the *formatting*. The same trick works if you paste data in from another source, like Microsoft Word or an email message. If the text comes with formatting you want to lose, just do that undo voodoo that you do right after you paste.

Paragraph Formatting

FileMaker doesn't stop with text (or *character*) formatting. It also has some paragraph formatting tools that come in handy. Well, they're handy if you can find them. You have to go through the Line Spacing dialog box to get there. To see the dialog box in Figure 2-13, choose Format→Line Spacing→Other.

There you see all the stuff you'd expect to be able to do to a paragraph in a field. You can align the paragraph, indent it from the left or the right, and give it a first-line indent. You can change line spacing and add space above and below a paragraph. There's even a handy Apply button so you can examine how it's going to look before you close the dialog box. Finally, a Tabs button gives you access to another dialog box, this time for setting tab stops.

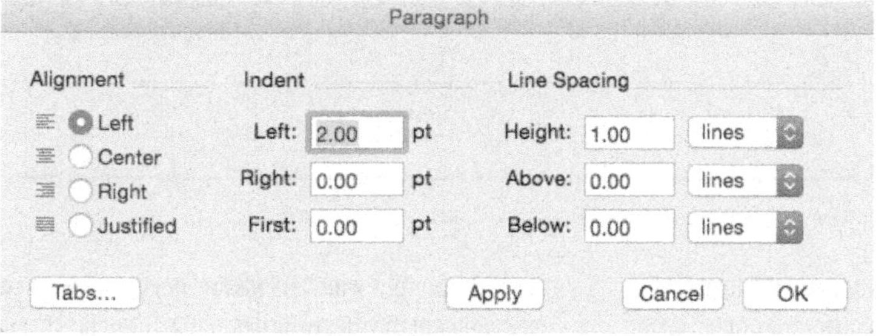

FIGURE 2-13

This hidden dialog box can make text in a field more legible. In your sample database, you may have noticed how the text stands a little away from the left edge of the field border (see Figure 2-12). That formatting was done on the layout, but you can add this effect to a field in one record with the settings shown above.

Remember, just as with text-formatting commands, any paragraph formatting you apply in Browse mode changes only the record and the field that's active when you choose the command. This ability comes in handy sometimes, but people use the Layout cousins of these commands far more often.

The Text Ruler

The Text Ruler is a visual version of the Paragraph formatting dialog box. Use the ruler to set indents and tab stops. The ruler has an arrow icon for the Left, Right, and First Line indent settings (Figure 2-14), which you just drag to the spot on the ruler where you want the indent set. You'll learn how to set tab stops on page 66.

Choose View→Ruler, and the ruler appears below the Status toolbar. When you're in a field, the ruler is a white area the width of the field, with the zero point on the ruler lined up with the left edge of the field. When you're not in a field, the ruler measures the width of the content area.

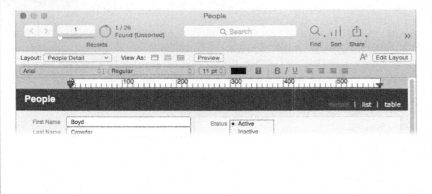

FIGURE 2-14

The text ruler lets you change paragraph margins. The Margin marker (on the ruler's bottom left) also moves the First Line marker (the bar above the arrow). To move them separately, drag the margin marker first and then move the First Line marker. Or hold down the Alt (Option) key as you drag.

What's the Point?

In FileMaker the default unit of measurement is "points," abbreviated as "pt." If you're still designing for the printed page, there are 72 points per inch. And traditionally, computer screens have 72 pixels per inch. So you can treat a point as the equivalent of a pixel on your computer (or mobile device's) screen.

If you just like the old ways, you can change FileMaker's unit of measurement to either inches or centimeters. But you'll need to be viewing layout rulers to do it. Here's how:

1. Choose View→Layout Mode. The status area changes to show FileMaker's layout tools.

2. Choose View→Rulers. A horizontal and a vertical ruler appear at the top and left edge of the layout.

3. Click where the two rulers intersect (you'll see the abbreviation "pt," which stands for "points"). The unit of measurement changes to inches ("in"). The rulers change to the new measurement system. Click a second time to change to centimeters ("cm").

Your rulers aren't the only things that change. The Inspector, which is FileMaker's main method of formatting objects on a layout (page 120), also changes its measurement system. Once you're familiar with the Inspector, you'll probably prefer to use it to change measurements, even though the method isn't obvious. You'll see the "pt" abbreviation to the right of the Position and Size fields. Click any one of those abbreviations, and the units rotate from points to inches to centimeters.

Formatting Tabs

Since a field can hold just about any kind of text, you may eventually need to use tab stops *within* a field. For example, you could have a nice large field into which you paste rows of text from a spreadsheet. To make things line up properly, you can set tab stops for each column of text. To type a tab into a field, press Ctrl+Tab (Option-Tab). This is a special keystroke, obviously, because in FileMaker pressing Tab usually jumps you to the next *field*. See page 305 to learn how Field Controls make plain old tabs work the way you're used to.

Like most word processing programs, FileMaker gives you two ways to create tab stops: the ruler and the Tabs dialog box.

■ SETTING TABS IN THE TEXT RULER

With your cursor in a field, you can insert a new tab stop simply by clicking anywhere in the ruler. A small bent arrow appears where you clicked, representing a *left* tab stop. (The arrow's tail shows you what direction text goes when you start typing.) The tab stop may not land exactly where you want it; just drag it into place. Once you've created a tab stop, you can edit or delete it at will. Drag a tab around on the ruler to move it, or drag it off the bottom to delete it. FileMaker also supports other kinds of tab stops, but to get them, you have to visit the Tabs dialog box, described next.

■ SETTING TABS IN THE TABS DIALOG BOX

The Tabs dialog box is a laborious way of setting tabs, but it gives you more options because you can control all aspects of each tab stop manually. Here's the drill:

1. **With your cursor in a field, choose Format→Line Spacing→Other.**

   The Paragraph dialog box makes its entrance.

2. **Click Tabs.**

   It was a long way to go, but you've found the Tabs dialog box (Figure 2-15).

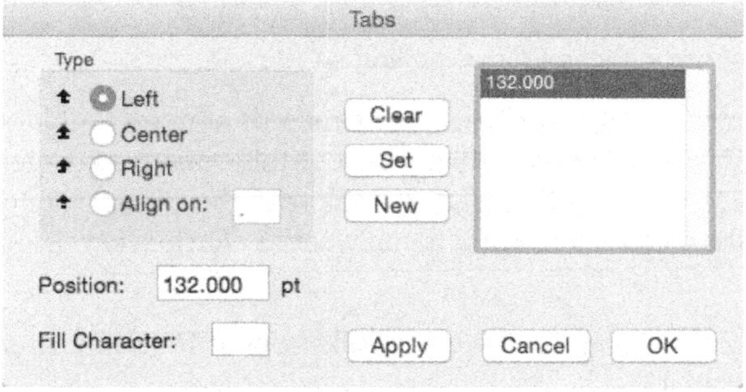

FIGURE 2-15

The Tabs dialog box lists all the tab stops set for a field in the list on the right. Each stop must have Type and Position values, but Fill Character is optional. Use it in situations like a table of contents where you want periods to fill the space between text and the page number. The character you enter in the Fill Character field "fills" the space before the tab.

3. **Select a tab stop type and enter a number in the Position field. This value is measured in points. Use the ruler to figure out the proper value.**

   If it's not exact, you can always fine-tune it by using the ruler later.

4. **Click the New button.**

   The new tab stop appears on the ruler and your text is adjusted accordingly. You can click OK to dismiss the dialog box or continue adding or editing tab stops. To change the settings for an existing tab stop, first select the tab stop, edit the settings, and then click OK.

You can create up to 20 tab stops, after which the New button is turned off. If you try to add a tab stop at a ruler position where one already exists, then the new stop replaces the old one. Use the Clear button to delete a tab.

TIP If the text ru ler is showing (Figure 2-14), then you can get to the Tabs dialog box quickly. Just double-click any tab stop in the ruler. The Tabs dialog box opens with the clicked tab preselected.

■ Checking Spelling

Before printing out your database or otherwise sharing it with the greater public, you want to make sure your spelling is correct. Nothing screams "amateur" louder than a City field that reads "Chciago." All the spell checking commands are found under the Edit→Spelling submenu.

Spell Checking with Menu Commands

Sometimes you want to fly through data entry and then do your spell checking later. If this is your preference, you have three choices:

- Choose Edit→Spelling→Check Selection to spell check selected text only. This method comes in handy when you're pretty sure a short passage, or even a single word, is wrong. Highlight the text you want to check and then choose the menu command.

- To check an entire record, choose Edit→Spelling→Check Record.

- Finally, you may want to check spelling on many records at once. In this case, choose Edit→Spelling→Check All. When you choose this option, you're telling the spell checker to look at every field of every record in the current found set (choose Records→Show All Records first if you want to check *every* record in the database).

No matter how many records you're checking, FileMaker opens the same Spelling dialog box shown in Figure 2-16.

NOTE Even if, by the magic of planetary alignment, you have no misspellings, FileMaker still opens the Spelling dialog box. In this case, though, it says, "Status: Finished Spelling" in small print in the middle of the busy window. You're supposed to spot this right away and know the program is done. Of course, if you're like most people, you stare blankly at the screen for 30 seconds trying to figure out what went wrong. Save yourself the confusion: Check the Status line when the window first appears. If FileMaker is finished, click Done.

When you're checking a word, the Spelling window says, "Status: Questionable Spelling." The Word text box displays the word in question. Things can proceed a few different ways:

- Usually the correctly spelled word appears in the list of suggested spellings. If it does, click the correct spelling and then click Replace. (Or just double-click the correct word.)

- If you don't see the right spelling, correct it yourself. Type the correct spelling into the Word box. To confirm that your new spelling is correct, click Check; the status line changes to say "Correct Spelling" if you got it right. Otherwise, you're back where you started, with a misspelled word and a few suggestions below it.

- If you spelled it right originally, but FileMaker doesn't agree, click Ignore All to tell FileMaker to skip this so-called misspelling. Better yet, click Learn to teach FileMaker the word so it doesn't bother you in the future. (Clicking Learn adds the word to your current user dictionary, which is explained on page 70. Ignore All ignores the word only temporarily; if you quit FileMaker and come back later, then it thinks the word is misspelled again.)

- If you change your mind and want to stop the spell checker, just click Cancel. This doesn't undo your changes; it just closes the dialog box.

- When the spell checker has finished, the status line changes to say "Finished Spelling," and the Replace button says "Done." Click the Done button to close the dialog box.

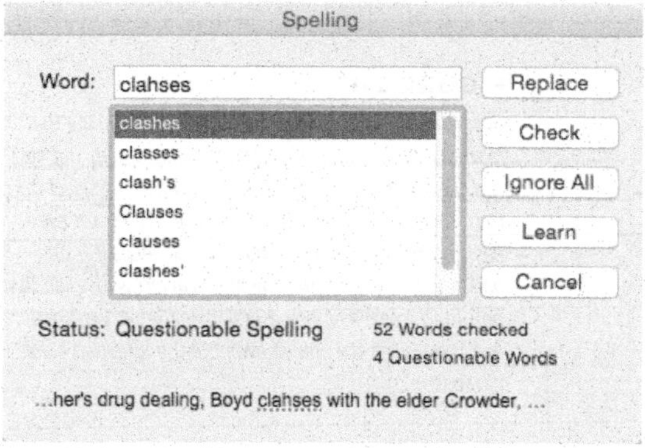

FIGURE 2-16

The spell checker found a typo—"clahses." You can see the misspelled word in the Word box, and underlined in red in the box at the bottom of the window. If FileMaker figures out the correct spelling, then, in the list under the Word box, It selects the spelling. And if you're the type who calculates your gas mileage every time you fuel up, you'll be delighted to discover that FileMaker keeps track of how many words you've spelled wrong so far and tells you at the bottom of the window.

Spell Checking as You Type

FileMaker's spell checker also works automatically as you type. This *visual* spell check is a per-database setting, so you control it from the File Options dialog box. Choose File→File Options and then click the Spelling tab. You find two options that you can mix and match to help you spell better, run faster, and jump higher. Well, you'll spell better, anyway.

The first option is "Indicate questionable words with special underline." If you miss your word processor, this one can make you feel right at home. You see that familiar red line underneath any word FileMaker doesn't like the looks of. Plus, if you right-click the underlined word and choose Suggested Spellings, FileMaker offers suggestions for spelling the word properly. If you see the correct spelling among the suggestions, just click it and FileMaker replaces the misspelled version. From the same shortcut menu, you can also tell FileMaker to learn the word or ignore it.

If red lines don't get your attention, then you can turn on "Beep on questionable spellings," and FileMaker makes your computer beep when you type a space after a misspelled word. Unfortunately, it's just the same old alert beep that your computer makes in all kinds of other situations—so you can easily miss it. But in combination with the red line, this pair can be a formidable reminder to spell better.

> **TIP** Visual spell checking can be handy. But often in a database your data entry includes things that don't need to be spell checked (inventory codes, abbreviations, email addresses, and the like). Luckily, when you design your own databases, you can turn off the as-you-type version of spell checking for any particular field. See page 307 for details.

Managing Spelling Dictionaries

FileMaker comes with spelling dictionaries for various languages, and you can easily choose among them. Just choose Edit→Spelling→Select Dictionaries. The Select Dictionaries window lets you choose the language to use for all spell-checking operations. You can see it in Figure 2-17.

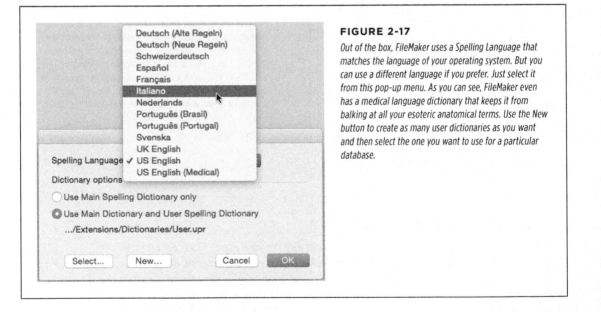

FIGURE 2-17

Out of the box, FileMaker uses a Spelling Language that matches the language of your operating system. But you can use a different language if you prefer. Just select it from this pop-up menu. As you can see, FileMaker even has a medical language dictionary that keeps it from balking at all your esoteric anatomical terms. Use the New button to create as many user dictionaries as you want and then select the one you want to use for a particular database.

◼ USER DICTIONARIES

Remember from page 69 when you clicked the Learn button to teach FileMaker a new word? When you did so, behind the scenes, FileMaker actually added that word to the *user dictionary,* which is separate from the normal dictionary that comes with FileMaker.

You can even have multiple user dictionaries for different purposes. For example, if you have two databases, one that tracks your apparel products and one that stores information about tools, you could keep two user dictionaries. The tools version may include words like "mm" and "pcs" while the apparel version would have "XXL" and "CottonPoly."

> **TIP** In reality, it's nine times easier to just use one user dictionary, so you don't have to worry about which one is selected. It doesn't hurt to have thousands of words in your user dictionary, but not having enough makes spell checking more time consuming. Nothing is more boring than wading through the same dozen correctly spelled words over and over. But if you want more than one dictionary, you can have it.

POWER USERS' CLINIC

Rewriting the Dictionary

You've already learned how to add to your dictionary by using the Learn button in the spell checker. Well, if you've ever wanted to just *tell* it what words you want it to skip, you can. Just choose Edit→Spelling→Edit User Dictionary to open the User Dictionary dialog box. Here you can add new entries to the dictionary (type the word and then click Add), or remove existing entries (select the word and then click Remove).

You can also export all the entries to a text file where you can edit them to your heart's content. When you click Export, FileMaker asks where it should save the export file. The file is a plain text file with one word on each line, which you can edit in a text-editing program.

If you already have a file that has words you want, then you can import those words into your user dictionary in one shot. For instance, if you use a lot of technical terms, then you may be able to download a list of terms from your industry and load them into a dictionary. The file has to have each word on its own line, so if it's in some other format, then you need to clean it up first. (For example, use your word processor's Find/Replace function to turn a comma-separated list into one with a carriage return between each word.) Don't worry about alphabetizing the list, though. FileMaker does that for you when you import the list.

Also, make sure the file is plain text. A Microsoft Word file (.docx) or other special format won't work. Making a plain-text file in Windows is a breeze: Just use Notepad, the simple text editor in the Accessories folder in your Start menu. On a Mac, however, you need a little more care. You can use Text Edit—it's in your Applications folder—but you have to tell it you want plain text. Just choose Format→Make Plain Text before you save the file.

Using the Import and Export features together can be particularly useful. You can export your user dictionary, edit it manually in the text-editing program (where making lots of edits may be easier), and then import it back in.

■ Preview Mode and Printing

It's a cruel fact of life that eventually you need to put your data on paper. You may want mailing labels for all your customers in Canada, or a special printed form pre-filled with patient information for insurance filing. Sometimes you just need your data with you when you're away from your computer. As you'll learn in Part Two, you can arrange the data any way you want in FileMaker, and make certain *layouts* that are particularly suitable for printing. But for now, remember that FileMaker lets you print *anything* you see onscreen (just choose File→Print). Its Print dialog box has a few special options. Figure 2-18 shows the Windows version. You can see the Mac version in Figure 2-19.

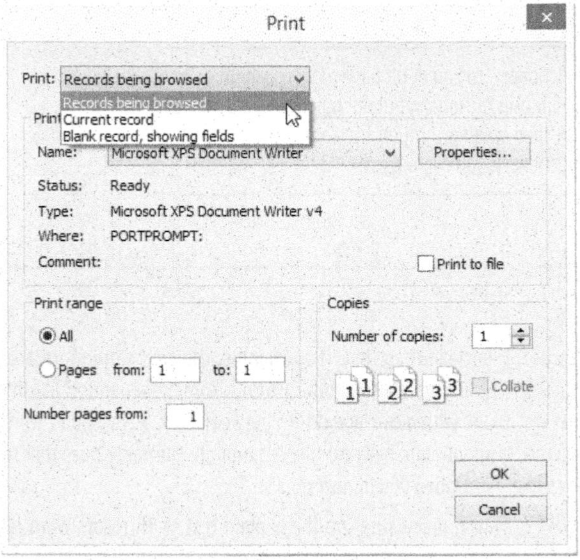

FIGURE 2-18

FileMaker's Print dialog box gives you all the standard options, plus a little more. The Print pop-up menu (at the top in the dialog box, as shown in Windows) lets you tell FileMaker which records to print. To print more than one record, as you would for a layout that uses a list or table view, choose "Records being browsed" from the Print pop-up menu. But choose "Current record" to print a single record no matter which view you're in.

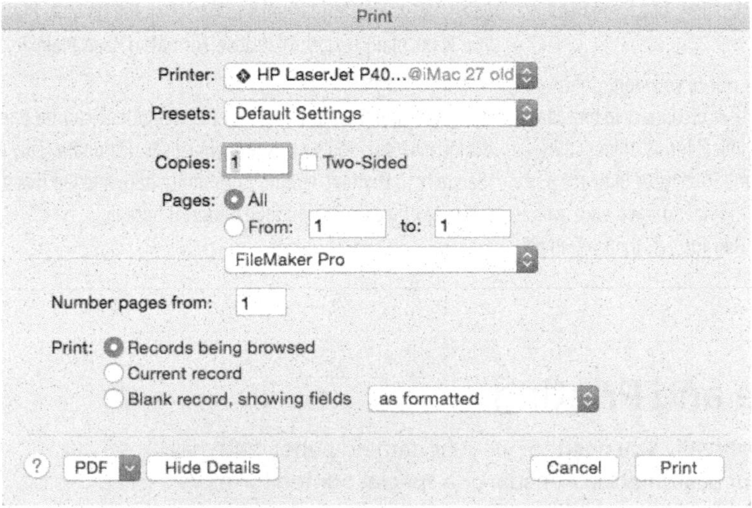

FIGURE 2-19

On the Mac, FileMaker's special print options may be tucked away in a not-so-obvious place. First make sure all the dialog box's options are showing. Look for a Show Details button to expand the dialog box to display all the options. Then if necessary, choose FileMaker Pro or FileMaker Pro Advanced from the unnamed but very important pop-up menu in the middle.

- **Records being browsed** tells FileMaker to print every record in the found set. To print all your Canadian customers, for example, find them first and then choose this option.

- **Current record** prints just the current record, which comes in handy when you just want to print *one* thing: your doctor's contact information to keep in the car, perhaps, or maybe the Form view of the record for the person you're meeting for a sales call later today.

- **Blank record, showing fields** tells FileMaker to print what's onscreen with no data at all. You can change the look of each field to a box or an underline if you want (from the pop-up menu shown in Figure 2-19). Choose this option if you want to hand out pages for people to fill out with a pen (it's a kind of antique writing device), and later type their responses into the real database.

To see how the printout is going to look without committing trees to it, you can use *Preview mode* (Figure 2-20). You access Preview mode via the View menu, the Mode pop-up menu, or Ctrl+U (⌘-U).

NOTE When you first go to Preview mode, the total page count says "?" instead of the number of pages. FileMaker doesn't know how many pages it'll print until you force it to count them. If you drag the Page slider all the way to the right, then FileMaker shows the last page. On its way there, FileMaker counts the pages, and updates the display, too. The process may take some time in a large document, but FileMaker catches up eventually.

On some computers and printers, you can reduce the printout by a percentage by using File→Print Setup (Page Setup on Mac). When you do, Preview mode shows the page proportionately larger or smaller so you can see how the content area fits on the page. The scaling options you get vary by computer, operating system, and printer, so trial and error may be necessary to find just the right setup.

NOTE Instead of printing, you can use one of the buttons in the Status toolbar to save the records you're viewing as an Excel file or a PDF.

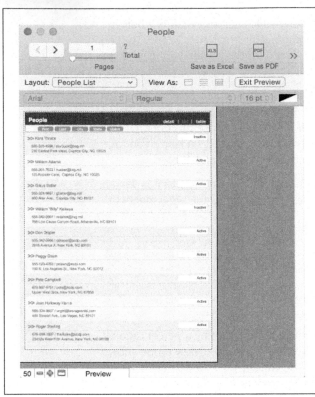

FIGURE 2-20

Preview mode shows you how a layout will look if it's printed. Here the People List layout is zoomed out to 50% of actual size so you can see the whole page in a smaller than life-sized window. Preview mode shows you where your page edges are—anything beyond them won't be printed. You can flip through a multiple-page list using the arrow buttons. The current page number appears where the current record number is displayed in Browse mode. When you get to the last page, a page count is displayed.

Getting to Know FileMaker Go

The first two chapters were all about FileMaker Pro on a Mac or PC. When you create databases, that's where you spend most of your time. But these days, technology users are less inclined than ever to be bogged down by a desktop—or even laptop—computer. In 2010, FileMaker responded to this desire by introducing FileMaker Go for iOS. A free download from the App store, Go lets you use FileMaker solutions on an iPad, iPhone, or iPod Touch. In FileMaker Go, you can do just about everything you did in Chapters 1 and 2, but because Go is built to work with the strengths and limitations of the touchscreen interface, everything will look a bit different. Don't worry, however—you already know the foundational concepts. This chapter simply illustrates how they're applied in the iOS.

> **NOTE** The figures in this chapter are taken from FileMaker Go on an iPad. Everything shown here works the same on an iPad Mini, iPhone or iPod touch, it's just a bit smaller.

■ Hello Go

At its heart, FileMaker Go is a FileMaker client application. Any database built with FileMaker Pro's built-in set of tools will open in Go and run as intended. Given the complexity FileMaker is capable of, and the restrictions inherent in a handheld device, that seamless compatibility is a laudable achievement. Still, it's important to recognize that FileMaker Go doesn't replace FileMaker Pro. Because Go is strictly a client app, you can't use it to create new databases or modify layouts or scripts. You can only create databases with FileMaker Pro (preferably FileMaker Pro Advanced). Once you've created a database in Pro, anyone with Go can open your databases to create, edit, and delete records; run reports; find and sort—all the usual stuff you do when using, not building, a database.

> **NOTE** To follow along in this chapter, you'll find it helpful to download the sample databases from this book's Missing CD page at *www.missingmanuals.com/cds/fmp14mm*.

Getting the App

You've dropped more than a few dollars on FileMaker Pro or Pro Advanced. Mercifully, FileMaker has opted to simply give FileMaker Go away for free. To get it, merely tap the App Store icon that came pre-installed on your iOS device. When the App Store is on your screen, tap into the search box in the upper-right corner, type *FileMaker Go,* and then tap Search. When selecting the app to download, make sure you're not paying money for it. The FileMaker Go app is free, unlike a couple of third-party FileMaker Go training apps you'll see in the Store. Once you've located the right app, tap Get to download and install it.

When download and installation are complete, tap the FileMaker Go icon. Upon first launch, you'll be offered a tour. If you don't feel like walking through it right away, just tap Close in the top-right corner. You can come back to the tour by tapping the Options button (the one that looks like a gear) and selecting Welcome Tour.

Loading Databases

Fresh from the App Store, FileMaker Go comes with the four sample databases shown in Figure 3-1. These files are sufficient for learning how to use the app, but you'll quickly want to see your own solutions in there. Go provides two methods for accessing databases.

▩ COPYING TO THE DEVICE

For databases that need to go on only one mobile device, your best bet is to copy the FileMaker file to that device. When you create a database using FileMaker Pro (which you'll learn how to do in the next chapter), it's saved to your hard drive as a file with an .fmp12 extension. Copy that file to your iOS device, and FileMaker Go will be able to open and run the database.

There are a number of ways to achieve the transfer. If the file is small enough, you can email it to yourself from your PC or Mac, then open the message on your device and voila, your file is attached and ready for FileMaker Go. File hosting services such as Dropbox and Google Drive have iOS apps that make transferring database files relatively easy too. The most reliable method to move a file is to use Apple's free iTunes application on your PC or Mac.

1. **If you don't already have it, download and install iTunes from *www.apple.com/itunes/download/*.**

2. **Using your PC or Mac, download the example file for this chapter from the Missing CD page at *www.missingmanuals.com/cds/fmp14mm*.**

   It's called *CH03 People.fmp12*.

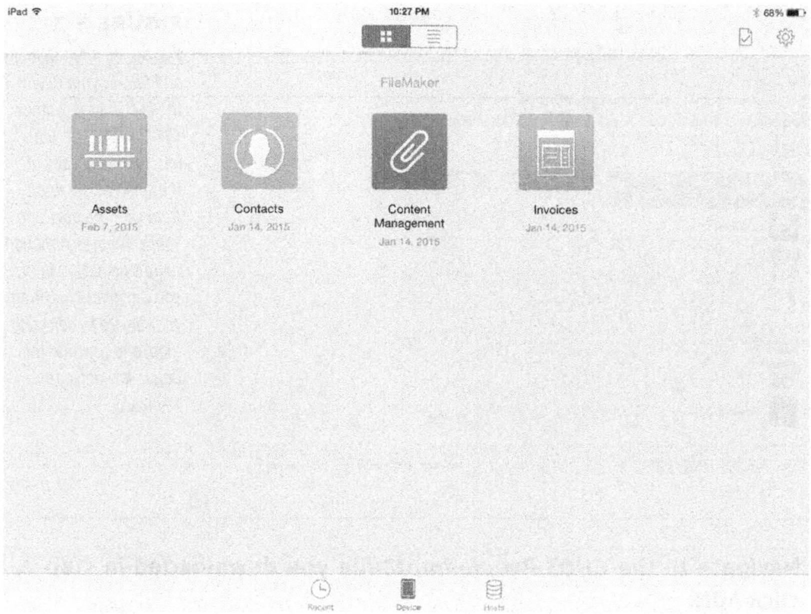

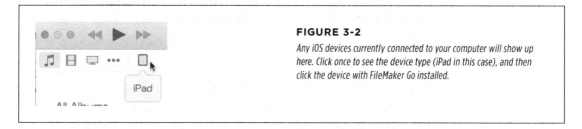

FIGURE 3-1

The Launch Center serves as a home base. From here, you can quickly access recently opened files, peruse a list of all databases on your device, and connect to databases hosted on FileMaker servers.

3. **Near the top-left corner of the iTunes window, click the icon for your device.**

   The device management view opens with Summary selected in the Settings column (Figure 3-2).

FIGURE 3-2

Any iOS devices currently connected to your computer will show up here. Click once to see the device type (iPad in this case), and then click the device with FileMaker Go installed.

4. **In the Settings column on the left, click Apps. In the content area to the right, scroll down to the File Sharing section and then click FileMaker Go.**

   Listed on the right under FileMaker Go Documents, you'll see four sample databases (Figure 3-3).

5. Below the list of databases, click the Add button.

A standard Mac or Windows dialog box opens for you to select the database that you'll be transferring from your computer to your iOS device.

FIGURE 3-3

You can do more than just add files to your device in the File Sharing window. The "Save to" button lets you pull a copy of the selected database from your iOS device to your computer. Although there's no button for it, you can delete files from your device by selecting them and pressing the Delete key on your keyboard.

6. Navigate to the *CH03 People.fmp12* file you downloaded in step 2, and click Add.

Back in the File Sharing window, confirm that the file was added to the list of databases.

7. At the lower-right of the iTunes window, click the Sync button.

iTunes syncs files with your device.

8. When synchronization is complete, go back to FileMaker Go. In the Launch Center, tap the Device icon in the bottom row.

You should now see *CH03 People* on the list of databases residing in your device (Figure 3-4).

■ OPENING FILES HOSTED ON A SERVER

Storing a database on your iOS device is fine if you're the only person who's ever going to use it. But FileMaker is all about sharing information among many users, whether they're on computers, iOS devices, or the Web (see Chapter 20 for more on that). So the more common way to access a database from your device is to open a file that's hosted on a FileMaker Server or via FileMaker Pro peer-to-peer sharing.

Regardless of the method used to share the file, you open it the same way in File-Maker Go. In the Launch Center, tap the Hosts icon in the bottom row. In pop-up list (Figure 3-5), you'll see a list of the computers on your local network that are currently hosting FileMaker databases.

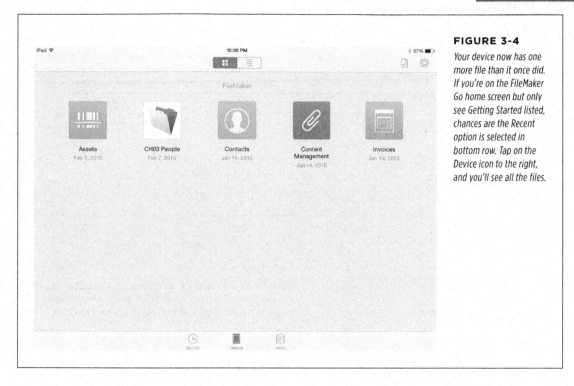

FIGURE 3-4

Your device now has one more file than it once did. If you're on the FileMaker Go home screen but only see Getting Started listed, chances are the Recent option is selected in bottom row. Tap on the Device icon to the right, and you'll see all the files.

If you *don't* see the host you need, it may not be on your local network, which means you have to take a few extra steps. First, ask the person sharing the database for the server's name or IP. At the top right of the Hosts pop-up menu, tap the + icon. FileMaker Go will prompt you to enter the server's name or address (Figure 3-6). While you're here, take a few seconds to add a short, descriptive title for the host computer in the space provided.

TIP The server's name would look something like *fmserver.myplaceofwork.org*. The IP (Internet Protocol) address would be four numbers with a dot between each—192.168.1.52, for example.

Now that you've found or added the desired FileMaker host, tap the host's name to reveal the available databases. Tap a database name to open it, and you're in business. As long as you can maintain a network connection, you can use that database as though it were stored on your device. All of your changes are saved to the server as you make them, and any other users who are connected to the database will see your edits as they happen.

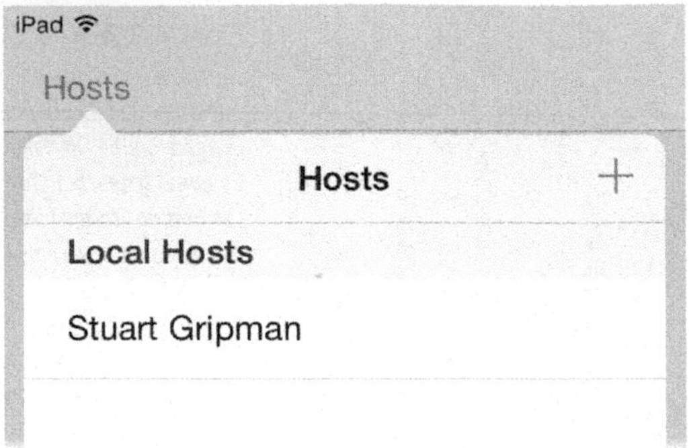

FIGURE 3-5

When you're just getting started, chances are you won't see any hosts in the Launch Center. That's OK, it just means there aren't any computers on your network hosting FileMaker databases.

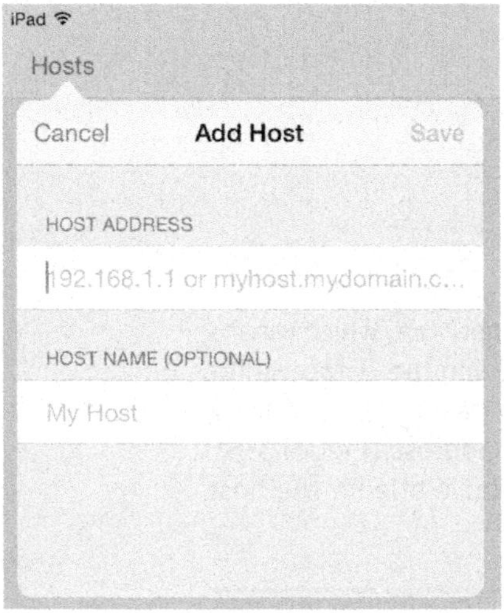

FIGURE 3-6

Whether you're entering an IP address or a server name, spelling counts. Being off by a single character will prevent a successful connection. If it doesn't work the first time, double-check your entry.

> **NOTE** When you're using a hosted database, things may run slower than when you're using a database that's right on your device. That's because you have to wait for the server to communicate with your device—and the devices of any other connected users.

■ CLOSING FILES

On an iOS device, you can always get out of an app by pressing the Home button. Sure, it's the quickest way to leave an app, but it's less than ideal when you're closing FileMaker Go with an open connection to a hosted file. Abruptly exiting FileMaker Go while, say, a script is running or an unsaved edit is onscreen can cause problems.

For that reason, you're strongly encouraged to close the files you've opened before exiting FileMaker Go. Simply tap the Action icon at top left (it resembles a file folder) and then tap Close File.

POWER USERS' CLINIC

Developing for FileMaker Go

When you create or develop a database in FileMaker Pro on your Mac or PC, you can get a pretty good idea for how the databases will look and work in FileMaker Go, there's really no substitute for testing your database on the intended device as you're building it. But who has time to stop every few minutes to copy the latest changes to an iPad or iPhone using iTunes? Or has a FileMaker Server up and ready to host development projects?

Fortunately, FileMaker Pro's *built-in sharing* gracefully solves this problem. First, make sure your iOS device and your File-Maker Pro computer are on the same local network. With your

database open in FileMaker Pro, activate peer-to-peer sharing following the instructions on page 786. Now switch to your iOS device and open FileMaker Go's Launch Center. At the bottom of the window, tap the Hosts icon. If all is working properly, you'll see your computer listed as a Host and when you tap it, you'll see your databases listed. Tap the database's name to open it.

From then on, changes you make in FileMaker Pro/Advanced will appear on your iOS device within a second or two. You'll be able to develop on the computer and test on the mobile device without interruption.

Getting Around

If you followed the instructions starting on page 76 or 77, you've loaded the *CH03 People* example file onto your iOS device. Time to open it up and kick some tires. In FileMaker Go's Launch Center, tap the Device or Hosts icon and then tap *CH03 People* from the list of databases. When the database opens up, it looks a whole lot like it did on your computer. But the menus and commands aren't all across the top; instead, they're nested along the top and bottom edges of the screen. Take a look at Figure 3-7 to get your bearings.

■ CHANGING LAYOUTS

The layout you land on the first time you open *CH03 People* is the People Detail layout designed for use on a Mac or PC. Its fields and buttons are much too small to be any use on a touchscreen. Fortunately, you're not stuck with the default. Other layouts, including a couple in the example file created just for touchscreens, are only three taps away.

1. **Tap the Action icon (the one that looks like an open folder) in the top-left corner of the screen.**

2. **Tap Layout (near the bottom of the list).**

3. **Tap the name of the layout you wish to view.**

The sample database has Details layouts optimized for the iPad and iPhone, as shown in Figure 3-8. If you're using an iPod Touch, select the iPhone layout for best results. You'll also see the same three View As options—Form, List, and Table—discussed in the previous chapter. Not every layout has every View As option enabled, but if you'd like to try it out, switch to the Notes layout, which has no restrictions.

The Show Toolbar toggle switch at the top of the Layouts menu gives you the ability to suppress the bottom row of icons shown in Figure 3-7. Hiding the toolbar gives you a bit more content area to work with, at the expense of convenient access to those functions.

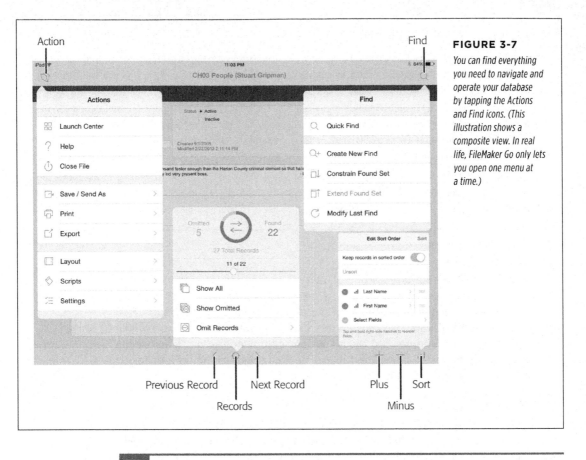

FIGURE 3-7

You can find everything you need to navigate and operate your database by tapping the Actions and Find icons. (This illustration shows a composite view. In real life, FileMaker Go only lets you open one menu at a time.)

TIP Toggling the toolbar doesn't require a trip to the Layout menu. A three-finger upward swipe on the screen will hide both the toolbar at the bottom and the title bar at the top. Three fingers swiped downward will bring them back.

■ MOVING AMONG RECORDS

FileMaker Go gives you three ways to navigate among records in detail view. To move one record at a time, simply tap the Previous Record or Next Record icons at bottom center (Figure 3-7). You can get the exact same previous/next effect by swiping with two fingers across the screen. A horizontal swipe from right to left navigates to the next record; swiping left to right takes you to the previous record.

If you need to get to a record more than four or five records away, navigating one by one is going to get tedious. Give the preceding techniques a miss and head straight for the Records icon at center bottom. Tap the icon and you'll find a slider indicating which record number you're viewing. Dragging that slider left or right is your express lane to distant records.

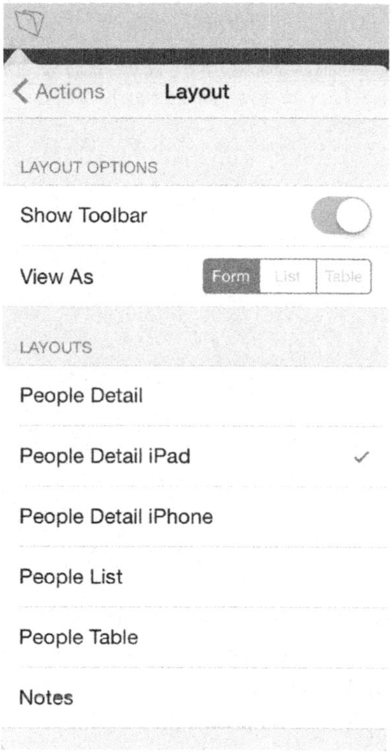

FIGURE 3-8

Disabling Show Toolbar hides the tools along the bottom of the screen (the ones shown in Figure 3-7). When the View As buttons below that are gray, it's because the database developer elected to disable them—a setting that can be changed in FileMaker Pro but not Go.

Finding and Sorting

Getting to the records you need isn't practical by browsing alone. So all the various ways you learned to search for your information using FileMaker Pro in Chapter 2 are represented in FileMaker Go as well. Your entrée to all of them is the Find icon in the top-right corner of the screen (Figure 3-9).

■ QUICK FIND

The first option in the Find menu is Quick Find. Tap it, and the menu changes to a one-line search box where you may enter a search term or phrase. When you tap Search on your onscreen keyboard, FileMaker Go checks for your search term across every field that appears on your current layout. Not unlike web searches, Quick Find is a blunt instrument, and you'll likely have to rifle through the found records to locate precisely what you were seeking.

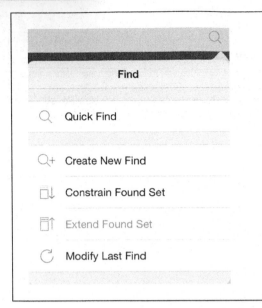

FIGURE 3-9

The Find menu offers no fewer than four ways to track down records in your database. If you ever need to see the last find you performed, tap Modify Last Find at the bottom of the list. It sets up your most recent find, but leaves you in Find view so you can tweak the parameters before starting the search.

Find

Q Quick Find

Q+ Create New Find

□↓ Constrain Found Set

□↑ Extend Found Set

C Modify Last Find

■ FINDING FROM THE LAYOUT

Tapping Find→Create New Find is the FileMaker Go analog to entering Find mode in FileMaker Pro. You'll get to a blank record where you can enter a search term in one or more fields. Type your search terms, tap Go, and watch the results roll in. The number of matching records briefly flashes on your screen (Figure 3-10).

FIGURE 3-10

If you're not watching for it, you might miss it. Immediately after each find is executed, FileMaker Go shows you how many records matched your search criteria. It also shows how many didn't match and the total number of records in the table being searched. If you can add numbers in your head really, really quickly, that last bit of info is superfluous.

Omitted 16   Found 11

27 Total Records

Just as in FileMaker Pro, entering search terms in multiple fields sets up an AND search (page 44). If you want to add additional find requests for a broader OR search, tap the tiny price tag icon with a plus symbol. When you've added all the requests you need, tap Go to execute the find.

NOTE If you need a refresher on concepts like OR searches, find requests, and constraining the found set, revisit Chapter 2 where all these FileMaker search concepts are exhaustively related.

If you want FileMaker Go to *exclude* the records that match your find, tap the Find Request icon at center bottom. The icon looks like a tiny blue price tag and displays the number of the find request you're currently viewing. (If a keyboard is currently onscreen, the Find Request icon will be just *above* it.) The top two items in the Find Request menu are Include Matching (the default) and Omit Matching. Selecting one will deselect the other. Choose Omit Matching to find every record that doesn't match your search terms.

If you create a new find only to realize that you'd really regret losing your current found set, don't panic. Just tap Cancel at top right, and everything goes back to the way it was.

Like FileMaker Pro, Go provides a way to search within an existing found set of records, though the order of operations is reversed. Just tap Find→Constrain Found Set. FileMaker Go sets up a new find request. Enter your terms and tap Go to execute that search within the records in your current found set.

The obverse, extending the found set, works just the same way. Tap Find→Extend Found Set. Any matching records are appended to records you're already viewing.

■ SORTING

Once you've perfected your find and corralled the records you require, you'll probably want to get them arranged in the right order. In FileMaker Go, it starts with a tap on the Sort icon in the bottom-right corner. Here's how to sort the *CH03 People* records in alphabetical order by last name.

1. **Tap Action→Layout→People List.**

   You land on a list layout where you can easily see the record order.

2. **In the bottom-right corner, tap the Sort icon.**

   If you see any field names in the menu (as shown on the right side of Figure 3-11), tap the red circle next to each field name and tap Remove.

3. **You must tell FileMaker which field you need the records ordered by, so tap Select Fields (the menu choice near the bottom with the green circle).**

   FileMaker Go presents you with a list of the fields that appear on your layout.

4. **Tap Last Name and confirm that the order is Ascending.**

   Ascending, for a text field like Last Name, means A comes first and Z comes last.

NOTE See page 25 for much more information about how FileMaker sorts different types of data like dates, times, and numbers.

5. **Confirm your selection by tapping Back at the top-left corner of the menu.**

   Back in the Sort Menu, Last Name should now appear with a red circle, much like you see on the right side of Figure 3-11.

6. **In the top-right corner of the Sort menu, tap Sort.**

   Your records snap into alphabetical order with William Adama at the top and Kara Thrace at the bottom.

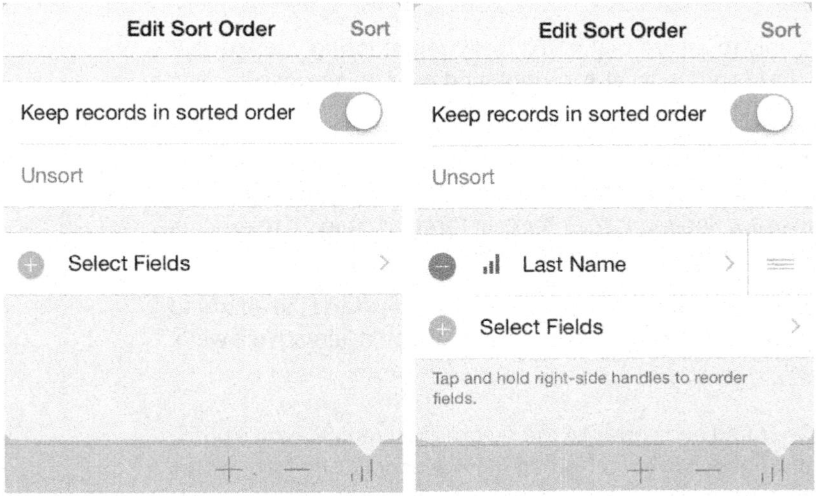

FIGURE 3-11

Left: If you've never sorted your records before, the Sort menu doesn't have much to display. Right: The field or fields checked off after clicking Select Fields now appear, and you're ready to put your records in a new order.

You're not limited to a single sort field. FileMaker Go lets you sort by any number of fields. So in step 3 on page 85, you could have tapped several other field names. Every field you tap gets a checkmark, and when you tap Back, they're all added to the sort order.

When FileMaker Go executes a multifield sort, it prioritizes the fields based on the order they appear in the Sort menu. Say you have Last Name at the top of the list, followed by First Name and then Middle Name. When you tap Sort, the records are lined up alphabetically by last name. Then FileMaker examines all the records with the same last name and arranges those by First Name. If any records share the same last and first names, FileMaker orders those based on the middle names. You can rearrange sort field rank by dragging the space to the right of a field name up or down.

The toggle switch for "Keep records in sorted order" reorders records as you create or edit them. Flip back to page 27 to see more about how that works and why you may or may not wish to use it.

Editing Information

Entering and editing field information in FileMaker Go works much like it does in other iOS apps. Tap in an editable field, and the keyboard slides up from the bottom. Press and hold on some text to move your cursor, and double-tap text to select it.

With a word or phrase selected, tap once to invoke the menu shown in Figure 3-12. Here you can cut, copy, paste, and so on. If you have copied styled text (text that includes multiple font colors, or some bold or italic words), that formatting will come through when you paste. If you'd prefer just to have plain, uniform text, opt for Paste Text Only instead of the regular Paste choice to keep the words but jettison the embellishments.

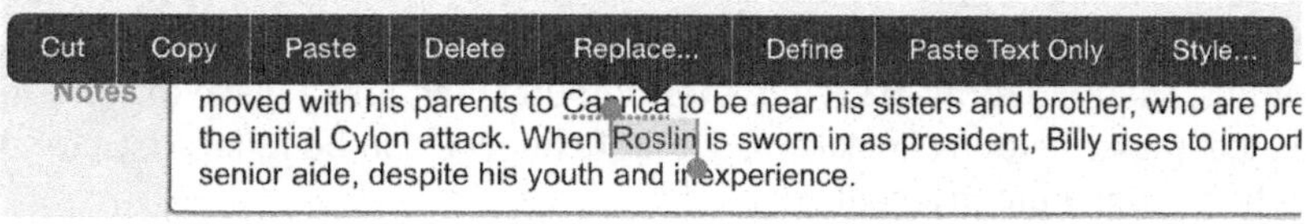

FIGURE 3-12

Once you've selected a word, FileMaker Go offers quite an array of options for doing things with it. The Replace option should not be confused with the Find/Replace feature in FileMaker Pro. Here it simply offers up to three predictive text guesses as to the word you may have wanted.

On the other hand, if embellishment is what you're looking for, the Style option is your friend. Tap Style to reveal the formatting menu shown in Figure 3-13. It lets you rework the look of the selected text in font, size, and color. You can also toggle bold, italic, and underline formatting. When everything is just so, tap Done.

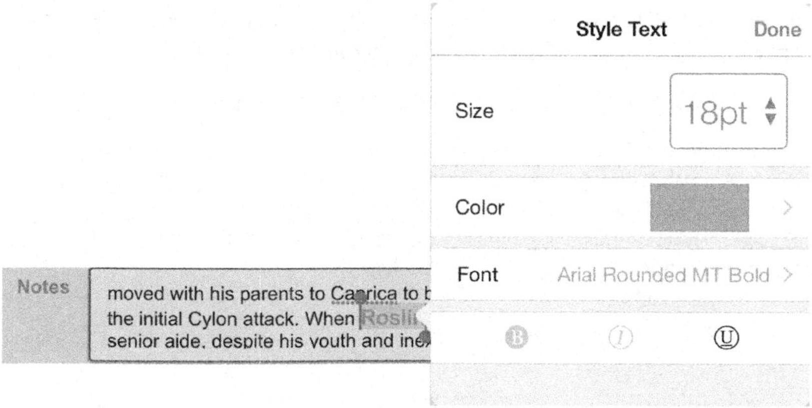

FIGURE 3-13

FileMaker gives you a multitude of ways to jazz up your text. However, do your users' eyes a favor and be sparing with the fancy formatting.

Container Fields

Container fields (page 103) let you store media files like images, videos, and music. They can also store pretty much any kind of file you throw at them, from CAD to Word to PDF. In FileMaker Go, container fields get some special tricks that FileMaker Pro on your Mac or PC can't match.

> **NOTE** The next set of screenshots and examples use the *CH03 Containers.fmp12* sample file. Download it to your computer from *www.missingmanuals.com/cds/fmp14mm* and transfer it to FileMaker Go using iTunes as described on page 76.

■ SIGNATURES

Signatures are still the gold standard for sealing agreements, but paper forms are a real wrench in your well-oiled digital workflow. You've got to print the forms, ink the signatures, scan the forms back into the computer, and find a place to store them. With a container field in FileMaker Go, that headache can be relieved. Here's how to capture a signature in a container field.

1. **Open the *CH03 Containers* file in FileMaker Go.**

   It opens to the layout you see in Figure 3-14, but without the signature or photos. It's all set up and ready for you to add a signature.

2. **Tap the Signature field.**

   It's the top-left field, just below the word Signature.

3. **In the Import menu that pops up (Figure 3-15), select Signature.**

   The screen changes to show a line with the words Sign Here.

4. **Using a finger, sign your name.**

   Or draw a happy face—FileMaker doesn't really care.

5. **If you like what you see, tap Accept in the top-right corner of the screen.**

   If you want to try again, tap Clear near the top-left corner. You can back out entirely by tapping Cancel, also near the top-left corner.

After you Accept, your autograph will fill the Signature field.

> **NOTE** The signature procedure described in the previous steps is fine, but it doesn't clearly state *what* you're agreeing to. There's a way to improve that. If you tap the button just above the Signature field, a script uses the Insert From Device script step to customize the experience with a title and some text summarizing the agreement. You'll learn about scripting in Parts Two and Three.

■ BARCODES

For decades, people have been using FileMaker Pro to create and print barcodes. Libraries, warehouses, bulk mailing operations, and retail stores have all benefited from FileMaker-generated barcodes. But until the advent of FileMaker Go, FileMaker didn't have a built-in way to *read* those barcodes. Nowadays, barcode scanning is a snap.

As with signatures, scanning a barcode starts with a tap in a container field. Then tap Import→Bar Code, and aim your device's camera at a barcode. It may take a few seconds, particularly in low light, but FileMaker Go will recognize the barcode, snap a picture of it, and beep its confirmation.

A photo of a barcode isn't much good if you can't do anything with it, so FileMaker offers a way to extract the contents of that barcode into plain numbers and text. In the *CH03 Container.fmp12* example file, a smaller field under the Barcode field uses this method to display the barcode's encoded contents. In Figure 3-14, you can see the content of a scanned QR code.

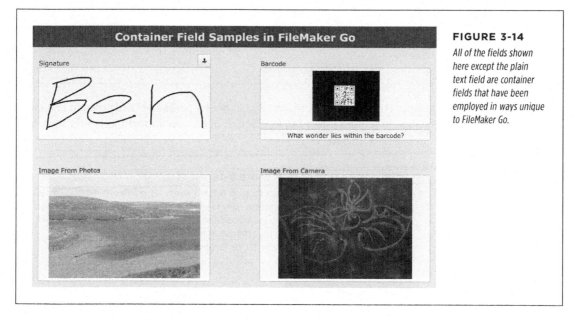

FIGURE 3-14

All of the fields shown here except the plain text field are container fields that have been employed in ways unique to FileMaker Go.

There are scores of barcode varieties out there, and FileMaker can't recognize all of them. But it does understand 17 of the most commonly used barcode flavors, which together make up the vast majority of the barcodes in use today.

■ PHOTO ALBUMS

Phones and tablets have come to replace the wallet full of family photos. Increasingly, business users are taking pictures with mobile devices too. Recognizing this, FileMaker has an easy way to place device photos into databases. Using the increasingly familiar Import menu (Figure 3-15), select Photos. In your photo collection, tap an album name and choose an image to place a copy in your container field.

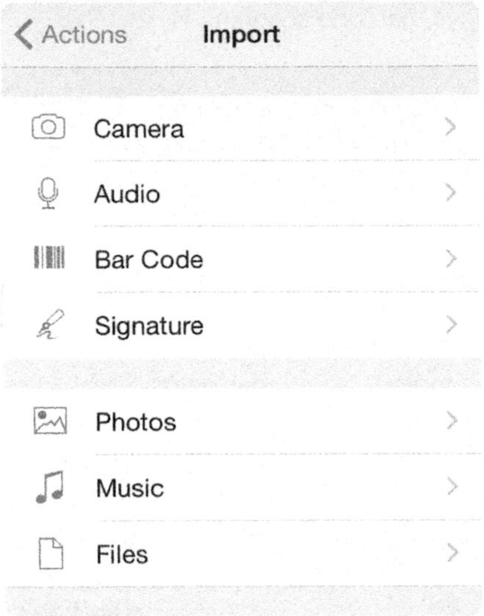

<Actions   **Import**

📷 Camera   >

🎤 Audio   >

▮▮▮ Bar Code   >

✒ Signature   >

🖼 Photos   >

🎵 Music   >

📄 Files   >

FIGURE 3-15

The Import menu appears when you tap an empty container field. In this case, the term "import" means adding something to a container field. Elsewhere in FileMaker Pro, "import" can also refer to adding a batch of records from an external source like a spreadsheet.

If you tapped the wrong photo, simply tap on the container field again to display an Actions menu (Figure 3-16). Tap Replace to get a new Import menu and start over.

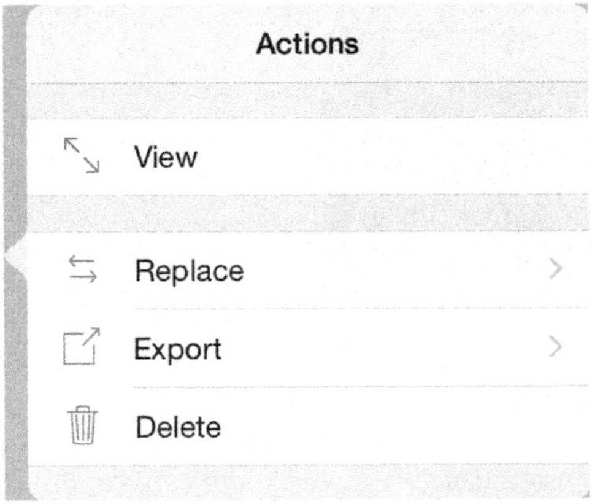

Actions

↖↘ View

⇆ Replace   >

↗ Export   >

🗑 Delete

FIGURE 3-16

Tap a container field that already has something in it, and you see this Actions menu. Tap View to see the field's media in full screen. Replace lets you pick something new to drop in, while Export offers some ways to share that content with other apps or people. Or use the Delete option to clear the container field completely.

■ CAMERA

If you like to capture the action as it happens, FileMaker Go has you covered there too. Tap Import→Camera, and snap a photo as you normally would. The image appears onscreen for your approval. If you want to try again, tap Retake at bottom left. When you get a keeper, tap Use Photo on the right, and FileMaker places your image in the container field.

■ OTHER MEDIA

As you saw in Figure 3-15, FileMaker Go can store a few other things in your container fields, including audio from your device's microphone, prerecorded audio files from your Music app, and any other files stored on the device.

Building Your First Database

Creating a Custom Database

I n Part One, you learned that you can work organically, flowing smoothly from finding to sorting and then to editing data as your needs dictate. In Part Two, you'll learn that FileMaker lets you create databases in a natural order, too. For starters, you'll create some fields for storing data about your property leasing business, and then you'll learn how to control layouts so they display data the way you want to see it.

NOTE The tutorials in Part Two serve as a general introduction to database creation. You'll go through the basics of all the major tasks associated with creating databases. Later sections go into more detail on the bigger topics, but you'll get a solid foundation by reading Chapter 4 and Chapter 5 straight through.

Creating a New Database

When you create a database from scratch, you'll see both familiar territory and some brand-new concepts right away. For example, when you launch a word processing program and then open a new document, you can type a lot of text before you get around to saving your document. But when you create a database, you need to give your document a name and some basic structure before you can enter any data. That's partly because of the automatic saving feature you learned about on page 33. Another reason is that you have to tell FileMaker about the fields you're going to use to store your data.

Here's how to create a new database file:

1. **Launch FileMaker Pro.**

   The Launch Center screen appears. It lets you open existing databases or start a new one (Figure 4-1).

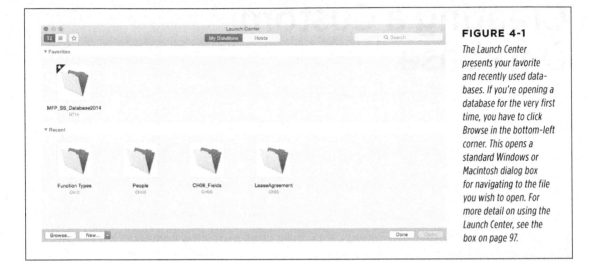

FIGURE 4-1

The Launch Center presents your favorite and recently used databases. If you're opening a database for the very first time, you have to click Browse in the bottom-left corner. This opens a standard Windows or Macintosh dialog box for navigating to the file you wish to open. For more detail on using the Launch Center, see the box on page 97.

2. **At bottom left, click the New button and choose New Solution. In the Save As field, type *Lease Agreement* and then choose a location to save your file.**

   The New File dialog box is very similar to a Save dialog box. You can name your new file and navigate through your folders to find your favorite storage spot.

3. **Click Save when you're done.**

   A new database window appears in Form view ready for you to start creating fields.

NOTE It may seem odd to name the file "Lease Agreement" (singular) and not "Lease Agreements" (plural). After all, the file is meant to store many agreements. True enough, and for that reason many developers always use plural for their file and table names. But at the record level, you'd never put two peoples' first names in one field, so it doesn't make sense to name the field "First Names." It's easier to remember never to use plural than it is to remember different rules for different database parts, so in this chapter, you'll stick to singular.

Mastering the Launch Center

Don't let its sparseness deceive you; the Launch Center abounds with possibilities. When you select the My Solutions button in the title bar, you'll see two classes of files:

- **Favorites.** You determine which files appear in this list. Point to an icon on the Recent Files page, and in the top-left corner, click the gray star that appears. Its background turns black to indicate that it's now a favorite and will appear in this list the next time you open the Launch Center.

- **Recent Files.** FileMaker remembers which files you've opened recently. Set the number displayed in the list (it's automatically set to 10) by choosing Edit→Preferences (Windows) or FileMaker Pro→Preferences (Mac) and then type the number you want in the "Show recently opened files" field.

You'll also see two buttons in the lower-left corner of the Launch Center:

Browse invokes the standard Open File dialog box, where you can navigate your computer or network to the file you need.

New contains three ways to create a new database:

- **Create New Solution** opens a fresh, new database file, as described in the steps on page 96.

- The **New From Starter Solution** option gives you access to FileMaker's handy templates (page 113), including business, academic, and personal solutions.

- **New From Existing** converts files from older FileMaker versions (those with .fp7 file extensions) to the .fmp12 format used by FileMaker 14. This command also converts databases from other sources, like Excel or comma-separated text files.

Select the Hosts button in the title bar to view databases hosted on other computers. The left column lists your favorite hosts. Click the + button to add a new favorite host, as described on page 790. Click a host's name to see the available files.

■ Creating and Managing Fields in Form View

When you create a new database in FileMaker Pro 14, the file starts out in Form view and Layout mode. Since the file has no fields or records, FileMaker opens the Field Picker, shown in Figure 4-2, which lets you get right to the business of creating your initial fields.

When FileMaker created your blank layout, it made it a fixed height and width. The sample database you'll create in this chapter will only have a few fields in it, so the next step is to reduce the layout to a more compact, manageable size. This is how you resize the layout:

1. **Choose View→Rulers.**

   The rulers appear at the window's top and left edges. The default measurement system for a new file is inches.

2. **Click anywhere in the gray area outside the Field Picker.**

   The layout area becomes active, so you can change it.

3. **Expand the window or scroll right to view the layout's right edge.**

   When you first create a layout, the Header section is solid black. The edge of the layout is where the Header section ends; the area to the right of the layout is a darker gray.

4. **Grab the right edge of the layout and move it left to the 8-inch mark on the top ruler.**

   Your mouse pointer changes to a double arrow when it's directly over the layout's edge.

You're almost ready to start making fields. But first, you need to think about the fields the database needs for storing data in a logical manner. The box on the next page has some suggestions.

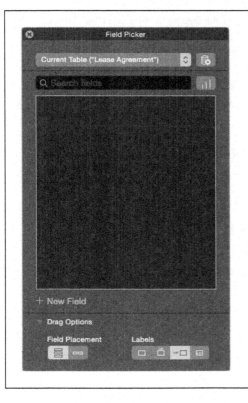

FIGURE 4-2

The Field Picker lets you create a batch of new fields (or just one) and then drag them onto your layout. Click the + symbol to add new fields. Click the Drag Option triangle at bottom to see two choices that determine how FileMaker arranges the new fields and labels when you drag them to your layout. Because the two options work together, you have good control over how your fields appear when they land on the layout.

NOTE To follow along in this chapter, you'll find it helpful to download the sample database *CH04 Lease Agreement.fmp12* from this book's Missing CD page at *www.missingmanuals.com/cds/fmp14mm*. You'll also find PDFs and other files that you can use as you work through the steps.

Creating Fields in the Field Picker

The Lease Agreement database will track the names of people to whom you lease houses and record how much money you can expect to receive for rental fees over the life of each lease. Your first task is to create the fields you need to run your growing empire. Here's the list of fields:

- First Name
- Last Name
- Rental Fee
- Lease Duration
- Date Signed
- Lease Document

Creating fields with the Field Picker is quick and easy.

1. **Click the + button labeled New Field.**

   A field—labeled Field—appears in the list.

2. **Type *First Name* and then press Enter.**

   The field's name is accepted.

Repeat the process to create the Last Name and Rental Fee fields. See the box below for more information on how to decide which fields your database needs.

UP TO SPEED

A Field = Individually Significant Data

Your database tracks lease documents, and its fields will include all the important attributes about those documents. How do you decide which fields to create?

For example, you may create a single Name field to hold lease signers' first and last names—but you'd be making a mistake. What if you need to sort your data by last name? If you've entered names the way you might type them in a word processor (first name and then last name), you'd only be able to sort by the person's first name.

It's usually a bad move to have different kinds of information in the same field. Instead, think about what elements—no matter how small—are important to how you'll search, sort, analyze, and otherwise access your records later. In database lingo, those bits of information are *individually significant,* and each one should get its own field.

For example, a U.S. address often contains several pieces of information: street name, optional suite number, city, state, and Zip code. If you stored all that data in one field, you'd have a hard time searching for all the people in Washington state. Your search results would include records with streets or cities called Washington. So when you're deciding which fields you need, ask yourself: "Which bits of my data are *individually significant?*"

It's usually not necessary to split off a suite number from a street address field, but it's usually best to split off the city, state, and Zip code. It's a rare case, but if you have a compelling reason to split off a bit of data (say you have to do targeted mailings to people with street numbers ranging from 1000 to 1500), then it may make sense for you to split street addresses into two or even more fields.

Managing Field Types

People's names are considered text, because they're made up of alphabetical characters. When you created fields using the simple technique in the previous section, you didn't have to do anything special to create a field that's ideal for storing text. FileMaker automatically creates text fields unless you tell it otherwise. When you need to store numbers, dates, or times, you should create fields meant to store those types of data.

In the Field Picker, click the word "Text" to the right of the Rental Fee field name to view the Field Type menu (Figure 4-3). The Rental Fee field will hold a monetary amount, which is a number. So select Number from the menu.

Now create your remaining fields and set their field types. Here's a list of the fields you need and the field type for each:

- Lease Duration: number

- Date Signed: date

- Lease Document: container

As you add new fields with the Field Picker, it remembers the type of field you created previously and gives each new field you add the same type. You can change the field types as you go along or go back and assign all the proper field types at the end.

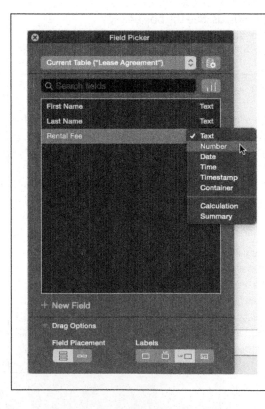

FIGURE 4-3

This menu lets you select among the various field types as you create them in the Field Picker. You can also change a field's type after you create it.

Now that you've created all of your fields, you need to place them on the layout. Select all the items on the list (using standard list selection techniques) and drag them into the layout. You're creating a Form view, so it makes sense to arrange the fields in the order you created them, with labels to the left of each field. The Field Picker is also useful later on in the creation process. As you create new fields, they'll all appear in the field list, where you can drag them—individually or as a group—onto any new layout you create.

> **TIP** While FileMaker's default Drag Option settings—fields in columns with labels on the left—work for the current example, it's not the only choice. Click Drag Options triangle to choose how fields are arranged when you drag them in. These options also let you determine where the labels go or skip labels altogether.

The Field Picker is a handy way to create fields and set their types. But it's not the only way. To view one alternative, click the Exit Layout button on the right side of the Status toolbar. FileMaker asks if you want to save the changes you made to your layout (Figure 4-4). After you click Save, choose View→"View as Table" to switch to Table view, where your data is presented like a spreadsheet.

Spreadsheets have rows, which are equivalent to the records in your table, and they have columns, which are equivalent to the table's fields.

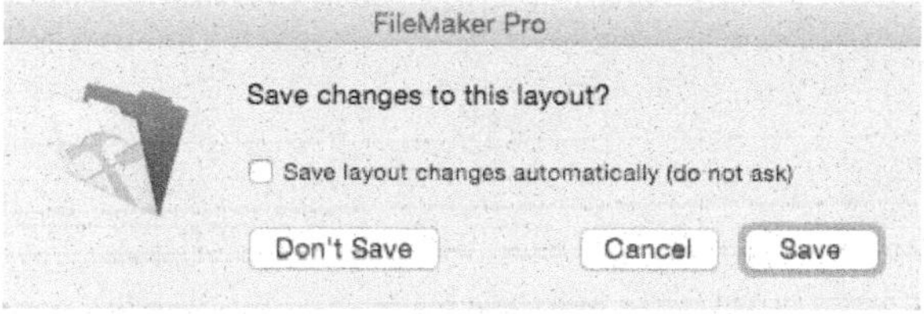

FIGURE 4-4

Once you feel comfortable editing layouts, you can tell FileMaker to stop asking you about layout changes by turning on "Save layout changes automatically (do not ask)." An option in FileMaker's preferences lets you turn the Save dialog box back on if you decide you need it. In Windows, choose Edit→Preferences, on a Mac, choose FileMaker Pro→Preferences, and then click the Layout tab.

In Table view, all your fields are shown in the same order as they appeared in Form view. At the right side is a + sign, which you can use to create a new field. To change a field's type, click the tiny triangle to the right of the field's name. A hierarchical menu appears that lets you change the field's type (Figure 4-5).

You can even change a field's type after you've started entering data in your database. But since some field types have stringent data entry requirements, some of your data may change if you do. For example, text fields can hold more data than number fields, so if you change a text field that contains a lot of data to a number field, some of that data could be lost. So it's definitely safer to make sure you've chosen the right field type *before* you enter any information. See page 242 for details on other field types and how to decide which field type is right for your data.

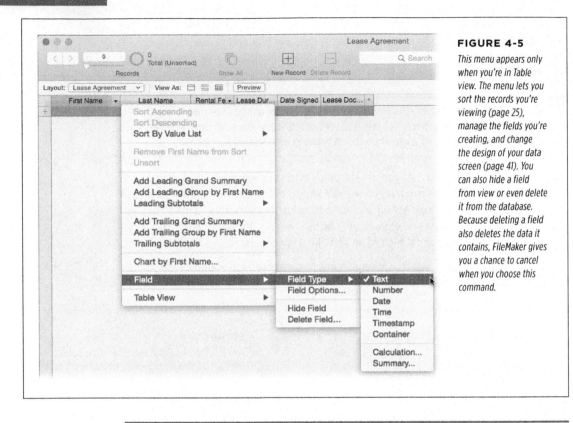

FIGURE 4-5

This menu appears only when you're in Table view. The menu lets you sort the records you're viewing (page 25), manage the fields you're creating, and change the design of your data screen (page 41). You can also hide a field from view or even delete it from the database. Because deleting a field also deletes the data it contains, FileMaker gives you a chance to cancel when you choose this command.

NOTE   If you change a field type, you'll get a warning message box. FileMaker is making sure you know about the ways existing data will be changed. At this point, you don't have any data yet, so those warnings don't matter.

Creating Records in Table View

Now that you've created your fields, your first database is ready to use. Entering data in Table view isn't much different from entering it in Form view. Get started by clicking in the First Name column heading. As soon as you click, FileMaker creates a place for your next new record, and the gray row moves down a place.

Be careful, though. That gray row is just a placeholder. While it looks like a new record has been created, the record count in your Status toolbar tells you that the number of records in your database hasn't increased. The record doesn't get created until you actually click in that gray space. It might seem confusing at first, but this process keeps you from creating blank records in your database.

Type this information into your first record:

- First Name: Antoine
- Last Name: Batiste
- Rental Fee: 985
- Lease Duration: 12
- Date Signed: 9/22/2015

Notice that you can use the Tab key to move from field to field. But unlike a spreadsheet, where you might expect to go to a new row after you get to the last field in that row, the cursor cycles back to the first field of the record's row instead. To move down, click in the gray row. When you click, FileMaker again creates space for the next record.

Embedding a File in a Container Field

When you first created your database, you made a container field called Lease Agreement. Container fields can hold pictures, audio clips, videos, or even other files. In this case, you'll use the field to store a digital copy of each renter's lease agreement for quick reference. It's time to learn how to place a PDF file in your container field.

1. **Click in the Lease Document field.**

   The field's borders have a blue outline, showing that the field is active.

2. **Choose Insert→File.**

   The Insert File dialog box appears. It looks like a standard Open dialog box.

3. **Go to where you downloaded the sample files for this chapter, and select the one called *aBatiste.pdf*.**

   Alternatively, you can use any PDF file on your hard drive.

4. **Click Open (Windows) or Insert (Mac).**

   A small icon and filename appear in the Lease Document field.

The PDF file is now stored inside your database, and better yet, it's linked to a specific record. See page 168 for a way to view the PDF from inside FileMaker. And on page 775, you'll learn how to let FileMaker manage externally stored files you insert into container fields.

Inserting a File with a Reference

Using container fields for storing your files gets you a little closer to the paperless office. But when you embed files in your database, you're increasing the database file's size by the size of the file you've embedded. Text files aren't very large, so embedding them isn't too much of a problem. But if you're storing graphics files, PDFs, or videos, you know those files can be enormous. And in some solutions, like a database that stores your photographs and keeps track of the clients who've bought the rights to use those photos, you could easily end up with a multiple-gigabyte file. But container fields let you link to a file without embedding it in the database and swelling its size. All you have to do is choose the "Store only a reference to the file" option when you insert the file into the container field. It'll look and behave just like an embedded graphic, but it won't make your database into a lumbering ox that clogs up your computer or network.

> **NOTE** Since you're storing a link to the file instead of placing it inside the database, FileMaker will lose track of the document if you move or rename it after you create the link in the container field. Instead, you'll see a message that says, "The file cannot be found:" followed by the file's name. So make sure that you have a file organization system in place before you start storing your files as references.

Exporting Field Contents

If you ever need a copy of the original PDF file, you can open the *CH04 Lease Agreement.fmp12* file, find the record containing the document you need (you'd probably search by first and last name), and then export the record. When you do, FileMaker creates a new copy of the file, outside of your database. Here's how it works:

1. **Click in the Lease Document field to select it.**

   You have to tell FileMaker which field contains the file you need.

2. **Choose Edit→Export Field Contents.**

   The "Export Field to File" dialog box appears.

3. **Navigate to the folder into which you want to save the file and then click Save.**

   You don't even need to type a new file name. FileMaker knows the file's original name and is ready to recreate it exactly as it was. Of course, you're free to change the name if you want.

It doesn't matter whether your container field contains embedded or linked files (as long as a linked file was never moved or renamed). Either way, your file will be exported. See the box on page 106 for information on the handy options at the bottom of the "Export Field to File" dialog box.

■ Understanding Layouts

Tables help you organize and store your data, but layouts determine how that data appears. Layouts determine the text formatting of your data and even where each field appears onscreen. Layouts are so critical to the way your database performs that FileMaker automatically creates a layout to go with each table you create. When you created the Lease Agreement file at the beginning of this chapter, FileMaker made a layout to hold the fields you created.

You already know one way that layouts give your data visual structure. For example, when you switch from Table view to Form view, the data changes from a spreadsheet-like list to a record-by-record version of your data. But a more powerful way to change your data's appearance is to use Layout mode. There you get access to graphics and designing tools that let you change fonts, add color, paste in your logo, or move your fields around so that your database can match your company's branding. Many of FileMaker's most powerful features are set up in Layout mode, so it's not just about making your database pretty.

One database file can contain as many layouts as you want. So you can create one layout for data entry and another for printing. Indeed, it often makes sense to create one List layout for an onscreen report and a separate report layout meant for printing that same information.

NOTE Layout mode has so many features that this book devotes two entire chapters to designing layouts (Chapter 8 and Chapter 9). In your real working life, you'll switch frequently between Browse and Layout modes, so this first section begins by helping you identify the basic tools and commands you'll use for layouts.

The Layout Bar

The Layout bar is tucked between the Status toolbar and the content area of your window (Figure 4-6). At the left of the Layout bar is a Layout pop-up menu so you can switch between your layouts (once you get more than one layout, that is). Form, List, and Table view buttons are to the right of the Layout pop-up menu. Click the Edit Layout button to switch from Browse mode to Layout mode. (Or you can use the View menu commands, or the Mode pop-up menu near the bottom-left edge of the window.)

TIP If you can't see the Layout bar, it may be because the Status toolbar is hidden. Click the Status toolbar control button at the bottom of your window to show it (look between the Zoom controls and the Mode pop-up menu).

POWER USERS' CLINIC

Getting the Most Out of Your Fields

The Edit→Export Field Contents command isn't limited to container fields. With very few exceptions, you can export the contents of almost any field to a file (if you can't click in the field, you can't export its contents). To understand why you can't click in some fields, read about field behavior in Chapter 7, and about security in Chapter 19.

Here are some examples of how to export to your advantage:

- Use Edit→Export Field Contents to create a file without having to retype what you've stored in FileMaker. But if you just whiz by the "Export Field to File" dialog box without looking, you'll miss a couple of options that'll save you buckets of time. If you want to watch a QuickTime video at a size larger than the skimpy container field, just select the "Automatically open file" option as you export the contents of your field. FileMaker creates a duplicate video file for you and then opens a QuickTime player for your viewing pleasure.

- If you choose the "Automatically open file" option when you export a file, FileMaker can open the right program for whatever you've exported. You'll get a text editor

for text, a PDF viewer for a PDF, or a graphics viewer for graphics. You don't have to scramble around looking for a program that can handle your file, because FileMaker figures it out for you.

- If you want to spread the wealth around—let your colleagues know about a customer who always makes a big order at the beginning of the new quarter, for instance—then turn on the "Create email with file as attachment" option when you export your field contents. FileMaker makes a file and then launches your email program, starts a new email message, and attaches your newly exported file to it. All you have to do is type a name, subject, and some text, and then send the email on its merry way. FileMaker can send email through Microsoft Exchange (Windows only), Microsoft Outlook, and Apple Mail (Mac only).

Let FileMaker really impress you by clicking both options at once. You'll get a copy of the file open for reference and a fresh, shiny email nearly ready for sending. If you've got the screen real estate, you can look at both of these little jewels while you're checking out the FileMaker record that spawned them.

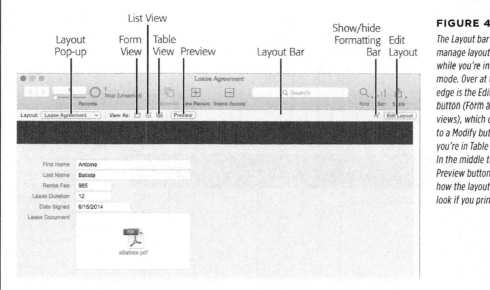

Layout
Pop-up

List View

Form   Table
View   View   Preview

Layout Bar

Show/hide
Formatting   Edit
Bar   Layout

FIGURE 4-6

The Layout bar helps you manage layouts even while you're in Browse mode. Over at the right edge is the Edit Layout button (Form and List views), which changes to a Modify button when you're in Table view. In the middle there's a Preview button to see how the layout would look if you printed it.

The Layout Status Toolbar and Layout Mode

When you switch to Layout mode, the Layout and Status toolbars change to show the tools you need to customize your layout. Even the menu choices and available commands have changed. Two new menus (Layouts and Arrange) have appeared, the Records menu is gone, and if you scroll through the other menus, you'll see that they have many new commands in them.

Before you start designing, it makes sense to get familiar with these new tools. Figure 4-7 shows what your database looks like in Layout mode and points out the tools and objects you need to identify when you're doing basic layout design.

TIP Since the tools in Layout mode are different from those in Browse mode, you can customize each toolbar separately. Choose View→Customize Status Toolbar to see the collection of buttons and tools available in each mode.

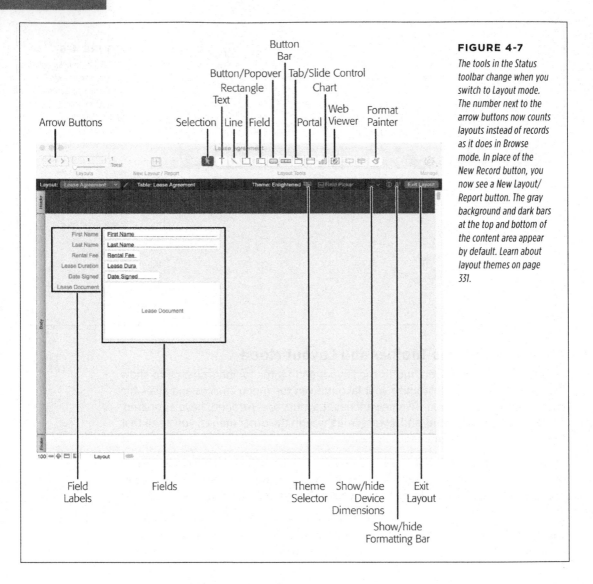

FIGURE 4-7

The tools in the Status toolbar change when you switch to Layout mode. The number next to the arrow buttons now counts layouts instead of records as it does in Browse mode. In place of the New Record button, you now see a New Layout/ Report button. The gray background and dark bars at the top and bottom of the content area appear by default. Learn about layout themes on page 331.

Layout Objects

The items you see in the content area of a layout are called *objects,* and they're the basic building blocks for all layouts. You can click individual objects to move, resize, or format them. You can use your favorite technique for selecting multiple objects (see the box on page 110) and apply formatting to groups of objects at one time. There's even a Format Painter tool to copy formatting from one object to other objects of the same type.

A layout features nine types of objects, and each has its own specific uses and behaviors. Here's an introduction to each type:

- **Text objects.** Text objects appear on nearly every FileMaker layout. Field labels are text objects that can be moved and formatted separately from the fields they identify. All the formatting you learned about in Chapter 2 can be applied to text objects. The spell checker even works in Layout mode, except it checks text objects instead of data inside fields. And if you're using the visual spell-checking feature (page 69), you'll see dotted red underlines if you make a typo or misspell a word.

- **Lines and Shapes.** FileMaker has some tools for creating basic lines and shapes. You can create a colored box and place it behind a group of fields to help your database's users understand which bits of information belong together, or add lines to reports to make them easier to read.

- **Images.** For more graphic power than FileMaker provides, use a program like Photoshop, Illustrator, or GIMP to create your graphics, and then place them on your layout. You can place your company's logo on a layout created to print invoices, or you can use a tiny icon next to an Email field and turn it into a button for sending email.

TIP Don't get carried away importing too many graphics onto a layout, though. If you're sharing a database to a mobile device or over the Internet (page 821) your database can slow down.

- **Fields.** Fields are the heart and soul of your database, so expect to put them on every layout you create. You can easily tell the difference between fields and text objects, because fields have solid borders around them to show their shape and dimensions (unless someone has turned them off). Each field's name appears inside the borders, so you can tell which is which. Just as with text objects, you can apply text and paragraph formatting to fields; the formatting you choose will apply to all the data that appears in your formatted field.

TIP Fields are so important that FileMaker's normal behavior is to add any new field you create to the current (active) layout without even asking you. That's helpful in the beginning stages of creating a database, but it can become annoying after you've honed your layouts to look just so. You can turn off this behavior by choosing Edit→Preferences (Windows) or FileMaker Pro→Preferences (Mac). Click the Layout tab and then click "Add newly defined fields to current layout" to deselect it.

- **Buttons.** Buttons can run automated tasks for you. You'll learn about them on page 177.

- **Tab Controls and Slide Controls.** Both of these objects help you make use of the limited space on your layouts. Tab Controls are discussed on page 162; Slide Controls are examined on page 378.

- **Portals.** Portals are like miniature list layouts within a layout. They display records from other related tables. Find out how they work on page 154.

- **Charts.** Charts let you convert your dry data to visual form. See page 652 to learn how to create and manage them.

- **Web Viewers.** Web viewers are simple web browsers you place right on a FileMaker layout. See page 642 for more information.

Selecting Lots of Objects

Selecting objects on a layout is such a common task that FileMaker gives you several ways to do it. You can always click an object to select it, but you can use any of the following methods as well:

- If you want to select more than one object (so you can operate on them all at once), select the first object, press Shift, and then click each additional object. As you click, each object joins the selection. If you accidentally select an object you don't want, Shift-click it again to deselect it.

- To select *everything* on the layout, choose Edit→Select All or press Ctrl+A (⌘-A).

- You can even select every object of a certain type (every field, for example). First select one object of the type you want. In Windows, press Shift and then choose Edit→Select All. On a Mac, press Option and then choose

Edit→Select Same. FileMaker selects every object that's similar to the one you selected yourself.

- If you have more than one type of object selected when you choose this command, FileMaker selects every object like any of the selected objects. For example, to select every field *and* every text object, select one field and one text object, and then choose this command.

- Finally, you can easily select objects that are close together on the layout with the selection rectangle technique. When you click an empty place on the layout and drag, FileMaker shows the selection rectangle. Drag the rectangle, and anything it touches is added to your selection. Or hold down the Control key (Windows) or the Command key (Mac) to select just the objects that are completely inside the rectangle.

■ Customizing a Layout

FileMaker gives you so many tools for customizing layouts that you can while away hours making each layout look just the way you want it to. Don't mistake this time as wasted effort. The principles of good design and software usability apply to even the most basic database. After all, if you're going to be staring at your database for hours every day, it should look and feel polished. And few databases have just one user (see Chapter 20 to learn how to share your database), so when you're customizing layouts, you have to keep other people's needs in mind, not just your own.

Good design isn't just about how things look. It's also about helping people figure out how the database works. For example, when you're storing data for contact management, you want to arrange objects like address fields in forms that people are familiar with. Most U.S. addresses are shown in a standard form like this:

Name

Street Address

City, State Zip

To make other people—your database's *users*—feel at home in your database, you should arrange your fields as close to that standard arrangement as possible. So a good arrangement of basic fields on a layout for your Contacts would be to have your First Name and Last Name fields on the same line, with the Street Address on the second line, and the City, State, and Zip fields arranged on the third line and resized to the relative widths each bit of data usually takes up. That is, state names are almost always stored as two-letter abbreviations, so the State field can be very narrow compared with the City field. Finally, you'd group the name and address fields together in a "chunk" and add a little space between the name/address chunk and other chunks of data on your layout (Figure 4-8).

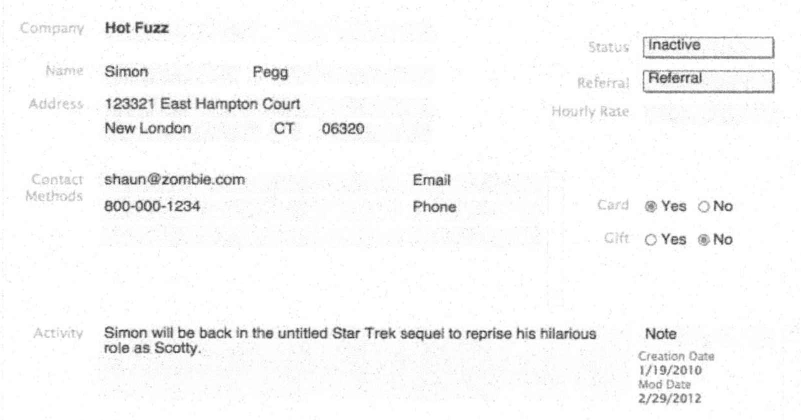

FIGURE 4-8

This sample layout shows data grouped in related "chunks" to help orient users to the layout's purpose. The company name is bolded and slightly separated from everything else. The name and address fields are grouped together and arranged in a familiar pattern. Phone and email are chunked together. Metadata (information about the record itself) is chunked near the lower right.

The principles for good software design have filled many books and websites. Despite their massive usefulness, most of those principles are beyond the scope of this book. However, as you're trying to decide how to arrange your layouts for maximum efficiency and impact, you can take a look at FileMaker's Starter files. See the box on page 113 for more information. The sample files for this book aim to keep good design principles in mind, too.

Editing Text Objects and Fields

Looking at your Lease Agreement layout, you can see that FileMaker placed all your fields in a column when it created your layout. It's up to you to arrange the objects so they make sense. You need to learn how to move, resize, edit, and delete objects to chunk your name fields and labels. You also need to learn how to import a logo to brand your database and add a splash of color. Before you get started, take a look at Figure 4-9 to see the end result you're shooting for.

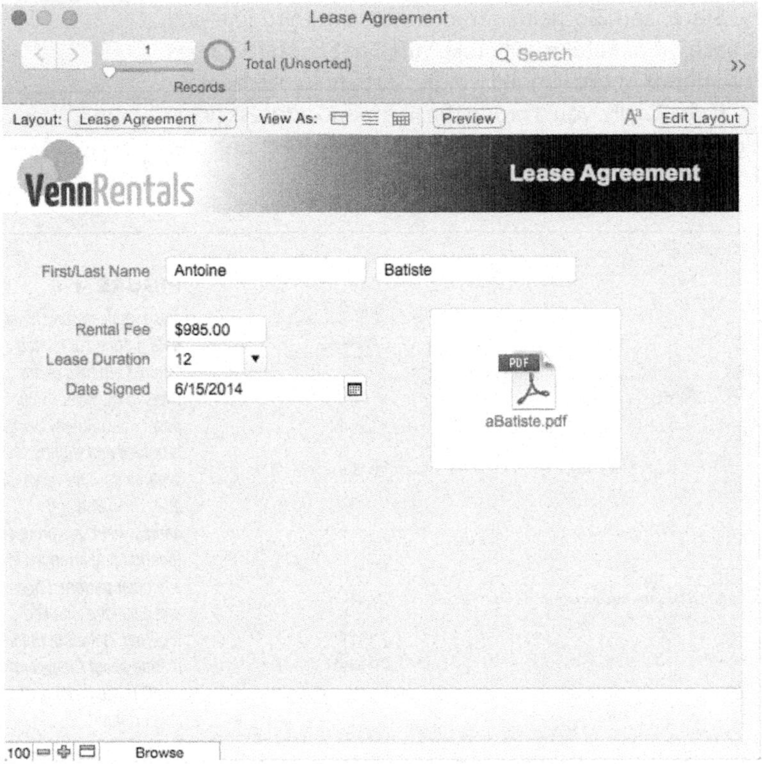

FIGURE 4-9

Here's a preview of your finished layout in Form view. The layout features a logo and title, and the data has been chunked together to help make visual sense. The Lease Document container field is larger, and you can see a thumbnail version of the file itself. The Rental Fee field has been formatted for currency, and the Lease Duration and Date Signed fields have field controls that make data entry quick and consistent.

■ MOVING AND RESIZING FIELDS

To chunk your data on the Lease Agreement layout, put the First Name and Last Name fields on the same line. To save space and be more helpful, you can change the field label for the First Name field to read "First/Last Name." Here's how:

1. **Switch to Layout mode.**

   Use the Edit Layout button, the View menu, or the Mode pop-up menu.

2. **Click the First Name field to select it. Then press Shift as you click the Last Name field to add it to your selection.**

   A single set of handles appears around all your selected objects.

3. **Click the handle in the middle of the right edge of your selected fields and then drag toward the left side of the layout to shorten the fields.**

   As you drag, a tooltip shows you the fields' new measurement, and dynamic guides help you resize objects. See Figure 4-10 for more info.

4. **Shift-click the First Name field to deselect it.**

You want to leave just the Last Name field selected.

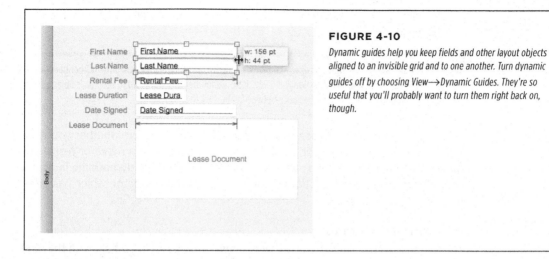

FIGURE 4-10

Dynamic guides help you keep fields and other layout objects aligned to an invisible grid and to one another. Turn dynamic guides off by choosing View→Dynamic Guides. They're so useful that you'll probably want to turn them right back on, though.

GEM IN THE ROUGH

Explore Starter Solutions

FileMaker's starter solutions are grouped in general categories, like Business, Education, and Personal. They cover common database uses, like Invoices, Expense Reports, Event Management, Product Catalog, and Contacts.

These starter files are a good showcase of FileMaker's features, but because they're generalized templates, they aren't meant to meet *your* specific business needs. Even if you think about starting small, these files may need a lot of retrofitting to work well as your business grows. However, poking around in these files is a great way to spark ideas about features you want to learn how to create, as well as get a handle on some good ways to organize your data and create layouts.

So feel free to take a look at a few starter files and then come back to this book to learn how to make a solution that's tailored to your business rules and procedures. Here's how:

1. To create a new database from a starter solution, choose File→New From Starter Solution.
2. The Starter Solution dialog box appears, displaying the 16 solution choices.
3. Click the Content Management solution in the top row and then click Choose.
4. You see a standard Save dialog box with the name of the sample you chose in the Save As field.
5. If you want to change the file's name, type the new name and then select a location for saving the file.
6. Finally, click Save. The new database appears onscreen.

You can start entering data and exploring the file right away. As you move through the chapters in this book, you'll be able to understand what you're seeing under the hood of these starter solutions.

5. **Drag the Last Name field up so it's in line with and a bit to the right of the First Name field.**

The dynamic guides come into play again: As you drag, FileMaker shows a baseline indicator on the Last Name field to help you line it up with the First Name field.

> **TIP** Pressing Shift as you move an object constrains it so it moves in one direction only—either horizontally or vertically. You determine which direction when you drag. Remember this handy tip to keep your objects nicely lined up when you want to create a little space between your data chunks.

Switch to Browse mode to see your changes. If FileMaker asks whether you want to save changes to the layout, click Save. You can select and move or resize any object on a layout; only fields and text objects have the handy baseline indicator line, though. Later in this section, you'll learn about the Inspector, which has other tools for aligning objects.

■ USING OBJECT GRIDS

The dynamic guides were helpful as you aligned the Last Name field with the First Name field. But the grid has more ways of helping you—giving you visual feedback for aligning objects and providing a magnetic pull that snaps objects into alignment as you drag them near the gridlines. Reveal the grid by choosing View→Grid→Show Grid. Turn on the magnetic pull by choosing View→Grid→"Snap to Grid." You don't have to use the snap-to feature if you just want to use the grid for eyeballing alignment. But the grid *must* be visible for the snap-to feature to work.

You can also show or hide the grid, toggle the snap feature, and specify the grid's spacing on the Inspector, at the bottom of the Position panel. The grid is divided into 1-inch squares, but you can change this measurement in the Major Grid Spacing box. Each large square is divided into eight parts horizontally and vertically—the Minor Grid Steps. If you don't like inches, you can change the measurement system by clicking on the "in" label to the right of the Major Grid Spacing field. It toggles through inches, centimeters, and points.

> **TIP** If you don't want to see all those tiny lines between each large grid square, type *0* in the Minor Grid Steps box.

The grid is a big timesaver, unless you *don't* want an object to align with it. But you can work around the grids in several ways:

- To skirt the grid temporarily, press Ctrl (⌘) as you drag the object. As long as the key is down, you can drag the object smoothly to any spot on the layout.

- Choose View→Grid→Snap to Grid to turn the grid off (or use the Inspector, as described earlier). (You can always turn it on again any time you want by repeating this menu command.)

- Press any arrow key to move the selected object (or objects) one point in any direction. You can press an arrow repeatedly to carefully nudge an object into place.

■ VIEWING SAMPLE DATA

If you make a field too narrow, the data inside it will appear cut off or truncated when viewed in Browse mode. Don't worry—the data is there, it just doesn't all show up. So to help you figure out how wide a field needs to be to show its data comfortably, choose View→Show→Sample Data. The field names are replaced with data from the record that was active when you switched to Layout mode. If some of the fields were blank at the time you switched to Layout mode, FileMaker will make up some data (possibly in Latin!) to display. When you want to see the field names again, choose the same command to turn the feature off.

> **NOTE** Even if the field is too narrow to display all its data, you can still type lots of text into the field. When you're in Browse mode, the field expands as you type, but once you leave the field, it snaps back to size. It can't display all that lovely data at once (unless you widen the field, or make it multiple lines high). See page 293 to learn how to add a scroll bar to a field.

UP TO SPEED

Exercising Constraint

FileMaker has a few tricks up its sleeve to make moving and resizing objects easier. You already know how to press Shift to constrain mouse movement. Here are a few more goodies:

- With an object (or objects) selected, press any of the arrow keys to move the object one point in the appropriate direction.

- Duplicate an object by pressing Ctrl (Option) while you drag it.

- Choose Edit→Duplicate to create a new object that's nine points to the right and nine points below the original. Shortcuts are Ctrl+D (Windows) and ⌘-D (Mac).

- Choose View→Grid→"Snap to Grid" to turn another alignment feature on or off. Instead of moving with point-by-point freedom—which can make things nearly impossible to line up—things on the layout automatically align themselves to an invisible grid as you drag them.

Once you're familiar with the Inspector (page 120) you can control your grid by setting spacing. Its controls are on the Position tab.

You can also use the Inspector to move objects. If the position palette says the left edge of an object is two inches from the ruler origin, you can type 4 into the Left Position field to move it two inches farther into the layout.

■ EDITING TEXT OBJECTS

The text objects you're concerned about now are field labels. They're usually created along with the fields they describe. But they're separate objects, so you can apply one font and size to a field and a different font/size combo to its label.

Here's how to edit a text object:

1. **In Layout Mode, click the Text tool to select it. It's a button with a capital T on it (Figure 4-7).**

   The pointer turns to an insertion point as you move across your layout's content area.

2. **Click in the text label, between "First" and "Name."**

   A dotted outline appears around the text object to show you've hit the mark. The cursor will blink where you clicked.

3. **Edit the label to read *First/Last Name*.**

   The slash indicates to the user that there are two separate fields provided for data entry.

4. **Click any other layout object or onto the blank space of the content area to switch back to your pointer tool.**

   You've just edited your text label.

There's a shortcut for selecting the Text tool and clicking into a text object—just double-click the object. Double-click where you want the insertion point to appear. If it's off by a character or so, just use your arrow keys to move it and then start typing. A triple-click selects a whole word within a text object.

After you've edited a text object with the Text tool, the Selection tool (the arrow) is automatically reactivated. FileMaker assumes you wanted to work with just one text object and saves you the trouble of switching back to the Selection tool. If you need to edit several text fields in a row, give the tool icon a double-click instead of a single-click. The icon on the button turns a slightly darker shade of gray to let you know the tool is *locked.* With a locked Text tool, you can create as many text objects as you want: Click to create the text box, type the text, click again for another text box, and so forth. When you're finished, click the Selection tool again to make it active, or just press Esc. This trick works for the other drawing tools, too.

NOTE If you never edit a field label, the label will stay in sync with the field name if the field name is changed. But once you edit the field label, that connection is broken, and you'll need to edit it manually if you change the field name.

On your layout, the name fields are in place and their label reads correctly. But now there's a stray field label taking up valuable real estate.

■ DELETING OBJECTS

To delete any object on a layout, select it and then press the Delete (or Backspace) key. Now that the Last Name field label is a solo act, select it and then delete it. If you prefer using the mouse, you can select an object and then choose the Edit→Clear command, but that's extra steps.

Find and Replace Revisited

If your assistant thought he'd be helpful and add a colon (:) to the end of every field label on your layout, you don't have to visit every text object one by one to clean up the mess. Use Find/Replace to fix every field label in just one shot. When you're in Layout mode, the Find/Replace command searches through text on the *layout* rather than the data in fields and records.

The slightly pared-down dialog box you see when you choose Edit→Find/Replace→Find/Replace in Layout mode works just like its Browse mode counterpart, aside from the lack of "Search across" and "Search within" options.

The other commands on the Edit→Find/Replace submenu—Find Again, Replace & Find Again, and Find Selected—also work exactly as they do in Browse mode. (See page 59 for details on Find/Replace.)

■ ADDING TEXT OBJECTS

Text objects serve more purposes than just field labels. Even relatively simple databases can have many layouts, so it's helpful to put a title at the top of each layout to help you remember what the layout is for. Or you can add helpful hints, like "use the format mm-dd-yyyy" beside a date field to remind data entry folks to enter dates with a four-digit year. Here's how to add a descriptive title to your layout.

1. **In Layout mode, select the Text tool and then click near the top-right side of the layout, where the title should appear.**

   A dotted outline with a blinking insertion point appears where you clicked.

2. **In the text box, type *Lease Agreement*.**

   The text appears as you type, and the dotted line expands to fit.

3. **Click the selection tool (arrow) and then click the text block to select it. Choose Format→Text Color and then choose the lightest gray block from the color swatch that appears.**

   The text color changes to match your selection.

4. **Choose Format→Size→18 Point.**

   The text size increases. If the text block is too close to the right edge of the layout, it may disappear off the screen. To fix that problem, just drag it back toward the left.

> **NOTE** You can also increase font size with the keyboard shortcuts Shift+Ctrl+> (Windows) or Shift-⌘-> (Mac). Each time you use the shortcut, the font size increases to the next measurement in the font size menu. Use the same shortcut, but with the "<" to decrease font size.

5. **Drag the text block into place using Figure 4-9 as a reference.**

The dynamic guides appear as you're moving the text, and if you have "Snap to Grid" turned on, it snaps into place as you drag.

For short bits of text, like a title for your layout or a completely custom field label, just click and then start typing. But if you want to add a block of text that might need paragraph-style formatting (like automatic line breaks and alignment), then you should drag to define the height and width of the text block before you start typing in the new text object.

NOTE You can choose any font you want from your computer's system, but every font you choose has to be installed on the computer where your database is used. If FileMaker can't find the font you choose, it'll substitute a plain one instead. So unless you're the only person who'll ever use your database, it's best to stick with the old standbys most folks are likely to have, such as Helvetica, Times, and Verdana.

■ CREATING A NEW STYLE

In the last section, you changed the font size and color of a text block to make it useful as an orienting headline on your new layout. If you create another layout in the same file (as you will later in this chapter), you can create consistency by making the layout titles look the same. To do so, you could try to remember the font, size, and color you used on the form layout's title. But it's a lot easier to let the Inspector do this work for you, by creating a style that you can apply to other text blocks.

If the Inspector isn't showing, choose View→Inspector. Select the Styles tab. Then follow these steps:

1. **Click the Lease Agreement text block to select it (select the object, not the text itself).**

The Inspector's style options change to show available text styles. The Default style is selected, and at the right side you see a circle with a red triangle.

2. **Click the circle with the red triangle.**

A pop-up menu appears (Figure 4-11).

3. **From the pop-up menu, choose "Save as New Style."**

The Specify Style Name dialog box appears.

4. **Type *Layout Title* into the field and then click OK.**

The Layout Title style is added to the Inspector's list of styles. The circle with the triangle at the top of the Style panel turns red to show you've made changes to the file's theme.

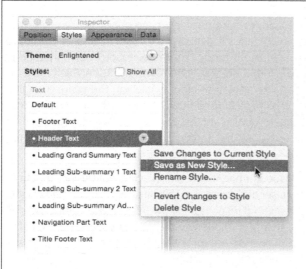

FIGURE 4-11

The Inspector's Styles tab lets you manage the styles that store formatting for items on your layouts. Once you've applied a style to layout objects, any changes you make to the style's definition will change the formatting of all objects you apply the style to.

5. **Click the circle with the red triangle beside the theme's name and then choose "Save Changes to Theme."**

   The triangle turns black to show that the changes are saved. However, FileMaker doesn't actually save changes to its default themes; instead it creates a new *Custom* theme with the same name. To avoid confusion, you should change your Custom theme's name.

6. **Click the circle with the black triangle beside the theme's name and then choose Rename Theme.**

   The Specify Theme Name dialog box appears.

7. **Type *Venn Enlightened* into the field and then click OK.**

   The theme's new name appears on the Styles palette and in the Layout Bar. Your custom theme contains all the styles from the default, plus the edited style you've just made.

> **NOTE** You can explore FileMaker's default themes by choosing Layouts→Change Theme. The Venn Enlightened theme appears at the top in the Custom section. FileMaker's default themes are grouped below. See page 331 for more details.

You've just created a style for a text block, but you can create or edit a style for any layout object. Explore by clicking on objects on your layout while the Inspector's Styles panel is active. The list of styles changes based on the object that's selected.

Read on to learn more about the Inspector, which is FileMaker's most important layout tool.

Using the Inspector

The Inspector is the central clearinghouse for controlling nearly every property of your layout objects (Figure 4-12). Since it deals with layout objects, the Inspector is only available when you're in Layout mode. There's so much information on the Inspector that it's broken down into four tabs' worth of information. Each tab is also divided into sections that you can display or hide by clicking the white triangle to the left of the section's title. When you hide or show a section, the Inspector shrinks or grows to fit the appropriate options. And since those options change based on the object (or objects) selected, don't be alarmed if your Inspector seems to have a life of its own.

You can even open multiple Inspector panels, each displaying a different tab. Choose View→New Inspector to get a second, or even a third Inspector, and then click the tab you want to see on each one. All Inspectors show information about the same object (or group of objects), so any changes you make to any Inspector will affect every selected object. Multi-Inspectors are meant to let you view all of an object's properties at once, without needing to switch tabs.

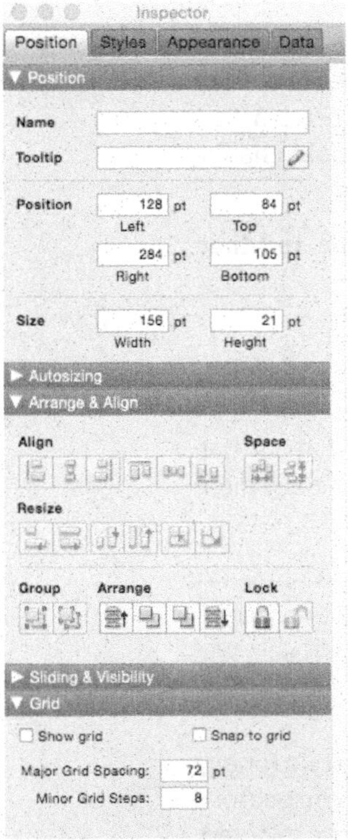

FIGURE 4-12

The Inspector shows the properties of the active object. If many options on the Inspector read 0 or if the buttons are grayed out, you probably don't have anything selected. Or if you have a group of objects selected, you may see some options dimmed because they can't be applied to some of the objects in the group. If you don't see what you need, just change what you've selected on your layout.

If the Inspector isn't showing on your layout, make sure you're in Layout mode, and then choose View→Inspector. If no information is showing in the Inspector when it appears, make sure you have at least one object selected.

The Inspector doesn't just show you an object's properties; it lets you change them, too. For example, the layout title you created in the last tutorial may not have enough space around it. You can give the title a little breathing room by making the layout's Header a little taller. Here's how:

1. **In Layout mode, click the Header label to select it (the label is sideways on the left edge of the Header).**

   The Header label turns a darker gray to show that it's selected.

2. **If the Inspector isn't showing, choose View→Inspector.**

   The Inspector appears, and it's showing the Header's properties. (If the Inspector is in the way of the objects you're focusing on, move it out of the way by dragging its title bar.)

3. **If the Position tab isn't active, click it.**

   The fields you need for changing the Header's height are on the Position tab. Measurement systems are shown to the right of each position and size field.

4. **Click any measurement label to change the measurement system to points.**

   You may have to click a few times to get to the system you want. All the labels change when you click any one. The measurement choices are inches (in), centimeters (cm), and points (pt). Since font sizes are measured in points, it makes sense to use it as a screen measurement system. (Plus, a point is roughly the same as an onscreen pixel.)

5. **In the Size section of the Position tab, click in the Height field. Type *60* in the Height field and then tab or click out of the field to make the change.**

   The Header increases in height.

Alternatively, you can drag the dividing line between the Header and Body to resize it. Keep your eye on the Inspector's display to see when you get to the right height. Either way is fine. Use the method you find easier.

You may need to move the layout title's text block now that the Header height has changed. Make sure that the text block fits completely within the Header. If it overlaps the Body part by even 1 point, you may get unintended display problems. You'll learn more about Layout Parts on page 277.

Inserting a Picture on a Layout

You've already seen how to insert a file into a container field, but that's not the only way to use outside resources in FileMaker. You can put your company's logo on your layouts to make them look more customized and professional. Use any common graphic file format: .jpeg, .gif, .png, .eps, .tiff, .bmp, or .wmf. For a complete list of supported formats, see FileMaker Pro Help (page 35) for details.

Formatting Text

Fields and text objects both show text. You can change the font, size, color, and style of both types of objects. First, select the objects. Then go to the Format menu. The first seven submenus let you manipulate the text formatting of the selected object.

- The Format→Font menu shows fonts installed on your computer. (In Windows, you may need to choose Format→Font→More Fonts and then add the fonts you want to your font list. On a Mac, every font you have installed is automatically listed.)

- You can dress up your text in any font, size, and style you like. But don't forget that any computer your database is *used* on has to have the font installed. You might have fancy $300 fonts on your computer, but your employees may be using the database on stripped-down PCs. So you'll either need to pick a font that comes standard with the operating system or buy and install your custom fonts on each machine that will use your database.

- From the Format→Size menu, you can choose a size. If you don't see the one you want, choose Format→Size→Custom instead. In the window that appears, type any number from 1 to 500.

- If you're designing a database on the Mac for use on PCs, you need to make all your text objects 15 to 20 percent larger than you (and FileMaker) think they need to be, because PCs display fonts larger than their Mac brethren do. You should check your layouts on a PC, since any text object that isn't wide enough flows over onto another line or may be cut off, which probably isn't what you intended.

- FileMaker includes all the standard styles (bold, italic, and so on) in the Format→Style menu. You can pick from three different types of underlines (Word Underline underlines words, but not the space between them, and Double Underline puts two lines under your text). You can also choose Upper Case, Lower Case, or Title Case to format the case of text no matter how you typed it.

- The options in Format→Align Text let you align the text left to right and top to bottom. For instance, if you choose Bottom, the text sticks to the bottom of the text object when you make it taller. This setting makes sense only if you type multiple lines of text into a text object. For instance, you may want your company address to appear at the bottom of all your invoices. You'll get better alignment if you format the address text block with Bottom alignment.

- Choose Format→Line Spacing→Double to apply double-spacing (or choose Format→Line Spacing→Other to specify the spacing more precisely).

- The Format→Orientation menu applies only to text in Asian languages and lets you run text either vertically or horizontally.

- To color your text, point to Format→Text Color. A color palette appears, and the color you select is applied to the selected text.

You can apply each of these options to an entire text object (just select the object first) or to a run of text *inside* the object. To style just a portion of the text, use the Text tool to select a portion of the text first. In this way, you can mix fonts, sizes, and styles inside a single text object. All of these options, except Orientation, are also available on the Inspector.

NOTE If you downloaded the sample files earlier in this chapter, you have a sample logo file you can use for this tutorial. If not, go to this book's Missing CD page at *www.missingmanuals.com/cds/fmp14mm*.

Here's how to place a graphic on a layout:

1. **In Layout mode, click Insert→Picture and then navigate to the folder where you've stored the sample files from this chapter.**

   If you didn't download the files earlier, you can place any GIF, JPEG, or PNG file, but your results won't be the same as Figure 4-9.

2. **Select the *Venn Logo.png* file and then click Open (Windows) or Insert (Mac).**

   The logo appears on your layout, but it's not in the right spot. Luckily, though, it's already selected.

3. **In the Inspector's Left Position field, type *10* and then press Tab. Then type *0* in the Top Position field and press Tab.**

   The logo graphic moves into place.

Alternatively, you can use your computer's Copy and Paste commands to place a graphic onto a layout. Most of the time, they work just fine. But for some file formats, you may get unexpected results. If you do, delete the funky graphic and then use Insert→Picture.

Adding a Gradient

You've got a nice logo in the header, but it gets a little lost in that black background. You can switch the solid background to a gradient that fades to white—perfect for making your logo pop off the screen. As usual, make sure you're in Layout Mode and you can see the Inspector.

1. **Click the Header label to select it.**

   The Header's label turns darker gray to show that it's selected.

2. **Click the Inspector's Appearance tab. In the Graphic area, use the Fill pop-up menu and choose Gradient.**

   When you change a solid-colored item to a gradient, you'll see a slider with two color swatches (Figure 4-13). The swatches tell FileMaker how to make the color change you want. Initially, both swatches will be white.

3. **Click the color swatch on the left.**

   When the Color palette appears, click on the black square. Should you desire a color that isn't in the palette, you can click the Other Color button to open your OS's color picker.

4. **The color swatch changes to match the color you selected. In the Angle field, type *110* and press Tab.**

   The gradient's angle changes so that the gradient fades to white near the logo.

5. **Click the Inspector's Styles tab.**

   You've made changes to the Header's style, so you need to save those changes to the style. Then you can apply it to headers on other layouts.

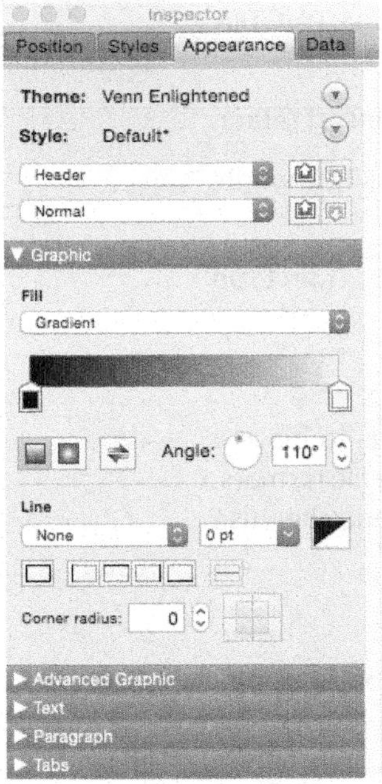

FIGURE 4-13

You can use the Gradient to fill any object you create. But with great power comes great responsibility, so use this effect with restraint. FileMaker gives you lots of tools for creating beautiful effects on your layouts. But your data is the most important thing in your database, so each time you add a new object or effect, switch back to Browse mode and cast a critical eye over your changes. If the layout's design makes it hard to make things out, then start removing nonessential details that take focus away from your information.

6. **Click the circle with the red triangle beside the style's name and then choose "Save Changes to Current Style."**

   The default Header style for this layout has been changed.

7. **Click the circle with the red triangle beside the theme's name and then choose "Save Changes to Theme."**

   The new style is now saved inside the file's theme. It will be available in the Inspector when you need to apply it to another header on another layout.

Formatting Fields

For most layout objects, the Inspector's Data tab is a dim, gray dud. But when a field is at stake, that fourth tab comes into its own (Figure 4-14). There you can set up data formatting controls that display currency, percents, and negative numbers the way you want to see them. You can also give a field a pop-up menu, drop-down list, or drop-down calendar, or assign a checkbox or radio button set to the field. Chapter 8 gives details about all the Data tab's options, but you'll meet a few of them here.

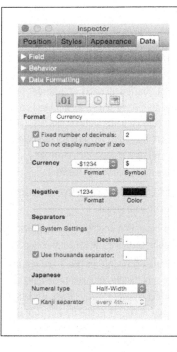

FIGURE 4-14

The Inspector's Data tab as it appears when the Rental Fee field is selected. The Field and Behavior sections have been closed to focus on Data Formatting. Since this section is at the bottom of the Data tab, it's helpful to collapse the sections you're not focused on if you have a smaller monitor or are working on a laptop. The options in the Data Formatting section change depending on the type of the selected field. You can use options here to add currency signs, thousands separators, and colored negative numbers. The Japanese section is useful if you're using a copy of FileMaker that's localized for Japan and you're using Japanese fonts for data display. Otherwise, you can ignore those options.

▪ FORMATTING A NUMBER FIELD

The Rental Fee field contains the amount of rent each Lease Document specifies. Because it will contain numbers, you made it a number field when you created it. Now it's time to learn about the Inspector's suite of formatting options for number fields.

Since a Rental Fee is currency data, that's the format you'll apply. Number formatting doesn't change the value in the field, it just changes the display of that data. By applying a format, you can save keystrokes and make the data more consistent. Here's how to apply the currency format to a number field:

1. **In Layout mode, click the Rental Fee field to select it and then click the Inspector's Data tab.**

   If the Inspector has disappeared, choose View→Inspector. Once the Data tab is selected, you'll see all the options you can apply to the Rental Fee field. Data Formatting is down near the bottom.

2. **Choose Currency from the Format pop-up menu.**

   The Data Formatting section changes to show all the options for the Currency format.

3. Choose the "Fixed number of decimals" option.

The number 2 is the unsurprising automatic setting. That means you'll get two places to the right of the currency's decimal point.

The Right Tool for the Job

FileMaker has some basic line and shape drawing tools, which are always available in the Status toolbar (in Layout mode)—unless you've customized it and removed them (page 16) or if your window is very narrow (just widen it to see all the tools). A companion to the toolbar—the Formatting bar—gives you more control over your drawn objects. If you can't see a Font pop-up menu and some alignment tools just below the Status/Layout toolbar, then the Formatting bar isn't showing. Choose View→Formatting Bar to display it.

Four drawing tools let you create simple shapes, like lines, rectangles, rounded rectangles, and circles. Here are some tips:

- Use the Graphic section of the Inspector's Appearance panel to add a fill to an object or to change its line type, width, or color.

- The border icons let you toggle parts of a border on and off. They work on all two-dimensional objects on your layout (drawn objects, fields, buttons, portals, tab controls, and slide controls). So you could place two fields side by side and turn off their inside borders to make your layout look like some forms you see on the Web.

- These same fill and line controls can also change the appearance of fields on your layout.

- Add shadows to two-dimensional objects with the options in the Advanced Graphic section of the Appearance panel.

- Press the Ctrl (Windows) or Option (Mac) key while creating or resizing a rectangle, rounded rectangle, or oval to make a perfect square or circle. When working with a line, this key makes it perfectly horizontal, perfectly vertical, or exactly 45 degrees from one of these directions.

TIP The most common reason to change this option is to suppress the display of numbers to the right of the decimal place, even if you enter those characters. So if the entry in the field is "985.99," the field will show "986" instead. FileMaker uses normal rounding rules to display the formatted data. Enter *0* in the "Fixed number of decimals" field to get this format.

4. Choose the "Use thousands separator" option.

The standard character for a thousands separator is a comma, but you can use any other character you'd prefer. Another common choice is a period, which is used in some European countries.

5. Switch to Browse mode to view your handiwork. Click Save if FileMaker asks whether you want to "Save the changes to the layout."

You can tell FileMaker to stop asking you about layout changes by choosing the "Save layout changes automatically (do not ask)" option.

Click in the Rental Fee field. You can see that the data appears just as you entered it. But when you're not clicked in the field, the display changes according to the formatting options you just set.

ADDING A FIELD CONTROL STYLE AND A VALUE LIST

Consistent data entry is critical to a well-behaved database. If you're tracking students for your school district, and the best half of your data entry folks type a school's name as "Glenwood Elementary School," and the mediocre half type "Glenwood School," and the lazy third half barely manage to peck out "Glnwod," you're going to have a mess on your hands. But you can control what users put into fields that should contain only specific bits of data. Figure 4-15 shows the Inspector's Field panel, where you control how fields look and behave.

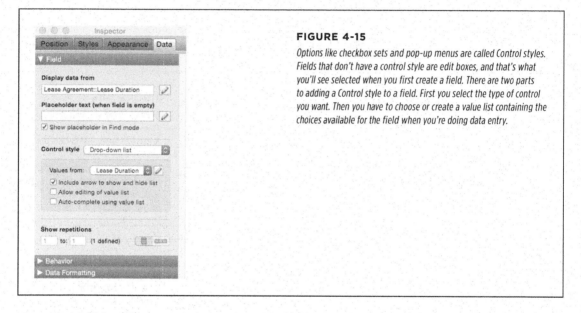

FIGURE 4-15

Options like checkbox sets and pop-up menus are called Control styles. Fields that don't have a control style are edit boxes, and that's what you'll see selected when you first create a field. There are two parts to adding a Control style to a field. First you select the type of control you want. Then you have to choose or create a value list containing the choices available for the field when you're doing data entry.

Your database doesn't store school names, but you do limit your properties' leases to durations of 1, 2, or 3 years, and you want the data entered in months only. Here's how to create a value list that lets your data entry people know what values belong in the Lease Duration field:

1. **In Layout mode, click the Lease Duration field to select it and then click the Inspector's Data tab.**

   If the whole Inspector has disappeared, choose View→Inspector.

2. **In the Field section of the Inspector, choose "Drop-down list" from the "Control style" pop-up menu.**

   The "Values from" pop-up menu appears, but there's nothing in it. You have to create a value list for the field to display.

3. **Click the pencil icon next to the "Values from" pop-up menu.**

The "Manage Value Lists for 'Lease Agreement'" dialog box appears.

4. **Click the New button.**

The Edit Value List dialog box appears.

5. **In the Value List Name field, type *Lease Duration*.**

A simple descriptive name is the best policy for database elements. In this case, you're matching the value list's name to the field you'll be assigning it to.

6. **Click in the "Use custom values" field and then type the numbers *12, 24,* and *36,* without any commas, and press Enter (Return) after 12 and 24, so each number is on its own line. (Figure 4-16).**

You're typing the number of months in 1, 2, and 3 years, and each has to be on a separate line. Each line represents one item in the drop-down list you're creating.

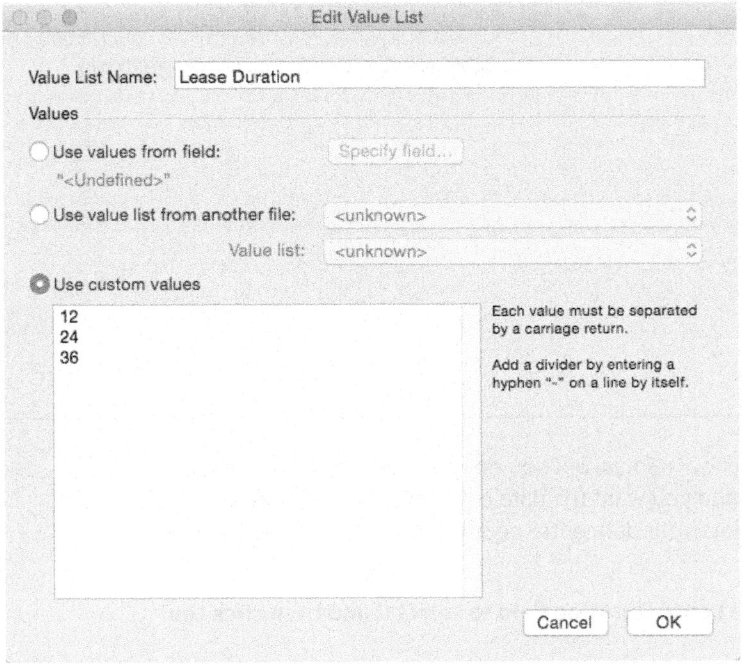

FIGURE 4-16

When you name elements in your database, it helps to give them descriptive names. In this case, the new value list will be used to limit the data entry in the Lease Duration field, so even though it's the same name as the field itself, that's the best name to give the value list. Notice that each value is on its own line. Take care not to accidentally type an extra return at the end of your list. If you do, you'll get a blank line in your value list. That's not a big deal for a drop-down list, but it's pretty confusing if you choose a radio button or a checkbox set.

7. **Click the OK button until you're back on the layout.**

The Lease Duration value list now shows in the Inspector's "Values from" pop-up.

8. **Click the "Include arrow to show and hide list" option.**

The arrow gives users a visual clue that the field contains a drop-down list.

Switch to Browse mode to see the new drop-down list in action. Click its arrow to see the drop-down list and then make a selection to see how data is entered into the field.

▦ EDITING A VALUE LIST

If your business rules change and you need to change the values that display in the value list, it's easy to edit. Select the field your value list is attached to (Lease Duration, in this case), open up the Inspector to the Data tab, and then click the pencil icon next to the value list's name. Click Edit and then make the appropriate changes. Click OK until you're back on your layout. Finally, switch to Browse mode to see the new values.

> **NOTE** Changing the value list has no effect on any data that's already in that field. But now you have the option to select the new value going forward.

▦ ADDING A DROP-DOWN CALENDAR TO A FIELD

FileMaker is picky about how you store dates in date fields. To make data entry easy, you can add a handy visual calendar to your date fields. Here's how:

1. **In Layout mode, click the Date Signed field to select it, and then click the Inspector's Data tab, if it isn't already the front tab.**

   If the whole Inspector has disappeared, choose View→Inspector.

2. **In the Field section of the Inspector, choose "Drop-down calendar" from the Control Style pop-up menu.**

   It's the last item on the list.

3. **Choose the "Include icon to show and hide calendar" option.**

   The calendar will drop down even if you don't choose this option, but this way your users can tell it's there.

Switch to Browse mode. You'll see the calendar icon at the right edge of the Date Signed field (Figure 4-17). Click the icon to view the calendar pop-up menu. If there's data in your field, the calendar will be set to show that date. The calendar's left and right arrows move the display to the previous and next month. Its up and down arrows go to the next and previous year on the Mac, or click the Month/Year title to change years in Windows. Your keyboard arrow keys move through the calendar's dates. To enter the current date, just click the Today line at the bottom of the calendar.

After all your refinements, this layout is starting to look and behave like something you can use to make your property leasing business hum. But it's the rare database that can function with a single layout. Find out how a list layout can help you in the next section.

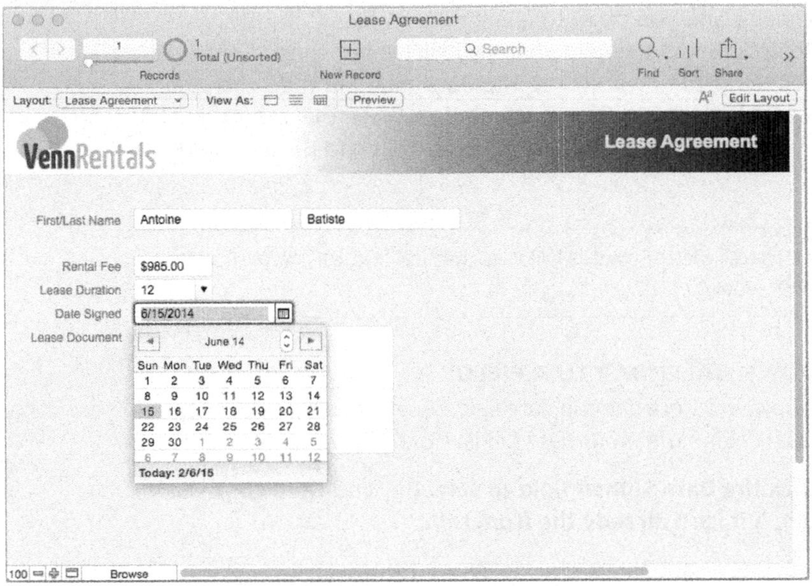

FIGURE 4-17

A drop-down calendar ensures that dates are entered according to FileMaker's rules. In Windows, drop-down lists or calendars may pop up instead, if the window isn't big enough to contain all their glory. You don't have to use the calendar to enter data even if a field has been formatted to show one. Just click in the field and type away, but be sure to enter a FileMaker-approved format (7/21/2014, 7.21.2014, or 7-21-2014, for example).

■ Creating a New Layout

Your first layout gives you a detail view of each Lease Document record. It's a good place for doing your basic data entry and viewing a thumbnail of the document's PDF. Once you have lots of data in the file, it'd be nice to have a list of all your lease documents. But the List view button isn't very useful because of all that blank space below your fields. What you need is a new layout that's designed with a list in mind. FileMaker has a Layout Assistant that walks you through the process. Here's how it works:

1. **In Layout mode, choose Layouts→New Layout/Report.**

   The New Layout/Report window of the Layout Assistant appears.

2. **Type *Lease Agreement List* in the Layout Name field.**

   Because most databases end up with lots of layouts, it's helpful to give them descriptive names.

3. **When the assistant asks you for device options, select Computer. From the layout options, select List.**

   When you're done picking options, click Finish.

4. **Back in Layout mode, on the Layout bar, click the Field Picker. Select all the available fields in the list, except the Lease Document field.**

   Since a list is meant to be a compact display of your records, it doesn't make a lot of sense to show a large container field on the new list. You can drag the field names to rearrange the list.

5. **In the Drag Options, select horizontal orientation for field placement and choose the icon that puts labels above the fields. Drag the fields into the body area of the layout.**

FileMaker has created a layout that's suitable for a screen list. The fields are in columns, based on the order you chose in step 5. Switch to Browse mode to see how your layout looks.

> **NOTE** If you can't see more than one record on the list layout, first make sure you have entered data for multiple records. If you have, click the "List view" button. The finished sample file for this chapter has several records, so you don't have to worry about spending time on data entry.

To make your new layout fit in stylistically with the custom form view you made earlier, you'll need to add the layout title ("Lease Agreement List") in the header and apply the Layout Title style to it, adjust field widths, format the Rental Fee with currency, and add your field control styles (Drop-down list and Calendar). Make the control style changes only if you'll be using the List view for adding records and/or editing data. (Check out page 305 to learn how to change field behavior to keep data in those fields from being edited.)

Making Two Layouts Match

Your database will be more polished if your layouts look alike. Whenever possible, put some of the same elements in exactly the same place on each layout. That way, people can use those familiar objects to get oriented as they switch from one layout to another. The logo and layout title are perfect candidates for creating a sense of consistency among your layouts. You can use the Insert→Picture command to put your logo on the List layout, or just copy and paste it between layouts.

■ APPLYING STYLES

Making the two layout titles look the same is easy because you already saved the style back on page 118. Now you just need to apply your saved style to the text block. Make sure the Inspector is visible and select the Styles tab. Click the Lease Agreement List text block to select it and then choose Layout Title from the list of styles in the Inspector. The text block's formatting changes.

> **WARNING** If you're familiar with the Format Painter from previous versions of FileMaker Pro, you'll be tempted to use it to make your layouts match. It's still there for old times' sake, but you should rarely use it in your new databases. If you use the Format Painter instead of applying styles, your database may increase drastically in file size and become inefficient. This is especially important if you'll share your database on iOS or on the Web (page 821).

This text block has more text in it than the one you copied the style from, so you may need to resize it after the new formats are applied.

Now that you've formatted two layouts—Lease Agreement and Lease Agreement List—switch back to Browse mode and then switch between layouts. Although the text blocks are now the same font and point size, you can see that they're not in exactly the same spot on the two layouts. Making sure objects look alike and are in the same location is another way to make your database more polished. When objects are in nearly the same location on different layouts, but are off by a few pixels, you'll notice an annoying flash in that spot when you switch between layouts. But if they are in exactly the same spot, that flash goes away and you'll have a seamless transition as you switch.

Use the Inspector to find the Left and Top positions of the logo on one layout, and then switch to the other layout to apply those position measurements to the second logo. Use the same technique for matching the title text blocks—except that for the title blocks, you'll match up the right and top edges. Make the new layout's Header part 95 points high. That's a lot taller than the other layout's header, but this one needs to have room for your column heads. Select the Field labels and move them down near the bottom of the Header part.

> **TIP** To move an object more precisely, press the up, down, right, or left arrow keys on your keyboard. The selected object(s) move 1 point at a time.

◼ COPYING OBJECT AND PART STYLES

Back on page 121, you customized the header part to make your logo stand out from the background. That process required several steps, including a trip to the Color palette. If you followed the tutorial and saved the changes to the header's style and the file's theme, your header part will already have the customized style. But if you've forgotten to save changes to a style you'll have to get that style some other way. One fix is to go back to the layout that has the changes and then save style and theme changes. But there's a pair of buttons on the Inspector that can easily move a style onto a new layout for you. Make sure you're in Layout mode and that your Inspector is visible.

1. **On the Lease Agreement layout, click the Header label to select it. On the Inspector's Appearance tab, click the blue button with the up arrow (Figure 4-18).**

   This button copies the style of the selected object, or in this case, the selected layout part.

2. **Switch to the Lease Agreement List layout and then select its Header part.**

   The blue button with the down arrow is highlighted, telling you that the style is ready to be copied to the selected object.

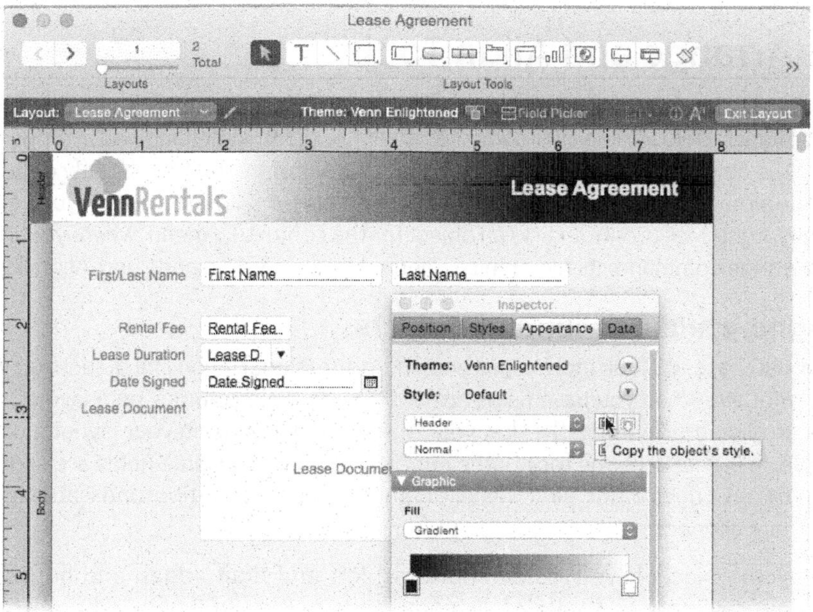

FIGURE 4-18

The Copy/Paste Style buttons on the Inspector work on both layout objects and layout parts. As with the other tools on the Inspector, you can get information about the Copy/Paste Style buttons by pointing to them. Wait a second or so, and a tooltip appears.

3. **Click the blue button with the down arrow.**

   It sure would be easier if this button had a name. But your styles are safely copied to the new layout's Header.

4. **Click the circle with the red triangle beside the style's name and choose "Save Changes to Current Style."**

   The changes to the default Header style are now saved.

5. **Click the circle with the red triangle beside the theme's name and then choose "Save Changes to Theme."**

The new style is now saved inside the file's theme and will be available in the Inspector when you need to apply it to another text block. The Header and its logo look great, but those gray field labels on the left get lost as the gradient turns to white. Draw a rectangle in the header the width of your layout that's about quarter of an inch tall. Then use the Alignment tools (see next section) to send the object behind your field labels to help them stand out from the gradient. If you want to enter data on the list layout, you'll need to add field control styles to the Rental Fee (page 125) and Date Signed fields (page 129). See page 306 for a way to keep folks from clicking in fields and entering data.

NOTE   All objects, not just text blocks, have styles. Applying them consistently is important, especially when you'll be sharing your database using FileMaker Go or on the Web. See page 332 for details.

◼ Arrange and Align Tools

Designing custom layouts requires lots of moving and resizing layout objects. It's such a frequent task that FileMaker dedicates an entire menu to helping you arrange and align the objects on a layout. You can find the same commands in a slightly different form on the Inspector's Position tab, in the Arrange & Align section (Figure 4-19). Finally, right-click (Control-click) an object for the contextual menu, where you'll find an Arrange command. Its hierarchical menu contains the Arrange and Align tools.

Aligning and Distributing Objects

Your database will look more organized and professional if you line objects up with one another. When you have fields arranged in multiple columns on a layout, take care to align the fields neatly. *How* you align them depends on your layout. For example, in Figure 4-19, the tops of the First Name and Last Name fields are aligned, and the left edges of the First Name, Rental Fee, Lease Duration, and Date Signed fields are aligned.

All layout objects have tops and bottoms, left and right edges, and horizontal and vertical centers. A suite of six commands (shown in Figure 4-19 or on the Arrange→Align submenu) helps you align multiple selected objects on any of their edges or centers. When you align objects on an edge, all the objects move to align with the object that's farthest in the direction you chose. When you align objects on their centers, they line up on an invisible line through the center of every object.

If the spaces between objects are uneven, use the Distribute commands. Distribute works by measuring the space between the two outermost objects and then distributing the rest of the objects between those first two. For this command to work, you have to select at least three objects. Then click the appropriate Space button shown in Figure 4-19, or choose Arrange→Distribute Horizontally or Arrange→Distribute Vertically.

Resizing Objects

Back on page 111, you learned how to "chunk" data into related bits and to align edges for better organization. A related concept is to make fields that are near one another, or in the same chunk, the same height and/or width.

You can resize any layout object manually by dragging one of its handles, or by using the Inspector to type a measurement into a size field. But FileMaker gives you a set of menu commands and Inspector tools that make the task more efficient and consistent. You can select multiple objects and resize them to match either the smallest or the largest object's height or width. There's even a command to resize objects to match both width and height. No matter where they are on the layout, selected objects aren't moved with this command; they're only resized.

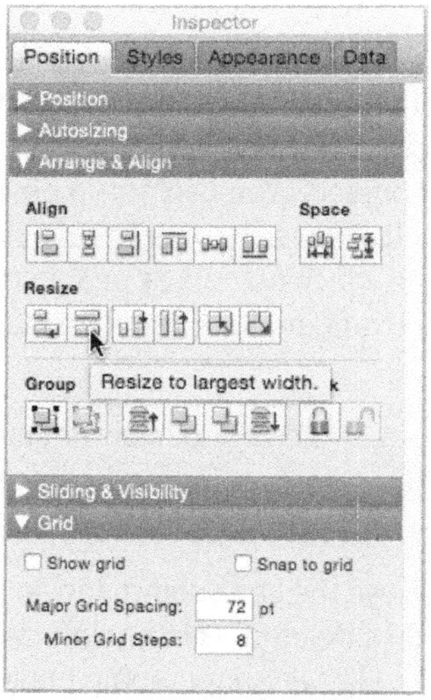

FIGURE 4-19

The Inspector's Arrange and Align tools have icons that indicate their purpose. If you're not sure which tool to use, point to a tool to see the tool's pop-up tooltip. Here the mouse is pointing to the "Resize to largest width" tool. If you get unexpected results, just choose the Edit→Undo Resize command, and all your objects return to their original sizes.

Fine-Tuning Aids

When you do the kind of fine-tuning work it takes to finish up a layout, you need (and probably want) all the help you can get. For instance, it sometimes helps to have rulers to guide your work. You may also want to group objects together, or to lock them in place while you fine-tune things around them.

Choose View→Rulers to see a ruler running along the top of the layout, and another along the left edge. As you move and resize items, markers on the rulers show you how large your objects are and how they line up with other objects on your layout.

You can drag custom guides down from the top ruler or over from the left margin ruler. They're helpful when you have a large number of items that have to be manually aligned and the alignment commands don't work because the objects are coming from different locations on the layout.

If you have a group of objects that you're done tidying up and you want them to stick together, select them all and then choose Arrange→Group. Then, if you need to move them, you can just drag the whole group around as if it were one object. To break the group apart again, choose Arrange→Ungroup.

Other times, it's hard to work with some items because it's too easy to accidentally select objects nearby. Select the objects that don't need editing and then choose Arrange→Lock. Locked objects can't be moved, and their formatting can't be changed. When you're done (or to change the objects), select them and then choose Arrange→Unlock.

Grouping and locking commands are also available on the Inspector and the context-sensitive menu for each object. There's much more on grids and guides starting on page 343.

TIP See page 355 to learn how to let objects resize automatically when you resize a window.

Grouping and Locking Objects

These commands are often used when you have lots of objects on a layout. By grouping objects, you can control many objects as one. Locking objects makes it harder to add an unintentional format change to them. You can see the Inspector's buttons in Figure 4-19 (they're the padlock symbols), or find them on the Arrange menu.

- **Group.** Select multiple objects and then group them so you can work with them as a single object. You can copy and paste grouped objects as one item, and you can align them to another object or a group of objects. You can group objects in series. That is, you can add new objects to a grouped set to create subsets of groupings. You can also group objects to control which objects appear in front of or behind other objects. See the section on Arranging for more information on moving objects from back to front.

- **Ungroup.** Choose a grouped object and then select the Ungroup command to work with the objects or subgroups individually. If you've grouped objects in subsets, they'll ungroup in those same layers.

- **Lock.** Choose an object or objects and then choose the Lock command so that the objects can't be moved, resized, reformatted, or deleted. This is helpful when you have objects stacked on top of one another, like with a rectangle behind a group of fields to chunk them together.

- **Unlock.** Choose a locked object or a group of locked objects and then choose the Unlock command so you can move, change, or ungroup them.

NOTE The Align, Distribute/Space, Resize, and Group tools work on multiple objects only. So if the commands in the Arrange menu or the buttons in the Inspector appear dimmed, make sure you have enough objects selected.

Arranging Objects

When you create objects on a layout, each new item appears in front of the older objects in an invisible stacking order. You can change this stacking order with the stacking commands.

- **Arrange→Bring to Front** moves the selected object on top of everything else on the layout.

- **Arrange→Bring Forward** moves the selected object up one level in the stacking order. You may have to issue this command a few times to get the effect you want.

- **Arrange→Send to Back** moves the selected object behind all other objects.

- **Arrange→Send Backward** moves the selected object down one level in the stacking order.

TIP The Inspector has buttons for these Arrange commands.

Rotating Objects

You can rotate most layout objects using the Arrange→Rotate command. Each time you choose the command, the selected object rotates 90 degrees clockwise. So to rotate a text block so it reads from bottom to top instead of left to right, issue the command three times. It's most common to rotate field blocks when you're trying to make a lot of labels fit into a tight space.

> **NOTE** Portals, Tab Controls, and web viewers can't be rotated.

You can edit rotated text blocks in Layout mode. Just click the block and it flips to normal orientation while you're editing. Then when you deselect the block, it flips back to the orientation you set. Oddly enough, fields do the same thing in Browse mode. But unless you're trying to confuse your users, it's usually best to leave fields in their normal orientation.

Adding Power to Your Database

In the previous chapter, you created a custom database for storing lease documents. You learned how to create fields of the appropriate type to store your data and then you customized two layouts—one for viewing the data as a form and a second for viewing the data in a list.

If you never went any further than that, you'd still have a database that tracks documents. But now that your business is more efficient, it's time to teach the database some new tricks. You're already storing the signing date and lease duration data for each lease. In this chapter, you'll create a field that lets you know when each lease is ending. Then you'll create a new table and all the supporting mechanisms for recording monthly payments.

▉ Creating a Simple Calculation

On page 100, you learned about field types as you created them. You chose a field type based on the kind of data you wanted to enter into each field. But calculation fields can create data under their own power. For instance, your database already stores monthly Rental Fee and Lease Duration data. If you wanted to figure out the value of that lease over its life, you could punch the numbers into a calculator and then manually enter the result into your database. But a calculation field calculates and enters data automatically and can even update if the data in either field changes. All you have to do is write a formula that tells the calculation field how to get the answer you want.

NOTE   This tutorial picks up where Chapter 4 left off. If you didn't complete those tutorials, or you want to start with a clean file that's already got some data in it, download the sample database *CH05 Lease Agreement Start.fmp12* from this book's Missing CD page at *www.missingmanuals.com/cds/fmp14mm*.

Creating Fields with Manage→Database

In the last chapter, you created fields with the Field Picker (page 100). But for creating fields with more control, call up the Manage Database window (Figure 5-1). That's how you'll create your first calculation field:

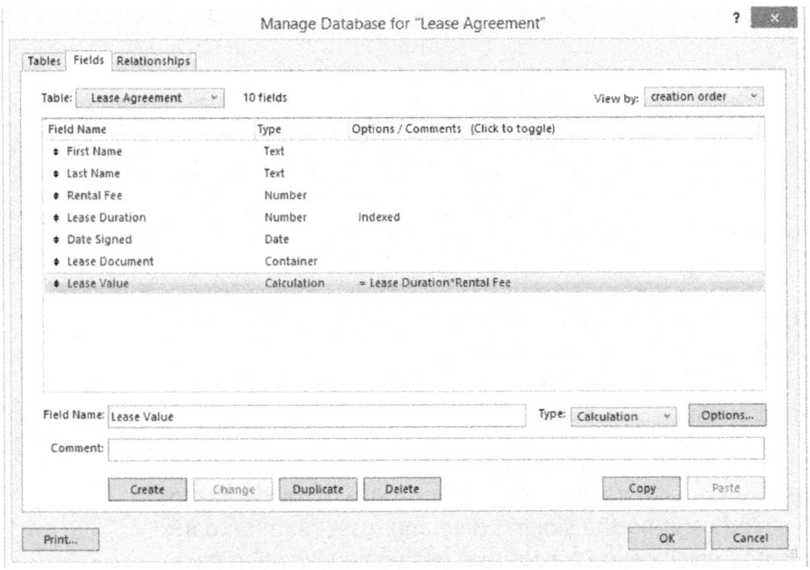

FIGURE 5-1

The Manage Database window is the most efficient way to create and manage fields. You can also Duplicate or Delete fields here. To rename a field, select it in the list, type the new name, and then click Change.

1. **Choose File→Manage→Database and then click the Fields tab (if it isn't already active).**

   The Fields tab is where most of your field creation takes place. (See the box on page 142 for more information about using this window.)

2. **In the Field Name field, type *Lease Value*.**

   As with other database elements, it's best to use simple, descriptive names for your new calculation field.

3. **From the Type pop-up menu, choose Calculation and then click Create.**

   The Specify Calculation window appears. Here's where you'll write the formula that gives you the Lease Value. It's based on data in the Lease Duration and Rental Fee fields.

4. **In the Current Table list (the left column of Specify Calculation window), double-click the Lease Duration field.**

The field's name appears in the calculation area of the window. You can also start typing the name of the field you want until you see its name in the list of suggested fields and calculation functions. For a small database like this one, it's easier to double-click it from the Current Table list on the left.

5. **In the Operators column along the right edge of the main calculation area, click the * sign.**

The asterisk means multiplication.

6. **In the Current Table list, double-click the Rental Fee field.**

The formula now reads *Lease Duration * Rental Fee.* Your calculation should look like Figure 5-2.

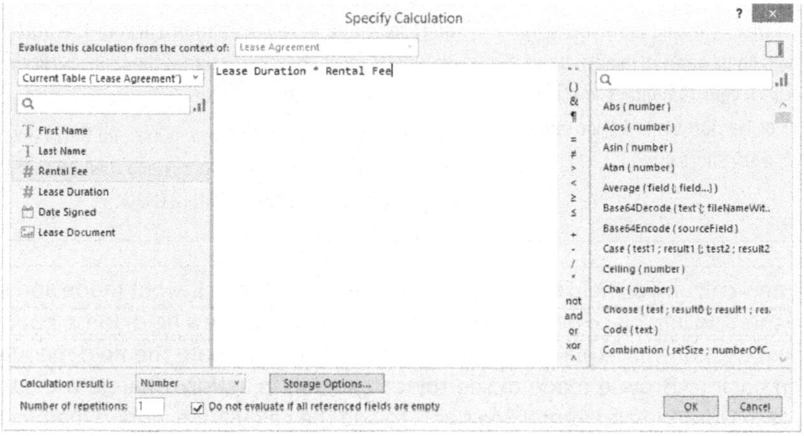

FIGURE 5-2

The Specify Calculation window lets you write a formula that's attached to a calculation field. You can perform calculations on text, number, date, time, timestamp, or container fields and get results of each of those types, too. The option "Do not evaluate if all referenced fields are empty" can speed up your database, because FileMaker doesn't have to try to calculate a value if data is missing from all the fields that make up the calculation.

NOTE Number is automatically selected for the "Calculation result." But if you create several calculation fields in one session, the default result type changes to match the last type you created. So always check this setting when you're creating calculations, since some calculations don't work as you intend if the calculation result type isn't set properly. You'll see one such example in the next tutorial.

7. **Click OK and then OK again to close both windows.**

Depending on the settings in your Preferences window, you may not see the new calculation field appear immediately on your layout.

Use the Keyboard

You can get to almost everything in the Manage Database window's Fields tab from the keyboard alone. If you're a speed freak, you can avoid the mouse almost entirely. Here's how:

- In Windows, use the Tab key to move among buttons, text boxes, and pop-up menus. On a Mac, you can press the Tab key to move between the field list, Field Name, and Comment boxes. (Unfortunately, FileMaker doesn't honor Mac OS X's Full Keyboard Access settings.)

- While the field list is active, use the up- and down-arrow keys to select the next and previous fields.

- Hold down Ctrl (Control) while pressing the arrow keys to move the selected field up or down in the list. If this doesn't work for you, check your computer's keyboard shortcuts (PC and Mac) or Mission Control (Mac only), which can override FileMaker's shortcuts.

- Use the keyboard shortcuts to assign field data types. (Look in the Type pop-up menu to see them.)

- When a field is highlighted, press Alt+N (⌘-O) to see the field options dialog box for the selected field.

- Press the Delete key to delete the selected field. Then, when you're asked if you're sure you want to delete the field, press D (Windows). Mac works the same, except the D key doesn't dismiss the dialog box; you have to click the Delete button.

- Press the first letter of a button name in any of FileMaker's alert message boxes instead of clicking the button (Windows only). Pressing Return is the same as clicking the highlighted button on a Mac.

- To close the Manage Database window and throw away all your changes, press the Esc key and then press D to discard (Windows) or press Return (Mac).

If the new calculation field appears on your layout, switch to Layout mode and then move the field into place below your existing fields. (If the new field doesn't appear, the next section will explain why and show you how to create the field manually.) Switch back to Browse mode to see the calculation in action. Change the data in the Lease Duration and Rental Fee fields to see the calculation work dynamically.

TIP Now that you've created fields using the Manage Database window, you may never want to go back to creating them in Table view. If so, you can change FileMaker's Preferences by choosing Edit→Preferences (Windows) or FileMaker Pro→Preferences (Mac) and turning on the "Use Manage Database dialog to create files" option. The next time you create a new database, you'll get the Manage Database dialog box instead of a table. Note, though, that once you set Manage Database as your preferred method for creating fields, new fields no longer automatically appear on your layouts when you create them in Table view unless the Preferences option "Add newly defined fields to current layout" is also turned on.

Adding New Fields to a Layout

When you create new fields using the Manage Database dialog box, you can have them automatically appear on your layout—or not. It's up to you. To find this setting in Windows, choose Edit→Preferences; on a Mac, choose FileMaker Pro→Preferences; and then select the Layout tab to see the "Add newly defined fields to current layout" option. When this option is turned on, FileMaker plops the field down at the bottom of your layout and, if necessary, increases the Body part to accommodate the new field. Since you're going to invest a lot of time making layouts look just so, you'll usually work with this option turned off. That means you have to place any newly created fields on your layout manually.

Once you've created fields, FileMaker provides many ways to add one to a layout, all of which require you to be in Layout mode. First of all, you can just choose Insert→Field. When you do, FileMaker asks which field you want and then drops it on the layout for you to move into place. The Field/Control tool (Figure 5-3) gives you more control, so it's used more often than the menu command. It lets you create an edit box, drop-down list, pop-up menu, checkbox set, radio button set, or drop-down calendar instead of a plain vanilla edit box. Another version of the field tool—the third tool from the right—lets you drag a field onto the layout. This tool doesn't give you the option of choosing a control type, though.

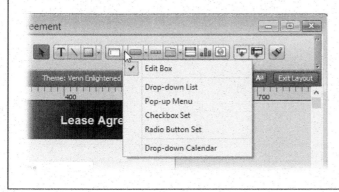

FIGURE 5-3

In Windows, an arrow to the right of the tool lets you view the pop-up menu. On a Mac, press and hold the Field/Control tool to reveal this menu. The Field/Control tool icon changes to reflect your choice, and then you use the crosshair cursor to drag on the layout and create the new field. When you're creating fields, turn on dynamic guides, so you can see the size, shape, and location of the new fields. The dotted horizontal line represents the field's baseline.

The Field Picker is the best method when you need to add several fields at once, because you can select all of the fields you need and then drag them onto the layout where you can start arranging them. This method also lets you choose where the fields' labels appear.

Finally, you can copy an existing field. Use the Edit menu's Copy and Paste commands (or their keyboard shortcuts). But to really work like the pros, Shift-drag (Option-drag) an existing field to copy it as you move it. Fields you create this way have all the formatting of the original, so you can save lots of trips to the Inspector.

To add the Lease Value field to the layout, in your Lease Agreement database, follow these steps:

1. **Click the Field/Control tool.**

    The Field/Control tool will darken to indicate it's the active tool. When you move your cursor down to the work area, it changes to crosshairs.

2. **Click in the layout and drag to create a new field.**

    As you drag, FileMaker shows dynamic guides to help you size and line up the field.

3. **When the field is the size you want, release the mouse button.**

The Specify Field window appears (Figure 5-4), showing a list of the fields in your current table.

4. **Choose the Lease Value field.**

Make sure the "Create label" checkbox is turned on.

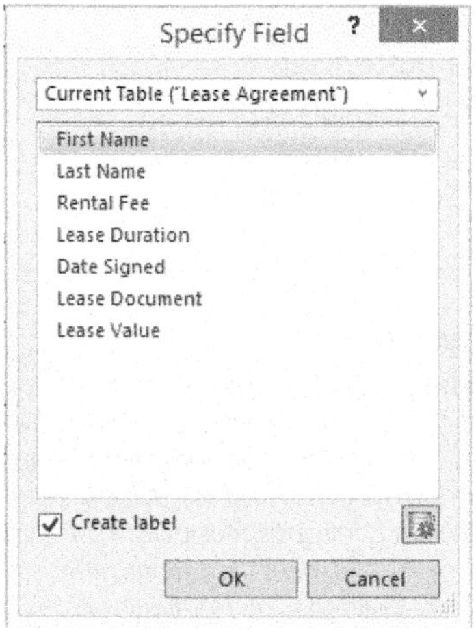

FIGURE 5-4

When you add a field to the layout, FileMaker asks which field you want by showing you the Specify Field dialog box. Another way to quickly create a field with the formatting you want already on it is to copy and paste an existing field and its label. Double-click the new field to show the Specify Field dialog box. Select the field you want, and then turn off the "Create label" checkbox before you click OK. Finally, manually change the field's label.

5. **Click OK.**

The field and its label appear on the layout. If either the field or the label doesn't appear in the format you want, make sure you've saved the changes to the proper style (page 119) and then apply the style to the object.

The new field isn't quite as wide as the original, so now is a good time to notice that your other currency field, Rental Fee, is much wider than it needs to be. Make the Rental Fee and Lease Value fields the same width as the Lease Duration field. Don't forget to use the Inspector's Data tab to apply Currency formatting. Most people prefer to see currency data aligned to the right. You can do that in one of three ways:

- Choose Format→Align Text→Right.

- Click the Right Align button in the Formatting bar (page 64).

- Go to the Inspector's Appearance tab, Paragraph section, and then click the Right Align button.

Now you're ready to switch to Browse mode to view the data in your new calculation field. The Date Signed field is also wider than it needs to be, so switch back to Layout mode and make it a little smaller as well, but not quite as narrow as your currency fields.

Deleting a Field

In the Manage Database window, you can delete a field (and its contents in all records of the current table) by selecting it and then clicking Delete. You'll see a dialog box asking you to confirm that you really do want to delete the selected field. There's a caveat, though: Calculation fields (like Lease Value) make reference to other fields. That is, the formula for Lease Value is *Lease Duration * Rental Fee*. If you try to delete either Lease Duration or Rental Fee, FileMaker shows you a warning dialog box and refuses to delete the field. If you absolutely, positively have to delete either field, you have a choice: Either change Lease Value's formula so it doesn't refer to the field you want to delete, or delete Lease Value first. Then when you try to delete the field again, FileMaker still asks you to confirm that you want to delete the field, but it doesn't need to warn you about the other ones that refer to it—because there aren't any.

> **NOTE** You'll also get a warning if you try to delete a field that's used in a script. But in that case, you get the choice to proceed anyway or cancel the delete. If you delete a field used in a script, be prepared to do some repair work. The script can't do its work properly once a field it needs is gone from your database.

■ DISCARD CHANGES

There's a fallback position if you delete or change fields and then change your mind or realize you've made a mistake. Click the Manage Database dialog box's Cancel button. FileMaker asks whether you want to "Discard ALL changes made in this dialog to tables, fields, and relationships." Click Discard, and FileMaker performs *none* of the changes you've made since you opened the Manage Database dialog box. You may lose work you would have preferred to keep, but that's often a better option than losing a field with a tricky calculation that you can't quite remember.

■ Creating a Related Table

Now that you've got the basic information stored for your leases, you realize that you can centralize your data if you record rent payments in the same database as the lease documents. Your first thought might be to create a field or two (Date Paid and Amount Paid) to record each payment, but you quickly realize that since some leases last 36 months, you'll have to create 72 fields and then place them on your layout. Worse yet, for your 12- and 24-month leases, most of those fields will be empty.

If you start signing 48-month leases, you'll have to create a whole slew of new fields and start rearranging your layout again. And what if your tenants make more than one payment each month? It'd be so much more efficient if each record could have only the fields it needed, and no more.

You're on the right track—instead of adding fields in the Lease Agreement table, what you need is a set of new records in a related table (see the box on page 147 for a definition of *table* and other terms you'll need to know for this section). That's where a relational database comes in. You need separate tables to store each type of information. Because when you think about it, monthly payments aren't really part of a Lease Agreement table. Date Paid and Amount Paid data pertain to a specific lease agreement, but they don't belong with the name of the tenant or the PDF of the lease agreement itself. What you need is a new Payment table, where you can add 12 records (one per month, of course) to the 12-month leases, or 24 records to the 24-month leases. With a separate table, even if you start offering 5-year leases, you'll never have to add more fields or stretch a layout to accommodate a change in the way you do business.

And you don't even have to create a new file for your new table. FileMaker lets you put dozens, even hundreds, of tables into the same file. There's an art and science surrounding how to figure out which tables you need and how to relate them to one another. You'll learn that in Chapter 6. For now, you'll learn about the tools you need to create a related table and enter monthly Payment records on the Lease Agreement layout.

Understanding the Elements of a Relationship

Now that you've decided to store lease information in the Lease Agreement table and payment information in a new Payment table, you need to make sure payments match the right Lease Agreement record. First, you start with a unique identifier called a *key field,* which uses the auto-enter field option to create a serial number that's unique for each record in the table. Then you use the *Relationships* graph to match the two tables' key fields. Finally you create a special layout object, called a *portal,* that lets you view, create, and edit records from a related table. In this case, you'll use a portal to show Payment records on the same layout where you store data about each lease agreement.

Creating a Key Field with an Auto-Enter Serial Number

To ensure that Lease Agreements and Payments records match properly, you need a unique identifier in the Lease Agreement table. One of FileMaker's field options, called *Serial Number,* automatically assigns a unique number to each record when it's created. Here's how to create a key field and then apply an Auto-Enter Serial number option to it:

1. **Choose File→Manage→Database and then, if it's not active, click the Fields tab.**

   The Manage Database window appears, with the Lease Agreement table's fields in a list.

2. **In the Field Name field, type *agreementID*.**

   This field name may seem odd (no spaces and a mix of upper- and lowercase letters), but it's one of many naming conventions used by developers to help them quickly identify fields that they've created to make the database work. In this naming convention, the field name starts with the name (or one-word abbreviation) of the table for which it is the key field. The "ID" at the end confirms that the field is used as a key.

These Terms Are Relational

Before you dive into creating a relational database, you'll find it helpful to review some vocabulary and learn a few new terms, as they apply to FileMaker:

- A *database* is a collection of tables, layouts, and other features that form an organized system.

- A *table* holds information about one kind of thing, like the two tables in your database: lease agreements and payments. Another database might have four tables: people, products, invoices, and payments. Each table is like a single worksheet in a spreadsheet program.

- A *field* holds one bit of information about something: lease duration, the date a payment was made, the person's first or last name, the order date, the color of a product, or the supplier's address. It's like a single column in a spreadsheet.

- A *record* is the collection of data (a set of fields) in a table that describes one unique thing. It's like a single row in a spreadsheet.

- An *attribute* is an individual characteristic. For example, a bicycle might have several attributes: color, size, style, and price. In a database, each of these attributes gets its own field. Remember the term "individually significant" from the box on page 99?

- An *entity* is one kind of thing. If you track information about your customers, the concept *People* is an entity; so is a Payment or an Invoice or an Invoice's Line Item. Remember, though, the individual thing itself isn't the entity. The person Philip J. Fry isn't a database entity; neither is the November 2016 payment for a specific lease. If this is confusing to you, don't get hung up on it. Focus on this: Each entity (People) gets one table in a database and each instance of an entity (Philip J. Fry) gets one record in that table.

- A *key field* uniquely identifies each record so that each related record knows which record it matches, like an Employee ID Number for a person. You'll create a key field using FileMaker's Auto-Enter Serial number option in this chapter and learn about their finer points on page 206.

- A *relationship* describes how the records in two tables match each other (page 194).

The most common relationships are called *parent-child relationships*. That's because one parent record can have many children, but each child record can have only one parent. So in your database, the Lease Agreement is the parent record and each Payment record is a child.

3. **From the Type pop-up menu, choose Number.**

   Key fields are most often number fields. (See page 206 for more information on choosing and creating a good key field.)

4. **Click the Create button and then click the Options button. See Figure 5-5.**

   The "Options for Field 'agreementID'" window appears.

5. **Turn on the "Serial number" checkbox and then click OK until you're back on the Lease Agreement layout.**

   A serial number is created in the agreementID field for each new record you make.

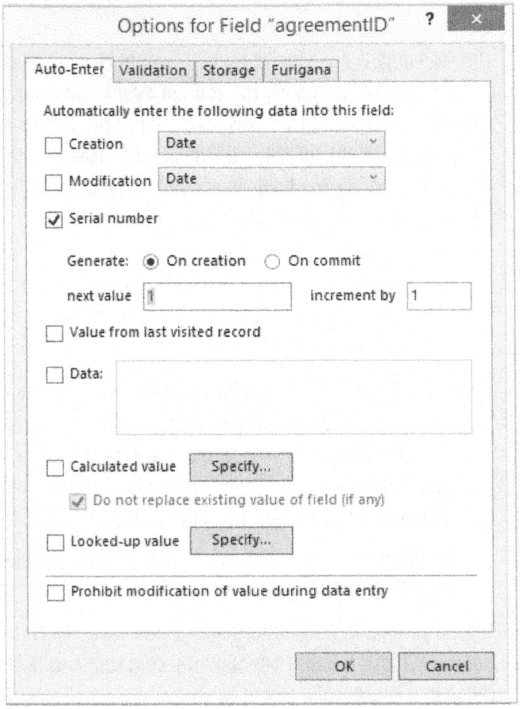

FIGURE 5-5

When you first set up an auto-enter serial number field, the next value is always "1" unless you change it. Auto-enter serial numbers are most often assigned as a record is created ("On creation"), but if you choose "On commit" instead, FileMaker doesn't generate the number until the first time the user commits the record. Usually, you use the "On commit" option when your database has multiple users (as you'll learn on page 250). For instance, a user might create a record but then delete it instead of filling out its data. In that case, there would be a gap in the serial numbers, because the numbers assigned to deleted records are never reused. If you're importing data from another source, you should find the highest serial number in the imported data and then set your field's "next value" to one number higher than the imported data. And while the most common "increment by" value is 1, you can make the numbers increase by any other number you choose instead.

It's important to know that even if you can't see the agreementID field, the serial number is added to it when you create each new record. And if you still haven't turned on the "Add newly created fields to current layout option" in the Preferences dialog box, do that now. Create a few new records to watch serial numbers being created. Notice, though, that the records that were already in your database don't have serial numbers yet.

■ USING REPLACE FIELD CONTENTS TO ADD SERIAL NUMBERS

When you create a key field after data has been entered, you don't have to go to each record and manually enter a serial number. You can use the Replace Field Contents command (page 58) to add in the missing serial numbers and reset the field option's "next value" counter at the same time. Since you have to have a field on a layout in order to use the Replace Field Contents command, you may have to put the agreementID field on the Lease Agreement layout if it isn't already there.

1. **In Browse mode, choose Records→Show All Records.**

   Every record has to have data in its key field in order to relate to another table, so make sure you aren't looking at a found set of just some of your records.

NOTE   If you're using this tutorial on a database where some records have serial numbers and some don't, make sure you don't replace the value in the records that already have numbers. First, find just the records without serial numbers. Then make sure you set the "next value" higher than the largest number in the record with serial numbers.

2. **Click in the agreementID field.**

   If you don't click into a field first, the Replace Field Contents command will be dimmed.

3. **Choose Records→Replace Field Contents.**

   The Replace Field Contents window appears. See Figure 5-6.

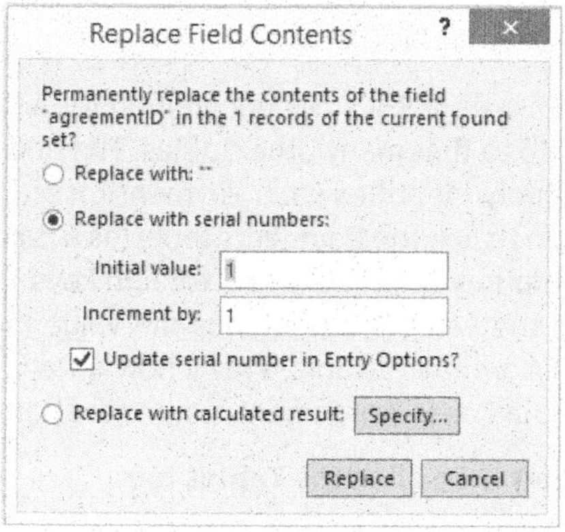

FIGURE 5-6

In the Replace Field Contents dialog box, the default button is not the one that does the action you've just set up. The Replace command can't be undone, so FileMaker is saving you from unintentionally destroying good data if you hit Enter too soon. Instead, pressing Enter cancels the replacement and leaves everything as it was. Replace Field Contents is a lifesaver when you have to retrofit a table with a key field after you've created records. However, replacing data after you're created relationships between tables is risky—if the value in the key field in either table changes, the child record gets disconnected from its parent.

4. **Select "Replace with serial numbers," and then turn on "Update serial number in Entry Options," if it isn't already turned on.**

   "Replace with serial numbers" tells FileMaker how you want the numbers created in your existing records. "Update serial number in Entry Options" ensures that records you created after the Replace don't reuse any of the numbers entered in the current found set. If you didn't choose this option, you'd have to look through your records to find the highest number and then return to the Manage Database dialog box to change the "next value" setting for the agreementID field manually after the replace is done.

5. **Click Replace.**

   Serial numbers are created in all the records of your database.

Flip through the records to see the serial numbers. You can go back to the Manage Database dialog box and check the auto-enter options for the agreementID field to see that its "next value" has been updated. While you're there, select the "Prohibit modification of value during data entry" option at the bottom of the window. You don't want people changing your carefully crafted serial numbers. Create a new record to see the next value appear automatically in the agreementID field.

> **TIP** Because it can be cumbersome to create a key field and populate it with data months or even years later, it makes sense to create a key field in every table you create even if you have no immediate plans to relate the table to any other table. That way, you don't have to deal with all that rigamarole if your needs change. Plus, a unique serial number is very helpful if you're trying to troubleshoot missing or duplicated records.

Creating a New Table

Your Payment table needs to store information about each monthly payment for a specific Lease Agreement. The Payment table's attributes are the date the rent was paid and the amount paid. You also need a key field for hooking up Payments to the Lease Agreement table. And since it's good practice to create a key field in every table, just in case, you'll also add a paymentID field.

Two key fields in one table? It may sound crazy, but it's not uncommon for a table to have 10 or more key fields that let it relate to that many other tables. The first key field you'll create (called paymentID) uniquely identifies each Payment record and could be used when you figure out a reason to link the Payments table (as a parent) to another table. (See page 207 for information on primary and foreign keys.) The second key field (agreementID) will hold the value that matches the value in the key field of a specific record in the Lease Agreement table. That's how a Payment record (the child) matches up with the proper Lease Agreement record (the parent).

1. **Choose File→Manage→Database and then click the Tables tab.**

   This tab is where you create, edit, and manage your tables.

2. **In the Table Name field, type *Payment* and then click Create.**

   Remember: When you created the Lease Agreement table, you decided to use the singular case for your database elements, so stay consistent. The Payment table appears in the Tables list.

3. **Click the Fields tab.**

   You're viewing the field list for the new Payment table. FileMaker is smart like that and switched to the selected table for you. But if you need to, you can switch tables using the Table pop-up menu above the list of fields.

4. **In the Field Name field, type *paymentID* and then select Number from the Type pop-up menu. Click Create.**

   It's a good habit to create a table's key field first thing. That way, you won't forget to do it.

5. **Click the Options button and make the paymentID field an auto-enter serial number.**

All your Payment records will have serial numbers because you created a key field right at the beginning, before you created any records. And since you have no records yet, the next value should be "1."

6. **At the bottom of the Options window, turn on "Prohibit modification of value during data entry."**

This prevents users (even you, the developer) from changing the data in a field. Protecting the data in a key field is critical to keeping your records properly related to one another. But if you ever do need to change this data, just head back to the field's options and switch off this option.

7. **Click OK.**

You're ready to finish creating the rest of the fields for the Payment table.

Use the skills you learned earlier in this chapter to create these fields (their types are in parentheses):

- Date Paid (Date)

- Payment Amount (Number)

- agreementID (Number)

Click OK when you're done. Because you're still viewing the Lease Agreement layout, you don't see evidence of your new table yet. But it's there.

■ VIEWING THE NEW TABLE'S LAYOUT

If you click the Layout pop-up menu (in either Browse or Layout mode), you'll see a new layout called Payment. FileMaker created it for you when it created your new table. And much like the boring layout you got when you created the Lease Agreement table, there's nothing there except the standard lineup of layout parts and your newly created fields. In Browse mode you can see that this new table doesn't have any records yet. If you click in a field as if to enter data, you'll see the warning message in Figure 5-7.

FIGURE 5-7

When you see this message, just click OK. But don't bother creating a record. You'll do that later—from the Lease Agreement layout.

You can dress this layout up any way you want to. For instance, you could turn it into a list layout so you can report on your payments. But since you'll be creating Payment records and entering data from the Lease Agreement layout, for now just note that the Payment layout is here, and go back to the Lease Agreement layout.

Creating a Relationship Between Two Table Occurrences

You just saw that when you create a table and then add fields to it, FileMaker makes a bare-bones layout for that table. It also makes a Table Occurrence for the new table on the Relationships graph. That graph is found on the only tab of the Manage Database window that you haven't seen yet. And true to its name, that's where you create the relationship between the Lease Agreement and Payment tables.

> **NOTE** Your Relationships graph can have more than one instance of any table, and each instance is a different view into the table. Each instance of a table is called a *table occurrence*. It's important to know whether you're referring to the table itself or an occurrence of the table. A word of caution, though: FileMaker isn't all that consistent about using the term in its own windows and help files, so it's not your fault if you're confused.

Also true to its name, the Relationships graph is a visual representation of your file's tables and how they relate to one another. And you create relationships in perhaps the easiest way possible: You drag from one table to another to create a line. Here's how to create a relationship between two tables, using their key fields:

1. **Choose File→Manage→Database or use the shortcut Shift+Ctrl+D (Shift-⌘-D) and then click the Relationships tab.**

   You'll see two table occurrences: one for the Lease Agreement table and the other for the Payment table. You need to draw a line between the agreementID fields in each table, but that field is not visible in the Lease Agreement table occurrence.

2. **Click and hold the tiny triangle at the bottom of the Lease Agreement table occurrence.**

   That scrolls the field names so that you can see the one you need. Or you can drag the bottom border of the table occurrence to make it tall enough to show all its fields.

3. **In the Lease Agreement table occurrence, click the agreementID field and then drag to the agreementID field in the Payment table occurrence. Release the mouse when it's pointing to the proper field.**

   As you drag, you'll see a line with a box in the middle, and the key field is highlighted to help you stay oriented. The pointer changes shape to show that you're creating a relationship. As you point to any field, it's highlighted. When you release the mouse, the two fields you've connected jump above a new divider at the top of each table occurrence. They still appear in the list below and are italicized to show that they're used as keys (Figure 5-8).

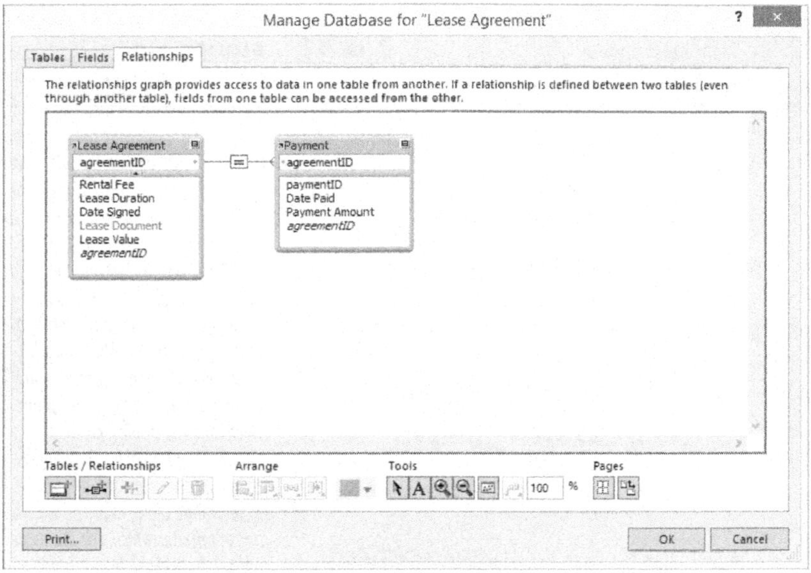

FIGURE 5-8

*The line between the
two Table Occurrences
Is straight on the Lease
Agreement end and has
a "fork" at the Payment
end. This crow's foot
helps you know which
is the parent and which
is the child side of the
relationship. But how
does FileMaker know?
It's an educated guess
based on the fact that
the Lease Agreement end
is an auto-enter serial
number field (typical for
a primary key field) while
the Payment end is not.*

4. **Double-click the box in the middle of the relationship line.**

    The Edit Relationship window appears (Figure 5-9). The window is divided into halves, showing Lease Agreement on the left and Payment on the right.

5. **On the Payment side of the relationship, turn on "Allow creation of records in this table via this relationship" and "Delete related records in this table when a record is deleted in the other table."**

    This setup is typical of the child side of a relationship. Here's how to think about it: You'll be creating Payment records from the Lease Agreement layout, so the relationship's options need to allow record creation. And if you delete a Lease Agreement record, there probably isn't much use for the Payment records, so that second option deletes Payment records that would otherwise be "orphaned" when the parent record is deleted.

6. **Click OK until you return to the Lease Agreement layout.**

    Or the Payment layout, if that's the one you were viewing at the start of this tutorial.

    If naming fields in both tables with the same name seemed confusing as you were doing it, you've just seen why it's a good idea. In a large or complex database, some tables can have many key fields for relating to other tables. But if you use the same name in the child table as the key field in the parent table, it's very easy to find the proper key field and then drag a line between the two tables.

NOTE Purists will say that the "tables" you just connected by their fields are really *table occurrences*. Turn to page 602 to find out why.

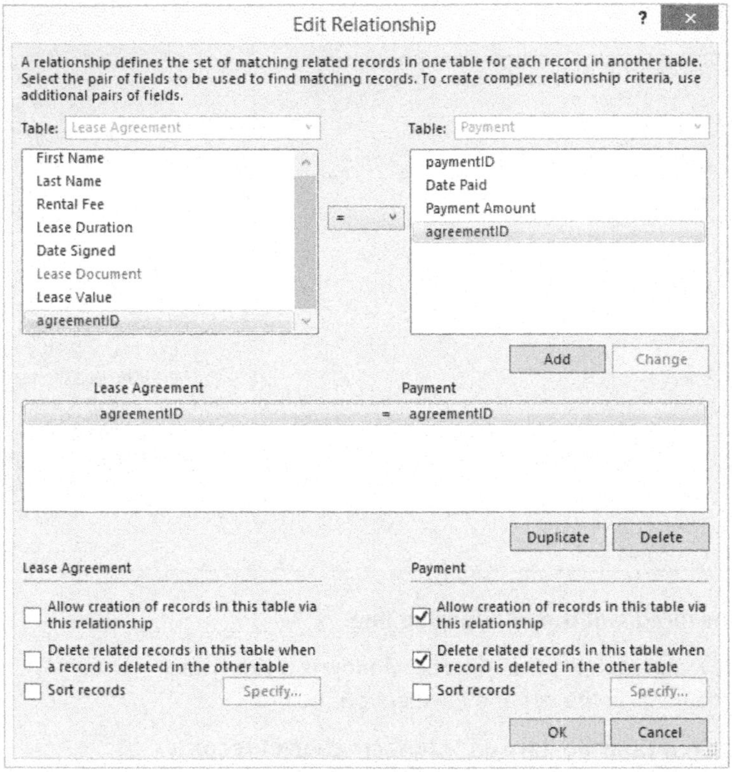

FIGURE 5-9

The Edit Relationship window lets you define how a relationship works. It's divided in half vertically, with one table's information on the left and the other table's information on the right. For most people, it's easiest to visualize a relationship when the parent table is on the left and the child table is on the right. If your window is flipped (Payment on the left and Lease Agreement on the right), it's because your table occurrences are flipped on the Relationships graph. To change the display, close the Edit Relationship dialog box and then drag the table occurrences to rearrange them. In practice, it doesn't matter which side the tables appear on because relationships are bidirectional (you'll learn what that means on page 235).

Creating and Using Portals

Once your tables are related to one another, you can freely display related fields on layouts. For example, say you want the Date Paid and Payment Amount fields from the Payment table to appear on your Lease Agreement layout. You could simply add those fields to the layout, but you'd quickly find a big problem. There's only a single instance of each field, and the point of this related Payment table is to have *multiple* records from the child table related to the parent table.

The problem is solved with a *portal,* which is a layout object that displays multiple records from a related table. Not only can the portal display related records, but you can also use a portal to create, edit, and delete related records.

Adding a Portal to a Layout

A portal can display as many related records as you want, limited primarily by the size of your layout and the height of the portal. As with other layout objects, you can format portals to match your database, using fills and lines the way you would with other drawn objects. Here's how to create a portal on the Lease Agreement layout:

1. **In Layout mode, drag the bottom edge of your Body part to make room for your portal. Or use the Inspector to make the Body 500 points high.**

    Figure 5-10 shows you how much space you'll need.

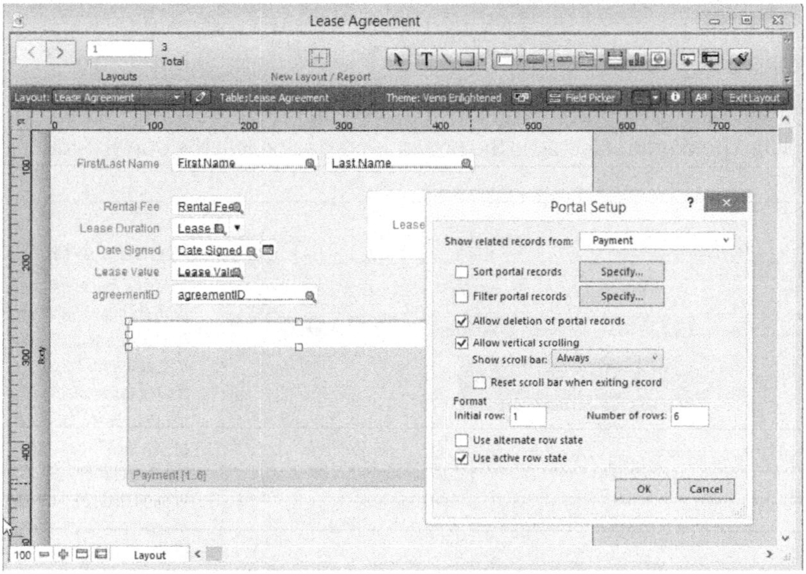

FIGURE 5-10

In the upper right of the Status toolbar, you see the Portal tool selected. On the layout you can see an outline where the portal will be when you finish creating it. The settings shown in the Portal Setup dialog box above, along with the relationship's setting to allow record creation, let you create, edit, and delete Payment records without ever having to visit a Payment layout.

2. **Click the Portal tool to select it and then drag on the layout to create a portal.**

    As with all drawn objects, it's usually easiest to start in the upper-left corner and drag to the lower-right corner where you want the portal to appear. When you release the mouse, the Portal Setup window appears.

3. **From the "Show related records from" pop-up menu, choose Payment.**

    This is the Payment table occurrence you saw when you hooked up the Lease Agreement and Payment tables in the Relationships graph (page 152).

4. **Check "Allow vertical scrolling" and set "Show scroll bar" to Always.**

    A scrollbar lets you see more related records in a smaller space.

5. **Turn on "Allow deletion of portal records" and then click OK.**

    The "Add Fields to Portal" window appears.

6. **From the list of available fields on the left, select and move the Date Paid, Payment Amount, and agreementID fields.**

Each field appears in the list on the right as you move it. It isn't necessary to add a related table's key field to a portal. In the real world, you *don't* usually want to see that data. But while you're learning about portals and relationships, it's very helpful to display the key field so you can see how portals work.

> **TIP** Pay attention to the way the field name appears in the available fields list. You're seeing the parts of a *fully qualified field name*. That is, the field is represented by its table name followed by a pair of colons, and then the field name itself. It's kind of like you being called by both your first and last names. This nomenclature helps you and FileMaker keep the Lease Agreement and the Payment tables' agreementID fields straight.

7. **Click OK.**

FileMaker adjusts the portal object to show the number of rows you specified, and the related fields you selected in the previous step appear in the portal (Figure 5-11).

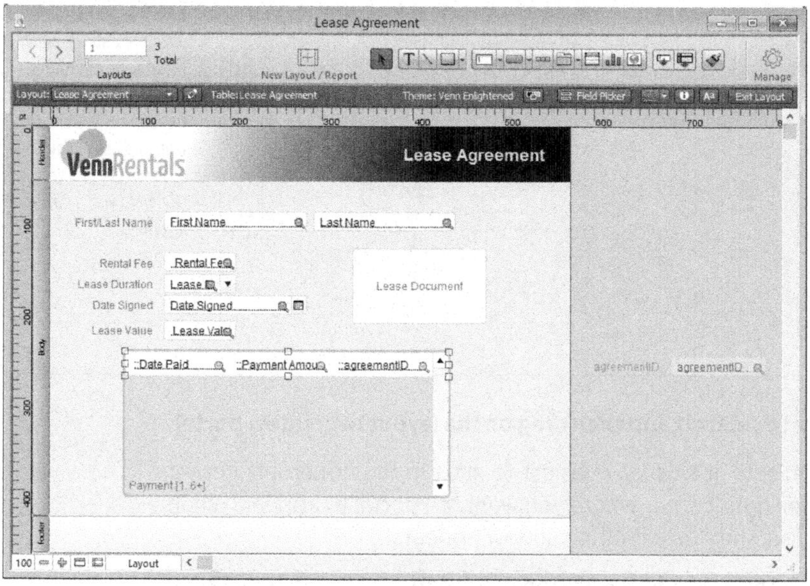

FIGURE 5-11

In Layout mode, the portal displays information about the data it contains along its lower-left edge. The related table's name (Payment) appears, followed by "[1...6+]." That means that the portal is tall enough to display six rows of related records, starting with the first record. The + sign means that the portal can be scrolled when it contains more than six child records.

> **NOTE** In Figure 5-11, the Lease Agreement::agreementID field is moved out into the gray space beyond the edge of your layout. Objects in that space don't show up in Browse mode, so it's a handy place to put things you might need for troubleshooting but you don't want to see while you're entering data.

No matter how many rows the portal is set to show, you see only one row of fields in Layout mode, and they're always in the portal's first row. Notice that the fields fit

...

precisely in that top row. In fact, FileMaker used the height of your fields to figure out how many rows it could fit in the space you drew with the portal tool.

The Payment fields are evenly divided within the width of your portal. You'll likely need to do some fine-tuning of the fields for best presentation. Adjusting field widths to neatly fit the data, right-aligning number fields, and adding field labels are all common tasks with freshly created portals.

NOTE Sometimes you'll want your field labels to properly convey their field's function to users rather than adhere to the internal naming conventions. For instance, it's okay to make the label for the agreementID field say "Agreement ID" or "Agreement No."

Resizing and Moving a Portal

Just like any other layout object, a portal shows selection handles when you click to select it. But the location of its bottom selection handles may surprise you. They're at the bottom of the portal's first row, not at the bottom edge of the portal. If you drag the bottom middle selection handle downward, you change the row height and *not* the number of rows the portal will display. That's useful where you want to show lots of data from each related record and a single row of fields won't get the job done. You can change the width of a portal by dragging one of the middle handles on either side or by using the Width box on the Inspector's Position tab.

To move a portal, click to select it and then drag it to the new location. When you do, all the fields move along with it. So it's safest to click in the gray area below the fields, because if you click a field and then drag, only the field you click will move. You may want to move fields within their portal—say to rearrange their order or to scoot them around to make room for new fields—but make sure they stay inside the border of the portal's top row. If they're off by even a point, two problems can occur. First, only one row of data from the related table will appear, no matter how many related records there are. Second, if you try to move the portal, the fields that stick their necks up get left behind when you drag the portal.

Delete a portal by clicking it and then pressing the Delete key (or choosing Edit→Clear). The portal and its fields are deleted together. You can copy a portal and its fields with the Copy and Paste commands or keyboard shortcuts. But the Shift-drag (Option-drag) shortcut is quickest. See the box on page 158 to learn why you might want to copy a portal.

ADDING ROWS TO A PORTAL

Making a portal taller doesn't give you more rows. If you want to add more rows, change its options. Do that by double-clicking on the portal to make the Portal Setup dialog box appear. That's the same one you saw when you created the portal. To add or remove rows, just type the number you want in the "Number of rows" field. When you click OK, the portal will resize to accommodate its new settings.

Power to the Portal

On page 155, you learned about how the Portal Setup dialog box works. Now it's time to dig a little deeper. To see the settings for your portal, in Layout mode, select it and then choose Format→Portal Setup. Here's how some of the options break down:

- **Portals can be sorted by any field in the related table.** Click "Sort portal records," and you'll see the Sort Records window for the related table. You can sort the portal's records by any field in the related table—as long as it can be sorted; container fields can't be used to sort. Sorting portal rows has no effect on the underlying table itself, so your Payment layout can have a completely different sort order than the Payment portal has.

- **Portals can be filtered.** You can write a calculation that decides which records show up in a portal. For example, you may want two portals on your Lease Agreement layout: one to show rental payments and another to show a deposit or repair payment. You could add a Type field to the payment table and then use the field to filter your portals. Details on page 599.

- **Portals can have scroll bars.** By default, the scrollbar is always showing—though not active—until the number of related records exceeds the number of portal rows.

- **You can assign an "Alternate row state" to a portal.** When you turn this option on, every even-numbered portal row has a different background color and pattern. You can make every other row green, for example. The *odd*-numbered rows have whatever background color you assign to the portal itself on the layout. Assign custom colors using the Inspector's Appearance tab.

- **You can use "Active row state" on a portal.** Active row state highlights the background of a portal row when any field in the row is active. It's the default choice when you create a new portal, and you'll almost always want to leave it turned on because it gives great visual feedback

about which related record you're dealing with.

- **If you change the "Initial row" value, the portal skips some rows.** For example, if you put *5* in the box on a nine-row portal, the portal shows records 5 through 13 instead of records 1 through 9. If it suits your needs, you can even put the same portal on your layout more than once and give it different initial rows. Your layout could show the first six payments in one portal, and payments 7 through 12 in a second portal so they look like columns.

In addition to the options in the Portal Setup dialog box, portals have other features you may find useful:

- **Each row in a portal can hold multiple fields,** and it's no problem to add an extra field after you've walked through the initial setup. First widen the portal, then copy and paste a field that's already in the portal, and then change it to the field you want. Double-click the new field to view the Specify Field dialog box. It's already set to the proper table, so you just have to choose the field you want and then click OK.

- **You can draw objects and place graphics in a portal row.** Just drag or insert them into the first row, taking care that their boundaries are completely inside the first row. Because buttons (page 177) are so useful, you can add them to a portal row, too. Or if you have a portal with a tall row height and you've arranged fields two rows high within that first row, you could draw a horizontal line in the portal to help organize the data.

- **Portals also have special automatic resizing powers.** If you anchor the bottom of a portal vertically, you get to decide whether FileMaker *adds more rows* or just *makes each row bigger*. Here's the trick: If anything *in* the portal is anchored on the bottom, then the portal rows get bigger when you enlarge the window. Otherwise, FileMaker keeps the rows the same height and adds more visible rows as your window grows larger.

NOTE If the layout isn't tall enough to fit the adjusted portal, you'll see a warning message that tells you that the layout size needs to be increased. If you don't want FileMaker deciding how tall your layout should be, click No in that warning dialog box, and the portal will stay the height you drew it. Then you'll have to increase the layout size manually and then try to change the row display again.

Context

Back in Browse mode, you can see the portal, but there's no data in it. That's because the Payment table doesn't have any records yet. If you're thinking about choosing the New Record command, don't act on that thought, because it won't work. At least it won't create a new Payment record. It will continue to work as it always has, by creating a new Lease Agreement record. To understand why, backtrack just a bit to take a look at your layout's setup. Switch to Layout mode and then choose Layouts→Layout Setup (Figure 5-12).

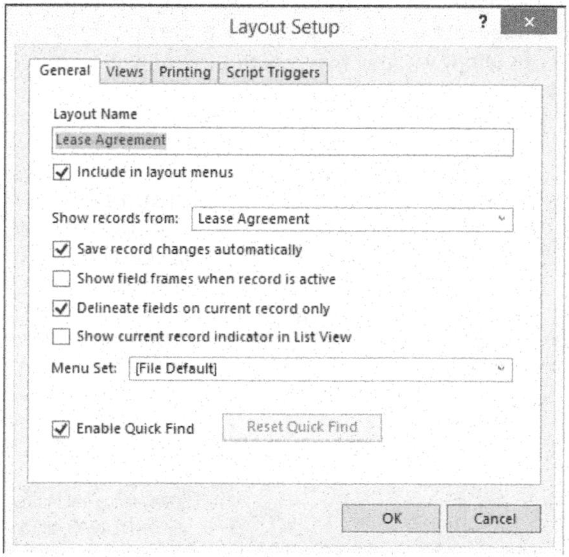

FIGURE 5-12

The Layout Setup dialog box tells you that the Lease Agreement layout shows records from the Lease Agreement table occurrence. The "Include in layout menus" option lets you determine which of your layouts show up in the Status toolbar's Layout pop-up menu. Deselecting this option is a good way to keep users off a layout you don't want them to see, like your Payments layout or layouts you create for printing envelopes or mailing labels.

Each layout is tied to one, and only one, table occurrence. That table occurrence tells the layout which table's records it can show. Another way of saying the same thing is that the table occurrence gives the layout its *context*. Context is fundamental to many aspects of your database, because without the proper context, the layout can't show you the records you want to see. Layouts have context, and so do portals. The portal you added to the Lease Agreement layout has the context of the Payment table. Keep context in mind as you're reading the next section, which covers the things you can do with related records by using a portal.

This database has only two tables and only one occurrence of each table, so context seems obvious. But real-world databases often have dozens (even hundreds) of tables, and they may have several occurrences of each table. So if you get used to thinking about context now, you're laying a good foundation for working with more complicated databases later. No matter how complicated a database gets, though, you can thread your way through the most tangled mess by answering two simple questions: Where am I, and what records do I need to see? Right now, you're on the Lease Agreement layout, and you need to see Payment records. The relationship you created on page 152 shows you the records you need.

Creating Records Through a Portal

Once you've set up a portal on a layout, you can create records without going all the way back to the Payment layout. On a Lease Agreement record, in Browse mode, click in any field. You can now tab into the Payment portal's fields, just as if they were a part of the Lease Agreement table. The fields are active even though there aren't any related records, because when you defined the relationship between the Lease Agreement and Payment tables, you chose the option that lets related records be created. View your related table by choosing Window→New Window. A new window appears that's a duplicate of the original. Move the new window over to the side so you can see both windows and then switch the new window to the Payment layout (Figure 5-13).

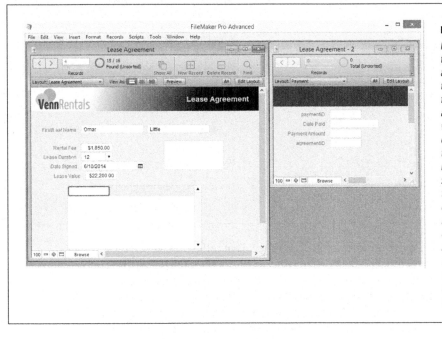

FIGURE 5-13

In the window on the left, the Omar Little record is active, and you can see that the portal shows a field boundary as if there's a new record. But in the window on the right, you can see that the Payment table doesn't have any records yet. Keep your screen set up like this for the next tutorials, so you can watch how and when related records are created, edited, and deleted. This is also a good troubleshooting tip when something is wrong with a relationship and you're trying to figure out how to fix it.

1. **On the Lease Agreement layout, go to Browse mode, click in the Payment portal's Date Paid field, type a date and then press Tab.**

   As soon as the insertion point moves to the next field, you'll see the record appear in the Payment window. Even though you didn't enter it, the new record's agreementID field now has a value, and it matches the value in the Lease Agreement::agreementID field.

2. **Type a number in the Payment Amount field and then press Tab again.**

   The agreementID field in the portal is active. Because it's a child record key (sometimes called a foreign key), it's not set up to prohibit data entry. Try this experiment: Change the number in the Payment::agreementID field (it's in the portal). Click outside the portal to commit the change and the Payment record disappears. After you commit the change, the Payment record is no longer related to the Lease Agreement record. It might even be related to the wrong parent record now. Luckily you have the Payment window open, and you can just change the Payment::agreementID information back to match the value in the parent record you're viewing. When you commit the Payment record, it will show back up in the portal.

Use the portal to create a few more Payment records just to watch how the process works behind the scenes. Notice how the Tab key travels through the rows in the portal, much as in a spreadsheet.

Remember you wouldn't usually put a foreign key field in a portal because as you just saw, the child record disappears from the portal when you changed the field's value; it's no longer related to the parent record you're viewing. It's confusing to users, since the value in every child record is, as it should be, exactly the same. Still, viewing an ID field in a portal, along with a second window opened to a layout that has the context of the related records, is a good way to learn how relationships work. Plus it's a great way to troubleshoot when something is not working the way you expect.

Editing Records Through a Portal

You can edit any related record by clicking in the field you want to change and then typing the new info. Tab to the next row, or if you're on the last row in the portal, click into a blank space on the Lease Agreement record to commit the changes.

■ DELETING RECORDS THROUGH A PORTAL

Unlike the New Record command, the Delete Record command *can* work on a portal record—if you've formatted the portal to allow related record deletion (luckily, you did just that back on page 152). But you have to click in a portal row first to set up the context so FileMaker knows which related record you want to delete.

1. **Click in any field of the portal row you want to delete.**

   You'll see the insertion point blinking in the field you clicked in.

2. **Choose Records→Delete Record.**

The delete related record warning appears (Figure 5-14).

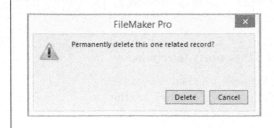

FileMaker Pro

⚠ Permanently delete this one related record?

Delete   Cancel

FIGURE 5-14

As long as a portal row is active, FileMaker will display this message. You can activate a row by clicking into a field or just clicking some empty space on the row. Either way you do it, the Delete Record command will be applied to the related record represented in the active portal row.

3. **Click the Delete button.**

The related record is deleted.

Performing Finds with Related Data

You can search in related fields just as easily as you can search in the "local" table's fields. So if you wanted to find all Lease Agreements with April 2016 Payment records, just switch to Find mode, click in the Payment portal's Date Paid field, type *4/2016* and then click Perform Find. You get a found set of all the Lease Agreement records that have related Payment records dated April 2016. Each Lease Agreement record will still show all its related records in the portal, and not just the ones that match your search criteria. As you flip through your found set of Lease Agreement records, you might think that some records shouldn't be in the found set because you can't see April 2016 dates in the portal. But remember, if there are a lot of Payment records for a Lease Agreement, you may need to scroll to see more records. So if you think a record showed up when it shouldn't have, scroll down in the portal. You'll find an April 2016 Payment record in there somewhere.

But if what you wanted was a list showing only the April 2016 Payment records, you have to search using the Payment layout, which is set to show records from the Payment table occurrence (because it has the context of the Payment table occurrence). That way, your found set *will* contain just the records with April 2016 payments.

■ Using Tab Controls

Adding a portal to the Lease Agreement layout may have streamlined your workflow, but it required you to increase the size of your layout. And if you want to add a large Notes field, you'll have to increase the size even more. Plus, the Lease Document container field would be more useful if it were larger. But if you make it *too* big, that field will dwarf all the other data on the screen, making it hard to focus on the text data.

That's where Tab Controls come in. Like the tabs that let you open multiple websites in one browser window, Tab Controls let you organize data on a layout so you can focus on a few chunks of data at a time. Tab Controls also let you put far more information on the same layout without making it gigantic or cramming it with data. For example, FileMaker's own Inspector uses four tabs to organize all the information it holds. A layout Tab Control works much the same way (although without the collapsible sections). Figure 5-15 shows the Lease Agreement layout reorganized using a Tab Control.

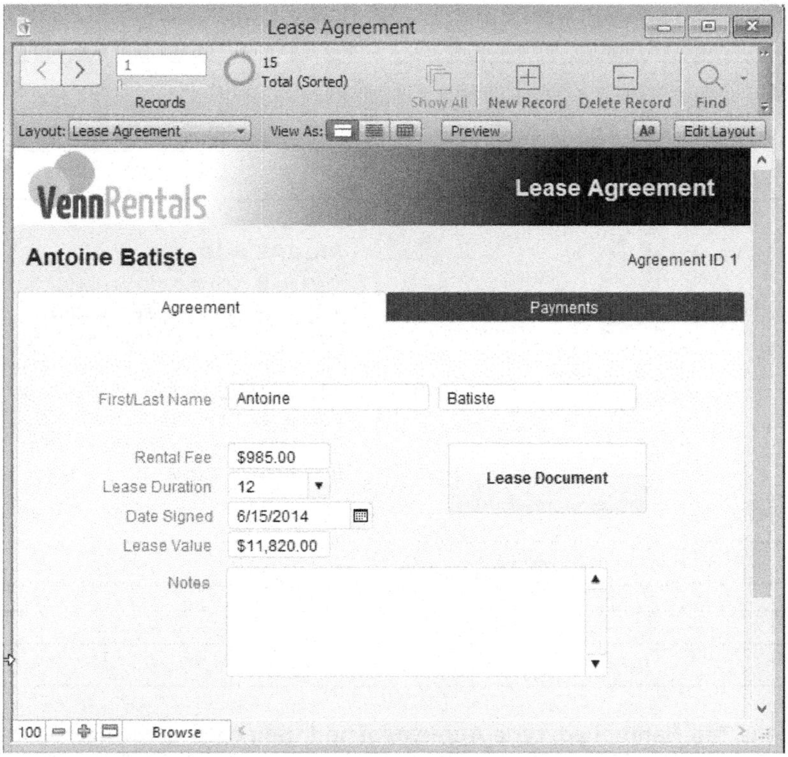

FIGURE 5-15

This version of the Lease Agreement layout has a large Tab Control covering most of its area. The Tab Control has two tabs, with the existing fields divided between them. The Agreement tab has the basic data, plus a Popover button for the Lease Document (more on popover buttons on page 168). The Payment portal has been moved to the Payments tab. Check the finished sample database to see what those tabs look like.

Creating a Tab Control

Tab Controls are easy to draw, but since it can be tricky dividing the objects on an existing layout among the new tabs, you'll need to do a little prep work. The process is easier on a larger monitor, but you can do it even on a small one. First, expand the database's window as large as your monitor will allow. If it's not big enough to show you about double the width of space as you currently have showing, try zooming out. Next, follow these steps:

1. **In Layout mode, drag all of your fields and field labels over in the gray space to the right so they're past the visible edge of the Lease Agreement layout.**

   If you don't move your fields, the new Tab Control will be on top of them in the layout's stacking order, and it won't be easy to select them afterward. Although you'd think that the "Send to Back" command would fix things, it doesn't always, so it's better to empty out the space first.

2. **In the Status toolbar, click the Tab Control tool. (It looks like a tiny tab control, with just one panel.) Then draw a large tab control on the layout.**

It should be as wide as the Body part and nearly the height of the Body. Put the left edge of the Tab Control on the left edge of the layout, and its bottom edge on the bottom edge of the Body part. When you finish drawing, the Tab Control Setup dialog box (Figure 5-16) appears.

NOTE You can also create a Tab Control by selecting Insert→Tab Control. The Tab Control tool lets you predefine the size and placement.

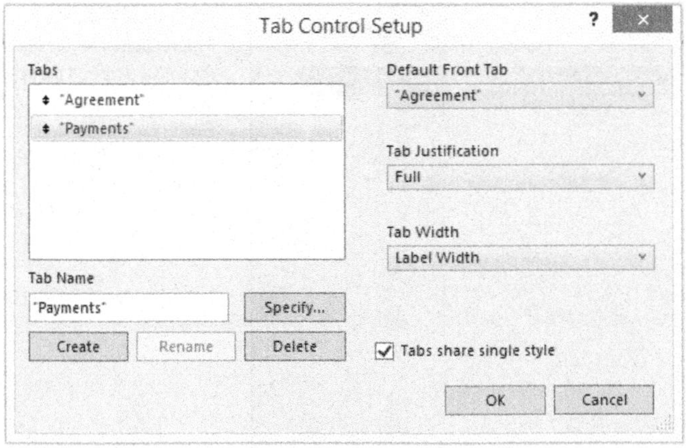

FIGURE 5-16

These are the settings for the Tab Control shown in Figure 5-16. Tab widths are automatically determined by the length of their names. But you can use the Tab Width pop-up menu to add extra space, set a minimum or fixed width, or make all tabs the width of the widest label. All Tab Width options are overridden if you select Full justification, though.

3. **In the Tab Name field, type *Agreement* and then click Create. Repeat this step and name your second tab *Payments*.**

FileMaker adds the two tab names to the Tabs list. The first tab you create is set as the Default Front Tab. That means the Agreement tab will be the active one whenever you switch to the Lease Agreement layout—no matter which tab was active the last time you left it.

4. **From the Tab Justification pop-up menu, select Full.**

The Full option will make the tabs appear all the way across the top of the Tab Control itself.

5. **When you're done, click OK to close the Tab Control Setup dialog box.**

Your new tab panel, complete with two tabs, sits highlighted in place on your layout.

Notice the selection handles and a dark box around each of the tabs. Any formatting changes you make with this selection will affect both tabs. It's easiest to make formatting changes to the Tab Control right after you set it up, because it's a bit of a pain to reselect all your tabs later. Try it now: Click outside the Tab Control to deselect it. Then click the Agreement tab. To select the others, you have to press Shift and then click twice on the other tabs. Pause slightly between clicks—if you click too fast, your computer will think you're double-clicking and open the Tab Control Setup dialog box.

Switch to Browse mode, where you'll see that your Tab Control is already working. You can click tabs, and each one comes to the front, just as you'd expect. But a Tab Control without objects is pretty useless.

Switch back to Layout mode to divide your objects and move them onto their proper tabs. First, select the fields and field labels that belong on the Agreement tab (refer back to Figure 5-16, if you need a refresher). Then drag those fields onto the Agreement tab. Choose File→Manage→Database to create a Notes field (Text type) in the Lease Agreement table and then put it on the Agreement tab, too. Use the Inspector to add a vertical scroll bar to the Notes field.

Click the Payments tab and move the Payment portal and its fields to the Payments tab. Double-click the portal to view the Portal Setup dialog box and then increase the number of rows to nine. Finally, now that the tabs are filled, put copies of the Name fields above the Tab Control (you may have to reduce the height of the Tab Control to make room for the Name fields above it). That way, you know whose record you're looking at, no matter which tab is selected.

NOTE If you use the Arrange→"Send to Back" command for an object that's on a Tab Control, the selected object goes behind other objects *on the same tab*, but not behind the Tab Control itself.

Editing Tab Controls

As you just saw, you can add a Tab Control any time you need to fit more stuff on a layout. And once it's there, you can add or delete panels or change the control's appearance. Edit a Tab Control by double-clicking it in Layout mode to summon the Tab Control Setup dialog box.

ADDING, REMOVING, AND REORDERING TABS

In the Tab Control Setup dialog box, you can add new tabs by typing a name and then clicking Create. The new tab appears at the end of the list of tabs and to the right of the existing tabs in the control. You can also rename an existing tab: Select it in the list, enter a new name, and then click Rename.

To delete a tab, select it in the list and then click Delete. When you delete a tab from a layout, you also delete all the objects on that tab, so be sure to move any objects you want to keep to another part of the layout first. (If the tab you select for deletion has objects on it, FileMaker warns you first, and asks whether you're sure you know what you're doing.)

Finally, you can control the tab panels' order. FileMaker draws the tabs in the order they appear in the Tabs list. The leftmost tab panel is the one that appears at the top of the list, and so on. Rearrange the list using the arrows to the left of each name. FileMaker is smart enough to move the objects on each tab along with the tabs themselves when you reorder.

▪ DEFAULT FRONT TAB

When you first switch to a layout but before you've clicked a tab, FileMaker needs to decide which tab to show automatically. You tell it which one by choosing the appropriate tab name from the Default Front Tab pop-up menu in the Tab Control Setup dialog box. While it's possible to choose any of the tab panels, be aware that most places where tabs appear, the leftmost tab is usually the front tab. If there's a compelling reason for a tab to always be in front when you first see a layout, it's pretty likely that that tab should be on the left, too.

▪ TAB JUSTIFICATION

If the total width of all your tabs is less than the width of the Tab Control itself *and* you haven't chosen Full justification, then FileMaker lets you choose where the grouping of tabs should be positioned. It's a lot like aligning a paragraph of text: Choose from Left, Center, or Right, and the tabs will bunch up according to your selection.

> **NOTE** If you have more tabs than can fit given the size of the Tab Control, then FileMaker simply doesn't show the extras. You can either force the tabs to be narrower using the Tab Width option (see the next section), make the Tab Control itself bigger, or make the tab names shorter.

▪ TAB WIDTH

The Tab Width pop-up menu has several choices to influence the width of the tabs:

- The standard setting, **Label Width,** makes each tab just wide enough to hold its label, so each tab could be a different width.

- **Label Width + Margin of** adds the amount of additional space you specify around the label text. You can choose your favorite measurement system (as long as it's either inches, centimeters, or points). The label's text will be centered within the tab.

- If you prefer all your tabs to be the same width, choose **Width of Widest Label.** FileMaker figures out which label is biggest, sizes that tab appropriately, and then makes the others match. This setting may push some tabs out of view if they won't all fit with the new width.

- If you'd like all your tabs to be a nice consistent width, but with the ability to accommodate the odd long label, choose **Minimum of.** Enter a minimum width (75 points, say), and every tab will be that width, unless the label is too big to fit, in which case that one tab will widen enough so the label fits.

- If you want the utmost in control and uniformity, choose **Fixed Width of** and then enter a width in the box. Every tab is exactly that width. If the label's text is too big, then FileMaker cuts it off at the edges.

NOTE Full tab justification overrides some settings in the Tab Width pop-up menu, so if you're making changes and don't see what you expect, make sure you haven't selected Full in the Tab Justification pop-up menu.

▥ TABS SHARE SINGLE STYLE

This option pertains to the styling of the your Tab Control's constituent panels. Out of the box, this setting is turned on, so formatting you apply to *any* panel is instantly propagated to all of them. Most of the time, this setup saves time and helps you maintain a consistent design. If you feel the need to style each panel individually, uncheck this box and customize away. But be warned: if you come back to the Tab Control Setup dialog box and turn "Tabs Share Single Style" back on, all tab panels will be set to match the *leftmost* panel. FileMaker gives you no warning and no way to undo this change, so approach this checkbox with caution.

▥ FORMATTING A TAB CONTROL

Out of the box, Tab Controls are matched to the theme you chose when you created the layout. But as with other objects on a layout, you can change their formatting. Use the Line and Fill tools on the Inspector's Appearance tab (or use the Formatting bar, if you prefer). Change the setting in the Corner Radius tool to make the tabs squared off or rounded. Usually, you'll format all panels in a given Tab Control the same way. See the preceding section for how to format panels individually.

Deleting a Tab Control

If you don't want a Tab Control after all, just select it and then choose Edit→Clear, or press Delete or Backspace. FileMaker warns you that it's about to delete all objects on the tab panel as well. If that's all right with you, click OK. If you need to keep fields or objects on the tab panels, though, click Cancel and then move the keepers off the panel for safekeeping.

Tab in a Tab

If your layouts have more doodads than the bridge of the *Enterprise,* take heart. You can *nest* a Tab Control on another tab for even more space savings. That's right. You can put tabs inside tabs inside tabs. So long as the new control sits entirely *inside* an existing tab, it behaves just like any other object on a panel. It sits there quietly behind the scenes and doesn't make an appearance until you click its enclosing panel. Only then is it visible, in all its tabbed glory. Needless to say, the more you use the tab-within-a-tab technique, the more complex your layout becomes—and the more potentially confusing to anyone using your database. Because they can hold so much data, multiple nested tabs can also dramatically increase the amount of time it takes your computer to draw a layout when you're sharing a file, using FileMaker Server (page 783). The speed decrease usually isn't an issue for FileMaker Pro running on a wired network. But if you're sharing your database using FileMaker Go (page 836) or through a browser (page 837), you can see dramatically slower speeds. If your database is likely to be used on a mobile device, use Tab Controls sparingly. Nested tabs are not recommended for iOS or mobile.

Adding a Popover Button

When you created the Lease Document container field (see page 100), you made a simple container that stores a copy of an external file and shows an icon to let you know what type of file has been stored in the field. But it might be handy to view the contents of that file from your database. You might think you'd need to make a giant field that uses massive screen real estate. But with a *popover button,* you can create a temporary overlay that only appears when a user clicks that button. The rest of the time, the overlay is hidden, letting users focus on the stuff they use most frequently.

To create a popover button, switch to Layout mode and follow these steps:

1. **Click the Agreement tab to select it. Drag the Lease Document field into the gray area to the right of the layout.**

   In this example, you're going to put a popover button for the Lease Document onto the Agreement tab.

2. **In Windows, click the arrow to the right of the Button tool. On a Mac, press and hold the Button tool in the Status bar.**

   A pop-up menu appears, giving you the option to create a button or popover button.

3. **Choose "Popover button" from the menu and draw a button on the upper right of the Agreement tab.**

   A popover window appears, along with the Popover Setup dialog box. In the dialog box, the Title field is selected (Figure 5-17). In the background, the button you created has a blinking text insertion point, which lets you add text to your button later on.

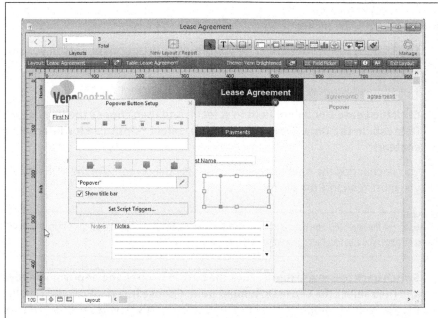

FIGURE 5-17

*The Popover Setup
dialog box automatically
appears when you first
create a popover button,
letting you label the
popover button, title
the popover window,
and determine where
the window opens in
relation to its button. To
access the Popover Setup
dialog box again later,
double-click the popover
window's title bar.*

4. **In the dialog box's top field, type *Lease Document*.**

   A row of icons in the middle of the Popover Setup dialog box lets you choose
   where the popover window appears in relation to the button when the user
   clicks the popover button.

5. **Select the far left icon.**

   The popover window's title appears at the top, and it scoots over to reflect the
   position you chose.

> **NOTE** If you click outside the Popover Setup dialog box, it closes. Double-click anywhere on the popover
> window to get it back.

6. **In the Popover Title field, type *Lease Agreement*.**

   In step 4 you named the button. This step defines the title of the popover window.

7. **Click the button you created in the step 2 and change the text style to bold
   so it stands out. Drag the Lease Document field into the popover window.
   Resize it to fill the window.**

   If you didn't draw your popover window large enough back in step 3, you may
   need to make it bigger and then resize the Lease Document field. Your popover
   window is complete.

Switch to Browse mode to see the popover in action. Find the record for Antoine Batiste, whose record contains a lease document file. When you click the popover button, the popover window opens, displaying a file icon—just like the Lease Document field did before you made the popover. You need to change the Lease Document field to display the file's contents instead. Here's how:

1. **Switch back to Layout mode and double-click the popover button you just created.**

   The popover window appears with the Lease Document field inside.

2. **Click the Lease Document field to select it and then choose the Inspector's Data tab. In the Data Formatting section, select "Optimize for Interactive content."**

   You've changed the field's behavior to display the contents of the PDF file, but you must reimport the file for it to work.

> **NOTE** For the next step, you need a PDF file to insert. If you didn't download the samples from this book's Missing CD page, you can find them at *www.missingmanuals.com/cds/fmp14mm*.

3. **Switch back to Browse mode, click the button to open the popover window, and then select the Lease Document field. Choose Insert→PDF and find the file you want to import (the Missing CD folder gives you sample PDFs for the first six records in the Lease Agreement database).**

   The PDF document appears in the popover window. You may need to expand the popover window and the lease document field to see the PDF controls. Figure 5-18 shows how it should look.

> **NOTE** If you can't see the PDF in your new popover window, you can try a few fixes. Make sure you've installed Adobe Reader (available at *http://get.adobe.com/reader*) and launched the program at least once. You'll be asked to accept the license terms. (Just installing Reader isn't enough.) Also, make sure your web browser is set up to allow plug-ins.

■ Adding Merge Fields

The Lease Agreement table's First Name and Last Name fields are up above the new Tab Control so you can tell which record you're dealing with as you switch tabs. But all the rest of your fields are on the Tab Control, and if you're chunking data, it's not the best idea to have some of your data entry fields up there above the Tab Control. That's one place merge fields come in. You can create a text object that contains merge fields to display the data from each record's First Name and Last Name field. A *merge field* is a text block containing the field's name, surrounded by a pair of double angle brackets like this:

```
<<First Name>>
```

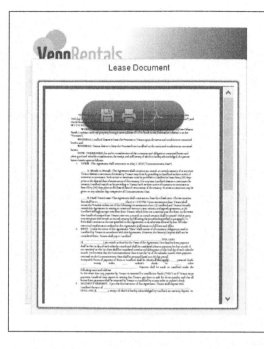

FIGURE 5-18

Because the PDF you've inserted has multiple pages, the container field gives you a scroll bar to view all of them. The field's controls also include up and down arrows for scrolling and + and – buttons for zooming. Alternatively, you can view the PDF in Adobe Reader by clicking its icon.

Besides being useful for displaying data on layouts, merge fields are often used for things like form letters, labels, or envelopes. Either way, merge fields expand and contract to use only the actual amount of space required by data inside the fields they represent. You can't enter or edit data using a merge field, nor can they be searched in Find mode (but the Quick Find in Browse mode will search merge fields). But that's no problem here—you have the normal First Name and Last Name fields down on the Agreement tab where you can edit and search them. In this case, a pair of merge fields help orient you as you switch tabs and are a more attractive way to display data than using normal fields would be. Start by deleting the copies of the name fields you placed above the Tab Control.

1. **In Layout mode, select the Text tool, click in the blank space above the Tab Control and then change the formatting to 18-point bold and the text color to black.**

   The click tells FileMaker where you want the merge field to land. Setting the format here saves you a trip back to the toolbar.

2. **Choose Insert→Merge Field, Or use the shortcut Ctrl+M (Windows) or Option-⌘-M (Mac).**

   The Specify Field dialog box appears.

3. **Double-click the First Name field and then press the space bar.**

   The First Name merge field, "<<First Name>>," appears inside your text block. The space is so the Last Name doesn't run onto the First Name.

TIP If you know the exact name of the field(s) you want, you can type it instead of using the Insert→Merge Field command. Just be careful to get the angle brackets and name of the field exactly right. If you make a mistake, all you'll see in Browse mode is what you typed, and not the data you expect.

---

4. **Make sure that the insertion point is still blinking after the First Name and space in the text block and then Choose Insert→Merge Field again. Double-click the Last Name field.**

   The text "<<First Name>> <<Last Name>>" now appears inside the text block.

Click outside the text block to switch back to the pointer tool and then move the text block if necessary. Switch to Browse mode to see that the field's contents appear inside the merge fields there.

The agreementID field is another good candidate for a merge field, since it can be useful to see the agreement number. Make a text block near the top of the layout and use *Agreement ID <<agreementID>>* for its contents. Align the text to the right, put it at the right side of the header, and make sure it lines up with the merge field showing the name.

You can format merge fields just like any other text block. But since they also contain data, if you apply formatting from the Inspector's Data tab to text blocks that contain merge fields, FileMaker displays the data according to your formatting. So if you put a merge version of the Rental Fee field on the Payment tab (so you can see what the Rental Fee is supposed to be as you record each payment), don't forget to format the text block as currency.

You can use merge fields to create a form letter (you'll get one copy for each record in the found set, with appropriate data for each record). Just create a new layout, select your context, and then type the text of the letter inside a large text block, and insert merge fields within the text as appropriate. Because your new layout shows you records from a specific table occurrence, you'll never have to run another "merge" operation. Just find the records for the folks who should get a letter and then print all the records in your found set (page 324). You'll also see heavy use of merge fields if you use the Layout/Report Assistant to create label or envelope layouts for sending out your merged letters.

Using Symbols to Show Important Info

Merge fields aren't the only things FileMaker can use to show dynamic information. You use one of a handful of special *symbols*—stand-in characters that are replaced with info when you view your database in Browse, Layout, or Preview mode. For example, see Figure 5-19, where each record on the Lease Agreement List layout is numbered. The record number symbol displays an automatic number for each record.

FIGURE 5-19

The number to the left of each record on the Lease Agreement List layout comes from a special symbol placed on the layout. Sort the list, and notice that the records change order, but the record numbers themselves stay in sequence. The record number is meant to help you figure out where the record is ordered in a list, but not to identify any specific record. See page 146 for a way to assign a permanent ID number, or key, to a record.

NOTE FileMaker offers a host of other symbols besides the record number symbol. See the box on page 175 for details.

To add a record number to your Lease Agreement List layout, you'll need to slide your fields and their labels to the right to make space. Then click the Text tool to select it and click in the space you've just made. Choose Insert→Record Number Symbol. You now have a text object that contains "{{RecordNumber}}". It takes up way more space than it needs to in Layout mode, but it'll be fine in Browse mode. It's annoying having it cover part of the First Name field, so select the text block and then choose Arrange→"Send to Back" to place it behind the Name field. It'll work just fine there without being distracting. If you want to format the record number, just select it and apply the changes you want. You don't need to bring it forward first. Switch to Browse mode, where you see that FileMaker puts the current record number in place of the symbol.

As with Merge Fields, you can insert symbols into existing text objects. Just click in the text object first, as if you're going to type. Then, when you choose Insert→Record Number Symbol, FileMaker adds the record number symbol to the existing text.

■ Writing a Basic Script

Now that you have a record number on the Lease Agreement List layout and have sorted the list, you can start to see how useful the layout really is. The Lease Agreement layout is great for revealing detail, but when the Lease Agreement List layout is sorted by Last Name, it's a cinch to scroll to the record you need without entering Find mode, typing in search criteria, and then performing a find. But it could be easier to sort the records on the layout. As it is, you have to choose Records→Sort Records, select the field you want to sort by, and then click Sort. Doing this routine is easy, but not a good use of your time. The solution is to write a script to do these things automatically.

If you're familiar with *macros* in other programs, then you already have the idea of scripts in FileMaker—you set up scripts to perform tasks for you. The task at hand—sorting—is just one command, but it has several steps. They're all quick steps, but when you have to repeat them several times a day and so does everyone else in your office, all that wasted time adds up to real inefficiency. Also, any manual process leaves room for human error. When you make a mistake, no matter how harmless, you have to undo or redo what you just did. A script that handles your sort is more efficient and less susceptible to error.

Creating a Sort Script

Here's how to write a script that sorts the records on your list layout alphabetically by Last Name and then First Name:

1. **Choose Records→Sort Records. Set up the window to sort by Last Name and then First Name (page 25) and then click Sort.**

   Every time you open the Sort window, your most recent sort order is already in the window. So save yourself some time by performing the sort before you start creating your script. That way, the order will already be in the Sort window.

2. **Choose Scripts→Script Workspace.**

   The Script Workspace window appears.

3. **Click the + button in the top-left corner of the window to create a new script.**

   A new, blank script is created (Figure 5-20).

Other Symbols

On the Insert menu, FileMaker includes symbols for several special values you may want to show on a layout. In Browse mode (or Preview mode), FileMaker replaces the symbol with the up-to-the-moment correct value. You can read about the record number symbol on page 172. Here are the other symbols:

- The **Date Symbol** ({{CurrentDate}}) is replaced by the current date. You'd include this symbol on printed reports so you can easily see when the reports were printed.

- The **Time Symbol** ({{CurrentTime}}) is replaced by the current time. If your reports needed to be identified down to the hour and minute they were printed, add this symbol to a report's header or footer.

- The **User Name Symbol** ({{UserName}}) is replaced by the current user's name. FileMaker takes the user name of whoever's logged into your computer (or the custom User Name if one is entered in FileMaker's Preferences).

- The **Page Number Symbol** ({{PageNumber}}) is replaced by the page number in Preview mode and when you print. Otherwise, it just shows as a question mark.

- **Other Symbol** opens up a whole host of dynamic values, called *Get functions*, that you can place on the layout. Like PageNumbers or the CurrentDate, these functions change as appropriate to show you the latest information. To use them, you'll need to understand calculations. Chapter 10 is where you'll get the basics.

The Insert menu has three related options as well, but unlike symbols, these don't get replaced by anything in Browse or Preview mode. When you use the Insert→Current Date command, for instance, FileMaker simply adds today's date to the text object in Layout mode. It's a static value (that is, it never changes) and shows the same date in any mode. In fact, the Insert Date, Time, and User commands remain in the menu when you're in Browse mode so you can use them for entering data into a field.

You can use the Insert menu to place symbols where you need them, but just like merge fields, you can type them in manually too. So once you've seen that {{CurrentDate}} makes a page number, forget about mousing around, and just type away.

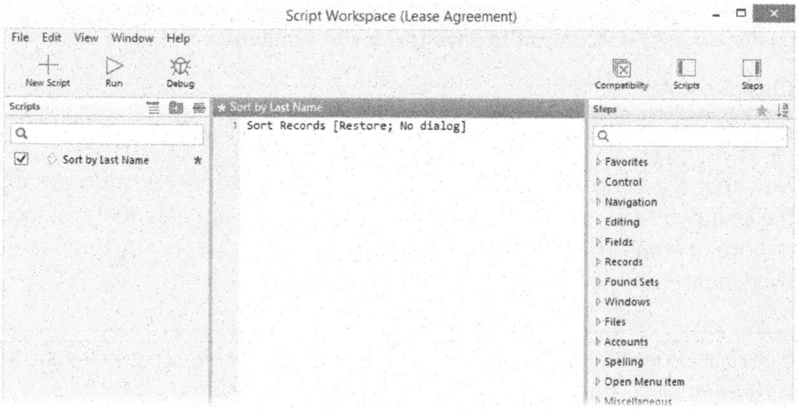

FIGURE 5-20

The Edit Script window contains everything you need to write a script. Many of the script steps available are the same as the commands in FileMaker's menus. If you know how to use those commands manually, you know how they'll behave as script steps. But there are some commands that you can access only through scripting, and the subject is so deep and wide that this book has three Chapters—12, 13, and 18—devoted to the subject.

4. **Double-click the words "New Script" to rename this script. Select and delete the words "New Script," type *Sort by Last Name,* and then press Enter to save the change.**

Always use descriptive names in FileMaker. Mature databases can have hundreds of scripts, so good naming is the first step in keeping things organized.

5. **Begin typing *sort.***

As you type, a list of matching script steps appears.

6. **Select the Sort Records script step from the list of suggestions, using arrow keys or your mouse, and then press Enter.**

The Sort Records script step is added to the script.

7. **Press Enter again to reveal the script options. Use the down arrow key to move the focus to "Perform without dialog," and then press the space bar to select it.**

Without this option selected, you'd see the regular Sort window every time you run the script. Don't turn on this option when you're writing a script that lets the user choose a custom sort as the script runs.

8. **Use the down arrow again to choose "Specify sort order," and then press the space bar to select this option.**

The regular Sort window appears, with Last Name and then First Name set up already. As you know, FileMaker remembers your most recent sort order, but it's good practice to verify *everything* when you're scripting. And if you want a different sort order, you can change it and the script will remember your changes.

9. **Click OK to close the Sort window and then close the Script Workspace window.**

FileMaker asks if you want to save the script's changes.

10. **Click Save All.**

FileMaker saves the script and closes the Script Workspace.

Now that the Script Workspace window is closed, you need some way to run the script you just wrote. Look in the Scripts menu. It appears there, along with a shortcut. You can run the script by choosing Scripts→"Sort by Last Name" or by using the shortcut.

> **TIP** You can save scripts before closing the Script Workspace window by choosing Scripts→Save Script or using the keyboard shortcut Ctrl+S (⌘-S).

You've finished writing the script and it's time to test it to see if it works as intended. Unsort your records (choose Records→Unsort) and then run the script.

Creating a Button

Running the script from the menu saved you a few steps, but you can make it even more convenient by attaching the script to a layout object, which then becomes a button. Then whenever you click the button in Browse mode, the script runs automatically. Here's how:

1. **In Layout mode, click the Last Name Field's label to select it.**

   It's a common convention to click a column label to sort a column, so help your users out by adopting that principle.

2. **Choose Format→Button Setup.**

   The Button Setup window appears (Figure 5-21).

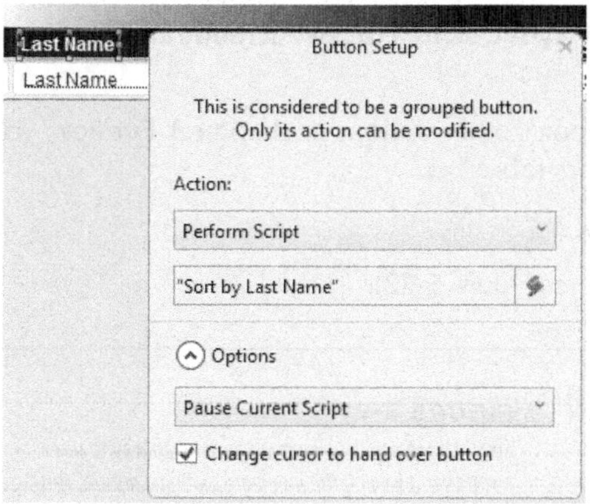

FIGURE 5-21

The Button Setup window lets you choose from most of the same steps you see in the Edit Script window. The difference is that you can only choose a single script step when you define a button this way. Any time you need a process that requires two or more script steps, create a script and then attach it to the button. But even if the process is a single step, you may still want a script, so you can set it to appear in the Scripts menu. Even better, if you apply a script to several buttons throughout your database, you can change the script, and all the buttons will run the edited script automatically. But if you had attached a single action to each of those buttons instead of a script, you'd have to change each one manually.

3. **From the Action pop-up list, select Perform Script.**

   The Specify Script window appears, showing a list of all the scripts in your database. You've only got one, but it's not uncommon to have hundreds.

4. **Click the "Sort by Last Name" script and then click OK. Click anywhere outside the Button Setup Window to dismiss it.**

   Your button is ready to use.

Switch to Browse mode and then Unsort your records, if they're sorted. Finally, click the Last Name field label to see the script run. You haven't put anything on your layout to indicate to your users that the field label does anything useful. FileMaker changes the pointer to a hand icon when it's positioned over any button, but you have to give users a visual clue that there's something useful besides text. So change the label's formatting (make it a contrasting color, or put a border around it so that it looks like a button) to help users out. (Learn more about buttons on page 365.)

NOTE If your pointer *doesn't* change to a hand when you put your cursor over a button, go to Layout mode and double-click the button. Select the "Change hand to cursor over button" option and then click OK.

Applying a Script Trigger

The script was nice, and the button improved things, but you're still not done learning how useful and intuitive scripts can be. Since the point of going to the List layout is to quickly scan a list so you can find a particular Lease Agreement record, it'd be even more convenient if the list just knew to sort itself every time you switch to the layout. And that kind of thing is what Script Triggers are for.

You've just seen that you can run a script from the Scripts menu or from a button. But you can also tell a script to run when you do other things, like enter data in a field or go to a specific layout. Here's how to make the "Sort by Last Name" script run every time you go to the Lease Agreement List layout:

1. **On the Lease Agreement List layout, switch to Layout mode and then choose Layouts→Layout Setup.**

   You'll learn about this dialog box's other options in Chapter 8. For now, you're interested in the Script Triggers tab.

2. **Click the Script Triggers tab.**

   The Script Triggers tab appears (Figure 5-22).

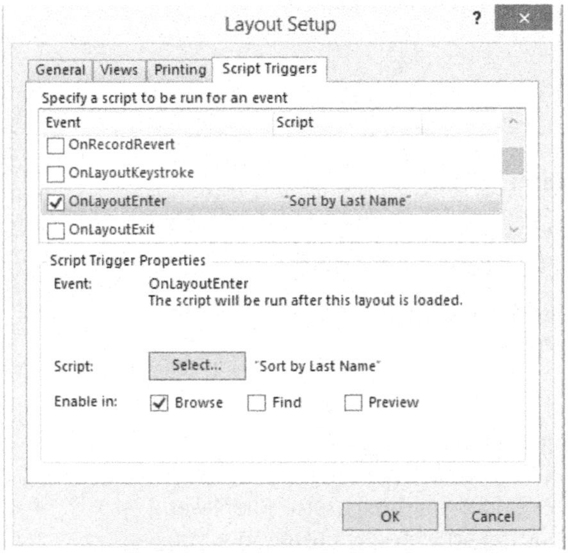

FIGURE 5-22

Script triggers give you a more automated way to run a script than by using the menu or creating a button. This script trigger will run a script called "Sort by Last Name" every time you view the layout in Browse mode. When you apply a script trigger with the Layout Setup dialog box, it affects only the layout you apply it to. Script triggers are enormously powerful, but they can be tricky. Learn more about them on page 455.

3. **Select the OnLayoutEnter option in the Event list. Windows users may need to scroll the list to see that option.**

Selecting an Event tells FileMaker *when* to run a script. Once you make a selection, the Specify Script window appears.

4. **Click the "Sort by Last Name" script to select it and then click OK.**

The Script Trigger tab is now set up. Notice that you're letting the script run only while you're viewing the layout in Browse mode.

5. **Click OK.**

The script will run each time you switch to the Lease Agreement List layout.

To test the script trigger, switch to Browse mode and unsort your list, and then switch to the Lease Agreement layout. Then switch back to the Lease Agreement List layout. The script runs and sorts your list for you.

Creating a Dynamic Report with the Assistant

Your database is getting pretty smart now. It can do math and perform some housekeeping duties on its own. But one of the main purposes of storing data is to be able to analyze it. You're storing information about lease agreements, but so far, there's no way to take a look at any trends that might show up. For instance, you offer leases of 12, 24, or 36 months. If you sort and count your leases by duration, you may be able to spot interesting trends, like people who are willing to sign longer leases are also willing to lease your more expensive properties, for example. Or, maybe the opposite is true and they're less willing. If so, you'll want to come up with some incentives to get the high rollers to sign longer leases. But you'll never know until you create a report.

You've already seen how the Layout/Report Assistant makes it a breeze to create a new layout (page 130). Many of the assistant's panels are already familiar to you. But the assistant can also build some special layout parts and create fields for you that summarize your data. Better still, the report you'll build is dynamic. If you add a new record to the list while you're viewing the onscreen report, the record is automatically sorted into place, and your summary data updates immediately. Here's how to create a dynamic report:

1. **In Layout mode, choose Layouts→New Layout/Report.**

The New Layout/Report dialog box appears.

2. **In the "Show records from" pop-up menu, make sure the Lease Agreement table is selected. In the Layout Name box, type *Lease Agreement Report*. Click the Computer icon and then choose Report from the layout type list in the lower half of the screen. Click Continue.**

After you click Continue, the "Include Subtotals and Grand Totals" panel appears.

3. **If they're not already selected, choose "Include subtotals" and "Include grand totals" and then click Next.**

   After you click Next, the Specify Fields panel appears.

4. **Move the First Name, Last Name, Rental Fee, and Lease Duration fields to the "Fields shown on layout/report" box and then click Next.**

   This should be familiar territory by now. Remember that you can use the arrow to the left of each field to move it up and down in the list on the right. After you click Next, the "Organize Records by Category" panel appears.

5. **Move the Lease Duration field into the Report categories list and then click Next.**

   The sample report icon changes as you move fields into the Report categories list. After you click Next, the Sort Records panel appears.

6. **Move the Last Name and First Name fields into the Sort order list and then click Next.**

   Lease Duration is already in the list, because that's how the report will categorize the list. But you want records with the same Lease Duration value to be sorted alphabetically by Last Name and then by First Name. After you click Next, the Specify Subtotals panel appears (Figure 5-23).

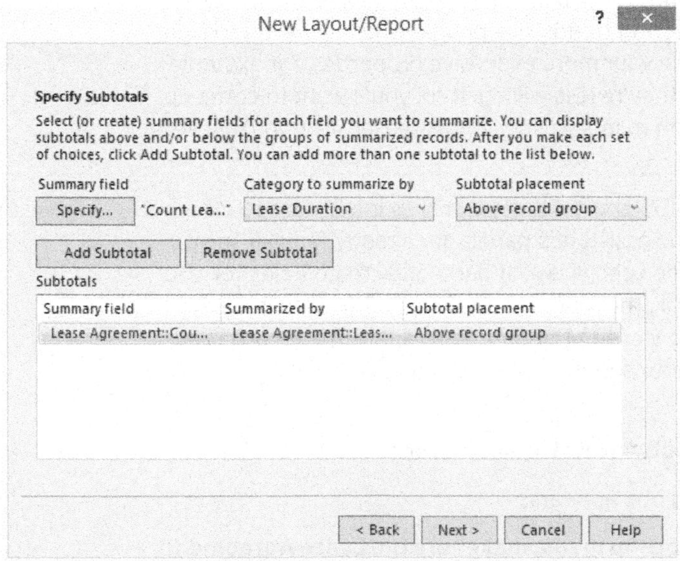

FIGURE 5-23

Choices you make in this window determine how many subtotals your report will have. You can also place the subtotal above or below the records it's summarizing. You need to have at least one Subtotal line item in the Subtotals box at the bottom for the summary to work, though, so make sure you click Add Subtotal after you create or choose a summary field (you'll learn about those later in this tutorial).

7. **From the Subtotal Placement pop-up menu, choose "Above record group" and then click Specify under "Summary field."**

The Specify Field window appears.

8. **Click Add.**

The "Options for Summary Field" window appears (Figure 5-24). You'll create a special field that counts the records in each category. The field will appear above the record group it summarizes because of the choice you made in step 7.

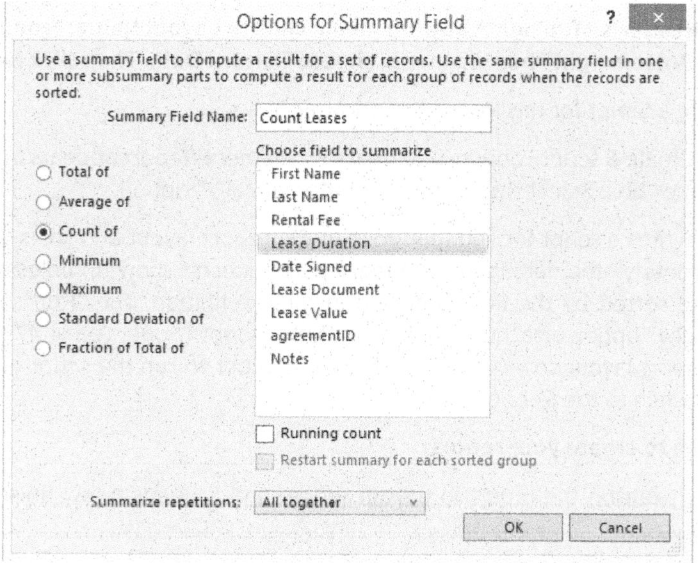

FIGURE 5-24

You'd see a nearly identical window if you used the Manage Database window to create a summary field. Summary fields do just what their name implies: They summarize groups of data. You can apply one of several mathematical operations to the fields, including Totals, Averages, and Counts. You can count any field, but you can't apply math to text fields. So if you're trying to select a field, but it's grayed out, check the operation you're trying to perform. It may not be the right option for the field you want to summarize (or the field's definition may be set to the wrong type).

9. **In the Summary Field Name box, type *Count Leases* and then select "Count of." Now choose Lease Duration from the "Choose field to summarize" list and then click OK until you're back on the Specify Subtotals panel. Now click Add Subtotal. Click Next.**

FileMaker creates a new Count Leases field (Summary type) and adds it to the Subtotals list. At the end of this process, you'll see a Subsummary part (you'll learn how to create them manually on page 631) based on the options you just chose. The summary field counts each record in the sorted category group you selected and displays a count of records for each group in its own Subsummary part. Make sure the Lease Agreement::Count Leases field appears in the Subtotals list at the bottom of the window. After you click Next, the Specify Grand Totals window appears.

10. **Click Specify.**

The Specify Field window appears. The Count Leases field you just created appears in the list.

11. **Click the Count Leases field to select it and then click OK. Leave the "Grand total placement" pop-up menu set to "End of report," and then click Add Grand Total. Make sure the Lease Agreement::Count Leases field appears in the Grand Totals list at the bottom of the window. Finally, click Next.**

Summary fields are smart enough to display different data depending on the layout part they're placed in. So you can use the same summary field in a Sub-summary part and a Grand Total part, and it will display appropriate data in each part. This version of the Count Leases field will appear at the end of the report and will give you a grand total count of all the records you're viewing. After you click Next, the "Header and Footer Information" window appears.

12. **From the Header's "Top right" pop-up menu, choose Layout Name. From the Footer's "Bottom right" pop-up menu, choose Current Date. Then click Next.**

The "Create a Script for this Report" window appears.

Click the "Create a script" option, and *Lease Agreement Report* appears in the "Script name" box. Select the "Run script automatically" option.

FileMaker writes a script for you that goes to the report layout and sorts your records properly—the data in Subsummary parts doesn't show up unless the records are sorted by the field specified in their definition. The "Run script automatically" option attaches an OnLayoutEnter script trigger (page 475) to the new report layout so you don't have to remember to run the script every time you switch to the Report layout.

13. **Click Finish to create your report.**

You're now viewing the report in Layout mode, and it needs a few finishing touches.

14. **Choose Layouts→Change Theme. Select Enlightened and click OK.**

The custom Venn Enlightened theme doesn't lend itself to this layout, but the original theme will work just fine.

15. **If necessary, resize the text box at the top right so it displays the full layout name.**

You may also wish to drag the Layout Name and Date objects to the left so they're not hanging out so far to the right of your data.

16. **Switch to Browse mode.**

Your report appears, but the subtotals don't show up. The script wasn't triggered because you weren't in the Lease Agreement Report layout, even though you just created it.

17. **Switch to the Lease Agreement layout, then switch back to the Lease Agreement Report layout.**

Your sorted report appears (Figure 5-25).

There were a lot of steps and a lot of selections to make. But the hard work's been done for you. In Chapter 16, you'll learn how to create a sorted subsummary report completely by hand. Once you've done that, you'll appreciate how much easier it was to make selections in an assistant. However, you need to format your fields and generally beautify the layout so that it matches the rest of your database.

When you've got the layout looking fine, switch to Browse mode so you can see how the report updates dynamically. For example, click the Toni Bernette record to select it and then click the New Record button in your Status toolbar. Finally, enter the following data in the new record:

- First Name: Janette

- Last Name: Desautel

- Rental Fee: 1295

- Lease Duration: 12

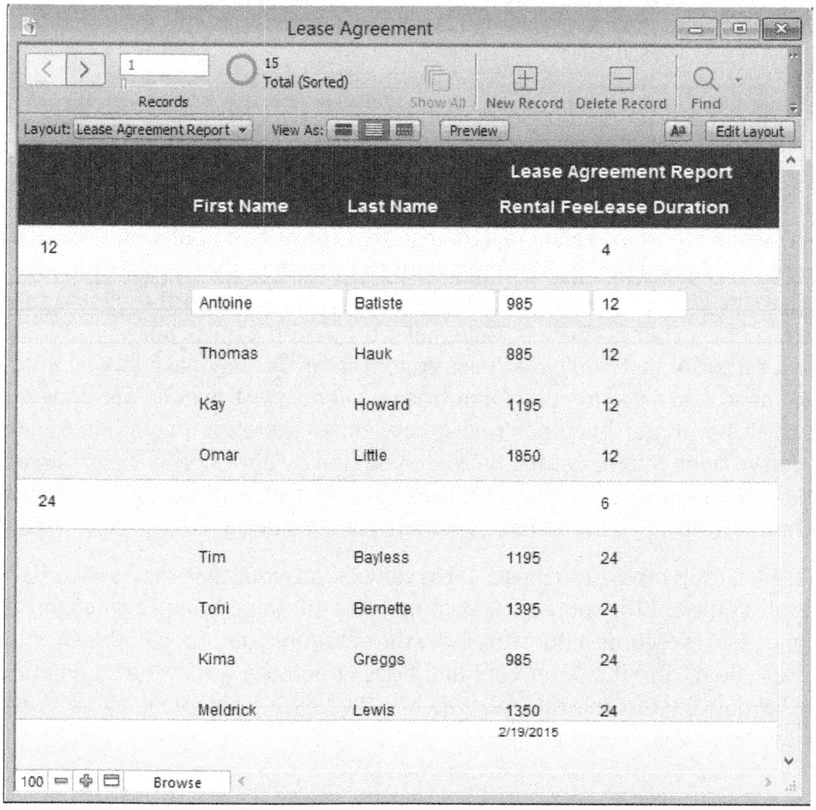

FIGURE 5-25

Graphically speaking, the report as created is nothing to write home about, so you'll need to put your layout design skills to use on this layout. However, the Layout Assistant gave you some nice tools to help you start analyzing your data. You can see that your current group of tenants trend toward longer leases. And it looks like your higher-priced properties are leased out longer, too. Except for that one guy with the $1,850 lease who's only signing on for 12 months. (While you're learning FileMaker, have your assistant find out what it'll take to get that guy signed up for another couple of years.)

Your new record is created right below your active record. When you commit the new record, it's sorted into the 12-month group, and the Count Leases field is updated immediately in both the Subsummary and Grand Total parts. The same thing is true if you edit data in the field on which the sort is based (remember that this report is always sorted by the Lease Duration field and then by Last Name and First Name). Change some data in a Lease Duration field and then commit the record. It will sort into the proper group. If you add data that's not in an existing group (say you type *48* in the Lease Duration field), a new group will be formed with a Count of "1."

Subsummary layouts show their summary data only when your records are sorted by the field that's attached to the Subsummary part (explained on page 631). So if you unsort your records, or do a sort that doesn't include the Subsummary part's field (say you sorted by Last Name and First Name only), the groups and subtotals don't show on the layout. To get them back, sort the records again, and this time, make sure you include the proper field (in this case, it's Lease Duration) in the sort order.

NOTE Sorted subsummary reports are great for looking at trends in your data, but you probably wouldn't usually use them as the primary way to add new records or edit existing ones. But on those occasions when it's suitable (say the sorted report makes it clear that some data wasn't entered correctly), it's convenient that you don't have to leave the report layout to make corrections.

■ Creating a Trailing Group Report

The dynamic report you just created is perfect for printing out when you want to analyze your data. Even if they don't want to print the report, your users can just switch to the Lease Agreement Report layout and get an up-to-the-minute catego-rized report on your properties. But what if they need a quick analysis of the data using a category that you haven't set up for them? Do they have to wait until you have time to add a new report? Or maybe you need a last-minute, one-time report that won't be printed (you don't even have time—there's a meeting in 5 minutes and you've been told to get the data), so you don't want to bother creating a new layout and spending time making it match the rest of your database. Either way, FileMaker's Trailing Group reporting feature is the solution.

A Trailing Group report requires a Table view on a layout that shows records from the table you want to report on. It accomplishes the same thing as a dynamic sub-summary (sorts records automatically by the category you choose, with an optional summary field), but it's temporary and doesn't actually add a Subsummary part to the layout. To start this tutorial, switch to the Lease Agreement layout and then click the Table View button.

1. **Click the triangle to the right of the Lease Duration field's column heading. (The triangle appears when you place your mouse over the heading.) Choose "Add Trailing Group by Lease Duration" (Figure 5-26).**

   The Lease Duration column's pop-up menu appears when you click the triangle, and then when you choose the Trailing Group command, a gray summary row appears on the table and the records are automatically sorted by Lease Duration.

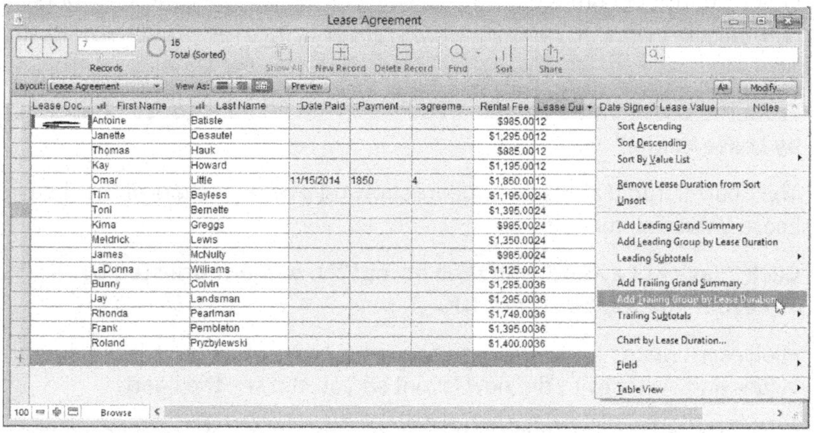

FIGURE 5-26

The contextual menu for column heads in Table view lets you create quick Trailing Group reports, but it also lets you change field options, delete the field, add new summary fields, or sort the records you're viewing. You can even change the way the Table view behaves by adding, resizing, or deleting columns.

2. **From the Lease Duration column's pop-up menu, choose Trailing Subtotals→Count (Count Leases).**

   The count appears in the summary row below each Trailing Group.

FileMaker sorts and groups the records for you, so you can get the information you need from the ad hoc report without fuss. As with the dynamic report in the previous section, the records must be sorted by the Trailing Group you chose for the summaries to show up. So if you switch back to Form View and sort your records another way, you won't see the Trailing Group Report when you return to Table View. Select Sort Ascending from the Lease Duration column pop-up menu to sort the records, and the Trailing Groups reappear.

If you switch to Layout mode, you'll see that the layout *doesn't* have a new part added to it. Nor does the Count field actually appear on the layout. That's why this type of report is temporary. It's meant to let you get a quick, bird's-eye view of your data and then get right back into your other tasks (or to the meeting on time and with the data you were told to have at your fingertips).

You can get creative with your ad hoc reports by adding multiple Trailing Groups at the same time. In a small database like the one you're working on, you may find that nearly every record gets its own group. But in a database with lots of records, you can use this technique to get fine-grained reports very quickly. Remove a Trailing Group by clicking the column head menu associated with that group. Choose "Remove Trailing Group by Lease Duration," and the group no longer shows up.

Creating Charts in Table View

Text-based reports, whether they're meant for print or screen, are not the be-all and end-all of data analysis. Most people find information easier to read in the form of a chart over a bunch of numbers. So FileMaker gives you a quick method for creating charts from Table view. To see it in action, on the Lease Agreement layout, start in Table view.

1. **From the Lease Value column head's pop-up menu, choose Chart→"Chart by Lease Value."**

   The Chart Setup dialog box appears showing a column chart of the data in the Lease Value column.

2. **Click "Save as Layout," and then accept the name suggested by the "Save as Layout" dialog box. Click OK.**

   FileMaker creates a new layout showing a chart of all your lease agreement values and switches to the new layout so you can see the chart.

   FileMaker creates a column chart by using the context of Lease Agreement and the Lease Value field. If FileMaker created it too large to see all at once, you can resize it like any other object. Currently, the chart displays *all* the records from the table, so if you had *hundreds* of records, this chart wouldn't be very useful. But there's a quick trick for making it show you just some of your records. As you might expect, the solution is found in Layout Mode. All you need to do is put a field on the layout so you can do a search to limit the number of records in the found set.

3. **Switch to Layout mode, click the Field tool to select it, and then drag to create a field down in the gray area to the right of the chart.**

   If you've resized your chart and didn't resize the layout to match, there will be a light gray area (the original dimensions of the chart) and a darker gray area. You need to drag the field into the darker gray area.

   Anything in the gray area doesn't appear when you're in Browse mode. When you release the mouse, the Specify Field window appears.

4. **From the Specify Field window, choose Lease Duration, click OK, and then switch to Browse Mode.**

   The chart looks just like it did before, but now you have a way to change the records you're viewing.

5. **In the Quick Find field (Figure 5-27), type *36* and then press Enter.**

   FileMaker searches the only field on the layout (Lease Duration— even though it's hidden in the gray area, Quick Find still knows it's there and can search its contents) and finds the records with 36-month leases. The chart changes dynamically with the found set.

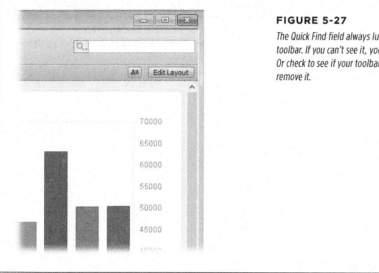

FIGURE 5-27

The Quick Find field always lurks on the right side of your Status toolbar. If you can't see it, you may need to make your window wider. Or check to see if your toolbar has been customized (page 16) to remove it.

Changing the Default Account

You know that FileMaker creates a lot of elements for you when you first create a new database. One thing you may not know is that it even created a login account for you *and* it assigned that account name to be entered automatically each time you open the file. You can see that setting and then turn it off by choosing File→File Options (Figure 5-28).

This default account is created in every database FileMaker creates, so to protect your new database from prying eyes, turn off the option to log in using the automatic account, and then change the default account's name and password. Here's how to change the default account:

1. **Choose File→Manage→Security.**

   A warning pops up about having a blank password on your Admin account.

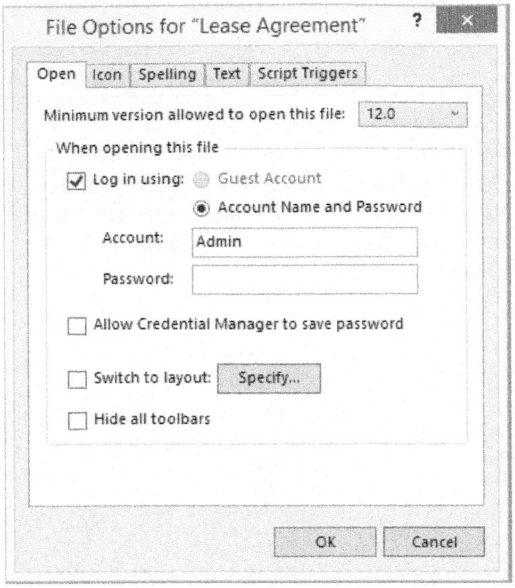

FIGURE 5-28

It's not industrial-strength security, but FileMaker created an Admin account for you and has been secretly using it every time you open the Lease Agreement database. Really it's not that much of a secret, because you have to figure that at least half of FileMaker's millions of users know about this account and the hackers among them would try the "Admin" account name (it doesn't even have a password) if they wanted to break into your database. One of the first things you should do to make your database more secure is to turn off the "Log in using" option of this window. Then change the default account to a custom name and password.

2. **Click the Ignore button.**

   The Manage Security window appears. It shows two built-in accounts, but only the Admin account is active, as shown by the checkmark in the Active column (Figure 5-29).

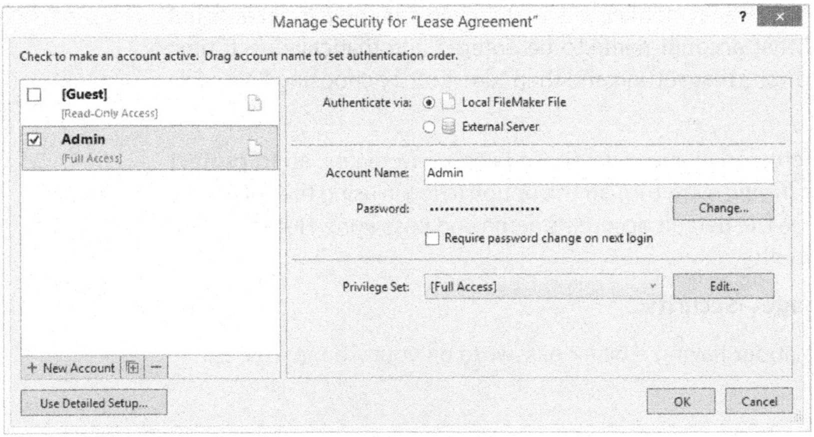

FIGURE 5-29

Account Names appear in the Account Name box just as you type them, but characters in the password box are obscured by a password font. That keeps your typing safe from wandering eyes, but it does mean that you have to be very careful as you type. Once you add a password to an account, even you can never see it. (Go to Chapter 19 to read all about security.)

3. **Click the Admin account and then, in the account box, type your first initial and last name.**

   This first initial/last name scheme is commonly used for creating account names. But you can use whatever scheme you like, so long as you can remember it.

4. **Click the Change button to create a password.**

   Technically you're adding a password where there was none before, but the button always says Change.

5. **Enter your desired password twice.**

   After you enter your password in the top field, FileMaker will offer its opinion of just how strong a password it is. You'll find FileMaker's password standards are rather rigorous. For example, the password "^UKPatA>92kEo@N4dUt" is considered *moderate.* You're the one who has to remember that password, so don't get too hung up on pleasing the password judge here.

   > **NOTE** Case doesn't matter for account names, but it *does* matter for passwords.

6. **Click Set Password to close the Password dialog box.**

   You've just changed the Full Access account for the file.

   > **NOTE** If you forget a file's Full Access account name and password, you may not be able to use or access the file. Even FileMaker Tech Support can't retrieve it for you. You may want to write it down before you enter it the first time and store it in a safe location.

7. **Click OK to close the Manage Security dialog box.**

   The Confirm Full Access login dialog box appears.

8. **Type the Account Name and Password to confirm that you want to make change to the file's security.**

   You'll have to type this information every time you make a change to your file's security. Chapter 19 gives you the full scoop on this important topic. If you can't quite get the combination right, go back into the account you've just edited and then retype your password. Once you get the combo correct, the window closes, and you're back on your layout.

You know that you've got the account name and password right, because you were able to close the window. But you should test the new login account by closing the file (if you still have multiple windows open, make sure you close them all) and then opening the file again. This time, you'll be asked to enter the new account name and password.

FileMaker guesses that the account name used for each file it opens is the same as the name you entered when you first installed FileMaker. But you can change this name in the program's Preferences window. Choose Edit→Preferences (Windows) or FileMaker Pro→Preferences (Mac) to get the window shown in Figure 5-30.

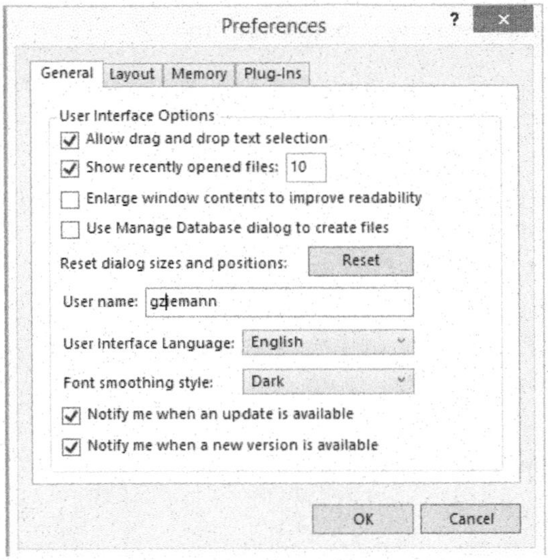

FIGURE 5-30

Type the account name you want to appear in the User Name box, and FileMaker will use that as the automatic account name from now on. On the Mac these options are a little different. You can choose from the System's Admin Account name or choose Other, and then type a custom name. Either way, it saves you a few keystrokes every time you open the database.

◼ Summing Up

Over the last two chapters, you've created a database from scratch. In that process, you've learned the basics of FileMaker's major features. You know how to create tables and fields, and you can create relationships between them. You can create layouts and layout objects, and you can change the format of the most common layout objects. You've even tried your hand at writing a script, creating some data analysis reports, and adding security to your file. Before you delve deeper into these topics, it's time to switch gears and learn more about planning a database. In the next part, you'll learn how to think like a database developer.

Thinking Like a Developer

Creating and Managing a Relational Database

I n Part Two, you learned the fundamentals of creating a custom database. You saw that you could create tables and fields whenever you need them. You learned how to polish layouts and add features and designs that make your data easy to maintain and analyze. You even learned how to harness the powerful combination of buttons and scripts.

And you did all those things in an organic fashion; as the need arose, you created elements that gave your database more power. FileMaker's flexibility let you make these improvements without much advance preparation. But as the databases you create get more sophisticated and the tasks you need them to perform get more complex, you'll find that the right kinds of planning and preparation make development go more smoothly. It's time to start thinking like a database developer, so your database can grow as your needs grow.

In this chapter, you'll learn how to create a road map for the tables and fields that comprise your database. (Database nerds called this map their database's *schema*.) Before you define the first table in your database, it pays to sit down and think about the kinds of data you'll be storing. Think about the basic tasks the database handles and how those tasks get carried out. This chapter shows you how to plan your database schema and then start putting that plan into action.

TIP   Go back and read the box on page 147 if you want to review basic database and relationship terms before you plunge into the theoretical material ahead.

Understanding Relational Databases

You got your feet wet with relational databases on page 150 when you created a Payment table to track monthly payments for the Lease Document database. You needed to attach a new Payment record to a specific lease document as each payment was made. So you created a second table and then used a key field in each table to create the relationship between the two tables. Those two points are what define any relational database:

- The database contains more than one table.

- Those tables are related to one another by a key field.

Both conditions have to be true; just putting more than one table into a FileMaker database doesn't make it relational. Say you have a Customer table and an Antiques Collection table. There's no point putting them in the same database unless there's a relationship between those two things. But if you're selling antiques to your customers, you can create a database that tracks your inventory and sales to specific people.

Why not just keep two databases—one for customer info and one for sales tracking? There are several benefits to creating a relational database instead:

- **You don't have to enter data twice.** Think back to the Lease Document database. Without two related tables, the Payment table would need a lot more fields in it. It would need to track the name of the person making the payment and the name of the property for which the payment is made. But because the Payment record is related to a Lease Document record, that relationship tells you where the payment belongs and who signed the lease. The relationship also lets you display Payment data on the Lease Document record and vice versa.

- **Your data is easier to maintain.** Since the data really "lives" in only one table (although you can display it in any related table), you can change data in one place, and those changes are immediately reflected everywhere. When the same data is stored in unrelated tables, you may have dozens of places to find and fix data when it changes.

- **Relational databases are easier for users to understand.** Other databases (not FileMaker, lucky you) use complex queries and reports to show users their data. Spreadsheets are simpler, yet often require manipulation of rows of data to get meaningful information from them. But even a new user looking at the Lease Document record can see that the list at the bottom of the layout is for tracking payments. One reason it's so obvious is because the relationship in the database is an onscreen representation of a real-world relationship.

Keep these benefits in mind as you plan, because efficiency and clarity can help you make decisions as you draw your road map.

This chapter teaches you how to plan the schema for a database that'll track time and expenses for jobs you do for your clients and then create invoices for those jobs. Although the database you'll design has specific sets of tasks that may not pertain to your real-world database, the concepts you'll learn can be applied to any tasks you need your custom database to do.

Modeling Your Database

When you model your database, you decide what entities you'll be tracking, which ones deserve a table, and how they relate to one another. It's easier to create the right tables and connections the first time than to go back and change them later, especially if you need to change tables that already have data in them. The point of this exercise is to build a "blueprint" to follow as you build your database. The pros call this blueprint an *entity relationship* (or ER) diagram.

Choosing Entities

The first step in modeling a database is to forget there's going to be a database. Focus on what you *do*—the things you need to achieve and the information those tasks require. During your workday, what do you need to produce for yourself? For your coworkers or customers? If you hit a wall, what information might get you going again? Write down what you do, what you *wish* you could do, and the results you require. Figure 6-1 illustrates a first take at this process.

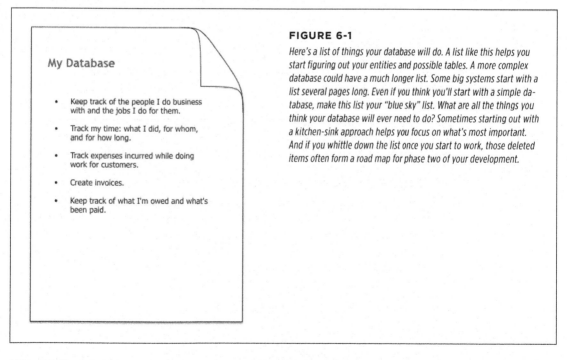

My Database

- Keep track of the people I do business with and the jobs I do for them.

- Track my time: what I did, for whom, and for how long.

- Track expenses incurred while doing work for customers.

- Create invoices.

- Keep track of what I'm owed and what's been paid.

FIGURE 6-1

Here's a list of things your database will do. A list like this helps you start figuring out your entities and possible tables. A more complex database could have a much longer list. Some big systems start with a list several pages long. Even if you think you'll start with a simple database, make this list your "blue sky" list. What are all the things you think your database will ever need to do? Sometimes starting out with a kitchen-sink approach helps you focus on what's most important. And if you whittle down the list once you start to work, those deleted items often form a road map for phase two of your development.

With this list in hand, you can start to figure out what *entities* your database needs to track. For each item on your list, think of all the *things* it involves. Figure 6-2 shows a possible list. Add those things to each item on your list. For "Track my time," add "Time" and "Services," for example.

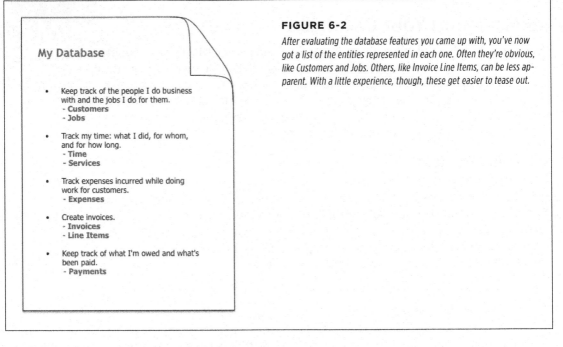

My Database

- Keep track of the people I do business with and the jobs I do for them.
  - **Customers**
  - **Jobs**

- Track my time: what I did, for whom, and for how long.
  - **Time**
  - **Services**

- Track expenses incurred while doing work for customers.
  - **Expenses**

- Create invoices.
  - **Invoices**
  - **Line Items**

- Keep track of what I'm owed and what's been paid.
  - **Payments**

FIGURE 6-2

After evaluating the database features you came up with, you've now got a list of the entities represented in each one. Often they're obvious, like Customers and Jobs. Others, like Invoice Line Items, can be less apparent. With a little experience, though, these get easier to tease out.

Your initial list should include all the entities you think are important. Try to evaluate every angle of the tasks and the information they require. Once you have a list of entities, the next step is to figure out which ones really matter. Consider each entity and get rid of the ones that essentially duplicate an existing entity, are excessively specific, or are simply not worth tracking in your database. This process will help you look at each entity from different perspectives as you come up with a final entity list.

Finding Relationships

Now that you have a list of entities, you need to figure out how they relate to one another. To get started, just pick two of your entities—Customers and Jobs, for example—and ask yourself how one instance of each entity relates to the other (if you need some guidance, see the box on page 199). You might come up with this answer: *Any given customer hires me to do jobs, and any given job is done for a customer.* That sentence tells you two important things:

- Customers and jobs *are related.*

- *One customer has many* jobs, but each job has only one customer.

By comparing different entities in this way, you can figure out how each entity relates to other entities. Your notes as you consider these relationships might look something like Figure 6-3.

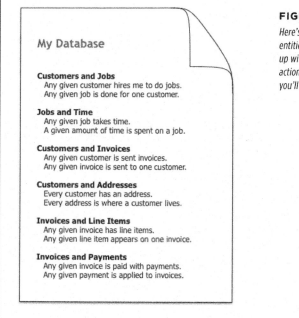

My Database

Customers and Jobs
Any given customer hires me to do jobs.
Any given job is done for one customer.

Jobs and Time
Any given job takes time.
A given amount of time is spent on a job.

Customers and Invoices
Any given customer is sent invoices.
Any given invoice is sent to one customer.

Customers and Addresses
Every customer has an address.
Every address is where a customer lives.

Invoices and Line Items
Any given invoice has line items.
Any given line item appears on one invoice.

Invoices and Payments
Any given invoice is paid with payments.
Any given payment is applied to invoices.

FIGURE 6-3

Here's a series of sentences that describe relationships between entities on your list. (You may have worded things differently, or come up with some that aren't on this list.) If you're writing good subject-action sentences, they'll usually tell you what kind of relationship you'll need between the two entities.

Now you need to convert your list of sentences into a graphic representation. You can show each entity in a sentence as a box with its name in it, and then draw lines to show the type of relationship each pair will have. For example, the sentence "A customer hires me to do jobs, and a job is for a customer" makes a clear case for what's called a *one-to-many* relationship. That is, one customer can have many jobs, and each job has only one customer. The line you see in the top pair of boxes in Figure 6-4 is the visual representation of a one-to-many relationship.

As you work down the list, you can see how entities like Invoices and Customers relate to one another. (I send invoices to customers.) But the relationship with the Time entity isn't so obvious. Is "Time" plural? For that matter, if Time is an entity, then it has to be a thing, so what is a *time?* You've just discovered one of the common challenges to good relational design—choosing names that are clear and helpful.

You added Time to your list of entities because you spend time working on a job. That's a little ambiguous, though, so think about what exactly you'll be putting in the database. You'll be logging the time you spend working: what you're doing, when you started, and when you finished. You could call it a work log entry, but that's pretty cumbersome. The standard term for this entity is *hours.* It says what you were doing for one period of time. That unit of time will always be linked to a specific job.

Using this language, your relationship description becomes clearer:

- Any given job has multiple hours worked, and any given hour record is for one job.

Now it's a lot more obvious: This relationship is one-to-many.

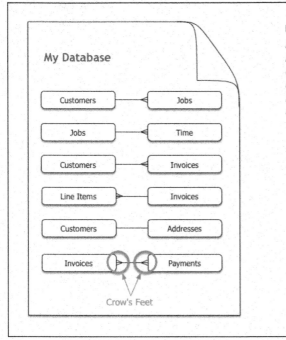

My Database

Customers — Jobs

Jobs — Time

Customers — Invoices

Line Items — Invoices

Customers — Addresses

Invoices — Payments

Crow's Feet

FIGURE 6-4

In this picture, boxes represent entities, and the lines between them indicate relationships. The little forked end on the relationship lines (called crow's feet*) means "to-many" as in "one-to-many." If the line doesn't have a crow's foot, it's to-one. So the relationship between Payments and Invoices is many-to-many, while that between Customers and Invoices is one-to-many.*

ONE-TO-MANY RELATIONSHIPS

Most of the relationships in your diagram are one-to-many, which is normal. One-to-many relationships outnumber all other types by a large margin in almost any system. See the box on page 199 for a description of the various types of relationships.

ONE-TO-ONE RELATIONSHIPS

Your list of entities and relationships shows a one-to-one relationship between Customers and Addresses. For the purposes of this database, one customer can certainly have one address, and vice versa. But if that's the case, are they really separate entities? In fact, Address is just an *attribute* of the Customer entity. That makes it a prime candidate for entity elimination. Put the address *fields* in the Customers table instead. You may argue that you *could* work for two people in the same household, and would therefore have to type the same address twice in your Customers table if you didn't have an Address table. The best answer to an argument like that is: "big deal." This situation doesn't arise often enough to justify a more complicated database just to eliminate duplicating one or two addresses. Even without a separate Address table, you can still separately handle all other tasks for these two clients.

Many for One and One for Many

Relationships tell FileMaker which records in two tables go together. Conceptually, relationships come in three flavors: one-to-many, many-to-many, and one-to-one. Your entity list (Figure 6-4) has examples of all three types. One-to-many relationships are the most common.

In a *one-to-many* relationship, one record in the first table relates to several records in the second. For example, one Invoice record has several line items, so it's a one-to-many relationship. Since relationships work both ways, a one-to-many is *always* a many-to-one as well. It's important to be clear about just what that means, though. Many different line items can be related to the same invoice, but each individual line item is related to only one Invoice record.

A *many-to-many* relationship means something quite different. A common example is registering students for classes. Each

student can be in many classes, and each class contains many students. That's a many-to-many relationship.

Finally, you can have two tables locked in a *one-to-one* configuration. If your database holds pictures of each product you sell, then you can create a Pictures table that would have one record for each product. Since the Products record also has one record for each product, the relationship is one-to-one. But in practice, you may need to have multiple beauty shots for at least some of your products, which means that your one-to-one relationship quickly changes to a one-to-many. For that reason, a true one-to-one isn't very common.

FileMaker doesn't make you learn a different method for creating each type of relationship. But each type has its own set of considerations that affect the way you design your database.

On the other hand, if you're managing a school, it's important to know which students share a home, and which parents they belong to. In that case, an Address entity makes sense. But as you start to think about the entity called Address, you start to realize that it's really a Household, and once again the Address is an attribute, but of the Household and not of the Student. This new way of thinking about your entities is one of the many realizations that can dawn on you as you're modeling your data, and it's a great example of why this sort of planning is so crucial. It's a lot better to make these types of mistakes on paper than in the database.

TIP If you expect to have to track several addresses for each customer, then you can create a one-to-many relationship between Customers and an Addresses table. For the current example, though, you'll stick to a single address built right into the Customers table.

As a general rule, unless you can articulate a good reason for its existence, a one-to-one relationship is a mistake: It's just two tables where one would suffice. You'll almost always want to combine entities like people and their addresses into one table.

■ MANY-TO-MANY RELATIONSHIPS

Ideally, you send an invoice to a customer, who pays the entire invoice with one check or credit card payment. It may even be the case that most of your customers do exactly that most of the time. But in the real world, customers will make partial payments on invoices, or sometimes they won't pay an invoice when it's due and a new one gets issued in the meantime. Then they'll cut a check to cover both invoices.

Your database has to be able to track those cases, even though they aren't the norm. A many-to-many relationship lets you handle all those situations.

But many-to-many relationships pose a special challenge. To understand why, think about how they're different from a one-to-many relationship, like an Invoice and a Line Item. One Invoice can have many Line Items, but each Line Item can belong to only one Invoice. The two tables are related by a key field, which holds the same value in all the records that relate to one another. And of course each record's key field has only one value in it.

With a many-to-many relationship, you need many records in each table related to many records in the other table. But you can't put multiple values in a key field to try to make it work. Instead, you add a new special-purpose entity between the two ends of a many-to-many relationship—called a *join table*. Think of it as chopping the many-to-many line in half and then inserting a new table in the middle. That new table has a one-to-many relationship to both of the original tables.

Here's how it works in your many-to-many relationship (Invoices and Payments): To split it up, you need to create a new entity. Since it doesn't have a decent name, just call it *Invoice Payment* (as in "This record represents one invoice payment—one payment on one invoice"). Now, instead of "Any given invoice is paid with payments, and any given payment is applied to invoices," you can say these two things:

- An invoice is paid with invoice payments, and an invoice payment is applied to one invoice.

- A payment is divided into invoice payments, and an invoice payment is part of one payment.

Figure 6-5 shows the updated diagram.

The Entity Relationship Diagram

Now that you have a list of entities and their relationships, you're ready to assemble your master plan: the entity relationship (ER) diagram. An *ER diagram* is a picture that shows all the entities in your database and the relationships between them. Unlike the diagram you've already drawn, each entity appears only *once* in an ER diagram.

Drawing the ER diagram has two purposes: first, to help you find relationships you missed, or relationships that don't belong; and second, to serve as a road map for your database. That is, you'll use the ER diagram when you create this database in FileMaker and again if you go back to make changes later.

> **NOTE** The diagram you're about to create isn't, in the most technical sense, a *real* ER diagram. The most formal kind deals with all kinds of technical details that simply don't matter in FileMaker. So some database big shots may chastise you for calling your beautiful picture an ER diagram. Never mind—just be glad FileMaker doesn't make you *care* about all that drivel.

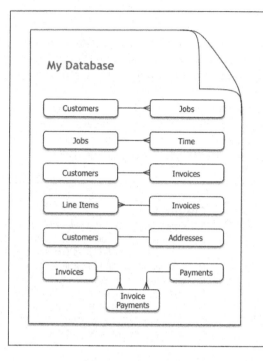

FIGURE 6-5

In this updated version of the diagram, the Invoice Payments join entity has been added. Now you have only one-to-many relationships—perfect. You're ready to move on to the next step.

■ CREATING AN ER DIAGRAM

When you assemble an entity relationship diagram, you have to put all your entities and relationships together in one big picture. Each entity appears on the diagram just once, but it may be connected to several other entities by lines that explain the relationship between each pair.

Your ER diagram is crucial to a successful database designing experience. First, you almost always find ways to improve your database as you create the diagram. Then when you set out to actually *build* the database, the ER diagram guides you through the process. Finally, a couple of years from now, when you need to add to your database design, the ER diagram will bring you—or your successor—up to speed on how your database fits together. So don't toss the diagram once you've moved from the planning phase to creation.

Here's a description of the general process: Make one box for each entity you've identified and then draw lines between them. Place the boxes on the page so there's some open space in the middle where your lines can roam free. When that's done, start drawing lines to represent each of the relationships you've come up with. For a simple database, you can usually get the lines in the picture without much difficulty. But creating a larger diagram without the right tools can be a real pain. If you work on paper, you may end up starting half a dozen times before you get a good arrangement. If you use a typical drawing program (the drawing capabilities in Word, for example), then you can spend copious hours reconnecting lines and entities, reshaping lines, and hand drawing crow's feet as you move things around. See the box below for some suggestions to solve this problem.

When you're done, you should have a single, unified diagram with each entity appearing only once, and every relationship indicated by a line. When you're thinking about relationships with just pairs of tables, you don't get the big picture. The ER diagram shows you how *everything* comes together, and when that happens, you often discover tangles of relationships just like those in Figure 6-6. Tangles like these aren't inherently bad; they're just usually completely unnecessary. Take the first tangled group—Expenses, Jobs, and Customers. The diagram tells you that customers have jobs, jobs have expenses, and customers have expenses.

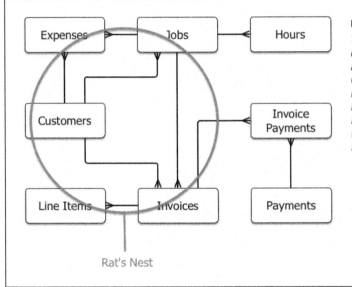

FIGURE 6-6

This diagram doesn't look all that bad—except for one thing. The circled area, labeled Rat's Nest, has a lot of lines among just a few tables. Expenses, Customers, and Jobs are all interrelated—there's a relationship between Jobs and Customers, another between Customers and Expenses, and a third between Expenses and Jobs. If you look closely, the same situation exists for Customers, Jobs, and Invoices. In both cases, you have a better way.

It's All about the Tools

If you plan on creating more than one ER diagram, or if you have a complicated one to create, diagramming software will save you lots of time and heartache. Microsoft Visio (available in the Microsoft Store) and SmartDraw (*www.smartdraw.com*) are two choices for Windows. Try OmniGraffle (*www.omnigroup.com/OmniGraffle*) or ConceptDraw for Mac OS X (*www.conceptdraw.com*). If none of these fit the bill for you, do a web search for *ER diagram* to see what new diagramming programs have hit the market. You'll even find some free, online-only diagramming tools, if that's what your budget calls for.

The beauty of all of these tools is that they *understand* ER diagrams. They can hook entities together with ease, draw crow's feet on your behalf, and keep everything connected as you move your entities around to find a good arrangement. One caveat: Some of these programs have built-in database diagramming features, but they're too complex for FileMaker work. The main capabilities your software package needs are drawing a box and labeling it and adding crow's feet to your lines.

If you're an unrepentant cheapskate, here's a tip: Write the entity names on a piece of paper, and cut out each one. Then arrange them on paper, draw lines, and see how it looks. You can slide the entity scraps around a few times to find a decent arrangement and then commit the whole thing to a clean piece of paper.

But you don't need all those lines to understand all the relationships, and neither does FileMaker. Now that you have an ER diagram, you can see that the line between Customers and Expenses is entirely superfluous. Even if it weren't there, you could still see all the expenses charged to a certain customer. Just find all that customer's *jobs* first (by following the line from Customers to Jobs). Once you've found those jobs, you can look at the expenses for each job. Since customers incur expenses only by way of jobs, you get exactly what you want without an extra relationship. In other words, if two entities are connected by a path along relationship lines—even *through* other entities—then they're related as far as FileMaker is concerned. Your database can show you the expenses for a customer just as easily as it can show the jobs for that customer. Figure 6-7 shows this concept.

When you're thinking about these implied relationships, pay attention to the crow's feet. If, when moving from one entity to another along the relationship lines, you *ever* go through a to-many relationship, then the larger implied relationship is itself to-many. This isn't just a clever trick; it's actually intuitive. If a customer has more than one job, and each job has expenses, then clearly a customer can have more than one expense.

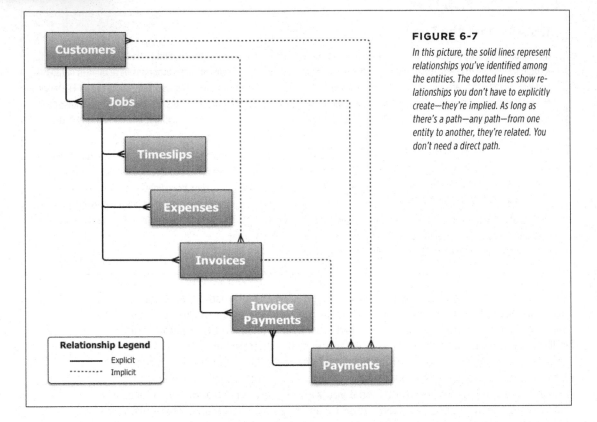

FIGURE 6-7

In this picture, the solid lines represent relationships you've identified among the entities. The dotted lines show relationships you don't have to explicitly create—they're implied. As long as there's a path—any path—from one entity to another, they're related. You don't need a direct path.

When you make your ER diagram, you should get rid of redundancy in your relationships. In other words, remove lines that show direct relationships when the relationship is already implied by other entities and relationships. If you don't do this now, you'll have trouble creating relationships when you finally get back to FileMaker (you'll see why on page 593). In your diagram, you can remove the relationship between Customers and Expenses. You can also axe the one between Customers and Invoices because Customers can find their Invoices by way of Jobs. With this revision, the ER diagram now looks like Figure 6-8.

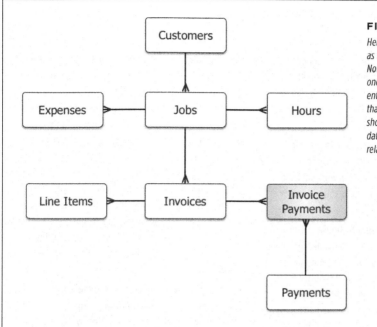

FIGURE 6-8

Here's the final ER diagram that you'll use as the road map for creating your database. Notice that every entity is related to at least one other entity in some way. Stray, unrelated entities are so rare in a real database system that if you see one in your diagram, then you should check to make sure it belongs in your database. Or did you just forget to draw the relationships it needs?

Now's the time to take one last look over your ER diagram. Keep these points in mind as you check for errors:

- You should have no undivided many-to-many relationships.

- If you have any one-to-one relationships, then make sure you can justify them (see page 198 for some ideas).

- Make sure you don't have any unnecessary entities hanging out all by themselves.

- Be certain you don't have any unnecessary lines or rat's nests.

If you discover an entity that has no relationships, you may not need it in your database at all. Read back on page 196, and see if that item ought to be a field in one of the other tables. Or if your diagram has two or more groups of related entities and no relationships *between* the groups, you might have forgotten to draw in a relationship, or, again, you might have one or more entities that your system doesn't need. Go back and make sure you're clear on your one-to-many and many-to-many relationships. (For more advice, see the box on page 199.)

Think Relationally

If you're dazed and confused trying to figure out how different entities relate, you're not alone. Understanding relational database design takes practice, plain and simple. Here are some ideas to improve your thought process:

- **Don't get hung up on technicalities.** At this point in your design, you shouldn't be thinking about database terms like primary keys, foreign keys, or join tables. Those things are all implementation details that you can work out later. Right now, just focus on the kinds of things you're keeping track of and how they fit together.

- **Use familiar words.** If you're trying to figure out how customers and jobs should be related, use words familiar to you, for example: "A customer hires me to do jobs," not "A Customer entity is related to a Job entity in a one-to-many configuration." As you get the hang of it, you'll discover that the simple sentences you use every day say a whole lot about relationships. For example, if a customer hires you to do *jobs* (note the plural), then you probably have a one-to-many relationship between customers and jobs.

- **Consider individual items first.** Don't think about what *customers* do. Instead, think about what *any given customer* does. The answer tells you whether a single customer has many jobs, or just one job. Then turn it around. Once you've decided a customer hires you to do jobs, ask yourself what a job has to do with customers. "Any given job is for a customer." This process tells you that each job is connected to just one customer. (If you didn't follow this advice, and thought, "I do *jobs* for customers," then you're not any closer to understanding the relationship.) By combining these results, you discover that a customer has many jobs, while a job has just one customer. So Customers and Jobs have a one-to-many relationship.

- **Don't let the word "many" hang you up.** It's just a standard term to help keep things simple and doesn't imply any particular amount. (Otherwise, you could have a *one-to-quite-a-few* relationship between Jobs and Invoices, a *one-to-a-handful* relationship between Customers and Jobs, and a *usually-just-one-or-two-to-rarely-more-than-three* relationship between Payments and Invoices. Yikes!) "Many" simply means more than one.

Keys

Back on page 146, you created key fields and used them to relate two tables. Now it's time to look more closely at how key fields and relationships work together. Take, for example, an Invoice table and its friendly neighbor, Line Items. The Invoice table probably contains fields like Due Date, Balance Due, and Terms—all attributes of the invoice itself. Then there's the *Invoice Number* field. Unlike the other fields, it's a made-up number. It does one thing—identifies a single invoice—and does it very well. Without it, you and your customers might have conversations like this: "I need a refund on one of my invoices...you know, the big one...yeah, in February...right, with the Renholm Industries products...no, the other one...." As soon as someone mentions an invoice number, though, everybody knows exactly which invoice to look at. More important, FileMaker knows which invoice it is, too.

The invoice number is good at identifying an invoice because it has three important characteristics:

- **It's unique.** No two invoices ever have the same invoice number.

- **It's unchanging.** Invoice #24601 is #24601 today, and it will be tomorrow, and the next day, and the next day.

- **It's consistent.** *Consistent* is a database term that means "never empty." All Invoice records have an invoice number.

Since it's a unique number, if you're talking about invoice #24601, and your customer is talking about invoice #24601, there's no question that you're both referring to the same invoice. Since it's unchanging, you can go back weeks, months, or even years later and find the invoice every time. And since it's consistent, you never have lonely invoices hanging out there without an identifying number. In database terms, the invoice number is called a *key*. So to sum up: A key is a field whose value uniquely, unchangingly, and consistently identifies one record.

FileMaker doesn't have a special field type for designating a key (although keys are typically number fields). As far as FileMaker is concerned, any field you use to link one table to another is a key field. Just make sure that you choose a field in which the data follows the rules you just learned.

■ PRIMARY AND FOREIGN KEYS

When a key field is in the same table as the records it identifies, it's called a *primary key*. In the Invoice table, the Invoice Number field is the primary key because the invoice number identifies an Invoice record. If you put the invoice number in some other table (like, say, the Line Items table) it's not a primary key there. Instead, it's called a *foreign key*. Foreign keys identify records in other tables.

> **NOTE** The terms "primary" and "foreign" may not seem like a match made in linguistic heaven. Wouldn't "domestic" and "foreign" make more sense? If those terms don't make sense to you, you're in good company. FileMaker avoids the terms in its software and its help files. But developers aren't so reticent, and the concepts of primary and foreign keys are extremely important to getting your database designed properly.

Clearly every table needs a primary key, but how do you know which tables need foreign keys as well? In the Invoices database, why did we put an Invoice Number field in the Line Items table? Why not create a Line Item ID key field in the Line Items table, and put it in the Invoices table? Wouldn't that accomplish the same thing? At first glance, it might seem like either method would produce the same relationship. After all, they sure *look* similar in a picture (Figure 6-9).

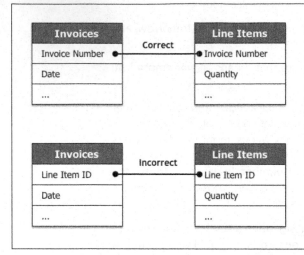

FIGURE 6-9

These two relationships look similar, but they show how a simple mistake can cause big headaches. In the top example, the primary key in the Invoices table matches a foreign key (Invoice Number) in the Line Items table. This arrangement lets one invoice have many line items because the same invoice number value can be in the foreign key field in many line item records. But in the bottom example, a foreign key in the Invoice table is related to the Line Items table's primary key (Line Item ID), which would let each invoice have just one line item.

Think about what a primary key means. Each primary key value identifies one, and *only one,* record in the table. If you were to build a relationship between the Invoice and Line Items tables based on a Line Item ID key, then each invoice could have only one line item. If it had two, you'd have two line items with the same line item ID, and it would no longer be unique. When you have a one-to-many relationship, you have to put the foreign key in the table on the *many* side. Luckily, keeping this information straight in your head is a breeze. Since foreign keys belong on the to-many side of a relationship, just remember this rule: When you see a crow's foot on your ER diagram, you need a foreign key in the table on the crow's foot side.

NOTE That rule bears repeating: *When you see a crow's foot on your ER diagram, put a foreign key field in the table on the crow's foot side.* The foreign key refers to whatever table is on the other end of the line. This is one of the very few absolute hard-and-fast rules in relational database design, so cling to this singular bit of simplicity when you start to have doubts.

■ CHOOSING A GOOD PRIMARY KEY FIELD

A primary key is most often a made-up serial number, like the one you made in your Lease Agreement database. You'll use that same technique a little later in this chapter, when you tell FileMaker to automatically make up a unique primary key value for each new record. This kind of primary key, based on purely made-up data, is called a *surrogate key.*

NOTE Unless you generate the value in your database, it's not a surrogate key, even if somebody else made it up. A surrogate key is made up *by your database.*

Occasionally, your table has a real value that meets the requirements for a key. For example, if your Product database has a field for your internal Inventory Control Number, you may be able to use that field as the primary key. If you use some real piece of data as a key, then it's called a *natural key*. Surprisingly, though, the vast majority of tables don't have a field that meets the criteria for a natural primary key. Take, for example, the Phone Number field in a contact database of people. Phone numbers are *usually* unique, and don't change *all that often*. But words like "usually" and "often" have no business in a discussion about good key fields. (See the box below for the reasons why.)

WORD TO THE WISE

Going Natural

Should I try to find natural keys for the tables in my database if I can?

This question has generated an eternal debate in the broader database world. Some ivory-tower theorists are convinced that natural keys are superior to surrogate keys for two primary reasons. First, they're *meaningful:* When you look at a natural key in your own database, it means something to you. Second, if a key is also real honest-to-goodness meaningful data, then in a relational database situation, your table always has at least one piece of good information from the table it relates to. If that happens to be the snippet you need, you save the software the trouble of going to another table and finding the right record. Thus, the theory goes, natural keys make database programs run a trifle faster.

But for the kinds of databases you're likely to build with FileMaker, neither of these concerns comes up very often. If a surrogate key isn't all that meaningful to the database user, just don't put it on the layout. It's perfectly normal to have utilitarian keys that users never see. And as for performance, the minuscule increase in speed is almost never significant enough to matter.

And there's a much more significant argument against trying to find an acceptable natural key; It's usually impossible. You almost never have a normal piece of data in a record that meets all the criteria for a good primary key.

Even natural keys that really seem like great choices often turn out to be problematic. Suppose you work for a company that assigns an employee ID to each employee. You're building a database to keep track of employee stock options. Just like a Social Security Number, Employee ID is a surrogate key to somebody, but it's a natural key to you. You decide to make it your primary key. Then you discover you need to track stock options for employees even if they quit and then return to the company. When they do this, their employee IDs change, and your database can't track them properly without some inconvenient upkeep. If you had used your own surrogate key instead, you wouldn't have this problem.

The penalty for a bad key choice can be huge: anything from lost connections in your data to the need for a major overhaul of the system. By contrast, surrogate keys are easy and always work. Once you accept the fact that your database will have an extra field that serves no other purpose than to be the primary key, the choice becomes a no-brainer. Don't bother with natural keys.

In fact, in most cases, the only fields that meet the requirements for a natural key are, in reality, surrogate keys from somebody else's database. Your database may contain employee numbers that come from your company's payroll system, part numbers from your supplier's catalog, or document numbers from your corporate knowledge base. All these numbers are surrogate keys in some system somewhere, but they may be natural keys to you.

Serial Text

As funny as it sounds, you can auto-enter serial numbers into text fields, and the values *themselves* can contain text. FileMaker looks at the text you've specified for "next value" and tries to find a number in it somewhere. When it comes time to generate a new value, it pulls that number out, increments it, and stuffs it back in its place.

Say your "next value" is C000LX, and "increment by" is set to 10. The first record you create gets C000LX. The second gets C010LX

and then C020LX, and so on. When you get to C990LX, FileMaker doesn't just give up. Instead, it makes more room: C1000LX.

If your "next value" has more than one embedded number (C000LX22, for example), then FileMaker uses only the *last number.* If you don't have a number at all, it simply adds one to the end.

Join Tables

A many-to-many relationship is more complicated than its one-sided brethren. Back on page 199, you learned that a join table is necessary to make the many-to-many relationship work. Remember: The database you're designing tracks payments from your customers. A customer could send a check to cover *two* invoices, or a check could cover *part* of an invoice only. So an invoice can have multiple payments, and a payment can be for multiple invoices: That's the concept that drives this many-to-many relationship.

How do you build a relationship like this? If you put the Payment ID in the Invoices table, then a payment can be applied to more than one invoice (just put the same Payment ID in each Invoice record). But an invoice could have only one payment, since it has just one Payment ID field. If you put the Invoice Number field in the Payments table, you get the same problem in the other direction. You may be tempted to try putting a foreign key field in *both* tables. In other words, add a Payment ID field to the Invoice table, and an Invoice Number field to the Payments table. Dig a little deeper, and you see that this has a whole *host* of problems:

- An invoice now has a field called Payment ID, but that field *doesn't* identify the payments for that invoice. To find the payments for an invoice, you have to search the Payments database, using the Invoice Number field. That's just plain confusing.

- Instead of one bidirectional relationship, you have two unidirectional relationships. The Payment ID in the invoice matches the Payment ID in the Payments table, but this tells you only which invoices belong to each payment. You need the other relationship (based on Invoice ID) to figure out which payments belong to each invoice. If you connect a payment to an invoice by putting the invoice number in the Payment record, then you also have to put the Payment ID in the Invoice record. If you forget, your data is no longer valid.

That's where a *join table* (Figure 6-10) comes in. A join table doesn't usually represent a real entity. Instead, each record in the join table represents a relationship between two records in the related tables.

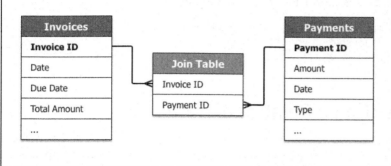

FIGURE 6-10

A join table's job is to create a many-to-many relationship. This one holds foreign keys for Invoice ID and Payment ID. To attach a payment to an invoice, add a new record in the join table, with the correct Invoice ID and Payment ID. Once the record is added, the payment and invoice are properly connected in both directions.

If it helps, think of join tables this way: Invoices and Payments both have a one-to-many relationship to the join table. So any given invoice can connect to many join records, each of which connects to one payment. Likewise, any given payment can connect to many join records, each of which connects to one invoice. So you get many related records in both directions. A join table always contains *two* foreign keys, one from each table it's joining.

NOTE The join table in the database you're building is the type that doesn't represent a real entity. But in some cases, a database may already have a real table that can act as a join table. Figure 6-11 shows an example.

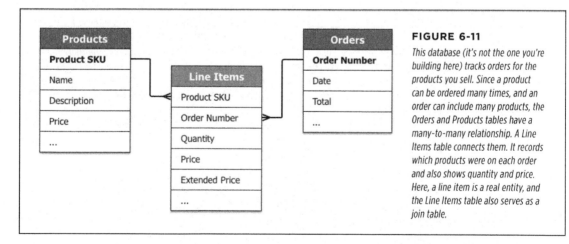

FIGURE 6-11

This database (it's not the one you're building here) tracks orders for the products you sell. Since a product can be ordered many times, and an order can include many products, the Orders and Products tables have a many-to-many relationship. A Line Items table connects them. It records which products were on each order and also shows quantity and price. Here, a line item is a real entity, and the Line Items table also serves as a join table.

Join tables can sometimes hold fields that don't quite belong in any other table. Suppose you wanted to record the portion of a payment that was applied to each invoice. For example, if a customer hands you a check for $100 and you have two outstanding invoices for that customer, for $80 and $30, then you may want to decide how to allocate the payment. Perhaps you apply $80 to the first invoice and $20 to the second. This dollar amount applied to each invoice can't be stored in the Invoice table because an invoice can have several payments. It can't be stored in the Payment table because you have *two* amounts and only one Payment record. The best place for it is right in the join table itself.

By adding a join table between Invoices and Payments, you've fleshed out the many-to-many relationship on your ER diagram. Now you know which foreign keys you need to make it all work. You're finally ready to build your database.

Creating a Relational Database

The planning is finally over. Now comes the fun part—actually making the database. And believe it or not, this part will go *much* more smoothly with your plan in place. You create a relational database in three steps. First, you tell FileMaker what tables you want and then you add the fields to each table. Finally, you add relationships.

> **NOTE** Some developers cut right to the chase by creating tables with only their key fields and one or two other fields in each table to get started. For example, you might create only the primary key field and the first and last name fields in the Customer table so you don't spend hours trying to create hundreds of fields before you hook up the first relationship.

So don't be alarmed if you forget a table or miss a field. Although the point of planning is to help you figure out which tables and fields you need from the start, you *can* go back at any time and make changes, even when your tables are loaded with data.

> **WARNING** Deleting a table is a dangerous operation. Right now there's no risk because you're working in a brand-new database. But imagine 2 years from now, when the database is full, if you accidentally delete a table, then you lose *all* the data in it. You'll also have a lot of work to do putting your relationships and layouts back together. FileMaker warns you before it lets you delete a table, but it's worth an extra measure of caution. Because there's so much potential for danger, there's one final fail-safe: In the Manage Database dialog box, if you click the Cancel button, FileMaker discards *all* your changes, including any table deletions. (You do keep regular backups, right?)

Creating Relationships

Once you've defined tables and keys, you have everything you need to create your relationships. In other words, you tell FileMaker how the tables in your database fit together by matching up key fields. In the Manage Database window, click the Relationships tab, shown in Figure 6-12.

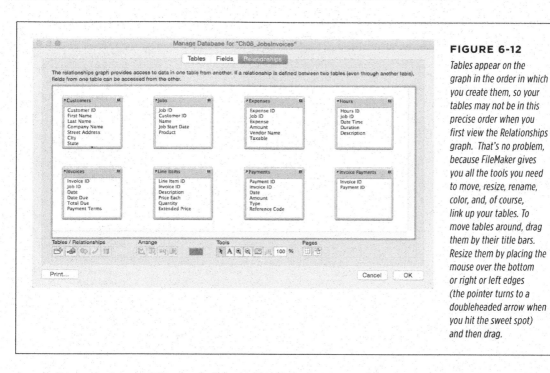

FIGURE 6-12

Tables appear on the graph in the order in which you create them, so your tables may not be in this precise order when you first view the Relationships graph. That's no problem, because FileMaker gives you all the tools you need to move, resize, rename, color, and, of course, link up your tables. To move tables around, drag them by their title bars. Resize them by placing the mouse over the bottom or right or left edges (the pointer turns to a doubleheaded arrow when you hit the sweet spot) and then drag.

As you learned on page 152, you define relationships between tables by dragging from one key field in a table to the key field in another. But if you just start dragging without rearranging, you may end up with a tangled mess in the graph. So take out your ER diagram and start by arranging the tables on the Relationships graph like the tables on your ER diagram. Refer to Figure 6-8 if you need a refresher. Once they're in place, it's a breeze to drag key fields from table to table. Here's a list of the relationships you need to create:

- Customers::Customer ID to Jobs::Customer ID

- Expenses::Job ID to Jobs::Job ID

- Invoices::Job ID to Jobs::Job ID

- Line Items::Invoice ID to Invoices::Invoice ID

- Invoice Payments::Invoice ID to Invoices::Invoice ID

- Invoice Payments::Payment ID to Payments::Payment ID

- Hours::Job ID to Jobs::Job ID

Remember, it doesn't matter whether you drag from Customers to Jobs (for example) or vice versa. What does matter is that you pick the right key fields to relate. When you're done, you should have seven relationship lines and your graph should look something like Figure 6-13.

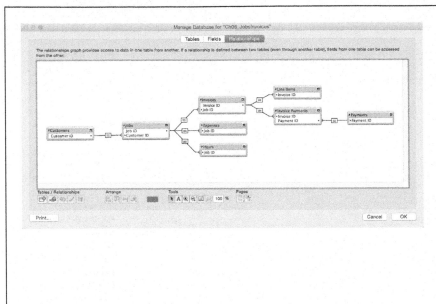

FIGURE 6-13

The table occurrences (TOs) have been collapsed so you see only key fields. Change the TOs' display by clicking the button at the right of each TO's title bar. Tables toggle through three settings—open, key fields only, and title bar only. On a complex graph, it's much easier to read relationships when your TOs are partly closed, as they are here. If you need to see a list of all the fields in a table, you can temporarily expand the appropriate TO or switch to the Fields tab.

FileMaker's Sixth Sense: Crow's Feet

I haven't done anything to tell FileMaker what kind of relationships I created. How does it know where to put the crow's feet?

You never have to tell FileMaker what type of relationship to create because it doesn't really matter. The work FileMaker performs to deal with a one-to-many relationship is no different from what it does for a one-to-one, so it doesn't care about the distinction.

However, it's useful to you as the database designer to know what kind of relationships you have. So as a special service to you, FileMaker tries to figure out where the crow's feet go. It helps you decide whether an invoice should have room for

one line item or a whole list of them, for example. So FileMaker assumes every end of every line needs a crow's foot unless it finds evidence to the contrary, like the following:

- The field used in the relationship is a serial number.
- The field used in the relationship has the "Unique validation" option turned on.

A line that connects to a field that meets either of these conditions does *not* get a crow's foot at that end. Since all your primary keys are serial numbers, FileMaker has no trouble figuring out where to leave off the crow's feet.

If you make a mistake (say you grab the wrong field or drag to the wrong table), double-click the box in the middle of the relationship line. Here you can adjust which field is at each end of the relationship. If you want to ax the whole relationship, click the box in the middle of the relationship line and then press Delete.

> **TIP** If you have a stray table occurrence (named the same as the database itself) on your Relationships graph, just select it and then press Delete. It's a useless artifact from when the file was first created. Since this table occurrence isn't part of your ER diagram, you can safely ignore FileMaker's protestations that deleting it will break things.

Sorting a Relationship

When you drag key fields to create a relationship, you get a plain vanilla relationship. That is, the relationship links two records together when the values in their key fields match exactly. You can't create or delete records through the relationship, and it isn't sorted. Without a sort order, records will appear in the order they're created, from the first created to the last. So if you're creating Line Items for an invoice, the line items will normally appear in a portal in precisely the order in which you create them. But maybe your company likes line items to appear sorted by an internal Part Number field because it makes fulfilling the orders easier for the warehouse. Or your employees may enter their hours at the end of the week instead of daily, and they sometimes enter them out of order.

The Edit Relationship window lets you sort a relationship by any field in either table (when you select the option, you'll see the regular Sort Records window). You can sort the relationship by any sortable field in the table to show related records in the order you prefer, but it's far more common to sort on the to-many side.

It's important to note that sorting a relationship doesn't just change the order of records in a portal. Remember that you can show related records without using a portal, but if you do, the related field shows only the *first* related record. A relationship's sort order can change that first record, which may not be what you intended, so be careful about sorting relationships. See the box on page 217 for more information on sorting relationships and portals.

Managing the Relationships Graph

Although the JobsInvoices Relationships graph is small and easy to understand, chances are it will grow as you power up your database by adding more tables (and even as you add new features, as you'll see through the course of the next few chapters). As it grows, your graph can easily get messy and hard to decipher. But the Relationships graph has lots of tools for keeping things uncluttered and easy to understand (Figure 6-14).

■ MANAGING TABLE OCCURRENCES USING THE TABLES/RELATIONSHIPS TOOLS

These tools help you create and edit *table occurrences* (TOs) on the graph. A table occurrence is a representation of a table on the Relationships graph. Each time you create a new table in the Manage Database Tables tab, FileMaker automatically adds a TO for your new table on the Relationships graph. But you're not limited to just that one. FileMaker lets you create multiple TOs of any given table in your database. They only caveat is that each TO must have a unique name.

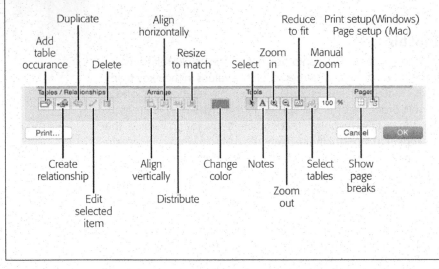

Duplicate

Add
table
occurance

Align
horizontally

Reduce   Print setup(Windows)
to fit   Page setup (Mac)

Resize
to match

Zoom
in

Manual
Zoom

Delete

Select

FIGURE 6-14

*The first group of tools
helps you create and edit
table occurrences and
relationships. When you
select more than one
table occurrence, the second group, the Arrange
tools, becomes available.
The tiny triangle in the
bottom-right corner of
each tool shows that you
can choose how the tool
behaves. You also have
standard zoom tools, and
printing tools for getting
the graph onto paper.*

Create
relationship

Align
vertically

Change
color

Notes

Select
tables

Show
page
breaks

Edit
selected
item

Distribute

Zoom
out

TIP Don't let the Tables/Relationships label on these buttons confuse you. You have a whole tab dedicated to managing *tables*. These tools are strictly for *table occurrences*, not the underlying tables the occurrences refer to.

The Tables/Relationship tools let you create new TOs or edit or delete existing ones:

- The **Add Table Occurrence** tool shows a Specify Table window where you select the table the new occurrence should refer to. You can also give the TO a name. If you choose a name that's already in use, then FileMaker appends a number to the end of the occurrence's name. If this happens, change the name to something more descriptive right away to save yourself from confusion later.

- The **Create Relationship** tool shows the Edit Relationship window as you saw it first on page 154, except you now have access to pop-up menus for selecting the TOs you want to relate to one another. Dragging a relationship is super easy, but you get only one flavor. Using the button instead lets you set up multicriteria relationships (page 595) and specify whether the relationship allows creation and/or deletion of related records and if the relationship should be sorted right from the onset.

- Copy/Paste doesn't work on the graph, so the **Duplicate** tool is the way to go. It can duplicate whole groups of TOs, called table occurrence groups (TOGs). See page 607 for details.

- The **Edit** button opens the controls for editing whatever object you've selected on the Relationships graph. Faster yet, double-click the object you wish to edit to get the same tools.

How Do I Know Where to Sort?

I saw that I can choose the sort order for a portal in the Portal Setup window. Now you're saying I can set the sort order in the relationship. What's the difference? Does it matter?

When you set a sort order in the Edit Relationship dialog box, it applies to the relationship itself. Any time you use that relationship, the sort order applies: in portals on any layout, when showing a single related field, when referring to a related field in a calculation or a script, and when finding a set of related records (page 233).

A portal's sort order, on the other hand, applies only to the portal itself. If you don't tell the portal to sort, then FileMaker uses the relationship's sort order (or, if there isn't one, the order in which the records were created) instead.

If you know that every time you look at your related data it should be shown in a specific order, then set the relationship to sort. But if you think the related data ought to be sorted different ways in different contexts (and thus in different portals), then don't sort the relationship, because that's making your database do extra work—FileMaker has to sort the records for the relationship and then sort them a different way for your portal. (You don't usually see this process happening, but FileMaker is doing it behind the scenes. With a portal displaying a lot of related records, across a slow network, you might sometimes see a Sort dialog box appear.) So when you're planning on viewing data in lots of different orders, rely on sorted portals instead of sorted relationships.

TIP You can tell when a relationship line is selected, because the line thickens, the box in the middle is highlighted, and the Edit tool becomes active.

- The **Delete** button has a trash can icon on it, making its purpose clear. You can also delete items by selecting them and then pressing Delete. Because deleting items from the graph is so potentially destructive (layouts, scripts and calculations that use the TO, and all other relationships that depend on the relationship will break), you'll see a warning message to confirm that you want to remove the selected items.

If you make changes on the graph that might be destructive, or if you just change your mind, then in the Manage Database window, click Cancel and then click Discard. You'll have to redo the changes you made since you opened the window, but it's easier to redo good work than to undo bad work.

■ ARRANGE THE GRAPH

The table occurrences in the graph behave like layout objects in Layout mode. You can Shift-click or drag across several to select them all. You can even press Ctrl+A (⌘-A) to select *all* the table occurrences. Just click empty space on the graph to deselect. Once you have some selected, you can use the Arrange tools to line them up.

After you've dragged a few table occurrences around on your graph, it can look pretty sloppy. Here's how to use the tools to inflict some order on the graph:

- The **Align Vertical** tool lets you choose whether to align the left edges, centers, or right edges of any highlighted table occurrences.

- The **Align Horizontal** tool lets you align the top edges, centers, or bottom edges of the highlighted table occurrences.

- The **Distribute** tool makes the space between three or more selected table occurrences uniform. You can choose horizontal or vertical distribution.

- The **Resize** tool makes short work of getting those manually resized table occurrences back in parade order. Select some table occurrences and then click the Resize tool to tell FileMaker whether you want all the highlighted table occurrences resized to the smallest width, height, or both, or the largest width, height, or both.

SELECTION TOOLS

The Relationships graph has a few selection tricks that make life easier. To help with selecting an entire group of connected objects, you can select just one. Click the Select Tables button and then choose "Select related tables 1-away." FileMaker automatically adds every table that's directly connected to your current selection. You can choose this same command again to extend the selection one more notch on the graph.

If you have multiple table occurrences that have the same underlying base table (you'll learn why on page 602), then click the Select Tables button and then choose "Select tables with same source table" instead. FileMaker highlights all the table occurrences that match those you've selected.

These tools are most useful on a large and complicated graph when you know you need a specific TO but just can't find it. Highlight one TO from the source table you're concerned with and then click the Select Tables button. Now you only have to look at the highlighted TOs to find the one you need.

COLOR YOUR TABLE OCCURRENCES

You can change the color of any selected table occurrence(s) by using a standard color pop-up menu. It looks just like the one you saw on page 123 when you learned about coloring layout objects. Adding color to table occurrences doesn't affect the database's behavior at all. It's just there to help you organize your graph. Some people like to color all TOs in a TOG the same color, and others like to color TOs from the same source table the same color, thus reducing the need to use the selection tools above.

ADDING NOTES

You can add comments about the graph with the Notes tool. Just select the tool and then drag out a rectangle on the graph to create the note. In the Edit Note dialog box that appears (Figure 6-15), type the text of the note and set its font, size, and text and background colors. If you want to revise an existing note, double-click it and the dialog box reappears, ready to do your bidding.

The Note tool lets you place floating notes anywhere on your graph. Make detailed notes about individual tables, or make them as wide as the graph, with a few words describing what kind of data is in the table occurrences directly underneath. Notes always appear under a table occurrence in the window's stacking order, so you can even put one behind a set of TOs as a visual grouping (like the one behind the Invoice Payments TO in Figure 6-15).

■ PRINTING THE GRAPH

Last but not least, FileMaker offers some tools to help you print the graph. Since the graph is a road map to your tables, some people like to print it and tape it up beside the computer for quick reference while building layouts. Graphs can run large, so FileMaker offers to shrink the whole thing so it prints on a single page.

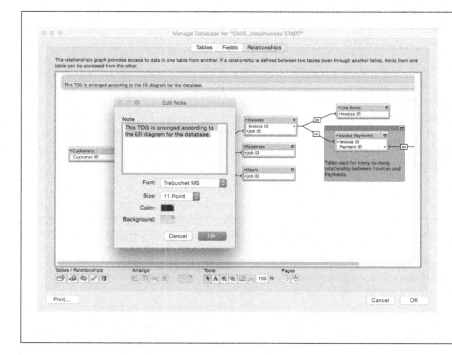

FIGURE 6-15

The Edit Note dialog box lets you pick font, size, and color, and type any text you want. When you click OK, the note appears on the graph, and you can drag it around, resize it, or use the alignment tools much like you do your table occurrences. Here the Edit Note dialog box shows the setup for the highlighted note in the background. You can also see a note that appears behind the Invoice Payments table. Both notes help show how things work at a glance without poking around in each relationship.

■ Using Relational Database Power

The essence of a relational database is its multiple connected tables. So far this chapter has focused on planning, creating, and managing tables and relationships. But the power of multiple tables trickles throughout FileMaker. It's time to learn how to take advantage of your database's relationships as you search records, build layouts, and create value lists.

NOTE For a refresher on creating, editing, and deleting related records by using a portal, see page 160.

One Table Occurrence, One Found Set

The most fundamental thing you should understand when using a multitable database is that each layout sees the entire database from a single perspective, or context (page 159). It's time to do a little exploration to see this concept in action. A layout is attached to a table occurrence on the graph, and that's how it sees the world. This means when you're looking at a record on the Customers layout, you're seeing a customer. If you switch to Table view, then you see a list of customers. You don't see Jobs at all. To see those, you need to switch to the Jobs layout.

Since each table holds different data, the concept of a found set changes a little as well. When you perform a find, the layout you're on determines which table FileMaker searches. Your new found set is associated with that layout's table occurrence, too. Just as when you had only a single table, the found set stays the same until you perform another find, or you tell FileMaker to show you all the records for that table occurrence (Records→Show All Records). But if you switch to a different layout (one tied to a different table occurrence), your found set no longer applies.

For example, if you find the six customers from New York and then switch to the Jobs layout, you won't have six records in your found set anymore. Instead, you have a separate *Jobs* found set. Switch back to Customers, and you see the six New Yorkers again. FileMaker remembers one found set for each table occurrence. It also remembers the *current record* for each table occurrence, so if you switch to a different layout and then come back, you're still on the same record that was active when you left that layout.

Of course, you can have more than one layout attached to the same table occurrence—Customer List and Customer Detail, for example. The found set and current record are associated with the *table occurrence,* not the layout, so a find on the Customer List layout affects the found set on the Customer Detail layout.

> **TIP** If you want more than one found set or current record in the same table occurrence; don't create a new TO, though. Use multiple windows, just like you learned on page 31.

If you want to see two kinds of records side by side (say, Customers and Invoices), you can create a new window (Window→New Window) and then switch one of them to a different layout.

Viewing Related Fields on a Layout

Think of the layouts FileMaker made for you as starting points from which you'll put relationships to work. You saw this in action on page 155, when you put a Payment portal on the Lease Agreement layout. With this more complicated database, you have more opportunity to show related data. Portals will be very useful: You'll probably want to start by creating a Jobs portal on the Customer layout. Then edit the Customers to Jobs relationship to allow for creation and deletion of related records (page 153) so you can enter a few new Jobs records. See the box below to learn how to create related records without a portal.

After you've created a Jobs portal on the Customers layout and viewed the two jobs for Jerald Tabb (Figure 6-16), you realize that you have expenses to enter on that job. So head for the Expenses layout, where you find that the Expenses table has a Job ID field, but not a Job Name field, which would help you make sure you're chalking expenses up to the right job. Instead, you'll use the related fields from the Job table, and let FileMaker display the correct *related* data using the relationships you created.

Auto-Creation Without a Portal

You don't have to have a portal to get automatic creation of related records. Auto-creation works when you put data in *any* related field as long as the relationship is set up to allow it. Suppose you have a one-to-one relationship with one table for Bicycle Team Members and another for a photo of each racer. Both tables have a Rider ID field, but only the Riders::Rider ID field is a serial number. The relationship between the two tables is set to allow creation of related Photo records.

Your Bike Rider detail layout doesn't need a portal to create the related record in the Photo table. It just needs to display the container field from the related Photo table. Since the relationship is set to auto-create Photo records, you can insert a new picture of the rider in the Picture field, and FileMaker creates the related record for you automatically. This process works only for one-to-one relationships. You can change the picture you insert in the related record, but you can never create a second record with this technique.

If you don't have Auto-creation turned on for the relationship, then you can't click into the Picture field. FileMaker shows the dotted field outline as if the field is there and active, but it doesn't let you in.

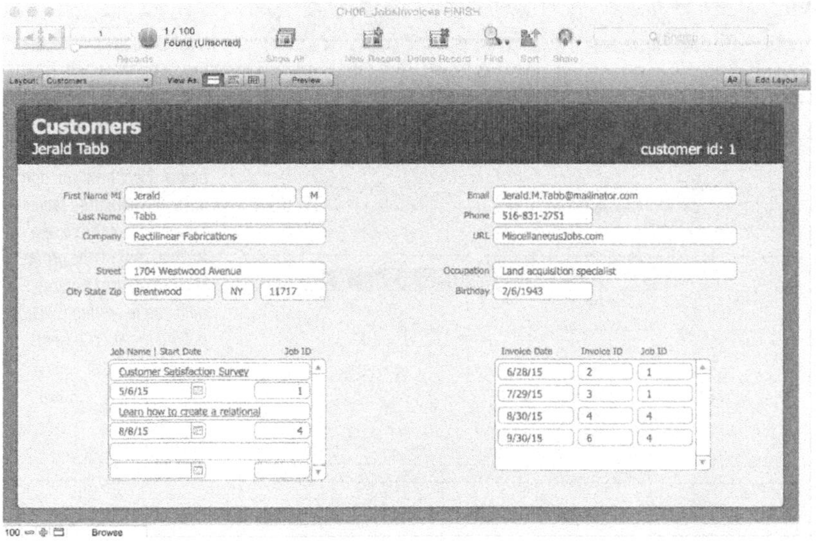

FIGURE 6-16

The sample database for this chapter has been set up with data so you can focus on the relationship you're creating. To see the relationships working, make sure you're viewing the first few records in each table. Here's the first Customer record, showing one way you can arrange the new Jobs and Invoices portals you'll create as you work through the next sections. You may find it helpful to compare the finished version of the database to your work to see how all the pieces fit together.

Here's how to add a Jobs Name field to the Expenses layout:

1. **On the Expenses layout, switch to Layout mode.**

   That's where the tools that let you put fields on layouts are.

2. **Click at the beginning of the Expenses merge field to place the insertion point in the text block.**

   You want the text block with the angle brackets around it. It reads: "<<Expense>>". Make sure your cursor is to the left of all the angle brackets, since they belong with the Expenses merge field. You'll add a merge field for the Job Name in front of the Expense name. That way, you can tell at a glance which job an Expense is for.

3. **Choose Insert→Merge Field.**

   The Specify Field window appears, displaying a list of fields from the table you worked with the last time you opened the window.

4. **From the Current Table pop-up menu, choose Jobs.**

   Here's where you venture into unfamiliar waters. The Current Table pop-up menu lets you pick any table occurrence on your graph (Figure 6-17).

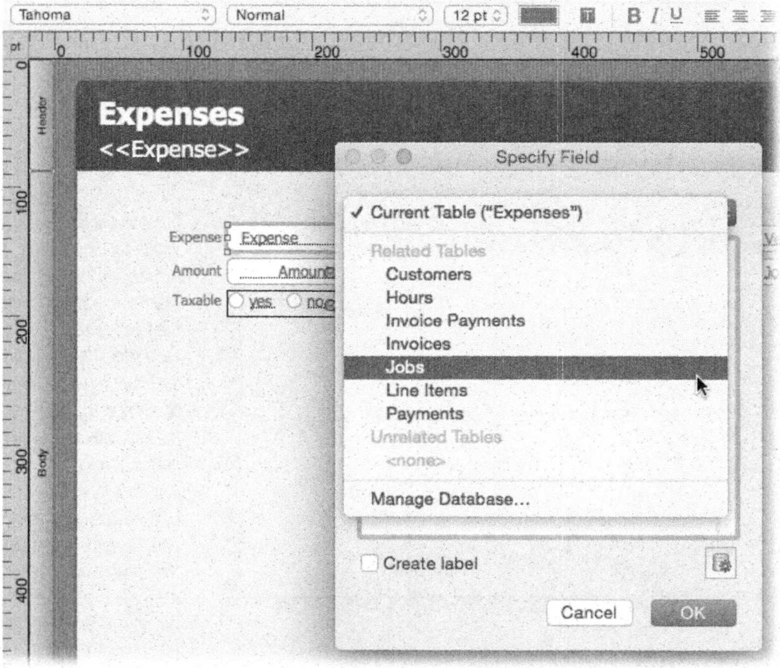

FIGURE 6-17

Here you see the Specify Field dialog box's Current Table menu popped up, with a list of all the table occurrences on the graph. The ones related to the current layout are at the top, and all unrelated tables are grouped below. Right now you don't have any unrelated tables because the entire graph is connected in one group. The <<Expense>> merge field you're editing is visible behind the Specify Field window.

5. **Select the Name field from the Jobs table and then click OK.**

FileMaker adds the Jobs::Name field to the text block. It should read "<<Jobs::Name>><<Expense>>." The Expense field is local, so it doesn't have to include its table name in the text block. But the related field shows its full name, just so everybody is clear on where the data is coming from.

6. **Type a colon (:) and a space between the two merge fields.**

The text block contains the text "<<Jobs::Name>>: <<Expense>>." The single colon here is just punctuation, and doesn't mean anything special to FileMaker. The double colon (::) inside the Merge field, on the other hand, is used by FileMaker to show that the field Name comes from the Jobs table occurrence.

Now when you view an Expense record in Browse mode, you'll see data from the Jobs table on the Expenses layout. You could have used a regular field instead of a merge field. In fact, sometimes that makes more sense, like when you might want to edit data from both contexts. But in this case, the related data appears in a text block that serves as a title for the record and doesn't need to be editable. So a merge field (which you can't click into in Browse mode) is the best solution. See page 306 for a way to make regular fields non-enterable.

If you were to use a regular field instead of a merge field to display related data, you wouldn't see the fully qualified name, in this case "Jobs::Name", in the field. Instead the name will appear as "::Name" to show it's a related and not a "local" field. To see where a regular field comes from, select it and look at the Inspector's Data tab. The "Display data from" box shows the field's fully qualified name.

FREQUENTLY ASKED QUESTION

Portal or Related Field?

So far I've used a portal and a merge field to display related data on a layout. How do I know when to use each one?

It's pretty simple, really. Remember that most relationships are one-to-many. To keep it straight, think of the one side as the parent side of a relationship, and the to-many side as the child side. On a layout that shows the parent record—Customers, for example—you used a portal because you wanted to show the to-many line item records from the child table—Jobs.

Over on the child side, you wouldn't use a portal back to Customers, because there will only ever be one Customer related to any one Job. So there, you'll just use a related field or a merge field, as you did on page 220.

This rule of thumb is true for any parent-child relationship: Invoice to Line Item, Jobs to Expenses, or Jobs to Hours. You'll almost always use a portal on the parent layout and a related field on the child layout.

As you flip through the records, you'll see that the first few expenses show a Job name. That's because the sample database had Expense records with Job ID values in them, and once you defined the relationships, the proper records were linked. But how do you go about entering a valid Job ID into an Expense record as you log expenses? That's where *value lists* come in.

Creating a Value List Based on a Related Field

You've already seen value lists based on custom values—on page 127, you created a value list to make sure only certain values were entered in the Lease Duration field. In a relational database, valid data entry is even more critical, particularly when you're not using a portal to create related records. Remember, a portal automatically adds the primary key value to the child table when you create a related record; that way the proper foreign key value is created in the to-many side of the relationship.

But what if you don't want to use a portal for creating records? For example, even though each invoice needs to be attached to a Job record, it doesn't make sense to create an Invoice in a portal on the Jobs layout. Although you could create an *Invoice* record this way, there's no good way to create the proper *Line Item* record for the new invoice using that same portal. You really need to be viewing the Invoice record on a layout that shows Invoice records when you create the invoice's Line Item records.

Here's the solution: On the Invoices layout, create a new record and then use a value list to enter the proper Job ID. The value list ensures that only valid values (those from existing Job records) are entered into the foreign key field in the Invoices table. Here's how to create the value list you need:

1. **Choose File→Manage→Value Lists and then click New.**

   Name your new value list *All Job IDs*. Since you're likely to have lots of value lists in a finished database, descriptive names help you keep things straight.

2. **Select "Use values from field."**

   The "Specify Fields for Value List 'All Job IDs'" window appears (Figure 6-18).

3. **In the pop-up menu under "Use values from first field," choose Jobs.**

   This selects the table that holds the Job ID field.

4. **In the list of fields, select Job ID.**

   Job ID is the key field that relates an Invoice record to a specific Job record, so you'll use that field to make sure the information entered is accurate.

5. **Turn on the "Also display values from second field" checkbox. Then, from the right-hand field list, choose Name.**

   To avoid having to remember Job IDs, display the job's Name, too. That way, you can easily find the right Job ID. The second field's data won't be entered into the field, though—it's just for show.

> **TIP** The "Show values only from second field" option is really handy when you're using the value list to enter key field values and you don't want people to be confused by a number that might not mean much to them. They see only the value in the second field, even though the field really stores the key value.

6. **In the "Sort values using" radio button set, turn on the "Second field" option.**

   It's probably easier to find the Job you need if it's sorted by Name and not ID.

7. **Click OK until all the dialog boxes are gone.**

Your value list is now defined, but FileMaker isn't displaying it anywhere yet. Read on to see how to apply the list to a field.

Now that you've created the value list, you can attach it to the Job ID field in all the to-many layouts in the database. First, you'll put it on the Jobs ID field on the Expenses layout.

1. **Switch to Layout mode and then, if it's not already showing, choose View→Inspector. Finally, click the Inspector's Data tab to select it.**

That's where you add a value list to a field.

2. **Click the Job ID field to select it and then, from the Control style pop-up menu, choose Pop-up Menu.**

The pop-up menu looks like menu choices you see in most dialog boxes, so its behavior and appearance are already familiar to most users.

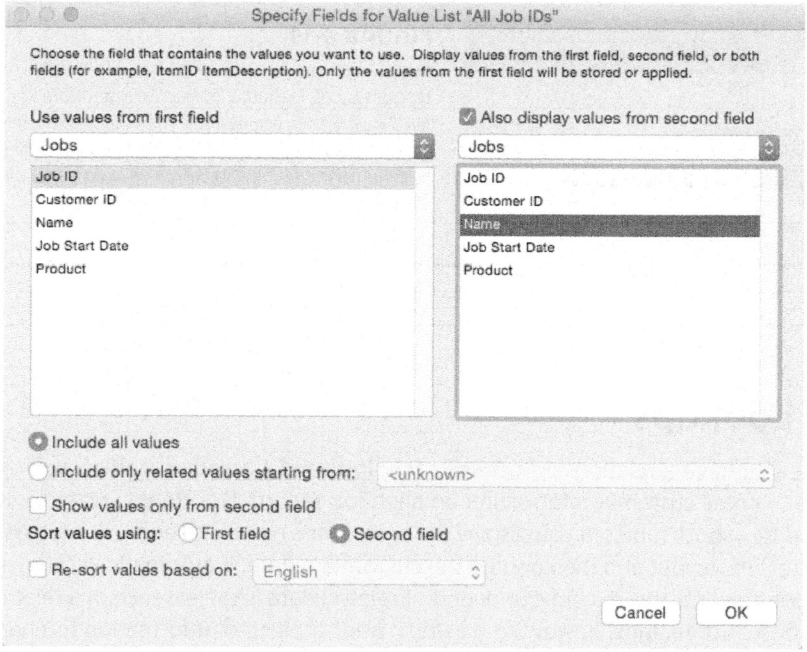

FIGURE 6-18

In the "Specify Fields for Value List" window, the "Use values from first field" option gives your value lists shape-shifting power: Instead of a dull list that never changes, your value lists automatically update as your data changes. So if you add a new job, it automatically shows up in the All Job IDs value list. Delete a job, and it drops off the value list.

3. **Choose All Job IDs from the "Values from" pop-up menu.**

The Job ID field's appearance changes to show that it's now a pop-up menu instead of an edlt box.

Switch to Browse mode, and flip to a record that doesn't have a Job ID. Choose a job from the Job ID pop-up menu (Figure 6-19), and you'll see the Job name change in the merge field. (See the box on page 227 to learn how to make a value list show only related values.)

> **TIP** Sometimes showing just one field's data in a value list isn't the best way to find the right record—say you want to show a customer's first and last name in a drop-down list. But the dialog box lets you pick just one field. See page 387 for a calculation that puts data from multiple fields into one field.

When you combine a relationship that allows the creation of related records, a portal and a value list from a related table, you have a solid technique for creating child records. Start to think about other places to apply the technique. For example, the Invoice layout could use a portal for creating Line Item records; similarly, you can make creating Expenses easier with an Expenses portal on the Jobs layout. You can have a portal for entering Hours on the Jobs layout, too. If a layout starts getting crowded, a Tab or Slide Control might cut down on the clutter.

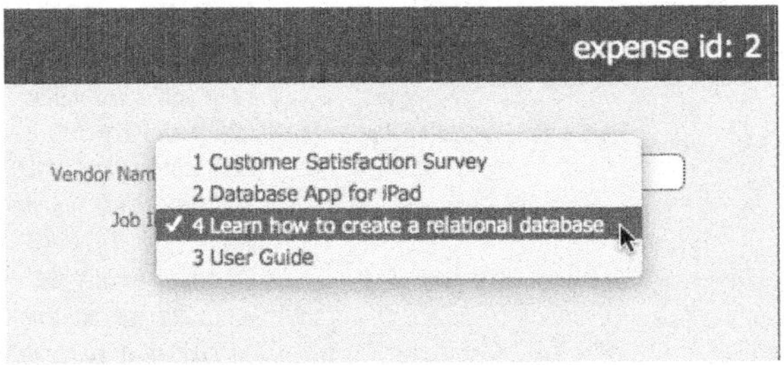

FIGURE 6-19

Here's the new pop-up menu for the Jobs ID field on the Expenses layout. To attach a job to an expense, choose a Job ID from the new pop-up menu. When you do, FileMaker places the ID of the job you choose in the Expenses::Job ID field. The name is displayed in the pop-up menu to help you pick the right ID but is not entered into the Job ID field.

Lookups

Since you have a relationship between the Jobs and Customers tables, you don't have to enter customer information on each job record. Nor do you want to store that data in both tables. If you display the customer's name and address information on the Jobs layout and then update the customer's data, it automatically shows on the Jobs layout. This dynamic updating of related data is the essence of a relational database. Sometimes, however, you *don't* want a piece of information to change; you want FileMaker to remember the way it was at a certain point in time. *Lookup fields* use relationships to do a one-time copy and paste of data from one table to another. Once the looked-up data is in its new table, you can edit it, if necessary, but it doesn't change automatically if the related data changes.

Take a look at the Invoices table, for example. When you create an invoice, you attach it to a job. The job is in turn attached to a customer. When it comes time to mail the invoice, you could easily put the address fields from the Customers table occurrence on the Invoice layout and see the customer's address. But this method is a bad idea for two reasons:

- **It doesn't allow for special circumstances.** If a customer tells you she's going to be in Punakaiki for a month and to please send her next invoice there, you have no way to enter an alternate address on just one invoice. You have to change the address in his customer record, send the invoice, and then change the address back.

- **It destroys relevant information.** When you *do* revert the customer record with her original address, you lose any record of where you sent the invoice. If you go back to the special-case invoice 2 years from now, it'll *look* like you sent it to his home address.

POWER USERS' CLINIC

Related Value Lists

On page 225, you saw how to make value lists that change when you add, edit, or delete records in a table. You can also decide whether the list includes values from every record in the table, or only from the related records. You start creating both types of value lists the same way: You choose a field to base the value list on, and then tell FileMaker whether you want to use values from a second field in the value list (you can even use a related field for the second value). As with regular field-based lists, you can sort the list by the first field or by the second one.

But when you select the "Include only related values" radio button, the value list behaves differently. The list shows only the records related to the one you're sitting on. For example, you can use this option to show only a specific customer's Job ID on the Invoice layout. (But you'd have to add a Customer ID field to the Invoices table to make it happen.) Then when you enter a Customer ID on an Invoice, the related value list for Job

ID would show only the Jobs that have the same Customer ID value as the one you just entered.

For this method to work, FileMaker has to know which table occurrence you're using the value list on (there's that concept of *context* again). In other words, if you ask for only the related Jobs, do you mean jobs related to the Customer record or to the Invoice record? It can get confusing, but in this example, you want to use the jobs that are already related to the Customer table, even though you're using the value list on a layout that uses the context of the Invoice table occurrence. That way, the list's values change if you change the Invoice's Customer ID.

Careful, though: When you create a value list using related values only, the list works properly only when it's attached to a field on a layout associated with the same table occurrence selected in the "related values starting from" menu. If you try to use it on a layout that shows records from a different TO, it will be out of context, and FileMaker can't show the right values.

These problems arise because invoice data is *transactional*—an invoice represents a single business transaction at one specific point in time. But your customer record doesn't represent a single transaction with your customer: It represents an association you have with that customer. If the association changes (the customer moves and you need to store a new address), then your data should change accordingly. However, transactional data should *never* change once the transaction is complete, since it has to serve as a record of what happened during the transaction. Lookup fields solve the problem of saving transactional data.

While related fields automatically show new data, lookups use a semi-automatic approach. If you change a customer record, it *doesn't* affect the fields in existing

Invoice records at all. But any new Invoice you create *does* get the updated data and you can change the data in a field configured to Auto-Enter Lookup at any time—for a one-time address change, for example. This semi-automatic approach to updating data turns out to be just the right thing for transactional data like address fields on invoices: When you change the *transaction* record, its fields update appropriately, but when you change *source* records (the address fields in your customer record), FileMaker leaves the transaction alone.

Creating Lookups

To create a lookup, you define a field normally but add an auto-enter option called *Looked-up value.* You can also add a lookup to an existing field. Simply click the field in the field list and then click Options. The following steps explain how to create a new lookup field:

1. **Choose File→Manage→Database and then, if necessary, click the Fields tab. Finally, from the Table pop-up menu, choose Invoices.**

   You see the fields in the Invoices table—and you're ready to add a new one. You start by adding a lookup field for the customer's street address.

2. **In the Field Name box, type *Street Address*, and make sure the Type pop-up menu is set to Text. Click Create.**

   FileMaker adds the new field, but it's still just an ordinary field.

3. **Click the Options button. In the Field Options dialog box, click the Auto-Enter tab.**

   The Options dialog box appears. You'll create the lookup here.

4. **Turn on the "Looked-up value" checkbox.**

   The Lookup dialog box appears (Figure 6-20).

5. **Make sure the "Starting with table" pop-up menu is set to Invoices.**

   It is almost certainly set properly, because in this case, the context is clear. You're defining a field in the Invoices table, so that's the field's context. If you have multiple occurrences of a given table on the graph, then you might have to change the "Starting with table" pop-up menu to reflect the context of the layout on which you'll use the newly defined field, which influences how the lookup finds related data.

6. **From the "Lookup from related table" pop-up menu, choose Customers.**

   As soon as you choose a table, the "Copy value from field" list is populated with all the fields in the Customers table. You're interested in the Street Address field's value.

7. **In the "Copy value from field" list, choose Street Address. Turn off the "Don't copy contents if empty" checkbox.**

When you turn off "Don't copy contents if empty," FileMaker dutifully copies the empty value, wiping out data in the lookup field. If you turn this option on instead, then FileMaker leaves the lookup field untouched—its value before the lookup remains in place.

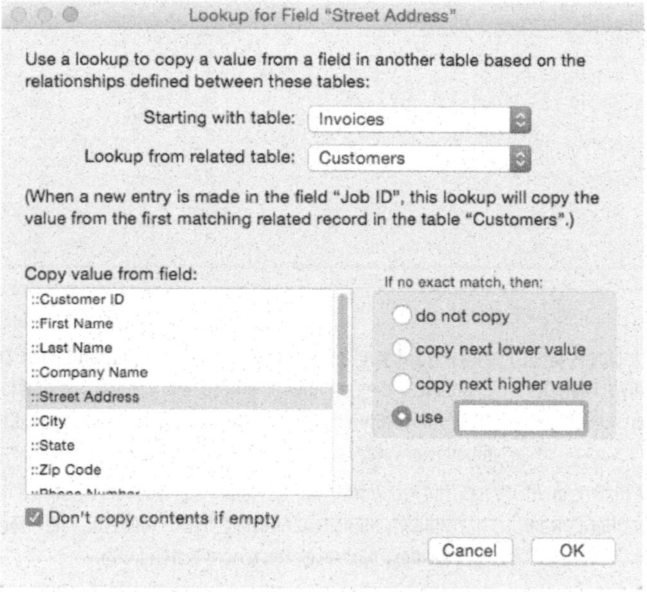

FIGURE 6-20

Here's what your Lookup dialog box looks like when you've set up the Lookup for the Invoices::Street Address field. In other circumstances, you might not want to copy over existing data if the related fields are blank. Imagine you have a table of currency exchange rates. If some currencies don't have data available the day you gather the rates, then those rate fields are blank. If you use a lookup to refresh exchange rates in your Products database, you don't want to wipe out any existing exchange rates. To keep last week's value, select the "Don't copy contents if empty" option.

8. **In the "If no exact match, then" group, turn on "use," and leave the associated text box empty.**

If there's no customer record, the Street Address field should be blank. If you leave this set to "do not copy," then any existing address (for a different customer, perhaps) is left in the field. (See the box on the next page for other "If no exact match, then" options.)

9. **Click OK to close all the dialog boxes.**

You have other fields to create, but first, you'll see how this one works.

Now switch to the Invoices layout and then add the new field to it (page 142). When you choose a job from the Jobs table, the Street Address field looks up the appropriate address from the Customer table. If you create an invoice and give it a valid Job ID number but no data shows up, check the Customer record to make sure you've entered addresses for your customers.

To finish your Invoices layout, create lookup fields for the remaining customer data you'll store in the Invoice table (see the following list). Use the same options as in the steps on the previous pages, or—to save clicks—duplicate the Street Address field, change its name, and then just change the field from which it looks up. That way, you get all the other lookup settings for free. Then put the new fields on the layout and create a few new records to watch the lookups in action:

- Company Name
- First Name
- Last Name
- City
- State
- Zip Code

Empty Lookups

Lookup options give you some control over what happens when you don't have a matching related record. Normally, if FileMaker tries to find a related record to look up data from and it can't find one, it just leaves the lookup field alone.

That's what happens when, in the "If no exact match, then" group of radio buttons, you turn on "do not copy." Here's what the others do:

- The "copy next lower value" option looks at the closest *lower* related record. For example, if you turn it on for the Invoices::Street Address field, and there's no matching related customer, FileMaker copies the address of the customer with the next lower Customer ID alphabetically. In this case, it makes absolutely no sense.

But what if you're looking up price information based on quantity? If the customer orders 38, but you have pricing for 30 or 40, you might want to get the price for 30 items, the next lower value.

- The "copy next higher value" option works just like its similarly named counterpart. It just copies the value from the next *higher* related record instead.

- The "use" option lets you specify any value you want to substitute for a missing related value. For example, if you're looking up customer age information and you don't have an age for one person, you can tell FileMaker to use "N/A" instead.

Using a Relookup

A lookup is triggered whenever you change the data in the key field on which the relationship is based. That's why changing the Job ID field makes FileMaker look up the customer information again.

Sometimes you want a lookup to trigger *without* changing the key field. For example, suppose a new customer hires you. You work for her for 3 months but never receive payment—despite sending three invoices. You finally decide it's time to ask her what's up, and that's when you discover you've been sending them to the *wrong address*. You mistyped her address in the Customers layout, and now all your invoices are incorrect, too. She agrees to pay you as soon as you mail the invoices to her correct address. You correct her address in the Customers table, but that doesn't affect the old invoices.

Luckily, you can easily update them—with the Relookup Field Contents command. First, find just the three bad Invoices for your customer and then click the field that normally triggers the lookup—the Job ID field in this case. Then choose the Records→Relookup Field Contents command. You see the message shown in Figure 6-21.

FileMaker is asking whether you want to copy the correct address onto the six bad invoices. Click OK, and FileMaker executes the lookup for those invoices.

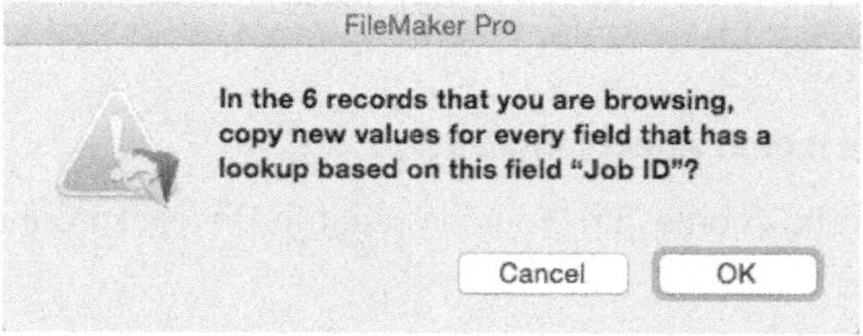

FIGURE 6-21

When you run the Relookup Field Contents command, FileMaker shows this message. The program reminds you how many records you're updating, since you can't undo this action. If you look up new address information into old invoices accidentally, you lose historical data. If you're sure you want to proceed, click OK.

> **TIP** To get into the Job ID field, click it—and be sure to choose the job that's already selected from the pop-up menu. Your goal is to make FileMaker think you're changing the data so the lookup retriggers without changing the data that's in the field. After you make your choice, the Relookup grabs the updated data.

Navigating Between Related Records

With pop-up menus and auto-creating records, adding data to your new database is now a breeze. But you still have to do some serious work to navigate the system. For example, if you're looking at a job and you want to see details about the related customer, you have to note the Customer ID or name, switch to the Customers layout, and then find the customer. That's two steps too many.

Simplify this process with a button (page 177) on the Invoice layout—one that uses the *Go to Related Record* (GTRR) command. GTRR does the obvious, plus a little more. It goes to the related record *and* changes the layout appropriately. It can also find all the related records and then sort them (if the relationship you're using has a sort specified). It can even create a new window, while it's at it. That's a lot of work for one little command. If that weren't enough ways to use this little powerhouse, you can also set an option that shows all records related to your found set instead of just the record you're currently on.

■ GO TO RELATED RECORD

Here's one way to create a button that activates the "Go to Related Record" command. On the Customers layout of the JobsInvoices database, the customer's name appears at the top of the layout in a merge field. In the following steps, you'll create a button on the Jobs layout that goes to the left of the customer name. When you click the button, it takes you to the proper customer record.

1. **Switch to the Jobs layout and then go to Layout mode.**

   You always add buttons in Layout mode.

2. **Select the text tool, click just to the left of the customer's name, and then type a > symbol. Use the Inspector (page 124) to make the symbol's font match the text block it'll sit next to.**

   The > symbol is a commonly used button for revealing detail or navigating to a related page.

3. **With the text block still selected, choose Format→Button Setup.**

   The Button Setup panel appears.

4. **From the Action pop-up menu, select Single Step.**

   The Button Action dialog box comes up. You can see it in the background of Figure 6-22.

5. **Type *gtrr* and press Enter.**

   The "Go to Related Record" step is selected. You could have started typing *Go to Related Record* to bring up the step you need, but FileMaker has built-in shortcuts for many steps.

6. **Press Enter again to open the "Go to Related Record" Options dialog box shown in the foreground of Figure 6-22.**

   Clicking the gear icon is an alternative way to get to this dialog box.

7. **From the "Get related record from" pop-up menu, choose Customers.**

   You're specifying which table occurrence you want to go to.

8. **From the "Show record using layout" pop-up menu, choose Layout.**

   The Specify Layout window appears. In this case, there's only one layout in the list, because you have only one layout associated with the Customers table. But in a database where there's more than one layout associated with a table, you get to choose which one to show. For now, leave both Result Options choices nchecked.

9. **Click OK until you're back to the Button Setup panel, and then click its Close button to dismiss it.**

   The button is set up. Use the View→Show→Buttons command to display an identifying badge on all of the current layout's buttons. (These badges appear only in Layout mode.)

Switch to Browse mode. Make sure you have a customer related to this job. If you don't, click the Customer ID field and then choose one. Once you assign a customer

ID to the Jobs record, the relationship is valid, and your button will work. Click it and you're transported directly to that customer's record.

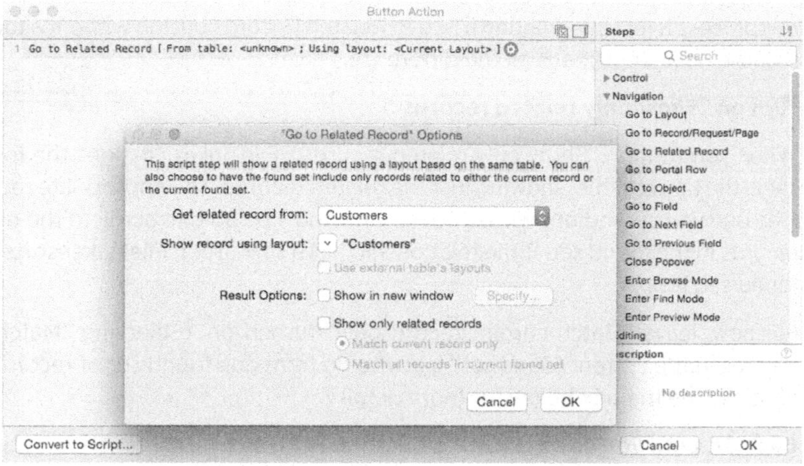

FIGURE 6-22

In the "Go to Related Record" Options window, "Get related record from" determines which table occurrence to use and "Show record using layout" determines which layout is shown. In the JobsInvoices database, you have only one table occurrence for each table, so once you choose a TO, there's only one layout to select.

Current Layout is the automatic option in the "Show record using" pop-up menu. If you forget to make a selection there, you may have trouble. After all, if you're going to a related record, it's got to be from a different table occurrence. If your current layout isn't associated with the target TO, you'll get an error message. Check your "Show record using layout" settings and then try again.

NOTE The "Use external table's layouts" option in the GTRR Options window applies only when you're linking multiple *files* together. You'll learn about that on page 620.

▓ USING GTRR TO CREATE A FOUND SET

If you're looking at a Customer record, then you can see all that customer's jobs, since they're right there in the Jobs portal. But what if you want to see those jobs (and only those jobs) in a sorted found set on the Jobs layout? It would take a bunch of steps if you had to do it manually. But the "Go to Related Record" command does all those steps for you—when you add a few new options to the setup you just learned.

1. **On the Customers layout, switch to Layout mode and then select the Jobs::Name field.**

   It's in the Jobs portal.

2. **Choose Format→Button Setup. In the Button Setup dialog box, from the list, select the "Go to Related Record" command and then click Specify.**

   The "Go to Related Record" Options window pops up.

3. **From the "Get related record from" pop-up menu, choose Jobs. From the "Show record using layout" pop-up menu, choose Layout, choose the Jobs layout, and then click OK once.**

   You need a layout that shows you meaningful data from the Jobs table. So far, this process is just like creating a "Go to Related Record" button without a found set. The next steps make all the difference.

4. **Turn on "Show only related records."**

   When you turn on "Show only related records," FileMaker changes the found set in the target table, showing just the related records. The appropriate record (the one you clicked on) will be active, and you'll be able to scroll to the other records in the found set. If the relationship has a sort order, FileMaker sorts the found set, too.

   For now, leave "Match current record only" turned on. (Selecting "Match all records in the current found set" lets you go from one found set of records to another. See the box below for more detail.)

5. **Click OK until you're back on the Customers layout.**

   If the Button Setup dialog box is still showing, you can click the close button at its top-left corner, or simply click anywhere outside of the box.

6. **For good measure, make sure the Jobs::Name field is blue and underlined (so it looks like a link).**

   Training time is cut down when you provide clues that the field is clickable.

Switch to Browse mode to admire your work. Now you have a way to move from a Job to its Customer and from a Customer to a found set of all her Jobs. To see the real power of a button in a portal, use the arrow buttons to navigate to a customer record that has more than one related job. Click the *second* portal record. Since you're on the second row, the button takes you to the second record in your found set, not the first one. Then click the Customer Name button again and see how the results change when you click in the first portal row.

What you're seeing is another example of context. In this case, the context of the *button* (the row you click) determines which record is active when the GTRR is complete. When you click the GTRR button on the Jobs layout, you see the Customer that's related to that job, but without changing the found set on the Customer layout (because you didn't select the "Show only related record" option). But when you click a button in the Jobs portal, you get a found set of only the job records you just saw in the portal.

GTRR Deluxe

The "Show only related records" option of the "Go to Related Record" window lets you display a found set of records from a related table. But what if you want to do something really cool and complicated, like find a group of invoices that don't have anything in common other than being unpaid, and then see the Customers for those Invoices in a found set—without writing down the list of customers and then performing a complicated search?

Here's how you do it: Make a button on your Invoices layout and then give it a GTRR step that goes to the Customers table occurrence by using the Customers layout. Then in the Options window, select "Show only related records" *and* "Match all records in current found set."

The starting found set on the Invoices layout determines which Customer records you'll see. So if you were viewing 10 Invoice records from six different customers, you'd get a found set of those six customers when you click the GTRR button. The cool thing is that you don't have to know how many customers are related to the Invoices found set, because the relationship tracks that for you. Now that you have a found set of late-paying customers, you can send them all an email diplomatically requesting that they cough up the dough.

Apply GTRR (deluxe) liberally throughout your database, and people won't need to do as many complicated searches to find the data they're looking for.

Reviewing Relationship Concepts

Wrapping your head around relationships and how they work in FileMaker is a little like trying to play chess on a multilevel playing board. Though the Relationships graph is flat, it has powers that may not be apparent at first. For example, when you created Lookup fields (page 226), you used the graph to tunnel through one table to get to a table beyond, grab some data, and then come back to put it in a local field. In this section, you'll go into more depth on some concepts you've touched on earlier in this chapter.

Bidirectionality

You've started to tap the power of that one little line you drew between the Customers and Jobs tables. But one very important aspect of that line is worth paying extra attention to—a line describes a relationship that works in *two* directions. You saw that in action when you used the same relationship to make GTRR buttons that navigate between the tables at either end of one relationship.

Notice that the GTRR command behaves a little differently depending on which table you start from, since the tables are on either end of a one-to-many relationship. But the key concept is that the relationship works both ways. That's why one Edit Relationship window (Figure 6-23) lets you set options for both tables in the relationship.

Remember that Table Occurrences appear in the Edit Relationship window based on their relative positions on the graph. Left and right don't matter here, but if it's easier for you to visualize the relationship with the "one" TO on the left, then make sure the "one" TO appears to the left of the "to-many" TO. But because a TO might appear in the Edit Relationship window on either side of the relationship, options are shown on both sides of the window even though you'll rarely set those options on the "one" side.

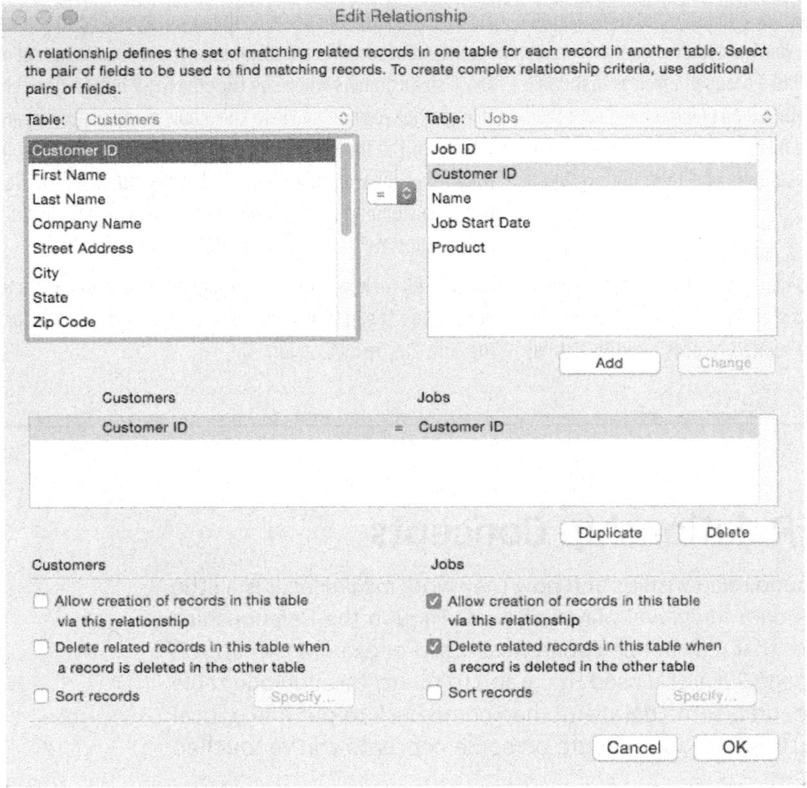

FIGURE 6-23

You can set options for both tables involved in a relationship with the Edit Relationship window. It's important to understand which options make sense for which table, though. It would be extremely rare, for instance, to allow creation of a parent record from a child table. And since each child record only has one parent, clicking the option to sort the records in a parent table is a waste of time.

NOTE Here's a list of refreshers on the options you can set in the Edit Relationship window: allow record creation (page 154), delete, and sort (page 215). See the box on page 238 to learn about the hidden danger of using the delete option for related records.

Implicit Relationships in Action

When you modeled the JobsInvoices database, you learned about *implicit* relationships. These relationships are when tables are connected to one another through other tables. For example, when you create a lookup field in the Invoice table that can enter data from the Customer table, you're leveraging an implicit relationship. Specifically, Invoices and Customers don't relate to each other directly (Figure 6-24). They relate to each other through the Jobs table. So you didn't create or need a

Customer ID in the Invoice table to pull the data from Customers. FileMaker uses the Job ID field to find the right Customer and then put the right data into the Invoice table's name and address fields. Because it can feel like having a direct pipeline into a table, using these implicit relationships is sometimes called *tunneling*.

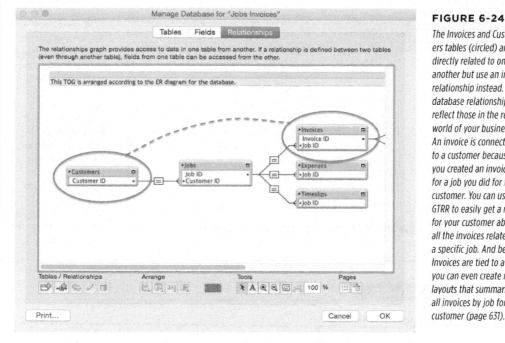

FIGURE 6-24

The Invoices and Customers tables (circled) aren't directly related to one another but use an implicit relationship instead. The database relationships reflect those in the real world of your business. An invoice is connected to a customer because you created an invoice for a job you did for that customer. You can use GTRR to easily get a report for your customer about all the invoices related to a specific job. And because Invoices are tied to a job, you can even create report layouts that summarize all invoices by job for any customer (page 631).

You can use tunneling to show a list of all a customer's invoices on the Customers layout. So on the Customers layout, create an Invoice portal and place the Invoices::Date, Invoices::Invoice ID, and Invoices::Job ID fields in the portal. Normally, you *wouldn't* put an ID field in a portal. In fact, it would probably be a bad idea because it would confuse users and raise the possibility that the data in a key field could get changed, thus stranding the related record or connecting it to the wrong parent record. But for this experiment, you want to see the ID fields so you can see how data tunneling works. While you're violating standard procedure, throw the Jobs::Job ID field into the Jobs portal. When you're done, your layout will look something like Figure 6-25.

NOTE The sample database for this chapter has Job and Invoice records that already have IDs for Customer Mary Reynolds. If you've created Invoice records that are related to Jobs, they'll show up too, so long as the Jobs are related to a customer record.

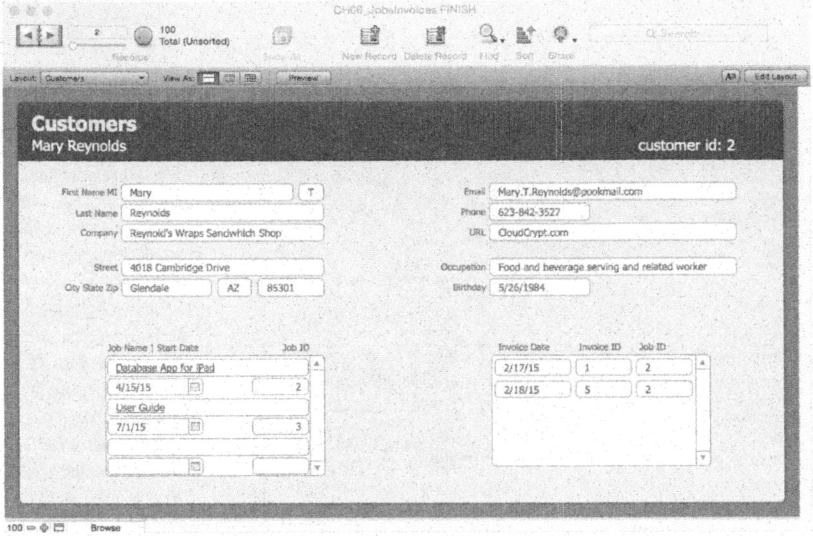

FIGURE 6-25

The Invoice portal shows all invoices that are attached to either of Mary Reynolds' two jobs (Database App for iPad and User Guide). Placing the ID fields in a portal is a good way to see how relationships work in theory. It's also a good troubleshooting tip if a portal or relationship isn't working the way you think it should be working. Once you see the values in those ID fields, it's easier to figure out what the problem is and how to fix it.

WORKAROUND WORKSHOP

Cascading Deletes

The "Delete related records" option can be dangerous for a couple of reasons. First, if you turn it on where it should be turned off, then you can find yourself in an odd situation: Records keep disappearing for no apparent reason. You'll get frustrated if you don't realize how this option works.

But even if you *want* it on, keep this fact in mind: FileMaker can't bring back a record you delete. It's one thing if someone accidentally deletes a Jobs record—you just have to look up the Job Name and then enter it again, being careful to give the job the same ID it had before.

It's something else entirely if you also select the "Delete related records" option in the Jobs-to-Customers relationship,

and the Customers-to-Invoices relationship, and again in the Invoices-to-Line Items relationship. You've set up the Towering Inferno scenario called *cascading deletes*. Because now, when you delete one Job record—perhaps thinking that the job is finished and you don't need the record anymore—FileMaker also obeys your "hidden" instructions and deletes the Customer record attached to that Job record, *all* the Invoices attached to the Customer, and *all* those line items, too!

Some people decide it's not worth the risk and leave the "Delete related records" option off even when it *should* be on. For a better solution to the cascading deletion problem, read up on how access privileges can limit who's allowed to delete records on page 755.

The records displayed in the Invoice portal show all Invoices that are related to any of the customer's jobs. So if a customer has 20 jobs, the invoices from all those jobs appear in the portal. When you think of *this* Invoices portal, it helps to think of it as a one-to-many-*to-many* relationship. That's not a term you'll hear database developers using, but it makes the concept more clear—one Customer is related to many Jobs, each of which in turn is related to many Invoices.

Context is the key. From a Customer record, the context of the Invoice table is always through the Jobs table. Because Customers are implicitly related to Invoices through Jobs, you can copy the Invoices portal from the Customer layout and then paste it on the Jobs layout, where it will behave perfectly without any extra work on your part. It will show slightly different data in its new context, though. On the Customers layout, the portal shows invoices from all jobs related to the customer. On the Jobs layout the same portal shows Invoices related to the current job only. The move works because you're moving a portal to a new context along the same relationship line.

The Invoice table isn't the only one in the database that shares these properties. For example:

- You can put an Expenses, Line Item, Hours, or even a Payments portal on the Customers layout. For instance, you might want to see all the expenses incurred for a specific customer. And like the Invoices table, you can use calculations to sum up all those related records (page 398).

- You can put a GTRR button (page 233) on the Invoice portal so you can quickly see a found set of a Customer's invoices without performing a find.

- Using the principle of bidirectionality, you could put a Customers::Full Name field on a Payment record or use a GTRR button on an Expense record to jump through hyperspace directly to the proper Customer record.

WARNING The options you set in the Edit Relationship window (Figure 6-23) don't pass through implicit relationships, with good reason. For example, the Customers-to-Jobs relationship is set to allow the creation of related Jobs records. However, when you're on a Customer record, you can't create an Invoice record from the Invoice portal unless you also turn on the option to create related records for the Invoice table in the *Jobs-to-Invoices* relationship. If you do that, though, all Invoices you create through the Invoices portal on the Customers layout will get the Job ID from the first record in the Jobs table. That's probably not what you want. More likely, you'll have multiple jobs going on for at least some of your customers, so you should create Invoices only when you're on a record in the Jobs table. Implicit relationships have some limitations, and you should be aware of them as you're designing.

When you're figuring out how best to add a new feature to your database, take a gander at your Relationships graph, and trace the line between all the tables that'll be affected. Take notice of the key fields in each table and the options set for each relationship. This simple preparation will often help you come up with solutions faster, and with fewer oddball behaviors.

You'll learn more advanced relationship techniques in Chapter 15. But now that you've mastered the fundamentals of relationships, you'll be switching gears to learn more about how to make fields work.

Field Options

In Chapter 4, you learned a couple of ways to create fields and how field type helps define the kind of data you're storing. In this chapter, you'll learn more about the field types you already know, and then you'll learn about some types you haven't come across before. But type is only one of the options you can choose when you create a field. For example, lookup fields (page 226) are one way FileMaker can automatically enter data into a field, but they're not the only way. FileMaker gives you so many other ways to get automatic data into fields, the Field Options window has a whole tab dedicated to those options.

Other times, you need to limit the types of information people can enter in a field, but a value list (page 127) is too restrictive. So FileMaker lets you decide what kind of data—date, text, or whatever—a field can accept. That's called field *validation,* and once again, there's a whole tab full of options.

After you've put your data into fields, FileMaker lets you decide how to store it and do more advanced tricks—like create a field that has the same value for every record in a table or repeat the same field multiple times on one record. And you'll learn how container fields let you store entire files from other programs within a FileMaker record.

NOTE   To follow along in this chapter, you'll find it helpful to download the sample database *CH07 Field Options.fmp12* from this book's Missing CD page at *www.missingmanuals.com/cds/fmp14mm.*

Understanding Field Types

FileMaker has eight different field types. Each one has its strengths and best uses. Selecting the right field type for your data is fundamental to getting your database to behave the way you want it to, so here are some tips for figuring out which field type to choose.

Text

Text fields are the most commonly used field type. Each text field can store about 2 GB of letters, numbers or symbols, including carriage returns, so long as your computer's memory allows that much storage. That's about one *billion* characters. The figure is approximate because it's partially based on your computer's RAM and disk space. Use text fields for names, addresses, and even phone numbers.

Number

Use a number field if you intend to perform math on its contents. If you're creating invoices, you'll need number fields so other fields can tally up the invoice total. You can type letters and even symbols in a number field, but if you do, FileMaker may change your data in unexpected ways. For instance, if you create a field to store a Part Number and then put data like 234A111, FileMaker will treat that entry as the numeric value "234111," so it's usually safest to store data with letters and symbols in text fields.

Numbers can be very large or very small. And to help people who use FileMaker for scientific or mathematic solutions, here are some limits for number fields:

- Numbers must be greater than -10^{400} and less than 10^{400} (it's actually 9.99999999^{399}, because -10^{400} itself isn't included). If you're counting something reasonable—say, the number of protons in the universe—you'll be just fine.

- You get 800 significant digits in all. In general, though, any nonzero value is a significant digit. That is, the digit contributes to the number's precision. For example, the leading zeros in the number "00042" are *not* significant. That's probably all you need to know about significant digits. If you're still curious, ask a high-school algebra student.

- Only the first 400 digits are indexed in all, significant or otherwise. So if you're searching for numbers, then you have a little less precision to work with.

You can enter numbers in FileMaker as you would in almost any program. Type the number and any symbols that define it, like a negative sign or a decimal point. You can also use *scientific notation*. For example, to record the number of air molecules in your living room, you can type *6.02E23* into a number field, which is a lot easier to type than 60,200,000,000,000,000,000,000,000. Of course, the exponent part (after the E) can be negative if you need really small numbers instead.

Number fields can't contain paragraph breaks. If you try to hit Return, FileMaker will beep at you.

NOTE Number fields can also contain Boolean values. See page 311 to learn about them.

UNDERSTANDING
FIELD TYPES

Date

Unlike text or number fields, you can store only valid Gregorian dates in date fields. Data entry has to be as month, day, and year, but you can use several different punctuation marks as separators. That is, you can type: "11/7/2015," "11-7-2015," or "11.7.2015."

NOTE Computers in Europe and other areas use system settings that expect different day, time, and number formats. FileMaker uses the settings that are in effect on the computer where the file was created. So if you ever open a file created by a Japanese user (for example), FileMaker will ask you which settings to use the first time you open that file. Choose File→File Options and then click the Text tab to change the file's Data Entry settings.

The first possible date you can store is 1/1/0001, and the current format is good until the end of the year 4000 AD. If you enter a two-digit year (like 15 or 75), FileMaker puts either 19 or 20 in front, using the current year as a decision point. For example, if the year is 2015 and you type *46*, FileMaker enters 1946. However, FileMaker won't go more than 70 years into the past. So if you type *45*, FileMaker enters 2045. If you really want a two-digit year (because you're entering a date from ancient history), then enter it like this: 6/17/0034.

If the date you're entering is in the current calendar year, you can save a few keystrokes by typing the month and day only. Use only a single separator, though. For example, in 2015 you can type "11/7" to get the date November 7, 2015, Save even more time with the Insert→Current Date command. Press Ctrl (⌘) and then the hyphen key (–) to enter the current date. (This command actually works in a text field, too, or even in a block of text on a layout.)

NOTE Although FileMaker lets you enter and display dates in a format that humans find meaningful (September 26, 1957, or 11/11/11), the program actually stores them as numbers. That gives you the power to perform mathematical operations on date fields when you create calculations. Figure 7-1 shows what those values look like.

Date	4/12/2012		734605
Time	2:20:18 PM		51618
Timestamp	2/27/2012 2:20:18 PM		6.3466e+10

FIGURE 7-1

In the left column, you see a date, a time, and a timestamp field. In the right column, you see the results of calculation fields that display the values as numbers instead of dates or times. That number represents the number of days between January 1, 0001 and the date in your field. The time calculation is the number of seconds since midnight. The timestamp calculation is the number of seconds since midnight on January 1, 0001.

Time

Like date fields, time fields require precise entry. Separate hours, minutes, and seconds with a colon. You don't have to enter seconds if you don't want to, but you have to include both hours and minutes. You can put "am" or "pm" in the field to indicate which 6:00 you mean (FileMaker will assume a.m. if you do not specify p.m.) or you can use military time and enter 18:00 instead of 6:00 p.m.

Time fields are most often used for time of day, like 4:30 a.m. or 6:13:27 p.m. But you can also enter a *duration* instead, like 123:38:22 (meaning 123 hours, 38 minutes, 22 seconds). You don't even have to limit yourself to a 60-minute hour. A time like 0:82:17 is perfectly valid (it means 82 minutes, 17 seconds, and is exactly equivalent to 1:22:17). On page 315, you'll learn how to force a field to always show a valid time value in the format of your choice.

NOTE When entering time values, you *always* start with hours. If you're trying to enter just 12 minutes, 37 seconds, then you have to enter *00:12:37* or *0:12:37* so FileMaker doesn't think you mean 12 *hours*.

Time values are also quite precise. If you're recording the time it takes for somebody to complain about changes in your company's insurance plan, you can enter *00:00:27.180* for 27 seconds, 180 milliseconds. You can put up to six digits to the right of the decimal point. Time data is stored as numeric data and is counted by seconds elapsed since midnight of the current day.

Timestamp

A *timestamp* field is basically a date field and a time field combined. It has to hold *both* a date *and* a time. As with its companion types, Date and Time, data needs to be precise. All the rules for date and time entry apply: *7/4/2014 2:45 am*. Because they're so picky, you usually don't want people typing directly into timestamp fields, so use auto-enter options (page 245) to create their data instead. You can also use Insert→CurrentTime, and FileMaker is smart enough to enter the date and time in a timestamp field.

A timestamp is stored as a number. A timestamp represents the number of seconds elapsed since January 1, 0001, at 12:00:00 am (midnight).

You can use this kind of field to record when an event happened, or when it will happen. You may be tempted to use two fields (a date field and a time field), but that road leads to only heartache and pain when you try to reference those fields in calculations. If something happens on a specific date and time, you should use a timestamp field for it.

Timestamps support the same fraction-of-a-second accuracy as time fields. They're displayed as a date followed by a time with a space in between.

NOTE If you're formatting a timestamp field, you have to apply *both* a date and a time format. If you apply only one type of format, then that formatting change won't show up.

Container

Use container fields to store graphics, movies, sounds, or files—text documents, spreadsheets, PDFs, or even other FileMaker files. Container fields have such specific behavior that a whole section in this chapter is dedicated to explaining how to use them.

Calculation

Unlike the other field types discussed so far, you don't enter data in *calculation* and *summary* fields. Calculation fields' values are based on settings you define when you specify a *formula* that determines its value. For instance, if you had a field called Birth Date, you could create a calculation field that shows the person's age. The Age field automatically updates to stay correct as time goes by, so you don't have to change it. Three chapters of this book are dedicated to calculations; you'll start plumbing their depths in Chapter 10.

The results of calculation fields have types. Choosing the right type is important, since the wrong type can change a calculation's results. Calculation results can be text, dates, and even the contents of another field.

Summary

Calculation fields typically perform math on fields that are in the same record. But Summary fields collect data from across sets of records. So even though summary fields can be defined in a table, and thus may seem as if they refer to a specific record as other fields do, summary fields get their values from found sets of records. You used New Layout/Report to create a summary field in the tutorial starting on page 179, and you'll learn how to create them manually in Chapter 16.

■ Auto-Enter Field Options

Most fields are empty when you create a new record. Often, but not always, that's what you want—a completely blank slate into which you can type the information pertinent to a record. But auto-enter options put data into fields for you, saving time and reducing human error. Auto-enter options can create serial numbers for a primary key (page 249) or can store data about your records (Figure 7-2).

NOTE If you don't see any options in the Fields tab of your Manage Database window, click the Options/Comments column heading. That toggles it between showing comments and showing options.

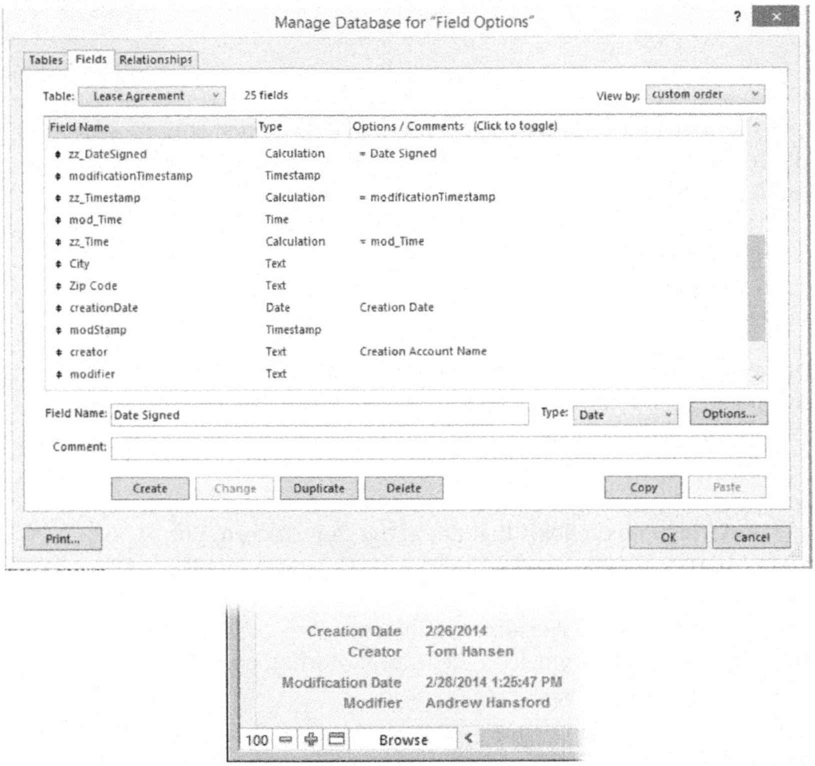

FIGURE 7-2

Top: The Manage Database window's field list shows auto-enter options in the Options/Comments column. The "modStamp" field tracks the date and time that any field in a record gets changed. In conjunction with the "modifier" field, you can figure out who's entered stuff into this record and when.

Bottom: This layout shows four auto-enter fields that store information about who creates and modifies each record and when they do so.

On the "Options for Field" dialog box's Auto-Enter tab, the first two auto-enter options (creation values and modification values) let you create and maintain metadata. Many developers find these fields so useful for peeking behind the scenes that they create primary key fields and the four metadata fields shown in Figure 7-2 in each table before they create any other fields.

> **TIP** The information that describes a set of data is called *metadata*. In this chapter, fields like Invoice Number and Customer Name are your data. Auto-enter creation and modification fields are metadata describing the database record—not the invoice itself. Metadata fields let you do some simple forensics on your database. For example, if there's a question about an Invoice, you can see at a glance who created it and then ask that person to solve the mystery. Plus, when data entry folks know you're tracking this kind of metadata, they may start being more careful, since they know you can track their mistakes back to them.

Creation Values

When a record is *first created*, FileMaker can enter information about the circumstances under which it was created. It can record the date, time, or timestamp at the moment of creation, and who created the record. You can search such fields to find recently created records, all records that are over a year old, or even records that were created on a Tuesday.

You can apply an auto-enter option to a newly created field or to one that already exists. Just make sure that the field type and option match each other. For example, make sure that an auto-enter Creation Date option is applied to a Date field. Strictly speaking, you can apply a Creation Date option to a text field, but if you do, the result will be sorted as text and you may not get reports sorted in the order you want. You'll get more predictable results if you match types consistently. Here's how to set an auto-enter creation date field:

1. **In the *CH07 Field Options* database, go to File→Manage→Database, make sure a date field is selected in the field list and then click the Options button.**

   The "Options for Field" dialog box appears (Figure 7-3).

2. **Click the Creation checkbox.**

   You use this option for any data specifically related to the creation of a record like, say, the date or time it was created.

3. **From the Creation pop-up menu, choose Date.**

   In this case, you want the field to contain the date the record is created.

4. **Turn on the "Prohibit modification of value during data entry" checkbox.**

   Because this field automatically gets the right value, you never need to change it manually after a record is created. Plus, you don't want folks accidentally (or worse, *intentionally*) editing this data. The whole point of the exercise is to have FileMaker create an official date for each record that's reliable. Figure 7-3 shows the settings you need.

5. **Click OK until you're back on your layout.**

   You're now ready to test your new field. Any existing records don't have the creation date, because they were created before the field's option was set. But every record you create from here on will have a creation date.

NOTE If you already have a lot of records in your table before you create the Creation Date field, you can enter dates manually by turning off the "Prohibit modification of value during data entry" option temporarily. Just be sure to turn it back on when you're done to prevent future mistakes.

FIGURE 7-3

Turn on the Creation option and then choose Date to get data showing the record's date of birth. You can save yourself a little time and skip the Creation checkbox altogether. It's turned on automatically when you choose an option from the pop-up menu next to it.

In this case, a creation date is specific enough. But sometimes you need to know the date and time of an event. While you could create two fields (one Date field with an auto-enter creation date and a Time field with an auto-enter creation time), a Timestamp field with an auto-enter timestamp value is a lot easier to use in a calculation.

Auto-enter creation date fields are also useful for things like invoice dates. For most invoices, their date is the date they're created, so go ahead and apply an auto-enter creation date option to that field. But just make sure you don't turn on the "Prohibit modification of value during data entry" option. You want to have the ability to change the date, in case you don't have time to create an invoice the same day you delivered the product or service.

▦ USING CREATION NAME AND ACCOUNT NAME

When you're tracking who created a record, you might be tempted to choose Name from the Creation menu to store metadata about who created a record. But this option uses the FileMaker user name and has a couple of weaknesses. First, people can change their user name in the operating system or in FileMaker preferences. (In Windows, choose Edit→Preferences; in Mac OS X, choose FileMaker

Pro→Preferences). Second, someone can sit down at another user's computer and enter some information; you really only know which computer the information came from, not which person. A more reliable method of tracking the "who" part of metadata is to create database Account Names instead. To learn how to set up and manage accounts, see page 745.

Modification Values

It's useful to know when a record was *created*, and also to know when it was *last changed*. That way, you can quickly find everything that temp you hired last week entered, or see how stale the info you have on your best customer is.

To see how FileMaker records changes or modifications to a record, make a new timestamp field called modificationTimestamp. Then in the field's Auto-Enter options, turn on the Modification checkbox and then, from the pop-up menu, choose "Timestamp (Date and Time)." Don't forget to click on "Prohibit modification of value during data entry." As with creation metadata, you want FileMaker, and not the data entry people, determining what goes into this field.

> **NOTE** In Chapter 13, which covers scripting, you'll discover other ways to change a field that don't involve data entry. The "Prohibit modification" option applies only to the process of a human being interacting with a field in Browse mode. FileMaker can still update the value for you.

Serial Number

Back in Chapter 1, you learned that record numbers (as viewed in the Current Record Indicator) can change as records get deleted or sorted. Then on page 146, you saw that when you want to assign a unique number to your record, you use the "Serial number" auto-enter option. Here's more detail on how that works: A serial number is a field whose value goes up for each new record. Typically, it goes up by a count of one, so the first record might be 1, 1001, or INV0001. In the second record you create, the serial number field would be 2, 1002, or INV0002. The numbers don't have to go up by one with each new record—you can provide any "increment by" value you want. But the value always goes up by some fixed amount.

In the Field Options dialog box, once you turn on the "Serial number" checkbox, you can specify the "next value," which is the value FileMaker uses for the next record that you create (usually, the starting value). The "increment by" value tells FileMaker how much to add with each new record.

You can specify non-numerical values for "next value." For example, if your field is a text field, you can put INV00001 in the "next value" box. Your first record would then get INV00001, followed by INV00002 and INV00003.

The Generate radio buttons under "Serial number" control *when* the serial number is assigned. If you select "On creation," then as soon as you create a record, FileMaker puts the serial number in the field. If you decide you don't want the record, even if you delete it right away, that serial number value has been *used up,* and the next record you make has a new serial number. Most times, losing a serial number poses no problem at all, and it's convenient to have the serial number value available before you commit the record because serial numbers are so often used as key fields when you're creating relationships.

If you select "On commit" instead, then the serial number doesn't show up in the field until you exit the record. In other words, you can delete this new record without *committing,* and you haven't used up a serial number. Still, unless you have a good reason (like a stringent government regulation that requires you to record every single transaction with a string of unbroken serial numbers), you should use the "On creation" option. See the box below for more on committing records.

UP TO SPEED

Committing: Making Changes Permanent

The word *commit* refers to a database concept that means your data is saved. When you create a new record, you haven't actually added a record to the table yet. Instead, you get a blank record on the screen, and the information you enter is stored in a temporary working area in your computer's memory. When you exit the record, the information in that working area is *committed*—or written—to the database.

When you edit a record, the same principle holds: As soon as you enter the record, it's copied to the working area. While you edit it, you're actually editing this copy. When you exit the record, FileMaker puts your edited copy back in the table. In general, think of *committing* a record as the same thing as *exiting* a record. When you exit the record, you commit it.

You use serial numbers most often when you create relationships between tables. Serial numbers also come in handy when the items in your database don't have a convenient name. In a database of invoices, it can be tough to talk about one particular invoice. ("You know, that one we sent last Thursday. No, not that one, the *other* one.") People often use serial numbers to clarify such things.

Value from Last Visited Record

Some databases need a lot of repetitive data entry. For example, if you're entering scores into a grade book database, you have to enter the same assignment information and date for each student's paper—only the grade changes. In cases like this, FileMaker's "Value from last visited record" auto-enter option is very handy. When this option is selected and you make a new record, FileMaker automatically fills in the same data as the record you last created or edited.

It's important to understand that "Last Visited Record" has a specific meaning. It's not the last record you were *looking* at. It's the last record that was *active*. In other words, you can flip to a record and view it, but if you don't click into one of its fields, it wasn't *visited*. If you're using this option but getting unexpected data, remember this distinction.

As with the auto-enter Date option, you can easily change the values FileMaker enters after you create the record. When you do, the next record you create copies the new, changed values from the record you just edited. Entering multiple sets of repetitive information becomes a breeze—you modify the Assignment field only once per set of papers, for instance.

NOTE This auto-enter option is so handy that there's also a menu command you can issue at will. Choose Insert From Last Visited Record or use the keyboard shortcut Ctrl - ' (⌘ - ').

Data

The Data option on the Auto-Enter tab is useful when you have a field that usually has the same data in it but occasionally needs to change. Suppose most of the properties you manage are in Portland. FileMaker can put *Portland* in a City field for you—but you can still change it when appropriate. Or if all your part numbers start with the same prefix, say "TPS-," then set up your part number field to enter that data automatically. Then you can type the rest of the numbers in manually.

Calculated Value

Auto-enter calculation fields are different from calculation fields. With calculation fields, the data is entered for you, and you can't override the value. You can click into a calculation field, but if you try to type, you'll get a warning telling you the field isn't modifiable.

But auto-enter calculations give you the power of calculations, along with the ability to change the result. For example, say you have a regular calculation field called Invoice::Due Date. Its calculation—Invoice Date + Payment Terms—adds Payment Terms to the Invoice Date field to come up with the Due Date value. Invoice Date is set as the creation date of the record, and Payment Terms are auto-entered data (say Net 10 Days). The Due Date field is filled in when you create each Invoice record. With a normal calculation field, the only way to change the Due Date is by changing the value in the Invoice Date field or the Payment Terms field, and then FileMaker updates the calculation. But you can't type the date you want directly in the Invoice::Due Date field.

NOTE Yes, you can add the Payment Terms field's value of "Net 10 days" to a date, *if* the Payment Terms field is defined as a number field. That way, FileMaker can ignore the text when asked to do math with the field's value. But to reduce ambiguity, stick to straight numbers in fields that are referenced by calculations.

That's where the "Calculated value" option comes in. You can specify a calculation, which enters a date when FileMaker creates the record, but then you can click into the field and change it to another date. Plus, if you convert a calculation field to another field type with an auto-enter calculation option, FileMaker automatically moves the calculation formula you wrote into the auto-enter calculation box for you. You don't even have to rewrite the calculation. Even better, you can get the field's calculated value to reset later by changing the value in either the Invoice Date or Payment Terms fields. Just make sure you *don't* turn on the "Do not replace existing value of field (if any)" option when you set up the field (Figure 7-4).

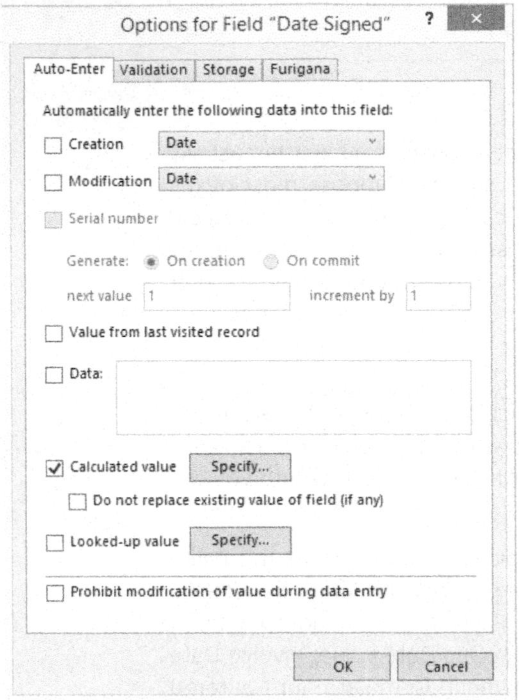

FIGURE 7-4

The Auto-Enter tab of the "Options for Field 'Date Signed'" window is where you select the Calculated value option and then turn off the automatic "Do not replace existing value of field (if any)" option. With these settings, if you change the value in any field referenced in the Date Signed field's calculation (Date Paid), the Date Signed value will be updated. But if you leave the "Do not replace" option turned on, the calculation kicks in only when data is entered into the referenced fields the first time. Either way, you can change the value at will unless you also choose "Prohibit modification of value during data entry," which defeats the purpose of an auto-enter calculation field.

NOTE Don't worry if all this calculation talk seems mysterious. You'll learn more about how to create calculations in Chapter 10.

Looked-Up Value

As you've learned, FileMaker lets you relate multiple tables together in various ways. When you've done that, you can tell FileMaker to automatically fetch a value from a related record in another table and plop it in the field. This feature is called a *Lookup,* and it's explained on page 226.

■ Validation Options

Auto-enter options tell FileMaker to enter data for you. *Validation* options tell File-Maker what *not* to let you put in a field. You decide what kind of information *should* go there, and FileMaker warns you when you enter something that doesn't look right.

In your sample database, you may want to make sure the Zip Code field always looks like a real Zip code. (This example uses American 5-digit Zip codes. You may need to adjust the validation settings for your country's postal codes.):

1. **Go to File→Manage→Database, and in the Lease Agreement table, open the Field Options dialog box for the Zip Code field.**

   Don't change the field from a text field to a number field. See the box on page 254 to learn why not.

2. **Go to the Validation tab. Make sure that the "Allow user to override during data entry" checkbox is turned on.**

   As you can see in Figure 7-5, there are many options for field validation.

3. **Turn on the "Strict data type" checkbox and then, from its pop-up menu, select Numeric Only.**

   Even though you've formatted the field as a text field, you can use a validation setting to accept only numerals in the field.

4. **Click the "Maximum number of characters" checkbox and then type *5*.**

   You can do better than just require numbers. This option tells FileMaker to accept no more than five digits in the Zip Code field.

5. **Turn on the "Display custom message if validation fails" checkbox.**

   FileMaker automatically shows a message when a value in a field doesn't match the validation settings, but it's often more considerate to give the message in your own words. That's what this setting does.

6. **In the text box below this checkbox, type *The Zip code you entered has too many digits. Is this correct?***

   FileMaker displays this message if the validation fails. (For a little guidance on what these messages should say, see the box on page 256.)

7. **Click OK until you're back on the Lease Agreement layout.**

   Switch to Browse mode (if necessary); it's time to test. Try entering too many characters into the Zip Code field, and you see your message when you exit the field, as shown in Figure 7-6.

NOTE It's true that the validation settings you selected in the previous steps aren't perfect. For example, they don't allow Zip+4 codes (46077-1039). At the same time, they would let you enter something like *123*, which isn't a valid Zip code at all. To handle the nuances of the simple Zip code, you need to use the "Validated by calculation" option, which lets you set more specific validation standards by using the Specify Calculation dialog box.

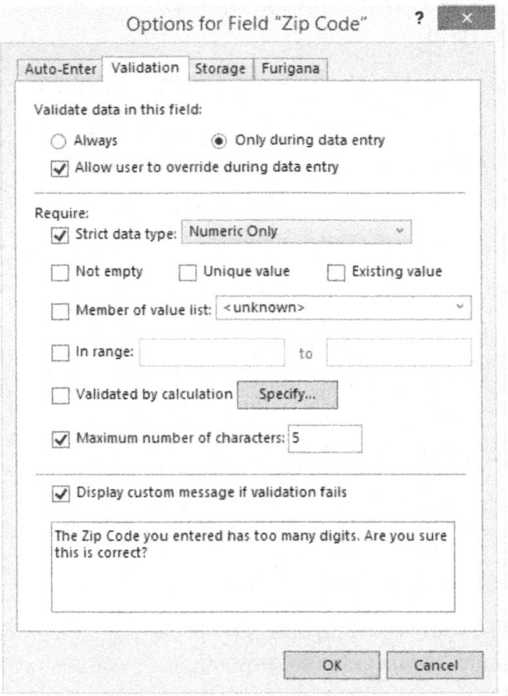

FIGURE 7-5

The "Options for Field" dialog box's Validation tab lets you check for errors before the data is committed. You can, for example, make sure only numbers are entered, or that the first name is no more than 30 characters. You can apply as many validation rules as you want, and FileMaker checks each one whenever someone modifies the field. However, overdoing validation can put an extra burden on your data entry people. Each validation is handled separately, so if an entry violates more than one validation, the user will have to correct each one in turn, which can be frustrating and inefficient.

FREQUENTLY ASKED QUESTION

Numbers and Text

You have to set an awful lot of validation options to make sure people enter only Zip codes into a text field. Can't I just make the Zip Code field a number field instead?

No, you can't. Zip codes are numeric characters, but they're not *numbers*, and that makes a big difference as far as FileMaker is concerned. For example, number fields don't recognize leading zeros—like the ones at the beginning of 01247 and scores of other perfectly valid Zip codes. If you enter *01247* in a number field, FileMaker thinks you meant to type the number *1,247* and will treat it as the number 1,247 for almost all uses, including searches, sorts, and if saved to an Excel spreadsheet. But "almost all uses" may not get your mail to North Adams, Massachusetts on time. FileMaker is kinda, sorta forgiving on

this point, but when you absolutely, positively have to rely on the Zip code entered in a field, text type (with a numeric validation) is the way to go.

The Numeric Only validation option lets the field stay a text field (which preserves all entered characters) but still accept only numerical digits on entry, which is exactly what you want for a Zip code.

Some people also assume that a phone number should be stored as a number field. Wrong again. Phone numbers contain numerals and dashes, parentheses, and sometimes other special characters—all mere text to FileMaker. As a general rule, make a field a number field only if it's expressing a mathematical value like height in inches, or the price of a cup of tea.

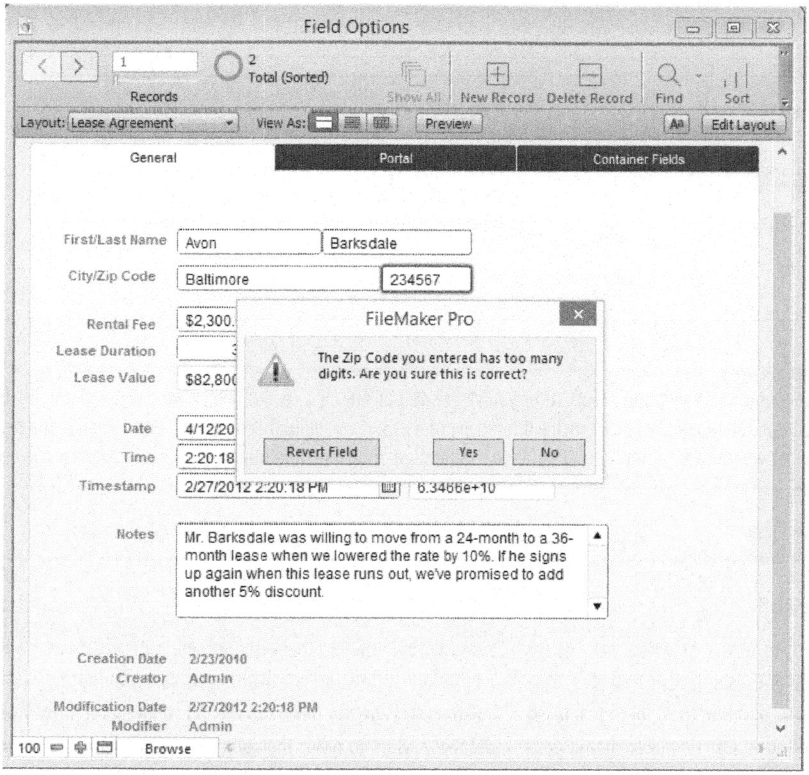

FIGURE 7-6

*If you enter a bogus Zip
code in your database
(background), you see
your custom message.
Click Yes to keep the
invalid Zip code. If you
want to fix it, click No and
you'll be back in the field.
If you click Revert Field,
the field value changes
back to what it was before
you started editing.*

Making Validation Stricter

Your Zip Code field validation options work, but there's a glaring problem: Anybody
can enter just about anything they want and then click Yes to tell FileMaker to accept
the invalid data. It may help prevent mistakes, but it doesn't ensure good information.

To make FileMaker more restrictive, revisit the "Options for Field" dialog box's
Validation tab and then turn off the "Allow user to override during data entry"
checkbox (it's near the top of the window). Since this change removes the "Yes"
and "No" choices when entering data, you should reword the custom message you
entered. Change it to something more informative, like *Zip Codes must contain no
more than five numerals. Letters and symbols are not permitted. Please check your
data entry and try again.*

With these settings in place, if someone enters a bad Zip code, then he sees the
error message shown in Figure 7-7.

NOTE The Validation tab has two other related options. Under "Validate data in this field" you can choose "Always" or "Only during data entry." If you switch to the stricter Always setting, FileMaker enforces your validation rules even when data is modified by a script (Chapter 13). The Always option also enforces validation when you import data in bulk (page 880).

FIGURE 7-7

When you turn off the "Allow user to override during data entry" validation option, FileMaker won't present a Yes button to accept an invalid value. So don't phrase your custom message as a question Express the error as a statement or a suggestion instead.

WARNING Validation occurs *after* you've created or edited a record, which may cause problems if you create a special data entry layout with a limited set of fields. If you validate a field, but don't include the field on the layout where users enter data, they'll see a validation error message but have no way to correct the error.

POWER USERS' CLINIC

Validation Messages

If you don't provide a custom message when you set up field validation, then FileMaker uses a generic message. This message explains the validation option that's being violated in language more suited to a software engineer than a data entry person. By writing your own messages, like the ones in Figure 7-6 and Figure 7-7, you can explain things in a way that relates to the exact type of information you're dealing with. Custom messages make your database a pleasure to use and give it a professional quality.

Bear in mind, though, that although you can turn on as many validation options as you want, you can provide only one custom message per field. Unless you can depend upon your database users to enter the correct format every time, your message should explain exactly how to fill in the field. A message that says, "Your widget description is invalid" gives your database users no help in fixing the problem and could prevent them from getting their work done.

Validation Requirements

When you added validation to the Zip Code field (see page 253), you asked FileMaker to accept only numbers and to allow only five digits.

But data type and character count are just two of the eight kinds of validations FileMaker has up its sleeve. In the Field Options window's Validation tab, you have six more checkboxes. Most of them work much the same way: They compare what you type against some specific condition. But one option, "Validated by calculation," offers a completely flexible way to describe exactly what you're looking for. To use it, you need to learn how to perform *calculations* (mathematical or logical formulas) with your data. They're covered starting in Chapter 10. Until then, here's what the other options do.

STRICT DATA TYPE

This option lets you pick one of three specific validations. You've already seen "Numeric only," which requires that every character in your field be a number. "4-digit Year Date" tells FileMaker to expect a date value, and that the year has to be four digits long (2015 instead of 15). This choice works with text, date, and timestamp fields.

"Time of day" tells FileMaker that only time values that represent real clock times are acceptable. Since time fields can hold any number of hours, minutes, and seconds, you can enter something like *237:34:11* to mean "237 hours, 34 minutes, 11 seconds." But if the field is *supposed* to be the time of your lunch meeting, that value doesn't make sense and this option prevents its entry. It applies to text and time fields (timestamp fields *always* require a time of day).

NOTE   The "4-Digit Year Date" and "Time of Day" options also work on Number fields.

NOT EMPTY

If you insist on having *something* in a field, select the "Not empty" validation option. This option makes FileMaker show a message if you try to commit the record without entering *anything in the field.*

UNIQUE

The "Unique value" option prevents you from putting the same value in a field for two different records. It comes in handy for things like product codes, account names, or course numbers.

EXISTING VALUE

"Existing value" is just the opposite of "Unique value"; it doesn't allow any value that isn't already in that field on some other record in the database. Imagine you've been using a Book database for a while, and you've built up a representative list of Category values. You can turn on the "Existing value" validation option for the Category field to be sure any books you add in the future get one of the categories you've already specified, so that typos are prevented.

This option doesn't make sense until after you've put data in your database. Like all the field options, you're free to turn it on or off whenever you want.

MEMBER OF VALUE LIST

In Layout mode, you can attach value lists to fields to restrict data entry to the values in the list (page 127). But you can also make that list a validation requirement. You'd usually do that if the people using your database have found a way around using your value lists (like using a field on another layout that doesn't have a value list attached to it, for instance). That way, even if the value list doesn't appear on the field, you can set the validation message options as a tighter control over data input.

When you select the "Member of value list" option, a pop-up menu lets you choose which value list to use as a validation. You can choose an existing value list or use the Manage Value Lists command in the pop-up menu to create a new list.

▦ IN RANGE

"In range" lets you specify a minimum and maximum allowable value. FileMaker then protests if you enter a value outside this range. This method works for all the standard data types, since they all have a concept of order. For example, if you specify a range of *A* to *F* for a text field, validation fails for *Sara*. Range validation is most common, however, with number, date, and time values. You can require the Age field to be between 0 and 100, for example, or the Birth Date to be between 1/1/1900 and 12/31/2015.

▦ MAXIMUM NUMBER OF CHARACTERS

As previously mentioned, this option enforces a limit on the number of characters you can enter into a field. FileMaker fields can normally hold a huge amount of text. This option lets you keep things under control. You can use it to require specific kinds of information, like the five-digit Zip code above, or to prevent abuse of the database (for example, by limiting the First Name field to 30 characters so someone doesn't get carried away and paste the complete works of Shakespeare into it).

When you define a container field, "maximum number of characters" changes to "maximum number of kilobytes." Set the value to 1024, and FileMaker won't let you put any file larger than a megabyte in the field.

WORKAROUND WORKSHOP

Minimum Number of Characters

You can set validation for a maximum number of characters, but FileMaker doesn't provide a built-in validation option to enforce a minimum number of characters in a field. If you need to do so, use the "Validated by calculation" option.

To create this calculation, click the Validation Tab and then select the "Validated by calculation" option. In the window that appears, type the following calculation:

```
Length(My Field) ≥ 5
```

Change "My Field" to the exact name of your field. If you want a minimum number of characters other than 5, just change it in the calculation. When you're done, click OK and then try out your new validation.

If you want *more than* five characters, change ≥ to >. If you want *exactly* five characters (no more, no less), then change ≥ to =. See Chapter 10 for much more on using calculations.

▦ Storage Options

It's time to get a little technical. Choose File→Manage Database and select any field. Then, in the Field Options dialog box, the Storage tab (see Figure 7-8) lets you control aspects of a field related to the concept of *storage.* Like a highly organized attic, FileMaker holds onto your information *and* makes it easy to take out again.

There are several options for storing data in a field, and you can even use more than one of them at once. For instance, you can tell FileMaker to store a single value in a field that is the same in every record, no matter how many records you have, or to allow one field to hold more than one value in each record. Plus the Storage tab gives you control over indexing, which can have a profound impact on how your database performs and behaves.

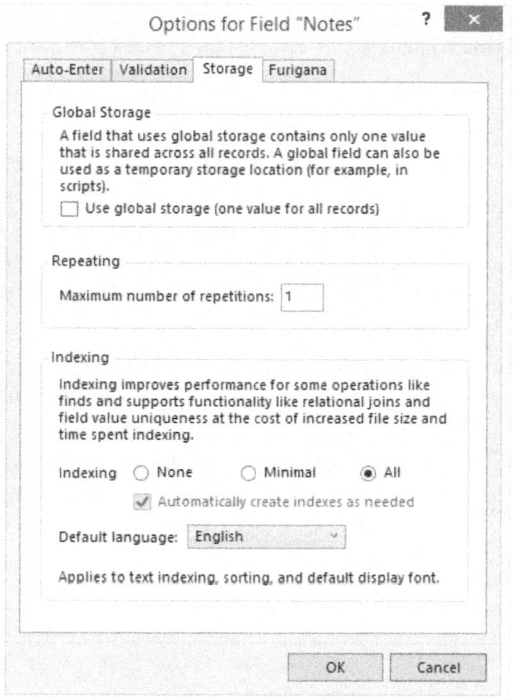

FIGURE 7-8

The Storage tab is where various behind-the-scenes field settings lurk. Here, you can make a field Global so it has only one value for the whole table, or make it Repeating so it has several values in each record. Many of these options are most useful when writing scripts (Chapter 12) or for very advanced purposes.

Global Storage

When you use the "Use global storage" option, everything you learned about tables goes out the window. As a bit of onscreen text explains (Figure 7-8), a *global field* isn't like a column in a table at all. Rather, it's a single bit of storage that can hold one value, no matter how many records you have. If you show a global field in Table view, you'll see the same value in every row (record). And if you change the value in one of those cells, they'll all change when you commit the record. A common use for a global field is as a key field in a relationship (page 146). You can also use a global field as a fixed value in a calculation, or to store preference-type data like your company logo or address. To use the contents of the field, just place it on your layout instead of typing the data in a text block. Then if your company moves, you only have to change the address in one place to update all your layouts.

Repeating Fields

You can turn any field into a *repeating field*. These fields can hold more than one value, each kept in a separate spot (and each shown in its own little box in Browse mode). In the Storage tab section of the Field Options dialog box, you specify the maximum number of repetitions the field can hold. When would you want to use repeating fields? Almost never for normal data storage. See the box below for more info.

Repeating Fields: No Substitute for Related Tables

In a database that's not relational (called a *flat file database*), you have no good way to track lots of different kinds of entities in one database, so in its prerelational days, FileMaker came up with repeating fields to let you store more than one kind of thing in a single record.

FileMaker is fully relational now, but it's also really understanding about supporting all your ancient databases, so the software still supports repeating fields today.

If you're new to databases and are thinking that repeating fields might work for line items in an invoice, go back and read Chapter 6 before you create a repeating field. Never use a repeating field when what you really need is a related table. That path leads only to pain and heartbreak. That said, repeating fields are *occasionally* useful when writing calculations (Chapter 10) and scripts or for some very advanced uses like storing temporary data in arrays or storing resource graphics

for use elsewhere in your file. Other than that, you should avoid them when storing most data for a few reasons:

- **Repeating fields are uniquely FileMaker.** If you want to take data out of your database and put it in some other program (like a spreadsheet or another database program), repeating fields can produce one serious pain in the neck. Likewise for getting data from other programs *into* repeating fields.

- **Repeating fields are inherently limited.** If you create a field with 20 repetitions, then you get 20 spots for data. If you need less, you're saving space for empty fields all the time, which is wasteful. If you need more, you have to modify your fields and then make room on your layout. A relational database, on the other hand, can grow and shrink as needed without modifying the database structure at all.

Furigana

Furigana is a Japanese reading aid that converts complex Kanji characters into syllabic characters for aid in pronunciation. To use this feature, you must have a Japanese keyboard and fonts. A Furigana field watches a data-entry field and updates its display something like a calculation field does. Options on this tab let you select a field to display the guide characters and choose the field to watch.

Indexing

An *index* is a list of all the words or values in a field. FileMaker uses the index to find records quickly, perform the "Unique value" validation, and keep track of how tables are related to each other. All fields have an index, but since these indexes increase the size of your database, there are times when you want to control how they behave. In some limited situations, you may even want to turn the index off entirely. See the box on page 261 for more information on when it makes sense to turn off indexing.

FileMaker's indexing feature takes notes about the data in your fields *as you commit your data,* so that when you enter Find mode, or scroll in a portal (page 155), you'll get faster results.

■ AUTOMATIC INDEXING

Every field starts out with no index, to keep things as lean as possible. Then, as you're working in your database, if you do something that would be faster with an index—like relating two tables using a field, adding Unique validation to it, or using it to find some records—FileMaker automatically turns indexing on for that field. So the first find on a field may be slow, since FileMaker looks through records one by one and builds the index as it's searching. On a really large file, you may even see a progress bar. But once the field is indexed, subsequent finds happen quickly. You almost always want this automatic behavior.

FREQUENTLY ASKED QUESTION

The Dark Side of Indexing

If indexing makes searching faster, why not just index every field?

Indexes have disadvantages as well. An index is useful only if it's up to date. When you change a field value, FileMaker has to store that new value in the table. If the field is indexed, FileMaker has to change the data you've typed, and it *also* has to update the index so that it knows about the changes to the field. Updating the index takes time (not much time, mind you, but it does take time). When all your data is entered manually, you won't even notice the nanosecond lag time. But if your database routinely imports lots of records, the index has

to be updated while all that data is coming in, making large imports painfully slow.

Also, indexes take up space. A database file that has indexing turned on for every field will be much larger than the same file without indexes. For most users, the storage space isn't an issue, but if you have a very large file, and saving space is a priority, you can turn off FileMaker's automatic indexing where for any field. However, you won't be able to use an unindexable field in a relationship, and finds on those fields will never get the benefit of added speed that an index provides. Take care to turn off indexing only for fields that you know won't, or rarely, be searched.

■ MANUAL INDEXING

In very large databases, there may come a time when you want to adjust indexing manually. For instance, if you know you only very rarely search by a person's middle name, you can tell FileMaker not to index that field. Searches that include that field may seem slower, but that's acceptable since you hardly ever do it. On the Field Options Storage tab, select None to turn indexing off for any field. If there is an index, FileMaker dumps it. But if you leave the "Automatically create indexes as needed" option selected, FileMaker will rebuild the index the next time someone searches on the field.

You can also optimize your database by understanding the type of index you need. FileMaker can create two types—value and word. Value indexes are created for text, number, date, time, and timestamp fields, or for calculation fields that return those result types. Since they only store the first 100 characters in a field, Value indexes are smaller than word indexes, and are suited for fields used as keys in related tables.

Word indexes are created for text fields and calculation fields with text results. Each individual word in each record in the table is stored once in a word index. They're best used on fields you'll search, but they can increase your file's size significantly.

The rule of thumb is simple: To search a field efficiently, select the All index, and FileMaker creates a word index for the field. If you'll be using it in a relationship, select Minimal, and you'll get a value index instead. What if you're searching in a field *and* using it in a relationship? It's best to let FileMaker handle it; turn that index back to automatic because you need both types on indexes.

NOTE FileMaker uses the field index when you do a find from Find mode, but *not* when you use the Find/ Replace command. The index points FileMaker to *records,* and since Find/Replace doesn't find records (it finds text inside a record or records), the index does it no good. Therefore, when you do a Find/Replace, you don't make FileMaker automatically index a field.

■ INDEXING LANGUAGE

To keep its indexes as small and tidy as possible, FileMaker doesn't actually store all a field's text (or dates or numbers) in the index. Instead, it performs a little cleanup on the field values first. Most notably, it gets rid of the notion of uppercase and lowercase letters: "Peter" and "peter" become the same entry in the index.

The index also splits the field value up into individual words and removes any characters that aren't generally part of a normal word. In order to do that, it needs to know what language the text in the field is in. If your computer's regional settings are for English, then FileMaker's field indexes use English, too. Usually, that's exactly what you want. But in some cases, FileMaker's following the same language rules as your computer can cause a problem. For example, if you enter another language in a field without changing the index, then your searches can give you unexpected results. If you search in an English-indexed field for *lang* (German for "long"), then you get both "lang" and "länger" ("longer"), but if you set the index to German, you only get "lang." (In German, "ä" is a different character from "a.")

You can select a default language for a field's index using the pop-up menu on the Storage tab of the Options dialog box. A field's language setting also comes into play when you sort records. To use the example given above, when you're sorting in ascending order (A–Z), "länger" comes before "lang" in a field indexed as German (in accordance with rules for German alphabetizing), but after it if the field's index is set to English. See the box on page 263 for using Unicode Indexing instead of a human language.

Unicode Indexing

One language option, called Unicode, isn't a language at all. It's a method of standardizing characters across platforms. If you choose Unicode Indexing, FileMaker forgets everything it knows about languages and uses the internal code numbers for each character instead. When indexing with this option, FileMaker doesn't remove special characters from the index, and it doesn't ignore uppercase and lowercase letters.

A find in such a field is *case-sensitive*. When sorting, FileMaker also uses the character code numbers. Whichever code is lower comes first in the sort order, so capital "Z" comes before lowercase "a."

This option isn't commonly used, though. You're more likely to use Unicode indexing when you want to easily search for punctuation. For example, a field that holds text from a business-to-business Electronic Data Interchange (EDI) document can be well served by Unicode indexing so you can easily find the records that contain "-BIG."

The Web is full of details about Unicode characters. Do a web search for "Unicode table" if you want to find the code for a particular character (*http://unicode-table.com* is a good example).

■ SEEING THE INDEX

When a field is indexed, you can get a glimpse of what's in it and even put it to use. Just click in an indexed field in Browse mode and then choose Insert→From Index. You see the window in Figure 7-9.

FIGURE 7-9

Left: If indexing is turned on for a field, you can click into it and then choose Insert→From Index. FileMaker shows the View Index window. There's one line in the list for each unique value in the field. The list shows the Minimal, or Value index.

Right: If the index's storage options are set to All or to "Automatically create indexes as needed," you can select the "Show individual words" option, and the list shows the word index instead—one line for each unique word or number in the field. When you show individual words, you're also switching the Indexing setting to All, even if you click Cancel after making the selection. But selecting "Re-sort values based on" a different language doesn't change the field's automatic language. It's just a way to temporarily re-sort the index.

This window is handy when you want to quickly enter something you know you've entered in a previous record. Just select the entry you want and then click Paste to have the value inserted into the current field. This trick works in Find mode, too, where it lets you quickly see a list of things for which you may want to search. See the box on page 264 to learn how to use the index to clean up inconsistent data entry.

POWER USERS' CLINIC

Using the Index as a Housekeeping Tool

The View Index window is useful when you want to quickly paste data that's already in another record, but it has another power-user trick up its sleeve—helping you search out and clean up oddball values. For example, you might need to clean up the data in a Street Address field because users have entered their own unique versions of street abbreviations: St, ST, Str, Stt, Bld, Boul, and other creative variations. Here's how you could do the cleanup:

1. In Find mode, use the View Index feature to select a non-standard value (Stt, for example) and then click Paste to use it as your find criteria. Perform the Find to show all the records with that value.

2. Make sure you're still clicked into the Street Address field and then choose Records→Replace Field Contents. The Specify Calculation window appears.

3. Choose the "Replace with calculated result" option to show the Specify Calculation window. In the calculation box, type *Substitute (Street Address; "Stt"; "St")*. This formula tells FileMaker to look inside the Street Address field and find all instances of "Stt" and then replace them with "St" instead. See page 425 for details on how this calculation works.

4. Click OK to close the Specify Calculation window and then click Replace to perform the replace. The found set is clean.

5. View the field's index. The stray entry "Stt" is gone from the index.

Lather, rinse, and repeat for each bad abbreviation.

■ CONTAINER FIELD OPTIONS

Container fields can't be indexed, but they do have a couple of storage options. In the Field Options dialog box, you can turn on "Store container data externally," which tells FileMaker to store and manage container field data outside of the database. Your two storage options are Open, which stores the container field files exactly as they were uploaded; and Secure, which carves up and encrypts the files. Secure storage helps protect your container field data in case someone nefarious gains control of your computer. Outside of the database, securely stored container files are just gibberish. Databases with thousands of container-stored files get a side benefit when using secure storage: The nature of how FileMaker structures the files on the hard drive can make them faster to write and retrieve in spite of the extra work that encryption requires. The next section is all about Container Fields, so read on to learn more about how to create and use them.

NOTE If you're viewing the Fields tab in Manage Database, you have to select at least one field for the Print button to become clickable. Then when you click Print, you'll get details for any field that's highlighted. To select and print just a few, Ctrl-click (⌘-click) each field you want to print and then click Print. If you want a printout of *all* the fields in the table, first select one field and then choose Edit→Select All. Now every field is selected, and the Print button prints them all.

Printing Field Definitions

Now that you've learned how to add auto-enter and validation options to your fields, you may want to create a list of what you've done. The Field Options window is the best reference for the current set of options you've applied to fields, but if something goes wrong with a calculation or auto-enter option, it helps to have a printed snapshot of your original settings so you can see if anything has changed. Even better, you can use the printout as a map for putting things right. Or you can print a field list to send to an associate so she can send you a file with the right bits of data to be imported into your database.

To print a list of all a table's fields and their options, choose File→Manage→Database, switch to the Tables tab and select the table, if needed, and then click Print (it's in the lower-left corner of the window). The printout looks like the field list, except that it's expanded to make room for *everything* about a field.

You don't have to print all of a table's field definitions, though. To print a list of just some fields, switch to the Field tab. The Print button is grayed out until you select at least one field. Now Ctrl-click (⌘-click) each field you want to include in the list. To print all field definitions from the Field tab, select one field and then choose Edit→Select All before you click Print.

Beyond Text: Container Fields

Text and numbers are the backbone of most databases, but as you saw when you placed a PDF of a lease agreement right in the record with its data (page 103), you can also store graphics and other multimedia files in your database. For example, you can store a photograph of each employee along with their personnel record, or add product shots to your inventory database. In either case, you use the graphics much like data. You could print picture badges or product catalogs using your new container fields.

Unlike all the other field types, container fields don't accept typed text. Instead, you use the Insert menu to insert just about any file you want, including pictures, sounds, animation, music, and movies. You can put any file from your hard drive into a container field, like a PDF file, a Word document, or even a FileMaker database.

NOTE Unlike with text and other kinds of fields, you can't sort records by using a container field, and you can't perform finds on them. (But you can create a companion text field with *metadata* or manually entered keywords that will let you find and sort.)

The Insert menu shows four commands for placing items into a container field: Picture, Audio/Video, PDF, and File. Once you select a command and then choose a file to insert, you can also choose whether to store the file inside FileMaker, or just store a reference to the file. In the next sections, you'll learn how you can use these commands to get what you need.

NOTE   This section is about *using* container fields. See page 103 to learn how to create them. And see Appendix A for detail on how to decide which insert command works best for your situation.

Pictures

A *picture* can be in any of more than a dozen formats, including the common kinds like JPEG, GIF, PNG, TIFF, PICT, and BMP (but not, alas, RAW or DNG). FileMaker will also accept Photoshop (PSD) and PostScript (EPS) files. When you put a picture in a container field by using the Insert→Picture command, the field displays the picture itself. But if you use the Insert→File command, you'll just see a file icon and the file name. The four commands work very similarly—you choose a file and select the proper options as shown in the Insert Picture section next. But each command has some variations, which are discussed in their own sections following the tutorial.

■ INSERT→PICTURE

Use the Insert→Picture command to put graphics into your records. Here's how:

1. **Click in the Graphic field.**

   It's on the Picture Field tab of the Lease Agreement layout in the sample database. You've now entered the record, and the Picture field is active.

2. **Choose Insert→Picture.**

   The Insert Picture dialog box appears. This window looks like a typical Open File dialog box in Windows or Mac OS X. Use it to find the picture you want to insert. The sample database for this chapter contains the files shown in Figure 7-10.

3. **Select a picture or other graphic from your computer and then click Insert.**

   FileMaker stores the picture in your database and shows a thumbnail of picture you chose in the Graphic field.

The other insert commands work the same way as Insert→Picture, but what you see in the field varies. Insert→Picture shows a thumbnail of the picture, but the same picture inserted with Insert→File shows only a file icon and the file name.

NOTE   If you need to insert *lots* of pictures into a database, you can save yourself a lot of trouble by using the File→Import Records→Folder command. See page 880 for the full explanation.

■ REMOVING A FILE FROM A CONTAINER FIELD

If you don't need a file anymore, you can remove it from a container field by clicking in the field and tapping Delete. Or choose Edit→Clear to remove it. But you don't have to remove a file first if you want to replace it with another one. Just click in your container field and choose the proper insert command. The new file replaces the old one with no fuss.

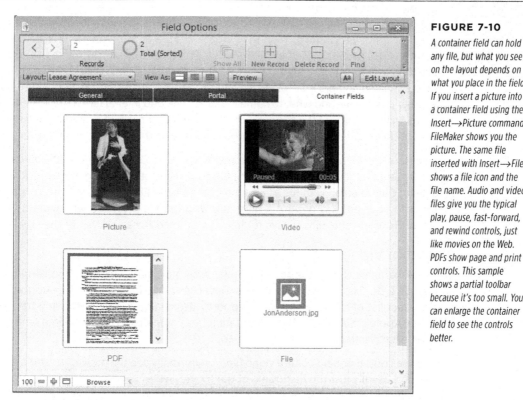

FIGURE 7-10

A container field can hold any file, but what you see on the layout depends on what you place in the field. If you insert a picture into a container field using the Insert→Picture command, FileMaker shows you the picture. The same file inserted with Insert→File shows a file icon and the file name. Audio and video files give you the typical play, pause, fast-forward, and rewind controls, just like movies on the Web. PDFs show page and print controls. This sample shows a partial toolbar because it's too small. You can enlarge the container field to see the controls better.

■ STORING A FILE REFERENCE

The process you just learned is a very simple way to store files along with the appropriate data. But when you place a file inside the database, the database's file size balloons with each graphic you place. Sure it's safe and easy, but there's a better way. Instead of storing the file in the container field, you can store a reference to the file, which describes the path to where the graphic is stored. To store a reference to a file, select the "Store only a reference to the file" option at the bottom of the Insert dialog box before you click Insert.

Even though you've only stored a reference to the file, you can still see the graphic displayed in the container field. But it's important to remember that the real content of the field is a text version of the file path you showed FileMaker when you selected the file. So if the file is edited, your container field will display the changes in the picture. But if the file gets moved or renamed, you won't be able to see the picture unless you insert it again, from the new location or with the new name. Or you could restore the file to its original name or location.

■ EXPORTING DATA FROM CONTAINER FIELDS

Sometimes you're storing a file in a database just to remind you that you have it. But more complex solutions use the database as a document management system. That is, you use the database to keep track of all your files. For instance, a court reporting company may have a database to schedule, track, and create the transcripts for court or affidavit sessions. Then they create a table to store all the related documents—exhibits, transcripts, even invoices for service—that are related to the job. To use the file (for example, if you need to edit the exhibit sheet), click in the container field and then choose Edit→Export Field Contents. FileMaker asks you where you want to put the file and what to name it. Click Save, and FileMaker creates a new file that's an exact copy of the one you put in the container field. After you've edited the exhibit sheet, delete the version in your database and then insert the edited version.

Two handy options make file management a breeze. Choose "Automatically open file" to launch the app that created the file so you can start editing more quickly. Or select "Create email with file as attachment" to have FileMaker hand off the document to your email program. A message with the file attached will open in your email program, and all you have to do is type the address and text of the email.

Audio/Video

FileMaker uses QuickTime to help it deal with multimedia files, so you can insert any file type that QuickTime supports. Because QuickTime is frequently upgraded, the exact list of formats FileMaker supports also changes. If you're having trouble, check Apple's website for the list that matches your version of QuickTime or check FileMaker's Help files (page 35).

When a container field holds a video file, you normally see the movie's *poster frame*, which is usually just the first frame of the movie. When you click the movie, a standard movie controller appears, so you can play, pause, fast-forward, and rewind it. The controller also has a button to adjust the volume and a little knob that shows you where you are in the movie.

Use the Insert→Audio/Video menu command to select a movie or audio file from the hard drive. If the command isn't available, check to make sure you have Quick-Time installed on your computer and that you've formatted the container field to be interactive (Figure 7-11).

Because audio and video files are so large and require so much computing power to play, FileMaker *never* stores these types of files in the database. So you won't see the option to store a reference to the file, because that's the only behavior allowed with this command. Then when you click play, FileMaker loads the data from the file as needed. As with other files that are stored as references, if you move or delete the original file, you'll see a message in your container field telling you FileMaker can no longer find the file. And as with other lost files, you'll need to show FileMaker where the file has been moved with another Insert command. To help avoid losing these files, consider using FileMaker Server. That way, FileMaker will always know where the files are. Also, because it has much more processing power for streaming audio and video, FileMaker Server will give you much better performance than if you're depending on a desktop machine.

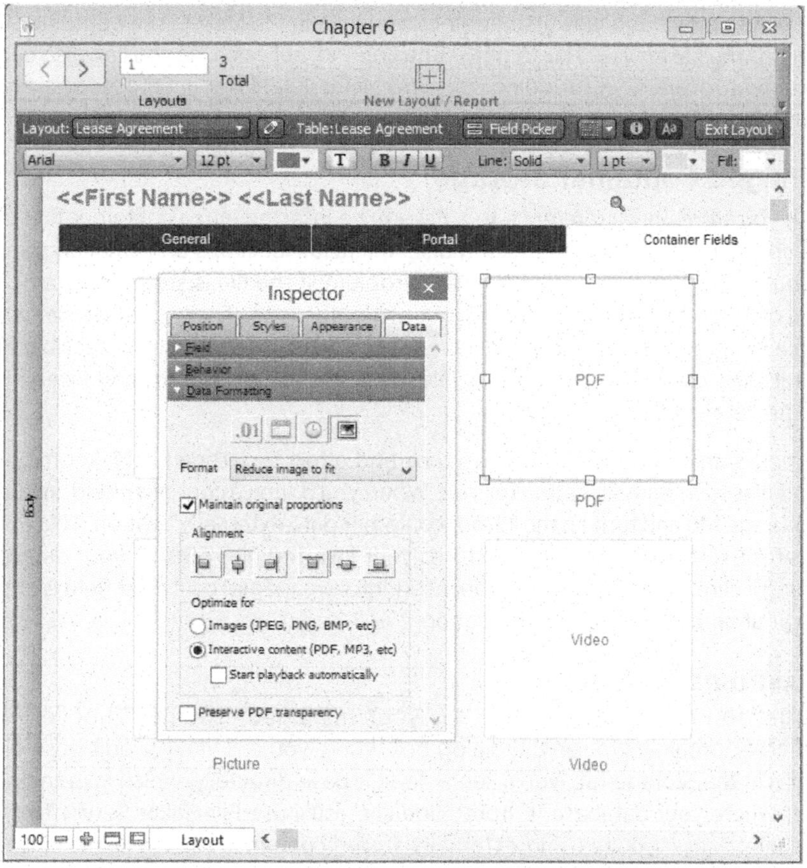

FIGURE 7-11

Container fields must be optimized for "Interactive content" before you can use the Insert→Audio/ Video or Insert→PDF command. If you don't need to see the contents of a PDF displayed inside the container field, you can skip this process and just use the Insert file choice instead.

PDF

As with Insert→Audio/Video, this command is only available if your target container field is formatted to be interactive. You can still insert a PDF into a non-interactive container, but you have to use the Insert→File command. In that case, you won't see the playback controls, and instead of a thumbnail, you'll just see a file icon. So most of the time, you'll insert PDFs into interactive containers. When you do, you get the playback tools, plus a couple of bonuses. If your container field is big enough to read the PDF's text, you can click on the thumbnail and select text so that you can copy and paste it. Just use the proper keyboard shortcut for Copy (Ctrl+C or ⌘-C). Then click into the field (or other app you want to paste into) and Paste (Ctrl+V or ⌘-V).

As with audio and video files, PDFs are rendered more quickly when you're using FileMaker Server because the server can send thumbnails of the pages as you scroll.

File

A plain vanilla container field can also hold a *file*. Since FileMaker doesn't know what the file is supposed to be, it just shows you the file's name and icon. Unfortunately, you can't do anything with a file like this while it's in FileMaker. You can't edit it. You can't even open it and view its contents while it's in FileMaker. The container field just holds the file for you. This might sound limiting, but because you can also export the contents of any field, including container fields, FileMaker databases make good document tracking or retrieval systems.

Managed Container Storage

When you store only a reference to a file you've inserted into a container field, you save space in the database, which makes for faster backups and smaller, peppier database files. But now you have a new problem: If the file is stored on your computer, only users who have access to your computer—specifically to the folder where the file is stored—can see your file. One way to make inserted files accessible to all a database's users is to upload your files to a shared server and then insert them into the database.

But there's an even better way. Save time and effort by letting FileMaker move inserted files to a central location for you. When you define a container field, switch to the Storage tab and turn on the "Store container data externally" option. This option activates External Storage, which stores your inserted files outside your database, keeping it slim and trim. Each file you insert into a managed container field is copied from your computer to another location.

■ BASE DIRECTORIES

You get to choose the location for your managed storage. Choose File→ Manage→Containers to see the dialog box where you can view or edit base directories. On the Storage tab, you'll see a default base directory, which is in the same folder where your database is stored. Ideally, you'll use FileMaker Server to share your databases if you're using externally stored container fields. FileMaker Server protects your externally stored files by backing them up along with your database (page 810).

But you can change that location to a shared volume on a server if you're using peer-to-peer sharing (page 785). Or you can add new base directories and store files from different container fields in different directories. Just make sure you choose a location that everyone using the database has access to, and that they use FileMaker to retrieve the files. It's good practice *not* to give users shared access, so they don't forget and try to grab the files directly from the shared location instead of through the database. If someone does access the file outside of FileMaker, even if he puts it back in the same place when he's done, FileMaker can lose track of it. In some cases, the loss might be due to a name change. But if you're encrypting your files, FileMaker sees those changes as enemy action and, as a safety measure, will refuse to open the edited files. You'll see an error message in the container field telling you the file's been tampered with.

That encryption is another benefit of managed container storage. FileMaker encrypts files as it moves them to your base directory. That way, even if some hacker gets access to your server and finds your external files in your base directory, she won't be able to open secure files, because they're no longer in their original format. And if someone opens and edits an encrypted file, you'll know about it because of the file tampering message.

But if security isn't your top concern, you can turn off Secure storage and use Open storage instead. This leaves your files in their original format in your base directory. However, you should still use the Edit→Export Field Contents command if you need to edit or print externally stored files, since editing files on a shared volume can cause problems with FileMaker Server's progressive backups (page 816).

■ THUMBNAILS

The Thumbnail tab of the Manage Container dialog box lets you control how File-Maker creates and renders thumbnails for your stored files. By default, this option is turned on, with Temporary storage selected. With this setting, appropriately sized thumbnails are created and stored in the cache when you insert each file. As long as the thumbnail remains in the cache, you'll see it in the container field immediately as you're viewing records. If you flip through lots of records at a time, or need to print a large number of records showing thumbnails, the cache can get full. If this happens, the first thumbnails are dumped to make room. So if you need to view or print large sets of records showing thumbnails, switch thumbnail storage to Permanent. It might take a few nanoseconds longer as you're importing each file, but you'll see better performance when you go to view your records.

Layout Mechanics

I n Chapter 3, you learned how easy it is to design a database using FileMaker's tools. You started with a blank layout and then added the elements you needed to make your database run. Now it's time to learn more about how layouts work, and how to use layout tools to make your databases more user-friendly. FileMaker provides different *layout types* for different tasks, like entering data, viewing lists, or printing reports. Each layout is made up of different parts, each with its own job to do, like a body, header, and footer. You'll learn how to add field controls like checkbox sets and drop-down menus, format sets for data display, and automate database processes by creating buttons that run scripts.

> **NOTE** To follow along in this chapter, you'll find it helpful to download the sample databases from this book's Missing CD page at *www.missingmanuals.com/cds/fmp14mm*.

■ Layout Types

You first saw FileMaker's New Layout/Report dialog box when you created the List layout in Chapter 3, but you won't always want to look at your data in a simple list. So before you start building a layout, it's time to learn about layout types and how to select the best one for the task at hand.

Creating a New Layout

To create a new layout, switch to Layout mode and then choose Layouts→New Layout/Report. The New Layout/Report dialog box is divided into four sections (Figure 8-1).

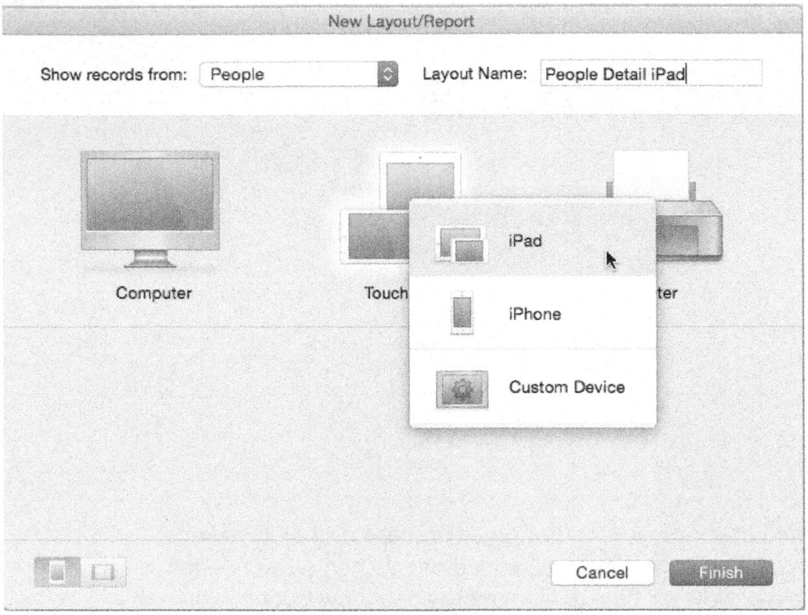

FIGURE 8-1

Click the Touch Device icon, and a pop-up menu lets you choose the appropriate device for your layout. If you choose the Custom Device option, a pair of fields appears at the bottom of the window, where you can type your device's width and height in pixels.

In the top section, you specify the table occurrence you want to use on the new layout and give it a name. All layouts have a *context,* or table occurrence, and the default is the one used on the layout that's active when you create the new layout. (You can read more about context on page 159.) Since even moderately complex databases will have many layouts, choose a simple, descriptive name that will help you identify this layout from a list of all layouts you create for the database.

The second section lets you choose a device where you and your users will view the new layout. The icons let you choose from:

- **Computer.** This option covers all desktops and laptops.

- **Touch Device.** You can choose from built-in Apple iPad and iPhone options, or Custom Device for all other tablets and smartphones.

- **Printer.** This option is the way to go if your layout is destined for paper.

After you've selected a device, the third section shows you the layout types appropriate for that device. Finally, at the bottom left, you can set a layout orientation and click Cancel or Finish. When you click Finish, FileMaker creates the layout using your specs.

For Printer and Report layouts, FileMaker adds extra panels for helping you choose, and even create, the fields you need for the layout type you've chosen. For the Form and List types, you'll use the Field Picker (page 98) to place the fields you need where you want them on the new layout. For a Table layout, you'll use the Modify Table View window (page 42) to add the fields you need to the layout. Read on to learn more about each layout type.

Computer and Touch Device Layout Types

After you select a device, layout type options appear in the New Layout/Report window. Here's the lowdown on each type:

■ FORM

The Form layout type is just like the one FileMaker creates automatically when you start your database—a simple detail layout. It's best suited for data entry, but you can use it in any situation where you need to view a single record at once, like when a customer walks in and the receptionist needs to pull up all of that customer's info. In situations like this, you usually want to display all or most of the fields in the table occurrence, and the Form layout is perfect for that.

■ LIST

To show lots of records on the screen or page at one time, choose List. List layouts show only a small subset of the fields for each record—usually just the ones you need to do a quick search or sort the found set. FileMaker sets up the new layout with the proper layout parts in the right locations, and when it's done, you can use the Field Picker (page 98) to move the fields you need into place.

■ TABLE

When you select Table, FileMaker creates a layout much like Form, but the layout is set to Table view automatically. In Browse mode, you can choose View→View as Table to see *any* layout in Table view, so you rarely need to create a separate layout of this type. But if you want a layout that looks and acts like the spreadsheets you're accustomed to, then a Table view layout gets you there. After you click Finish, the Modify Table View window appears, and you can start adding the fields you need.

■ REPORT

Report layouts are List views, with subtotals and totals to group and summarize your records. FileMaker guides you through the options that determine how your records are grouped and tallied, and then sets up the layout with the Subsummary or Grand Summary parts required. You'll learn how to harness the power of these fields in Chapter 16.

Printer Layout Types

When you click the Printer button, the layout type choices show some typical report layouts, like labels, envelopes, and subsummary reports. Read about each type below.

▪ LABELS OR VERTICAL LABELS

If you need to print a sheet of peel-and-stick labels from your database—to make nametags for every attendee at your conference, or address labels for all those follow-up letters, for example—the Labels layout type is your best friend. FileMaker knows how to set up a layout for most of the standard Avery label types (and a few DYMO ones). You just pick your type on this screen, as shown in Figure 8-2, and then click Next. On the next screen, you choose the fields to print on the labels. FileMaker creates the layout with all the pieces perfectly positioned to fit the labels. The layout may look strange at first, because each field is surrounded by << and >>. (These brackets indicate merge fields—see page 170 for details.)

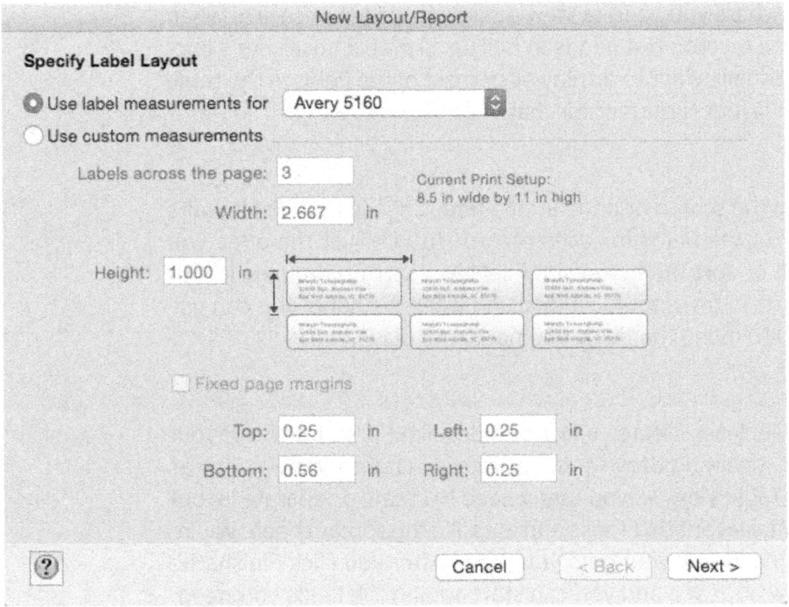

FIGURE 8-2

When you create a Labels layout, FileMaker lets you pick a standard Avery label from a pop-up menu, or if the type you need isn't on the menu, you can enter custom measurements. Look on the label package for that info. It's a good idea to do a test run on plain paper first, in case you need to make minor adjustments for your printer's quirks.

NOTE The "Vertical labels" type applies only to databases that use Japanese text. This layout type rotates the text to create *vertical* labels.

▪ ENVELOPE

If you'd rather print right on the envelope than stick a label on it, use the Envelope layout type. As with labels, FileMaker lets you choose the fields for the address area of the envelope, and then it manages the merge fields for a standard Number 10 envelope (see Figure 8-3). But you can customize the layout with your company's logo and return address by adding text and pictures to the layout.

Since every printer handles envelopes a little differently, the layout probably needs some adjusting to print perfectly. Sometimes deleting the Header part from the layout does the trick. Also, don't forget to choose the right paper size (File→Print Setup in Windows; File→Page Setup on Mac) and orientation for your envelope. On more persnickety printers, you may have to leave the header in place and even adjust its height. Getting things lined up always involves a few test prints, but once you've got it working, you never have to fuss with it again. (Well, until you get a new printer.)

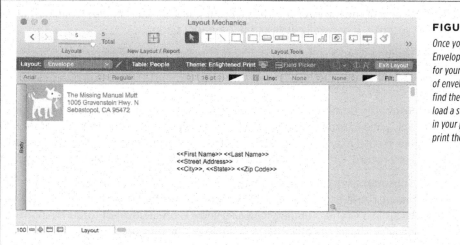

FIGURE 8-3

Once you get your Envelope layout dialed in for your printer, a print run of envelopes is easy. Just find the people you want, load a stack of envelopes in your printer, and then print them out.

REPORT

Choosing a Report layout from *any* of the device types (Computer, Touch Device, or Printer) will take you through the process described in detail in Chapter 16.

Layout Parts

A layout is made up of one or more parts, each of which define how and where your data is displayed. The Body part controls how much space to devote to each record. In Form view, the Body part is usually fairly tall, so it can display fields from the same record from top to bottom. But in a list the Body will be quite short, because it may only display one row of fields per record. Here's how part types work:

- **Top Navigation.** In Browse and Layout modes, the Top Navigation part stays anchored to the top of your screen. Top Navigation appears in Browse mode, whether you're in Form or List view, but it doesn't appear in Table view by default (see the note on page 278 to learn how to turn it on). Put navigation buttons or a button bar (page 373) in a Top Navigation part so people can move around in the database, no matter what record they're looking at.

- **Title Header.** Put objects in the Title Header that should appear at the top of the first page of a printed report. The Title Header appears only in Preview mode and when printed. Some common Title Header objects are the report's title, a company logo, large column headings, and general information about the report itself. If you make a Title Header the height of a full page, it can act like a cover page for your report.

- **Header.** Objects in a Header will appear at the top of every page in a report, *unless* there's a Title Header. In that case, Header objects appear from the second printed page onward. When you're in Browse mode, objects in the Header appear at the top of your screen. Layout titles, column headings, and navigation buttons are generally well suited to Header parts.

- **Leading Grand Summary.** This part appears below the Header and above the Body onscreen and in print. You'll usually place special fields, called summary fields (page 245) in a Grand Summary part.

- **Body.** The Body shows data from each record. In Form view, the Body appears only once in Browse mode. In Preview or Print modes, the Body for more than one record may fit on a page. In List or Table view, the Body repeats once for each record. Other parts are optional, but all layouts must include a Body part.

- **Subsummary.** Subsummary parts work like Grand Summary parts, but they summarize subsets of your data. For example, a sales report showing worldwide totals in a Grand Summary can also show a breakdown of totals by individual country. Unlike the other parts, a single layout can contain more than one Subsummary. See page 631 for more info.

- **Trailing Grand Summary.** Just like a Leading Grand Summary, except it appears below the records it's summarizing.

- **Footer.** A Footer is like a Header, but it appears at the bottom of every screen or printed page, unless you use a Title Footer. Place page numbers, copyright notices, small report titles, and anything else you want to appear at the bottom of your screen or page.

- **Title Footer.** The Title Footer appears at the bottom of the *first* page when printed or viewed in Preview mode. If you have information you want to appear only on the *last* page of your printed document, use the Trailing Grand Summary part.

- **Bottom Navigation.** Like Top Navigation, except it's anchored to the bottom of the screen.

> **NOTE** To show a navigation part in Table view, switch to Layout mode and the choose Layout→Layout Setup. Click the Views table, and then click the Properties button. A checkbox set lets you display Top Navigation, Header, Footer, and Bottom Navigation parts.

Parts in Form View

In Browse mode, and while viewing the layout as a form, you see most parts (Subsummary parts are a special exception, as you'll learn in Chapter 16). As you learned in the previous section, the Body part is essential for showing data from your records.

But most Form view layouts will also have at least one navigation part and either a Header or Footer. Use these parts to make your Form layouts consistent. Ideally, you'll create a Button Bar for your Top or Bottom Navigation part (page 373) and put repeating elements like company logos and layout titles in the same place on every form layout.

Parts in List View

The whole idea of List view is to show many records at once. List layouts have a Body part, and may also include Header and Top or Bottom Navigation parts for consistency and a professional look. To make a simple list into a report, you may also include one or more Subsummary parts and a Grand Total part. Subsummary parts appear once for each category of item the report is sorted by (page 631). Grand Total parts appear either before the first record or after the last record, depending on whether they're Leading or Trailing types. Title Headers and Title Footers don't appear in Browse mode, only in Preview and Print modes.

Parts in Preview Mode

Almost all the parts you see in Layout mode appear in Preview mode. Top and Bottom Navigation parts are the exception, since they're used to help users get from layout to layout and shouldn't contain other information (like layout titles). As in List view, the Grand Summary parts appear before the first record and after the last record (Figure 8-4). Finally, scrolling in Preview mode scrolls only the current page. To see other pages of your report, use the arrow buttons to scroll through the pages of the report.

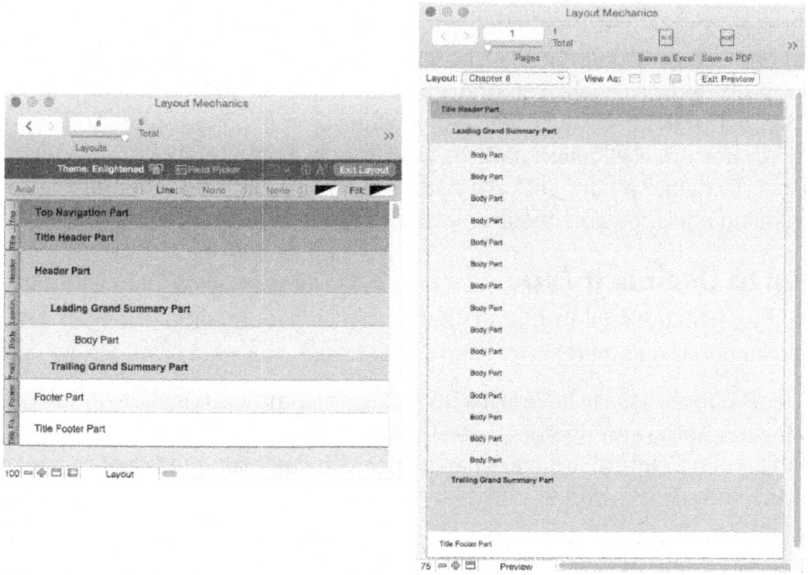

FIGURE 8-4

Left: In Layout mode, you see a Top Navigation, Title Header, Header, Leading Grand Summary, Body, Trailing Grand Summary, Title Footer, and Footer part.

Right: In Preview mode, the navigation part doesn't appear. If this were a multiple page report, the Title Header and Title Footer would appear on the first page of the report and the regular Header and Footer would appear on subsequent pages.

Part Setup Dialog Box

When you choose Layouts→Part Setup, FileMaker shows you the Part Setup dialog box (see Figure 8-5). In this dialog box, you can create new parts and edit, delete, and rearrange existing parts.

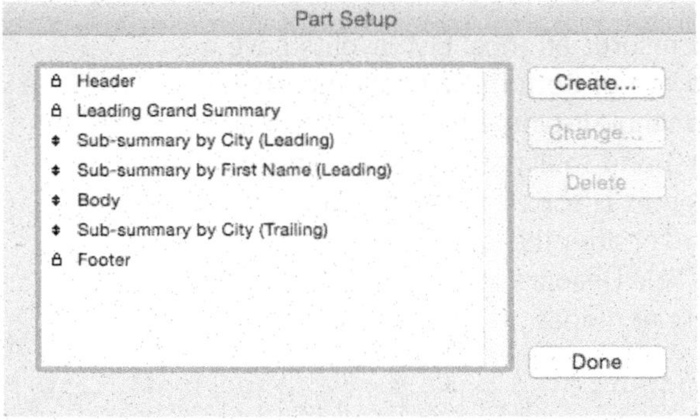

FIGURE 8-5

The Part Setup dialog box gives you options for creating and rearranging layout parts. Parts that can't be reordered have a lock icon to the left of their names. Click the arrow to the left of a part name to drag it to another position in the list to rearrange it on the layout. When you release the mouse, you'll see the layout part switch order in the background. Click Done to dismiss the dialog box.

To add a new part, click Create. To view or edit the part definition for an existing part, select it in the Part Setup dialog box and then click Change. Both buttons bring up the Part Definition dialog box. You'll learn its secrets in the tutorial on page 282. To delete a part, select it and then click Delete. If the part contains any objects on the layout, then FileMaker asks you if you're sure, because when you delete a part, you delete everything on it as well.

You can do some of this dialog box's tasks more simply from the layout. Use the Part tool to drag a new part onto your layout. FileMaker will skip the Part Setup dialog box and go straight to Part Definition. It'll even preselect the part it thinks you want, based on where you drag the new part. For example, if you drag the new part below the body, you need either a Subsummary, Trailing Grand Summary, Footer, or Bottom Navigation part. To view or edit a part's definition, double-click the label. To delete a part, click the part's label to select it and then press Delete. Rearranging parts requires the dialog box, though.

When to Use Each Type

While it's perfectly legal to put any parts on any layout, some arrangements are more common than others:

• Detail layouts usually have just a Body part, or some combination of Navigation, Header, Body, and Footer. These layouts show only a single record, so there isn't much point to Summary parts since you can't see the list of records that would be summarized.

• List layouts usually have Navigation parts, a Header, a Body, and sometimes a Footer. Occasionally, you want a Trailing Grand Summary on your List layout too, since it can show summary information after all the records without taking up space on every page like a Footer does.

Getting Table View to Mind Its Manners

Table view is a real boon if you want a quick and easy way to make your data look like a spreadsheet. With one command, your layout displays data in rows and columns, which you can rearrange and sort. But if you dig a little deeper, then you find that you have a lot of control over how Table view works. These controls lurk under the Layout Setup command. When you click the Views tab, you see that the Table View option has a button that leads you one dialog box deeper—into Table View Properties.

- With the Grid controls, you can show or hide Table view's horizontal and vertical gridlines. Try switching off the vertical gridlines to make rows more prominent. This way, you can more easily read across the data pertaining to a single record.

- The Grid Style option comes with two customizations. You can choose a new color for the grid lines by clicking on the color square and selecting a suitable hue, and you can apply a pattern to them from the adjacent pop-up menu. Keep in mind that setting the pattern to None has the same effect as turning off both the Horizontal and Vertical checkboxes.

- Under Parts, you control the header, footer, and column headers. Headers and footers anchor to the top or bottom of the screen while the records scroll through long lists. Column headers are the field names at the top of each column.

- Headers and footers are normally suppressed when a layout is in Table view. Choose "Include header part" or "Include footer part" to display those parts of the layout. (For obvious reasons, these options have no effect on a layout in which you don't have those particular parts.)

- Since the column headers tell you what information you're looking at, you don't often find a reason to turn off their display. But you can do it if you want to, by turning off "Include column headers."

- More often, you may want to turn off some of the column headers' other features. Stop users from resizing columns by turning off "Resizable columns." Turn off "Reorderable columns" to keep folks from rearranging their order in the table. That way, nobody can move the First Name field so far away from the Last Name field that the data loses its meaning.

- Choose "Use custom height" to set rows to a specific height.

- Printed reports come in many forms. It's common to use many layout parts in a single report: a large Title Header for the first page, and a smaller Header for each additional page; a Leading Grand Summary that shows below the Title Header and before the first record; a Body part for each record; a Trailing Grand Summary to show totals from all records; and a footer to show page numbers and the like.

- Envelopes and labels often need headers or footers just to get the record data to align properly on the printed item. These parts are generally empty.

- You use a List layout to browse records, but you might print it as well. Make the layout do double duty by adding a Title Header or Title Footer. These parts will appear *only* when you print, and you can save valuable screen real estate that way.

Arranging Parts

Building a layout isn't always a linear process. Most people tend to bounce from task to task as they mold the layout to match their vision. You might create and arrange some parts, arrange fields, do some designing, and then revisit field formatting. It is, after all, a creative process.

But usually, you start by getting the parts roughed out. The main thing you need to know is which device you're designing for, so you can take size constraints into account. Although you can scroll on all devices to see more of a layout, scrolling usually only makes sense on a list layout, where people intuitively understand that they need to scroll down to see more records. It isn't critical that you get all the parts exactly the right size at first, but you do want to decide which parts you'll be using, get them in the right places, and then adjust as your layout develops.

> **NOTE** FileMaker only lets you move objects into parts—you can't put them in the gray area below the lowermost part. Sometimes, as you're arranging things, your layout can get cramped, so it's helpful to start with parts that are a little bigger than you really need. You can shrink them again later when you've finished laying things out.

Adding and Removing Parts

Open this chapter's sample database, *Ch08 Layout Mechanics Start.fmp12,* and view the People layout in Layout mode. You'll see three parts: a header, body, and footer. If you were to print this layout, the header would appear on the top of each page, and the footer on the bottom of each page. Right now, though, the header and footer are both empty.

Since this layout is designed for Form view, headers and footers may not be important to you. But you might consider using a Title Header just in case you decide to print this layout. That way any information or graphics you have on the top of the layout, like the ones shown in Figure 4-9, print only at the top of the first page, leaving more room for record data, and using less ink. Here's how to fix it:

1. **If necessary, go to the People layout and then switch to Layout mode.**

   You're now ready to work on your layout.

2. **Choose Insert→Part.**

   The Part Definition dialog box appears (Figure 8-6) and the part types are listed in the order in which they appear in Layout mode.

3. **Make sure Title Header is selected and then click OK.**

   FileMaker adds a Title Header part at the top of your layout, per the Part Definition window's order.

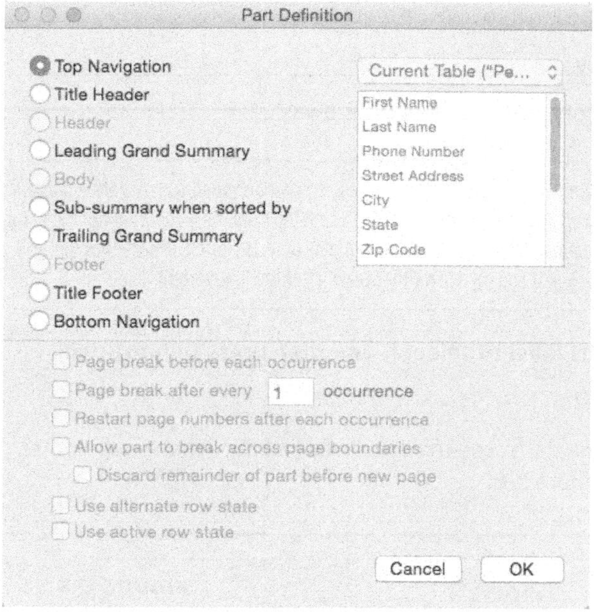

FIGURE 8-6

The Part Definition dialog box appears when you add or modify a layout part or when you double-click a part label. It includes a radio button for each of FileMaker's part types. The options at the bottom of the dialog box don't apply to all part types; the ones that don't apply to the highlighted part are grayed out. Most of these options control how and where page breaks occur in printed reports. But the last two options control visual feedback on List layouts. "Use alternate row state" lets you delineate records by applying a color to even numbered records. "Use active row state" highlights the current record in a list. Make sure to select this option if you've turned off Layout Setup's "Show current record indicator in List View" option. If you forget, it will be hard for users to see which record they're clicked into.

4. **Drag the Title Header part separator straight down to make the Title Header slightly larger.**

   Use Figure 8-7 as a guide.

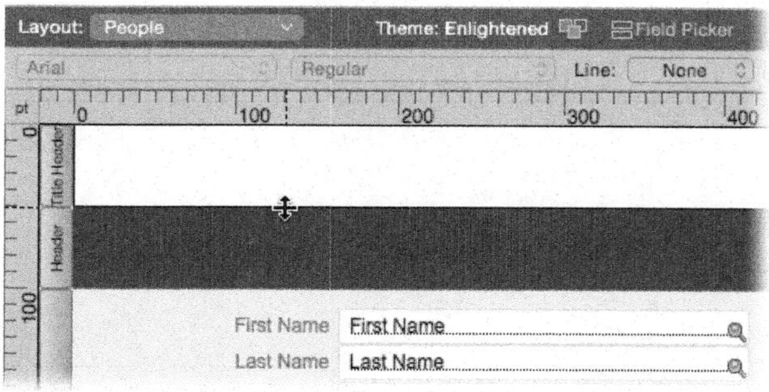

FIGURE 8-7

To resize a part, drag the thin part separator line that extends from the part label across the layout.

Now that the Title Header is in place, you can get rid of the Header and Footer parts. This step is a snap:

1. **Click the Header part label to select it.**

   FileMaker darkens the label to show it's selected.

2. **Press the Delete key.**

   Since this part is empty, it disappears right away.

WARNING If you delete a part with objects on it (like the Body part on your layout), FileMaker asks you for confirmation. If you agree, then the part *and every object on it* are deleted from the layout (but not the database). The good news is that the Undo command will restore the part and its objects. Since FileMaker has multiple levels of Undo, you can restore the part even if you do a few other tasks after the inadvertent deletion.

---

3. **Click the Footer part label to select it and then press Delete again.**

   The Footer disappears.

For more tips on arranging parts, see the box on page 286. When you're done, your layout should look like Figure 8-8.

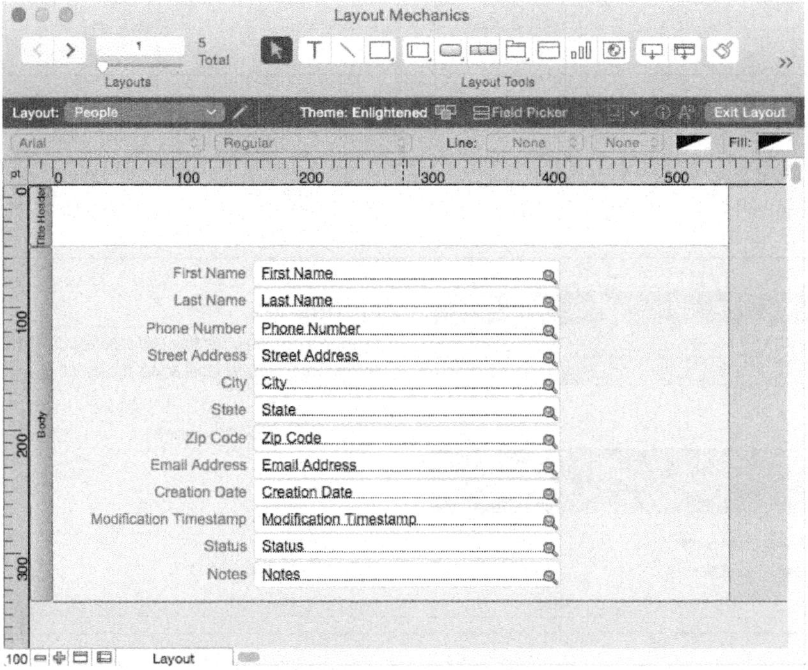

FIGURE 8-8

Once you've added a Title Header and removed the header and footer, your layout will look like this.

Renaming a Layout

If you're looking over your list of layouts and finding some of those names aren't descriptive enough, you can change them. To rename a layout, you need the Layout Setup dialog box. Here's how to find it:

1. **If you're not already in Layout mode, click Edit Layout at the right end of the Layout bar.**

   The window switches to Layout mode. You can tell at a glance because the Layout bar turns black. It also gets several new buttons, including the one identified in Figure 8-9.

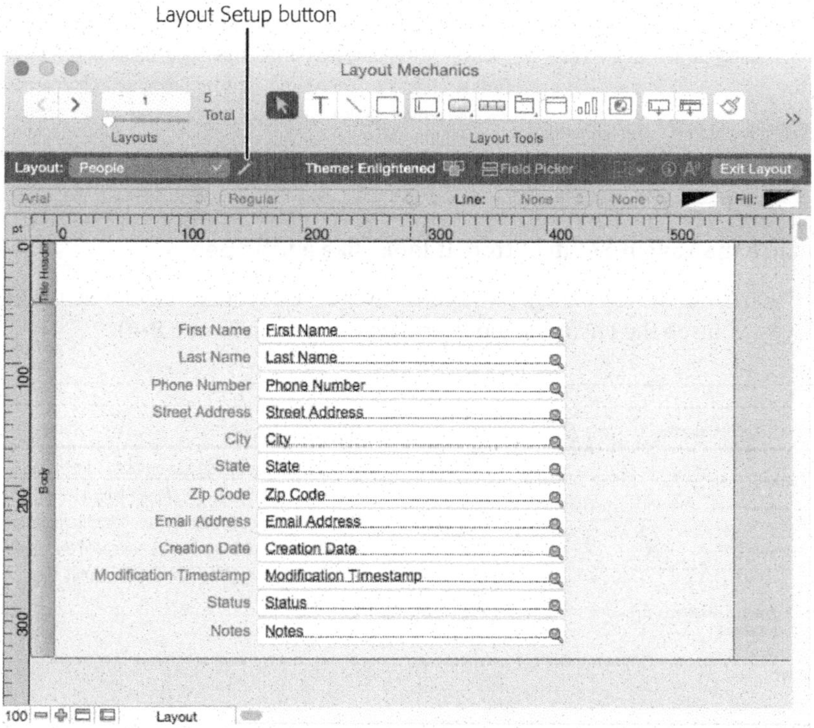

Layout Setup button

FIGURE 8-9

When you switch to Layout mode to edit a layout, the Layout bar turns black. This strong visual cue helps you know where you are. It also adds several buttons, most of which you'll learn about individually, as they are introduced. To rename a layout, click the Layout Setup button, shown here.

Part Manipulation

Sometimes when I try to drag a part's separator line up, it won't go. It seems to get stuck. What am I doing wrong?

FileMaker won't let a part get smaller than the objects on it. For example, if you try to shorten the Body part on your People layout, then you discover you can't go farther north than the bottommost field. Once the part separator touches this field, it simply doesn't go higher no matter how far you drag, because FileMaker won't simply push the objects up to accommodate the smaller size.

Fix this problem by moving things out of the way or resizing them before you resize the part. For instance, if you want a

shorter body, move the fields around first and then shorten the body.

If you want to be cavalier about it, you can press Alt (Option) while you drag instead. When you do, FileMaker changes the way it moves parts. Instead of moving everything below the part up or down to compensate for its new size, everything stays put, and just the dividing line between the two parts moves. In this way, you can move part boundaries right through other objects to, for example, resize the body to encompass newly added fields that landed on the footer.

2. **Click the Layout Setup button. It looks like a little pencil.**

   If you're not the toolbar type, you can also choose Layouts→Layout Setup. Either way, you see the Layout Setup dialog box, shown in Figure 8-10.

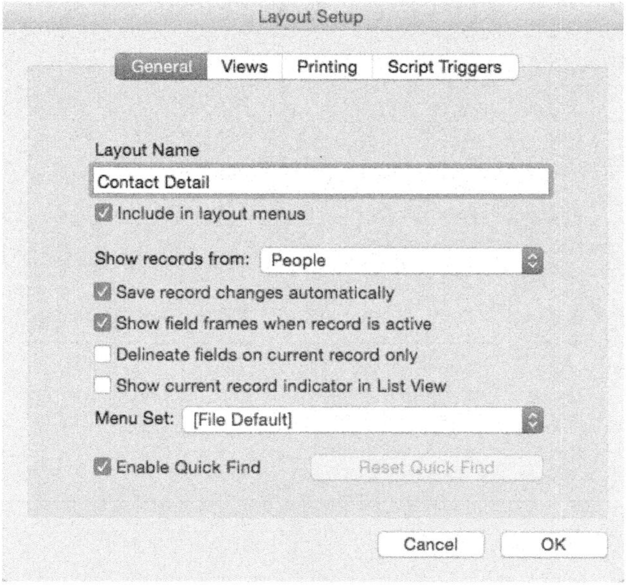

FIGURE 8-10

The Layout Setup dialog box organizes the options for your layout. You can configure which views should be allowed for the layout, how big the print margins are, and which menus appear in the menu bar. And, of course, you can type to change the layout's name.

3. **In the Layout Name box, type a more descriptive name, say, *Contact Detail*.**

   Contact Form or Contact Entry would also work. Choose a naming scheme that works for your company, and then use it consistently. If this were the real world, you would check all the other layouts based on the People table and change their names consistently. For example, you'd change People List to Contact List.

4. **Click OK and then, in the Layout bar, click Exit Layout.**

   When you click Exit Layout, FileMaker asks if you want to save the change you've made to the layout.

5. **Click Save.**

   Now the Layout pop-up menu shows the new layout name.

Setting Layout View

When you create a layout, you get complete freedom to make the layout look just the way you want. By default, there's nothing stopping you (or anybody using your database) from switching your carefully crafted Form view layout to List view, or Table view. Since it doesn't make sense to see this layout in either view, you can tell FileMaker to disable the List and Table view for this layout:

1. **Switch to Layout mode and then choose Layouts→Layout Setup.**

   Remember, Layout mode is where you make changes to a layout.

2. **On the Views tab, uncheck List View and Table View.**

   You've just told FileMaker to make these two menu choices off-limits in Browse and Find modes.

3. **Click OK to close the dialog box and then switch to Browse Mode.**

   In the View menu, "View as List" and "View as Table" are grayed out. So are the corresponding buttons in the Toolbar. Now no one can switch to a useless view of the data.

Found Sets and Layouts

FileMaker knows that the People List and People Detail layouts are showing the same records. In fact, you might use the People List layout to find someone you want and then switch to People Detail to make some changes.

To make switching back and forth as smooth as possible, FileMaker remembers which record you're looking at and which records are in your found set as you switch layouts. Prove it to yourself:

1. **Switch to the People List layout.**

   Nothing new here. Your records appear in a list.

2. **In Browse mode, perform a simple search. For instance, find someone by typing a first name in Quick Find or in the Search field in the heading area.**

   The list changes to show only the matching records.

3. **Click one of the records.**

   Even in List view, FileMaker has the notion of a *current record*. Since you can see several records at once, the program indicates which one you last clicked with a little black marker along the left edge of the record. You can see the marker in Figure 8-11.

4. **Switch to the People Detail layout.**

   Notice that the record you're looking at is the one you clicked when on the List layout. Also, if you use the arrow buttons to change records, then you see that you have the same found set as you did on the List layout. If you perform a different find now and then switch back to People List, FileMaker lists the records of your new found set. In other words, the found set does not change when you change layouts based on the same table occurrence.

Because FileMaker keeps all this in sync, you can use multiple layouts with ease. When you want to find records, use whatever layout makes it easiest. Need to print a sheet of labels? On the List layout, find what you want first and then go to the Labels layout and print.

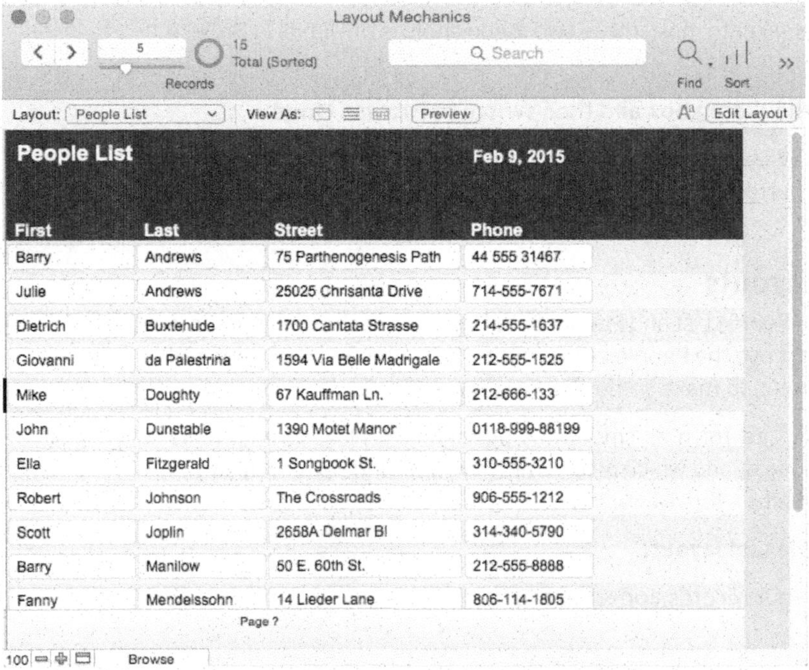

FIGURE 8-11

When you're in List view, FileMaker puts a little black marker next to the record you last clicked (in Table view it's a darker gray square) and highlights it— Mike Doughty's record in this example. That's what FileMaker folks call the current, or active record.

Layout Setup

FileMaker has a few more layout options that haven't appeared in this chapter so far. These options let you control overall aspects of the layout. To see them, go to the Contact List layout, switch to Layout mode and then choose Layouts→Layout Setup. You see the window in Figure 8-12:

- The "Include in layout menus" option lets you determine which layouts show up in the Layout pop-up in the Browse mode toolbar. You might have special utility layouts that are just for you to use for data maintenance. To keep prying eyes out, don't show them in menus. Or if all your reports are run through scripts (if you automate monthly reports, for example), hide those print layouts from view, too.

- If you create a layout and then realize that you chose the wrong context (table occurrence), you can change it with the "Show records from:" pop-up menu.

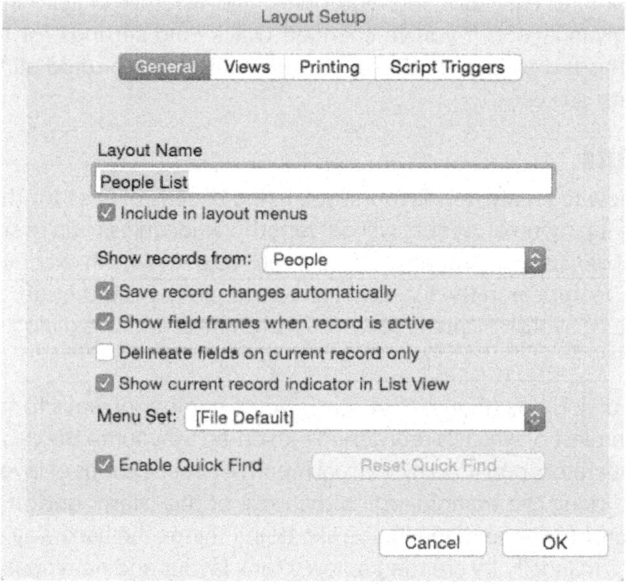

FIGURE 8-12

The Layout Setup dialog box (Layouts→Layout Setup) holds options that apply to the layout as a whole. They range from critical (which table's records this layout shows) to the cosmetic (whether or not FileMaker shows flashy outlines around fields when you edit records).

- The "Save record changes automatically" option is turned on with every new layout. If you turn it off instead, then FileMaker won't automatically commit the record. Whenever you click out of a record after making changes on this layout, FileMaker pops up a window asking if you want to save your changes. You can save, cancel the commit and keep making changes, or revert instead, and toss out all the changes you made since the last commit. You typically use this option when you're working on a small layout where you edit complex data. Normally, of course, FileMaker saves the record changes automatically without bothering you.

- When you're actively editing a record in Browse mode, FileMaker draws a dotted outline around enterable fields, making it immediately obvious where you can enter data because each field is outlined. But some people find this feature unsightly. Turn off "Show field frames when record is active," and FileMaker cuts it out.

- The "Delineate fields on current record only" option suppresses field borders on every record except the one you're working in. This can create a cleaner-looking list layout.

- The "Show current record indicator in List View" option lets you decide whether or not to show the black marker at the left edge of the current record. Since mobile devices are so small, this option gives you back a few critical pixels to show important stuff, like data.

- The Menu Set pop-up menu lets you pick a custom *menu set*. You'll learn all about customizing menus in Chapter 14.

- The Enable Quick Find checkbox lets you determine whether Quick Find is permitted on a given layout. If you've changed Quick Find settings for individual fields on this layout, use the Reset Quick Find button to undo all that customization with one click.

Managing Layouts

Now that you know how to create new layouts, you'll find dozens of uses for them. Pretty soon, your pop-up menu of layouts will get lengthy. And, unless you're some kind of organizational genius, you probably won't create your layouts in exactly the order you want them to appear in the list. You can rearrange the list, though. Just choose File→Manage→Layouts or press Shift+Ctrl+L (Shift-⌘-L). The dialog box is shown in Figure 8-13.

The Manage Layouts dialog box (Figure 8-14) gives you a number of ways to tame your layout list, the simplest of which is reordering—just drag a layout to the desired position on the list. Separators provide a nice visual break between groups of layouts. Add a separator by clicking the triangle just to the right of the "New" button and then selecting Separator from the menu. If you like doing things the hard way, you can create a separator manually by creating a new, blank layout and naming it "-."

Perhaps the most useful organizational tool here is the Layout Folder. Add a folder using the triangle next to the New button and naming the folder when prompted. A layout folder can contain any number of layouts and subfolders. Drag a layout from the list onto a folder to place it inside. When viewing the Layout pop-up menu in the toolbar, you'll then see your folders listed with arrows pointing to submenus of the layouts they contain. Once you have your layouts placed in folders, you can simplify the list by closing the ones you aren't working with.

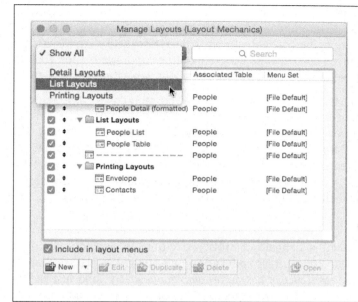

FIGURE 8-13

This version of the Manage Layouts dialog box, has more layouts than your sample file for illustration purposes. The pop-up menu at the top of the window contains a list of your Layout folders. Pick a folder from that menu to temporarily hide all other folders and layouts from the list. Drag the double arrow to the left of a layout's name to reorder the list and thus rearrange layout order. And so you don't have to visit each layout and its Layout Setup window individually, the checkbox in the left column lets you determine whether a layout appears in the Layout pop-up menu.

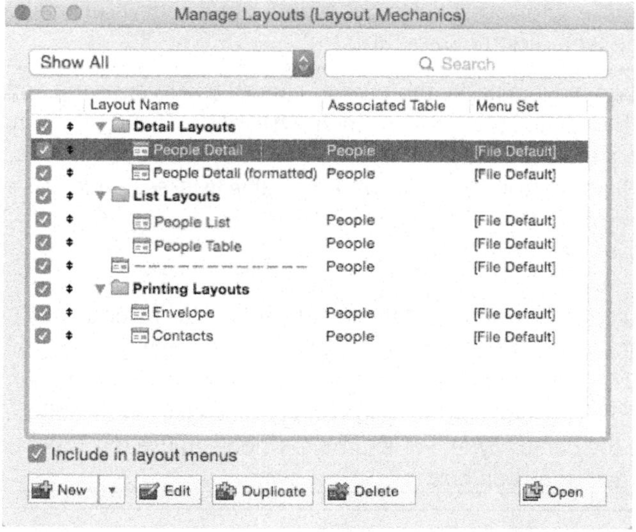

FIGURE 8-14

When you select a layout in the Manage Layouts dialog box, the four right-hand buttons at the bottom of the window become available. Click Edit to open the Layout Setup dialog box. Duplicate creates a new layout just like the selected one with the word "Copy" appended to the layout's name. Click Delete, and you have one opportunity to change your mind. If you don't cancel, FileMaker deletes the selected layout for good; the Undo command won't bring it back. Open, off to the bottom right of the dialog box, will bring up the selected layout in Browse mode and in a new window.

■ Formatting Fields

Field formats range from controls, which let you add checkbox sets or pop-up menus to a field, to simple date or currency formatting. All field formatting is done on the Inspector's Data tab. Most of those options are grayed out unless you have a field selected. Specific options that aren't applicable to the type of field you have selected may also appear grayed out. Other objects, like buttons or drawn shapes, can't be formatted as fields, so they won't activate field options when they're selected.

At the top of the Data tab is the Field section, where you apply controls like checkbox sets or pop-up menus. The Behavior section lets you decide whether users can click in a field to enter or edit its data. The Data Formatting section changes how data is displayed, as for Date or Currency formatting. You always apply formatting the same way: Select the field or fields that you want to format and then click whatever options you want. Or, if you need to check formatting that you've applied previously, select the field and then read the Inspector to see the options you've set.

Field Controls

FileMaker supports all the standard controls you're used to, like pop-up menus, checkboxes, and radio buttons. It also offers pop-up calendars. And if you want to type with just a little assistance, it has *auto-completion,* which works just like the address bar in your web browser: As you type, FileMaker gives you options based on other values you've typed in the field before.

Make the selections you need on the Inspector's Data tab (Figure 8-15). If you can't see your Inspector, make sure you're in Layout mode, choose View→Inspector or press Ctrl+I (⌘-I), and then click the Data tab.

Field Controls have two moving parts: the type of control you're applying and the value list that shows the choices the user sees in Browse mode. Since some controls have different options, those also appear after you've selected a control style. For a refresher on apply field control styles and creating value lists, see page 127. You'll learn about each control's options in the next section.

■ EDIT BOX

Most of the fields you've used so far have been *edit boxes.* These fields are the click-and-type variety that some other programs call a *text box.* No matter what you call it, this sort of control isn't limited to just text. You can use an edit box with number fields, date fields, and so on. Most of the fields on your layouts will be edit boxes, which is why they're the default type. For example, when you use the Tool button to create a field, it starts as an edit box.

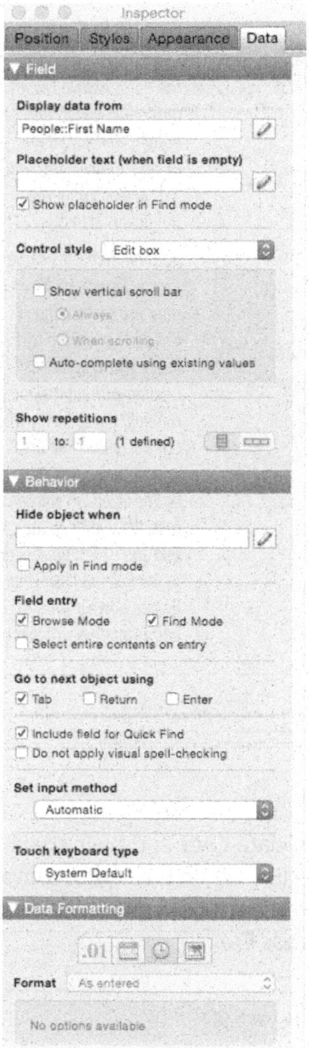

FIGURE 8-15

The Data tab on the Inspector palette lets you configure the type of control people use to enter data into the field. You can collapse or expand the sections by clicking on the triangle to the left of a section's name.

Show vertical scroll bar

If you want to limit the size of an edit box on the layout, but still let people type lots of text, select the "Show vertical scroll bar" option (Figure 8-16). Then you can decide if the scrollbar always appears or is only visible when the user is actively scrolling in the field. The "When scrolling" option cuts down on the visual clutter of the ever-present scrollbar, plus it's become an expected behavior on mobile devices.

Since the space on mobile layouts is already limited, you'll probably make heavy use of the "When scrolling" option on layouts designed for mobile access.

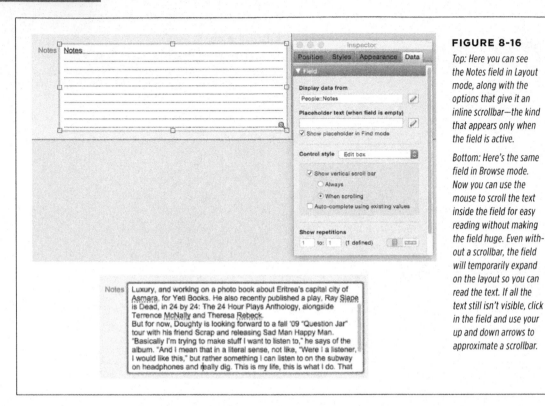

FIGURE 8-16

Top: Here you can see the Notes field in Layout mode, along with the options that give it an inline scrollbar—the kind that appears only when the field is active.

Bottom: Here's the same field in Browse mode. Now you can use the mouse to scroll the text inside the field for easy reading without making the field huge. Even without a scrollbar, the field will temporarily expand on the layout so you can read the text. If all the text still isn't visible, click in the field and use your up and down arrows to approximate a scrollbar.

Auto-complete

There are times when you'll enter mostly the same data over and over again in a field, but you don't want to the restriction of a value list. When the "Auto-complete using existing values" option is selected, FileMaker will suggest entries for you as you type. When it presents the option you need, press Enter.

NOTE To learn more about how auto-complete does its work, see page 300.

DROP-DOWN LIST

This field type *looks* like an edit box, but when you click into the field, a list of available choices appears just below it (see Figure 8-17). It can get annoying to have lists flashing at you just because you happen to be tabbing through the data in a record, so FileMaker lets you stop the list waving by choosing "Include arrow to show and hide list." Now the list is a little more polite; the list doesn't drop down until you click the arrow. When you make a choice from the list, it disappears. Or, if you don't want to enter anything into the field after all, just click the arrow, and the list disappears.

NOTE If you don't apply borders to a drop-down list, then the show/hide arrow appears only when the field is active. Add field borders (at least a right border) to make the arrow show.

FIGURE 8-17

A drop-down list like the one here, showing cities, gives you a list of choices to save you the trouble of typing the one you want. Just click an item in the list, and FileMaker enters it into the field. You can also use the up and down arrow keys to select an item in the list. Finally, you can type the first few letters of an item's name to select it. Once you have an item selected, press Enter to accept it.

Finally, turn on "Allow editing of value list" if you want your users to be able to easily modify the list of choices. When you choose Edit (always the last item in the list), the window in Figure 8-18 shows up so you can modify the value list.

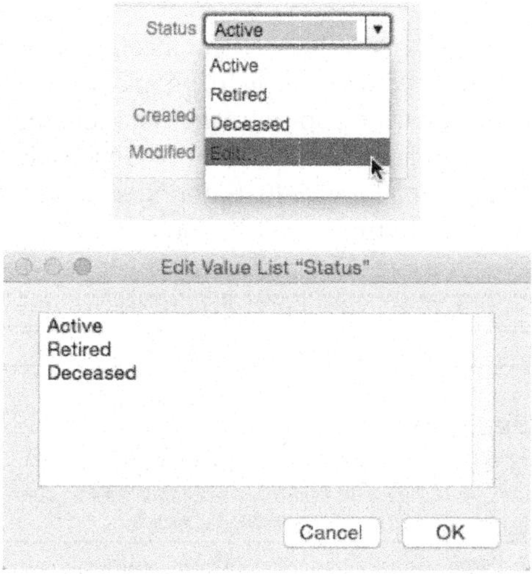

FIGURE 8-18

Top: If you include an Edit item in a drop-down list, you'll see an Edit Value List window when you select Edit.

Bottom: The Edit Value List window lets you add or delete items, or edit items in the list—all by typing in the text box. The name Edit here is significant—you're actually editing the value list. The next time you see the drop-down list, you'll see the changes you made to the list. See the box on page 296 for details. All of this assumes that your value list was created with the "Use custom values" option. You can't edit the items in a value list based on field values.

Drop Down, Pop Up, Turn On

You may wonder how a drop-down list differs from a pop-up menu. They're similar in purpose but have three differences:

- A pop-up menu requires you to make a choice when entering data—you can't type into the field. But with a drop-down list, you can always dismiss the list and type directly into the field instead. When the list pops up, click the field again to make the list go away and then start typing. From the keyboard, press Enter (Return) to make the list go away, or press Esc to toggle the list on and off.

- Drop-down lists work just fine with *thousands* of items in them. Since the list scrolls, it doesn't much matter how long it is. Pop-up menus, by contrast, get very cumbersome with more than a dozen or so items.

- Finally, you can make selections from a drop-down list by using just the keyboard, while a pop-up menu requires a trip to the mouse. The drop-down list's keyboard ability makes it preferable in cases where speed of entry is the priority.

■ POP-UP MENU

When you format a field as a pop-up menu, the look changes significantly, as shown for the Status field in Figure 8-19. Rather than type into the field, people have to click the menu and make a choice. Like drop-down lists, pop-up menus let mere mortals edit value lists, plus they up the ante by including an Other item. When people pick Other from the menu, they see the window in Figure 8-19. Entering a value in this window puts it in the field but *doesn't* add it to the value list. Turn on "Allow entry of other values" to grant this power to your users. (See the box below for advice on the ramifications of letting people edit or bypass your carefully crafted value lists.)

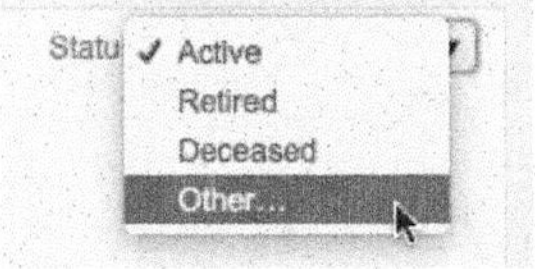

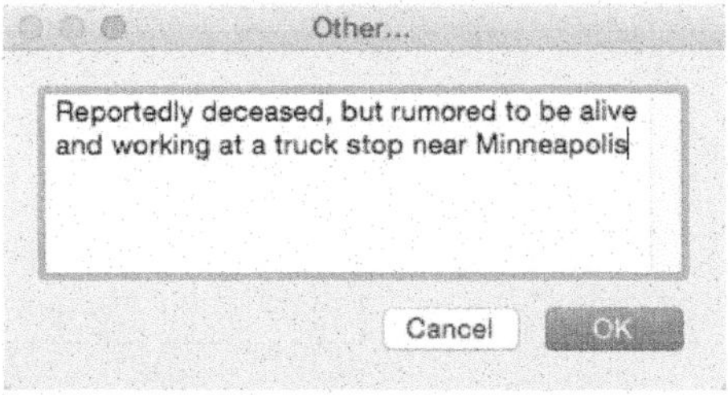

FIGURE 8-19

Top: With a pop-up menu, choosing the Other option lets you add a one-time custom entry in the field. Unlike when editing a drop-down list, this option doesn't change the underlying value list.

Bottom: The Other dialog box has plenty of space (some would say too much space) to type at will. For that reason, and because users can type anything they want into the field, this option should be used sparingly. You wouldn't use it on a field where you're sorting data for a report, for example. If you did, you can expect to get lots of nonstandard entries that may not sort as nicely as they would if you used a field control with more restrictions.

A Cautionary Tale

Not even the smartest database developer can think of everything his users might want to enter in a database, and a drop-down list with a handy edit option might seem like an flexible solution. But use it with caution. When some villainous or misguided soul chooses Edit, she's editing *your value list,* and potentially defeating the purpose for which you created it. Furthermore, if other fields in your database are formatted to use the same value list, *their* list of choices changes, too, because the value list itself has changed.

So remember that value-list-based fields serve two purposes: simplicity and consistency. If you make it easy for folks to add their own items to a value list, you're also making it easy for the value list to become inconsistent and disorganized.

Adding an Other item can undermine consistency even more, because it encourages quick-handed mousers to simply bypass the value list entirely.

If your value list's primary purpose is to gain consistency, then you should consider leaving the Edit and Other options turned off. You can always add new choices to the value list yourself at any time as the need arises.

■ CHECKBOX SET

Figure 8-20 shows two versions of the same field—one is formatted as a checkbox set and the other is an edit box, showing how FileMaker stores the data. With a checkbox set, people click each item to turn it on or off. As they do, the data in the field changes to reflect the checked items. Data is stored as a return-separated value list, which is often more suitable for printing or onscreen reporting than the checkbox version. But don't let people enter data into an edit-box version of the field. If they do, they're likely to enter values that aren't in the value list, and so FileMaker won't have a way to display that value in the checkbox-formatted version of the field. Since text fields are the only kind that support paragraph returns, checkbox sets only work properly when applied to text fields. You'll get squirrelly results if you try to use them on any other field type.

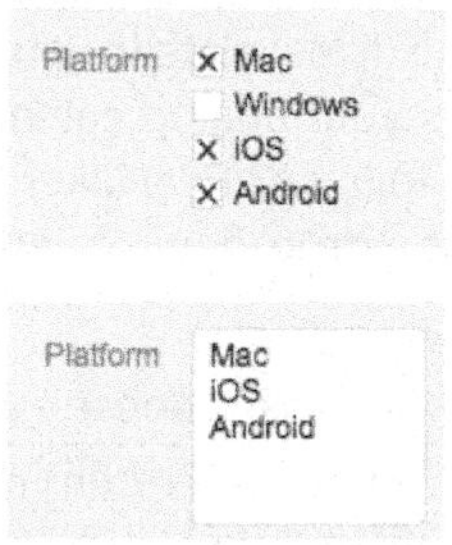

FIGURE 8-20

Top: When you format a field as a checkbox set, it looks like the Platform field shown here. People can select all the platforms they use. FileMaker adds one checkbox for each item in the value list and arranges them to fill the boundaries of the field.

Bottom: A second copy of the Platform field shows data in a return-separated list. Data appears in the order in which you click the items in the value list. If you deselect an item, it disappears from the list.

Checkbox sets can include the Other item, just like a pop-up menu. If someone enters a value that isn't in the value list, FileMaker turns on the Other checkbox to indicate that the field has something more in it.

Checkbox icons

The Icon option lets you decide whether the checkboxes display a checkmark (√) or an X in each box. Choose the icon that makes the most sense for the situation. For example, you might have an Expired field with a checkbox set that uses a value list with a single item—Expired. In that case, you'd want to mark records that show expired products, and it makes sense to show an X, since that symbol denotes something negative. By contrast, if you're giving people a list of all platforms they use at work, the checkmark is more appropriate.

■ RADIO BUTTON SET

A radio button set (see Figure 8-21) works much like a checkbox set. The only distinction is that you can select only *one* item. Click one value, and the previously selected value is cleared out. These buttons work much like old-timey car radios—when you change the channel from, say, smooth jazz to light rock/less talk, the station you were listening to is dropped and the new station takes its place.

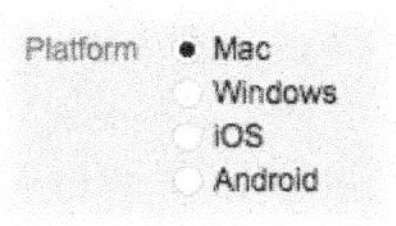

Platform ● Mac
          ○ Windows
          ○ iOS
          ○ Android

FIGURE 8-21

Here the Platform field is formatted as a radio button set, as would be appropriate if you want to select just one option—the platform you use most frequently. Now you can click the right option to set the field, making this one of the fastest field formats for mouse-based entry.

WARNING Some sneaks out there know they can Shift-click to select multiple items in a radio button set. See the box on page 299 to learn how calculations can control these people's urge to get around the system.

Just as with checkbox sets, you can add an Other item to the radio button set. But it's still not a great idea if you need consistent data entry.

■ DROP-DOWN CALENDAR

Typing properly formatted dates into a date field is notoriously tricky. If you don't get just the right combination of numbers and separators, FileMaker tells you the date you've just typed isn't valid. And if somebody swipes your analog calendar, how are you supposed to know what date Thursday next falls on? FileMaker can handle both these problems. It lets you give your date fields a drop-down calendar where anyone can point and click to enter a date.

When you first format a field with a drop-down calendar, FileMaker doesn't give you any visual feedback letting you know a calendar is lurking there, waiting to drop down when you tab into the field. If you want to provide a visual clue, select "Include icon to show and hide calendar." Then you see a mini calendar icon at the right side of your field. That's just to show you it's there; the drop-down calendar itself is a useful size (see Figure 8-22). Tiny as it is, the calendar icon still takes up some room, so you may have to make the field a little wider to display the entire date plus the icon.

One or Many?

Strange as it sounds, pop-up menus and radio buttons both allow *multiple selections*, just like checkbox sets. Just hold down the Shift key while you select an item, and FileMaker dutifully turns it on without turning off the item that's already selected. Chances are you don't want anyone to use this trick to choose more than one value—if that was what you wanted, you'd have used checkboxes to make it obvious that multiple choices are okay.

Unfortunately, there's no direct way to turn off this undocumented feature. If you want to prevent people from picking multiple items, you have to get creative.

Here's one way to do it: Auto-enter calculations (page 405) let you automatically change the value in a field, based on the results of a calculation. You'll use an auto-enter calculation to restrict data entry to the *most recent* choice made in the field.

Here's how to limit your fields to a *single* value:

1. In the File→Manage Database window, select the field you want to fix and then click Options. The Field Options dialog box appears. If it isn't already selected, click the Auto-Enter tab.

2. Turn on the "Calculated value" checkbox. The Specify Calculation dialog box appears.

3. In the big free-entry box on the middle of the window, type RightValues (Self ; 1). This calculation tells FileMaker you want to keep only the rightmost—or most recent—value in the field.

4. Click OK. You're now back in the Field Options dialog box.

5. Turn off the "Do not replace existing value (if any)" option, click OK, and then click OK again to close the Manage Database window.

Now if you try to Shift-click a second item, FileMaker deselects your first choice, effectively short-circuiting the keyboard shortcut. To the user, it *looks* like you can't Shift-click.

You can use a variation of this technique to limit the number of choices users can make in a checkbox set. If you want them to select only three choices, use this calculation:

    RightValues (Self ; 3)

This calculation will only accept the three most recent items a user clicks.

FIGURE 8-22

The drop-down calendar makes entering dates a snap. It has some sweet controls, too. When the field is empty, the current date is highlighted when the field drops down. Or, if there's data in the field already, then FileMaker highlights that date when the calendar appears.

NOTE Like the show/hide arrow on drop-down lists, the calendar icon shows up in an inactive field only if the field has a border. If you're a minimalist on the field-border issue, you can format your field with only a right border to force the icon to appear.

The calendar itself is a little dynamo. You can click the month and year display at the top, and you see a pop-up menu that lets you jump to a specific month in the current calendar year.

Right-click anywhere on the calendar, and the pop-up menu changes to read "Go to today." The calendar closes and plunks the current date into the field.

You can also change the month with the right and left arrows at either side. The left arrow icon moves you backward in time, and the right one moves you forward. Finally, you can move the highlighted date with your keyboard's arrow keys. Tap the down arrow key a few times to see how fast time flies.

But if you get carried away playing with the controls ("Is my birthday on a Friday in 2022?"), remember that the calendar's footer always displays the current date. Just click that display to enter the current date and then click to open up the calendar again. It reorients to today's date.

■ AUTO-COMPLETE

Auto-complete is a strong ally, both for database designers who care about data consistency and for data entry folk who hate to type. Unlike the other field/control styles, you can apply this little beauty to a regular edit box. Once you've turned on the option to "Auto-complete using existing values," the field gets ESP and tries to figure out what you want to enter. Where do these superhuman powers come from? From that old friend, the field's index (page 260). But auto-complete behaves a little differently on edit boxes than it does on drop-down lists. You'll learn the differences in the following sections.

Auto-complete in edit boxes

To turn on auto-complete for an edit box field control, visit the Inspector's Data tab and turn on "Auto-complete using existing values." (The Auto-Complete checkbox shows up only when the field's control style is set to "Edit box" or "Drop-down list.")

When you start typing into an auto-complete field, FileMaker scans the field's index and drops down a list of matching entries. There *is no value list* in this case—it always draws from field values on other records. If you type *T*, for example, then you see a list of entries that begin with the letter T. If you type *R* next, then the list shortens to only words beginning with "TR." Once the list is short enough for you to find what you want, just click the list item to select it.

> **NOTE** The auto-complete list behaves just like a regular drop-down list, so if you prefer, you can highlight an item using the arrow keys and then press Enter.

When Is Auto-Complete Not Useful?

With such a cool feature, one that seems to know what people want to type before *they* do, you may be tempted to add auto-complete powers to most of your fields. But sometimes it just isn't very helpful.

Auto-complete depends on the index to know what to show in its list. At least one record has to have data in the field for FileMaker to have any entries in the index. And indexes increase the size of your file, so if you index a lot of fields just for auto-complete, you may find that the file size balloons. Remember, this feature comes with all of indexing's dark sides as a tradeoff for its power (see the box on page 261).

Another weakness: When someone types a letter that's not used—like X, J, or Z—auto-complete can't show a drop-down

list. This lack of a list doesn't mean auto-complete is broken. It just means the index doesn't have any entries beginning with that letter. The index saves no time in such cases and may be confusing if you don't know why there's no list.

Auto-complete works best in databases with lots of records. And it's usually most effective if the records have a fairly wide range of data in them. For example, if a field is going to have only a few possible values (G, PG, PG-13, R, NC-17), then a drop-down menu or a pop-up menu is a better choice than an auto-complete edit box.

None of these cautions means that you shouldn't use auto-complete. Just be aware of its limitations and the overhead it places on your file.

Auto-Complete in Drop-Down Lists

If your field is formatted as a drop-down list, you can make it even smarter by adding auto-complete behavior. Visit the Data tab of the Inspector, make sure "Control type" is set to Drop-down list and then turn on "Auto-complete using value list." When used in conjunction with a drop-down list, auto-complete uses the values from the associated value list. In fact, in many ways, it works just like an ordinary drop-down list. Now, though, you get the automatic type-ahead behavior you've come to know and love: As you begin to type, FileMaker automatically narrows the list to include items that start with what you've entered so far. This can make your drop-down lists even faster and easier to use.

NOTE When you click into an auto-complete drop-down list that's formatted with a show/hide arrow, the list doesn't appear until you click the arrow or press the Esc key. If you want the list to display as soon as the field is entered, then don't select the "Include arrow to show and hide list" option.

Repetitions

On page 260, you learned about repeating fields, which let you put several values in one field, with a separate edit box for each one. When you put a repeating field on a layout, you get to decide how many times it shows up. No matter how many repetitions a field's definition provides, you don't *have* to show them all on the layout. You can show just the first 10. Or just the last 10. Or numbers 3 through 8.

To control how repeating fields display, use the "Show repetitions" option in the Inspector's Data tab. Enter the number of the first repetition you want in the "Show repetitions" box, and the last one in the "to" box. You can't show noncontiguous repetitions here—you have to enter one beginning and one end, and FileMaker shows those and every repetition in between. If you need to show non-contiguous repetition numbers, put multiple copies of the field on the layout, but specify that each copy displays a different range of repeats.

TIP If the "Show repetitions" and "to" options are grayed out and you see "(1 defined)," it means your field isn't defined as a repeating field. Change that by visiting File→Manage→Database, selecting the field, and then clicking Options. On the Storage tab, set the "Maximum number of repetitions" to any number greater than one.

Once you've figured out which repetitions to show, you get to pick an orientation. Your choices are Horizontal and Vertical, and Figure 8-23 makes sense of them. See the box on page 303 to learn about special formatting considerations for repeating fields.

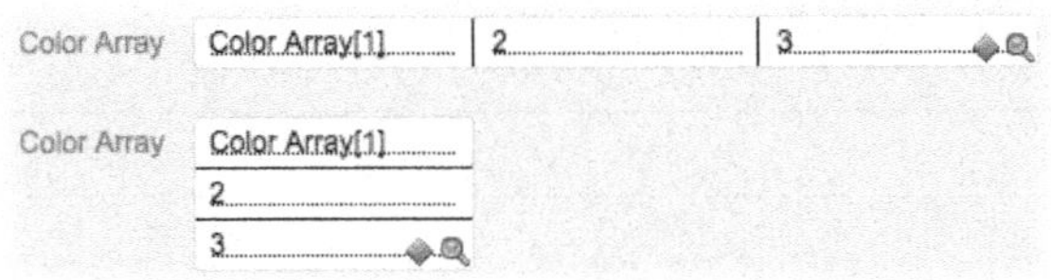

FIGURE 8-23

This layout shows the same repeating field twice, once with horizontal orientation, and once with vertical. In Layout mode, FileMaker numbers each repetition in a repeating field to let you know which one it is. The first repetition shows the full field name and—if there's room—the repetition number in brackets.

Display Data From

Now that you've learned about the most frequently used options in the Field section of the Inspector's Data tab, it's time to look at top of the section, where you can define where the data in a field comes from. To understand how this works, think about the most basic way to create a field: You click the Field button in the toolbar and then drag a rectangle onto your layout. When you start to drag it, you get a dialog box asking which field you need. The "Display data from" option does the same thing. It lets you change the data shown in your field. This option comes in handy if you've got a field formatted just the way you want it and then realize that you need another one just like it. You can start from scratch, or you can Ctrl-Drag (Option-Drag) the field to make a copy and then click the pencil icon to the right of the option to change to the field you need.

Borders and Repeating Fields

While you've got repeating fields on the brain, there's one more formatting choice worth talking about. You can put a border around a repeating field just as with any other field. But this border goes around the entire set of fields, not each individual repetition. You wind up with what looks like one big field, and it can be a surprise when someone clicks it and discovers those repetitions. Wouldn't it be nicer if you could format those repeating fields to look like a standard set of individual fields?

To do so, in Layout mode, select a repeating field, open the Inspector (View→Inspector), and then click its Appearance tab. See that row of six rectangular buttons in the Graphic section of the Inspector? Click the one furthest to the right, and you'll get your border *between* each repetition.

Placeholder Text

Just below "Display data from" is an option that's a champion at saving space on your layout. The "Placeholder text (when field is empty)" option lets you specify static or dynamic text that will appear in the field if there's no data in it (Figure 8-24). That is, you can type text that never changes, like the field's name, or you can write a calculation that changes based on some other condition in your database. For example, if several departments use the same layout for data entry, you could change placeholder text for the Document Name field with a calculation. If the design department thinks of documents as Projects, but Quality Control thinks of them as Policies, you could use this formula to change the placeholder text based on the user's Privilege Set (page 744), like this:

```
Case ( Get ( AccountPrivilegeSetName ) = "Design" ; "Project Name" ; "Policy
Name" )
```

To enter static text, just click in the Placeholder field and start typing. When you tab out of the field, FileMaker puts quote marks around your text for you. If you need to harness the power of the calculation engine, click the pencil icon to the right of the Placeholder field. The Specify Calculation dialog box appears. For a refresher on how it works, see page 144.

Placeholder text is easy for users to understand too, since it's a common design feature on websites and mobile apps—you just click in the field to start entering data. In an edit box, the insertion point appears at the beginning of the placeholder text, and disappears when the user starts typing. If data is deleted from the field, the placeholder text reappears.

If you applied this option to all your fields, then you'd save considerable screen real estate, which is especially helpful if you're designing a layout for use on a mobile device. And since labels are equally helpful in Find mode, there's a secondary option for showing placeholder text when you're searching.

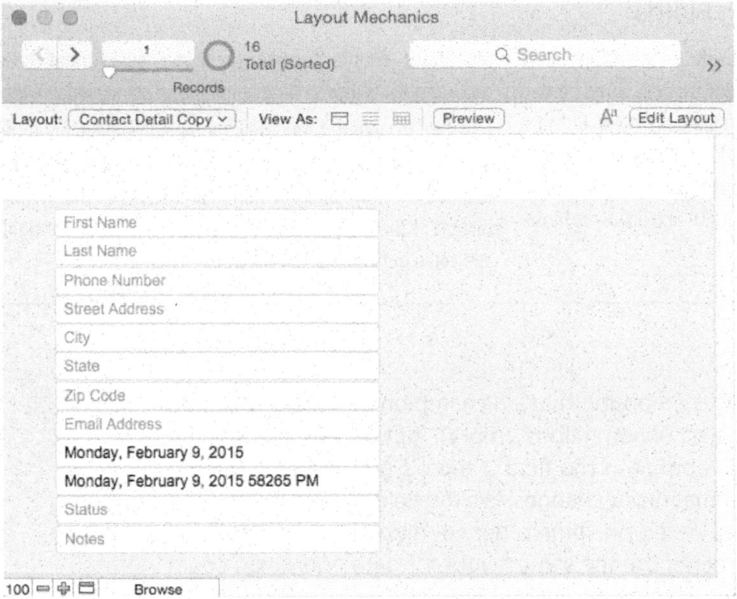

FIGURE 8-24

Here's the layout you saw back in Figure 8-9, now with field labels removed and placeholder text added. Without labels, you can make the layout narrower, making it more suitable for use in a popover or on a mobile device. Placeholder text appears in a medium gray by default, but you can change that using styles (page 333). While it saves space for mobile layouts, placeholder text is also helpful on desktop Form views, because it reduces visual clutter that can take focus away from the data. However, placeholders repeat on each record, so you wouldn't add placeholder text in a list view because you rarely offer data entry on them. Since placeholder text appears in every empty field, you'd increase visual clutter instead of reducing it. Column heads are a better design choice.

You can apply placeholder text to fields with some, but not all, controls. Checkbox sets and radio buttons don't lend themselves to placeholder text because they already show value list data. However, you can apply placeholder text to the following controls: edit box, drop-down list, pop-up menu, and calendar.

All field types can accept placeholder text, but it can be especially helpful for Container fields, because it isn't always clear to new users how to get data into them. So consider making the container field's placeholder into a tip with placeholder text like "Click to insert a graphic" to help users understand how to interact with the container field. For a Date or Part Number field, you might use the field's name and then include some helpful formatting information like one of the samples below:

    Date (xx/xx/xxxx)

    Part Number (PWC-xxx-xxxx)

■ THE FIELD PICKER AND PLACEHOLDER TEXT

If you use the Inspector to assign placeholder text, you must select each field individually and then enter the text. But the Field Picker (page 98) has a super timesaver that you should use heavily when you're first designing a layout. The Labels button bar (Figure 8-25) has an option for creating labels inside your fields as you drag them onto your layout. When you drag fields onto your layout this way, FileMaker uses the field's name for the placeholder text. So if you take care when naming your fields so the names make sense to users who have to figure out what data to enter, you won't even have to edit the placeholder text FileMaker creates for you.

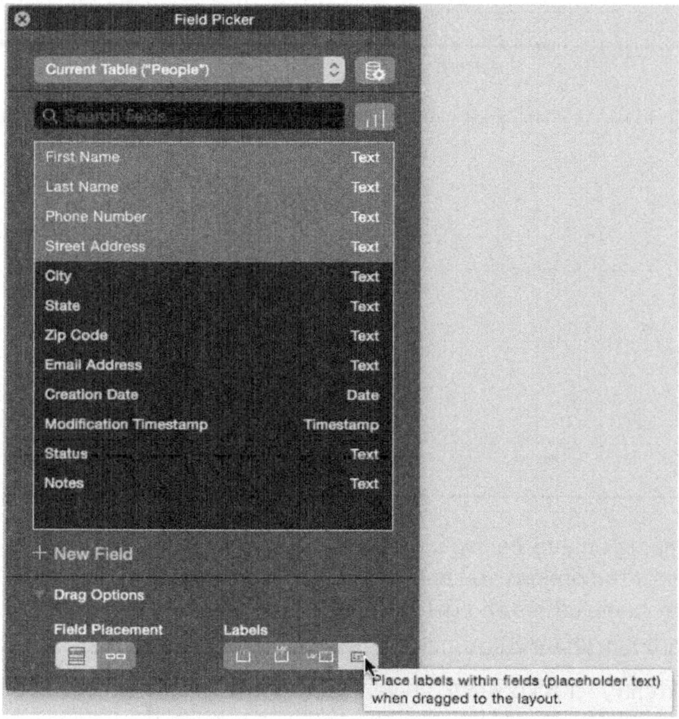

FIGURE 8-25

The placeholder label option is the last one on the button bar. It's not labeled, but the mouse is shown hovering over it, and you can see its tooltip here. This option makes creating layouts for mobile data entry a breeze because you just select the fields you need, choose the Vertical field placement, and then click the inline label option (the button on the far right). Drag the selected fields onto the layout. Except for adding a layout name and the buttons you need, you're nearly done!

Field Behavior

The Field section of the Inspector's Data tab lets you determine how a field looks and how it's controlled. But the Behavior section lets you change the way fields act. You can control whether they show up in Browse mode, whether users can click into them, and what the Tab, Return, and Enter keys do when a field is active. Plus, you can specify how data is entered into a field, and for mobile layouts, you can specify which keyboard type users see when they click into a field. Check out the options in Figure 8-26.

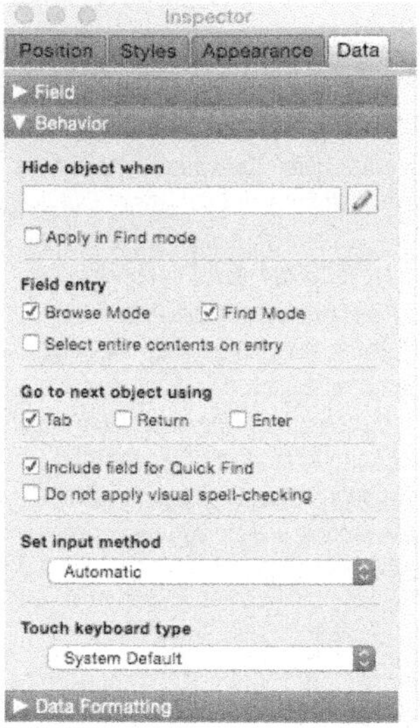

FIGURE 8-26

The Inspector's Behavior section lets you control how fields behave when users interact with them. The most common options are the first two: conditionally hiding the object and determining whether the field is enterable.

Most behaviors apply only to fields, and you add them the same way: Select the field and then select the options you need. The first option ("Hide object when") is a little different from the others and gets its own section on page 308. Here's more on how the other behaviors work:

- Use the "Field entry" checkboxes to prevent users from clicking into specific fields. When you turn the Browse Mode checkbox off, clicking into the field in Browse mode doesn't work. Users can see the data; they just can't click inside the field to add or edit it. Since you often want a field that can't be edited, but can be searched, you'll frequently turn off Browse mode and turn on Find mode. But you're free to turn on or off either checkbox in any combination that suits your needs.

> **NOTE** When you can't enter a field, you can't select its text to copy and paste. So if you want to let people copy the information from an uneditable field, then you can leave a field enterable, but remove their ability to edit using field options (page 241) or security (page 759).

- Normally when you click into a field, the insertion point appears right where you clicked. But sometimes you *always* want to edit the entire field value. For instance, you might have a set of records you update monthly with new sales projections, and you're always replacing what's there with new numbers. In that case, turn on "Select entire contents on entry." Now, when you click in the field, FileMaker selects the entire value, and you can start typing to replace what's there. You can always click a second time to get an insertion point, or start making a new selection. Figure 8-27 shows this subtle difference in action.

- You can press the Tab key to move to the next field in Browse mode or Find mode. The Return key (or the Enter key by your main keyboard) inserts a new line into the field, and the Enter key by the number keypad commits the record and takes you out of any field. But if you prefer, you can configure any or all of these keys to go to the next record instead. Just turn on the appropriate checkbox under "Go to next object using." If you turn a checkbox *off*, then the key goes back to its normal behavior, so if you turn off the "Tab key" checkbox here, then the Tab key inserts a tab into the field instead.

- Quick Find searches all the fields on a given layout automatically. Uncheck "Include field for Quick Find" if you prefer to leave a particular field out.

- Turn on "Do not apply visual spell-checking" to turn off the dashed red lines that appear under misspelled words in that field. Many fields hold data that the spell checker doesn't like, like part numbers, email addresses, and launch codes. Since the red underlines are distracting in those fields, you can turn them off. You can see the change in Figure 8-27.

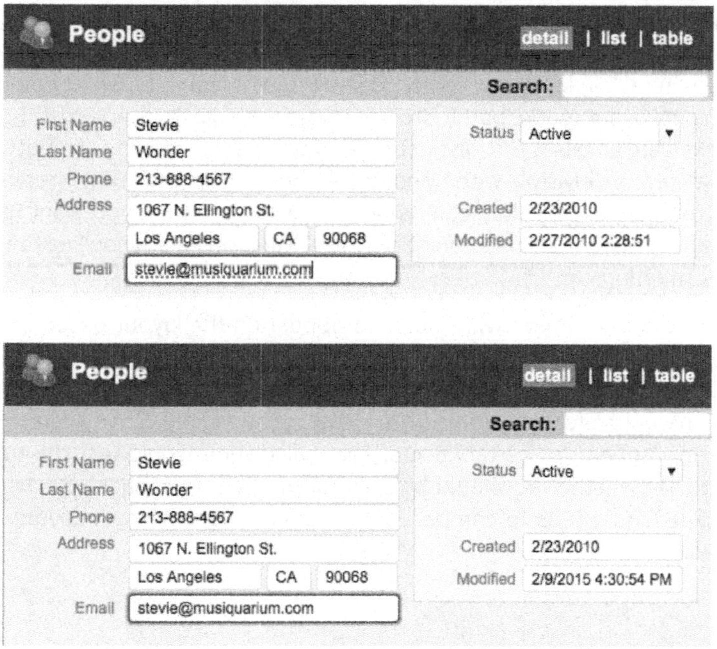

FIGURE 8-27

Top: When you click a field, the blinking insertion point appears where you clicked. In this image, you clicked at the end of the email address. Also notice that FileMaker has underlined the address because it thinks it's misspelled.

Bottom: By changing field behavior settings, a click in the Email Address field selects the whole address, making it a breeze to copy or replace. And the visual spell checker has been turned off for this field, so you're no longer bothered by an underline. You'll also notice the Created and Modified dates no longer appear as editable.

- The "Set input method" option deals with text entry in Asian languages. When this option is on, you can control which text "input method" is used for this field. Your operating system must be configured to allow alternate inputs, and you need appropriate Asian character fonts to use this option.

• The "Touch keyboard type" option lets you choose the keyboard that appears on mobile devices when users tap a field. This option has no effect in FileMaker Pro on a desktop or laptop. Onscreen device keyboards, especially the default System Keyboard, take up a lot of screen space. If people need to see data in one field as they're entering data in another, some keyboards can make that hard, so choose carefully. For example, in a number field, choosing the Number Keypad keyboard not only saves space, but it limits the keys users have to hunt through.

NOTE To keep those keyboards from flying open when you switch layouts on mobile devices, take all fields out of the tab order. Page 321 explains how.

Hide Object When

At the top of the Behavior section, the "Hide object when" option lets you write a calculation that checks a condition to see whether to display the object or not. Despite the fact that this behavior control appears on the Data panel, you can actually apply it to other layout objects, like drawn shapes, tab controls, and text blocks. The "Hide object when" field expects a Boolean value (page 311), so although you can type static text in the field, you should use a calculation instead. When you switch to a layout that contains a conditionally hidden object, FileMaker evaluates the calculation and then decides whether to show the object. You will always see hidden objects in Layout mode, but in Browse mode the objects don't exist if their calculations evaluate as false. This distinction is important for objects like buttons, which might *seem* to be invisible with Conditional Formatting (page 648), but users can still click on them even if they can't see the button. So when you want make an object disappear under certain conditions, use "Hide objects when" instead of Conditional Formatting.

Use "Hide objects when" if you want fields to appear on the layout based on the data entered in other fields. For instance, in an Expenses database you might have a Travel Expenses field that doesn't appear if an event is held locally. In that case, your calculation would refer to the data in an Event Location field. Or you can create buttons that only appear for certain users. That calculation would test the user's privilege set to see whether he should be able to run the script that's attached to your button. See Figure 8-28 to compare how hidden objects look in Layout and Browse modes.

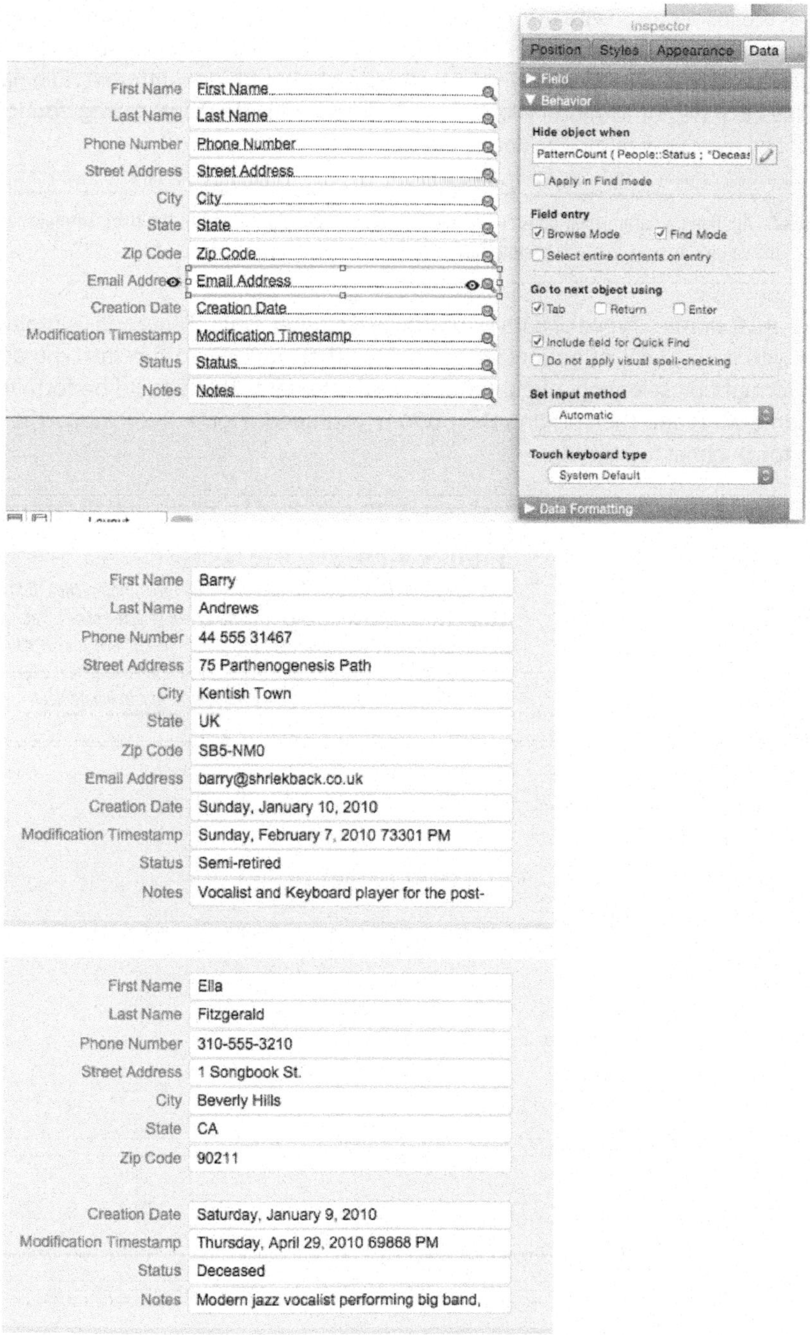

FIGURE 8-28

Top: Hidden objects show a badge when you're in Layout mode. That way you can tell that the object appears conditionally and may be missing when you switch to Browse mode. (For a complete list of layout badges, see Appendix B.)

Middle: The object appears when the calculation evaluates as false.

Bottom: The object doesn't appear when its calculation evaluates as true.

■ Data Formatting

You've learned about field controls and field behavior in the last two sections. Now it's time to tackle *how* the data inside a field is displayed. That's handled at the bottom of the Inspector's Data tab, in a section called Data Formatting. Here's why you might need to format the data in a field: Number fields can store both prices and weights, but they're different types of values and should *look* different. FileMaker provides a series of formatting options for the data inside fields, giving you loads of control over how numbers, dates, times, and pictures look.

NOTE Applying a data format doesn't change the underlying value stored in the field. Formatting only changes the value's display. To see the actual value, click in the field.

There are four main types of data formatting—Number, Date, Time, and Container—each with its own set of options. As with the other options on this tab, you apply data formats by selecting a field (or even multiple fields that should be formatted the same way) and then picking the options you need. Figure 8-29 shows the options for Decimal formatting.

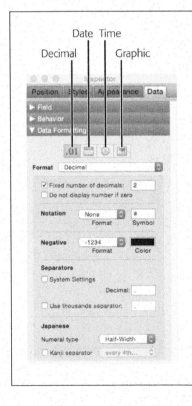

FIGURE 8-29

Here the Inspector's Data tab shows the Data Formatting section. If the option you want is grayed out, then check your selected object. Data formatting can only be applied to fields, or to text objects that contain merge fields (page 170). Also, formats appear only where they're appropriate. That is, you can't apply a Number format to a Date field.

Number Formatting

Use Number formatting to select the best method of displaying the data from fields that are formatted as Number fields. There are six main choices, each of which has a different set of options.

■ GENERAL

The default format is called General, and it either rounds its value or converts it to scientific notation so that the value can be displayed. If you entered 3.141592653 589793238462643383279502884197169 into a narrow field, the value might be rounded to 3.14169157 to fit in a field that's only a few pixels wide.

■ AS ENTERED

If you don't want the automatic rounding and scientific notation you get with General format, simply choose "As entered." FileMaker leaves your numbers alone, so they appear exactly as typed. In this case, if there are too many digits to fit in the field's width, the value is truncated instead of rounded.

■ BOOLEAN

Boolean data has only two values: true or false (see page 672 for more on how Boolean logic works). Unlike some other database programs that have Boolean as a field type, FileMaker lets you format any number field as a Boolean value. Then you use the field as a test for some condition or marker that you want to be able to search your data for. For example, you might mark a People table to flag customers who get holiday cards.

When you format a number field as Boolean, you get to determine how the true and false (or zero and non-zero) values are displayed. The default settings are Yes for true (or non-zero) and No for false (or zero). In the holiday card example, you may be tempted to turn this option on, and use Send Card and Don't Send Card as the display values. Unfortunately, FileMaker lops off anything past the first *seven* characters for each display value. So you have to stick with short and sweet values, like True and False.

TIP Use the Boolean format to make an indicator dot for display in a list or other area where space is at a premium. In the non-zero field, type "•" (or another bullet character) and remove the settings for the zero display. Now you can put a tiny field in a list and only true values show in the list. This reduced clutter can really help you scan a long list of records and find the ones that meet specific criteria.

■ DECIMAL

The Decimal format has a large number of options. If your Inspector can't show all the Decimal options, you can either drag the Inspector's bottom edge to make it taller, or click the triangles to the left of the Field and Behavior section titles to close them up.

- Select **Fixed number of decimals** if you want to force every number to have the same number of decimal places, and then enter a new number if the default value of 2 isn't what you need. If the number in the field doesn't have a decimal part, FileMaker just fills in zeros after the decimal point. To see integers only, set the number of decimals to zero.

- **Do not display number if zero.** Suppose you have a report with lots of numbers, where many of those numbers are zero. For example, a financial report that shows who owes you money (like an Aging Receivables Report) often has more zeros than anything else. All those zeros can make the report cluttered and hard to read. Turn on the "Do not display number if zero" option to make the zeros go away and draw attention to the deadbeats.

- **Notation** lets you associate a unit description with your number field. To display temperatures, enter a degree symbol in the box, and FileMaker will display it with the numbers in your selected field. The drop-down options where the symbol appears are: not at all, before the minus sign (if any), between the minus sign and the number, or after the number.

- The **Negative** line gives you control over how numbers below zero are displayed. You can set a color and choose any one of six negative number formats:

  - –1234 puts a negative sign before the number in the most common U.S. fashion.

  - 1234– puts the sign on the *end* instead.

  - For that oh-so-financial look, choose (1234) instead. It puts negative numbers in parentheses.

  - <1234> is similar, but it uses angle brackets instead of parentheses.

  - The 1234 CR option makes accountants feel right at home when crediting those accounts.

  - The last choice puts a small triangle before negative numbers.

NOTE   The Color option for negative numbers may seem redundant considering you can get the same effect with conditional formatting (page 648). In FileMaker's early years, the "Use color" option was the only way to apply a different color to negative numbers. These days, you can use whichever method you prefer.

- **Separators** are used to partition parts of a number. The box labeled Decimal contains the symbol used to demark the point between the whole and fractional parts of the number. It's traditionally a period, but you're free to change it to whatever single character you want. Turning on "Use thousands separators" will group large numbers into sets of three digits. Here too, you can change the default comma to a different character. Activating the System Settings checkbox takes the matter out of your hands and displays the default separator characters supplied by the current user's operating system.

- The **Japanese** subsection lets you choose among half-width, full-width, traditional kanji, or modern kanji for your numerals. You can also turn on kanji-specific separators.

■ CURRENCY

The Currency option is almost exactly like Decimal, except that the Notation label changes to Currency. It's not immediately apparent, but you can configure Decimal and Currency settings independently so you don't lose those oddball decimal settings you slaved over every time you need to use currency. See Figure 8-30 for more detail.

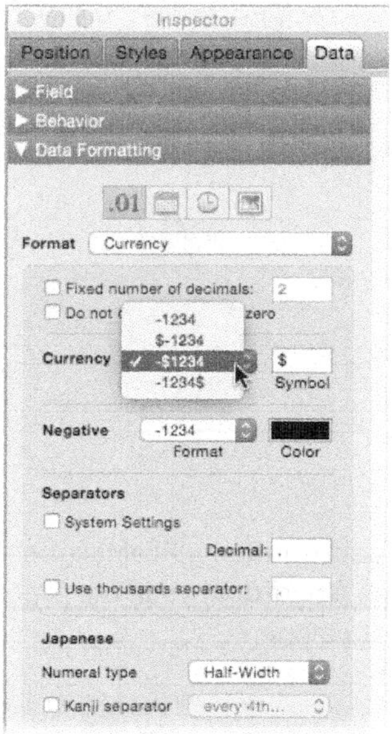

FIGURE 8-30

Currency formatting offers four choices for the placement of the currency symbol (a dollar sign in this example). The first option leaves it out entirely. The second and third place it before the number and before or after the negative symbol if present. The final option places the currency symbol immediately after the number. To use an alternate currency symbol, just type it into the Symbol field.

■ PERCENT

Choose Percent to turn the number into a percent value. FileMaker automatically multiplies the number by 100, and puts a percent sign after it. That way, people can enter *.1* for 10 percent. (Entering the number this way makes math with percentages easier, since your calculations can simply multiply the values instead of converting them first. The other choices under Percent work the same way as under the Decimal option.)

NOTE If you've entered percent and dollar signs into your fields, don't worry. Because the field is defined as a Number type, FileMaker ignores that information when it's performing math on the values. But if you print those fields, you may see duplicated symbols (like $$49.99), so you might want to use the Index technique on page 264 to clean up those stray marks.

Date Formatting

Date formatting works a lot like its numeric sister, but they can only be applied to Date or Timestamp fields. For example, the date at the top of a letter may look best spelled out, but the due date on a list of 25 invoices may be easier to scan displayed in a numbers-only format. Figure 8-31 shows the Date Format pop-up menu.

FIGURE 8-31

The Format pop-up menu gives you nine canned formats, plus a custom one, to pick from. As with other Data Formatting options, some choices in this menu change the options that are available below. For example, if you choose one of the options showing a slash, you can choose something other than the "/" symbol to go between each number by typing it in the "Numeric separator" box. You can also add a leading zero or a space to single-digit day and month numbers by picking from the "Leading character" area's pop-up menus.

▦ AS ENTERED

When you choose "As entered" from the Format pop-up menu, FileMaker shows the date *almost* the same way you type it. If you type a two-digit year, the program changes it to four digits. Otherwise, it leaves the data alone.

▦ PRESET STYLES

The next six choices in the Format pop-up menu offer the most common ways dates are formatted. If you pick one of these choices, you can still configure it slightly, by adding leading characters.

▦ CUSTOM

If one of the canned choices doesn't do the trick, choose Custom. When you do, nine new menus and boxes appear (Figure 8-32), one for each main part of a date display. By selecting different parts of a date from the pop-up menus and adding your own text as appropriate to the boxes, you tell FileMaker exactly how you want the date formatted. For example, if you're in the United States, FileMaker suggests date formats that follow typical U.S. standards (month, then day, then year). But if people in Europe use your database, you may want to construct a custom format in line with their expectations (day, then month, then year).

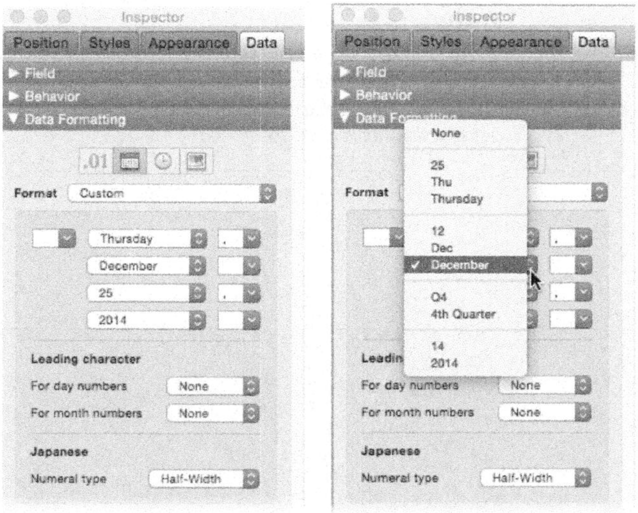

FIGURE 8-32

Left: The Custom date format options consist of a series of text boxes and four Date Value pop-up menus. You can put anything you want in the text boxes, and it appears between portions of the date.

Right: Each pop-up menu includes the same set of choices. The first three let you show the day portion of the date. You can show the day-of-month number, or the day-of-week name as an abbreviation or a full name. Next, you get the same three ways to display the month. If you're so inclined, you can add a quarter to your date in one of two ways. Finally, you can pick between a two-digit and a four-digit year. FileMaker strings the text and date values together to produce the final result.

When you tell FileMaker to format a date with the Custom option, it assembles the final date value from all nine controls, starting from top to bottom, and then from left to right. So whatever you type in the Start Text box (just to the left of the word "Thursday" in Figure 8-32, left) comes first, followed by the first date value. FileMaker then adds the text from the top Between Text box (just to the right of the word "Thursday" in Figure 8-32, left).

If you're getting unexpected spaces in your assembled date, check to make sure you haven't accidentally selected or typed a space into one of these controls. The easiest way is to view the field to figure out where your stray space or character is, and then choose "<None>" from the appropriate pop-up menu.

■ SHORT SYSTEM DATE AND LONG SYSTEM DATE

These options force the data in the field to be formatted as Short or Long settings as defined by the operating system. Both OS X and Windows have system settings that can be configured to display dates in either short or long formats. Examples:

- Short System Date: 12/13/2015

- Long System Date: Tuesday, December 13, 2015

Time Formatting

Compared with dates and numbers, formatting time values is a breeze—FileMaker gives you just a few simple choices. Figure 8-33 shows the Inspector's time formatting options (click the clock icon to activate them).

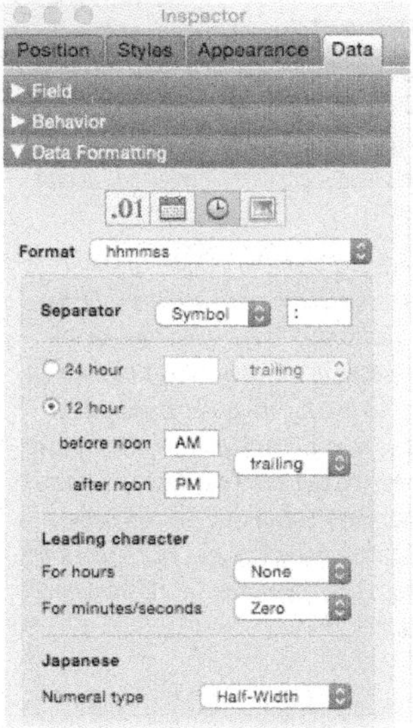

FIGURE 8-33

To have FileMaker show your time values exactly the way you type them, choose "As entered" from the Format pop-up list. If you want to standardize the display of time values, select any other option and customize the settings as you see fit.

Except for As Entered, the Format choices let you narrow down how much detail is displayed. Use the pop-up menu to choose what time information you want to include:

- **As Entered** shows the value exactly as you typed it.

- **hhmmss** tells FileMaker to show hours, minutes, and seconds.

- **hhmm** says you want hours and minutes, but no seconds. If your time value has seconds, FileMaker doesn't display them.

- **mmss** limits the display to just minutes and seconds. If the time value has hours, then the minutes are increased accordingly. For instance, if your field has *1:13:27* and you format it without hours, then you see *73:27.*

- **hh** gives you a field that shows just the hours. Any minutes and seconds are left off.

- **mm** tells FileMaker to show the number of minutes. Again, any hours in the time value are counted as 60 minutes, and any seconds are not displayed.

- **ss** shows a time as just a number of seconds. Every minute counts as 60 seconds, and every hour as 60 minutes. They're added up along with the seconds themselves to produce the final number.

- **Short System Time** shows a time as defined by the operating system and can be configured in your system settings (Windows or Mac). Typically, the Short System time shows hours and minutes, with AM or PM (*8:23 AM*).

- **Long System Time** is also defined by the OS, and typically shows hours, minutes, and seconds, with AM or PM (*8:23:54 AM*).

Normally time values show a colon between each number. You can change this by typing something else in the Separator box. To leave out the separator entirely, clear the box. (This method lets you make military-style times, like *0730*.)

When displaying clock time, FileMaker can use 24-hour or 12-hour notation. In other words, do you want to see *14:23* or *2:23 PM?* When you choose "24 hour," you can add text before or after the value (23:00UTC, for instance). When using 12-hour notation, you get to decide what text you want to represent a.m. and p.m. by typing in the "before noon" and "after noon" boxes.

You can choose from the pop-up menu to the right of these labels to put them on either side of the time value. Like a date value, you get to tell FileMaker how to handle single-digit numbers. Again, you can leave them as a single digit, add a leading space, or add a leading zero.

Timestamp Formatting

Although FileMaker has a timestamp *field* (page 244), the Inspector doesn't have a timestamp option. Remember that timestamp fields really contain two values: a date and a time. So, you use the Date formatting options (the button with the calendar icon) to control how the date part of a timestamp looks, and the Time formatting options (the button with the clock icon) for the time portion. If you add formatting to Date, you must also set formatting for Time, and vice versa. If either format is set to "As Entered," FileMaker won't show your display options until you've selected both Time and Date formats.

POWER USERS' CLINIC

International Super-Date

If people all over the world use your database, you'll quickly discover that date formats can lead to unending confusion. A date like 1/11/15 could mean January 11 or November 1, depending on your location. To avoid confusion, consider a date format that strikes a nice balance between efficient display and unambiguous interpretation: 1-Nov-2015.

To get this format, select a date field, head over to the Data Formatting portion of the Inspector's Data tab, and then choose the Custom option. Configure it like so:

- In the first pop-up menu, choose the number version of the day. (It's the number in the first group of options, right below "<None>.")

- In the top text box immediately to the right, enter a hyphen (–).

- In the second pop-up menu, choose the abbreviated month name.

- In the next text box, enter another hyphen (–).

- In the third pop-up menu, choose the year (you can use either the two- or four-digit version).

- Clear the contents of the two remaining text boxes and then, in the last pop-up menu, choose "<None>."

Now switch to Browse mode. Your date field shows the new format.

NOTE Timestamp formats are a little tough to read because the date and time sort of run together with a scrawny single space separating them. Make a custom date format with " at" (that's *space*-a-t) in the last placeholder, and you get "Fri, May 6, 2005 at 12:30 pm." Much better.

Graphic Formatting

In Chapter 4 you learned how to put pictures, audio/video, PDFs, and files into container fields. Remember that, where it can, FileMaker shows the content right on the layout. When you design that layout, you have some control over how that content is displayed (see Figure 8-34).

NOTE If someone puts a file (Insert→File) in your container field, then you have no control over how FileMaker displays it. FileMaker automatically shows the appropriate icon and leaves it at that.

The pictures and movies you put in the field may not always be exactly the same size and dimensions as the field control itself, so FileMaker has to decide how to make things fit. Should it shrink a big picture down so the whole thing shows, or let it get cut off on the edges? FileMaker lets you decide. With the graphic format options (the rightmost button in the Inspector's Data Formatting Section), you can control scale, position, and proportions.

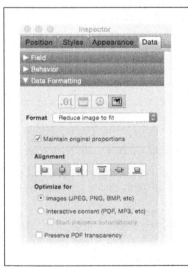

FIGURE 8-34

Using the Inspector's formatting options, you can tell FileMaker to shrink or enlarge a picture to fit the field boundaries, or to crop it—showing only what fits. If you don't mind wildly skewed images, you can also tell FileMaker to stop keeping your pictures properly proportioned. You can align the graphic inside the container field and set options for interactivity with PDFs and audio/video.

■ FORMAT

The Format pop-up menu for the container field lets you decide how FileMaker should handle pictures that aren't exactly the right size. Figure 8-35 illustrates a few of the possibilities:

FIGURE 8-35

*Here's the same photo shown in three versions of the
same container field, but formatted three different
ways.*

*Top: Set the Format to "Reduce or enlarge image to
fit" and check "Maintain original proportions" to see
the whole photo. You may see space on the edges,
though, if the container field has a different aspect
ratio than the image you're inserting.*

*Middle: If you turn off "Maintain original propor-
tions," FileMaker stretches the photo to fill the whole
field.*

*Bottom: Setting the Format pop-up to "Crop to
frame" causes FileMaker to display the image in
its native size. Here the photo's native size is much
larger than the dimensions of the container field, so
whatever doesn't fit isn't displayed.*

- Choose **Crop to frame** if you want FileMaker to crop large pictures, showing
  only what fits. "Crop" might not be the best word choice here. FileMaker doesn't
  actually alter the image—even if you don't see the complete image onscreen,
  it's safely stored in the database record.

- Choose **Reduce image to fit** if you want FileMaker to shrink large pictures to fit but leave small pictures alone. This is the default setting.

- Choose **Enlarge image to fit** to make small pictures grow so they fit the field but are as big as possible. (The more FileMaker has to enlarge the image, the blockier it looks for low-resolution graphics.) Large pictures get cropped.

- Choose **Reduce or Enlarge image to fit** if you want FileMaker to shrink big pictures and enlarge small ones. This setting ensures that every picture in the field (on each record) is about the same size.

TIP When FileMaker reduces or enlarges a picture, it keeps the picture's aspect ratio the same. In other words, a picture that's 4 × 6 inches may not be that *size* in the container field, but its height *is* two-thirds of its width. If you'd rather FileMaker make the picture *exactly* the size of the container field, even if it means distorting it, then turn off "Maintain original proportions."

■ ALIGNMENT

If the picture is small and one of the enlargement options isn't selected, the alignment buttons control *where* in the field the picture appears. For example, select the third button from the left (right-align) and the fourth (top-align) to nestle the picture in the field's top-right corner.

If a picture has been reduced or enlarged so that it fills the field, it might still be smaller than the field in one dimension. In this case, the alignment pop-up menus tell FileMaker where to put the picture along this dimension.

Finally, for large images that have been cropped, alignment controls which portion of the larger image you see. If you align to the top and left, for instance, you see as much of the top-left corner of the image as possible. You can see the same cropped picture with each possible horizontal alignment in Figure 8-36.

Align Left   Align Middle   Align Right

FIGURE 8-36

A cropped photo is shown aligned three different ways: left, center, and right. FileMaker cuts off each image, but the alignment setting determines which portion of the image is visible.

■ OPTIMIZE FOR

Container fields can hold just about anything, but the type of database you're designing often determines what kind of file you'll store in its container fields. For example, the containers in your sound-effects database probably won't ever store spreadsheets. And since you'll want to be able to play back your sounds inside FileMaker, you'll Optimize your container fields for the type of data they'll store and display. Choose Images for regular pictures, like JPEGs and PNGs. Choose "Interactive content" if the container field will store audio, video, or PDFs. When you do, FileMaker will display the appropriate controls for starting and stopping the content or turning PDF pages. If you insert interactive file types in a container field optimized for images you won't do any harm, but instead of seeing the video or hearing the sound, you'll see only an icon and file name.

Tab Order

When you press Tab while editing a field, FileMaker moves the insertion point to the next field. But what does *next* mean? Normally, FileMaker moves through fields in a left-to-right, then top-to-bottom direction. That works well in many cases, but sometimes it falls short. For instance, on your People Detail layout, when you tab from the First Name field, it doesn't go to the Last Name field next. Instead, it goes to the Status field (a pop-up menu, so you can't type into it), which is probably not what you want. And what if you want to be able to tab to a button? You need to customize the *tab order* to make that work. In other words, you tell FileMaker in what order it should tab through the fields and other objects on a layout.

Customizing the Tab Order

You can customize the tab order for any layout. To fix the tab order on the Detail layout of your People database, switch to Layout mode and then choose Layouts→Set Tab Order. A few things happen onscreen: You see the arrows indicating tab order, and the Set Tab Order dialog box appears (Figure 8-37). You tell FileMaker what order to use by putting appropriate numbers into the tab order arrows. Put a *1* in the arrow that points to the button or field that should get your attention when you first press Tab. Put a *2* in the next object in line, and so forth.

Chances are, all the arrows that point to fields already have numbers in them reflecting FileMaker's automatic tab order. Clearing and typing into each arrow can be tedious on a layout with many fields. To ease the pain, FileMaker shows the Set Tab Order window, which lets you make a wholesale changes to the tab order.

First of all, you can clear the numbers from every arrow by clicking Clear All. This trick is great because once all the arrows are empty, then you no longer have to type. Just click each arrow in succession, and FileMaker enters the numbers for you.

To quickly add all the unnumbered fields to the tab order, select "Fields only" from the "Add remaining" pop-up menu and then click the Add button. FileMaker numbers them for you using the same left-to-right, top-to-bottom philosophy that the automatic tab order uses. This option comes in handy if, for example, you want to set up a specific tab order for a few fields first and then use the automatic ordering for all fields thereafter.

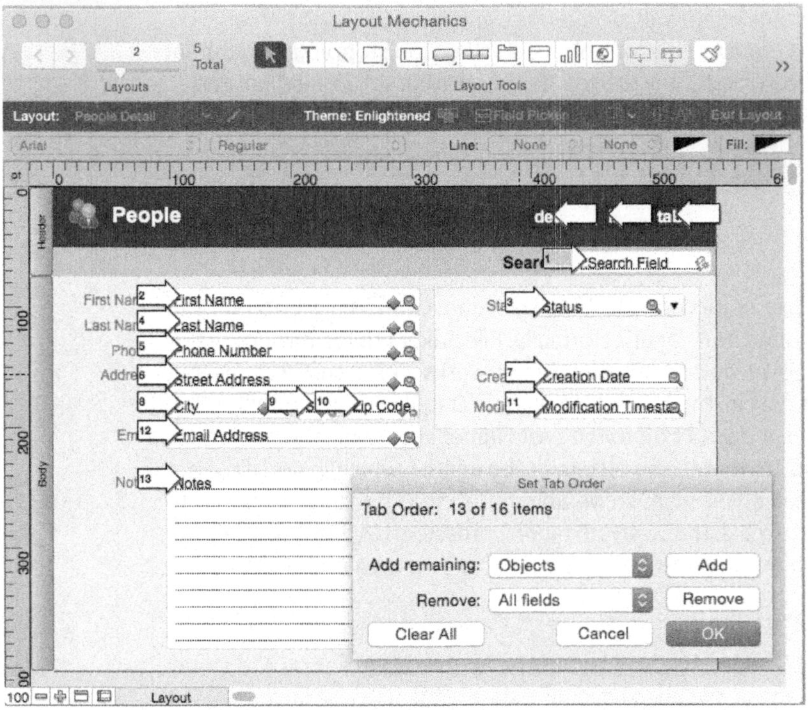

FIGURE 8-37

When you choose Layouts→Set Tab Order, the Set Tab Order window appears. Meanwhile, FileMaker also adds arrows to the layout while this dialog box is open. From here, you can make bulk adjustments to the tab order, clear it, and start over, or manipulate the numbers one by one to get exactly the order you want.

When you're done making changes, either in the window or by editing the arrows directly, click OK. If you decide you've caused more harm than good in this tab-order editing session, then click Cancel instead, and the tab order reverts back to the way it was before you opened the Set Tab Order box.

On your sample database for this chapter, view the People Detail layout. You want to fix the tab order so that Last Name comes after First Name. You can approach this task in several ways, but the following steps show you a trick that makes it easier. You may be tempted to Clear All and then renumber all the arrows yourself. But since you're only *removing* a field from the tab order (the Status field) you can save yourself the trouble. Here's how:

1. **Choose Layouts→Set Tab Order.**

   The Set Tab Order window and its flock of arrows appear.

2. **Click the arrow pointing to the Status field and then delete the number.**

   The arrow pointing to Status is now empty. Your order also now goes straight from 2 to 4, skipping right over 3. Pay no attention to this problem (that's the trick).

3. **Click OK in the Set Tab Order window.**

   If you switch to Browse mode and try out your tab order, then you see that you can now tab right from First Name to Last Name.

This trick works because FileMaker establishes the tab order by following the numbers in the arrows in order. It doesn't give a hoot if there are gaps in the sequence. You've fixed your layout with a minimum of clicks. The same basic trick applies if you need to *insert* a field into the tab order, too. For instance, if you add a new field that should go between 2 and 3 in the tab order, just give it the number 3 spot. When you do, FileMaker automatically bumps number 3 up to 4 (and so on) for you.

Tab Order and Repeating Fields

FileMaker treats each repetition of a repeating field as a separate item in the tab order. It's perfectly legal to have the *last* repetition come right after the *first*—if you're into aggravating the people using your database. But it can be a real drag to have to click each and every one of those repetitions when you set the tab order. FileMaker has a nice feature to save you the trouble.

While setting tab orders, first make sure your repeating field is not in the tab order yet (its arrow is blank). Now click on the field's first repetition: FileMaker gives it a number and the arrow begins to flash. If you click this flashing arrow *again*, then FileMaker numbers that field's additional repetitions for you, in the logical order.

But the magic doesn't stop there: Suppose you have a series of repeating fields. The standard tab order would go *down* each column before moving to the next one, but you'd prefer to tab *across* the rows first. Then once you've completed a row, you want the next tab to take you to the next one.

FileMaker can automatically do this kind of numbering for you, too. When setting the tab order, click the top field in your first repeating field. It gets a number and begins to flash. Now click the top field in the second repeating field. The arrow in the first field continues to flash. Once you've done these three clicks, click the flashing arrow again. FileMaker now numbers all your repetitions properly.

Summed up, you click the repeating fields in the order you want them tabbed to. When you're done, click the *first* one again to let FileMaker know to auto-number them. FileMaker fills out each row of repetitions matching this order.

Preserving the Automatic Order

Until you choose the Set Tab Order command on a particular layout, FileMaker automatically manages the tab order for you. For example, if you add a Middle Name field to the layout, and place it between the First Name and Last Name fields, it automatically goes into the right spot in the tab order—between First Name and Last Name. If you switch the positions of the First Name and Last Name fields, Last Name becomes the first field in the tab order, and First Name comes next.

Once you click the Set Tab Order window's OK button, though, FileMaker hands full responsibility thereafter over to you. If you add a new field to the layout, then it just gets stuck to the *end* of the tab order, no matter where you put that field on the layout, and it's up to you to update the order. If you move fields around so that the tab order makes absolutely no sense, FileMaker doesn't care. It keeps the tab order exactly as you specified in Set Tab Order. So remember that once you make a custom tab order on a layout, you have to maintain it manually if you add new fields.

Buttons and Tab Order

Since buttons (page 365) are an important part of how people interact with your database, FileMaker makes activating buttons as convenient as possible. It even lets folks operate them from the keyboard. When you set the tab order for your layout (Layouts→Set Tab Order), you can put buttons in the mix. If a button is in the tab order, you can tab to it in Browse mode (it gets a thick black outline) and then press the space bar to "click" the button.

While you're at it, you can put Tab Controls in the tab order, too. Once again, the space bar switches tabs.

If you include important buttons and tabs in the tab order, then people can breeze through complex data-entry tasks without using a mouse. They'll thank you.

■ Creating Layouts for Printing

By now you've probably knocked out a few good layouts. Layouts like these meet many typical database needs: You've got a Form layout for finding and viewing individual records, and a List layout for rapidly scanning many records at once. You also want to do *reporting,* an equally important task in a typical database. A report is no different from any other layout as far as FileMaker is concerned. But Report layouts are designed from the ground up to be *printed.* For example, instead of using screen size for its dimensions, a print or report layout uses a sheet of paper. And fonts might be smaller, since you won't be reading details onscreen. Almost no database gets by without some kind of a Report layout, and most important databases have several, from straightforward lists to powerful snapshots of your data's important statistics, like sales by region or inventory by product category.

NOTE If you craft an elegant Report layout and then discover it's printing only *one* of your records (or none of them) instead of the entire found set, you probably need to make a change in the Print dialog box. Choose File→Print and then turn on the "Records being browsed" option. This tells FileMaker to print all the found records.

Here's your guided tour of how layout setting choices will help you use the People database to print a list of people. You can print a report and then file it as a hard copy backup, take it with you on a trip, or mail it to an associate. But FileMaker's reporting powers go far beyond simple lists. Chapter 16 introduces FileMaker's powerful data summarization and reporting capabilities.

Preview Mode

First, you need a rough idea of how your layout should look, since the physical constraints of a piece of paper dictate the working space you have. FileMaker's Preview mode makes it easy to visualize your layout without printing. From the Preview illustration in Figure 8-38, you can get a pretty good idea of how the People List layout is going to come together. It has a header, a body, and a footer. The header includes a title, the date, and some column labels, and the footer has just a page number (these parts print on the top and bottom of each page). The body is the most important part: It has all the fields that show your information.

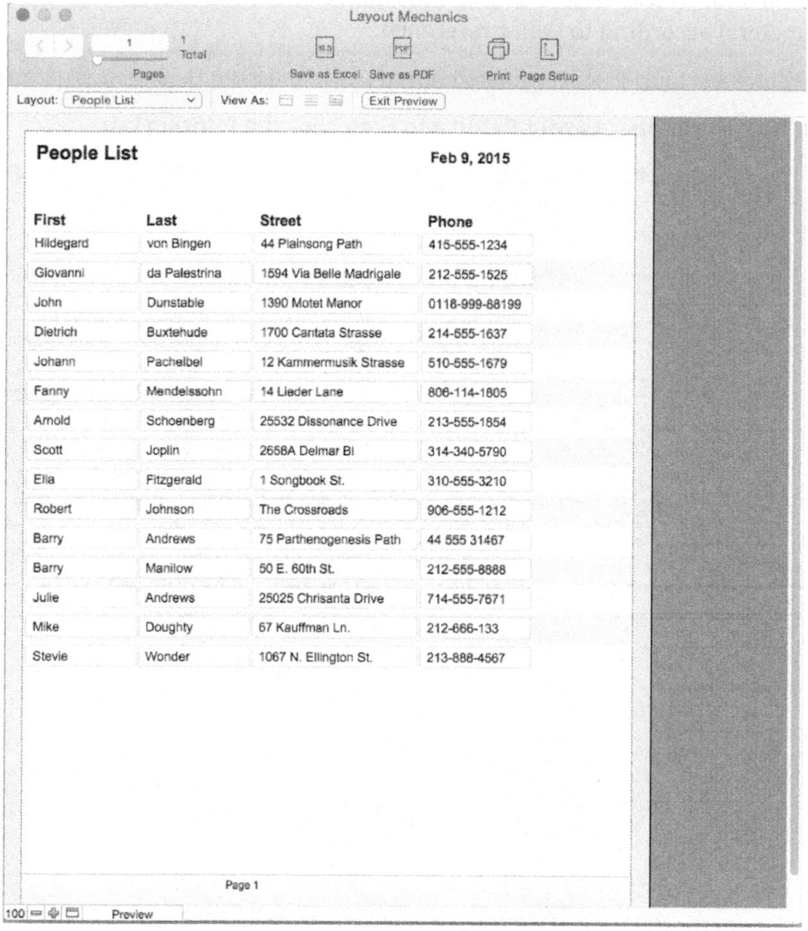

FIGURE 8-38

This is your starting point. It's already a halfway decent printable layout. It's black and white to avoid wasting color ink, it fits nicely width-wise, and it includes a concise list of records. But you can improve it in several ways, as outlined in the following pages. To see your layout in Preview mode, click the Preview button in the Layout bar, or choose View→Preview Mode.

Print Margins

Margin configuration is the first problem you need to solve. Usually when you print from FileMaker, the page margins are set to the minimum size your printer allows. This arrangement provides the most usable space possible, but at a cost: The margins—and the printable area—change as you switch printers. For a report that may be printed on a variety of printers, all of which could have different margins, you don't want to deal with that kind of inconsistency.

Luckily, you can override this behavior and set explicit margins. First, you need to make sure FileMaker is using units that make sense for page margins. Follow these steps to set the units and the margins:

1. **In the People List layout, choose View→Rulers.**

   The Rulers appear at the top and left side of the layout's content area.

2. **Click in the corner where the top and side ruler meet to cycle between the unit abbreviations (in, cm, pt), and choose either in (inches) or cm (centimeters) according to your preference.**

   You've just told FileMaker your preferred unit of measurement for this database.

3. **Choose Layouts→Layout Setup and then click the Printing tab.**

   The printing options associated with this layout appear, as shown in Figure 8-39.

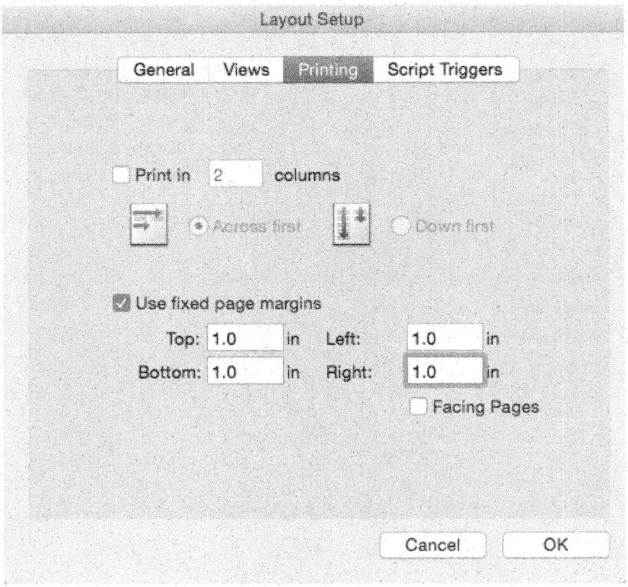

FIGURE 8-39

The numbers you see on your computer are the margins associated with the printer selected in your Page Setup dialog box, so they may look different from the ones shown here. Use the boxes under the "Use fixed page margins" option to enter custom page margins when the defaults don't work with your printer. The facing pages option changes the Left and Right field labels to Inside and Outside so you can set a wider gap between two pages (sometimes called a page gutter) if you're using FileMaker to print a book or a printed brochure instead of a loose-leaf or stapled report.

4. **Turn on the "Use fixed page margins" checkbox.**

   The Top, Bottom, Left, and Right text boxes start out grayed out. As soon as select this checkbox, you can type into them.

5. **In each of the Top, Bottom, Left, and Right text boxes, type *1.0*.**

   Don't forget to type the decimal point and the trailing "0." FileMaker balks if you just type a "1."

6. Click OK.

If your printer's driver software hogs too much margin space, you'll see a warning message, but it doesn't tell you *which* margin setting is too narrow. Tweak the margins until the warning no longer appears. The Layout Setup dialog box disappears, and you're looking at your layout again.

If you're having trouble identifying the page margins on your layout, check out Figure 8-40. If you still can't see them, select View→Page Breaks to turn them on. Now that you've fixed the usable space on the layout, you can rearrange the fields so they fit nicely in the available width.

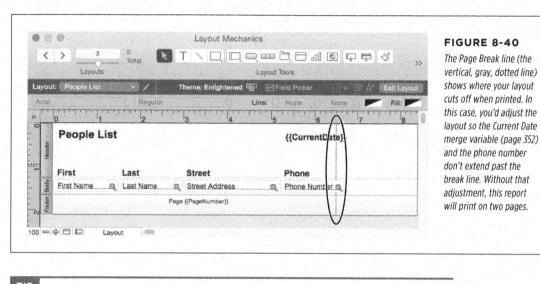

FIGURE 8-40

The Page Break line (the vertical, gray, dotted line) shows where your layout cuts off when printed. In this case, you'd adjust the layout so the Current Date merge variable (page 352) and the phone number don't extend past the break line. Without that adjustment, this report will print on two pages.

TIP If you like working in points and don't want the bother of switching units, take heart. You can probably do the math in your head even faster. Remember, you have 72 points per inch: A one-inch margin would be 72 points, and a half-inch margin would be 36. (If you like centimeters, then figure 28 points per centimeter.)

Columns

Sometimes your printed page needs to spread records across more than one column. For example, when you print on address label sheets, the sheets you buy usually have two or three columns of labels on one page. Columns are set up automatically when you create a Label layout, but a List or even a very small Detail layout can save paper by printing two records side by side. To change a layout to print multiple columns, choose Layouts→Layout Setup, switch to the Printing tab and then select the "Print in" checkbox. Now you can tell FileMaker how many columns you want by typing a number in the field by the checkbox. When you turn on column printing for a layout, FileMaker shows you what's going on in Layout mode (Figure 8-41).

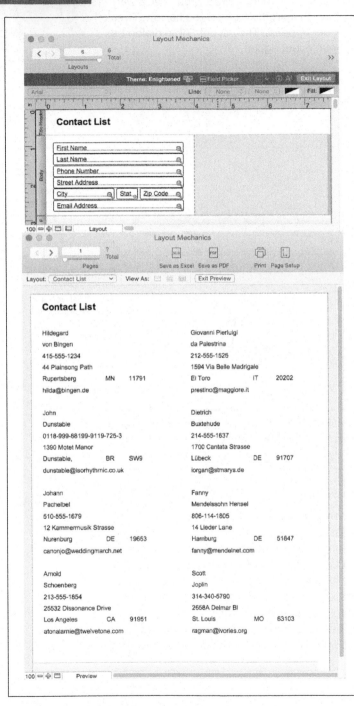

FIGURE 8-41

Top: FileMaker draws a dashed line through your layout to show you where the columns will appear on the printed page. It also covers every column but the first with a gray pattern. This pattern is its way of saying, "Don't expect anything you put here to print." Since every column is identical, you just have to lay out the first. FileMaker repeats it for the rest.

Bottom: With the layout set to print in two columns, everything comes together in Preview mode or when you print.

The column setting has no effect on your layout in Browse or Find modes. But if you print or switch to Preview mode, then you see the effect. Instead of repeating the Body part just vertically, FileMaker *tiles* the Body part both horizontally and vertically so that it fills the page.

Every column will be the same width (this makes sense because every column contains the same kind of information). FileMaker automatically sets the column width based on the settings in the Print Setup (Windows) or the Page Setup (Mac) dialog box *at the time you turn on columns*. If you later switch to a different paper size or orientation, then you may need to resize the columns. Just drag the first (leftmost) dashed line on the layout. When you finish, FileMaker makes every column the same width as the first one, with no space between them. (You can simulate padding or a *gutter* between columns by keeping the things you add to your layout away from the column edges.)

Lastly, FileMaker gives you two choices for the way it arranges records in the columns. Choose "Across first" in the Layout Setup dialog box if you want the second record to be at the top of the second column. Choose "Down first" if it should be the second item in the *first* column. The flow arrows on the icons in the Layout Setup dialog box show how the data flows onto the printout.

Layout Design

In Chapter 8, you learned to create and manage layouts and fields. Now it's time to learn about FileMaker's design tools. Some tools, like Themes and Styles, help you create consistency and reliable flexibility between your database's layouts. Grids and guides help you place objects accurately. Some tools, like merge fields and merge variables, let you place data on a layout without using a field. And since buttons are the primary way users run scripts that automate data management, you'll also learn about buttons and button bars and how they can make your users' work easier.

NOTE To follow along in this chapter, you'll find it helpful to download the sample databases from this book's Missing CD page at *www.missingmanuals.com/cds/fmp14mm*.

Layout Themes

If you're familiar with page layout, then you've probably run across *styles*, which are stored definitions of how page layout elements (like headlines, footnotes, and body text) should look. As you create your document, you just apply one of these styles to some text, and all the formatting is applied at once. A group of styles is sometimes called a *style sheet*. FileMaker's layout themes are similar to a style sheet—a theme is a set of definitions that you can apply to layout objects with a click instead of choosing multiple formatting options over and over again.

Each layout has one theme attached to it. When you create a new layout in FileMaker, the theme is automatically applied. If you're creating a database from scratch, the default theme—Enlightened—is applied to your first layout. If you don't change the theme in the New Layout/Report dialog box (page 179), then each new layout gets its theme from layout that was active when you issued the New Layout command.

If you're not trained in design or information presentation theory, don't worry. FileMaker gives you a set of professionally designed themes to choose from. But if you like dipping into design, you can customize these themes and even create your own.

Theme Families

Themes can be device specific, so you'll see a set of related themes for mobile devices and for printed reports (Figure 9-1). These theme families are meant to work well together for typical databases where you have desktop and mobile users who need to create reports. Themes with "Touch" in their names are made to work well on mobile devices. They have large font and object sizes that are better suited to finger-based navigation and data entry on the go. Themes with "Print" in their names have smaller fonts and fewer colors, and like their name implies, they're designed to look best on the printed page.

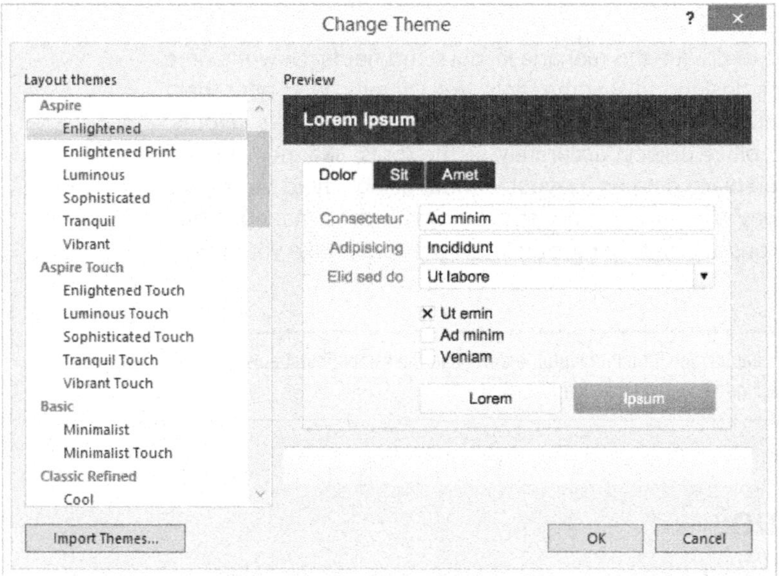

FIGURE 9-1

The Change Theme dialog box shows the themes that you can use with any database—52 in all. The Enlightened theme, selected here, is the default theme when you create a new database. Themes are grouped by device, and the designation "Touch" or "Print" suggests the kind of tasks they're best suited for. Some of the styles have been around a while, and are included even though they feel dated stylistically. They're included so when you upgrade from a previous version of FileMaker, your old theme will still work.

If you've been developing your database for a while without delving into themes, you may be wondering how all those different themes were applied to your layouts. FileMaker automatically applies a theme to get you started. For example, when you create a new layout and choose a mobile device, FileMaker silently applies the Enlightened Touch theme. If you choose a report layout, then you'll get Enlightened Print. Each theme has a set of styles appropriate to the layout type you've chosen.

■ CHANGING A LAYOUT'S THEME

Now that you know how themes work, you can always change the theme your layout uses. Choose Layout→Change Theme. In the Change Theme window, scroll through the list of themes to find one that matches your device or output. You can preview themes by selecting one from the list. The sample on the right side of the dialog box shows how some common layout elements look in the selected theme. When you find the one you want, click OK and your theme is applied to your layout and its objects.

NOTE Although you can mix and match Theme families, it could be jarring to your users, who may think they've suddenly moved to a different application. It's best to stick with one family, especially when you're getting started.

■ Styles

Changing a layout's theme lets you give the elements on the layout a unified look with minimal fuss. It works by applying sets of format definitions, called *styles*, to each layout object. A *style* is a set of formatting attributes that apply to a category of layout object, like a field, tab control, or button. Depending on the layout object, a style can define its fill color, line size, corner roundness, font size, and many other characteristics. Almost anything you can define on the Inspector's Appearance tab can be part of a style.

Each object has a Default style defined in the theme, and when you add a new object to a layout, FileMaker automatically formats it with the default style for the object type in that layout's theme. If your layout uses the Enlightened theme, for example, any new text field will have a 1-point black border with slightly rounded corners and 12-point Arial text in black on a solid white background—all the characteristics of the Enlightened theme. If you drop the same field on a layout that uses the Sophisticated theme (or if you change the current layout's theme to Sophisticated), the field will have a 1-point gray line with square corners in 11-point Helvetica Neue in dark gray on a cream background.

There are two reasons for using styles. First, formatting an object is infinitely easier when you apply a style instead of all the individual options, like font, size, color, border, and fill. Second, just as it's easier for you to applying formatting, it's also quicker and easier for FileMaker to show all the elements on a layout if similar elements share the same definition. That's a good thing when you're sharing a database using FileMaker and FileMaker Server. But when you're sending complex data to FileMaker Go on an iPhone, or through a web browser, it's critical that all those definitions be as streamlined as possible. In other words, using styles on all your layout's objects improves performance.

Applying a Style to an Object

Each theme contains a Default style and a few alternate styles for each object type. There are styles for portals, buttons, text blocks, and even each type of layout part. Since fields can be formatted with different kinds of controls (edit box, pop-up menu, checkbox set, and so on), each of those field formats has its own Default style too. When you create a new object using the regular object tools, the theme's Default style is applied. But you can change an object's style using the Inspector's Style tab. Here's how:

1. **To change the fields on a List layout, open the sample file called *Ch09 Styles Start.fmp12*, and go to the People List layout. Switch to Layout mode.**

   You want to remove some visual clutter from the list layout to put focus back on the data.

2. **Go to the Inspector's Styles tab.**

   The Styles tab shows a list of all styles for the selected object type.

3. **Select the four fields on the Layout.**

   You could apply the style to each field one by one, but since all four fields are edit boxes, it's faster to do them all at once.

4. **Click the Minimal Edit Box style.**

   The fields change formatting.

Switch to Browse mode to see the changes. Now the list is less cluttered.

Customizing Styles

As you've learned, all the layout objects you create have a theme's Default style applied as you create them. But you can add custom changes on top of the style. For example, if you change the font on a single field, you're adding custom formatting to the style. But that comes at a slight cost. If you change the layout's theme, your customized field retains its additional formatting, and unlike all the other objects on the layout, it won't change to the new style. However, if you update the style's definition to include the font change, then your custom field changes—and so do all the other fields on the layout that have the same style applied.

NOTE See the box on page 337 for more about customizing styles and performance.

Here's how that works. Take a look at Figure 9-2. This layout uses the Enlightened theme, and five of the six fields have the default style. The First Name field has been customized with a new and bigger font, a gradient background, and a blue border.

You need to apply your custom appearance to the Default style definition so all the fields update to match your custom field.

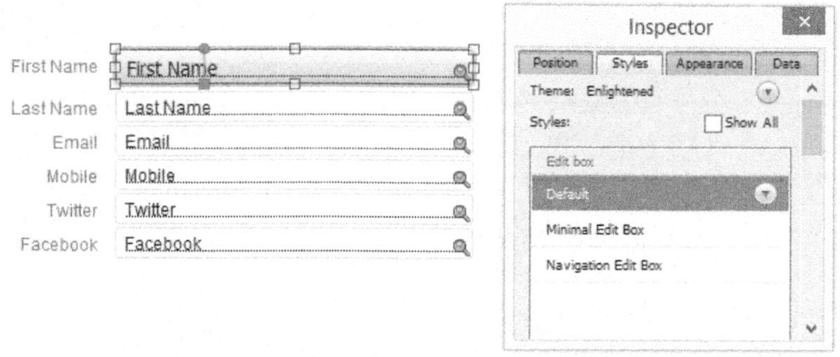

FIGURE 9-2

Here you see fields on a layout and the Inspector's Style tab. Since an edit box is selected on the layout, the Styles tab shows a list of the theme's styles for that object type. The red triangle to the right of the Default style tells you that custom formatting has also been applied to the selected object.

Saving Custom Formats to a Style

To save the First Name field's custom formatting to the Default style, go to the layout named Styles in *CH09 Styles Start.fmp12*. Then follow these steps:

1. **Switch to Layout mode and make sure the Inspector's Styles tab is showing. Click the Last Name field.**

   On the Inspector, of the three styles available, the field style is set to Default.

2. **Click the First Name field.**

   It also shows the Default style selected, but the button just to the right of the style name has a red triangle, indicating that the object has been customized. Instead of a solid white background, the First Name field has a gradient.

3. **Click the red triangle next to the style name. The Styles pop-up menu appears (Figure 9-3).**

   Here's how the menu commands work:

   - "Save Changes to Current Style" updates the selected style to the appearance of the selected object.

   - "Save as New Style" adds this new style as a choice within the current theme.

   - Rename Style comes in handy if you want to give your styles more descriptive names than Default and Minimal.

   - "Revert Changes to Style" discards the custom appearance and reverts the field to the Default style.

   - If you created a style by mistake, or if you're sure you aren't going to use it, choose Delete Style to delete it from the theme. All objects that were formatted with this style revert to Default style.

4. Choose "Save Changes to Current Style."

The red triangle beside the Default style's name disappears, showing you that the changes have been saved. In the background, the other five fields change to match First Name field's appearance.

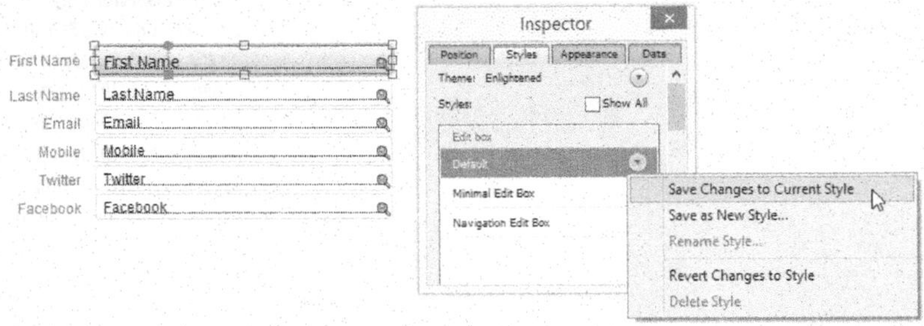

FIGURE 9-3

The Style pop-up menu lets you manage changes to the default styles included with themes. If you want to change themes significantly, you'll find objects with each of a theme's styles, customize them appropriately, and then save the changes to the style.

In your sample database, all edit box fields on the current layout changed when you saved your custom formatting to the style. Read on to learn how to send those changes to all the default-styled edit fields on all the other layouts in your database.

Saving Style Changes to the Theme

Saving a style's definition is the first step in propagating the change throughout your database. The Default style lost its red triangle as soon as you saved your changes, but those changes haven't been saved to the theme yet. Look at the theme's name, shown above the style list. As Figure 9-4 shows, it's now Enlightened* with an asterisk, and that red triangle appears to its right. This feedback shows that you've made changes to a style in the Enlightened theme, but those changes have not been applied to the whole theme. Put another way, changes made to a style apply to the current layout only. If you want the modified style to be applied across *all* layouts, you must also save it to the theme.

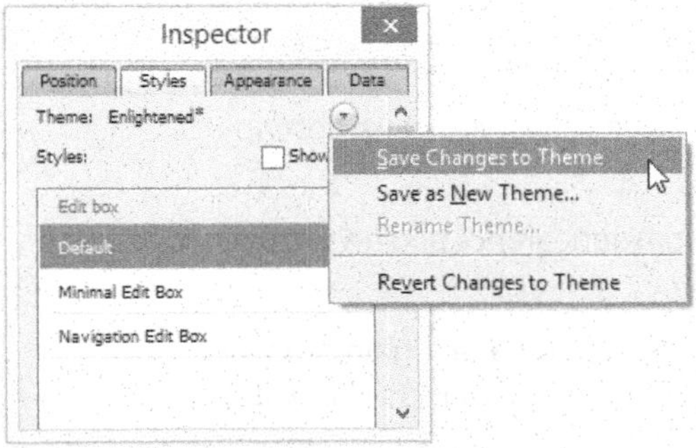

FIGURE 9-4

The red triangle by the theme's name indicates that you've made changes to one or more of the theme's styles. Until you update the theme, those edited styles are only available on the current layout. Update the theme to make those changes available throughout the database.

Styles and File Performance

I just need to add minor custom formatting changes to a few styles. Do I need to bother updating all my styles and themes?

Back on page 334 you learned about one cost of customizing styles without saving the changes. But there's a second cost that doesn't come into play until you share the file. Each change puts a slight nick in the layout's performance, because in order to show the field with its custom formatting, FileMaker has to render the object with the style's defined formatting and then add on your customizations. If you're the only person using your database, then you'll never see the effect of those small changes. But if you're sharing the file using FileMaker Server over a WAN, and especially if you have people using FileMaker Go or a web browser to connect to your database, you should be very careful about how you use styles. In those cases, all that style and custom format information has to be sent from the host to the client machine. You'll improve your file's performance if you save *all* your custom formatting to styles and then save the theme in turn.

Ok. But doesn't that mean I might have to make a lot of new custom styles? Don't all those new styles have an impact on performance too?

You're right, saving custom formats means that you'll have more styles for each object type than you would if you just made format changes to an object without saving the styles. For example, you may need to create a new custom style for

showing a field with bold text and another one for showing text in a light gray. But load tests on FileMaker Server–shared databases show that a layout that uses dozens, even hundreds, of styles per layout performs better than one with those same formats added without saving them to the style, especially when more than one object has the same custom formats added. So here's the rule of thumb for when to save a custom format to a style: If you're making a format change for a single object on the layout, you don't need a new style. But as soon a second object needs the same format change, that's your cue to create a new style to define the format.

Hmm. If that's the rule of thumb, why does the Inspector's Appearance tab have copy and paste buttons? Don't they let you copy an object's style and its custom formatting?

Yes, that's how they work. So that's a great question with no good answer. If you ever find yourself reaching for those buttons, it's a signal that it's time to create a new style that includes your custom formatting, too.

How will I keep all those new styles straight? Won't they have names like Default Bold and Default Gray?

Not if you're thinking ahead, they won't. Give your new styles simple, descriptive names that help you figure out where to apply them. Instead of naming a style "Default Right Aligned," call it "Default Number." Then you'll know to use it for all your number fields so they line up to the right instead of the left.

You can see this in action by switching to another layout called Theme Defaults. It contains the same six fields you saw on the original layout. But these fields show the old formatting for the "Edit box" style. Here's how to propagate the style changes that are currently confined to the Styles layout out all the other layouts that use the Enlightened Theme:

1. **Go to the Styles layout and then switch to Layout mode. If necessary, select the Inspector's Style tab.**

   In the Inspector, you should see an asterisk at the end of the theme's name and a red triangle on the button to its right.

2. **Click the red triangle and choose "Save Changes to Theme."**

   FileMaker warns you that you're about to update all layouts that use the current theme.

3. **In the warning dialog box, click Save.**

   In the Inspector, the asterisk goes away and the triangle turns from red back to gray. The layout, however, doesn't appear any different.

To see your handiwork, switch back to the Theme Defaults layout. The fields have been updated to match the ones on the Styles layout.

This section has focused on styling fields, but *every* object on every layout has a style applied to it—text, buttons, lines, shapes, portals, tabs, even backgrounds and the layout parts (header, body, footer, and so on). So while it's very easy to customize a theme by changing an object's appearance, updating its style and then updating the theme, there are many styles for each theme, and it'll take you a while to find and change each one.

Some people live for design and are happy to spend the first few hours of database creation customizing a theme's styles. Once you've invested all that time, you don't want to have to do it over again if you need to create a new database for your company. Read on to find out how you can reuse styles, and see the box below for more information on what happens to custom themes created in prior versions of FileMaker when you upgrade to FileMaker 14.

UP TO SPEED

A Short History of Styles in FileMaker

Themes and styles were introduced in FileMaker 12. At the same time, there was a format change, which meant that all pre-12 files needed to be converted to the new format. FileMaker's conversion tools automatically changed all the old individual formats to a new custom theme called Classic, because it retained all the old style borders, shapes, and other formatting from prehistoric versions of FileMaker. From there, you were free to customize the Classic theme any way you wanted to. However, the custom theme updater in FileMaker 13 overwrote those custom changes, so when you upgraded from 12 to 13, you had to do some customization work over again. And even though Classic had problems, you had to keep using it if you wanted to publish your databases through FileMaker 12's Instant Web Publishing, the precursor to WebDirect, the current web technology.

Version 14 has a new custom theme updater that retains your custom theme and style information. So don't hesitate to upgrade if you're concerned that all your custom style work will disappear. Don't bother looking for that old standby Classic theme; it's not included in FileMaker 14's theme set. If you open or convert an older file that uses Classic, the theme will appear in the list, but your new files won't have Classic as a choice. But if you're just now getting around to converting those pre-12 files, and you use FileMaker 14 to convert, they'll be converted to Enlightened.

Importing Themes

As you make more databases, you'll likely find yourself adopting certain design patterns and color palettes that become your database's signature look. But each time you create a new, empty database, you start all over again with FileMaker's stock themes. Luckily, that custom theme you poured your heart and soul into isn't locked into one single database. You can import themes from other databases, and it's easier than just about every other aspect of styles and themes.

1. **Open the database into which you want to import a custom Theme. Then choose File→Manage→Themes.**

   A list of the themes currently used in your database appears.

2. **In the lower-left corner of the dialog box, click the Import button. Select the database containing the theme you want to import.**

   FileMaker shows a list of available themes like the one shown in Figure 9-5. If the selected database has access restrictions, you need a Full Access login for this step (page 745).

3. **Select the theme (or themes) you want to import.**

   The imported themes are imported and then show up on the theme list.

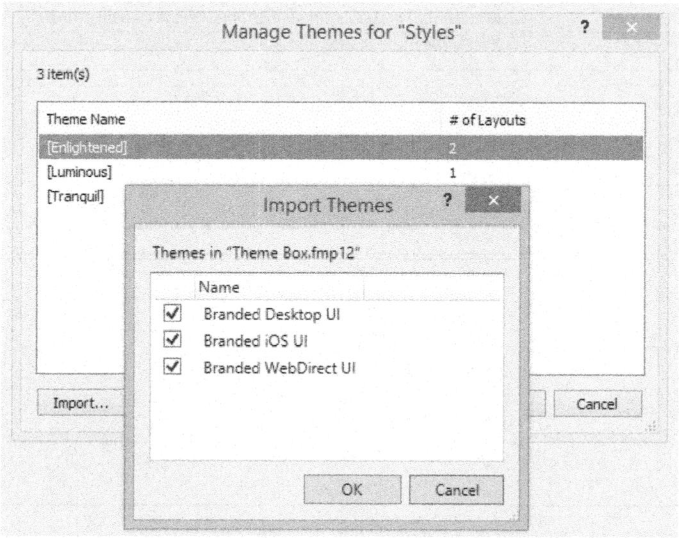

FIGURE 9-5

The Manage Themes dialog box lets you import themes from other files. Here you see the list of themes from a source database showing custom themes developed for a company's corporate brand. This dialog box also lets you rename, duplicate, or delete existing themes. If you're switching themes completely, use this dialog box to find all the layouts that are still using your old theme and then switch them to your new theme. You can't delete a theme until there are no layouts in the database using it.

If you import a theme that has the same name as an existing theme in your database, FileMaker appends a number to the imported theme's name.

◼ Formatting Object States

Just as themes and styles were ported into FileMaker from page layout, you may be familiar with the concept of *object states* from other applications or the Web.

Object states are a part of a style's definition that gives you visual feedback about the object. You've already learned about two of FileMaker's object states—active record state and alternate row state. *Active record state* highlights the active record on a List layout to help you keep track of the record you're in. Back on page 38 you selected an option in the Layout Setup dialog box to turn on active record state. But now that you know how to use styles, you can have more control over how the active record displays. Here's how to change the formatting for an object's state:

1. **Go to the People List layout and then switch to Layout mode. Select the Inspector's Appearance tab.**

   This panel is where you'll find the object state pop-up menus. You can also view the options set for each object's style.

2. **Click on the Body part's label to select it.**

   The Appearance panel shows the Body formatting (Figure 9-6).

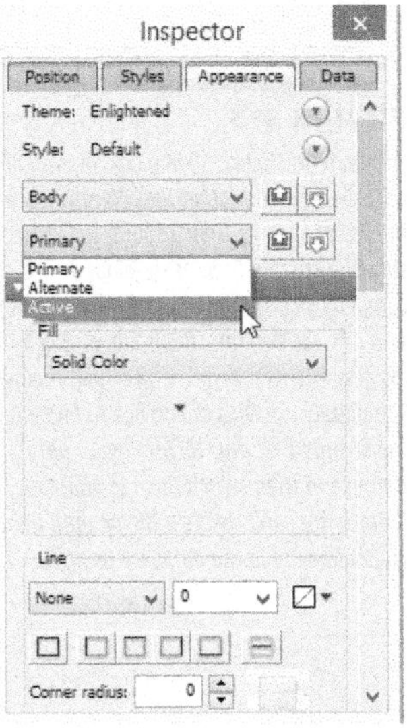

FIGURE 9-6

The State pop-up menu shows the object states for the selected object. Not all layout parts have more than one state, but a Body part has three: Primary, Alternate, and Active.

3. **In the State pop-up menu, choose Active.**

   The Style tab shows you the current formatting for the Body part's Active state. Enlightened's default is a light blue.

4. **Fill color swatch (under the Graphic section) swatch to view a drop-down color selector and then choose a blue color.**

   The swatch fills with the color you select. See page 341 to see how FileMaker helps you choose an appropriate tint of your blue.

If you want to perpetuate this change throughout your database—say if you've created 12 different list layouts that should all have the same active record state—switch to the Inspector's Style tab, save the changes to the Default style, and then save the changes to the theme. All your list layouts will show this style. Switch to Browse mode to see the changes on your list layout. Even though you changed the part's style, form layout Body parts don't have an alternate or active state, so you won't see the highlight on those layouts, even though it's now part of the style's definition.

FREQUENTLY ASKED QUESTION

Using Shades and Tints

The tutorial for formatting object states suggested that I pick a different blue. But how do I pick a good blue? I'm not a graphic designer.

FileMaker knows that people whose job is database designer (and especially those whose main job is business development, admin assistant, or one-man-shop) probably don't have design degrees. So FileMaker's color picker has some handy features that help you see a theme's existing colors and mix new ones with confidence. To see the color picker, go to Layout mode and select any object that has a solid-colored background. (If you can't find one already formatted that way, you can change the formatting temporarily and then revert layout changes at the end of this process.) On the Inspector's Appearance tab, click the color swatch below the Fill pop-up menu.

FileMaker's Color Picker tools appear at the top of your regular operating system color picker window. In the upper left, the magnifying glass icon lets you grab a color from anywhere on your computer screen. Click the magnifying glass and then move your mouse around the screen. Notice that the small swatch shows the color your mouse is pointing to. The field to

the right shows you the hexadecimal color definition FileMaker uses to create the color. Just click when you've found the color you want. The selected object changes color to match. So if you have a Photoshop document showing your company logo, you can easily bring the exact shade into FileMaker to use in your database.

The next three rows of colors are the Swatch Palette. It shows the 12 most commonly used colors in the current layout's theme. The primary color, which is used for an object's normal state, is in the middle row. The color in the top row is created by adding black to the primary color, and it's called a *shade*. It's suitable for an object's grayed-out state. The color in the bottom row is made by adding white to the primary color. In color theory, this is called a *tint*. A color's tint is often used for an object's hover state.

If the color you need isn't in the Swatch Palette, just click the color sample button (between the magnifying glass and the hex box). Drag the color onto one of the blank swatches and FileMaker mixes the shade and tint colors for you.

The Body isn't the only part with states. Most layout objects have multiple states. Here's a list of object states:

- **Normal** is the state of an object when it's visible, but not active.

- **Primary** is the Body part's version of Normal state.

- **Hover** is when you're holding your mouse over an object. Because of the touch screens, Hover state doesn't work on iOS.

- **Pressed** is the state when the mouse button—or, in iOS, a user's finger—is pressing on an object.

- **In focus** means the object has been selected by a click, a script, or by tabbing into the object.

- **Placeholder Text** applies only to fields. When a field is empty, text you specify appears in the field.

- **Active** and **Inactive** states apply to tab controls and buttons in a button bar. The Active state is like a radio button. When you click a button or a tab panel, it becomes active and all the others are inactive.

Buttons, fields, drawn shapes, portals, text blocks, web viewers, and charts all have states that you can custom format or style. To view the formatting for any object's state, select it and read the Inspector's Appearance tab. Two different pop-up menus let you view and edit object states. The top pop-up menu shows you the object type. Many objects just have one attribute with states, but a button has two attributes that you can style separately—the button and its icon. To format an object and all its attributes, select the attribute, then use the Status pop-up menu to switch states and then format each state separately. As you do, you'll see the selected object (or objects) change formatting on your layout and the Inspector's set of selected options change accordingly. See the box below to learn more about how object state formatting creates good user experience.

Object States Make Good UX

UX is designer-speak for User Experience. Simply put, the term UX refers to the feelings people have about your database as they're working in it. If mysterious things happen that don't make sense, that doesn't make for good UX. But if your database behaves in expected ways, and gives people clues about what they need to do to get their work done, people will have a good experience. Good UX is all about creating trust, and, believe it or not, formatting object states is one way you can instill immediate familiarity and trust in your users. Objects on the Web and in mobile apps have these states, so even without thinking about it, people know that when an object changes as the mouse waves over it, they can click that object and cause some action. This visual feedback is called *affordance*. It makes a website or app feel responsive to user input. When affordance is good, users feel competent and have an easy time learning to use the app.

Before FileMaker 13, the only way for a button to provide affordance was to change the pointer to a hand when the mouse hovered over it. But with FileMaker 14's improved object states, you can provide more and better visual feedback on buttons, fields, and other layout objects. With object states, the button changes appearance instead of the pointer changing shape. That's more in line with current user expectations. The good news is that if UX isn't your bailiwick, you don't have to give it another thought, because themes already include professionally designed object states that abide by current standards.

But if you change major elements of a theme, like the background of a part or object, the theme's object state formatting may stand out like a sore thumb, so you'll need to tweak it to match. As with all formatting, a little bit of affordance goes a long way. Affordances should be different enough to be noticed, but not enough to be startling, so FileMaker gives you another tool for making great choices. See page 341 to learn about the improved color palette.

Alignment Tools

One of the keys to visually appealing and usable layouts is keeping things neat. A jumbled layout detracts from your data and makes your database seem amateurish. Your tools for keeping the chaos at bay are grids and guides, plus the usual assortment of Arrange and Align buttons.

Grids

Every layout has a grid, even if you never use it. FileMaker uses the grid to help you place objects and keep them in place. To use the grid to your advantage, open the Inspector's Position tab and look at the Grid section at the bottom. Selecting Show Grid draws FileMaker's grid on your layout (in Layout mode only). Think of it as instant graph paper. The "Snap to Grid" checkbox lets you be a little lazy when you create or move objects. As you drag an object around a layout, you'll see a magnetic "pull" as you near an intersection of grid lines. "Snap to Grid" makes it a cinch to get objects evenly aligned and spaced.

CUSTOMIZING THE GRID

The grid's default setup is a 1-inch grid with eight divisions in each square. You can see those settings in the Major Grid Spacing and Minor Grid Steps fields at the bottom of the Inspector's Position panel. That's a lot of snap-to-it-iveness. You can change the grid, but first you may want to change your measurement scheme to better match the device you're designing for or even the theme you're using. Here's why: In the Enlightened theme, new fields dragged with the field tool have the height of 0.292" but are 0.611" tall on an Enlightened Touch layout. That seems a little random in inches, but if you switch to pixels, those same measurements translate to 21 and 44 pixels. Those measurements are not accidental. The Arial font at 16 points needs about five extra pixels of height to show the ascending and descending parts of letters, plus a little margin of space. Studies on usability have found that the fields and buttons on mobile devices need to be at least 44 pixels high for people to use them comfortably. None of those measurements divide nicely on a 1-inch grid, so it makes sense to change it to something that matches better.

After you change your measurement system to pixels (click a measurement label in the Inspector's Position section), you need to decide on a better grid system. One common method is to take the width or height of the screen you're designing for and divide it to arrive at a good number. If the device you're designing for has a width of 1280 pixels, then you could make the Major Grid Spacing 128, so you'll have 10 evenly spaced intersections across your page (Figure 9-7). That makes it really easy to place your fields in multiple columns across the screen. Another scheme says that you should use a multiple of the theme's field height, plus a few pixels for space between pixels so you can let grid-snapping place your fields evenly from the top to the bottom of your layout.

Guides

A guide is a horizontal or vertical line that appears only in Layout mode and helps you partition the space and place objects neatly. You create guides by dragging them from their respective rulers. That is, horizontal guides come from the horizontal ruler and vertical guides come from the vertical ruler. You can make as many as you want, and you can move them around or get rid of them completely once they've served their purpose. Remove a guide by dragging it back to the ruler from whence it came.

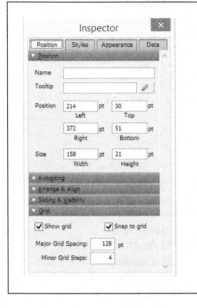

FIGURE 9-7

The Inspector's Position tab gives you the "address" of the selected layout object in the Position section. You can move an object by typing in the Position fields and resize an object by typing in the Size fields. The Grid section at the bottom lets you show or hide the grid, turn its snapping power on and off, and change the grid's spacing and steps. Whether the grid is on or off, most people prefer having two to four Minor Grid Steps. That way, you have a good place to stop if you have to adjust some object that won't fit perfectly onto the grid.

Although you can customize the grid's spacing, and even turn it off and on at will, it can be distracting, especially on complex layouts. So some people prefer to use guides instead of the grid. Here's how to create a set of guides that will help you create a more visually appealing layout.

1. **Switch to the Using Guides layout and choose View→Layout Mode. If the Inspector isn't open, choose View→Inspector.**

   Half the job is in the prep work.

2. **Click the Inspector's Position tab. If the unit of measurement is "in" or "cm," click it until it changes to "pt."**

   This layout is designed to be viewed onscreen, so pixels is the best measurement system to use.

3. **If you don't see the graphic rulers running along the top and left sides of the layout, choose View→Rulers.**

   Now you're ready to start the real work.

4. **Drag the vertical ruler (on the left side of the layout) to the right.**

A thin blue line comes out from the ruler. Release the mouse button when the line is 120 points from the left edge, as shown in Figure 9-8. After you've created all your guides, you'll place the right edge of your field labels on this guide.

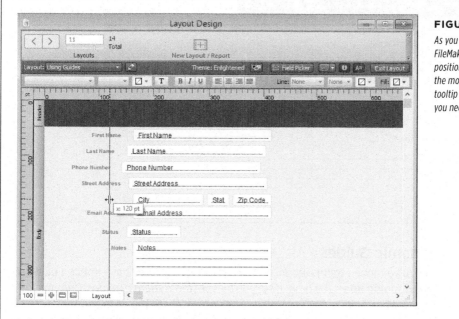

FIGURE 9-8

As you drag the guide, FileMaker shows a handy position tooltip. Release the mouse when the tooltip shows the position you need.

5. **Drag out a second vertical guide, and place it at 110 points.**

You'll place the left edge of your fields on this guide.

6. **Drag down two horizontal guides from the ruler across the top of the layout. Place the first one at 180 points from the top and the second at 200 points.**

Use the top guide to line up the bottom of the City, State, and Zip Code fields. Use the bottom guide to place the top of the Email Address field. This chunks your field in related bite-sized pieces that are easy for users to digest (Figure 9-9).

Now you can use the guides to move your fields and labels around. See Figure 9-9 for the finished product. Switch to Browse mode when you're done to see how much difference a little grouping and aligning makes.

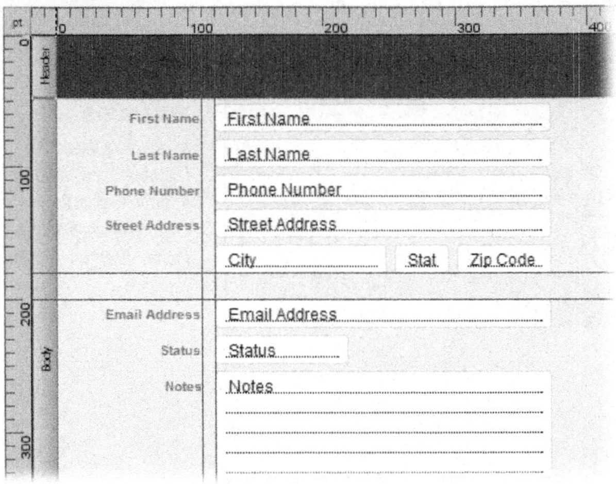

FIGURE 9-9

A simple four-guide arrangement can neatly partition a layout. If you don't need a guide any more, just drag it back to the ruler it came from.

Dynamic Guides

As you've moved things around in Layout mode, you may have noticed blue guidelines popping up as you drag. If so, you've spotted *dynamic guides*. Dynamic guides appear when an object you're moving has one of three things in common with other nearby objects: aligned centers, aligned edges, or equal spacing. Figure 9-10 shows you each of these scenarios. Even though dynamic guides alone won't make your layout perfect, they will help you keep things tidy without requiring frequent trips to the alignment and distribution tools. In Layout mode, choose View→Dynamic Guides to turn this feature on or off.

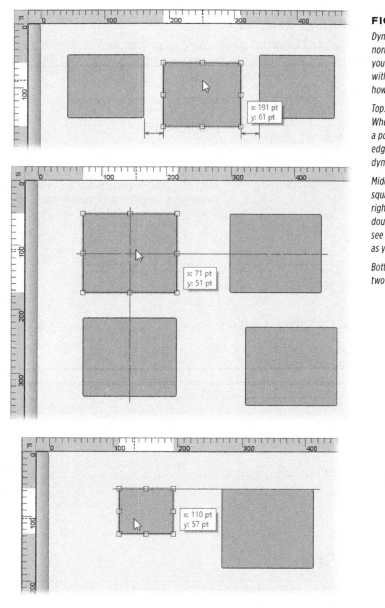

FIGURE 9-10

Dynamic guides are the same blue color as normal guides, but they only appear when you're dragging an object and it aligns with other objects on the layout. Here's how that works:

Top: Here you see the spacing guides. When the center square is dragged to a point equidistant from the nearest edges of its neighbors, the double arrow dynamic guide appears.

Middle: Here, the midpoint of the top-left square aligns with both the square to the right and the one below. Without this double alignment, though, you may only see either a vertical or a horizontal guide as you drag.

Bottom: The edge guide appears when two or more objects' edges line up.

NOTE You also see dynamic guides when you nudge objects into place using the up and down arrow keys. Since dynamic guides only appear on the precise pixel of alignment, nudging makes precision easier than dragging for many people.

Arrange and Align Buttons

As with most programs that let you create and move objects, FileMaker has a suite of tools for arranging and aligning objects on your layouts. You'll find them on the Inspector's Position tab, in the Arrange & Align section (Figure 9-11).

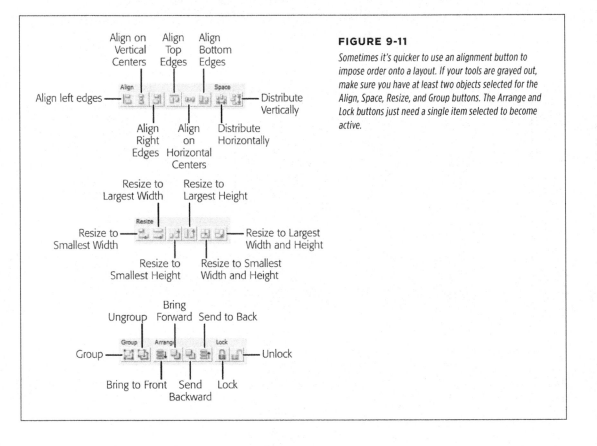

FIGURE 9-11

Sometimes it's quicker to use an alignment button to impose order onto a layout. If your tools are grayed out, make sure you have at least two objects selected for the Align, Space, Resize, and Group buttons. The Arrange and Lock buttons just need a single item selected to become active.

■ Screen Stencils

Rare is the database that's created and used exclusively on a single screen. Even if you're making a database solely for yourself, you might be able to use it on a couple different computers plus an iPad and an iPhone over the course of its life. If a database is shared, it could be on 10 different-size screens all at the same time! So the layout that you spent hours making work just right on your palatial 32-inch screen could turn out to be a real headache for the new hire down the hall who stuck with an 18-inch display. The most practical solution is designing layouts that fit the lowest common screen resolution. Luckily, you don't have to keep old monitors around to do it.

That's because FileMaker's Screen Stencil tool lets you overlay up to eight common layout dimensions on your layout. When you select a stencil in Layout mode, it appears on the layout like an orange guide—but stencils are rectangular and immovable. You can't drag them around like regular guides. As you work on your layout, you can be sure that if you keep within the orange lines, the content will fit your users' screens.

WARNING The name "Screen Stencil" can be a bit misleading. Screen Stencils help you manage layout content dimensions, not the dimensions of the screen. For example, a layout conforming to a 1024 × 768 screen stencil on a Mac will have an overall window size of 1039 × 889 pixels if the Status toolbar is showing. The fixed menu bar at the top of the screen is 22 pixels tall, and a permanently displayed dock can easily eat up another 100 pixels. That means a database user might need a total screen height of nearly 1200 pixels to see a content-area height of 1024.

To display a Screen Stencil:

1. **In Layout mode, click the white triangle to the right of Screen Stencil button in the Layout toolbar (Figure 9-12).**

   It's the one that looks like a dotted-line box within a dotted-line box.

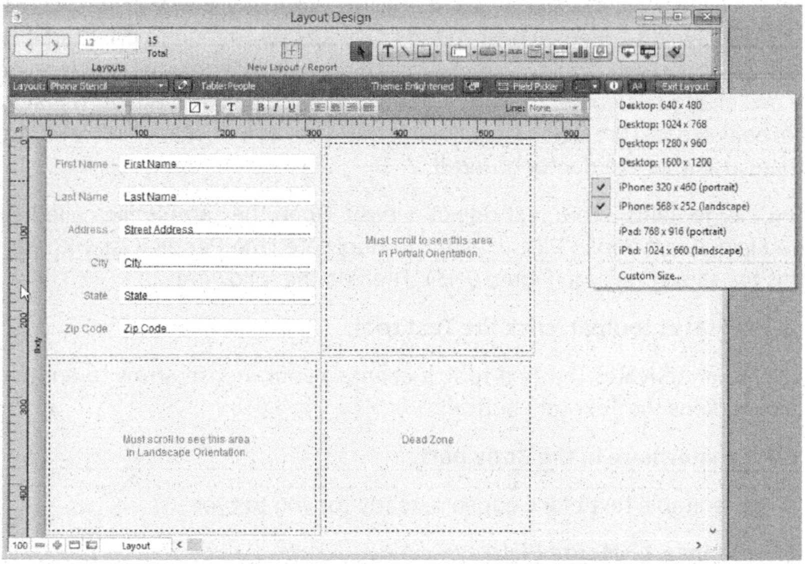

FIGURE 9-12

Designing layouts for the iPhone and iPod Touch presents unique challenges. Portrait and Landscape orientations don't just swap length and width measurements. When a user changes orientation, FileMaker doesn't automatically switch layouts—it just shows a different part of the current one. That means every iPhone layout has a dead zone in the bottom-right corner that is never displayed if the user doesn't scroll.

2. **Select the first iPhone choice, "iPhone 320 × 460 (portrait)."**

   The orange stencil lines appear onscreen.

3. **Return to the pop-up menu from step 3, and select the second iPhone option.**

   You have both iPhone stencils on the layout at the same time.

FileMaker provides one slot for you to define a custom stencil size. To set or change the dimensions of your custom stencil, choose Custom Size from the pop-up menu. If you want to temporarily hide all your stencils without having to reselect them from the pop-up menu, just click the Screen Stencil button (not the white triangle next to it) to toggle them on and off.

Merge Fields

Knowing what you know now, if you set out to build a layout yourself, you'll probably grab the Field tool and start dragging fields onto the layout. But look closely at Figure 9-13 first. When you put a field on a layout, you're putting it *exactly* where you want it. No matter what record you're on when you look at the layout, that field value is in the same spot. Usually, that's where you want it to be, but sometimes—like in a new List Layout—you want something a little more flexible. You want the Last Name field to start where the first name ends. Since some first names are longer than others, this spot changes from record to record.

In FileMaker, you solve this problem using *merge fields.* As you learned back on page 170, merge fields work a lot like a mail merge in a word-processing program. They're only for display and generally best suited to layouts you intend to print rather than to work with onscreen. You need a real field if you want people to be able to get in there and change its contents. Your database already has a layout with real fields just for editing data (the Detail layout), so in this case, as with many list views, merge fields are just what the doctor ordered.

Putting merge fields into a text object is easy. Open the sample file called *CH09 Merge Fields Start.fmp12.* Pick a layout to duplicate (the People List with regular fields is the same one as in Figure 9-13). Then do the following:

1. **In the Status toolbar, click the Text tool.**

   FileMaker activates the Text tool; it changes your mouse arrow to an I-beam, and darkens the Text tool button.

2. **Click somewhere in the Body part.**

   A new editable text block appears, ready for you to type.

3. **Choose Insert→Merge Field.**

   The Specify Field dialog box appears, listing every field in the current layout's table.

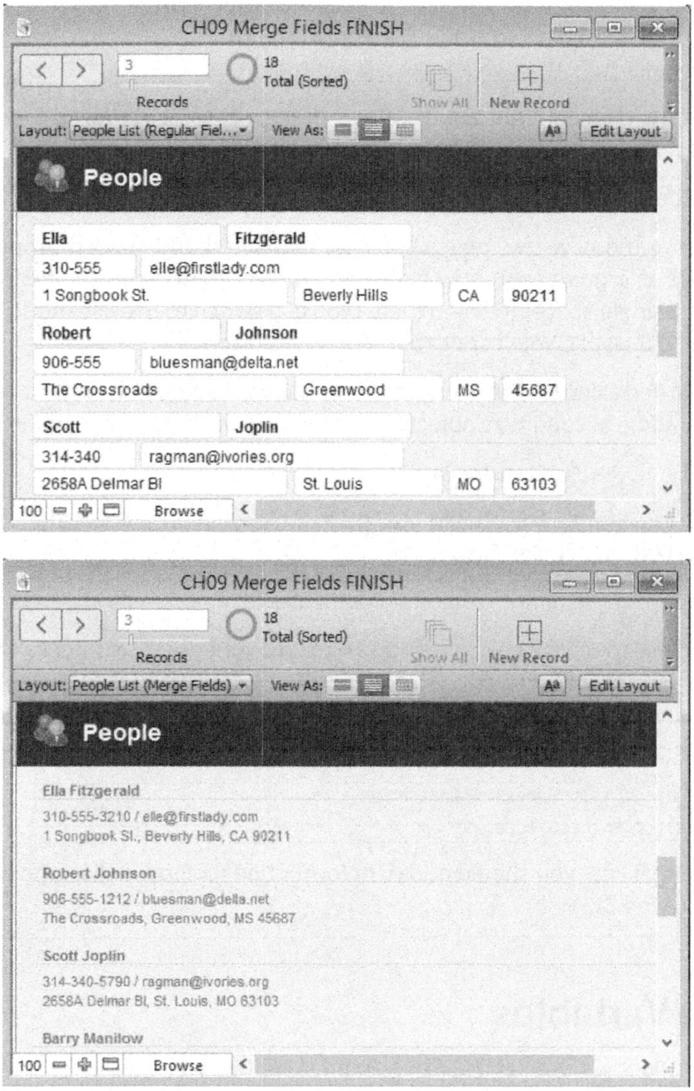

FIGURE 9-13

Top: This layout uses normal fields, which are always in the same place on the layout, no matter what record you're on. Notice how the spacing between the contents of each field, particularly the First Name and Last Name fields, looks odd because it's inflexible.

Bottom: By using merge fields, you can create a more professional-looking result. Plus, it can be a lot more efficient. With merge fields, you can usually get more information in the same space—along with some restful white space to divide your records.

4. **Select the First Name field and then click OK.**

   FileMaker inserts <<First Name>> into the text block for you.

NOTE Although you can *type* the merge field into a text object, this method can be error-prone. If your field data isn't showing in Browse mode (and you see <<MyFieldName>> instead), you probably misspelled the field name. So unless you know the exact field name, it's usually quicker to use Insert→Merge Field.

5. **Type a single space.**

   If you forget this step, the two names will run together.

6. **Choose Insert→Merge Field again. When the Specify Field dialog box returns, select the Last Name field and then click OK.**

   FileMaker adds the Last Name merge field to the text object.

If necessary, move the new text objects so they're aligned and spaced properly, using Figure 9-13 as a guide. You now have a text object that shows the first and last names with a single space between them (you can switch to Browse mode and then try it out if you want). You just need to put it into place.

Next, you need to add a line for the phone number and email address. Using the same steps as before, add a second text object below the first, with these merge fields:

```
<<Phone Number>> / <<Email Address>>
```

Finally, the address information should also be in a merge field. Repeat the steps above to build a text object like this:

```
<<Street Address>, <<City>>, <<State>> <<Zip Code>>
```

You can mix and match merge fields and normal text to your heart's content. When you were setting up the first and last name, you added a space between the merge fields. But you can also add text that acts like a field label or other helpful information, like so:

```
Customer Name: <<First Name>> <<Last Name>>
Invoice Total: <<Invoice Total>>
```

For the Invoice Total line, you should add data formatting to show dollar signs and decimal places (page 313).

■ Merge Variables

Merge fields are dandy, but FileMaker has another cool way to create layout text that changes under certain conditions: the *merge variable*. A variable is like a temporary field you can create with the Set Variable script step. You can choose from two kinds of variable, but if you want to use yours on a layout, it's got to be a Global variable. Global variables have two dollar signs at the start of their names—*$$found*, for example. Here are the steps to create a variable that displays the count of found records on a layout:

1. **Go to Scripts→Script Workspace.**

   The Script Workspace opens.

2. **Click + to create a new script, and name it *Set Merge Variable*. From the list of script steps on the right, double-click Set Variable (it's in the Control section).**

   FileMaker adds this step to your script and automatically selects it.

3. **Next to the script step, click the button shaped like a gear.**

   The Set Variable Options window appears.

4. **In the Name field, type *$$found*. In the Value field, enter the following formula and then click OK to save it.**

   ```
   "People found: " & Get ( FoundCount )
   ```

   This calculation lets people know about their found count of records even when the toolbar isn't open. It's very common to hide and lock the toolbar, especially if you're sharing the database on the Web. The part of the calculation in quotes gives some context to the calculation's result.

5. **From the list of script steps on the right, double-click Refresh Window (it's in the Window section).**

   This step tells FileMaker to redraw the window after the variable is set, so the change will show up onscreen right away. This script step doesn't need options, so you can ignore its gear button.

6. **Close the Script Workspace and save the script when you're prompted.**

   You're back on the People List layout.

7. **If necessary, switch to Layout mode, select the Text tool, and then click in the Header to create a text box. Choose Insert→Merge Variable.**

   FileMaker inserts "<<$$>>" and places your cursor just after the dollar signs.

8. **Carefully type *found* just as you entered it in step 4.**

   Spelling counts here, although case doesn't matter.

9. **Switch to Browse mode.**

   The variable's value won't appear until you run the script.

10. **Choose Scripts→Set Merge Variable to run the script and set the variable.**

    The current found count appears in your merge variable.

If all the text doesn't appear, your text block may not be wide enough. Switch back to Layout mode to tweak it. For more on how global variables work, see page 689.

Tooltips

Training people, either when you first launch a new database or when new employees arrive, is a big part of making your database successful. You can have beautiful layouts, bulletproof privilege sets, and complex, well-thought-out scripts, but if folks don't know how and when to use them, then they miss out on the benefits. To spare you the wrath of confused (or worse, frustrated) people, FileMaker Pro Advanced has a feature called *tooltips*. These onscreen labels can help guide people through the features you've created for them, and maybe even cut down on training time.

You can attach tooltips to any object, or group of objects, that you can select on a layout: fields, text, or graphics. To create a tooltip, go to Layout mode and then choose the object you want tipped. If the Inspector isn't open, choose View→Inspector. Click the Inspector's Position tab and then look for the Tooltip field, near the top. Enter the text for your tooltip here and then tab out of the Tooltip field. A "T" badge in a yellow swatch appears in the object's lower-left corner. The badge is there to help you quickly find all the objects on a layout that have tooltips. (See Appendix B for a complete list of object badges.)

Just to the right of the Inspector's Tooltip field is a small button with a pencil icon. Click this button, and you get all the power of calculations. The result of the calculation becomes the tooltip's text. If the calculation has an empty result, then FileMaker doesn't show the tooltip.

You can see the Tooltip in action in Browse mode. Save the changes to your layout if prompted. Point to the object in Browse mode. Just like tooltips in other programs, the tooltip doesn't appear immediately, so as not to inconvenience more advanced users. You can see a tooltip in action in Figure 9-14.

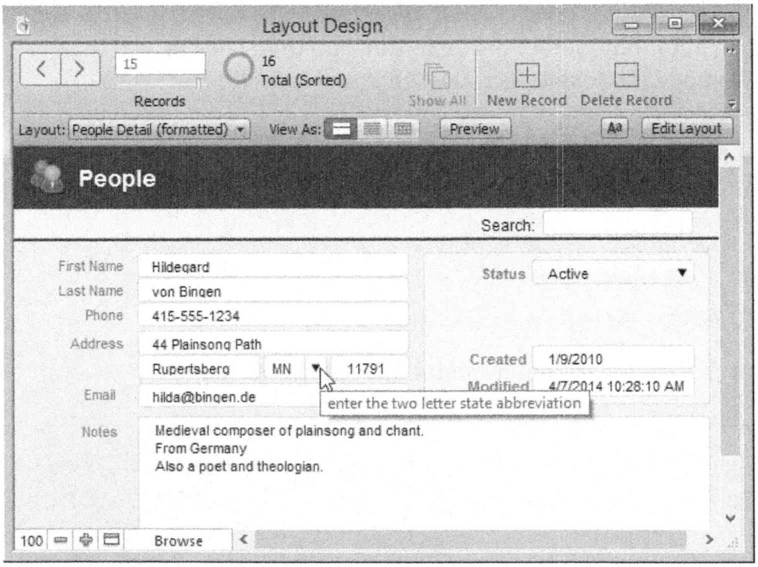

FIGURE 9-14

With a tooltip in place, you can point at the State field and wait a moment to get a little help. The tooltip shows just below the mouse arrow.

■ Autosizing

Take a look at the People Detail layout in this chapter's sample database. Your layouts are neater. Things are aligned, grouped, and sized in a pleasing way. But what happens if you make your database window bigger or smaller? Well, there's no need to guess. Have a peek at Figure 9-15 to see the not-so-great news.

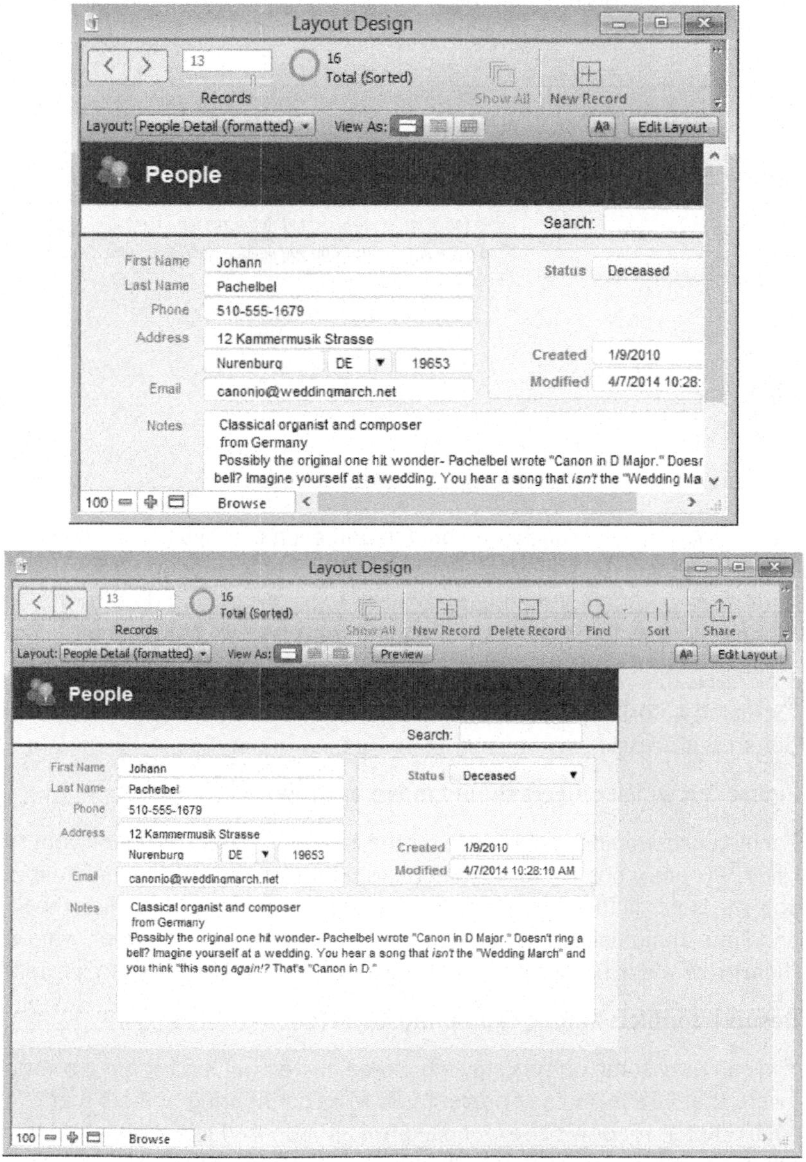

FIGURE 9-15

Top: When you resize the database window, FileMaker seems to make the worst choices possible. A smaller window leaves things out—like parts of the Notes, Status, Created, and Modified fields.

Bottom: A bigger window, on the other hand, is just a waste of space. You don't get any extra room where it counts (in the fields) so your window just takes up extra space for no good reason.

Every object on the layout has a hidden set of *anchors*. These anchors connect the object to one or more sides of the window, so when you move and resize the window, the objects know how to move. Out of the box, FileMaker anchors each object to the top and left, meaning if you move the bottom or right edges (by making the window bigger), then nothing happens.

But you can control the anchors. The Inspector holds the key—on the Position tab. The Autosizing section contains a sample object and four lock buttons that toggle off and on. Click any button, and the selected object or objects gets anchored to the associated side, as shown in Figure 9-16.

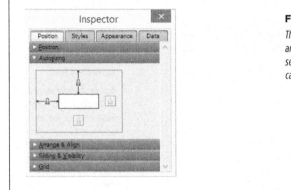

FIGURE 9-16

The Inspector's Autosizing control has four padlock buttons that can anchor the selected object to any side of the window. Right now the selected object is anchored to the top and left—the default setting. You can make any combination you need, anchoring no sides or all four.

There are a lot of ways to anchor an object, and each combination is useful in one situation or another. You can even anchor an object on competing sides (both top and bottom, or both left and right, or even all four). When you do this, the object doesn't just *move* as the window gets bigger—it *grows* too, as Figure 9-17 shows.

The problem is that growing and moving objects can run over the top of other objects. So using Autosizing correctly is something of a dark art. The easiest approach is a four-step process:

1. **Figure out which objects should move or grow.**

   For instance, would it make sense for the First Name field on your layout to get *taller?* Probably not. If you let something get taller, the best candidate is probably the Notes field, since you expect it to hold a lot of text. Likewise, the Status and Timestamp fields don't benefit from extra width, so you don't want to let them grow wider. But the remaining fields could all be bigger, space permitting.

2. **Resolve conflicts among expanding objects.**

   You can have some objects stay left, some move right, and some grow. But be aware that FileMaker can't prevent you from configuring objects that overlap each other as window size expands—after all, it doesn't know what the conflicts might be until you resize the window. For instance, the City, State, and Zip Code fields all occupy the same horizontal space. Anchoring all three on both the left and right will result in a confusing mess. So you need to decide which one should get the extra width. The obvious choice is the City field, since State and Zip Code always hold short values.

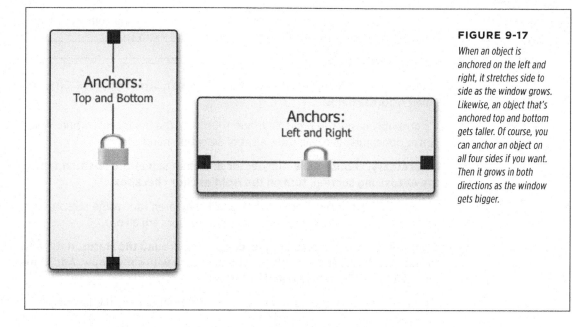

FIGURE 9-17

When an object is anchored on the left and right, it stretches side to side as the window grows. Likewise, an object that's anchored top and bottom gets taller. Of course, you can anchor an object on all four sides if you want. Then it grows in both directions as the window gets bigger.

WARNING If you have a series of side-by-side fields, then you might want them all to get a little wider together. But FileMaker doesn't give you that power, so you have to make a choice. If your company has big monitors for all employees, you can make your layout big enough to accommodate the data, and skip resizing windows altogether.

3. **Apply the anchors.**

   This process is tedious, but you can use the rubber band technique (see Figure 9-18) to grab collections of objects and then set them all at once.

4. **Test.**

   If you're like most of us humans, you'll miss something the first time through. So switch to Browse mode periodically, and resize the window. You'll instantly spot misbehaving objects. Return to Layout mode to fix them.

The best anchoring approach for *this* layout may be as follows:

- Anchor the First Name, Last Name, Phone Number, Street Address, City, and Email Address fields on the top, left, and right. This way, the fields stay near the top of the window and grow wider as you make the window bigger.

- Anchor the State, Zip Code, Status, and Timestamp fields on the top and right, but not the left, so they slide out of the way as the other fields get wider. You also need to anchor the Status, Created, and Modified fields and their labels to the right for the same reason.

- The Notes field will be anchored on all four sides. It's the one field that holds a lot of information, so it benefits the most from the extra space.

Here's how to make it happen:

1. **Select the First Name, Last Name, Phone Number, Street Address, City, and Email Address fields.**

   It's probably easiest to press Shift and then click the fields one by one. When you're done, the fields will show a set of selection handles.

2. **If necessary, choose View→Inspector and then select the Position tab. In the Autosizing section, turn on the right anchor checkbox.**

   The top and left anchors are already on (if they aren't for some reason, then turn them on so that the top, left, and right anchors are all on).

3. **Using the rubber-band technique, drag a box around the status, date, and timestamp fields, and their three labels. Figure 9-18 shows how. Additionally, select the Search field and its label.**

   Now the collection of fields and labels on the right side of the layout are all selected.

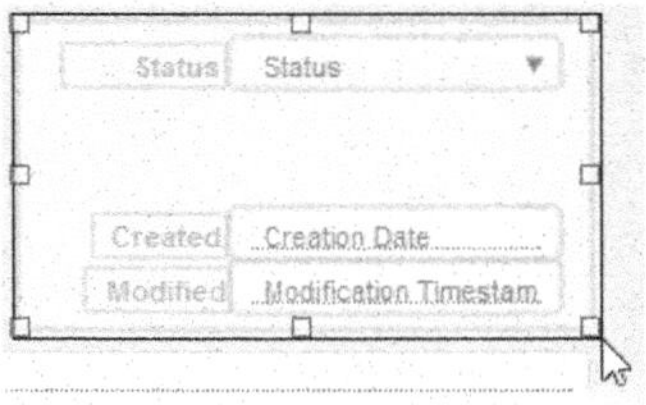

FIGURE 9-18

To select several objects that are close together, you can rubberband them. Click above and to the left of the objects and then drag down and right until they've all been touched by a side of the box. When you release the mouse button, everything the box came into contact with is selected.

4. **In the Autosizing controls, turn off the left anchor, and turn on the right anchor.**

   Once again, the top anchor should already be turned on, so make sure you have just the top and right anchors in play.

5. **Select the State and Zip Code fields and then anchor them to the top and right.**

6. **Select the Notes field and then turn on its bottom and right anchors.**

   This object should now be anchored on all four sides.

If you try your layout in Browse mode now, it should use space wisely when you make the window bigger. Compare your layout to Figure 9-19.

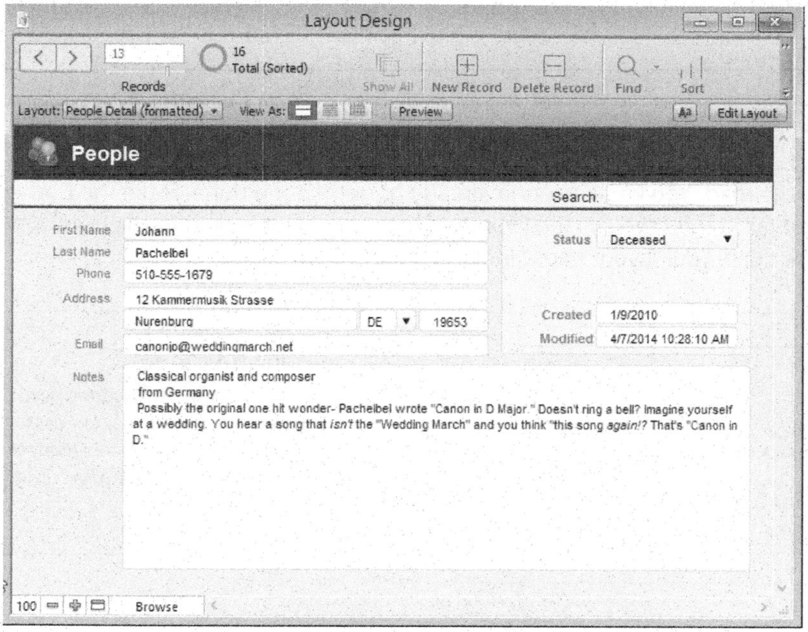

FIGURE 9-19

Now when you make the window bigger, the notes and address fields (State and Zip excepted) get bigger, too. If any of the expanding fields start to overlap another object on the layout, go back into Layout mode and make sure that all the objects to the right of the expanding field are anchored to the right but not the left. Similarly, anything below a vertically expanding layout object must be anchored at the bottom but not the top.

If you make the window *smaller,* the fields don't shrink beyond the size of your layout boundaries. FileMaker never lets the objects in Browse mode get smaller than they are in Layout mode. This behavior lets you establish a minimum size for your layout to keep things from getting too small, but it limits your flexibility. In general, design your layouts to be as small as they reasonably can be. That way, people who use your database can decide how big things should be by adjusting the window size.

Autosizing in List Layouts

You just learned how to use anchors so you can keep layout objects in check when users resize their windows. But in List view, anchors work a little differently. FileMaker never stretches records taller than the height of the Body in List view. If the window gets taller, you see more records instead. So top and bottom anchors have no effect in List view. But left and right anchors still work as you'd expect.

To get your People List layout with merge fields into shape, set the anchors as follows:

- Anchor the horizontal line on the left and right so it stretches the full width of the window.

- Anchor the three text objects with merge fields on the left and right. This way, if the window gets wider, then you can see more of the address, for instance.

- Anchor the Status field and Details button on the right, but not the left. They'll slide to the right and stay out of the way as the text object to their left gets bigger.

If you try things out in Browse mode now, as you make the window wider, the line should always span the full width, and the objects on the right should stay close to the right edge.

Sliding Layout Objects

Suppose you want to add the Notes field to the People Report layout so you can use it on the road. You know enough already to get the job done. Make the Body part a little taller and then use the Field tool to add the Notes field to the layout. When you're done, your layout might look like Figure 9-20.

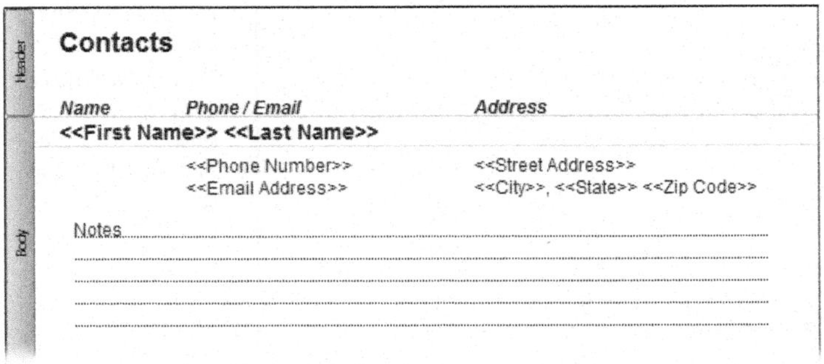

FIGURE 9-20

Here's a suggestion for adding the Notes field to your layout. It can take up the entire width of the page, yet clearly be related to the name and address data above.

If you preview this report, though, then you quickly spot a problem. Figure 9-21 shows the trouble.

Normally, a field on the layout takes up a fixed amount of space, no matter how much (or how little) data is inside. You might be tempted to try to fix this with a merge field, but that doesn't help here because no matter how tiny the text gets, the Body part is still just as tall as ever. You need some way for everything on the layout to *slide up* if the Notes field isn't full. Luckily, FileMaker's Inspector has the answer in the form of the Position tab's Sliding & Visibility section.

NOTE Sliding *only* takes place in Preview mode and when printing. Browse and Layout modes ignore the sliding configurations of layout objects.

■ UNDERSTANDING SLIDING

Normal field behavior doesn't always cause a problem. After all, you may *want* that empty space because you're printing onto a preprinted form, and everything needs to go in just the right spot on the page, or maybe your report design counts on consistent field sizes so things line up properly. But sometimes you can't get the effect you want without adjusting the layout based on the amount of data—usually when you're trying to tighten things up on the printed page to avoid wasted paper or excessive spacing around data, as with the Notes field example in the previous section.

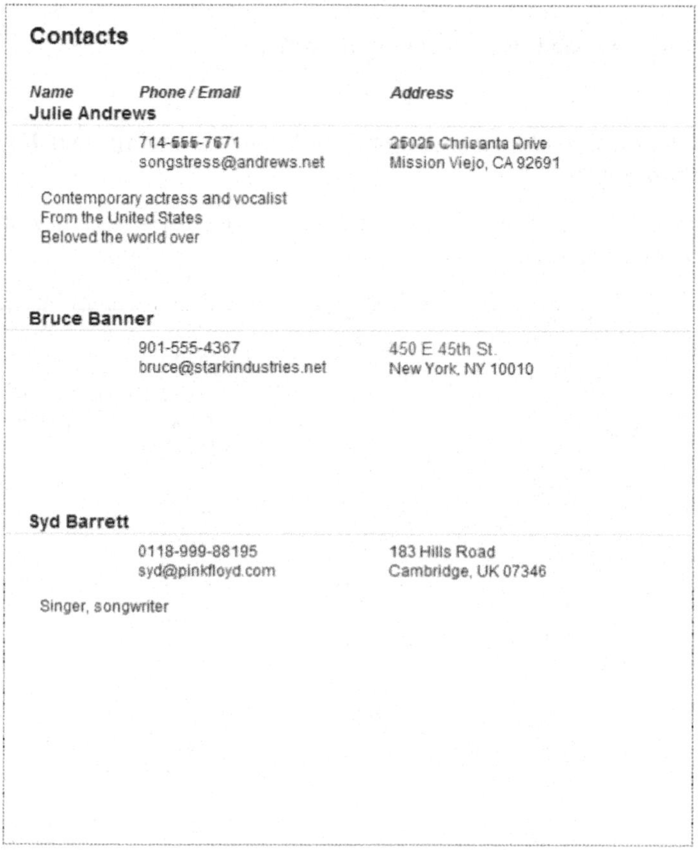

Contacts

Name	Phone / Email	Address
Julie Andrews		
	714-555-7671	25025 Chrisanta Drive
	songstress@andrews.net	Mission Viejo, CA 92691

Contemporary actress and vocalist
From the United States
Beloved the world over

Bruce Banner

901-555-4367   450 E 45th St.
bruce@starkindustries.net   New York, NY 10010

Syd Barrett

0118-999-88195   183 Hills Road
syd@pinkfloyd.com   Cambridge, UK 07346

Singer, songwriter

FIGURE 9-21

When you preview the report, you'll notice that your nice compact printout is now very space-inefficient. The Notes field may be empty, or hold just a line of text, but FileMaker reserves lots of space for it just in case. Also, if you have lots of notes in one record, then the field may not be big enough, so the text is cut off. But if you make the field even bigger, then you just waste more space. Sliding layout objects are the solution.

Sliding does three things to help in this situation. First, it lets fields shrink to just the right size for their data. After a field has shrunk, objects to the right or below the shrunken object will slide into place to fill the empty space.

TIP Sliding would be easier to understand if it were just called "shrinking" instead.

■ SETTING SLIDING OPTIONS

Here's how to make the Notes field on the People Report layout shrink (er, slide):

1. **Select the Notes field, click the Inspector's Position tab.**

   You need the Sliding & Visibility section.

2. **Select the "Sliding up based on" checkbox. Leave the default option of "Only objects directly above" selected.**

If you stop here, you don't quite have your problem solved. Even though the Notes field would shrink, the Body part wouldn't, and your report would still waste paper.

3. **Select the "Also resize the enclosing part" option.**

Body part also shrinks.

4. **Switch to Preview mode by pressing Ctrl+P (⌘-U), saving your layout changes if prompted.**

Now the Notes field and Body part take up only as much space as they need. Figure 9-22 confirms it.

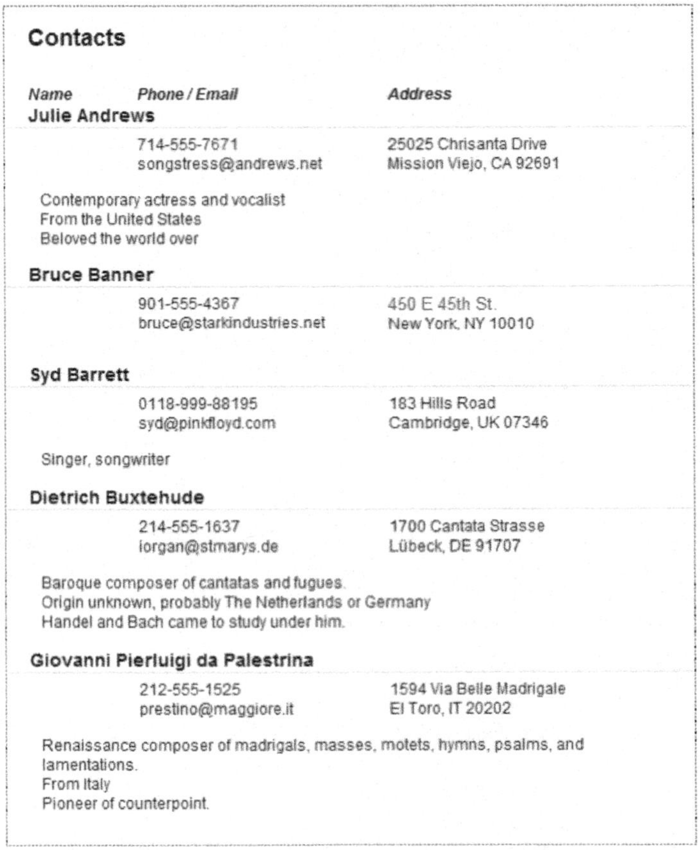

Contacts

Name	Phone / Email	Address
Julie Andrews		
	714-555-7671	25025 Chrisanta Drive
	songstress@andrews.net	Mission Viejo, CA 92691

Contemporary actress and vocalist
From the United States
Beloved the world over

Bruce Banner

	901-555-4367	450 E 45th St.
	bruce@starkindustries.net	New York, NY 10010

Syd Barrett

	0118-999-88195	183 Hills Road
	syd@pinkfloyd.com	Cambridge, UK 07346

Singer, songwriter

Dietrich Buxtehude

	214-555-1637	1700 Cantata Strasse
	iorgan@stmarys.de	Lübeck, DE 91707

Baroque composer of cantatas and fugues.
Origin unknown, probably The Netherlands or Germany
Handel and Bach came to study under him.

Giovanni Pierluigi da Palestrina

	212-555-1525	1594 Via Belle Madrigale
	prestino@maggiore.it	El Toro, IT 20202

Renaissance composer of madrigals, masses, motets, hymns, psalms, and lamentations.
From Italy
Pioneer of counterpoint.

FIGURE 9-22

With the Notes field set to slide up, your layout can now show long or short notes without wasting space.

Sliding objects have layout badges to help you remember their special behavior. If you can't see them, choose View→Show→Sliding Objects. FileMaker adds little up-pointing and/or left-pointing arrows to each object that slides. Now you can see at a glance what goes where.

■ MORE SLIDING & VISIBILITY OPTIONS

The Inspector's Sliding & Visibility section has several options to control just how the selected objects slide (and shrink if appropriate). In general, an object can slide left, up, or both.

If you want something to just slide left, as when you're displaying fields for City, State, and Zip Code on a single line, you're in luck. Just select all three fields, select the "Sliding left" checkbox, and you're done. When you print or preview the layout, the objects slide to the left when field data isn't long enough to fill the full width of the field.

Objects that slide up, on the other hand, require a second decision. When you select the "Sliding up based on" option, you also need to decide how objects below the shrinking object behave. Everything on the layout that's below the shrinker can slide up, or only those objects FileMaker considers "directly" below the object can slide. Since a picture is worth a thousand words, see Figure 9-23.

As you learned in the last section, if you turn on "Also resize the enclosing part," the part the object is on shrinks to fit its contents. Be sure to test and retest your layout. If you set a field to slide up and reduce the size of the enclosing part, all the layout objects below it have to be set to slide up, too. If you don't, the sliding object will still shrink, but the non-sliding objects below will obstinately hold their ground, and you'll end up with a gap between them. See the box below to learn how sliding and merge fields compare.

FREQUENTLY ASKED QUESTION

Merge Fields vs. Sliding

Why should I bother with sliding? Isn't that what merge fields are for?

It's true that merge fields and sliding objects have some things in common. Both adjust the data shown on a layout, squeezing things together in the process. But they have some major differences:

- Merge fields work everywhere, even in Browse mode. Sliding objects, on the other hand, have no effect on Browse mode (or Find mode). Instead, they do their thing only in Preview mode and when printing.

- Any object on a layout, including pictures, can slide. You can't show pictures using merge fields.

- Fields that slide act like normal fields in Browse mode, in that you can edit the data in them. Merge fields are just text objects; they're for data display, not data entry.

If you have a few fields that you want to display as a single block of text, then use merge fields. If your needs are more complex (incorporating graphics, for instance), or you need to be able to edit data on the layout, then use sliding objects instead.

Also, there's absolutely nothing wrong with using both on one layout. In fact, the People Report layout you've been working on could use merge fields for the name and address, along with the sliding Notes field. You can even set a text object containing merge fields to slide if you want.

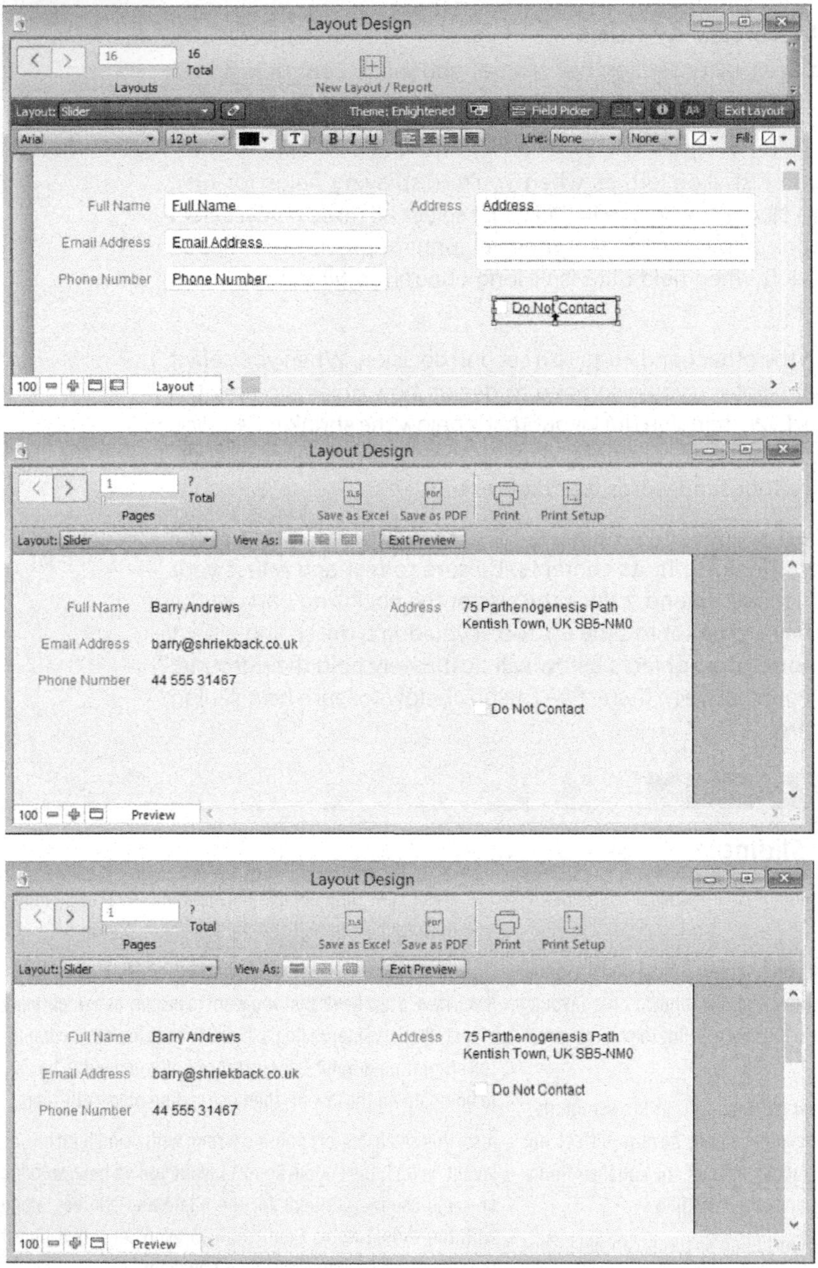

FIGURE 9-23

Top: Everything on this layout is technically above the Do Not Contact checkbox. But for the purposes of sliding, only two count. From FileMaker's perspective, the Address field is "directly above" it, but the Phone field is also considered above Do No Contact. If the Address field and the Do Not Contact checkbox are both set to slide up, then the "All Above" or "Only directly above" choice becomes important.

Middle: If you choose "All Above," then the checkbox never slides because the Phone field doesn't.

Bottom: If you choose "Only directly above," then the checkbox sticks with the Address field, even if that means sliding up alongside the Phone field.

Be cautious when sliding up based on "Objects above." "Above" includes items to the right of the vertical page break. When previewing and printing, FileMaker ignores layout items to the right of the vertical page break, so it's a handy spot to put onscreen notes or instructions that you don't need printed. But no matter how far to the right you place an object, it's still above any objects further down the printable area. In other words, a layout object off to the right that by definition can't be printed can still prevent an object from sliding past it. The simplest solution is to slide based on "Objects directly above."

■ OBJECT VISIBILITY

One more Sliding & Visibility option is pretty self-explanatory. If you turn on "Hide when printing," all currently selected objects will disappear in Preview mode and when printing. This option is handy for things like buttons that don't make sense on a printed page, or background graphics that would waste ink.

■ Buttons

So far in this chapter you've learned how to use themes and styles to format layout objects, how to use grids and guides to give layouts order, and how merge fields enhance data display. In this last section, you'll put all that experience together with a new skill that gives your layouts the power to run scripts. FileMaker's Button tool creates a special layout object that can display a label, an icon, or both, and the instructions to run a specific script when the button is clicked. You can turn other layout objects into buttons too. Plus, the Button Bar tool lets you make professional panels of buttons that can perform related tasks, like navigation, or tasks common to every layout in your database. But before you dive into learning how button tools work, an introduction to a few basic application design principles will help you use those tools to create an attractive and user-friendly database.

Designing Buttons

The main point of creating a button is to give users a way to run a script you've created. In other words, there's a task they need to perform, and you give them a way to do that task by providing a button they can click to do it. As with all your design decisions, the look and placement of your button can have an effect on whether users know how or when to click it. Before you can put your buttons in the right place, your database needs to be well organized and consistent from layout to layout. To start planning for this organization, it's helpful to think about the scripts you'll be creating for your users. Most of the scripts you'll assign to buttons can be broken into three main categories of tasks: navigation, layout-specific, and context-specific. Each task type has a corresponding button type that best suits it. The next sections will describe each task type. Take a look at Figure 9-24 to see what's in store.

■ NAVIGATION TASKS

People need a way to get around in the database. The Layout pop-up menu is a native FileMaker control that lets people move from layout to layout at will. But that process isn't intuitive to users. Nor are those controls aligned with modern expectations about moving from place to place on the Web, which has taught visitors to look for navigation controls at the top of every web page. So if you give users something that looks familiar—for instance, navigation buttons that look like ones you might see on a website and appear in the same place on every layout in your database—they'll feel comfortable from the first time they see your design. Even if they don't understand everything at a glance, they'll know how to get around.

Designing good navigation means thinking about your database's *information architecture* (that's another way of referring to the ER diagram described on page 194). The navigation buttons you choose may be a subset of all the tables in your database; a complete version of *CH09 Buttons.fmp12* would include Estimate Line Items, Invoices, Payments, Receipts, and other supporting tables. But users will interact with those records through the context of a Job or an Estimate record, so there's no need to give them a button on the main navigation bar.

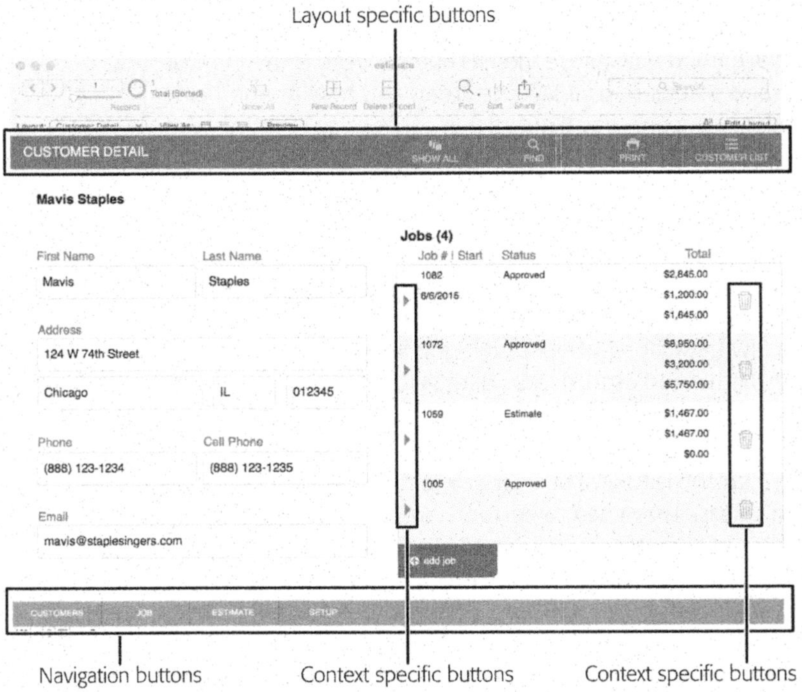

FIGURE 9-24

This image shows the Customer List layout from the sample database CH09 Buttons.fmp12. You can see three categories of buttons: navigation, layout specific, and context specific. The second two categories are well suited to button bars. This layout was created for FileMaker Go on an iPad, where many apps show navigation buttons at the bottom of the screen. Layout specific buttons are at the top. Context specific buttons make sense, based on where they're located. The Add Job, Trash can, and green triangle are all context specific because they perform actions based on their location. The green triangle shows detail about the job clicked on. The Trash can deletes the Job record, and Add Job creates a new Job record that's related to the current customer.

LAYOUT SPECIFIC TASKS

Layout specific tasks are also best created as button bars. Not only are they easy for you to create, they also provide consistency, which is extremely important in making your database professional and user-friendly. If people know that they can click a Find button on the same location on every layout, you only have to show them how once. If you didn't locate the Find button in the same spot, your users have to hunt for the right button before they can do a find. People do get used to inconsistency, but they're never as efficient, or as happy, as they would be with a thoughtfully designed database.

CONTEXT SPECIFIC TASKS

Context specific tasks are those that make the most sense when they're located in a particular spot on the layout. The Add Job button appears at the bottom of the Jobs portal, so its location (actually touching the portal, as though it's part of it) and its name each help make obvious what the button does. Use this concept throughout your database, and as with the Find button example described above, you'll only have to show users how to create new related records once, and they can carry the concept throughout the database.

While there's nothing wrong with putting the Add Job button in a layout specific taskbar, it's still separated from its context on this layout. Users are looking at the Job portal, but have to reach up to the top bar to click or tap to add a job. What if you wanted to also show an Invoice portal on this layout? Now it makes even less sense to have two Add buttons—one each for Jobs and Invoices—up at the top, away from their respective portals.

The mobile platform has lots of well-known conventions for dealing with list items. Anyone who's used a smart phone or tablet knows what to do with the icons that appear next to each item. So in this mobile layout, the green triangle lets users click or tap to show the Job record's detail. The Trash icon comes with similar user expectations: There's no doubt that clicking or tapping it deletes the item.

Creating a Button

The Button tool lets you create a drawn shape that can show a name, an icon, or both. Button objects also have scripts or button actions (page 177) attached, and they come with object states (page 339) that cue users that clicking on them will cause something to happen. Button actions are simple tasks, most of which are available in one of FileMaker's menus. See the box on page 370 to learn more about button actions and why it makes sense to use them instead of menu commands.

Here's how to create a button, and then assign it an icon and a script step:

1. **Open the sample file *CH09 Buttons.fmp12*. Switch to Layout mode and then go to the Customer Detail layout. Click the Button tool and then click and drag in the top row of the Jobs portal.**

   When you release the mouse button, the Button Setup dialog box appears (Figure 9-25).

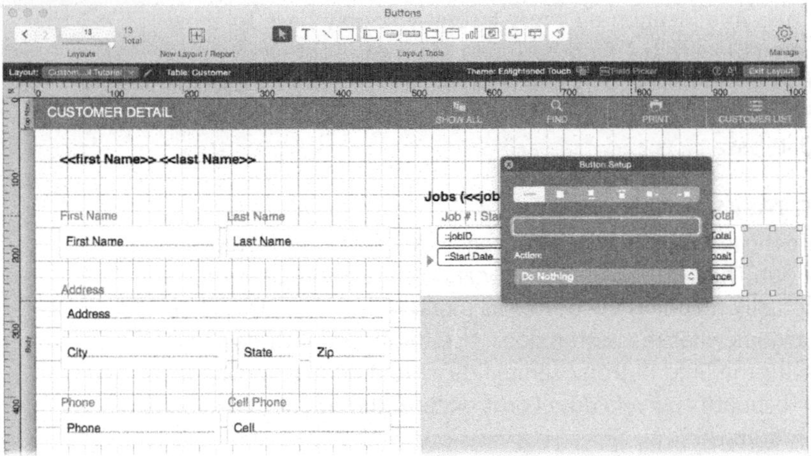

FIGURE 9-25

As you draw the new button, it appears in the theme's default style. You'll change that later in the tutorial, using a style that's been created for you. In real life, seeing the button in the wrong style might remind you to create a new style to fit your new button. As you've learned, designing in File-Maker is fluid, and you'll switch tasks frequently in the design process.

2. **In the Object Name text box, type *Trash*.**

   The name won't appear after you're done, but it's still helpful for the name to appear in the dialog box if you have to edit the button later.

3. **In the display bar at the top, select the "Display only an icon" button.**

   The icons make each button's effect clear, but you can point to the icons to display tooltips. The dialog box changes to show you the glyph palette. Scroll the palette to see the full array.

4. **Select the second Trash icon.**

   In the background, an icon appears on your button.

5. **Use the font size slider to change the icon's size to 24 points. Or type *24* in the size field.**

   You want the icon to be large enough to be instantly recognizable, but not so large that it's distracting.

6. **From the Action pop-up menu, choose Single Step.**

   The Button Action dialog box appears. Here's where you'll assign the button a task.

7. **In the Script Step box, type *d* to filter the list, and then choose Delete Portal Row. Click OK to close the Button Action window.**

   Figure 9-26 shows this process in action. Now the button knows what to do when it's clicked or tapped.

8. **If necessary, select the Inspector's Styles tab. Select the Trash style.**

The button changes appearance. It's light orange on a transparent background.

> **NOTE** The Button Setup's Option section still has the holdover option for changing the cursor to a hand when it's hovering over the button. But that hand cursor looks outdated. Most every layout object has object states, so use those instead. About the only layout object that doesn't have object states these days is an imported graphic. But if that's what you need, you're better off using a real button and then creating a new glyph (page 376) for your graphic.

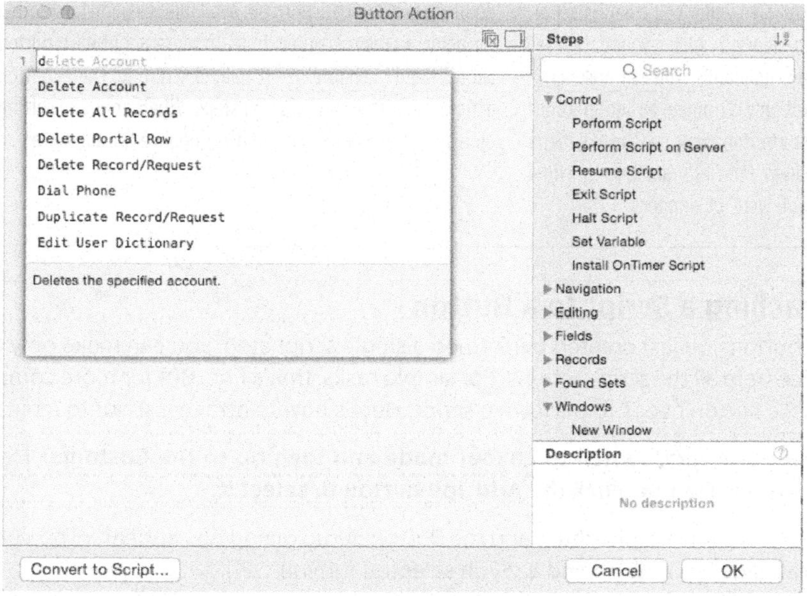

FIGURE 9-26

The Button Action dialog box works much like the Script Workspace, except you can only choose a single script step to attach to a button. But if you pick a script step and then realize that you really need to write a script, click the Convert to Script button. You'll see a dialog box that lets you name the new script. Once you do, the Edit Script dialog box appears, along with all its power. See page 825 to learn more.

Switch to Browse mode and test your button. Buttons work in Browse and Find modes, but not in Preview or Layout modes. Notice the button's object states: If you hover over it, the button gets a line around it. Clicking or tapping reverses its colors. These clues—called *affordances* in UX-speak—are part of the Trash style you applied in the steps above. You may need to adjust the button's size or location in the portal to polish the look. Don't forget that if you're designing for FileMaker Go, users interact with buttons with their fingers, and those buttons should be at least 44 × 44 pixels to be comfortable for most.

> **NOTE** Although the glyph palette contains almost 150 icons, you can add your own. Click the + button below the palette and then find the graphic you need. For best performance, the graphic should be SVG formatted, but PNGs will also work.

Button Actions

The Button Setup window has dozens of available actions, as you saw in the steps on page 369. There you made a Trash icon that deletes a portal row. Scan through these commands; you'll notice that many of them repeat the same functions you find in FileMaker's menus. In fact, the list of actions is almost identical to the list of script steps available when you create a script. That's not meaningless redundancy. By giving your databases buttons for lots of everyday commands, you can make File-Maker even easier to use. Not only is training easier—because common commands are just a button away, instead of a menu and even a submenu menu away. (And let's face it, by that time you probably forgot what you were looking for.)

For some sets of users, you might want to close and lock the toolbar and create custom menus (page 568) that hide all the potentially dangerous commands, like Delete Found Set and Import Records. If you do that, you have to give users a way to do basic tasks like searching, sorting, and printing. So having a good grasp of which actions are available is a good foundation for being a power scripter. To learn more about each button action, head to Chapter 12—it's about scripting. There, button actions are referred to as script steps. Whether you're setting up a button or writing a script, they behave the same way.

Attaching a Script to a Button

The button you just created performed a single script step: you can make only one choice from all the script actions. For simple tasks, that's fine. But for more complex tasks, a button needs to perform a script. Here's how to attach a script to a button:

1. **If necessary, switch to Layout mode and then go to the Customer Detail layout. Double-click the Add Job button to select it.**

   The button is highlighted and the Button Setup dialog box appears. The button already has a name and a glyph selected for you.

2. **From the Action pop-up menu, select Perform Script.**

   The Specify Script dialog box appears.

3. **Select the Create Job script and then click OK. Or double-click Create Job to select the script you need and close the dialog box at the same time.**

   Create Job appears in the Script field (below the Action field). The Script button lets you reopen the Specify Script dialog box if you've selected the wrong script. The Options section has a new option when a button runs a script instead of a button action. You can choose what happens to any currently running script when your button is clicked. The default option is Pause Current Script, and that's what you want here. You'll learn what the other options do in Chapter 13.

Converting a Layout Object to a Button

Drawn buttons are useful, but there are times when an existing object on the layout might serve better than a new drawn shape. For example, back in Figure 9-24, you saw a green triangle button that shows the Job Detail record. You can see the same button in the *CH09 Buttons.fmp12* file. It's a large, transparent button covering almost the whole portal row. Users click anywhere in the portal (except on the Trash icon) to view a Job's detail. But users also know that they can click blue underlined text. You could remove the existing button and convert the JobID field to a button instead. Is it a better design choice? If you need to allow data entry in a portal (a rare, but sometimes necessary, occurrence) or if the portal is just too tight to allow the extra space needed to display the triangle, then It might be. Here's how to convert an existing object to a button:

1. **If necessary, switch to Layout mode, then go to the Customer Detail layout. Select the JobID field and then choose Format→Button Setup.**

   The Button Setup dialog box appears, but this time its options are limited. You can't name the button or add a glyph to it. You can only attach an action to it.

2. **In the Action pop-up menu, choose Perform Script.**

   The Specify Script dialog box appears.

3. **Select the "Go to Job Detail from Portal" script and then click OK. Or just double-click the script.**

   The script you choose will perform the proper navigation from Customer Detail to the Job Detail layout.

4. **On the Inspector's Styles tab, click the Portal Link style.**

   The JobID field is now formatted in blue text with an underline.

You can switch to Browse mode without even bothering to close the Button Setup window. But click the X in the window's upper right corner first if you're bothered about that stuff.

■ MAKING A BUTTON NOT A BUTTON

Once you see the blue underlined text, you might decide you liked the transparent button better. Or maybe you've created a layout object button that you don't need anymore. All you have to do is change the object's Style back to what it was and then take the object's button action away. To do that, select the button and then choose Format→Button Setup. Or you can right-click the button and then choose Button Setup from the context sensitive menu. In the Action pop-up, choose Do Nothing. Again, you can switch directly to Browse mode afterwards without closing the setup window. Now the button has no action and nothing happens if you click on it.

NOTE   In Layout mode, you can choose View→Show→Buttons to view a small blue badge in the lower-right corner of every button on the layout. Choose the same command again to turn the badge display off.

Don't confuse undoing a button with graying it out to show that it's not available until some condition is met. If that's what you want, keep the button script, but make its script smarter. See the box below to learn about using conditional formatting to make your button appear unavailable or grayed out.

Making a Button Appear Grayed Out

Most programs and apps, FileMaker included, include buttons you can't always click. For example, you can't click Delete in the Manage Database window's Fields tab if you don't have a field selected. The universally accepted look for a button that isn't quite ready to be clicked is faded, or *grayed out*.

To extend that visual metaphor and so give feedback to your users, you'll want to mimic this behavior when users need to do something before a button can be clicked. Suppose you have a button that sends an email to the address in the Email field. The button should be grayed out if there's no address. That's where FileMaker's conditional formatting helps.

You'll learn more about conditional formatting in Chapter 16. Here's a sneak peek to whet your appetite: Create a button using what you've learned so far (there are two envelope glyphs suitable for an email button). Select the button and then choose Format→Conditional. Click Add to add a new condition. In the box next to the "Formula is" pop-up menu, type the following exactly as shown:

```
IsEmpty ( Customer::Email )
```

In plain English, the formula says "If the Customer Email address is empty…" The If part is understood, and the rest almost makes sense.

Use the text color settings in the Conditional Formatting dialog box to tell FileMaker to turn the button text *and the icon color* gray. You can also lighten the fill color of the button itself. You now have a button that automatically gives you visual feedback about the state of the Email field.

This technique only changes the button's *appearance*. Graying out the text doesn't cause a different response when you click the button. For that, you'll need a script that doesn't try to send an email if the field is empty. And it needs to tell users why the email wasn't sent, too. Chapter 12 will give you the pieces you need to put that together.

Popover Buttons

The buttons you've seen so far in this chapter aren't the only kind in the FileMaker kit. Popover buttons add depth to your layouts by displaying content only when the user asks for it. You can put just about anything you want into a popover. For example, you can use one to display a container field for signature capture on a mobile device. You can attach one to the bottom of a navigation button to create a FileMaker version of a hierarchical menu—the buttons are displayed only when you click a popover button. In this case, you'll load the popover with a set of buttons that act as a submenu. If you're going to make a tightly controlled solution, with locked, hidden toolbars and custom menus, you'll need to give users an alternate way to do a find. Figure 9-27 shows a popover used to display a limited set of fields suitable for finding customers.

NOTE If you can't see the Popover Button tool, press and hold the Button tool. A menu appears; from there you can switch the tool's behavior. Note that the icon changes shape to give you feedback on which button type the tool is ready to create.

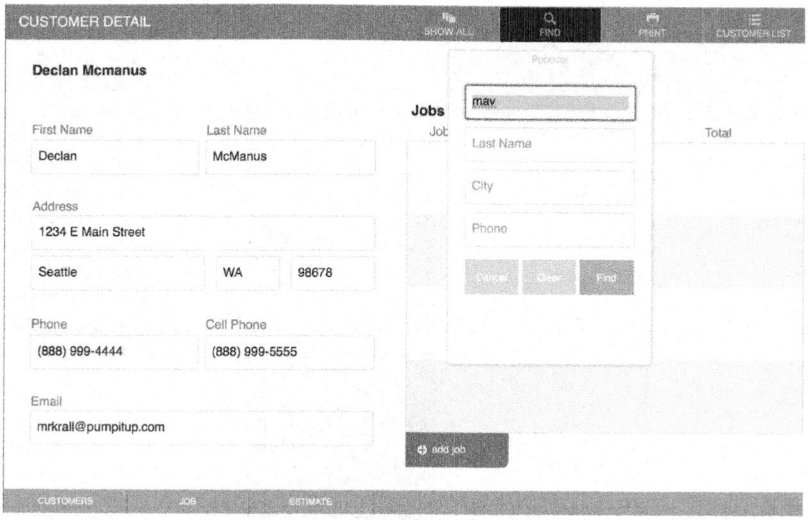

FIGURE 9-27

This popover holds a set of global fields that are used by a Find script. Take a look at the script to learn more about how it does its work. The popover provides a simple way for people to search on a limited set of fields from this layout. That way, they don't have to deal with figuring out how to enter appropriate search criteria in the Email field or in the Jobs portal.

Think of objects on the popover as being layered on top of it. As with portals, anything you want to place in the popover must be fully enclosed by it. And although you can put an object on a popover that's as big as the popover itself, you may see scroll bars momentarily when the popover is first displayed. To avoid user confusion, it's best to leave some padding space between a popover and its objects.

After you've created a popover button, you can resize it, rearrange its objects, or change its options. To do that, double-click the button in Layout mode and the Popover Button Setup window appears. There you can set the popover's orientation, name the popover, display that name in a title bar, and attach a script trigger (page 469). And see Figure 9-28 for the options you can set in your popover buttons.

Button Bar

A button bar is made up of two or more *segments,* each of which behaves like an individual button. Back on page 366 you learned that most tasks your buttons offer fall into one of three categories: navigation, layout specific, or context specific. These categories move from the least specific to the most. That is, navigation tasks are necessary throughout your entire database and they do the same work wherever they occur, so navigation functions are the most general. Somewhat less general are layout specific functions. They relate to a specific layout, but may have tasks in common with other layouts. For example, at the top of the Customer Detail layout in the *CH09 Buttons.fmp12* file, you see a group of tasks that all relate to the current record or to the layout as a whole (Show All, Find, Print, Customer List). Button bars are useful in all these cases.

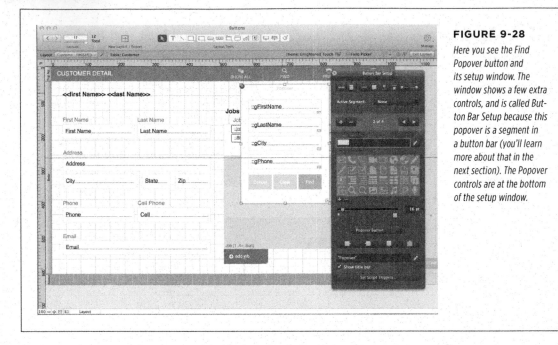

FIGURE 9-28

Here you see the Find Popover button and its setup window. The window shows a few extra controls, and is called Button Bar Setup because this popover is a segment in a button bar (you'll learn more about that in the next section). The Popover controls are at the bottom of the setup window.

So far in this chapter, you've created context specific buttons, those whose function is related to their immediate location. Back on page 368, you created a Trash button that deleted a specific record in a portal; that's a context specific button because FileMaker knows the button is located in a portal and even which record a user clicks on. It uses that information to figure out which record the user wants to delete. Context sensitive tasks aren't usually good candidates for button bars, but navigation and layout specific tasks are.

Here's why: Button bars make it easy to keep your layouts consistent. Once you've formatted a bar and given it tasks to do, you can save time by copying and pasting it throughout your database. You can often paste the same navigation bar on all of your layouts without making any changes to it. In this way, you can create a consistent interface for your users with little effort. Layout specific tasks are also good candidates for bars. Even if all the tasks aren't the same on every layout—in the example above, all the Detail layouts in your database will need Show All, Find, and Print buttons. Only the button on the right (Customer List) will need to behave differently on different layouts. That is, it shows the Customer List on the Customer Detail layout and the Job List on the Job Detail layout.

As in the entity-relationship exercise in Chapter 6, thinking about where to use button bars can help you crystallize the organization in your database. Here are some other attributes of button bars that can make them more useful than individual buttons:

- You can create up to 50 segments in a button bar. If you add or remove segments, FileMaker automatically adjusts the width of each segment.

- You can format each segment separately, with its own script or button action.

- Autosizing acts on the bar, and not on each segment, so button bars behave better on layouts where windows are resized.

- Segments have all the object states of regular buttons, and as you'd expect, the Active state only applies to one segment at the time.

- All segments of a bar share the same style, so consistency is baked in.

- Segments can have conditional formatting (page 648).

- Segments can have script triggers (page 469) in addition to their formatted button action or script.

- Segments can be hidden using the Inspector's "Hide object when" option.

- Unlike an individual button, a button bar segment can have a calculated name.

- Button bars can contain a mix of Buttons and Popover Buttons.

- You can arrange the segments horizontally or vertically.

- Unlike a regular button, you can switch a segment from a button to a popover (and vice versa).

Now that you know why they're useful, here's how to create a button bar that handles navigation. If necessary, open the *CH09 Buttons.fmp12* sample file and switch to the Customer Detail layout.

1. **In Layout mode, select the Button Bar tool.**

   Just to the right of the Button tool, it looks like three rectangular buttons in a row. Or a Tootsie Roll.

2. **Drag in the space below the Email field to create a small button bar. Then, using the Inspector's Position tab, enter the following dimensions to resize the bar and move it into the footer: Left = 0, Top = 616, Width = 484, Height = 32.**

   You could try to drag to approximate these dimensions, but it's usually easier to create your object roughly to size and shape, and then let the Inspector do the fussy work. When you're done, a button bar with three segments appears in the footer, and the Button Bar Setup window appears (Figure 9-29). Selection handles appear all around the button bar, and the first, or leftmost, segment is active.

3. **On the Inspector's Styles tab, choose the Bottom Nav style.**

   This style has already been created for you in the sample file. The style matches the footer, so the bar blends into the background.

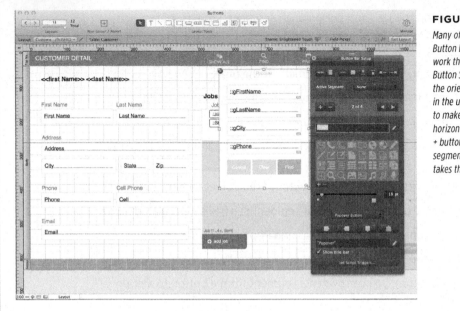

FIGURE 9-29

Many of the options in the Button Bar Setup window work the same as in the Button Setup window. Use the orientation buttons in the upper-left corner to make a button bar horizontal or vertical. The + button lets you add new segments and the - button takes them away again.

NOTE The Change a cursor to a hand over button option is outmoded. Most modern programs show object states instead. And since mobile apps don't support the hover state, the option doesn't work there anyway.

4. **In the Button Bar Setup window, type *Customer* in the Segment Name field.**

   This process is the same as when naming a regular button. The pencil icon to the right of the field lets you use the calculation engine to name a button dynamically.

NOTE It might seem odd to create a segment in a button bar that goes to the layout you're already on. Remember, though, you're creating this button bar once, so that you can copy and paste it throughout your database. The button action will run, but since it's already on the layout it's specified to go to, the user won't see anything happen.

5. **From the Action pop-up menu, choose Single Step.**

   The Button Action window appears, just as it does when you format an individual button.

6. **In the Button Action window, choose "Go to Layout" from the list of steps on the right.**

   The script step appears in the Action pane, along with the gear icon.

7. **Click the gear icon, and then choose Layout.**

   The Specify Layout window appears.

8. **Choose the Customer Detail layout, and then click OK to close the Specify Layout window. Click OK again to close the Button Action window.**

   The first segment of the button bar is formatted.

9. **Click the right triangle to move to the next segment.**

   The selected segment display in the Button Bar Setup window changes to show that the second segment is selected. In the background, the second segment is highlighted on the layout.

Use what you just learned to format the remaining two segments. Enter *Job* as the second segment's Name and give it a "Go to Layout" action that specifies the Job Detail Layout. The third segment's name is Estimate, and it should go to the Estimate Detail layout. When you're done, switch to Browse mode and test the button bar. Once you've got it working, you can copy and paste it to the other layouts in the database to create a working navigation system.

This tutorial uses mostly default button bar options. But all the regular button options—like label positions, icon positions, and glyphs—are also available in your button bars. And as with other layout objects, you can double-click a button bar as a shortcut for showing its setup window.

> **NOTE** A single dynamic script, like the one the Customer Detail Nav Script layout in the *CH09 Buttons.fmp12* file, can do the work of three different Button Actions.

■ Slide Controls

Efficient use of layout space is critical to your database design. Now that FileMaker Go is popular on small touchscreen devices, database developers have to make do with less real estate than ever before. And as with popovers, it's helpful to tuck information away until the user asks to see it. While tab controls (page 162) are a reliable way to layer content, you still need space at the top for clickable tab headings. Slide controls let you minimize the screen space given over to navigation between panels, or even remove it entirely.

In this example, you'll create a touchscreen-friendly interface that's small enough for an iPhone, courtesy of a slide control:

1. **In the *CH09 Styles Start.fmp12* file, switch to the Slide Control layout and then switch to Layout mode.**

   You'll build a slide control that covers nearly the whole layout.

2. **Press the Tab Control tool show to its menu. Choose the Slide Control option. Then drag a rectangle that takes up most of the layout—300 × 400 pixels.**

   Or you can choose Insert→Slide Control and then adjust FileMaker's work. Either way, the Slide Control Setup window appears when you're done (Figure 9-30).

3. **On the Field Picker, select horizontal alignment and the placeholder text label option (it's the last one of the four label buttons). Drag the First Name, Last Name, Address, City, State, and Zip Code fields onto the new slide control.**

   You've just placed all of these fields on the slide control's first panel.

4. **Click the middle navigation dot at the bottom of the slide control to display the second slide panel.**

   The dots behave in the same way in Layout and Browse modes. If you don't display them, you must use the right triangle on the Slide Control Setup window to advance the panels. Users on mobile can just swipe—a natural gesture for mobile device users.

5. **Drag the Email Address and Notes field on to the panel. Make the Notes field taller, so it fills most of the remaining space.**

   You'll want to give your users plenty of space to make and read notes.

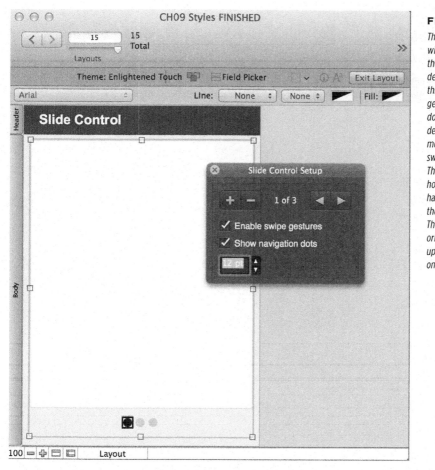

FIGURE 9-30

The Slide Control Setup window lets you choose the control's options. The default slide control has three panels, and swipe gestures and navigation dots are enabled. If you're designing a layout for a mobile device, then keep swipe gestures enabled. The dots help users see how many panels a control has, and which panel they're currently viewing. They're helpful for user orientation, but they take up space below the objects on the control.

6. **Click the right navigation dot and drag the Photo field into the panel. Adjust the height it to fill the panel, leaving a little breathing room at the edges.**

   The slide control lets you put the most important information on the first panel, while other data is easily accessible with a click or a swipe.

Switch back to Browse mode and click the navigation dots to see your slide control in action (Figure 9-31). Better still, open your database in FileMaker Go and use swiping gestures instead!

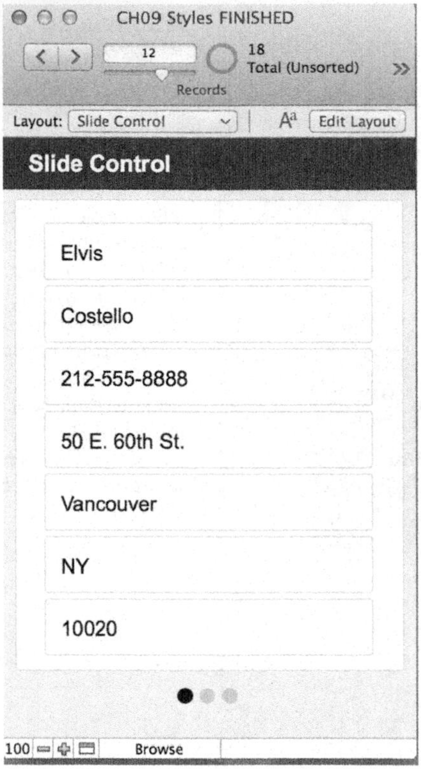

FIGURE 9-31

Slide controls let you show a manageable amount of information on each panel. Unlike tab controls, which require clickable tab objects across the top of the layout, swipe gestures let FileMaker Go users use their whole screen to navigate.

Understanding Calculations

When you learned about tables, fields, and relationships in the previous chapters, you dabbled in FileMaker's calculation dialog box. Most people first encounter the Specify Calculation window when they're creating a calculation field, so it's easy to think that's the only place it's used. True, writing formulas for calculation fields is probably the most common use of FileMaker's *calculation engine* (that's the fancy name for the code that handles math for your database), but that's far from the only use, as you'll see in this chapter.

No matter where you run into the Specify Calculation window, it works the same way. You use that window's field list, operators, and predefined functions to tell the calculation how to find the value you need. This chapter tells you how the basic concept works.

While calculations can make your database total invoices, analyze trends, and calculate dates and times, they aren't limited to number-crunching tasks. You can use them to find out about the computer your database is running on, track who's logged into the system, monitor their privileges, and then perform logical tests based on what you find. You'll start by learning how FileMaker handles calculations, and then you'll see how some common functions can take your database up to a new level of power.

■ Understanding Calculations

Way back on page 139, you saw how to create a field that's defined as a calculation. A calculation is a mathematical formula that manipulates the information in your database to give you the answers you need. For example, for a line item on an invoice, you need to multiply the price of an item by the quantity to get an extended price. To hand that task over to FileMaker, you create a calculation field and then write a formula that refers to the appropriate fields by name. FileMaker takes the information in the invoice fields and does the math.

FileMaker calculations can also do more than math. For starters, you can do calculations on time, date, timestamp, container, and text fields, too. (See the box on below for an example.) Calculation fields work just like any other FileMaker field, except that you can't type data into them. The calculations you give them determine what data they show. If you change the data a calculation refers to, you see FileMaker update the data automatically. Figure 10-1 shows where calculation fields can benefit your Invoice layout.

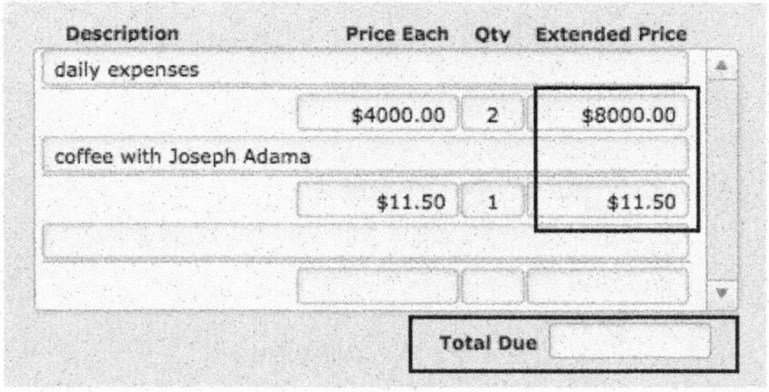

FIGURE 10-1

Without calculations, you have to manually calculate the extended price for each line item by multiplying the quantity times the price. And then, if the quantity changes, you have to visit your calculator again. But with calculation fields, the database does the math as soon as there's data in the fields the calculation refers to. Here the Extended Price field multiplies Price Each by Quantity. Plus, if data in either field changes, FileMaker updates the Extended Price automatically.

FREQUENTLY ASKED QUESTION

Text Calculations?

Aren't calculations just for numbers?

Many people see the Manage Database window's Calculation field type and assume it's for numbers. Too bad, because calculations can do all this:

- Calculations can pick apart text and put it together in different ways (on page 644, you'll use a calculation to make a web address that links to a customer's address map). You can even modify fonts, sizes, colors, and styles (turn every occurrence of the word "credit" to bold text, for instance).

- You can do math on *dates, times,* and *timestamps.* You can find out how old someone is based on his birthdate,

figure out how long you worked on a job, or see which payment came first.

- If you've stored a reference to a file in a *container* field, then you can use a calculation to retrieve the *path* to the original file.

You can even convert one kind of value into another when you use calculations. For example, if you have a text field that contains *"12/29/2016,"* then you can use a calculation to turn that date into a proper date value (such as December 29, 2016 or Dec. 29, 2016).

They're so useful that if you have a problem to solve, a calculation is likely to form at least part of the solution.

You can use a calculation field just like any other field: Put it on a layout, use it in Find mode, and even use it in *other* calculation fields. But as a calculation field, its value always stays up to date automatically.

Instant recomputation is what makes calculations useful for so many tasks. For example, you can use a calculation with the Records→Replace Field Contents command (see page 264). Instead of replacing the data in every record with the *same* value, a calculation can produce a unique value for each record. In the Manage Database dialog box, you can start using the "Auto-Enter Calculated value" and "Validated by Calculation" field options, making those features much more powerful. Scripts, as you'll learn in Chapter 12, use calculations in many of their script steps. Here are some other places you can use the Specify Calculation dialog box:

- **Auto-enter** field options let you put a calculated result in a field when someone creates a record or edits data (page 245).

- **Field validation** uses calculations to make sure the data entered in a field conforms to rules you set up (page 252).

- **Portal filtering** lets you show only some related records in a portal (page 599). For example, you can filter a portal so it shows only invoices with the status "Unpaid," or another portal could show only completed jobs.

- The **Send Mail** command can create email addresses or concatenate the body of an email (page 461).

- **Chart titles**, labels, and even x- and y-axes can be calculated (page 652).

- **Tooltips** can use calculations to determine the message that gets displayed (page 354). For example, you can show a list of related data, like the number of items remaining in inventory, or the total of all Invoices for a specific customer.

- **Conditional formatting** lets you apply logic to objects on a layout to change the way they look (page 648). On an invoice layout, for example, you can display the Total Due field in a bold red font *if* the invoice is more than 30 days overdue.

- **Scripts** let you use calculations to change the way script steps work. You can test conditions, create dynamic data, or even take different actions based on the results of calculations. Chapter 12 introduces you to scripts.

- The **Data Viewer** lets you preview your calculations without making a fake field or messing with an otherwise good calculation that needs a little tweaking. (You need FileMaker Pro Advanced to use the Data Viewer; see page 552.)

- **Privilege Sets** can use calculations to limit access to tables, records, and fields. Chapter 19 tells you how to use calculations for tighter database security.

Creating a Calculation

As the Jobs database now stands, when you add line items to an invoice, you have to type the quantity and price for each item. Then you have to multiply them together to get the extended price, and then you have to type the result. In this section, you'll learn how to tell FileMaker to do all that work for you, using a calculation that names your fields and uses computer shorthand to do the math:

1. **In the *CH10 Jobs Start.fmp12* sample database, choose File→Manage Database and then make sure you're on the Fields tab. From the Table pop-up menu, choose Line Items.**

   That's the table with your Extended Price field in it.

2. **In the field list, select the Extended Price field. From the Type pop-up menu, choose Calculation and then click Change.**

   FileMaker warns you that when it converts the field, it changes (read: overwrites) any information already in the field. See Figure 10-2.

FileMaker Pro

When changing the field type to Calculation or Summary, FileMaker will replace any data in the field with the result of the formula. Proceed anyway?

OK   Cancel

FIGURE 10-2

This warning is serious. Your new calculation overwrites existing data when you close the Manage Database window. But you're safe until you click OK to this warning and in the Manage Database dialog box. If you change your mind and don't want the calculation after all, just click Cancel instead, and you get the chance to discard all the changes you've made to this field.

---

3. **Click OK.**

   The Specify Calculation dialog box appears, as shown in Figure 10-3.

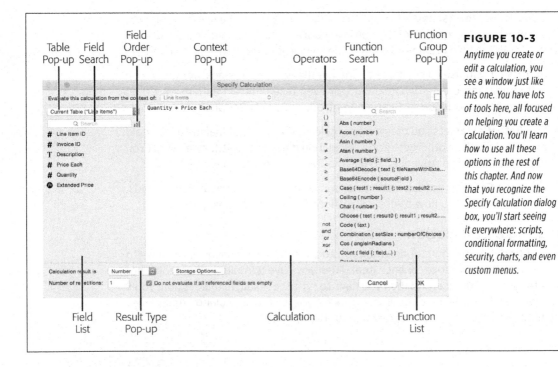

Table Pop-up   Field Search   Field Order Pop-up   Context Pop-up   Operators   Function Search   Function Group Pop-up

Field List   Result Type Pop-up   Calculation   Function List

FIGURE 10-3

Anytime you create or edit a calculation, you see a window just like this one. You have lots of tools here, all focused on helping you create a calculation. You'll learn how to use all these options in the rest of this chapter. And now that you recognize the Specify Calculation dialog box, you'll start seeing it everywhere: scripts, conditional formatting, security, charts, and even custom menus.

4. **In the Calculation box, type *Quantity * Price Each*.**

You've just added a brand-new calculation that multiplies the contents of the Price Each field by the contents of the Quantity field. The "*" is the same symbol you see on your computer's keypad, and it means multiply. See page 390 for details on other symbols (or operators) used for math.

> **NOTE** As you begin to type the name of each field, a list of options appears below your text. FileMaker is offering up the names of fields in your current table as well as calculation *functions* (which you'll learn about later in this chapter). When you've typed enough of the field name to see it selected in that list, just press Enter, and FileMaker will type the rest.

5. **Click OK.**

The Manage Database window updates itself, showing the calculation for the Extended Price field.

6. **In the Manage Database window, click OK.**

You're back where you started.

> **TIP** If FileMaker complains about not being able to find a field when you click OK, then check the spelling of your field names. And if you hate to type, you can double-click the fields in your field list instead of typing.

Switch to the Invoices layout and then add a line item. You see that the Extended Price field updates *automatically* once there's a value in both the fields you referred to in the calculation (Price Each and Quantity). If you try to manually edit the value in the Extended Price field, an error message appears, telling you the field is not modifiable.

The Structure of a Calculation

If you accidentally mistyped or misspelled a field name in the example in the previous section, you already know that FileMaker is picky about how you create a calculation. *Syntax*—the order of elements and punctuation—is critical when you're creating calculations. So before you learn more tricks, this section outlines common calculation terms and rules of thumb.

> **NOTE** Calculations are often called *calcs* for short, or *formulas*. Although some slight differences exist between a calculation and a formula, people usually use the terms interchangeably. Sometimes, a formula is so useful or common that FileMaker defines it as a reusable formula, also known as a *function*.

In the next examples, don't focus on what the example calculation does. You'll get to that. Right now, focus on structure. A calculation can be short and simple:

    Pi * Diameter

Or it can be more complicated:

```
Case (
  Shape = "Circle" ;
  Pi * (Diameter/2) ^ 2 ;
  Shape = "Rectangle" ;
  ShapeLength * Width ;
)
```

NOTE To avoid headaches, never give a field the same name as an existing function. The field containing the length of a rectangular object has the unwieldy name "ShapeLength" to avoid confusion with FileMaker's Length() function. The field name "Width" is fine, because there's no width function. A complete list of FileMaker functions can be found at *www.filemaker.com/help/html/help_func_alpha.html*.

In fact, calculations can be *really* long and complicated if you need them to be—up to 30,000 characters. Practically speaking, the only limit on the complexity of a calculation is your patience for creating it.

Regardless of its complexity, a calculation, or formula, is made up of three different elements: *field references, constants,* and *operators.* In the first example above, "pi" is a constant, "*" is an operator, and "Diameter" is the name of a field. The second example uses a function called a *case statement.* In that example, "Shape" and "Diameter" are field references, "Circle" and "2" are constants, and "=," "*," and "^" are operators.

Field references tell the calculation engine where to find the *values* it'll be working on. When the calculation is performed, or *evaluated,* first the field references are replaced with the actual values in those fields; then the operators tell FileMaker what to do to those values; and finally, FileMaker returns a *result* in your field.

NOTE FileMaker uses the value *stored* (not necessarily displayed) in a field. So if you have a number field with 3.1415926 as the stored value, but you've formatted the field on the layout to display only two decimal places, FileMaker still uses all the digits in the stored value to do its math.

Here are some helpful definitions of terms you'll see throughout the next chapters:

- **Field references** are just what they sound like. They refer FileMaker to the data in the field you specify. Since the data inside those fields can change on each record in your database, the values in each record can give a different result.

- **Constants** stay the same each time FileMaker does the calculation. Turn the page for details.

- **Operators** tell FileMaker what to do with the values in the calculation. See page 390 for a listing of operators and what they do.

- FileMaker has nearly 300 predefined **functions** that you can use as shortcuts when you create your formulas. You'll learn about some of the most common functions later in this chapter. Chapter 17 introduces you to more advanced functions and shows you how to create your own reusable functions, called *custom functions*.

- Each calculation has a **result.** This result is, in a sense, the "answer" to the calculation. The result of the first calculation above is the circumference of the circle. The second calculation is a little more complex: Its result is the area of a circle *or* a rectangle, depending on the value in the Shape field. (Don't worry if this calculation doesn't make sense to you now. It will before too long.)

- The result of a calculation has a **type** (just like every field has a type). The type can be any of the standard field types—text, number, date, time, timestamp, or container—or a *Boolean* yes/no result (page 311). Chapter 11 goes into more detail about calculations and data types.

UP TO SPEED

Evaluating Calculations: Now or Later

When you use a calculation, you're asking FileMaker to do something with your fields, constants, and operators and come up with a result. In technical lingo, FileMaker *evaluates* the calculation. *When* the evaluation takes place depends on *where* in your database FileMaker encounters the calculation. Sometimes FileMaker evaluates it right away, as when you're calculating an Extended Price. As soon as you type either a price or a quantity, FileMaker tries to multiply the value. But since one of the fields is empty, the Extended Price calculation has a result of zero. When you provide the second value, FileMaker immediately does the math and shows you your result:

- If you create a new calculation field after you already have data in your database, then FileMaker updates

the data for all records as soon as you close the Manage Database dialog box. You may see a progress bar if you have a lot of records.

- When you run the Records→Replace Field Contents command, FileMaker evaluates the calculation you specify once for every record as soon as you click OK. As above, this may take a couple of seconds, but it's happening just as soon as FileMaker can plow through your found set.

- Validation calculations evaluate whenever you change the field or exit the record (you get to decide). See page 407 for more on these.

- Calculations used in scripts are evaluated when the script runs.

NOTE Sometimes people call a Boolean value "True or False" or "One or Zero" instead. Which term you use doesn't matter much if you just remember that there's a yes-like value and a no-like value.

Using Fields in Calculations

It's very common to reference fields in calculations. For example, let's say a field has this calculation:

```
First Name & " " & Last Name
```

NOTE See page 127 to learn how to use this calculation to show data from more than one field in a value list.

When you look at the result of this calculation back in Browse mode, you see that FileMaker replaces the names of the fields with the actual First Name and Last Name data in the records you're viewing, adding a space between them.

Using Constants in Calculations

As handy as it is to refer FileMaker to a field to find the values in your calculations, you don't want to have to store everything in fields just to use it in a calculation. When a value is going to be the same for every record, it's time to call in a constant. You simply include that value right in the calculation.

■ NUMBER CONSTANTS

Sales tax is one of the most common constants. If you need to add sales tax to your order, you can just type the percentage right in the calculation, since it's the same for everybody:

```
Order Total * 1.0625
```

You can enter numbers in any of the formats supported by number fields:

- 37
- .65
- 28.3
- 6.02E23

■ TEXT CONSTANTS

You can also use a constant to have FileMaker plunk some text in with your results. If you want a text value instead of a number, put it in quotes:

```
Age & " years old"
```

Everything within the quote marks is a *text constant* (some people call it a *string,* as in "string of characters"). Those quote marks in the calculation are very important. Suppose you have a field called Car, and a calculation like this:

```
"You should see my Car"
```

The quote marks enclose the text that is also a field name, so the result of this calculation is always (*constantly*) "You should see my Car". FileMaker makes no connection whatsoever between the Car field and the word "Car" in the text, because the text is in quote marks.

Forgetting quote marks around a text string, putting them in the wrong place, or omitting operators can make FileMaker whiny. If you make the following calculation:

```
"You should see my " Car
```

FileMaker shows you a warning message that says, "An operator (e.g. +, -, *, ...) is expected here" when you try to click OK to close the Specify Calculation dialog box (Figure 10-4). The characters "Car" are highlighted in your calculation so you can tell exactly which part of the calculation confuses FileMaker. Add an ampersand to the end of the text constant, and FileMaker will stop complaining. Here's the correct formula that combines the text constant with the value that appears in the field named Car:

```
"You should see my " & Car
```

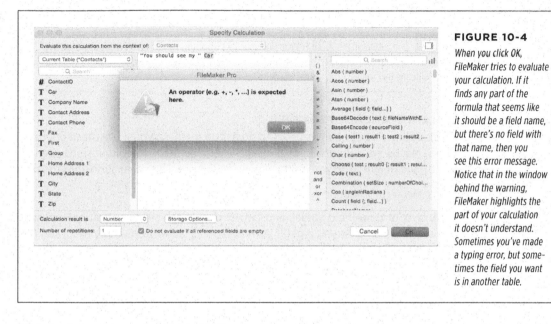

FIGURE 10-4

When you click OK, FileMaker tries to evaluate your calculation. If it finds any part of the formula that seems like it should be a field name, but there's no field with that name, then you see this error message. Notice that in the window behind the warning, FileMaker highlights the part of your calculation it doesn't understand. Sometimes you've made a typing error, but sometimes the field you want is in another table.

Using Operators in Calculations

The power of calculations comes from their ability to combine various values to come up with a new and meaningful value. Here's where *operators* come in. An operator takes the values on either side of it (the *operands*) and *does something* (operates) with them.

A special symbol or word stands for each operator. This calculation uses the + (addition) operator:

```
3 + 2
```

In this case, the + operator is given 3 and 2 as operands. When the calculation is evaluated, the operator and its operands combine to produce a single value.

Operators come in three flavors:

- **Mathematical and logical** operators combine two values into one. The + operator is a good example; it takes two number values, and adds them together. Its resulting value is the sum of the two numbers.

- **Comparison** operators compare two values. For example, the = operator tells you if two values are exactly the same. This kind of operator always produces a Boolean value.

- **Parenthesis** operators are used to group parts of a calculation together. Remember your eighth-grade math teacher carrying on about PEMDAS or the "order of operations" (working from left to right, calculating within parentheses starting with exponents first, then multiplication and division, and finally addition and subtraction)? FileMaker remembers, too, and it uses those same rules to figure out how to evaluate calculations. If the rules don't work for you, then parentheses let you take more control.

NOTE Two buttons in the Specify Calculation window's Operators section aren't really operators at all. The ¶ is a special character that tells FileMaker you want a new line in your calculation result, and the quotation marks are for entering text values.

■ MATHEMATICAL OPERATORS

A calculation's most obvious use is to do a little math, so you'll use these operators often. Maybe your database of products includes fields for dimensions (Length, Width, and Height), and you want to know the volume. This calculation does the trick:

```
ShapeLength * Width * Height
```

It consists of three field values and two copies of the * (multiplication) operator. The result is just what you'd get if you used a calculator to multiply the three field values together.

FileMaker includes operators for basic math:

- + for addition
- – for subtraction
- * for multiplication
- / for division
- ^ for exponentiation ("to the power of" a value)

■ THE CONCATENATION OPERATOR

While the mathematical operators combine numbers, the "&" (concatenation) operator works with text. It hooks together two text values:

```
ShapeLength & " inches"
```

If the ShapeLength field contains 36, then the result of this calculation is *36 inches.*

TIP FileMaker can mix numeric values and text together in the same calculation. If you use a number value or field where FileMaker is expecting text, it just treats the number as text and gets on with its business.

■ COMPARISON OPERATORS

You often need to compare two values to learn about them. For example, you may need to add an additional shipping charge if the total weight of an order is more than 20 pounds. All comparison operators result in a Boolean value.

FileMaker can compare things in several ways:

- = tells you if two values are the same.

- ≠ or <> tells you if the two values are different.

- > tells you if the first value is greater than the second.

- < tells you if the first value is less than the second.

- ≥ or >= tells you if the first value is greater than or equal to the second.

- ≤ or <= tells you if the first value is less than or equal to the second.

■ LOGICAL OPERATORS

The logical operators evaluate values and come up with a Boolean (Yes/No) result. Unlike the other operators, most of them are recognizable words:

- The and operator tells you if both values are Yes. The calculation below uses the and operator. It evaluates to Yes if the length is greater than 3 *and* the height is greater than 5.

  ```
  ShapeLength > 3 and Height > 5
  ```

- The or operator tells you if *either* value is Yes. The *or* calculation below evaluates to Yes if the length is greater than 3 *or* the height is greater than 5.

  ```
  ShapeLength > 3 or Height > 5
  ```

- The xor operator's function is as offbeat as its name. It stands for *exclusive or*. The xor operator tells you when *only one* of your two choices is Yes. Put another way, if you find yourself thinking, "I want one of two things to be true, but *not both* of them," then xor saves the day. For instance, you may want to track whether you've billed a customer *or* you've marked her character rating below 3. That formula looks like this:

  ```
  Invoice Sent = Yes xor Character Rating < 3
  ```

NOTE If you can't think of a use for xor, don't worry. Most of the time when you need an "or" calculation, you can handle it with plain old or and not *exclusive or.*

- The last logical operator, not, stands alone: It works only on one value, not two like every other operator. It simply reverses the Boolean value that comes after it. So the calculation below would evaluate to Yes if the length is *not* greater than 3.

  ```
  Not Length > 3
  ```

NOTE In practice comparison and logical operators are commonly combined with the *logical functions* you'll find on page 680.

■ PARENTHESES

FileMaker uses standard mathematical rules to decide in what order to evaluate things. The order of evaluation is exponentiation, then multiplication/division, and then lastly, addition/subtraction. If you need FileMaker to do part of your calculation *first,* before moving on to any other operators, put it in parentheses. The parentheses tell FileMaker to treat everything between them as a single unit.

In the calculation below, FileMaker multiplies 3 and 2 before adding 4, and gives you a result of 10:

```
4 + 3 * 2
```

Even though the + operator comes first in the calculation, FileMaker follows the standard order of operations. If you want to add 4 and 3 before multiplying, then you need to use parentheses:

```
(4 + 3) * 2
```

Thus, it sees that it needs to add 4+3 first, then multiply by 2, for a result of 14. You can see the value of parentheses in calculations like the one below, which calculates the interest on the sum of the balance and service charge. Without the parentheses, FileMaker would calculate the interest on only the service charge and then add that to the balance due, with an entirely different result:

```
(Balance Due + Service Charge) * Interest Rate
```

NOTE If you have trouble remembering (nay, understanding) the order of operations, then just use parentheses when in doubt. It certainly doesn't hurt to be *too* explicit.

Functions

The meat of calculations is found in the function list (which you saw briefly back in Figure 10-3). A *function* is a predefined formula, and FileMaker's list covers most common calculation purposes. If you find a function that already does what you want to do—like average all invoices—use it. When you add these tried-and-true formulas to your calculations, you save time and even help prevent errors.

For example, if you didn't know about functions, you could find your average with a series of fields. First, you'd need to create a calculation field to total all the invoices in your found set. Then you'd need another field to count the invoices in the set and a third one that divides the first field by the second. It would work, but it'd be clumsy and inefficient, since you'd have to create at least two fields that you didn't really need.

Because you often need to find averages, FileMaker gives you a *function* that handles the math in a given field. All you have to do is tell FileMaker *which* field you want to average. The function takes care of figuring out both the count and sum of the related values. It looks like this:

```
Average ( Line Item::Quantity )
```

The word *Average* is the function's name. *Line Item::Quantity* is a reference to a related field. This field reference is called a *parameter.* Parameters tell the function which values to use when performing the calculation. The Average() function requires only a single parameter, but many functions have two or more.

Parameters are always enclosed in parentheses. (A few functions—most notably, Random—don't need any parameters, so you leave the parentheses off altogether.) When there's more than one parameter, they're separated by a semicolon, as in the date function below:

```
Date ( Month ; Day ; Year )
```

FileMaker Pro 14 has 285 functions, divided into 18 groups, as described below. Later in this chapter, you'll learn how to use some of the more common functions. (Functions come into play in Chapter 11 and Chapter 17 as well.)

> **TIP** FileMaker has a lengthy help file (Ctrl+? or ⌘-?) that lists each function and some sample uses. If you want to explore a function that isn't covered here, open Help and then type the function's name.

▓ TEXT FUNCTIONS

Dozens of *text* functions let you work with text values. You can compare them; convert them into other types (like numbers); split them up in various ways; count the number of letters, words, or lines; change case; and replace parts of them with new text values. If you're trying to slice, mix, or examine words, look here first.

▓ TEXT FORMATTING FUNCTIONS

Text formatting functions let you adjust the font, size, style, and color of all or part of a text value. For instance, you could make the Account Balance field for a customer turn red if the customer owes more than $100.

▓ NUMBER FUNCTIONS

Number functions do everything with numbers—from the mundane (rounding) to the esoteric (combinatorics). In between, you can get rid of the decimal part of a number, calculate logarithms and square roots, convert signs, generate random numbers, and perform modulo arithmetic.

▓ DATE FUNCTIONS

Date functions make working with dates a breeze. You can safely create date values without worrying about the computer's date settings. You can also pick date values apart (for example, get just the *month* from a date), convert day and month numbers into proper names, and work with weeks and fiscal years.

TIME FUNCTIONS

Time functions are few: They create time values from hours, minutes, and seconds, and split times up into the same parts. You use these values most frequently when you're trying to find out how long something took. For instance, if you bill your services hourly, then you can create Start Time and Finish Time fields. Then, in a Duration field, you can subtract finish time from start time to find out how long you worked on a project.

TIMESTAMP FUNCTIONS

There's only one *timestamp* function: It lets you build a timestamp value from a separate date and a time. If you're creating your own data, then you already know that FileMaker needs both a date and a time for a valid timestamp field, and you've planned accordingly. But you may receive data from an outside source in which the date and time aren't already in a single field. No problem; just use the timestamp function.

CONTAINER FUNCTIONS

Most of the Container functions return information about the object in a given Container field. Two encode and decode container data into text representations that are compatible with other databases and one generates a thumbnail from an image stored in a Container field.

AGGREGATE FUNCTIONS

Aggregate functions calculate statistics like average, variance, and standard deviation. They can also count things, sum things, and compute minimums and maximums. By definition, aggregate functions *gather up* multiple values, and find results based on the group as a whole. (See the box below for more detail.)

SUMMARY FUNCTIONS

You have only one *summary* function—GetSummary(). Its primary purpose is to let you use the value of a summary field in your calculations. In the olden days, before FileMaker was the robust relational database it is now, the GetSummary() function was the best way to sort and summarize certain kinds of data. Now that FileMaker is relational, you usually use calculations through table occurrences to do that work.

REPEATING FUNCTIONS

Repeating functions work with repeating fields, and some of them work with *related* fields as well. You can make nonrepeating fields and repeating fields work together properly in calculations, access specific repeating values, or get the *last* nonempty value. Since repeating fields have limited uses in these days of related tables within files, so do these functions.

FINANCIAL FUNCTIONS

Financial functions make the MBAs in the audience feel right at home. Calculate present value, future value, net present value, and payments. Non-MBAs could calculate the cost of competing loans with these functions.

■ TRIGONOMETRIC FUNCTIONS

Trigonometric functions aren't common in business-related databases. But engineers and scientists know what to do with this bunch: sine, cosine, and tangent. They can also convert between radians and degrees. And if you need to, you can get pi out to 400 decimal places.

UP TO SPEED

Aggregate Functions

Aggregate functions work on groups of things. They can work on multiple fields within a record, a group of related records, or even multiple functions. The Sum function helps you add up the various charges on an invoice, using fields on the Invoice layout:

    Sum (Subtotal ; Sales Tax ; Shipping)

But since you can use an operator to get the same result (Subtotal + Sales Tax + Shipping), this type of use isn't very common. More often an aggregate function refers to a related field. In that case, FileMaker aggregates that field's values from *every* related record:

    Sum (Line Items::Extended Price)

An aggregate function can also reference a single repeating field, either a local one or a related one. As with a reference to a related field, a Sum function that refers to a repeating field adds the values in every repetition into a single value.

This special behavior for related or repeating fields works only if you use a single parameter. You can't, for example, sum two sets of related fields as one like this:

    Sum (Line Items::Extended Price ; Line
    Items::Shipping Charge)

If you refer to more than one field in a sum function, then it looks at only the *first* related value or repetition for each field. Of course, if you do want to total two related fields, you can do so by calling Sum twice and adding their results:

    Sum (Line Items::Extended Price) +
    Sum (Line Items::Shipping Charge)

■ LOGICAL FUNCTIONS

Logical functions are a powerful grouping. These functions can make *decisions* based on calculated values (if the due date is more than 3 months ago, add a late fee of 10 percent). FileMaker has functions to evaluate *other* calculations inside your calculations; functions to figure out if fields are empty or contain invalid data; performance-enhancing functions to create and use variables; and functions to perform lookups inside calculations. Chapter 17 is where you learn when and how to use these big dogs of the function world.

■ GET FUNCTIONS

Get functions pull up information about the computer, user, database, or FileMaker Pro itself. They make up the largest group (116 in all). You can, for example, find out the computer's screen resolution, the current layout's name, the computer's network address, the current user's name, or the size of any database window. This list just scratches the surface, though. If you're looking for information about the current state of the database, FileMaker, the computer, or the user, then you can probably find it with a Get() function.

■ DESIGN FUNCTIONS

Design functions tell you about your database's structure. You can get a list of tables, fields, layouts, or value lists, or details about any of these items. You won't need most of these functions until you become an advanced database designer indeed. ValueListItems() is one notable exception; it gives you a list of the values in a value list, separated by paragraph breaks.

■ MOBILE FUNCTIONS

Mobile functions are used with FileMaker Go to get the current latitude, longitude, and altitude of the iOS device being used, as well as the horizontal and vertical accuracy of the values returned and the number of minutes since the values were returned.

■ CUSTOM FUNCTIONS

If you have FileMaker Pro Advanced, then you can create your very own *custom* functions and have them show up on the list. Once you have them, you (or anyone you let create fields in your database) can choose them just like the built-in functions. (See Chapter 17 for details on creating and using custom functions.)

■ EXTERNAL FUNCTIONS

If you've installed any plug-ins ("mini-programs" that add extra features to File-Maker), they probably brought along some functions for their own use. FileMaker stores them in this category. (External plug-ins are covered on page 696.)

Expressions

Expression is a fancy name for a subsection of a calculation—one or more fields, functions, or constants, each connected with operators. When you made the first calculation in this chapter (page 384), you multiplied the contents of the field called Price Each by the contents of the field called Quantity. That's a calculation, but it's also an example of an *expression.*

An expression always reduces to a single value when you combine its individual values according to the operators. If you can't boil it down to a value, then it's not an expression. That's an important point, because it means you can use expressions as function parameters (page 564) just like any individual values—fields and constants. When used in a function, these expressions are called *sub-expressions.*

Here are some examples of expressions:

The following is a simple expression, which reduces to the value 6.

```
3 + 3
```

Below is a more complex expression. It might turn a name into something like "Moss, Maurice Q."

```
Last Name & ", " & First Name & " " & Middle Initial & "."
```

The following calculation is a function *and* an expression, because it reduces down to a single value:

```
Average ( L1 * W1 * H1 ; L2 * W2 * H2 ; L3 * W3 * H3 )
```

But if you look at just the stuff in parentheses, then you have this:

```
L1 * W1 * H1 ; L2 * W2 * H2 ; L3 * W3 * H3
```

That's *not* an expression because it doesn't reduce down to one value. It has three expressions in all, each separated by a semicolon. Each expression reduces to a single value—three values in all that become parameters passed to the Average() function.

You can put *any valid expression* in place of a parameter in a function. In the trade, that's called *nesting* expressions. For example, you can rewrite the expression 3 + 3 like this:

```
( 1 + 1 + 1 ) + 3
```

In this case, the sub-expression (1 + 1 + 1) has replaced the original value 3. The whole thing is a new expression, and it contains one sub-expression. While the nested expression example is very simple, the concept behind it gives you a lot of power when you work with functions. Instead of using individual fields or constants in a function, you can pass along whole expressions. You can even nest functions within other functions (see page 691).

UP TO SPEED

Think Like a Machine

If you've jumped right in and started making perfect calculations every time, then you can skip this bit of arcana. But if FileMaker throws up a warning dialog box every time you try to make a halfway complex calculation, or if the syntax seems fine, but you just aren't getting the math to work out right, then you might have to try thinking like FileMaker thinks. To understand how fields, constants, functions, and operators come together to produce a single result, you have to think very logically and in a straight line that inexorably leads to the end of a problem. When FileMaker evaluates a calculation, it looks for something it can do to simplify it—fetch a field value, perform a function, or evaluate an operation.

The calculation shown in Figure 10-5 has a function (average), several operators (* and &), a constant (cubic inches), and six fields (L1, W1, H1, L2, W2, H2). You might think the average function is the right place to start, because it comes first. But you quickly realize you can't compute the average until you figure out what its parameters are by performing the multiplication. The * operators multiply values on either side to produce a new value—but FileMaker needs to replace these fields with their values before it can do anything else.

In step 1, FileMaker identifies six fields. Step 2 shows how the calculation looks once FileMaker replaces them with values.

Now the * operators are all surrounded by values, and FileMaker is ready to do some multiplication. Step 3 shows the calculation once all the multiplication is finished.

At last, the Average() function has two parameters, which is just what it needs, so FileMaker performs this function, and the new calculation looks like step 4.

You have no more fields to replace and no more functions to perform, but there's one last operator. The & operator takes two values and puts them together (step 4). With all the steps completed, FileMaker can now display the final result. Finally, the & operator is evaluated, and the box below step 4 shows the calculation result.

If you apply the concepts outlined here to your problem calculations—find the answer to each step and then plod along to the next one—you can always figure out where your calculation has gone astray.

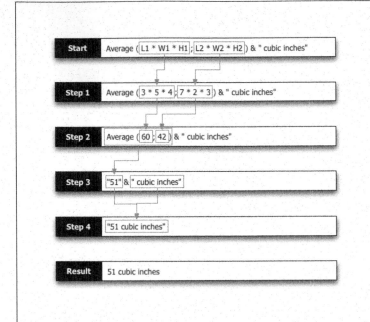

FIGURE 10-5

Taking a complex calculation one bite at a time helps you get the results you expect. Just chip away at the parts and check your logic at each stage to make sure you and FileMaker are in concert.

Using a Related Field in a Calculation

The invoice line items now calculate their extended prices automatically, because you created a calculation at the beginning of the chapter to handle that. But you still have to add up the extended price of each line item and enter the total amount due on the invoice itself. Another calculation solves this problem:

1. **In the *CH10 Jobs Start.fmp12* sample database from the steps on page 384, choose File→Manage→Databases and then go to the Fields tab. From the Table pop-up menu, choose Invoices.**

   The field list shows all the fields in the Invoices table.

2. **In the list, select the Total Due field.**

   It's currently a Number field.

3. **From the Type pop-up menu, choose Calculation and then click the now highlighted Change button. When FileMaker asks if you're sure you want to make this change (and replace any data in the field), click OK.**

   The Specify Calculation dialog box pops up.

4. **In the search box just above the function list, type *sum*.**

   The function list now shows just the functions containing the text "sum".

5. **Double-click the Sum (field {; field…}) function in the list.**

   FileMaker copies the full function example into the calculation box. To save you an extra step, it even selects everything between the parentheses (Figure 10-6). The next thing you type or click becomes the first parameter to the function.

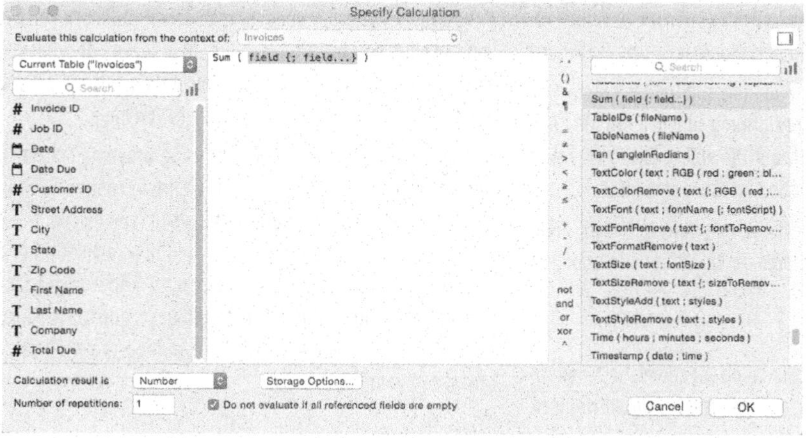

FIGURE 10-6

FileMaker gives you a handy syntax reference for each function you choose from the function list. When you double-click to place the function in the calculation box, FileMaker even highlights the parameters for you, so you can start building right away. Click OK in each dialog box to return to your layout.

TIP Anything within {curly braces} in a function is optional. In the Sum( ) function in step 5, you could reference several fields that all get summed up into one glorious total. But that doesn't make sense when you're trying to summarize line items on an invoice, so you're just replacing all the highlighted material with a single field reference.

---

6. **From the pop-up menu above the field list, choose Line Items to view the table occurrence you need and then, in the list of Line Item fields, double-click the Extended Price field.**

   FileMaker adds this field to the calculation, placing it between the parentheses that surround the parameters to the sum function. Your calculation should now read:

   `Sum ( Line Items::Extended Price )`

7. **From the "Calculation result is" pop-up menu, choose Number.**

   Because this field was a number type before you changed it, it's probably already set to have a Number result.

   Click OK and if you've done everything right, the Specify Calculation window disappears. If not, check the syntax of your calculation and then try again.

Your Invoice::Total Due field should now work perfectly. Since you modified an existing field that's already on your layout, you don't need to do anything else. Every layout that shows the Invoices::Total Due field now shows the new calculated value.

Switch to the Invoices layout to try for yourself. As you edit, add, or delete Line Item records, the Invoices::Total Due field changes automatically to reflect the correct total.

FREQUENTLY ASKED QUESTION

Result Type

Why do I have to tell FileMaker my calculation has a number result? I'm multiplying two numbers together, so isn't it obvious?

You're right; FileMaker can figure that out for itself. In fact, in a calculation where you're performing simple math, the field always has a number result. But the ability to set the result type for a field gives you a good measure of control.

For one thing, you and FileMaker may have different ideas about what type a result *should* be. Take this calculation, for example:

    1 & 1 * 3

Because you're mixing concatenation (&) and math (*) operators, it's not terribly obvious *what* that calculation will produce.

A number? Or just a numerical text value? So FileMaker lets you say what you *want* it to produce. If it doesn't do what you expect, then you can easily fix the calculation, but at least you don't have to wonder what type of field you have.

Furthermore, explicitly setting the type prevents FileMaker from changing it later. Imagine if a simple change to your calculation accidentally changed the result type from number to text. If you try to reference this field in a calculation or a relationship, then you get strange results. And it might take you a while to figure out that the problem is due to FileMaker calculating a text value instead of a number, rather than a mistake in your calculation.

◼ Understanding the Specify Calculation Dialog Box

As you saw in the previous tutorial, whenever you create a new calculation field, FileMaker shows the Specify Calculation dialog box (see Figure 10-3). This window is loaded with options, making it seem a bit daunting—but all those options are there to help you. FileMaker shows you the table occurrences, fields, operators, and functions, and all you have to do is point and click to build any calculation you have in mind.

Once you learn how this box works, you can write calculations like a pro without memorizing complicated functions and/or typing out long field names. The following pages give you a guided tour of each element in the window.

Table Occurrence Context

Since FileMaker sees your database from the perspective of one table occurrence at a time, you have to specify which context you want the calculation to be evaluated from. The Context pop-up menu lists every occurrence of the current table—the one you're adding a field to—on the Relationship graph. All you have to do is pick the one that works for your purposes. (If your calculation doesn't reference any related data, you can ignore the Context pop-up menu.)

NOTE Anchor-Buoy relationships (page 618) make it much easier to conceptualize calculations' context, since most calculations are created in the Anchor table occurrence, looking toward the Buoys.

Field List

Since most calculations include fields, and field names are often long and hard to remember, FileMaker lets you pick field names from a list. The Context pop-up menu shows every table occurrence in the graph, with the related tables at the top and the unrelated tables in a group below. The list below the pop-up menu shows the fields in the selected table occurrence. A calculation can refer to any related field in the database: FileMaker follows the appropriate relationships to grab the data it needs.

NOTE You can use Global fields (page 259) from unrelated tables in your calculations. But if you try to use a regular field from an unrelated table, then you get a warning message when you try to close the Specify Calculation window.

If you want to put a field in the calculation itself, just double-click its name in the list, and FileMaker does the typing for you. Anytime you're referring to a related field, the pop-up menu saves time and helps avoid error.

NOTE When you double-click a field from a related table occurrence, you create what FileMaker calls a *fully qualified field reference,* which contains the Table name, two colons, and the Field name (Invoices::InvoiceID). Because you might have similar field names in several tables, a fully qualified name makes sure you refer to the right one.

Operators

To help you remember all those operators, FileMaker shows them in the Operators column. Click an operator to add it to your calculation. For readability, many operators are inserted with a single space character on either side.

Function List

As you get familiar with the functions, you'll find it easier to start typing the name of the one you want and then picking it from the list of suggestions. But if you're uncertain of the name, the Function List is the way to find the one you need. It shows every function FileMaker understands, *and* all the parameters each function expects, in the right order. (See the box on page 403 for more detail.)

As usual, double-click a function to add it to the calculation. If you don't fancy an alphabetical list of every function, then you can narrow down your choices by using the Function Type pop-up menu. You can pick a specific function type and see a list of just those functions. To see all of the functions grouped with their kin, choose the second option from the top, "all functions by type." You can see the effect in Figure 10-7.

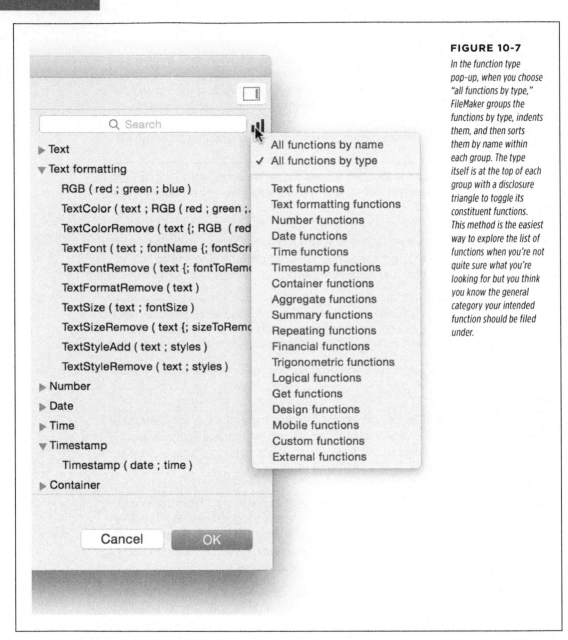

FIGURE 10-7

In the function type pop-up, when you choose "all functions by type," FileMaker groups the functions by type, indents them, and then sorts them by name within each group. The type itself is at the top of each group with a disclosure triangle to toggle its constituent functions. This method is the easiest way to explore the list of functions when you're not quite sure what you're looking for but you think you know the general category your intended function should be filed under.

The Function List

The function list doesn't show just a list of meaningless names—it also shows the syntax for the function. This prototype function includes everything you need to call the function in a calculation: name, the necessary parentheses, and a placeholder for each parameter. You just need to replace the placeholders with fields, constants, functions, or expressions.

Most functions are simple, and have a simple example to match:

```
Date ( month ; day ; year )
```

This function, called Date, expects three parameters: a month, a day, and a year. (If you're curious, it returns a date value based on the three numbers passed to it.)

The syntax of some other functions isn't as simple, and their syntax needs some explanation (you won't learn how the functions work here; just focus on syntax for now). Some functions don't have a predetermined number of parameters. The Average( ) function needs *at least* one parameter, but you can pass as many as you want. It looks like this in the function list:

```
Average ( field {; field...} )
```

The first "field" parameter shows that you need to specify at least one value. The second one is inside curly braces, meaning it's optional. And it's followed by "...", meaning you can add more copies if you want.

The Case function shows up like this:

```
Case ( test1 ; result1 {; test2 ; result2
; ... ; defaultResult} )
```

This shows that you can add additional test and result parameters, and you can put a final defaultResult parameter on the end if you want.

Finally, a few functions actually accept more than one value for a single parameter. The Evaluate( ) function is an example:

```
Evaluate ( expression {; [field1 ; field2
;...]} )
```

It always expects one parameter, called an *expression* (see page 396). You can also specify a field to go with it. The curly braces around the fields show you that it can take two parameters, but the second can be a square-bracketed list of multiple values. In other words, you can call this function in three ways:

```
Evaluate ( "<some expression>" )
Evaluate ( "<some expression>" ; A Field )
Evaluate ( "<some expression>" ; [Field 1
; Field 2 ; Field 3] )
```

In the first case, it receives only one parameter. In both the second and third cases, you're passing *two* parameters. In the third case only, the second parameter is actually a list of values. Functions like this are rare, but a few exist.

Result Type

Just as you specify field types when you create fields, you also specify result types for your calculations. If you change a field to a calculation type field, FileMaker uses its former field type as the automatic result type. But you can use the Result Type pop-up menu to override the automatic setting. And when you create a calculation field from scratch, the Calculation result is automatically set as "Number," but that's not always what you want. Your result type should match the function type. That is, if you're using a Date( ) function, set the result type to Date. If you're concatenating data from text fields, then Text is the result type you want. It's common to forget to change the result type when you create calculations, so if you're not getting what you expect from your calculations, check the result type setting.

Calculation Box

Your calculation itself goes in the Calculation box in the middle of the window. You can type right into the Calculation box if you're a codehead, but mere mortals usually use the field list, operators, and function list, and let FileMaker assemble their calculations for them. When you're getting started, you probably mostly point and click, but as you get more familiar with formulas and functions, you'll start typing more often. Most people end up using a hybrid of typing and clicking to create their calculations.

> **TIP** You can also copy and paste into the Calculation box. If you have a calculation in another table file that's the same or similar, you can paste and then update it for its new home, saving yourself some typing. See the Self() function on page 673. It can reduce or even eliminate editing when you reuse a calculation.

Changing the Standard Evaluation Behavior

At the bottom of the Specify Calculation dialog box is the standard option "Do not evaluate if all referenced fields are empty." Since the option is meant to improve performance, you'll leave it selected most of the time. When this checkbox is turned on and all referenced fields are indeed empty, the calculation result will be blank.

But sometimes "blank" isn't the right value. When you create a new invoice, its Total Due value is "blank" (there's no data in the field), but it should be zero dollars and zero cents, or $0.00. First, turn off the "Do not evaluate if all referenced fields are empty" option for Invoices::Total Due. Then change that field's calculation to:

```
0 + Sum ( Line Items::Extended Price )
```

The calculation's result isn't changed by the addition of the constant value "0," but there's now a value in the fields that'll trigger evaluation of the calculation, even when the invoice has no related items (Figure 10-8).

> **TIP** Still don't see that zero? Switch to Layout mode, select the Total Due field, and then take a look at the Data Formatting options in the Data tab of the Inspector. Make sure the "Do not display number if zero" checkbox is turned off.

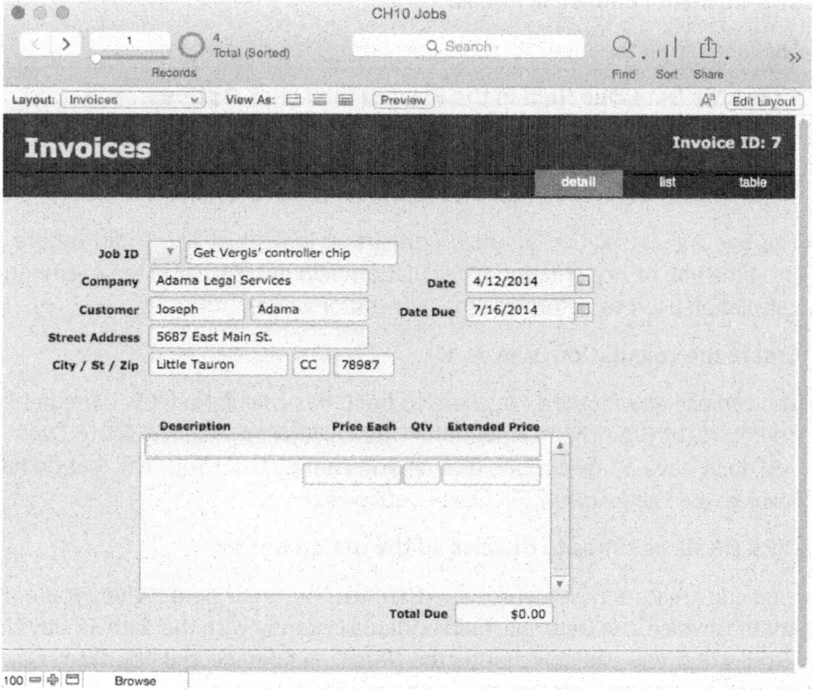

FIGURE 10-8

When you first create a record, the fields referred to in your calculations are usually empty, so your calculation results are blank until you enter data in at least one field that's referenced in the calculation. Turning off the "Do not evaluate if all referenced fields are empty" option and then editing the calculation displays a "0" in the field instead. Use the same technique on the Line Items::Extended Price field if you want a "0" to show there, even when both Line Items::Price and Line Items::Quantity are blank.

▦ Auto-Enter Calculations

Back on page 245, you learned about most of the auto-enter field options. Now that you know about calculations, it's time to learn how to combine the power of the calculation engine (accuracy and efficiency) with the ability to override a calculated value using auto-enter calculations. Calculation fields are fantastic—they save time and ensure error-free results. But they have one serious limitation: *You can't click into a calculation field and change its value.* Of course, you can adjust the calculation itself, or the data in the fields the calculation depends on, but sometimes you need to be able to override a field's calculated value on a record-by-record basis.

For example, it would be nice if your invoice's Date Due field automatically showed a date 30 days after the date of the invoice itself. But sometimes you may want to make an invoice due earlier or later. If you make the Date Due field a calculation field, then you don't have this flexibility. Use a normal Date field with an *auto-enter calculation.*

Here's how to create an auto-enter calculation:

1. **In the *CH10 Jobs Start.fmp12* sample database, bring up the Manage Database window and then switch to the now-familiar Fields tab. From the Table pop-up menu, choose Invoices.**

   The fields from the Invoices table appear.

2. **Select the Date Due field in the list and then click Options.**

   The Options for Field dialog box makes an appearance.

3. **On the Auto-Enter tab, turn on the Calculated Value checkbox.**

   The Specify Calculation window appears. It looks just like it did before, but this time you're *not* creating a calculation field. Instead, you're specifying the calculation used to determine the auto-enter value.

4. **Create the calculation Date + 30.**

   You can use any method you want to build this calculation: Click the field and operators, or type them. Notice that the calculation result is set to Date, and you don't have a pop-up menu to let you change that. Your calculation has to resolve to a valid date or FileMaker squawks at you.

5. **Click OK three times to dismiss all the dialog boxes.**

   Now you can create a new invoice and then test out your field. When you enter a date for the invoice, the Date Due field updates instantly with the date 30 days from now. Notice that you can still change the Date Due field value if you want. See the box above for more on auto-enter calculations.

POWER USERS' CLINIC

Do Not Replace Existing Value

Auto-enter calculation fields don't act *exactly* like other calculation fields. If you change the invoice date, the due date doesn't update to reflect the change. Instead, it keeps its original value, as in the example on the previous page. That's normally the way an auto-enter calculation works: It acts only when you first create a record or if the field is empty. Once the field gets a value, the calculation doesn't update it, even if the field it refers to changes.

Often, though, you *want* the calculation to change the field value every time any field used in the calculation is changed, just like a normal calculation. You can easily get this modified behavior by turning off the "Do not replace existing value of field (if any)" checkbox in the Field Options dialog box (shown in Figure 10-9). When you turn this checkbox off, FileMaker

dutifully updates the field value whenever the calculation evaluates—in other words, when any field it uses changes.

You choose your option depending on the situation. For the Date Due field, you probably want to turn this option off. After all, if you're changing the date of an invoice, it's reasonable to assume you want to rethink the due date as well.

But suppose you have a database of products and you use an auto-enter calculation to copy the distributor's product code into your internal product code field. If you then change the internal product code to something unique to you, then you probably *don't* want it to change again if you switch to a different distributor. In that case, you'd leave the "Do not replace existing value of field (if any)" option turned on, ensuring that once you've put in your own special value, it never changes.

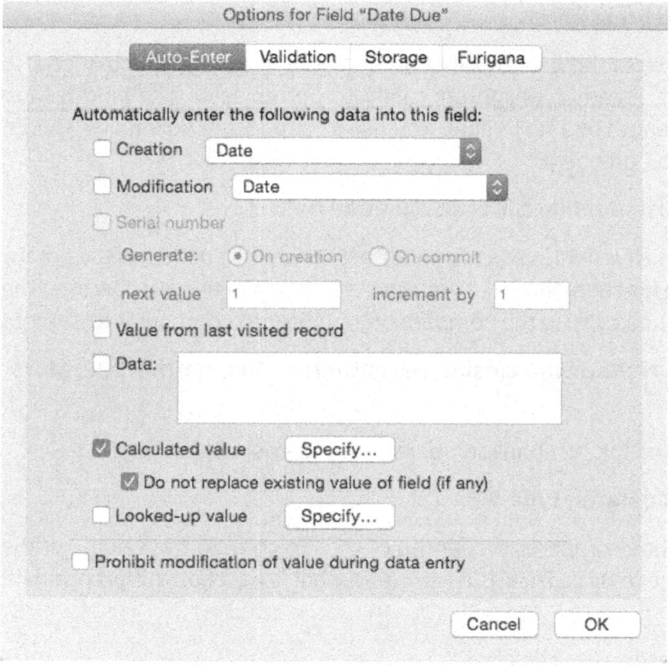

FIGURE 10-9

Auto-enter calculations let you protect data that's already in a field if you change the field the calculation refers to. The verbose setting here, "Do not replace existing value of field (if any)," is turned on for you. But if you want an auto-enter calculation to update any time the field(s) it refers to changes, then uncheck this option.

Validate Data Entry with a Calculation

In Chapter 7, you were introduced to several ways to validate data entered into a field. But what if the Validation tab in the Field Options dialog box doesn't have a checkbox to meet your needs? For example, you may want to use validation on the Zip Code field in the Customers table. A valid U.S. Zip code has *either* five characters or 10 characters (in other words, it can look like this: 94950, or this: 94950-2326). The closest validation option is "Maximum number of characters"—close, but not right.

This situation is just the kind where the "Validate by calculation" option comes in handy. Your job is to create a calculation with a Boolean result. It should return *True* when the data is valid, and *False* otherwise. Here's how it works:

1. **In the *CH10 Jobs Start.fmp12* sample database, choose File→Manage→ Database and then click the Fields tab. Then switch to view the field definitions for the Customers table. Select the Zip Code field and then click Options.**

   The Options for Field dialog box pops up.

2. **Click the Validation tab and then turn on "Validated by calculation."**

   The Specify Calculation window appears, ready for you to enter your validation calculation.

3. **Type *len* and press Enter.**

   FileMaker selects the Length function and adds it to your calculation. Notice that "text" is already highlighted, ready to be replaced. The length function returns the length of a text value. You use it here to see how many characters are in the Zip Code field.

4. **In the field list, double-click the Zip Code field.**

   FileMaker puts this field inside the parentheses, where it becomes the parameter to the length function. Now that you have a function to tell you how long the Zip code is, you need to use the comparison operator to compare it to something.

5. **Click to the right of the closing parenthesis. Then, in the Operators list, click =.**

   FileMaker adds the comparison operator (=) to your calculation.

6. **After the = operator, type *5*.**

   Your calculation compares the length of the Zip code to the value 5. If they're equal, then it returns *True*. But you also want to accept a Zip code with *10* characters.

7. **In the Operators list, click "or."**

   Remember that this operator connects two Boolean values and then returns *True* if *either* value is true. Next, you set up the second value.

8. **Add another length function like you did in step 3, then double-click the Zip Code field again, click to the right of the closing parenthesis, and then click the = operator.**

   This second check should also compare the length to some other value.

9. **In the Calculation box, type *10*.**

   Your calculation is complete. It should look like the one in Figure 10-10.

10. **Click OK until you're back on your layout.**

    You're now back in your database and ready to test. Try giving a customer a few different Zip codes to make sure the validation works.

Most validations happen as soon as you leave the field, even if you're just moving to another field in the record. But some validation types—including most validation calculations—don't happen until you exit the *record*.

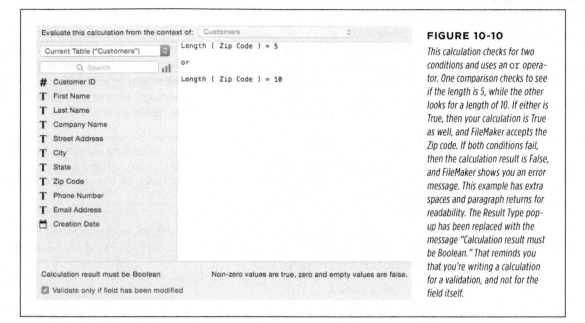

FIGURE 10-10

This calculation checks for two conditions and uses an or *opera- tor. One comparison checks to see if the length is 5, while the other looks for a length of 10. If either is True, then your calculation is True as well, and FileMaker accepts the Zip code. If both conditions fail, then the calculation result is False, and FileMaker shows you an error message. This example has extra spaces and paragraph returns for readability. The Result Type pop- up has been replaced with the message "Calculation result must be Boolean." That reminds you that you're writing a calculation for a validation, and not for the field itself.*

FREQUENTLY ASKED QUESTION

Validate Only if Field Has Been Modified

What's the "Validate only if field has been modified" checkbox for? I don't remember seeing this in the Specify Calculation window before. For that matter, where did the Result Type pop-up menu go?

Good eye. The Specify Calculation window can show up in lots of places—when defining a calculation field, when specifying an auto-enter calculation, and so on—and it can change slightly in some cases.

First, the Result Type pop-up menu shows up only when you're defining a calculation field, since it can produce any data type. Since a validation calculation always has a Boolean result, there's no need to ask you here.

In place of this pop-up menu, you often see some new options specific to the calculation type—like the "Validate only if field has been modified" checkbox in Figure 10-10.

Normally when you edit a record, FileMaker validates only the fields you actually change. Any field in the record that hasn't been changed is accepted even if it violates the validation rule. This violation can happen when you have your field set to validate "Only during data entry" and the records have been set some other way—from an import (page 869) or with a set field in a script (page 442). If you want to validate this field whenever you edit the record, not just when the field itself changes, then turn off this checkbox.

■ Commenting in Calculations

Everything you can put in a calculation has some kind of value—unless it's a *comment*. Comments are brief notes that you place *inside* a calculation. Professional database developers, like all good programmers, provide lots of comments for the benefit of people who might work on the computer code months or years later. Once you have a few sets of parentheses or nested function calls, you may have trouble understanding even your *own* FileMaker calculation when you have to go back and make changes. When it evaluates the calculation, FileMaker ignores all comments completely—it's as if they weren't there. (But you'll be glad they are.)

NOTE   You may have noticed that this book shows some extra spaces and paragraph returns that FileMaker doesn't throw into your functions automatically. These spaces are for ease of reading, and lots of developers type them into their calculations. Like comments, FileMaker ignores those extra spaces and blank lines, as long as all the other syntax is correct.

You can use two different styles for your comments. First, any text that comes after two consecutive slash marks (//) is considered a comment. This kind of comment goes all the way to the end of the line:

```
// this is a comment
3.14 * Diameter // and so is this
```

A comment is also any text that comes between the symbols /* and */. This symbol pair comes in handy in two places. It saves typing if you need to type a long comment across multiple lines:

```
/* this is a comment that runs across multiple
lines. To make life easier, you can use the second
comment style */
```

Also, this comment style lets you add comments *within* a line:

```
3 /*sprocket size*/ * 10 /*sprocket count*/ * 57 /*tooth count*/
```

In addition to comments, you can—and should—use white space to make your calculations easier to read. Calculations don't have to be strung together in one long line, even though that's the way FileMaker does it in the Specify Calculation window. Press the Return key or the space bar to add space anywhere, except in a field name, function name, text constant, or number. Comments and white space can make a world of difference. Here's a long calculation that doesn't use either:

```
Let([DaysToAdd=Case(DayOfWeek(theDate)=1;1;DayOfWeek(theDate)=2;0;DayOfWeek
(theDate)=3;-1;DayOfWeek(theDate)=4;-2;DayOfWeek(theDate)=5;-3;DayOfWeek
(theDate)=6;-4;Date(Month(theDate);Day(theDate)+DaysToAdd;Year(theDate)))
```

The calculation works just fine, but it's a nightmare to read and worse to edit. Here's the same calculation, written with a comment and helpful spaces:

```
/*Figure out what day it is and then add or subtract the
proper number to the DayOfWeek value to identify This Monday.*/

Let ( [
  DaysToAdd =
    Case (
DayOfWeek ( theDate ) = 1; 1; // Sunday
DayOfWeek ( theDate ) = 2; 0; // Monday
DayOfWeek ( theDate ) = 3; -1; // Tuesday
DayOfWeek ( theDate ) = 4; -2; // Wednesday
DayOfWeek ( theDate ) = 5; -3; // Thursday
DayOfWeek ( theDate ) = 6; -4; // Friday
DayOfWeek ( theDate ) = 7; -5) ] ; // Saturday
  Date ( Month ( theDate ); Day ( theDate ) + DaysToAdd; Year ( theDate ))
)
```

Sure, it takes up a bit more space, but this way, you can much more easily pick apart the pieces to figure out what the calculation does. In the next chapter, you'll learn about the functions used in this calc.

More Calculations and Data Types

The last chapter introduced the terminology and concepts behind FileMaker's calculations. You learned how to create them by using the Specify Calculation window's tools. The sheer length of the function list shows how big a role functions play in good calculation construction. FileMaker divides that long list into types so it's easier to find the one you need, and because the types usually share some common traits that make using them easier. The types are not listed in alphabetical order, but the functions within each type are. Choose "All functions by name" from the pop-up menu to the right of the search bar to get a purely alphabetical list, with no consideration for types. In this chapter, you'll learn about the most common functions for the various data types—text, number, date, time, timestamp, and container—and when to use them. To test a calculation, just create a brand new calculation field and then start building it using the techniques you've learned so far. If it doesn't work the way you expect, or if you don't need it after your experiment is done, then just delete the field.

NOTE To follow along in this chapter, you'll find it helpful to download the sample database *CH11 Function Types.fmp12* from this book's Missing CD page at *www.missingmanuals.com/cds/fmp14mm*.

■ Number Crunching Calculations

Although they don't come first in the function list, number functions are the most obvious application of calculations, so they're a logical place to start. Plus, many concepts you'll learn for number functions apply to other functions as well.

NOTE   See page 390 for a refresher on mathematical operators.

Number Function Types

Since FileMaker has so many number functions, the function list breaks them up into smaller groups with descriptive names. You can easily find the group you need (or skim by them without looking, if you might be traumatized by accidentally seeing a sine or cosine function). These are the function groups you use with your numeric data:

- Number functions

- Aggregate functions

- Financial functions

- Trigonometric functions

NOTE   This book doesn't cover the financial and trigonometric functions, which have highly specialized uses. If you need to use these brawny functions, you probably have the mental muscle to decipher the technical terms in FileMaker's Help file, where you'll find them explained.

Using Number Functions

As you saw on page 392, most functions expect one or more parameters. Number functions' parameters have to be number values, and all the number functions return a number result. In the next sections, you'll see examples of several of the most commonly used number functions. These examples are from the Number and Aggregate groups, but you might find them more easily if you sort your function list alphabetically.

ABS()

Abs is short for Absolute, and it returns the absolute value of a number, which is the positive value of the number or zero. For example, you might have a series of readings from a brainwave scan that range from negative to positive, but you just need to know how far each value is from zero. You could add an

to each field to find out. This calculation returns *343.7634:*

```
Abs ( -343.7634 )
```

This calculation returns *4:*

```
Abs ( 2 * 42 / -21 )
```

■ AVERAGE()

The Average() function can work with one or more of the following: constant values, regular fields, repeating fields, all related fields in a relationship, or just the first related field. For example, if you store a series of student test scores in several related tables, then you can use an `Average()` function to round them all up. This calculation returns *10:*

    Average (3 ; 6 ; 21)

When you use fields instead of numbers, FileMaker uses the values from those fields. This calculation returns the average of all test scores in the related table:

    Average (Tests::Score)

This calculation returns the average for each of the first related test records:

    Average (AIMS::Score ; Reading::Score ; Math::Score)

▩ COUNT()

The `Count()` function counts all non-blank values in a field, whether they're repeating fields, all related fields, or several nonrepeating fields. Because it's possible to have a record that doesn't have a value in a particular field, it's usually more accurate to count a related field that is guaranteed to have a value, like a table's ID field. This way, you can easily count related values, like the number of invoices for a customer or tests taken by a student. This calculation returns the number of invoices in the related table:

    Count (Invoice::InvoiceID)

This calculation returns the total number of fields in the list that contain data. The highest possible example result from this example is 3.

    Count (NameChanges ; DeptChanges ; LicenseChanges)

▩ FLOOR() AND CEILING()

The `Floor()` function is like a supercharged rounding function. It rounds any value down to the next lowest integer. It just takes a single parameter, so you can use a number, an expression, or a field reference. This calculation returns *3:*

    Floor (3.999)

Watch what happens with a negative number. This calculation returns *−4:*

    Floor (-3.1416)

The `Ceiling()` function is a close relative of `Floor()`, but it rounds a number up to the next highest integer. So, this calculation returns *4:*

    Ceiling (3.1416)

And this calculation returns *−3:*

    Ceiling (-3.999)

▩ LIST()

This aggregate function works with numbers, but is even more useful on text. `List()` gathers up all the values you specify and then returns them in a *return-separated list.* That is, each value appears on a line by itself, and each line has a paragraph symbol after it. So for this calculation:

```
List ( Line Items:: Description )
```

You might get:

```
Virtualizing software
Holoband
Batteries (for Serge)
```

The most common use of List() is to suck related data or values from repeating fields, or a series of nonrepeating fields into a single text block for easy display, reporting, or manipulation. You could display the results of a List() in a tooltip (page 354). Or, if you need to grab a list of related IDs, List() is your go-to function.

■ ROUND()

The Round() function rounds a value to the number of places you set. It takes two parameters: number and precision. So if you set the precision to 3, this calculation returns *3.142:*

```
Round ( 3.1416 ; 3 )
```

> **TIP** You might be tempted to simply use number formatting on a field to display a value to a specific number of decimal places. But remember, that method changes only what you see on a layout. If you perform math on that field, then FileMaker uses the real value (with all its decimal glory) in the calculation. But when you use the Round function, you're actually changing the value in the field, and any calculations acting on that field use the rounded value.

■ SETPRECISION()

Some calculations demand a high degree of precision, like those that track radioactive isotopes or other scientific data with lots of places following the decimal point. The SetPrecision() function extends FileMaker's automatic precision of 16 decimal places, up to a maximum of 400. To get more than 16 decimal places, add a SetPrecision() function to the calculation that produces the value that requires precision. You can use SetPrecision() with all other numeric functions, except trigonometric functions, which don't accept this extended precision (Figure 11-1).

The SetPrecision() function requires two parameters: expression and precision. The first parameter is a number, or any expression that results in a number. The second is the number of decimal places you want to see.

> **NOTE** The SetPrecision() function affects your calculation's result, but not necessarily the way FileMaker displays it. To save space on your layout, you can use Number formatting on the field to show only a few decimal places until you click the field, when you see the real, stored value.

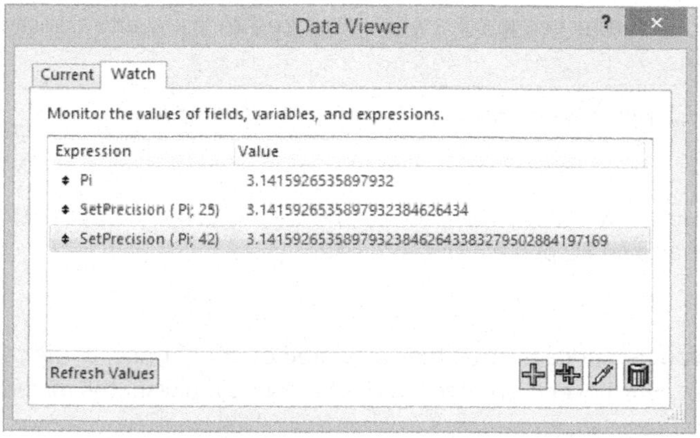

FIGURE 11-1

The first item in this window shows how FileMaker normally evaluates the value of pi. In the second, the SetPrecision() *function shows 25 decimal places. The third item shows 42 decimal places. You can see the formula on the left and the result on the right. This window is FileMaker Pro Advanced's Data Viewer, which lets you write a calculation and view its results without creating a field. It's a huge timesaver when you're writing a complex calculation. Read about it, and other developer features, on page 552.*

Going Beyond Basic Calculations

In the last chapter, you created two very simple calculation fields using numbers: Extended Price and Invoice Total. Now you'll build on those basic concepts and use some of the number functions you've just learned to make a set of calculations that fit an upcoming sales promotion.

Reviewing the Data and New Business Rules

You've decided to start reselling personal security products to your customers. To help keep track of things, you have a Products table in your database. The table has these fields:

- A text field called SKU (a retail term for a product ID code)

- A text field called Description

- A number field called Cost

- A number field called Price

Switch to that layout now and flip through the product records. To help drive sales to your larger clients, you want to implement a volume discount scheme; they should get a 5 percent discount if they buy enough. But some of the products you sell don't have enough markup to justify these discounts. You want to be sure the discount never reduces your markup below 20 percent.

First, the lawyers say you have to add a line to all your marketing materials: "Volume discounts not available for all products." You can make this line as small as humanly possible, and hide it way down in the corner. Next, you need to fix your database so it tells you the discounted price for each product.

Planning the Calculations

To implement this discount scheme, take what you need to know and translate it into calculation terms.

- First, calculate 95 percent of the price (a 5 percent discount):

  Price * .95

- Second, you also know the cost (in the Cost field) and you can figure out the lowest price by adding 20 percent to this cost:

  Cost * 1.2

- Finally, the discounted price is either the calculated discount price, *or* the cost + 20 percent price, whichever is *greater*. Put another way, you want the *maximum* of these two values:

  Max (Price * .95 ; Cost * 1.2)

Using the Max() function, the previous calculation results in either the discounted price or the minimum price, whichever is greater (see the box on page 419). That result is *almost* perfect. But suppose you have a product whose *normal* price is less than 20 percent above cost (hey, it's a competitive market). If you use the Max() calculation as it is now, then the new discounted price is *more* than the normal price. You need to go back and add to your calculation so that it takes the regular price into account, and uses *that price* if it's lower than the calculated discount. Read on to learn how to think through this calculation quandary.

Constructing the Calculation

When calculations start to get complicated like this discount price example, you can visualize the finished calculation by imagining that you have a calculation field that contains the value you need. You can use this pretend field in your new calculation and then, when you're all finished, put the original calculation in place of the pretend field. In this case, just pretend you have a field called Calculated Discount that holds the discount price. With that imaginary field in mind, create a calculation with this formula:

    Min (Calculated Discount ; Price)

The result of this calculation is either the calculated discount or the regular price, if it's lower. Now, just put the original calculation in place of the words "Calculated Discount" (since the original calculation *results in the calculated discount*):

    Min (Max (Price * .95 ; Cost * 1.2) ; Price)

The Max() and Min() Functions

Often, you need to know either the highest or lowest value in a series. The Max() function and its opposite, Min(), fulfill these needs, and you find them in the function list's aggregate functions category. Like all the aggregate functions, these functions expect at least one parameter and are glad to get more. Every parameter should be a number. Your parameters can be any of the following:

- Constant data
- Fields within a record
- Repeating fields
- All related fields
- Fields from the first of record from one or more tables

The max function looks at every number referenced and returns whichever is largest. Min(), on the other hand, returns the smallest value.

For example, look at this calculation:

    Max (10 ; 3 ; 72 ; 19 ; 1)

Its result is 72, since that's the largest parameter.

If you have a repeating field called Distances that holds the distances from your office to each Krispy Kreme store in your city, then you can use this calculation to find the closest sugar fix:

    Min (Distances)

The same is true for *related* fields, too. This calculation finds the most expensive line item on an invoice:

    Max (Line Items::Price)

With both repeating fields and related fields, you pass just one field to the Min() or Max() function, but FileMaker considers *all* the values in that field. If the field is a repeating field, then FileMaker considers every repetition. If it's a related field, then its value from every related record is considered. But you can refer to multiple related tables, too. If you have several tables of updates, each with a date the update was done, then you can find the first update this way:

    Min (Name::Update ; License::Update ;
    Department::Update)

TIP You don't even have to write the second formula in place of the words "Calculated Discount." Until you click OK, you can treat the calculation box like a big word processing page. Move the insertion point a few lines past the first calc and then create the second calc. Then when it's correct, cut and paste it into place in the first calc.

The entire Max() function, complete with its two parameters, is now the Min() function's first parameter. You might think it looks a little confusing at first, but with practice you become accustomed to looking at functions-inside-functions like this.

If it helps, you can add white space and comments to clarify the calculation, as Figure 11-2 shows.

If you want to test a complicated calculation, then spot-check a few records where you know the result. Sometimes the math is so complex that you just have to work it out on paper and enter dummy records to check the calculation. Usually, if a calculation isn't working, you can figure out how to fix it when you compare your math to the value in the field.

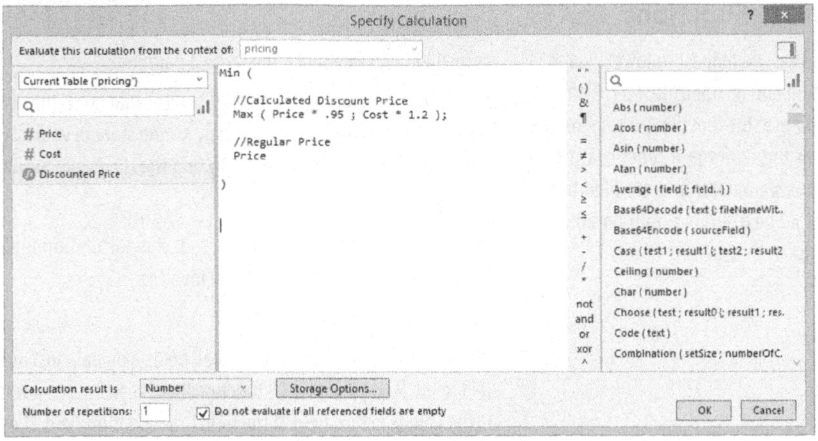

FIGURE 11-2

You may find it hard to write nested calculations, and hard to read them if you need to come back later and tweak them. In this case, though, the calculation is formatted with copious white space and plenty of comments. Chances are you understand this version better than the one shown in the text above.

Text Calculations

Although most people think of functions for doing dry stuff like math in a spreadsheet, you can also use functions in your database's text fields. Just as you can add and subtract numbers with number functions, you can use text functions to slice and dice the words in your database. For example, you might receive data from an outside source that needs major cleanup before you can use it. This data has people's first and last names in the same field; it's even got entire email messages crammed into a field—address, subject, and body—when all you need is the email address. You can equip a temporary database with fields and text calculations to *parse* (think of it as sifting) the data into the form your better-designed database expects.

> **NOTE** Fixing data with parsing calculations is called a *calculated replace,* since you use the Replace dialog box to enter the calculation. Since Replace works on the found set of records, you do a find first to isolate just the records that have the problem you're fixing, and then (and only then) do a calculated Replace Field Contents that fixes the error.

In contrast to the wide variety of mathematical operators for working with numbers, only one pertains specifically to text—the *concatenation* operator. Represented by the "&" sign (ampersand), it strings bits of text together. (When you need to chop and divide your text in order to parse it, you use a *function* instead of an operator, as described in the next section.)

To use this operator, put it between units of text, as in the expression below:

```
"This is a " & "test"
```

The result of this calculation is *This is a test.*

The concatenation operator lets you combine text from two different fields and make them work better together. Although you store First Name and Last Name in two separate fields, you often want to display them in a single field. When you're showing a second field in a value list, you can pick only *one* field to show along with the primary value. That example used the First Name field, but the full name would make the menu more useful. That's where concatenation comes in.

Create a new calculation field in the Customers table called *Full Name*. Set the calculation's result type to Text and then create this calculation:

```
Last Name & ", " & First Name
```

Some results are "Greystone, Daniel" or "Adama, Joseph." Note that the calculation includes a comma and the appropriate spaces for separating data between your fields. Now you can use the Full Name field instead of First Name in a value list. Figure 11-3 shows the result.

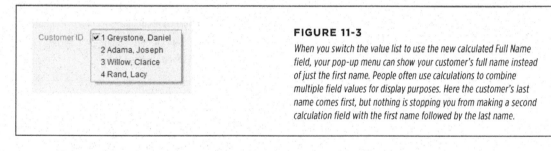

FIGURE 11-3

When you switch the value list to use the new calculated Full Name field, your pop-up menu can show your customer's full name instead of just the first name. People often use calculations to combine multiple field values for display purposes. Here the customer's last name comes first, but nothing is stopping you from making a second calculation field with the first name followed by the last name.

Text Functions

It's surprising to database newcomers, but text requires nearly as much manipulation as numbers do. That's because data frequently comes from another source, like Excel or Access. If you're lucky, the data is already in the form you need. Often, though, you have to massage the data to get it divided up to match your tables, fields, and field types. Sometimes, as with the Full Name calculation in the previous section, you just want to make the data display better. To know how to solve your problem, you need to know about text function types.

■ TEXT FUNCTION TYPES

FileMaker's text-handling functions come in two flavors: *text* and *text formatting*. Text functions handle tasks like finding whether a particular string of characters occurs in a field, or changing all instances of specific characters within a field, or counting text length. Text functions can break up text in three ways: by *characters, words,* or *values*. When FileMaker does the dividing, it gives you three ways to decide which parts you want: *left, middle,* or *right*.

Text formatting functions change the way your text looks, like making a part of the text in a field bold and red. These functions are a lot more flexible than just making a field bold and red on your layout, because you can tell the calculation to search *inside* the field, find just the characters "Propane Sale!" and make them red, but leave all the surrounding text untouched.

A Calculation in a Button

On page 177, you learned how to create buttons on a layout and program them to perform all kinds of database duties at a click. The only problem is, the more features you give your database, the more buttons you have to make. And some of the folks using your database need a completely different assortment of buttons. Fortunately, most button commands have one or more options you can set with a calculation. The calculation can adjust what the button does based on field data, user information, the current date or time, and so forth.

Suppose you have two different layouts to view the people in your People database. One is for the people who are *customers*, and the other is for *employees*. You might think that with two different detail layouts you'd need two buttons. But you

can summon the power of calculations to make one button do double duty.

If you take a peek at the options for the "Go to Layout" button action, then you see that in addition to all the layouts in your database, the pop-up menu includes two options you haven't used before: "Layout Name by calculation" and "Layout Number by calculation."

If you pick either of these options, FileMaker presents the Specify Calculation window. You simply write a calculation that evaluates to the correct layout name (or number if that's your persuasion), and FileMaker goes to the right one. For example:

```
If ( Person::Type = "Customer", "Customer
Detail", "Employee Detail" )
```

■ CHARACTER FUNCTIONS

Parsing by character comes in handy when you have data in a predictable format and you need to access pieces of it. You can use functions to grab the first three digits of a Social Security number, the last four digits of a credit card number, or the style code buried inside a product number.

FileMaker can work with individual characters inside a text value. The first letter in a text value is number 1, the second is number 2, and so on. Then you can ask for the first few characters, or the last few, or just the fifth, sixth, and seventh.

NOTE Every letter, number, punctuation mark, space, tab, carriage return, or other symbol counts as a character.

- The Left() function returns only the leftmost letters of a text value. You *pass* (that is, tell) the calculation the actual text value to parse, and the number of letters you want. For example, to get a person's initials, you can use a calculation like this:

```
Left ( First Name ; 1 ) & Left ( Last Name ; 1 )
```

To get the first three digits of a Social Security number, you can use this calculation:

```
Left ( SSN ; 3 )
```

- The Right() function does the same thing but starts from the other end of the text value. If you want to record the last four digits of someone's credit card number, then you can do it like this:

```
Right ( Credit Card Number ; 4 )
```

- If the information you want isn't on either end, you may need to use the Middle() function instead. This function expects *three* parameters. Just as when using Left() and Right(), the first parameter is the text value FileMaker's inspecting. The second parameter is the starting position. Finally, you tell FileMaker how many characters you want. (If you're not sure whether to use Middle() instead of Left() or Right(), see the box on page 424.

For example, suppose you have a product database that uses a special coding system for each item. The code "SH-112-M" indicates shirt style 112, medium size. To pull out just the style number (that 112 in the middle of the product code), you want your calculation to grab three characters from the Product Number field, starting with the fourth character.

```
Middle ( Product Number ; 4 ; 3 )
```

> **TIP** Use the Right() function to pad a number with leading zeroes (or any other character). For example, the calculation Right ("0000" & InvoiceID ; 5) puts two zeroes in front of InvoiceID #789 (#00789), only one in front of #6789 (#06789), but none at all in front of #56789 (#56789).

■ WORD FUNCTIONS

FileMaker also understands the concept of words. With word functions, you don't have to bother dealing with every single character.

In FileMaker's mind, a *word* is any stretch of letters, numbers, or the period character that doesn't have any other spaces or punctuation in it. Most of the time, this definition means FileMaker does exactly what you expect: It sees the real words in the text. For example, each of the following is one word:

- FileMaker
- ABC123
- This.is.a.word

Any sequence of other characters isn't part of a word at all. Each of these has two words:

- FileMaker Pro
- ABC 123
- A-Test
- Two *** Words

The Middle Way

It looks like you can tell the Middle() *function to isolate characters anywhere in a text field, just by telling it which characters to count. So why do we need* Left() *and* Right() *functions when you can do the same thing with* Middle()*?*

As the example on this page suggests, the Middle() function indeed provides all the power you need to pick text values apart character by character. For example, instead of:

    Left (Model Number ; 3)

You could do this:

    Middle (Model Number ; 1 ; 3)

It gets a little tougher to mimic the Right() function, but it's possible.

In *lots* of places, one function can do the same thing as another (or a few others).

For example, you can use Left() and Right() instead of Middle() if you want. This calculation:

    Middle (Product Number ; 4 ; 3)

can be rewritten like this:

    Right (Left (Product Number ; 6) ; 3)

The good news is, there's more than one right answer. Shorter is usually better, if only because you can often read it more easily. But if a few extra keystrokes make the calculation easier to understand, then they're usually worth it.

NOTE If your text value doesn't have normal words (like a long URL, for example), then you may have to pay special attention to the letters-numbers-periods rule to get the results you expect.

Along the same lines as the character functions, FileMaker has three word-oriented functions called LeftWords(), RightWords(), and MiddleWords(). You can use a word function to parse a person's first and middle names if you ever get a file with all three names unceremoniously dumped into a single field.

- LeftWords() returns all the text before the end of the specified word. For instance, this function:

      LeftWords (Preamble ; 3)

   might return *We the People.* But if Preamble contained "This *** Is *** a *** Test," it would return *This* *** *Is* *** *A* instead. In other words, it doesn't just return the words. It returns *everything* before the end of the third word.

- Likewise, RightWords() returns everything *after* the specified word's *beginning*, counting from the end. This calculation:

      RightWords (MagnaCarta ; 1)

   returns *reign.*

- What would LeftWords() and RightWords() be without MiddleWords()? You can probably guess how this function works: You pass it a text value, a starting word, and the number of words to return. It then returns everything from the beginning of the starting word through the end of the finishing word. The following calculation shows how it works; it returns *or not* because they're the third and fourth words.

```
MiddleWords ( "To be, or not to be" ; 3 ; 2 )
```

▉ TEXT EDITING FUNCTIONS

FileMaker includes dozens of text functions, but a few of them are worth special mention because you see them throughout the rest of this section, and because they're so useful for cleaning up messy data.

- The Substitute() function performs a find-and-replace within a text value. For example, if you want to turn all the x's to o's in your love letter (maybe you felt like you were coming on too strong), then you can do this:

```
Substitute ( Love Letter ; "x" ; "o" )
```

Substitute() is one of a few FileMaker functions that support a special *bracketed syntax*. You can perform *several* replacements on a piece of text with one substitute function. Each pair in brackets represents one search value and its replacement value. Here's how to remove all the vowels from a field:

```
Substitute ( My Field ; ["a" ; ""] ; ["e" ; ""] ;
["i" ; ""] ; ["o" ; ""] ;
["u" ; ""] )
```

> **NOTE** This example shows another nice fact about the substitute function: You can use it to *remove* something. Just replace it with empty quotes: *""*.

- While the substitute function can be used to change or remove what you specify, Filter() can remove everything you *don't* specify. For example, suppose you want to strip any non-numeric characters from a credit card number. You can *try* to think of all the possible things a person might type in a Credit Card Number field (good luck!), or you can use the filter function instead:

```
Filter ( Credit Card Number ; "0123456789" )
```

This calculation tells FileMaker to return the contents of the Credit Card Number field with everything except the numerals removed. In other words, simply put the characters you'd like to *keep* in the second parameter.

- The PatternCount() function tells you how many of a specific character string exist in the text. The function needs to know what you're searching, and what to look for. Consider:

```
PatternCount ( US Constitution ; "citizen" )
```

In this case, the calculation returns *11*. If the pattern doesn't appear in the text, then the calc returns a *0*.

- The Trim() function cleans up after those data entry folks who can't stop typing extra spaces before and after the important stuff. Just tell the function what to look at. From the calculation below, you get the string "Anyway" placed in your field.

```
Trim ( "Anyway " )
```

▓ TEXT VALUE FUNCTIONS

If a field holds more than one chunk of text, with a paragraph symbol putting each chunk on its own line, then it's very much like a value list. The data inside the list is called *return-separated values.* Text value functions let you grab individual lines from a value list. And since you can so easily grab a particular line from a value list, you can use the List() function (page 415) to put your data *into* a list to make it easier to grab.

Here's a simple example to show how parsing a value list works. Suppose you have a field called Colors with a list of data like this:

- Red

- Green

- Blue

- Orange

- Yellow

The LeftValues() function works like its counterpart LeftWords(). It takes two parameters: the list to examine, and a number to specify how many values you want. This function returns *Red* and *Green:*

```
LeftValues ( Colors ; 2 )
```

If LeftValues() doesn't do the trick, try MiddleValues() or RightValues().

Use the GetValue() function when you need to parse just one value from a list. The value you need has to be in a predictable place in the list, as in the whole-email-slammed-into-one-field example at the beginning of this section. Say the email comes to you like this:

- Email From

- Email To

- Subject

- Body

You could grab the Email To address with this function:

```
GetValue ( Email ; 2 )
```

You can figure out how many values in a list with ValueCount(). Just tell FileMaker which value list to count. The text parameter can refer to one or more fields or to static text. For example, this function returns *2*:

```
ValueCount ( "Tom Cruise¶Keith Urban" )
```

NOTE The value list doesn't need a paragraph symbol after the last value to return the proper count. So if you're building a return-separated list in order to grab data from it, then don't worry about adding that last ¶ symbol.

FilterValues() works like its plain cousin Filter(). You specify the text and then the values you want to allow. For example, the following function returns *Nicole* and *Katie,* each word on its own line:

```
FilterValues ( "Mimi¶Nicole¶Katie" ; "Katie¶Nicole" )
```

FileMaker has RightValues() and MiddleValues() functions, too. See the box on page 427 for ideas on how to use them.

■ TEXT COUNTING FUNCTIONS

You can also work with text by counting its individual parts. FileMaker has three related functions for finding out *how much* text your fields contain:

- The Length() function returns the length of a text value by counting characters.

- The WordCount() function tells you how many words are in a text value.

- Using the ValueCount() function, you can find out how many lines a field has.

These functions become powerhouses in combination with the various left, right, and middle functions. When the fields you're parsing contain varying amounts of text, you can have FileMaker count each one so you don't have to. For example, you might have a Parts Number field that contains parts numbers of varying length. Always, though, the last character is one you don't want. To return all but the last character in a field, use this calculation:

```
Left ( My Field ; Length ( My Field ) - 1 )
```

It uses the left function to grab characters from the field, and the length function (minus one) to find out how many to get. Just change the number on the end to chop off any number of junk characters from the end of a field. You're welcome.

When Data Doesn't Comply

Sometimes the text you need to break up doesn't come in pieces that FileMaker automatically recognizes, like characters or words. For example, suppose you have a URL:

music.site.com/Fishbone/Truth_and_Soul/Deep_Inside.mp3

You need to get the name of the file (Deep_Inside.mp3) and its parent folder (Truth_and_Soul). Unfortunately, this text value isn't divided into characters, words, or values. It's divided into *path components,* with a slash between each.

When you're faced with something like this, your best bet is to make it look like something FileMaker *can* deal with. If you can turn every slash into a new line symbol (¶), then you can simply use the RightValues ( ) function to pull out the last value. In other words:

```
Substitute ( File Path ; "/" ; "¶" )
```

The result of this expression is the list of path components, each on its own line:

```
music.site.com
Fishbone
Truth_and_Soul
Deep_Inside.mp3
```

To get just the filename, you can nest the Substitute function inside a RightValues ( ) function like so:

```
RightValues ( Substitute ( File Path ; "/"
; "¶" ) ; 1 )
```

Unless your data already contains multiple lines, you can always use the Substitute function to turn any kind of delimited list into a list of values. Bear in mind, though, that the substitute function is *case-sensitive.* You can read more about case sensitivity in the box on page 681.

Text Formatting Functions

Normally when you see data in a calculation field, it's displayed in the format (font, size, style, color, and so on) you applied in Layout mode. Every character in the field shares the same format, unless you want to manually search through all your records selecting the words "Limited Time Only" in your Promotion Notes field, so you can make that bold and red every time it appears. Not only does that method waste your precious time (especially if you're on salary), but it also plays havoc with your design when you try to print the field.

FileMaker's text-formatting functions let you specify exactly what bit of text you want in 18-point, boldfaced, red Verdana. And you don't have to visit a single record in person. You just write a calculation and FileMaker does the drudgework for you, without tampering with the real data.

Outsmarting the Smarties

LeftValues() and RightValues() are helpful when you need to pull some items from a return-separated list. But they're also helpful when you want to protect your database from people who know a few workarounds. Say you have a sales promotion going, where your best customers get to pick one free premium from a list of four items. So you've set up a field with a value list and a set of radio buttons. Everybody knows that you can choose only one item from a radio button set, right? Apparently not, because you've got some salespeople who know they can beat the system by Shift-clicking to select multiple radio buttons.

You just have to add an auto-enter calculated value to your Premiums field. Make sure you uncheck the "Do not replace existing value (if any)" option. Here's how the calculation goes:

```
RightValues ( Premiums ; 1 )
```

Now your savvy salespeople can wear out their Shift keys, but they still can't select more than one item in the premium field, because your calculation holds the field to a single value.

You can even add smarts to a Checkbox Set with a similar technique. Make this calculation:

```
LeftValues ( Premiums ; 2 )
```

People using the program can't select more than two checkboxes. FileMaker knows the first two items they selected and just keeps putting those same two back into the field, no matter how many checkboxes the salespeople try to select. For another twist, change the calculation to:

```
RightValues ( Premiums ; 2 )
```

Now FileMaker remembers the last two items selected, and very cleverly deselects the oldest value, so that the field always contains the last two items selected from the Checkbox Set.

FileMaker has six text-formatting functions, which we'll cover in the following sections.

> **NOTE** Since that big heading clearly reads "*Text* Formatting Functions," any reasonable person would assume that this formatting applies only to text. Luckily, unreasonable people rule the world. You can apply text formatting to any data type except a container.

◼ TEXTCOLOR() AND RGB()

The TextColor() function takes two parameters: some text and a color. It returns the text you send it in the right color. Like many computer programs, FileMaker thinks of colors in RGB code, which defines all colors as combinations of red, green, and blue, as expressed by numerical values. The second parameter to the TextColor() function is (almost) always the RGB function (and FileMaker automatically adds it when you add TextColor() to your formula).

This function returns a color based on three parameters: red, green, and blue. For example, if you want to change the Full Name field to show the first name in bright red, and the last name in bright blue, you use this calculation:

```
TextColor ( First Name ; RGB ( 255 ; 0 ; 0 ) )
& " " &
TextColor ( Last Name ; RGB ( 0 ; 0 ; 255 ) )
```

TIP For a crash course in RGB code—including how to avoid using it—see the box below.

■ TEXTFONT()

To change the font in a calculation result, use the TextFont() function. You just pass it the text you want to format and the name of the font to use. FileMaker returns the same text with the font applied:

```
TextFont ( "Dewey Defeats Truman!" ; "Times New Roman" )
```

UP TO SPEED

Color My World (with 16 million Colors)

What kind of data is a *color?* The explanation isn't very, er, colorful. FileMaker understands 16,777,216 distinct colors, each subtly different from the one before, and numbered from 0 to 16,777,215. Unfortunately, *learning* all those colors by number is beyond the reach of even the most bored developer. So FileMaker uses a standard (albeit entirely unintuitive) method of specifying a color as a mixture of component colors—red, green, and blue—with varying intensities.

Each parameter to the RGB function is a number, from 0 to 255. The number says how intense—or bright—the component color should be. A zero in the first parameter means red doesn't enter into the equation at all. The number 255 means FileMaker should crank the red component to the max. The RGB function returns a number, identifying one of those 16-odd million choices. To make it doubly confusing for anyone who doesn't have a degree in computer programming or television repair, the RGB system deals with red, green, and blue as sources of *light,* not the more intuitive red-yellow-blue primary colors of paints and pigments.

When colored lights mix (like those little pixels on a monitor), red and green make...yellow. In other words, to FileMaker and other RGB experts, it makes perfect sense to see bright yellow as the following:

```
RGB (255 ; 255 ; 0)
```

If, like most people, you don't think of colors as numbers, there are tools that can tell you the RGB numbers of any hue on your screen.

If you use a Mac, you have just such a tool in the Utilities folder (in your Applications folder). It's called Digital Color Meter. Launch the application and then, from the pop-up menu in its window, choose "Display in Generic RGB." The numbers now show the proper red (R), green (G), and blue (B) values for any color you point to on your screen. For example, in the status area (in Layout mode), pop open the Fill Color menu and then point to any of the colors there to see the RGB equivalent.

In Windows, you can see RGB colors in the standard color picker window. Just go to Layout mode and then, in the status area, click the Fill Color button. Choose Other Color. When you click a color, you see the red, green, and blue values listed in the window's bottom-right corner.

If FileMaker can't find the specific font you've asked for, then it selects another font in the specified script, so if you're on an English-based system and need to select a Chinese font, this parameter can help. (If you don't specify a script, FileMaker automatically uses the standard script on your computer. That's why you rarely have to worry about it—you automatically get what you probably want.)

■ TEXTSIZE()

The TextSize() function is simple in every case. Just pass some text and the point size you'd like (just like the sizes in the Format→Size menu in Browse mode). FileMaker returns the resized text.

■ TEXTSTYLEADD() AND TEXTSTYLEREMOVE()

Changing text *styles* (bold, italic, and so on) is a little more complicated. After all, a piece of text can have only *one* color, *one* font, or *one* size, but it can be bold, italic, and underlined all at the same time. With text styles, you don't just swap one style for another; you need to do things like take italic text and add bold formatting or even take bold-titlecase-strikethrough text and un-strikethrough it, leaving everything else in place.

To solve these problems, FileMaker gives you *two* functions for dealing with style: TextStyleAdd() and TextStyleRemove(). You use the first to add a style to a piece of text:

```
"Do it with " & TextStyleAdd ( "style" ; Italic )
```

Likewise, the TextStyleRemove() function removes the specified style from the text.

```
TextStyleRemove ( My Text Field ; Italic )
```

The text style parameter goes in the calculation without quotes, just like the examples above. You can use any and every text style in FileMaker: Plain, Bold, Italic, Underline, Condense, Extend, Strikethrough, SmallCaps, Superscript, Subscript, Uppercase, Lowercase, Titlecase, WordUnderline, and DoubleUnderline. And then there's AllStyles. When you use the AllStyles parameter, it adds (or removes) *all* existing styles.

With these two functions and all these style options, you can do any kind of fancy formatting footwork imaginable. Here are some guidelines:

- When you add a style to some text by using TextStyleAdd(), it doesn't change any style that you've already applied. The new style is simply layered over the existing styles.

- Plain style is the notable exception to the above point. Adding Plain style effectively *removes* any other styling. This style comes in handy when you need to remove a mess of styling and apply something simpler. Say your fields contain the words "Past Due," styled in uppercase, bold, italic, and double underlined, and you decide that modest italic would work just fine. Nesting the TextStyleAdd() function with the Plain parameter does the trick:

```
TextStyleAdd ( TextStyleAdd ( "past due" ; Plain ) ; Italic )
```

NOTE As you may suspect, using TextStyleRemove() with the AllStyles parameter does the exact same thing as TextStyleAdd() with Plain. They both remove existing styling, but as you can see above, when you add *Plain*, you can write neater expressions.

- When you add more than one style parameter, FileMaker applies them all to the text. You can use nesting, as shown in the previous point, or simply stack them up with + signs:

```
TextStyleAdd ( "WARNING" ; Bold+Italic )
```

- If you take a bit of text that was formatted with a text formatting function and then send it to another calculation as a parameter, then the formatting goes along with the text. With the substitute function, for example, you can format text that hasn't even been typed yet. If you add this function to a text field into which people can type letters to customers, then it changes every occurrence of "for a limited time" to bold italic:

```
Substitute ( Letter ; "for a limited time" ; TextStyleAdd ( "for a limited
time" ; Bold+Italic )
```

■ Date and Time Calculations

Before you start writing date and time calculations, think about how FileMaker keeps track of dates and times. FileMaker internally stores any date or time value as a single number that uniquely identifies every day and time of that day. Then when it needs to display a date or a time, it converts the number to a value people recognize, like "11/7/2014" or "10:23 AM." As with other numbers that it stores one way and displays another, FileMaker does the math on the stored value and then converts it for your convenience.

This secret to date and time storage isn't just a technicality. It actually tells you a lot about how you can use dates and times in calculations. For example, without this knowledge, you could spend ages trying to write a calculation that gives you the first day of the month following the date an invoice is due. But it's actually pretty simple:

```
Date ( Month ( Invoice Due Date ) + 1 ; 1 ; Year ( Invoice Due Date ) )
```

To break it down, you're just adding 1 to the month in question and then looking for the first day of that month. This section tells you what you need to know to analyze this calculation and then use its lessons in your database.

Math with Dates and Times

Because FileMaker looks at dates and times as numbers, you're free to use them right along with other numbers and operators in all kinds of mathematical functions. By adding, subtracting, multiplying, and dividing dates, times, timestamps, and numbers, you can come up with meaningful results.

■ DATES

You can use the information in your database's date fields to have FileMaker figure out due dates, anniversaries, and so on. You can use date fields and numbers interchangeably. FileMaker is smart enough to figure out that you want to add whole days to the date value it's storing. Here are some general principles:

- To get a date in the future or past, add or subtract the number of days. For example, if your policy is that payments are due 10 days after invoices are presented, then in your Date Due field, use this calculation:

```
Invoice Date + 10
```

- Of course, you aren't limited to adding constant numbers to dates. You can add the value in a number field to the value in a date field just as easily. If your video-rental database holds the checkout date and the rental duration, you can find the due date with this calculation:

  ```
  Checkout Date + Rental Duration
  ```

- To get the number of days between two dates, subtract them.

  Suppose your registration database holds arrival and departure dates. You can find the duration of the stay (in days) using this calculation:

  ```
  Departure Date - Arrival Date
  ```

NOTE   When you're adding a number to a date, the result is a brand-new date, and you should set the result type of your calculation accordingly. On the other hand, if you're subtracting two dates, the result is a number—the number of days between the two dates. In this case, set your calculation to return a number result.

■ TIMES

Although FileMaker's internal clock counts time as the number of seconds since midnight, a time value doesn't always have to be a time of day. Depending on the field format, a time value can be a time of day, like 2:30 p.m., or a *time* (as in duration, like 3 hours, 27 minutes).

TIP   FileMaker is savvy to the concept that time passes, but not all programs are. For instance, if you're exporting data to Excel, you may want to make calculation fields that convert time fields containing durations to a number field and then export the new field instead.

In both cases, times have a numeric value, in hours:minutes:seconds format. When you consider a time of day, 14:30:05 represents 5 seconds after 2:30 p.m., but if you look at it as a duration, it represents 14 hours, 30 minutes, and 5 seconds. If the time has fractional seconds (a decimal point), then the numerical value does, too.

You can record how long your 5-year-old takes to find her shoes (34:26:18), or how long she takes to find the Halloween candy (00:00:02.13).

The key to doing math with any kind of time value is to remember you're always adding and subtracting amounts of *seconds*. Here are the guidelines:

- To get a time in the future or past, add or subtract a number of seconds or a time value. If you know when a student finished her exam, and you know how long the exam took in minutes (1 minute = 60 seconds), then you can figure out when she started:

  ```
  Finish Time - ( Exam Duration * 60 )
  ```

- To get the number of seconds between two times, subtract one from the other. A Test Reporting database could store start and finish times for each exam. To find the duration, use this calculation:

```
Finish Time - Start Time
```

From Numbers to Times

If you can treat dates and times like numbers, then it makes sense that you can go the other way, too. Suppose you have a field called Race Time that holds each athlete's race time as a number of seconds. If you'd rather view this time in the Hours:Minutes:Seconds (or Minutes:Seconds) format, then you can easily use a calculation to convert it to a time value:

```
GetAsTime(Race Time)
```

When you pass it a number value, the GetAsTime() function converts that number into the equivalent time. (If you view the field on a layout, then you can use the time formatting options to display hours, minutes, and seconds in just about any way you want, as shown on page 315.) The GetAsTime() function has another purpose: It can convert *text values* into times. If someone puts "3:37:03" into a text field, you can use GetAsTime() to convert that text into a valid time value.

FileMaker has GetAsDate() and GetAsTimestamp() functions, too, which work just the same.

To get a time of day value in the future or past, add or subtract the number of seconds or a time value. Suppose you have a database of movie show times for your theater business. You use a timestamp field to record the date and time when each showing starts. You also use a time field to keep track of each movie's length. Now you need to know when each movie *ends*:

```
Showtime + Duration
```

NOTE If you store the date and time the movie starts in separate date and time fields, then the movie time calculation is much more difficult. Suppose a movie starts at 11:30 p.m. (23:30 in 24-hour notation) and runs for 2 hours. Adding these together, you get 25:30, a perfectly valid time value, but not a valid *time of day*. When you add to time values, they don't "roll over" after midnight. Timestamps, on the other hand, work as expected: You get 1:30 a.m. on the next day.

- You can subtract one timestamp value from another. The result will be given in seconds, so you'll have to do more math on the result to get minutes or hours. For example, you use timestamps to record the start and finish times for a job. To find out how long the job took, in minutes, use this calculation:

```
(Finish Time Stamp-Start Time Stamp) / 60
```

- To increase or decrease a time duration value, add or subtract the number of seconds or another time duration. Say you have a related Songs table with a Song Lengths field to hold the length of each song on a CD. This calculation tells you how long the entire CD is:

```
Sum ( Songs::Song Lengths )
```

- To double, triple, halve, or otherwise scale a time duration, multiply or divide it by a number.

If chilling your microbrew always takes twice as long as cooking, then you can determine the chilling time with this calculation:

```
Cooking Time * 2
```

Parsing Dates and Times

Just as you can parse bits of text from text fields, FileMaker lets you pull out parts of a date or time value. For example, you can keep track of all your employees' birthdays in a normal date field, but when you're trying to get statistical data from the year they were born, you're not concerned about the month or date part of that value. You have six functions at your disposal to pick those individual components from a date, time, or timestamp value. They are Year(), Month(), Day(), Hours(), Minutes(), and Seconds().

With a date value, you can use Year(), Month(), and Day(). If you have a time, Hours(), Minutes(), and Seconds() apply. You can use all six functions with a timestamp value.

These functions all have the same form. Each takes a single parameter—a date or a time—and returns a numerical result. For example, the day function returns the day portion of a date. This calculation returns *27*:

```
Day ( "7/27/2016" )
```

TIP   Just because FileMaker thinks of dates as numbers, you're not limited to using them that way. See the box below to see how to use parts of a date as text.

Name the Day (or Month)

Even when you're using the month number to group your data, you may prefer to see months by *name*. For example, if you produce a report of sales by month, you probably want the groupings labeled January, February, March, and so on, instead of 1, 2, and 3. You can use the MonthName() function to get this effect:

```
MonthName ( Invoice Date )
```

You can still sort all your invoices by the date field to get them in order, but you use your new MonthName() value to display in the Subsummary part. See page 631 to learn how to use Subsummary parts in reports.

Sometimes you need to see the day name (like Monday, Tuesday, or Wednesday). The DayName() function does just that. To get its numerical equivalent, use DayOfWeek() instead, which returns *1* for Sunday, *2* for Monday, and so forth.

Calculations that Create Dates and Times

Without even being aware of it, people do incredibly complex math every time they glance at a paper calendar or analog clock. When the boss said, "I want these invoices to go out two days before the end of this month," a human clerk knew exactly what to do. But how do you tell a computer to put "two days before the end of next month" in the Invoice Date field? The answer is at the end of this section, but first you'll learn the functions you'll need to calculate dates and times:

- The `Date()` function accepts three parameters—Month, Day, and Year—and returns the appropriate date value. For example, to get a date value of June 21, 2015, from a calculation, you use the date function like this:

  `Date ( 6 ; 21 ; 2015 )`

> **NOTE** To ensure accurate dates and date calculations, always use four digits when entering a year. You can configure date fields on layouts to just display the last two if that's how you want to see them.

- The `Time()` function wants three parameters as well: this time Hours, Minutes, and Seconds. It returns the time value. (The Seconds parameter can have a decimal point if necessary.) For example, you can construct the time value "8:00 p.m." like this:

  `Time ( 20 ; 0 ; 0 )`

> **NOTE** For time-of-day values, the time function doesn't let you specify a.m. or p.m., so you have to use 24-hour notation and format the field on the layout to display the time using 12-hour notation.

- The `Timestamp()` function takes just two parameters: Date and Time. It combines the two into a single timestamp value. It shows June 10, 2015, at 8:30 p.m. like this:

  `Timestamp ( Date ( 6 ; 10 ; 2015 ) ; Time ( 20 ; 30 ; 0 ) )`

■ THE SECRET POWERS OF DATE()

Although FileMaker doesn't look at calendars the way people do, that's not all bad. You see a calendar in absolute terms: April 30 belongs to April, May 1 belongs to May, and that's that. FileMaker, however, thinks of dates in relative terms and sees no such limitations. You can use this flexibility to your advantage in calculations—big time. You can give seemingly illogical parameters to the `Date()` function and have FileMaker produce a valid date anyway.

For example, this calculation actually produces a valid date:

  `Date ( 7 ; 0 ; 2015 )`

You might expect a nonsense result—July 0, 2015. But FileMaker looks at the same code and says, "No problem. Zero comes before 1, so you must mean the day that comes before July 1." And so it returns June 30, 2015.

These same smarts apply to the month as well:

```
Date ( 15 ; 11 ; 2015 )
```

That calculation produces March 11, *2016*. In other words, 3 months into the next year, since 15 is 3 months more than 1 year.

This behavior comes in super handy when you're trying to fiddle with dates in calculations. Suppose you have order records, each one with an order date. You bill on the last day of the month in which the order was placed, so your calculation needs to figure out that date, which could be 28, 30, or 31, depending on the month, or even 29 if it's February in a leap year. That calculation would take an entire page in this book. But here's a much easier approach: Instead of calculating which day each month ends, use the fact that the *last* day of *this* month is always the day *before* the *first* day of *next* month. To start with, you can calculate next month like this:

```
Month ( Order Date ) + 1
```

So the date of the first day of next month is:

```
Date ( Month(Order Date) + 1 ; 1 ; Year(Order Date) )
```

To get the value of 2 days before the end of any month, just subtract 3 from the whole thing:

```
Date (
  Month(Order Date) + 1; // the _next_ month
  1; // the _first_ day
  Year(Order Date) // the same year
) - 3 // subtract 3 days
```

It may look a little confusing at first, but it's much shorter than the page you'd need to work the calculation out longhand. And it works perfectly every month of every year.

■ Containers in Calculations

Although it isn't a typical calculation data type, you can do a few interesting things with container fields in calculations. You don't have the same vast options you do with other types. It would be great if you could subtract CousinClem.jpg from FamilyReunion.jpg to get the scoundrel out of the picture, but alas, the technology isn't quite there yet. Nevertheless, FileMaker doesn't leave containers entirely out in the cold when it comes to calculations.

Calculations with Pictures, Sounds, Movies, and Files

When you create a calculation field, you can set its result type to Container. You can't *create* container data in a calculation, but you *can* refer to other container fields. When you do, the picture, sound, movie, or file in the referenced container field shows in the new calculation field.

You can, for example, make a calculation field that shows the contents of one container field when you're in Browse mode, and another in Preview mode. This field lets you use low-resolution images when you view on the screen and higher resolutions when you view in print. (You'll learn how to create decision-making calculations in Chapter 17.)

You may also want to use container fields in a calculated replace. Suppose you have a found set of 30 records that don't have a low-resolution image. You have to have something in that field, so you decide to take the high-resolution image for those few records and plunk them down in the low-resolution image field. Choose Records→Replace Field Contents and then perform this calculated replace:

```
Graphics::High Resolution Image
```

The entire calculation consists of a reference to a field of that name in the Graphics table. The calculation does the grunt work of copying the high-resolution image into the low-resolution field in each record.

Calculations with References

If a container field holds a reference to a picture, movie, sound, or file instead of the object itself (see page 270), then you can do even more. When you treat such a field as *text,* FileMaker gives you some information about the referenced file.

If you have a field called Product Shot that holds a reference to a photograph file, then you can use this calculation:

```
GetAsText ( Product Shot )
```

The results you get depends on how the image is referenced. If you turned on "Store only a reference to the file" when you added it, the result will look something like this:

```
size:480,360
image:banjo.jpg
imagemac:/Macintosh HD/Users/sgripman/Desktop/banjo.jpg
```

If you're using FileMaker's secure container management feature, the result will be more akin to the following:

```
remote:space_ghost.jpg
size:396,284
JPEG:Secure/31/1C/4B1A4079/3DB25A4E/7685EA68/9B07
```

FileMaker tells you the size (width and height in pixels) and location of the file (if this weren't a picture, then you wouldn't see the "size:" line).

You can use this calculation to help you keep track of a set of images that the whole company needs to use. The calculation isn't dynamic, however, so the path serves as a reference of where the file *should* be, not where it really is. Company policy about putting things back where you found them has to reinforce your good data practices.

Understanding Scripts

When you created the Lease Agreement database in Chapter 4 and Chapter 5, you wrote a script to sort records viewed in a list (page 174). That script didn't do anything you couldn't have done manually. But since it remembers a sorting setup, the script runs faster and more accurately than with manual commands. To make it even more convenient, you attached the script to a button that your users could click to sort data without the need to understand how to set up a Sort window. For even more automation, you gave the list layout a script trigger that ran the Sort script every time that layout is viewed. It's almost like your database knows what your users need before they do.

That basic script introduced you to many of the advantages of scripting. Here are the main reasons to add scripts to your database:

- **Efficiency.** For just about any process, a script can run faster than you (or your users) can issue the same commands.

- **Accuracy.** Once you set it up, a script won't leave out a step or perform a series of steps out of order.

- **Convenience.** You don't have to remember how to do a process that you don't perform often.

- **Automation.** With script triggers, processes can run without you explicitly running the script. In many cases, users won't even know a script is running. They'll just see the results.

- **Complex processing.** Some processes just aren't possible (or maybe they're not feasible) without a script handling the grunt work.

Most scripts you'll write will combine more than one of these advantages. Scripts are so useful that complex databases often have hundreds of scripts (or even more). Even relatively simple databases benefit from scripts, since reports usually require a similar sequence of steps: finding records, sorting them, and showing a list layout in Preview mode. This chapter introduces you to the basics, but two more chapters (Chapter 13 and Chapter 18) dive deeper into scripting.

NOTE To follow along in this chapter, you'll find it helpful to download the sample databases from this book's Missing CD page at *www.missingmanuals.com/cds/fmp14mm*.

■ Understanding Scripts

A *script* is a series of steps bundled together. When a script runs, FileMaker carries out all the steps on your behalf, one after the other. You can create a script to automate almost any routine task, and once it's working the way you want it to, you decide how and when the script will run.

You can run a script from the Manage Scripts window or by selecting it from the Scripts menu. But more commonly, you put a button on a layout, and have FileMaker run your script when someone clicks the button. You can even use *script triggers* to make scripts run automatically in response to what someone does. For instance, you can make a script run every time someone goes to a particular layout, clicks into a certain field, or selects a specific tab panel in a Tab Control. Using the `Install OnTimer Script` script step, you can make a script run periodically or at a certain point in the future. Finally, you can run scripts on a schedule by using FileMaker Server to perform automated imports, send emails, clean up data, and so on. Scripting is FileMaker's real power feature, and there are as many ways to take advantage of its scripting prowess as there are databases.

Scripts can be simple—just the same few steps you'd go through if you printed a report manually. Or they can be much more complicated—and handle tricky or tedious tasks you wouldn't want to do manually. Advanced scripts can even incorporate calculations to do different things in different situations by making decisions based on the data in your database, the current time or date, or just about any other condition you want to test.

NOTE If you've worked with other scripting environments—like Visual Basic for Applications, AppleScript, or JavaScript—then FileMaker's scripting commands are pleasantly familiar.

■ Your First Script

To get a feel for how scripting works, you'll create a really simple script. Suppose you want to find all invoices with a balance due and view them in a sorted list. The following pages show how to go about preparing your database, planning, creating, and polishing the script, and finishing off with a way to run it.

Preparing the Database

Reports usually need their fields arranged differently from data-entry layouts. You'll usually use just a few of a table's fields, and they need to be positioned so they're easy to see and interpret. Also, reports usually need to be suitable for printing or PDF, instead of onscreen. As you're writing a script, you might realize that you need new calculation fields to get a report's summary data. FileMaker is flexible enough to let you create fields and layouts on the fly, but it's easier to focus on the script if you create all your supporting material before you even open the Script Workspace.

TIP In practice, you can't fully prepare a database until you've done some planning...and your preparation can reveal flaws in your plan. Work with the assumption that the plan and preparation phases of scriptwriting overlap and intertwine.

For this report, your list layout should include the Invoice ID, Job Name, Date, Date Due, and Balance Due fields. Figure 12-1 shows the List layout from the *CH12 Scripts Start.fmp12* sample database for this chapter. At the end of the chapter, you can compare your work to the Scripts End database. Both are available on this book's Missing CD page at *www.missingmanuals.com/cds/fmp14mm.*

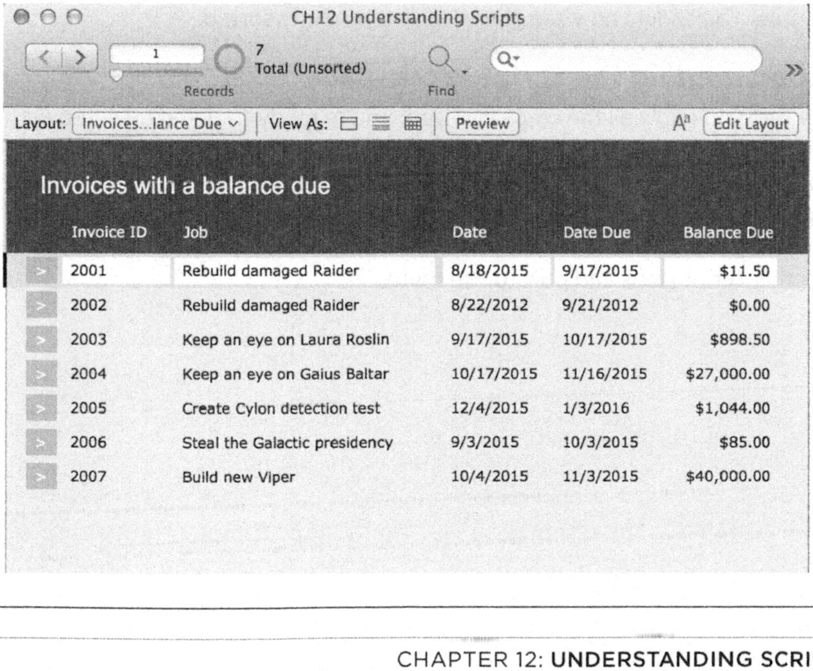

FIGURE 12-1

To follow along in this chapter, you need an invoice list layout like this one. You can use a report layout in your own database if you prefer, but the tutorials might not match precisely.

Planning Your Script

When you're planning a script, it often helps to manually work through the process the script should do first, so you can see how the process works. This trial run helps you clarify the steps you're scripting. As a bonus, some scripts are easier to write if you do the steps manually beforehand, since dialog boxes retain some settings. For example, if you manually set up the sort needed for your report, the *Sort* script step's dialog box will have the settings you need when you're actually creating the script.

So run through the steps necessary to find Invoices with a balance due, and take notes. You'll probably end up with something like the following:

- **Switch to the "Invoices with Balance Due" layout.** This layout has the fields the script needs to create the invoice list. It's also going to display the final list, so make sure the script runs in this layout.

- **Choose View→Find Mode.** Whether you're doing a find manually or by script, you have to start by switching to Find mode.

- **In the Balance Due field, enter ">0", and then press Enter.** FileMaker scripts use a step called Set Field to enter data into fields. Then a separate step performs the find and shows the correct records, just as if you'd performed the find yourself.

> **NOTE** If none of your invoices has a balance due, just click Cancel when the error message pops up and then choose Records→Show All Records so you can do the next step. Note that your script needs to account for this message box if it pops up when someone runs your script. In Chapter 18 you'll learn how to make your scripts account for errors like these.

- **Choose Records→Sort Records and then sort the records ascending by Date Due.** You should now see your final list, properly sorted.

Understanding the Script Workspace

Now that you know all the steps involved, you're ready to get acquainted with the Script Workspace window. Figure 12-2 shows a complete script to do the steps in this section. Because FileMaker Pro's scripting uses natural language in its script steps, even if you know nothing about scripting, you can probably read the script and get a general idea of what it does. Later scripting chapters will teach you about the other script steps and how to use them.

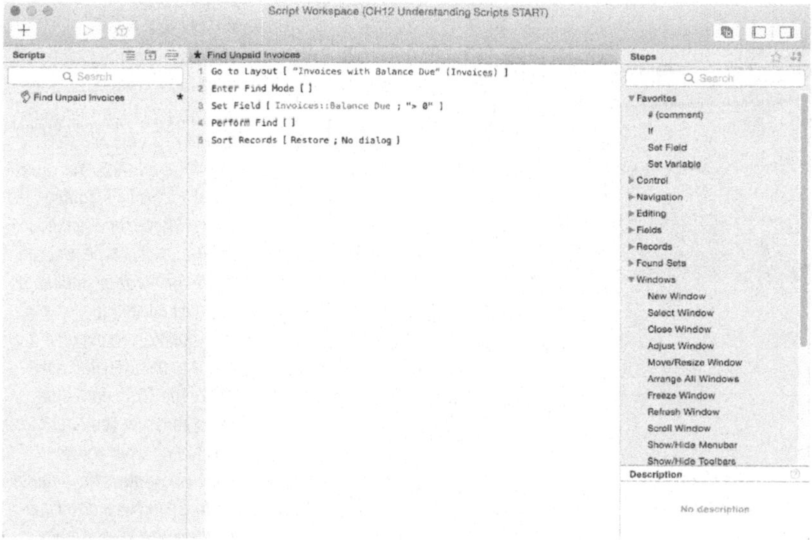

FIGURE 12-2

This script tells FileMaker to go to the "Invoices with Balance Due" layout, switch to Find mode, put a find criteria in the Balance Due field, perform the find, and sort the found records. It may not use exactly the words you'd expect, but it's easy to tell what this script does just by reading the "code."

But when you launch the Script Workspace for the first time, there are no scripts created yet. The only object available is a + button in the upper left. When you click it, the workspace adds a new script to the script list on the left. You can give the script a name in the middle of the workspace, and that's where you'll add the steps that make up a script. The right panel shows a list of all the script steps. See Figure 12-3 to learn more about the workspace and its tools.

The Script Workspace is made up of three panes: Scripts, Script Editing, and Steps. Before you create your first script, it helps to be familiar with each pane and to understand how it's used.

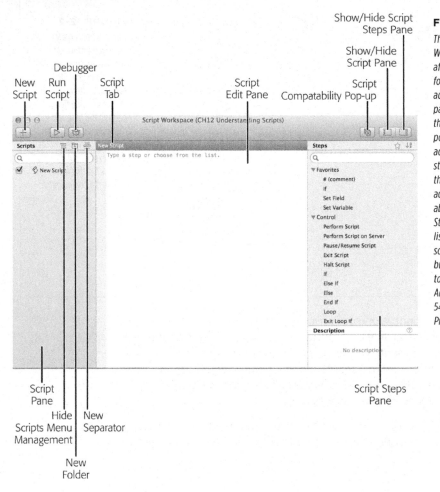

FIGURE 12-3

This version of the Script Workspace is what you'll see after you click the + button for the first time and start adding script steps. You adjust panel widths by dragging the dividers. If you're the point-and-click type, you can add script steps by finding the step you need in the list and then double-clicking on it to add it to the list. Filter boxes above the Script and Script Steps panes let you filter those lists to find what you need. This screenshot shows the Debugger button, which is a developer tool found in FileMaker Pro Advanced. The Debugger (page 544) is available in FileMaker Pro.

■ **THE SCRIPTS PANE**

The Scripts pane shows all the scripts in your database. Three buttons at the top of this pane let you control the clutter in the script list. The script management button (left) toggles the script list to show or hide script management tools. Script management is turned on by default, and shows checkboxes to the left of each script. Checked scripts appear in the Scripts menu. When they do, you can select a script from the menu to run it. The Folder button (middle) lets you create folders to organize your scripts. A common organization scheme is to put all the scripts for a layout into their own folder. That way, you can open only the folder you need as you're working on a specific layout. The Separator button (right) creates separators in the script list, much like in the Manage Layouts window. If you select a script separator, a separator appears in the Scripts menu. You'll learn more about these tools later in this chapter.

To keep all the scripts in a mature database straight, the pane gives you a filter field, for typing the field name. As you type, the script list gets shorter. You only have to type enough characters to see the script you need. To clear the filter, click the x at the right of the filter field.

■ THE SCRIPT EDITING PANE

The middle pane is where you'll do most of your work, so most of this chapter is devoted to how it works. In this pane, you'll give new scripts a name, add script steps, set options for those steps, and rearrange their order. You can have multiple scripts open for editing at one time. While you can create several new scripts at once, that's not likely to be your normal workflow. More often, you'll have two related scripts opened at the same time so you can compare or edit them—double-click on a script to open it in the Script editing pane. Then click the tabs to highlight the one you want to work with.

You can view scripts in separate windows, which is useful for side-by-side comparison. In the Scripts pane, select the script you want to see in the new window and then use the keyboard shortcut Ctrl+Shift+T (⌘-Shift-T). The Edit Script window appears, with your script in it. The Edit Script window doesn't have a Scripts panel, but otherwise works like the Script Workspace. Click the close button on a window or tab when you're done editing a script.

■ THE STEPS PANE

Scripts are made up of individual steps. As you learned on page 174, many script steps are automated versions of a command you can find in one of FileMaker's menus. The Steps pane has two buttons at the top. The star button lets you mark frequently used steps so they appear in the Favorites folder at the top. The Sort button lets you toggle between an alphabetical listing of script steps, or one that's grouped by category. The filter field works like its companion in the Script pane. Type the first few letters of a step's name to filter the list. Stop typing and select the step you need when you can see it in the list. To clear the filter, click the X button.

Creating Your Script

Now it's time to build the script. You'll use script steps to tell FileMaker to repeat each of the steps you went through when you planned the script. Here's how:

1. **Choose Scripts→Script Workspace, or choose File→Manage→Scripts. When the Script Workspace window appears, click the + button.**

   A New Script appears in the Scripts pane, and is opened in the middle pane.

2. **In the Script Name box, type *Find Unpaid Invoices*.**

   Your script's name is important. It's how you'll identify it when you want to run it later. As usual, a short, descriptive name is the best policy.

3. **In the Step filter box, type** *go* **in the Step filter box and then double-click the** `Go to Layout` **step to move it to your script.**

The step appears in the Open script pane. As they appear in the list, steps are numbered in a column on the left, making it easy to scroll to a specific location in a long script. Some steps have options that you must set before the step is complete. When that happens, part of the step is highlighted; clicking on the highlight shows a dialog box for setting step options. Click the Original Layout popup menu and then choose Layout. When the Specify Layout window appears, choose "Invoices with Balance Due."

That's the report layout you saw in the planning stages of writing this script.

4. **Click the x by the step filter field to clear it. Then click the Sort step button to sort the list alphabetically. Scroll down until you see the** `Enter Find Mode` **step. Double-click to move it to the list.**

The Options pop-up menu appears, showing options that make sense with the `Enter Find Mode` step. The Pause option at the left side of the Script Step Options area is turned *on*.

5. **Turn off the Pause option and then click the gear button to close the pop-up menu.**

Turning off this option tells the script not to wait for user input when it's run. You'll learn more about pausing a script in the box on page 516.

6. **Press the Enter key to create a new line in the script. Type** *set* **to filter the pop-up list of script steps. Use the down arrow key to select the** `Set Field` **script step, and then press Enter to add it to the script.**

You've used three different methods for finding and selecting script steps. The `Set Field` step lets you put (or set) data in a field. You can use `Set Field` in Browse or Find mode. In Browse mode, it enters data; in Find mode, it specifies find requests. Since this `Set Field` step comes right after an `Enter Find Mode` step, the script will specify a find request for the invoices.

7. **Click the Gear button in the Set Field step. Or press the Enter key.**

The step's options pop-up appears (Figure 12-4).

8. **Select the Specify target field option, or click its Specify button. Scroll the field list, and then double-click Balance Due to add it to the step's options.**

The Specify Field window appears, and because you're viewing a layout with the context of the Invoices table, that's the table you'll see. That's another benefit of planning your script—FileMaker saves you steps by guessing what you need. If you don't specify a target field, the result appears in the field that's active when the script runs.

9. **In the Set Field step options pop-up, click the bottom Specify button. Then in the Calculation box, type** *">0"* **(including the quotes) and then click OK.**

This step sets the Find mode version of the Invoices::Balance Due field to the appropriate value for finding unpaid invoices. Translated to English, this step reads, "Set the Invoices::Balance Due field to greater than zero," which is exactly what you did when you planned this script.

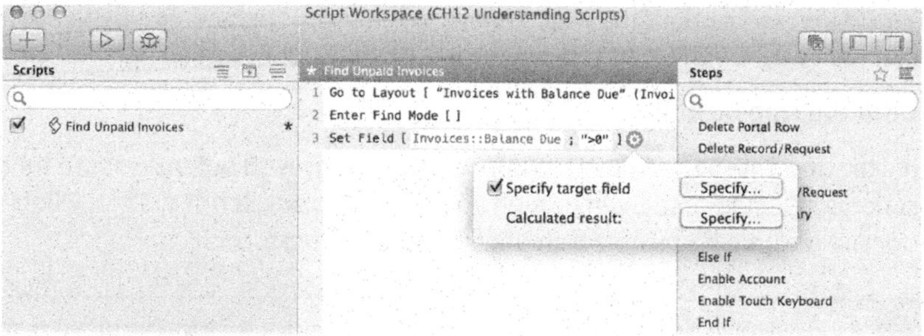

FIGURE 12-4

The Set Field step's option pop-up gives you two choices. First, specify the field you're setting data into, and then specify the data you're setting. The Specify Field window appears when you set the target field; use the Specify Calculation window to create the result.

10. **Add a** Perform Find **script step to your script.**

    Use the selection method of your choice and don't specify any options. This step will carry out the find operation. It's the equivalent of clicking Find or pressing Enter if you were doing it yourself.

11. **Add a** Sort Records **script step to your script. Then, in the step options pop-up menu, select "Perform without dialog."**

    This action tells FileMaker you want the script to sort without showing the Sort window when it runs. That way, the user won't have the opportunity to change the sort order when the script runs.

12. **Turn on the "Specify sort order" checkbox.**

    If you went through the script-planning phase, as described on page 442, the Sort dialog box is already configured properly. When you add a Sort Records step to your script, FileMaker configures it to match the *last* sort you performed. If you skipped the dry run, then set the dialog box to sort by Date Due, in ascending order.

13. **In the Sort Records window, click OK.**

    Unlike some other script steps, Sort Records doesn't show its settings. It just says Restore to indicate that you've set up sort criteria. To check the settings, click the Specify dialog box to view the Sort Records dialog box again.

14. **Choose Scripts→Save Script. Or use the shortcut Ctrl+S (⌘+S).**

    The Open Script pane has no Save button, but if you close it before you've saved your changes, you always see a warning dialog box that lets you save your scripts.

TIP In Windows 7, the Edit Script window has a File menu, from which you can choose Save Script. On a Mac, use the shortcut ⌘-S. If you're writing a long or hairy script, save often because it's not uncommon to be in this window for a long time as you're working out the script's logic.

The script is now complete. Flip back to Figure 12-2 to check your work. As with any new feature, you need to test your script to make sure it works as you intend. You'll learn more about the various ways to run scripts on page 454. But the most common way to run a script for testing is with the Script Workspace's Run button.

15. **Click the Run button.**

It's the one with a triangle in the upper left. If it's grayed out, make sure that the script is selected first. Even though you have only one script written, FileMaker doesn't assume it knows which one you want to perform.

NOTE If you did the trial run before you wrote the script, you may not see anything happen on screen. That's because your script repeats what you did. To be sure the script works properly, show all your invoices and unsort them. Then switch to another layout and perform the script again.

You should see the correct list of invoices, or, if you don't have any unpaid invoices in your database, you'll see an error message (see the box on page 449 for more about errors). In the next section, you'll refine your script to help deal with these message boxes if they pop up when someone runs the script.

TIP Since most reports follow these same steps, but with different options, you can adapt the basic structure of this script for a host of purposes. Use the Duplicate button to copy the script, give the new script a descriptive name, specify a different layout, and then change the find or sort criteria.

Improving Your Script

In the last section, you created a script that automates what you'd do to get an unpaid invoice list. Often, a script can get the results you want with *fewer* steps than it would take to do it yourself. For example, to see your unpaid invoice list, the manual steps are:

- Switch to the "Invoices with Balance Due" layout.

- Find the right invoices.

- Sort the records.

This version has just *three* steps instead of five because it assumes you can "find the right invoices" in one step. With just a small change, the Perform Find script step *really can* find what you want in one step. Here's how to revise your script to use the simpler form:

1. **In the Script Workspace window, select the Find Unpaid Invoices script, if necessary.**

   Selecting the script makes it active in the Script Editing Pane.

UP TO SPEED

To Be Continued

If your database has no unpaid invoices when you run the Find Unpaid Invoices script, then you see a message indicating that no records were found. The message is the same as the one you see if you perform the find manually, with one exception: This time you get a Continue button.

Since FileMaker was running a script when the error occurred, it gives you the choice to cancel the script (in other words, stop in the middle and return control to the user) or continue the

script (keep going and pretend nothing went wrong). In this case, Cancel and Continue do the same thing since the error happened on the *last* step in the script.

If you don't want the database user to make this choice, then you can tell FileMaker to *capture* the errors as they happen and let you deal with them inside the script. You'll learn about this process on page 723.

---

2. **Select lines** 2 **and** 3 **in your script (**Enter Find Mode **and** Set Field **).**

   You can select both by clicking Enter Find Mode in your script and then Shift-clicking Set Field.

NOTE Select the steps in your script (in the middle pane of the window), not the steps in the available script steps list (on the window's right side).

---

3. **Press Delete.**

   FileMaker removes the two selected steps from the script.

4. **Select the Perform Find step and press Enter (or click the Gear button) to show the step's pop-up options. Click the Specify button.**

   The Specify Find Requests dialog box (Figure 12-5) appears. Like the Sort script step in the previous tutorial, it's already set with the find you did when you planned your script. Since that's exactly what you want, you don't need to do anything in the Specify Find Requests dialog box except click OK and skip to step 8. But if you didn't do the recommended planning work on page 442, then you have to set your find request manually now, as described in steps 5–7.

5. **Click New.**

   The Edit Find Request dialog box appears. See Figure 12-6.

6. **In the "Find records when" pop-up menu, choose Invoices (if necessary) and then scroll through the list until you see the Balance Due field. Click to select it.**

   The Balance Due field is highlighted so you can remember which field you're telling FileMaker to search.

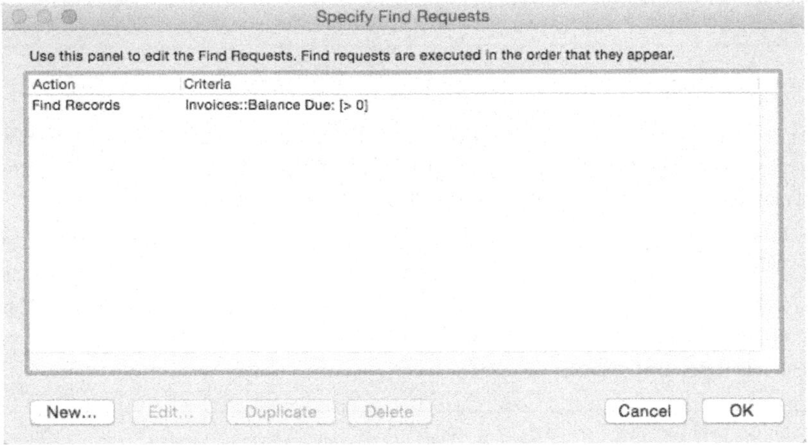

FIGURE 12-5

The Specify Find Requests window shows the requests you select in the Perform Find *step. You can add or edit find requests here. Doing your editing here is usually easier than adding* Set Field *steps like you did the first time 'round.*

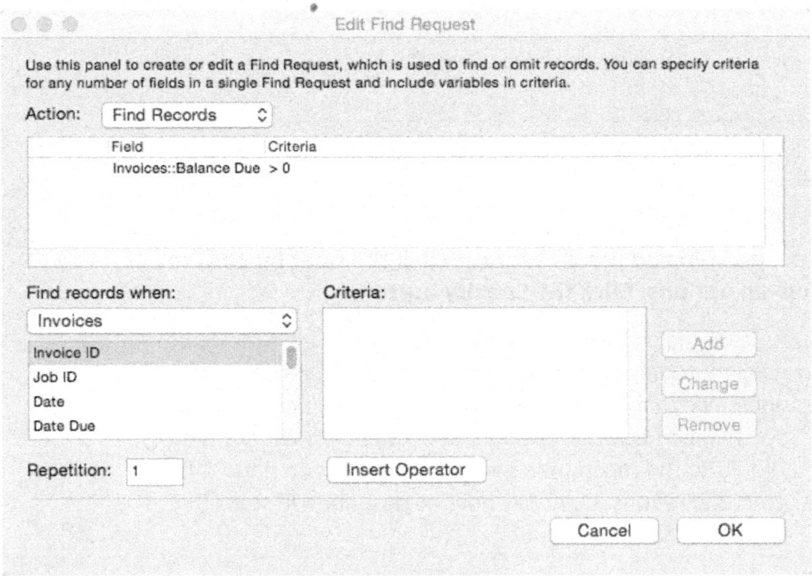

FIGURE 12-6

Here you see the finished Find request. The list at the top shows all criteria in the request. From the Find Records When list, you can pick a field and then enter your search terms in the criteria box. From the top list, you can also select requests and then edit them (click Change when you're done) or click Remove to remove them. Everything you do in this window has the same result as typing into fields in a single request in Find mode.

7. **Type *>0* (this time no quotes are required) in the Criteria list box and then click Add.**

    Your Find request is entered at the top of the dialog box, in the Action box.

8. **Click OK until you're back in the Script Workspace window.**

The Perform Find script step now has Restore options set (Figure 12-7), like the Sort step below it. Notice that the script has an * (or asterisk) at the end of its name in the script list. A second asterisk appears *before* the script name in the Open script pane.

9. **Click the X in the Script Editing Pane and then, in the dialog box that follows, click Save.**

Or choose Scripts→Save Script, or press Ctrl+S (Windows) or ⌘-S (Mac). The asterisks disappear, and the script is saved. You don't have to wait until you're done writing a script to save it. In fact the longer and harder a script is to write, the more frequently you'll want to save it to avoid the risk of losing your work.

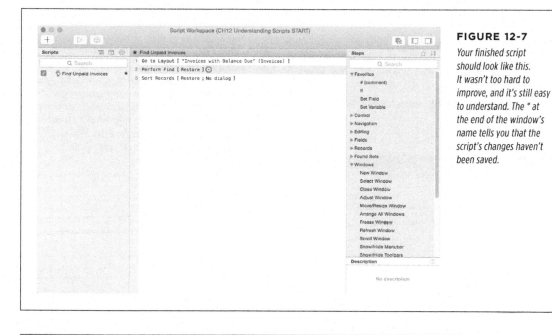

FIGURE 12-7

*Your finished script should look like this. It wasn't too hard to improve, and it's still easy to understand. The * at the end of the window's name tells you that the script's changes haven't been saved.*

TIP The Scripts menu also has a Save All Scripts command (yes, you can work on more than one script at a time) and a Revert Script command. These commands have no keyboard shortcuts, but you don't have to click the Close box on an Edit Script window to handle your save/revert chores.

Select your improved script in the Scripts list and then click the Run button. This new, simpler script does everything the first script did. It's simpler because you didn't have to script all the steps involved in performing a find: Enter Find Mode; Set Field; Perform Find. Instead, you let FileMaker do all that in one Perform Find step. You'll find that you can reduce *many* of FileMaker's common multistep operations to a single step.

Shortcuts to the Script Workspace

When you wrote the Find Unpaid Invoices script in the previous section, you opened the Script Workspace window by choosing Scripts→Scripts Workspace or File→Manage→Scripts. These multiple choices aren't just redundancy—they're meant to give you flexibility. But there are other ways to open the workspace that don't involve a trip to the menus.

Say you want to create a button on the Customer layout that finds unpaid invoices for the customer you're viewing. After you draw the button, the Button Setup window appears. If you select the `Perform Script` step and then click Specify, the Specify Script window appears, but the script you need isn't there (that's because you haven't written it yet). Just click the + button at the bottom of the Specify Script window (Figure 12-8) to open the Script Workspace.

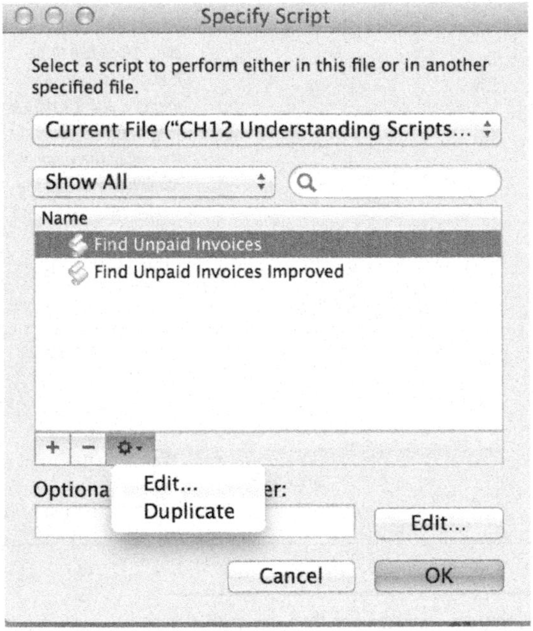

FIGURE 12-8

The + button opens the Script Workspace window. The - button deletes the selected script, but click it with extreme caution—you can't retrieve a deleted script. The pop-up menu (shown here) lets you edit or duplicate existing scripts. Edit opens the selected script in a floating Script Editing Pane, complete with a Steps pane (but no Scripts list). Duplicate creates a copy of an existing script. Then to edit the duplicate, select the Edit command.

> **TIP** Anywhere the Specify Script window appears you'll get these same shortcut buttons. Look for them in the File→File Options window (on the Script Triggers tab), the Layout Setup's Script Trigger tab, and the Edit Custom Menu's Action Option window.

■ The Importance of the Layout

In a script, the active layout is very important, since it determines the script's *context*. Context is critical when you do things like delete records. If you write a script that simply deletes a record without checking for context, then it deletes the current record from whatever layout someone happens to be on. That record may not be the right one at all. You could end up deleting a record from the Customer table instead of the single Invoice record you meant to delete!

Take the script you've created in this chapter, for example. Before it does anything else, your Find Unpaid Invoices script goes to the "Invoices with Balance Due" layout—but what would happen if you left that step out? `Perform Find`—like most other script steps—makes no mention of which table it should act upon. Just because you're asking it to "Find records when Invoices::Balance Due > 0" doesn't mean you're looking for *Invoice* records. These same search criteria yield different results on different layouts. If you did this search on a Customer layout, you'd end up with a found set of customers who owe you money. On a line item table, you'd see a found set of all the line items from invoices with balances due. So specifying a context within a script can be very important.

When to Switch

Don't assume that you *always* have to switch to a layout for your script to work. The fact that a script can do something useful from more than one context can be a good thing. In general, you have three choices when you write a script, and here are some guidelines on when to use each:

- **Switch to a layout associated with the table you want to work with.** The `Go to Layout` script step makes sense when you're showing certain results from a specific context, as in the Find Unpaid Invoices script. If necessary, you can then switch *back* to the original layout at the end of the script (`Go to Layout` has an Original Layout option).

- **Don't include a `Go to Layout` script step at all.** Just let the script go about its business, whatever the context. If you use this approach, then you have to make sure the script works and makes sense from any perspective. For instance, a script could switch to Preview mode, resize the window to show the whole page and then ask someone if he'd like to print. This script can run on nearly any layout and still do something useful: print.

- **Prevent the script from running on the wrong layout.** Using an `If` test in a script (page 549), you can make a script stop running if it's not working properly on the current layout. This is your best choice if you can't switch layouts within a script. For example, suppose you have a Refund Invoice script that carries out the steps necessary to pay someone back. Using `Go to Layout` to switch to the Invoices layout would ensure the right layout, but not necessarily the right *invoice*. It's best if this script runs only when someone's *already* open to the Invoices layout—presumably looking at the invoice she wants to refund.

NOTE When a script can do damage to your database if it's run from the wrong layout, use the fail-safe of the third option even if you're the only person who uses your database. If your mouse hand slips and runs the script because you're insufficiently caffeinated, then the script can show you an error message rather than running in the wrong context.

Running Scripts

You're probably starting to see how scripts can be really useful in your database. But so far, you only know how to run a script through the Script Workspace or by creating a button. There are other ways to run scripts, and you'll learn about them now.

The Scripts Menu

You can show scripts in the Scripts menu. If you have a script (or two) to which you want quick access from *anywhere*, then it makes sense to put it in the Scripts menu. That way, anyone can run it by simply choosing it from the menu. FileMaker even has keyboard shortcuts for the first 10 scripts in the Scripts menu: Ctrl+1 (⌘-1) through Ctrl+9 (⌘-9) for the first nine, and Ctrl+0 (⌘-0) for number 10. Figure 12-9 shows how to assign a script to this menu in the Manage Scripts window.

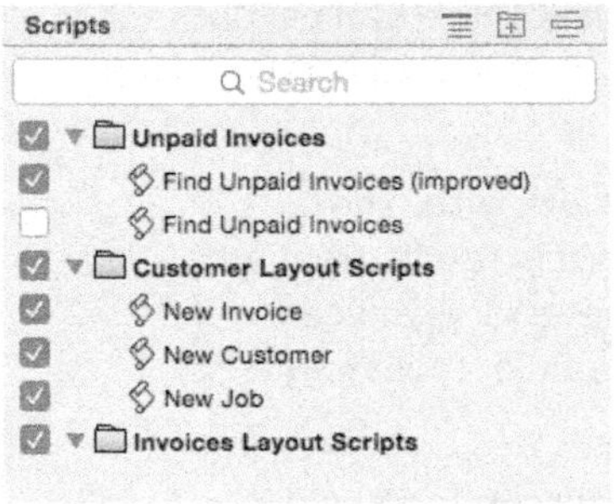

FIGURE 12-9

Top: In the Script Workspace's Scripts pane, every script has a checkbox by its name. If you click this box, the script appears in the Scripts menu, and you can run the script by selecting it as if it were a regular menu command.

NOTE If 10 scripts in a list isn't your idea of a highly organized command center, take heart. In Chapter 14, you'll learn how to completely customize the menus in your database.

Buttons

As you learned on page 177, you can add buttons to any layout—or turn existing fields, labels, and pictures into clickable buttons. As you saw, you can attach a single script step, or a Perform Script action to your buttons. When you click the button, the script or action you selected runs. See the box on page 455 to learn when to perform a script rather than run a button action.

Buttons are the most common way for users to run scripts, because the buttons sit right there on the layout reminding people that they're available. Many users, especially new ones, won't explore menus to find what they need, and they have an "out of sight, out of mind" mentality. That is, users can forget features when they're run from the scripts menu. But when buttons sit on the layout, and are well named, they become a training aid in helping people remember everything their database can do.

Script Triggers

You don't have to wait for someone to click a button to make a script run. Using *script triggers,* you can tell FileMaker to automatically run a script whenever someone performs a particular action. You can apply a script trigger to a layout or an individual layout object. For example, you might run a script when someone switches to a particular layout or trigger a script when she tabs into a field.

You learn how to use script triggers and more about how they behave at the end of this chapter.

A Script Action or a Script?

Attaching a single script action to a button is so easy that it's tempting to use that technique often. But even if your buttons do only one thing, you'll still save time in the long run if you create a single-line script, and attach that to your button instead. Yes, it's a little more work upfront, but scripts have a lot more flexibility over the long haul. Here's why.

Lots of the initial development work in a database has to do with helping the users get around. So many of the first buttons you create just go to a layout, or to a set of related records. But what if your business rules change—like from now on, only managers can see a customer's payment history? You have to figure out how to stop unauthorized folks from seeing

payment data. With an If statement (page 680) that checks Get(PrivilegeSetName), a script can see who's logged in to the file before it allows the Go to Layout script step to run. But you have to write the script and then find all the 14 places you created a button with a plain-vanilla Go to Layout script action and switch those buttons to Perform Script actions that run the new script. If you'd written a Go to Layout script in the first place, and attached that to your 14 buttons, you could handle this new wrinkle just by editing the script. No time wasted finding all those Go to Layout buttons, or worrying about what happens if you missed one, because the script can work the same way from every button.

Timer Scripts

Using the Install OnTimer Script script step, you can tell FileMaker to run a script periodically. For example, you can give the user feedback during scripts by setting a message that displays in a merge field on a layout. But you won't want to leave that message hanging around forever, so use the Install OnTimer Script step to clear the message.

OnTimer scripts work by setting a timer that starts ticking in the window that's active when the script is run. Then you set an "Interval seconds" option that tells FileMaker how often to run the script. OnTimer scripts run repeatedly until you stop them. So they can be alarming to work with until you get used to their ways. But OnTimer scripts run only in the window they were set in, so you can stop an out-of-control

OnTimer script by closing its window. More commonly, though, you'll stop an OnTimer script by installing a second one that doesn't actually call another script or express an interval. This technique clears the timer and stops the first script.

NOTE This chapter's finished sample file has a layout called Customer [OnTimer script] that demonstrates the technique of installing and uninstalling an OnTimer script. It uses the Set Variable script step, which is a mainstay of dynamic script writing. You learn how it works on page 518.

Running Scripts on the Server

FileMaker Pro is a robust program that can whip through complex scripted tasks quickly and efficiently. Because FileMaker Go (page 75) runs on a device with a lot less power than a desktop, it's similarly less powerful. So you should tailor FileMaker Go's scripted tasks accordingly. Sometimes, though, you need to let a mobile user run a heavy-duty process. In that case, you can use the Perform Script on Server step to shift the heavy lifting back to the server. But you might also want to offload some tasks to the server to let even desktop users click a button and then return to their own work without waiting for a script to finish. Server-run scripts support script parameters (page 716) and can return results (page 712).

You may be tempted to start shifting *all* the work to your server, but on a fast network with modern computers, the desktop will handle most tasks as quickly as the server can. Plus, if you have a lot of users, or if your database has a lot of scripts, you could overload the server. FileMaker Server is multithreaded, but even a fast server with multiple processors sometimes has to queue up tasks under heavy loads. Here are some places where a server script may run a script faster than a client script:

- Creating, editing, or deleting large numbers of records (including using Replace Field Contents).

- Summarizing large data sets into variables or using summary fields.

- Using the ExecuteSQL() function for large groups of records or across many related tables.

- Searching on unindexed fields (page 261).

In addition, there are some caveats you should be aware of before you run any script on the server. Obviously, the database must be hosted on FileMaker Server before you use this step (see page 793 for details). Second, scripts that are performed on the server run with the access of the user who runs the script. So make sure users who will initiate server-run scripts have the appropriate security access (page 777) to everything the script needs to do its work. Third, server-side scripts don't have the same context as client-run scripts. So scripts that will be performed on the server may need to go to specific layouts; find, sort, or activate records; or do other preparations that a client-side script might not require.

There are a few things that can make a server-run script fail:

- The script is run while the file is not hosted—say if you were trying to test it on a local computer or if the file is stored on an iOS device.

- Server-run scripts don't have access to global variables unless they're set in the script itself.

- Perform Script on Server is compatible only with FileMaker 13 or greater. So the script step will fail if it's run by any client older than FileMaker 13.

- Perform Script on Server doesn't work in peer-to-peer sharing (page 785).

- A Perform Script on Server step won't run in a Scheduled script (page 804).

■ WAITING FOR SCRIPT RESULTS

The Perform Script on Server step gives you two options. As with the regular Perform Script step, you can select the script you want to run. You can also decide whether the client machine waits for the script to finish before proceeding. Scripts that don't have the "Wait for completion" option turned on can't return results to client machine that initiated the script, so make sure you only use this option if the user (or the script itself) doesn't care what happens after the processing is done. For example, you might want your database to do some housekeeping tasks after everyone has gone home, but you don't have specific quitting times, so you can't just schedule the script to run on the server at a specific time. In that case, the last person leaving could click a button to start the housekeeping script and then shut his computer down. Just make sure the script doesn't need input from users before it finishes up.

■ Organizing Your Scripts

Most mature databases end up with dozens, or even hundreds, of scripts that make life a lot easier for the folks who use it. But developers don't usually have the luxury of creating scripts in an order that makes sense for display in the Manage Scripts window. That's why FileMaker gives you a suite of tools you can use to organize your scripts.

Creating Script Folders

In Figure 12-10, you can see the Manage Scripts window from a database with a lot of scripts. The window looks a little like a window on your operating system, where documents are organized in folders. FileMaker lets you create folders for organizing your scripts that same way. Not only can you give a new folder a descriptive name, but also, like folders on your desktop, you can collapse them, so you don't have to scan a lengthy list of scripts to find those under Reports.

Script folders make the Manage Scripts window nice and tidy, but they also organize the Scripts menu. Any script you place inside a folder appears in a hierarchical (or pop-out) menu when you click the Scripts menu. To see how all this works, you need to create a few extra scripts in your sample file. But they don't have to be real, working scripts. Just select your Find Unpaid Invoices script and then, in the Script Workspace, click the Duplicate button a few times.

1. **In the Script Workspace window, click the Folder button.**

   A new script folder appears at the bottom of the script list, and its name is highlighted so you can change it. You can control where a new folder lands by selecting a script *before* you create the folder. When you do, the new folder lands below the highlighted item.

2. **In the Folder Name box, type *Reports* and then press Enter.**

   Just like everything else in FileMaker, a descriptive name helps you figure out what's what. "Reports" is a little arbitrary, since this exercise is theoretical, but it's still a good habit to use descriptive names.

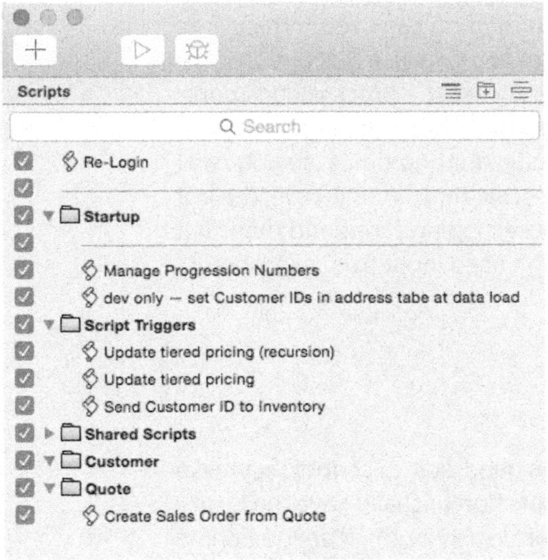

FIGURE 12-10

When your database has lots of scripts, like this one, organization becomes critical. Here, the scripts are arranged in a logical order, and grouped into folders, as described in the steps starting on the facing page. Some folders are open, and others are closed, to make it easier to scan the list when you're working with a particular script.

3. **Drag the folder to the top of the list. Then drag a few scripts on top of the folder.**

   When your pointer lands on the Reports folder, it's highlighted to show that the script is now inside. When you release the mouse, the script is indented to show it's part of the Reports folder.

Create and name several new scripts (with no actual script steps in them). The names aren't important, since you're creating them just to get familiar with how the folders work. Move a few scripts into the Reports group to get the hang of the technique. When you have some scripts in the new group, to the left of the group name, click the gray triangle to collapse it. A second click opens the group again.

When you have a nice list of organized folders, close the Script Workspace by clicking the window's close button. The scripts you selected appear in the Scripts menu.

Creating Menu Separators

Grouped scripts help you when you're plowing through a list of scripts trying to find the one you need to tweak. But you can also help people who use your database by giving them *menu separators*. It's a good idea to use them to organize sets of scripts that do different things. For example, the scripts that print reports could all be grouped together with separators. To create a menu separator, click to select the script that's just *above* where you want the separator to appear and then click the Separator button. If a separator isn't where you want it, then you can drag it into place.

You can also use the Duplicate button to copy multiple separators with just a few clicks. Each new separator appears just below the original; just drag them into place.

A separator is really just an empty script whose name is "–", so if you like to do things the long way, you can make one manually. Figure 12-11 shows how a well-organized list of scripts can make it easier to find the one you're looking for in a long list.

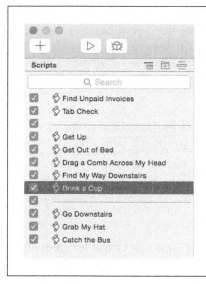

FIGURE 12-11

In the Script Workspace, separators show up as scripts named "–", but everywhere else, they turn into proper visual separators. Here, in the Scripts pane, one separator appears before the "Get Up" script and another appears after the highlighted "Drink a Cup" script.

▇ Branching and Looping in Scripts

Now that you have a basic foundation in what scripts do and how to run them, it's time to see some of scripting's more powerful features. The script you created at the beginning of this chapter was the simplest kind: It goes through a series of steps from start to finish every time. Sometimes your script needs more smarts. You can add steps to the script that cause it to take different actions depending on the situation (called *branching*), or make it do the same thing over and over again (called *looping*).

Branching with If, Else If, Else, and End If

Sometimes a script needs to take action based on certain conditions in your database. When you send an email to a customer manually, you look him up in the Customers layout, copy his email address, and then go to your mail program to create, address, and send the email. You'll add a button to the Customers layout that creates the email directly, saving you all the trouble of copying, switching, and pasting.

The Send Email to Customer script shown in Figure 12-12 creates a new email addressed to the current customer. But what happens if you *don't* have an email address for this customer? If the Customers::Email Address field is *empty,* then your script tries to send an email without a valid address through your email program, which complains mightily. Fortunately, you can head off this problem at the pass. If the Email Address field is empty, the script should let you know and then skip the Send Mail step entirely.

The If step is the answer; it tests a condition and can take action based on the result of its test. Here's how to add an If step to the Send Email to Customer script:

1. **In the Script Workspace window, create a new script called "Send Email" and then add the Send Mail step.**

   Use the settings shown in Figure 12-12 to set the proper options. This step is the heart of your script, so create it first. Even when you know you're creating a script that branches, it makes sense to write the "work" part first and then add the branching once the rest of the script functions.

2. **Add the If step to your script.**

   FileMaker adds this step *after* the Send Mail step. It also adds a third step: End If. You can't have an If without an End If, so you get both automatically.

NOTE If you accidentally delete the End If step from your script, then FileMaker shows an error message when you try to save the script. To fix the error, you need to add the End If step back to your script and then drag it to its proper place.

---

3. **In the If step's calculation box, type *Not IsEmpty(Customers::Email Address)* and then press Enter.**

   This calculation evaluates to True and sends your customer an email only if the Email Address field has data in it. See the box on page 463 for details on how this calculation makes these decisions.

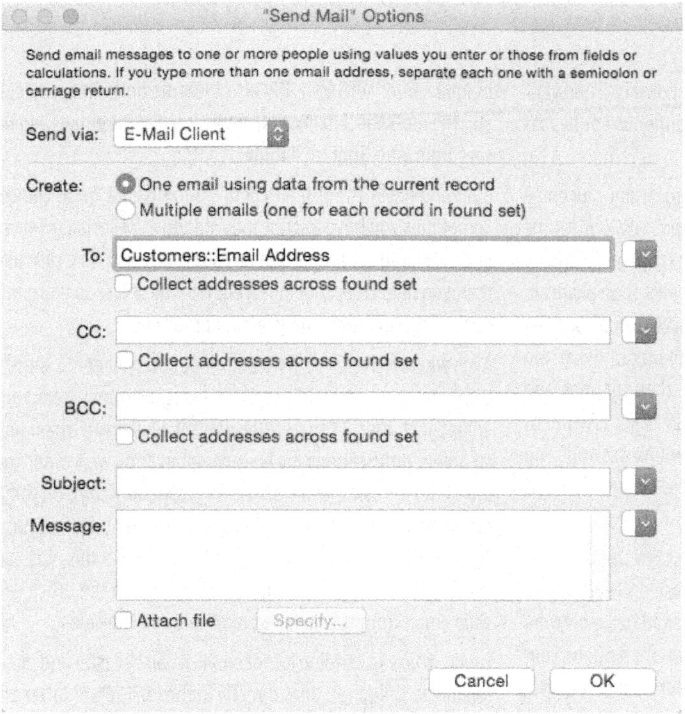

FIGURE 12-12

The "'Send Mail' Options" lets you set the options you need for scripting email. Click the triangle by any box and either pick a field or enter a calculation. Turn on the "Multiple emails (one for each record in found set)" checkbox to use this script step to send email to more than one person at a time. But remember, this option must be used for good, never for evil. You'd never send spam emails, would you? See the box on page 462 to learn about the Send Via options.

4. **Drag the If step up above Send Mail.**

   The Send Mail script step is automatically indented when it's nested inside the If/End If pair. Indents make your script more legible, which is especially important if you ever nest one If test inside another. Your script should look like Figure 12-13.

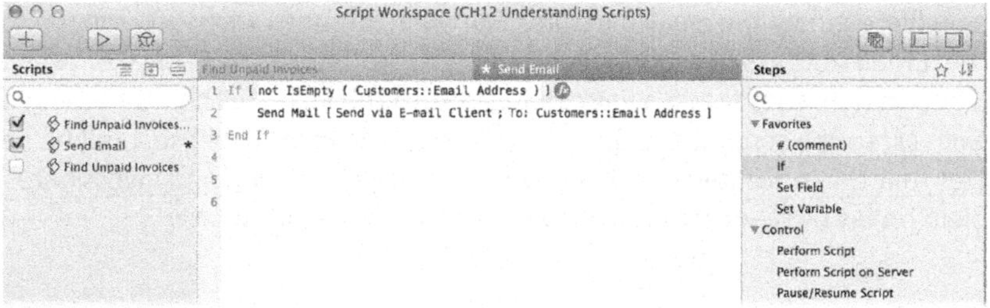

FIGURE 12-13

To prevent FileMaker from making an email message when the customer has no email address, wrap the Send Mail step inside an If test. Drag to make the workspace wider so that script steps are more legible.

Two Ways to Send Mail

The first option in the Send Mail Options window is "Send via," and it gives you two options, letting you either use or bypass the email program on your computer:

- Choose E-Mail Client to send the message using your email program. If you turn on "Perform without dialog" for the Send Mail script step, then the message goes directly into your mail program's outbox, and that program sends it the next time the send/receive mail process runs (which is automatic in most mail programs). If you leave "Perform without dialog" off, then the message goes into the Drafts folder instead. FileMaker also opens it up and switches to your mail program. This way, you get a chance to double-check the message and edit it as needed before you send it.

- Choose SMTP Server to send the message through your mail server. In other words, you're asking FileMaker to bypass your email program and go straight to the network post office. You have to put in information about your mail server, including its network address and any user name and password it requires. This configuration has no "Perform without dialog" option, so you can't edit the message before FileMaker sends it off, and it doesn't show up in your Sent mail folder.

Under most circumstances, you'll probably stick with the E-mail Client option. It's easier to use (because you don't need to put

in mail server settings). It's also more flexible since you can edit the message. Finally, you get a record of the emails you've sent from your Sent mail folder.

But sometimes the E-mail Client option isn't a good choice. Sometimes you have a script that runs on the FileMaker Server or on a shared computer that has no email client. In a case like that, you're better off going straight to the server so you don't have to set up and manage a mail program.

Also, when you use the SMTP Server option, you get to specify the From name and address. If the message comes from your email client, then it comes from you. But what if you're sending shipment notifications for your company? You may want the messages to come from *orders@mycompany.com,* or some other shared address instead of your personal email, as happens with the E-mail Client option. In a case like this, you can use the SMTP Server option, and everybody in the office can send email from the same account through FileMaker.

Finally, if you're sending lots of email, it can be faster and more reliable to send messages directly to the mail server (after all, its job is to send *lots* of email). As a general rule, it's fine to use the E-mail Client option unless you need the increased power (and hassle) of the SMTP Server option.

Now your script checks to see if the Email Address field has something in it before running off to create the email message. But what happens when you run the script and the Email Address field is empty? Right now, nothing at all. FileMaker evaluates the If condition, sees that it's False, and skips to the End If. There's nothing after the End If, so the script just stops and your user waits in suspense, until he finally realizes that the requested email message simply isn't coming and investigates the problem on his own—or chucks his computer out the window.

Inverting the Logic

In the script you wrote on page 460, the If script step runs the indented steps only when the whole calculation evaluates to True. To figure out when that happens, you have to deconstruct the calculation itself.

By itself, the IsEmpty() function returns True when the value you pass it is completely empty—in other words, when the Email Address field is empty:

    IsEmpty (Customers::Email Address)

But that action doesn't help you because you want the email sent only when there *is* data in the Email field. If you have no email address entered, then the calculation above returns True, and causes the Send Email step to run. If the Email Address field is filled in, on the other hand, then the calculation's result is False, and FileMaker skips the Send Mail step.

This behavior is exactly the opposite of what you want. To flip the result of the calculation around, you use the *Not* operator to invert the test's logic. It looks at the Boolean value to its right, and turns a True to a False, or a False to a True. Here's the calculation you need:

    Not IsEmpty (Customers::Email Address)

You can easily tell if you've got the right construction by reading the If step like a sentence: "If not is empty Email Address." It may not be grammatical perfection, but it gets the logic right.

If this kind of logic makes your head spin, then you have another option. Remove the "not" and then switch your steps around. If you read the script in pseudo-English logic, it'd go like this: "If the email address is empty, show a message, else send the email." This method may not have the cool factor of inverting a test's logic, but it's straightforward and less ambiguous.

In the interest of preventing property damage, your script should tell him *why* nothing is happening. For example, you can have your script show a message box saying, "Customer email address is empty." The Else step creates a place to put the steps that happen if the If test fails. Here's how to edit your script to include an Else step:

1. **In your script, select the Send Mail script step.**

   When you add a *new* step, FileMaker inserts it after the selected step. You want the Else step to go right after the Send Mail step, so you select that step first.

2. **Add the Else step to the script.**

   FileMaker inserts an Else step between Send Mail and End If.

NOTE Don't click the Else If step by mistake. You want the step called just Else. If you added the wrong step, select it, press Delete, and then try, try again.

3. **Right after the Else step, add the Show Custom Dialog script step to the script.**

   This step is found under Miscellaneous. Its job is to pop up a dialog box. You'll learn more about it on page 464.

4. **Press Enter to show the step's options.**

   The "'Show Custom Dialog' Options" window appears.

5. **In the Title box, type *No Email Address*.**

   This text will appear in the title bar of your custom dialog box.

6. **In the Message box, type *Customer email address is missing*.**

   This tells FileMaker what to put *inside* the dialog box as the message.

7. **In the Button 2 box, select and then delete the word "Cancel."**

   A custom dialog box can have up to three buttons. In this case, you want only one: an OK button. (If you don't type anything in the Button 2 and Button 3 boxes, then those buttons don't show up.)

8. **Click OK.**

   Your script should now look like the one shown in Figure 12-14.

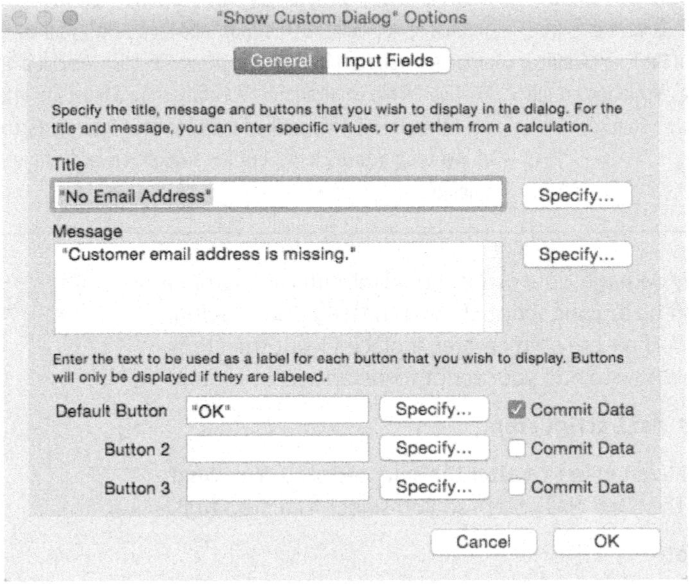

FIGURE 12-14

The Show Custom Dialog script step lets you provide feedback, like why an email script isn't behaving as expected. You can give your dialog box a title, a message, and up to three buttons for people to click.

Now return to your database and then try your script out: Find a customer without an email address (or just delete the email address for the Customer record you're viewing—this is just a sample database, so it's OK), and choose Scripts→Send Email. If you look at a customer record with an email address, then the script creates an email message in your mail program, ready for you to fill out. If the email address field is empty, then you see an error message instead, as shown in Figure 12-15. See the box on page 465 to learn why this script doesn't need to worry about context.

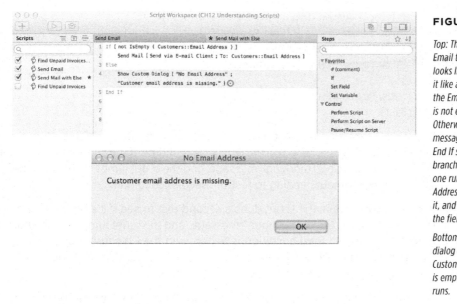

FIGURE 12-15

Top: The finished Send Email to Customer script looks like this. If you read it like a book, it says, "If the Email Address field is not empty, Send Mail. Otherwise show an error message." The If/Else/End If steps create two branches in the script: one runs if the Email Address field has data in it, and the other runs if the field is blank.

Bottom: This dialog box appears if Customers::Email Address is empty when the script runs.

Context Independence

You may be wondering why the Send Email script you created on page 464 doesn't go to the Customers layout first. After all, doesn't it only make sense from this context? Actually, this script is a perfect candidate for *context independence*. If you run this script from the Jobs layout, it creates a new email message addressed to the *related customer*. The same holds true from the Invoice layout. In fact, you can run this script from *any* layout, and get a useful result: FileMaker finds the related customer record, and addresses the message to her.

It's important to know who'll get the email if there's more than one related customer record. (Remember, the "Send Email to Customer" script is set to send only one email, even though the *Send Mail* script step lets you send multiple emails to all customers in a found set.) As you'd expect, the answer depends on the starting context when the script is run. If you run the script from the Scripts menu, FileMaker selects the *first* related customer for the active record on the current layout. If the relationship to Customers is sorted in the Relationships tab of the Manage Database window, then that customer sorts to the top. Otherwise, you get the first (oldest) customer record.

But if your layout has a portal of related customers, a button on the portal determines the context from which the script runs (you created a similar button in a portal on page 231). When you click this button, the script addresses the email to the customer in the portal line corresponding to the button you clicked.

The point is, you can put a button just about anywhere and tell it to run this script. FileMaker does something a little different depending on where you put the button.

Testing Multiple Conditions

If you have more than one condition to consider, you can use the `Else If` script step. You could have a script like this, for instance:

```
If [ Get ( CurrentTime ) < Time ( 12 ; 0; 0 ) ]
   Show Custom Dialog [ "Good Morning!" ]
Else If [ Get ( CurrentTime ) < Time ( 18 ; 0 ; 0 ) ]
   Show Custom Dialog [ "Good Afternoon!" ]
Else
   Show Custom Dialog [ "Good Evening!" ]
End If
```

When this script runs, it tests each condition in turn, deciding which custom dialog box to show someone, based on the actual current time. If the current time is before noon, she sees a "Good morning" message, and the script jumps to the end (the `End If` script step) without needing to test the second condition.

If it isn't before noon, the script does a second test to see if it's before 6 p.m. If it is, the user sees a "Good Afternoon" message, and the script jumps to the end. But if both tests fail, no third condition is tested, and the `Else` just shows the "Good Evening" message, like an automatic condition in a `Case` statement. However, you can add other `Else If` steps to test other conditions.

You can add as many `Else If` steps as you want, but they have to come between the `If` and `End If` steps. Each `Else If` can test a different condition. If you have an `Else` step, it should come after the `If` and every `Else If`, but before the `End If`. You can think of the `Else` condition as the default condition in a `Case()` or an `If()` statement when you write a calculation.

> **TIP** When you're writing multiple condition scripts, it can be hard to figure out when a condition tests as True. Read about the Script Debugger (page 544) to learn how to watch your scripts run step by step.

Looping

Sometimes you want to do the same thing over and over again, until you reach an end point. For example, people often write a script that does something to every record in the found set, one after another. This script is called a *looping script.* You make a script *loop through records* by using the `Loop` script step.

The `Loop` step comes immediately before the steps you want to repeat. Like an `If` test, the `Loop` step is part of a pair—you'll put an `End Loop` step at the end of the repeating steps. Sometimes, you'll also use an `Exit Loop If` step, which lets you write a calculation to figure out when the loop should stop. This step usually comes at the end of the steps that'll repeat each time the loop runs and just before the `End Loop` step. The `Exit Loop If` calculation is evaluated every time the loop runs. When the condition is met, the script proceeds to the `End Loop` step and then executes any steps that come after the loop is finished. FileMaker has three ways to exit a loop:

- The **Go to Record/Request** step has an "Exit after last" option when you go to the next or previous record. That way, you can easily loop through all the records in the found set, exiting the loop when you get to the last one.

- The **Exit Loop If** script step lets you provide a condition formula (just like If). If the condition evaluates to True, then FileMaker immediately skips to the first step after End Loop.

- The **Exit Script** and **Halt Script** steps both end a script immediately, even if you're in a loop.

NOTE If you forget to provide a way for a loop to stop, you can press Esc to stop it. Better yet, use the Script Debugger in FileMaker Pro Advanced (page 544) whenever you're creating and testing scripts.

◼ USING GO TO RECORD/REQUEST/PAGE TO EXIT A LOOP

The most common, and certainly the simplest, use for a loop is to repeat a process on a found set of records. Your script starts with the steps that do any preparatory work that needs to be done before the loop can start—often a find for creating a found set for the loop to run through. Use the Go to Record/Request/Page step to move through the found set, and turn on the "Exit after last" checkbox (Figure 12-16). The "Exit after last" option exits the found set (and stops the loop) after the loop's steps have run on the last record in the found set.

You can work through a found set backward by choosing Previous in the Specify pop-up menu and then selecting "Exit after last." This makes sense if you want to leave the user on the first record in a found set at the end of a loop.

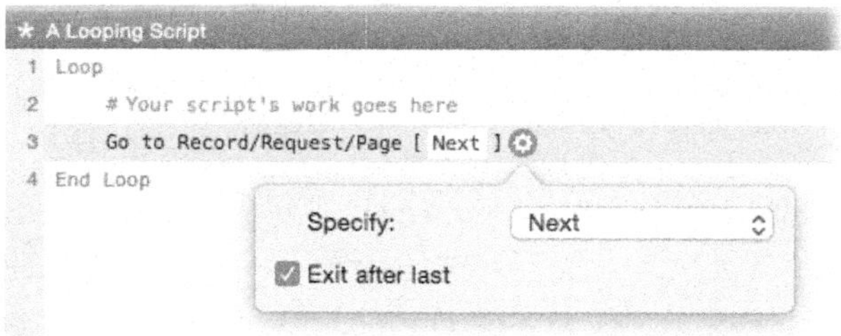

FIGURE 12-16

When Next is selected in the Specify pop-up menu, the Go to Record/Request/Page script step has an "Exit after last" option.

◼ USING EXIT LOOP IF TO EXIT A LOOP

There are times when an If test is a better way to exit a loop, as when you need to deal with the first few records in a found set. For instance, you might want to chart the data from your top 10 best selling products. You'd find all your products, sort them by sales volume, and then loop through them, setting the data the chart needs into global variables. The looping part of that script might look like this:

```
Loop
  Exit Loop If [ $counter > 10 ]
  Set Variable [ $counter ; $counter + 1 ]
  Set Variable [ $$chartData ; Value: $chartData & "¶" & Product::Sales ]
  Set Variable [ $$chartLabel ; Value: $chartLabel & "¶" & Product::Name ]
  Go to Record/Request/Page [Next]
End Loop
```

The first step inside this loop is a test to see if the looping steps should run. The first time through the loop, the counter hasn't been set yet, so the test will be false and the loop steps run. The counter increments 11 times before the Exit Loop If test evaluates as true and the loop ends. Take care to write a test that exits when you need it to. For example, if the test were written as $counter = 10, then the 10th record's data wouldn't be included. You don't have to put the test at the start of your loop, but if you do, make sure you test the script thoroughly before you release it into the wild. Learn about variables on page 687.

■ UNDERSTANDING TYPES OF LOOPS

A loop that works on a found set of records is called a *record loop*. A *field loop* works through fields within a single record. You can nest one loop inside another, as when you need to work on a set of parent records and then on each parent's child records. A nested loop's structure looks like this:

```
Loop
# Work on the first parent record here
Go to Related Record [From table: ChildTable; Using Layout: ChildLayout ; New
Window]
    Loop
      # Work on one set of child records here
      Go to Record/Request/Page [Next; Exit after last]
    End Loop
Close Window [Name: "Child Record Window" ; Current File]
  # Go to the next parent record and then start the process over
  Go to Record/Request/Page [Next; Exit after last]
End Loop
```

In this nested loop, the first loop works on a parent record and is called the *outer loop*. It runs once for each parent record. The one that works on the child records is called an *inner loop* and it runs once for each child record that's related to the currently active parent record. Nested loops work on many different found sets of records, so it's often easier to set them up and troubleshoot them by using Go to Related Record steps that open new windows for the child records and then close the child record window after each loop.

■ Script Triggers

Scripts are all about saving you (and your users) time. And what could be less time-consuming than something you don't have to do at all? As you learned earlier in this chapter, script triggers let you tell FileMaker to run a script automatically in response to something that already happens when people use your database. You'll get a brief introduction to each of FileMaker's trigger options here. Then, throughout the next chapters, you'll use these triggers in key places to make your database come alive. You can set up script triggers to run when you:

- Open or close your database

- View, commit, or revert a record

- Press a key on the keyboard when you're on a particular layout

- Switch to a particular layout

- Switch away from a particular layout

- Switch to or from Browse, Find, or Preview modes

- Switch to or from Detail, List, or Table views

- Enter an object (click or tab into a field, or highlight a tab panel or button with the Tab key)

- Exit a field that has field validation options

- Press a key on the keyboard while in a field, or while a button or tab is selected

- Change the contents of a field in any way

- Switch from one tab panel to another

- Leave a field or tab away from a button or tab panel

- Leave a field after you've made changes to it (in other words, when FileMaker has to save changes to the field).

- Play an audio or video that's stored in a container.

Script triggers come in three flavors:

- **File triggers** apply to the database file. They run when you open or close the file or when you open or close a window.

- **Layout triggers** apply to specific layouts. These triggers include actions like loading or committing a record, switching layouts, or pressing a key on the keyboard.

- **Object triggers** are tied to a single layout object (like a field, portal, Tab Control, or web viewer). These triggers fire when you interact with that object in some way, like editing the data in a field, or switching to a different tab panel.

- **Timer triggers** are attached to a specific window and set to run at a specific time interval.

Some triggers fire before their controlling action, and some fire afterward. And you can apply more than one trigger to a single layout or object, so it's critical to understand when they fire and in which order. So take care when you start to apply triggers. They're simple to apply but can be tricky to predict, and tricky to troubleshoot, unless you understand all their behaviors. You'll start this section by applying a simple script trigger and then you'll learn how each trigger works. You'll see other examples of script triggers in later scripting chapters.

Creating a Simple Script Trigger

Since you'd only view the "Invoices with Balance Due" layout when you want to find unpaid invoices, it makes perfect sense to run the Find Unpaid Invoices script every time you switch to that layout. You'll use an `OnLayoutEnter` script trigger to get the job done:

1. **Go to your "Invoices with Balance Due" layout and then switch to Layout mode.**

   You're creating a layout trigger (that fires when you switch to the "Invoices with Balance Due" layout), so you need to be on that layout.

2. **Choose Layouts→Layout Setup and then click the Script Triggers tab.**

   This tab is where you configure triggers for the layout. You can see it in Figure 12-17.

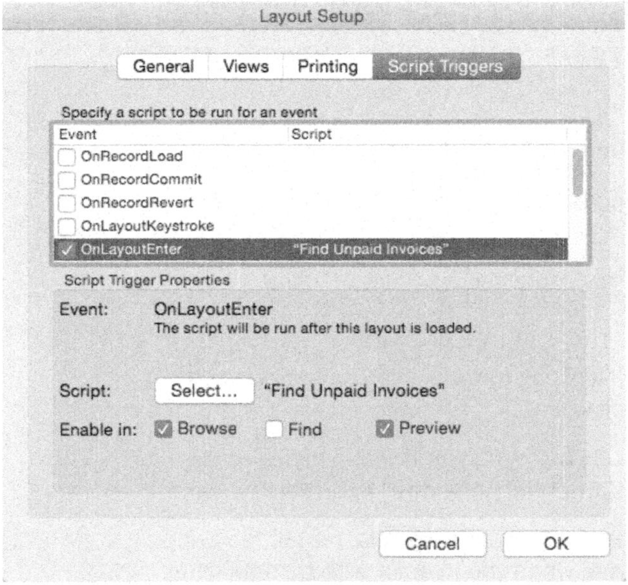

FIGURE 12-17

The Layout Setup dialog box has a Script Triggers tab. From here, you can turn on various triggers, pick which scripts run, and choose which modes the triggers apply to. You can turn on as many triggers as you want, but each trigger can have only one script. If you need to run more than one script for a trigger, write a script that has one Perform Script step (page 452) for each script you need to run, then select this new, master script.

3. **In the list, turn on the** `OnLayoutEnter` **checkbox.**

The Specify Script window appears.

4. **Select the Find Unpaid Invoices script and then click OK.**

In the list, the `OnLayoutEnter` trigger is highlighted, and, in the Script column, the Find Unpaid Invoices script shows. You can also see the script's name beside the Select button in the Script Trigger Properties section of the window.

5. **Select the Browse and Preview checkboxes and, if necessary, deselect the Find checkbox.**

Since it does a find, this script makes sense only in Browse mode and Preview mode, so you want it to trigger only in those cases.

6. **Click OK.**

Now your trigger is installed and ready to test.

To test things properly, go to the Invoices layout and then choose Records→Show All Records. Then switch to the "Invoices with Balance Due" layout. If all goes well, FileMaker will find only the unpaid invoices and sort them for you.

Now that you're on the List layout, you can do another Find if you want to see different records, or sort in a different way. As its name suggests, the `OnLayoutEnter` trigger fires only when you first come to the layout from somewhere else.

File Option Triggers

File option triggers run when something happens to your database file, like opening or closing it. You can use a file trigger if you want to be greeted with the list of unpaid invoices first thing every morning or see a list of open projects that need your attention. Or you could do some database housecleaning when you close the *last window* for your database. This option is a little less common, but it has its uses. For example, some solutions are made up of multiple databases; if you want to make sure other related files close whenever the main file closes (even if they have open windows), then you can write a script to close them whenever you close the main file. To set up file option triggers, choose File→File Options and then click the Script Triggers panel (Figure 12-18).

◼ ONFIRSTWINDOWOPEN

Just as it sounds, `OnFirstWindowOpen` runs when you open your database and its first window is drawn. This script trigger is very useful because it can run a setup script that finds and shows you specific data when you start work. But if a script from another database or a relationship opens your database, your database's first window may be hidden (page 526). In that case, the `OnFirstWindowOpen` script trigger won't run. When it does run, `OnFirstWindowOpen` is triggered before FileMaker enters a mode. That's important because layout triggers can be set to run in specific modes. So if your database's first window opens to a layout that has a layout trigger set, the `OnFirstWindowOpen` script will run and then the layout trigger script will run.

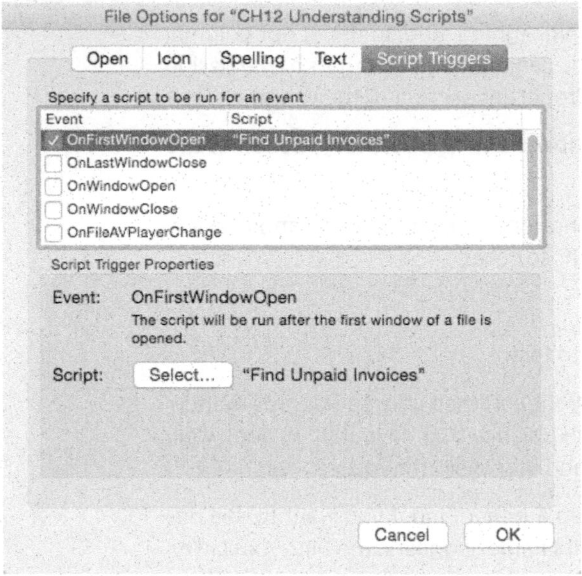

File Options for "CH12 Understanding Scripts"

Open | Icon | Spelling | Text | Script Triggers

Specify a script to be run for an event

Event	Script
✓ OnFirstWindowOpen	"Find Unpaid Invoices"
☐ OnLastWindowClose	
☐ OnWindowOpen	
☐ OnWindowClose	
☐ OnFileAVPlayerChange	

Script Trigger Properties

Event: OnFirstWindowOpen
          The script will be run after the first window of a file is
          opened.

Script: [Select...]   "Find Unpaid Invoices"

[Cancel]   [OK]

FIGURE 12-18

The OnFirstWindowOpen script trigger is set to run the Find Unpaid Invoices script when the database is opened. The "first" in the script trigger's name is important. The script won't run every time you open a new window for your database or if you manually hide all its windows and then show them again (Window→Show Window→[Your Window Name]). This trigger is only fired when the first window opens after you launch the database.

■ ONLASTWINDOWCLOSE

As you're working on your database, you'll often open several windows. The OnLastWindowClose script trigger fires just *before* the last window of your database is closed. In other words, the window stays open long enough to run the script you've specified, and *then* it closes. Your database's last window is closed if you quit FileMaker or if you manually close all its open windows. However, your database may stay open even if you've manually closed all its windows; when another database uses one or more of your database's tables in a relationship, FileMaker keeps your database open as long as it's needed by that other file. If FileMaker keeps a database open, OnLastWindowClose runs each time you close your database's last open window.

So now that you've worked through all that logic about when a window is open and when your database is open, why would you want to use an OnLastWindowClose script? You might want to do housekeeping chores like finding and marking incomplete records so an OnFirstOpenWindow script can find them for you the next day.

NOTE Exactly when a script trigger is fired is very important because it means your script can cancel the action that triggered it. You can use an Exit Script step (page 711) to check a condition that keeps your database from closing. For example, if you forgot to run the credit card for your last invoice, Exit Script could return a False, which would cancel the closing of that last window. The database stays open so you can finish the job.

■ ONWINDOWOPEN

OnWindowOpen runs every time a new window is opened in a database. It doesn't matter if a script opens the window or you do it manually (Window→New Window). The script you assign to this trigger runs every single time, no matter what context the window is opened to. As with OnFirstWindowOpen, this trigger runs before its window enters a mode. Because the script would need to be free of context (you might open a window for the Customer, Job, or Invoice layout) and will be run frequently while you're working, this trigger is not commonly used. But it can be used in combination with OnFirstWindowOpen, which runs first, then OnWindowOpen will run. And if that first window opens to a layout that also has a trigger, you can start a little Niagara Falls of scripts running to get your database all lined up and in marching order.

■ ONWINDOWCLOSE

OnWindowClose shares behavior with the other members of this trigger family. Like its sister trigger, OnWindowClose runs every time a new window is closed in a database. And like OnLastWindowClose, the trigger runs its script just before the window actually closes. OnWindowClose is cancelable; you can use an Exit Script step to check a condition that, when false, will keep the window from closing.

OnWindowClose runs even when the database stays open, as when another file is related to it and needs access to its data. You can use this trigger in combination with OnLastWindowClose. In that case OnWindowClose runs, and when it's finished, OnLastWindowClose runs.

■ ONFILEAVPLAYERCHANGE

OnFileAVPlayerChange fires if audio or video is playing (from a container field or in a web viewer) and the user changes the play state by clicking Pause, Play, or Stop. It also fires if the record is changed, which will stop the playback, or if the audio or video finishes playing. The trigger is fired after the action, so is not cancelable.

Layout Triggers

As you saw in the previous section, you configure layout triggers in the Layout Setup dialog box (Layouts→Layout Setup), in the Script Triggers tab (Figure 12-19). Layout triggers are performed when an action takes place that concerns a layout itself. For example, each time a new record is viewed, that's considered a layout trigger. That makes sense, given that the layout is FileMaker's method of showing you a specific record. When you think about it, you can see that the same trigger, running the very same script, can behave slightly differently depending on whether it's run on a Detail or a List type layout. Triggers can fire before their action or afterward.

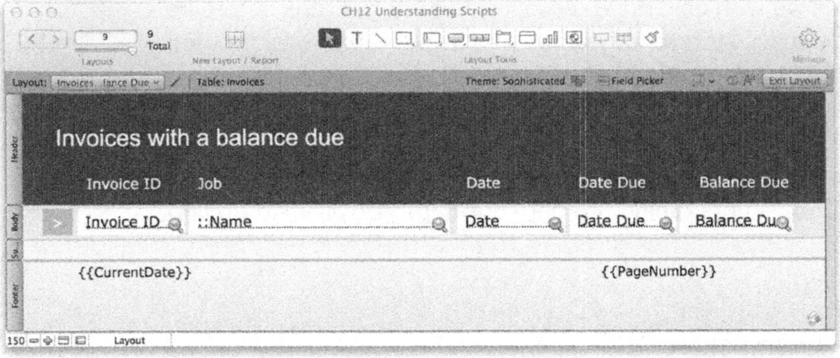

FIGURE 12-19

When you're in Layout mode, a small script trigger badge appears at the bottom-right corner of each layout that has one or more triggers attached. Toggle script trigger badge display with View→Show→Script Triggers.

■ ONRECORDLOAD

The `OnRecordLoad` trigger fires when a record is *loaded.* In other words, when you first visit a layout, switch to a new record, make a new record, or perform a find, a record is loaded. This trigger fires after the record is loaded and works in Browse and Find modes. You'll use this trigger in the next chapter to automatically sort a set of records. But it can also be used in tightly controlled databases where data is checked before you let a user view or edit it.

■ ONRECORDCOMMIT

`OnRecordCommit` works in Browse and Find modes. When you commit a record, the trigger fires. It doesn't matter how you commit (by clicking out of the record, switching layouts, or running a script, for instance). In each case, if this trigger is turned on, then the script runs. Even though the trigger is called `OnRecordCommit`, it actually fires *after* you make the action that would normally commit the record but *before* FileMaker commits it.

That means the script that's triggered can cancel the commit operation by returning a False value in an `Exit Script` step. If you cancel the commit, then you don't leave the record, and FileMaker doesn't save your changes. You can use this power to force the person using the database to make some kind of change to a record before saving, or require some kind of extra confirmation.

■ ONRECORDREVERT

When someone reverts a record (using the Records→Revert Record command, or the equivalent script step), the `OnRecordRevert` trigger kicks in. The trigger fires before the record is reverted and works in Browse and Find modes. It's cancelable with a false value in an Exit Script step.

◼ ONLAYOUTKEYSTROKE

The OnLayoutKeystroke trigger fires every time a key is pressed. Obviously, any script you trigger should be quick, because it will be called *very* frequently. The trigger fires before the keystroke is applied and works in Browse, Find, and Preview modes. You can use the Get(TriggerKeystroke) and Get(TriggerModifierKeys) functions to find out which key was pressed.

You can also cancel keystrokes. So if you want to stop allowing the letter L in your database, you could do that by testing for the letter in the field and then canceling the script with a False result in an Exit Script step. Truthfully, though, keystroke triggers aren't for beginners. People can press *lots* of different keys. Your script needs to be fast, and it takes a lot of knowledge to figure out which keys were pressed. For instance, this trigger fires even if someone presses an arrow key, or the Ctrl or ⌘ key, the Tab key, or a function key. You'll write a script using keystroke triggers on page 730.

NOTE One exception is Ctrl or ⌘ key combinations. These *don't* fire keystroke triggers. If you want to configure keyboard shortcuts to run scripts, then use custom menus (page 568).

◼ ONLAYOUTENTER

When you switch to a layout, the OnLayoutEnter trigger fires (you did just that on page 470). The trigger fires after the layout shows onscreen and works in Browse, Find, and Preview modes. You can do some initial tab setup, or sort the records, or even bounce to a different layout if you want. OnLayoutEnter is one of the bread-and-butter triggers for an advanced database that aims to streamline people's workflows.

◼ ONLAYOUTEXIT

When you switch away from a layout, OnLayoutExit fires. It runs its script before you leave the layout and works in Browse, Find, and Preview modes. It might seem as if you don't need this trigger if you've already got OnLayoutEnter, but it can make your scripting cleaner. That is, you can prevent a user from leaving a layout by checking some condition in your script. For example, you can return a False value in an Exit Script result. That keeps you from having to write a script that remembers where the user was before he tried to switch to a new layout, and then take him back if you want to cancel that switch to keep him where he was. This way, you prevent the switch until some condition (like entering data in all the required fields on a layout) is met.

◼ ONLAYOUTSIZECHANGE

OnLayoutSizeChange is triggered when a layout or a window is resized. It runs after the resizing action, is not cancelable, and runs in Browse and Find modes. OnLayoutSizeChange fires when a window is first opened on all FileMaker platforms, and after any of the following events:

- In FileMaker Go, when the IOS device is rotated, or when the status toolbar is hidden or shown.

• In FileMaker Pro and WebDirect, when the user changes the size of the layout or window, and by hiding or showing the status toolbar or formatting bar via a menu command, shortcut, or script step. Any script step that resizes the window or shows or hides the status bar also fires the trigger.

ONMODEENTER
The OnModeEnter trigger fires after you switch *to* a mode. So if you switch to Find mode, the triggered script can use the Get(WindowMode) function to look at the current mode and then branch accordingly.

ONMODEEXIT
OnModeExit fires after you *leave* a mode and is cancelable. As with the layout enter/exit triggers, if you use both triggers, then OnModeExit fires first, before you leave the current mode. Second, you enter the target mode, and finally, OnModeEnter fires after the switch. But you can intercept this whole process with an Exit Script step that checks a condition that keeps the user in the original mode.

ONVIEWCHANGE
OnViewChange fires after you switch between Form, List, or Table views, so it isn't cancelable. It works in Browse and Find modes. It doesn't activate when you first open a window or switch to a layout.

ONGESTURETAP
OnGestureTap fires when a tap gesture is received on a layout in FileMaker Go. It runs before the event is processed and can be used in Browse and Find modes. It's cancelable with a False value in an Exit Script step.

ONEXTERNALCOMMANDRECEIVED
OnExternalCommandReceived fires when a external audio or video controls are pressed *and* the user is using FileMaker Go. Examples of external controls are iPhone earbud buttons or special media control keys on keyboards. This trigger fires after the command is received. A companion function, Get (TriggerExternalEvent), helps you find out what kind of event fired the trigger.

Object Triggers
To configure an object's triggers, select the object and then choose Format→Set Script Triggers. The resulting window shows you the triggers available for the object (Figure 12-20).

You can apply triggers only to fields, tab controls, portals, buttons, and web viewers. For some triggers, the behavior of a script trigger may be slightly different, so expect to test scripts fired by triggers until you get used to their intricate ways. You can't attach a trigger to a text label, line, shape, or picture. The Set Script Triggers command will be grayed out when those objects are selected. The new OnPanel Switch script trigger is grayed out except when you have a tab control or other panel object selected.

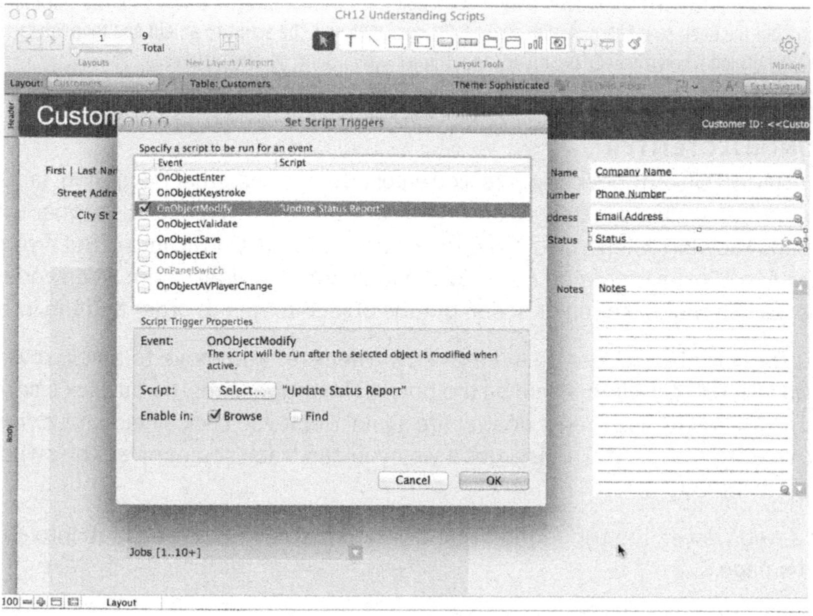

FIGURE 12-20

The Format→Set Script Triggers menu command lets you add triggers to the selected layout object. Behind the dialog box in this figure, notice the script trigger badge at the bottom right of the Status field. This trigger runs if the Status field is modified. If you copy an object that has a script trigger, the trigger is copied along with the object. So get in the habit of working with your script trigger badges visible so you don't get more than you bargained for when you copy objects.

Object triggers sound picky when you scan through their names (and to a degree they are), but that's just to give you as much control about when they fire as possible. As you read through this list, you'll see that object triggers appear in the same order as users interact with an object, in this case, say, a field. So for any particular interaction with a field, the following actions might take place:

- The object is *entered*—when you click in it.
- A keystroke is *detected*—users select an object and then start to type.
- The object is *modified*—you type new data into it.
- A field's *validation* kicks in—you click out of the field.
- A field's new data is *saved*—FileMaker's autosave makes the new data permanent.
- The object is *exited*—a new object is entered or the record is committed.
- A Tab Control's panel is *switched*—either because the user clicks on a panel, or if a script selects it.
- An AV player's state has *changed*—users click play, pause, or stop, or if any other process (like the video playing through to the end) changes the play state.

As you'll see in this section, the better you understand how FileMaker handles objects, the easier it is to apply the proper object trigger.

> **TIP** When you're trying to tease these triggers apart, it's helpful to write a very simple script that does nothing but the Beep script step. Assign an object trigger that runs the script to a field and then interact with the field, noticing when the beep occurs. Try each trigger—you'll soon get the picture.

◼ ONOBJECTENTER

The OnObjectEnter trigger fires *after* you enter an object, whether by clicking, tabbing, or script. It's available in Browse and Find modes. Usually you use this trigger with a field and knowing when a field is entered is easy—you click or tab into it. But if you set an OnObjectEnter trigger on a button or a tab control, it *doesn't* fire when you click it. To get the trigger to run its script, put the object in the tab order and tab into it.

An OnObjectEnter trigger on a portal fires whenever you move to a new row. For instance, if you click into a field on the portal, the trigger fires. If you click a second field on the same row, then it *doesn't* fire again. But if you click a field on a *different* row, then it fires again. This is a good way you can track someone as she switches from row to row.

For a web viewer, the trigger fires if you click into the web page or tab into a field on the page.

◼ ONOBJECTKEYSTROKE

Once you've entered an object, it can track keystrokes by using an OnObjectKeystroke trigger. When you press a key on the keyboard, the trigger fires *before* the keystroke is entered, which means it can be canceled. OnObjectKeystroke triggers are used to prevent data entry in a field. Usually the script looks for certain characters and then refuses to enter them. For example, you could disallow all data except numbers and the hyphen character in a Social Security Number field. You'll see an example of limiting data entry on page 731.

OnObjectKeystroke can be applied in Browse and Find modes. When attached to fields, the script runs repeatedly as you type or arrow around in the field. It also fires when you press the Tab key or Enter key to leave the field. For buttons and tab controls, you have to tab into the object for it to receive keystrokes. Since most people don't expect to type in a button or a tab control, you'd rarely use OnObjectKeystroke on them. Portals and web viewers never receive keystrokes, so this trigger never fires if you assign it to one.

◼ ONOBJECTMODIFY

The OnObjectModify trigger is frequently used to prevent data entry into a field. For example, you might want users to be able to enter or edit data in a Print Date field up until the date in the field. But once that date has passed, you don't want to allow any more data entry. An OnObjectModify trigger can run a script that compares the field's date to the current date and then taken the proper action. The trigger fires *after* data in the field changes but *before you've exited the field.* For instance, if you type into the field, then the trigger fires each time you add or delete a character. But it *doesn't* fire if you just use the arrow keys to move around in the field, or if you press Tab, Return, or Enter to leave the field. It also fires once each time you cut or paste in the field. It's available for Browse and Find modes.

On a tab control, OnObjectModify fires when you switch tabs, so if you used it in earlier versions you won't have to find and change all your tab control script triggers to the new OnPanelSwitch. But since its behavior is clearer, your new databases should use OnPanelSwitch instead. OnObjectModify never fires with buttons, portals, and web viewers.

> **NOTE** The OnObjectModify trigger doesn't fire if you modify the field without entering it. For instance, if a script runs the Set Field script step, then the field changes but the trigger doesn't fire. Nor does it fire when calculation, auto-enter, or summary fields are updated. Dragging text into a field *does* fire the OnObjectModify trigger. Take care with this trigger if you have a mix of versions, though. FileMaker Pro 10 doesn't run the OnObjectModify script trigger when data is dragged in its fields.

ONOBJECTVALIDATE

This trigger can be applied to any object, but is only triggered for fields that have field validation options (page 254). The trigger fires *before* the data in the field changes, and so isn't triggered just by clicking or tabbing into the field. Because it fires before its action, OnObjectValidate can be canceled. It's available in Browse and Find modes.

Not all changes to data in validated fields will cause the trigger to fire, however. Spell Check and Find/Replace don't fire OnObjectValidate. Whether you run them manually or by script, Import, Replace Field Contents, and Relookup Field Contents also don't fire this trigger.

ONOBJECTSAVE

While OnObjectModify fires as you modify a field, OnObjectSave fires after the field's data has been validated and saved, but before the field is exited. With this trigger, you can modify the field repeatedly without interruption. Then when you're done and you leave the field by tabbing, pressing Enter, clicking in another field, or by any other means, the trigger fires.

This trigger fires only if you actually make a change. If you click in a field and then leave the field without making changes, nothing is saved and the trigger doesn't run. And because it fires before its action, OnObjectSave can be canceled. If your script returns False in an Exit Script step, then it forces the user back into the field. It's available in Browse and Find modes but can be attached only to fields.

ONOBJECTEXIT

The OnObjectExit trigger is exactly the opposite of OnObjectEnter. It fires before you leave an object. For fields, this means tabbing away, committing the record, and so forth. For buttons and tab controls, "exit" means tabbing away. For portals, the trigger fires when you leave a portal row by using any method. Finally, for web viewers, it fires before you click away from an active web viewer. Any script step that causes an object to be exited will fire the trigger.

Many actions can trigger an exit from a field, portal, or web viewer. For instance, you might leave the layout, close the window, or quit FileMaker. In every case, the trigger fires, and in every case, if the script returns False, then the action is canceled. So you can even stop folks from closing the window before they attend to the demands of the script run by your trigger. It's available in Browse and Find modes.

■ ONPANELSWITCH

OnPanelSwitch lets you run a script when a tab control or other panel object is clicked. The trigger runs before the switch, so you can cancel it. Use this trigger to keep users from viewing a tab panel. For example, you can keep all users except your financial person from viewing the Invoice tab. The script in Figure 12-21 checks to see if the Invoices tab was clicked. The click proceeds normally for any tab except Invoices. When Invoices is clicked, the script checks Get(AccountName) to see who the user is (page 743). If the clicker isn't the right person, the script exits with a false result, which cancels the click and leaves the user on the currently active tab.

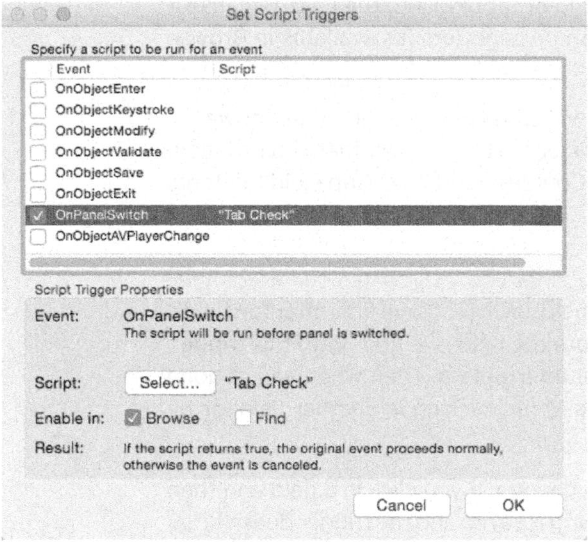

FIGURE 12-21

The OnPanelSwitch *trigger fires when any tab is clicked, so scripts should use* Get (Trigger-TargetPanel) *to find out which tab panel is targeted.* Get(Trigger-TargetPanel) *returns both the tab number and the title of the tab, so it is nested inside the* GetValue() *function, which lets you select the return value you need. A companion function,* Get (TriggerCurrentPanel) *lets you know which tab was active when the user clicked the new target.*

■ ONOBJECTAVPLAYERCHANGE

OnObjectAVPlayerChange fires if audio or video is playing (from a container field or in a web viewer) and the user changes the play state by clicking pause, play, or stop. It also fires if the record is changed, which will stop the playback, or if the audio or video finishes playing. The trigger is fired after the action, so it's not cancelable.

Exploring Script Steps

N ow that you know how to create scripts, it's time to expand your repertoire. FileMaker has a script step for just about everything you can do from the menus and Status toolbar. You can use any combination of these steps with script techniques like looping, branching, custom dialog boxes, and more to automate just about anything FileMaker can do. Major areas of scripting include working with field data and records; finding, sorting, and working with windows and files; and printing. This chapter is a reference for some of the most commonly used steps—and boatloads of scripting possibilities.

NOTE Download sample databases for this chapter from this book's Missing CD page at *www.missingmanu-als.com/fmp14mm*.

Go to Layout

You learned about the Go to Layout script step in the previous chapter. Its purpose is simple: Change layouts. It works just like making a choice from the Layout bar's Layout pop-up menu, except that the script can go to *any* layout (even if it doesn't show in the menu).

Go to Layout has just one option, a pop-up menu. Here's how the options break down:

- The **Original layout** option tells FileMaker to switch back to the layout that was active when the script started. After all, you can run lots of scripts anywhere, especially if they're on the Script menu. Since scripts often change layouts as they run, this option makes sure folks end up back where they started.

- The **Layout** option opens the Specify Layout window, from which you can choose any layout in the file. And since going to the layout may fire layout triggers, the dialog shows a badge on the layouts that have one or more script triggers attached.

- The **Layout Name by calculation** option lets you specify a typical FileMaker calculation. The result of the calculation has to be text, and it should match *exactly* the *name* of one of the layouts in the database. When the script runs, FileMaker evaluates the calculation and then switches to the specified layout. If nothing happens, double-check the spelling and spacing of the name.

- The **Layout Number by calculation** option is similar. You specify a calculation with a *number* result. FileMaker numbers every layout sequentially, in the order in which it's listed in Layout mode. The result of the calculation determines which layout to visit by number.

Like record numbers, layout numbers reflect the current state of the database and aren't reliable ways to identify a layout. First, layout numbers don't necessarily correspond to their positions in the Layout pop-up menu because not all layouts show in the menu (you can turn off their display—see page 287), plus you can re-order them manually. To find out a layout's number, you have several choices. The manual method is to switch to Layout mode and then go to the layout in question. In the Status toolbar look at the Layout box. It shows which layout number you're on. Better yet, use the Get(LayoutNumber) function in the FileMaker Pro Advanced Data Viewer (page 552). See the box below to learn when to use Go to Layout with Layout Name and when to use Layout Number.

FREQUENTLY ASKED QUESTION

Specifying a Layout

FileMaker has three ways to tell the Go to Layout step which layout to visit. Which one should I use?

The easiest, most foolproof way is to choose the layout directly from the Specify pop-up menu. When the script runs, FileMaker goes to the layout, period. The step only fails if the layout has been deleted since the script was written.

The other two options—specifying a layout by name or number—are trickier because calculation methods have soft underbellies. If you specify a layout name using a calculation, and later rename the layout, even just by adding an accidental space somewhere in the name, then the script can't find the layout anymore. If you use the layout number and then add or delete a layout, or rearrange your layout list, then the script goes to the wrong layout.

Still, you should consider using these options when you need flexibility. For example, if you use Go to Layout and specify by Layout Name, then you can use script parameters to name any layout in your database. With this technique, you can create a single navigation script and use it for all routine database tasks, as in a navigation Button Bar.

If you want to create a scripted process that's like a wizard or an assistant, then Layout Number is a godsend. Create the layouts that control your process and then make a Next button that you copy onto each layout. The button gets a Go to Layout script step, specifying a Layout Number that's one more than the current layout number [Get(LayoutNumber) + 1]. Naturally, the last layout in the series won't have a Next button; perhaps you can make a Finish button to take users back to an appropriate layout. As long as you keep the layouts arranged in the proper step-by-step order, the button always takes people to the right layout.

Go to Object

Go to Object is massively useful, because you can go to (or activate) any object on a layout, and set up the context for the steps that follow. You can also use Go to Object to activate a tab control that's not the automatic tab. Say you have a layout with a tab control, and the user clicks a button on the third tab. If the button's script has to leave the layout to run part of its process (say you need to run over to the Line Item layout and create a line item record before switching back to the original layout), then FileMaker will activate the automatic tab when it returns. But that's confusing and annoying to your user, who almost always wants her screen set up just like it was before she clicked a button. To smooth those ruffled feathers, name the tab where the button resides and then add a Go to Object step at the end of that button's script.

Naming Objects

Give objects a name with the Inspector (Figure 13-1). This name is in addition to any other name or identifier it has, such as a fully qualified field name (Invoices::InvoiceID or Customer::Full Name) or any internal FileMaker IDs. You can name any object on a layout, but there's usually no reason to unless you need to use the name in a script.

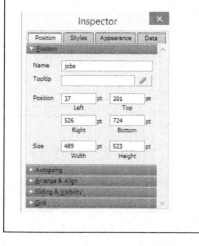

FIGURE 13-1

Here you can see the Inspector's Position panel. The Jobs tab on the Customer layout of this chapter's sample file is active, so the Inspector shows its name. Since you and your scripts are the only ones who'll ever see this name, you don't have to make it pretty for your users. Choose a simple and descriptive name, though. There's no list of named objects anywhere in FileMaker Pro, so there's no handy pop-up from which to choose the right name in the Go to Object script step's option field. Quick tip: After you name an object, select the name and copy it. Then go to the script step and paste. The process also works in reverse. That is, if you're writing a script and realize you haven't given your object a name yet, no worries. Go ahead and refer to the name you want to use in the script step. Copy it and then go to the layout, select the object and paste the name into the Inspector. FileMaker Pro is flexible like that.

Why, though, would you bother naming a field when you can just use the Go to Field script step? If there's only one copy of a field on a layout, then you don't need to name the field. But if you have two copies of a field on a layout, but need a script to go to a specific one, then name it, and use Go to Object instead. A common reason for having two versions of the same field on a layout is when you have two portals from the same relationship on a layout. You might have one portal show all the records in the relationship and the other portal filtered to show just records with "Active" in their Status fields (page 598). You might also need two or more copies of a field to show the same data on multiple tabs on a tab control.

You can use any naming scheme you want, but here are a few rules to keep in mind:

- **Object names have to be unique, but only within a layout.** That is, you can't have two objects named "jobs" on the same layout, but every layout could have an object named "jobs" on it.

- **Object names aren't case sensitive.** "jobs" and "Jobs" are the same name as far as FileMaker is concerned.

- **Names can be no longer than 100 characters.** That should cover most needs, though.

- **You can name objects or groups of objects.** If you group an object after you've given it a name, it retains the name, even if you name the group. You can't edit, or even see, the name of an individual object in a group unless you ungroup first.

- **If you copy an object that has a name, the name is copied also.** FileMaker appends a number after the object's name for you (jobs 2), since names have to be unique. If you start noticing that lots of fields have inappropriate names with numbers at the end, then you (or more likely your colleague) has unknowingly copied and pasted a named object all over the place.

Using Go to Object in a Script

The "'Go to Object' Options" dialog box (Figure 13-2) is where you put the name of the object you're targeting. You can type (or paste) the object's name, and if the object is a repeating field (page 260), you can also specify which repetition to select. Both options give you access to the Specify Calculation dialog box, so you can write calculations instead of typing or pasting static data.

Usually, FileMaker is really great about knowing that you've renamed an object. If you change your First Name field to Name_First in the Manage Database window, the name is reflected everywhere you see lists of field names. But if you change a field's layout object name, any script steps that refer to that old name will fail. If all you're doing is activating a tab for a user, that's not such a big deal. But the results could be disastrous if you're using Go to Object to set the context for doing something permanent to a bunch of records at once, like editing or deleting field data. To avoid harming your database with a bad script, avoid changing object names if at all possible.

TIP   Use the Database Design Report (DDR) in FileMaker Pro Advanced to get all the information you need about an object, including its name, before you change it (page 557).

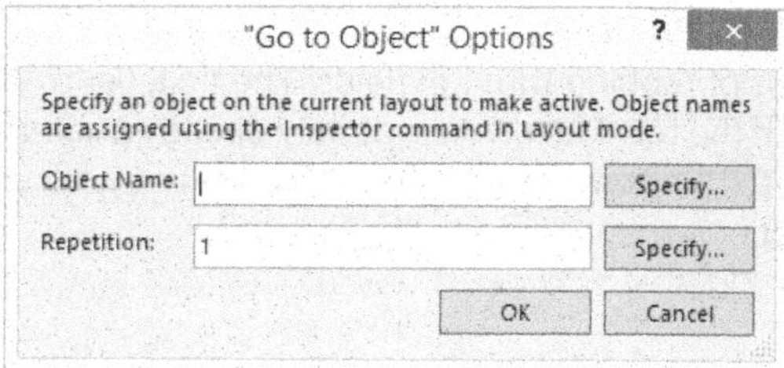

FIGURE 13-2

The "'Go to Object' Options" window's Object Name field lets you type, paste, or calculate the exact name of a layout object.

Scripting for Fields

Most people using FileMaker spend *a lot* of their time working with field data, so there are many script steps devoted to fields. Lots of them are grouped together in their own category—Fields—but they're also sprinkled in the Navigation and Editing sections. You can put someone in a specific field, select field text, and even play sounds and movies from container fields. You can perform a find and replace operation, run the Replace Field Contents command, and export field contents to a file. Finally, you get over a dozen ways to insert data into a field.

Navigating Fields

FileMaker offers a couple of ways to field-hop—pressing Tab to move to the next field in order, or just clicking the desired field. The Navigation group has script steps that mimic both techniques.

GO TO FIELD

The simplest field navigation script step is called Go to Field. It's really a two-purpose step, with two checkboxes to prove it. In its simplest form, you turn on the "Go to target field" checkbox and then pick the field you want to go to. When the script runs, FileMaker puts the cursor in the specified field (*if* it's on the layout).

NOTE The Go to Field script step overrides field behavior. So even if you've turned off field entry in Browse mode, users can enter or edit data in a field by running a script (which may have an If test to determine whether the data entered is ok). Or if you make a field into a button—for navigating from a portal to a detail layout, perhaps—but you need the field to be searchable in browse mode, then put an If test in the navigation script that goes to the field if the layout is in Browse mode.

The step also has a checkbox called "Select/perform." When this option is turned on, the script either *selects* the contents of the field it goes to or *does* what's in the field—if possible. For example, if the step goes to an *interactive container* field (page

269) that holds a sound or a movie, FileMaker *plays* the contents. If the container field holds a *reference* to a picture or a file, FileMaker *opens* the correct file, using the appropriate program.

◼ GO TO NEXT FIELD AND GO TO PREVIOUS FIELD

Two other steps mimic the process of tabbing through fields. The first, Go to Next Field, just goes to the next field in the tab order. You probably already figured out that Go to Previous Field goes to the *previous* field in the tab order. These steps don't have a "Select/perform" option—they just go to the field.

Editing Commands

FileMaker has all the classic commands in its Edit menu: Undo, Cut, Copy, Paste, and Clear. It also has a script step for each of these commands. The Undo step is the simplest. It has no options at all, and has exactly the same effect as choosing Edit→Undo. You rarely want to undo something you just scripted, so you rarely use this script step. It's useful, though, if you use custom menus (page 568) to control access to certain menu commands.

Cut, Copy, and Clear are slightly more complicated, with two options each. The first, "Select entire contents," lets you decide which part of a field's value gets cut, copied, or cleared. If you turn this option on, then FileMaker selects the entire field before acting. If this option is turned off, then FileMaker cuts/copies/clears whatever is selected in the field. So if nothing is selected when the step runs, nothing will be copied. (But see page 488 to learn why you should rarely use these commands.) You also get a "Go to target field" option, through which the script can tell FileMaker *which field* to act on. If it's not turned on, then it uses the *current field*—the one that's active when the step runs.

The Paste step is the most complicated of these four. In addition to specifying the field you want, and whether or not to select everything in the field before pasting, you get an option to "Paste without style." When you turn this option on, FileMaker pastes the text on the Clipboard but throws away any style information.

Selecting Text

FileMaker has two script steps to help you select text. The first, called Select All, selects everything in the current field, just like the Edit→Select All command. If you need more control, then use Set Selection instead. This step has two options. First, you can specify a target field so that FileMaker operates on the current field. The step also has a separate Specify button (unlabeled, but below the one associated with "Go to target field") that brings up the Specify Set Selection window (Figure 13-3).

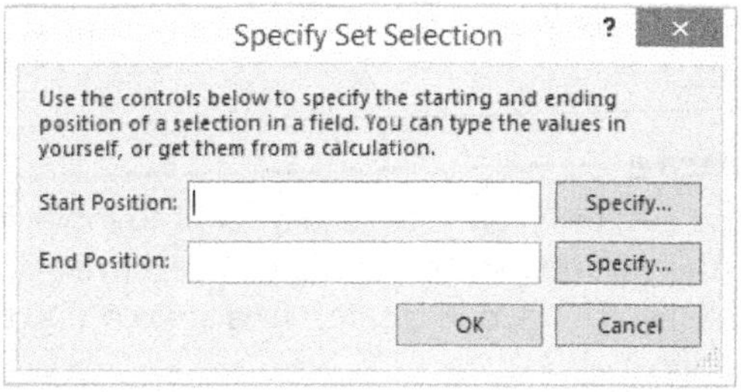

FIGURE 13-3

This window lets you tell FileMaker exactly what text you want the script to select. You can type numbers directly in the Start Position and End Position boxes, or click either Specify button to bring up the Specify Calculation window.

If you imagine the text in your field as a string of letters, numbers, spaces, and punctuation, then you can pretend each of these is numbered. For instance, the word "Avengers" has letters numbered one through eight. You tell FileMaker where the selection will *start* by putting the number of the first character you want selected in the Start Position box. Next, you put the number of the *last* character in the End Position box. When the step runs, FileMaker goes from start to end and selects everything in between. See the box below to learn how to position the insertion point in a field.

CODERS' CLINIC

Positioning the Insertion Point

You can use the Set Selection script step to put the insertion point anywhere in a field, too. The trick is to make sure *nothing* gets selected. When you specify a Start Position and an End Position, FileMaker selects the characters at each position, plus anything in between. If these two numbers are the same, then FileMaker selects just one character.

But what if the End Position comes *before* the Start Position? When you set the End Position one number lower than the Start Position, FileMaker doesn't select anything. Instead, it puts the little flashing insertion point right before the Start Position. Using this technique, you can get your script to put someone anywhere you want inside a field—say, at the beginning of a Notes field—so she can just start typing, without needing to move the cursor.

Editing Field Data

Editing field data is such an important part of FileMaker that it gives you 18 ways to put data in fields with a script step. Some methods reproduce what you might do manually, but others are meant to handle special cases, like inserting graphics, or pulling data from the Web or handheld device. So there's an art to knowing which script step best fits your need.

The first thing to understand is that, except for Set Field and Set Field by Name, the steps in the Editing and Fields sections *work only if the field is on the current layout*. This is no problem for scripts you use to structure data entry, but it can be a roadblock in other cases. Suppose you have a script that sets a "Paid in Full" flag on an invoice. You want this script to work no matter what layout you're on (as long as it's one that shows invoice records), and whether or not the field is on that layout. In that case, you need to use the Set Field script step (or its power-user partner, Set Field by Name).

■ AVOIDING CUT, COPY, AND PASTE

Your first inclination might be to use Cut, Copy, and Paste in a script to move data from one field to another, and it usually works. You can, for example, have a script copy the Customer ID field, go to the Invoices layout, create a new invoice, and then paste it into the Customer ID field there.

But most developers don't use this approach for two reasons. First, many developers consider people's Clipboards to be sacred ground. They argue you should *never* change what's on the Clipboard unless someone asks you to. So it would be OK to have a Copy button by the Address fields, for example, that copies the address to the Clipboard because the person would know exactly what's going into the Clipboard. But what if he manually copies a long product description to the Clipboard and then runs a script that has copied something else onto the clipboard? To keep from mystifying users, avoid Cut and Copy.

Worse for you, these steps don't work if the field isn't on the layout. People often show the customer's *name* on an invoice, but not his *ID*. So scripts that use Cut, Copy, or Paste and the Customer ID field won't work unless you put the field onto every layout on which the script might be run. For those reasons, the Set Field steps are almost always used to move or insert data.

■ SET FIELD

Set Field is the preferred method for editing data in a field because it works even if the field it references isn't on the layout. Set Field replaces the contents of a field with the result of a calculation. Its two options let you specify the field to set and the calculation to use. Its only (minor) weakness is that the calculation result must be the same type as the target field. For text, number, date, time, and timestamp fields, Set Field is usually the step of choice: It's flexible and reliable, no matter what's on the layout.

> **TIP** As with many other FileMaker processes, be aware of context when you use a Set Field script step. You can edit data through a relationship by using Set Field, but make absolutely certain the context is what you intend. If you aren't careful, you can edit data in the wrong record.

Like other steps you saw earlier, you don't have to specify a field. In this case, Set Field changes the field you're in *at the moment the step runs*. (This method works only with text results; otherwise, you have to specify the field so FileMaker knows what data type you have in mind.)

Set Field's normal behavior is to replace all the data in a field with the data in your calculation. But you can write a calculation that appends results to existing data: Just include the field's data in the calculation. If you want to add "Esquire" to the end of the customer's last name (in the Last Name field), then just use this calculation in your Set Field step:

```
Last Name & ", Esquire"
```

■ SET FIELD BY NAME

Like Go to Layout by Name, the Set Field by Name script step lets you make a single script more flexible because you can calculate the field's name instead of hard-coding it in a script. Other than that detail, though, Set Field by Name works just like its cousin Set Field. But how do you know which version to use?

Every once in a while, you need an extra jolt of flexibility. Suppose your script sets one of any number of possible fields, and which one varies from one running of the script to the next. For instance, imagine you have a script that puts a measurement into one of seven different fields in a database of statistical recordings, one for each day of the week. When your script goes to put the data in the right place, you might think you'll need a giant If/Else If block with six cases, and six nearly identical Set Field steps.

Instead, you can use the Set Field by Name script rather than an If/Else test. This way, instead of selecting the target field from a list, you use a calculation to produce the target field name. For instance, imagine your six fields are called "Measurement 1" through "Measurement 7." You could use a formula like this for your target field:

```
"Measurement " & DayofWeek ( Get ( CurrentDate ) )
```

This formula produces the name of the field for each given day, so a single Set Field by Name step can replace all those If conditions.

Set Field by Name has a downside, though: If you rename a field, the step stops working because the calculation uses a character string (static text) and not a reference to the field. To combat this problem, use a special function called Get-FieldName(;) it lets you refer to a field, and *will* update if you rename the field. So if you're inclined to rename objects without checking first to see if they're in use somewhere, use a formula like this to be safe:

```
Choose (
DayofWeek ( Get ( CurrentDate ) ) - 1;
GetFieldName ( Measurements::Measurement 1 )
GetFieldName ( Measurements::Measurement 2 )
GetFieldName ( Measurements::Measurement 3 )
GetFieldName ( Measurements::Measurement 4 )
GetFieldName ( Measurements::Measurement 5 )
GetFieldName ( Measurements::Measurement 6 )
GetFieldName ( Measurements::Measurement 7 )
)
```

NOTE See page 682 to learn how the Choose() function works.

The formula above checks the current date and then returns the correct field name for that day. And since it uses GetFieldName(), it returns the right name even if you rename the field it refers to. As a formula in the Set Field by Name function, it's still a lot shorter and easier to manage than those seven If steps would be. For instance, suppose you want to change what goes into the measurement field? With Set Field by Name, you have one calculation to update. With seven separate Set Field steps, you'd have to fix things in all seven script steps.

■ INSERT CALCULATED RESULT

Set Field overwrites the data in a field completely unless you calculate it to append the data instead. Insert Calculated Result lets a script put data in a field while keeping the data that's already there. It has three options. First, you can specify a target field. You can also choose "Select entire contents" in the field first (in which case it overwrites the entire field, just like Set Field). Finally, you get to specify the calculation. Here are some variations on these options:

- If you *don't* turn on the "Select entire contents" option, then FileMaker inserts the calculation result *after* whatever is already in the field.

- If you *don't* specify a field at all, and you *don't* turn on "Select entire contents," then FileMaker inserts the result of the calculation into the current field. If you select data when the script step runs, then the calculation result overwrites whatever is highlighted. Otherwise, the text goes in wherever the insertion point happens to be, just as though you'd typed it from the keyboard.

■ INSERTING OTHER VALUES

FileMaker has six other Insert script steps that work like Insert Calculated Result. Each step lets you specify a target field, and select the field contents if you want. They differ only in what gets inserted:

- **Insert Text** lets you specify any static text value and add it to the field verbatim. Use this step if you know ahead of time what you want your script to put in the field and don't need to calculate it.

- **Insert from Device** lets FileMaker Go users upload content to container fields from certain sources of the iOS device. Some sources have options that appropriate for the asset you're uploading:

  - **Music Library.**

  - **Photo Library.**

  - **Camera.** Select from the Front or Back camera, choose a Resolution.

  - **Video Camera.** Camera options, plus set a Maximum duration for recording and whether recording will Start Immediately.

- **Microphone.** Set a Maximum duration for recording and whether recording will Start Immediately.

- **Bar Code.** Choose from two sources: Camera (Front or Back) or another field in the database. Choose the type of encoding(s) you want to allow.

- **Signature.**

- **Insert from Index** makes your script show the same View Index window just like choosing Insert→From Index in Browse or Find mode. Someone picks a value from the list, and FileMaker inserts it into the field. This option is especially valuable in Find mode, both to keep people from having to type a value (and possibly making a typo) *and* to make sure the search always finds records, since if a value is in the index, then it's in a record somewhere.

- **Insert from Last Visited** grabs the value from the *same* field on the *last vis-ited* record, and inserts it. This step is particularly useful on data-entry layouts. Imagine, for example, you have to enter 300 people records from 15 different companies. You could use this step to create a button that pops in the *last* com-pany you typed into the Company Name field, rather than type it over again.

> **NOTE** You can't just take a peek at a record and call it visited, though. The record has to be entered or opened. An Open Record/Request script step helps ensure you get the record you intend.

- **Insert from URL** lets you use several Internet protocols (http, https, httppost, httpspost, ftp, ftps, and file) to insert data or copy files from the Web or a local computer into a container field. Step options include verifying a server's SSL certificate (and canceling the import if the certificate isn't valid), replacing the entire contents of the field, performing the step without a dialog box, specify-ing a target field, specifying the URL, and automatically encoding the URL to make it web-appropriate. In Windows, container fields optimized for images can render .gif, .jpg, .png, .bmp, and .tiff files. On the Mac, they can render all these, plus .jpg2, .tif, .fpx, .psd, .tga, .mac, and .qif files. Other images may show up as thumbnails. When a container field is optimized for interactive files, you can also insert PDF files on both platforms.

- **Insert Current Date** and **Insert Current Time** do just as they say. Unfor-tunately, there's no Insert Current Timestamp step; use Insert Calculated Result and the Get(CurrentTimeStamp) function instead.

- **Insert Current User Name** puts the user name from your operating system into the field. But if you change it on FileMaker Preferences' General tab, the step uses that name instead.

See the box on page 492 for advice on when to use Set Field and when to use an Insert step.

UP TO SPEED

Set Field vs. Insert

FileMaker's field editing script steps have a lot of overlap. For example, Set Field with no target field behaves the same way as an Insert Calculated Result step with no target field and the "Select entire contents" checkbox turned on. And you can use Insert Calculated Result with the appropriate calculation to do the same thing as Insert Date, Insert Time, Insert Text, and Insert Current User Name. In general, it doesn't matter one bit which one you use.

But you should think twice about using the Insert script steps with a target field specified *and* the "Select entire contents" checkbox turned on. With both options set, these script steps simply overwrite the value in some field—exactly what Set Field does.

Since these steps need the field on the layout, though, they're more *fragile:* The script can break if you make changes to a layout. You'll probably save yourself a headache tomorrow if you just use Set Field today.

Of course, if you're inserting *into* a field (without "Select entire contents" turned on), then it's easier to use an Insert step. But it's best to use this step in a script that'll be run if someone is already in the field. That way you know the field is on the layout and the step will run properly.

Finally, you can't accomplish some of the Insert steps from a calculation. Specifically, you can't access the last visited record or the View Index dialog box from a Set Field step.

■ PUTTING DATA IN CONTAINER FIELDS

With managed container fields you have great power to create solutions that can move files to a shared location, so they're available to everyone using the database (page 270). Even if you're not using managed container fields, you can either embed the files into the database (which increases its size dramatically when you're storing lots of files) or you can store a reference to the file (which should be moved to a shared server before you insert it into FileMaker). These script steps let you put files into container fields:

- **Insert Picture** lets the user choose an image file to insert into a container field that's optimized for images. Options let you specify a source file for insertion or store only a reference to a file. You can't specify a target field, so a container field must be active when the script runs for this step to work. Use a Go to Field step to activate the target container field or let the user click in a field before the step runs.

- **Insert Audio/Video** lets the user choose an audio or video file to insert into an interactive container field. Options let you specify a source file for insertion or store only a reference to a file. Like Insert Picture, the step has no option to specify a target container field, so it needs either a Go to Field step or user interaction.

- **Insert PDF** lets the user choose a PDF file to insert into an interactive container field. Options let you specify a source file for insertion or store only a reference to a file. The step has no option to specify a target container field, so it may require a `Go to Field` step or user interaction.

- **Insert File** has so many options that it needs a full section to describe them all. Read about it next.

■ USING THE INSERT FILE SCRIPT STEP

With great power comes great responsibility. There are so many options to choose when inserting files into container fields that unless you have a highly trained set of users, you usually won't let them insert files without a script that uses one of the steps above. The `Insert File` script step is the most powerful and flexible of them all, and you'll use it to help users make the right choice for inserting files. It has the option to specify a target container field and a source file. But the "'Insert File' Options" dialog box (Figure 13-4) lets you create a custom dialog box that can restrict the user to the choices you want him to see.

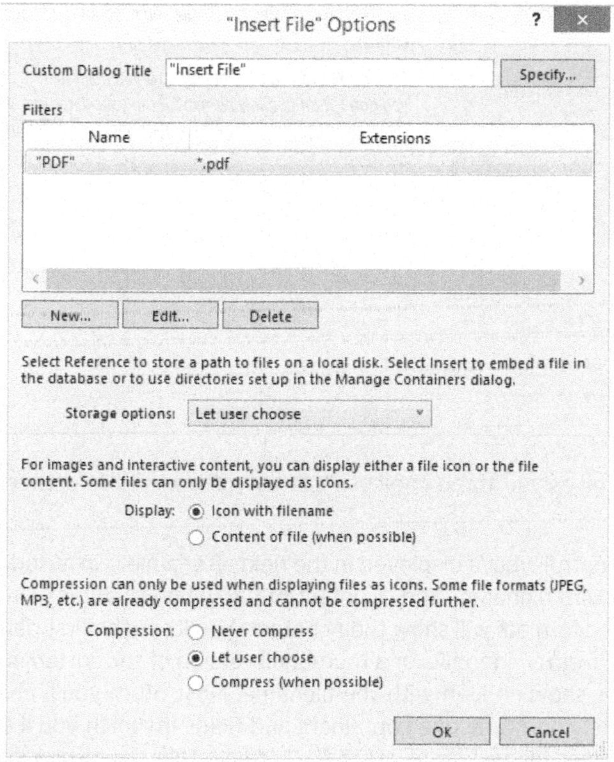

FIGURE 13-4

The "'Insert File' Options" dialog box gives you control over which options a user sees in the dialog box that appears when he chooses a file to insert into a container field. You can control the file's storage options, display, compression, and even file format. Here a custom filter restricts user choice to PDF files only.

The `Insert File` script step's Dialog options gives you the option to customize nearly every feature of the dialog box used to select a file for insertion. Here are the options you can set:

- **Custom Dialog Title** lets you type static text or use the Specify Calculation dialog box to write a formula for a dynamic title. For example, in a database that stores graphics files for an art department, you could display data from the Project::Name field in the dialog box's title bar.

- **Filters** lets you choose from a list of predefined filters (Figure 13-5) or create a custom filter like the one shown in Figure 13-4. You can give the user a set of filters to choose from by creating more than one filter. Use the New button below the Filter box to add new filters, or click the Edit button to change the default filter. Since this default filter lets you choose any file type, including those that FileMaker doesn't support, you'll almost always change it (see Appendix C for a complete list of supported file formats).

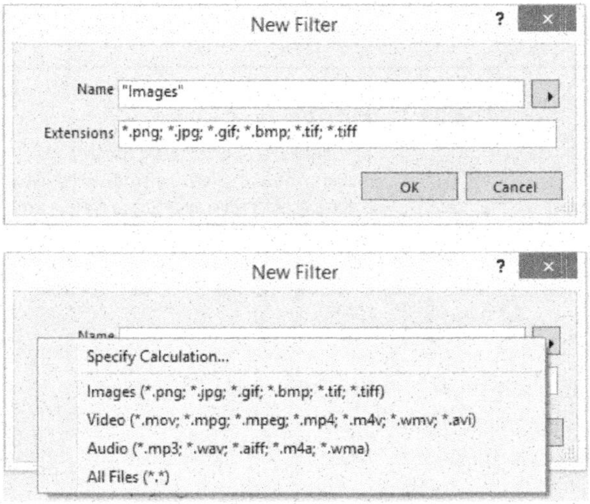

FIGURE 13-5

The New Filter window gives you access to the calculation engine or one of four predefined options.
Top: FileMaker creates the syntax you need for the Images options.

Bottom: You can edit the definition if you need to. If you don't want to allow bitmap files in your database, select the ".bmp;" part of the extensions data and then delete it.*

- **Storage options** gives you three choices: "Let user choose," "Reference," or "Insert."

- **Display** lets you control what's displayed in the field after a file is inserted. The choices are "Icon with filename" and "Content of file (when possible)." Image files with supported formats will show their content. You'll see the first page of a PDF file, a frame from a video file, or a thumbnail version of supported image files. All other files show an icon with the filename. Most often you'll choose "Content of the file" for interactive containers and fields in which you'll store images. If a container file will store other file formats (like word-processing documents or spreadsheets), then choose "Icon with filename."

- **Compression** lets you choose whether a file is compressed before it's embedded in a container field or moved to the base directory for the field's external storage. The choices are "Never compress," "Let user choose," and "Compress when possible." Some files can't be compressed. For example, if a file is already compressed, it can't be compressed further. Note that this option is grayed out if you've selected Reference in the "Storage options" section.

Creating a Field Script

The Customer table in the sample database has a Notes field that holds any information you think is important about the customer. Unfortunately, you soon realize this field is a little *too* unorganized. You have no idea if the note that says, "Customer already paid" is from last Tuesday or last year. You need a consistent way to keep track of *who* left a note, and *when.* You decide everybody should record this information along with any notes. To make things even easier, you want to be sure people add *new* notes *above* older notes. Thus, when a customer record has been around for a while, the Notes field looks something like this:

```
--- 6/12/2015 @ 1:45 PM by Mrs. Lovett ---

It's priest. Try a little priest.

--- 6/12/2015 @ 10:38 AM by Sweeney Todd ---

Is it really good?

--- 6/12/2015 @ 11:51 AM by Mrs. Lovett ---

Sir, it's too good, at least.
```

In this example, you create a script that helps organize the Notes field. This script adds a separator line with the date and time (plus a couple of blank lines) and leaves the insertion point under the separator. You also create a button next to the Notes field that runs this script. People just have to click and then type.

NOTE As with almost every problem you ever solve with a script, there's more than one right way to get the job done. One way is described next, and another in the box on page 496. You may come up with a different way, and that's OK.

Before you start creating your script, think about what you need to do in sequence. Here's a breakdown:

- Put the insertion point at the start (top) of the Notes field.
- Insert two blank lines to create some space before the previous comment.
- Put the insertion point back at the start, and add the separator line with the date and time.
- Move the insertion point below the separator line so the user can start typing.

Your next mission is to translate these plain-English steps into script steps, which you do in the next section.

Fewer Steps, Bigger Calculations

You can easily create the Add Note Separator script described on page 495, but it has one weakness: It uses four steps where two could accomplish the same thing. A more concise approach would be to put the separator and a few blank lines at the top of the Notes field first and *then* use the "¶" to put the insertion point after the separator. The drawback here is that you have more complex calculations to write. The choice is yours. Here's how:

In the Insert Calculated Results step, you need a calculation that builds the separator line, adds two blank lines after it, and finally adds the *old* contents of the Notes field to the end:

```
"--- " & Get(CurrentDate) & " @ " &

Get(CurrentTime) & " by " &
Get(AccountName)
```

```
& " ---¶¶¶" & Customers::Notes
```

To keep the contents of your field from being duplicated, make sure you leave the "Select entire contents" option on this time.

Now you need to get the insertion point in place after the first line, using the Set Selection script step. Use the same technique as before: Set the selection with an end position that's *smaller* than the start position. FileMaker puts the insertion point *before* the character at the start position. Since you want it *after* the end of the first line, you need to find the first new line symbol, add 1 to it, and put *that* in the Start Position field. Here's the calculation that does the trick:

```
Position ( Customers::Notes; "¶"; 1; 1 )
+ 1
```

Put this same calculation, but without the last +1, into the End Position field. Delete the extra script steps, and you're ready to test your script.

BUILDING THE SCRIPT

Switch to the Customers layout, if you're not viewing it already. Then proceed as follows:

1. **Choose Scripts→Script Workspace. Create a new script called Add Note Separator.**

   Give your scripts descriptive names so you can remember what you want them to do.

2. **Add a Set Selection script step to the script.**

   You can find this step under Editing in the list, or, from the View pop-up menu, you can choose "all by name" to see an alphabetical list. When you add the step, it appears in your script.

3. **Turn on the "Go to target field" checkbox. Set Customer::Notes as the target and then click OK.**

   The Set Selection step in your script updates to show the target field.

TIP The Customer::Notes field was already created for you, but in the real world you may need to create a field while you're writing a script. Click the Specify Field Table pop-up menu and scroll all the way to the bottom, where you'll find the Manage Database command.

4. **In the Script Step Options popup, click the second Specify button.**

   It's not labeled, but it's below the first Specify button. When you click it, the Specify Set Selection window appears.

5. **In both boxes (Start Position and End Position), type *0* (zero) and then click OK.**

   Zero in both boxes tells FileMaker you want the insertion point right at the start of the field, and you don't want any text selected.

6. **Add an Insert Text step to the script and then turn off the "Select entire contents" option.**

   You don't want the two blank lines you're about to insert to replace everything in the field.

7. **Click the bottom Specify button.**

   A window simply called Specify appears (Figure 13-6).

8. **In the Specify dialog box, add two empty lines (press Return twice) and then click OK.**

   You won't see the Returns you've typed in the dialog box, but the insertion point blinks down on the third line, and in the Insert Text script step you'll see two blank spaces inside quotes. Those returns tell FileMaker to add two blank lines to the top of the Notes field.

9. **Select the Set Selection step at the top of the script and copy and paste the step. You can use the menu, or use the keyboard shortcuts—Ctrl+C (⌘-C) and Ctrl+V (⌘-V).**

   Since this next step should repeat the first script step, you might as well reuse the work you've already done. FileMaker adds a second copy of the Set Selection step, right below the first.

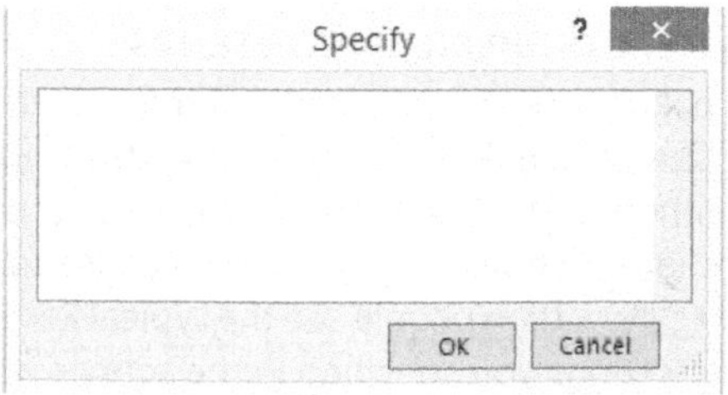

FIGURE 13-6

The Specify dialog box for Insert Text gives you no options to click. You just type the exact text you want the script step to insert. Note that this dialog box isn't a calculation dialog box—you can insert only static text. Use Insert Calculated Result if you need to insert dynamic text with a script step.

10. **Drag either** Set Selection **step to the bottom of the script.**

Keyboard junkies can use Ctrl+down arrow (⌘-down arrow) to move script steps. The shortcut won't work if the step's pop-up is open, so you may have to click the step to close the pop-up. If this *still* doesn't work on your Mac, check your Mission Control setup in System Preferences. Shortcuts set there override FileMaker's native shortcuts.

Your script now has Set Selection, then Insert Text and then Set Selection again.

11. **Add the** Insert Calculated Result **step to the script and then turn off the "Select entire contents" option.**

Make sure the step lands *after* the last Set Selection script. If it doesn't, drag it there. Turning off the selection option ensures that the calculation goes in at the insertion point (which is at the beginning of the field now).

12. **To the right of "Calculated result," click the Specify button and then, in the Specify Calculation window, enter this calculation:**

```
"--- " & Get(CurrentDate) & " @ " & Get(CurrentTime) & " by " &
Get(AccountName) & " ---¶"
```

You can use any method you want to enter the calculation, as long as your calculation looks like this one when you're done. See page 395 to learn about Get() functions.

13. **Save the script.**

Your new script is ready to test.

Now you just need to add a button near the Notes field that runs your new script. When you click the button, FileMaker adds the separator to the field and puts the insertion point in place. Your notes will be nicely organized and separated.

Other Steps that Work with Fields

Lots of times, you want to be able to write scripts that work on multiple records. You may need to change values across a found set of records, or you may want to let FileMaker handle the serial numbering of all the records in a table. The next script steps let you manage data in lots of records without lots of hassle.

▓ REPLACE FIELD CONTENTS AND RELOOKUP FIELD CONTENTS

The Replace Field Contents and Relookup Field Contents commands let you specify a field to act upon. If you *don't* specify a field, then they act on the current field. You also get the typical "Perform without dialog" checkbox. When you turn this checkbox on, the action happens immediately when the step runs. If you leave this option off for the Replace Field Contents step, then people see the typical Replace Field Contents dialog box (with all the settings you specified in the script—which they can change before the step runs). With the Relookup Field Contents step, they just see a confirmation message first, asking if they really want to perform the relookup operation.

■ SET NEXT SERIAL VALUE

The Set Next Serial Value script step is invaluable—in the rare cases it's needed. It's a one-trick pony: If a field auto-enters a serial number, then this step changes the "next value" stored in the Field Options dialog box. This process is so critical that you'll probably prefer to do it manually. But see the box below for an example of why you might want to let a script reset a field's serial value.

NOTE Use extreme care when you change a field that's used as a key in a relationship. You risk leaving related records orphaned if you don't change their key fields, too. See the box on "Referential Integrity" for a script that helps you change key fields without losing related records (or your sanity).

The step has two options. First, you can specify the field to update. As usual, if you don't specify a field, then it works on the current field. You tell FileMaker what to set the "next value" to by entering a calculation.

■ PERFORM FIND/REPLACE

When you use the Find/Replace command manually, you use it to replace text in one or more fields and across one or more records. But the Perform Find/Replace step has *extra* powers when you use it in a script (Figure 13-7).

UP TO SPEED

Why Set Next Serial Value

The Set Next Serial Value script step may seem odd to you. After all, if you want to set the next serial value for a field, you can just do it yourself from the Manage Database window. But this step can come in very handy in some situations.

Imagine you work in the auto parts business and you have 200 sister stores around the country. Each office has its own copy of your database, which gets updated periodically. You have to send a new empty database to each store with all the latest enhancements, and the folks at each store have to *import* all the data from their old databases into the new one (you'll learn about importing and exporting data in Chapter 21).

Now suppose this database includes an Orders table with an Order ID field. After the old orders have been imported, the database might have orders with IDs from 1 to 1000, for example. But since no *new* records have been created yet, the Order ID field still has a "next value" of 1. The store's first thousand orders use IDs that are *already used by other records*. That's a big no-no.

The solution is obvious: You need to fix the "next value" on the Order ID field after the import is finished. To save the store manager the trouble, you can put a script in the database to fix this glitch for her. (In fact, you can make a script that does *all* the work of importing old data and fixing next serial values in every table.)

The Quick Find feature (page 22) is great, but it searches *all* the fields you specify on a layout and returns a found set. What if your Notes field is so widely used that some customers' notes fields are full of pages of notes? What if people are complaining that it's getting hard to scroll through them to find the notes you made regarding specific topics? What you need is a way to find a word or phrase that's used somewhere in the current customer's gigantic Notes field.

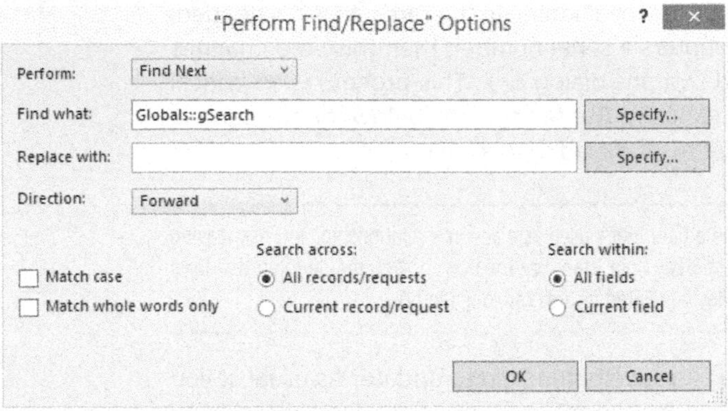

FIGURE 13-7

The window for the Perform Find/ Replace *script step looks a lot like the normal* Find/Replace *window. But this version has a new pop-up menu (called Perform) and a couple of new Specify buttons that let you specify calculated values for what you're looking for and what you want to replace the found results with.*

The script itself is simple, just two lines, but you need to do some prep work. First, create a new table in your database, and name it Globals. Give it one field: a global text field called "gSearch." Don't forget to set the field option to use global storage (page 259). Place this new field on the Customers layout above your Notes field. Set the field's behavior to be enterable in Find mode. The idea is that your users will type a word or phrase in this field and then click a button to run the script.

Here's how to write the script. Call it *Search Notes Field.*

1. **Add** Go to Field **as your first script step. Set it to go to the Customers::Notes field.**

    Find/Replace requires a field to be selected before it can work, so you're taking no chances with this script step. Script nerds call this being *explicit*. In this case, you're being explicit about where the script should take its next action.

2. **Add the** Perform Find/Replace **step to the script, and turn on the "Perform without dialog" checkbox. Click the Specify button.**

    The "'Perform Find/Replace' Options" window appears.

3. **Make sure the Perform pop-up menu is set to Find Next and then, to the right of the "Find what" box, click the Specify button.**

    The Specify Calculation window appears.

4. **In the list on the Left, choose the Globals table, and then double-click the Globals::gSearch field to add it to your calculation. Click OK.**

    This calculation tells FileMaker where to look when it runs the Perform Find/ Replace step—whatever the user has typed in the new field, in this case. Clicking OK when you're done returns you to the "'Perform Find/Replace' Options" window.

5. **In the Direction pop-up menu, choose All.**

This option tells FileMaker to look through the entire Notes field.

6. **Turn on the "Current record/request" and "Current field" radio buttons. Save the script and close the Script Workspace window.**

You don't want the search to spill into different fields or records. Since the script goes to the Notes field first, FileMaker searches only that field.

To finish the job, create a button next to the Global::gSearch field and then attach your script to the button. Type into the search field and then click the Find button to test your new script. The search word or phrase will be highlighted in the field. Click the Find button again (without changing the search terms) to find other instances of the same search criteria.

> **NOTE** If you're just getting started with the Script Workspace, you may be relying on the mouse to do most of your work. As you start to remember script steps, you'll find it much more efficient to use keyboard shortcuts instead. See the box on page 502 to learn how the pros write scripts without leaving the keyboard.

◼ Working with Records

You can get only so far with your scripts by working with field values. Eventually you need to deal with more than one *record.* FileMaker has script steps for creating, duplicating, and deleting records; navigating among existing records; and even managing the process of opening and editing a record, and saving (committing) or reverting the changes. You can also work directly with portal rows on the current layout—and the records they represent.

Creating, Duplicating, and Deleting Records

New Record/Request and Duplicate Record/Request have no options and do exactly what you'd expect. The first script step creates a new record, just like the Records→New Record menu command. The second duplicates the current record. In either case, the *new* record becomes the current record, just like when you do it manually. You use these steps most often on buttons, when you're taking away menu commands from people and providing them with buttons that appear only on the layouts where you want people to be able to create records.

> **NOTE** Duplicating a record from a script step works just like doing it manually—that is, the script duplicates the static (non-calculated) values in the record, too. If calculations depend on those static values, they also get duplicated, but they change if you edit the non-calculated values later. Serial numbers are *not* duplicated, but are recalculated at the time the duplicate record is created.

The Delete Record/Request script step deletes the current record. If you turn on its "Perform without dialog" option, then the delete happens with no warning. When this option is turned off, the manager sees the same "Are you sure?" message box he'd see when deleting a record manually.

> **NOTE** Each of these three script steps also works for *find requests* when a script runs in Find mode.

Ditch the Mouse

Until you start to memorize script steps, you'll spend a lot of your scriptwriting time seaching through the Script Workspace's Steps pane looking for what the steps you need. But you'll soon notice that you're using the same script steps frequently. For those steps, using the mouse is the slow lane. Once you know a script step's name, you can type the first few letters, and FileMaker will show you a filtered list right there in the Script Editing pane. Better still, you can select from the list using the keyboard. Here are a list of keyboard shortcuts for common scripting tasks:

- Ctrl+N (⌘-N) creates a new script. Just start typing to give the new script a name.
- Press Enter to complete a task, as after you've named your new script or selected options from a pop-up menu.
- Start typing a script step's name to create a filtered list of steps in the Script Editing pane.
- Use the arrow keys to select the step you need.
- Press Return to move a selected script step from the filtered list to your script.
- Enter (Enter) or the down arrow key creates a new blank line for a script step.
- Enter or Space (Enter or Space) opens the options popup *and* toggles options in the pop-up menu. Use the arrow keys to move through the options.
- Ctrl+S (⌘-S) saves the current script.
- Ctrl+R (⌘-R) runs the selected script.
- Ctrl+Shift+R (⌘-Shift-R) saves *and* runs the selected script.
- Ctrl+Alt+R (⌘-Option-R) debugs the selected script. See page 544 to learn how the debugger works.

- Ctrl + } and Ctrl + { (⌘-{ and ⌘-}) move through the opened script's tags.
- Ctrl+Shift+T (⌘-Shift-T) opens the selected script in a new Edit Script window.
- Ctrl+W (⌘-W) closes the current script (whether it's in a separate window, or is the current one in the Script Editing pane. Ctrl+Alt+W (⌘-Option-W) closes all open script tabs. If any scripts are unsaved, you'll see a message that lets you revert, cancel or save.
- Ctrl+Arrow Keys (⌘-Arrow Keys) moves a script step up or down in the list.
- Delete or Backspace (Delete or Backspace) to remove a selected script or script step.
- Ctrl+D (⌘-D) duplicates the selected script or script step.
- Ctrl+/ (⌘-/) disables the selected script step (FileMaker Pro Advanced only).
- Ctrl+P (⌘-P) prints the selected script.
- Esc (Esc) removes focus from script step options (in other words, the pop-up menu disappears).

Some script steps open dialog boxes, like those with a Specify button. The normal shortcuts that work with dialog boxes work in the Script Workspace. For instance, the Escape key closes an open dialog box without saving its changes, the tab key moves from fields to field, and the Return key activates the default button and accepts the changes you've made.

You can always pick your mouse back up if you just need to scroll through the Steps pane searching for some new-to-you step. But the less you leave the keyboard, the faster your scripts will come together.

Navigating Through Records

Two script steps let you switch to a different record. The Go to Record/Request step works a lot like the arrow buttons on the Status toolbar by taking you to the specific record you specify. Or you can switch to a related record, or a set of related records, using the Go to Related Record script step.

■ GO TO RECORD/REQUEST/PAGE

FileMaker has one script step that handles changing records, find requests, and pages. This may seem strange at first, but it makes sense because it's exactly how the Status toolbar's book icon works: If you're in Browse mode, then the step goes to a different record. If you're in Find mode, it switches between find requests instead. Finally, if you're in Preview mode, then it flips through pages.

NOTE   You can't run scripts in Layout mode, and scripts *can't* go to Layout mode, so Go to Record/Request/Page doesn't apply there.

The Go to Record/Request/Page step has just one option. You get to pick *which* record, request, or page to go to from a simple list:

- First
- Last
- Previous
- Next
- By Calculation

When you lock people out of the usual display and control everything they do through the script (see the box below), the First, Last, Previous, and Next options let you provide your own customized replacement for the Status toolbar and book icon.

POWER USERS' CLINIC

Controlling the Display

If you want to pull out all the stops, you can use a combination of layouts, custom menus (page 568), window styles (page 525), tooltips (page 354), and scripting to almost completely take over control of your database. You can hide and lock the Status toolbar and then give people buttons to go to the next, previous, first, and last records. You can make it so that when you click a customer on the List layout, a new detail window pops up named after that particular customer. You can even make your script so smart that it selects an existing detail window for the customer if one exists, and makes a new one

otherwise. In this way, you give people the impression that each customer has his own window, and you make comparing customers side by side a breeze.

This kind of high-level window management takes a fair amount of work, so most people stick with the normal every-layout-in-one-window approach and let people create windows as needed. Your approach depends entirely on how much time you want to spend writing scripts and how important the multiple-window display is to you.

Another common but more advanced use of this step is to provide a way for a looping script to end. When you choose the Next or Previous option, a new checkbox appears in the Script Step Options area, called "Exit after last." When it's turned on, FileMaker knows to exit the loop after it's finished with the last record (when you choose "Go to Record" [next]) or after the first record (when you choose "Go to Record" [previous]). When to exit a loop is no small matter, as page 466 explains.

When you choose By Calculation, you get the chance to specify a calculation with a number result. FileMaker goes to exactly that record, request, or page. You could use this option if the record number is in a field, or if you want to skip ahead 25 records each time the script is run, for example. This technique is more useful than it sounds.

GO TO RELATED RECORD

You were first introduced to this power step when learning about relationships (page 231). It can go to a different record, found set, layout, window, and even file—all in one step. This step's job is simple: It takes you to a related record. But when you click the Specify button, you get a wealth of choices, as shown in Figure 13-8. To go to a related record, you need to tell FileMaker which related table occurrence you're interested in by selecting it from the "Get related record" pop-up menu. For example, if you're on the Customer layout and you want to see a related job, then choose Jobs from the menu.

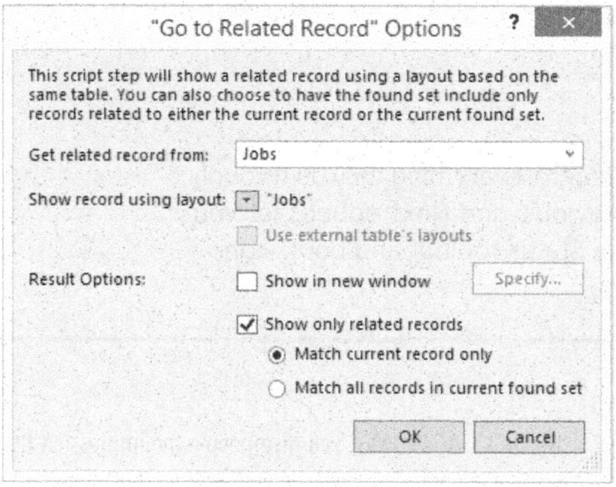

FIGURE 13-8

This window is the same one you saw when you attached a Go to Related Record script step to a button back on page 231. But inside a script, you wield a whole new level of power when you tie this command to other processes, like printing a report from a found set that changes based on whichever record someone is on when running the script.

With this done, FileMaker can find the right record. But if you're visiting related records, chances are you can't view them directly on the current layout, since the layout is associated with the wrong table occurrence. So a Go to Related Record command almost always involves changing layouts. Choose Layout from the "Show record using layout" pop-up menu to view the Specify Layout window, from which you pick the layout you want.

Specify Layout shows all the layouts associated with the Jobs table occurrence you chose above, as you'd expect. But it *also* shows layouts associated with any *other* occurrence of the same table. FileMaker uses the specified table occurrence to find the right related record and the specified layout to show it to you. You can show a job record from any layout that shows records from the Jobs table, no matter what *occurrence* it uses.

If the table occurrence you picked in the first menu is an occurrence of a table from a *different* file, then you can turn on "Use external table's layout" to see layouts in the file the table comes from. When you use this option from a button, FileMaker switches to a window for the other file instead of showing records in the current window. If you use this option in a script, though, then you need to add a Select Window script step (page 526) if you want the external file's window to be active.

> **NOTE** Using an external file's layout saves you from having to create a similar layout in your "local" file. But it's worth the effort of creating a local layout that shows data from that external file if you want to keep your users in the local file. They'll still need privileges to view the external file's data, though. See page 755 to learn about view privileges.

If you want a *new* window (whether you're using an external table or not), then turn on the "Show in new window" checkbox. When you do, you see the "'New Window' Options" dialog box, which is explained alongside the New Window script step on page 523.

Finally, you get to decide how to deal with the found set when the script step finishes. See the box on page 506 to help you decide when each option makes sense.

- If you don't turn on "Show only related records," then FileMaker goes to the related table, but you see all the records in the related table, not just those that are related to the formerly active record. The first related record is active in your new found set. So, from the Customer layout, GTRR without "Show only related records" shows all your jobs, and the active record is the first one for the customer that you're viewing when the GTRR script step runs.

- If you turn on "Show only related records" and "Match current record only," then FileMaker returns a found set of only those records that match the active record. The customer job GTRR set, as described above, shows you a found set of just the jobs for the customer record that was active when the script step ran. The active record will be the first related record.

- Choosing "Show only related records" and "Match all records in current found set" is most useful when you have a found set selected before the GTRR script step runs. In this scenario, FileMaker shows a new found set in which all the records are related to at least one of the records in the old found set. So, in the Customers layout, you've found your two highest-volume customers. Use GTRR, matching all records in the current found set to find all the invoices related to either of these two customers. The active record will be the first record that's related to the customer record that was active when the GTRR script step runs.

Opening, Reverting, and Committing Records

When you use your database in Browse mode, FileMaker does a lot of things automatically. When you start typing in a field, it locks the record. When you exit the record—click outside any field or press Enter—it commits the record. When you use a script, though, you're not really clicking fields and pressing Enter. So how does FileMaker know when to lock a record and when to commit? You have to tell it, by including the appropriate script steps: Open Record/Request, Revert Record/Request, and Commit Records/Requests.

▓ OPEN RECORD/REQUEST

The Open Records/Requests step tells FileMaker you're about to start editing a record. If the record is already open, then it does nothing—that is, it doesn't automatically commit the record first. It just locks the record so no other user can edit it, if it isn't locked already. But if the record is already open (by you via another window, or by someone else), then you get a record-locking error. (See page 723 to see how you can check for errors while a script is running.)

FREQUENTLY ASKED QUESTION

To Show or Not to Show

How do I decide when to turn on "Show only related records" and when to leave it off?

If you don't turn on "Show only related records," then FileMaker doesn't change the found set in the target table unless it has to in order to show the proper record. In other words, if the target table is showing all its records, FileMaker just makes the target record active without changing the found set. All the records are still in the found set, and the user can flip through them to see records that aren't related to the original record. But if the target table has a found set of records and your target record isn't in the set, FileMaker has to change the found set to show the target record.

But when the "Show only related records" option is turned on, the found set in the target table will always be related record(s) only. So use this option when you want to restrict the found

set, either for the users' convenience, or because the script must have a found set to do its work.

The tradeoff is performance. When you turn the "Show only related records" option off, FileMaker just makes the proper record active. It doesn't worry about the found set or the sort order. When the option is turned on, though, FileMaker has to find the correct records first and then show the one you asked for. If your relationship is sorted, then FileMaker also sorts the records. If your script just needs to visit a specific related record, do something to it, and then come right back, you can leave this option turned off to make your script run more quickly.

Whichever option you choose, you can avoid annoying your users when your untimely GTRR destroys their found set by choosing the "Show in new window" option. When you create a new window for the target table, your script won't tamper with the user's existing found set for the target table.

▓ COMMIT RECORDS/REQUESTS

Whether you've used the Open Record/Request step or just let FileMaker lock the record for you, you can explicitly commit the record with the Commit Records/Requests step. It has two options:

- The "Skip data entry validation" option tells FileMaker to commit the record even if it violates field validation. This option works only when you turn on the

"Only during data entry" radio button in the Validation options for the field. If you've set the validation to happen Always, then the script *can't* get around it.

- When the "Perform without dialog" option is turned off, and in the Layouts→ Layout Setup window's General tab you turn *off* "Save record changes automatically," FileMaker shows the message in Figure 13-9 when the step runs.

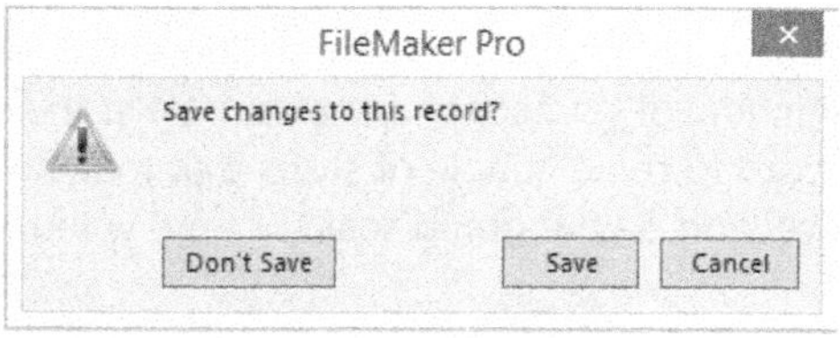

FIGURE 13-9

If the layout isn't set to save record changes (page 289) and you don't turn on the "Perform without dialog" checkbox, then you see this warning when the Commit Records/Requests step runs. Click Save to commit the record. If you click Don't Save, then FileMaker reverts the record instead. The Cancel button leaves the record open and locked.

NOTE Most database designers try to avoid requiring people to interact with FileMaker's normal dialog boxes while scripts are running, especially when people could make a choice that circumvents the purpose of the carefully crafted script.

■ REVERT RECORD/REQUEST

The Revert Record/Request step has only one option: "Perform without dialog." When this option is turned off, someone sees a confirmation message. Otherwise, FileMaker reverts the record immediately when the script runs.

These steps are easy to understand, but *when* to use them is harder to figure out. Here are some things to keep in mind when you're trying to decide when you need to open or commit a record in a script:

- When you use a script step that *inserts* data into a field (and leaves someone in the field), FileMaker locks the record when the step runs but doesn't commit the change. You can then do *more* work with fields if you want. FileMaker commits the record later, when the user exits the record.

- If your script changes to a different layout, switches to Find or Preview mode, or closes the window, then FileMaker automatically commits the record if needed.

- If you use a script step that modifies several records—Replace Field Contents, for example—FileMaker commits the records in batches as it goes. When it's finished, every record that was modified is committed.

- If you perform a series of Set Field steps in a script, and you're *not* in the record when the script runs, then FileMaker locks the record and makes the field changes. When the script is done, you're not in the record (no field is active), but the record is still locked and uncommitted. In other words, you can use the Records→Revert Record command to revert all the changes made by the script, which probably isn't what you want. Add a Commit Records/Requests script step at the *end* of the script to avoid losing the data your script enters.

- If your script changes some records and includes a step to revert them if something goes wrong, then you should probably make sure to commit any changes someone was making before your script changes anything. That way, the script doesn't undo any of her work. Thus, put a Commit Records/Requests step at the *beginning* of your script.

And if you're still not sure if your script really needs an Open or Commit step, go ahead and open the record at the beginning of your script and commit it at the end. Sure, it takes a nanosecond or two extra to run a couple of steps that may not be strictly necessary. But what's a nanosecond on the grand scale of time when your data may be at risk?

Copying Records

FileMaker has two record-related script steps that do something you can't easily do manually in Browse mode: copy an entire record to the Clipboard. One version copies just the current record, while the other copies every record in the found set at once.

◼ COPY RECORD/REQUEST

The first, called Copy Record/Request, works on one record at a time. It copies data from *every* field on the layout and puts it on the Clipboard. FileMaker puts a tab character between each field value. Then you can switch to another program, like Word or Mail, and paste the data from the record. Since there are tab characters in the copied data, you may need to format it or manually delete the tab characters.

NOTE As usual with FileMaker, you have more than one way to get things done. See page 863 for two other ways to export data. Remember, using a scripted Copy, Cut, or Paste command violates your sacred trust not to mess with the contents of someone's Clipboard unless he knows it's happening.

◼ COPY ALL RECORDS/REQUESTS

While Copy Record/Request copies the entire *current* record, its brother—Copy All Records/Requests—copies *every* field on the current layout for every record in the found set. Each individual record is added to the Clipboard in the same format as the Copy Record/Request command produces, with one record on each line. Each record is separated by a paragraph character.

Suppose, for example, you want to get all the Invoice IDs for a particular customer and put them in an email to a coworker. Or perhaps you're compiling a list of all the Zip codes in Phoenix where you have customers. Using Copy All Records/Requests, you can do this job with ease.

Why Open a Record?

Why would I ever use the Open Record/Request step? Doesn't FileMaker automatically lock a record as soon as my script starts editing it?

For simple scripts, this step is almost always unnecessary. FileMaker does, indeed, do the right thing. But as you'll learn in Chapter 20, you can set up your FileMaker database so multiple people can use it at the same time, each on her own computer. When you set up FileMaker this way, lots of interesting things can start happening.

For example, a record can change while you're looking at it. Suppose a new area code is added in your area, and you write a script that looks at the phone number and decides, based on its exchange code, whether or not to change the area code. The script might look like this:

```
If [ Exchange Code = 555 or Exchange Code
= 377 ]
  Set Field [ Area Code, "602"]
|End If
```

You probably find this hard to believe, but technically, someone could change the Exchange Code field after the If step runs but before the Set Field happens. (Remember that other people are editing records on other computers, so they're free to make changes while the script is running on your computer.) If this scenario happens, you end up assigning the customer an incorrect phone number.

To fix this, you need to lock the record before you start looking at it:

```
Open Record/Request
If [ Exchange Code = 555 or Exchange Code
= 377 ]
  Set Field [ Area Code, "602"]
  Commit Records/Requests [No Dialog]
Else
  Revert Record/Request [No Dialog]
End If
```

Now nobody else can edit the Exchange Code field because the record is locked. In general, if many people use your database, then you should open a record before you start looking at it in a script. This technique can be particularly useful if your script needs to deal with groups of records, any one of which might already be open by another user or might be opened while your script is running. In that case, loop through your working found set and open each record in turn. Then you can either process the group of records or take some other action, like canceling, if the script finds that one or more of the records can't be opened.

This script reverts the record when it didn't make any changes. FileMaker does this reverting for two reasons. First, committing a record means saving the data, and that's unnecessary here. Second, suppose a field has had validation turned on since this record was created. It's possible that this unmodified record has now-invalid data. If you try to commit this data back, then you get a validation error. Reverting avoids this error since nothing is being saved. Moral of the story: Try to commit a record *only* when necessary.

The trick is to create a *new* layout that has only one field on it. For example, make a new layout with just the Invoice ID field, or just the Zip Code field. Write a script that switches to this layout and then runs the Copy All Records/Requests command to get a simple list of values on the Clipboard.

Working with Portals

You'll often need to deal with related records in a script, and portals can come into play when you do. Because they're like a mini ist on your layout, portals need their own navigation scripts to select a portal row. And to help them display work done in a script, a special Refresh Portal step lets you tell a portal to update itself, which you'll learn about on page 511.

GO TO PORTAL ROW

Go to Portal Row is critical when you're dealing with portals, because when you use the Go to Field script step to target a field in a portal, the step goes to the *first* portal row, which may not be the one you need. If you want to select the field on a *different* row, you need to go to that row first and then select the field you need.

Plus, when you use data from a related field, or put data in a related field, and you have *multiple* related records, FileMaker grabs the value from the *first* record. If you want to tell FileMaker to work with a different related record instead, then use a portal and go to the correct row. See the box on page 511 for tips (and a warning) on working with portals.

The Go to Portal Row works a lot like Go to Record/Request/Page. You can go to the First, Last, Previous, or Next portal row, or specify the row *number* with a calculation. It even has an "Exit after last" option to help when looping through portal rows.

This step includes an option you can use to make what's happening onscreen more obvious to people: "Select entire contents." When you turn this checkbox on, File-Maker highlights the whole portal row. Otherwise, it goes to the portal row without highlighting it onscreen. When a script continues running after this step, you don't want the screen flashing—it can cause confusion or concern for users.

One setting you *don't* get with Go to Portal Row is *which portal to use.* The guidelines below are how FileMaker knows which portal you have in mind:

- If the current layout has only one portal, it's used automatically.

- If the layout has more than one portal, the currently active portal is used.

- If the layout has more than one portal but no portal is active, the one that's in the front of the stacking order is used.

NOTE In general, a portal is active whenever a person (or a script) puts the cursor in one of its fields. If you aren't sure what someone will be doing before your script runs, then throw in a Go to Field or Go to Object script step, just to be safe.

Beware the Portal

Technically, you can do all kinds of things through a portal by using a script—but it's not always wise. For example, if you want to discount every line item on an invoice by 10 percent, then you can write a looping script that can loop through portal rows, applying the discount to each Line Item::Price field. Unfortunately, the active portal row is too transient to rely upon. A script can do all kinds of things that make FileMaker forget which portal row you're on (change modes, change layouts, go to another field, commit or revert the record, to name a few).

When this happens, the script can loop forever because you never reach the end of the portal. Or it can work repeatedly on the same portal row. It's much safer to find the appropriate related records and work with them directly. Use the Go to Related Records script step to find all the line item records and then loop through the records directly with Go to Record/Request/Page, and avoid the perils of the portal. To leave the context of the current window intact, set the Go to Related Records script step's option to open a new window that the script can work in. Then use a Close Window script step to tidy up when the script is done.

▪ REFRESH PORTAL

Sometimes work you do in a script doesn't trigger FileMaker to refresh the screen to show the updated work. Portals are a prime example—they don't always realize that you've added a new record. To make sure they check, add a Refresh Portal step near the end of your script. You have to name the portal, and then address it by name in the step's options. You can use static text for the name, or create a calculation (usually one that names a variable you've set earlier in your script). The step is faster than Refresh Window, because FileMaker doesn't have to redraw the whole screen, just the records in the portal. This is especially important on mobile devices, where data often has to come across a cellular network.

NOTE   In FileMaker WebDirect, this step must run the Refresh Window step, which sends the entire contents of the window to the browser. So you won't gain performance by using it instead of Refresh Window. Do an If test to check the platform so that you can still use Refresh Portal on FileMaker Go and FileMaker Pro.

▪ Finding Records

FileMaker has three nearly identical script steps to handle the grunt work of finding records. You can let people tell the script what to find, you can decide what the script finds (a *hard-coded* find), or you can script a dynamic find using calculations.

Deciding which one to use depends on whether people know what they're looking for—or how much work you want to save them. The upcoming sections go into this topic in detail. You'll also see a find script in action and learn how to make a script pause and wait for information.

Pausing for Users' Find Requests

The Perform Find script step is like switching to Find mode and then clicking the Requests→Perform Find menu command. Perform Find's single option lets you specify what find requests to use, but, surprisingly, you can skip it entirely. If you *don't* turn this option on, then Perform Find assumes you're already in Find mode with one or more requests, and works just like the Requests→Perform Find menu command (and the Status toolbar's Find button). It looks for records that match the already-defined find requests. All the matching records become the new found set.

But where do those find requests *come from?* Either someone creates them or your script does. For example, many developers like to add special "Find" layouts to their databases. These layouts can show just the right fields, along with helpful text, to make things easier for people. Figure 13-10 shows a Find layout for the Customers table.

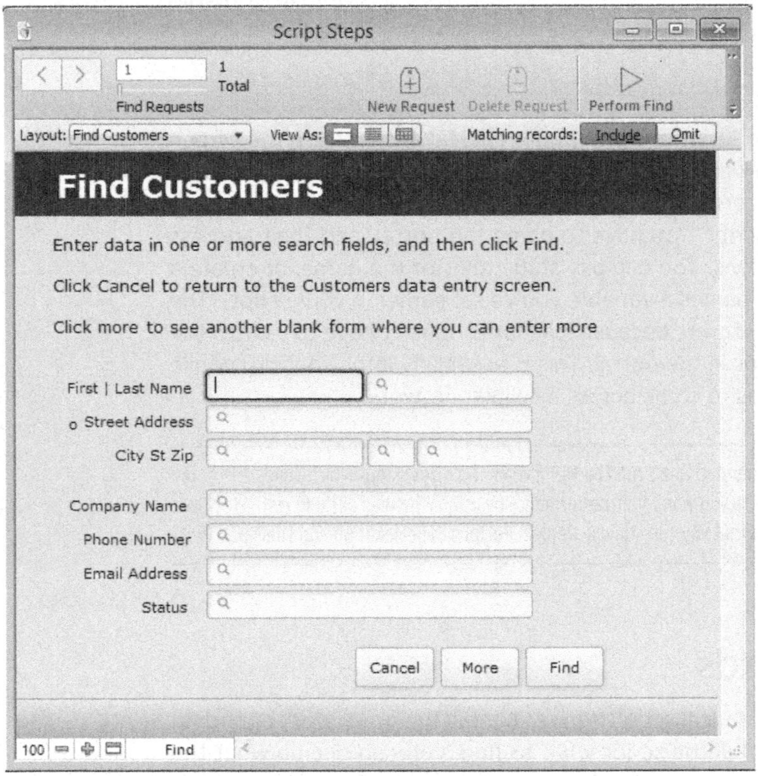

FIGURE 13-10

This layout is designed specifically to be used only in Find mode. A list of instructions helps people figure out what to do. The Find button resumes your script. The More button runs a New Record/ Request script step. Since this layout is for Find mode only, the script puts the layout in Find mode and returns to a different layout when it's done.

To go along with this custom layout, you'll write a script that goes to the Find layout and puts your user in Find mode. The script then *pauses,* giving her a chance to enter find requests. When she's done, she clicks a button to *resume* the script, which performs the find and then switches back to the Customers layout. To get started, choose Scripts→Manage Scripts, click New, and then name your script appropriately. Here's how to create the script you need:

1. **If necessary, open the Script Workspace. Create a new script and type _Find Customers_ in the Script Name box.**

   Choosing a good name is the standard prep work for every new script.

2. **Add the `Go to Layout` script step, targeting the Find Customers layout.**

   You want to make sure the person is in the right context—the new Find Customers layout—before the script enters Find mode.

3. **Add an `Adjust Window` script step, and from the pop-up menu, choose Resize to Fit.**

   Your Find layout is a different size than the Customers layout and you want the new window to fit. Learn more about this script step on page 527.

4. **Add the `Enter Find Mode` script step to the script.**

   The step already has its Pause option turned on and its "Specify find requests" option turned off. That's just what you want.

NOTE   If you want to start someone off with some basic criteria, you can specify them in the `Enter Find Mode` step. Because the step pauses, the user is free to modify or delete your requests as he creates his own. To create a request the user can't change—say, to limit them to a single product category or to just active customers—create a new request before the Perform Find step.

---

5. **Add the `Perform Find` script step to the script.**

   Once the script continues, you assume she has added the necessary find requests, so you're ready to use the `Perform Find` step with no find requests specified. (Be careful not to choose the `Perform Find/Replace` script step, which isn't what you want for this script.)

6. **Add another `Go to Layout` script step to the script. This time, pick the Customer Detail layout as the target.**

   This step returns to the Customer Detail layout after FileMaker finds the records.

7. **Duplicate the `Adjust Window` script step, and move it to the end of your script.**

   You resized the window for the Find layout; now you need to set it back to fit the Customers layout.

To complete your layout, on the Find Customers layout, create a Find button. You don't even have to write a script for this button. Since the user is always in the middle of a paused script when she sees this layout, just set the button action to run a Single Step: the `Resume Script` action. If you're feeling adventuresome, you can also create a More button with a `New Record/Request` script step.

Finally, the Cancel button should run a new script that switches back to the Customers layout, switches to Browse mode, and adjusts the window (step 2 above). Since your user will click this button in the middle of a paused script, you need to think about what will happen. She will go back to the Customers layout in Browse mode, but she'll still be in the middle of a paused script. That's a recipe for confusion the next time she presses Enter.

When you assign a script to a button, think about what happens to any running script when the button is clicked. Your choices are shown in Figure 13-11.

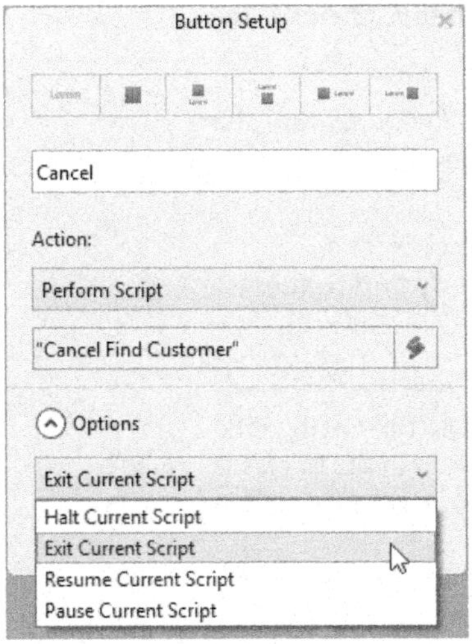

FIGURE 13-11

When a button runs a script, a paused script may already be running. This pop-up menu lets you decide what should happen to it. Choose Halt or Exit to have the running script immediately stop and the new script takes over. On page 711 you'll learn about the subtle difference between these two. If you choose Resume, the button's script runs and then the paused script resumes. If you choose Pause, then the paused script stays paused. You may need to use another Resume step, on a button or within another script, to start the paused script up again.

In this case, set the Current Script pop-up menu to Exit so the paused script is stopped. That way, when someone clicks Cancel, she gets back to a normal state.

TIP It's a good idea to hide the Find Customers layout from the Layouts pop-up menu so people don't accidentally switch to it without running your script. In the Layout Setup dialog box (or Manage Layouts, if you need to hide multiple layouts at one time), turn off the "Include in layouts menu" checkbox.

■ TRIGGERING A FIND SCRIPT

Once you have your scripts and layout in place, you need to consider how the script will be run. You could put a Find button on the Customer Detail layout. But what happens if people try to find another way (like the Mode pop-up menu on the bottom of the window, or the View→Find Mode menu command, or a keyboard shortcut, or the Status toolbar's Find button)? If you want to make sure that the only way people can find customers is through your script, then a layout script trigger is the key. OnModeEnter runs whenever you enter a mode on a particular layout. You get to decide which modes you care about, and which script to run.

Setting it up is a snap:

1. **Switch to Layout mode and then go to the Customers layout.**

   Script triggers are always associated with a particular layout or object, so you need to get to the proper layout first.

2. **Choose Layouts→Layout Setup and then switch to the Script Triggers tab.**

   You see the list of layout script triggers.

3. **Scroll down the list and then select** OnModeEnter.

   The list is too long to show every trigger, so you have to scroll to find the one you want. Once you select it, the bottom portion of the window shows the trigger's properties.

4. **Click Select and then choose the Find Customers script you just created.**

   The Select button shows the same Select Script window you see when you're setting up buttons.

5. **Turn off the Browse and Preview checkboxes (and leave the Find checkbox turned on).**

   The OnModeEnter trigger normally fires when you first go to any mode (except Layout mode, which is script-averse). In this case, you want the trigger to fire only when you enter Find mode. When you're done, the window looks like Figure 13-12.

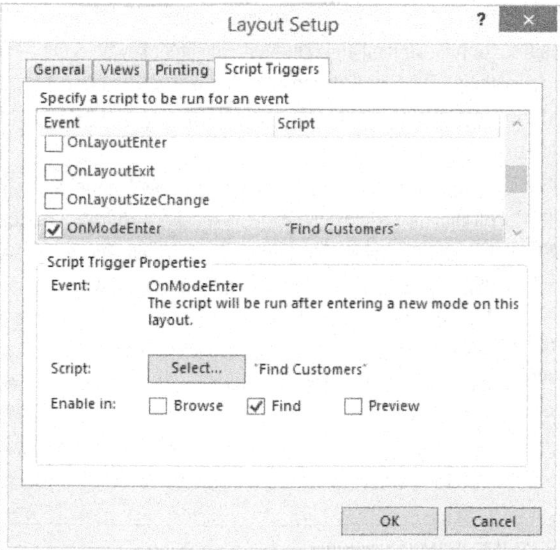

FIGURE 13-12

Here's how your OnModeEnter trigger looks once you've configured it. To recap, whenever someone enters Find mode on this layout, the Find Customers script runs automatically.

When you're done, click OK to go back to the Layout Setup dialog box, save your layout, and then switch to Browse mode. Now switch to Find mode by using any available method and bask in the glory of script triggers, as FileMaker automatically starts your stylish find process.

> **NOTE** This script runs perfectly as long as the user searches for and finds a record. But if no records are found, or if the user wants to change his mind, your script has to get smarter so that it doesn't leave the user on the Find layout or choke on an error. You'll learn about handling errors on page 723. Combine that knowledge with an If script step, and you'll be able to put your user back on the right layout, and in the right mode, no matter what happens.

Static Find Requests

With the script you created on the previous few pages, people can search for customers by entering find requests. More often than not, you *don't* want to make people enter the find requests manually. After all, the whole point of a script is to have FileMaker do things so people don't have to. If you know ahead of time exactly what you want the script to find, use the Perform Find step all by itself: Just turn on the "Specify find requests" option and create the settings for the request; the search options stay the same each time the script runs. When you specify find requests in a script, you see a pair of windows that let you set up a scripted request.

Pausing a Script

Normally when you run a script, FileMaker performs its steps one by one as fast as it can. When they're all finished, the script is done. But sometimes a script should pause, usually to wait for someone to do something (like enter Find criteria) or to show the user something (like a Preview mode for a report). The Pause/Resume Script step, and some other steps (like Enter Find Mode) can pause the script automatically when their Pause options are turned on. When FileMaker gets to a step like this, it stops executing the script but remembers where it left off. Later, the script continues, starting with the next step in line. While a script is paused, you're free to edit records, switch modes, change layouts, and so forth. You *can't* open the Manage Database, Manage Value Lists, Manage Custom Functions, or Manage Scripts windows, though, until the script finishes running.

While a script is paused, FileMaker adds two new buttons to the Status toolbar. The Continue button causes the script to continue immediately (pressing the Enter key does the same thing). The Cancel button tells FileMaker you don't want to run the rest of the script. Your script stops, and you get back full control of the program.

If you want to, you can tell FileMaker how long to pause by clicking the Script Step Options area's Specify button when the Pause/Resume Script step is selected. The dialog box that appears has two choices: Indefinitely and For Duration. If you choose For Duration, you get to enter the number of seconds you want the script to pause, or you can click *another* Specify button to use a calculation to set the number of seconds. If you have set the script to pause for a specific duration, then you can still do things with your database while the script is paused, including clicking the Continue or Cancel buttons.

When you turn on the option Specify Find Requests or click the Specify button for the `Perform Find` script step, you see the Specify Find Requests window (Figure 13-13). Click New and you'll see the Edit Find Request window (Figure 13-14). To edit an existing request, select it first and then click Edit. You can also delete or duplicate the selected step by using the Delete and Duplicate buttons. Using the Specify Find Requests and Edit Find Request windows, you can tell the `Perform Find` step to perform any find you can set up from Find mode.

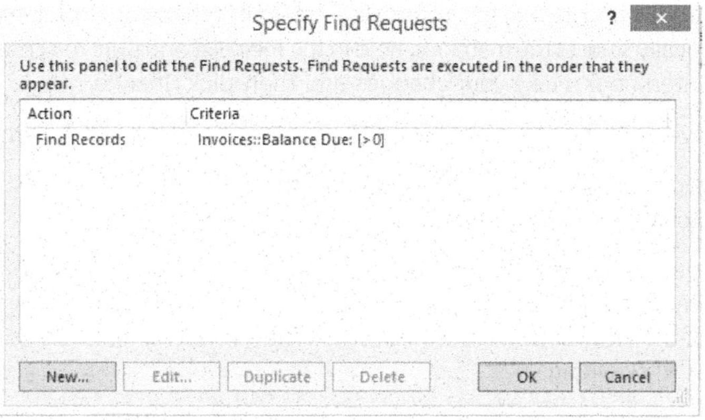

FIGURE 13-13

The Specify Find Requests window appears when you tell FileMaker you want the `Perform Find` *script step to perform a predetermined find. (Developers call this technique hard-coding.) FileMaker automatically fills it with all the requests you used the last time you were in Find mode. If you have different requests, select them all and then click Delete.*

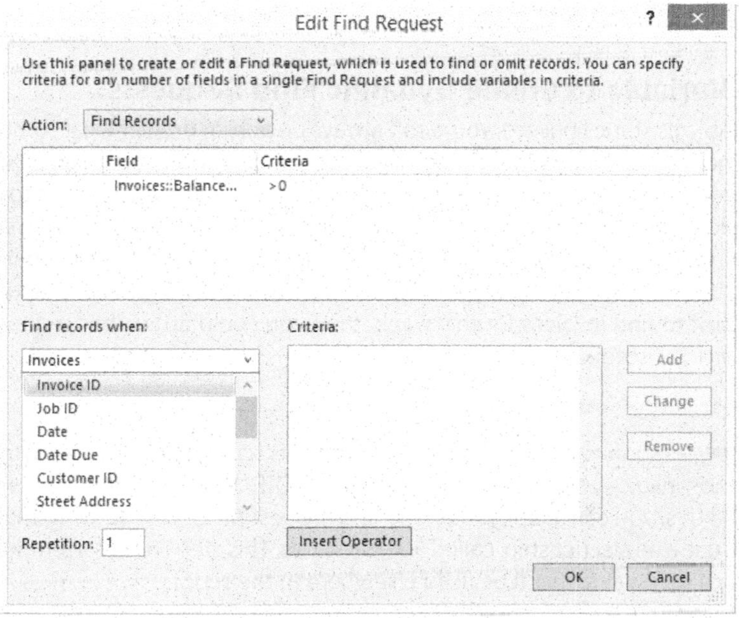

FIGURE 13-14

When you add a new find request or edit an existing one, you see this dialog box. It's just a more structured way to type data in fields in Find mode. Instead of using your layouts, you use this window, which gives you direct access to every field in the database (the Fields list at the bottom left). You can type what you're search for in the Criteria field.

Here's how the options work:

- To create a find request, from the "Find records when" list, select a field (if it's a repeating field, then you can specify the repetition number in the Repetition box) and then, in the Criteria box, enter text. The Insert Operator button gives you quick access to the same symbols you see in the Status toolbar in Find mode, and the Criteria box accepts all the standard symbols if you prefer to type them manually. Once you've finished entering the criteria, click Add to add it to the Criteria list.

- To edit an existing item in the criteria list, select it. When you do, FileMaker automatically selects the matching field in the Field list and puts the criterion in the Criteria box. Make your changes and then click Change.

- To remove a criterion from the list entirely, select it and then click Remove.

- At the top of the window, choose whether this request should be used to *find* matching records or to *omit* them (see page 45).

- When you've finished adding criteria, click OK. Just like Find mode, you can add more find requests if you want. In the Specify Find Requests window, just click the New button a second time. When you're all finished adding requests, click OK again.

> **TIP** The Edit Find Requests dialog box is confusing until you get used to it. But there's a way you can learn how it translates requests into its own particular syntax. Perform a find manually and then write a test script with a Perform Find script step. FileMaker sets the dialog box with the criteria for the search you just did. Now you can pick it apart to see how it works.

Using a Variable to Create Dynamic Find Requests

As dependable as static finds are, you won't always be able to predict what someone wants to find. Or the criteria for finding the same thing over and over can change, like when you're searching in a date field. For example, suppose you want to find all the invoices created a week ago. You can easily do that in Find mode: Enter a "≥" and then put the date from a week ago in the Invoices::Date field. But what you put in that field *changes every day.* For example, if today is November 7, and you create a script to find invoices for this week, then you could attach this request to the Perform Find step:

```
Invoices::Date = "≥10/31/2015"
```

Unfortunately, as soon as November 8 rolls around, this script doesn't work anymore. It always finds invoices created since October 31, 2015. When you're faced with a situation like this, you can adapt your static find request process slightly. To make it work, you'll use a new script step, called Set Variable. This step creates a temporary holding place for a value that'll be used elsewhere in the script.

> **NOTE** You'll learn more about script variables on page 720.

Here's how to write a dynamic find script by using a variable in a Find request:

1. **Create a new script called *Find This Week's Invoices*.**

   Always use short, descriptive names for your scripts.

2. **Add a Set Variable script step to the script.**

   It's in the Control section of the script steps list.

3. **Click the gear button to see the step's options.**

   The "'Set Variable' Options" window appears (Figure 13-15).

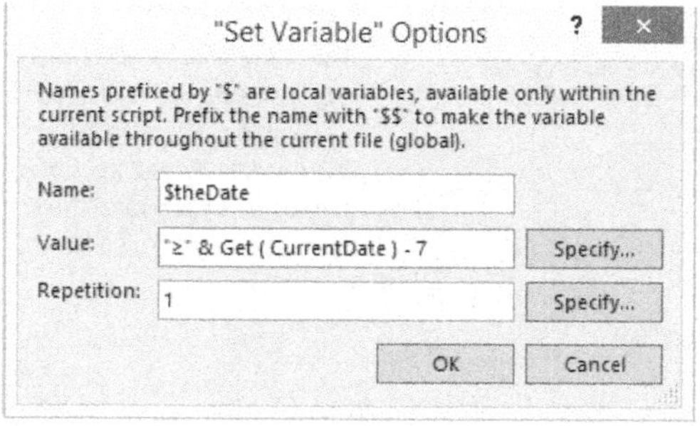

FIGURE 13-15

To set a variable, you give it a name and tell it what value to store. Both Specify buttons show the Specify Calculation window, where you can create calculations. You'll use the first one to set the value most often. The second Specify button lets you put more than one value into a variable, much like a repeating field can hold multiple rows of data.

4. **In the Name field, type *$theDate*.**

   Variables' names have to start with a $ symbol. As with all things FileMaker, the name should be short and descriptive. In this case, the variable is called $theDate because there's a function called Date, and you should avoid using function names.

5. **In the Value field, type *"≥" & Get (CurrentDate) - 7*.**

   Do include the quote marks, but don't include the period at the end. You're typing the proper search criteria into the variable's value box, just as you'd type into a date field. That is, you're telling FileMaker that the date value is "greater than or equal to today, minus 7 days."

6. **Add a Perform Find script step to the script.**

   Now it's time to tell FileMaker how to use the date you've just defined.

7. **Open the step's options, click Specify and then click the Specify Find Request window's New button.**

   The Edit Find Request window appears.

8. **In the "Find records when" list, choose the Invoices::Date Due field.**

   That says which field to search.

9. **In the Criteria box, type *$theDate*.**

FileMaker will use the dynamic date value to search each time the script is run.

10. **Click the Add button, check your window against Figure 13-16 and then click OK.**

You're back in the Script Workspace window.

11. **Save the script and then close the Script Workspace window.**

Attach your script to a button on the Invoices layout and test your new button.

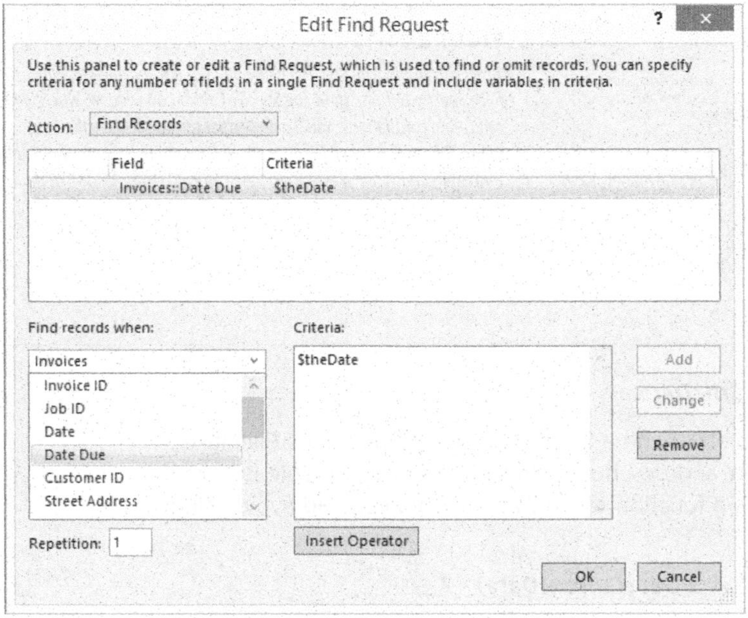

FIGURE 13-16

With this setting, FileMaker uses a dynamic date value to find an invoice where the Invoices::Due Date is within the past week. The value in the $date variable will be set appropriately each time the script is run.

Constraining and Extending the Found Set

You may have already noticed that Perform Find doesn't have an option for the Requests→Constrain Found Set and Requests→Extend Found Set commands. That's because each of these is a separate script step. It makes sense, really, because to constrain or extend a find, you need to do a find first. In other words, this process always takes two separate steps to complete.

The Extend Found Set and Constrain Found Set script step options work like Perform Find. Everything you just learned about Perform Find still applies: You can hard-code the find requests, pause the script and then let the user enter them, or build them in the script.

Omitting Records

The Omit Record script step lives a dual life. If you're in Browse mode when it runs, it omits the current record from the found set. If you're in Find mode, it turns on the Status toolbar's Omit checkbox.

Omit Multiple Records works only in Browse mode and does the same thing as the Records→Omit Multiple command. As usual, you can specify the number of records to omit in the script, either as a number or as a calculation. You also get a "Perform without dialog" option so you can decide whether or not people get to enter the number of records to omit.

Finally, the Show Omitted Only script step has the same effect as the Records→Show Omitted Only menu command. See the box below to learn more about when to how to use the various Find script steps.

UP TO SPEED

Mix and Match

You have three basic options when performing a find in a script: You can let someone enter the find requests, hard-code the requests right in the Perform Find step, or use a variable to set dynamic requests. But these choices aren't mutually exclusive: You can mix and match techniques.

For example, suppose you need a relatively complex set of find requests that, for the most part, never change, but one value in one field on just one request needs to be based on the current date. It would be tedious to have to add dozens of Set Field and New Record/Request steps to your script when all but one use a hard-coded value.

Other times, it would be nice to let people specify the find requests but add a little more to it when they're done. You can start on the Enter Find Mode script step, by turning on the "Specify find requests" option. This step tells FileMaker to go to Find mode *and* load it up with the requests you specify in the Specify Find Requests dialog box.

Once you're in Find mode, though, you're free to use Set Field, New Record/Request, and Go to Record/Request to modify the prefab requests to your heart's content. Just go to the right request, and use Set Field to work the dynamic date value into it.

Suppose you want to let people search for invoices. You create a Find Invoices layout and a script like the one for Find Customers, except for the Invoice layout. This time, you want to restrict people to invoices created only in the last year. Before the Perform Find step, you can add these two steps:

```
New Record/Request
Omit Record
Set Field [Invoices::Date; "<" &
Get(CurrentDate) - 365]
```

Now the script finds just what someone asks for but omits records more than 365 days old. You've used the script to add a new request to the ones she created. What's more, she doesn't even know you've controlled her find.

Modify Last Find

The simplest find-related script step is Modify Last Find. It has exactly the same effect as the Records→Modify Last Find command: It puts you in Find mode with the same requests you created the *last* time you were in Find mode.

■ Sorting Records

After all that fuss about finding records, the sorting script steps are refreshingly simple. There are only two and you already know how to use both. The Sort Records script step behaves in a now-familiar way. By default, it brings up the Sort dialog box when the script runs. If you turn on its "Specify sort order" option, then you can specify the sort order but allow users to change it. Finally, turn on the "Perform without dialog" option to sort the records without giving users a choice about the sort order.

If the records are already sorted, then you can *unsort* them from a script. For instance, you might sort records for a report, but you want to return them to their unsorted order when the report is finished so people don't get confused. Just use the Unsort Records script step. It does its job with no options.

Sorting Records with an OnRecordLoad Trigger

When you first encountered a Sort script, you learned how to attach it to a layout with the OnLayoutEnter script trigger (page 475). That sorted your records whenever you viewed the List layout. But if you switch that trigger to OnRecordLoad, you'll get different behavior with that same script. OnRecordLoad fires whenever a new record is loaded, but you can still sort the records a different way any time you need to.

If you do a find on a layout when the OnLayoutEnter trigger is set, the results come back unsorted. OnRecordLoad changes the layout to automatically sort when you first view the layout *and* when you find new records. The OnRecordLoad trigger fires whenever a new record is loaded, which always happens after a find. True, it happens when you switch records too, but FileMaker is smart enough to know it doesn't need to sort an already-sorted list, so this doesn't cause a slowdown. But whenever you visit the Customers layout, your records are presorted. If you sort manually, then your new sort order sticks until you leave the layout and come back (or sort manually again).

___

TIP Use OnRecordLoad for list views, where you're not likely to do much data entry. But on a Form view or a Detail layout, where you're creating lots of records, this script may trigger so often it affects performance. In that case, use OnLayoutEnter instead.

___

■ Working with Windows

Scripts give you complete control over the database windows on the screen. You can create new windows, close existing windows, bring any window to the front, and move or resize any window. The most common reason for controlling windows is to work in a found set without disturbing your user's screen. In that case, your script will create a window, navigate to a new layout, find some records, do the work, and then close the window. In this section, you'll learn more about the script steps that you'll use.

Creating Windows

To make a new window on the screen, use the New Window script step. The step shows a dialog box for selecting all its options (Figure 13-17)

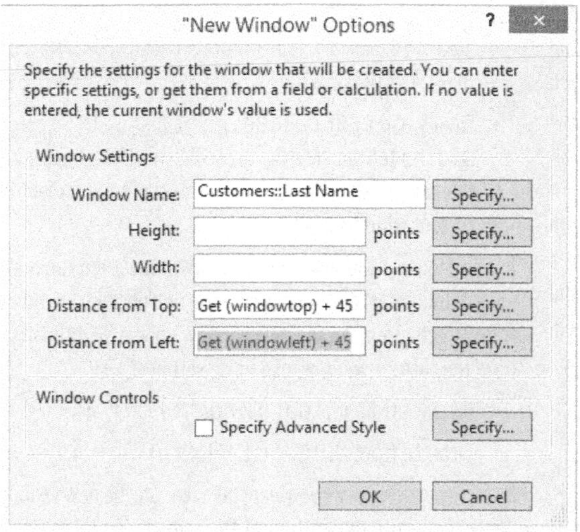

FIGURE 13-17

The New Window Options dialog box lets your script create windows in a specific size and location on your screen. Each box in this window has a Specify button that leads to the Specify Calculation window. The settings shown here could be used in a script that runs from a list layout to show detail about a specific customer. The window will show detail for the customer record the user clicked on, and the title bar will contain that customer's name. Because the Height and Width are left blank, the new window will be the same size as the window that's active when the script step runs. The window will be created 45 pixels down and to the right of the window that spawned it. See the box on page 524 to learn more.

The Window Name box gives your script control over the name of the window. You can also tell FileMaker how big the window should be (Height and Width), and where to put the window on the screen ("Distance from top" and "Distance from left"). The Advanced Style options are so important that they warrant their own section below.

Here are some tips on using the main "'New Window' Options" dialog box:

- If you leave any of the values blank, FileMaker uses the value from the *current* window. It adds a number to the end of the window name so the new name is different, though. For example, if the current window is called "Vergis Corporation" and you run the New Window script step without specifying a name, then the new window's name is "Vergis Corporation – 2."

- If you don't specify a size and position, FileMaker puts the new window right over the top of the current window (with the same size and position).

> **TIP** To avoid confusing people, it's best to offset the new window at least a little so they can see the new window on top of their existing ones.

- You can set each value directly by typing in the box in the New Window Options dialog box, or set them from a calculation by clicking the Specify button by any box. See the box on page 524 for more info on window size and position options.

Window Size and Position Calculations

The fact that you can set a new window's size and position using a calculation may seem a little strange. After all, do you really need a bigger window for someone named Kirk than you would for Janeway? Do you want your windows in a different place on Thursdays?

In fact, though, you can do a lot of interesting things with window size and position calculations. FileMaker provides a handful of functions that let you find out about the size and position of the current window, and of the computer screen, and use that information in calculations:

- The Get(WindowHeight) function, for instance, returns the height of the current window, in screen pixels (the little dots on your screen). Its brother, Get(WindowContentHeight) returns the height of just the window's content area; that is, the area inside the title bar, scroll bars, and Status toolbar. The Get(WindowWidth) and Get(WindowContentWidth) functions are similar.

- The Get(WindowTop) and Get(WindowLeft) functions tell you where the window is on the screen. The first returns the distance from the top of the window to the top of the screen. The second tells you the distance from the window's left edge to the screen's left side. Both distances are measured in pixels.

- The Get(WindowDesktopHeight) and Get(Window DesktopWidth) functions tell you how much desktop space you have. In Windows, it's the

area of FileMaker's main program window. On a Mac, it's the size of the desktop.

- Finally, Get(ScreenHeight) and Get(Screen Width) tell you how big the screen is. (If you have more than one screen, then they tell you about the screen the current window is on.)

By combining these functions in creative ways, you can make your scripts smart about how they size and position windows. For example, to make the new window appear slightly offset from the current window, use these settings:

- Distance from top: Get(WindowTop) + 45
- Distance from left: Get(WindowLeft) + 45

If you're particular, and you want to make sure the new window never hangs off the bottom of the screen, use this Let() function calculation for the "Distance from top" value:

```
Let (
  [Limit = Get(WindowDesktopHeight) -
Get(WindowHeight);
  Offset = Get(WindowTop) + 20;
  Best = Min(Limit; Offset)];
  Best
  )
```

Similarly, you can use the "Distance from left" value to make sure it doesn't hang off the screen's right edge. Just substitute WindowDesktopWidth, WindowWidth, and WindowLeft for WindowDesktopHeight, WindowHeight, and WindowTop.

■ SPECIFYING ADVANCED STYLE OPTIONS

By default any new window you create is just like the window that was active when the new window appeared. But you can change the window's style and restrict users' ability to control new windows by using the "'Specify Advanced Style' Options" dialog box (Figure 13-18). Here's how the styles break down:

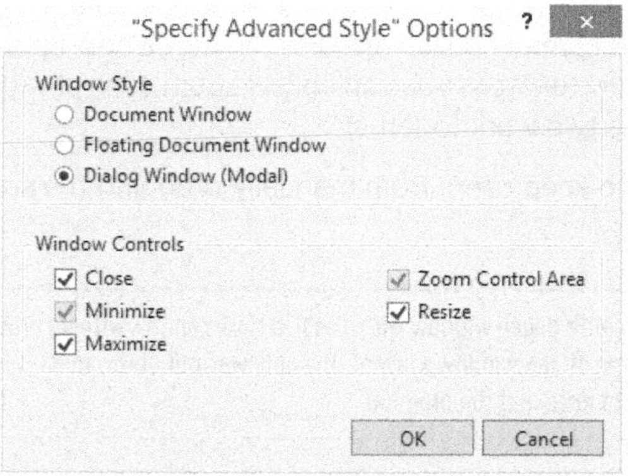

"Specify Advanced Style" Options   ?   ×

Window Style
○ Document Window
○ Floating Document Window
◉ Dialog Window (Modal)

Window Controls
☑ Close   ☑ Zoom Control Area
☑ Minimize   ☑ Resize
☑ Maximize

OK   Cancel

FIGURE 13-18

FileMaker gives you near-complete control over new windows you create with the Specify Advanced Window Style Options dialog box. If the Show Custom Dialog script step doesn't give you the options you need, turn to this powerful script step to build a layout that will get the custom job done.

- A **Document Window** is the default type, and it's used most often. Its behavior is called *modeless,* which means that you can minimize, hide, or activate it as you're working with other FileMaker windows.

- A **Floating Document Window** is also modeless, but it stays on top of all other windows until it's closed. Use a floating document window to make a button palette with your database's most commonly used scripts. That way, the buttons are always available, and the palette can't get lost, because a floating window always stays on top of all open windows.

- A **Dialog Window** is *modal,* which is the way a dialog box behaves. That is, when a dialog box appears, you have to deal with it before you can work in windows underneath it. Users can't select other windows, switch modes, open a new file, or run a script until the window is closed. Use this option to create a custom dialog box with as many data-entry fields, text blocks, and other layout objects as you need.

Setting a window's style is just the first part of the control you get. You can also do away with the native buttons that document windows normally show. For example, if you create a custom layout for entering customer data and then call that layout in a script using a dialog window, you should turn off the user's ability to close or minimize the dialog window. If you don't, they could short-circuit your script by closing the window without entering the data the script needs, or minimize the window and then be stuck because they can't do what the script requires. Here's the scoop on the options:

- Turn off the **Close** control when you want to keep users from closing the window before you're ready. If you turn off the Close control, you'll need to give users some other way to close the window, like a custom Close button that runs a script.

- Turn off the **Minimize** and **Maximize** controls when you don't want users changing the size of your custom window by using the buttons that appear in default windows' title bars.

- Turn off the **Zoom Control Area** if you don't want users to be able to zoom the window. Surprisingly, this command also disables the mode pop-up menu next to the zoom control. Unfortunately, you can't allow zoom control without allowing mode control. These two work together.

- Turn off the **Resize** control to keep users from manually dragging the size of your custom window.

> **NOTE** You can get into trouble if you create a dialog window with disabled close controls without providing another way to close the window, like a button on the window's layout. The only way out of this mess is to quit FileMaker. On the Mac, you might even have to force quit the program.

All the window control options are available for regular and floating document windows, but the Minimize and Zoom Control Area options are not available for dialog windows. When you disable one of a window's title bar buttons (Close, Minimize, Maximize) the corresponding menu command is disabled, too.

Bringing a Window to the Front

The Select Window script step lets you bring a window in front of all open windows. It has one option, which lets you select the current window or specify one by name, as shown in Figure 13-19. It may seem silly to select the current window—after all, if it's *current,* it should be the one in front, right? Not always. If you're running a script in another database (you'll learn how in Chapter 18) then the script will run in another window that's current, but that won't be selected. If you need to see the window, or to insure that the script's context is correct, use Select Window and select the Current Window option. You also use this script step to show a hidden window and bring it to the front.

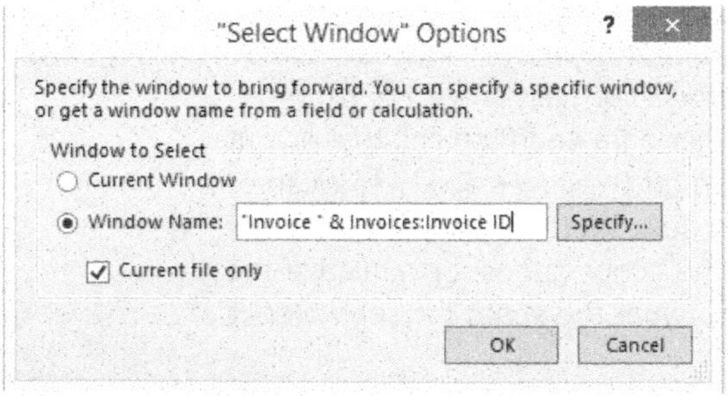

FIGURE 13-19

This dialog box appears when you click the Specify button with a Select Window script step selected. From here, you can specify the Current Window, or choose Window Name and then put the name of the window you want in the box. This calculation looks for a window with the name "Invoice" and the current Invoice's InvoiceID.

If you choose the Window Name option, you must address the window by its exact name. So it's best to use this option when you've named the window previously in a script. To be sure you don't introduce spelling errors, copy the text or calculation you used to name the window into the Window Name option. It's a little extra work, but the safety factor makes it worthwhile.

Closing a Window

The `Close Window` script step has the same options as `Select Window`. You tell FileMaker which window to close: the current window or one you specify by name.

Moving and Resizing Existing Windows

FileMaker has three ways to move and resize a window. You can opt for one of its canned window maneuvers, or you can set the exact pixel size and location of the window just like you can with the `New Window` step. You can also *hide* the current window.

■ ADJUST WINDOW

The `Adjust Window` script step always operates on the current window, and it gives you just five simple choices:

- Choose "Resize to Fit," and FileMaker makes the window exactly the right size to fit its contents.

- Choose Maximize to make the window as large as possible.

- Choose Minimize to shrink the window to a little bar (Windows) or a Dock icon (Mac).

- Choose Restore to switch the window back to the *last* size it was, just before it was most recently resized.

- Choose Hide to hide the window (Just like the Window→Hide Window command).

NOTE The Maximize options have slightly different behavior on Windows and Mac. For example, when you maximize a window in Windows and then select a different window, the second window also gets maximized. On a Mac, the second window keeps its original size. Also, a maximized window on a Mac fills as much of the screen as possible. In Windows, it fills FileMaker's outer window, whatever size it may be, and you can't adjust the window from a script.

■ ARRANGE ALL WINDOWS

The `Arrange All Windows` script step is the equivalent of the four window arrangement options in the Window menu. You can tile windows horizontally or vertically or cascade them (see page 33). On a Mac, you can also bring all FileMaker windows to the front. This command doesn't change the active window.

■ MOVE/RESIZE WINDOW

The `Move/Resize Window` script step can move and/or resize any window with pixel-perfect precision. Its Specify button shows the dialog box in Figure 13-20, where you can choose the window's size and position. As with New Window, you can leave any of the size or position values empty. Empty fields don't change their corresponding part of the window's size or position. For example, if you specify a new value for Width but leave Height blank, FileMaker makes the window wider or narrower, but its height doesn't change.

NOTE Move/Resize Window also selects the window it acts on, which always brings the window to the front, and, if it's a hidden window, shows it.

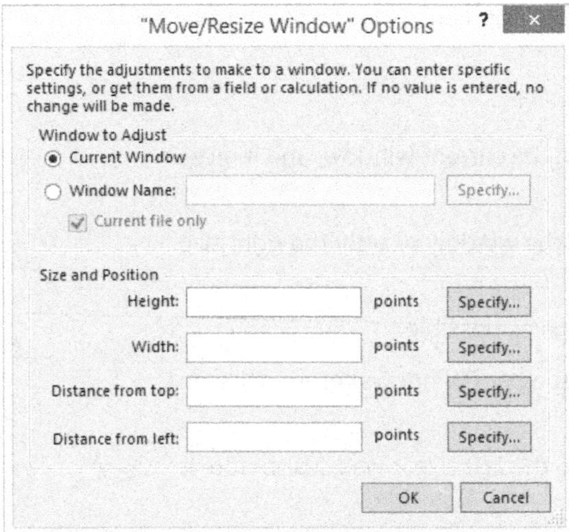

FIGURE 13-20

The Move/Resize Window settings look like a combination of the Select Window settings and the New Window settings. First, you pick which window you want to work on (Current Window, or a window selected by name). You then specify the new size and position for the window.

Other Window-Related Script Steps

FileMaker has a handful of other window-related script steps, listed below. These steps come in handy if you need to exert more control over what people see (not to imply that you're a control freak or anything):

- **Freeze Window** tells FileMaker to stop showing changes in the window while the script runs. For example, if your script is looping through all the records in the found set, then you normally see each record on the screen as it runs. If you add a Freeze Window script step before the loop, then people see only the first record while it runs. When the script is finished, FileMaker updates the window again. Looping scripts that have to visit lots of records run much faster when the window is frozen, which is an even better reason to use this script step.

- **Refresh Window** forces FileMaker to update what's inside the window when it normally wouldn't. This action can be because you previously ran the Freeze Window step, or because FileMaker is simply being conservative. If you want to make sure someone sees a particular record or field value on the screen while a script is running, then add a Refresh Window step after making the change.

- **Scroll Window** lets you simulate a vertical scroll bar click in a window. You can scroll to the Home (top) or End of a window, or move up or down one screen-ful. You also get a To Selection option, which scrolls the window so that the selected record and field value both show. You'll design most of your windows so that scrolling isn't necessary, which means you may never need this step.

- **Show/Hide Menubar** lets you decide whether people should see the Menubar, which is the equivalent of the Toolbar in FileMaker Go and WebDirect. The script step has no effect in FileMaker Pro. You can show or hide the Menubar, or toggle it (show it if hidden, and hide it if shown). And since users have the ability to show or hide it at will, you also have the ability to lock your choice. When you lock the Menubar, the control is visible, but grayed out. Create a Login script that checks for the user's platform (page 835) and then use File Options to run the script OnFirstWindowOpen. That way, the Menubar is tucked away before users have a chance to notice it's missing.

- **Show/Hide Toolbars** lets you decide if people should see Toolbar, which is part of FileMaker Pro, FileMaker Go, and WebDirect. As with the Show/Hide Menubar, you can show, hide, or lock the Toolbar. More commonly, though, the Status toolbar is turned off and locked during a process, such as a scripted find. You don't want people using the Cancel button during a Pause step to cancel a script and then end up dumped on a layout that you meant them to see only while a script is running. If you hide the Status toolbar, though, you should provide a button that cancels the process, in case people change their minds. That way, they don't have to go all the way through a process if they get an urgent phone call and need to do something different from the script's agenda.

NOTE When you're sharing your database using WebDirect (page 822), you may want to hide and lock toolbars to control what users can do for a couple of reasons. You might want to limit their access to some commands, but just as often, you limit what they see to increase the database's performance. In that case, your login script can check to see if users are accessing the file via WebDirect. Use the Get(ApplicationVersion) function to find out if they're using FileMaker Go (the function returns "Go" on the iPhone or iPod Touch and "Go iPad" on an iPad) or through a browser (the function returns "Web Publishing Engine").

- **Allow Formatting Bar** lets you disable the formatting bar and all its tools. It only affects the window that's active when the script runs. Since the formatting bar takes up space, add a Resize Window step to avoid blank space at the bottom of the window. This step works only in FileMaker Pro (not on the Web or in FileMaker Go).

- **Show/Hide Text Ruler** can toggle, show, or hide the Text Ruler. Unlike Show/Hide Status Toolbar, this step doesn't have a Lock option. Someone can always override your setting, so this step is rarely worth the trouble.

- **Set Window Title** lets you change any window's name. You can specify the current window, or any window by name, as well as the window's new name. FileMaker normally names a window with the file's name, but you can tailor each window to show the user's login name, for example. Write a script that runs when the file is opened, and use the Set Window Title script step with this calculation: Get(FileName) & "" & Get(AccountName).

- **Set Zoom Level** sets the window zoom level, just like the zoom controls in the window's bottom-left corner. You can pick a specific zoom level, or choose to zoom in or out to the next level. Again, you get a Lock option. If you set the zoom level and then turn on the Lock checkbox, people can't manually change the zoom level.

- **View As** is in the Windows section of the script step list, but it isn't really a window-related step. It changes the view option for the current *layout.* You can pick Form view, List view, or Table view. You also get a choice called Cycle that tells FileMaker to switch to the *next* view setting in the list. If you really want to control how people see your database, use Layouts→Layout Setting (View Tab) to turn off the views you don't want them seeing. You can then let folks override those settings with this script step.

■ Working with Files

In the Script Step list, the Files section contains some of the least used script steps in all of FileMaker. But if you work in a school, say, the day may come when you need to automate the process of formatting files or saving backup copies of your database for every student in a class. You can also script the process of converting older databases to FileMaker's .fmp12 format and recovering damaged databases, but these processes are sensitive and usually better handled manually.

Opening and Closing Files

Because the Open File script step lets you open another FileMaker file, it's used more than the others in this group. You can pick any of your existing file references (see page 622) or create a new file reference if necessary. When the step runs, the specified file opens and appears in a new window. If the file has a script set to run when it opens, it runs. If you want the file to open, but you don't want to see a window on the screen, then turn on the "Open hidden" option for this step. The file opens, but it's listed in the Window menu's Show Window submenu, with its name in parentheses.

The Close File script step closes a specific open file. You have the option to choose the current file, or any file that has a reference in the current file (page 589). When the script step runs, then all of the specified file's windows close, and any scripts triggered by its closing will fire.

NOTE In general, FileMaker is very smart about when to open and close files. It opens a file when it needs to (usually to display data from related tables) and closes it again when it no longer needs it. You usually don't need to open and close files from a script, but there's one important exception: when the file has an opening script that should run before someone can see the file. If you jump directly to a related record in another file, then FileMaker bypasses the opening script, so use an Open File script step to ensure that the open script runs.

Save a Copy As

If you need to make a copy of an open database, use the Save a Copy As script step. It works just like the File→Save a Copy As command. When you're working on a set of files and want to back them up without a lot of manual muss and fuss, just add a Save a Copy As script to each one. Then, from your main file, call that script in each file, and you've made a backup with one script.

NOTE This script step (or menu command, for that matter) doesn't work on files shared by using FileMaker Server. See page 812 to learn how to create automatic backups.

Other File-Related Script Steps

The rest of the file-related script steps are almost never used, but that doesn't mean *you* won't find a good reason to use them.

- **Convert File** lets you convert an older FileMaker database (as long it's in .fmp7 format or later) to the .fmp12 format. Since this process requires a lot of preparation and manual checking, it's rarely scripted.

- **Set Use System Formats** toggles the Use System Formats file option on or off. When you first create a database, FileMaker remembers how your system expects dates, times, and numbers to be formatted. If someone opens the file on a computer with different settings (usually a different language), then FileMaker has to decide if it should use the original format settings for the file, or those specified by the new system. You can set this choice manually in the File→File Options window.

- **Recover File** runs FileMaker's automatic file repair process on a selected database. Recovering a file is a rare thing in general since FileMaker is careful to avoid damaging databases even when your computer crashes. It's more rare, and even inadvisable, to do this on the same database so often you'd need a script to do it for you.

Printing

Printing typically involves two specific commands on Windows or Mac: File→Print Setup (or File→Page Setup) and File→Print. The Script Workspace window gives you those same two choices.

You'll use these steps often, since they're the meat-and-potatoes part of printing a report. Use the `Print Setup` script step to set the options in the Print Setup or Page Setup dialog box. Turn on "Specify page setup" to see the standard dialog box. Pick the option you want to associate with the script step. When the script runs, FileMaker restores the options you chose. When this option is off, a person sees—and can change—the Page Setup dialog box when the script runs. If you want to set the options without user intervention, select "Perform without dialog."

The Print script step works similarly. You can set the options and retain them by selecting "Perform without dialog," or let users choose by leaving the option turned off. FileMaker Pro's Print window has some options that aren't common to other programs. "Records being browsed," "Current record," or "Blank record, showing fields," change what's printed. If the print job depends on making the right choice, you may need to suppress the dialog box because users won't remember, or understand, the choice.

> **NOTE** Many of the options you can set in the Print dialog box are specific to a particular printer model. For example, some printers let you pick color or black-and-white printing or have settings for different kinds of paper. Be careful about setting these proprietary options, though. When someone uses your database and script on a different printer, these options won't work.

Working with FileMaker Go

Several script steps work only in FileMaker Go, like those for the touch keyboard and the orientation controls. The keyboard controls can make user experience better by keeping them out of the way for certain fields where they might obscure too much screen real estate. Orientation controls can detect how the screen changes, and help you limit the changes if the user flips her mobile device 90 degrees.

ENABLE TOUCH KEYBOARD

`Enable Touch Keyboard` gives you three options: On, Off, and Toggle. It lets you enable or disable the keyboard in fields only. It has no effect on the keyboard display in dialog boxes. It also works with Windows 8 touchscreen technology. Use the `Get ( TouchKeyboardState )` function to detect the keyboard and then disable it if it's enabled.

SET ALLOWED ORIENTATIONS

`Set Allowed Orientations` has four parameters: Portrait, Portrait Upside Down, Landscape Left, and Landscape Right. You can turn each one off or on independently of all the others, but at least one option must be on. If only one option is on, the step has the effect of locking screen rotation completely.

■ INSERT FROM DEVICE

Insert from Device lets you control mobile devices special files, like photos, videos, and music. You specify the container field the file will be inserted into and then choose a source for the file. There are seven choices: Music Library, Photo Library, Camera, Video Camera, Microphone, Bar Code, and Signature. Camera, and microphone options let you choose the front or back camera, and can set resolution or time limits. The Bar Code option lets you choose a camera to scan from and choose an encoding scheme. You can display a title on the Signature Capture screen, and display a message and a custom prompt that replaces the "Sign Here" boilerplate under the signature line.

■ SET ZOOM LEVEL

Set Zoom Level works as you'd expect in FileMaker Pro and on WebDirect. But it lets you control whether users can change the zoom in FileMaker Go. For example, some users zoom their screen in so far that they get motion sickness as they tab around the layout. But if you lock the zoom, then they can't pinch or expand the layout.

■ Other Script Steps

You've now seen most of the often-used script steps (and a few of the not-so-often-used ones). You'll see even more as they come up in the next few chapters. The rest of this chapter covers a few oddball steps that are mostly found in the Miscellaneous section of the step list.

Upload to FileMaker Server

Users can upload files to the server by clicking on a prominent button on the Status toolbar (page 4). This might provide a little too much convenience for your liking, so you can disable the button using custom menus (page 568). Then you can write a script that lets only specific users to upload files, or lets everyone upload, but only after certain conditions are met. To do that, you'll need to use the Upload to FileMaker Server script step. This script step opens the same dialog box the toolbar button or menu command (File→Sharing→Upload to FileMaker Server) provides.

The script step itself has no options, but you can choose the settings you need in the dialog box it shows. This step is only supported for FileMaker Pro. It doesn't work on iOS or in a browser and can't be run on the server itself.

Get Directory

Get Directory shows a dialog box that lets users select a folder, and then it sets a variable to the fully qualified path of the selected folder. You have four options: you can let the user create a new folder (instead of selecting an existing one), you can name the variable (in fact, you must), you can specify the dialog box's title, and you can set a default directory, which the user can override. You could use this script step to export files from a found set of records into a specified folder.

Set Layout Object Animation

Animations are visual effects that let you know something's happening, like the swiping effect you see as you move from panel to panel on a slide control. They're pleasing and useful for users, but scripts that deal with animated objects can take longer to run if they have to wait for animations to finish before they can go on to the next step. Animations can also be distracting to users, so unless your script contains user interaction and its animation is critical to their understanding of what's happening onscreen, set animation to Off. This disables all animations that would normally show while the script runs. Disabling animations can speed up performance on mobile devices.

Refresh Object

Like its companion Refresh Portal, Refresh Object lets you refresh a single object instead of an entire window's contents. This step can be faster and more effective than Refresh Window, especially for FileMaker Go or in a browser, because you're sending less information over the network. You must specify a named object that's on the current layout. You can also specify a specific repetition number of a repeating field, but that is optional. The step will update an object's contents, conditional formatting, and visibility state.

Open URL

When FileMaker runs this step, it asks your computer's operating system to open the URL you specify. Most often the URL is a web address (http or https), but it can be any URL type your computer supports, including ftp, mailto, ldap, and even fmp (to open a file on a network server). As usual, you can specify the URL or let someone else do it, and you can use a calculation if needed.

Dial Phone

The Dial Phone script step tells your modem to dial the telephone. You can use a calculation to specify the phone number or enter it directly.

> **NOTE** This script step doesn't work on a Mac. If you choose the step and try to set the options for it from a Mac, a warning message lets you know the feature is unavailable.

Set Web Viewer

Web viewers are pretty cool on their own, but the Set Web Viewer script step (Figure 13-21) can make your FileMaker layouts look and behave even more like a web browser. With this flexible script step, you can make a series of buttons:

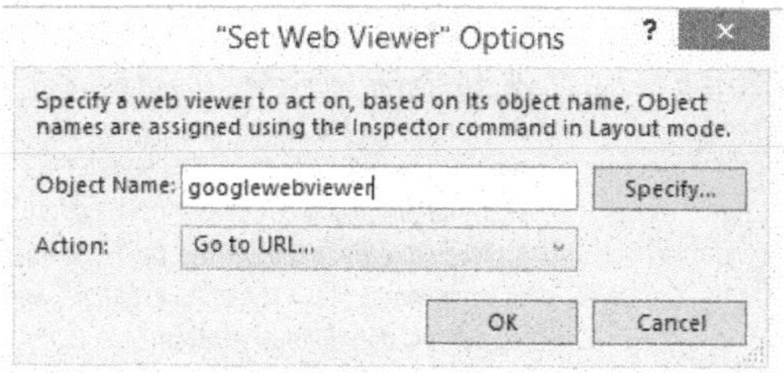

FIGURE 13-21

This Set Web Viewer dialog box is set to work on a web viewer with the name "google webViewer." When you select the "Go to URL" option, you see the same Set Web Viewer dialog box that comes free with every web viewer.

- **Reset** sets the web viewer back to the web address that's specified in its Web Viewer Setup dialog box.

- **Reload** gets you a fresh copy of the web page you're currently viewing.

- **Go Forward** lets you move forward through your web page history.

- **Go Back** lets you move backward through the web pages you've been browsing.

- **Go to URL** lets you specify any new web address via the Specify Calculation window.

But to use this script step, you have to refer to your web viewer by name. One cool thing about referring to a web viewer by name is that you can display more than one web viewer on a layout, and then, by using its name, choose which one your scripts address.

Execute SQL

If you need to manipulate data in an ODBC data source, like Oracle, SQL, or MySQL, then this script step is at your service (Figure 13-22). Unlike many other script steps, this one requires some setup. You'll need an OBDC driver installed on any computer that runs an Execute SQL script. Each driver is a bit different, so use the drivers' documentation for installation and setting up data sources. Finally, if you don't write SQL queries, then you need help from someone who does, to make sure you get to the data you want. See page 851 to learn how you can use SQL data almost as easily as native FileMaker data.

> **NOTE** The Execute SQL script step has nothing to do with the ExecuteSQL() function. The *script step* works with data outside FileMaker. The *function* uses SQL to query FileMaker's data.

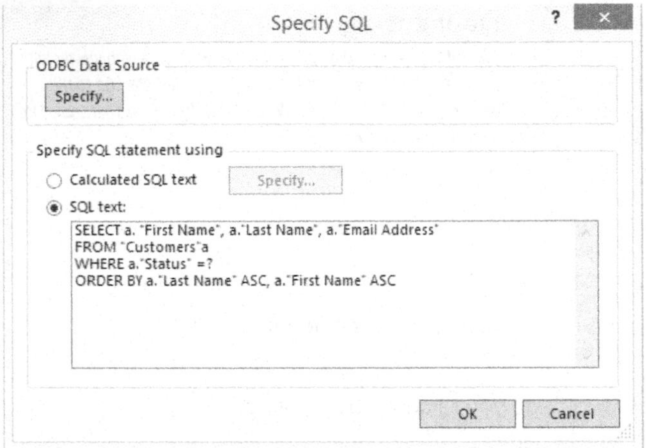

FIGURE 13-22

Once you prepare your computer, and select an ODBC data source, the source name shows up beside the top Specify button. Then you can use the Calculations dialog box to assemble a query, or just type directly in the SQL text field. The query shown here grabs the First Name, Last Name, and Email Address data for every customer record where the status is dynamic. The data would be sorted by Last Name and subsorted by First Name, all in ascending order.

Flush Cache to Disk

Any time changes are made to a record, FileMaker records those changes in your computer's memory first and writes the change to the hard drive later—when it gets some free time. If you want to *force* the changes to be written to disk immediately, then you can run the Flush Cache to Disk script step. For instance, you might add this script step after a script that creates a new customer order. That way, if your computer crashes while you're busily taking orders, then you lose only the last order you were working on. It's also commonly used to refresh the contents of a window, because sometimes the Refresh Window script step (page 528) isn't doing its job. This script step can really bog down performance, especially on databases shared using WebDirect (page 822). Use it sparingly. In most cases, the Refresh Object step is a better choice for maintaining speed.

Exit Application

Exit Application quits the FileMaker program. Every open window and file is closed before FileMaker quits. People often use this script step when they have just one database, and they never use FileMaker unless they're in that database. But if you're locking down your solution and providing custom menus that suppress the Exit (Quit) command, then you'll need to write a script and give users a way to run it when they're done.

TIP Use an Exit Application script as part of your logout routine when you're sharing a database using WebDirect or FileMaker Go. This step clears a browser's virtual windows (a temporary window some browsers draw to do behind-the-scenes work), which might otherwise keep them logged into the database. This step can free up WebDirect connections for other users.

Becoming a Power Developer

Applying Developer Utilities

A s you've learned in previous chapters, FileMaker Pro gives you lots of power to create databases that help you and your company get on with your jobs. But as your database's needs, and your skills, get greater, you'll start to hunger for tools that help you develop more powerful databases. So if you consider yourself a developer of databases—whether that's your actual title or just your function—you'll start to wonder where the developers' tools are. That's when FileMaker Pro Advanced comes in. It has power not included in FileMaker Pro. You wouldn't show up at the Tour de France with a tricycle, and you don't become a power developer without FileMaker Pro Advanced. Here are some highlights of the pro tools you'll learn about in this chapter:

- Import, or copy and paste, tables and fields from other FileMaker files

- Trace script errors and run your scripts step by step

- Analyze data referenced in your scripts and calculations

- Create custom functions that aren't found in the calculation engine's function library

- Create custom menus that hide native FileMaker features or provide new ones

- Create runtime versions of your database that people can use without their own copy of FileMaker

- Create a Database Design Report (DDR)

These pro tools cost a little more, but the value in time saved is well worth it. For a couple hundred dollars more ($549 for Advanced vs. $329 for Pro), you get developer tools to make your life easier, your work more efficient, and your databases better. While you can get a demo version of FileMaker Pro, and even FileMaker Server, there is no demo version of FileMaker Pro Advanced. But read this chapter even if you don't have the software. If you've gone through the previous chapters (or have enough experience to have skipped them), you'll be able to follow along in FileMaker Pro. If you can see the usefulness of even one of the features you'll learn in this chapter, the extra cost for FileMaker Pro Advanced will be a good investment.

> **NOTE**   The example database for this chapter contains custom functions that you can analyze when you get to that section. If you have a copy of FileMaker Pro Advanced, you can follow the text using a copy of any FileMaker file. You can download the example database, *CH14 Dev Tools.fmp12*, at *www.missingmanuals.com/cds/fmp14mm.*

Copying Database Structure

The beginning work of creating a new database is fairly repetitive, so FileMaker Pro Advanced provides some tools that let you take shortcuts through the tedious process of creating tables, fields, and scripts. By copying work you've already done, you can spend less time defining fields or recreating complex scripts, and more time doing the creative work of designing a database. You can import tables and fields—without copying data—between tables in the same file and even between different files.

FileMaker Pro Advanced also provides Copy and Paste capability in several major dialog boxes so you can reuse fields in the Manage Database window, scripts and script steps in Script Maker, and even entire tables.

> **NOTE**   You need full access privileges in both the source file and the target file to import or copy and paste tables and fields. You need at least script modification privileges to import or copy and paste scripts.

Importing Tables and Fields

If you have tables in one file that would also be useful in another, then you can *import* the table and field information. Importing a table doesn't copy record data—it copies the table's fields, including field names, types, comments, calculations, and other options. To import a table, choose File→Manage Database and then click the Table tab. Click Import and then locate the file that contains the table you want to copy. You'll see the Import Tables window, as shown in Figure 14-1.

FIGURE 14-1

After you select a file, you'll see a simple list of all tables in the file. You can select as many as you need. Turn on the checkbox by all the tables you want to import. You don't get to specify which fields are imported—they all come in. So if you don't need a few of those fields, just delete them when the import is finished.

Select the tables you want to import and then click OK. When FileMaker Pro Advanced has finished importing the tables and fields, it displays a dialog box similar to the one you see when you import data. You see a summary of the items that were imported. FileMaker creates a log file, which is shown in the dialog box. It's helpful to view the log file, since some items, like calculation fields, may be listed as *broken* in the log file. In other words, they won't work. There's a good reason for this: When you import tables, you're not importing table occurrences. And since calcuations must refer to field values using a fully qualified name (which includes table occurrence names), the calculations won't work until you recreate the relationships between tables. But you can also find broken calculation fields by scanning the Fields tab. You'll see the calculation enclosed in comments like this: (like /* this */).

In practice, though, broken calculation fields aren't as much trouble as they sound. Although the tables in your new file match (say you've imported a People table from your contact management solution), your new database's features may not be the same. In other words, the calculation you wrote to tally up all contacts with a person probably doesn't make sense in your new Invoicing database. Instead of repairing those calculation fields, you'll often just delete them.

Copying and Pasting Tables

If you prefer, you can copy and paste tables in the Manage Database window instead of using the Import button. In the Tables tab, just select a table and then click Copy. If you want to copy the table in the same file, just click Paste. To put the table in another file, click OK to close the Manage Database window, open your target file, bring up its Tables tab and then paste the table there. As usual, you can use the Shift key to select several items next to one another in the table list. Use the Ctrl (⌘) key to select tables that aren't right next to one another.

Copying and Pasting Fields

You can avoid the fuss with broken calcs by just copying some of a table's fields. Just as with tables, select one or more fields and then click Copy. Then open the table where you want to create the new fields, and then click Paste to move the fields into your database.

When you copy *calculation* fields, it helps to plan ahead. Make sure the field references already exist in the target table before you copy and paste. In other words, if a calculation refers to an Invoice::Total field, make sure it exists before you paste the calc. That way, FileMaker won't consider it broken and it'll just work in its new table.

But you can always paste the calculation fields and clean up the references later, especially if you intend to use different field names anyway. Here are some general rules:

- If fields matching the references in your copied calculation don't exist in the target table, then FileMaker pastes the calculation as a comment (for example, `/*Products::Amount * LineItem::Quantity*/`), since it can't find matching fields in the new table. Simply edit the calculations to use the new field references, delete the comment markers (/* and */), and then click OK.

- To save yourself some editing work, *first* paste into the target table (or create) fields with names that match the ones in the calculation you're transferring. Then, when you paste the calculation field, FileMaker resolves the field references automatically.

- If the field references are local (that is, they refer to other fields within the same table), then you can copy the fields referenced in the calculation *and* the calculation field at the same time. When you paste the set of fields, FileMaker resolves the field references automatically, and there's nothing to edit.

- If you're copying a calculation field that contains a fully qualified field reference (containing both a table name and a field name, like Expenses::Job ID), the calculation transfers just fine, *if* a table occurrence exists with the same name in the target file.

Importing Scripts

Scripts are also reusable from file to file, and with the same caveats as with tables and fields. Table occurrences and field references should already exist in your target field before you move the script. If not, you'll need to repair the respective steps. Fortunately, it's simple. For complex scripts, it's much easier to repair a few broken fields or layout references than it is to start from scratch. To import scripts from another file, open the Script Workspace and choose Scripts→Import. Use the Open File window to locate your source file. After you select it, the Import Scripts window appears (Figure 14-2).

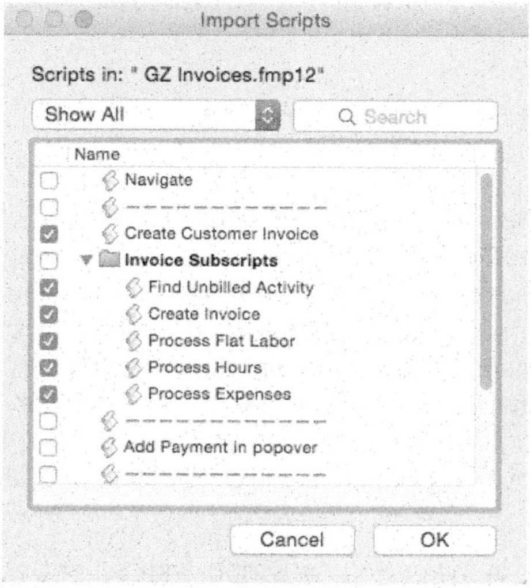

FIGURE 14-2

As with importing tables, you can choose just one or all the scripts from a source file. If any of your scripts refer to other scripts, make sure you select them too. View the log when the import is done so you can check for, and repair, broken references.

Copying Scripts

If you prefer, you can copy and paste scripts instead. Open the file that contains the scripts you want to copy and then, in the Manage Scripts dialog box, use Copy (Ctrl+C [⌘-C]) to grab the scripts you need. Then switch to the target file and open its Script Workspace. Then Paste (Ctrl+V [⌘-V]). As with importing, you should check all pasted scripts to see if any field, layout, or other reference needs to be pointed to another element in its new location. Copying or importing scripts works best when you need the whole script, and all the elements referenced in your script are already in place, so that no script steps break on the way in.

> **TIP** These features, once the domain of FileMaker Pro Advanced, are now part of normal FileMaker Pro's toolkit, too.

Copying Script Steps

You can also copy script steps individually or in chunks. Usually, you'll be copying them between scripts within the same file, but you can also copy script steps between files. In the Edit Script dialog box, select the script steps you want and then Copy. Then you either create a new script or open the script that needs your copied steps. Select the script step just *above* where you want the next steps to land and then Paste. Your pasted steps appear below the selected step. Fix any broken references as needed.

You don't even have to move to a new script to find Copy and Paste useful. Sometimes you'll want to reuse a sequence of steps more than once in a single script. You can also use the Duplicate command on a step or selected group of steps (Ctrl+D [⌘-D]). They'll appear in a chunk below the bottommost duplicated step. Drag them as a group to their new location.

Script Debugger

When you write a script using FileMaker Pro, your testing and troubleshooting routine is pretty simple. You perform the script and wait to see what happens at the end. In a simple script, like one that prints a report, you can easily enough see what went wrong, and fix it: Your script just went to the wrong layout, didn't find the right records. But when you're creating a complex script that sets variables and works with different sets of records that you can't verify before the next script step whizzes past, it's devilishly hard to figure out where your script veers off course. Even simple scripts can go wrong in puzzling ways that you can't detect by reading over your steps.

That's where Script Debugger comes in. When you run scripts with Script Debugger turned on, FileMaker performs scripts at human speed, so you can see exactly what's happening each step of the way (Figure 14-3).

> **NOTE** To run Script Debugger, you must be logged into the file with a password that has script editing privileges or full access (see page 744). But if you need to figure out how a script runs for lesser accounts, then you can log in as someone else and then use the Authenticate/Deauthenticate button to login with higher privileges.

To see the Script Debugger, click the Debugger button in the Script Workspace. The selected script opens in the Script Debugger, with the first script step highlighted. Use the buttons to control the script and watch each step work. If you choose Tools→Script Debugger, the window opens, but without a script. But whenever this window is open, the Debugger will "catch" every script you run.

The Script Debugger shows the name of the script you're running near the top and the complete contents of that script in the main pane below. You can even see the value of any parameter that was passed to the script down in the Call Stack section. The Debugger is high-powered, but it doesn't tell the whole story. Just as important as stepping through the script is setting up your screen so you can see your database in the background. For example, you need to be able to verify that the script is doing what you need it to do: is it changing to the right layout, finding the right records, grabbing the right value?

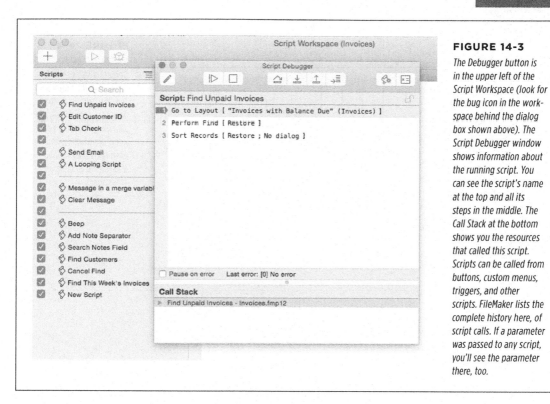

Controlling Script Execution

Unlike most windows, Script Debugger stays on top of your work, giving you constant feedback about any script that runs while it's open. When a script starts running, it shows up in the Script Debugger, but is paused. FileMaker waits for you to tell it to perform the first step. You control the running script by using the buttons at the top of the window (Figure 14-4).

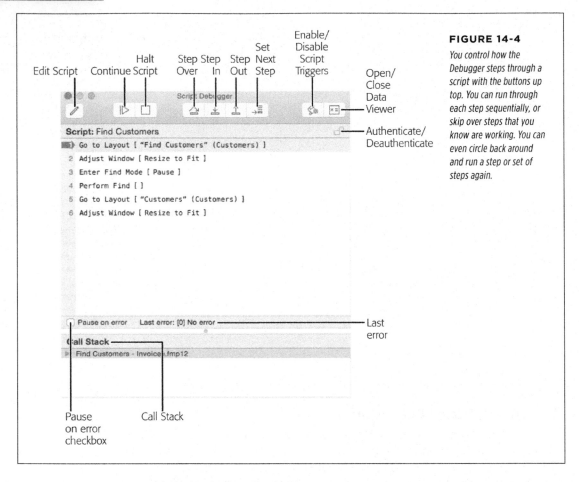

Edit Script   Continue   Halt Script   Step Over   Step In   Step Out   Set Next Step   Enable/ Disable Script Triggers   Open/ Close Data Viewer   Authenticate/ Deauthenticate

Script: Find Customers

1 Go to Layout ["Find Customers" (Customers)]
2 Adjust Window [Resize to Fit]
3 Enter Find Mode [Pause]
4 Perform Find [ ]
5 Go to Layout ["Customers" (Customers)]
6 Adjust Window [Resize to Fit]

Pause on error   Last error: [0] No error ————— Last error

Call Stack
   Find Customers - Invoices.fmp12

Pause on error checkbox   Call Stack

FIGURE 14-4

You control how the Debugger steps through a script with the buttons up top. You can run through each step sequentially, or skip over steps that you know are working. You can even circle back around and run a step or set of steps again.

Button behavior is described below:

- The **Edit Script** button is one of the Script Debugger's handiest buttons. If you're debugging a script and you spot the problem in the debugger, just click Edit Script. The Script Workspace window moves to the front (or opens, if necessary) with the debugged script's tab active. The script step that was current is even highlighted—a great help in a long sequences. Make the change and then run the script again to test it.

- **Continue** starts the script running normally; the Debugger stops only if you've set a *breakpoint* (which you can read about in the next section). If your script doesn't have a breakpoint, the script runs all the way through without stopping.

- If you need to stop the script completely, click **Halt Script,** which works just like the Halt script step. The Script Debugger window clears the script, and FileMaker returns to normal behavior.

- Click **Step Over** to run the *current* script step. The current step is marked with a highlight and a blue arrow along the left edge of the script steps. FileMaker runs the current step, moves the arrow to the next step, and then pauses, waiting for further instruction from you. Often, you'll check in the database to make sure the results were what you expected, then come back and run the next step.

- **Step Into** works just like Step Over, with one caveat. If the current step happens to be a `Perform Script` script step, then Step Into goes into that script and stops at its first line. This way you can step through the subscript line by line. The Step Over button, on the other hand, executes the subscript without opening it in the Debugger—the next line in the calling script is highlighted.

- Use **Step Out** when you're running a subscript. The Debugger runs the subscript to the end, takes you back to the calling script, and then stops. If the script you're running wasn't called by another script, then Step Out just finishes the script normally. Use Step Out if you accidentally step into a script you don't need to see in full detail, or if you're finished investigating a subscript and want to get back to the calling script quickly.

- If you want to skip a portion of a script, or run some steps over again, select a script step and then click **Set Next Step**. This button moves the little current step arrow to the selected step, running any steps between. For example, you might have an `If` test that know will fail, but you still need to run the steps inside the `If`. Select the first step inside the `If`, then click **Set Next Step**. That way, you can check the work without running the `If` test. You can also back up and run a section of steps over again by moving the current step up in the list.

WARNING   Anytime you use the Set Next Step button, you're changing the normal flow of the script. The results you get when you use it may not match what would happen if you ran the script normally. For instance, if you back up and start part of a script over again, things may be different this time through because the script already changed something it had tested previously. You may end up with a different found set or a different current record. Or script variables may be different this time through. All kinds of things could be different, so be watchful to make sure your script doesn't do something desctructive to your data while you're debugging.

- When doing serious debugging, triggered scripts can sometimes become a hassle. For example, an OnRecordLoad trigger will run its script every time you switch from Layout mode to Browse mode. When that happens, the script you were debugging is paused while the triggered script pops into the Script Debugger window, and now you have to step through it instead. The **Enable/Disable Script Triggers** button exists to suppress these interruptions and let you focus on what's important.

WARNING   If you've disabled script triggers you must keep the Script Debugger window open. Closing it will automatically *and silently* re-enable the triggers.

- You use the **Set/Clear Breakpoints** button to add or remove breakpoints in your script. You'll learn about these in the next section.

NOTE When you click the Edit Script button, FileMaker opens the script for editing but keeps it running in the Script Debugger. You're free to jump back to the Script Debugger window and then click any of the buttons to step the script forward further. So you can also use the Edit Script button to see more details about a script (like the exact calculation in a Set Field script step) while you're debugging. However, if you *save* a change to any open script, FileMaker halts all scripts to do the save.

- The **Open/Close Data Viewer** button shows FileMaker Pro Advanced's Data Viewer window, where you can examine the current value of referenced fields, calculations, or variables. You'll learn more on page 52.

- The **Authenticate/Deauthenticate** button (padlock icon) lets you debug a script when you're logged in with a lower-level privilege set. Scripts can behave differently for your users (who don't have full access to the database) than they do for you. To see what's happening, log in as one of the users who are having problems. You can still open the Debugger, but FileMaker won't open the script in the Debugger until you authenticate with your high-level account. That way, the script runs as your user experiences it, and you can hunt down the problem.

TIP Each button in the Script Debugger window has a menu command counterpart in the Tools→Debugging Controls submenu. If you prefer the menus, or want to learn the keyboard shortcuts, this menu is your friend.

Breakpoints

In some situations, the click-the-step-button-for-each-step approach can become unacceptably tedious. For example, you may have a long script, and you know the problem part is near the end. To make your life simpler, the Script Debugger includes *breakpoints.* You set a breakpoint on any line you want and then click the Run/Pause button. FileMaker cruises through the script steps at full speed. When it reaches the step with the breakpoint, it stops so you can step through manually.

You can set a breakpoint three different ways:

- In the Script Debugger window, select the script step and then click the Set Next Step button.

- In the Script Debugger window, click next to the script step in the gray stripe along the left edge of the script steps.

- The same gray stripe appears in the Script Editing pane of the Script Workspace. Click next to any step to set a breakpoint. Using this method, you can set a breakpoint in a deeply nested subscript before you debug the main script. Then if you click Run/Pause, FileMaker runs through the script and its subscripts until it hits your breakpoint, saving you a lot of clicking.

A gray arrow appears to the left of any script step that has a breakpoint. To remove a breakpoint, click it again. The arrow disappears.

When you click the Run/Pause button, FileMaker runs to the *next* breakpoint it encounters (even if it's in one of the subscripts this script calls). If you hit a breakpoint before the one you want, click Run/Pause again to jump to the next one. Adding breakpoints at key places in a complex script (and leaving them there) can make it easy to quickly debug the script later, as you Run/Pause your way through the major chunks, stopping to step through only the parts that currently interest you. Breakpoints have no effect on scripts that run without Debugger, so you needn't worry that they'll mess with your users.

WORKAROUND WORKSHOP

Conditional Breakpoints

Some programs have a feature called *conditional breakpoints* that let you tell the debugger to stop on a certain line only when some condition is met. For example, you may want to stop only if the $count variable is bigger than 100, or if the found count is more than 1000.

FileMaker doesn't have built-in conditional breakpoints, but you make a workaround. Just add an If script step to your script that checks the condition you need. Then put a comment inside the If block and set a break point on the comment. The Debugger goes into the If block only when the condition is met; otherwise it skips right past it and its breakpoint.

For example, you can add this to a long loop in your script, so you can break only after the loop has run 100 times:

```
If [$count > 100 ]
# break here
End If
```

Make sure to set a breakpoint on the line with the "break here" comment, and you'll get what you need.

Examining Errors

Coping with errors can be a significant part of debugging a script. As you step through your script line by line, the debugger updates the Last Error display with each script step (Figure 14-5). Most script steps don't produce an error, so the display will be "[0] No error." But if you *do* encounter an error, the error number appears right after the step runs, making it a breeze to see what error number a certain situation produced so you can handle it in your code.

Pause on Error

If you know your script is producing an error *somewhere* (perhaps because an error message pops up when you run it), but you don't know where it's coming from, then the "Pause on error" checkbox is your friend. Just turn this option on and then click Run/Pause. FileMaker runs the script full speed until a step produces an error.

Then the Debugger stops the script so you can examine it, see the error number, and check what's happening in the background with your database. In these cases, it's useful to click the Edit Script button to jump to the trouble spot in the Edit Script window.

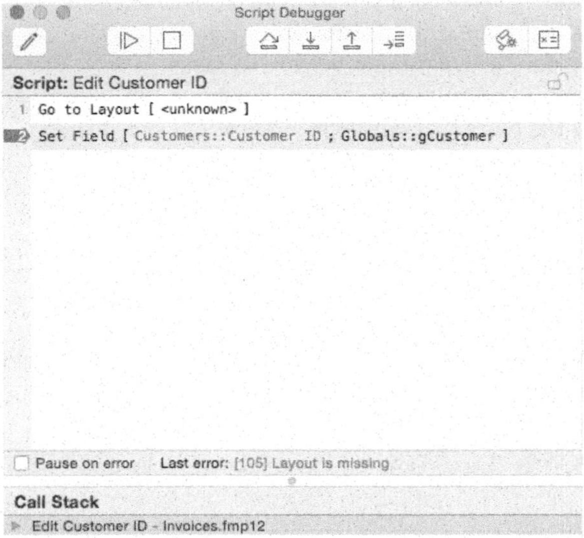

FIGURE 14-5

Every script step generates an error display, even if no error occurs. For steps that run correctly (at least according to the Debugger), the "Last error" display will read: [0] No error. But if the step doesn't run correctly, you'll see one of FileMaker's error codes instead. Here, the Go to Layout *step is clearly broken—its target layout is <unknown>. Even though the* Set Field *step is highlighted, it hasn't run yet. The error display is always for the very last step that ran. Refer to Appendix D for a list of FileMaker's error codes.*

This feature works whether or not error capture is turned on, so it may spot errors you're already handling. For example, a loop script that moves through a found set of records will throw an error when you get to the last record. While technically an error, FileMaker needs it to properly end the loop-, and it's rarely a problem that you need to address. When the debugger pauses on one of these, just click Run/Pause again to run to the next error. Keep going as necessary until you find the error you're looking for.

TIP "Pause on error" isn't just a checkbox, it's also the name of an occasional developer conference! Visit *www.facebook.com/PauseOnError* to learn more.

The Call Stack

The bottom part of the window shows you the call stack. *Call stack* is a nerdy term for the list of actions that got you to the currently running script. Although you may run a script from the Script Workspace window, users run it from a button, which triggers a main script that then performs a subscript; the call list lets you examine how subscripts are being triggered. Every time one script calls another one, the calling script moves down in the list to make room for the new script's information. FileMaker puts the topmost—and current—script in boldface at the top of the stack.

Below it, you see the script that came before. Then as each script finishes running, it drops out of the stack and all the calling scripts move up a notch. You can see how this looks in Figure 14-6. Of course, scripts don't run spontaneously. Some action puts things in motion, like a script trigger or the click of a button. At the very bottom of a call stack, you can find that action with an icon to indicate what it is.

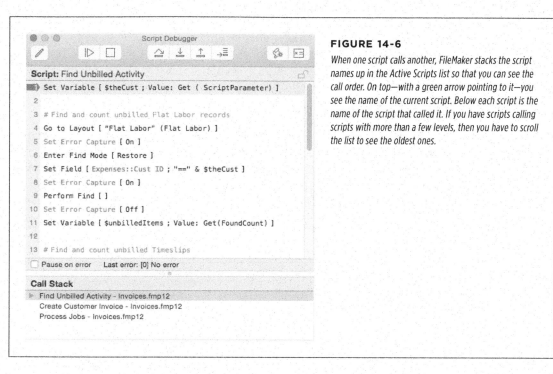

FIGURE 14-6

When one script calls another, FileMaker stacks the script names up in the Active Scripts list so that you can see the call order. On top—with a green arrow pointing to it—you see the name of the current script. Below each script is the name of the script that called it. If you have scripts calling scripts with more than a few levels, then you have to scroll the list to see the oldest ones.

Click a script in the list to switch the debugger's view to that script. The Current Position arrow changes color (white with blue outline) to indicate that you're viewing a script that doesn't include the current script step.

Working with the Debugger Window

The Debugger window doesn't work like FileMaker's other dialog boxes. First, it's always on top of all other windows, so you may want to move it to the side so that you can see what's going on in your database. Plus, you can still interact with your database. When the Debugger has your script paused, you can move database windows around, switch layouts, and even type data into records. That way, you test and see how things are progressing. Careful, though: You could mess up your script by putting it in a state it would normally never reach, like an inappropriate layout, or by putting bad data into a global field. And although you can edit existing records, you can't create new records, delete records, or open new windows.

You're free to arrange the debugger and database windows on the screen so you can see as much as possible while your script runs. You can also resize the debugger window at any time to make more space.

WARNING Before you get too hung up trying to fit your layouts on the screen so you can see field values and the like, read about the Data Viewer in the next section. It's often a better choice if you're trying to watch the data or variables change.

As long as the Script Debugger window is showing, FileMaker debugs *every* script that runs. Close the Debugger window (or choose Tools→Script Debugger) to return to normal script execution. If a script is running when you close the debugger window, it will complete all its steps. If that's not what you want, click the Halt button first and then close the Debugger.

The Data Viewer

In the Debugger section you learned how important it is to check in on your database while you're debugging a script. The *Data Viewer* grants you under-the-hood access to field data, variables, and calculations. It's usually the easiest way to watch values change as the Debugger runs your script. Click the Data Viewer button (the last one on the right) to open the Data Viewer. Or choose Tools→Data Viewer (Figure 14-7).

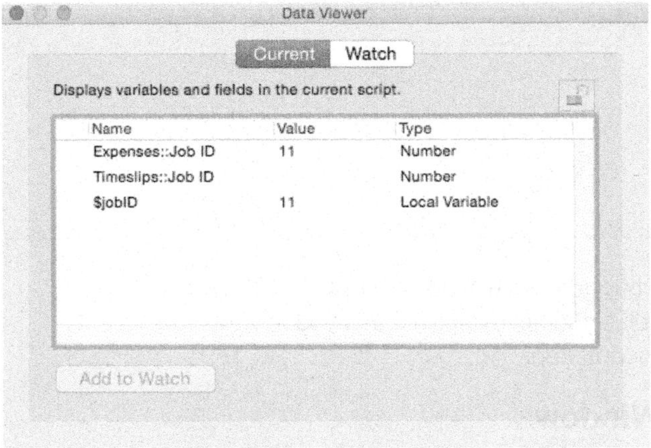

FIGURE 14-7

The Data Viewer has two tabs, Current and Watch. Current shows information related to the script that's currently running in the debugger. Two fields and a variable are referenced here, along with their current values and their data types. Under Watch, you can use the calculation engine to create any calculation you need to see.

The Current Tab

If you open the Data Viewer (Tools→Data Viewer) and then switch to the Current tab, FileMaker shows you pertinent information about the script you're debugging. As a script runs in the Debugger, the Data Viewer lists every field that the script uses in any way. For instance, if you use the Set Field script step to modify a field *anywhere* in the script, that field appears in the Current tab list, no matter which step is running. In addition to the name of each important field, the Data Viewer shows its current value (in the Value column) and its data type.

As you step through the script, the Data Viewer updates the value column appropriately, so it always reflects the current field value. It also helps to draw your attention to fields you should be watching, as Figure 14-8 attests.

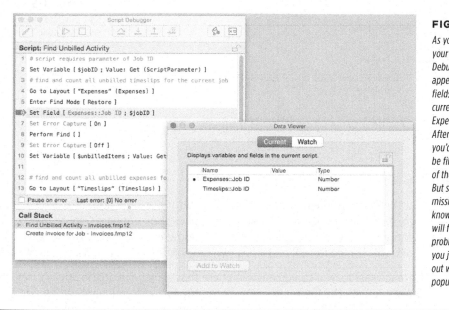

FIGURE 14-8

As you step through your script in the Script Debugger, a black dot appears to the left of fields referenced in the current script step. Here Expenses::JobID is blank. After you run this step, you'd expect the field to be filled with the contents of the $jobID variable. But since that variable is missing from the list, you know that the script step will fail. You've found the problem in your script: you just have to figure out why $jobID didn't get populated.

The Current tab also shows information about script variables. Instead of showing every variable the script uses as soon as the script starts, the window shows a new line for each new variable *as it's created.* For example, when you use the Set Variable script step to set a $customerID variable, $customerID appears in the Data Viewer, along with its type and value.

NOTE The $customerID variable has a single $ in front of its name, and is a *local variable*. That means that it's created within the context of a script and will no longer exist after the script stops running. Global variables (which have two $$s) remain, and are visible even after a script has exited and the Debugger window is closed.

The Current tab almost always shows you just what you need to see while you debug. It can be a huge timesaver, pointing out everything your script is using and what it's doing with data, so you don't have to run calculations in your head or scramble around different layouts. Open it early and often when you debug.

The Watch Tab

The Watch tab, shows the same kind of information as the Current tab, but you get to configure it yourself. Instead of showing the fields and variables your script is using, it shows the fields and variables you tell it to show, whether they are being evaluated in the Debugger or not. And it can show the result of arbitrary calculation expressions as well. You can see a sample Watch list in Figure 14-9.

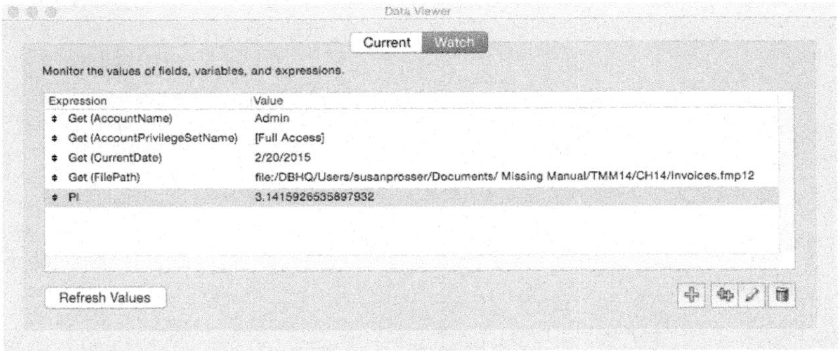

FIGURE 14-9

The Data Viewer's Watch tab is like a silent, unresting sentry. It shows the results of whatever you tell it to watch. Load the Watch tab with any calculation you can come up with, and it evaulates the results for you—the Debugger doesn't even need to be running.

To add an item to the Watch list, click the Add button; it's the one with a single green + sign. When you click, the Edit Expression dialog box appears (Figure 14-10). This window works like the Specify Calculation window, except it has an extra text box at the bottom labeled Result, and it has two new buttons: Evaluate Now and Monitor.

Differences aside, you can do anything here that you can do in the Specify Calculations window. In the Expression box, enter any formula you want. When you click Evaluate Now, FileMaker performs the calculation and shows the result in the Result box at the bottom of the window. But if your calculation's syntax has an error, the formula isn't evaluated until you fix the problem.

When you're satisfied with the formula, click Monitor. FileMaker adds the expression to the Watch list, with its value beside it. FileMaker attempts to keep the values up-to-date, but it can't auto-refresh some kinds of calculations (typically those that use Get functions). If necessary, you can click Refresh Values to automatically recalculate each Watch expression.

NOTE The Data Viewer's Edit Expression window comes in handy when you're trying to write a calculation, even if you're not debugging a script and don't need to keep an eye on the results. Just click the Add button and fiddle with the formula until you have it right (clicking Evaluate Now whenever you need to see how it's doing). When you're happy with the results, copy the formula (Edit→Select All followed by Edit→Copy) and then click Cancel. You can now paste the tested-and-working formula into a field calculation or a script step.

The Data Viewer isn't attached to a specific file, so its Watch list contents don't change when you open and close files. The viewer can even be open while you have no databases open. Since all files and scripts share the same Watch list, it can quickly get long and hard to monitor. Select items you aren't using and then click the Trash can icon to delete them.

Finally, if you need to see how certain calculations behave for people who don't have full access, log in as the person in question. In the Data Viewer, select the Current tab and then click the Authenticate icon to unlock its powers. You can now monitor values and edit expressions even though you don't have full access.

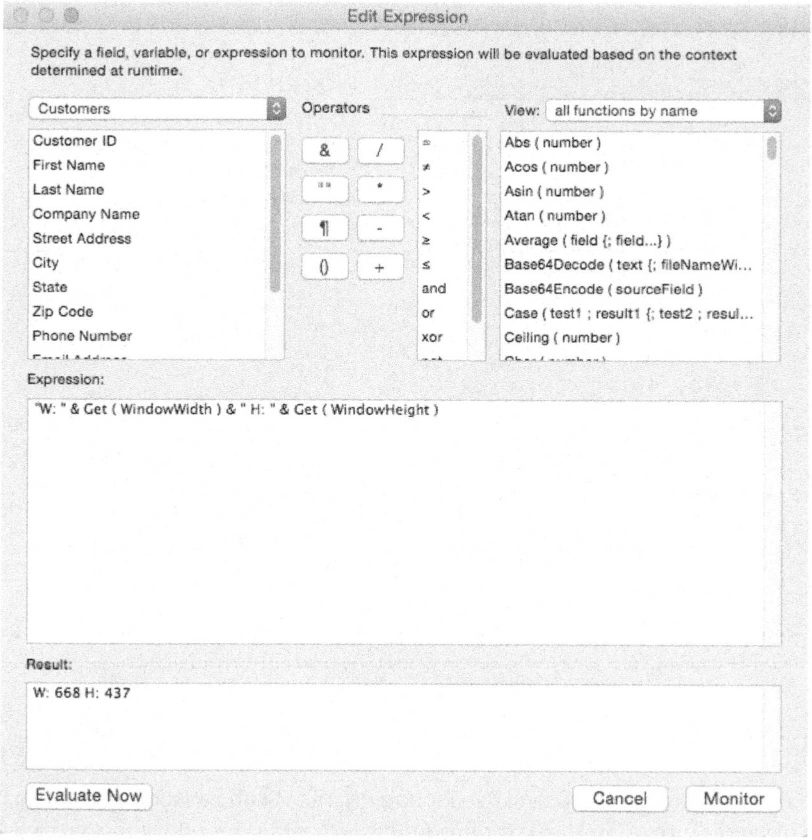

FIGURE 14-10

The Data Viewer's Edit Expression window should look familiar—it's similar to the Specify Calculation window. Although the panes and tools don't look the same, they behave nearly the same way. But the Data Viewer version can run the calculation in place and show you the result on command (just click Evaluate Now).

■ Disable Script Steps

The Set Next Step button in the Script Debugger lets you manually skip script steps while debugging, but it's not much help unless *you* remember to click it at the right time. Sometimes you have a script step (or several) that you always want FileMaker to skip. You could just delete them, but maybe you're not quite ready to. Perhaps it's code that isn't working yet, and you intend to come back later to fix it. Or perhaps you're moving the code somewhere else, and until you're sure you've got it moved and working, you don't want to delete the original. Whatever the reason, you may want to temporarily turn off a group of steps.

To turn off a script step (see Figure 14-11), open the script and then select the step you want to turn off. Choose Edit→Disable (Edit→Enable/Disable). Or use the keyboard shortcut Ctrl+/ (⌘-/). FileMaker puts two slashes in front of the script steps and grays them out so you can identify them. To turn a step back on again, first select it and then reissue the command. As always, you can select *multiple* script steps at once and turn them on or off all in one shot.

Create Invoice for Job

```
 1  // Perform Script [ "Tab Check" ]
 2  // Perform Script [ "Clear Message" ]
 3
 4  # find unbilled line items
 5  Perform Script [ "Find Unbilled Activity" ; Parameter: Jobs::Job ID ]
 6  Set Variable [ $unbilledItems ; Value: Get ( ScriptResult ) ]
 7
 8  # make sure there are unbilled timeslips or expenses
 9  If [ $unbilledItems = 0 ]
10      Show Custom Dialog [ "No Unbilled Items" ;
        "No invoice was created because there are no unbilled items… ]
11  Else
12
13      # create an invoice record
14      Perform Script [ "Create Invoice Record" ;
        Parameter: Jobs::Job ID ]
15      Set Variable [ $invoiceID ; Value: Get ( ScriptResult ) ]
16
17      # TODO: process timeslips
18      Perform Script [ "Process Timeslips" ; Parameter: $invoiceID ]
19      # TODO: process expenses
20      Perform Script [ "Process Expenses" ; Parameter: $invoiceID ]
```

FIGURE 14-11

Two steps in this script—the highlighted Perform Script steps at the top—turned off, as you can see by the double slashes in front of the names and their grayed-out appearance. When the script runs, FileMaker skips the steps you turned off.

Turning script steps off is useful for debugging, but it can have long-term use, too. Any step you turn off in FileMaker Pro Advanced gets skipped whenever someone runs it—even in FileMaker Pro. Say your company has a semi-regular promotion that creates discounts for a limited period. You don't have to write two different scripts, one with the discount and one without, and then worry about some kind of test to make them available on a button or in the script menu at the proper times. Write one script, making sure the discount creation steps are separate from the main process. Then you can turn on the pertinent steps when the promotion starts and turn them off when it's over, with very little fuss.

Keeping Watch

Some functions are very handy to keep in your Data Viewer's Watch tab all the time. When debugging a multifile or multiuser database, consider giving these expressions long-term residency:

- **Get (FilePath).** Shows the name of the current database and where it resides on your drive or which server is hosting it.
- **Get (AccountName).** The account you're currently logged in with.
- **Get (AccountPrivilegeSetName).** Your current privilege set.

- **Get (LastError).** Lets you see errors even when the Script Debugger is closed.
- **Get (LayoutName).** For those times the toolbar is hidden.
- **Get (LayoutTableName).** Displays the name of the table occurrence the current layout is based on.
- **Get (WindowWidth)** and **Get (WindowHeight).** Useful to keep an eye on when designing a database for someone with a smaller screen than you.

The Database Design Report

Sometimes you inherit a large database from somebody else, and you simply don't see how it comes together. (OK, be honest. Sometimes *you* create a large database and can't quite remember how it's all put together.) While FileMaker's point-and-click display makes it easy to build databases, teasing things out later is a different story. You can look at a script, field, layout, table occurrence, or even an entire table in FileMaker Pro and have no idea whether the database actually uses or needs it.

With FileMaker Pro Advanced, however, you've got help. Its built-in internal analysis tool, the Database Design Report (DDR), gives you an overview of your database, where you can easily see how database items are connected and other details, all in one place. You run the report, tell it what kinds of things you're interested in, and FileMaker presents the information in a series of web pages.

Unlike the reports discussed in Chapter 16, the DDR is a report about the *structure* of your database, *not* about the data inside. It tells you what tables and fields you have, which fields are used on each layout, what properties those fields have, where scripts are available, and a whole lot more.

Generating the DDR

The Database Design Report window lets you tell FileMaker what you want it to report on. You get to pick which files and table occurrences to include, what kinds of things you want to report on, and what format you want the report to use. You also get to decide whether you want to open the report right away or just save it for later use. To get started, choose Tools→Database Design Report. Up pops the Database Design Report dialog box (Figure 14-12).

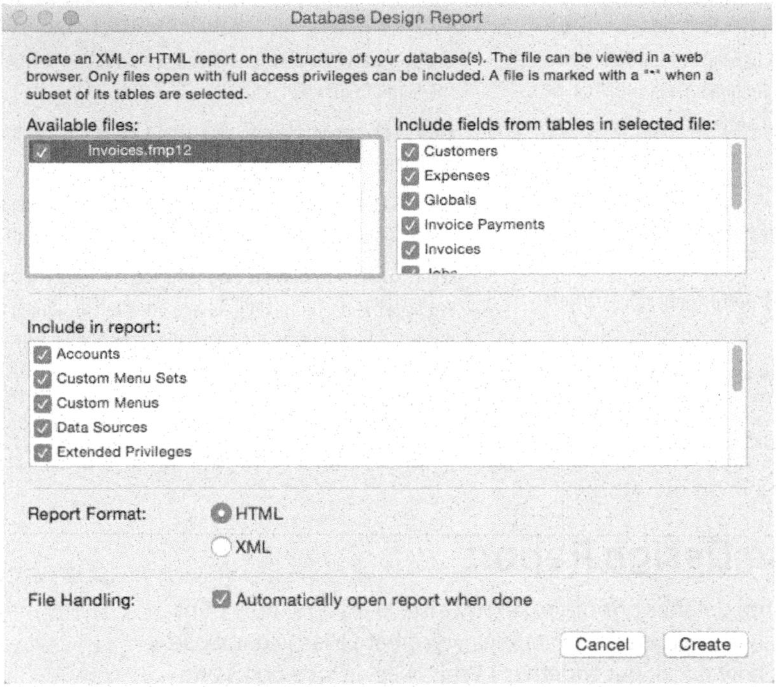

FIGURE 14-12

The Database Design Report dialog box lets you tell FileMaker what to include in the report. First, choose from among the open files. When you select one, all its tables appear to the right. Select the ones you need with the checkboxes. In the "Include in Report" section, you can decide what other elements you want to report on. Finally, you can opt for an HTML or XML report and ask FileMaker to open it for you when it's done.

The Available Files list in this window shows every open file. To include a file in the report, turn on the checkbox by its name. FileMaker assumes you want every file at first, so you may have to do more turning off than on if you have a lot of files open.

> **TIP** You can Shift-click to select more than one file. Then if you turn off one file's checkbox, every selected file turns off as well. This same approach works in all three lists.

The report includes field information for tables in each file. Select a file in the list to see all its tables in the "Include fields from tables in selected file" list. Again, you can use the checkboxes in this list to tell FileMaker which tables you want included in the report.

The "Include in report" section has a checkbox for each kind of database element the DDR can report on. Again, FileMaker assumes you want everything, but you're free to limit the report to just certain information. The less you report on, the faster the report runs, and the smaller the final files.

Normally, FileMaker saves the report in HTML format so you can read and navigate it in any web browser, but it also offers a more structured XML format. XML files aren't easy for *humans* to read, but if you're already working with XML, you probably own software that lets you process the XML and integrate information about your database into other systems. But you don't have to learn XML to harness this power. Some third-party companies make DDR analysis tools that process the XML version of your DDR and provide extra tools for browsing, finding, and reporting on the information it contains. Google "filemaker ddr tool" to shop around.

When you're done making decisions, click Create. FileMaker asks you what to name and where to save the report. (For simplicity's sake, it's probably best to keep the automatic name "Summary.") The DDR is made up of several files, so you probably want to make a new folder to hold the report. The more complex your files, the longer it takes to create the DDR. In a file with dozens of tables, each of which may have dozens or even hundreds of fields, this could take a minute or more. FileMaker displays a progress bar for you, so you can gauge how long the process will take.

NOTE A DDR is a snapshot of the database at the moment you create it. So it's good to make periodic DDRs as your database evolves. You can create a record of when you added or changed various parts of the database. A DDR can also help with troubleshooting broken elements or for figuring out if it's safe to delete a script or a field.

Using the DDR

If you turned on "Automatically open report when done" when you create an HTML-formatted DDR, then FileMaker launches your browser and shows you the DDR Report Overview (Figure 14-13) as soon as the progress bar disappears.

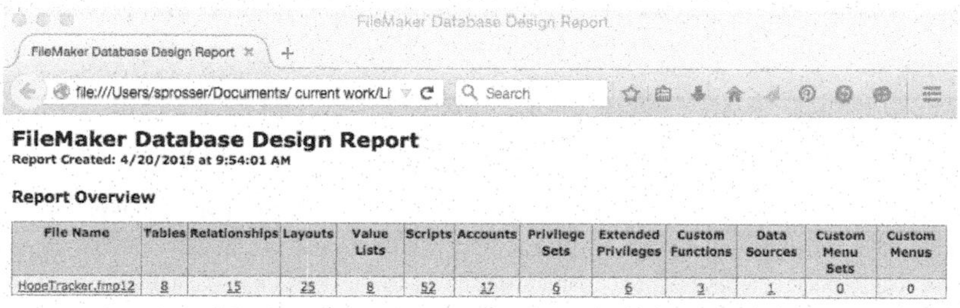

FIGURE 14-13

Report Overview is the first thing you see when you open a DDR. The header lists the DDR's creation time and date so you can compare it with the current state of your database, or with other DDRs. It's a table, with one row for every file you included in the report, and a column for each option you checked when you created the DDR. Each cell has a link leading to details.

This window shows the main report file, and it has links that bring up the detail pages. It's a table, with one row for every file you included in the report, and a column for each option you checked when you created the DDR. Each cell has a link leading to more details. To view the DDR later, go to where you saved it and then open the primary file, usually called "Summary," although you can name it whatever you wish at the time you create the DDR. (You also see a folder named for each file you selected when you created the DDR.)

On the overview page, the DDR tells you which elements you chose when you created the DDR. If you click a file name, then you see the file detail page (Figure 14-14), with lots of information about that file. The links in each column go to the same file detail page, but each link scrolls you to the relevant section. On large databases with lots of fields, this option can save you a lot of time scrolling through the page, looking for what you want. For instance, if you click the number in the Relationships column, you see the Relationships section of the file detail page.

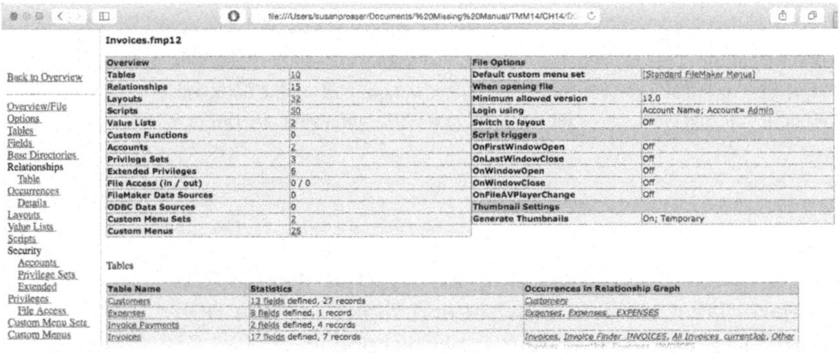

FIGURE 14-14

On the Report Overview page, when you click the File Name link, you see this page. The top link on the left leads back to the Overview page. All the others just scroll the page to various important parts. The report itself is also loaded with links. You can click any link to go to more details about that item.

Getting the Most from the DDR

At first glance, you may not appreciate the true value of the DDR. It appears to tell you the same things you can find out in other FileMaker windows, like Manage Database, Script Workspace, and so on. But once you run your first DDR, you understand it has vistas those windows never dreamed of.

For example, the DDR information for a script helps you determine how the script functions in and interacts with the rest of the database. In a neat chart, you can see every field, layout, table, table occurrence, and custom function the script uses.

More importantly, you can see every script or layout button that runs this script. That kind of information would be very hard to nail down without the DDR. You'd basically have to go to each layout in your database, click anything that might be a button, and see if the script you're interested in is attached to it.

If you've created custom menus, you'd have to check them individually, too. The DDR gathers up all that information for you—not just for scripts, but for tables, layouts, value lists, and other kinds of database elements as well.

Use the DDR to help you figure out what parts of your database can safely be edited or deleted. Since you can so easily create tables, fields, and layouts in FileMaker, you may well end up with extras that you don't need when your database reaches completion. You can make your database easier to understand, and more efficient, by deleting these extra elements. But even if a database is the last word in efficiency, running a DDR is one of the best ways to trace the designer's thinking process.

To see if—and how—a particular element is used, look at its detail. Suppose you have a bunch of fields you'd like to delete from your database, and you want to find out whether it's safe to do so. First, click the Tables link; fields are part of tables. You see a list of tables, with information about how many fields each table contains, along with a list of occurrences of each table in the Relationships graph (Figure 14-14). Click the link for a table's fields, and you see a list of all the fields in that table.

Details appear in the Field Name, Type, and Options columns for every field. Comments, if there are any, show up in the Comments column. Any layouts or scripts that use the field are listed in the On Layouts and In Scripts columns, respectively. You see the information in the "In Relationships" column only if it's a key field. Fields used in layouts, relationships, and scripts are called *dependencies* of those elements.

NOTE Even if you don't use a "Go to Field" script step for a specific field, a field may be listed in the scripts column or any other step that uses a relationship, also requires the use of that relationship's key field, so it also has that field as a dependency.

Finding Broken Elements with the DDR

Suppose you've deleted a field, unaware that it's used in a script. Your script could be run numerous times, not *quite* working, without your knowledge. The DDR is a great way to check for errors like this. Say, for example, you unwittingly delete a field used in a script. If you open the script to edit it, then you can see the words "<Field Missing>" right in the script:

```
Set Field [Expenses::<Field Missing>; "==" & Get ( ScriptParameter )]
```

To spot every error like this, though, you have to open every script and read through it. FileMaker has no facility to let you search through your scripts.

But you *can* search the DDR page in your web browser. (Pressing Ctrl+F or ⌘-F does the trick in most browsers.) In the Find field, type the text you're looking for and then click Next (or whatever button your browser uses) to start the search. You see the first instance of your search criteria highlighted. Click the button again to find other instances.

The whole list of errors you might search for appears below. If you have any inkling what kind of error you're looking for, start with that one:

- **<unknown>.** This is a catch-all for lost references.
- **<Missing Field>.** Referenced field is missing.
- **<Missing Table Occurrence>.** Referenced table occurrence set is missing.
- **<Missing Base Table>.** Referenced base table is missing.

- **<Missing File Reference>.** Referenced file reference is missing.

- **<Missing Layout>.** Referenced layout is missing.

- **<Missing Valuelist>.** Referenced value list is missing.

- **<Missing Custom Function>.** Referenced custom function is missing.

- **<Missing Script>.** Referenced script is missing.

- **<Missing Account>.** Referenced account is missing.

- **<Missing Privilege Set>.** Referenced privilege set is missing.

- **<Missing Extended Privilege>.** Referenced extended privilege is missing.

- **<Missing Custom Menu>.** Referenced custom menu is missing.

- **<Missing Custom Menu Set>.** Referenced custom menu set is missing.

Once you find a broken element, return to your database and then fix it manually. The DDR doesn't update itself to show your fix until you run another one. And since you can't mark up the electronic version of your DDR, a good way to keep track of your work is to print it out and then mark off each item as you fix it. Then, when all the broken elements are fixed (or you've deleted all the unused stuff), run another DDR. This time it should be clean, but if it's not, you've got the tools to fix it.

An Ounce of Prevention

Why use the DDR to fix your mistakes when you can prevent them in the first place? Here's a technique you can use next time you want to delete a field, script, layout, or any other important element. If you're not completely certain you don't need the element, you can use the DDR to check for you.

First, in FileMaker, *rename* every element you plan to delete. Put something noticeable and consistent in each name. For example, you might put "TO_BE_DELETED" before each element's name.

Once you've renamed every doomed element, run a fresh DDR. Choose the HTML type. When the report is finished, search it for the code words you put in each name ("TO_BE_DELETED," in this example). FileMaker should find each element you've marked for deletion. But it also finds this element in the list of dependencies if it's still in use. For example, a field you're pondering deleting might show up in a script. Unless that script is also marked for deletion, you have a situation you need to investigate further. Once you're sure the things you're deleting aren't used by anything else, you can delete them with confidence.

■ Custom Functions

No FileMaker feature is quite so pervasive as the calculation. Calculations show up in field definitions, scripts, custom menus, security settings, and conditional formatting. Chapters 10, 11, and 12 are all about employing FileMaker's calculation engine to manipulate your data. But FileMaker Pro Advanced lets you take calculations to a whole new place.

Functions are the primary building blocks of a calculation. Many calculations use two or three of FileMaker's 250 or so built-in functions. But as your databases grow more complex, you'll inevitably find yourself using some of the same calculations over and over again. Enter the custom function. With a custom function, you can centralize oft-used calculations and avoid rewriting them (and introducing errors) again and again. Better still, if you have to make a change to your calculation weeks or months after it was created, you won't have to track down and modify it in every place you used it. Just change the custom function, and the update ripples through your database instantly

You create custom functions in the Manage Custom Functions dialog box (Figure 14-15). Custom functions have to follow the same syntax as FileMaker's regular functions. That is, you provide a name and, optionally, one or more parameters.

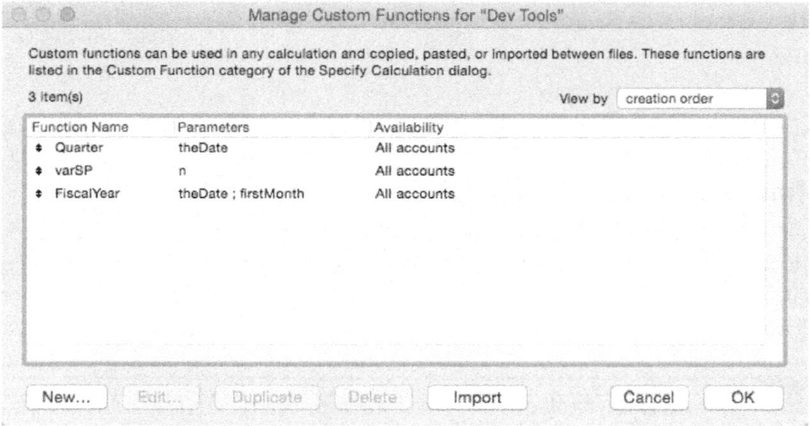

FIGURE 14-15

The Manage Custom Functions window (File→Manage→Custom Functions) shows a list of any custom functions you've defined, plus buttons for creating, editing, duplicating, deleting, or importing custom functions. Sort the list by making a choice from the "View by" pop-up menu. Click OK to save all your changes or Cancel to close the window and ignore any changes you've made.

Rules for custom function names and their parameters are similar to the rules for naming tables and fields. Specifically, function and parameter names may not:

- Contain + - * / ^ & = ≠ < > ≤ ≥ (, ;) [ ] " :: $ {}

- Contain AND, OR, XOR, NOT

- Begin with a digit or period

- Have the same name as another function, parameter, or keyword

If you violate any of these rules, FileMaker shows you a warning message. Unlike the slight leeway you get with table and field names, the program doesn't let you finish creating your custom function until you comply with the naming rules. You're safest sticking with alphanumeric characters.

Once you've created them, you can see Custom Functions in a special category of the Specify Calculation window's functions list (Figure 14-16).

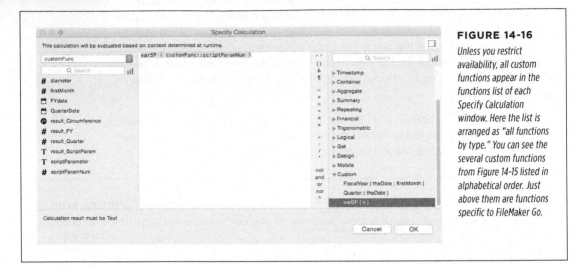

FIGURE 14-16

Unless you restrict availability, all custom functions appear in the functions list of each Specify Calculation window. Here the list is arranged as "all functions by type." You can see the several custom functions from Figure 14-15 listed in alphabetical order. Just above them are functions specific to FileMaker Go.

Defining a Custom Function

To get started, you'll add a new function that can calculate the circumference of a circle. Since a circumference is derived by multiplying the circle's diameter by pi, it makes sense to use the words "circumference" and "diameter" in your function. That way, your formula will be easy for other people to use later.

NOTE You may not actually need to calculate circumferences in your own databases much, but this example shows important concepts common to creating any custom function. Plus, it's easier to type than most real-world examples. See this chapter's sample file, *CH14 Dev Tools.fmp12*, on this book's Missing CD page at *www.missingmanuals.com/cds/fmp14mm* for other examples.

1. **In FileMaker Pro Advanced, choose File→Manage→Custom Functions.**

   The Manage Customer Functions window appears. If you've never created your own function before, the list is blank.

2. **Click the New button.**

   The Edit Custom Function window appears. You can see it in Figure 14-17.

3. **In the Function Name box, type *Circumference*.**

   You've just given your function a name, which you'll call upon later when you want to use this function in calculations.

4. **In the Function Parameters box, type *diameter* and then click the Add Parameter button.**

   FileMaker moves "diameter" into the parameter list.

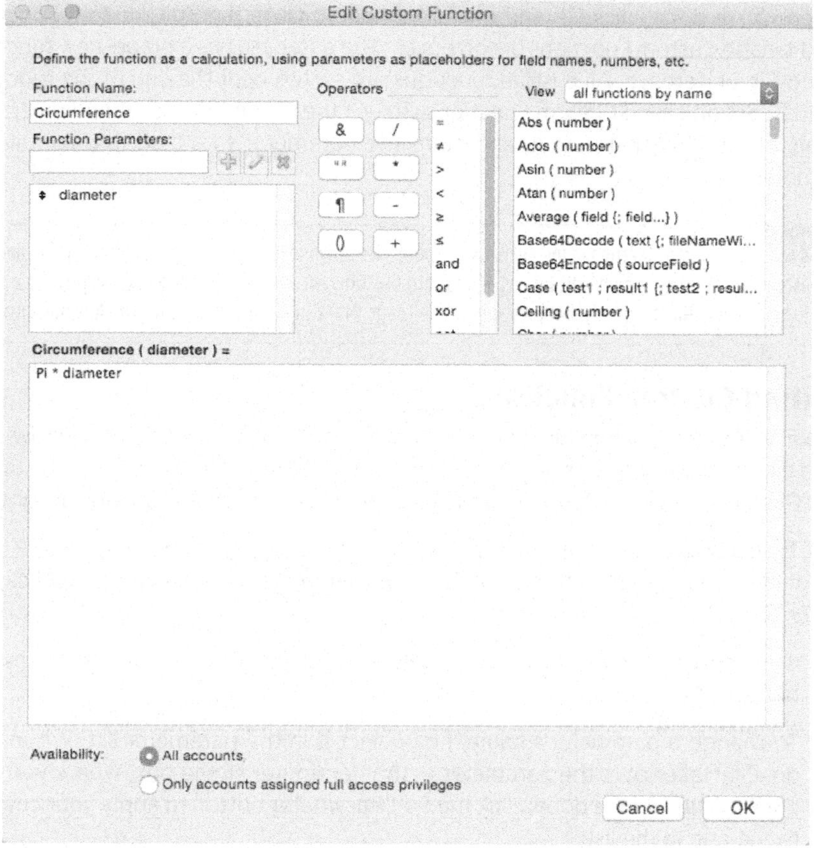

FIGURE 14-17

The Edit Custom Function dialog box is similar to the regular calculation dialog box, but where Specify Calculation shows tables and fields, Edit Custom Function has spaces for the name of the function and its parameters.

TIP When you add more than one parameter to the Function Parameters list, you can use the arrow icon by each item to move it up or down in the list. The order here is important: It determines the order in which you want the parameters appear when you write a calcuation that uses the new custom function.

---

5. **From the View pop-up menu (above the function list), choose "Trigono-metric functions."**

   The function list changes to show just the relevant options.

6. **In the function list, double-click the `Pi` function and then click the * operator button (or type *).**

   The function calculation area now reads `Pi  *`.

7. **Finally, in the parameter list, double-click** `diameter`.

FileMaker adds the word `diameter` to the end of the calculation, like so: `Pi *`
`diameter`.

When you're done, click OK and then OK again to close the Edit Custom Function
and Manage Custom Functions dialog boxes. The database has a brand-new function
called Circumference. All custom functions are sorted near the end of the function
list in a section called Custom Functions. To use the Circumference function, create
a calculation field that uses it, and point the parameter to a field that contains a
diameter value.

> **NOTE**   The standard setting in the Availability options lets anyone who accesses your database see and use
> the custom function in her own calculations. If you turn on "Only accounts assigned full access privileges," the
> function still works for everybody, but only superusers (page 744) can see the function in the functions list.

Editing Custom Functions

To edit an existing custom function, open the Manage Custom Functions window, and
then either double-click its name, or select it from the list and then click Edit. In the
Edit Custom Function window, you can modify the definition of a function as follows:

- Type a new name in the Function Name field to change a function's name. You
  can add new parameters: Type the new parameter's name and then click the
  + button.

- If you no longer need a parameter, select it and then click the Delete Parameter
  button (X).

- To change a parameter's name, first select it in the parameter list. When you
  do, FileMaker puts the parameter in the Parameter Name box, where you can
  edit it. When you're done, click the Edit Parameter button to apply your change
  to the one in the list.

- You can reorder parameters by dragging them up or down in the list.

> **NOTE**   Be careful adding, reordering, or deleting parameters for an existing function. If the function is being
> used in a calculation somewhere, then that calculation breaks because it no longer passes the parameters in the
> right number. On the other hand, it's safe to *rename* a function or its parameters—FileMaker updates any existing
> calculations when you do.

- If you click Duplicate, then FileMaker makes an exact copy of the selected function. That way, you can use a custom function as a starting point for creating
  a new one.

- If you don't need a function anymore, select it and then click Delete.

NOTE Unlike built-in functions, custom functions can be *recursive*, meaning a custom function can run itself repeatedly until a given condition has been met. To learn about recursion, find yourself a nice, quiet place where you can concentrate, and skip ahead to page 691.

Sharing Custom Functions

Custom functions are created in individual FileMaker database files. So if you've come up with a custom function you want to reuse in another database, you'll have to move it. As with tables, fields, and scripts, you can either import custom functions or use copy and paste.

WARNING Whichever method you choose for sharing Custom Functions among databases, be certain to test each function at its new location. Custom functions can reference other custom functions, but if you copy or import one custom function without the others it relies on, *FileMaker doesn't warn you of your omission.* It does, however, comment out the imported function's calculation, a sure sign something is awry. As you bring custom functions into a new file, select each one in the Manage Custom Functions dialog box and then click Edit. If you see the calculation wrapped in /* comment markers */ you've got a missing reference to track down.

The Manage Custom Functions dialog box sports an Import button: It's the third button from the right. Click Import and then select another FileMaker database file. The Import Custom Functions dialog box appears (Figure 14-18). It lists all of the custom functions in the selected database. Simply turn on the ones you'd like to bring into the current database file and then click OK.

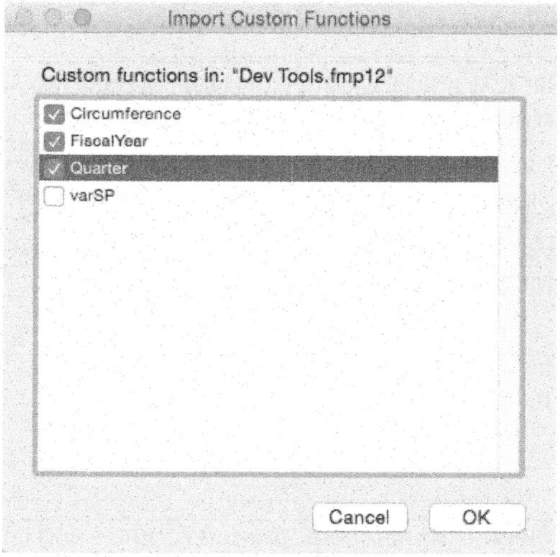

FIGURE 14-18

Select the custom functions you need and then click OK. As whenever you import structural elements, check your imported functions to make sure that no references have broken. If you have a repertoire of custom functions you frequently use, consider keeping them all in one database and importing them into your new databases as needed.

Building on Custom Functions

You can use custom functions just like any of FileMaker's built-in functions. When you're in the Specify Calculation window, choose Custom Functions from the View pop-up menu to access the functions you've made. (When you create a custom function, you're adding it to the FileMaker file you're working in. It isn't available in other files unless you add it to them as well.)

Just like other functions, custom functions can also use other custom functions to do their job.

For example, if you want to add a new function that calculates the surface area of a cylinder, then it can take two parameters (diameter and height) and use your custom Circumference function, like so:

    Circumference (diameter) * Height

With this in mind, you can create functions that build upon one another—to keep each one simple, or to provide different but related capabilities.

The second, secret way to move custom functions is to simply copy and paste. If you select one or more functions and then press Ctrl+C (⌘-C), the custom function, along with all its parameters, is copied to your computer's Clipboard. You can then click OK, switch to another database file, choose File→Manage→Custom Functions to open the Manage Custom Functions dialog box, and then press Ctrl+V (⌘-V) to add the function to that file.

Think Locally, Share Globally

There's a world of FileMaker developers out there, and chances are that one of them has already written the custom function you need, or at least one like it. Here are a couple websites where you can search custom functions created by others in the FileMaker community and share your creations, too.

The oldest depository of custom functions is at: *www.briandunning.com/filemaker-custom-functions/*.

The folks running fmfunctions.com have an entire website dedicated to custom functions: *www.fmfunctions.com*.

A terrific all-around resource, fmforums.com, has a modest library of custom functions available: *http://fmforums.com*.

FileMaker Today, another discussion website, offers a custom function thread: *http://filemakertoday.com*.

■ Custom Menus

FileMaker's menus are all about power. Through them, you can control—and limit—people's access to the whole feature set. As the developer, you need all those commands to do the design and development of your database. But some commands give too much power to people, particularly to folks who don't have much computer experience or who aren't shy about experimenting with commands they don't completely understand.

With FileMaker Pro Advanced, you can completely customize the menus people see. You can remove the Delete All Records and the Replace Field Contents commands for everyone, or you can remove them from only certain people's privilege sets. If you're the type of developer who likes to take charge of the onscreen display, custom menus are your dream come true.

Here are just a few of the things you can do:

- Remove potentially destructive items from menus: Delete All Records, for example.

- Edit menu commands: Like changing Modify Last Find to read Repeat Last Find.

- Add, edit, or remove keyboard shortcuts: If you can't remember that Ctrl+S (⌘-S) does *not* mean Save in FileMaker, then you can at least prevent that pesky Sort dialog box from popping up every time.

- Remove entire menus, like the Window menu, which can be confusing for folks new to FileMaker Pro.

- Run a script from a new or edited menu item: Substitute a custom Delete Record script (complete with a custom warning) for FileMaker's normal Delete Record command.

- Change menus when a user changes layout: Create a special menu that runs commands or scripts that pertain to invoices and shows up only on the Invoice layout.

- Make one set of menus for Mac and another for Windows.

- Make menu sets that match privilege sets: Give people with administrative privileges a special menu showing the scripts only they can run.

You can create and edit custom menus only in FileMaker Pro Advanced, but anyone can use them. These menus don't transfer to files you publish on the Web, though (Chapter 21). When you create custom menus for a database, you may want to provide a user guide or similar documentation explaining what your custom commands do, since people can't look up the commands you add in FileMaker's help system.

You can use custom menus to supplement, and even go beyond, privilege set features. For example, if you want to limit data entry people to using the copy and paste buttons that run your scripts, then remove the Edit menu for people with that privilege set. They can't use keyboard shortcuts to cut, copy, or paste. Removing the View menu prevents the Mode pop-up menu, toolbar, and all related keyboard shortcuts from working. (But you need to do some work providing replacement commands in your buttons and menus.)

NOTE As powerful as custom menus are, they're no substitute for good security practices, as discussed in Chapter 19. For example, just because you don't see a Delete command right in front of your face doesn't mean you can't delete records. For example, if you turn off the ability to delete records by using only custom menus but forget to attach your menu set to a particular layout, FileMaker's standard menus, including Delete Record, will be present and available. If you need to prevent someone from doing something, *you must restrict it by privilege set.*

Tricky Terminology

The terms used in creating custom menus can be very similar, but they mean very specific things. Just in case it gets a little confusing, this mini-glossary and Figure 14-19 should help keep things straight.

- **Custom menus** refers generally to FileMaker Pro Advanced's ability to create your own menus.

- A **custom menu** *set* is a complete group of menus (like File, Edit, View).

- A **custom menu** is just one of the individual menus that comprise a custom menu set.

- A **custom menu item** is the thing you actually choose from the custom menu. FileMaker provides three types:

  - The **command** is the most common. When selected it performs some kind of action.

  - A **separator** is simply a horizontal line used to group similar commands within a given custom menu.

  - A **submenu** is like a custom menu nested within a custom menu. You can add menu items to a submenu that appears onscreen only when the submenu is selected.

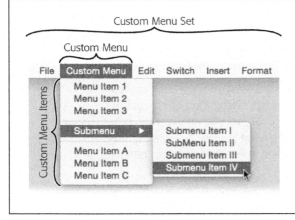

FIGURE 14-19

FileMaker lets you create all kinds of custom menu items. The process of creating custom menus is relatively straightforward; not so the terms for the items that make up your custom menus. Here's a handy cheat sheet for the terms you'll need.

Editing a Menu

All new files use FileMaker's standard menu set until you tell them to use a custom set. Every new file comes with one set of custom menus that you can edit to suit your needs. Some items are in brackets; they can't be edited or duplicated, but you're free to create new menus with the same name and customize them.

In this exercise in customizing menus, you want to remove menu items that may confuse people. When people are just learning FileMaker, simplified menus are less intimidating than masses of unfamiliar commands. You can also help protect your database from damage by someone unwittingly choosing the wrong command. You start the process by editing the View menu so that only a few items show up:

1. **Open the example file *Dev Tools.fmp12* and choose File→Manage→Custom Menus and then click the Custom Menus tab.**

   You can see this in Figure 14-20.

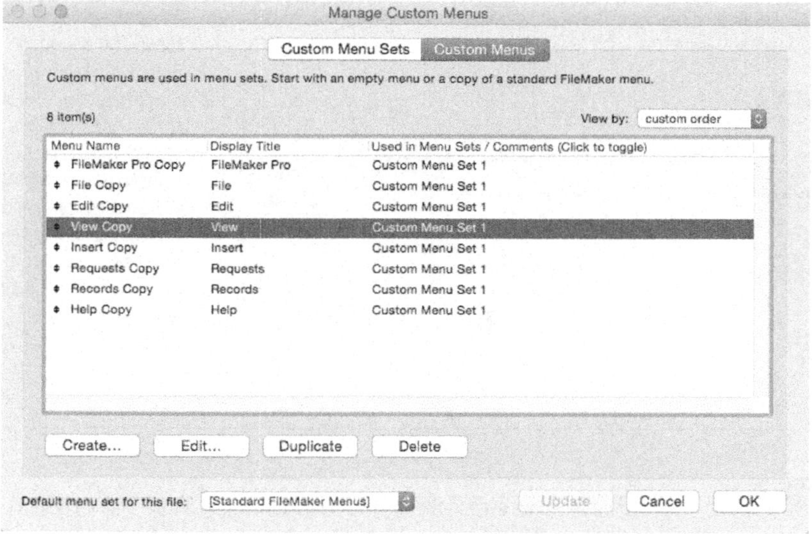

FIGURE 14-20

You can sort the items in the Custom Menu list with the "View by" pop-up menu. You can also click each of the column headers to sort the list. This window's most important item is the small pop-up menu at the bottom that determines when the custom menu set loads. If you forget to load the custom set, no one will ever see it.

2. **Click "View copy" and then click Edit. Or you can double-click an item to edit it.**

   The Edit Custom Menu window appears (Figure 14-21). Here you tell the custom menu what it should look like and how it should behave.

3. **Select the radio button beside the Override Title field and then, in the field, type *Switch*.**

   The Override Title option changes what someone sees in his menu bar. You changed it to Switch since the word "View" is too vague for beginners. Plus, you don't want them getting confused if they pick up FileMaker's manual (or this book) for help. The changed menu name should clue people in that they need to look at your custom documentation for help.

   The menu's name *in this dialog box* remains View Copy; that's how you know it originated from the normal View menu, not from scratch.

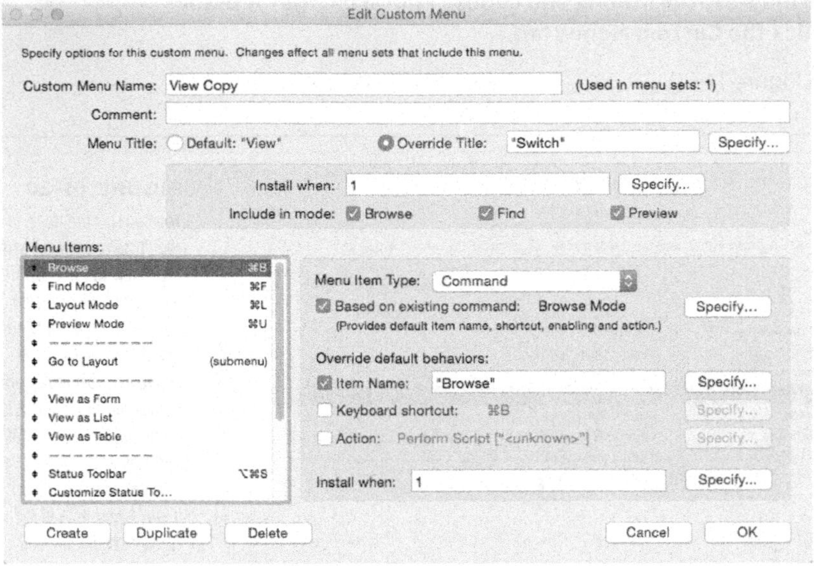

FIGURE 14-21

The Edit Custom Menu dialog box is jammed with options. Work from top to bottom to make sense of it. Among the best choices: You can specify that a menu appears only when someone is on a Mac, or only when she's in Find mode. You can add, change, or remove keyboard shortcuts. You can delete commands entirely. The most powerful choice is to replace a command's normal action with a script.

WARNING   If you customize menus even in the slightest, consider turning off the built-in Help menu as well. It opens FileMaker's online help file, which can't answer people's questions about *your* custom menus. If you need documentation, then you can add your own Help menu that leads people to the custom-crafted help on your website, for instance.

4. **Select the dashed line in the Menu Items list just below "Go to Layout (sub-menu)" and then press Shift as you select the last item in the list. Click the Delete button. Select Layout mode and then delete it too.**

   All highlighted items disappear when you click the Delete button (those hyphens represent divider lines in menus). You should be left with three mode menu items, a divider, and a "Go to Layout" menu (a total of five items) remaining in the list.

5. **Click the Browse mode menu item. Turn on the Item Name checkbox in the "Override default behaviors" section and then change the title to "Browse."**

   This menu item title replaces the text that appears in the list. People see a command called "Browse", not Browse mode. Notice the quotation marks around "Browse." If you forget (or refuse) to type the quotes, FileMaker obstinately puts them back in for you. This behavior is your indication that FileMaker considers that text a character string, and that's a further cue that the Specify button gives you access to the Calculation dialog box.

6. **Repeat the previous step for Find mode, Preview mode, and "Go to Layout."
   Change Find mode's title to "Find," change Preview mode's title to "Print
   Preview," and then change the title of "Go to Layout" to "Show." When
   you've made these changes, click OK.**

   Use terms that folks can easily comprehend. Most people already understand
   what Print Preview does, but Preview mode's meaning is a little murky.

7. **From the "Default menu set for this file" pop-up menu, choose "Custom
   Menu Set 1" and then click OK.**

   You've just told FileMaker to display the customized version of your View menu.

   The View menu now says "Switch." When you click it, you see four choices and
   one separator. Notice that the Edit Layout button is grayed out, and Layout mode
   has disappeared from the Layout pop-up menu at the bottom of your screen.

By editing menus to suppress items that might confuse those who haven't had in-
depth FileMaker training, you've made your database a friendlier place to work. But
don't stop there: In the next section, you'll learn how to create menus that show lists
of commands, like your scripts, that you *do* want people to see.

Creating a New Menu

Using the steps described in the previous tutorial, you can edit FileMaker's menus to
your heart's content, renaming them and deleting extraneous commands to make
room for new ones. If you don't necessarily want to delete any existing menus or
commands, or even if you do, you can always create *additional* menus from scratch.

1. **In Manage Custom Menus, select the Custom Menus tab and then click Create. In the Create Custom Menu window that appears, choose "Start with
   an empty menu." Click OK.**

   If an existing menu is similar to what you need, you can use it as a template
   when you create new menus. But in this case, you don't need any existing menu
   commands because you'll attach your scripts to a new menu. When you click
   OK, the Edit Custom Menu window appears, like Figure 14-21 but without any
   menu items just yet.

2. **In the Custom Menu Name field, type *Invoices*. Also type *Invoices* in the
   Override Title field.**

   Since you started with an empty menu, FileMaker assumes you want a custom
   name. If you don't type a name, then the word "Untitled" appears in your menu bar.

3. **Next to "Include in mode" uncheck Find and Preview.**

   You don't want your scripts run from either Find or Preview modes, so by telling the menu not to even *show up* in those modes, you're adding another layer
   of security.

4. **Click the Create button.**

   In the set of options that appears to the right, confirm that Menu Item Type is set to Command.

5. **Turn on the Item Name checkbox and then type *Create invoice for unbilled expenses*. Turn on the Action checkbox.**

   The Specify Script Step dialog box appears.

6. **Select Perform Script and then click Specify. Select the script named "Create Invoice for Job" and then click OK. Click OK once more to close the Specify Script Step dialog box.**

   To add more commands to this menu, repeat the last three steps until you've created a new menu command for each script you want to make available. The arrows to the left of each item let you rearrange them.

   To add a divider line between groups of menu commands, click Create and then set the Menu Item Type to Separator.

7. **When you've created all the commands you wish to include in your new Invoices menu, click OK.**

   You have to include your shiny new Invoices menu in a custom menu set in order to use it.

8. **In the Manage Custom Menus dialog box, click the Custom Menu Sets tab. Select "Custom Menu Set 1" in the list and then click Edit.**

   The Edit Custom Menu Set window appears.

9. **Click Add. Down at the bottom of the menu list, you'll find Invoices (Figure 14-22). Click it and then click Select.**

   "Invoices" appears at the bottom of the Custom Menu Set menu list.

10. **To the left of the Invoices menu, click that little double arrow and then drag it up until it's positioned between Records Copy and [Scripts].**

11. **Click OK until you're back in your database.**

    The Invoices custom menu is now a part of the new custom menu set, and it appears between the Records and Scripts menus of Figure 14-23.

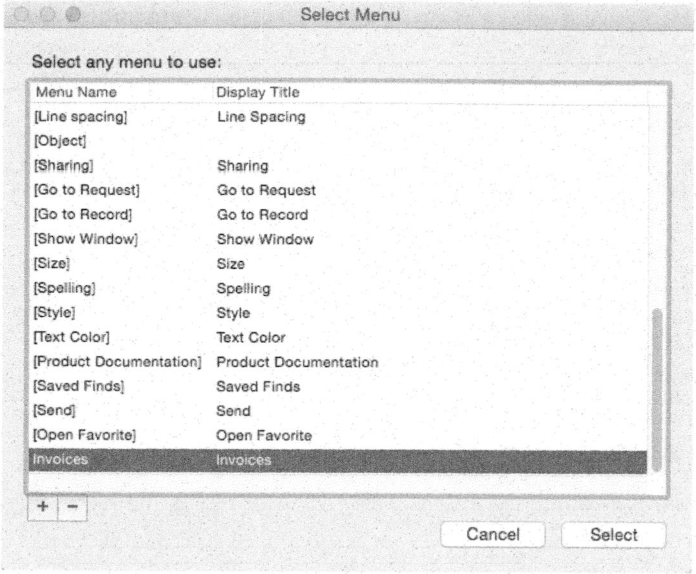

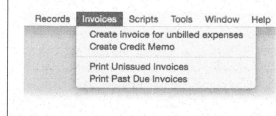

FIGURE 14-22

When you select a menu to add to your custom menu set, FileMaker's built-in (and unchangeable) menus appear in square brackets: [ ]. Custom menus are unencumbered.

FIGURE 14-23

This custom menu has two menu items for creating invoices and two for printing with a separator between them. The separator appears as a row of hyphens in the Edit Custom Menu dialog box, but it appears in the actual menu as a clean horizontal line.

Using Existing Commands

While there's great power in attaching scripts to custom menu items, if you just need a menu item that's already in FileMaker's standard menu set, you can save yourself the trouble of writing a script for it. When you're creating or editing a menu item in the Edit Custom Menu dialog box, try turning on the "Based on existing command" checkbox. FileMaker offers up a list of all the built-in menu items, along with the menu where each one typically resides. Figure 14-24 depicts the process. When you select an existing command, your menu item is automatically imbued with the same name, keyboard shortcut, and behaviors as the original it's based on. That's handy, but you're free to customize those settings as much as you see fit.

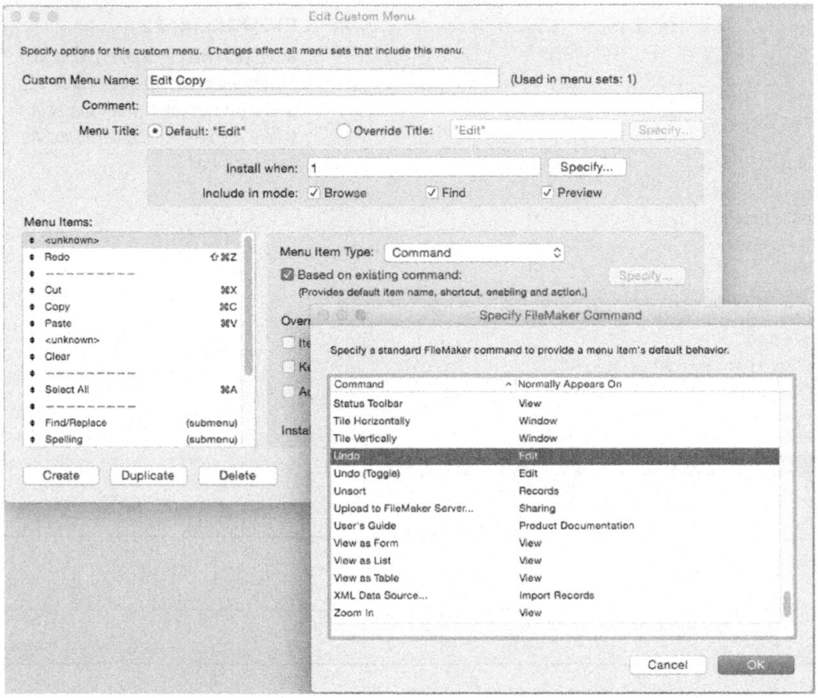

FIGURE 14-24

The Specify FileMaker Command dialog box (front) automatically pops up when you turn on "Based on existing command" (highlighted in the background) in the Edit Custom Menu dialog box.

Examine the list of existing commands closely, and you'll find that one command has a blank space in the "Normally appears on" column. FileMaker's Quick Find feature comes with a Perform Quick Find command that isn't available in any standard menu. But you can use it in a custom menu item to let your database's users trigger a Quick Find.

Submenus

If a custom menu starts getting too lengthy, you can use submenus to consolidate its options. A submenu is a custom menu nested within a custom menu. (Flip back to Figure 14-19 to see an example of a submenu.) Creating a submenu is a combination of two things you already know how to do: making a custom menu and adding a menu item.

Say, for example, you have a custom menu called Reports, and you want one class of reports—call them "TPS Reports"—to appear in a submenu. You can do this example in any FileMaker database you'd like. First, create a new custom menu, using the steps on page 570, and then add a menu item for each report you want in the submenu. Click OK when you're finished.

1. **Back in the Manage Custom Menus dialog box, select the custom menu in which you want the submenu to reside and then click Edit.**

   The Edit Custom Menu dialog box appears.

2. **Click Create to add a new menu item, and set the Menu Item Type to Submenu (Figure 14-25). Then click the Specify button immediately below Menu Item Type.**

   The Select Menu dialog box appears with a list of all the built-in menus and those you've created.

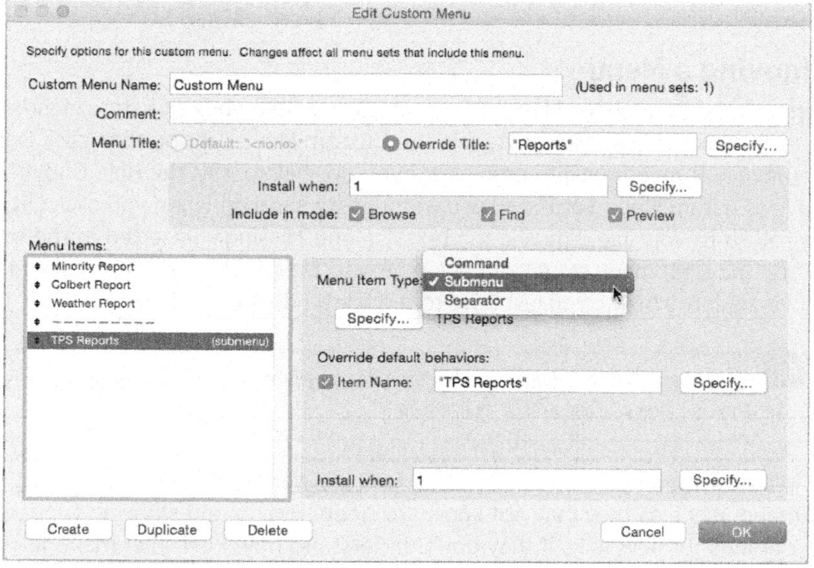

FIGURE 14-25

Adding a submenu is as simple as setting the Menu Item Type to Submenu. You have to create that submenu as a custom menu first. Only then can you add it as a Submenu.

3. **Scroll down to the bottom of the list to locate the "TPS Reports" custom menu you just created, and double-click it. Click OK to return to the Manage Custom Menus dialog box.**

4. **Select the Custom Menu Sets tab and add your Reports menu to your custom menu set.**

5. **Click OK until you're back to your database window.**

   With your custom menu set active, you'll see your new submenu, like the one in Figure 14-26.

So far, you've simplified one of FileMaker's menus and created a custom menu from scratch. Now you need to get rid of a menu that strikes fear in the hearts of even experienced FileMaker users: You're going to *completely* suppress the Window menu.

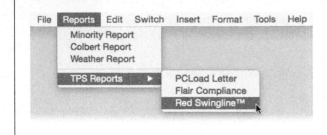

FIGURE 14-26

A submenu is simply a custom menu nested inside another custom menu. When judiciously applied, submenus can help keep menu commands organized and accessible. That way, if you've got four bosses, each of whom needs three different TPS reports, you could go ahead and come into the office on Saturday, or you could group them neatly into subfolders and knock off work early.

Removing a Menu

At first glance through the Manage Custom Menus dialog box's Custom Menus tab, you may think you just click an item in the Custom Menu list and then click Delete to remove it. But you run into problems if you do. Delete, say, the Help Copy menu used in "Custom Menu Set 1" and you get a nasty surprise when you click OK and then return to your file. You see the text "<Menu Missing>" inserted in the menu bar, and the Help menu stays right where it was. Despite these obstacles, you *can* remove an entire menu; you just have to dig a little deeper to do it.

> **NOTE** You can troubleshoot a file for missing menu items by running a DDR (page 557) or by checking Get(LastError) after you load a menu set in a script.

The Window menu can cause problems for new people. For example, the Show command lists files they may not know are open. Hiding and showing windows is also perilous for new folks if they don't understand how FileMaker manages windows. Instead of bothering people with stuff they don't need to know, you can just suppress this menu entirely by removing it from the menu bar.

1. **In the Manage Custom Menus dialog box, click the Custom Menu Sets tab. Select "Custom Menu Set 1" and then click Edit.**

   The Edit Menu Set dialog box appears.

2. **In the Menu Set Name field, type *Data Entry*.**

   This descriptive name helps you remember the menu set's purpose. Optionally, type additional information in the Comment box.

3. **In the "Menus in 'Data Entry'" list, click the "[Window]" menu. Click Remove and then click OK until you're back in your database.**

Back in your database, the Window menu is gone entirely from the menu bar. This menu configuration is ideal for your data entry people, but not so great for people with administrative privileges, who understand the Window menu and use it all the time. Read on to find out how to tailor *sets* of menus for people with different privilege levels.

Hiding or Showing a Menu by Calculation

You've already seen how to choose which mode a menu appears in and how to make it go away entirely. But if you really want to get fancy about when to show a menu, you can do it with a *calculation*. In "Custom Menu Set 1," there's a menu called FileMaker Pro Copy. Double-click that menu to open the Edit Custom Menu dialog box (Figure 14-27). Halfway down, you see a text box labeled "Install when:" Here's where FileMaker looks to decide whether or not to display the menu. If you always want the menu to be displayed, put a *1* in there. When your needs are more complex, enter a calculation that resolves to a zero when you want the menu hidden, or any non-zero value when the menu should appear. In the case of our FileMaker Pro Copy menu, the calculation uses a Get(SystemPlatform) function to determine whether the database is running on Mac or Windows. If it's a Mac, the menu is displayed; otherwise it's suppressed.

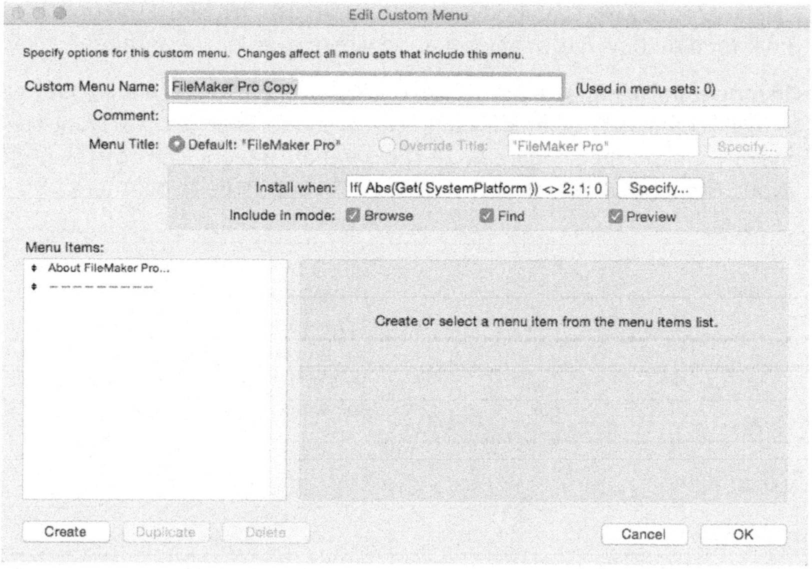

FIGURE 14-27

The "Install when" box determines when a menu is displayed onscreen. It applies to the whole menu, and you can't use it to toggle its constituent menu items.

The key to writing calculations here is that the result must be Boolean. If the calculation result is blank or the number zero, then the menu will not be displayed. If the calculation result is 1, -42, chai, or *anything* else, the menu will appear onscreen.

> **WARNING** Never leave the "Install when" calculation blank; an empty calculation means your custom menu won't ever display. When creating a new menu, FileMaker sets the calculation to "1" so it always displays by default, but it won't display a warning if you clear the calculation and save the menu.

Installing Custom Menu Sets

FileMaker Pro Advanced lets you create a set of custom menus and use it as the *standard* for a file, meaning everyone who uses your database sees it, every time. But since the people using your database may have different levels of skill (and trustworthiness), you may want your custom menus to adapt accordingly. In fact, if you've read this book's chapters on layouts and privilege sets, you have all the tools you need to make the right menus appear to the right people at the right time. It's a simple matter of assigning menu sets to these existing features. You can conceal certain menus and commands from people who don't need them, but keep them available for everybody else. Or maybe you just want menu items to show up when they make sense for the active layout.

Once you've created menu sets by using the steps outlined earlier in this chapter, you can install them in any of several ways:

- **By calculation.** That's what you did in the tutorial on page 571. Unless you tell FileMaker otherwise, everybody sees the same custom menus. This option works great for a runtime file, or any situation where everyone is at the same level.

- **On individual layouts.** In this scenario, when someone switches layouts, either by menu command or through a script, the menu set changes to a layout-specific one of your choosing. Figure 14-28 shows where a menu can be attached to a layout; in Layout mode, choose Layouts→Layout Setup to get there.

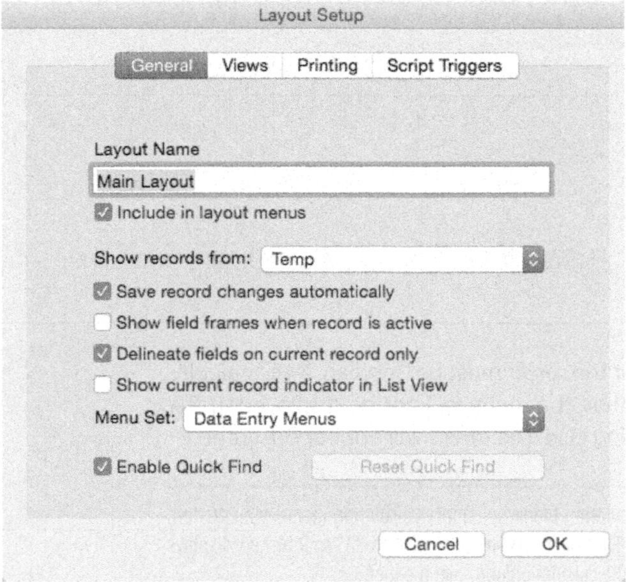

FIGURE 14-28

Custom menus can be tied to specific layouts. That way, you can control the features users have access to—give them only what they need to do the work and nothing that might get them into trouble.

- **By mode.** This option offers the ultimate in elegance. It lets you do things like create a set with only one menu and just a few items, and make it the *only* menu people see when they're in Find mode. Instead of a gaggle of buttons to perform and cancel finds, write the appropriate scripts, and display them in the one menu, short and sweet.

- **When a script is run.** By checking the privilege set in a script that runs when someone logs into your file, you can load a set of menus customized to that person's level of privilege. Use the Get(PrivilegeSetName) step to check privileges (page 777) and the Install Menu Set script step to specify which menu set installs. (If you have a re-login script, then you need to make sure the right menu set is installed each time people re-login.)

NOTE Since you're effectively removing features for people when you customize menus, thorough testing is a critical part of the process. Be sure to test menus with all affected layouts, privilege sets, and scripts, and across platforms. In FileMaker Pro Advanced, choose Tools→Custom Menus to switch among sets as you test them. If you get stuck, you can always get back to familiar ground by choosing Tools→Custom Menus→[Standard FileMaker Menus].

Developer Utilities

The Tools→Developer Utilities command looks insignificant and benign to the unsuspecting person, but behind it lurks a vast array of powerful features. You have developer utilities for the following techniques:

- Rename one file in a system of interconnected files, and have every file reference in the *other* files automatically update to the new name.

- Turn your database into a *kiosk* system. You can use this feature to make interactive programs that run on publicly accessible computers. In this setup, FileMaker hides the menu bars, the Windows taskbar or Macintosh Dock, and all other screen decorations that aren't part of your layouts.

- Create a *runtime solution*—a special version of your database that anyone can use, even if he doesn't have FileMaker Pro.

- Permanently remove full access to files so you can send your database to people you don't know, and be sure they can't tamper with your hard work, including your scripts, table and field definitions, and Relationships graph.

- Create an error log to help you troubleshoot problems that happen when FileMaker generates runtimes.

In fact, you can (and often want to) do several of these things at once. Here's an example: You build a beautiful interactive product catalog, complete with pictures and an easy-to-use ordering screen. You then want to set up a kiosk computer at a trade show where attendees can use the database to see what you have and place their orders. Using the developer utilities, you could do all this:

- Add "Kiosk" to the end of every file name, so you can keep this copy separate from the one you use in the office.

- Make the database run in Kiosk mode so people at the trade show can't exit FileMaker, switch to other programs, or otherwise cause mischief.

- Make the whole thing run by itself so you don't have to bother installing File-Maker on the computer you're renting just for this job.

- Lock out full access so if someone manages to steal a copy of your database while you're not looking, she can't see how it works or steal your product's beauty shots.

Using the Developer Utilities

Close your databases before you work with them. Then choose Tools→Developer Utilities. The Developer Utilities window appears (Figure 14-29).

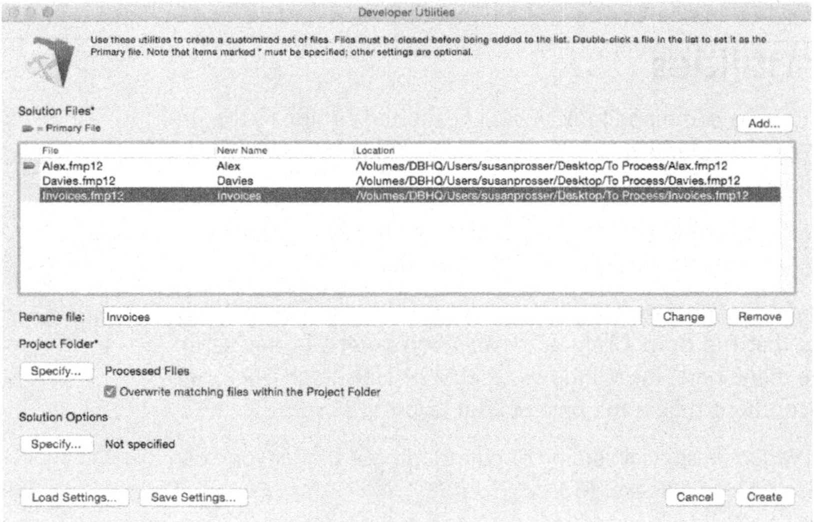

FIGURE 14-29

The Developer Utilities window (Tools→ Developer Utilities) lets you gather the files you want to change and then tell FileMaker what changes to make. When you're done, click Create, and FileMaker builds new versions of your files (in a new location) with all the changes in place.

In the Developer Utilities window, choose which files you want to work with. Click Add to put a file on the list. In the Open File dialog box, you can select several files at once by using your Shift and Ctrl (⌘) keystrokes. Keep on adding until every file you want to change is in the list. If you accidentally add the wrong file, select it and then click Remove.

You have to pick one file to be your *main* file, which really just means the one that opens first. Your navigation scripts can move between files if necessary. To set the main file, in the list, just double-click it. FileMaker shows a red icon by the main file.

■ RENAMING FILES

Of course, you can always rename a file in Windows Explorer or the Mac's Finder. But doing this lets you change *only* the file name. Developer Utilities makes that look like child's play. When it changes a file name, it also looks inside the file and updates any internal file references to match the file's new name. If you've ever tried to open two versions of a multiple file solution at the same time (to test some scripts that delete data on a copy of the files, say), then you know FileMaker sometimes gets confused and keeps multiple copies open even after you try to close one set. You can eliminate the crossover problem by renaming one set in Developer Utilities. You can test your scripts without a problem, since the scripts in the copied files automatically inherit the correct new file names.

To rename a file or set of files, add them to the Solution Files list. Select a file; in the "Rename file" box, type the new name and then click Change. FileMaker shows the new name in the New Name column.

Next, you need to pick the *project folder*. FileMaker saves the finished files in this folder. Under Project Folder, just click the Specify button and then pick any folder you wish. If the folder already contains files with the same names as the ones you're about to create, then you get an error message—unless you turn on "Overwrite matching files within the Project Folder." When you click Create, FileMaker Pro Advanced makes copies of the files with their new names, leaving the originals untouched.

■ CREATE RUNTIME SOLUTION APPLICATION(S)

To create runtime solutions, add the files to the Solution Files list and then select a project folder, just as you did above. Don't type a new name for the runtime in this window, though. Under Solution Options, click the Specify button. You see the Specify Solution Options dialog box, as shown in Figure 14-30.

When you tell FileMaker you want to build a runtime solution, it generates a special program you need to include with your databases. This program can do most of what FileMaker Pro can do, but it can't modify tables, fields, layouts, or scripts. You get to decide what this program is called—in the Runtime Name box, just type it. Along with the runtime program, FileMaker creates new copies of each of your files to go with it, and changes all the file name extensions to something other than .fmp12. Tell FileMaker which extension to use in the Extension field.

> **WARNING** Your computer's operating system uses filename extensions to figure out which program files belong to. The Developer Utilities let you assign any extension you want, but you should avoid common extensions like .doc, .jpg, .mp3, and so on. You know computers—they get confused easily.

The new files don't just have a new name; they're also modified internally so they're *bound* to the runtime program, and the runtime program in turn can open only properly bound files. In other words, when you send people a runtime program, they can't use it to open any other FileMaker Pro file.

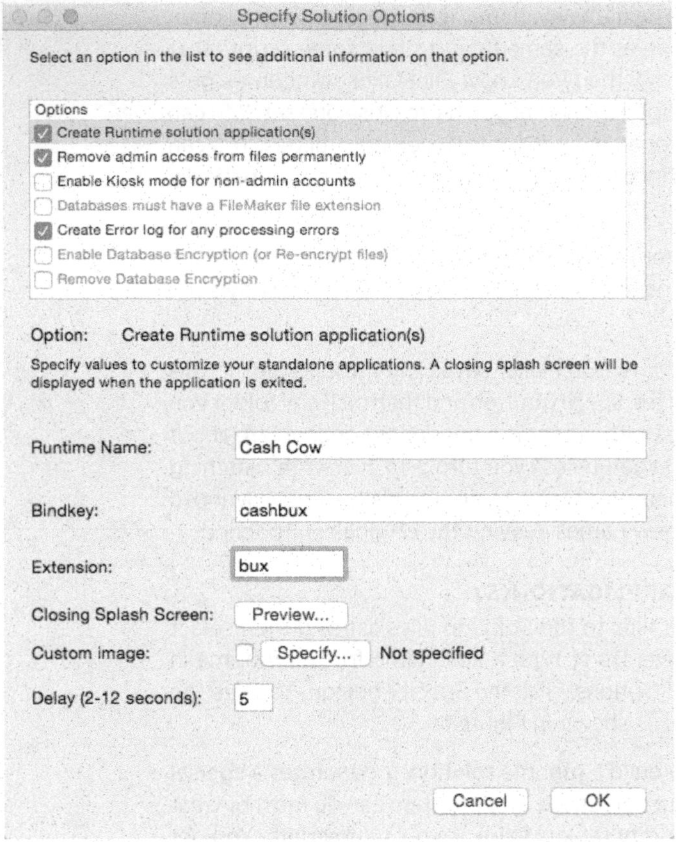

FIGURE 14-30

The Specify Solution Options window lets you tell FileMaker what you want done to the files. Turn on a checkbox in the options list to tell FileMaker you want that thing done to your files. Most options need to be configured, and when you select an item in the list, the bottom half of the window lets you change the appropriate settings.

To facilitate the binding process, FileMaker asks you to provide a *bindkey.* FileMaker stores this value in both the runtime program and any database files in the Developer Utilities window. The value you use for the bindkey is entirely unimportant, and you don't have to keep it secret. But if you later want to bind *new* databases to the same runtime program, then you have to use the same bindkey.

Finally, when people exit the runtime program (in other words, when they close your database system), they see a "Made with FileMaker" splash screen like the customized version shown in Figure 14-31. Are you among the 3 percent of computer users who *enjoy* splash screens? If so, you'll be delighted to learn that the splash screen can't be turned off. However, you can't admire that screen for more than 12 seconds at a time.

FIGURE 14-31

When you quit a runtime solution, this window pops up for a few seconds. You can't get rid of the "Made with FileMaker" logo, but you can override the big FileMaker Logo that usually appears in the top half of the screen. Just turn on "Custom image" and then, from your hard drive, pick a .jpg or.gif file. FileMaker stretches the picture to fit in the window, so to avoid distortion, you should create a picture that's exactly 382 pixels wide and 175 pixels high.

NOTE If you build a runtime solution with FileMaker Pro Advanced in Mac OS X, it runs *only* in Mac OS X. Likewise, if you build from Windows, your runtime solution is limited to Windows. If you need a runtime solution for *both* platforms, then you have to buy FileMaker Pro Advanced for Mac OS X *and* for Windows, and build a separate runtime solution on each kind of computer. Runtimes on Windows must install the required version of Microsoft .NET. Visit *www.microsoft.com* for details.

▓ REMOVE ADMIN ACCESS FROM FILES PERMANENTLY

The "Remove admin access from files permanently" option doesn't actually remove the accounts that have full access. Instead, it modifies the [Full Access] privilege set so it no longer truly has full access. If you log in with an account that used to have full access, it will no longer have access to the Manage Database window, Layout mode, or ScriptMaker, and its access to Accounts & Privileges is limited to the Extended Privileges tab. This option has no settings.

▓ TURN ON KIOSK MODE FOR NON-ADMIN ACCOUNTS

If you turn on Kiosk mode, and open the file, using an account that has full access, it won't look any different. But if you log in with a lesser account, *everything* changes. The screen goes completely black, except for the content area of your database window. When you use Kiosk mode, you typically hide the Status toolbar and let people control everything by using the buttons on layouts. Alternatively, you can use Custom Menus to hide all the menus and commands that would let nosy people poke around in your file. Remember to troubleshoot your file before creating a custom runtime from it, because any problems in your file (broken links, missing data, bad scripts) also show up in the runtime. Once you've suppressed all the normal FileMaker commands, folks have no way of getting around these problems.

■ DATABASES MUST HAVE A FILEMAKER FILE EXTENSION

Sometimes people, Mac types especially, create databases without the .fmp12 file extension, only to regret that decision later. An extension is the computer's most compatible way to identify a file. So turn on "Databases must have a FileMaker file extension," and FileMaker adds ".fmp12" to the end of every file name that doesn't already have it.

■ CREATE ERROR LOG FOR ANY PROCESSING ERRORS

While FileMaker processes your files, applying your options, building runtime programs, or renaming files, it may encounter problems. Turn on "Create error log for any processing errors" so you can see what went wrong. FileMaker saves error messages in a file on your hard drive (you get to pick where it goes and what it's called).

■ LOADING AND SAVING SETTINGS

If you maintain a database system that other people use, you may well run your files through Developer Utilities every time you send out a new version. To save you the tedium of configuring the Database Utilities dialog box again and again, FileMaker lets you save all your settings to a special file—just click Save Settings. Later, when you're ready to process your files again, click Load Settings and then select the same file. FileMaker sets up everything in the dialog box for you. All you have to do is click Create.

■ File Maintenance

With normal use and good backup strategies, computer files are reliable and dependable. But they are subject to accident: a computer crash, power surge, power outage, or malfunctioning hard drive can corrupt your digital files. FileMaker databases are just as susceptible to corruption as any other file. For best practice and automatic backups, use FileMaker Server (page 793).

File corruption may be obvious—like an error message telling you to recover the file when you try to open it, or FileMaker crashing when you navigate to a particular layout or record. There are subtler forms, too, like gibberish text suddenly appearing in a field or a record that never sorts into the right position. With appropriate care and maintenance, however, you can head off and even repair injury to your databases.

1. **Choose File→Recover.**

    The Select Damaged File dialog box opens.

2. **Click the problematic database and then click Select.**

    The "Name new recovered file" dialog box appears (Figure 14-32).

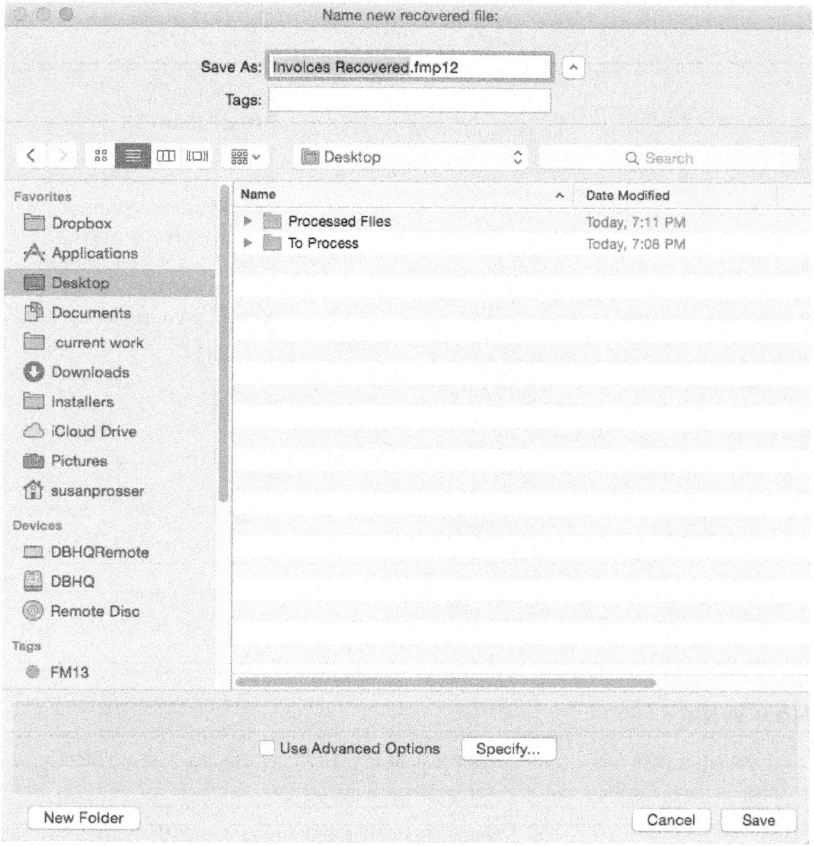

FIGURE 14-32

Recovery doesn't fix a file in place. Rather, it reads the damaged file and builds a new copy of it, fixing as much as it can in the process.

3. **Choose a location to save the recovered file. Turn on the Use Advanced Options checkbox.**

   The aptly named Advanced Recover Options dialog box opens (Figure 14-33). You see three methods for making that new copy of your file.

   - **Copy file blocks as-is.** Copies the database as-is without scanning for damage.

   - **Copy logical structure (same as Compacted Copy).** This choice creates an optimized file that contains all your data, but takes up less space on your hard drive and operates more efficiently. It's a good choice for keeping a file in shape *before* corruption shows up, but it doesn't check for structural damage.

- **Scan blocks and rebuild file (drop invalid blocks).** The heavy hitter of the bunch, this process reads every piece of data (those are the "blocks" it refers to) and removes those that appear to be damaged. It's a blunt instrument designed to salvage data even at the cost of structure like layouts and scripts. Use this only when a file won't open normally.

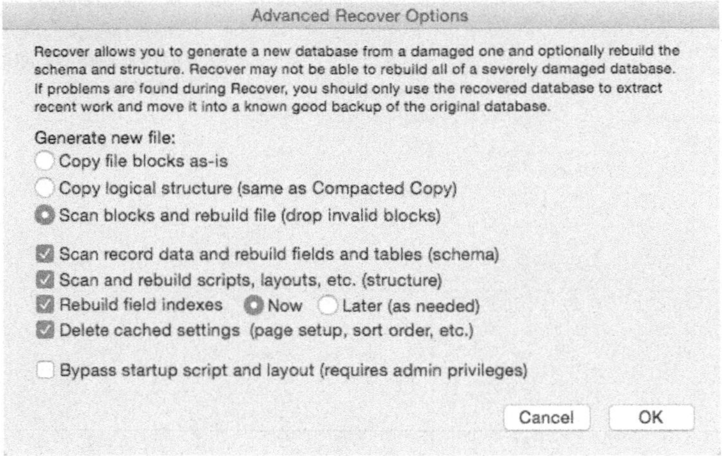

FIGURE 14-33

When good databases misbehave, the Advanced Recover Options are your instruments of discipline. Still, file maintenance can be an exercise in patience. If your database runs into many hundreds or thousands of megabytes, recovery can take hours.

UP TO SPEED

File Recovered. Now What?

The Recover command has reanimated your recalcitrant database, but at what cost? Although the command is called Recover, the process doesn't actually fix everything it finds wrong. Instead, it can delete corrupted blocks in the file, which may leave a hole in the definition on an object or a piece of data. When the recovery is done, FileMaker places a file called Recover.log in the same directory as the recovered file. Inside you'll find painstaking documentation of every step taken in the recovery process. It's here where you may learn a bit more about the file's problems. Scan through Recover.log's Error column. If you see anything but a zero, a problem was encountered on that step.

Regardless of what went wrong, putting the recovered file into service is not recommended. Your best bet for a happy, healthy database is to pull a backup copy of the database that was saved before it corrupted. Make a clone of the backup (page 35) and then import the data from the recovered copy into the clone. This process combines your most current salvageable data with your cleanest database structure.

The next four checkboxes are automatically turned on, but you can toggle them to provide more refined control of the recovery process:

- **Scan record data and rebuild fields and tables.** A corrupt field may show gibberish where sensible text once appeared, or crash the database when clicked into, or even abruptly disappear leaving a "<field missing>" everywhere it was used. This option meticulously sifts through the damage and resurrects those wayward fields whenever possible.

- **Scan and rebuild scripts, layouts, etc.** Like the record data option, this choice provides first aid to the file structure components.

- **Rebuild field indexes.** Indexes are like invisible databases within a database. FileMaker relies on them to perform finds and sorts, display related data, and execute certain calculations. A classic case of index corruption is when you perform a find for a value you're certain exists, only to have FileMaker claim no records match your request. Rebuilding the indexes typically alleviates this problem.

- **Delete cached settings.** If FileMaker keeps reverting to an old print setup (page setup on the Mac) configuration no matter how often you change it, try deleting the cached settings.

The final option is useful when a startup script isn't functioning as intended and you can't seem to stop it. "Bypass startup script and layout" ignores the corresponding settings under File→File Options, thus allowing you to take corrective measures. You must, however, have a full-access login or your attempts will be thwarted.

Advanced Relationship Techniques

I n Chapter 14, you learned how to use the tools in FileMaker Pro Advanced to make your development tasks—like debugging your database and creating custom menus—easier. That's a great start on thinking like a developer. Now it's time to turn your attention back to relationships and delve into some of the more powerful features in the Relationships graph. Your first relationships, like the ones you created on page 146, were of the most basic type: They used a single key field pair, and the value in those key fields matched exactly. But you can also create relationships that work when values don't match, by using an operator other than the = sign. And just as you can add more criteria to a search, you can also add multiple criteria to a relationship. You do that for the same reason you add more criteria to a search: because you want the results to be more specific, as when you need a customer ID *and* a date field each to match corresponding fields in a related table. And just as you can sort a portal separately from the underlying relationship's sort order, the Portal Setup dialog box also lets you filter related records to show only some related records.

You'll also delve deeper into table occurrences. FileMaker lets you create as many instances of a table as you need on the graph. Once you know about more complex joins, you have the tools you need to start making those multiple table occurrences. But as your graph grows, so does the potential for problems, so you'll learn some organizing and structural concepts that'll help keep you on the right path as your table occurrences multiply.

NOTE Sample databases for this chapter are available on this book's Missing CD page at *www.missingmanuals. com/cds/fmp14mm*. Use the *CH15 Invoices Start.fmp12* file to work through the chapter's tutorials. At the end of the chapter, you can compare your work with *CH15 Invoices End.fmp12* or use the file to get extra help as you work.

▆ Advanced Relationships

A portal on a layout makes creating related records as simple as entering data. But another common use is to help your users avoid performing a find. Finds are relatively easy, but it can mean switching modes *and* layouts, especially when finding related records. So in addition to the relationships you create that act as your ER diagram (page 194), you'll also want to create relationships and portals that show specific related records. Then when you add buttons or scripts that navigate to those layouts using a "Go To Related Record" step, users won't need to enter Find mode as often to see the data they need.

Self-Join Relationships

The Invoices layout of the *CH15 Invoices Start.fmp12* database has a Line Items portal and a Payments portal. You can get a better picture of a Job's total costs by creating a third portal that shows all the other invoices related to the current invoice's job. Sure, there's already such a portal on the Job layout, but if you're researching the way a particular job was billed, you can see that data on each invoice, plus a button on the new portal can move you through a Job's invoice records without needing to go back to the Jobs layout or do a find on the Invoice layout.

You'll need a special type of relationship called a *self-join* to make this portal. A self-join relationship is one in which a table is related to itself instead of to another table. Since you want the portal to show all invoices from the same job, you'll use the Job ID field as the key for the self-join relationship. Follow these steps to create the self-join you need to show all invoices for the current Invoice's job:

1. **Choose File→Manage Database and then click the Relationships tab.**

   The Relationships graph appears.

2. **Click the Invoices TO (table occurrence) to select it and then click the Duplicate button.**

   The Duplicate button has two plus signs on it. A copy of the Invoices TO, named Invoices 2, appears on the graph.

3. **Drag the Invoices 2 TO under the Invoice Payments TO and then double-click Invoices 2.**

   The Specify Table dialog box appears. Because you duplicated an Invoice TO, this new TO has the same data source as the original. It's from the Invoices table.

4. **Change the TO's name to *Invoices_currentJob* and then click OK.**

   As with all things FileMaker, use a descriptive name.

5. **Click the Expand button on the Invoices_currentJob TO and then drag the Invoices::JobID field to the Invoices_currentJob::JobID field.**

   You're creating a relationship between invoices that share the same Job ID. Compare your graph with Figure 15-1.

6. **Click the OK button.**

   The new relationship is ready to use.

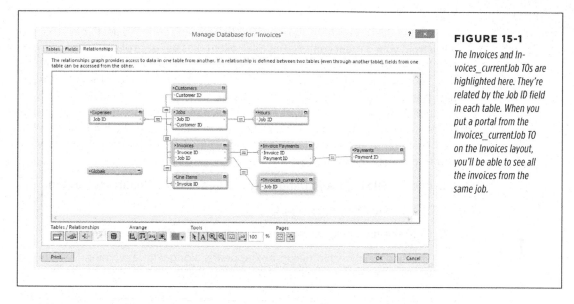

FIGURE 15-1

*The Invoices and In-
voices_currentJob TOs are
highlighted here. They're
related by the Job ID field
in each table. When you
put a portal from the
Invoices_currentJob TO
on the Invoices layout,
you'll be able to see all
the invoices from the
same job.*

Now that you've created the Invoices to Invoices_currentJob relationship, put a portal from the Invoices_currentJob TO on the Invoices layout (see page 154 for a refresher). Add the Invoices_currentJob::Date and Invoices_currentJob::Total Due fields to the portal. To make the portal more functional, create a button that uses a "Go to Related Record" step (page 231) and place it in the portal. The GTRR step has to use the same relationship as the portal: Invoices_currentJob. This is one of those rare instances where a GTRR step can use the current layout. When you're done, you can click the button to travel between all the invoices that are related to a particular job. To show financial information for the Job below the portal, create a Sum( ) calculation using this new relationship and then display it on the layout below the portal.

■ AVOIDING AMBIGUITY

FileMaker won't let you create any relationships that would make the graph ambiguous. To understand what this means, recall the concept of *context*. That is, every TO is an instance of a particular table, which provides the context for any layout that shows records from that TO. So if you put the Jobs::Job Name field on the Invoice layout, it's as if FileMaker stands on the Invoice TO and looks through a window (or a portal...get it?) into the Jobs table to get the proper name for the job that's attached to the current invoice. Getting the job name is easy, because the Jobs TO is only one table occurrence away from the Invoices TO. But remember, you can also have FileMaker stand on the Invoices TO and get the Customer's name and address data, which is two TOs away. And to the degree that you have an unbroken line of TOs, it's possible to get data from many more "hops" away from the current context. In the sample database, you could "stand" on the Payments TO and get data from the Customer TO, four hops away. And since most relationships are bidirectional (page 235), you could also stand on the Customer TO and view data from the Payments table or any point in between.

Some other databases make you jump through flaming hoops to get to data that's far away from your current context. But FileMaker takes its "ease of use" label seriously, so it handles the complexity for you. In exchange, though, you can't create ambiguous (or circular) relationships. For example, you can't create another relationship between the Expenses and Payments TOs because they are already related to one another through Jobs and Invoices and Invoice payments. So in any Relationships Graph, there is always one, and only one, unambiguous path between any two TOs. Now that you see what ambiguity means, it's time to learn how FileMaker prevents you from creating it in your graph.

1. **Choose File→Manage Database and then click the Relationships tab.**

   The Relationships graph appears.

2. **Drag the Invoices_currentJob::JobID field to the Jobs::JobID field.**

   The Add Relationship dialog box appears, along with a warning that you are trying to make a relationship that won't be allowed. See Figure 15-2.

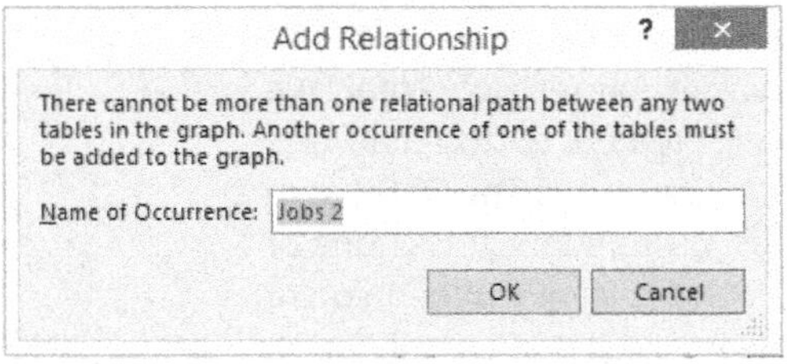

FIGURE 15-2

FileMaker keeps you from creating any relationship that would introduce ambiguity into the Relationships graph. If you try to make a relationship between two TOs that are already related, you'll see the Add Relationship dialog box.

3. **Click OK to create the TO.**

   A TO with the name "Jobs 2" appears on the graph. Its source table is Jobs. FileMaker makes a guess about which table you need an occurrence for, based on where you dragged. You can learn more about how this works in the box on the facing page. This behavior is so reliable that some people intentionally drag to an ambiguous spot on the graph because it's quicker than clicking the Add Relationship button and then setting up the relationship.

4. **If you don't like FileMaker's guess, click Cancel.**

TIP   The Add Relationship and Edit Relationship dialog boxes are two of the many places where FileMaker itself doesn't make the all-important distinction between tables and table occurrences. If you're not sure, take a look at the items in the Table pop-up menu. If you see names like Invoice_currentJob, or if the names listed in the Table pop-up outnumber the tables you've created, you can be sure that you're looking at a list of TOs, and *not* tables themselves.

When Dragging Doesn't Do It

Dragging isn't the only way to create a new relationship on the graph. Some folks like to click the Add Relationship button to start with a clean Add Relationship window. It's just like Edit Relationship, except that since it starts out blank, the Table pop-up menu at the top of the window isn't grayed out. That is, you have to start out by selecting the two table occurrences you want to relate. Then you can select your key fields and all the other options that get the relationship job done.

Using this method doesn't circumvent the rule forbidding ambiguity or circularity (page 593). But say you're trying to create a new relationship between the Invoices table and the Customers table by using the Add Relationship window. In that

case, you'll get all the way through the process of selecting tables and key fields and operators before FileMaker can warn you that the relationship won't work and you need a new table occurrence.

You might wish the warning had been offered a little earlier in the process. But you do have control over which table gets the new occurrence. FileMaker creates the new TO for the table listed on the right side of the window. When you drag, FileMaker uses the direction you drag to decide which table to create a new occurrence for. That is, if you drag from Customers to Invoices, FileMaker will create a new TO for Invoices.

Multiple Criteria Relationships

Just as you can add extra search terms when you're performing a Find, you can also add criteria when you're defining a relationship. For example, the Invoices_Current-Job relationship is one place you might want to add another match field. Your new portal is convenient for jumping around to see the detail for other invoices related to the same job, but there's a slightly confusing element to that list. The invoice you're viewing on the layout also appears in the portal of "other" invoices. So if you're viewing Invoice #2014001, and you glance at the "other invoice" portal while you're distracted, it's easy to think that there are two invoices for $8,011.50. Just as bad, when you view a record that doesn't have any other invoices for the same job, the current invoice still appears in the list. The situation would be clearer if that list *didn't* show the current invoice. In this case, a multiple criteria relationship will remove the current invoice from the portal.

■ EDITING A RELATIONSHIP

You define extra conditions in a relationship so that records match only when they're all met. In this case, you want to add another criterion to the relationship that says, "Don't show the record if it's the current invoice." Here's how to add a new criterion to an existing relationship:

1. **Choose File→Manage Database and then click the Relationships tab.**

   The Relationships graph appears.

2. **Double-click the line between the Invoices and the Invoices_currentJob TOs.**

   It's easiest to double-click the box with the = sign in it rather than trying to hit the line itself.

The Edit Relationship window appears. The Job ID to Job ID criteria appears in the list section.

3. **Click the Invoices::Invoice ID field and then click the Invoices_current Job::Invoice ID field.**

   You're selecting the key fields for the new criterion.

4. **From the operator pop-up menu (it's between the two table occurrence lists), select the ≠ sign.**

   You want every record that has the same Job ID, but that *doesn't* match the current Invoice ID. In other words, don't show the current record in the "other" invoices portal.

5. **Click the Add button.**

   The new criterion appears in the list. Your window should look like Figure 15-3.

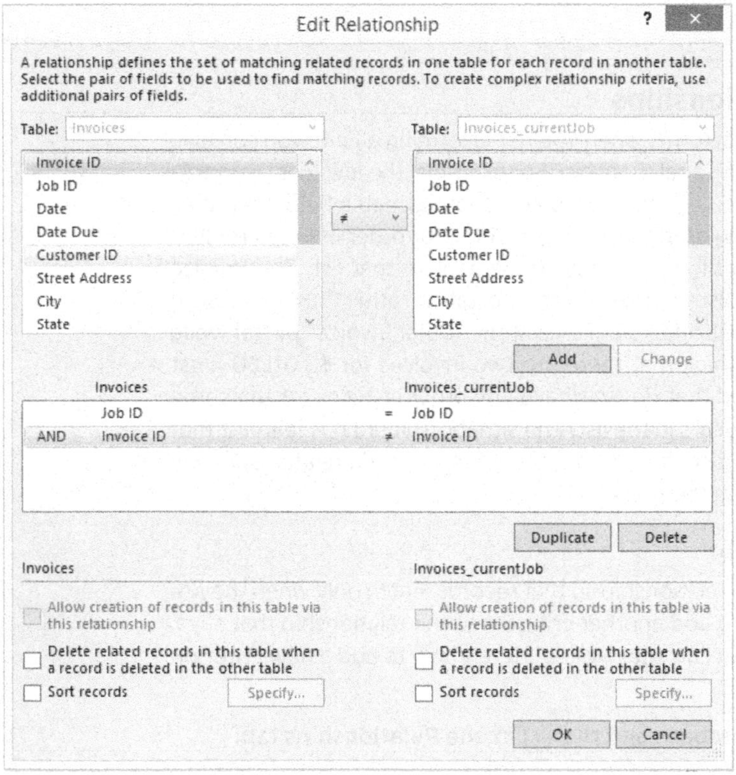

FIGURE 15-3

This is a relationship with two criteria, sometimes called a multi-key (or multi-predicate) relationship, because it uses two sets of key fields in its definition. Notice the "AND" in front of the second criterion. In order for two records to relate, they have to meet both criteria. If you wanted to translate this relationship's description into words, you could say something like, "Show all records where the Job ID matches AND where the Invoice ID does not match." It doesn't quite trip off the tongue, but it's accurate. Multiple criteria relationships are always AND conditions, never OR.

6. **Click OK.**

Notice that the box on the line between Invoices and Invoices_currentJob has a new symbol, and both ends of the line are forked to indicate that it's a multiple criteria relationship (Figure 15-4).

7. **Click OK.**

You're back on the Invoice layout. The current invoice no longer appears in the Invoices_currentJob portal.

After you perform these steps, the portal shows invoices only where there's more than one invoice related to the same job. And the current invoice (the one you're viewing on the layout) never shows up in the portal.

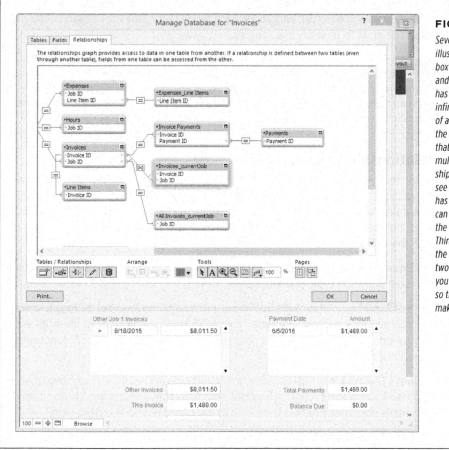

FIGURE 15-4

Several concepts are illustrated here. First, the box between Invoices and Invoices_currentJob has a sort of squared-off infinity symbol instead of an equal sign, like all the rest. That tells you that the relationship is a multi-criteria relationship. Second, you can see a new relationship has been created so you can use it to sum up all the invoices for each job. Third, the layout behind the dialog box shows the two sum fields and how you can arrange them so that the portal's data makes sense.

If you created a Sum( ) function after the steps on page 592, you may notice that you solved one problem but have created a new one. That is, the current invoice no longer shows up in the list, and the calculation field shows the wrong total amount for the job. Because it's excluded from the relationship used by the portal, the current invoice isn't included in the sum calculation based on that relationship.

You can fix the problem by adding a new self-join relationship for the Invoice table (follow the tutorial on page 592, or copy the existing self-join TO and then edit as appropriate). This one should be set to your original criteria of matching Invoice::Job ID to Invoice::Job ID (without the multiple criteria). Then create a new Sum( ) calculation that uses the relationship you just created. That way, the calculation takes the current invoice into account, and you get an accurate Job cost total, but since it uses a different relationship to show an invoice list, the portal *doesn't* include the current invoice. See the results in Figure 15-4.

And you thought you'd only ever need one table occurrence for any particular table. You have three Invoice TOs on your graph, and you've only just started finding reasons to create new ones. Later in this chapter, you'll learn a better way to control what shows up in a portal, and you'll learn some techniques for organizing a graph when TOs start to multiply like rabbits.

> **TIP** If you prefer, you can convert a single criterion relationship to a multiple criteria one by dragging between a new pair of fields. But you always get an = operator for this second pair, and the Edit Relationship window doesn't open automatically when you do. So if you need anything nonstandard, you may as well just open the Edit Relationship window straightaway.

Relationship Operators

As you learned in the last section, sometimes you want a relationship to work when the values in key fields are different. But you might also want to show all Invoices after a particular date. In that case, you want to match dates when the values are greater than (>) or greater than or equal to (≥) the value in a key field. Here's a list of all the comparative operators:

- **Equal (=).** The keys on both sides of the relationship match exactly. This is the most common type of relationship.

- **Not Equal (≠).** All records but those with matching keys relate to one another. You just saw a good example: You want to show all related invoices except the one you're viewing. This operator is most often used in conjunction with another criterion.

- **Less Than (<).** Keys in the table on the left side of the dialog box have to be less than keys in the table on the right side. Use this operator to show all records with a date that's before the value in the date field on the right side.

- **Less Than or Equal To (≤).** Keys in the table on the left side of the dialog box have to be less than or equal to the keys on the right side of the table. Use this operator to show all records with a date that's before or on the value in the date field on the right side.

- **Greater Than (>).** Keys in the table on the left side of the dialog box have to be greater than keys in the table on the right side. Use this operator to show all records with a date that's after the value in the date field on the right side.

- **Greater Than or Equal To (≥).** Keys in the table on the left side of the dialog box must be greater than or equal to the keys on the right side of the table. Use this operator to show all records with a date that's after or on the value in the date field on the right side.

- **Cartesian Join (x).** All records in the table on the left are related to all records in the table on the right, regardless of the value in their key fields. A Cartesian join is the only one where it doesn't matter which fields you choose as keys. But if you like things nice and neat, pick the primary key in each table. It may be hard to think of reasons why you'd want this type of relationship, so here's one example: Suppose you need a count of all the invoices you've ever created. By creating a Cartesian join from any table to your Invoices table, you can keep a running count of how many invoice records exist. A calculation field in the parent table with the formula **Count (Invoices::InvoiceID)** would do the job.

As you go through the rest of this chapter, you'll see some of these operators in action. Now it's time to learn another way to show just some of the related records in a portal.

Portal Filtering

Using a multiple criteria relationship as you did on page 595 is one way to change what displays in a portal. But when you change the relationship's definition, every portal, script, or calculation that uses the relationship will change, even if that's not what you intend. And if you create a new TO every time you need a slight variation on a relationship, your graph can easily become a cluttered mess. But with an option in the Portal Setup dialog box, you can tell a portal to show records only under certain circumstances (say they're unpaid invoices) without changing the underlying relationship.

In the Invoices database the Customers layout has an Invoices tab, containing a portal that uses the plain-vanilla Invoices table occurrence. If you look on the Relationships graph, you can see that from the starting context of the Customers TO, the relationship travels through the Jobs TO to get to the Invoices TO. That means the portal currently shows all Invoices for all the current customer's jobs. Looking at it another way, when you view a customer record, you can see all Invoices related to any job that's in turn related to the current customer.

If you wanted to see just the invoices that have a balance, you may think that adding another criterion to the relationship would do the trick. But that approach has its own problems. First, there's no direct relationship between the Customers TO and Invoices TO, so you'll have to go through the Jobs-to-Invoices relationship to change what appears on the Customer layout. If you changed that relationship's rules, everything that depends on the Jobs-to-Invoices relationship would change, too. Calculations that use the relationship would change to reflect the new rules, so the summary fields that show up at the bottom of the Jobs layout would change to show just those Invoices that are unpaid. Not only would your calculation amounts change, but the Job layout's portal would change, too, as would any scripts that use that relationship. Making a change to a relationship can have widespread, unintended consequences that are time-consuming to find and fix.

Or you may decide that you need a new occurrence of the Invoices table connected directly to the Customers table. You plan to use the ≥ operator on the Invoices::Balance Due field as your key for the new criterion. But you don't have an appropriate field on the Customer side to match with it. You *could* create a field called Zero, give it the calculated value of "0," and then use that as a key. But that plan adds two pieces of extra overhead (an extra field and an extra TO) to your database that don't really do anything except make a single portal work. Maybe you're willing to live with some cruft (that's the nerd term for the overhead your plan requires). But portal filtering gives you a non-crufty way to get the job done.

Here's the rule of thumb: If you want to change the records shown in a *specific* portal on a *specific* layout, portal filtering is usually your best bet. That's because it doesn't require you to add any complexity to the graph. Instead, you tell the portal which related records you want it to show. Portal filtering brings the power of the Specify Calculation window to a portal without changing its underlying relationship. The *filter* part means that the relationship still determines which records are properly related to one another. But with filtering turned on, FileMaker analyzes each record individually to decide if it should show up in the portal. Some of them will get through, and some won't. You write a calculation that decides how to let records through the filter. Here's how to set up the Customer layout's Invoices portal to show only invoices that have a balance:

1. **In Layout mode, double-click the Invoices portal.**

   The Portal Setup window appears.

2. **Click the Filter portal records option.**

   The Specify Calculation dialog box appears.

3. **In the calculation box, type *Invoices::Balance Due > 0*. Or if you prefer, double-click the field name to enter it into the box and then type *> 0*.**

   However you do it, the calculation checks the value in the Invoices::Balance Due field before deciding whether to show each record in the portal. Click OK to return to the Portal Setup.

4. **Click the Sort portal records option and then move the Invoice::Date field to the Sort order list.**

   That way, the oldest invoice record will appear at the top of the portal.

5. **Click OK until you're back on the Customers layout.**

   The label at the bottom of the portal changes to show that it's filtered (Figure 15-5).

6. **Switch to Browse mode.**

   That's where you'll see the real changes.

Make sure you're viewing a Customer record with at least one invoice showing a Balance Due amount. Customer Kara Thrace in your sample database will work.

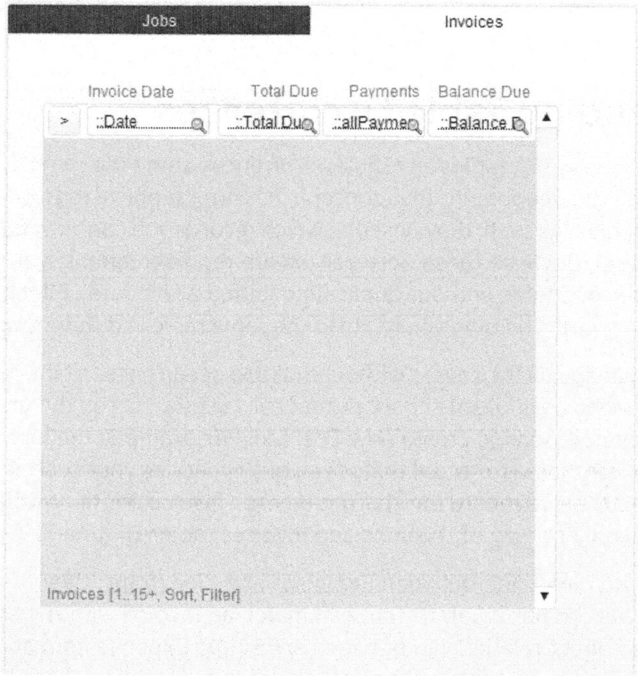

Jobs		Invoices	
Invoice Date	Total Due	Payments	Balance Due
> ::Date	::Total Due	::allPaymen	::Balance

Invoices [1..15+, Sort, Filter]

FIGURE 15-5

This portal's label reads "Invoices [1..15+, Sort, Filter]." There's a lot of information packed away in those few characters. "Invoices" is the name of the related table occurrence the portal uses to show the proper records. It shows the first 15 related records (the "1..15" part) and has a scroll bar to show more (the "+" sign), where appropriate. The words "Sort" and "Filter" mean that you've selected those options for this specific portal. To see the sort order or the filter calculation, double-click the portal to show the Portal Setup dialog box.

> **NOTE** If the zero-balance invoice doesn't disappear immediately, you've been bitten by a portal refresh issue. Since it's based on a calculation, a portal filter kicks into effect when the values in the referenced table have changed. But changing data isn't possible or desirable here, so you can take any action that causes the window to refresh instead. Flip to the next record and right back, switch tabs, or if the portal refresh bug bites you when you're scripting, add a Refresh Portal script step.

You can't set up more than one filter per portal, but you can write a calculation that tests more than one condition. The calculation *Invoices::Balance Due > 0 and Invoices Total Due > 10000* would filter the portal to show only invoices with a total of over $10,000 and that still have a balance due amount. You have all the power of the calculation engine at the service of creating the filter you need. For instance, you could use a Case statement (page 681) to test a condition before deciding whether to apply a filter. You can even use a variable to filter a portal dynamically. That is, the portal's contents could change each time the script runs if the value in the variable changes. Let your calculation wizardry rule the day.

> **NOTE** Portal filtering is most helpful where you expect the set of records to be fairly small—say, fewer than a couple hundred or so. There's no hard-and-fast rule, but since FileMaker has to look at every related record to decide if it can pass through your filter, performance can suffer with large numbers of related records. If a portal doesn't display records quickly, you may have to live with whatever cruft it takes to make a multiple criteria relationship to do the same job. All that extra overhead does yield a speed increase, so performance is a good determining factor in which method to use.

■ Understanding Table Occurrences

As you first learned on page 152, tables and table occurrences aren't the same thing. Now it's time to dig a little deeper into that concept. TOs are graphical representations of their source tables. As such, they describe which records you can view based on your current context. Because these occurrences are representations, you can make new occurrences of a table without duplicating it (and all its data). FileMaker isn't trying to confuse you; it's helping you relate to the same table in different ways.

Few databases can manage all their tasks without multiple occurrences of the same table. You've already seen a couple of situations that call for new TOs on the graph. But there are functional reasons to create new TOs, too. For example, the Invoices database has an Expenses table to record things you buy to service your customers. It also has a Line Items table to record the charges on each Invoice. Right now these tables are connected only by way of the Jobs and Invoices tables (Figure 15-6).

Even though there's no direct line between Expenses and Line Items, they *are* related. Each Expense record has a Job ID that can match an Invoice with the same Job ID. But there's no direct relationship between any single Expense item and its corresponding Line Item, so you can't look at an Expense record to see if it has been billed, or, if it has been billed, which Invoice Line Item bills it. Of course you *could* type some text into the Line Items::Description field to help you remember, but that's not very convenient from the Expenses point of view, nor would that create a relationship between the tables. You really need a whole new relationship—one that connects Expenses and Line Items directly. This new relationship lets you display Line Item data on the Expenses layout to make it completely clear that the item has been billed. And you can use a "Go to Related Record" command to navigate between expenses and line items.

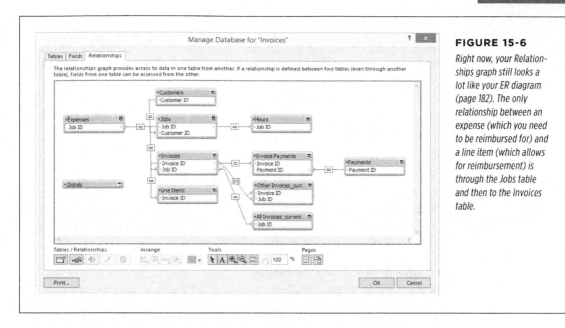

FIGURE 15-6

Right now, your Relationships graph still looks a lot like your ER diagram (page 182). The only relationship between an expense (which you need to be reimbursed for) and a line item (which allows for reimbursement) is through the Jobs table and then to the Invoices table.

Your new relationship will be one-to-one. In other words, one Expense Line Item is related to one, and only one, Invoice Line Item. One-to-one relationships are fairly rare birds. This new one-to-one relationship—Expenses to Line Items—is purely about how your database functions. It exists for one purpose only: to give your database a convenient way to record which Line Item an Expense has been billed on. To create this new relationship and make it work properly, you need three things:

- A new primary key (page 146) to hook the two tables together.

- A way to represent the new relationship in your Relationships graph without throwing the whole thing into disarray. That's right—a new table occurrence.

- New fields on one of your layouts (the Expenses layout in this case), to show the newly related data.

The next section covers the entire process.

Deciding Which Table Needs a New Occurrence

When you create a new occurrence of a table, you're giving that table a new meaning in the relational structure of your database. But when you're thinking about the problem of creating a direct relationship between the Expenses and Line Item tables, how do you know which table to make a new occurrence for? To answer that question, ask yourself this one: What layout do I want to view the related data from, and which table has the information I need to see? Here are the three possible scenarios:

- If you want to display Expense data on the Line Item layout, then the Line Item table will be the parent and the Expenses table will be the child. You could use Line Item::Line Item ID as one key, but you'd need to create a Line Item ID in the Expenses table.

- If, on the other hand, you want to display Line Item data on the Expenses layout, then the opposite is true. The Expense table would be the parent, and the Line Item table would be the child. You'd hook up the existing Expenses::Expenses ID field with a newly created Expenses ID in the Line Item table.

- In some instances, you might want to display data from both layouts. In that case, you'll need two new TOs and two new key fields.

All three scenarios are valid, depending on what you're trying to achieve. In this case, you want to display Line Item data on the Expenses layout, so you'll create a Line Item ID field in the Expenses table. In the Invoices database, choose File→Manage Database, switch to the Fields tab and then select the Expenses table. Create a new number field called Line Item ID and then click OK when you're done. You'll use this new field to relate the Expenses table to Line Items.

■ ADDING A TABLE OCCURRENCE

Since you want to display line item details on the Expenses layout, you'll create a new TO for the Line Items table. And you need to make a new relationship between the Expenses TO and the Line Items TO by using your new Expenses::Line Items ID key field. Figure 15-7 shows what that Relationships graph looks like with the new Line Items TO.

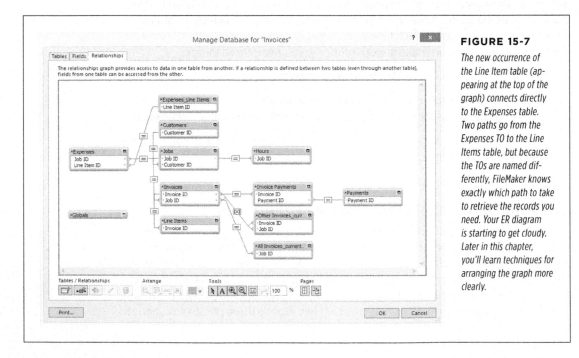

FIGURE 15-7

The new occurrence of the Line Item table (appearing at the top of the graph) connects directly to the Expenses table. Two paths go from the Expenses TO to the Line Items table, but because the TOs are named differently, FileMaker knows exactly which path to take to retrieve the records you need. Your ER diagram is starting to get cloudy. Later in this chapter, you'll learn techniques for arranging the graph more clearly.

With the new graph in mind, here's how to create the new Line Item TO in your database:

1. **On the Relationships tab of the Manage Database dialog box, click the Add Table Occurrence button (on the bottom left).**

   The Specify Table dialog box appears (Figure 15-8).

2. **Select the Line Items table from the list and then, in the Name box, type *Expenses_Line Items*.**

   You want a descriptive name so you can pick it out of a lineup later.

3. **Click OK.**

   FileMaker adds the new table occurrence to the graph and selects it for you.

4. **Drag the Expenses::Line Item ID field to the Expenses_Line Items::Line Item ID field.**

   FileMaker creates the relationship.

> **NOTE** If you don't see the Line Item ID field in the TO, it may be because your table occurrences are collapsed and they show only fields used in relationships. In the upper-right corner of the TO, click the little button to expand it. Since the button cycles the TO through three states, you might have to click twice before you see all the fields.

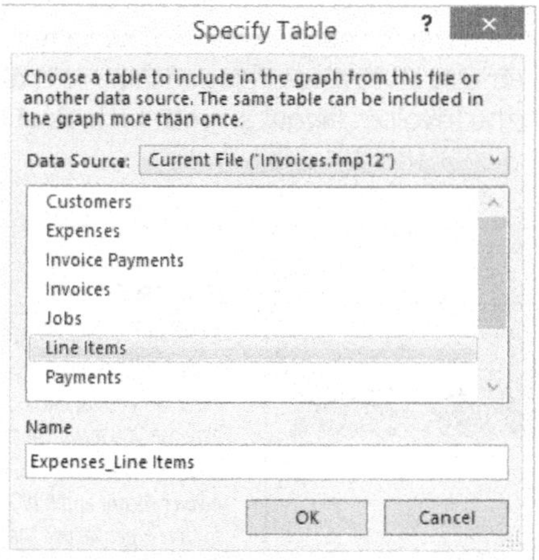

FIGURE 15-8

The Specify Table dialog box lets you tell FileMaker what table to use when you make a new table occurrence. You also get to give the new occurrence a name. When you name a new table occurrence, the goal is to help you remember the source table for the new table occurrence. The new TO's name is Expenses_Line Items. The "Expenses" part of the name helps you remember that this occurrence of the Line Item table is attached to the Expenses TO.

5. **Click the OK button.**

   You're back on the layout.

Now it's time to add fields from your new table occurrence to the Expenses layout.

■ ADDING FIELDS FOR NEW TABLE OCCURRENCES

To put your new relationship to work, you add the Invoice ID, Description, Price Each, Quantity, and Extended Price fields to your Expense layout. Here's how:

1. **In Layout mode, switch to the Expenses layout.**

   Or you could go to the Expenses layout and then switch to Layout mode.

2. **Open the Field Picker. In the pop-up menu at the top, choose Expenses_Line Items.**

   The fields from the Line Items table appear. Remember, you'll get the exact same list if you choose the plain Line Items TO, since it's the same table. But you may not see the right data if you choose the wrong TO.

3. **From the list, choose the Invoice ID, Description, Price Each, Quantity, and Extended Price fields. Set the Drag Options to a row with labels on top and drag the fields into the Expenses layout.**

   With these fields on the Expenses layout, you can see the details of each line item and verify that it's the right one before moving on. (You may have to widen the layout to fit everything in.)

4. **Add the Expenses::Line Item ID field to the layout and then in Browse mode, enter 1 in the sample Expense record.**

   When you enter a valid ID into this local field, the relationship is completed, and related data shows up on the Expense record.

Back in Browse mode, you can start entering expenses. Make some expense records and then create a Job ID pop-up to choose a job for each expense. The sample file has a few invoices with line items you can use to test the relationship. To make it easier, open a new window and switch to the Invoices layout so you can look at Line Items (Figure 15-9).

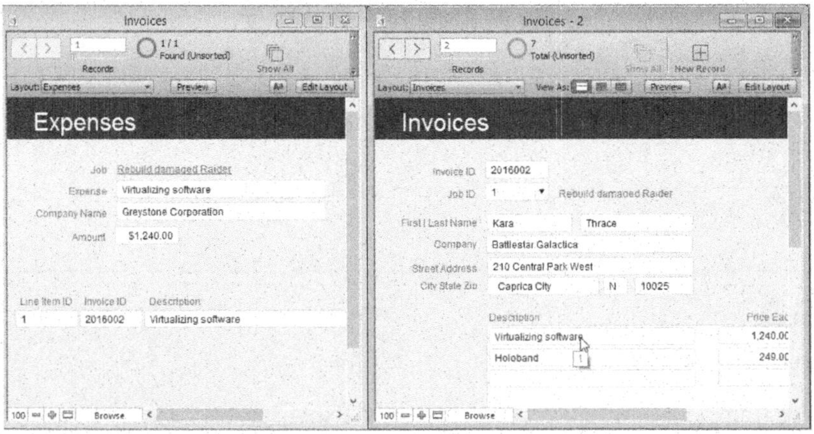

FIGURE 15-9

To the left is the Expenses layout, where you can enter data about each expense you incur. Then, after you create an invoice record and bill for the expense, use the Invoices layout (shown on the right with a tooltip showing the Line Item ID) to find the Line Item ID for each expense.

■ Table Occurrence Groups

The relationship between expenses and line items you created in the last section is *functional*, but as you added Line Item IDs, you probably discovered that it isn't very easy to work with. You had to view invoices and their line item IDs to figure out which Line Item ID to add to your Expense record. A value list of Line Item IDs might help, but as your database grows, so do the value list *and* the problems. First of all, your database could have *thousands* of line items. And even if it doesn't, line items don't have a very good name—their descriptions aren't unique, and their IDs aren't very meaningful.

It would improve the process if you could type an Invoice ID *right there on the Expenses layout* and then see that invoice's Line Item IDs. A new layout called Assign Expenses (Figure 15-10) uses a new set of table occurrences, called a Table Occurrence Group (TOG), to let you manage line item data from a new Assign Expenses layout.

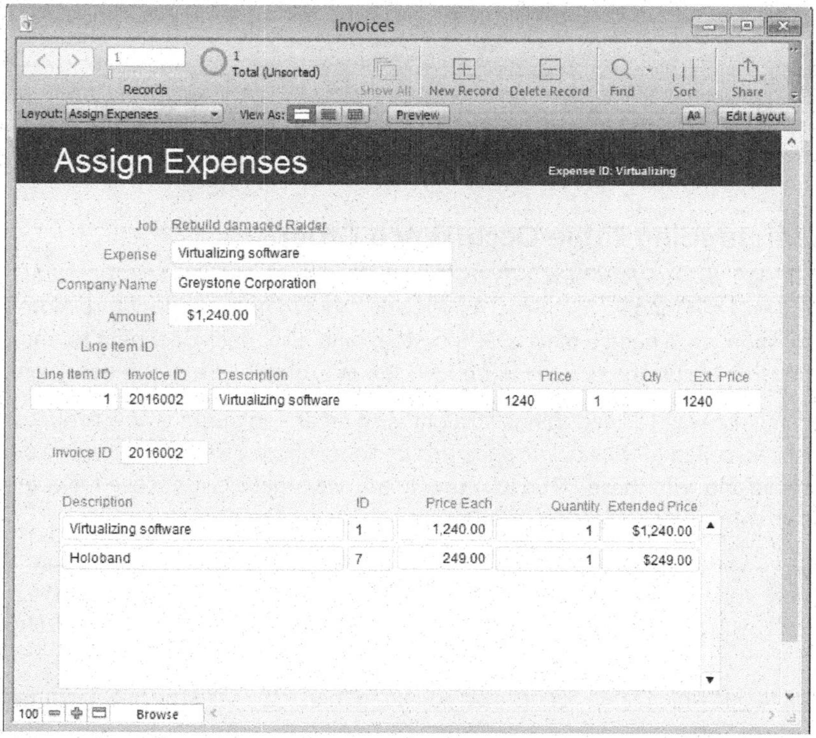

FIGURE 15-10

This layout provides a nice interface for assigning line items to an expense. First, you enter an Invoice ID into a global field. Then the invoice's line items show up in a portal that shows you the data you need to choose the proper Line Item record to assign to each Expense record. As before, when you type a Line Item ID, you see the Description, Price Each, Quantity, and Extended Price that was invoiced for the Expense.

Planning the New Elements You'll Need

The Assign Expenses layout will provide a special set of tools, or an *interface,* to expedite a certain *process.* In this case, the process is matching line item records to expense records so you can record the Line Item ID that billed out each expense. For the new interface to work, you need several new elements. They're listed here to avoid confusion as you start creating them; you'll learn more about the role each item plays as you build the interface. You need:

- A new group of table occurrences that you'll create specifically to handle this task.

- A field in the Expenses table to type in the Invoice ID. Because this field doesn't hold information about any particular entity in your database, it's a perfect candidate for *global* storage. Global fields, as you remember from page 259, have the same value across every record of their table.

- A relationship between the Expenses table and the Invoices table, using Expenses::Global Invoice ID and Invoices::Invoice ID as the key fields.

- A new layout similar to the original Expenses layout, but with the context of your new table occurrence group and a portal showing Invoice Line Items.

To get these elements to work together, you first have to revisit your Relationships graph and decide which table occurrences to use in the new group. Read on.

> **NOTE** You can download a finished copy of the database (called *Invoices End.fmp12*) from this book's Missing CD page at *www.missingmanuals.com/cds/fmp14mm*. Use the file to see how the completed process works, and as a reference as you go through the exercises that create your new layout.

Understanding Table Occurrence Groups

If you tried to add your new TOs to the existing group of table occurrences, you could easily get tangled in a mess. As you add more features that require more TOs, pretty soon you'll need a map, a GPS system, and a six-pack of aspirin to untangle all the table occurrences. See Figure 15-11 for an example of a graph gone wild.

The simplest way to keep things straight is to create an entirely *new* group of occurrences, called a *table occurrence group,* somewhere *else* in the graph. You can assemble and wire these TOGs together in any way that makes sense for your new display, without complicating or otherwise changing the existing group.

> **NOTE** You can create as many TOGs as you like without making your database any larger. Still, performance may start to suffer if you create more than about 25 occurrences of tables that contain tens of thousands of records.

To figure out which table occurrence you need to use to make the new layout, think about what you need it to do. You start by finding an expenses record on the Expenses layout, and then you need to get to the new Assign Expenses layout—via a button, perhaps. Once you're on the new layout, you'll view an Invoice and decide which Line Item goes with the current Expense. Everything takes place from an expense record's context.

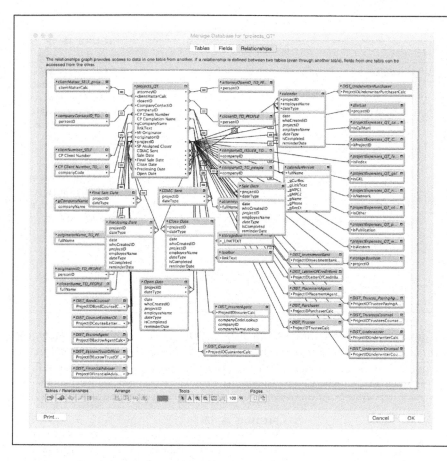

FIGURE 15-11

This relationship graph debacle shows plainly (and painfully) how quickly a good database can go bad. This database has just a handful of tables, but over 50 TOs are thrown together in one Gordian knot. If you had to tweak this database after a long absence, it could take a while to find the TO you need and then recreate the logic you used to assemble the thing.

Because your new layout lets you edit an expense record, you'll attach it to an occurrence of the *Expenses* table. The other tables you need are the same ones you used to show a related Line Item on the Expense layout: Jobs, Invoices, and Line Items. To keep things simple, you'll create new TOs of the tables needed for the new layout and then position the new group below your other table occurrences, as shown in Figure 15-12.

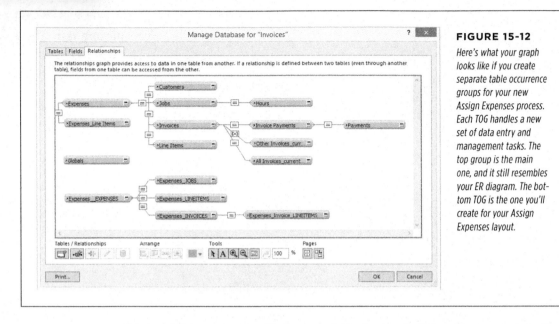

FIGURE 15-12

Here's what your graph looks like if you create separate table occurrence groups for your new Assign Expenses process. Each TOG handles a new set of data entry and management tasks. The top group is the main one, and it still resembles your ER diagram. The bottom TOG is the one you'll create for your Assign Expenses layout.

The graph lets you work with the two distinct sets of relationships separately. That way, you can tailor each relationship to fit the specific needs of the new layout, and you get the added boon of a more organized table occurrence menu (Figure 15-13).

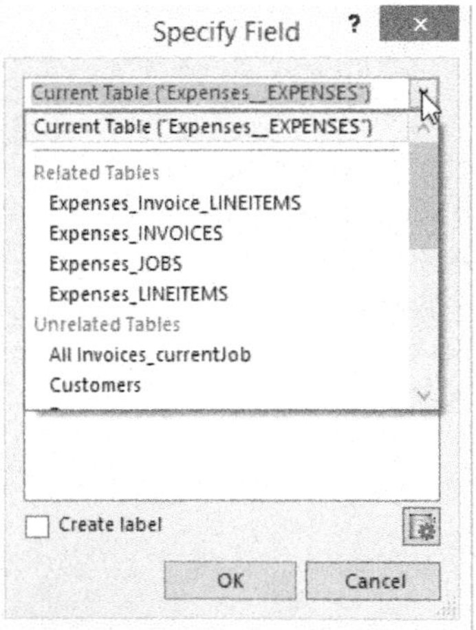

FIGURE 15-13

More TOs can actually reduce the overall confusion because now they aren't lumped together in a long list. Here's the Current Table menu from the Specify Field dialog box. TOs are grouped by Related and Unrelated Tables. When you're selecting a TO for a layout that shows records from the Expenses__Expenses TO, you only need to pay attention to the top group. Typing the Table name of each TO in all caps makes it easy to pick the TO you need. Finally, when you include the names of the intermediary TOs in a name (Expenses_Invoices_LINE ITEMS), you can easily tell which one is directly connected to Expenses, and which one is connected through the Invoice table. Note, though, that this menu should really refer to "Table Occurrences" and not "Tables." Just because FileMaker is confused, that doesn't mean you have to be too.

You can create many occurrences of a table, but each TO name has to be unique. Just as the graph can become a mess without a TOG plan, you need a TO naming scheme (or naming convention, as it's also called) to avoid creating wacky names that don't make sense in the clear light of day. Here you'll use a convention that gives each TO name a prefix identifying its TOG and that capitalizes the actual table name (Expenses_INVOICES) so you don't have to guess which source table the TO uses. The new Expenses TO will become the context of the new layout you'll create, so you'll type two underscores in its name (Expenses__EXPENSES). That way, it appears at the top of the TOG group in a menu list, as in Figure 15-14.

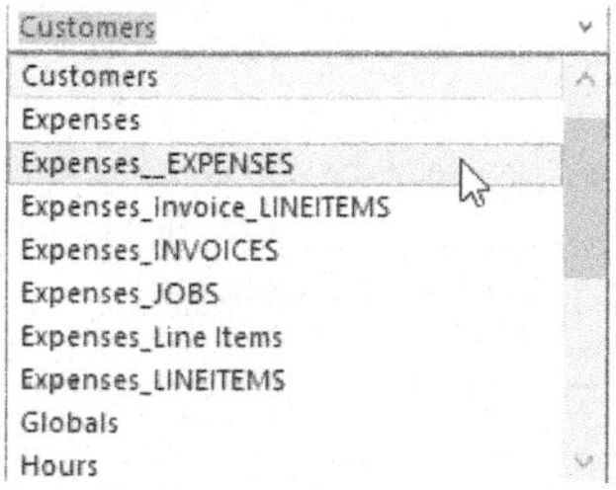

FIGURE 15-14

Not all menus that list TOs group them in related and unrelated chunks. By using a double underscore "__" in the name of the TO that provides the context for the new layout, it will appear at the top of its group, as you see with the Expenses__EXPENSES TO here. You can also see the result of not picking a good naming scheme earlier in your development because you have two very similarly named versions of the Expenses_Line Items TOs. Now that you know about naming conventions, you can see why it would be worth the time it takes to rename all the TOs in your ER diagram group. Things will only get worse as your graph grows. Renaming TOs won't break anything, so no worries there. If you rename your ER group with an "ER" prefix, then they'll all appear together in the list, instead of scattered, as they do here, plus you'd eliminate the confusion between the two similarly named Expense Line Items TOs.

NOTE This naming scheme is one of many out there. Many developers use a similar scheme, but abbreviate the layout names/prefix part of the TO name (Exp_INVOICE), so the names don't get too lengthy. Others refuse to use underscore in their TO names, and use a modified camel case instead (ExpensesINVOICE, for example). Feel free to make up your own scheme. Just use it consistently—it's your breadcrumb trail home.

Now that you've grasped the basic concept of the TOG, it's time to start the actual construction.

Managing Table Occurrences

When you use descriptive names for your TOs, they can get pretty long. Fortunately, you can easily resize any table occurrence so its entire name is visible. No matter how the table occurrence is configured, you can drag the right or left edge to make it wider or narrower. If it's set to show all its fields, then you can also drag the top or bottom edge to change its height. A table occurrence that's too short to show all its fields has little arrow icons above and below the field list. Click these arrows to scroll through the list. (When a table occurrence is set to show just the key fields or no fields at all, its height is fixed.)

To see which table an occurrence represents, just point to the arrow icon to the left of the occurrence name. FileMaker pops up an information window that tells you everything you need to know. And if long names and tooltips aren't enough, then you can use the note tool (it's the tool marked with the letter "A"). Use the note as a reminder of the purpose of your new table occurrences that's more detailed than a naming prefix. Notes behave themselves, staying in the background behind all your TOs, so some designers make large notes that enclose a new TO group to visually unite them on the graph.

Creating a New Table Occurrence Group

Before you start creating the new TOs, review your goals. Since the Assign Expenses layout needs the context of the Expenses table, it's easy to see that you need a new Expenses TO. Its purpose is to show invoice line items based on an Invoice ID you enter in a global field, and to show the job name when you've decided which job an expense belongs to. You also want to show the line item attached to that expense, so you need a second new TO for line items. With these TOs, you'll be able to see and manage the following information:

- The name of the job associated with an invoice

- The line items attached to that invoice

Figure 15-15 shows all the new table occurrences you need to create and the way you'll arrange them to make the new layout work.

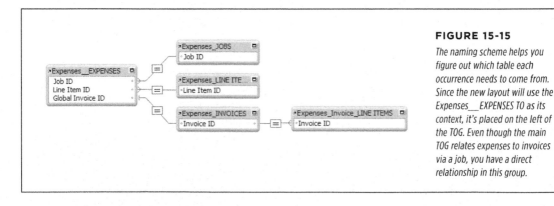

FIGURE 15-15

The naming scheme helps you figure out which table each occurrence needs to come from. Since the new layout will use the Expenses__EXPENSES TO as its context, it's placed on the left of the TOG. Even though the main TOG relates expenses to invoices via a job, you have a direct relationship in this group.

The steps are simple if you take it one table at a time:

1. **If necessary, click the Manage Database window's Relationships tab.**

   You need to see your existing Relationships graph.

2. **Click the Add Table Occurrence button. When the Specify Table window appears, select the Expenses table.**

   When you create your layout later, it'll have the context (or viewpoint) of the Expenses table, so it makes sense to create it first.

3. **In the "Name of Table Occurrence" box, type *Expenses__EXPENSES* and then click OK.**

   That's two underscore characters, to put this TO at the top of the list when it's sorted alphabetically. When you click OK, FileMaker adds the new table occurrence to the middle of the graph. Move it out of the way to get ready for the next steps.

Repeat the steps above (adjust step 2 to choose the appropriate table) to create the following TOs:

- Expenses_INVOICES

- Expenses_LINEITEMS

- Expenses_Invoices_LINEITEMS

- Expenses_JOBS

You now have five new table occurrences on your graph. Since the names are so long, you might have to stretch your new TOs so you can read their names.

TIP   If you use the Duplicate button to copy an existing set of TOs, you get their existing names and relationships. Then you can move the new TOG and change its names and relationships as appropriate. Or you can use a hybrid method of creating a new TO with the steps above, but copy/paste the prefix part of the name from the first TO. With practice, you'll find your own favorite style.

Once you have your TOs in place, you need to hook them together properly. Here are the relationships you need:

- From Expenses__EXPENSES to Expenses_JOBS, using the Job ID fields as keys. This relationship lets you display the Job Name on the Assign Expenses layout.

- From Expenses__EXPENSES to Expenses_LINE ITEMS, using the Line Item ID field as keys. The relationship will let you show a Line Item's detail on the layout.

- From Expenses_INVOICES to Expenses_Invoices_LINEITEMS, using the Invoice ID fields as keys. This relationship will show an Invoice's Line Items on the new layout.

- From Expenses__EXPENSES to Expenses_INVOICES, using Global Invoice ID and Invoice ID as keys.

After you create the Expenses__Expenses::Global Invoice ID to Expenses_Invoices::Invoice ID relationship, notice that the global relationship shows a little bar on the Expenses side. That's to remind you there's a global field on that side of the relationship. See the box below to learn more about naming global fields.

TIP Remember, if you like things lined up nice and neat, you have Arrange tools that let you resize and align a selected group of TOs together (page 217).

Building the Assign Expenses Layout

Now that you've finished the new table occurrence group and hooked up its relationships, you're ready to create the Assign Expenses layout. Since this new layout has a lot of objects, you'll have to repeat some processes a few times. Figure 15-16 shows what you're trying to accomplish.

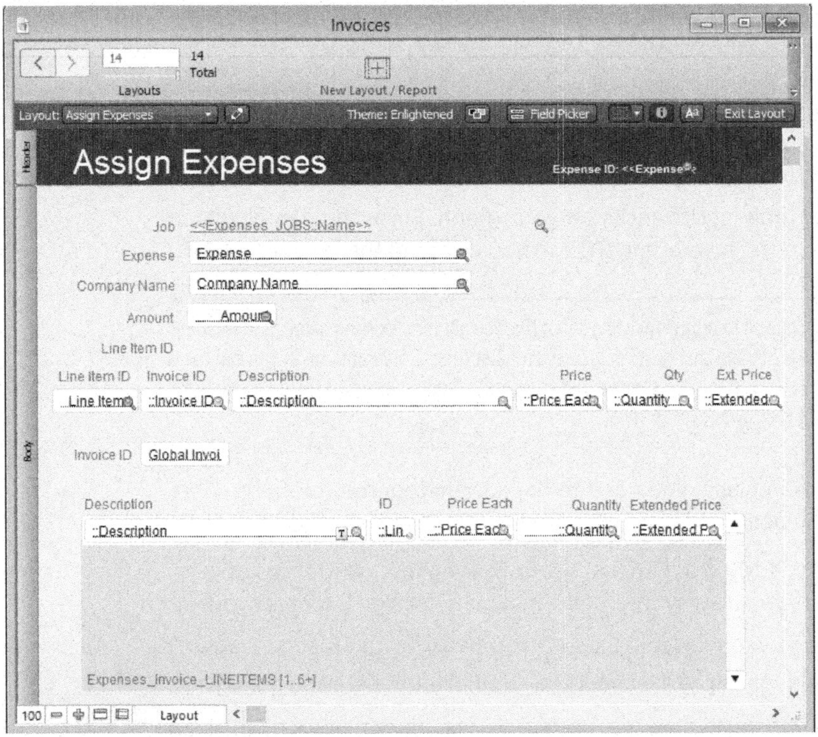

FIGURE 15-16

The new layout is similar to your existing Expenses layout. To get a jump start, you duplicate that layout and then change some objects to fit the new context. You'll also create brand new objects from scratch. Much of your real-world development will follow a similar mix of copying and editing existing elements and adding new ones from scratch.

POWER USERS' CLINIC

One (Global) Field to Rule Them All

You know that fields set to use global storage have the same value across every record in the table that holds them. Since these fields are so different from other fields, many database designers give them special names so that the fields stand out in a list. That way, they're less likely to get used inappropriately—say, in a context where they don't have much meaning—or plopped down on a layout where someone can edit the values when they should stay static.

You can just preface the names of all your global fields with the word "global," like you did in the steps above. But in the real world, people commonly just use a lowercase "g" as a prefix. With this scheme, you can name your global field "gInvoice ID" and save a few keystrokes. Plus, you look like a guru.

Some developers also use the lowercase "g" in the names of their TOs, to indicate that the relationship uses a global field as a key. It can be a handy extra reminder that the relationship doesn't work bidirectionally, as relationships that are based on normal fields do.

◼ DUPLICATING AND EDITING AN EXISTING LAYOUT

Even though they're from different contexts, the Expenses and Assign Expenses layouts have many of the same objects on them. Your databases will look more polished, and you'll save time, if you copy similar elements whenever you can. In this case, duplicating a layout will keep a handful of elements in the exact same locations, so that when you switch from layout to layout, you're immediately oriented by seeing similar onscreen elements in the same spot on every layout. Here's how to copy a layout and change a field reference:

1. **Go to the Expenses layout and then switch to Layout mode.**

   You're setting up the element you want to copy.

2. **Choose Layouts→Duplicate Layout.**

   The layout is duplicated along with all its objects. The new layout has the same name as the original, except the word "Copy" is appended to the name.

3. **Choose Layouts→Layout Setup and then change the new layout's name to *Assign Expenses*.**

   That'll make it easy to remember what the layout is for when you see it in a long list later on. Change the layout title in the header, too.

4. **In the "Show records from" pop-up menu, choose the Expenses__EXPENSES table occurrence and then click OK.**

   Now you can see another benefit of your naming convention—it's easy to spot the TO you need. All the fields on your layouts have changed from local fields to related ones. You'll have to switch each field to the proper TOG.

5. **Double-click the Expense field.**

The Specify Field window appears.

6. **From the "Table occurrence" pop-up menu, choose "Expenses__EX-PENSES."**

The "Table occurrence" pop-up menu is divided between related and unrelated tables. Expenses__EXPENSES is at the top of the list and is labeled as the Current Table (because you selected that TO in step 3). FileMaker is well mannered enough to know that you still want the Expense field, so you won't have to change that part of the field name reference.

7. **Click OK.**

The "::" disappears from the Expense field, and you can be sure that it will show data from the proper context now.

Repeat the process for each field on the layout. Remember, you're just switching the TO from the unrelated TO to the related TO, and you're keeping the same source table when you do. Don't forget to change the merge fields, too: Expenses_JOBS::Name and Expenses__EXPENSES::Expense ID (in the header). And there's a script step on the Jobs::Name merge field that needs to be set to use the new TO. If you absolutely hate this process of switching a whole bunch of fields from one TOG or TO to another, you're in good company. But to avoid it, you'll have to create all your layouts from scratch instead of duplicating and editing.

■ COPYING A PORTAL FROM ANOTHER LAYOUT

Just as you duplicated the Expenses layout to save time and (some) trouble, you already have a Line Items portal (over on the Invoice layout) that's formatted and organized nicely. Copying it and then changing its context also orients your users, because the portal on the Assign Expenses layout looks just like the one they use to create Invoices. They don't have to get used to a new arrangement of data just because they're performing a different task. Here's how to copy and edit a portal.

1. **Switch to Layout mode and then go to the Invoices layout.**

That's where the portal you need is found.

2. **Use your favorite technique for selecting multiple items. Grab the Line Items portal, all its fields, and their labels. Then choose Edit→Copy or press Ctrl+C (⌘-C).**

Make sure they're all highlighted, because it's a pain to come back here if you've missed something.

3. **Switch to the Assign Expenses layout. Make the Body part larger to accommodate the new portal. Click in the approximate spot you want the portal to land and then choose Edit→Paste or press Ctrl+V (⌘-V).**

   If the layout's Body part is big enough, your copied objects will land centered on the spot where you clicked. Refer back to Figure 15-16 if necessary for guidance on where to place the new portal.

4. **Double-click the portal and then choose Expenses_Invoices_LINEITEMS from the "Show related records from" pop-up menu.**

   You need the version of the Line Items table that goes through the Invoice table, and not the one that's directly connected to Expenses__EXPENSES. The benefits of a well-chosen naming convention are well worth the extra time and thought you put into using it.

5. **Double-click the Description field in the portal to show the Specify Field window. Change the "Show related records from" pop-up menu to the Expenses_Invoices_LINEITEMS TO and then click OK.**

   Repeat this step for the portal's other fields.

The major elements of the layout are in place. Add the Expenses::Global Invoice ID field and a label to the layout, and you're ready to test. Switch back to Browse mode and then enter invoice number *2016002* in the Global Invoice ID field. When you enter the number into the field, you'll see the invoice's line items appear in the portal below the expense data. You could add a tooltip showing the Line Item ID to the Description field, or because it actually makes sense to show an ID field on this layout, just add it to the portal. See page 306 for a refresher on making the field safe from accidental editing; see the box on page 618 to learn more about how global relationships work.

■ USING GTRR TO SWITCH TOGS

The layout you've just created is pretty slick, but there's one problem. Suppose you're on the Expenses layout looking at an expense. You decide you want to assign an invoice line item to it, so you use the Layout pop-up menu to switch to the Assign Expenses layout. Unfortunately, when you do, you won't always see the same record. That's because each table occurrence has its own current record, found set, and sort order. Users will find this situation frustrating, since they may have to do a find on the new layout to see the expense they were just looking at.

It turns out the "Go to Related Record" command has an unexpected power: It can transfer a found set—complete with current record and sort order—from one table occurrence to another. The "Go to Related Record" Options window has a "Get related record from" pop-up menu that shows every table occurrence in the database, not just the ones related to your current context. It shows layouts attached to *any* occurrence of the same table. In other words, when you ask to go to a record in the same table occurrence you're already viewing, you can pick the Assign Expenses layout, even though it's associated with a different occurrence of the Expenses table.

If you want to get all geeky about it, you can call this technique "TOG jumping," just like the pros do.

Globals and Relationships

I don't get it. I thought relationships were supposed to hook different records together, but a global field has the same value throughout a table and isn't associated with any specific record. Why can I use a global field to create a relationship?

As the Assign Expense example on page 614 shows, relationships can be created to support a layout that performs a specific task. When you use a global field in a relationship, it works just fine. You'll see related data just as you normally would.

This kind of relationship doesn't create a permanent connection between records—it just gives you temporary access to related records when there's a value in the Expenses::Global Invoice ID field. If you clear out that field, the relationship doesn't work anymore (it's called *invalid*) and no line item records will show in the portal. In this case, that's an asset, since you can reduce visual clutter on the layout by clearing Global Invoice ID field.

Since FileMaker doesn't index global fields, the relationship doesn't work the way you'd expect when you look in the other direction—from the normal-field context back toward the global field. From the Expenses::INVOICES direction, the relationship behaves like a *Cartesian join* (page 599), show-

ing every record in the other table. That makes perfect sense, because every record in the Expenses table has the same value in that global field. This behavior isn't important in situations like the Assign Expenses layout, because you only care what happens from the global side of a relationship. So unlike regular relationships, where you can pull data reliably from either direction, global relationships work in only one direction. As Figure 15-15 shows, FileMaker doesn't connect the relationship line in the graph directly to the global field. This visual cue lets you know this relationship works only from the global side to the "normal" side.

One last point: You can display a global field's data in another table *without* a relationship. Since global fields aren't associated with any record, you can view and modify them from anywhere, including unrelated tables. It's common to create a table to hold values you need to use from many different tables in a global table (say, your company's logo, name, address, and other contact information) and then use those fields on printed reports. That way, if any of that data changes, you can change it in the global table, and it's immediately changed on all your reports.

When you use this technique, FileMaker shows the records dictated by the relationship but uses the layout you choose. To make the connection, add a button to the Expenses layout that runs the "Go to Related Record" command. When you set up the button, choose the Expenses table occurrence and the Assign Expenses layout. Also, make sure you turn on "Show only related records." FileMaker does all the rest of the work for you.

You can also add a button to the Assign Expenses layout that transports you *back* to the Expenses layout. This time you configure the "Go to Related Record" command to use the Expenses__EXPENSES table occurrence and the Expenses layout.

■ Understanding Graph Arrangements

The first TOG in your graph still looks and behaves like the ER diagram you drew on page 194, even though it has a few extra TOs in it. But you can see that the more TOs you add to this group, the quicker its intended meaning will get lost in the visual clutter. That's not to say that the TOG's behavior would change, only that you'd have a harder time seeing the main tables' relationships at a glance. Because the graph's complexity increases along with the features you add to your layout, finding an appropriate graph arrangement early in your development is critical. Without a plan, you could end up with a labyrinth, like the one in Figure 15-11.

> **NOTE** If you do end up creating (or inheriting) a messy graph, you can rearrange TOs or change their relationships. But calculations, script steps, and other processes that depend on the changed item could break in the process. These types of developer-introduced bugs are time-consuming to trace and fix, so most developers run a DDR (page 557) first and then use it as a map for fixing the clutter.

However, FileMaker has two commonly used graph arrangement models: spiders and anchor/buoys. Both have their strengths and weaknesses. Spider graphs are simpler, because you can use relationship bidirectionality to use each TO for several different purposes. This technique tends to keep the need for extra TOs to a minimum. Anchor/buoy graphs are easier to understand, but you give up the flexibility of bidirectional relationships in return for legibility. Plus you'll end up creating two or three times as many TOs as a spider graph.

The first arrangement of TOs you made (the one that looks like an ER diagram), is sometimes called a *spider* because there's often a central table occurrence from which most other TOs are connected. If you're adopting this model, you may decide to keep the central spider free of extra TOs and then create free-floating TOGs whenever you need new relationships between tables.

> **NOTE** There's no one-size-fits-all rule for graph arrangement, but there are general rules of thumb. Plus, you can adapt formal data models to handle time-tested processes like inventory control or student registration databases. Those concepts are complex, though, and beyond the scope of this book. Do a Google search for *data modeling* to find out more, but don't get too bogged down in theory. As you already know, FileMaker is easier to use than most any other database out there, so some of those concepts won't apply to your FileMaker solutions.

Anchor/buoy graphs also get their name from their appearance. The second TOG you created (page 612) is an anchor/buoy TOG. That is, the TO on the left end of the group provides the context for the TOG's layout. All the other TOs flow out to the right in lines (or *buoys*) that are "anchored" by the main TO. Because these lines can be three or more TOs long, they can start to look like tentacles, which is why some folks call these graph arrangements *squids* instead. Since a layout's context almost always comes from the anchor in a TOG, there's no ambiguity about which TO to use. And calculations are easier to write because the TOGs are rigidly arranged. New developers find that this predictability helps them get up and running more quickly.

Some developers always work with one of these models, and asking them to consider change is like starting a discussion on politics or religion. If you're interested, search the Web for *anchor buoy, FileMaker data model,* or *FileMaker Relationships graph.* If you join the FileMaker Community site (page 901), you'll get access to white papers, including one on the pros and cons of several different graph arrangement schemes for FileMaker. With time and experience, you'll find that some databases work better with one arrangement, but others work just as well with a hybrid of spider and anchor/buoy, or another arrangement.

The graph in Figure 15-17 has been converted to something that looks more like an anchor-buoy. This arrangement retains all the benefits of the spider model and also makes it easier to see multi-hop relationships. What's not so clear, though, is how two tables like Expenses and Invoices relate to one another. The second TOG (bottom) is fully anchorbuoy, in that only one of its TOGs has a layout, and the others are used merely to display related fields on that layout.

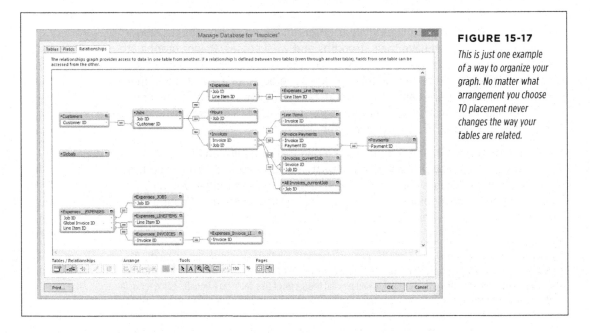

FIGURE 15-17

This is just one example of a way to organize your graph. No matter what arrangement you choose TO placement never changes the way your tables are related.

NOTE Rearranging your TOs doesn't change the way your tables are related, although it can change where they appear when you open a relationship's Edit Relationship dialog box.

Connecting Database Files

In FileMaker, you can make two database files work together as easily as you work with multiple tables. Using the techniques you already know, you connect tables from another file (often called an *external data source*) without the overhead of copying all that data into your file. You just put a table occurrence from your external file onto your Relationships graph, and that defines the relationship to all your other tables.

For example, suppose you have a Zip Codes database that you want to connect to the Invoice system. You want to let users type in a Zip code, and the Customer table's

City and State fields will use a lookup to automatically enter their data. You'll need a table occurrence from the external file to your "local" file's Relationships graph. See the box on "Systems with More than One Database" to learn more about why you might keep some tables in separate database files.

NOTE If you downloaded the sample files for this chapter, you'll have a file called *SW Zip Codes.fmp12*. Or find the file on the book's Missing CD page at *www.missingmanuals.com/cds/fmp14mm*.

Adding a Table Occurrence from Another File

Once you have a Zip Codes TO on the Invoice file's Relationships graph, it begins to act like a first-class citizen in its new environment: You can create relationships to it, create layouts that are based on it, and do just about anything else you can do with the tables in this database. Here's how:

1. **In the Invoices database, choose File→Manage Database and then click the Relationships tab. Then click the Add Table Occurrence button.**

   The Specify Table dialog box appears.

2. **From the Data Source pop-up menu, choose Add FileMaker Data Source.**

   A standard Open File dialog box appears—just like you see when you're opening a database.

3. **Browse to the *SW Zip Codes.fmp12* database, select it, and then click Open.**

   The Specify Table dialog box now shows tables from the Leads database. There's only one, and it's called Zip Codes. FileMaker selects the Zip Codes table and suggests the TO name *Zip Codes* for it. Since it doesn't duplicate any TO name in your file, you don't have to change it.

4. **Click OK.**

   FileMaker adds the new occurrence to the graph. As Figure 15-18 shows, you can tell at a glance that it's an occurrence of what FileMaker calls an *external* table, because it shows you the table occurrence's name in italic.

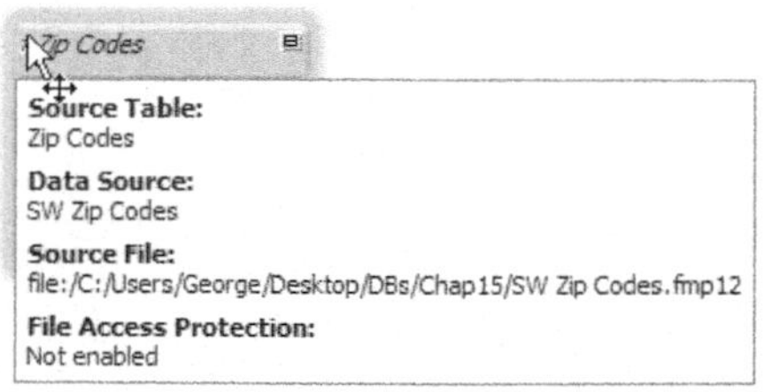

FIGURE 15-18

External tables' names display in italic. To find out which database it comes from, press on the little arrow to the left of the TO's name to show the information window. FileMaker displays the source table's name, the Data Source (or file name), the Source File's path and whether the file's access protection (page 774) is turned on.

5. **Drag the Zip Code::Zip Code field to the Customer::Zip Code field.**

   You've created the relationship you'll need to change Customer::City and Customer::State to lookup fields. See page 226 for a refresher on creating lookups.

Once you have the lookups set, click OK to close the Manage Database dialog box. Switch to Browse mode and type a Zip code to test the lookups.

Defining Data Sources Using a Path

When you added the Zip Codes TO to your graph in the previous section, FileMaker created an External Data Source reference. That's the path FileMaker uses to manage the data, so you never have to think about the connection. But these references aren't dynamic. That is, if you move the *Zip Codes.fmp12* file from the location recorded in your file reference, FileMaker won't be able to show you the data in the file until you update the reference. Choose File→Manage→External Data Sources and then double-click the file reference to edit it.

You use this same set of dialog boxes to create a data source manually. Give the data source a logical name and then click the Add File button to navigate to the file's location. If you prefer typing to pointing and clicking, you can type the path from scratch, but you have to follow strict form. Acceptable form varies, based on what platform you're using and how you access the external file. You'll see examples of the acceptable file path formats at the bottom of the Edit Data Source dialog box (Figure 15-19).

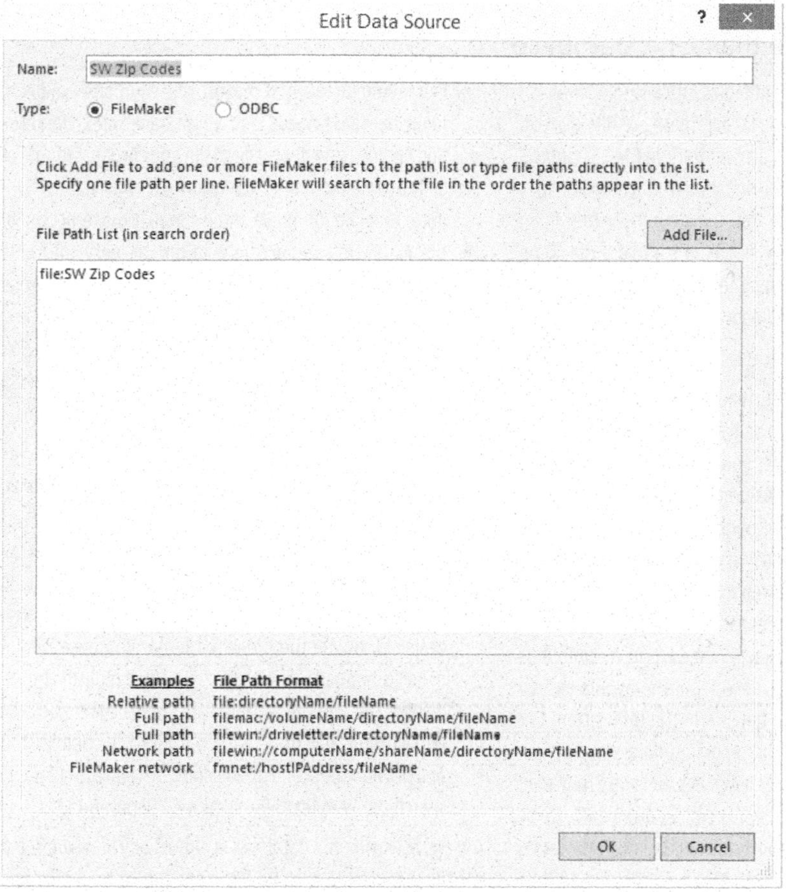

FIGURE 15-19

Here's the Edit Data Source dialog box. The data source's name is the same as the filename, since you let FileMaker handle it when you created the TO for the external file in the previous section. But you can edit the source name if you prefer. Here the file path indicates that the data source is in the same folder as the Invoice file. The Add File button lets you browse your system or network. In this case, you could use that button to find a file that's been moved and update its path.

You can even give a file reference more than one path. When you do, FileMaker looks for the file at the first path. If it doesn't find the file, then it tries the second path. The search continues until it finds the file or has tried every listed path. (If it never finds the file, then you see an error message.) Using this technique, you can have a database that opens files from different locations depending on which computer it's opened on. Or you can ask FileMaker to use your local copy of the Zip Codes database if it finds one, but use the network copy otherwise.

Systems with More than One Database

Just because you can put a lot of tables into a single database file doesn't make it imperative. In fact, there are lots of good reasons to divide your system across multiple files. Chapter 6 mentions a common reason: You might be storing large images or other files in your database. You can keep these files in an external table so the database file itself isn't so large. Then you can back up, copy, and email the information about the images without including the images themselves.

Here are some other reasons to use more than one file:

- You can create a database for each kind of layout you need. For example, if you need to track sales, you can create a database with the tables you need to store the actual data: orders, line items, customers, shipments, products, and so forth. Your company might use the database in two ways: Salespeople do data entry (creating and managing orders) and managers do reporting on those sales (daily, monthly, and quarterly sales reports; trend and promotion analysis; and so on). To keep your system as simple as possible, you can create these separate layouts as two distinct databases. Since they share the tables from the central sales database, the reporting data stays up-to-date as FileMaker processes new sales. But since they're in two databases, the layouts you need for order entry don't get in the way of the reporting layouts, and vice versa. Even better, it's easier to keep managers from seeing stuff that might confuse them, because those day-to-day task layouts just don't exist in their file.

- Expanding on this first reason, one company usually has many database needs. You might have Sales, Marketing, and Engineering departments in your organization. Each of these departments has a unique way it deals with data, and the database should match those needs. But the Marketing Department might be very interested in sales data, and the Sales Department needs access to engineering information. You can create a separate database for each department but share some tables between systems. This way you get a layout *and* sets of tables that are tailored to each group, but the important data is shared.

- When you can use external table occurrences, you have a very flexible design metaphor. A database—or file—can hold display elements (layouts, scripts, value lists) or data (tables and fields) or both. Some developers always separate their data and display because it can make it easier to update the file when major database changes need to happen. In that case, you can replace the new display file without needing to import masses of data into a brand-new file. Data separation is a complex topic and beyond the scope of this book. To read more about it, search the Web for "FileMaker data separation."

You can construct the database in almost any way you see fit: one file for each table, all tables in one file, or tables in logical groupings; all the layouts in one database, or several databases to break things up. A FileMaker file is a very flexible unit of organization: Use it as you see fit.

Going to External Records

Now that you've got a file reference and a table occurrence from an external file, what do you do with it? You *could* create a new layout attached to the Zip Codes table occurrence. But there already is a layout for viewing the details of a Zip Code record: the Zip Code database's Zip Codes layout.

Once again, as long as you have a valid relationship between any table and the Zip Codes table, "Go to Related Records" comes to the rescue (see Figure 15-20). Create a button that performs the "Go to Related Record" command. In the "'Go to

Related Record' Options" window, choose the Zip Codes table occurrence. Since this occurrence is from a table in another file, the "Use external table's layout" checkbox comes to life.

When this checkbox is turned on, the "Show record using layout" pop-up menu lists layouts from the Zip Codes database rather than the current database. Turn the checkbox on and then choose the Zip Codes layout. Don't forget to turn on "Show only related records." Now when you click the button, the Zip Codes database pops up and shows you the Zip code record.

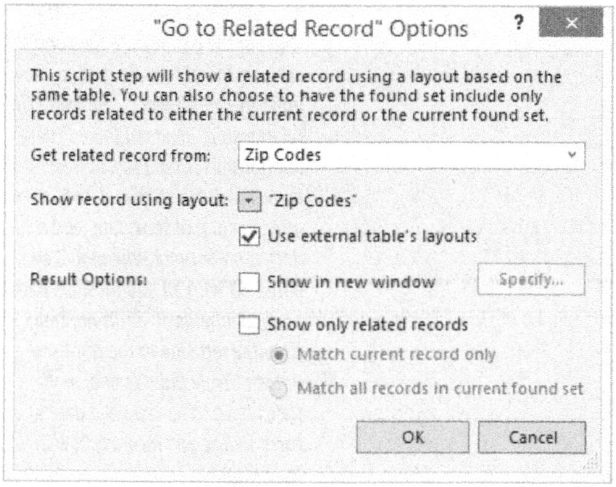

FIGURE 15-20

The "Use external table's layouts" option is available only when you choose an external table in a "Go to Related Record" command. When you choose this option, you see a list of layouts, from which you can choose the one you want as your target. Reuse work you've already done by showing data in its original form—its native layout in its source file. Whether or not you choose the "Show in new window" option, selecting an external layout will always show the related records in a window belonging to the other file. If "Show in new window" is turned off, FileMaker reuses an open window from the other file to display the records. If no window is already open, FileMaker creates a new one.

Using Multiple Relationship Techniques

Each technique you've learned in this chapter is useful on its own, but when you combine techniques, you can really start to get creative. For example, using two global date fields and a multiple criteria relationship, you can create a layout that lets users enter dates in a pair of fields and then see a list of invoices that fall between the dates they enter. You'll call this layout an Invoice Finder.

Creating the Invoice Finder Layout

To set up your new Invoice Finder layout, you need to add two new global fields to your Globals table. You also need a new relationship that matches fields in the

Invoices table using these global fields. This sort of job benefits from its own table occurrence group. Call this group *Invoice Finder*.

To get the portal to show the right invoices, you need a relationship that uses your new global fields, and it'll have slightly more complicated rules than you've seen before. See Figure 15-21 for the setup.

TIP If the logic in Figure 15-21 is confusing, remember that if you temporarily move the Invoice Finder__GLO-BALS TO to the right of Invoice Finder_INVOICES so that the relationships read Date ≥ gStart Date AND Date ≤ gEnd Date instead. Then when you switch the Invoice Finder__GLOBALS TO back to its anchor position at the left edge of the TOG, FileMaker switches the logic for you.

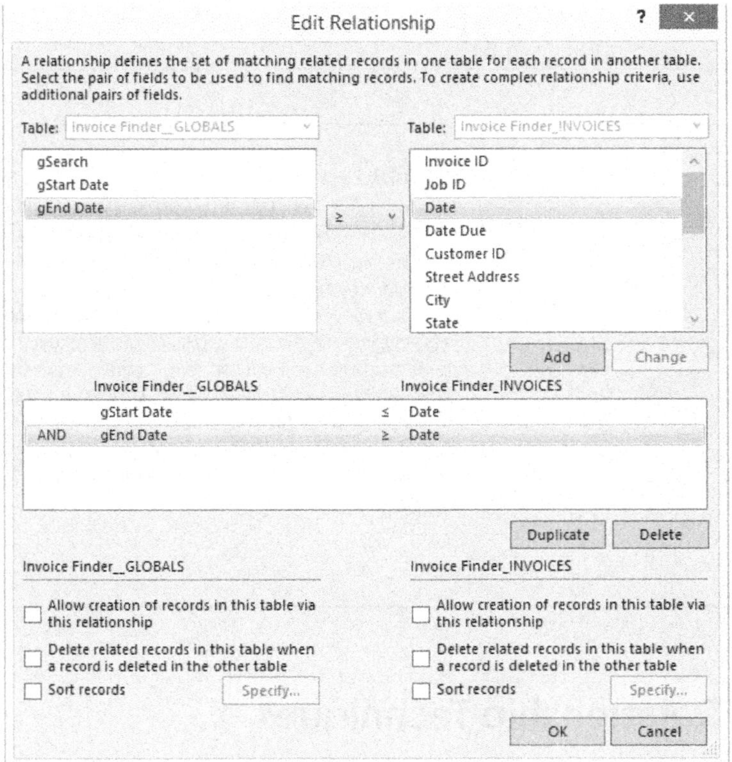

FIGURE 15-21

The relationship between Invoice Finder__GLOBALS and Invoice Finder_INVOICES connects two global date fields to one regular date field. An invoice has to be between the value in the gStart Date field and the value in the gEnd Date field to show up in the portal you create using this relationship. Read out loud: "These relationship criteria say that an invoice will match if its date is on or after the global start date, and if the date is on or before the global end date." As with all relationships based on global fields, it works normally from the left side to the right side but isn't truly bidirectional. Both fields have to have a valid date in them before any records show in the portal.

Below are the steps for creating a new table, defining some global fields in that new table, and then using your creations in a new table occurrence group. You've done most of this stuff before in other tutorials, so although you have to follow a lot of steps, they should all be familiar:

1. **In the Invoices database, go to the Manage Database window's Fields tab and select your Globals table. Then, in the Field Name box, type *gStart Date*. Make the field a Date type and then click Create.**

   The "g" prefix reminds you that the field is a global.

2. **Click the Options button. When the Field Options dialog box appears, click the Storage tab and then turn on the "Use global storage" checkbox. Click OK.**

   Since this field isn't holding data about an entity, but is used to change the records that display in a portal, you need to use a global field.

3. **Repeat steps 1 and 2 to create another global date field called *gEnd Date*.**

   Both fields appear in the list.

4. **Switch to the Relationships tab. Drag the Globals table occurrence down below your existing TOGs. Then double-click it, and change its name to *Invoice Finder__GLOBALS*.**

   This new TO will be the anchor in a new TOG, so place it near the left edge of the graph. You may also need to stretch the TO so its whole name appears.

5. **Add a new occurrence of the Invoices table called Invoice Finder_INVOICES and a new occurrence of the Jobs table called Invoice Finder_JOBS.**

   Since your portal shows invoices and the job name associated with each invoice, you need these tables in your group as well.

6. **Drag the Invoice Finder_INVOICES::Job ID field onto the Invoice Finder_ JOBS:: Job ID field to create a relationship.**

   When an Invoice record matches a Job, the Job Name shows in the portal.

7. **Refer to Figure 15-21 to create the multi-criteria relationship shown there between the Invoice Finder__GLOBALS and Invoice Finder_INVOICES TOs.**

   Because FileMaker uses both criteria, the portal you'll build using this relationship will show Invoices that have dates equal to or between the gStart Date and the gEnd Date.

8. **Click OK.**

   FileMaker returns you to the graph. Your Invoice Finder TOG should look like Figure 15-22.

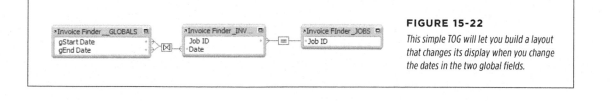

FIGURE 15-22

This simple TOG will let you build a layout that changes its display when you change the dates in the two global fields.

Click OK to accept your changes and start testing your new relationship. Create a new layout and then show records from the Invoice Finder__GLOBALS table occurrence. Add the two global fields and a portal based on the Invoice Finder_INVOICES relationship. For extra credit, add script triggers (page 469) to the global fields that commit the records. When it's all done, put values in the two global fields, and the portal updates to show the matching invoices. See one possible arrangement in Figure 15-23. See the box below to learn another way to create this same type of relationship.

FREQUENTLY ASKED QUESTION

Global Table or Global Fields?

I've already got relationships to my Invoice table all over my graph. Why can't I use one of them instead of creating yet another Invoice TO? For example, I could put my global date fields into the Jobs table and then use a portal filtering calculation on the Jobs-to-Invoice relationship to create the same Invoice Finder. Is there a problem with that?

Not really. In fact, that approach would save you from creating the Invoice Finder table and the whole TOG that made the layout work. The Invoice Finder layout would be based on the Jobs table, and the portal filtering calculation would look a lot like the multiple-criteria relationship you set up in the tutorial on page 595.

Using an existing relationship in a new way seems like a cleaner solution than adding new structure to the database and graph.

If you're comfortable with the fact that gStart Date and gEnd Date have nothing whatsoever to do with a Job record and exist only to keep the graph streamlined, then your plan will work just fine.

The main downside is that it might not be clear to another developer who has to work in your system why you made that choice (unless you make a note on the graph, of course). The benefit of creating a global field table is that as a separate table and TOG, it's completely clear what its function is. In fact, you might find other reasons to use global relationships, and then that table could become a repository for all the global fields that make similar features work. It would be rare indeed that any changes you make to the database's other structure would affect this standalone global table or any TOGs you hang from it. But it's your call.

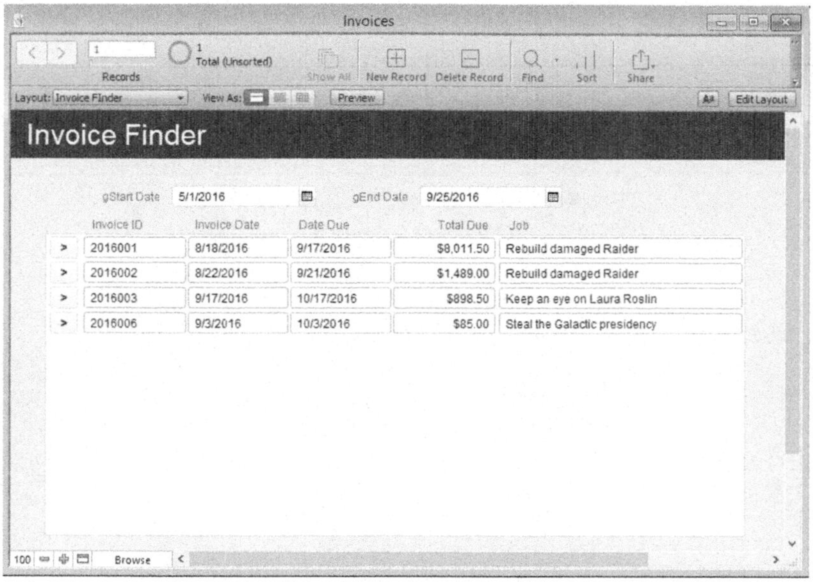

FIGURE 15-23

You can create a new layout that makes it easy to see the invoices you need at a glance. As you enter new dates in the global fields, the invoice portal updates on the fly, thanks to the global multiple-criteria relationship that powers it.

NOTE The Invoice Finder table has no records. You might think this would be a problem, but it isn't. However, in some older versions of FileMaker Pro, portals don't work properly when you have no records. If you run into this problem, just create a new empty record.

Do I Really Need a Relationship?

Those new TOGs I made in the Invoice Finder tutorial seem like so much cruft in my database. Isn't there a way to find Invoices that doesn't involve a portal?

Yes, there is, but this chapter is about relationships, so that's the technique covered here. And it's a perfectly legitimate technique. But you're right to wonder whether the end result is worth the cruft. In a relatively simple database, like the one you've been working on, a few new TOs aren't going to be a problem, so the Invoice Finder TOG is just fine. And in a system where people are used to seeing search results in a portal, it might make sense to stick with that same visual solution. That

way, when you roll out their new layout, they'll understand what to do without training.

But in a large database where performance is a primary concern, you'll need to spend time and energy keeping the file, and its relationships graph, slim and trim. In that case, you could give users the same effect as the Invoice Finder, by putting the two global date fields on an Invoice list layout. Write a script that finds invoices with dates that fall between the start date and end date the user enters in the global fields. Use a script trigger to run the script, and you've given your users a new way to find invoices that didn't require adding cruft to your relationships graph

---

Reporting and Analysis

A database excels at keeping track of things—itsy-bitsy, teeny-tiny details about hundreds, thousands, even millions of little things. But the point of keeping track of all those details is to understand them: You need to know what all those data points mean. For example, if you want to understand your customers' music tastes, a line item report of 200,000 individual MP3 sales doesn't do you much good: The information is in there somewhere, but a feeble human brain stands no chance of ferreting it out. A report that divides that information into 25 music genres, each with sales totals, and then further broken down by gender, would help you interpret all that data at a glance. In other words, a well-designed report, like the one you saw on page 179, summarizes the data for you. Now that you've learned how to create a vessel for all your data, it's time to learn how to analyze what it all *means*.

■ Summary Fields and Subsummary Parts

Analysis doesn't mean you need a degree in statistics. You only need to know how to create reports. FileMaker's flagship report is the summary report. The report uses a list layout, along with two special tools for categorizing and totaling the data. First, Subsummary parts create categories, and then you place summary fields in the Subsummary parts to figure out the math. At its simplest, a subsummary report could print your contacts database, grouping and counting all your contacts by city.

> **NOTE** To follow along in this chapter, you'll find it helpful to download the sample databases from this book's Missing CD page at *www.missingmanuals.com/cds/fmp14mm*.

Summary Fields

A summary field doesn't hold one value per record like the other field types. Instead, summary fields gather up and process data from a set of records—either in a found set or within a group of sorted records. A summary field always refers to some other field in the database—usually another one in the same table. Summary fields do their work on all the records in a group that contains data in the referenced field. Here's how to create a summary field:

1. **In the *CH16 People Start.fmp12* database, choose File→Manage→Database.**

   You're about to add a field that counts the people in your database. This action is one of the most common ways to summarize database information.

2. **In the Manage Database window, choose the Fields tab. Then, in the Field Name box, type *sumCount*.**

   This field name is different from the ones you've seen so far. It has no spaces, and it's in *camel case* (mixed upper and lower case). The "sum" prefix tells you that the field is a summary field. The Count part tells you what the summary field does.

3. **From the Type pop-up menu, choose Summary and then click Create.**

   The "Options for Summary Field" window appears (Figure 16-1).

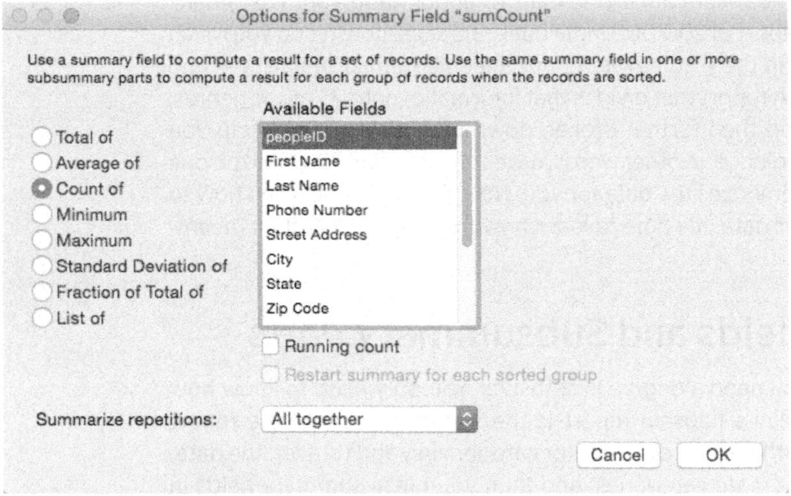

FIGURE 16-1

The "Options for Summary Field" window appears when you make a new summary field. Unlike the field types you've used so far, a summary field has options that aren't optional, so FileMaker shows you those options as soon as you create the field. As with any field options, you can revisit this window if you need to review or edit the settings.

4. **Select the "Count of" radio button.**

   A summary field can perform one of eight summary calculations. In this case, you want it to *count* the records in a group.

5. **From the Available Fields list, choose peopleID.**

   Because you want to count all your records, pick a field that will have data in it (for example, don't pick Phone Number if you don't have that information for everyone). Since key fields' data is created at the same time a record is created, it won't ever be empty, so it's common to use an ID or key field for a count summary.

6. **Click OK.**

   FileMaker adds the new field to the field list. You'll use the field on a subsummary report later.

If you add this field to the People Detail layout and then have a look in Browse mode, you can see the summary field at work. It gives you the same information on every record—the total found count. If you do a find, you'll see the count change.

> **NOTE** Since you already have this information in the toolbar, you won't often use summary fields on detail layouts. Instead, you'll use them in reports, as described next.

Subsummary Parts

The real power of summary fields becomes apparent when you combine them with Subsummary parts. Instead of counting all the people in your database, you might want to count how many you have in each city or state (or both). Maybe you need to know how many are still living, or get counts by Zip code. Or you may want to see how your contact list breaks down by city, gender, status, or any other field in the table.

All you need to do is create a Subsummary part for the field to live on and then sort the records by one of the fields you want to count. Here's how to create a Subsummary part on an exiting layout:

1. **Switch to the People List layout, enter Layout mode and then choose Insert→Part.**

   The Part Definition dialog box appears (see page 283 for a refresher).

2. **Turn on the "Subsummary when sorted by" radio button.**

   The list of fields on the right side of the window becomes active. Like a summary field, a Subsummary part always references a field. The part won't appear unless your records are sorted by a field you specify.

3. **In the field list, select the Status field.**

   You're telling the part to appear when the records are sorted by the Status field.

4. **Click OK.**

   FileMaker asks if you want this part to summarize the records above it or below it. When you add group totals to your layout, they can appear before or after the records they summarize.

5. **Click Print Above.**

FileMaker adds a new Subsummary part to your layout, between the header and the body. (If you had opted for Print Below, then it would be between the body and the footer instead.)

6. **Add a text object to the new part with this for content:** *Status: <<Status>> (<<sumCount>>).*

You're creating a text object that merges in the Status field and "Count of People" field. Type it, or use Insert Merge Field to select Status and then sumCount.

Switch to Browse mode. The Subsummary part doesn't appear because the records aren't sorted. Sort by the Status field to review your work. Your layout should look like Figure 16-2. Scroll through the records to see the grouped and counted data.

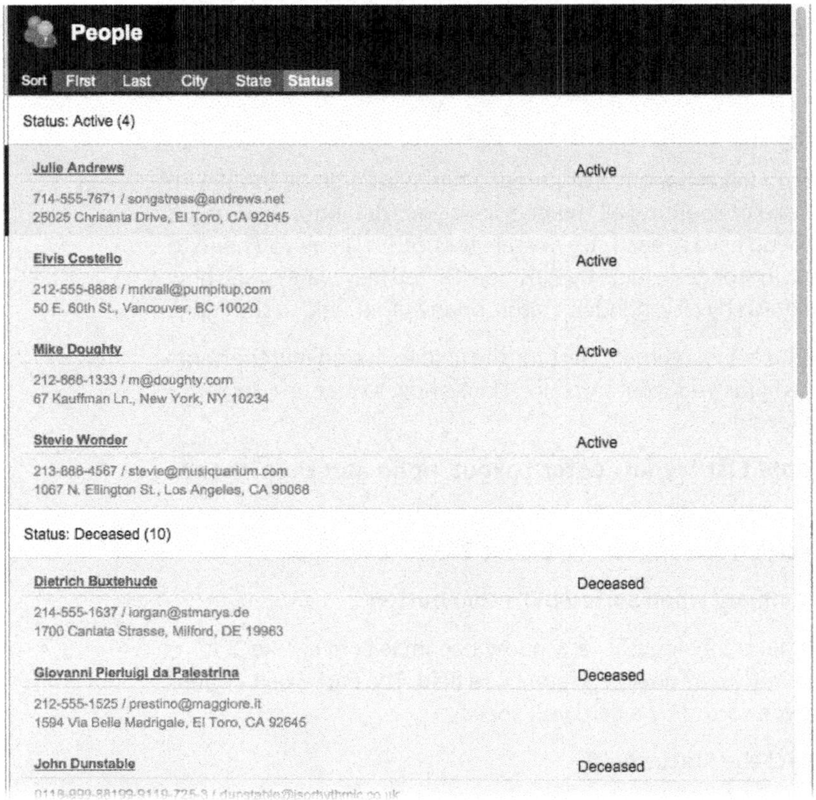

FIGURE 16-2

The People List layout now summarizes records by Status. As you can see here, a new visual separator appears between the two groups of musicians. The "Count of People" field now shows the count just for the group because it's in a Subsummary part.

You could make this layout even more informative by adding other Subsummary parts for City, State, Zip Code, or any other field you wanted to add to the table. As long as the field can be sorted in a meaningful way (it doesn't make much sense to sort by the Notes field, for example), you can use it on a Subsummary report. Place the same sumCount field in each new part (change the label to "City: <<City>> (<sumCount>>)" and so on) and then sort by each field in turn. Only the Subsummary part that references the field you sort by appears. Now a single layout can do several jobs.

Other Summary Field Types

Now that you know how summary fields and Subsummary parts work, it's time to look at other summary field options. Using the summary field's various options, you can perform a lot of powerful analysis on your data. Figure 16-3 shows a Subsummary report from a hypothetical sales database. This report uses several summary field options. The next sections describe how each choice works.

TOTAL OF

Use the "Total of" option to *sum* (add) number fields. In Figure 16-3, the Revenue field is a total of the Sales Amount field. For each group (state or region), you see its total.

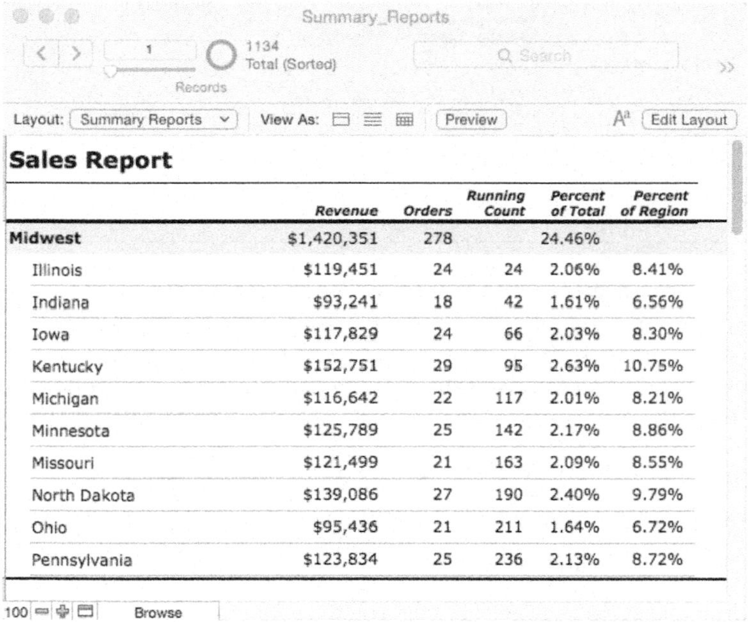

	Revenue	Orders	Running Count	Percent of Total	Percent of Region
Midwest	$1,420,351	278		24.46%	
Illinois	$119,451	24	24	2.06%	8.41%
Indiana	$93,241	18	42	1.61%	6.56%
Iowa	$117,829	24	66	2.03%	8.30%
Kentucky	$152,751	29	95	2.63%	10.75%
Michigan	$116,642	22	117	2.01%	8.21%
Minnesota	$125,789	25	142	2.17%	8.86%
Missouri	$121,499	21	163	2.09%	8.55%
North Dakota	$139,086	27	190	2.40%	9.79%
Ohio	$95,436	21	211	1.64%	6.72%
Pennsylvania	$123,834	25	236	2.13%	8.72%

FIGURE 16-3

This report shows summary fields in action. The Revenue column uses a "Total of" type summary field to add up sales numbers. Orders uses the Count type to show the total number of orders. The Running Count column, on the other hand, continues to count up the orders from one state to the next. Finally, two Percent fields use the "Fraction of Total of" summary field type to determine how much each state contributes to its region, and how much each region contributes to the total. You'll learn more about these options on the next few pages.

When you have this option selected, a "Running total" checkbox appears below the Available Fields list. When you use a summary field in a Subsummary part—total sales by Zip code, total sales by state, and so on—you normally see just the totals for each group in the report. If you turn on "Running total," FileMaker changes things slightly. Instead of individual totals for each group, the totals add up from group to group, much like the Balance column in your checkbook register.

■ AVERAGE OF

Obviously, the "Average of" choice calculates the average of the values in a number field. The option also has a "Weighted average" checkbox. When you turn it on, another field list appears (see Figure 16-4). From this list, you choose the field by which to *weight* your average.

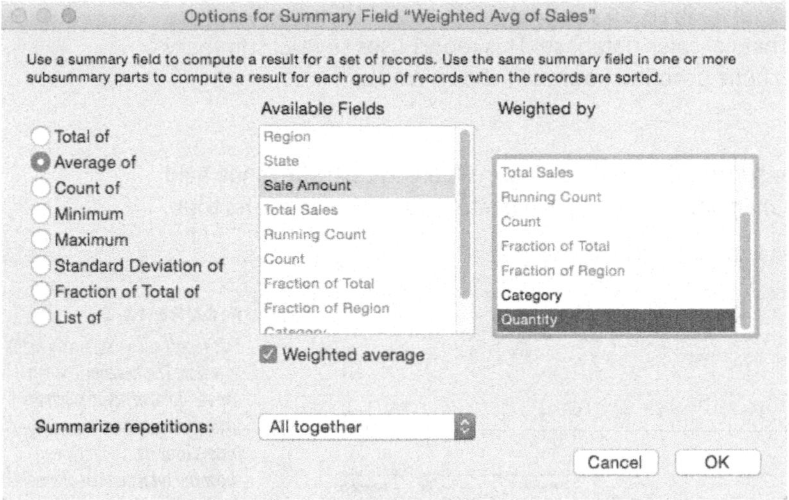

FIGURE 16-4

When you turn on the "Weighted average" check-box, FileMaker adds a second field list—"Weighted by"—to the window, where you can pick another number field. FileMaker averages the data in the first field and weights each record's input by the second field.

You use a weighted average when the things you're averaging have an associated quantity. For example, suppose your database has a record for each product sale. It records which product was sold, how many were sold, and the unit price. If you want a summary field that calculates the average sale price, then you probably want to turn on the "Weighted average" checkbox. Imagine you have these sales figures:

- You sold three laptop computers for $2,500 each.
- You sold 18 more laptops for $2,200 each.
- You sold a single laptop for $2,800.

If you use a simple average, FileMaker tells you the average sale price for laptops is $2,500 ($2,500 + $2,800 + $2,200, divided by 3). But that's not exactly right. You sold 18 of those laptops at just $2,200 each, but it counts only *once* in the calculation. In fact, you really sold 22 laptops in all, at three different prices. To calculate the correct average, you need to take quantities into consideration. In FileMaker, turn on the "Weighted average" checkbox and then, in the "Weighted by" list, choose the Quantity field. Now it reports the correct average: $2,268.18.

■ COUNT OF

Choose "Count of" to *count* items without totaling them. Since this option doesn't involve actual math, you can pick *any* field type, not just numbers. FileMaker counts each record in which that field isn't empty. If a field is empty, that record doesn't contribute to the count. As you learned, you should choose a field that's *never* empty if you want to be sure you count *every* record. You can use this property to your advantage, though. If you want your count to reflect just the flagged records, then count the Flag field instead. In Figure 16-3, the Orders column uses this option.

This option gives you a "Running count" checkbox. It works like running total but has an option that running total doesn't offer. When you turn on "Running count," the "Restart summary for each sorted group" checkbox becomes available. This option lets you produce a column like Running Count in Figure 16-3. This column counts up with each state, keeping a running count. But it's set to restart numbering based on the Region field. Notice that the running count starts over with each new region.

▓ MINIMUM AND MAXIMUM

If you want to know the *smallest* or the *largest* value in a group, use Minimum or Maximum. Both are very simple: Just pick the field you want to evaluate. No check-boxes, no extra lists. Number, date, time, and timestamp field types are available for minimum and maximum summarization, as are calculation fields with number, date, time, and timestamp results. You can use these to see the largest number of orders in your database, or the date of the earliest sale.

▓ STANDARD DEVIATION OF

A Standard Deviation summary field helps you figure out how your data is distributed. Put another way, it helps you know what's most common in your data, and how much a single data point varies from the mean value of the data. Standard deviations aren't commonly used in FileMaker, outside of specific types of statistical analysis, but two varieties of a standard deviation formula are provided. Click the "By population" option when your data represents the entire population of the dataset. Leave that option off when your data is a just a sample from all the data.

▓ FRACTION OF TOTAL OF

"Fraction of Total of" is the most complex summary option. It looks at the total for the *group* you're summarizing, as well as the total for the entire database. It then reports what portion of the overall total the group represents, as a decimal number. If all your sales were in California, it shows *1*. If California accounted for only 5 percent of your sales, on the other hand, it says *.05*.

The Subtotaled checkbox that comes with this option is also a little confusing. When you turn it on, FileMaker lets you pick another field from a list called "When sorted by." The name of this list serves to inform you that you have to *sort* the record by the selected field for this summary field to work. If you don't sort the records yourself before you view the report, then the field stays empty.

WARNING That problem is not as big as it may seem at first. As you learned on page 184, you have to sort records to do a lot of things with summary fields.

FileMaker looks at the selected field, figures out which records have the *same* value in them as in the current record, and calculates the fraction based only on the total of *those* records. In Figure 16-3, the "Percent of Total" field is a normal "Fraction of Total of" field, while the "Percent of Region" field uses "Fraction of Total of" subtotaled by Region.

■ LIST OF

Technically, generating a list of values doesn't really summarize anything, but lists of field values can be useful when wrangling data, so FileMaker gives you the option. For every record in the summarized group, it displays the value in the selected field. It correctly reflects sort order but ignores blank values, so you'll never see blank lines in the summary field. It does show duplicate values, however. For example, if you have 150 records all with the word "wonky" in the field being summarized, "List of" will present you with 150 lines of "wonky" in one summary field.

■ SUMMARIZING REPETITIONS

When you summarize a repeating field, you have another choice to make. Do you want *one* summary value that aggregates every repetition, producing a single value? If so, then choose "All together." If you want a repeating summary value that aggregates each repetition individually instead, then choose Individually.

> **NOTE** You may notice that the "Summarize repetitions" drop-down list is available all the time, although the items in it don't do anything unless you've selected a repeating field. Don't waste your time clicking them unless you're working with a repeating field. This is just one of those FileMaker mysteries for the cocktail-party circuit.

Advanced Subsummary Parts

As you know, a layout can have more than one Subsummary part. You can even have two versions of each Subsummary part: one printing above the body (where you would place the category name, or sort field) and a second one below the body (where the totals would appear). So you have lots of flexibility when formatting your reports. You can also sort by more than one field, so that more than one Subsummary part appears in the report. You can even create subsummary reports that don't have a body at all. Sorting still works on these layouts, but you don't have to wade through hundreds of records to see the summarized information you're looking for.

■ MULTIPLE SUBSUMMARY PARTS ON ONE LAYOUT

You can make your People List layout even more flexible by adding other Subsummary parts for City, State, and Zip code. As long as a field can be sorted in a meaningful way—you can't sort Notes or Phone numbers usefully, for example, because no two would group together in a category—then you can use it on a subsummary report. For each new type of report you want, you need a new Subsummary part that sorts by the field you want to report on. To report on City, State, and Zip code, add three parts to the layout—one for each field. Keep it organized by adding each part above the Body part, as you did in the tutorial on page 632. Place a copy of the sumCount field in each new part, but change the label appropriately ("City: <<City>> (<sumCount>>)," and so forth). When you're done, compare your layout to Figure 16-5.

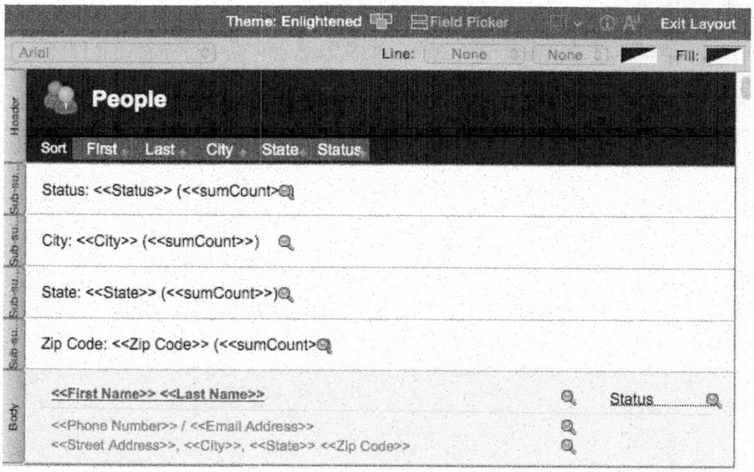

FIGURE 16-5

When you add more than one Subsummary part to your layout, FileMaker stacks them up in the order in which they were added. You can put the same summary fields in each one, and get totals appropriate to each group.

NOTE The labels of Subsummary parts aren't big enough to show you their full names. Click and hold the part label, and it displays its full name. Or double-click a part label to open the Part Setup dialog box, where you can view or change the part's settings.

Back in Browse mode, sort by each field in turn. Only the Subsummary part that references the field you sort by appears. Now a single layout can do several jobs (see Figure 16-6).

NOTE Records that are empty in one of your sort fields will go to the top of the list. Blank data isn't a big deal if all you're doing is counting sets of data. But as you start to analyze your data, you can see how important data entry is. To get the real picture, you need accurate and complete data.

Leading and Trailing Grand Summaries

Sometimes you want to see the totals for the found set as a whole. For example, you may have interesting summary fields that show averages or other statistics about your data, and you want to highlight them in your layout. FileMaker calls these layout parts *Grand Summary* parts.

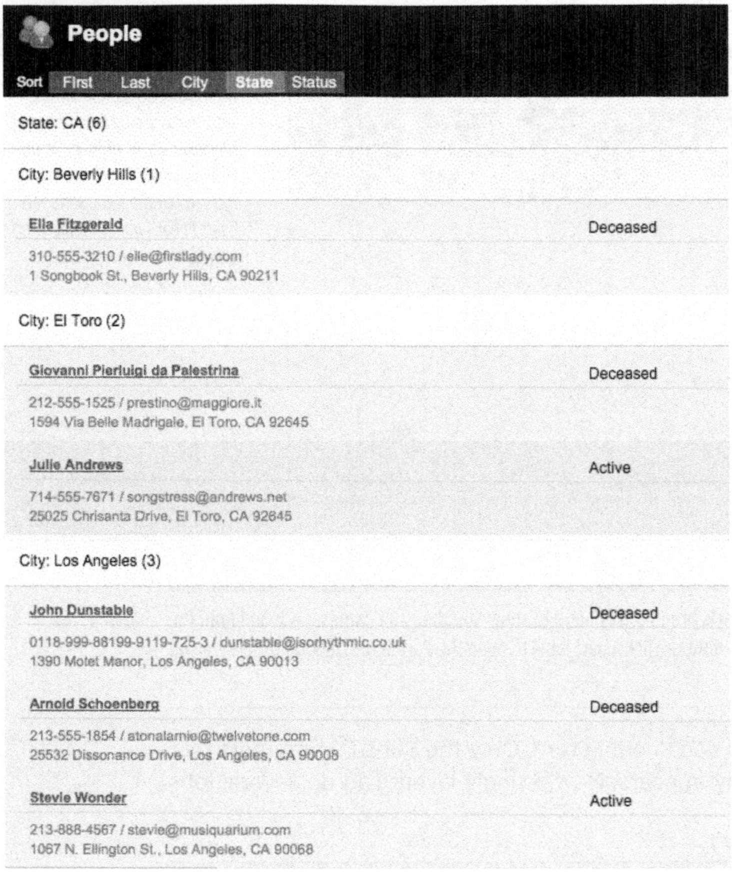

FIGURE 16-6

A report with multiple Subsummary parts has many talents. You can sort by any of the fields referenced in a part to see your data grouped and summarized by a different category. But if you do a multi-key sort, you're calling multiple parts into action, and you'll get major and minor groupings. For example, if you sort by State and then by City, your report will show you a count for all a state's contacts, along with subcounts for each city in that state.

If you want a grand total *above* all the records, then add a *Leading Grand Summary* part to the layout, and put your summary fields in it. If you use a *Trailing Grand Summary* part instead, then the grand totals appear after the last record. You can see a leading Grand Summary in Figure 16-7.

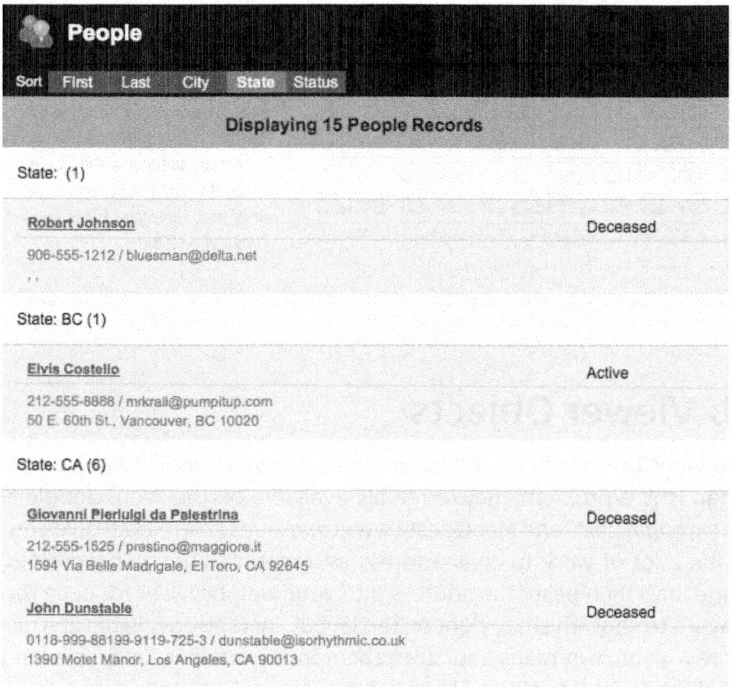

People

FIGURE 16-7

The People List layout now has a Leading Grand Summary part to show the overall total at the very top. If you scroll down to see more records, this total scrolls off the top of the list (unlike the Header part, which never scrolls away).

Subsummary Parts and Printing

You can use Subsummary parts to build high-level reports that break the data down by multiple nested groups and then roll up all the totals. For instance, your database of product sales may show order count, revenue, and share information. Using three Subsummary parts, you can break these down by region, then state, and finally category.

For a bird's-eye view of your sales, you can leave the Body part out of the layout entirely. When you do, FileMaker doesn't show the individual records. It shows just the summarized data. Figure 16-8 shows just such a layout in Layout mode.

> **TIP** You can find the database pictured in Figure 16-8 on this book's Missing CD page at *www.missingmanuals. com/cds/fmp14mm*. It's called *CH16 Summary Reports.fmp12*.

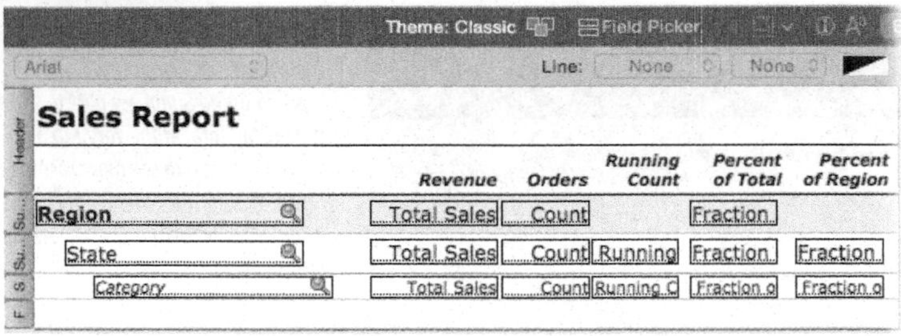

FIGURE 16-8

This layout has three Subsummary parts and several summary fields. The data is intended so that when multiple Subsummary parts show at once, you can see how the groups fit together. Also notice there's no Body part. This report shows only summarized data.

■ Web Viewer Objects

Imagine you want to view a map of someone's address in your People database. Getting a map isn't a problem; they're readily available on the Web. Google Maps (*http://maps.google.com*) and MapQuest (*www.mapquest.com*) both give you free maps. Still, it's a lot of work to copy address information, change programs, find the right page, and then paste the address into your web browser for each record. Maybe you want to show the map right on the layout, instantly available at a glance. You could draw your own maps and store them in a container field, or even take screenshots right off of Google and then paste them in. But those aren't dynamic. If somebody moves, you've got to repeat all that work.

Instead, you can tell FileMaker to go get the maps from the Internet for you. Using a *web viewer,* you can fetch almost anything available on the Web and display it on the layout. FileMaker even takes care of keeping things up-to-date: Every time you visit a record on the layout, it checks to see if newer information is available and automatically fetches the most up-to-date version, just like your web browser would.

You create web viewers with the web viewer tool. It's in the Status bar in Layout mode (look for the global inside a rectangle). It works like most layout tools: First, in the Status toolbar, click the button and then, on the layout, drag a rectangle to tell FileMaker where to put the web viewer and how big to make it.

Putting a Web Viewer on a Layout

Your People database could use a map on the People Detail layout. Here's how to put one there.

1. **Switch to the People Detail layout and then switch to Layout mode.**

   Since a map can be large, it makes sense to put it on the Detail layout, where you have some room to work with.

2. **Make the Body part much taller by dragging its label downward.**

The idea is to make room for the web viewer below your regular fields.

3. **In the Status toolbar, select the Web Viewer tool and then draw a rectangle on the page roughly the same width as the Notes field and a few inches tall.**

As usual, you're free to tweak the exact size and position of the web viewer anytime you want, so you don't have to be perfect here. As soon as you release the mouse button, FileMaker shows you the Web Viewer Setup dialog box (Figure 16-9).

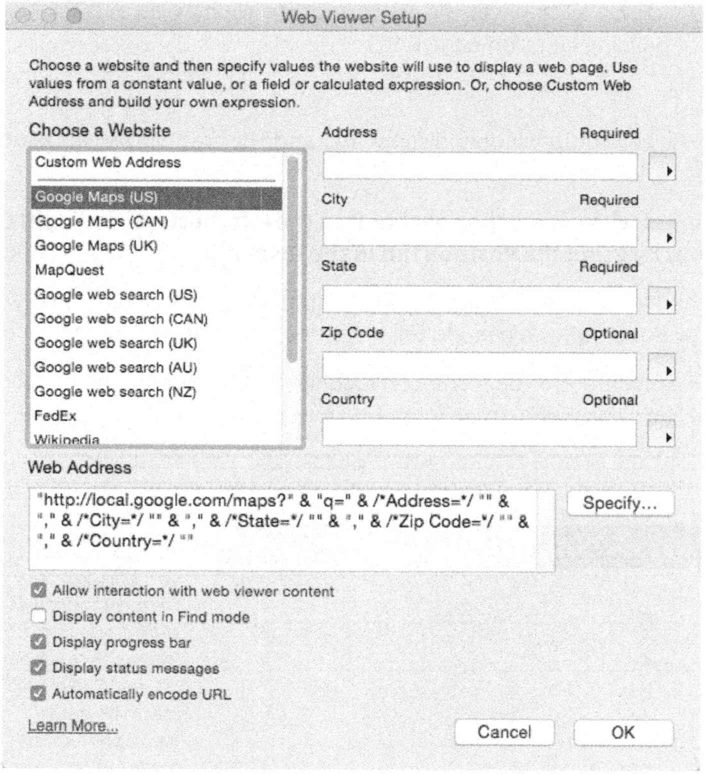

FIGURE 16-9

The Web Viewer Setup dialog box several canned options. First, from the list on the left, pick the website you want to show. Then fill in the appropriate boxes on the right. As you make choices, FileMaker builds the URL you need in the Web Address box. Or if you choose Custom Web Address, you can type or paste any URL you want.

4. **In the "Choose a Website" list, select Google Maps (US).**

You're telling FileMaker you want this web viewer to show information from the Google Maps website. As soon as you make this selection, several entry boxes appear on the dialog box's right side.

5. **To the right of the Address entry box, click the square button and then, from the resulting pop-up menu, choose Specify Field Name.**

   FileMaker pops up the standard Specify Field dialog box. Here you tell FileMaker which field to pull the street address from when it goes to find a map.

6. **In the Specify Field window, select Street Address and then click OK.**

   FileMaker now knows the first piece of information it needs to find the appropriate map. Notice that the Address box now shows People::Street Address.

7. **Repeat steps 5–6 once for each of the City, State, and Zip Code boxes.**

   As you make selections, FileMaker fills in the various boxes and builds the URL (Uniform Resource Locator) in the Web Address window at bottom. (Learn more about building URLs on page 647.)

8. **Click OK.**

   The Web Viewer Setup window disappears, and the web viewer appears on the layout.

9. **Select the web viewer and then anchor it to the left, bottom, and right (but not the top) by using the Position tab in the Inspector.**

   To keep the web viewer from bumping into the expanding Notes field when the window is resized, you need to tell it to stick to the bottom of the window.

Switch to Browse mode, and if your computer is connected to the Internet, you should see the Google Maps page with a map for the current person's record (Figure 16-10).

FIGURE 16-10

The People database now has a Google Maps web page showing right on the detail layout. FileMaker's web viewer lets you embed any web page on the layout, so you can save countless trips to your favorite web resources. Unfortunately, web pages tend to be big. You'll learn how to give this map more breathing room on page 645.

(See the box below for more on where the web viewer gets its power.) You may need to make the window bigger for the map to display properly. If you fiddle with the database a bit, then you notice a few important things:

- When you switch to a new record, the web viewer changes its contents to reflect the address information on the new record. Likewise, if you *change* the data in any of the address fields, then the map instantly updates to show the new address.

- Status information shows at the bottom of the web viewer while the page loads.

- You're free to click links in the web page, and the web viewer dutifully follows your clicks and shows a new page.

- Although the web viewer isn't a full-fledged browser (it doesn't have a Back button, for instance), you can access most typical browsing commands by right-clicking anywhere on the web page. In fact, the menu that appears when you do is just like the one you'd see if you did the same in your real web browser. (For instance, choose Back from this menu to go to the previous page.)

FREQUENTLY ASKED QUESTION

FileMaker's Web Browser

Is the web viewer a modern browser? Is it standards-compliant? Can it run JavaScript, or use browser plug-ins? Should I be worried about compatibility with various pages?

FileMaker doesn't actually have a web browser of its own. Instead, it calls upon the services of the web browser engine most readily available—the one that came with your computer. In Windows, FileMaker uses Internet Explorer as its browser technology. In Mac OS X, it uses Safari. This arrangement has a few important implications:

- FileMaker is using a tried-and-true browser technology, so you know it works well with most web pages. It has

support for all the major web technologies, just like its real web browser counterparts.

- If you install any plug-ins for your web browser, FileMaker web viewers can utilize them as well.

- If you upgrade your operating system or web browser, FileMaker's web viewer gets the benefits of the upgrade as well. For example, if you install Internet Explorer 8, then the web viewer gets all its page-handling capabilities. If you have Internet Explorer 6 installed instead, your web viewer has its limitations.

Web Viewer Options

FileMaker offers up a few configuration options for web viewers in addition to the page they should load. The bottom of the Web Viewer Setup dialog box (flip back to Figure 16-9) includes five checkboxes to adjust the behavior of this particular web viewer. (See the box on page 646 for more information on using the canned URLs in the dialog box.)

■ ALLOW INTERACTION WITH WEB VIEWER CONTENT

When the "Allow interaction with web viewer content" option is turned on (as it is for your map), FileMaker lets you actually *use* the web page it loads. Specifically, you can click a link on the page to navigate to a new page. You can also use shopping carts, send email messages, watch video, or use any other features on the page.

When you turn this option off, all page behavior is deactivated. Clicking the page produces no more response than clicking a blank spot on the layout. You can't even scroll the page. If a page is too big to fit in the space you've given it on the layout, then FileMaker just cuts it off.

Turn this option on when the page you're showing is just a starting point (like the login screen for your Orders web page, or the first step in the application process). You should also leave this option on when the page is larger or its size is variable. On the other hand, you can turn "Allow interaction with web viewer content" off when you're showing a small page that contains all the information needed.

UP TO SPEED

Using the Web Viewer's Built-in Sites

When you added a Google Maps page to your layout, you didn't have to figure out how Google expects to receive address information. Instead, you simply picked Google Maps from a list and then filled in the blanks. These canned approaches work because FileMaker has some under-the-hood smarts about how to handle Application Program Interface (API) for common websites, even though each website may have its own rules for connecting to it and getting information back out. The Web Viewer's canned sites contain different options, like the US, Canadian, and UK versions of Google Maps, for example.

These APIs are easy to use because you're probably already storing address information for your contacts. But some options may require you to create fields for data that you might not normally store, like tracking numbers for FedEx package tracking, or search-term keywords for Wikipedia. So depending on what you're trying to accomplish, you could link each record in your database to a Wikipedia entry, or you could create a generic layout with a global field and a large web viewer that lets your users type search terms for on-the-spot research.

Remember, though, you can type any URL you want into a web viewer's Web Address field. But you may have to do some research on the website's Help pages to figure out exactly how data should be entered. As long as you can use a calculation to create a properly formatted URL, you can make a web viewer do nearly anything a browser can do.

■ DISPLAY CONTENT IN FIND MODE

Normally, when you switch to Find mode, the web viewer just goes blank. Which makes sense, since a web viewer is usually showing a page associated with data in the current record. After all, if you go to Find mode, where you're no longer necessarily looking at a particular record, then FileMaker may not be able to tell which web address goes in the web viewer.

You can change this behavior, though, by turning on "Display content in Find mode." When you do, FileMaker makes its best effort to display the web page, even when you're in Find mode. For example, if you've typed a URL directly into the Web Viewer Setup dialog box, then FileMaker can continue to display the page properly no matter which mode you use (except Layout mode). If you're using a website that needs information from the database, then FileMaker feeds it the data from the find request instead. This behavior could come in handy if the web page information would be helpful to a person trying to construct a find request, but usually you want to leave this option off. It can be jarring to watch a web viewer constantly refresh itself as you enter your find criteria.

DISPLAY PROGRESS BAR

Unlike everything else on your layout, web page content isn't always immediately accessible by FileMaker. The program has to go to the Internet and pull up the page, which can take some time (just as it takes time for a page to load in your browser). If you turn on "Display progress bar" (it's on until you turn it off, in fact), then File-Maker shows a subtle progress bar at the bottom of the web viewer (Figure 16-11).

FIGURE 16-11

The web viewer can show a progress bar (a black line just above the Status toolbar) as the web page loads. If you prefer a minimalist look, in the Web Viewer Setup dialog box turn off both "Display status messages" and "Display progress bar."

DISPLAY STATUS MESSAGES

Another option that FileMaker automatically turns on is the "Display status messages" checkbox. This option tells the web viewer to reserve a little space along its bottom edge to show status information (Figure 16-11). Status information typically means the "Loading" messages you see at the bottom of a web browser window. Turn this option off if you'd rather not sacrifice precious layout space for not much more information than what the progress bar already gives you. That way, the web viewer can use all its space on the layout for web page content.

AUTOMATICALLY ENCODE URL

The "Automatically encode URLs" checkbox is FileMaker's effort to shield you from the rules about which characters can and can't be included in a URL. The following URL contains three verboten characters: `http://crookedarm.com/an\oddly|named%page.html`. Attempt to load that page in a Web Viewer with automatic encoding disabled, and it simply won't work. The page will never load. Switch that encoding checkbox on, however, and FileMaker finds those problem characters and replaces them with their encoded counterparts. The resulting URL, `http://crooke-darm.com/an%5Coddly%7Cnamed%25page.html`, loads as if nothing were ever wrong.

■ Conditional Formatting

Reporting isn't always about finding and sorting records. Sometimes you want to make the state of a field's data more obvious to users by making an object *look* different. For example, you may want a contact's name to change color depending on the person's status—gray out the name text if the person is inactive, for example. In an Invoice database, you may want any invoice with a balance that's over 30 days old to turn red. Our you may want a special format for empty fields to remind your data entry folks which fields shouldn't be left empty.

Conditional formatting makes it easy to provide these visual cues. It lets you attach an If test to a layout object and specify the formatting you want to appear if the test evaluates as True. Conditional formatting isn't limited to fields—you can apply formatting to almost other objects, like the icons on buttons (page 368). Conditionally formatted objects have a layout badge to make it easier to spot them.

Conditional Formatting of Fields

You can apply conditional formatting to any text object, button, field, or web viewer. Follow these steps to make your status field more dynamic:

1. **On the People List layout, select the Status field and then choose Format→ Conditional.**

   You see the Conditional Formatting dialog box pictured in Figure 16-12.

2. **Click Add.**

   A new condition appears in the list at the top of the window. Also, the dialog box's Condition and Format sections become active.

3. **From the first pop-up menu under Condition, make sure "Value is" is chosen.**

   You can configure your condition in two different ways. Either you place simple rules on the value of a field, or, if your needs are more complex, you use a *formula*. You'll start with the easy kind.

4. **From the second pop-up menu under Condition, choose "equal to."**

   In this case, you want the conditional formatting to apply when the Status is "Deceased," so you tell FileMaker that's the kind of comparison it should do.

5. **In the box to the right of the pop-up menu, type *Deceased*.**

   Here's where you enter the comparison value. (If you choose a comparison type other than "equal to," then the dialog box may show you different options.)

   FileMaker adjusts the display of the dialog box so that the condition line reads like a meaningful sentence: "Value is→equal to→Deceased."

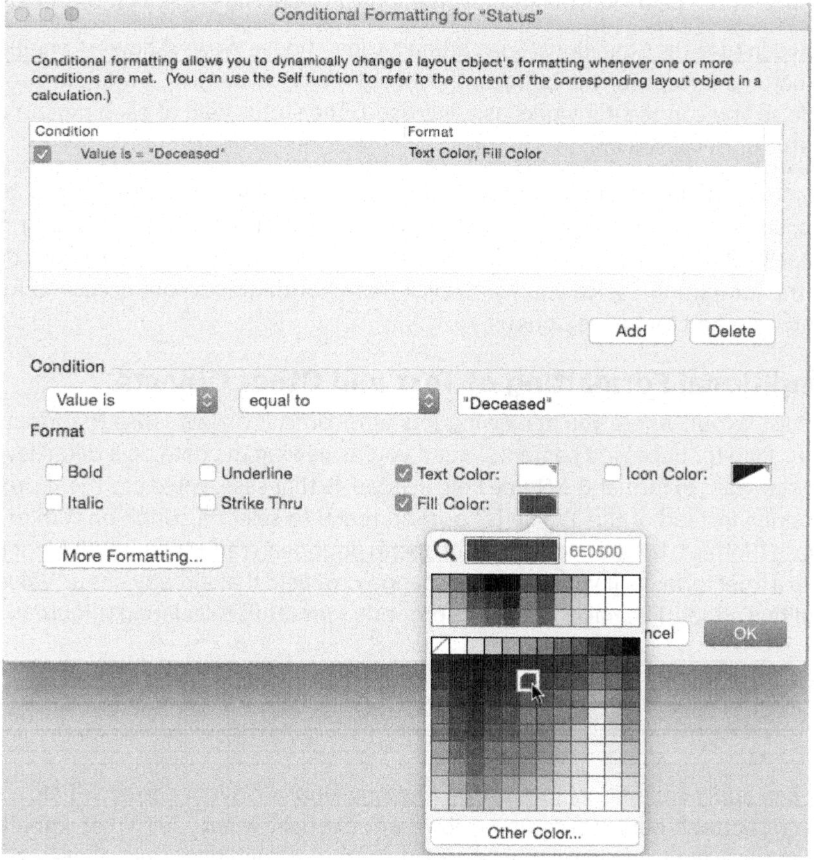

FIGURE 16-12

The Conditional Formatting dialog box lets you assign formatting to a field, button, or text object that applies only when specific conditions are met. You can add as many conditions as you want, but some tests may contradict each other. In that case, the last condition in the list will prevail.

6. **From the Fill Color pop-up menu, choose a dark red color. Then from the Text Color pop-up menu, choose white.**

   You could select the checkbox and then make your selections instead, but this way, FileMaker checkmarks the boxes for you. If you change your mind and don't want a fill color after all, just turn off the checkbox; you don't have to undo your selection.

NOTE You don't have to provide any formatting rules for other values in the Status field. When none of the conditions in the Conditional Formatting dialog box apply (you can add as many as you want), FileMaker leaves the object formatted as it is in Layout mode, so you don't need to add a condition for the *normal* case.

---

7. **Click OK.**

   The Conditional Formatting dialog box disappears, and your field now shows a Conditional Formatting badge. That little red and blue diamond on the right side of the field lets you know Conditional Formatting is used on this field.

If you don't see the Conditional Formatting badge, choose View→Show→Conditional Formatting. Except for the badges, the layout looks unchanged. Switch to Browse mode so you can see if it works as advertised. The status field of each person with a status of Deceased appears in red.

The most popular conditional formatting options include text and fill colors, bold, italic, underline, and strikethrough. You can even change a button's icon color conditionally. But there are a few more options another dialog box deep. If you don't see the formatting choice you want, click More Formatting to get access to fonts, point sizes, and font style options.

Conditional Formatting of Text and Other Objects

On a list layout, where you're viewing lots of records, it makes sense to format the Status field for deceased contacts. But if you're viewing the data on a detail layout, you may want to format the Name field instead. In that case, you'd use the "Formula is" option instead of the "Value is" pop-up menu to select a condition. When you choose "Formula is," the middle pop-up menu disappears, and you get a field for typing in a brief formula. If you make this change on a field that already has a "Value is" condition added, FileMaker displays a properly formatted calculation (Figure 16-13).

> **TIP** If the relatively small space isn't enough to write the calculation you need, click the Specify button, which gives you access to your old friend the Specify Calculation dialog box.

You can apply conditional formatting to many kinds of layout objects—fields, text objects, buttons, button bars, and web viewers. Usually when you format something other than a field, you need to use a formula for the condition, since those objects don't have values that change.

Advanced Conditional Formatting

In the tutorial on page 648, you added only one condition to the list in the Conditional Formatting dialog box. But you can add as many conditions as you need to check. In a list of conditions, FileMaker looks at every condition on the list and makes the formatting changes for each one that applies. As a result, you can easily create several different formats for several different conditions. For example, you can make numbers in your budget database turn red when you're getting behind, stay black when you're right on target, and turn green when you're beating expectations.

Two matching conditions may have competing formatting rules. For instance, you can set the text color to something different in each rule, even though they both apply to the same values. In that case, FileMaker chooses the format from the condition that comes *last* in the list. You can move these conditions around using their little arrows to influence the outcome. Just put the condition that should take precedence lowest in the list.

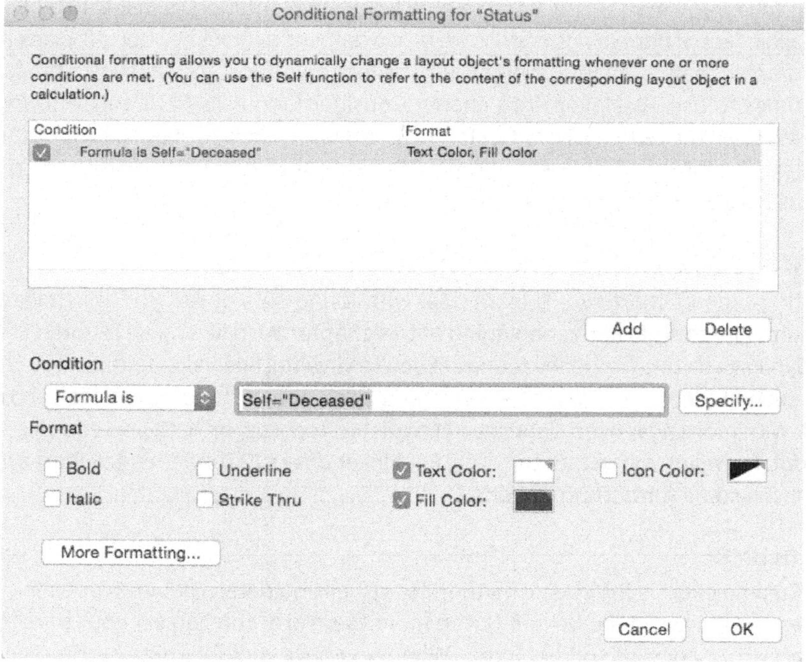

FIGURE 16-13

The Status field from the People List layout has been changed from "Value is" to "Formula Is." FileMaker converts the "Value Is" pop-up choices to a calculation that accomplishes the same task. The "Self" in the formula refers to the value in the field you're formatting. This makes it portable—you can write it in one place and then paste it elsewhere and it'll work without editing. Read more on page 673.

Removing Conditional Formatting

If you no longer want to see the visual feedback of conditional formatting, you can easily remove it. Select the object, choose Format→Conditional, and then delete the conditions from the list. You can Shift-click to delete them all at once, or just click the first and then click Delete repeatedly until they're all gone.

> **NOTE** If you duplicate a layout object, you also copy its conditional formatting. If the formatting doesn't make sense in the copied object's location, then remove it.

If you spent long hours adding complex conditions and you're not quite ready to let go of them forever, then you can *turn them off* instead. Each condition in the list has a checkbox beside it. If you turn off a condition's checkbox, FileMaker no longer uses that condition. You can always get the condition back later by turning it back on. You can turn multiple checkboxes on or off at once as well: Just Shift-click the conditions you want to switch so they're all selected. Then turn off the checkbox beside *one* of them, and FileMaker turns all the others off as well.

■ Basic Charting

Summary reports are useful, but sometimes, the people who want the summary information don't take the time to study and interpret the numbers you give them. Other times, you may simply need to punch up a presentation to make a point. And it's a plain fact of human nature that we grasp data more quickly when it's presented as a graphic than as a table of numbers or a lengthy report. All those examples are fine times to use FileMaker Pro's charts. Consider Figure 16-14. If you're trying to impress upon the Lawnmower Museum's curator just how little enthusiasm the public is displaying for the "Pull Cords Through the Ages" exhibit, which approach do you suppose will have the greater impact?

Chart Types

The first type of charts you'll learn deal with found sets of records, much like the subsummary reports at the beginning of this chapter. Also like those reports, charts are dynamic. If you change the found set you're viewing, FileMaker updates the chart. This section focuses on how to set up these basic charts. Later, you'll learn how to work with more advanced data sets, like related records, or data you compile with a script. However you gather the data, FileMaker offers 10 fundamental chart types, each with some formatting options.

■ COLUMN

The Column chart is the classic method for visualizing data: a column for each thing you're counting, and the taller it is, the more there are. You can set your Bars to be flat or 3-D, shaded or solid-colored. When you have multiple data series (see the steps on page 664), FileMaker will group and color them together.

■ STACKED COLUMN

Stacked charts are used to illustrate how multiple series of data combine to create a whole. For example, if each column represents a month of sales, each series making up a column could represent one particular product's share of the sales.

■ POSITIVE/NEGATIVE COLUMN

A normal Column chart will accurately show negative values. The Positive/Negative Column variant offers contrasting background colors for the positive and negative areas of the chart. It also lets you set a custom midpoint under the Y-Axis options if, say, you want to treat everything below 100 as negative.

■ BAR

Distinguished by their lateral proclivities, Bar charts are the same as Column charts described above, just turned by 90 degrees. All the formatting options are identical.

■ STACKED BAR

A knocked-over Stacked Column.

British Lawnmower Museum
Exhibit Popularity

Exhibit	VisitDate	Unique Visitors	Repeat Visitors
Pull Cords	1/31/2016	14	2
Pull Cords	2/15/2016	4	0
Pull Cords	3/2/2016	6	1
Pull Cords	3/17/2016	0	0
Pull Cords	3/1/2016	2	0
Pull Cords		**26**	**3**
The Gardener's Mistress	1/16/2016	8	1
The Gardener's Mistress	1/13/2016	110	38
The Gardener's Mistress	2/8/2016	85	21
The Gardener's Mistress	2/18/2016	72.5	7
The Gardener's Mistress	3/10/2016	77.5	15
The Gardener's Mistress	3/20/2016	62.5	13
The Gardener's Mistress		**415.5**	**95**
Turing meets Toro	1/29/2016	96	7
Turing meets Toro	1/19/2016	80	13
Turing meets Toro	2/12/2016	134	9
Turing meets Toro	2/28/2016	142	65
Turing meets Toro	3/14/2016	148	26
Turing meets Toro	3/30/2016	156	42
Turing meets Toro		**756**	**162**

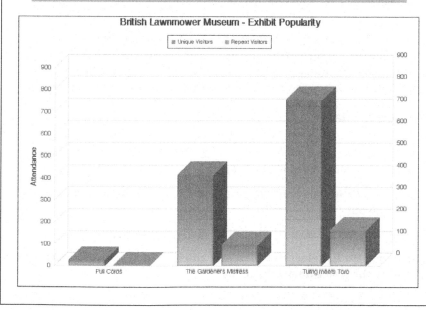

FIGURE 16-14

Top: The Lawnmower Museum's attendance figures are presented as a summary report. The data is presented neatly in a tabular arrangement. If your goal is to see specific details, like the number of visitors in the Turing exhibit on March 14, for example, then tabular data is usually the best presentation method. But you'll have to engage your brain to find the data that helps you see which is the most visited exhibit. You have to find a number, remember it while you search for other numbers, and then compare them all. Not only does this work require concentration, but it's not even terribly accurate. Most people just aren't that good at comparing numbers to each other without graphical aides.

Bottom: The same data presented as a chart with bars showing a rollup of total visitors for each exhibit. It's instantly clear which is the most popular exhibit, even if you're barely paying attention. All you have to do is read the category name below the tallest column to see where sales are the greatest, losses are the highest, or attendance is the best.

■ PIE

Pie charts always display one thing—the relative portions that make up a whole. Throw a set of data at it, and FileMaker helpfully calculates each item's percentage contribution and slices the pie for you. The usual flat/3-D solid/shaded formatting choices apply here as well. By their very design, Pie charts can visualize only a single series of data. See the Stacked options if you need to illustrate portions for multiple series.

■ LINE

Line charts are a classic tool for showing change over time. Trending information like historical stock market performance or annual snowfall is particularly apt for Line charts. FileMaker can draw your lines in smooth curves or sharp angles, but that's about all you can customize.

■ AREA

A close cousin of the Line is the Area chart. In fact, it's just an angular Line chart with color filled in beneath the line. Like the Bar charts, Area charts can be flat or 3-D. If the data you're plotting ever crosses (say you're showing digital music sales rising and CD sales falling), you'll want to take advantage of the "Semi-transparent" option to ensure all series remain visible.

■ SCATTER

The Scatter chart is useful for plotting many points of data. By seeing where points cluster on the chart, you can infer trends from large sets of information. Scatter charts are useful when a line chart gets hard to read. They're essential if you're trying to prove a correlation between two things.

■ BUBBLE

Akin to the Scatter chart, the Bubble chart illustrates the magnitude of each data point by drawing a corresponding radius. So while a Scatter chart could show you, say, the number of eggs your ostriches are laying each hour of the day, a Bubble chart can also show how large those eggs are by sizing those dots accordingly.

Creating a Chart

For this exercise, you can download the *CH16 Charts.fmp12* file from this book's Missing CD page at *www.missingmanuals.com/cds/fmp14mm*. Here's how to set up a simple Bar chart for the museum attendance database:

1. **Open the *CH16 Charts.fmp12* database and then switch to the Facility Bar Chart layout.**

   The layout has the context you'll need to create the chart.

2. **In Layout Mode, select the Chart tool and then drag to create a chart, using most of the space below the fields.**

   If you don't see all your tools, it usually means you need to make the window a bit wider. The Chart Setup dialog box appears. Leave the Chart Type set to Column.

3. **In the right column under the Chart heading, type *Museum Attendance* into the Title box.**

4. **Tab down to the Data field under Horizontal (X) Axis, click the button to the right of the field, and select Specify Field Name from the pop-up menu shown in Figure 16-15.**

   A list of fields appears.

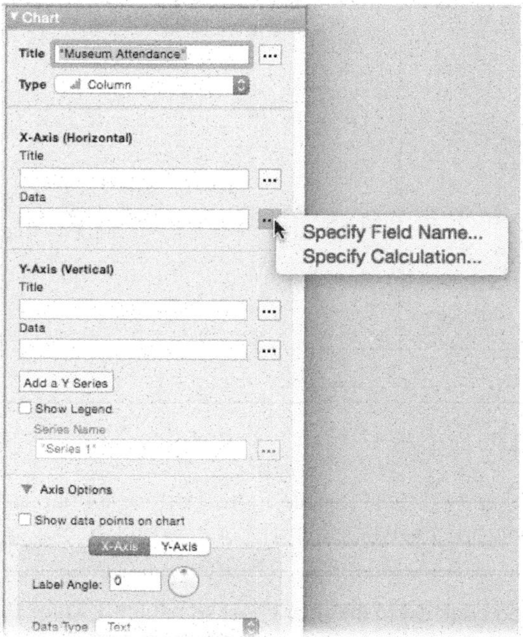

FIGURE 16-15

The axes of a chart can draw their data from a particular field as shown here, or from a calculation you construct.

5. **Click the Facility Name field and then click OK.**

   You see Facility::Facility Name in the X-Axis (Horizontal) field.

6. **Tab down to Y-Axis (Vertical), click the button to its right, select Specify Field Name, and then choose the field named Visitor Sum. Click OK.**

   Facility::Visitor Sum appears in the Vertical (Y) Axis box and a prototype of the chart appears in the Chart Setup dialog box.

7. **In the Chart Setup dialog box, click Done and then switch to Browse mode.**

   You should see a chart like the one in Figure 16-16. The bars are accurate, but the chart isn't usable yet.

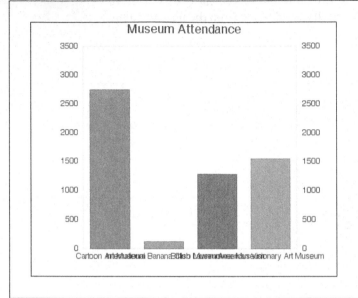

FIGURE 16-16
Sure it's a chart, but is it a good one? This chart's x-axis contains some unfortunately long museum names, so although you know which column is the tallest, you can't tell what the column represents. You'll fix the labels in the next exercise.

Editing a Chart

Some flaws are immediately apparent. The labels along the bottom overlap so you can't read them, there's no legend, and the whole thing is squished into a small space. A few edits will make this chart more legible. Here's how to edit a chart:

1. **Return to Layout mode and click once on your chart to select it. Over in the Inspector window, select the Position tab and, in the Autosizing section, activate the bottom and right anchors.**

   All four anchors should now be active. This will cause your chart to stretch with the size of your window when you're back in Browse mode.

2. **Before you switch to Browse mode, however, select Format→Chart Setup (or double-click the chart).**

   The Chart Setup dialog box appears.

3. **In the X-Axis Title box, type *Museum Name*. In the Y-Axis Title box, type *Attendees*.**

   They y-axis graphs the number of people who visited each museum.

4. **In the X-Axis Data field, change the field specified to Facility Abbreviation.**

   It's common to create fields that hold abbreviated data that is suitable for display in a chart. But if you don't have such a field, you could use a calculation to create an abbreviation.

5. **Click Done and then switch back into Browse mode to admire your handi-work.**

Now you've got a usable chart that's clean, readable, and appropriately labeled, your chart should look something like Figure 16-17.

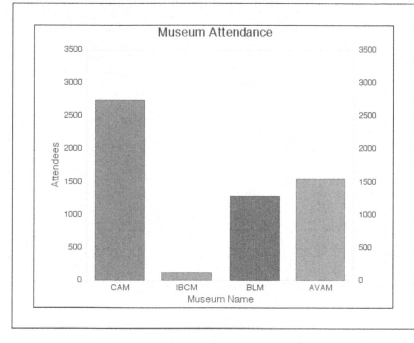

FIGURE 16-17

With abbreviated labels, the columns are now clearly identified. The axis titles you added make it clear that museum names run along the x-axis, and attendance numbers the y-axis.

Chart Formatting

Now that you've got the basic mechanics of chart creation and display, it's a great time to try out some formatting possibilities. As with other layout objects, your charts come with a default style (page 333). You can change the style's font, color scheme, and background, or create new styles for different types of charts. You have wide artistic latitude here, but remember, your goal is to enhance your chart and make it easier to read. Some formatting choices actually make charts harder to read, rather than easier. Remember: Less is more.

To dig into the possibilities, switch to Layout mode and then double-click your chart. In the Chart Setup dialog box, click the Styles heading. In the Chart Text area shown in Figure 16-18, you can change chart styles or color schemes and add background fills—but again, your goal is to be readable, not fancy.

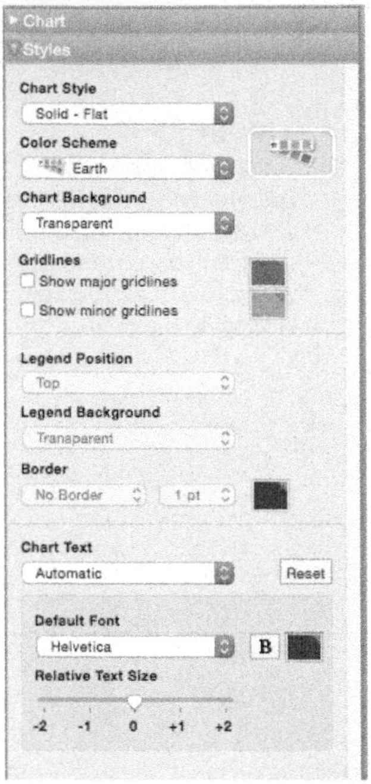

FIGURE 16-18

The Styles area of the Format Chart dialog box is where you can format your chart. FileMaker gives you wide latitude to customize your chart however you wish, but this isn't the place to abandon restraint. All of the distinct font settings in the custom areas of the Styles panel are best used to make your existing font smaller or larger. As with all chart formatting, choose your font and colors carefully so as to clarify your data, not distract from it.

The Chart Style pop-up menu varies depending on the chart type, but it generally offers solid or shaded coloring, and flat or 3-D style presentation. One advantage of the trend toward flat design is that there's less detail taking attention away from the important information. Flat purists even point out evidence that 3-D charts cause people to misinterpret data.

Moving down to the Color Scheme pop-up menu, you'll see a single color choice plus 20 color schemes. These schemes don't necessarily match your database's themes, so take care. You can't set colors for individual graph elements, and you can't create your own themes or styles. For clarity's sake, it's usually best to choose Single Color and then use the swatch to choose a color from your database's style palette.

The default background for charts is Transparent, for good reason. A background color can compete with your data. However, you can choose a solid color or a variety of gradients. If you choose a gradient, you get two color swatches: one to set the gradient's start color and the second to set its end color.

You can also set major and minor gridlines, but for most charts, they don't do much more than cause clutter. Use gradients if you have so many data points that the eye gets lost trying to find a value from the y-axis. But remember, the point of most charts is to give you a quick snapshot and not fine-grained data points. If people need to understand exact values, as opposed to relative values, a table may work better. Or maybe you need the best of both worlds: a very simple chart to give folks the quick picture, and a table if they need to know exactly how many ¾″ torque nuts were sold in the western region the third week of last quarter.

Down near the bottom, you can change fonts, make text bold, and change font size. The black color swatch shows the familiar color palette, along with the style's color swatches at the top. Use it to help you choose a color that's already in use in your style.

> **TIP** By default, the preview chart displayed on the Chart Setup dialog box uses the data from your database. Usually this is what you want. But if you have a very complicated chart with a huge data set, chart refreshes happen with every formatting change you make, and each one can take a long time. In that case, you can click the tiny Pause button below the sample chart, which prevents FileMaker from trying to update the preview while you're working. If you prefer to keep the preview updated, you can improve refresh speed by changing the "Use actual data" pop-up menu to "Use sample data."

Visualizing Data

Throwing together a simple chart is easy enough, but creating a *useful* and *meaningful* chart takes thought. Indeed, a poorly conceived chart can obscure or even contradict the information you want to communicate. Visualized data is subject to cultural context and your users' expectations about how data is arranged. Imagine you've invested in an ostrich ranch and the company has presented you with a chart showing your financial return in the form of Figure 16-19. If you're from a Western culture and read from left to right, that chart looks like bad news. Because the data isn't arranged the way you'd expect, you'd have a hard time understanding that the chart is actually good news.

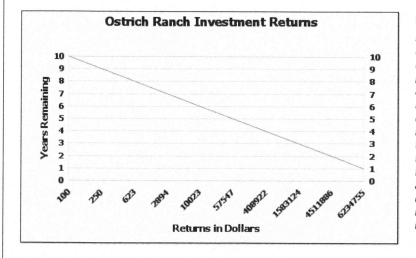

FIGURE 16-19

At first glance, this chart of returns on your 10-year investment in an ostrich ranch looks pretty grim. But it's actually accurate. This chart shows a return of over $6 million, but a downward-trending line denotes bad news. The natural assumption of the untrained eye is that time is displayed horizontally from left to right and values are in the vertical axis. This ill-conceived chart subverts those norms and risks being gravely misinterpreted.

Here are a few basic charting concepts to consider:

- The passage of time is usually charted in the x (horizontal) axis, starting with the earliest date or time on the left and proceeding to the most recent on the right.

- Numerical values are best suited to the y (vertical) axis, with the lowest values at the bottom of the chart range. FileMaker won't even let you order values any other way. If you sort your values in descending order, the y-axis won't change.

- Multiple items in the y-axis of a chart are called *series.* Consider a line graph with one line showing a particular stock's performance over time and a second line showing overall market performance. The stock is one series and the overall market is the second. Series are terrific for comparing multiple entities, but all the entities have to use the same unit of measurement. An individual stock and the whole stock market are both measured in currency (dollars, yen, euros, and so on), making them well-suited to being series on the same chart. Other series just don't pair up, like a commute (measuring distance) and the capacity of a gas tank (measuring volume). One final thought about series: Sometimes, even series that share the same unit of measurement don't chart well together. For example, if your database calculates the distances from various Italian cities to other Italian and South African cities, your unit of measurement will be the same. But most Italian cities are within a few hundred kilometers of each other, while South Africa is at least 7,000 kilometers away. If your data starts to show those kinds of gaps, consider whether you need two or more charts to show series.

- Pies portray percentages, or how one data point relates to others in the same series. That "whole" can be second quarter sales, Ray Bradbury's oeuvre, or your retirement savings. The slices can represent sales reps, editors, or mutual funds. The important thing is that you clearly define what the slices are and how they add up to 100 percent of something. FileMaker helps you stay clear of the temptation to use raw numbers instead of percentages for your pie charts by computing and displaying each slice's percent contribution automatically.

■ Charting and Reports

Charts and graphs are classic tools for boiling a whole lot of data down to easily understandable information. When it comes to FileMaker, concisely presenting a large data set often involves summary fields, and Summary parts on layouts.

Like other special layout objects, charts are useful in summary reports. But they don't behave as you might expect if you don't understand their quirky way of looking at your data. Take a look at Figure 16-20. The two charts are drawn from the same data. With no other changes, the two charts show different data. While you can use this to your advantage, it can be confusing when you aren't getting the results you expect. Ultimately, producing an accurate chart comes down to three main rules: Pick the right fields, place the chart on the appropriate layout part, and use the correct sort order.

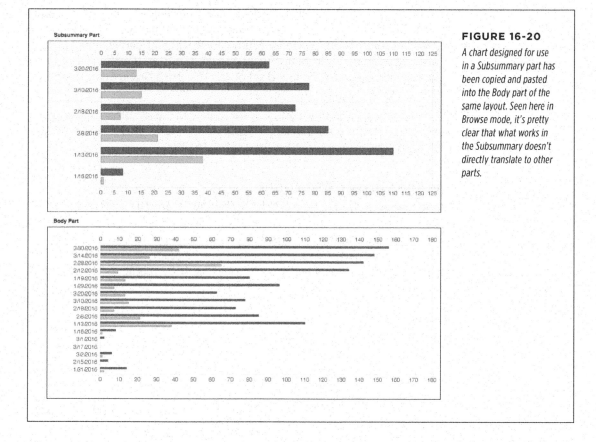

FIGURE 16-20

A chart designed for use in a Subsummary part has been copied and pasted into the Body part of the same layout. Seen here in Browse mode, it's pretty clear that what works in the Subsummary doesn't directly translate to other parts.

Picking the Right Fields

Choose fields that have accurate and consistent data. You can make the most beautiful, easy-to-read chart in the world, but if it's based on bad data, your message won't be clear.

If your chart appears in a layout's Body part, be sure you're not trying to use a summary field for one of the axes or you'll end up displaying the same values in every record. Charting related data carries a similar warning—see page 664 later in this chapter for details.

Choosing an Appropriate Layout Part

You just saw how putting two copies of the exact same chart into different parts of a layout can lead to very different data being displayed. Still, selecting the appropriate layout part needn't be a headache.

Here are the basic rules: If you're charting data from different fields on a single record, the Body part is your best bet. If you want to summarize data for groups of similar records (much like the sorted subsummary report you learned about on page 632), add a Subsummary part to the layout and stick your chart in there. If you want to show summarized data for a found set of records, use a Grand Summary part.

> **TIP** When working with related data, that is, fields from another table in your database, the guidelines here don't apply quite so rigidly. For example, it's possible to display summary data for related records in a Body part by using calculation fields—no summary fields or Summary parts necessary.

Using the Correct Sort Order

Regardless of *where* you place a chart, unsorted or incorrectly sorted records can make a good chart go bad. If your chart is located in a Subsummary part, you already know that you have to sort the records to make the part show up. Any chart you place in that layout part should also sort by the field associated with the Subsummary part. With Body part charts, you'll usually sort by the fields charted in the x-axis. See Figure 16-21 for more details.

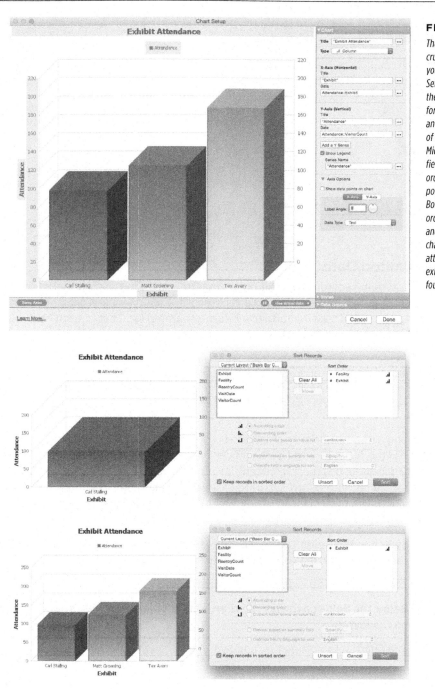

FIGURE 16-21

The correct sort order is crucial to the accuracy of your charts. Top: The Chart Setup dialog box specifies the field named "exhibit" for the x (horizontal) axis and "Summarized groups of records" is selected. Middle: When the exhibit field isn't first in the sort order, you get a rather pointless one-bar chart. Bottom: Change the sort order to put Exhibit on top, and the chart instantly changes to reflect total attendance for the three exhibits in the current found set.

■ Advanced Charting

So far, you've been charting data from multiple records in a single table, but File-Maker offers two other data sources: delimited data and related records. To set those options, you'll need to see the Data Source section of the Chart Setup dialog box (Figure 16-22).

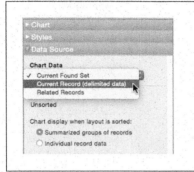

FIGURE 16-22

The Chart Data pop-up menu (found in the right column of the Chart Setup dialog box) is where you tell the chart to look for its data. You can also specify how your data is summarized, and so how it's charted, when records are sorted.

Delimited Data

The "Current Record (delimited data)" option in the Chart Setup dialog box tells FileMaker to look at fields in the current record when drawing a chart. The data to be charted has to take the form of a *return-separated list.* That is, each value has to be separated from other values by a return character.

> **NOTE** If you have repeating fields in your database, they might seem like a natural source for delimited data. Quite often, a repeating field even looks like a return-separated list on a layout. Alas, repeating fields aren't return separated, and you can't use them for delimited data when charting.

Creating a chart of delimited data is straightforward. Create the chart on a layout that has the context of the data you want to visualize. In the *CH16 Ostrich Ranch. fmp12* database, use the "Delimited" layout, shown in Figure 16-23. Here you'll find two text fields with return-separated lists already in them. The Chart Labels field contains the names of five ostriches. Chart Data shows the average number of eggs each bird lays each month. You're going to chart that data.

1. **Switch to the Delimited layout, choose View→Layout Mode and then select the Chart tool from the Status toolbar.**

   The layout holds the data you'll be charting.

2. **Below the fields on the layout, draw a chart object that fills the empty space on the layout.**

   The Chart Setup dialog box appears.

3. **Click the Chart heading in the column on the right.**

   Start by telling the chart object which fields hold its data.

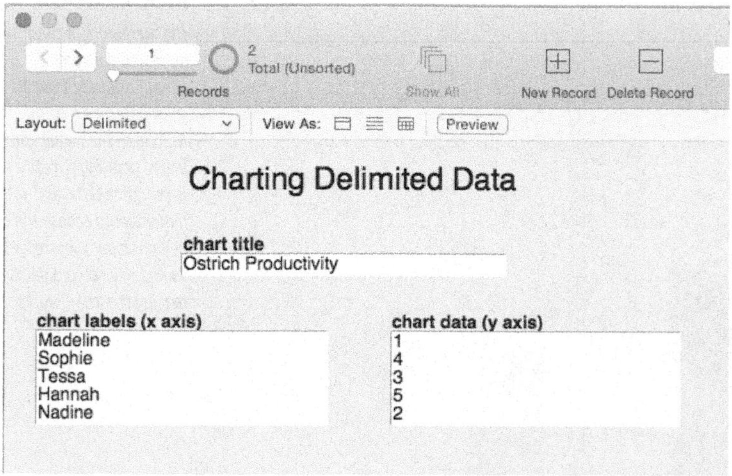

FIGURE 16-23

Delimited data is a list of values with line breaks between each one. Charting delimited data isn't very difficult technically, but it has an inherent fragility. If you rearranged the names on the left to be in alphabetical order, the numbers on the right wouldn't automatically change with them. That means you have to take care when you assemble your delimited lists.

4. **Click the box to the right of the Chart Title field and then select Specify Field Name from the list of fields that pops up. Choose "chart title" and then click OK.**

   All the data for this chart is found in fields in this table.

5. **For the X-axis Data, select the "chart labels" field. For the Y-axis data, choose the "chart data" field.**

   These two items, X-Axis Data and Y-Axis data, are the bare minimums you must set in every chart. All other settings should illuminate the data you're displaying.

6. **Click the Data Source heading in the column on the right and then choose "Current Record (delimited data)" from the Chart Date popup. Click Done.**

   The finished chart should resemble the preview pane seen in Figure 16-24.

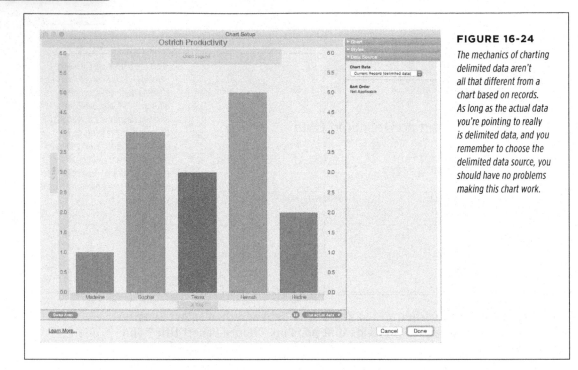

FIGURE 16-24

The mechanics of charting delimited data aren't all that different from a chart based on records. As long as the actual data you're pointing to really is delimited data, and you remember to choose the delimited data source, you should have no problems making this chart work.

Switch back to Browse mode to view your chart. If you modify data in any of the fields, the chart will reflect your new data as soon as you commit the changes. You can even add new data points by adding new values in the lists. In the real world, though, you probably won't create a chart that relies on manually entered data. You'll usually use a calculation or a script to gather the data. Since FileMaker draws the data in the order in which it appears in its source fields, delimited data charts don't require a sorted found set. The trick is making sure that your labels and data are gathered in exactly the right order.

NOTE   Placing a Delimited data chart outside a Body layout part can result in some unexpected behavior. Generally speaking, the chart will show data from the currently active record. But Delimited data charts inside Subsummary layout parts can show different results depending on your found set and sort order. Bottom line: Keep your Delimited data charts in the Body of your layout.

Related Records

Much of FileMaker's power comes from its relational database capabilities (Chapter 6); some of your most powerful charts will also come from related records. You can point a chart at a related table to graph the values related to the record you're viewing, which opens up some interesting possibilities. Navigating from one record to the next means your chart will change to reflect the data related to the record you're viewing. Depending on how the relationship is set up, you can also have a chart that filters its display based on selections you make. And in a multiuser setting, a chart of related data could serve as a real-time monitor to database activity.

Consider a museum attendance database. Figure 16-25 shows the relationships among the tables in this system. Charting related records will let you be on a museum's record in the Facilities table, but graph attendance trends using data from the Attendance table. Here's how to create a chart based on related record data:

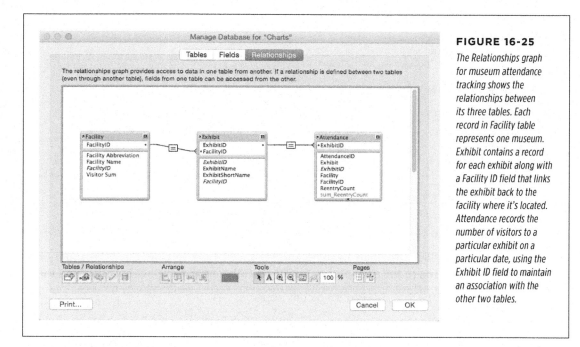

FIGURE 16-25

The Relationships graph for museum attendance tracking shows the relationships between its three tables. Each record in Facility table represents one museum. Exhibit contains a record for each exhibit along with a Facility ID field that links the exhibit back to the facility where it's located. Attendance records the number of visitors to a particular exhibit on a particular date, using the Exhibit ID field to maintain an association with the other two tables.

1. **Go to the Related Data Line Chart layout and switch to Layout mode. In the Status toolbar, select the Chart tool.**

   This layout is from the context of the Facility table.

2. **Below the fields on the layout, drag a chart object that fills the available space in the layout.**

   The Chart Setup dialog box appears.

3. **Under Data Source in the right column, change the Chart Data value to Related Records.**

   A new Related Table pop-up menu appears.

4. **From the Related Table pop-up menu, choose Attendance.**

   You want to chart Attendance data.

5. **Below "Sort Order of Related Records," click the Specify button and then double-click the VisitDate field on the left to place it in the sort order. Click OK.**

   This tells the chart how to display the related data. It's similar to choosing a sort order in a relationship.

6. **Set "Chart display when sorted" to the Individual record data option.**

   The Data Source settings should now match Figure 16-26.

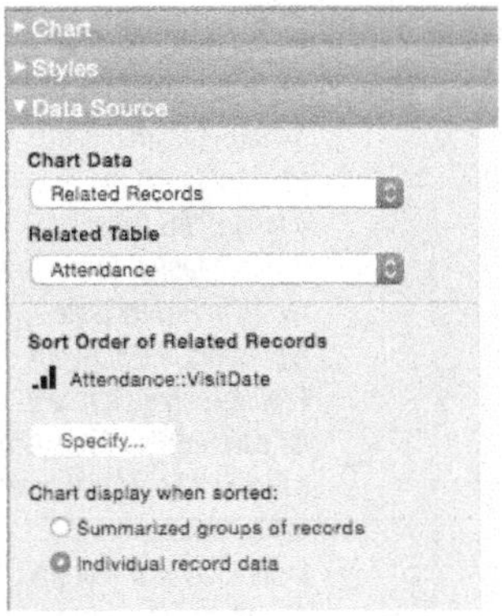

FIGURE 16-26

Choosing Related Records for your data source isn't enough. You also have to specify which related table's records you want charted.

7. **Click the Chart heading and set Chart Type to Line. Click the square button to the right of the Chart Title field and then select Specify Field Name.**

   The Specify Field dialog box appears.

8. **Set the pop-up menu to Facility. Click Facility Name field and then click OK.**

   Each record's chart title will be different.

9. **Under X-Axis, type *Date* into the Title field.**

   This text is the legend for the x-axis.

10. **Click the square button to the right of the X-Axis Data field and then select Specify Field Name. In the Specify Field dialog box that appears, set pop-up menu to Attendance.**

    This field contains your data. You'll almost always use a field from the table you specified in step 4 above.

11. **From the field list, select VisitDate and then click OK.**

    You'll see one data point for each related record in the Attendance table.

12. **Under Y-Axis, type *Visitors* into the Title field. Because this will be a two-series chart, click the "Add a Y Series" button.**

You're setting up the your two series.

13. **In the box on the left, click "Series 1." In the Series Name box, type *Repeat*. Click the button next to the Data box and choose Specify Field Name. In the Specify Field dialog box that appears, set the pop-up menu to Attendance, select the ReentryCount field, and then click OK.**

The first series is defined.

14. **In the box on the left, click "Series 2." In the Series Name box, type *Unique*. Click the button next to the Data box and then choose Specify Field Name. In the Specify Field dialog box that appears, set the pop-up menu to Attendance, select the VisitorCount field, and then click OK.**

The second series is defined.

15. **Turn on Show Legend. Under Axis Options, select X-Axis and set the Label Angle to 45.**

This option prevents the labels that run along the bottom of the chart from overlapping one another. While this is a simple solution, it may make the labels tough to read. However, because line graphs are meant to show change over time, actual dates are not the most important part of this visualization.

Your Chart Setup should resemble the one in Figure 16-27. Optionally, you may change the legend formatting.

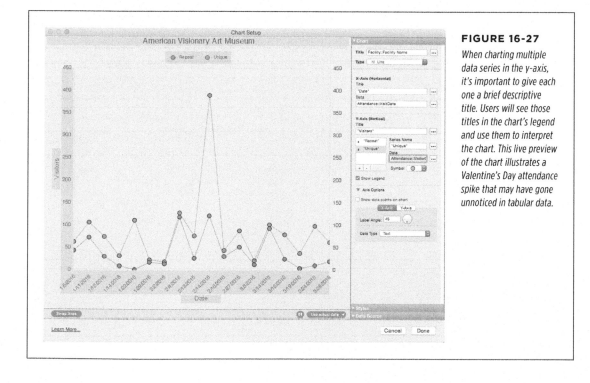

FIGURE 16-27

When charting multiple data series in the y-axis, it's important to give each one a brief descriptive title. Users will see those titles in the chart's legend and use them to interpret the chart. This live preview of the chart illustrates a Valentine's Day attendance spike that may have gone unnoticed in tabular data.

16. **Click Done to save your Chart Setup.**

Hop back into Browse mode by using Ctrl+B (⌘-B) to admire your multiple series, related record chart.

Your new chart shows attendance data that's related to the active Facility record. Flip through the four records in the table to see attendance trends for each facility. See the box below to learn how context can change how a chart displays related data.

Copy with Context

FileMaker lets you copy and paste charts among your various layouts, but do so with care. A chart of related records that works just fine on layout A may show wildly different results or none at all when copied and pasted onto layout B. Context is just as important for a chart as it is for a portal. (See page 159 for a refresher on context.)

Consider this metaphor: Looking out the front window of your house, you can see about half of your next-door neighbor's lawn but none of her house. If you move to a side window, you can now see almost all of her lawn and one entire side of her house. Whether your "context" was the front window or the side window, what you saw varied significantly, even though it was the same property. Copying and pasting a chart of related data from one layout to another can be like moving between the windows. You won't always get the same view. If you find that you're having difficulty with related data charts, go back to page 145. A solid grounding in the fundamentals of FileMaker's relational model will serve you very well when charting.

Advanced Calculations

In the earlier calculation chapters, you learned how calculations can make your databases work harder for you. But the functions you've learned so far can't make your databases work much *smarter*. For example, what if you want to add a 5 percent delinquency charge to invoices over a month old? You could create a special "past due balance" field on a special layout that you use only when you've searched for late invoices, but that's just extra complexity to create and then maintain, if the late fee rules change later on. On the other hand, if you create a calculation that makes a *decision* based on current data, you can let the database itself figure out when to apply late fees, and it works for every invoice, not just the late ones. This chapter shows you how to give your calculations that brainpower by using logical functions and other advanced techniques.

The calculation engine can also be used to give FileMaker features it doesn't have. You (or someone you hire) can create a *plug-in* in a programming language like C++. But you don't have to create a plug-in yourself. Lots of great ones are available from third parties (page 697). Whether you write a plug-in or buy it, each plug-in adds new functions, like file handling, credit-card processing, or web services, to FileMaker's Specify Calculation window.

> **NOTE** To *create* plug-ins, you need FileMaker Pro Advanced (Chapter 14). Once you've installed a plug-in, though, it can be *used* in any version of FileMaker.

But before you learn any of those new concepts, you'll revisit Boolean logic and learn more about how the Self() function can make your calculations reusable in other fields. And you'll finally find out how and when to set a calculation field's storage options.

■ Understanding Boolean Functions

Boolean functions aren't a distinct group like Text or Number functions. Nor is "Boolean" a choice in the "Calculation Result is" pop-up menu. It's the *result* of a calculation that makes it Boolean. Regular calculations return results like 3.14 or 753 or "Dread Pirate Roberts." Boolean results refer to the theory of logic, and can always be reduced to either "true" or "false," "yes" or "no," "not empty" or "empty." Conditional formatting calculations are always Boolean, since FileMaker needs to know if a particular condition is true before it can decide when to apply the formatting you set up. You can learn a lot about Boolean calculations by exploring the Conditional Formatting dialog box (Figure 17-1). See the box on the next page for more on using Conditional Formatting.

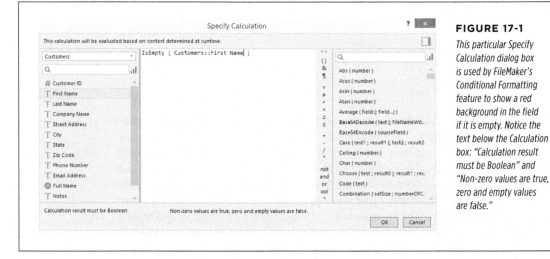

FIGURE 17-1

This particular Specify Calculation dialog box is used by FileMaker's Conditional Formatting feature to show a red background in the field if it is empty. Notice the text below the Calculation box: "Calculation result must be Boolean" and "Non-zero values are true, zero and empty values are false."

Even though it may be explicit to add the equal sign and empty quote marks, it isn't necessary because "empty" means False in the Boolean world. Plus, some developers don't like the inverted logic required when you check for the presence of nothing in a field.

If you're uncomfortable with the idea of nothing in a field being "true," you can come at it from the other direction. This calculation is True when the First Name field contains anything at all:

```
not Customers::First Name
```

Separating Formatting from Data

Why would a math major like me use lowly, layout-based conditional formatting when I can make a whole bunch of very cool, very complicated calculations using text-formatting functions?

It's true that conditional formatting doesn't give you a whole bunch of options that you don't have with text-formatting functions. However, you do get a giant leap closer to something that's been difficult to do in FileMaker—separating the presentation layer from the data layer of your file.

In programmer-speak, the *presentation layer* is anything having to do with showing your data. It's the layout and all the stuff you put on a layout to make your data easy to understand. Even the fact that you can move fields around in relation to one another is part of FileMaker's sophisticated presentation layer. Boldface fields, portals, buttons, and web viewers are presentation tools, as well. Custom menus and tooltips, which help you help your users work with their data, are also forms of presentation.

The *data layer* is just what it sounds like—the tables and fields of actual information. Most calculations also fall onto the data layer. For example, when you multiply the Quantity and Price Each fields together, using a calculation in the Extended Price field, that's the data layer.

So is adding a 5 percent surcharge to late payments.

Adding another 5 percent 30 days later, when those deadbeats have come up with more excuses, is still the data layer.

But when you use number formatting to display the results of any of those calculations with dollar signs, commas, and decimal places, that's presentation-layer territory. And if you use a text function to display the late penalty in red boldface at 18 points, then you're treading in the presentation layer, even if you use a sophisticated calculation to see if the penalty is due before you apply the format.

Furthermore, when you rely solely on calculations for formatting, you've got to add more *complexity* to your calculations to *simplify* some layouts. Say you use a text formatting function to display unpaid invoice totals in red after 30 days. The field *always* displays the red text where appropriate, even if that's not the purpose of the layout. For example, if the Marketing Department needs a list of invoices over $500 to decide who gets special offers, the red invoice amounts make no sense—and may violate customers' privacy. But if you separate presentation and data by using conditional formatting, you can apply the format on a layout-by-layout basis. So all in all, it makes life easier down the road if you confine your use of calculations to mathematical operations *on* your data and use conditional formatting to handle the display *of* your data.

So is one method better than another? Probably not. But when you look at other developers' calculations, you may see all these forms, so it helps to know how they work. If you're the only developer working on your files, then you're free to use the construction that makes most sense to you. But when you develop in a team, you might want to develop a standard for constructing your Boolean calculations. In either case, it's a good idea to comment your Boolean calculations, so those who follow you can save time trying to retrace your logic.

Using the Self() Function

You got a peek at the Self() function back in the box on page 299. The Self() function simply returns the contents of the object to which it's applied. FileMaker's engineers created the Self() function to make calculations portable—that is, you don't need to retrofit them if you move them from one field or object to another.

Here's one example of how it works. The five volunteer data entry folks keeping up with your theater group's subscription and donor list are expressing their artistic temperaments by using different formats for phone numbers. So when you print out the contact list, you've got (800) 555-1212, 800-555-1212, 800.555.1212, 555-1212, and every other variation under the sun.

FileMaker's auto-enter calculations can help you transform self-expression into standard formats. To straighten things out, you could add this calculation to your Phone field:

```
"(" & // start with an open paren sign
Left ( Filter ( Phone ; "0123456789" ) ; 3 ) & // grab the area code
") " & // finish the area code with a close paren and a space
Middle ( Filter ( Phone; "0123456789" ) ; 4 ; 3 ) & // grab the exchange
"-" & // give me a hyphen
Middle ( Filter ( Phone ; "0123456789" ) ; 7 ; 4 ) // the last four digits
```

This calculation takes the data entered into the Phone field and imposes its own order onto the data. As the comments show, one part of the phone number format is assembled from each line of this nested calculation.

NOTE This formula uses several techniques covered in Chapter 11: The `Filter()` function (page 425); `Left()`, `Middle()`, and `Right()` functions (page 424); and nested functions (page 418).

This calculation solves the problem for one phone field, but what if all your records contain three phone fields? Plus, you've got three phone fields in your Employees and Vendors databases, too. To transfer this calculation, you have to paste it into each field's auto-enter calculation dialog box, select each instance of "Phone," and then change it to "Mobile" or "Work Phone" so the calculation can work properly in each new context. Don't you have *real* work to do?

With the `Self()` function, which takes no parameter, and therefore doesn't need its own set of parentheses, you can write the calculation this way instead:

```
"(" &
Left ( Filter ( Self ; "0123456789" ) ; 3 ) &
") " &
Middle ( Filter ( Self; "0123456789" ) ; 4 ; 3 ) &
"-" &
Middle ( Filter ( Self ; "0123456789" ) ; 7 ; 4 )
```

The `Self()` function knows that it's referring to the field it's in, so you can copy and paste this function as many times as you want, and you'll never have to edit it for its new context. Good as it is, this calculation still has a couple of loopholes. See the box on page 675 for another way to clean up stray data entry in a Phone field.

WARNING Unfortunately, `Self()` doesn't work in every setting, script parameters (page 716), for one. When `Self()` won't work, FileMaker shows an error message.

Field Formatting Calculations

Now that you understand most of FileMaker's calculation power features, you're ready to see something really powerful. You've already seen how an auto-enter calculation can clean up a phone number during data entry (page 674). This calculation, which consolidates a lot of techniques you've covered in this section, goes one step further:

```
Let (
 cleanPhone = Filter ( Self; "0123456789"
 ) ;

Case (
Length( cleanPhone ) = 10 ;
"(" & Left ( cleanPhone ; 3 ) & ") " &
Middle ( cleanPhone ; 4 ; 3 ) &
"-" &
```

```
Right ( cleanPhone ; 4 ) ;

Self
 )
 )
```

First, the calculation uses the Filter function to remove any non-numeric characters from the entered phone number and puts the result in a variable called cleanPhone. Then, if cleanPhone has exactly 10 digits, the calculation breaks it apart according to the format you want. Otherwise, it just returns the phone number the way the person entered it.

To make the calculation work properly, in the Field Options dialog box, be sure you turn off "Do not replace existing value (if any)."

Using Storage Options

Calculation fields have storage and indexing options, just as other field types do. The results of most calculations are stored when you define the calculation field and again each time the value in a field that's referenced in the calculation changes. Storage options let you control that behavior (Figure 17-2).

Understanding Stored and Unstored Calculation Fields

Values in calculation fields are updated when the values in fields referenced in their formulas change. So even though the value in a calculation field can change, it's considered a *stored* value. When you create a calculation field, the value is automatically stored, and in most cases you'll leave it that way.

But you can also require a calculation to evaluate whenever it's displayed; for example, when you switch to a layout that contains the calculation field. Such calculations are considered *unstored,* and they have some special uses, as well as some drawbacks.

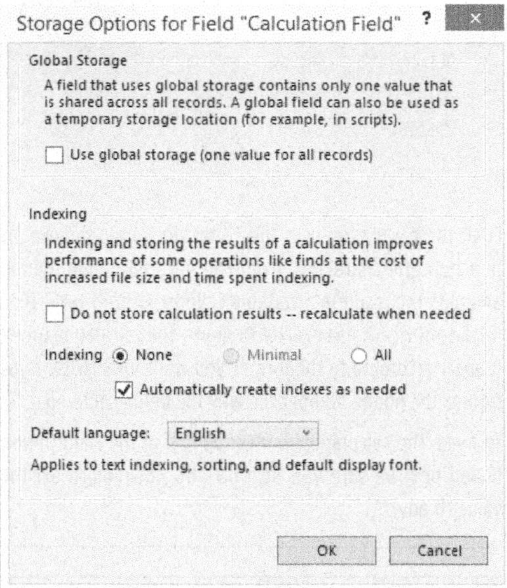

Storage Options for Field "Calculation Field" ? ✕

Global Storage

A field that uses global storage contains only one value that is shared across all records. A global field can also be used as a temporary storage location (for example, in scripts).

☐ Use global storage (one value for all records)

Indexing

Indexing and storing the results of a calculation improves performance of some operations like finds at the cost of increased file size and time spent indexing.

☐ Do not store calculation results -- recalculate when needed

Indexing ⦿ None ○ Minimal ○ All

☑ Automatically create indexes as needed

Default language: English ▾

Applies to text indexing, sorting, and default display font.

OK Cancel

FIGURE 17-2

In the Specify Calculation window, when you click the Storage Options button, you can set global storage and indexing options, just like any other field type. You also get a choice you haven't seen before: "Do not store calculation results." This example shows the storage options for the Invoice::Total Due field, which isn't stored because you want FileMaker to update if you add, delete, or edit any line item on the invoice. Notice, though, that you can't index unstored calculations and you can't use an unstored calculation as a key field (page 146).

Whenever the data in a field changes, FileMaker also works behind the scenes, finding all the *stored* calculation fields that depend on the changed field, and *recalculates* them (even if they aren't on your current layout), storing the new value in the field. Whether it's stored or unstored, a calculation field usually changes because a field used in the calculation has changed, as you'll see next. Understanding *when* fields recalculate and how dependencies work can help you decide whether it's appropriate to make a calculation field's value unstored.

NOTE When you use a field in a calculation, you can say the calculation depends on the field (or, in other words, it has a dependency on the field).

◼ FIELD DEPENDENCIES

Take a look at the example in Figure 17-3 to see how FileMaker knows when to recalculate fields. Calculation fields often use other calculation fields in complex arrangements, as this hierarchy of field dependencies shows.

First Name and Last Name are the only editable fields in Figure 17-3. But they aren't the only fields that can change. When someone edits a customer's name, FileMaker sees that it needs to recalculate Full Name, which in turn triggers a recalculation of the Full Address value. The recalculation trickles down through all the dependent fields as soon as someone makes the change, and then exits the First Name field.

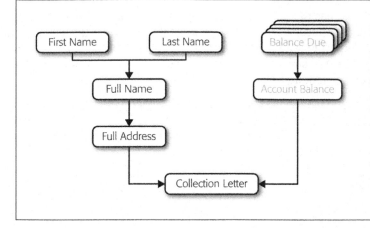

FIGURE 17-3

This picture shows a series of interdependent fields. The Full Name field is a calculation field that uses First Name and Last Name. The Full Address field uses Full Name (and some others not shown here). The fields in gray are unstored calculation fields. Collection Letter uses Account Balance and Full Address. Account Balance in turn uses Balance Due. Since an account can have several invoices, each with a balance due, Account Balance actually uses several balance due values—one from each related invoice.

By contrast, since Collection Letter is an *unstored field,* FileMaker *doesn't* recalculate it right away. (It doesn't need to recalculate if you aren't displaying the value anywhere on the current layout.) Instead, the program waits until someone brings up the field onscreen, and *then* it runs the calculation on the current data and displays the result.

That recalculates the Collection Letter value as FileMaker grabs the stored value for the Full Address field. But it also needs the Account Balance, which isn't stored. So *that* field is recalculated first. That calculation requires the new Balance Due on each invoice in turn, and then they're added up to get an Account Balance. Finally, the database has the values it needs to show you the Collection Letter.

Happily, FileMaker keeps track of these dependencies internally, so when you use *unstored* calculations, it pulls the necessary data down through the hierarchy of dependencies when your edits call for it. But if you understand how dependencies work, you can make good decisions about when to store data.

■ DECIDING WHEN TO STORE

When you first create a calculation field, FileMaker makes it a stored field automatically, *if possible.* Some field values aren't eligible for storage:

- If a field depends on any other unstored fields

- If a field depends on any global fields

- If a field depends on any related fields

- If a field depends on any summary fields

If your calculation meets any of these criteria, then FileMaker automatically turns on the "Do not store calculation results—recalculate when needed" option for you, and it doesn't let you turn it off. Otherwise, FileMaker automatically stores the field.

- An unstored field has to be recalculated every time it appears onscreen or in a report. All that recalculation can slow your database down, especially if the unstored field is part of a summary field or a calculation that aggregates many records. So it's best to store a field unless you need a freshly calculated value every time you see that data.

- If you perform a find based on an unstored calculation field, then FileMaker has to go through all your records one by one, calculating each one as it goes. The result is a slow search process. If you plan on searching a field, then store it. (For more detail, see the box below.)

FREQUENTLY ASKED QUESTION

I Want to Store My Field

What if I want to search on a field that FileMaker won't let me store?

Just because you can't store a field doesn't mean you don't wish you could. For example, in your Invoices layout, you probably do want to be able to search for invoices with a balance due. But since that field uses related data, it's not storable.

The good news is, you don't have to store a field in order to search it; the search is just a little slower. You don't notice the slowdown until you've amassed *lots* of invoice records. Sadly, there's no easy way to speed it up.

One remedy is to change the way people work with your database. You have to make your Invoice Detail layout *read only*—meaning people can't change data on the invoice directly (see page 306). Instead, they use a special layout and a script to make invoice changes.

When they're finished, your script can calculate the balance due and update a number field on the invoice appropriately. This way, the Balance Due field is a normal, nonrelated field, eligible for indexing and quick searches.

Also, remember that FileMaker can't search a calculation field that refers to related data very quickly, but it can search the related data *itself* with lightning speed. For example, to find an invoice that has payments applied to it, don't search the Amount Paid field in the invoice. Instead, search for invoices where Payments::Amount is greater than zero. That search turns up every invoice with a related payment record that's not negative. You get exactly what you want, and FileMaker can carry it out using indexed fields.

Even if FileMaker can store a certain value, you may not always want it to. Here are some reasons you might turn *on* that "Do not store" option:

- Stored fields automatically recalculate as needed when *other fields* change. But FileMaker has no such automatic behavior for other kinds of information. For example, when you use the Get(CurrentDate) function in a calculation, FileMaker doesn't recalculate it when the date changes. In general, when you use any of the Get() functions, you usually want to make your field unstored to "get" the most up-to-date information.

- A stored field takes up space on disk, while an unstored field doesn't. FileMaker 14 files can hold 8 TB of data, so space isn't a major consideration for most people. But if you're into slim and trim files, then you can save space by making calculations unstored.

- Lots of stored calculation fields can really slow down *record creation*. That's usually not a big deal, but if you often import data (Chapter 22) or use a script to regularly create lots of records, then you can speed things up by reducing the number of stored calculations.

> **NOTE** Obviously, you have some gray area here. When in doubt, store the field. You can always make it unstored later. Choose File→Manage Database, switch to the Fields tab if necessary, select your calculation field from the list, click Options, and then click Storage Options to find the "Do not store calculation results–recalculate as needed" option.

■ INDEXING CALCULATIONS

Unless they're global fields or unstored fields, you can set indexing for calculation fields just like any other field, as discussed on page 261. The available options and their effects depend on the result type of the calculation: text, number, date, or time.

Global Calculation Fields

A calculation field can use *global storage* (page 259) just like most other fields. When you turn on "Use global storage" (see Figure 17-2), FileMaker calculates just one value for the entire table, rather than a value for each record. If your calculation uses other global fields—and *no* other fields—then it works just as you expect. That is, when you modify one of the global fields it depends on, FileMaker automatically recalculates its value.

If the calculation uses non-global fields, on the other hand, things get a little tricky. Whenever you change one of the fields referenced in the calculation, FileMaker recalculates the global calculation field by using the values from the current record. For example, if you turn on "Use global storage" for your Full Name field, then it shows the name of the person you're looking at when you dismiss the Manage Database window. If you were on the first record, that's whose name you see in the field, just as expected. But as you flip through the records, you see that first person's name on every record. You're changing records, but with global storage, the Full Name value stays the same. That's because nothing it depends on has changed.

Now imagine you switch to the *last* record. If you then change the First Name field, Full Name recalculates. This new value displays the first and last name from the last record, since FileMaker reevaluates the calculation in its entirety.

This behavior may seem kind of odd, but it has a really cool use. If you need to track the data in the last record you *changed*—maybe you need an informal audit of which record just got changed while you were scanning through other records—throw a global calculation field on your data-entry layout. Then, no matter which record you're looking at, you see the value from the last *edited* record in that field.

■ Logical Functions

The logical function group is diverse and powerful. You get functions for making decisions (called *conditional functions*), learning about field values, and even evaluating calculations *inside* other calculations. This section covers all those possibilities. Along the way, you learn how to define and use *variables*, which act as placeholders while complex calculations go through their many steps.

> **NOTE** Though you learned about it at the beginning of this chapter, you find the Self( ) function (page 673) in the functions list, under the "Logical functions" heading.

Conditional Functions

This chapter began by posing an interesting challenge: You have a calculation field in the Invoices table called Total Due. It calculates the total amount due on an invoice by subtracting the sum of all payments from the total amount of the invoice. Can you modify the Total Due calculation to add a 5 percent penalty when an invoice is past due?

The answer lies in the three conditional functions. Each one lets you specify more than one possible result. The functions require one or more parameters—called *conditions* or *conditional expressions*—that tell them what result to pick. The conditional functions—If( ), Case( ), and Choose( )—differ in how many possible results they support, and what kind of conditions they expect.

■ THE IF() FUNCTION

The first and most common conditional function is simply called If( ). The If( ) function is the basic unit of decision making in FileMaker calculations. It's the ticket when you have to decide between two choices, based on some criteria. It looks like this:

```
If ( YourTestCondition ; True Result ; False Result )
```

When you use the If( ) function, FileMaker evaluates the condition looking for a Boolean result (True or False). If the condition has a True value, the function returns its second parameter (True result). If the condition is False, though, then it returns the False result instead. Here's an example:

```
If ( First Name = "Dominique" ; "Free" ; "$299.00" )
```

For example, the result of this calculation returns "Free" if the First Name field matches "Dominique." If it *doesn't* match, then it returns $299.00 instead. (See the box on page 681 for more details.)

Matching Text Values

What do you mean by "First Name field matches 'Dominique'?" What constitutes a match?

When you use the = operator with text values, FileMaker compares the two values on each side, letter by letter. If every letter, number, space, punctuation mark, and so on matches, then you get a True result. But the comparison isn't case-sensitive. In other words, this expression has a True result:

    "TEXT" = "text"

If this function is too forgiving for your needs, then you can use the Exact() function instead.

Exact takes two text parameters, compares them, and returns True if they match exactly—including case. This expression has a False result:

    Exact ("TEXT"; "text")

It's perfectly legal and quite common to use the Exact function (or any other function, field, or expression) as the first parameter of the If() function, like this:

    If (Exact (First Name ; "Dominique") ;
    "Free" ; "$299.00")

This version of the calculation will return "$299.00" if the First Name field contains "dominique," since the case on the letter D doesn't match.

■ THE CASE() FUNCTION

Sometimes you need to pick from more than just two choices. Luckily, the If() function has a cousin named Case() that simply excels at such problems. For example, suppose you want to show one of these four messages on the top of your layout:

- Good Morning

- Good Afternoon

- Good Evening

- Go To Bed

FileMaker chooses a message based on the time of day. The If() function doesn't work very well for this problem because If() allows only one condition and two possible results. You *can* nest If() statements one inside the other, so that the False result is really another If() statement. But nested If() functions are really hard to read and even harder to tweak, so if you find that your business rules require a change in your calculation, you may rue the day you decided to use four nested If() functions to decide which greeting method to display.

The Case() function has this form:

    Case (test1 ; result1 ; { test2 ; result2 ; ... ; defaultResult })

You can add as many parameters as you want, in pairs, to represent a condition and the result to be returned if that condition is True. Since the conditions and results are sequential and not nested, you can easily read a Case() statement, no matter how many conditions you pile on. You can even add an optional parameter after the last result. This parameter represents the *standard* result—the one FileMaker uses if none of the conditions are True.

> **NOTE** Since the `Case()` function accepts several conditions, more than one condition can be True at the same time. If so, FileMaker chooses the *first True* condition when it picks a result.

A calculation using the `Case()` function might look like this:

```
Case (
Get ( CurrentTime ) > Time ( 4 ; 0 ; 0 ) and Get ( CurrentTime ) < Time ( 12
; 0 ; 0 ) ;
"Good Morning" ;

Get ( CurrentTime ) ≥ Time ( 12 ; 0 ; 0 ) and Get ( CurrentTime ) < Time ( 18
; 0 ; 0 ) ;
"Good Afternoon" ;

Get ( CurrentTime ) ≥ Time ( 18 ; 0 ; 0 ) and Get ( CurrentTime ) < Time ( 22
; 0 ; 0 ) ;
"Good Evening" ;

"Go To Bed"
)
```

In this calculation, the `Case()` function checks first to see if the current time is between 4:00 a.m. and 12:00 p.m. If it is, then the "Good Morning" value is returned. If not, it then checks whether the time is between 12:00 p.m. and 6:00 p.m., which would produce the "Good Afternoon" message. Again, if not, it checks to see if it's between 6:00 p.m. and 10:00 p.m. If so, the user sees "Good Evening."

You don't need to specify a condition for the last result—"Go To Bed"—because if all the previous conditions are False, then it *must* be time for bed. In other words, if it *isn't* the morning, and it *isn't* the afternoon, and it *isn't* the evening, then it must be late at night. (If you need further help deciphering the above calculation, then see the box on the next page. On the other hand, if you're so far ahead that you can see a better way to do it, then see the box on page 683.)

■ THE CHOOSE() FUNCTION

The `Choose()` function is sort of the forgotten third member of the conditional trio. People don't immediately grasp how to use it—so they don't. But if you think of it as a value list with the choices coded into a calculation, then you see how the `Choose()` function can turn an awfully ugly `Case()` function into a specimen of neatness.

It looks like this:

```
Choose ( Condition ; Result0 {; Result1 ; Result2...} )
```

A Complex Case

The Case( ) function on page 681 expresses a familiar concept—do Plan A in one case, do Plan B in a different case, and so on. But you might not immediately know how you get from that simple idea to the more complicated calculations shown in this chapter. Here's how it breaks down:

Remember that semicolons separate the parameters you pass to a function. So the first parameter is *all* of this:

```
Get ( CurrentTime ) > Time ( 4;0;0 ) and
Get ( CurrentTime ) < Time ( 12;0;0 )
```

That whole expression forms the first condition. Remember that the and operator works on two Boolean values. It returns a True result if the values on each side are *both True.*

So really, you can split this condition in two. First, this expression must be True:

```
Get ( CurrentTime ) > Time ( 4;0;0 )
```

If that expression is True, then FileMaker checks to see if this expression is True, too:

```
Get ( CurrentTime ) < Time ( 12;0;0 )
```

These subexpressions are much simpler. Each has the same form, comparing the current time to a time you construct with the Time function. The first makes sure it's after 4:00 a.m. The second makes sure it's *before* 12:00 p.m. The other two conditions in the calculation are exactly the same—except they look at different times.

Unlike the other conditional functions, Choose( ) doesn't expect a Boolean expression for its condition. Instead, it looks for a *number.* The number tells it which of the results to choose: If the Condition is zero, then the function returns Result0; if it's one, then it returns Result1; and so on.

Imagine you have a Student table, and one of its fields is called GPA. This field holds the student's current grade point average, as a number. You'd like to turn this number into a letter grade on the printed report.

Many FileMaker developers would immediately jump to the Case( ) function to solve this problem. They'd do something like this:

```
Case (
GPA < 0.5; "F";
GPA < 1.5; "D";
GPA < 2.5; "C";
GPA < 3.5; "B";
"A"
)
```

While this calculation gets the job done, you can do it more succinctly with the Choose( ) function:

```
Choose ( Round(GPA; 0); "F"; "D"; "C"; "B"; "A" )
```

Clever Case Conditions

If you were one of those students who handed in homework early and always sat in the front row, you may be jumping up and down in your chair right now, waving your hand in the air. What you're *dying* to say is, "I can make that Case() function simpler!" Well, you're probably right. In fact, this calculation does the same job:

```
Case (

Get ( CurrentTime ) <= Time(4;0;0) or
Get ( CurrentTime ) > Time(22;0;0);
"Go To Bed";

Get ( CurrentTime ) < Time(12;0;0);
"Good Morning";

Get ( CurrentTime ) < Time(18;0;0);
"Good Afternoon";

"Good Evening"
)
```

This version takes advantage of the fact that the Case() function returns the result associated with the first True condition. FileMaker looks at the first condition, which checks to see if it's before 4:00 a.m. or after 10:00 p.m.

If either is True (note the or operator), then the function returns Go To Bed.

If both *are not* True, then FileMaker moves on to the second condition, which asks if it's earlier than 12:00 p.m. If so, it returns *Good Morning*. (What if it's 3 in the morning? That *is* earlier than 12:00 p.m., but you don't see "Good Morning" because FileMaker never gets this far. If it's 3:00 a.m., then the search for truth stops after the first condition.)

If it still hasn't found a True condition, then FileMaker moves on to the next: Is it before 6:00 p.m.? Again, the structure of the Case() statement *implies* that it must be after noon at this point since any time before noon would've been caught in the previous conditions. So this condition is *really* looking for a time between noon and 6, even though it doesn't say exactly that.

If you're comfortable with this kind of logic, then you can save yourself some clicks and a little typing. (Technically, you also make a more efficient calculation, but unless you're using the abacus version of FileMaker, you don't see a speed increase.)

Many people, on the other hand, find a calculation like this one utterly confusing. In that case, just use the longer version, and find something else in your life to brag about.

First, you turn the GPA value into an integer (using the Round() function), so the Choose() function can use it. When the GPA is 3.2, FileMaker rounds it to 3 and selects the result that represents the number 3: "B." (Remember that the first result is for *zero,* so 3 is actually the *fourth* result parameter. For more detail, see the box below.)

Constructing a Conditional Calculation

Now that you've seen the three conditional functions, it's time to take a stab at that calculation way back from the beginning of this chapter: Add a 5 percent penalty when the due date has passed.

When you're trying to come up with a logical calculation, think about what information FileMaker needs to make the decision and what action you want FileMaker to take after it decides. Then consider how best to do that using your database's existing fields and structure. First, decide which conditional function to use.

No Zero

The Choose() function insists that the first parameter should be for a zero condition. What if I don't want zero? My condition values start with 1.

You're in a common predicament. Luckily, you have two equally easy ways to get what you want from the Choose() function. Perhaps the most obvious is to simply add a dummy zero result:

```
Choose ( Door ; "" ; "European Vacation" ;
"New Car" ; "Wah Wah Wah" )
```

In this calculation, there's no Door number zero, so you just stick "" in the spot where the zero result belongs. You could just as well put "Death by Boredom" there, since it never gets chosen anyway. Just make sure you put a set of empty quotes there, so your first real result is in the number one spot.

If you just don't like having that dummy result in your calculation, then you can take this approach instead:

```
Choose ( Door - 1 ; "European Vacation" ;
"New Car" ; "Wah Wah Wah" )
```

This version simply subtracts one from the Door number. Now Door number one gets the zero result, and Door number two gets the one result. This approach becomes more appealing when your choices begin with an even higher number:

```
Choose ( Year - 2000 ; "Dragon" ; "Snake" ;
"Horse" ; "Sheep" )
```

Since this calculation uses the year as part of the condition, it would be a real drag to enter 2000 dummy values. Instead, you just subtract enough to get your sequence to start with zero.

TOTAL DUE CALCULATION #1: USING THE IF() FUNCTION

Most people's first thought would be to use the If() function, since the calculation needs to check *if* one condition is True:

- Is the value of the Date Due field earlier than today's date?

The calculation then takes the result of the If() function and returns one of two possible results:

- If it's *true* that the due date has passed, then add five percent (.05) of the Total Due to the value in Total Due.

- If it's *not true* that the due date has passed, then display the Total Due normally.

In plainer English, the If() condition checks to see if the due date has passed. If so, it adds 5 percent to the Total Due amount; if not, it returns the Total Due amount.

The full calculation might look like the following:

```
If ( // test
Get ( CurrentDate ) > Date Due
 and // Calculate the total due here to make sure it's not zero
Sum ( Line Items::Extended Price ) > allPayments ;
// True Result
 Sum ( Line Items::Extended Price ) + ( Sum ( Line Items::Extended Price )
 * .05 ) ; // add a 5% surcharge if Invoice is past due
 // False Result
```

```
  Sum ( Line Items::Extended Price ) // display the Total Due normally
  )
```

When the due date has passed, the value in your smart Total Due field changes to reflect a late payment penalty.

NOTE Since the Total Due field already calculates the due balance, you may be tempted to create a *new* field that calculates 5 percent of every invoice and then adds that value in only if the invoice is past due. But that would clutter your database with a superfluous field. Also, it's far better to have all your math in one place in case your business rules change.

■ TOTAL DUE CALCULATION #2: USING THE CASE() FUNCTION

Lots of people like the Case() function so much that they always use it, even in places where the If() function is perfectly competent. You might choose to use Case() if there's any chance you'll want to add some conditions to the statement later on. Instead of editing an If() expression later, you can save time by using Case() from the start.

The same calculation using Case() (and minus the helpful comments) looks like this:

```
Case (
 Get ( CurrentDate ) > Date Due and Sum ( Line Items::Extended Price ) >
allPayments ;
 Sum ( Line Items::Extended Price ) + ( Sum ( Line Items::Extended Price )
 * .05 ) ;
 Sum ( Line Items::Extended Price )
 )
```

NOTE With a single condition and standard result, the syntax for If() and Case() are the same. So if you do need to change an If() statement to Case() later, then simply change the word "If" to "Case," and add the new conditions.

This calculation works as advertised, but it has a couple of weak points. First, it has to calculate the total amount due *three times.* That's twice too many places to make typos and places to edit the Sum(Line Items::Extended Price) expression if you change the calculation later.

Second, allPayments is an unstored calculation based on the sum of related records. That's one of the slowest things you can ask a calculation to do. It may not matter much in this database, but in a more complicated situation, a calculation like this could slow FileMaker to a crawl.

In the next section, you'll learn how FileMaker helps you write leaner calculations that are easier to read—and quicker for FileMaker to work through.

■ The Let() Function and Variables

The Let() function creates a temporary holder for a value, called a *variable,* which can be plugged into a calculation over and over again. You have to do a little more work upfront to set up a variable, but that effort pays off with faster calculations that are easier to read, edit, and troubleshoot.

Defining Calculation Variables

In a Let() function, you define a value, give it a name and then use that name as often as you need throughout the calculation. In this case, you can calculate the amount due once and then store the result in a variable called AmountDue.

The Let() function is unique among functions because it controls the way you write your calculation, not the result. Here's an example:

```
Let ( [ L = 5 ; W = 10 ; H = 3 ] ; L * W * H )
```

Like the Substitute() function described on page 425, Let() uses bracketed notation. It really takes just two parameters. The first is a list of variable definitions. Each variable gets a name and a value using this format:

```
Name = Value
```

If you have more than one variable to define (as in the example above), put a semi-colon between each one and then put them all between a pair of square brackets. You can use any calculation expression as the value.

In fact, the expression that determines the value of a variable can even use other variables defined earlier. For example, the next calculation is perfectly legal. Its Hours variable has a value of *240:* 24 times the value of the Days variable:

```
Let (
[ Days = 10 ;
Hours = 24 * Days ;
Minutes = 60 * Hours ];
Minutes & " Minutes"
)
```

The second parameter can be any calculation expression. This parameter is special because you can use any of the variables you've defined inside the expression, just like fields. The first example above has three defined variables (L, W, and H); the expression then multiplies them together.

When FileMaker evaluates the Let() function, it determines the value of each variable just once and then plugs this value into the expression every time that variable is used. The result of a Let() function is simply the result of its expression.

■ TOTAL DUE CALCULATION #3: USING THE LET() FUNCTION

Your Total Due calculation can use the Let() function to solve all its problems. Just put the Amount Due in a variable, and use it throughout the calculation:

```
Let ( AmountDue = Sum ( Line Items::Extended Price ) ;
 If (
 Get(CurrentDate) > Date Due and AmountDue > 0;
 AmountDue + ( AmountDue * .05 );
 AmountDue
 )
 )
```

This version of the calculation is simpler, easier to change, and more efficient when it evaluates. You can't beat that.

The Life of a Variable

Most variables last only as long as it takes FileMaker to work through the calculation, and then they're gone. These variables are called *local variables* because they aren't valid outside the Let() function that calls them into existence. But you can also create a special variable called a *global variable,* which lives beyond your calculation. Read on to see when to use each type.

■ LOCAL VARIABLES

The variables you've written so far have all been local variables. Now it's time to learn that local variables have shockingly short memories. Local variables can lose their values even before a calculation is finished. If you write:

```
Let ( AmountDue = Sum ( Line Items::Extended Price ) ;
 If (
 Get(CurrentDate) > Date Due and AmountDue > Total Paid;
 AmountDue + ( AmountDue * .05 );
 AmountDue
 )
 ) & If ( AmountDue < 0 ; "CR" ; "" )
```

the calculation tries to use the AmountDue variable after the end parenthesis in the Let() function (that's the first one in the calculation's last line). Anything that happens after that in the calculation is outside the Let() function's *scope* (a technical term that refers to when the variable exists), so when you try to close the Specify Calculation window on this calculation, FileMaker complains that it doesn't know what that last AmountDue is supposed to be. Here's one way to rewrite that calculation by using a local variable:

```
Let ( AmountDue = Sum ( Line Items::Extended Price ) ;
 Case (
 Get ( CurrentDate ) > Date Due and AmountDue > Total Paid;
 AmountDue + ( AmountDue * .05 ) ;
 AmountDue < 0 ; AmountDue & "CR" ; AmountDue
 )
 )
```

In this example, you're including the last test condition within the scope of the Let() function, and you've switched to a Case() function, so that you don't have to read a set of nested If() functions.

If you want the local variables you set inside calculations to follow the same naming conventions as variables you set in scripts, then prefix their names with $. In that case, you'd write the calculation you just saw like this:

```
Let ( $AmountDue = Sum ( Line Items::Extended Price );
Case (
Get ( CurrentDate ) > Date Due and $AmountDue > 0;
$AmountDue + ( $AmountDue * .05 ) ;
$AmountDue < 0 ; $AmountDue & "CR" ; $AmountDue
)
)
```

NOTE When you create a variable with a $ prefix in a calculation that evaluates while a script is running, you extend its lifespan beyond the Let() function. In this case, the variable's scope is now the script. This can cause problems if you accidentally give two variables the same name. In that case, one variable will overwrite the other, and your script can go off the rails. Use this technique with extreme care. See page 720 for more information on how variables work in scripts.

Notice that you have to include the $ prefix in the Let() function, *and* in the formula that follows it.

■ GLOBAL VARIABLES

FileMaker gives you global fields; it also gives you *global variables*. Unlike local variables, global variables hold their results after the Let() function is finished. To create a global variable, add a $$ prefix to its name. Here's the same calculation rewritten with a global variable:

```
Let (
$$AmountDue = Sum ( Line Items::Extended Price ) ;
Case (
Get ( CurrentDate ) > Date Due and $$Amount Due > 0 ;
$$AmountDue + ( $$AmountDue * .05 ) ;
$$AmountDue < 0 ; $$AmountDue & "CR" ; $$AmountDue
)
)
```

The $$ prefix is the only difference you can see in the calculation. But the practical difference is vast: Global variable values remain until you change them (through another calculation or through a script), or until you close the file.

You could run a script that checks to see if a payment was made within 10 days of the invoice date, and if it was, apply a 1 percent discount to the $$AmountDue field. Sure, you can do something similar with a straightforward calculation field, but in that case, it gets a little trickier to apply the discount to some of the records, but not to others. With a script, you can find the records you want to give a spur-of-the-moment discount, run the script on that found set, and you're done.

Another reason to set a global variable with a calculation is to use that variable to filter portals (page 598). Portals that are filtered by variables may not always refresh when you expect them to because portals don't change their display unless a change of context (like moving to a new record) also occurs. Portal filtering by variable is usually safer in a script, because you can add a Refresh Portal script step or a change of context to the script to make sure the portal refreshes when the variable is changed. But using a calculation may fit the bill in some situations, so you should know that it's possible.

Nesting Let() Functions

As with other functions, you can nest Let() functions inside one another. In fact, you can define a variable once and then *redefine* it inside a nested Let() function. The variable's value changes while inside the nested Let() function and then changes back when it ends. By the same token, you can define a variable with the same name as a *field,* and FileMaker uses the variable's value while inside the Let() function. (These techniques aren't commonly used except by programmers who want to use the same techniques in FileMaker as they use when they write code.)

Here's a very simple example of a Let() function *inside* another Let() function:

```
Let ( X = 3 ; // only X is defined here
 Let ( Y = 4 ; // X and Y are both defined here
 X * Y
 )
 // Only X is defined here, too
 )
```

You can also use the Let() function more than once in a single calculation without nesting:

```
Let ( [ X = 3; Y = 4 ] ; X * Y ) &
Let ( units = "inches" ; " " & units )
```

◼ Recursion

As described in the box on page 568, you can create custom functions that call other custom functions, creating whole strings of mathematical wizardry that perform to your exact specifications. Even more interesting, a custom function can *use itself,* a technique known as *recursion.* With recursion, you can create calculations that repeat a process over and over again until they reach a result—called *iterative calculations.*

NOTE Recursion is a notoriously complicated topic, and many *very* capable FileMaker developers are stymied by it. Fortunately, recursion is rarely the only solution to a given problem, so you can certainly get by without it. For example, consider using a script instead.

Imagine you need a function that removes duplicate lines from a list. For example, if a field contains a list of colors, then you want a new list with only each *unique* color name, even if it appears in the original list several times. You can't do that with a normal calculation, because you just don't know how many words you need to pull out. A recursive function solves the problem by repeating its work until it takes care of all items.

Although the concept of a recursive function is simple, creating one can be tricky. To implement a recursive function, you're best off tackling the calculation in three distinct steps. First, solve the initial problem; second, call that first formula over and over again (that's the recursive part); and third, tell the formula how to stop.

NOTE If you have trouble getting through the following recursion example on your own, you can download a sample database from this book's Missing CD page at *www.missingmanuals.com/cds/fmp14mm.* It's called *CH17 Recursion.fmp12.*

Step 1: Solve the First Case

Rather than think about how to solve the entire problem, just figure out how to deal with the *first* line in the list. If you have a field called Values, for example, and you want to make sure the *first* line appears only once in the list, you can use this calculation (Figure 17-4):

```
LeftValues ( values ; 1 ) & Substitute ( values ; LeftValues ( values ; 1 ) ;
"" )
```

Suppose the Values field contains the following items with a blank line at the end:

```
Red
Green
Orange
Red
Orange
Yellow
```

The Substitute() part of this expression does the lion's share of the work, so start with that to figure out how the formula works. The Substitute() function sees that "Red" is the first item in the Values field and takes it out of the field everywhere it occurs. If Substitute() were the whole shooting match, then "Red" would disappear entirely from the Values field. But the LeftValues(values; 1) piece of the expression also notices that "Red" is the first item in the Values field, and it puts "Red" back at the top of the list. When both are put together (using the & sign), the result is the first item in the list, then the rest of the list with Red removed. Here's the result you see if you make a calculation field with the formula on the previous page:

Red
Green
Orange
Orange
Yellow

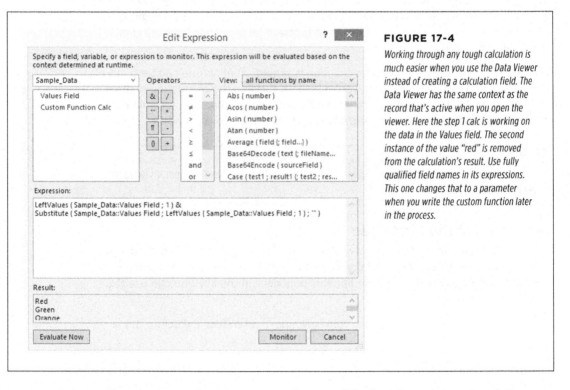

FIGURE 17-4

Working through any tough calculation is much easier when you use the Data Viewer instead of creating a calculation field. The Data Viewer has the same context as the record that's active when you open the viewer. Here the step 1 calc is working on the data in the Values field. The second instance of the value "red" is removed from the calculation's result. Use fully qualified field names in its expressions. This one changes that to a parameter when you write the custom function later in the process.

Now you're ready to move on to the rest of the function, where you call the same action over and over again—and things start to get interesting.

Step 2: Assume Your Function Already Works, and Use It

You're ready to take the *recursion leap of faith*. A recursive function, by definition, calls itself. So at some point, it depends on its own resources to work. But when you're *writing* the recursive custom function, it obviously doesn't work yet. You'll be at a total impasse if you don't *assume* it already works, and just get on with writing.

So since you're writing a new custom function called RemoveDuplicates(), write its syntax as if you already have a function called RemoveDuplicates() that does what you want (Figure 17-5). If such a function did exist, you could use it in the above calculation like this:

```
LeftValues ( values ; 1 ) & RemoveDuplicates ( Substitute ( values ;
LeftValues ( values ; 1 ); "" ) )
```

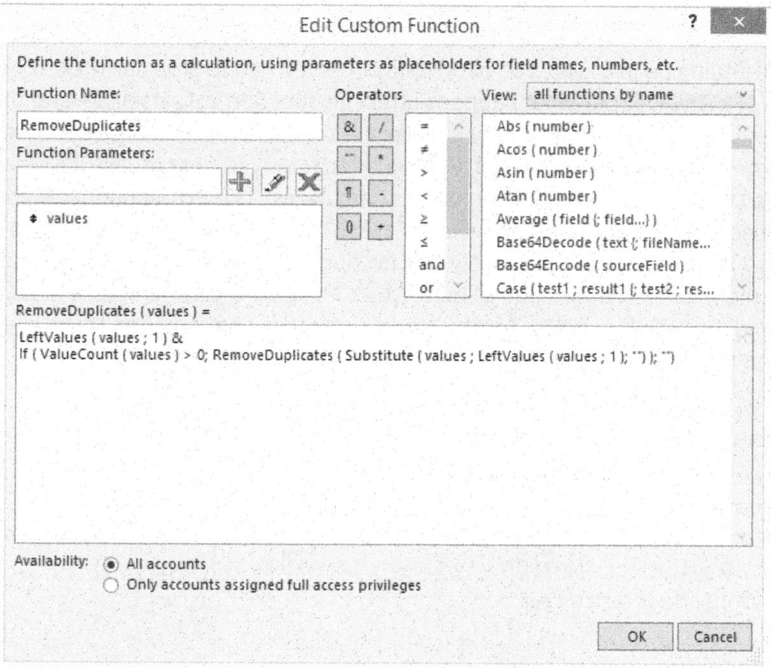

FIGURE 17-5

You can switch to the Custom Function window in step 2 if you want to, or you can wait until you've got the whole thing working. Like the regular Specify Calculation window, Edit Custom Function will analyze your calculation when you click OK, so make sure to define the function's parameter(s) to avoid an error message telling you that the parameters can't be found. You'll finish this function in step 3.

This new version works a lot like the last one. It first pulls the first item from the list and then adds it to the result. It also removes duplicates of the first item from the rest of the list (using Substitute()). But instead of adding that to the result, it sends the entire remaining list through RemoveDuplicates(). If you assume RemoveDuplicates() already works, then it removes duplicates from the rest of the list. You take care of the *first* line using your calculation skills. Then you rely on the function itself to take care of all the rest. Notice that the new list that's passed to RemoveDuplicates() starts with the *second line* of the original list. So when the function runs again, the second line becomes the first, and the function takes care of it. Unfortunately, this process goes on forever, which is probably not exactly what you want.

Step 3: Find a Stopping Point

You now have two of the three critical components of a recursive function: You're manually doing the *first* part of the job, and you're telling recursion to do the rest. If you leave the function like this, though, you're in trouble. If RemoveDuplicates() calls RemoveDuplicates(), which in turn calls RemoveDuplicates() (ad infinitum), then you have a problem: This function just keeps going forever.

> **WARNING** When you work on recursive functions, you inevitably create such *loops* accidentally. When you do, FileMaker thinks for several seconds and then gives up and returns *invalid* (a question mark in the field). If FileMaker seems to be hung, wait a few seconds; recursion is limited to 10,000 cycles, and FileMaker gives up eventually.

To avoid ending up in a loop, you need to figure out when to *stop* calling RemoveDuplicates(). Think about what happens after this function calls itself several times. Each time it's called with a slightly smaller list than the time before (because the first item—along with any copies of it—have been removed). Eventually it's going to get called with just one item (or sometimes zero items). When that happens, you no longer need the services of RemoveDuplicates(). Instead, you can just return that last word by itself, since it obviously has no duplicates. You use an If() function to help the recursion figure out when to stop. Make sure your list has a blank line at the end. See the box below for the reason why. The final function looks like this (with comments added):

```
// Start the result with the first item in the list
LeftValues ( values ; 1 ) &
// If there are items remaining in list...
If ( ValueCount ( values ) > 0;
// ...then remove duplicates from the remaining items
RemoveDuplicates ( Substitute ( values ; LeftValues ( values ; 1); "") );
// ...otherwise we're done
""
)
```

Now you just have to create the RemoveDuplicates() custom function. RemoveDuplicates() needs one parameter: the values from which you're sifting duplicates. A descriptive name, like "theList" (you can't use "list" because there's already a function with that name), helps you remember what this parameter does. Finally, create a calculation field using your new custom function, and create a reference to the field containing the list of duplicated values.

The Point of No Return

RemoveDuplicates() works great for finding unique values in a list, so long as the last item in the list has a ¶ (paragraph return) following it. If it doesn't, then the function gets confused and will not remove the last line, even if it's a duplicate. You can adjust for lists that don't have a trailing ¶ by adjusting your calculation field slightly:

```
RemoveDuplicates ( values & "¶" )
```

You could also modify the custom function itself to guard against this possibility. Doing so makes the formula more complex, but here it is in case you want a challenge:

```
Let ( [

    cleanList = If ( Right ( values ; 1 ) =
```

```
"¶" ; values ; values & "¶" ) ;

    first = LeftValues ( cleanList ; 1 )
  ] ;

    first &
    If (
        ValueCount ( cleanList ) > 1 ;
        RemoveDuplicates ( Substitute (
cleanList ; first ; "" ) )
        )

  )
```

Figure 17-6 shows an example of a recursive calculation calling the RemoveDuplicates() custom function to remove all duplicate colors it finds in the list. (It takes four iterations to remove all the duplicates and return a unique instance of each item in the list, in the order in which they appear.)

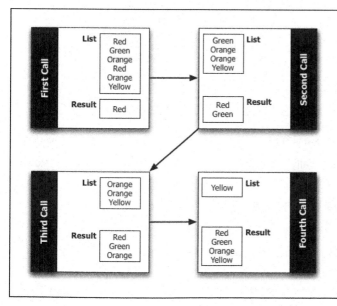

FIGURE 17-6

In the top-left corner, the box shows how RemoveDuplicates() is first called. It receives a list of colors as its one parameter. It returns the first item in the list, and the result of the second call. This time, though, Red has been removed from the list. The second call returns Green and the results of the third call. This progresses until the fourth call, when the script passes a single item to RemoveDuplicates(). This time RemoveDuplicates() simply returns the item without calling itself again. When it returns, the third call has all it needs, so it returns as well. This process goes back up the chain until the first call is reached and the final result is returned. If you join up the results of each call, then you see the correct list.

▉ Plug-Ins

Some things just can't be done (or can't be done *well*) using calculations and custom functions. When you run into this situation, you may consider looking into *plug-ins,* tiny applications that live inside FileMaker to help it do specific tasks that it can't do on its own.

Many plug-ins focus on doing certain things: processing credit card transactions or interacting with special devices like cameras, bar code readers, and so on. Although plug-ins work through calculation functions, scripts (which the next chapter covers) generally control them.

Plug-ins can convert, resize, and otherwise modify images in container fields, or perform complex mathematical, scientific, or financial calculations that would be difficult or inefficient in a calculation. Although this book doesn't cover any specific plug-ins, this section shows you how to access the functions provided by any plug-in you install.

Installing Plug-ins

A plug-in comes in a file bearing a special FileMaker plug-in icon (shown in Figure 17-7). In order to use plug-ins, FileMaker needs to *load* them—that is, it has to put the plug-in code into its own memory. Every time you launch the program, it searches for plug-ins in a folder called Extensions, and loads all the plug-ins it finds.

FIGURE 17-7

FileMaker plug-ins come in many varieties—with many names—but they all look more or less like this. Occasionally Windows displays a generic icon for FileMaker plug-ins. Don't panic if that happens. Just right-click the icon and choose Properties and make sure that the "Type of file" line starts with "FileMaker Pro Plug-in."

Installing a plug-in is thus a simple matter of making sure it's in the right folder:

- In Windows, it's typically C:→Program Files→FileMaker→FileMaker Pro 14→ Extensions.

- On Mac OS X, plug-ins can live in one of two places:

  - Applications→FileMaker Pro 14→Extensions

  - Home→Library→Application Support→FileMaker→Extensions

NOTE If you're using FileMaker Pro Advanced, then the FileMaker folder is called FileMaker Pro 14 Advanced, not FileMaker Pro 14.

Once you've found the folder, just drag the plug-in file into it and then restart FileMaker. To see which plug-ins FileMaker has actually loaded, visit the application preferences (FileMaker Pro→Preferences on Mac OS X or Edit→Preferences in Windows). In the Preferences window, click the Plug-ins tab, or look at Figure 17-8.

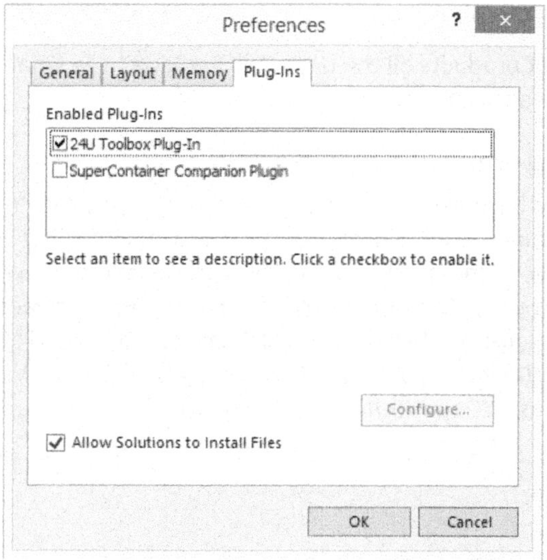

FIGURE 17-8

In FileMaker's Preferences window, The Plug-ins tab shows you the configurable plug-ins you've installed. (Some plug-ins, like the Web plug-in, aren't configurable, so they don't show up in this list.) Disable a plug-in by turning off the checkbox by its name. If a plug-in requires any configuration, select it in the list and then click Configure. When you have a plug-in selected, you see a description of it below the list.

Once you've installed plug-ins, you can find their functions in the Specify Calculation dialog box by choosing "External functions" in the View pop-up menu. For details on how to use these functions, consult their developer's manuals or websites. In most cases, you use Set Variable script steps to trigger plug-in actions.

Finding Plug-ins

You can hire a programmer to create a plug-in to your specifications, but you can often find one on the market that already does what you want. There's a comprehensive list of available plug-ins on FileMaker's website. Just choose Solutions→"Made for FileMaker" from the site's main navigation bar. The link to the plug-in section is at the top center of the page.

You can also visit the more prolific FileMaker plug-in vendors' websites:

- 24U Software (*www.24usoftware.com*)
- 360Works (*www.360works.com*)
- CNS Plug-ins (*www.cnsplug-ins.com*)
- Draconventions (*www.dracoventions.com*)
- Goya Pty (*www.goya.com.au*)

- Monkeybread Software (*www.monkeybreadsoftware.de*)

- New Millennium Communications (*www.nmci.com*)

- Productive Computing (*www.productivecomputing.com*)

- Qutic Development (*www.qutic.com*)

- Troi Automatisering (*www.troi.com*)

New vendors come up with great products all the time, so if you don't see what you want, then head over to Google and get your search on.

Creating Your Own Plug-ins

If you're feeling adventurous (or have helpful programmer friends), you can create your own plug-ins. To do that, you need FileMaker Pro Advanced, and the FileMaker Pro Plug-in SDK (Software Development Kit), which you can download at *www.filemaker.com/support/technologies/*. The download includes a sample project for Mac and Windows and sample plug-in code to get you started. You also need a C++ development environment. In Windows, you're best off with Visual C++ or Visual Studio.NET. On OS X, you can use XCode (a free download when you sign up for Apple's developer program).

Advanced Scripting

In Chapters 12 and 13, you learned about the Script Workspace and some of the most useful script steps. Some scripts, like creating reports or navigation, are simple to create, and to maintain if your needs change. But other scripts handle processes that would be difficult, or even impossible, for mere mortals to do without scripted aid. To give you the confidence to tackle tougher scripting chores, this chapter will build on what you already know, and also introduce you to some more powerful scripting tools. By the end of this chapter, you'll know how to:

- Add comments to your work
- Add user feedback to your scripts
- Create parameters to make a single script behave different ways
- Store temporary values using script variables
- Plan for and handle errors
- Use advanced script triggers
- Create modular scripts

NOTE Download this chapter's sample file from this book's Missing CD page at *www.missingmanuals.com/ cds/fmp14mm*. Use *CH18 Invoices_Start.fmp12* to work in and use *CH18 Invoices_End.fmp12* to see the completed examples.

■ Commenting Scripts

When you look at a script someone else created—or one you created a long time ago—you can't always tell what the script does just by reading the steps. To help keep things clear, add comments to your script. You add each comment by using a Comment script step. This step has just one option: the text of the comment itself. The Comment step is special for two reasons. First, it doesn't *do* anything. Second, it appears in green when you view your script in the Script Workspace window.

NOTE Comments appear green by default, but you can change the color under View→Syntax Coloring.

Use comments to document anything important about the script. Here are some things you may want to include in a comment or set of comments:

- What the script does

- Who wrote the script

- The date the script was written

- The date, if any, the script was last edited

- Who edited the script

- Anything special about how or when the script should be run, like whether only some database users can run it, or if the script requires parameters to do its work

Documenting scripts is standard operating procedure among FileMaker developers for a couple of reasons. First, if something is wrong with the script, or it needs to be changed, you've got extra information that may help. Good comments tell you exactly what the script should do and any setup necessary to make the script run properly. Plus you have a list of people who've worked on it and can give you background or pointers. Also, the date can help identify whether a particular business rule was in effect that made certain parts of a script necessary. Or if you see that a script is really old, you may decide to rewrite it with some of FileMaker's newer features. Comments don't slow down your scripts when they run, but it does take a little time to make good comments. Still, there's nothing so helpful as writing out your thought process as you're scripting, to save you time later. You can see a commented script in Figure 18-1.

TIP There's another way to indicate what your scripts are doing: Put comments in any embedded calculations. When a script has an If( ) statement that uses a complex calculation for its condition, comments in the calculation itself can demystify the calculation's purpose and the way it gets its work done. See page 422 for a refresher on calc comments.

■ Communicating with Database Users

Sometimes a script needs to give people feedback as it runs. You may, for example, need to let users know that there weren't any invoices with line items for ¾" lag bolts for May 2015, or ask whether they want to print their report or create a PDF. Depending on what you're trying to accomplish, you have several choices for exchanging information with users. You can show a custom dialog box, use a merge variable to show a message on a layout, or build a custom layout that guides users through a highly structured process.

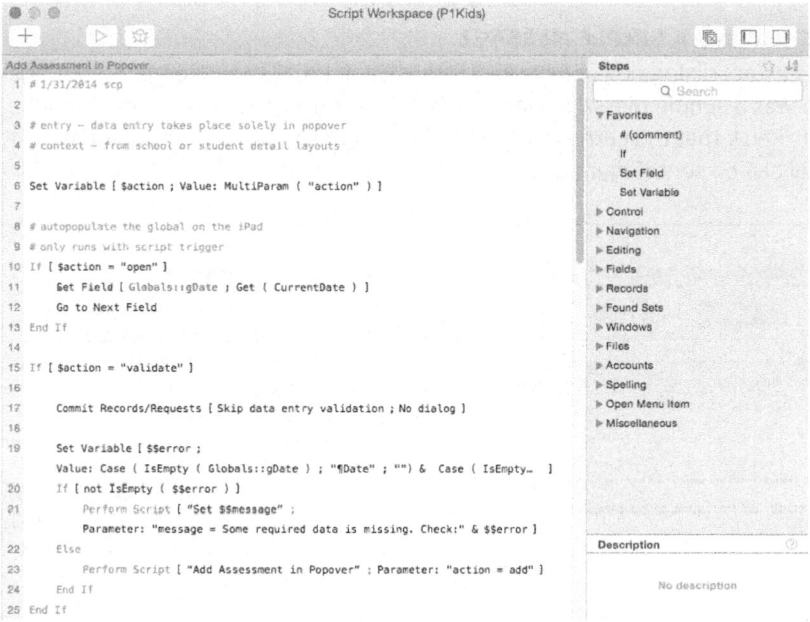

FIGURE 18-1

Script comments appear in green and with a # symbol in front. The first comment says who created the script and when. Blank comments create white space in the script to make it easier to read. A pair of comments talk about what the script does and the context in which it should run. The last pair of comments talk about the chunk of code that starts the script, which only runs when a popover is opened.

Showing Custom Dialog Box

The Show Custom Dialog script step lets you write a message and display it in a dialog box. Calling it a *Custom* dialog box may be a bit too generous—you don't have much say in how it looks—but you can at least give information to people using your database and ask them simple questions. The Show Custom Dialog script step has three basic uses. Custom dialog boxes can do the following:

- **Show a simple message.** Users don't get to make a choice, but like a warning dialog box, they have to click a button in response to your message.

- **Ask a simple question.** Users can make a choice by clicking one of the buttons you provide.

- **Providing input fields.** Users can enter data into fields provided by the dialog box.

To use a custom dialog box in a script, move the Show Custom Dialog step into place in your script and set the appropriate options for the type of message you need to show. When the dialog box pops up, your script waits for user response (he has to click a button) and then continues with the next step.

NOTE The title, message boxes, and button names each have a Specify button that brings up the calculation engine so you can make those items more dynamic. For instance, if someone wants to see all open invoices for a particular customer, but the script doesn't find any, you can show a calculated message that checks the Customer::Full Name fields and shows, "Kara Thrace's account is paid in full," instead of something equally true but less helpful, like "No records were found."

■ SHOWING A SIMPLE MESSAGE

The custom dialog box you created in the "Send Email to Customer" script on page 460 was a simple message with one button for user response. That message lets users know that the current customer record doesn't have an email address, so no email can be sent (Figure 18-2).

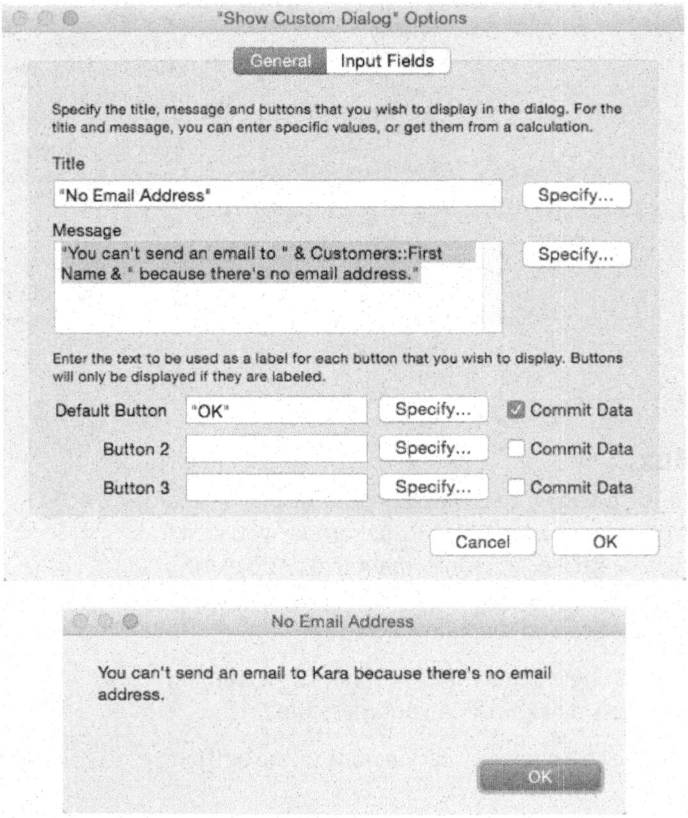

FIGURE 18-2

Top: The "Show Custom Dialog" Options window has two tabs. The General has three parts: Title, Message, and the buttons. In its most basic form, a custom dialog box shows a message with one, two, or three response buttons users can click. You must enter text in the Default Button box, but you can leave the other two blank. Buttons you leave blank won't appear in the dialog box. In this case, the standard text of OK makes most sense—it's not most common to change this text when you're giving users a message and don't want a response. By default, the Commit Data option is selected for each button. But when you're just giving the user information, you should turn this option off. Learn more on page 706.

Bottom: The dialog box that results from the settings shown above. This, the simplest version of a custom dialog box, has a title, a message, and a single button—just the basics for getting a message to folks using your database. The title appears along the top of the dialog box, the message in the middle, and the button at the bottom.

Button text is customizable, and you can even use the Specify Calculation dialog box to write a calculation that makes the button's text dynamic. But you should limit their text to short words like OK or Cancel. The technical limit is 32 characters, but anything longer than about 10 characters gets chopped off, and there's no way to make a button larger. See the box on page 703 to learn how to think like a programmer when you're showing your users a message.

THINK LIKE A DEVELOPER

Testing Multiple Conditions Redux

Back in Chapter 12, you learned how to write a script that tested multiple conditions. Now it's time to learn how to take a more advanced approach to the problem. Instead of calling three different custom dialog boxes that are each hard-coded, you can set your message in a *local variable* and then call a custom dialog box that that uses a value that's set when a condition tests as True.

Why go to all that trouble? It's certainly not because FileMaker gives you a limited number of Show Custom Dialog boxes and makes you ration their use. The rationale behind this exercise is to give you a taste of the software engineer's approach to using variables. By thinking in terms of storing temporary data inside a local variable (which exists only as long as the script that created it is running), you're well on the way to solving more advanced problems as they arise.

Here's how the new process looks:

```
If [ Invoice::Status = "Complete" ]
Set Variable [ $Message ; Value:
"Invoice Complete" ]
Else If [ Invoice::Status = "PO" ]
 Set Variable [ $Message ; Value: "PO form
emailed" ]
Else
 Set Variable [ $Message ; Value:
"Invoice Routed to Customer Service" ]
End If
Show Custom Dialog [ "Invoice Disposition"
; $Message ]
```

ASKING A SIMPLE QUESTION

Up one level of complexity, you can create a dialog box that asks a simple question and gives users a choice of responses. Then your script can take action based on that response. This process is very similar to the warning users get if they delete a record: FileMaker asks if the user if he wants to delete the record and gives him the option to cancel the delete action. Users are very familiar with this process, so if you have a script that posts a customer payment, you could show a custom dialog box to ask, "Are you sure you want to post a payment?" and you'd include Post Payment and Cancel buttons for feedback (Figure 18-3).

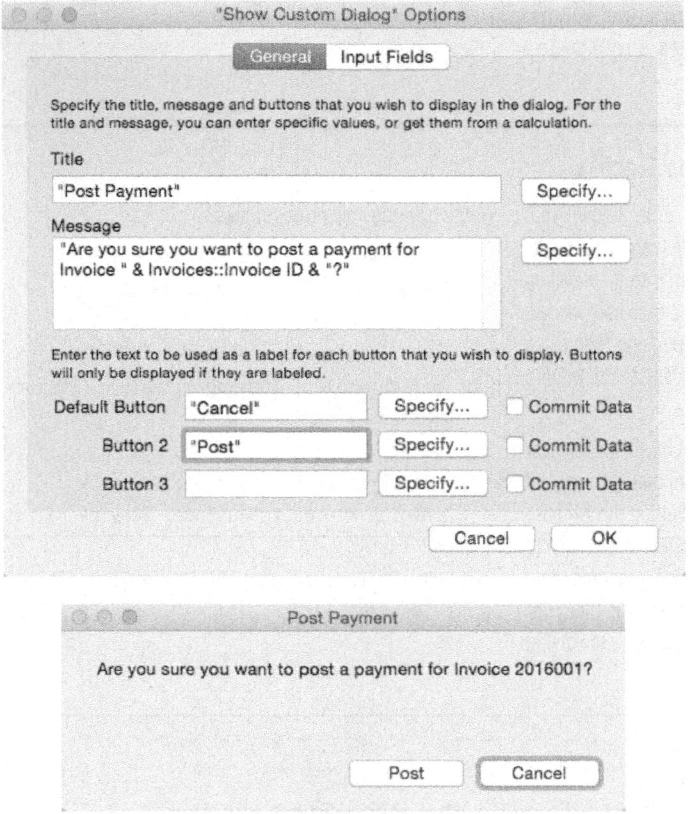

FIGURE 18-3

Top: This custom dialog box asks the user a question and offers two choices—Post or Cancel. Notice that the text in the Default Button box is Cancel.

Bottom: In the resulting dialog box, Cancel is automatically highlighted. This acts as a safety device, since people often reflexively hit the Return or Enter key when they see a dialog box. By making Cancel the default button, you can prevent potentially destructive processes when people fail to read your instructions. If you use this method all the time, you might even find that users start reading your dialog box messages to make sure they make the right choice.

When the dialog box appears, your script waits for a click of one of its buttons and then continues. FileMaker knows which button the user clicked, but your script should use an If test with a Get(LastMessageChoice) function to see what happened. Then the script can branch appropriately. Get(LastMessageChoice) returns 1 for the default button, 2 for Button 2, and 3 for Button 3. So your script will do the Post Payment script steps only if the function returns a 2. See Figure 18-4.

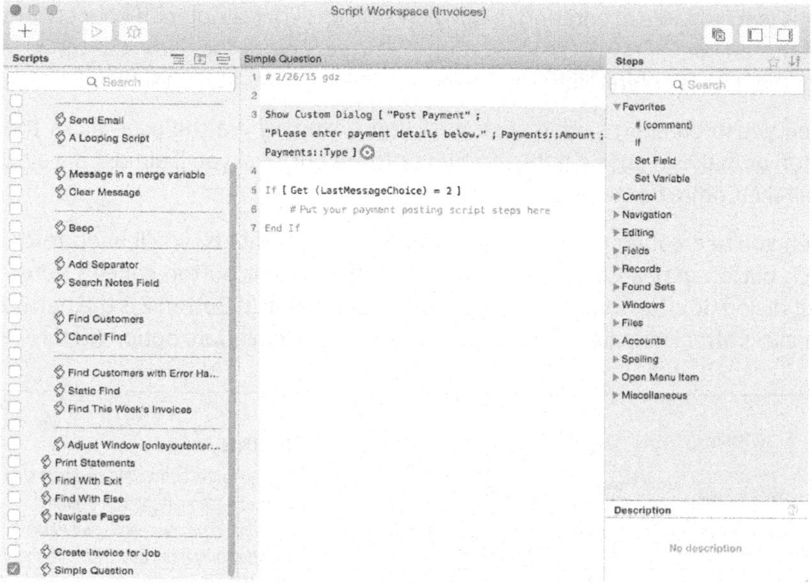

FIGURE 18-4

This script asks a question using a Show Custom Dialog *step, then an If statement with a* Get(LastMessage Choice) *function decides what to do. If someone clicks Post, then the function result is 2, and the script does whatever magic you create between the* If *statements. To give users two choices, plus a Cancel button, your script needs an* If *statement that checks for a value of 2 and an* Else If *that checks for a value of 3.*

PROVIDING INPUT FIELDS

If you need user input that goes beyond two or three button choices, like data that should be entered into specific fields in a specific record, you can add input fields to the dialog box so the user can provide the data in the controlled environment of your script. You can specify any existing text, number, date, or time field from your database. Since these input fields can't contain field controls, like value lists or pop-up calendars, you may want to avoid these input fields where consistency of data entry is important. For example, without a calendar, a user can enter a date without correct date formatting, in which case he'd get a validation error (page 252). Although you can specify calculation or summary fields, data won't be inserted into them. For these reasons, input fields are best used for text or number fields.

Context is important, too. You can't just show a dialog box with input fields and expect FileMaker to be able to put the data in the right record. You must craft your script carefully so it goes to the right layout and the right record. This technique is useful for controlling data input when a new record is created. In that case, input fields appear blank in your custom dialog box. But if the input fields you specify already have data in them, the data appears in your custom dialog box when the script step runs. In that case, the user can replace the record's existing data by typing in the custom dialog box.

■ UNDERSTANDING THE COMMIT DATA OPTION

The Commit Data option is a little deceptive because it actually performs two tasks. First, it enters data the user has typed into the fields you've specified, and then, if the record was *not open* when the script step runs, it commits the record. But if the user is in the middle of entering data when she runs your script, or if your script step contains an Open Record/Request step that runs before the Show Custom Dialog step, the data is entered into the fields, but the record is not committed.

When you're creating simple custom dialog boxes, where the user clicks the OK button or makes a choice between two or three buttons, you'll almost always turn off all the Commit options under your buttons.

When you're creating a custom dialog box with input fields, you'll need to decide which button gets a Commit Data option. If the default button cancels your data input dialog box, turn off Button 1's Commit Data option. If Button 2 is the button the user clicks after he's entered data, then turn on its Commit Data option (Figure 18-5).

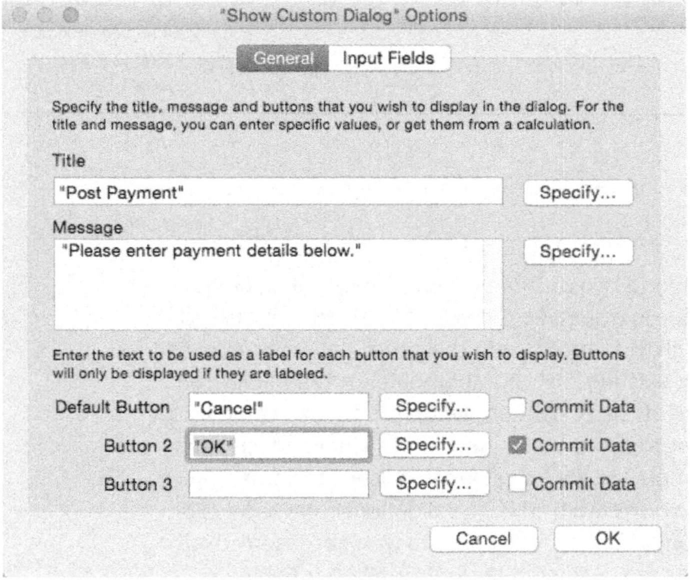

FIGURE 18-5

Since the Cancel button lets your user stop the script's action, it shouldn't commit the record. In this case, you want data committed only if the user clicks OK, so turn that option on. Note that it's not what the button says that's important; it's what it does. If your users expect the button that commits the data to say "Enter" instead of "OK," make your dialog box match their expectations. Just make sure the Commit Data option is turned on.

> **NOTE** If you're not providing data-entry field(s) in the dialog box, you can usually turn off all the options for committing the current record.

Once you've set up button text and commit options, select the Input Fields tab shown in Figure 18-6 (top). The "'Show Custom Dialog' Options" window's Input Fields tab lets you add up to three fields to your custom dialog box. To add a field to a custom dialog box, select the Input Fields tab and then turn on one of the "Show input field" checkboxes. When you do, FileMaker shows a Specify Field dialog box, in which you can pick the field to use.

You can also give the field a label, like "Payment Amount" and "Payment Type" shown in Figure 18-6 (bottom). A label can be the result of a calculation. If you don't enter text in the label boxes, no label appears. If you turn on "Use password character" for an input field, the field works like a typical Password box: It shows * (Windows) or • (Mac) instead of the letters you type, so someone watching over your shoulder can't read what you're entering.

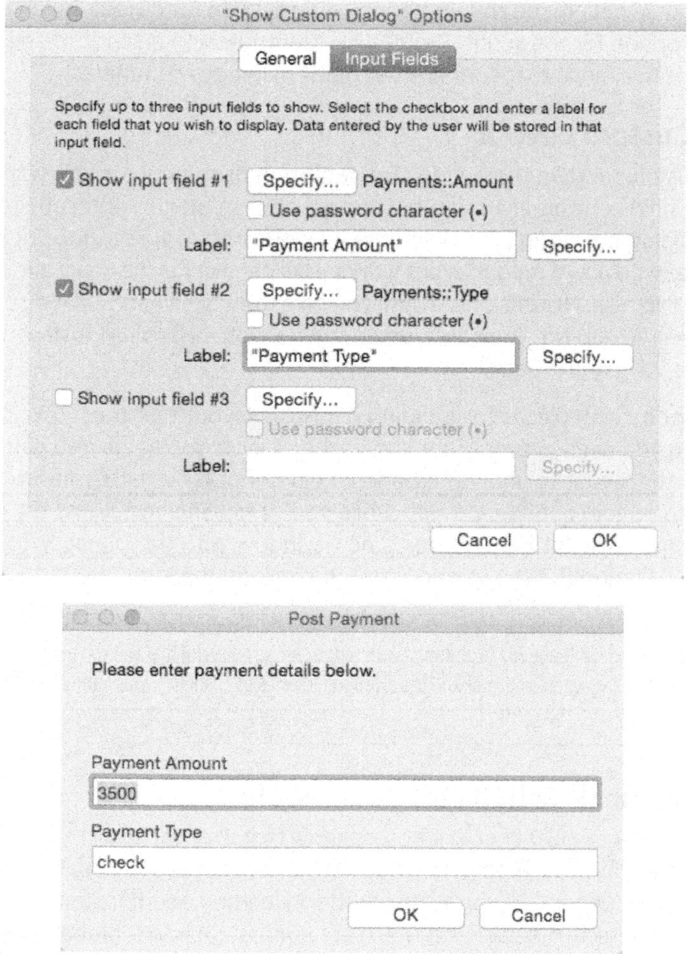

FIGURE 18-6

Top: The Input Fields tab lets you add fields to a custom dialog box so users can supply more information than they could just by clicking a button. You can use input fields for actual data input into the current record. In this case, you might script data entry for posting a payment on an Invoice.

Bottom: Here's the dialog box people see when the script runs. If you turn on the Commit Data option for button 2, FileMaker puts the data into the fields you've specified and then commits the record.

The fields you add to a custom dialog box have some limitations, including these:

- Show Custom Dialog can have only free-entry fields like those shown in Figure 18-6. You can't use radio buttons, checkboxes, calendars, or pop-up menus. You also have no control over the size of the field, so you can't specify, say, short fields for dates or tall fields for lots of text.

- "Data-entry only" validation doesn't apply to fields in custom dialog boxes. If you use a dialog box to gather data for a record, either use the Always option in the field validation, or check the validity of the data in your script (page 459).

- Data can't be inserted into fields that the users' privileges don't give them access to. You can get around this limitation by turning on the "Grant Full Access Privileges" option for the script. Right-click (Control-click) a script to see the context-sensitive menu that contains the grant privileges command.

Building a Custom Layout

If you need to use more than three fields for capturing user input, or you want to provide regular field controls like radio buttons or pop-up menus, you can create a fully custom dialog box using a new window, a layout, and some scripts. Back on page 702, you learned how a modal layout works. This behavior is the heart and soul of a dialog box: "No rush. I'll just sit here until you give me what I want. No, you can't click on that other layout. No, you can't run another script. Just follow instructions and then I'll give you control back."

There are a lot of moving pieces for building a custom layout that functions like a dialog box. First, you need a layout that shows the objects you need. You can use text objects on the layout to show messages, field controls to gather input, and layout buttons to run or continue a script. Once you've got the layout just the way you like it, you need a script that creates a new window with the Dialog Window option turned on. Figure 18-7 shows one script that will do the job.

> **NOTE** Modal dialog windows (page 702), combined with scripts, are so powerful that you can build a process like FileMaker's Layout Assistant, where you walk the user through a series of "panels," where they'll enter data and make choices.

Showing Feedback with a Merge Variable

The script shown in Figure 18-7 should let users know that they can't post a payment on invoices that have already been paid. You saw the concept of showing the user a message on their layout back on page 455 when you learned about Install OnTimer scripts. Here a similar script beeps and then sets a message into a global variable that's been placed on the layout and formatted in red to make it noticeable. The message appears if the Invoices::Total Due amount equals Invoices::allPayments. The message gives the user feedback about why she's not seeing a payment window when she clicks the + button on the Invoice layout. See the result in Figure 18-8.

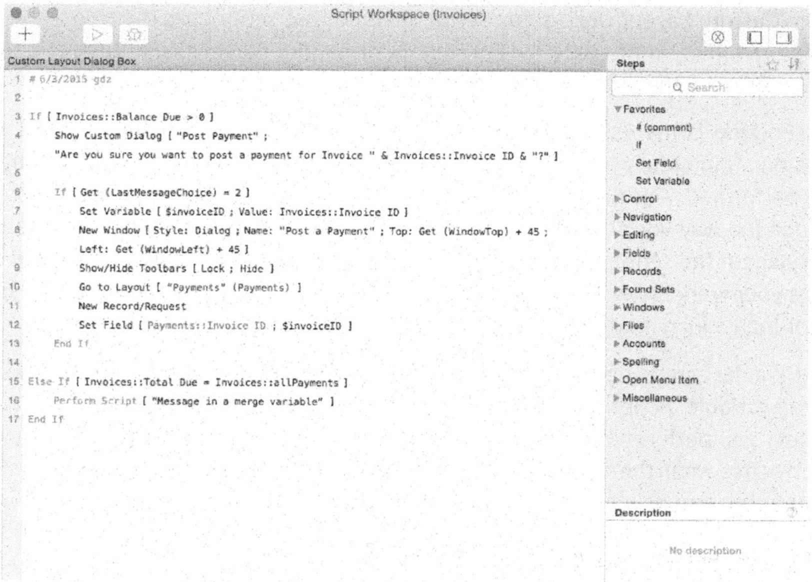

FIGURE 18-7

Run from a button on the Invoice layout, this script lets users enter payment data through a scripted process. First, the script shows a custom dialog box asking the user to confirm that she wants to post a payment. If the user clicks the Post button, then the script creates and shows a modal dialog window. Users can't do anything else until they click a button on the Payment layout.

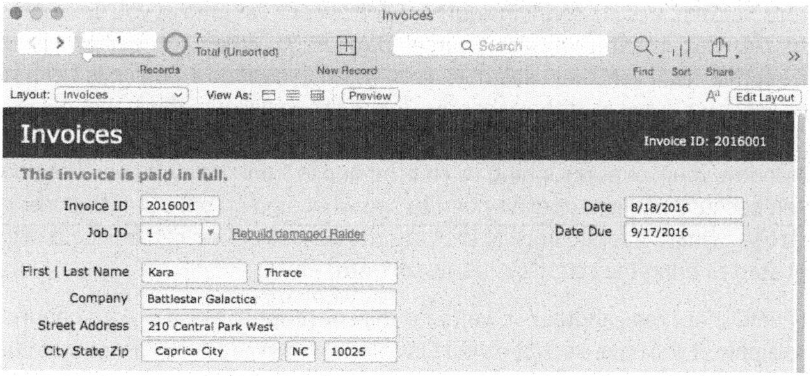

FIGURE 18-8

Putting a message in a merge variable lets your users work more efficiently, since they don't have to click OK to close a dialog box. But this method isn't suitable for scripts that need to take action based on user feedback. Be consistent about where you put the merge variable. Users shouldn't have to hunt to read the message before it's cleared.

■ Creating Modular Scripts

In the last section, you saw a script that shows a message in a merge variable if no money is owed on an Invoice. But the script steps that show the message aren't in the Custom Layout Dialog Box script. Instead that script calls the "Message in a merge variable" script, using the Perform Script step. When you Perform one script from within another, the script you perform is called a *subscript.*

Subscripting is the essence of *modular scripting.* You write a simple script that does one thing really well and then you call that script anytime you need that action performed. This process saves you work in two ways. First, if you ever have to change the way you show messages in a merge field, you can change it once, and everywhere the script is called it will run with the edited behavior. Second, it can make your work faster and less prone to error because it's far easier to test a short script than a long, hairy one.

But modular scripts need to be able to run in multiple contexts. The "Message in a merge variable" script has no context at all. The only thing it needs to work in any context you perform it in is a merge variable named <<$$message>> on the layout that's active when the script runs. In this section, you'll learn more about the Perform Script step and how all these scripts relate to one another as they run.

The Perform Script Script Step

When you add the Perform Script step to your script, you get only one option: a Specify button. Figure 18-9 shows how to use the Specify Script dialog box to tell your script which subscript you want to run and what file to find it in.

Perform Script can call a script in another FileMaker file, as long as you've connected to the file with an External Data Source (page 620). When you perform a script from another file, FileMaker uses that file's frontmost window (which is behind the user's window) to run in. If the other file doesn't have any windows, then FileMaker creates one, but won't activate it. Either way, you're in a unique scripting situation: The window your script is running in isn't the one in front. Many times, that doesn't matter, because the user doesn't need to see what's going on. But if the user does need to see what's happening, use the Current Window option in the Select Window script step to bring the script's window forward.

When one script runs another, it waits for the subscript to finish before continuing. For example, if you have a script called Find Unpaid Invoices, then a Print Statements script could start off by performing the Find Unpaid Invoices script. Then, once Find Unpaid Invoices is done, Print Statements can sort and print the found invoices. In this example, Print Statements is the main script, or *calling* script, and Find Unpaid Invoices is the subscript.

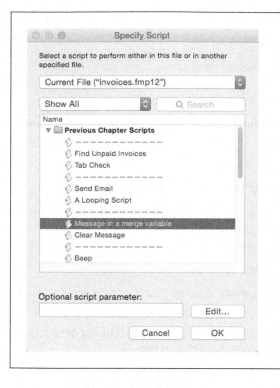

FIGURE 18-9

The Specify Script Options dialog box is where you tell the Perform
Script *step which script to run. It's the same window you get when
you tell a button which script to run. You can pick a script from the
local file or from any file you have a reference to using the File pop-up
menu (choose Add FileMaker Data Source to add a reference to a new
file). The script list shows every script in the selected file, complete
with its groups and separators. Just select the script you want, add the
appropriate parameters (page 716), and then click OK.*

Halt Script and Exit Script

When processes are broken up in this way, with parts of the whole performed by
different scripts, it's often important to know what happened in each script. To understand how to track script results, you need to think about what happens whens
scripts stop running.

Normally a script ends, or stops, when its last step runs. But you can force a script
to end early if you want to. FileMaker actually has *two* script steps that end a script
prematurely: Exit Script and Halt Script. If you run a script directly—from the
Script Workspace, by clicking a button, or from a script trigger—the two steps behave
the same way. But if the current script was run by *another script*—via the Perform
Script step—then they do different things. The Exit Script step tells FileMaker
to stop the current script and then continue the script that ran it. Halt Script, on
the other hand, causes *all* script execution to stop immediately, no matter how the
current script was started. Since halting a script could stop a process before it's
finished, use Halt Script only when you're absolutely sure it won't leave the user
dazed and confused.

■ EXIT SCRIPT (RESULT)

Exit Script has a powerful option that Halt Script doesn't have—a script result. This feature lets scripts communicate with each other. You set a value in the Exit Script step that becomes available to any script that calls it as a subscript. The calling script uses a Get (ScriptResult) function to find out what happened in the subscript, and from there the calling script can decide what to do. For example, if the Find Unpaid Invoices subscript doesn't find any invoices, the Print Statements calling script shouldn't try to sort and then print an empty found set. Here's how to add an Exit Script step to an existing script:

1. **In the Script Workspace window, double-click the Find Unpaid Invoices script.**

   The script opens in the Script Edit pane.

2. **In the script step list, double-click the Exit Script step.**

   If you had no script steps highlighted, the new step is added to the end of your list. If necessary, move it to the bottom of the list. (You don't want the script stopping before all the work is done.)

3. **Click Exit Script's gear button.**

   If you don't see the gear button, make sure the Exit Script step is still high-lighted. The Specify Calculation window appears.

4. **In the Calculation pan search field, type *get(fo* to filter the list of functions. Press Enter to choose the Get(FoundCount) function.**

   You only need to type enough of the function's name to find the one you need. The function appears in the calculation field. The script will record the number of unpaid records it finds when it's done.

5. **Click OK to return to the Script Workspace, and then choose Scripts→Save Script.**

   Find Unpaid Invoices is ready to tell calling scripts how many invoices it found.

Setting a result for the Exit Script step is the first part of the process. You also need to test those results in the main script. That script needs an If test, and the aptly named Get(ScriptResult) function to see if any records were found that should be sorted and printed. See Figure 18-10 for a script that calls Find Unpaid Invoices and then checks its results.

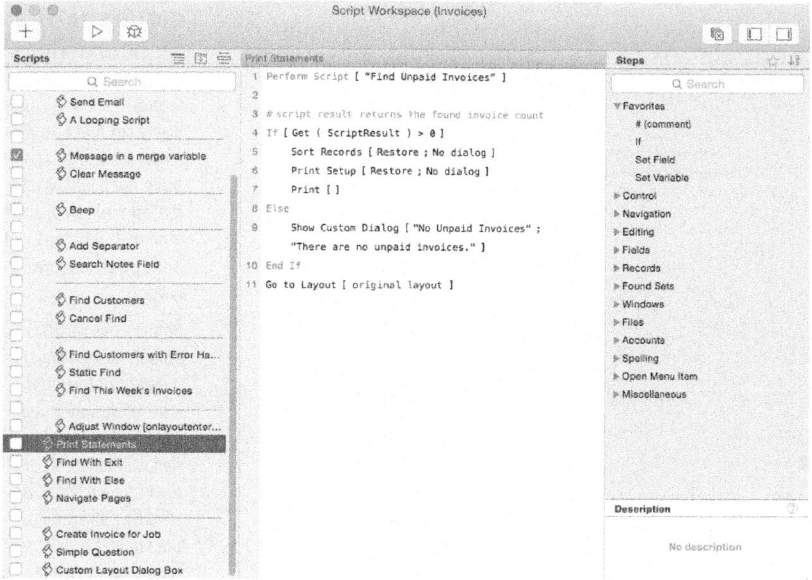

FIGURE 18-10

*The Print Statements
script calls the Find Un-
paid Invoices subscript, to
which you've just added
an Exit Script step.
Next, a comment helps
you remember what's
going on in the subscript,
so you don't have to
open that script to figure
it out. Then, an If test
checks the results of the
subscript to see whether
it should sort and print
invoices. If no invoices
need to be printed, a
dialog box tells the user
what's happening, (or
in this case, what's not
happening).*

■ ORGANIZING SCRIPTS THAT USE HALT SCRIPT OR EXIT SCRIPT

The Halt Script and Exit Script steps are useful exit strategies when you want
to abort a script's execution because a problem has come up. But if you're trying
to stop a script to *avoid* a problem, you're usually better off without them. Take, for
example, the two scripts shown in Figure 18-11.

Suppose you revisit this process later and want to add some more steps to the end of
the script that should happen *last,* every time the script runs—not just when records
are found. If your script looks like the one on top, you have a problem. You either have
to add your new steps to the script *twice* (once before the Exit Script, and again
at the end of the script), or reorganize the entire script to support the changes. But
the script on the bottom is easy to fix: Just add the new steps to the end. In general,
if a script ends in more than one place, it will come back to bite you later. You're
much better off organizing your script so it always reaches the same ending place.

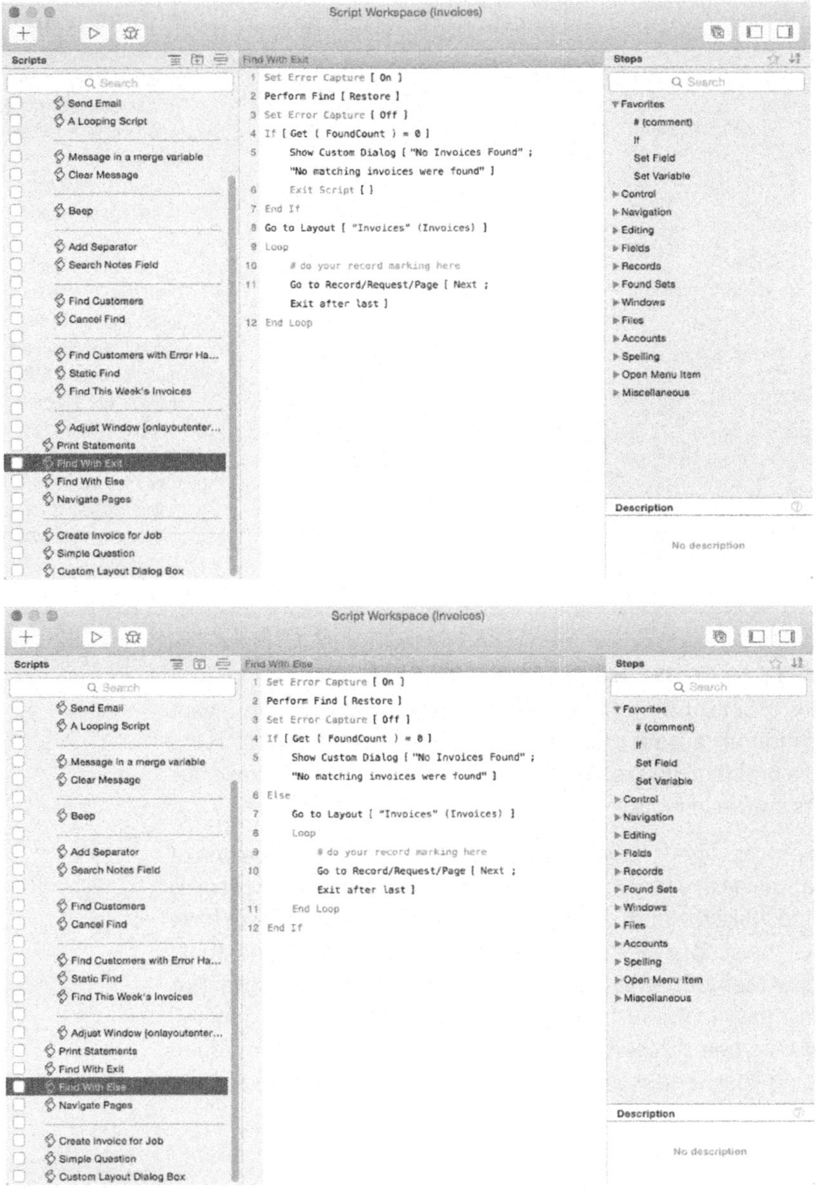

FIGURE 18-11

Top: This script performs a find. Then, if it finds no records, it shows a custom dialog box and exits the script. The end point of this script might be after the last script step, which is normal, or at the Exit Script step, which is not.

Bottom: This version does the same thing, but doesn't exit the script if no records are found. Instead, it puts all the remaining script steps in the Else section of the condition. The result is the same—the extra steps run only if the script finds some records—but the bottom script always ends after the last step.

NOTE Halt Script has an even bigger downside. Since scripts can run other scripts, and most databases grow and change over time, you never know for sure if the script you're writing today is going to be run by another script someday in the future. It's rarely a good idea to run another script that could halt before reaching its normal end. It gives your new script no opportunity to recover if something goes wrong, so use Halt Script sparingly.

Indirection

Script parameters let you write multipurpose scripts that you can use under many different circumstances. You just pass the script a parameter that triggers the branch that runs the parts you need, based on the circumstance.

To take your FileMaker skills to the next level, you need to learn *indirection*. That term means referring to things—usually fields, but also named objects (page 483)—without specifically naming them. The point is to make your scripts more reusable. For instance, a script that finds a record by ID needs to search the CustomerID field in the Customers table, but the InvoiceID in the Invoice table. Without indirection, you'd have to write two different find scripts, pointing to two different fields, even if every other script step is exactly the same.

A special script step called "Set Field by Name" lets you put data in fields by indirection. To understand how it works, look at the normal Set Field script step, which lets you specify a field to receive the result of a calculated value. For example, you might set the Zip Code field to a known value, for instance, or set the Balance Due field to the sum of costs minus the sum of payments.

By contrast, "Set Field by Name" step lets you specify two calculations. The second determines the value to store, just like Set Field. But the first calc evaluates to the name of the field you want to set. In other words, if the result of the calculation is "Customers::First Name," then the step stores its value in the First Name field. If the calc returns "Customers::Last Name" instead, then it puts the calculated value in the *Last* Name field. Here's a formula that assembles a field name:

```
Get ( LayoutTableName ) & "::First Name"
```

This formula targets the First Name field in the table associated with the current layout. So this step can work in a Customers table and an Employees table. To make it work, you use a script parameter to pass the complete field name and then "Set Field by Name" uses that parameter to identify its target.

You can also fetch data from a field indirectly by using the GetField() function:

```
GetField ( LayoutTableName ) & "::First
Name" )
```

This formula grabs the value from the First Name field based on the current layout you're viewing.

Finally, the GetFieldName() function helps you grab field names reliably. Suppose you need a script that finds Invoices with today's date in either the Invoice Date or the Date Due field. You create two different buttons to run that script, and type one field's name as the script parameter in each button. Then you use "Set Field by Name" to put today's date into the specified field with Get(ScriptParameter).

You've used indirection, but this approach is unsafe. Since you're passing the field name in a calculation text value, FileMaker doesn't see it as a proper field reference and won't update the script parameter if you rename the field(s). Now your scripts refer to a nonexistent field, and they won't run properly. To solve this problem, use the GetFieldName() function. (It's in the Logical section.)

```
GetFieldName ( Invoices::Due Date )
```

This formula returns the text value "Invoices::Due Date," which may seem like extra work to accomplish the same thing. But using the function to pass the field name instead of static text ensures that if you ever rename the field, FileMaker corrects the formula for you, and your script keeps working properly. If you ever want to pass the name of a field as a script parameter (or otherwise refer to a field's name directly in a calculation), use GetFieldName() to protect against name changes.

■ Script Parameters

When you call a script by using the Perform Script step or attach the script to a button, the Specify Script window shows a box labeled "Optional script parameter." You can type a static value in the box, or you can click Edit to create a dynamic calculation that FileMaker evaluates when the script starts to run. FileMaker stores the value, and you can check it anywhere inside the script with the Get(ScriptParameter) function and then branch the script based on the result.

For example, you might make a script that can sort records in three different ways. That way, three different buttons can run the same script, with three different results. The script parameter that's attached to each button tells the script which sort order to use. The benefit is similar to modular scripting: If this process has to change later—say you want to add one more sort order to the process—you have only one script to change and one new button to create. This technique can drastically reduce the number of scripts you have to write and maintain.

> **NOTE** Script parameters don't automatically pass on to subscripts. If the subscript needs to know what's in your main script's parameters, set Get(ScriptParameter) as the subscript's parameter.

Testing for Script Parameters

Suppose you want to put a button bar on the Customer List layout to sort your Customer records by Name, City, or State. Start by writing a script that tests for those three parameters. Here's how:

1. **Create a new script called Sort Customer List.**

   This script will handle a few common sorts, but you start with a branch.

2. **Add the If step to the script.**

   FileMaker adds two new lines—If and End If—to your script.

3. **Click the gear icon, and then click the Specify button. From the View pop-up menu, choose "Get functions."**

   The function list now shows all the Get() functions.

4. **Find Get(ScriptParameter) in the list and then add it to your calculation.**

   The Get(ScriptParameter) function returns the parameter value that was specified when this script was called. If the parameter was a calculation, it returns the *result* of the calculation, which is now in the Calculation box.

5. **In the Calculation box, after Get(ScriptParameter), type = "Last Name" and then click OK.**

   You're back in the Script Workspace window, where the If step shows your calculation. Your calculation should look like this: Get(ScriptParameter) = "Last Name". Its result is True if the parameter sent to this script is "Last Name," and False otherwise.

6. **Add the** Sort Records **script step to the script and then turn on "Perform without dialog."**

    Insert it after the If step and before the End If step. (If yours is somewhere else, move it between these two steps.)

> **NOTE** FileMaker inserts new script steps just below any highlighted step. If no script step is highlighted, then the new script step lands at the end of your script.

7. **Turn on the "Specify sort order" checkbox, add the Last Name field, and then add the First Name field to the Sort Order list. Then click OK.**

    You've written your first test. The rest of the script will be variations on this theme.

8. **Add the** Else If **script step to the script.**

    You want Else If to come after the Sort Records step and before the End If step. (If it doesn't land there, move it.)

9. **Click Specify. In the Specify Calculation box, type** *Get(ScriptParameter) = "City"* **and then click OK.**

    You're setting up a new test, this time checking to see if "City" is the script parameter. If it is, then you want a Sort step following this parameter to sort by—you guessed it—city.

> **NOTE** Sometimes it's quicker to copy an existing If test and then paste and edit it in the Else If steps.

10. **Add another copy of the** Sort Records **script step to the script. Turn on "Perform without dialog." Set the sort order to City and then click OK.**

    Your second test, and what to do if that test is True, is now complete.

> **NOTE** Now you can select the Else If and its Sort and then use the Duplicate button to make copies of both steps. Then edit the Else If test and the Sort order.

11. **Add one more copy of the Else If script step, this time with** Get(Script Parameter) = "State" **as the calculation.**

    Your finished script should look something like Figure 18-12.

> **NOTE** When you're making a series of tests like the ones in this script, it's more efficient to put the condition that most often tests as True at the top. That way, the script doesn't have to test conditions that usually fail.

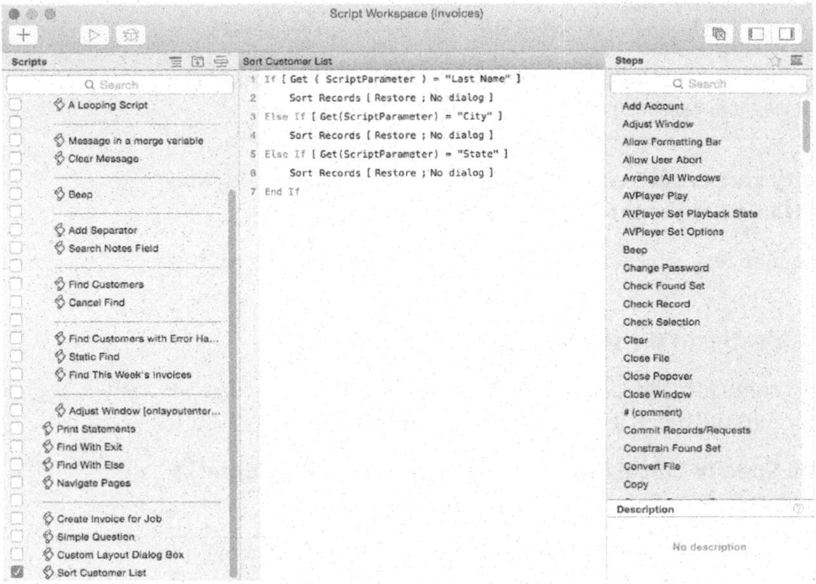

FIGURE 18-12

Your finished sort script should look like this example. It has three branches (one for each of the possible sort orders). Now you need to add buttons on the Customer List layout to run this script.

Adding Script Parameters to a Button

Now it's time to format a button bar on the Customers List layout to make it easy for people to run the script.

1. **Double-click the Last Name button to select it.**

   The Button Bar Setup dialog box appears, and the Last Name button is active.

2. **In the Action pop-up menu, choose Perform Script. In the Specify Script window, select Sort Customer List.**

   That's the branching sort script you created in the last tutorial.

3. **In the "Optional script parameter" box, type *Last Name* and then click OK.**

   If you check the text in the Optional script parameter box, you see that File-Maker put double quotes around "Last Name" because it's static text and not a dynamic reference. If you like to be thorough, you can type the quote marks yourself. When you click this button, "Last Name" will be passed to the Sort Customer List script. The first part of the If test will evaluate as True, and the records will be sorted by Last Name.

NOTE You can add parameters to triggered scripts, too. But if you run a script from the Script menu, there's no Specify Script window, and so no opportunity to attach a parameter. The same is true when you run a script from the Script Workspace (with the Run button). So if the script needs parameters to run properly, make a button to run it, even if you're still in the writing/testing phase.

Repeat the steps above for the City and State buttons. Change script parameters to "City" and "State" as appropriate. Switch to Browse mode to test your buttons. If a sort doesn't work, compare the spelling in your buttons' script parameters against the spelling in the script. Case doesn't matter, but spelling and spacing do.

More on Using Script Parameters

In the two preceding sections, you first wrote the script and then added the script parameters to your buttons. This process might feel backwards, but there's a reason some developers prefer doing the steps in that order: You can't add parameters to a button without selecting a script. The Specify Script window does have a + button that lets you create a new script in the middle of defining your button. But when you do, you don't get the full Script Workspace; you get the Edit Script window instead. That may not matter to you—you may even prefer that workflow. Either way you decide to work, it's helpful to think about the names you're giving to your script parameters as you write the script. Then if you forget the exact parameter you're testing, you can always go back to the If test and then copy the parameter to paste it into the button's script parameter field. Copying and pasting ensures that a typo won't derail your script.

NOTE If you copy a button (or a button bar) that has a script attached to it, you're copying the script and its parameter along with it. You can use this fact to your advantage if you're copying a button that uses the same script, but in different locations, for example. All you have to do is copy a button with the script and parameter that you need, and then edit the parameter appropriately for the new location. But it *may* be a problem if you unknowingly copy a button that has a parameter and then forget to change it. If the script the button runs doesn't check to see what the parameter is, then there's no harm done. But if the button's script expects one parameter and gets a different one, the script will fail (or at least it won't run as you expect it to).

Finally, adding new tests to a script that checks parameters is really easy. For example, to add a new sort to the Customer List layout, you add an appropriate Else If and a Sort step to the Sort Customer List step. Add a button to your button bar with a script parameter that matches the new test you added to the script. Except for some minor adjustments to make space for the new button, you're done.

Passing Multiple Parameters

A script can have only one parameter, and its result type is always text. But the parameter itself can be multiple values, if you're willing to use your calculation skills. To pass multiple parameters, string your values together with a separator character and then pull them apart again in the script.

For example, if you want a script to have a pair of static values, you could type this text as the script parameter:

    Molly¶Bloom

Since the separator is the ¶, each value is on its own "line," and that makes it easy to grab the bits you need using the GetValue() function. A calculation to pull "Molly" out from the script parameter would look like this:

    GetValue (Get (ScriptParameter) ; 1)

Just change the number in the second parameter of the function to grab other values from the list. Here's how to assemble a set of dynamic values into one script parameter:

    Customer::First Name & "¶" & Customer::

    LastName & "¶" & Customer::Phone & "¶"
    & Customer::Email

The GetValue() function above can pull apart the pieces of your multivalue parameter.

Although this process works well, it's what developers call *brittle*. That is, it won't take much more than sloppy typing to break your script. In the dynamic example above, Customer::Email is the fourth value. If your script looks in the third value of the parameter instead (you had a fat-finger moment and typed a "3"), then you won't be able to send an email. To get around this, developers have created various custom functions that let you send and parse name/value pairs of parameters in any order. Since the custom function looks for the value of a parameter by its name instead of its position in a list, those custom functions won't break as easily. This chapter's sample file has a custom function you can use for that purpose. But you can come up with your own, or find one on the Web.

Script Variables

You've used global fields to store a value that's not tied to a specific record in a table. Script variables are similar: Use them when you need to store a temporary value for your script to use, like when you're testing a condition. But variables are better than globals in one important way: You don't have to add a field to a table to use them. Instead, variables are created as a script is running and can vanish again when the script is finished, leaving no impact on your data's structure. (See page 687 for a refresher on using calculations to create variables.) Figure 18-13 shows you the Set Variable script step used in the Custom Layout Dialog Box script. It grabs an Invoice ID so it can set it in the new Payment record that's made a few steps later in the script.

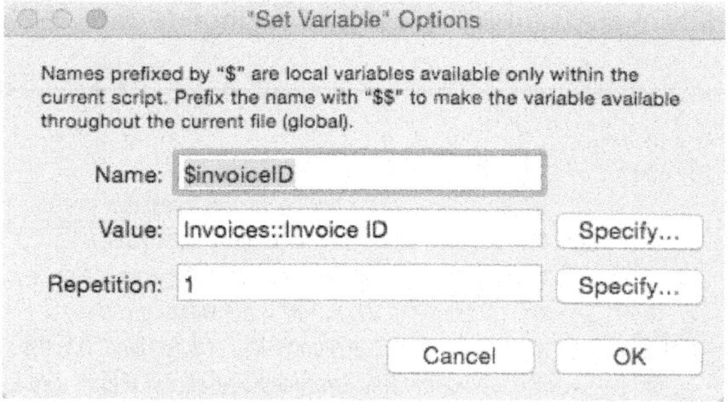

FIGURE 18-13

The "Set Variable" Options dialog box lets you create a variable by giving it a name and assigning it a value. Since you can use variables inside calculations, their naming rules are similar to those of field names. Don't use characters like a comma, +, -, *, or any other symbol that has a mathematical meaning and might confuse a calculation. You should also avoid names like "Date" or "List" that are also the names of functions. It's common to use camel case and no spaces in variable names.

The Set Script Variable script step has three options:

- **Name.** Choose a short, descriptive name. All script variable names require a $ prefix. If you forget to type the prefix, FileMaker adds it for you. But get in the habit of typing the prefix, since it determines how long the value in the variable is available. A single $ means the variable is local and lasts only while your script is running. Local variables aren't sent to subscripts. A double $$ prefix creates a global variable, and its value persists through subscripts and even after all scripts have finished running. Global variables are cleared when you close the database.

- **Value.** Here's where you define the value you want to store in the variable. Values can be static text or the dynamic result of a calculation.

- **Repetition.** A variable can store multiple values, like a repeating field does. Repetitions are optional, and not common. But if you know what a data array is, and want to create one, variable repetitions are one way to get that job done.

Since you can pass the value in a local variable with either a script result or a script parameter, some programmers consider global variables sloppy housekeeping, because once the script finishes running, variables just lie around your database full of values that have no meaning outside a script. One good reason to use a global variable is when you're using a merge variable to display a message on a layout after the script has finished running (page 708). In that case, you have to use a global variable.

WARNING Global variables are potential security risks, since the Data Viewer in FileMaker Pro Advanced will reveal their values to anybody who knows their names and has enough privileges to run scripts. If security is a big consideration in your business, make sure you don't leave sensitive data lying around in global variables by resetting their values to "0" or "" when the script is done. In practice, though, it's usually a lot easier, and cleaner, to use only local variables and rest assured that FileMaker is cleaning up after you.

■ Handling Errors

When an error occurs during a script (a `Perform Find` finds no records, for instance), FileMaker shows an error message almost like the one it would if you were doing the steps manually. The one difference is a button called Continue (Figure 18-14).

FIGURE 18-14

When an error occurs during a script, FileMaker gives the user all the normal choices he'd usually see in a warning dialog box, plus the option to ignore the error and continue the script. This is the warning you see if no records match the request in a scripted Find. It's just like the normal Find error message, except there's also a Continue button.

If a user clicks Cancel in an error message, the script stops immediately and leaves him wherever the script was when it stopped. If he clicks Continue instead, FileMaker ignores the error and moves on with the script. In the `Perform Find` example, for instance, the script continues with no records in the found set. Some errors, like when no records are found in a search, give users a third choice. The Modify Find button goes to Find mode on the current layout and then pauses the script.

Sometimes this error-handling approach is just fine. If the script is simple and everyone using it knows a little about FileMaker, it's not a big problem. But often, you need more control:

- If your system is complex—or your database's users aren't experienced with FileMaker—all sorts of confusion can result. First, the error message may make absolutely no sense to the person reading it. Maybe your script searches for a Customer record before making a new invoice. If a message complains about not finding any records, the person reading it thinks, "I just wanted to create a new invoice for this job. Who said anything about finding records?" Even worse, if she clicks Cancel, she could wind up just about anywhere: some layout in some window on some record. It could be a layout (like a developer-only layout you created to make the script run) that she's never even seen before.

- If an error happens in the middle of a larger multistep process, it might be really important that the script know about it and deal with it appropriately. But if you don't take control, it's the *user,* not the *script,* that decides whether to continue or cancel. You may want to make sure the script *always* continues, so it can get on with important work.

Luckily, you can opt for more control over error handling if you want it. FileMaker gives you three functions for finding and dealing with errors that may happen when scripts run.

The Set Error Capture Script Step

The Set Error Capture script step lets you turn on *error capture*. That way, instead of displaying potentially confusing error messages to your database's users, FileMaker keeps track of error information (*captures* it) so you can pull it into your script and handle it there. Although error capturing is a great feature, it's not part of FileMaker's normal behavior. You have to activate it by adding the Set Error Capture step to your script, and choosing the On option. At any time in the script, you can turn it back off again by using the step a second time and switching the option off.

If a script turns error capture on and then uses the Perform Script step to run another script, the second script also runs with error capture on. In other words, the error capture setting sticks around as long as scripts call other scripts. But as soon as script execution stops for good, FileMaker turns off error capture. Understanding this behavior helps you determine when you need an Error Capture script step and when it would just be redundant. Figure 18-15 shows a script that turns on error capture before performing a find and then turns it back off when it's done.

As discussed in the box below, you can just turn error capture on so that your script ignores any and all errors—but that's not good script writing. The best way to use Set Error Capture is hand in hand with the Get(LastError) function, described next, to achieve error-free results.

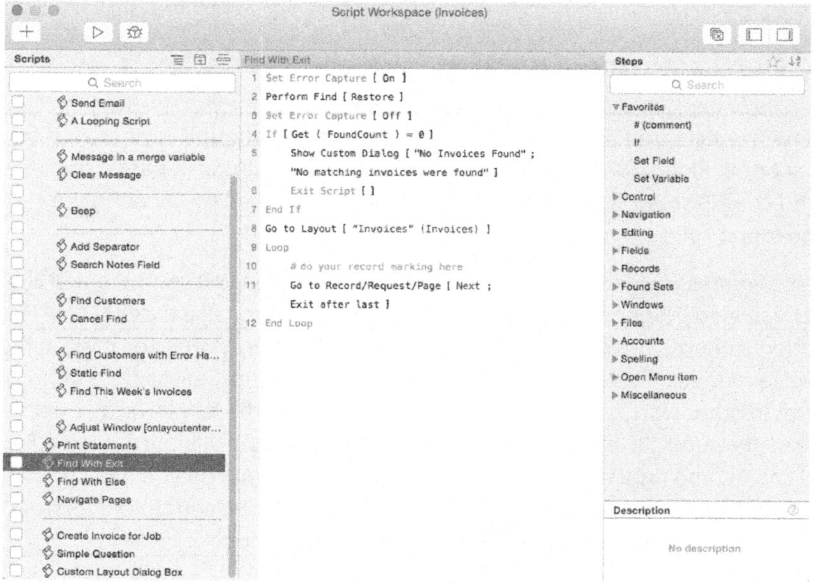

FIGURE 18-15

This script turns error capture on and then performs a find. That way, if the find fails, the script doesn't produce an error message. The script itself handles the error by checking for no found records in the If step, and then displays a more helpful, customized error message if an error did occur.

Capturing and Handling Errors

Using Set Error Capture to eliminate those pesky dialog boxes sounds so cool, you may be tempted to turn it on at the start of every script. You can't anticipate every error, but at least you can keep FileMaker from casting doubt on your database skills by throwing error messages in people's faces. But if all your script does is turn error capture on, and then never checks to see *which* errors are happening, you're not doing your database's users—or yourself—any favors.

If odd error messages pop up, people may let you know about it (perhaps via cellphone while you're trying to relax on the beach). But that's not your best chance to figure out the problem and improve your script. With error capture turned on, a script might seem to be working because no warning dialog box shows up, but really, something's gone kablooie

and error capture suppresses the dialog box that would have explained the problem.

You have little hope of figuring out what went wrong—especially if no one realizes there's been a problem until long after the script has run.

Usually, you find errors when you're developing your scripts, and you can use a custom dialog box along with error capture to deal with them. Remember two rules for using error capture: First, don't turn error capture on unless you've already anticipated an error and figured out how your script can handle it. Second, turn it off right after the error-producing part of the script has finished. That way, *unanticipated* errors don't get swept under the rug. In general, you should have just a few steps between Set Error Capture [On] and Set Error Capture [Off].

The Get(LastError) Function

When error capture is on, FileMaker doesn't show error messages. But it still knows which error occurred and gives you the chance to ask about it if you're interested. The script in Figure 18-15, for example, *isn't* interested. It doesn't ask if an error occurred at all. Instead, it just checks to see if the find worked by counting the records in the found set.

But sometimes you can use such error information within your script, much like any other value, to trigger other script steps. To check an error, use the Get(LastError) function to find out what happened. This function returns an *error code,* which is always a number. If there was no error in the previous step, Get(LastError) returns a zero. In other words, it doesn't return the number of the last error that occurred. Instead, it returns the error number for the last step that ran. If your Get(LastError) step can't come right after the issue you're checking (maybe you have to check a couple of steps for errors before your branching starts), you can store the error code in a variable and then check its contents later in the script.

In FileMaker, just about everything that could possibly go wrong has its own error number or code. This feature gives you a lot of flexibility, but it also makes it a real pain to figure out which errors you should check for. Luckily, most of these errors are pretty obscure, and chances are you'll never have to worry about them. Here's a list of the most common error numbers you should take note of:

- **Error 9, 200–217, 723–725.** Assorted security-related errors (see Chapter 19).

- **Error 112.** Window is missing (you get this error if you try to select, close, or move/resize a window that doesn't exist).

- **Error 301.** Record is in use by another user (you get this error when a script tries to modify a record that's locked in another window or by another user).

- **Error 400.** Find criteria are empty (if you let users enter find criteria during a script, the `Perform Script` step gets this error if they don't enter anything).

- **Error 401.** No records match this request (this is the actual error that happens when no records are found; most people choose to check `Get(FoundCount)` instead since it's easier to understand).

- **Errors 500–507.** Assorted field validation errors (you get these errors when you try to modify a field in a way that violates its validation setting and it's set to Always validate).

- **Errors 718 and 719.** XML processing errors (see Chapter 22).

- **Errors 1200–1225.** Calculation-related errors (you see these errors in conjunction with the `EvaluationError()` and `Evaluate()` functions).

- **Errors 1400–1414.** Assorted ODBC or SQL errors (see Chapter 22).

See Appendix D for a complete list of error codes.

TIP To capture an error by number, try this: Turn on error capture before the step that's producing the error and then add a Show Custom Dialog step right after the offending step. Set the dialog box to show `Get(LastError)`. When you run the script, instead of the error message you've been seeing, you'll see a custom dialog box with the real error number. You can then modify the script to handle this particular number.

But it's much easier to use the Script Debugger (page 544) in FileMaker Pro Advanced. The debugger automatically shows error numbers as they happen—no need to write junk steps into your scripts that you just have to strip out again. There's even an option to set your scripts to pause when an error (page 549) occurs so you can analyze the situation and fix the problem.

The Allow User Abort Script Step

One more script step has ramifications when dealing with errors: `Allow User Abort`. This step lets you turn off a user's ability to cancel the script. `Allow User Abort` has only two options: on and off. Its normal state is to be turned on, unless you specifically turn it off with the script step. Like `Set Error Capture`, when you turn user abort off or back on within a script, the setting carries through any subscripts called by the main script. `Allow User Abort` always turns back on again when the script finishes running.

If you turn user abort off, but leave error capture on, the Cancel button In error messages is removed, so the person is forced to continue the script. Turning off user abort also prevents the user from pressing Esc (Windows) or ⌘-period (Mac) to cancel a running script. Finally, if the script pauses, he doesn't get a Cancel button in the status area. Instead, the only choice is to continue.

NOTE When a script turns off user abort and pauses, the database user also can't switch to a different window, close the window, or quit FileMaker.

◼ Advanced Script Triggers

On page 455, you got an intro to using *timers* with the Install OnTimer Script step, which lets you schedule a script to run repeatedly. Now you'll get the full Install OnTimer story, and learn how the OnKeystroke trigger lets you respond to every keystroke your user makes.

NOTE These are power-user triggers that require a lot of expertise to use properly. They give you a lot of power, but they're more complex than the script steps you've seen so far. Approach them with a clear head and a fresh cup of coffee.

Install OnTimer Script

The Install OnTimer Script step has two options. First, you specify the script you want to run (along with an optional script parameter). Then you specify the number of "Interval seconds." For instance, you can schedule your Find Unpaid Invoices script with an interval of 10 seconds. If you then run the script with the Install OnTimer Script step, your Find Unpaid Invoices script runs every 10 seconds forever.

Of course *forever* is a long time. How do you stop a timer like this? In two ways:

• Timers are associated with the window that was active when the timer was installed. If this window closes, the timer stops running. So you can close the database window to stop its timer.

• A window can only have one timer running. If you install a new timer in the same window, it *replaces* the one you last installed. So if you run the Install OnTimer Script step with no script specified, then you effectively turn off the timer entirely. This way, you can keep the window open but stop its timer.

TIP Timers can be trouble (after all, if you accidentally schedule a complicated script to run every second, it can keep your database so busy that it's tough to do anything else, including unschedule it). While you're working out the kinks in your timer-based process, make a new window to work in. Then if you accidentally get a timer running that won't stop on its own, just close the bad window.

Here are some situations where a timer might come in handy:

• You have a series of informational layouts you want to display on a wall-mounted monitor (like shop operation information or information for customers standing in line). Using a timer, you can automatically switch layouts periodically, so your monitor shows each one for 30 seconds, like a repeating slide show.

- Your editing process is time sensitive. For example, say you have lots of people working in your database, and lots of people have to edit the same record. To keep someone from keeping a record locked too long (see the box on page 32), install a timer when she switches to the edit layout. It can switch back to the read-only layout after a few minutes in case she walks away from her computer.

- You want to set up a computer to run periodic tasks. Maybe you have to import order information from your company's web server every 10 minutes, or you want to send shipment notifications every hour. You can install FileMaker on a computer, and schedule a timer to run the appropriate scripts periodically, with no intervention from anyone.

You'll see an example of a timer in action in the next section.

Keystroke Triggers

The keystroke trigger is probably the most complex FileMaker scripting technique. The basic concept is simple, though: A script runs every time any key is pressed. It's the scripting part that's complicated, since the script needs to test for all the keystrokes you want to Intercept and then take action when they're pressed. Keystroke triggers can apply to the layout, or to a specific layout *object*.

You might use an OnLayoutKeystroke trigger to add direct keyboard navigation (for example, pressing C to switch to the Contacts tab, or using the arrow keys to switch between records, and so on). An OnLayoutKeystroke trigger is also useful if you want to cancel keystrokes layout-wide. For instance, you can prevent the entry of punctuation into any field, or keep the arrow keys from working. To configure a keystroke trigger for the layout, view the Triggers tab of the Layout Setup dialog box (Layouts→Layout Setup). Select the OnLayoutKeystroke option and then select the script that should run.

Most often, you apply the OnObjectKeystroke trigger to fields, where you can limit which keys your users can press, jump to the next field when they press the space bar, or some other specialized field-type action. To use an object keystroke trigger, select a layout object and then choose Format→Set Script Triggers. Select the OnObjectKeystroke trigger and then select the script that should run. This time, the trigger fires only if the object has keyboard focus when the key is pressed.

■ DETECTING KEYSTROKES

Suppose you have a report you show in Preview mode. As a convenience to the people using the database, you want the up and down arrow keys to jump to the previous and next page respectively (they just can't get the hang of the arrow buttons). It's a perfect job for an OnLayoutKeystroke trigger.

> **NOTE** If you want Control or arrow key shortcuts for your database, you should use custom menus, not keystroke triggers. See page 568 for details.

When FileMaker calls your script from a keystroke trigger, it remembers which key the person pressed. The script uses an If statement with the Get(TriggerKeystroke) function to find out what key was pressed. Then the script can take appropriate action based on the value that's returned. For instance, if the "a" key is pressed, Get(TriggerKeystroke) returns "a" to the script. If "A" (using the Shift key) is pressed, the script gets a capital "A" instead.

NOTE If you care about uppercase vs. lowercase in your script, you can use the Exact function. This function compares two values, and returns True only if they're exactly the same, including case. So instead of this:

    If (Get (TriggerKeystroke) = "a"; "Yes"; "No")

You should do this:

    If (Exact (Get (TriggerKeystroke), "a"); "Yes"; "No")

The first example results in "Yes" if the user presses "A" or "a," while the second gives you "Yes" only if she types a lowercase "a."

There are characters you can't type in FileMaker's Specify Calculation window, like an up or down arrow. But you can use the Code0 function with Get(TriggerKeystroke) to figure out what key was pressed. Here's the calculation for testing for the up arrow key:

    Code (Get (TriggerKeystroke)) = 29

The numeral 29 is the Unicode *code point* (or number) for the up arrow key. The codes are listed in FileMaker's online help (search for "Code") or right here:

- Backspace: 8
- Tab: 9
- Enter: 10
- Return: 13
- Escape: 27
- Left arrow: 28
- Up arrow: 29
- Right arrow: 30
- Down arrow: 31
- Space: 32
- Forward Delete: 127

TIP To find the code for an alphanumeric character or string of characters, use the Code( ) function. For example, Code ("c") returns the value 99 and Code ("sp") returns 11200115.

There's one more wrinkle to keystroke detection. What if someone presses Shift plus the Tab key? Since this is a common need, FileMaker has one more keystroke function: Get(TriggerModifierKeys). This function, plus a little math, tells you which of the modifier keys was pressed. Once again, special codes represent each key:

- Shift: 1
- Caps Lock: 2
- Ctrl (Windows) or Control (Mac): 4
- Alt (Windows) or Option (Mac): 8
- Command ⌘ (Mac only): 16

This list may seem to be missing some values, like 3 and 5. That's because Get(TriggerModifierKeys)—and its sister function Get(ActiveModiferKeys)—*add* the values of all modifier keys to get their results. For example, Shift + Ctrl pressed together result in a value of 5. And, if you do some experimenting, you'll see that that's the only way to get 5. This way, every combination of modifier keys results in a unique number.

To figure out which number to test for, decide what key combination you want to trigger something in your script—Alt and Shift, say. When you write the script, add them up yourself: 8 + 1 = 9. Then you can do a check like this:

```
Get ( TriggerModifierKeys ) = 9
```

> **NOTE** The Code( ) function has an alter ego called Char( ). Given a code (or series of codes) this function returns the original character equivalents. This function is far less useful than Code( ) (which is commonly used for keystroke triggers). Use it, for instance, if you need to force a tab character into a calculation—Char(9)—or something equally esoteric.

■ CREATING A SIMPLE KEYSTROKE TRIGGER

Now that you've worked through the concepts, you're ready to create your page navigation trigger. You can already use Ctrl-up arrow and Ctrl-down arrow to navigate through your records. But it'd be more convenient if the arrow keys worked without the modifier keys. You want to be able to use the trigger in Browse and Preview modes, so you'll need a way to short-circuit the arrow keys' behavior in Preview mode. The script you need navigates to the previous or next page, depending on which key is pressed (Figure 18-16).

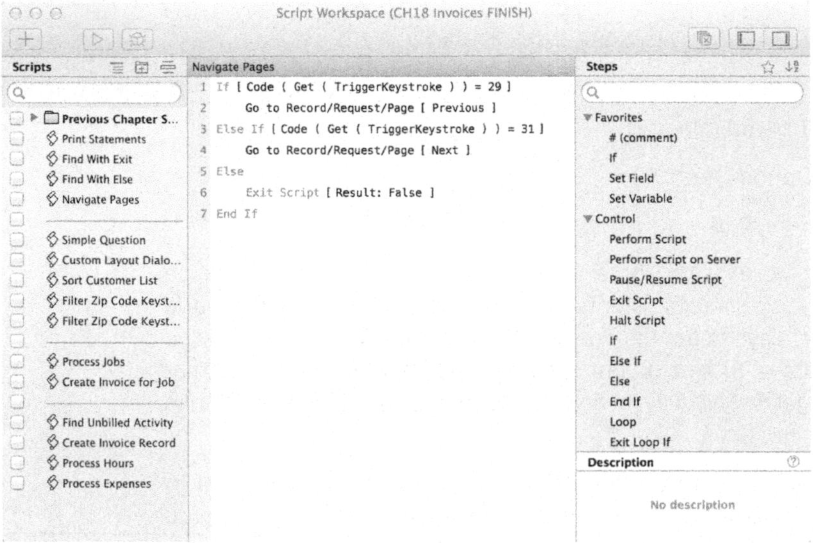

FIGURE 18-16

This script checks for the key that was pressed (it's looking for the up and down arrow keys only) and navigates records appropriately if it detects one.

Once you've written the script, you need to set up the keystroke trigger:

1. **Switch to the Customers layout and then go to Layout mode. Choose Layouts→Layout Setup and then click the Script Triggers tab to select it.**

   Since you're applying a layout trigger, you start in Layout mode.

2. **Select OnLayoutKeystroke.**

   The Specify Script Options window appears. Here's where you tell FileMaker which script to run.

3. **Choose the Navigate Pages script and then click OK.**

   You're now back in the Layout Setup dialog box.

> **NOTE** The sample file already has two triggers for the Customers layout. In this case, it's safe to apply a new trigger, because it doesn't conflict with the existing ones. But other triggers may not play well together, so make sure to test your triggers thoroughly.

4. **If necessary, turn on the Browse and Preview checkboxes.**

   You get to tell FileMaker which modes your trigger should run in.

5. **Click OK and save your layout if necessary.**

   Now you're ready to switch to Browse mode and test your trigger.

Press the up and down arrow keys to see FileMaker switch pages as the keystrokes trigger the script. Switch to Preview mode and test there, too. Since the arrow keys already do something in Preview mode (they scroll the page up or down a bit), each test has an Exit Script step with the result of False. The exit steps tell FileMaker to skip the normal behavior and let the scripted behavior take over. Without the exit steps, both actions would happen.

■ CREATING A MORE COMPLEX KEYSTROKE FILTER

Keystroke triggers also let you limit what users can type into a field. You know how to use validation to show an error message if something inappropriate is typed in a field (page 252). But with validation, users don't get feedback until after the wrong data has been entered. Alternatively, you can write a script and set an OnObjectKeystroke trigger that can refuse certain data and beep to warn the user.

The script will check *each* key your users press and cancel all invalid keystrokes. Careful, though: Writing a keystroke trigger takes special care. First of all, you have to decide what makes a keystroke invalid. Here are the rules for the Zip Code field:

- If the keystroke isn't a number (0 through 9), then don't allow it.

- If the field already has five digits in it, then cancel any keystroke.

With this in mind, switch to Layout mode and then select the Zip Code field. Choose Format→Set Script Triggers and then select the OnObjectKeystroke option. Then click the + button to create a new script. The new script consists of two If statements. First you check for non-number keys with a formula like this one:

```
Get ( TriggerKeystroke ) ≠ 0 and
Get ( TriggerKeystroke ) ≠ 1 and
Get ( TriggerKeystroke ) ≠ 2 and
Get ( TriggerKeystroke ) ≠ 3 and
Get ( TriggerKeystroke ) ≠ 4 and
Get ( TriggerKeystroke ) ≠ 5 and
Get ( TriggerKeystroke ) ≠ 6 and
Get ( TriggerKeystroke ) ≠ 7 and
Get ( TriggerKeystroke ) ≠ 8 and
Get ( TriggerKeystroke ) ≠ 9
```

Inside the If statement, you add a script step to let users know something is happening and then exit the script with a result of False. Your second If statement checks for *excess* keystrokes. It has a simple calculation:

```
Length ( Customers::Zip Code ) ≥ 5
```

Once again, inside this If statement, you add a Beep step and exit with a False result. You can see this script in Figure 18-17.

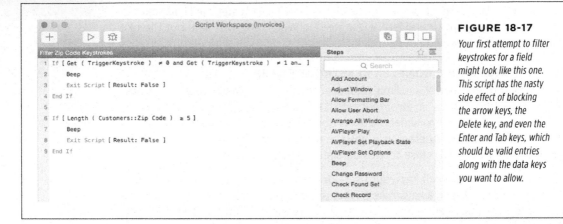

FIGURE 18-17

Your first attempt to filter keystrokes for a field might look like this one. This script has the nasty side effect of blocking the arrow keys, the Delete key, and even the Enter and Tab keys, which should be valid entries along with the data keys you want to allow.

When you test the Zip Code field script trigger, you'll see that the script is a little too aggressive. Since it cancels every keystroke that isn't a number, you can't use the Delete key to clear an accidental entry. Plus, it blocks the Enter, Tab, and arrow keys, and you can't exit the field easily. You've created a monster—a field that can't be edited.

The fix is easy, though. If you refer back to the list of special key codes on page 728, you see that most of the special navigation keys have codes less than 31. The notable exception is Forward Delete, which is 127. So instead of adding a special case for each and every key, you can allow all the special keys in one block with a simple formula. Add an If test to the top of your script, using this formula:

```
Code ( Get ( TriggerKeystroke ) ) < 32 or Code ( Get ( TriggerKeystroke ) ) =
127
```

You also need to improve your formula in the If statement that checks the Zip code's length so it lets users highlight the text in order to delete it. Edit that calculation to add a new test:

```
Length ( Customers::Zip Code ) ≥ 5 and Get ( ActiveSelectionSize ) = 0
```

This tactic is perfectly safe because every normal key (letters, numbers, space, and punctuation) has code 32 or above. You can see your new and improved script in Figure 18-18.

To finish up, take a look at the modes you're applying the trigger in. You might be tempted to assign the trigger for both Find and Browse mode, but remember that you might want to find a range of Zip codes (46077–90201) or use a wildcard in your Zip Code search (852*). So you're probably better off applying this trigger only in Browse mode.

Now when you test the script trigger, you should see better behavior. If you type text or punctuation into the Zip Code field, FileMaker beeps, and nothing appears in the field. But if you type a number key, it goes right in. And once the field has five numbers, it rejects any additional entry.

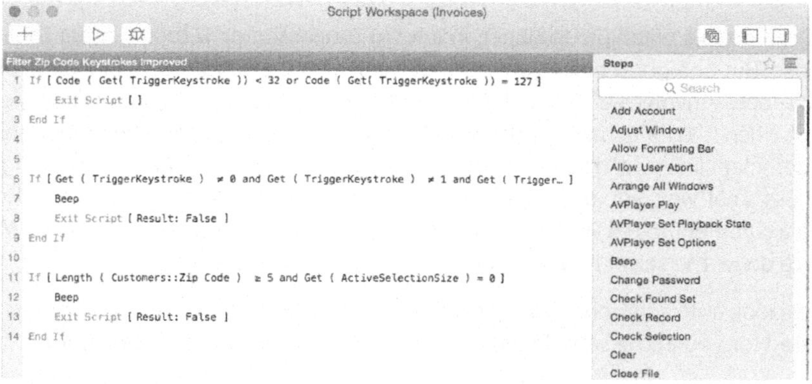

FIGURE 18-18

This script improves on the one in Figure 17-18. It allows for standard editing keys. If any other key is entered, the script uses the same logic as before to reject non-numeric keystrokes, and any entry beyond five digits. Now people can edit the field with ease. (Check the completed scripts in Invoices_End.fmp12.)

Putting a Complex Script Together

Building a complicated script takes more than just knowing how to use all of FileMaker's scripting tools. It takes time and planning. Because scripting gives you so much flexibility, you often have many ways to solve the same problem. Your job is to find the way that best meets your business needs and is the simplest to understand, fix, and maintain later. Plus, as your skills grow, the approach you take to solving problems will change.

Imagine that you need to write a script that generates an invoice for a job. You want to gather all the unbilled expenses and hours for the job and then add the appropriate line items to the invoice. To make a script like this, you need to cover all your bases:

- **Planning.** Before you even start writing the script, you have to decide upon a general approach. Outline all the things your script will do, and in what order. This process usually evolves from the general to the specific. The most specific version is the script steps, where you tell FileMaker *exactly* what to do.

- **Exceptions.** What kinds of things can go wrong? Think about how you'll check for errors and prevent problems.

- **Efficiency.** Are you doing the same things in several places in the script? Do you already have scripts that do part of the process that you can call without reinventing the wheel? Are there other reasons to break your script into multiple smaller scripts?

Planning the Script

Planning a big script is usually an iterative process. You start by outlining the steps the script will take in very general terms. You then go in and fill in more and more detail with each pass. When you're done adding detail, you know exactly what steps your script will use. Using the invoicing script as an example, you'll see how FileMaker gives you the tools to plan and execute your new script.

You can do this planning on paper, in a word processor, or with any other tool you choose. But one good place you may *not* think of is the script itself. Since the planning process involves a series of steps, and since it naturally produces the finished script when it's done, make notes with comment script steps. As you work, replace the comment lines with real script steps, and perhaps more comments explaining the process. That way, you never get lost or forget essential steps because you always have a comment to tell you what you still need to add and where it should go. When you're done, the script is written and commented for posterity.

Take a look at the sample script shown in Figure 18-19. To save you time, it's already created for you in the sample database for this chapter (*Invoice Start.fmp12*).

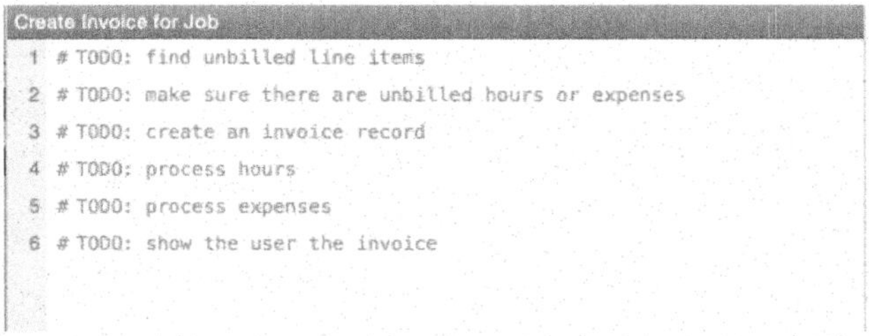

FIGURE 18-19

This first draft of your script doesn't do anything yet. It's just a series of comments that map out, at the most general level, what the script will do. You'll add more and more details as you go. Since these comments are placeholders for the real steps, perhaps even subscripts that you'll build separately, each one starts with the word TODO. Use any marker you want, as long as you can easily tell these placeholder comments apart from the real comments you'll add later.

Considering Exceptions

One of the most critical steps in script writing—planning for exceptions—is often forgotten. But the old saw "A stitch in time saves nine" truly applies to scripting. Spend a few minutes at the beginning of the process thinking ahead to what might go wrong and planning how to prevent problems. These few minutes can save you hours of troubleshooting and repair work on your data later.

Look at what your script is supposed to do and try to think of reasonable *exceptions*—situations where your script might not be able to do its job. Thinking of exceptions is important for two reasons:

- If your script always assumes ideal circumstances, it can wreak havoc if your assumptions are wrong when it runs. The last thing you need is a wild script running amok in your data, changing and deleting the wrong things.

- If a script gets halfway through its job and then discovers that it can't continue, you may be left with half-finished work. It's usually best to look for the problems up front, so the script can simply refuse to run if it won't be able to finish. (For more detail, see the box on page 737.)

For example, the Invoice creation script may run into two potential problems:

- How does the script know which job to create an invoice for? This problem is easy to solve: Make the script available only through a button on the Job layout. That way, people can run the script only from the right context. In other words, the script always runs on the job record the user is looking at. Make a comment at the top of your script that reminds you how the script is run.

- What if the job has no hours or expenses that haven't been billed? You wind up with an invoice that has no line items, and you don't want to send *that* to your customer, nor do you want it lying around in your database. You can go ahead and create the invoice and then delete it if it's empty. But this approach uses up an invoice number, and it means your script has to go through all the work of creating an invoice only to throw it away when it's done. Instead, have the script check first to be sure there's something to bill. Then it can display an informative message and skip all the hard work when there's nothing to bill.

Figure 18-20 shows how you could edit your script to take these two problems into account. Notice that you don't even have to write the real test yet. You can just make a calculation comment as a further To Do list.

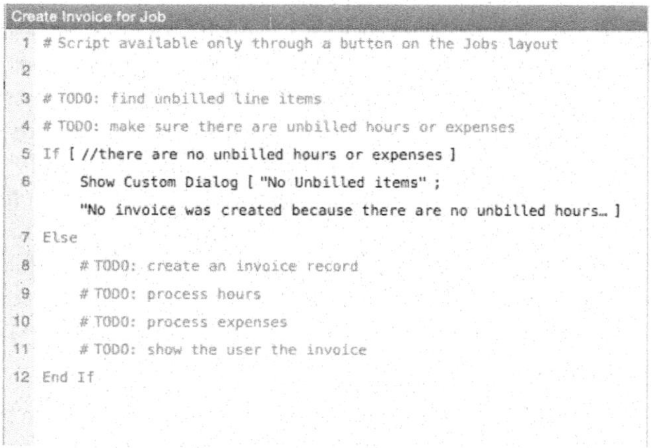

FIGURE 18-20

Your first pass at editing the script shows where you'll put the test that determines whether an invoice needs to be created. And since you want to show the user a message If no invoice is made, add the Show Custom Dialog script step to the If part of the test.

- **The If step doesn't need a fully realized test yet.** Put a commented calculation (page 410) as your test for now, just to remind yourself what needs to be tested. You can put the real test in later.

- **Add feedback by putting a custom dialog step in the True part of the If step.** If you don't give feedback here, the person using the database may get confused, since nothing happens when he clicks the button to create an invoice for the job. The dialog box should explain why FileMaker isn't creating an invoice.

- **Add an Else step.** Since you don't want to create an invoice if there aren't any billable items for the job, put an Else step after the Show Custom Dialog step and put the remaining TODO items in the Else part of the If test. The End If step should be at the end of the script.

Creating Subscripts

Now that you've figured out how to solve problems your script might encounter, you've come to a fork in the road. You can write a single script containing hundreds of steps, but it'll be long and hard to follow. For example, the End If steps at the end of the script may be a long way from their If and Else counterparts, making it hard to figure out where they belong. The script will be easier to read and troubleshoot if you break it up into smaller, more manageable pieces.

When you're trying to decide whether to write one long script or several shorter ones, you might consider a few other things. If you have several small scripts, you can run any one of them individually. This method gives you the chance to try out parts of the script to see if they work properly. Also, since you can pass errors, or script results to scripts via script parameters, using subscripts to do some jobs often saves trouble later on. But in the end, either approach is perfectly valid. Some people really like short, simple scripts, even if it means more of them. Others prefer to put everything controlling a single process into the same script, no matter how long the script gets. See the box on page 739 for some tips on breaking scripts into subscripts appropriately.

Once you've decided how to break up a process into appropriate subscripts, it's a good idea to put a Perform Script step in the place where the process will run. Then you can either write the subscript immediately or create a "skeleton" subscript that's just made up of the comments to remind you of the steps you need to add to the script (Figure 18-21). Either way, you have a script that you can specify in the Perform Script step. If you decide not to do the subscript, just make a comment that reminds you that it isn't done yet. FileMaker is very flexible about letting you create scripts in whatever order fits with the way you think and like to work. Just make it easy on yourself by leaving lots of commented breadcrumbs you can follow as you're working on the pieces of your scripts. Here are some more tips for making sure you cross your Ts and dot your Is:

- Add an Exit Script step to the end of every subscript. Even if there aren't any testable conditions in the script (that's uncommon), you can take a page from FileMaker's own error tracking and pass a value of "0."

- The corollary to the first rule of thumb is to use Get (ScriptResult) after every Perform Script to make sure the subscript did its work properly.

The Problem with Problems

Although detecting problems up front is usually best, it isn't always possible. Sometimes you can't find out about problems until your script has run partway through.

Most database systems handle this problem with something called a *transaction,* a chunk of work that's held in limbo until you tell the database to make it permanent. In a nutshell, you open a transaction, and you then can do anything you want, but your changes don't get saved until you commit the record. If you decide you don't want the changes after all, you can undo the transaction.

FileMaker uses this transaction concept under the hood to handle record changes, but unfortunately you have no easy way to tap into the transaction system from a script. Here's why: When you first enter a record—using the Open Re-cord/Request script step, for instance—FileMaker begins a transaction for you. When you exit the record—Commit Records/Requests—FileMaker commits the transaction, writing all changes to the database. If you revert the record instead—Revert Record/Request—FileMaker essentially rolls back the transaction, leaving the database untouched. Just remember that each transaction is linked to a record. For example, you can't begin a transaction, then make changes to five different customer records and 11 invoices, and then roll back all those changes—you can only roll back the last one.

But if you create, edit, or delete records in *portal rows* while you're still in the record, all your changes happen in one transaction.

Try this exercise in the Invoices file to explore how the transaction works. Have two windows open (Choose Windows→New Window)—one showing the Invoice layout and the other showing the Line Items layout. Create a new invoice record and add a few line items. Notice that FileMaker creates the new line item records when you add items to the Line Item portal on the Invoice layout. Being very careful not to commit the record (that is, don't hit the Enter key or click anywhere outside the fields onto your layout), choose Records→Revert Record. The parent invoice record disappears, *and* all the child line items disappear, too. You've just witnessed FileMaker's version of transactions.

Knowing this, you can use the Open Record/Request script step on an invoice record and then make changes to dozens of line items. Then if your script detects a problem, you can revert the invoice record and toss out all your line item changes as well. If you absolutely, positively must have control over your transactions, arrange your scripts so they do everything through relationships from one single record.

- When tackling a Looping script, write the "work" part of the script first. Don't add the Loop/End Loop pair until you know the guts are working. That way, if there's a problem, it's most likely because you didn't enter the loop with the proper preparation. For example, maybe you failed to find the right records, or you didn't set a variable the loop needs to do its work.

- It's common for lengthy processes to do the same kinds of work several times. You might need to process a set of Hours records and then process a set of Expenses records. Once you have the first process working, copy and paste your script steps and then update the field's references, context, and any other items that differ. It's almost always much faster than starting again from scratch.

- Pay attention to script parameters. Check the value you're setting when the script runs, and then make sure that value is passed along to any subscript that needs it. One of the most common reasons subscripts fail is that they don't get the script parameters they need. The best way to see and trace script parameter values is to use FileMaker Pro Advanced's Data Viewer (page 552).

```
Create Invoice for Job
 1  # Script available only through a button on the Jobs layout
 2
 3  # TODO: find unbilled line items
 4  # TODO: make sure there are unbilled hours or expenses
 5  If [ //there are no unbilled hours or expenses ]
 6      Show Custom Dialog [ "No Unbilled items" ;
        "No invoice was created because there are no unbilled hours… ]
 7  Else
 8      # TODO: create an invoice record
 9      Perform Script [ <unknown> ]
10      # TODO: process hours
11      Perform Script [ <unknown> ]
12      # TODO: process expenses
13      Perform Script [ <unknown> ]
14      # TODO: show the user the invoice
15  End If
```

FIGURE 18-21

Each empty Perform Script step marks a place for a subscript you'll create later. The first subscript will find the unbilled expenses and hours; the second will create the new invoice record that's related to the job; the third will loop through all the hours and add the necessary line items; the fourth will do the same thing for each expense.

Testing Scripts

Testing a script is as important as planning and writing it. In fact, the more complex a process is, the more time you should budget for testing the script after you think it's finished. To test the "Create Invoice for a Job" script (it's in the *CH18 Invoices End.fmp12* file), first go to a job record that has unbilled hours and expenses. Or create a new job record, plus new unbilled hours and expenses, if necessary. Back on the job record, run the "Create Invoice for Job" script. To make your testing as much like the conditions your users will see, create a button for running the script. In a flash, you should see a new invoice, properly assigned to the customer and containing line items for each unbilled item.

NOTE If the script doesn't work, you have options. First, check your data to make sure you have appropriate hours and expenses for the script to process. But if you have FileMaker Pro Advanced, you should also read about the Script Debugger and Data Viewer in Chapter 14. These tools make hunting down script problems much easier, and few serious scripters work without them. Stepping through this script, even though it should run without errors if your data is set up properly, will teach you a lot about how you can use the Debugger to troubleshoot a misbehaving script.

The "Create Invoice for a Job" script processes a lengthy task where the steps and outcome were known. Out there on the mean streets of development, you won't always have a roadmap to follow. Still, the concepts of planning, exception handling, and efficiency will get you out of a lot of sticky script situations.

TIP And even if your database doesn't handle invoicing, it's very common to create related records and move data via scripts so that you can retain control over data. Just adapt these scripts to meet your needs.

UP TO SPEED

The Right Way to Create Subscripts

When you think about ways to break your script into smaller pieces, you should be thinking about tasks. It makes good sense to create a script to do one of the self-contained *tasks* needed in a lengthy process. It doesn't make sense to simply take a long script and break it in two pieces, so that the last step in the first script simply performs the second script. Breaking scripts up that way has all the disadvantages of multiple scripts (more windows to work in, more scripts to scroll through) and none of the advantages (neither script is particularly simple or self-contained, and neither can be run individually for testing purposes). Also, as you look for places to use subscripts, look for opportunities for reuse. In other words, look for things the script has to do more than once in two different places. It almost always makes sense to use a subscript in this situation. You'll often save lots of time down the road, as when a new process needs to do that same small subroutine: You already have a snippet that you can reuse with a Perform Script step.

In most cases, the right way to subdivide a script is to create one master script that starts *and* finishes the process. The "Cre-

ate Invoice for Job" script in the End version of this chapter's sample file does that. It starts by finding unbilled line items and finishes by showing the invoice. Along the way, it relies on other simple scripts to get the whole job done.

There's no problem with a subscript having subscripts of its own. In fact, subscripts often do. But you should structure the entire set of scripts so that the top-level script implements the highest-level logic and behavior of the entire script itself. Each subscript should, in turn, do some particular task from start to finish. If the task is particularly complex, then the subscript itself might implement only its highest level of logic, calling on more subscripts to handle parts of the task. Since you're in the habit of naming scripts descriptively, each subscript's name can provide nearly as much information as a comment. If you read through the "Create Invoice for Job" script, you can easily follow its structure, even though it's fairly complex. The script almost reads like a book, describing exactly what it's doing.

When you're first learning to write scripts, or if you're attempting to do something that you aren't quite sure will work, following an approach like the one above will serve you well. In addition to creating your scripts in comment and subscript form, you can break scripting down even further. Create a few script steps and then test them to make sure they behave as you expect. If they don't work properly, tweak them until they do. Then add a few more script steps and test again. If a new problem arises, you know it's in the new steps you've just added.

Finally, don't forget that the state of your database can influence what happens when you test a script. For example, a button on the Jobs layout ensures that your users can run the "Create Invoice for Jobs" script only from the proper context. But in the heat of testing, you might accidentally run the script from the Script Workspace window while you're on the wrong layout. If you do, the script won't have a Job ID to work with, and all kinds of havoc will be loosed in the script: It won't know which unbilled items to search for and could create an Invoice that's not attached to any job at all.

As you gain experience, you'll find that planning, finding exceptions, and subscripting becomes second nature. You'll start envisioning scripts of increasing complexity, and soon you'll be making them your own way, without following a rigid plan.

Security and Integration

Adding Security

F ileMaker is all about easy access to information. But that's a double-edged sword. If you don't add security, every person who uses your database has unrestricted access and can add data, tables, and scripts as freely as you can. Of course, you can take all the usual precautions (give your computer a password, install virus-protection software, lock your office door, and so on). But the minute you let anyone else into the database, you have all kinds of security challenges. Mike in Accounting is free to rename or edit all your scripts if he so desires. And Kelly in Sales can delete all those "old" order records that are getting in her way. Fortunately, FileMaker gives you a fine level of control, so you can give different people, or different sets of people, access to the data they need to do their jobs, while keeping important information, and your database's structure, out of harm's way.

> **NOTE** You may be tempted to think you don't have to worry about security. But the best time to protect your data is *before* you have a problem. If you wait until your database grows big and complex before adding security, then it'll take you longer to build the security you need.

■ How Security Works

FileMaker's security system has two primary levels of control: *who* can get into your database in the first place; and *what* they can do once they're there. You determine who gets access to your database by setting up *user accounts,* and you control what each person can do by assigning *privilege sets* to each account.

Understanding Accounts

FileMaker understands that different individuals access your database. The *who* part of security is important for several reasons. For instance, Dwight and Pam each need access to the database, but their manager Michael doesn't. When you give each user of your database an individual account, you can keep track of who's using the file. Plus, if Pam leaves the company, then you can keep her from accessing the database without locking anybody else out. Likewise, when Pam's replacement is hired, you can give him access, too.

You control access by creating an account for each person who uses the database. Each account has a user name and a password. Users have to type their account name and password when they open the file. If they don't know the right combination, then they can't get in.

NOTE When FileMaker asks for an account name and password, propeller-heads say it's *authenticating* the user. In other words, it's making sure the user is for real. And the account name and password taken together are often referred to as *credentials*. This book, for the most part, dispenses with this jargon, but you may run across the term elsewhere. The more you know.

WORKAROUND WORKSHOP

Spying by Script

Once you've set up database accounts, FileMaker remembers the account name of whoever is currently signed in. Find out what FileMaker knows using the Get(AccountName) function. For example, if you want to record the account name in a table called Access when someone runs a particularly important script, the script can create an Access record and take notes before the script goes into its main work. To keep track, you could include a script step like this:

```
Set Field [Access::Notes ; Get ( Account-
Name )
```

```
& " ran the script on " & Get ( Current-
Date )
& " at " & Get ( CurrentTime )]
```

Then every time the script runs, FileMaker looks up the name of whoever is signed into the file at the moment, and puts the person's account name and the date and time in the Notes field.

FileMaker also knows the name of the privilege set used when someone logs in. The Get(AccountPrivilegeSetName) function tells you which one it is.

Understanding Privileges

But who gets into your database is only half the story. You also control *what* they can do. You decide which layouts users can see and which scripts they can run. You can let them see only certain records, and even just a few fields from those records. Each bit of access is called a privilege. Every person is unique, but you probably don't need to grant each person a unique set of privileges. For example, you may have one privilege set for Accounting and another for Sales. People with the Accounting privilege set can run reports, but they can't enter new orders. People with the Sales privilege set can enter and edit data, but they can't run reports. You can make as many—or as few—privilege sets as you need. And you can give lots of accounts the same privilege set, or make a privilege set just for one account.

■ Managing Accounts

Since the "who" part of the security equation is the easiest one to set up and manage, FileMaker puts those controls at front and center when you're managing your security. And like layouts that are created for you when you define the first tables in a database, each new database file comes with a pair of starter accounts, called "Guest" and "admin."

NOTE There are three sample databases for this chapter on this book's Missing CD page at *www.missingmanuals. com/cds/fmp14mm*. Use the file *CH19 Invoices Security.fmp12* for the exercises in this section.

Adding a Password to the Admin Account

You never knew it, but all this time you've been using an account called "admin." This account gives you have full access to the file without a password for those beginning stages of development when you aren't ready to think about security yet. Unfortunately, the rest of the FileMaking world knows this little "secret" too. So the first time you open the Manage Security window, you'll see a Security Alert, telling you that the Full Access account doesn't have a password (Figure 19-1).

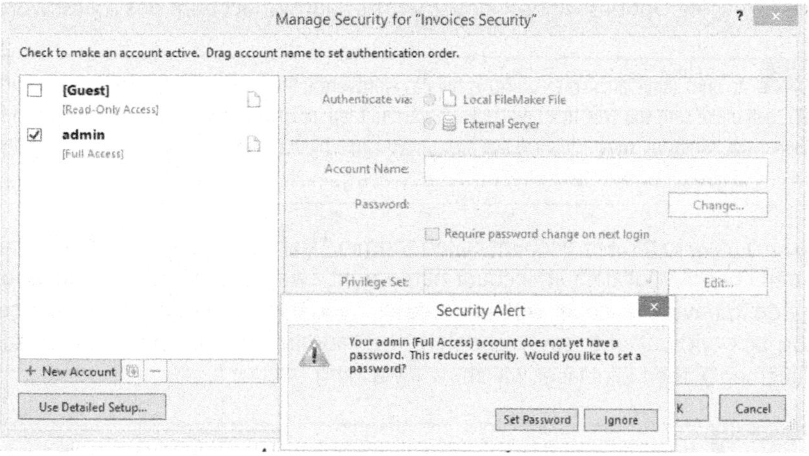

FIGURE 19-1

FileMaker puts some minimal security into each new file, but it's up to you to create a password for your Full Access account. You can click Ignore in the Security Alert window, but if you do, the warning appears every time you open the Manage Security Window.

Here's how to add a password to the "admin" account:

1. **Choose File→Manage→Security.**

   The Manage Security window and the Security Alert dialog box appear. There are two preconfigured accounts. The "admin" account is active, as shown by the checkbox to the left of its name.

2. **In the Security Alert dialog box, click the Set Password button.**

   The Set Password window appears.

3. **In the New Password field, type *citiZen 4!*.**

   This password includes a mix of upper and lower case, and a mix of alphanumeric and special characters. FileMaker shows you a password strength indicator. Its feedback doesn't use the same measures as some other strength indicators. If you're concerned about this disparity, you can ignore this feedback.

4. **In the Confirm Password field, type *citiZen 4!* again.**

   This confirmation helps ensure that you didn't make a typing error when you entered the password the first time.

5. **Click OK.**

   The password is saved.

If you didn't use the password suggested above, write yours down and keep it somewhere safe, because you'll need to enter a full-access account name and password when you close the Manage Security dialog box. And from now on, you'll have to enter the password whenever you open the Manage Security window. You'll have to do this even after you've opened the file using a full-access password. That little bit of extra security protects you if you walk away from your desk with the database open. Nobody can sneak over and create an account if they don't know a full-access password. See the box on page 747 to learn why you should change the settings in the File→File Options window now that the "admin" account has a password.

> **NOTE**   Account names aren't case-sensitive, but passwords are. If the Account Name or the password includes spaces, then make sure you type them precisely or you can't log in. FileMaker gives you five chances to log in and then it stops showing you the login dialog box. But you aren't blocked permanently. You can try again right away.

You don't have to have an account called "admin," so most people avoid the security risk and change that default account name right away. On the other hand, you *are* required to have an account with full access. If you try to close the Manage Security dialog box without one (say you delete the "admin" account but didn't create a replacement), then FileMaker will show a warning.

> **WARNING**   Make sure you don't forget your [Full Access] privilege set password. FileMaker uses industry-standard and ultra secure techniques to manage passwords; you simply have no way to bypass them. Some third-party hacks out there can promise to change your passwords for you, but steer clear of them—the process has been known to remove all accounts and can even damage your file. If you forget a more restricted password, the fix is simple. Just open the database with a full-access password, visit the Manage Security dialog box and then change the forgotten password.

Automatic Login

If I've been using the Admin account all this time, how come FileMaker never asked me to log in? Does it just skip the authentication dialog box when some account has no password?

Actually, FileMaker has been logging in for you. Every new database is set up to log in automatically using the Admin account and a blank password. Once you give the Admin account a password for a given database, automatic login stops. But you can set your database to log in with any account automatically, or you can turn off automatic login entirely, which is a much more secure option.

Change the setting by choosing File→File Options. The File Options dialog box appears. Turn off the "Log in using" checkbox to stop the automatic login process. Or, you can type a different account and password in the appropriate box to log in with another account. But this means no one will have to enter the account name and password when they open the file, so this option provides very little security. Finally, you can have FileMaker automatically log into the file using the guest account (see the box on page 748).

If you set your file to automatically log in with an account that doesn't have full access, then you can't come back to this window to turn it off while you're logged into the file with that lower privilege set. You may think you've just locked yourself out of your file completely, but you haven't. If you hold down the Shift key (Option key on a Mac) while a file opens, then FileMaker asks you for an account name and password even if the file is set to automatically log in.

Adding a New Account

You can add a new account almost as easily as you can edit an existing one. Since it's so easy to add accounts, there's no reason not to follow best security practices and give everyone an individual account. You can even give people more than one account. For example, you can designate some people as super-users who mostly do data entry and editing but sometimes need to create layouts. As much as you trust them, you just want to make sure they don't inadvertently damage layouts and scripts while they're doing other work. So you require them to log in with higher-level access when switching from data entry to tasks that require more care, like database design. (See page 781 for more detail on re-login.)

1. **If necessary, choose Manage Security and then click the +New Account button (bottom left).**

    A new account is added to the list, and the area to the right of the list changes to this new account's information.

2. **In the Account Name field, type *aswartz* and then click the Change button to the right of the Password area.**

    The Password area displays "<no password>".

The Guest Account

FileMaker has one built-in account called Guest that you can't rename or delete. By default, it's assigned to the Read-Only Access privilege set, but you can change it to any privilege set you want. The Guest account is also *inactive*. In other words, it exists, but it doesn't work unless you turn it on.

If you want to let some people access your database even if they don't have an account, activate the Guest account by turning on the checkbox by its name. When the guest account is turned on, the normal Log In dialog box includes a Guest Account radio button.

Someone can choose this option and then click OK without entering an account name or a password. FileMaker gives her access according to the privilege set you assigned to the guest account. Since anybody with FileMaker Pro can open your database by selecting this account, don't activate your guest account unless you have controlled conditions, like a special set of layouts that are the only ones available to the guest, or you're retaining the Read-only Access.

3. **In the New Password field, type *white H4t*. Type it again in the Confirm Password field.**

   No warnings appear if you type the password the same way in both fields.

4. **Click Set Password.**

   Bullets appear in the password area to show that a password has been set. You can't view or retrieve this password, so now is a good time to write it down. Remember that you can change the password, as long as you have a full-access account.

5. **In the Privilege Set pop-up menu, choose "[Data Entry Only]."**

   The new account can do data-entry chores, but no development work. You'll more about privilege sets later in this chapter. The Manage Security window should look like Figure 19-2.

If you want to let each person manage his own password, turn on "User must change password on next login." When this option is selected, you can create an account for someone with a generic password and then email the account information to him, with instructions to create a more secure and secret password when she first opens the database.

You can also make an account inactive. When you do, FileMaker keeps the account—and all its information—in the Accounts list, but it doesn't let people open the database using that account. For example, you can make an account inactive if a person goes on leave, but will return. That way you can easily reactivate the account when you need to. You can also use this option to create accounts for new employees before they start.

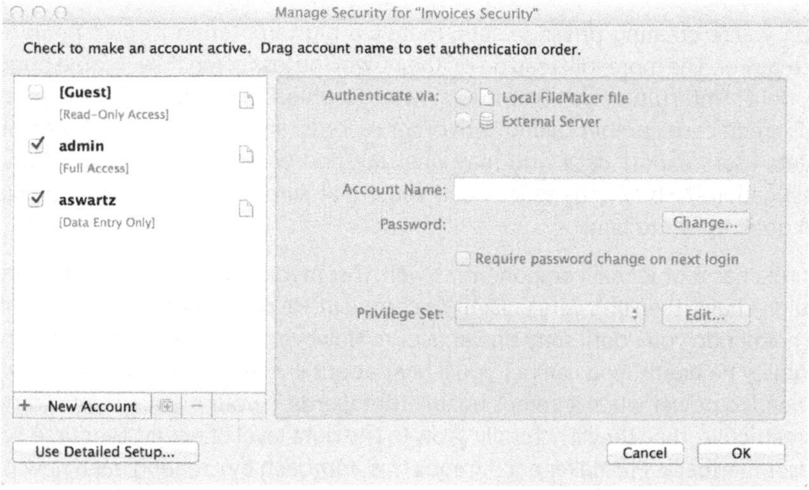

FIGURE 19-2

You now have two active accounts in this database. The smaller button to the right of the New Account button duplicates an existing account, FileMaker appends a digit to the end of the duplicated account's name. Use the third button to delete an account.

■ TESTING YOUR NEW ACCOUNT

Creating smart security involves many options and settings. And even with the process for confirming a password, it's still possible to mistype a password the same way twice. So it makes sense to test each new account and privilege set you create before you send that information out to your users. Then close and reopen the file. When prompted to log in, enter the new account name and password. Now experiment. Try modifying or deleting old invoices, or editing product records. You should see your new security settings in action. When you're done, close the file again and then open it one more time. This time use the [Full Access] account to log in.

> **TIP** Make this process easier by creating a script that lets you log in with a new account without opening and closing a file (page 781). You can even run Script Debugger (page 544) while you're testing a low-access account, as long as your account's privileges let you modify scripts.

■ Managing Privilege Sets

When you created your new account, you used one of FileMaker's canned privilege sets. But you'll gain much more control by creating your own sets. To do that you need to understand the concept of user roles. Each person who accesses your database is performing a *role,* or set of tasks. At the beginning of this chapter, you learned that the Accounting Department staff gets to run reports, but creating Invoices is left solely to the Sales staff. In this example, "Sales" and "Accounting" are two different roles that have no overlapping tasks. When you set up security, you need to understand what each user needs to do so you can give them access to the proper layouts, scripts, and even records.

When you're creating privilege sets, there's a big temptation to give people too much power. The more folks can do on their own, the less often they'll come bugging you, right? Unfortunately, this attitude invites trouble. For instance, if your database holds credit card numbers along with order records, and your Order Entry privilege set lets users export data, you may one day find yourself the subject of an FBI investigation. To be on the safe side, if you aren't *sure* someone needs a privilege, then don't give it to him.

This rule has a practical component as well. If someone has access to a feature he shouldn't have, then he's very unlikely to complain. He probably doesn't even notice, and neither do you—until someone abuses it. However, if you lock someone out of a capability he needs, you can bet you'll hear about it right away. You can easily add the needed power when it comes up. In other words, if your privilege sets start out too restrictive, then they'll naturally grow to the right level of power over time based on user feedback. FileMaker encourages this approach by creating each new privilege set without any privileges at all. Your job is to add each privilege a user needs.

Understanding Privilege Sets

Every FileMaker database has three built-in privilege sets: [Full Access], [Data Entry Only], and [Read-Only Access]. You can only make a few minor edits to these sets. The brackets make it easy to pick them out of a list with your custom sets. You can see the Privilege Sets tab in Figure 19-3.

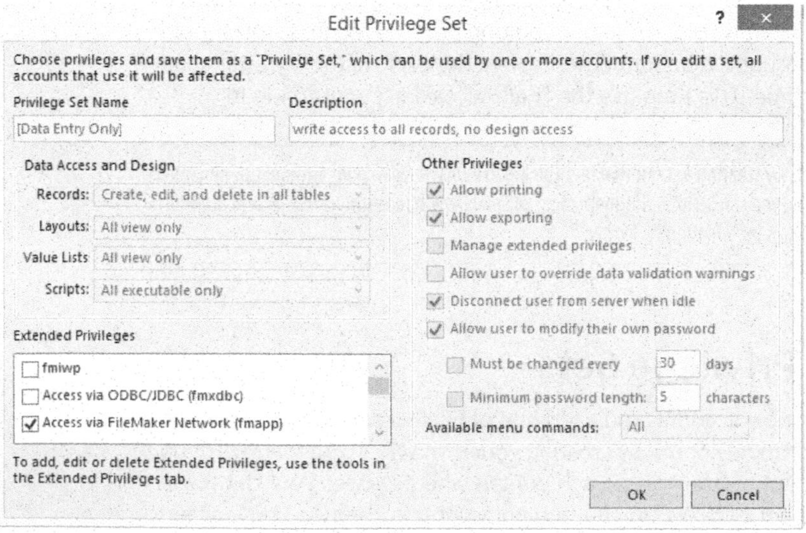

FIGURE 19-3

You can't edit a file's default privilege set, but it's instructive to look at the privileges it's assigned. Users can create, edit, and modify records in the database; they have access to all layouts, value lists, and scripts; and they can print, export, and change their own passwords. They can also access the database from FileMaker Server, as shown in the Extended Privileges section of the window.

Those brackets around the default sets' names are actually part of the name, as you'll soon find out when you use the Get(AccountPrivilegeSetName) function. So although they're awkward to look at and bothersome to read, get used to seeing them.

THE BUILT-IN PRIVILEGE SETS

The standard privilege sets cover three very common access levels, and you're welcome to use them if you want, but you have to live with the way they work out of the box, because FileMaker doesn't let you change anything except their extended privileges (page 771).

- Although you probably didn't realize it, you've been using the [Full Access] privilege set all along. As the name says, it gives you full access to the file with absolutely no restrictions.

- The [Data Entry Only] privilege set is much less powerful. Accounts assigned to this privilege set can't create or modify tables, field definitions, scripts, or layouts. But they can add, edit, and delete records in any table; print; change their own passwords; and export data.

- The least powerful built-in privilege set is [Read-Only Access]. Not only does it prevent all developer activities, but it also prevents modification of the data. Accounts with this privilege set can't create, edit, or delete records. They can view, print, or export the data that's already there, and change their passwords.

CUSTOM PRIVILEGE SETS

Those built-in privilege sets provide basic security, but they don't give you a full range of possibilities. Using just FileMaker's standard privilege sets, you can't give Dwight full control of some tables but let him just enter data in others. In developer's lingo, you don't get a lot of *granularity*.

NOTE Think of granularity as a medium for sculpture. If you're building a statue from boulders, then you can't create delicate details like the nose or eyelashes. If you're building with grains of sand (get it?), then you can work at a much finer level. Similarly, granularity in security lets you control specific access to your database.

In FileMaker, you can exercise precise, granular control over security by creating your own privilege sets and assigning them to the appropriate user accounts. When you create a new privilege set, it starts out with just one privilege. In other words, accounts attached to this set—if left alone—can't do *anything* in the database. You have to turn on all the privileges you think the user should have.

Understanding Individual Privileges

Since FileMaker has a privilege for almost every single thing you can do, you have *lots* of them.

To help you navigate the maze of privileges, the Edit Privilege Set dialog box (Figure 19-4) is divided into three primary sections:

- In the **Data Access and Design** section, you control access to the data via records and layouts. You also decide what kinds of developer operations the user can perform. For example, can she create new layouts? Or edit your scripts? Create value lists? Numerous dialog boxes and dozens of options live behind the pop-up menus in this section.

- **Other Privileges** includes a block of simple checkboxes controlling access to assorted database-wide features like printing, exporting, and password restrictions.

- The **Extended Privileges** section shows a scrolling list of checkboxes. For the most part, FileMaker adds these to control how you share your data, but you can also add your own custom extended privileges.

You'll learn more about each of these sections in the following pages.

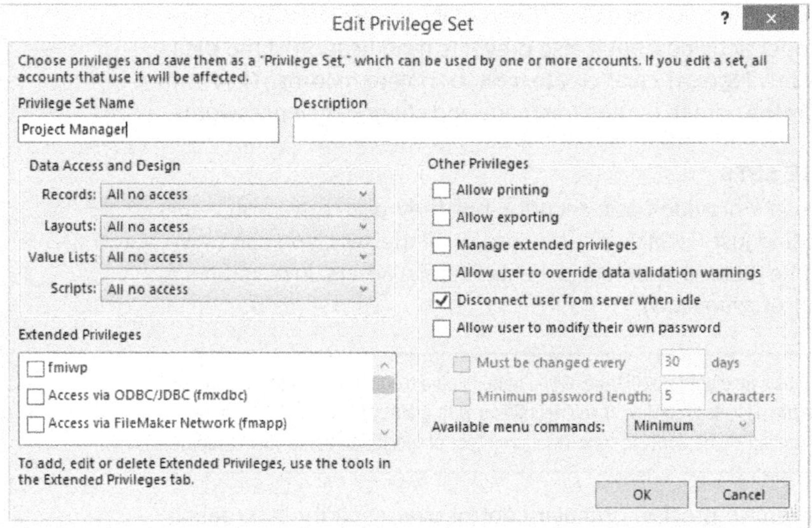

FIGURE 19-4

When you create a new privilege set, you see FileMaker's granularity of control in action. Notice how many things aren't turned on, or say "All no access." You set each privilege one by one, until you've built up a set that's appropriate for the kind of user you have in mind—in this case, a project manager.

TIP Even if you turn a privilege off, a script that's set to run with full access privileges can work around the restriction (page 745).

OTHER PRIVILEGES

With just a set of checkboxes to turn options on or off, the Other Privileges area is the easiest section, so it's a good place to start. Here's where you select basic FileMaker features:

- **Allow printing.** Turn this option on, and the user can print layouts. If it's off, then the Print menu command is grayed out, and the Print script step fails.

- **Allow exporting.** This option lets people access the Export Records command. Again, if it's off, the menu command is grayed out, and the Export Records script step doesn't work. Though the command's name appears to control exporting only, users without this privilege can't import records either.

- **Manage Extended Privileges.** Normally, only accounts with full access can manage security settings. Extended privileges are the exception. You'll learn more in a later section, but if this option is turned on, then people can assign extended privileges to different privilege sets themselves.

- **Allow user to override data validation warnings.** This option is a companion to the "Allow user to override during data entry" option on the Validation tab of the Field Options dialog box, which you can turn on if you want to let people ignore the error message that's displayed if they enter invalid data in the field. But when this privilege is *not* selected, people can't override the errors even when the field options say they should be able to. In other words, this privilege trumps that field option.

- **Disconnect user from FileMaker Server when idle.** This isn't actually a privilege. It's more of an *un-privilege,* and it's turned on when you create a new privilege set. When it's on, people are kicked out of a shared database if they don't use it for a while (you get to decide how long when you configure FileMaker Server). Turn it *off* if you want to give these people the power to stay connected right through their lunch breaks.

- **Allow users to modify their own passwords.** FileMaker lets you implement some typical password management features. First, you get to decide if someone can change his account password at all. If you want to give him this power, then turn this option on. Once it's on, you can choose "Must be changed every" and then enter a number of days to force him to change his password periodically. You can also enforce a minimum password length.

NOTE You want to turn this option off if people *share* accounts in the same database. If you have just one account for each group, for instance, then you don't want one wisenheimer changing the password on everybody else just for laughs.

- **Available menu commands.** Menu commands that users don't have privileges for are always unavailable, so this setting controls the ones you don't control elsewhere in the Edit Privilege Set window. The three levels of available menu commands are "Minimum," "Editing only," and "All." Minimum is the most restrictives and it's the automatic setting for new privilege sets. Choose "Editing only" to give people access only to the Edit menu and basic formatting commands in Browse mode. The All command makes all commands that aren't covered by other settings in this window available.

Creating a Privilege Set

In this chapter, you'll start adding security to your database by creating a privilege set in your Invoice Security database for project managers. PMs set up jobs and create invoices for those jobs, so you'll design a privilege set with appropriate privileges. Since so many steps are involved, this exercise spans several sections.

1. **To create a new privilege set that you'll attach to the "aswartz" account, choose New Privilege Set from the Privilege Set pop-up menu.**

   The Edit Privilege Set dialog box appears.

2. **In the Privilege Set Name box, type *Project Manager,* and in the Description box, type *create and edit jobs, create new invoices.***

   If the privilege set name matches the department name or personnel role, it's a lot easier to apply it later on when you're creating accounts. Use the description to help you remember the basic rules for the set.

3. **Select these checkboxes:**

   • Allow printing

   • Allow user to override data validation warnings

   • Disconnect user from FileMaker Server when idle

   • Allow user to modify their own password

4. **Set the "Available menu" pop-up menu to "Editing only."**

   People can't get into trouble exploring if they can't even open dialog boxes that are above their pay grades.

That's it for the Other Privileges part of the dialog box. But if you leave the Project Manager privilege set with these settings, people still can't do anything very useful. Next, you'll look at the section where all the granularity is hiding, so you can start adding real privileges to the list. Leave the Edit Privilege Set window open while you read through the introductory material below. The next tutorial takes up where the last one left off.

NOTE   You may have noticed there's no checkbox for "Allow user to manage the database" or "Allow user to create tables." Only accounts with full access can open the Manage Database window and use its features. The same goes for the Security window's Accounts and Privilege Sets tabs.

DATA ACCESS AND DESIGN PRIVILEGES

The Edit Privilege Set dialog box's "Data Access and Design" section is where you control access to your specific database elements. Records, Layouts, Value Lists, and Scripts each have pop-up menus where you'll set those privileges. Right now, the Project Manager privilege set doesn't allow access to any of these. To start adding privileges, click the Records pop-up menu. Figure 19-5 shows all your choices.

Record privileges

If the three built-in privilege sets form the first level of granularity in the security system, then the options in this pop-up menu are part of the *second* level. Without much fuss, you can pick one of the accurately named prebuilt options:

- **Create, edit, and delete in all tables** is the level you're accustomed to. People can do anything they want with the records—including delete them all.

- **Create and edit in all tables** is almost as good. It just prevents people from *deleting* records.

- **View only in all tables** is for the folks who just browse your data. They can *see* anything they want, but they can't *change* anything.

- If, for some reason, you want to give somebody access to your *database* but not your *data,* then keep "All no access" selected. This option isn't commonly used, though.

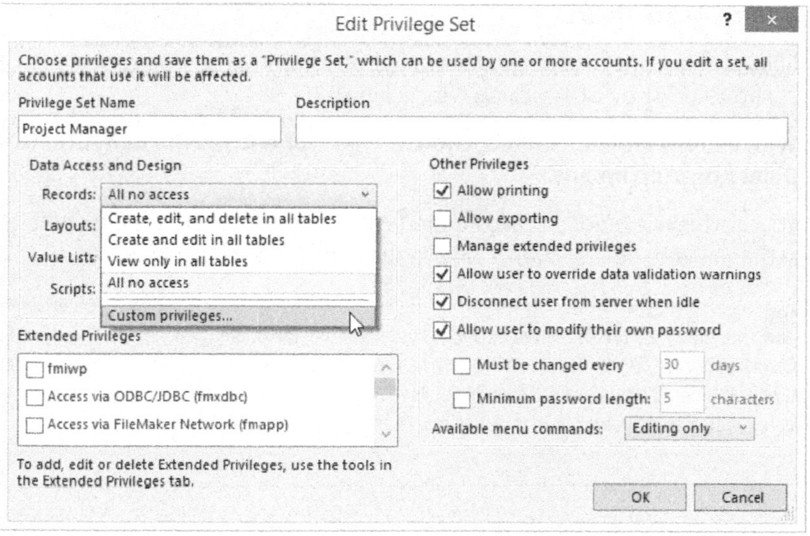

FIGURE 19-5

Here you see the Records pop-up menu in the Edit Privilege Set window. Like privilege sets themselves, you get the default no-access option, a few canned choices, and a custom privileges dialog box. Often, one of the canned choices works just fine, but for the utmost control—like letting people see only the records they've created themselves—you have to dive into custom privileges.

Each of these options applies to *every* record in *every* table. But you may want to let some people "Create, edit, and delete" only in *some* tables, and let them "View only" in others. For instance, you can let part-timers create new customer records, but not tamper with the Payments table. For that kind of control, choose "Custom privilege."

To modify privileges for a particular table, you first have to select it. But don't waste time: You can select *several* tables if you want to and then modify the settings for all of them at once. FileMaker even gives you a Select All button so you can easily make a change to *every* table.

For the Project Manager privilege set, you want to give *at least* View access to every table. PMs should be able to create, edit, and delete records in the Customers, Jobs, Expenses, and Hours tables. Here's how to set that up:

1. **From the Records pop-up menu (under "Data Access and Design"), choose Custom privileges and then click Select All (at the bottom left).**

   FileMaker selects every table in the list. You can apply the same privilege to them all at one time.

2. **From the View pop-up menu, choose "yes."**

   In the View column, the word "yes" appears for every table. Accounts with the Project Manager privilege set can see data in every table in the file.

3. **From the Field Access pop-up menu, choose "all."**

   The word "all" appears in the Field Access column. Now project managers can see the contents of every field in all of the tables.

4. **Click the list to deselect the group. Click the Customers table and then press Shift and click Hours.**

   Shift-clicking selects a continuous range of items in a list. You can select a non-contiguous list by Ctrl-clicking (⌘-clicking).

5. **With all four tables selected, choose "yes" for each of the Edit, Create, and Delete pop-up menus.**

   Your settings should look like Figure 19-6. You'll add more granularity to these settings in the next section, so leave the window open for now.

NOTE   The table list starts out sorted by creation order. Clicking the column headings in the Custom Record Privileges dialog box re-sorts the list. Click the column heading a second time to switch the sort between ascending and descending order. The column head stays highlighted to remind you which sort is in effect. The only way to get back to creation order, though, is to close and reopen the Custom Record Privileges dialog box.

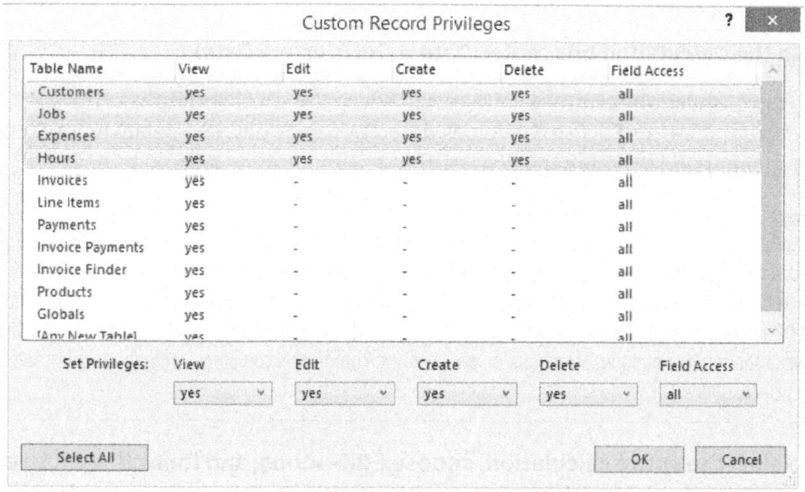

FIGURE 19-6

Now you're starting to see some real granularity. The Custom Record Privileges window lets you control view, edit, create, and delete privileges on each individual table. You can also control exactly which fields people have access to by choosing options from the Field Access pop-up menu.

CREATING RECORD-LEVEL ACCESS

Invoice privileges are a little more complicated. You want project managers to be able to create invoices, but invoices involve multiple tables and processes, which you have to translate into a set of privileges. They need to create invoice records, of course, but they also need to be able to create line item records. And once they've added items to an invoice, they should also be able to edit those items. You decide, however, that they *shouldn't* be able to edit items on invoices from last year. In fact, they probably shouldn't change any invoice that doesn't have today's date. You can handle even a complicated security requirement like this easily in FileMaker: Just add a simple calculation to the mix.

To limit access to individual records, FileMaker lets you use a calculation to decide which ones people can edit. This calculation gives you tremendous control over the security system. You can use data from the record itself, information about the current date, time, or account name, and even global field or global variable values. Your calculation must return a Boolean result: True if the record should be editable, and False if it shouldn't.

Here are the steps to set up the invoice privileges described above:

1. **In the Custom Record Privileges window, select the Invoices table. Then, from the Create pop-up menu, choose Yes.**

   FileMaker puts "yes" in the Create column, meaning that managers with this privilege set can create invoice records. From here on, things get more complicated.

2. **From the Edit pop-up menu, choose "limited."**

You don't want the person to be able to edit *any* invoice record. Instead, you're giving her *limited* edit privileges. Your old friend, the Specify Calculation window, appears.

3. **In the Calculation box, enter *Date ≥ Get(CurrentDate).***

This calculation returns a True result when the invoice date is on or after the current date. It's False for invoices dated before today, so FileMaker lets project managers edit today's invoices or those with a future date.

NOTE This security calculation has a significant weakness: Someone can simply change the date on his computer to bypass the restriction. Luckily, in most cases, a secured multiuser database is shared with FileMaker Server (Chapter 20). When that's the case, you can use a more robust calculation: `Date ≥ GetAsDate (Get(CurrentHostTimeStamp))`. The `Get(CurrentHostTimeStamp)` function gets the date and time from the server computer. Since you, or your IT folks, control this computer, ordinary people can't fiddle with its clock.

4. **Select the entire calculation, choose Edit→Copy, and then click OK to close the Specify Calculation window. (In Windows, the entire menu bar is disabled, limiting the ability to copy and paste in this dialog box.)**

You've copied the calculation so that you can paste it into another privilege calculation. The word "limited" shows in the Edit column for Invoices.

5. **From the Delete pop-up menu, choose Limited.**

The Specify Calculation window returns. This time, you're going to limit the managers' ability to delete invoice records. The rule is the same: They can only delete invoices dated on or after today.

6. **Choose Edit→Paste to use the calculation from step 3 here.**

FileMaker adds the calculation to the Calculation box. Click OK when you're done.

7. **Repeat the above steps for the Line Items table. In this case, though, you want to let managers edit or delete line items when the invoice they're attached to contains today's date. So use the following in steps 3 and 6:**

```
Invoices::Date ≥ Get ( CurrentDate )
```

Project managers at your company have no business creating or editing payments or products, so you can leave Edit, Create, and Delete set to "no" for Invoice Payments, Payments, and Products. You'll add more granularity to these settings in the next section, so leave the window open for now.

NOTE FileMaker shows a "-" instead of the word "no" when you turn off a privilege. The dashes make the denied privileges easier to spot when you're looking at a long list.

■ FIELD-LEVEL ACCESS

The Payments table has a field for Credit Card Number. This type of information falls into the *need-to-know* category: Unless someone *needs* it to do his job, he has no business seeing it. Even though project managers can view payment records, you can still control access to individual *fields* in that table. You're about to exercise field-level granularity:

1. **Select the Payments table and then, from the Field Access pop-up menu, choose limited.**

   The Custom Field Privileges window appears (Figure 19-7). FileMaker offers three field-level privileges: *Modifiable* means people can see *and* edit the field data; *view only* means they can see the information in the field, but can't change it; and *no access* means they can't even see it.

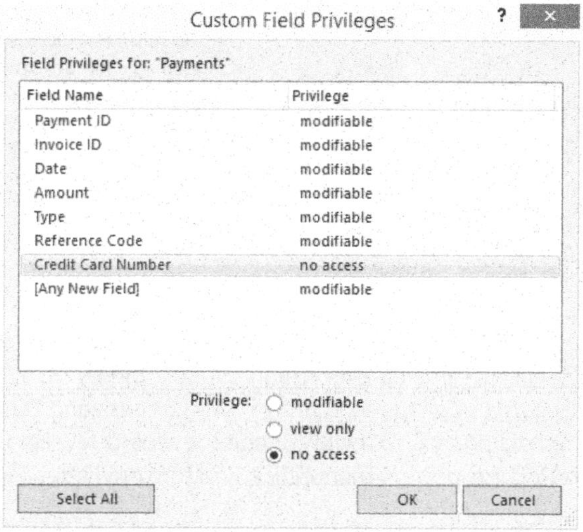

FIGURE 19-7

The Custom Field Privileges window lets you control access to individual fields. Select the fields you want to change and then select one of the Privilege radio buttons. FileMaker dutifully changes every selected field accordingly. Click Select All to quickly select every field.

2. **Click the Credit Card Number field to select it and then choose the "no access" radio button.**

   And indeed, the words "no access" appear in the Privilege column for the selected fields.

3. **Click OK.**

   The Custom Field Privileges window closes, and you can see that Field Access is now limited. Leave the Edit Privilege Set window open; you'll be adding more privileges in the next section.

> **NOTE** Even though the other fields in this list say "modifiable," the entire record isn't editable for this privilege set, so people can't change field data. The table-level security settings trump those at the field level.

The Invoice Finder table has only global fields, so it doesn't need records at all. But you still have to turn on the Edit privilege so the managers can change values in the global fields. Select it and then, from the Edit pop-up menu, choose "yes." When you're finished, your Custom Record Privileges dialog box should look like the one in Figure 19-8.

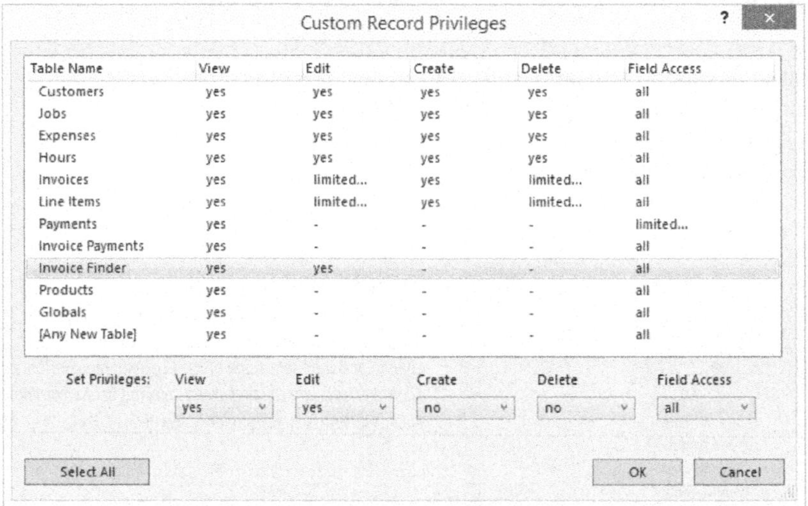

FIGURE 19-8

Project managers have wide-open access to some tables, limited access to others, and view-only access to a few. Notice that if you create a new table, then PMs can view data in all its fields, but they can't edit, create, or delete records. If that's not what you want, you need to edit this privilege set when your database changes. See the box on page 760 for more info.

When you're done looking, click OK to close this dialog box. Because you just made a set of complex choices, FileMaker sums up everything you just did by displaying "Custom privileges" in the Records pop-up menu in the "Data Access and Design" section of the Edit Privilege Set dialog box. To review or edit the record-level or field-level access you've set, in the Records pop-up menu, click "Custom privileges" again.

Any New Anything

The list in each Custom Privileges window has an unusual last item: [Any New Field], [Any New Layout], [Any New Table], [Any New Value List], and [Any New Script]. These privileges refer to any of those elements you create after the privilege set is created, and they all start out turned to "no access." That's right—any new layout, value list, or script you create is automatically unavailable to users with accounts tied to these privilege sets.

Administering security is an ongoing process, and this setting means that you can add a new feature that works perfectly well for you, but not for users whose custom privilege settings haven't been opened up for those new elements. So each time you add an element to your database, remember to select the appropriate custom options for the new element in every privilege set in your database. Yep, it's time-consuming, and you may be tempted to crank those [Any new] privileges up, thinking it'll save work. Often, though, those settings give users *too* many privileges, and it'll come back to bite you later.

Also, there's a downside to using the Select All button to make changes in the custom privileges windows—that button selects the [Any New...] item as well as the "real" items in the list. So if you use the Select All button, you may also need to manually deselect the [Any New] item before you make changes.

Would you ever want to turn these options on intentionally? Maybe. It's fairly common to let users create new value lists, but you have to give them editing privileges on some layouts to apply their new list to a field. You might also create a privilege set for users who are allowed to create report layouts. In that case, you'll need to turn on the "Allow creation of new layouts" option at the top of the Custom Layout Privileges window, along with letting those users modify any new layouts, which includes your new layouts. You'll also have to make sure that they have access to all menu commands, so they can enter layout mode and create new layouts.

But take care when considering whether to give users privileges to create and edit scripts, which is safe only when people know what they're doing. Remember, you can let users create and edit new elements but still keep them from editing *your* elements by setting their custom privileges to "view only."

Layout privileges

If you've been following along in this section, you've given project managers access to data that lets them do their jobs. But if you stop now, then they still can't get very far. They don't have access to any *layouts* yet, and without layouts, a FileMaker database isn't of much use. If someone were to open the database with this privilege set now, she'd see something like Figure 19-9.

FileMaker uses layouts to display your file's data, which means you need to add layout access to your privilege sets. To give people all-important access to the various database layouts, use the Edit Privilege Set window's Layouts pop-up menu:

- **All modifiable** means people can use *and* edit every layout. (Here, "edit" means "Add fields, delete portals, resize parts, and generally manipulate objects on layouts.")

- **All view only** gives people access to data on every layout but doesn't let them change the layouts themselves.

- **All no access** prevents *any* layouts from showing, as shown in Figure 19-9.

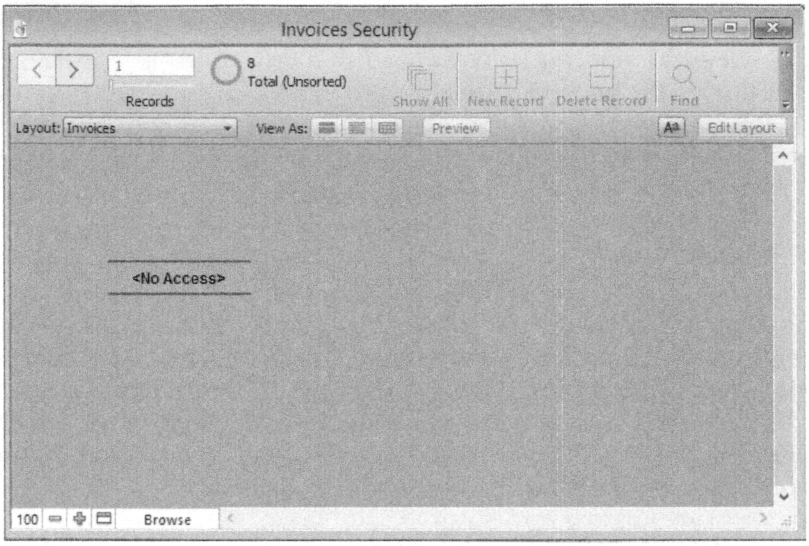

FIGURE 19-9

When people try to view a layout they don't have access to, this blank screen is what they see. FileMaker tries hard to avoid this situation, though; if you haven't already removed the layouts the user can't access from the Layouts pop-up menu, it removes them for you. But one of your scripts can still put users somewhere they don't belong. And in this case, they don't have access to any layout, so FileMaker doesn't have much choice but to show this grayed out layout and an alarming warning.

The final option—Custom Privilege—lets you exercise the greatest control over access to specific layouts. Since layouts are a vehicle for the other database items *on* the layout, you have two distinct layers of privilege:

- **Layout.** These privileges control people's ability to view or edit the layout itself. They're basically the same as the All layout privileges described above, but they apply only to the selected layout. Choose *modifiable* if you want to let people edit the layout (enter Layout mode and then move fields and things around), *view only* if you want them to only see it, and *no access* if you want them to see that gray screen that prompts tech support calls in Figure 19-9 instead.

- **Records via this layout.** Use this option to determine whether or not people should be able to see or edit data in fields on a particular layout. If you make records from the Customer layout "view only," then users can still edit them from the Customer List layout.

NOTE If you want to prevent editing of customer data altogether, it makes more sense to use the record-level privileges instead. The "Records via this layout" setting is available just in case you want to restrict editing from one particular layout, even though the data in the table can be edited elsewhere.

Figure 19-10 shows the Custom Layout Privileges dialog box. This window has something else that didn't exist on the Custom Record Privileges dialog box: The "Allow creation of new layouts" checkbox lets you decide if these people can create their own new layouts. In fact, you can let people who can't even add or edit data create layouts. For example, you might have a whole class of people—the Accounting Department, say—who shouldn't be editing customer records or adding product information, but who need to create monthly and annual reports (read: layouts) *from* that data. See the box on "Any New Anything" for more info.

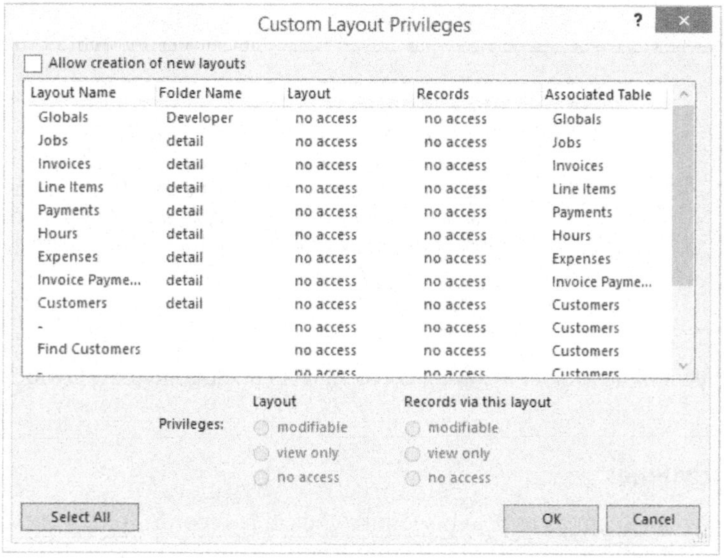

FIGURE 19-10

The Custom Layout Privileges window looks a lot like its records counterpart. You get a list of layouts and some privilege choices. As usual, select the layout (or layouts) first and then make changes. This window's columns can help you set up privileges. For example, you may have hundreds of layouts, and a layout's name alone isn't enough; seeing the layout folder name can help you remember which layout you're looking at.

In the current example, you want project managers to be able to use any layout (and edit records through them). But you also want them to be able to create their own layouts in case they need to do some custom reporting. These new layouts should, of course, be editable. Here's how to set Layout privileges for the project manager privilege set in *Invoice Security.fmp12*:

1. **In the Edit Privilege Set window, choose "All view only" from the Layouts pop-up menu.**

   You intend to make custom privilege settings, but when you first visit the Custom Layout Privileges dialog box, everything is turned off. Since you want most options on, save your wrist by choosing "All view only." FileMaker turns them all on for you. In the next step, you'll just turn a few options off.

2. **From the Layouts pop-up menu, choose "Custom privileges."**

   The Custom Layout Privileges window appears. Every layout, including the [Any New Layout] item, is set to "view only" with "modifiable" records.

3. **At the top of the window, select "Allow creation of new layouts" and then, in the layout list, select the [Any New Layout] item.**

   You may have to scroll down to see it, as it's always at the bottom of the list.

4. **Under Layout, select the "modifiable" radio button.**

   Turning this setting on tells FileMaker you want new layouts to be modifiable. Click OK when you're done. See Figure 19-11 to see the warning you'll get if you forget this option.

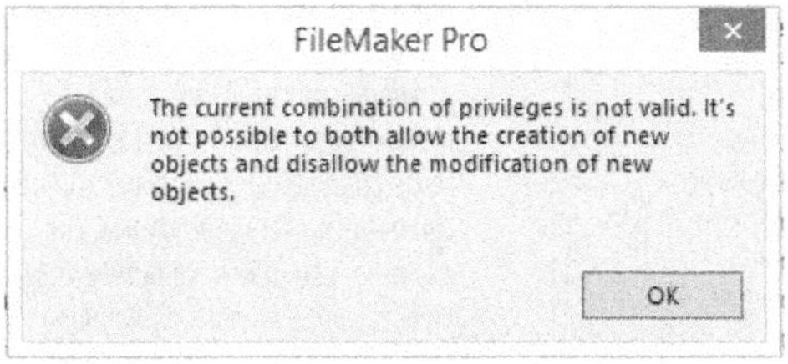

FIGURE 19-11

If you select "Allow creation of new layouts" without making new layouts modifiable, then FileMaker complains that it doesn't make sense to let someone make a new layout she can't edit. You can't close the window until the privileges do match one another. Either turn off "Allow creation of new layouts" or make [Any New Layout] modifiable.

Now, anybody with the Project Manager privilege set can edit any new layouts she creates.

Value list privileges

Value lists may not seem as critical a security choice as records and layouts, but since value lists help people enter consistent data, you want to pay attention to these choices. If you put a pop-up menu on a field to limit data input, but give people the ability to modify the value list underlying the pop-up menu, then they can circumvent your control.

You can see the Custom Value List Privileges window in Figure 19-12. This window lets you assign any of three privileges to each value list: modifiable, view only, or no access. You can also let somebody create new value lists with an "Allow creation of new value lists" checkbox, and set the privileges to be assigned to any new value lists.

You can control access to value lists in much the same way you manage record and layout privileges. And like record and layout privileges, you have three canned choices in the pop-up menu, plus Custom privileges:

- **All modifiable** means people can use and edit every value list.

- **All view only** lets people only see and select from your value lists, but not change them.

- **All no access** prevents people from seeing value lists at all.

- **Custom privileges** gives you a dialog box where you can create your own set of privileges.

In the business rules you're applying to your database, project managers should have view-only access to all value lists, so, from the Value Lists pop-up menu, choose "All view only."

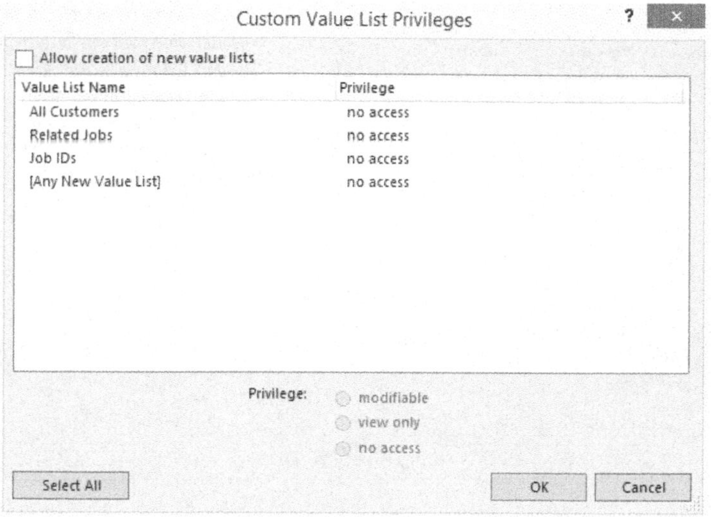

FIGURE 19-12

The Custom Value List Privileges window is even simpler than the Custom Layout Privileges version. It works just like the others: Select a value list or two and then choose a privilege as appropriate.

NOTE If you select all value lists in the dialog box and then make them "view only" there, then your settings say "Custom privileges," which may be confusing down the road.

The Value List access you assign to a privilege set overrides layout designs. That is, even if you set up a pop-up menu with the option of "Include 'Edit' item to allow editing of value list," then people with the Project Manager's privilege set can't edit values in the list.

Script privileges

The final option under "Data Access and Design" lets you control access to your scripts. As with layouts, you can have a class of people who can create new scripts but can't edit data. If it's the accountants mentioned in the example on page 763, they need to write scripts to run the reports on the layouts you're letting them create. You could also create a privilege set that lets people at one level run most scripts, but doesn't let them run certain scripts that do destructive activities like deleting sets of records. You could save those scripts for higher-level accounts instead. Figure 19-13 shows the control choices you have.

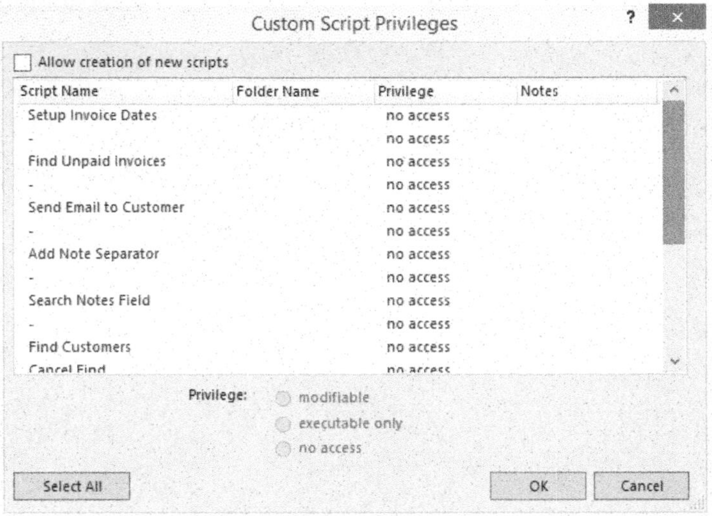

Custom Script Privileges   ? ☒

☐ Allow creation of new scripts

Script Name	Folder Name	Privilege	Notes	⌃
Setup Invoice Dates		no access		
-		no access		
Find Unpaid Invoices		no access		
-		no access		
Send Email to Customer		no access		
-		no access		
Add Note Separator		no access		
-		no access		
Search Notes Field		no access		
-		no access		
Find Customers		no access		
Cancel Find		no access		⌄

Privilege: ○ modifiable
               ○ executable only
               ○ no access

[Select All]   [OK] [Cancel]

FIGURE 19-13

The Folder Name column refers to the organizer folders you can create in the Manage Script window (page 458). The Notes column tells you when a script is set to "Run with full access privileges." You'll learn about this later in this chapter.

Again, the pop-up menu gives you three canned choices and a custom option:

- **All modifiable** means people can run *and* edit any script.
- **All executable only** lets folks *run* scripts, but not edit them.
- **All no access** keeps people from running any scripts at all.
- **Custom privileges** brings up the now-familiar Custom Privileges dialog box.

Here's how to choose the script settings for your Project Manager privilege set:

1. **From the Scripts pop-up menu, choose "All executable only."**

   With this change, you've finished creating your privilege set. Your window should look just like Figure 19-14.

2. **Click OK to close the Edit Privilege Set window.**

   FileMaker adds Project Manager to the list of privilege sets in the Manage Security window.

For the final tweak in the Project Manager privilege set, read about Extended Privileges on page 771. They determine how users can connect to your shared database (the most common setup option is "fmapp," which lets project managers open a database shared on FileMaker Server). In the past few tutorials, you created all the set's privileges. But you don't have to create everything in the same session. At any time, you can click OK to close all the Security windows and then return to regular work. FileMaker will remember the settings you have chosen and then you can resume setting up options later. But when you click OK to close the Manage Security window, you'll have to enter an account and password that has Full Access privileges. Since you haven't changed that account yet, use "admin" as the Account name and leave the password field blank—that's the not-so-secret "admin" account and password in every file. Read page 187 to learn how to change the default account.

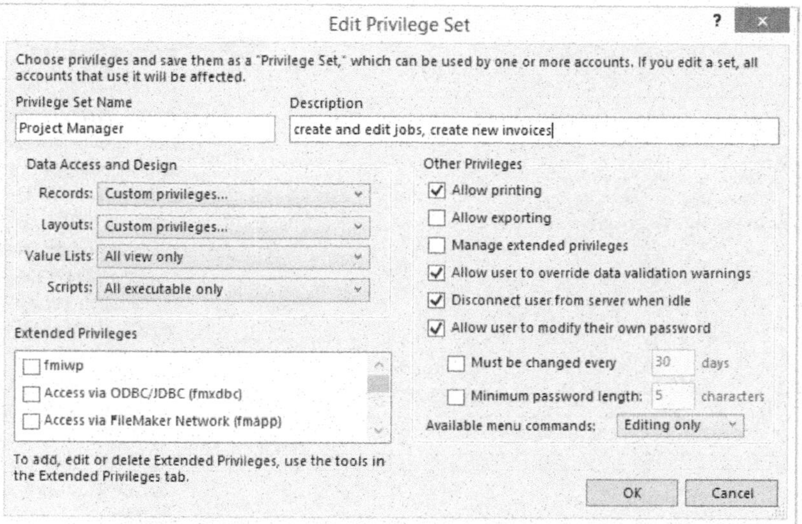

FIGURE 19-14

When your privilege set is finished, it looks like this. You have so much detail there that you can't see all your settings in one screen, but the "…" in the Records and Layouts pop-up menus lets you know there's more detail to be seen if you need it. Just choose the appropriate pop-up menu if you need to review or edit.

NOTE When you give an element—a record, field, layout, value list, or script—the "All no access" setting, it disappears from the user's view. Scripts disappear from the Scripts menu, layouts from the Layouts pop-up menu, fields from sort dialog boxes, and records from lists and portals. That way, people aren't tempted to run a script or go to a layout to which they don't have access.

◼ EDITING A PRIVILEGE SET

If you need to make changes to a privilege set later (maybe you've added new fields, layouts, or scripts to the database, and you have to make sure all your privilege sets give each group its proper access), just come back to this window, select the privilege set you need from the list, and then click Edit. You see the Edit Privilege Set window again, and you're free to change anything you want.

You can't edit FileMaker's built-in privilege sets. To change a set, duplicate it first and then change the duplicate. Remember, though, that you can't duplicate [Full Access].

Using Detailed Setup

Throughout this chapter, you've been using the Basic Setup in the Manage Security window. It's a simplified approach that's designed to let you add one or two new accounts, or to create one privilege set at a time. But there's another view of your security with more detail. It gives you an overview of your settings, and is better suited for the initial setup of your security when you're creating lots of privilege sets, and only a few basic accounts for testing each privilege set. Also, there are some tasks, like creating extended privileges and setting file access, that you can only do in this view. To see it, click Use Detailed Setup at the bottom left of the Manage Security window. A tabbed window appears (Figure 19-15).

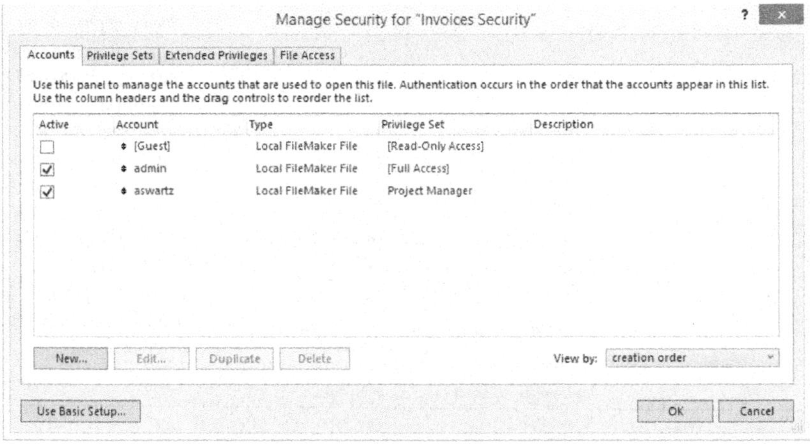

FIGURE 19-15

The Detailed Setup for Manage Security has four tabs: Accounts, Privilege Sets, Extended Privileges, and File Access. The Accounts tab is active by default. As in Basic Setup, you see a list of all the file's accounts, but in a more tabular arrangement, with columns for the account name, type, privilege set, and description. A checkbox to the left of each account lets you make them active or inactive.

The Privilege Set tab in Detailed Setup is similar to the list on the Accounts tab. This tab is the only place where you can see all your privilege sets. By default, they're sorted by creation order, with the default ones at the top. There are columns for Privilege Set name, Active Accounts assigned to each set, and Description. Check Figure 19-16 to see the Privilege Set tab.

Once you've clicked the Detailed Setup button, the Manage Security window always open in detail view. If you want to switch back to Basic View, click the Use Basic Setup button. You'll learn about the other two tabs—Extended Privileges and File Access—later in this chapter.

External Authentication

If you work for an organization that uses Windows Active Directory or Open Directory in Mac OS X, then you can take advantage of the fact that your coworkers *already* log in to their computers each morning. Since everybody already has a company-wide user name and password, you can use *external authentication,* which tells FileMaker to hand off the chore of identifying people to one of those other services. This setup has two advantages. First, you can save yourself the trouble of creating scads of accounts in all your database files. And when your IT department creates a new user, or removes someone who's left the company, access to FileMaker is automatically adjusted as well. Additionally, in Windows, your users can take advantage of Single

Sign-on: They don't have to enter a password to access FileMaker if they're already logged in to their computers with their own user names and passwords.

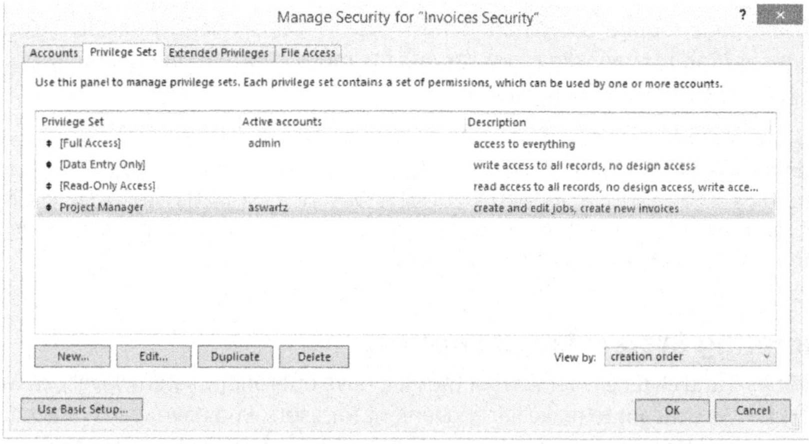

FIGURE 19-16

The Privilege Sets tab gives you an overview of all the privilege sets in a file. Buttons along the bottom let you create new sets, or edit, duplicate, and delete existing ones. (Remember that you can't delete the default privilege sets, though.) The "View by" pop-up menu lets you sort the list. To arrange the sets in a custom order, drag the arrows to the left of the sets' names.

Since these external accounts aren't actually stored in FileMaker, you don't need to add the accounts themselves to your database. Instead, you tell FileMaker which *groups* in the external system should be granted access. For example, if your Windows Active Directory already has a group for Accounting and another for Customer Service, you can tell FileMaker what privileges people in each of these groups have.

If you don't have appropriate groups in the external system, then you can have the system administrator add a new group (or several new groups) just for you. You can then assign a privilege set to each group that should be given access, and the system administrator assigns individual people to each group.

To assign a privilege set to an external group, you create a single account in File-Maker. But instead of entering a user name and password, from the "Account is authenticated via" pop-up menu, choose External Server. The Account Name and Password boxes disappear, and a new Group Name box appears instead. Just type the name of the Active Directory or Open Directory group in this box.

You can set up external authentication in two ways, but both require a working directory server and FileMaker Server (see Chapter 20):

- **Local accounts on your FileMaker server.** You can manage account names and passwords on the server itself and have them apply to every database. This method saves you the trouble of creating individual FileMaker accounts in every file.

• **Domain accounts.** FileMaker Server communicates with the directory server on your company's network to authenticate users. This approach centralizes account management *and* lets people log in with the same account names and passwords they use for every other computer system on your network.

Both methods require coordination with your IT department. Consult IT (or the documentation for your directory server) for more information on setting up and maintaining external authentication.

> **NOTE** You're free to use a mixture of normal FileMaker accounts and external authentication accounts. In fact, you *must* have at least one full-access FileMaker account in every file. If you need to extend access to someone who's not in the directory server, then you can add a FileMaker account for that person, too. People from the directory server can log in, and so can this special person.

Operating System Login Support

Windows 8 and all recent versions of the Mac have operating system–level password savers that are meant to make life convenient for users who have scads of accounts to remember. On Windows the program is called Credential Manager. On the Mac, it's called Keychain Access.

With these programs, you don't need to use external authentication to let users bypass the password dialog box. Each user controls whether or not to add each program's account to a password saver. The operating system adds an option to add the account to the manager the first time you log into an app or file that has security. Most security experts don't approve of these types of password savers, since when they're enabled, anybody who sits in front of a computer can open any program, file, or database that uses them. It's not good practice to use an OS password-managing utility if you're storing sensitive data unless the computer also requires you to log in at startup and after a short period of inactivity. Really picky security experts won't accept even a short period of inactivity. They require you to explicitly log out (or switch to a password-protected screen saver) if you go grab lunch or a cup of coffee.

Because this is a potential security risk, you can suppress the option to let users save their account names and passwords to their keychain programs. Choose File→File Options to see the File Options window (Figure 19-17).

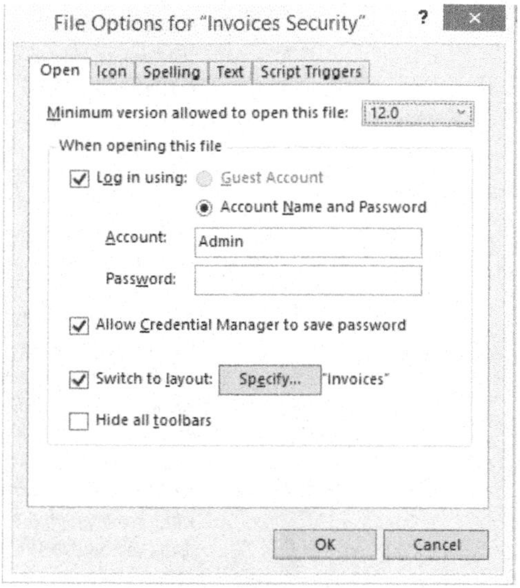

FIGURE 19-17

Turn off the "Allow Credential Manager to save password" option to make sure users actually log in to your file instead of letting their operating system's password manager handle FileMaker security. If you're viewing the window on a Mac, the option reads: "Allow Keychain Access to save password." The outcome is the same.

▊ Extended Privileges

Extended privileges come in two flavors. A set of standard extended privileges lets you determine how people and some technologies, like web publishing and ODBC/JDBC access, are allowed to interact with shared databases. Even if you aren't using those technologies, you must tell each privilege set the ways they're allowed to access the file. For example, if you're creating a database where most of your users are using a web browser out in the field to connect to your FileMaker Server shared files, you have to give them an extended privilege that lets them connect via WebDirect. Even the folks who work from the office must have access via FileMaker Network, if you're using FileMaker Server. You can see the complete list of privileges in Figure 19-18.

TIP   The only situation in which you don't need to include at least one extended privilege in a privilege set is if each of your users have their own copy of the database. This isn't a common setup. Forgetting to turn on the "fmapp" extended privilege on is the most common reason users can't see a shared database even though you *can* see FileMaker Server on the network.

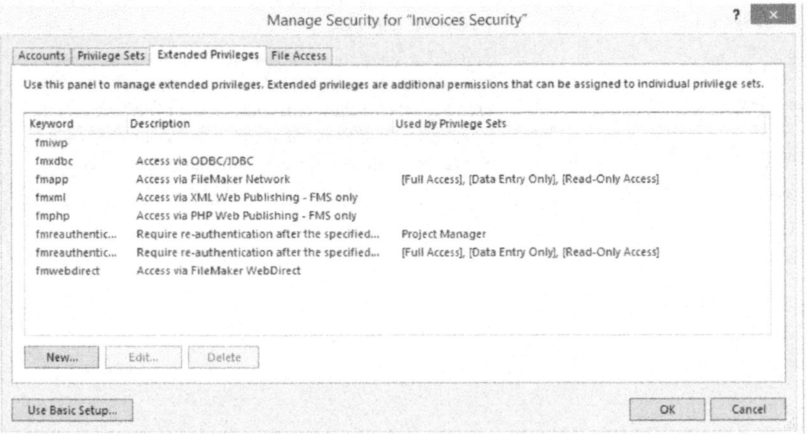

FIGURE 19-18

The Extended Privileges tab shown lists the default privileges that come with every FileMaker database file. There are three columns: The first column, Keyword, is used internally by the server to help track all the various connections it's hosting; the middle column, Description, tells you what the extended privilege does; and the right column, "Used by Privilege Sets," tells you which privilege sets use each extended privilege.

You can also create custom extended privileges of your own, using the Extended Privileges tab of the Manage Security dialog box. These custom extended privileges don't actually add any capability on their own. But using scripts, you can check to see whether the active privilege set has an extended privilege before you let anyone do anything important or irreversible. The next section takes you through one example.

Creating an Extended Privilege

Suppose you've decided to let project managers delete records directly, and you give them that power in their privilege set. When other people try to delete a customer record, you want FileMaker to *flag* the record instead, so that a manager can find and delete the flagged records later. To automate the process, you write a Delete script that checks for the new extended privilege before deleting the records. Here's how to set up the extended privileges in *Invoice Security.fmp12* so you can use them in the script.

1. **Open the Manage Security window, and if necessary, click the Use Detailed Setup button.**

   Extended privileges can only be managed in Detailed Setup.

2. **Click the Extended Privileges tab and then click New.**

   You see the Edit Extended Privilege window on your screen (Figure 19-19). This extended privilege controls a user's ability to delete customer records.

3. **Type *Delete customer records directly* in the Description box. For the keyword, type *delcust* as an abbreviation. While you're here, turn on the checkbox next to [Full Access].**

   For now, only those people with full access can delete customer records. You'll write and test an extended-privileges-checking script before you add the extended privilege to the Project Manager privilege set.

4. **Click OK to close all dialog boxes.**

You aren't prompted for full-access credentials because you didn't edit any accounts.

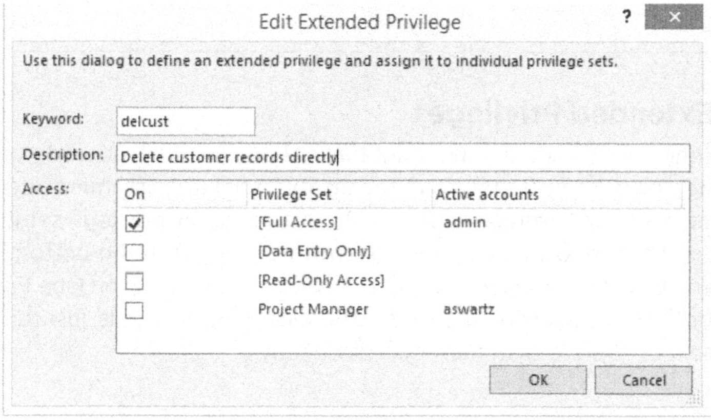

FIGURE 19-19

The Edit Extended Privilege window lets you give your extended privilege a keyword and a description. The description should say what the extended privilege is for. The keyword can be any few characters you want; it's what you'll look for in your scripts, so if you change it later, the script will break. Activate an extended privilege for one or more privilege sets by clicking the appropriate checkboxes.

Checking for an Extended Privilege

To use this new custom extended privilege, you need to write a script that checks to see if the user has access to it. Use the Get(AccountExtendedPrivileges) function to ask FileMaker for the list of extended privileges turned on for the active privilege set (in other words, the privilege set assigned to the account name the user opened the file with). The script checks to see if this list includes "delcust," and takes the appropriate action. While creating this script, you need to add a new text field called DeleteFlag to the Customers table. You can see the finished script in Figure 19-20.

Try out your script by running it from the Customers layout. Your [Full Access] account should delete the customer record, since you have the [Full Access] privilege set. Close the database and then open it again. This time, log in as someone assigned the Project Manager privilege set (you may need to create a new account or just assign the privilege set to an existing account). Project Manager *doesn't* have the "delcust" extended privilege turned on, so when you run the script this time, it sets the DeleteFlag field instead of deleting the record.

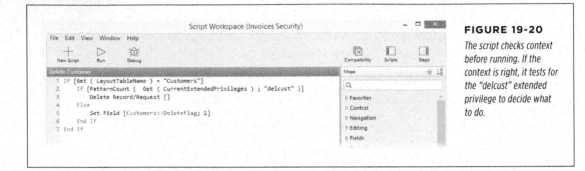

FIGURE 19-20

The script checks context before running. If the context is right, it tests for the "delcust" extended privilege to decide what to do.

Assigning Extended Privileges

You have an extended privilege, and the script that checks the privilege works properly. The final step gives project managers the ability to delete customers directly. You have two options: First, you can edit the Project Manager privilege set itself. The Edit Privilege Set window has a list of extended privileges in the bottom-left corner, where you can control which extended privileges are turned on (see Figure 19-21). To give project managers the power to delete customer records, just turn on the checkbox next to "Delete customer records directly."

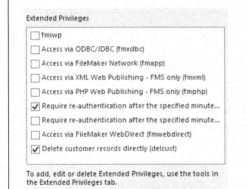

FIGURE 19-21

The list of extended privileges at the bottom left of the Edit Privilege Set window shows every extended privilege in the database, with a checkbox beside each one. If you turn one of these checkboxes on, then you're giving this privilege set access to everything controlled by that extended privilege.

If you have a few privilege sets that need the same extended privilege, there's a faster method: Go to the Manage Security window's Extended Privileges tab and then edit the "delcust" extended privilege instead. This way, you see all the Privilege Sets in a list. In the Edit Extended Privilege window, you can turn the extended privilege off or on for any privilege set by clicking the checkboxes in the list of privilege sets.

To test the "delcust" extended privilege, turn it on for the Project Manager privilege set and then close the database. Then open it, log in as a project manager, and run the Delete Customer script. This time it deletes the customer right away.

■ Managing External File Access

FileMaker databases can take table occurrences (TOs) from other files and then use that data almost as if it "lives" in the local file. And some design functions can glean information about your file's data and metadata, even when a user doesn't have full access privileges. To prevent these types of unauthorized access to data, you can create lots of record-level and individual script access privileges to keep those external reference folks from viewing and editing data remotely. Sometimes, even if you do create restrictions in your file, motivated folks using external file references can gain access to your information. So if you have a database that contains sensitive data, you can use FileMaker Pro's File Access protection. It lets you give only certain files access to a protected database.

File Access works by creating a special authorization token as part of the External Date Source. So even if a hacker tries to create a new file with the same name as the one you've authorized, it won't work. There are a few caveats, though. You can't set up File Access protection for a file that's being hosted by FileMaker Server. Instead, open the file on your local computer to protect it and then put the file back on the server. Also, turning on File Access protection doesn't lock out files that are *already* linked to the file you want to protect. And you have to be the only user of the file when you restrict external access. Finally, to turn on File Access protection, you must have full access privileges in both the file you want to protect and the file you want to authorize. Here's how to restrict external access to a file:

1. **In the *Invoices Security.fmp12* file, choose File→Manage Security and then select the File Access tab.**

   You must use Detailed Setup view to see this tab. Add each external file you want to authorize in this window's list.

2. **Turn on the "Require full access privileges to create references to this file" checkbox.**

   The Authorize button becomes available.

3. **Click Authorize.**

   A standard Open window appears.

4. **Browse to and select the *Access.fmp12* sample file you downloaded earlier (that's the one you'll authorize) and then click Open.**

   The file's login window appears.

NOTE Use the Remote button if the file you need is shared using FileMaker Server. You can *authorize* shared files for access to file you're protecting, but you can't activate internal protection for shared files.

5. **Enter a Full Access account name and password.**

   The account name and password for this sample file are both *access* (not great for security, but suitable for testing). The account name and password don't have to match the protected file's account name and password. However, both accounts need to have full access to authorize any file. When you enter appropriate account info, the file name, date and time you authorized the file, and the account name you used to authorize it appear in the list (Figure 19-22).

6. **Click OK and then, when you're prompted, enter a Full Access account name and password for the protected file.**

   You're done setting up File Access for the Access file.

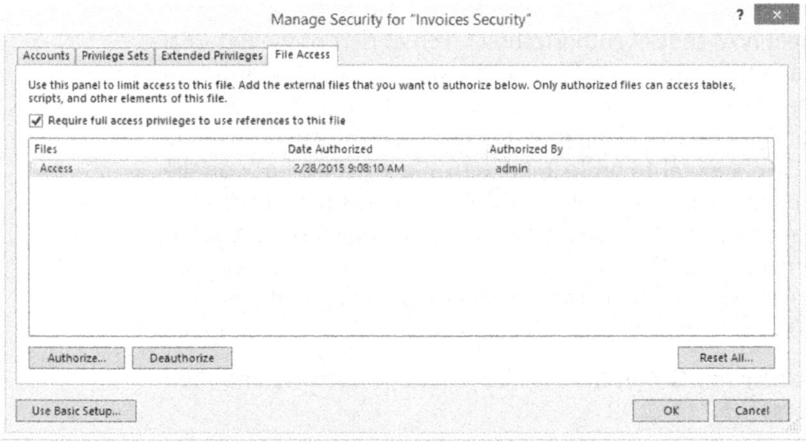

FIGURE 19-22

When a file is protected from external access, unauthorized files can't be used to sneak into a file. Without this protection, anyone with access privileges to a file can sneak around older privileges to create external references and use design functions, like ValueListItems() *or* ScriptNames(), *to get metadata about your database.*

In a closed system (one where several FileMaker databases work together), you may want to authorize other files in the protected database. Or another file (or set of files) may need its own list of authorized files. You don't have to authorize all the files in a system with one another, though. As with the rest of your security settings, take the pessimistic approach and authorize only the files that specifically need access to protected databases. You can always add more access later.

To test the *Invoice Security.fmp12* database's File Access settings, close it and *make sure all your database windows are closed*. If you open a protected database with a [Full Access] account and then leave it open on your computer, another user could sneak into your office while you're away and authorize a file without knowing the proper account information. So if your databases contain sensitive data, take all normal precautions: Close files when you leave your office, lock your door, and so on. And make sure protected files are closed when you're testing access. If you don't, you could accidentally authorize another file without noticing, so get in the habit of closing the files before you test your new access setting.

Now open a nonauthorized file (use the *No Access.fmp12* sample file: Account Name and Password are both "noaccess") and try to create a table occurrence from *Invoices Security.fmp12* on the *No Access.fmp12* Relationships graph. You see the standard login dialog box. The only way out of the Specify Table dialog box is to click Cancel or to enter a full access account name and password. If you enter valid information for an account that doesn't have full access, you'll see a warning like the one in Figure 19-23.

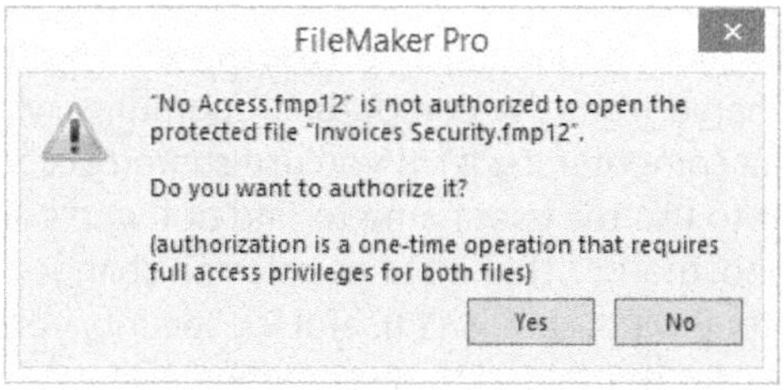

FIGURE 19-23

Even if a file is authorized for access to a protected file, you have to enter a full access account name and password before creating a TO from the protected file. You see this message when you first try to create a TO and again if you enter an account without full access privileges.

NOTE   The wording in the File Access dialog box is a little confusing. You can still create an EDS reference (page 620) to a protected file from an unauthorized file without a full-access password, but you can't create a TO from it, or use design functions to grab data from the file.

Now open the authorized file (*Access.fmp12*—account name and password are both "access"). Again, enter a full-access password for the Invoice file. This time, enter the account name and password you set up in the steps on page 745. Ta-da! Your authorized file can create TOs and then work with the flle's external data normally.

■ Scripts and Security

Security and script-writing intersect in two areas. First, you need to take into account the level of access people have, and whether or not your scripts override some or all of their privileges. Second, FileMaker lets you automate some of the security features described earlier in this chapter with scripting. A handful of script steps are dedicated to security-related tasks, and this section shows you how to use them.

Detecting Privileges in a Script

The first way to handle security in your scripts is to deal with it directly. In the last section, you learned how to check for extended privileges and take appropriate actions. If you want, then you can check for specific privilege sets, or even specific account names:

- To check the privilege set, use the Get(AccountPrivilegeSetName) function. It returns the name of the privilege set assigned to the current user. Bear in mind that if you change the name of a privilege set, then you have to modify any scripts that use this function.

- If you need to restrict an action to a particular account, then use Get(AccountName) instead. As you probably expect, it returns the name of the account with which the user logged in. The same warning applies here: Beware of renamed accounts.

NOTE If someone logged in with external authentication, then Get(AccountName) gives you her real account name in the external directory server.

- Finally, FileMaker has one more tempting function: Get (UserName). This function normally returns the user name from the computer's operating system (the name you use to log into the computer itself). If you use shared accounts in FileMaker, then you may want to use the user name to find out who's actually doing something. Bear in mind, though, that most people can change their user name settings to anything they want, so it isn't useful for security-related purposes because it's easy for a user to pretend to be someone else.

You can easily use these functions, but they have some drawbacks. Chances are that, at some point in the future, you'll need to change the account names, privilege sets, or users who can do certain things. Every time you do, you have to check and probably edit all your scripts.

If you want to secure a scripted process, then the extended privilege feature described on page 771 is safer and lets you update accounts and privilege sets much more easily.

Handling Security Errors

If your script tries to do something the person isn't allowed to do, then FileMaker shows the error message in Figure 19-24. If you turn error capture on in your script, then this error doesn't show on the screen. Instead, you can use the Get(LastError) function to check for an error. That way, you can have the script display a custom message box, email you the name of the misbehaving person, or take some other action. The most common security-related error is number 200: "Record Access is Denied." (If you're interested in learning more about error codes, check out the resources in Appendix D.)

Granting Full Access Privileges

Sometimes you *want* the script to do its duty even though the user doesn't have the necessary privileges. For example, you may want to remove an accountant's ability to delete invoice records since she's not supposed to delete any orders. But you may still want to let her run a script that finds old completed invoices, exports them to an archive and then deletes them. Since this script is careful to delete only invoices that are ready to go, the accountant can safely run it when necessary.

FIGURE 19-24

*When someone tries something your security setup doesn't allow,
he sees this message—even if it's a script that's breaking the rules.
Unfortunately, FileMaker doesn't tell him—or you—what the script is
trying to do.*

For those kinds of circumstances, FileMaker lets you specify when a script should run with full access privileges for *anyone*. In other words, the script overrides the normal restrictions you set up in the user's privilege set. Right-click (Ctrl-click) on a script to show the context-sensitive menu, and then choose the Grant Full Access Privileges command. With this option turned on, the script dutifully deletes the invoices even though the accountant running it isn't allowed to delete records in the Invoice or Line Item tables with her account's privilege set.

Even when you set a script to run with full access privileges in this way, you can still prevent some folks from running it by switching it to "no access" in the Custom Script Privileges window for a privilege set. You can also make the script check for an extended privilege and then take appropriate actions for different people.

Managing Security with Scripts

The Steps pane of the Script Workspace has an entire section called Accounts. It includes six steps that give you some control over the security system from your scripts. All these steps require full access privileges to work. If you don't manage a lot of accounts in your database, then you might not find much use for these steps. But if you have a large organization, or one that has lots of turnover—like a school system that's constantly adding new teachers or graduating a whole class of students who no longer need access to databases for classwork—these script steps can save tons of time and effort.

■ ADD ACCOUNT

FileMaker lets you add new accounts to a database from a script—and for good reason. If you build a system that uses several databases, and you can't use external authentication, then the Add Account step is your best friend. Instead of adding each account to all your files manually, try this: Write a script that asks for the account name and password with a custom dialog box, and stores them in global fields. Then use scripts in each file to add the same account to every file at once. When you're all done, be sure to clear the password from the global field to protect it from prying eyes.

Or, if you have to populate your brand-new file with a huge number of people when you're first installing your database, then you save tons of time creating accounts if you have an electronic list of user names and passwords. Import them (page 880) into a table and then use a looping script to create hundreds of accounts in a few seconds.

> **TIP** The Add Account step lets you specify the account name and password by using calculations, but you have to select a specific privilege set for all users in the loop. If you want to script the creation of accounts with different privilege sets, use the If/Else If steps and several copies of the Add Account step, each with a different privilege set selected.

■ DELETE ACCOUNT

If you're going to create accounts with a script, why not delete them, too? The Delete Account script needs only an account name—and you can supply it with a calculation. With this script, you can build the other half of your multifile account-management system.

> **WARNING** If you write a script that adds or deletes accounts, then pay special attention to its security settings. You can all too easily give a database the tightest security FileMaker allows and then leave a gaping security hole through a script. Customize privilege sets so that only you (or a trusted few) can run the script, and *don't* put it on the Scripts menu.

■ RESET ACCOUNT PASSWORD

If lots of people use your database, then forgotten passwords will undoubtedly become your worst nightmare. You could spend all day changing passwords for people. Why not write a script that can reset a password to something generic and then email it to the person? If you set the script to run with full access privileges, then you can even delegate password resetting to someone else. The Reset Account Password step needs an account name and a new password to do its job.

■ CHANGE PASSWORD

You'll probably use this script step only in cases where you're creating a special layout that lets people who don't have full access privileges manage security. For example, you may have someone on staff who should be able to manage accounts, but you don't want him to have full access privileges. So you can build a special layout (or two), and write scripts that run with full access privileges to manage all your security tasks. That way, you can even do special workarounds like allowing some members of a privilege set to change their passwords without giving this power to each of them. To do so, you usually need a user's table with a field that controls who can and can't run your Change Password script.

ENABLE ACCOUNT

Once you've created a bunch of new accounts using the Add Account step, the Enable Account step lets you turn them on and off at will. That way, you can create accounts for, say, an entire class of students, and later turn on accounts for those who've arrived on campus. This step sets the appropriate Account Status, and it works only when there's a valid account name that matches your script settings.

RE-LOGIN

The most useful step (for you, as the developer) in the Accounts section is Re-Login. It provides a function that doesn't exist anywhere else in FileMaker. It lets you switch to a different account without closing the file, which makes testing security settings a lot more convenient. Instead of opening and closing the files until your mouse button wears out, just run a Re-Login script. Add steps in the script that set global fields on pertinent layouts to Get(AccountName) and Get(AccountPrivilegeSetName) so you can keep track of what you're testing as you re-login over and over. To get the most realistic testing conditions, make sure your Re-Login script calls any script that runs when your file opens.

You can also use Re-Login when someone inevitably calls you to his desk to show you a problem in the database. Just re-login as an account with full access and then you can poke around and find out what's happening *on his computer*. When you re-login, you're not just saving time by not closing and reopening the file: You can actually work in the same window, on the same record, with the same found set and sort order without all the trouble of recreating the situation back at your desk.

> **TIP** If you have a login script that changes that setup, you usually don't want that process running when you troubleshoot. So turn on Script Debugger before you run the Re-Login script. Then skip over the parts of the login script that would change that all-important setup.

Just make sure don't leave the file open with your super-privileges when you're done. Either close the file entirely, or run the Re-Login script and let the user enter his login information. Since you can re-login only from a script, most developers add a Re-Login script to the Scripts menu in every database they create. It does no harm to leave the Re-Login script available to users if they only know one account name and password. That way, it's available to you from the menu even while they're logged in with lesser privileges than yours.

Sharing Data Using FileMaker Server

U p to this point, you've been learning how to create a database that works for you and your users. But you haven't learned how to let all your users connect to the file at the same time. For that, you have to *share* your database file. But before you dive in, you need to consider where you're going to keep the shared file and how people connect to it. You can choose from three main types of sharing: FileMaker Network, FileMaker Server, and Internet sharing. Internet sharing comes in two versions—Custom Web Publishing and the new WebDirect, which lets users with FileMaker Go (those who have an iOS device) or a browser (everybody else) connect to your database. Chapter 21 deals with Internet and FileMaker Go sharing, but in this chapter you'll learn about how to share your database with people who are using FileMaker Pro on your local network. You have two options:

- **FileMaker Network.** This type of file sharing is also called *peer-to-peer*—you don't use a server or any special software. You share files by using ordinary computers. Peer-to-peer sharing is limited to five users at once. Everyone using a computer to access the files will need a copy of FileMaker Pro or FileMaker Pro Advanced.

- **FileMaker Server.** This is the preferred method for database sharing, even if you have fewer than five users. FileMaker Server offers protection for your files in case of a crash, automated backups, and tremendous speed and stability boosts over peer-to-peer sharing. Theoretically, you can have an unlimited number of FileMaker Pro users connected to a FileMaker Server-hosted database at one time. In the real world, 250 users is the tested limit.

NOTE You can use any FileMaker database as a sample file for this chapter.

■ Understanding Database Sharing

With a shared database, users who connect to it can all work in the file at the same time. They each have access to any table, record, or layout specified in their access privileges (page 771). For the most part, you can have users adding, editing, and deleting records; performing finds; printing; and running scripts without stepping on each other's toes. But there's one big exception—no two people can work in the same *record* at the same time. So to understand what problems you might run into, take another look at the topic of record locking.

Reviewing Record Locking

Back in Chapter 1, you learned about record locking by trying to edit the same record in two different windows. When you start editing a record, FileMaker locks it, so you (or anyone else) can't change it in another window until you commit it in the first one. When several people share the same database, record locking is a constant concern. Once anyone starts editing a record, nobody else can edit it. So if Joan types a few lines in the Notes field, then heads off to lunch without clicking out of the record first, she keeps it locked from everyone else until she returns.

While record locking may be a minor annoyance to the user, it can be a real problem for the database developer. If you've designed all your scripts with the mistaken notion that you can *always* edit *any* record you want, then you'll get an unpleasant surprise the first time a script tries to modify a locked record. Your script will throw an error, but the results of the error will vary, depending on what your script is supposed to do. Some record locking errors can stop your script cold, while it's partway through a process. Or if the script was looping through a set of records, it might skip any that are locked, but process the rest normally. But unless the script marks the records it *can* process, you won't know which ones got skipped.

Sometimes a process just won't work for multiple users. For example, say two people flag a set of records and then run a script that *finds* all flagged records and loops through them. The script will conflate the two sets of records, which probably isn't what you intended. You could fix this problem by making each person's flag unique, say by entering the person's account name in the flag field. The script could then find just that person's flagged records for processing. But this solution only works if there's no chance that any two people might need to flag the same record at the same time. Or, to avoid the issue altogether, you could make it so only one person can use certain scripts and use privilege sets to keep everyone else away from them. See the box on page 785 to learn about precautions you should take if you do development tasks on shared databases.

Developing on Shared Files

Just as many users can work on a shared file, you can do development work in the file while users are connected. You—or anyone with the proper privileges—can add or modify tables and fields, manage relationships, add or edit value lists, add or edit data source references, manage security, work in Layout mode, and even write scripts. But the one-at-a-time rule again applies: Only one person can do each task at one time. For example, two people can't edit the same layout at the same time. If you try to switch to Layout mode when someone else is editing that layout, you'll see a warning letting you know who's using it, and then you have to wait until he's done to make your changes.

Plus, your work as a developer can conflict with users. For example, you can add new fields or change their definitions while users go about their daily business. But if someone has a record locked when you click the Manage Database's Done button, you'll see a warning letting you know which person hasn't committed their changes. You can send him a custom message, like asking him to finish editing his current record so you can do your work. But what if several users each have records locked? You have to ask each one in turn to stop working while you finish up. In a busy work environment, it can be costly to disrupt several people's workflow just so you can change the calculation on a field.

The safest practice is never to do development work on a database while users are connected to it. But since that might limit development work to late nights and weekends, many developers end up working on databases while others are using them. So common sense and a few rules of thumb are in order. First, remember that the changes you make will affect users as soon as you save them. For example, if you move a layout object while users are on that layout, they may see objects appear to jump as soon as you switch to Browse mode. If no one's currently using the database, saving a script incrementally as you work is a good idea, but if you make a change, save the script, and then make another change, users who run the script will be running it in a semi-edited condition, which could be disastrous.

If you do have to do development work on a database while people are using it, first make sure to let them know about your planned changes and work schedule ahead of time. Second, if you have more than about 25 users connected, the risk of corrupting the file is greatly increased. If you absolutely can't work at night, or if your manufacturing plant runs shifts around the clock, then you may have to schedule down time for file upgrades. Third, if you're using FileMaker Network Sharing instead of FileMaker Server, it's just not safe to make changes on shared files. Don't do it.

FileMaker Network Sharing

If you already have a network in your office and a few copies of FileMaker, then you're ready to share your database with *FileMaker Network Sharing*. First, put all your databases on one computer. Then open those files, configure each file to be shared (read how in the next section), and call that computer the *host*. Each computer that opens those files is called a *guest*, since it opens the same databases that are on the host. Up to five guests can connect to one host.

Using FileMaker Pro on an ordinary desktop computer to host your files is easy and inexpensive, but it has some considerable drawbacks. The main hurdle is the limit on the number of users it can handle—no more than five guests at once. If you need six people to share the same file, the last person has to wait until somebody else is done.

If you're going to use Network Sharing, consider the following:

- In small offices, a computer used as the host is usually also someone's work computer. So in addition to sharing the FileMaker database, the computer is sending email, editing video, and who knows what else. That's a recipe for instability. If the host computer crashes or freezes, everybody connected to the host will crash or freeze, too. Computer crashes while databases are open are not just inconvenient; they're dangerous because each crash can corrupt the database.

- A slightly safer alternative is a dedicated host. That's a computer that nobody uses as an everyday machine. It's set up just to share files. But there's a danger lurking here, too. Contrary to what most people assume, you should never share the databse file using the computer operating system's sharing methods. Instead, you should install a copy of FileMaker Pro should be installed on the dedicated host, and then FileMaker Pro should open the file and handle the sharing for the other five users. This setup is safer, but there's still no crash protection. Furthermore, open databases must never be copied, either manually or with an automated backup system. Copying an open database is a formula for file corruption.

- As you remember from page 35, you should close databases before you back them up. But if they're open on a host computer, you must also disconnect all the guests before closing the files. This precaution makes midday backups safe but inconvenient.

FileMaker Pro is designed primarily for *using* databases, not hosting them. It does a decent hosting job, but it simply wasn't built for speed or large numbers of simultaneous users. See page 793 to learn about FileMaker Server, the Cadillac of FileMaker database sharing.

Setting Up a Host Computer

To set up the host, open the databases you want to share and then choose File→Sharing→Share with FileMaker Clients. The FileMaker Network Settings dialog box appears (Figure 20-1). The top part of the dialog box lets you turn on Network Sharing, which sets up the computer as the host. Note the TCP/IP address shown in this section; you'll need it to set up a favorite host on all your guest computers (page 790 tells you how). The settings you make in this part of the dialog box apply only to the computer you're working on.

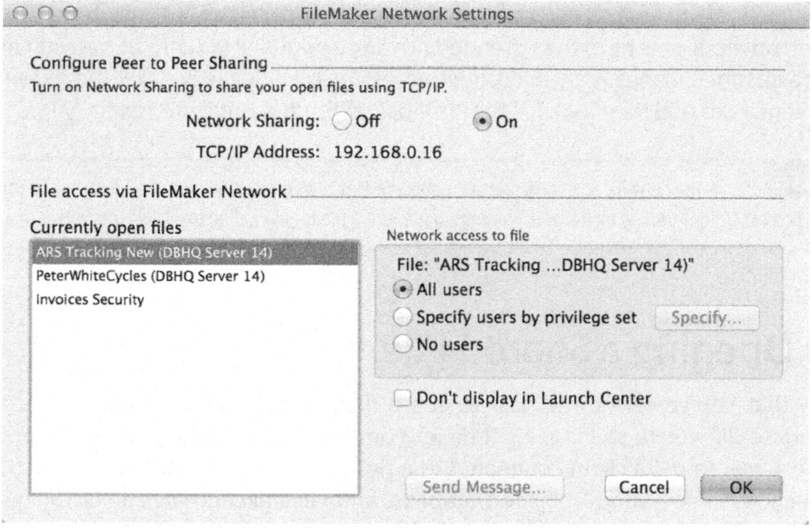

FIGURE 20-1

The FileMaker Network Settings dialog box lets you turn on the Network Sharing and control who gets access to the file. When the Network is on, FileMaker shows the computer's TCP/IP address, if it's connected to the network. (If you don't see a valid TCP/IP address, then you may have network problems.)

The "File access via FileMaker Network" section of the dialog box applies to each file you share, and these settings stay with the file even if you move it to another computer. This section shows a list of all currently open databases and lets you choose which privilege sets get to access each file. (If one or more of the files you need to share are missing, click OK, open the databases you need, and then choose File→Sharing→Share with FileMaker Clients again.) You must turn on network access for at least one privilege set in each file you want to share. First, from the "Currently open files" list, select a database. Then choose one of the following three settings to control who gets access to the file:

- **All Users** means that anybody on your network with a copy of FileMaker and a valid account can get in—up to the limit of five concurrent users.

- **Specify users by privilege set** lets you decide which users can access the database. When you choose this option, you see a dialog box listing all your privilege sets (see page 744). Turn on the checkbox to the left of each privilege set that you want to have access to the file.

- **No users.** If a file needs to be open on the host, but you don't want it shared, choose this option.

The "Don't display in Launch Center dialog" option lets you share a file without users seeing it. Turn on this option if you have a multiple file solution but want users to open a specific file first. To make this work, all the files in the solution must be shared, but make your primary file the only one visible in the Open Remote File dialog box. That way users can open the solution only through the file you intend.

When you make changes to the Network Access settings, it's a slightly easier way of making changes to each file's privilege set using File→Manage→Security. When you turn on "All users," FileMaker adds the "Access via FileMaker Network" extended privilege to every privilege set. If you choose "No users," it removes this extended privilege for every set. When you specify people by privilege set, you get to decide which privilege sets have this extended privilege added. If you prefer, you can make these changes manually by choosing File→Manage→Security. Click the Extended Privileges tab and then look for the "fmapp" extended privilege (page 771).

NOTE Since the network access changes you make in this dialog box stay with the file, you can use this same process (minus turning on Network Sharing) to prepare a file for uploading to a FileMaker Server machine.

■ Opening a Shared File

Now that you've set up the host to share files and set network access for each database file you're sharing, it's time let your users know how to open them. The easiest way to get a client connected to a newly shared database is to send a link. Just choose File→Send→Link to Database, and FileMaker creates an email in your usual email program with a clickable link that finds and opens the database. Your colleague must have FileMaker Pro for this link to work. If the recipient doesn't have an email program, all is not lost. Just use the handy Copy button to copy the link and then send him the info through chat, text message, or any means that lets you send a clickable link.

NOTE You open shared files the same way, whether you're using FileMaker Network Sharing or FileMaker Server.

Opening a Shared File with the Launch Center

Links are a convenient way to open a shared database for the first time, but it doesn't make sense to go back to an emailed link every time you need to open a database. The Launch Center's host tab is here to help. Here's how to use it:

1. **Choose File→Open Remote. Or if you're already looking at the Launch Center, click the Hosts tab instead.**

   Either way, you see the Launch Center's tools for tracking and opening your shared databases (Figure 20-2). FileMaker shows a list of the hosts it finds on your local network.

2. **If necessary, from the Hosts list on the left, select the appropriate host.**

   The host's shared files appear in the pane on the right. (If the host computer you're looking for isn't in the list, see page 790 to learn how to add a favorite host.)

3. **Select the file you want to open and then click Open. Or double-click the file.**

Even if there's only one file on a host, you have to click to open it. If you've added accounts to the file, then FileMaker asks you for an account name and password. When you give it what it needs, the database opens.

When a database opens from a host, FileMaker puts the host name in parentheses after the file's name in the window's title bar to help you remember which host you're using.

> **NOTE**   If you use the Set Window Title step (page 529) to change the window's name, then the host's name no longer appears automatically. Use Get (HostName) to add it back in.

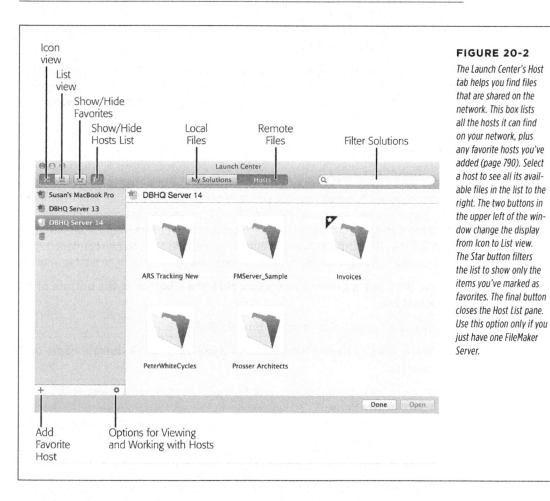

Icon view
List view
Show/Hide Favorites
Show/Hide Hosts List
Local Files
Remote Files
Filter Solutions

Add Favorite Host
Options for Viewing and Working with Hosts

FIGURE 20-2

The Launch Center's Host tab helps you find files that are shared on the network. This box lists all the hosts it can find on your network, plus any favorite hosts you've added (page 790). Select a host to see all its available files in the list to the right. The two buttons in the upper left of the window change the display from Icon to List view. The Star button filters the list to show only the items you've marked as favorites. The final button closes the Host List pane. Use this option only if you just have one FileMaker Server.

Understanding the Launch Center's Hosts Tab

It doesn't matter how you share a database. Whether you're using FileMaker Network Sharing or FileMaker Server, the Launch Center helps you find and open all databases shared with you. The Launch Center's Host tab (File→Open Remote) has more tricks up its sleeve, mostly geared toward folks with a lot of databases. To help you organize all the various hosts and remote files you deal with, you can change the tab's display, mark favorites, and add or edit host-tracking information.

FINDING FILES

If your selected host has *lots* of databases, then you can find the one you want by typing in the Filter box. FileMaker reduces the list to show each file whose name contains the letter or phrase you enter. For example, if you type *inv,* then the list shows only the Invoices and Inventory files.

MARKING FAVORITES

If you find yourself opening the same hosts or files often, you can mark them as favorites. To do so, click the icon to the left of the host's name. A star appears; hosts are sorted with your favorites at the top.

To mark a databases as a favorite, point to the upper-left of the database's icon and click the star that appears. The favorite then appears in a new section at the top of the My Solutions tab. So once you've marked all your favorite files, you won't need to use the Hosts tab as often.

ADDING A FAVORITE HOST

FileMaker is pretty good at showing you the hosts on your network, whether they're shared via FileMaker Network or FileMaker Server. But occasionally, a local host doesn't show up automatically. Or you may be connecting to your work computer from home or while you're on the road. If you have an Internet connection and you know the External IP address of your FileMaker Server (ask your IT person if you don't know it), you can add you server to your Hosts list so you can connect to your databases when you're out of the office. Here's how to add a favorite host to your list:

1. **On the Launch Center's Hosts tab, click the + button at the bottom of the Hosts list.**

   The Add Favorite Host window appears (Figure 20-3).

2. **In the Host's Internet Address field, type your host's domain name or IP address.**

   If you're using FileMaker Network Sharing, this number appears at the top of the FileMaker Network Settings window (File→Sharing→Share with FileMaker Clients). If you're using FileMaker Server, the number appears at the top of the Admin Console's Status panel.

3. **In the Favorite Host's Name field, type a name for the host.**

   The name is optional, but if you don't enter a name, the IP address or domain name appears here instead. Assign a descriptive name that's more helpful than a string of numbers.

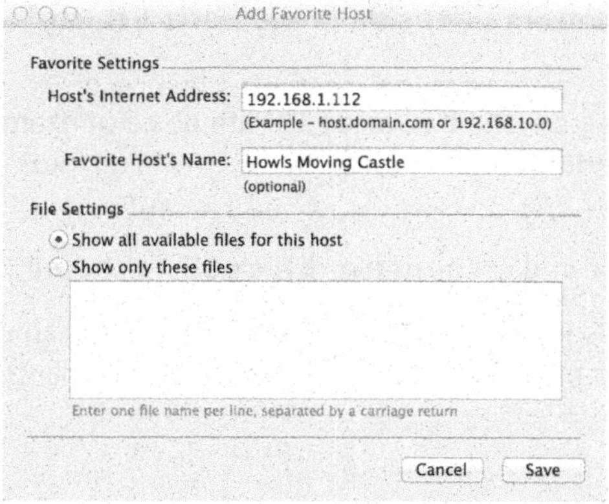

FIGURE 20-3

Use this window to add FileMaker hosts to your Launch Center. You can use the File Settings section to show all available files, or just some of a host's files. For example, if you have several databases that work together, and you may want to show only the main file, so that's the one people open.

4. **Click Save.**

The new host appears in the list.

Click the new host to view its files. If no files show up, check your domain name or IP address for typos. If it's correct, make sure that the host has shared files available.

NOTE The IT folks may have to do some port forwarding to make your FileMaker Server computer available from behind your firewall. You'll need port 5353 for Host Discovery and port 5003 to access the data. If your IT department doesn't allow port forwarding, you'll need to connect to your office network via VPN. Once you're on the network, you can open remote files as if you were in the office.

■ CONFIGURE LDAP

In a large organization with a lot of FileMaker servers, users don't have to manage their Favorites list manually if there's an LDAP server that stores available host information. Setting up that service is beyond the scope of this book, but if your organization uses an LDAP directory, you can connect to it using one of the options you see when you click the gear button. Choose Configure LDAP to view the Specify LDAP Directory Service window. You'll need the server address, port, and information about the service's login requirements. Ask IT if you need help with the settings; that department runs the LDAP server.

■ USING A NETWORK FILE PATH

Sometimes you may need to open a file that doesn't show in the list. For example, you might have an ancillary file that you've configured to share but not show in the Launch Center's Host tab. That setup is fine for your users, who never need to open this file directly. But you may need to open the file to look under the hood.

1. **In the Hosts list, select the host computer, if necessary.**

   Under the hood, FileMaker adds the host's address to a hidden Network File Path box.

2. **Click the gear button at the bottom right side of the Hosts list, and then choose Network File Path.**

   Your host's fmnet address appears in the Network File Path box. For example, if you select a host with the address 192.168.1.10, then FileMaker puts *fmnet:/192.168.1.10/* in the box.

3. **Add your database name to the end of the network file path (after the "/").**

   Since the file you want doesn't show in the list, you have to type its name directly. You're actually creating a network file path, which FileMaker will use to open the file for you.

4. **Click Open.**

   If you typed the name correctly, FileMaker opens the file.

If you get an error, then check to make sure you spelled the file name correctly, and that the file really *is* shared and open on the host computer. You may need to use FileMaker Server's Admin Console to do that (see page 803).

TIP You don't need to put the *.fmp12* in the network file path. FileMaker knows you're looking for a FileMaker database.

■ RECONNECTING TO FILEMAKER SERVER

No network is completely reliable, and sometimes as little as a flicker in power can cause a connectivity issue between FileMaker Pro and FileMaker Server. Whenever possible, FileMaker Pro works under the hood to stay connected, and if the disruption is slight, the file will be reconnected without your even noticing the break. For example, laptops sleep when you close their lids, plus they're more subject to WiFi interruptions than desktops, which typically connect via Ethernet cables, and both sleeping and WiFi loss create a disruption in network connectivity. But if you wake your laptop before the server times your session out, you probably won't notice FileMaker spinning under the hood to reconnect you. However, if your session has expired and you click in a field to start editing a record, you may see a spinning beach ball icon while the file reconnects—all without making you log in again.

But sometimes the disruption is too large for FileMaker to handle the reconnection seamlessly. In that case, your FileMaker window will remain visible in the background, but you'll see a Reconnection dialog box with boxes for you to re-enter your account name and password. You can either cancel the dialog box or enter your login info and let FileMaker reconnect you.

FileMaker Server

Back on page 785, you learned that sharing files by using peer-to-peer networking is cheap and easy, but it's also limited and risky. Even if you don't have more than five users in your office, you're better off using FileMaker Server to host your databases. That's because it's a special piece of software designed for one thing: turning a dedicated computer into a lean, mean, and *stable* database host. When FileMaker Server hosts your databases, you can have large numbers of guests connected at once—FileMaker, Inc. has tested up to 250 connections. Theoretically, there's no limit to the number of connected users, but performance may suffer after the tested limits, especially if your database is complex. Since it runs on a dedicated server, it tends to be much more stable (and you can put it in a safe location, where nobody will pull the plug or close the files accidentally as might happen with FileMaker Network Sharing).

FileMaker Server isn't just jacked up FileMaker Pro; you *can't* launch FileMaker Server and use the database directly. Instead, it's a true *server* (sometimes called a *service* or a *daemon*), designed specifically to share data over the network. Finally, it's loaded with special server-only features, including an automatic backup feature that can safely back up files while people are connected. And all that manual configuration you had to do before sharing your files with FileMaker Network Sharing? FileMaker Server handles that automatically for you.

So what's the catch? Money. FileMaker Server costs about three times as much as FileMaker Pro. Don't be tempted by false economy, though. This is money well spent if your database is at all important to your business.

Preparing to Install FileMaker Server

As with peer-to-peer sharing, FileMaker Server (FMS) runs best on a dedicated computer. The recommended installation calls for a dedicated server computer with fast hardware and a server-class operating system. FileMaker Server is multithread aware, so throw as many processors at the computer as you can afford. The more users you have, and the more complicated your database is, the more it will benefit from the recommended setup. Plenty of organizations run safe, happy FileMaker Server systems that meet the minimum technical specifications, but allow a limited set of other services on their host machines. Since there are so many variables, you should consult an IT person who's familiar with FileMaker, servers, and networks before you plunge in. See page 818 for some general guidelines.

Global Fields and Multiple Users

When many people share a single database, you might be worried about global fields. If one person changes a global field, does it change for *everybody?* In a word, no. FileMaker keeps global field information on the *guest* computer. That's right: Globals are local to each user. If one user changes the value in a global field, it has no effect on what's in that global field for anybody else.

This characteristic is, in general, a very good thing. But it does have an annoying side effect. If you open a shared database and change a global, then you lose your changes when you close the database. The next time you open that database, the globals have the same values as the *host* computer.

If you're using peer-to-peer sharing, then you can change the globals on the host directly to make them stick. But since FileMaker Server has no real interface, you can't directly modify

the initial value for a global field. You have to close the files on the server, move them to another computer, open them with FileMaker Pro, make the change, and then copy them back to the server. In other words, it's a pain. To make this a little easier, you can install FileMaker Pro on your server and modify the process slightly. To do that, close the files on the server, open them with FileMaker Pro, change your global values, and then re-open the databases on the server.

If you need to change globals permanently in a shared system, then it's often easier to simply set them from a script that runs when the database opens. Then you're sure they have the right value, the script acts as documentation of what values are in the global fields, and you can always modify the script the next time you need to change the starting value while the databases are still hosted on the FileMaker Server.

NOTE You can't run two copies of FileMaker Server on the same computer. You can't even *install* two copies of FileMaker Server and just run one of them. So if you're upgrading from a previous version, you have to uninstall the old version first. Don't try this task manually, though. The installer package comes with an uninstaller that removes the server for you. It leaves your databases and managed container files (page 270) intact for the new installation. See the FileMaker Server 14 Tech Specs web page for more details (*http://www.filemaker.com/products/filemaker-server/server-14-specifications.html*).

■ UNDERSTANDING INSTALLATION TYPES

Once your hardware is set up, the next step is to decide how you'll install the software. You can install FileMaker Server on one, two, or three computers. Most organizations will use the Single Machine option, which puts all the parts of FileMaker Server on the same computer. But if your organization has hundreds of users and some of them will be using a browser to share a FileMaker database, then you may want to break up the installation onto two or even three computers. Here are the most common multiple computer installations:

- **FileMaker Server and Web Server.** Install FileMaker Server and the Web Publishing Engine on one computer, and use an ordinary web server computer as the "front end" for your web publishing. This configuration works well if you already have a web server in your organization and you want to add some FileMaker-based web content. You can keep all the FileMaker parts together in one place, with minimal impact on the web server computer.

- **Web Server and Database Server.** Install FileMaker Server on one computer and the Web Publishing Engine on another. The database server handles all your pure data-serving needs. The Web Server handles both ordinary web pages and the FileMaker web publishing system.

- **Web Server, Web Publishing Engine, and Database Server.** Install the File-Maker Server on one computer, the Web Publishing Engine on another, and use a third as a web server. In this configuration, the load of the Web Publishing Engine doesn't interfere with ordinary web server tasks and doesn't slow down the FileMaker Server. This configuration is generally the fastest for maximum load.

NOTE   A multiple machine installation may require the help of a network specialist and a web server technician to make sure the web server is running and all the ports you need are opened properly. If you think you're a candidate for a multiple-machine setup, check out the FileMaker Server 14 Getting Started Guide for details.

Installing FileMaker Server

Like most software these days, you can still buy a boxed product, but more often, FileMaker Server is delivered electronically. Once you've paid for the software (or received your upgrade notice), you'll receive an email from FileMaker, Inc., with instructions for downloading the installer. Follow those instructions and then make a backup of the installer program to store somewhere safe. Then copy the installer on your server and double-click to launch it. After you accept the licensing agreement, you'll see the Installation Type window, shown in Figure 20-4.

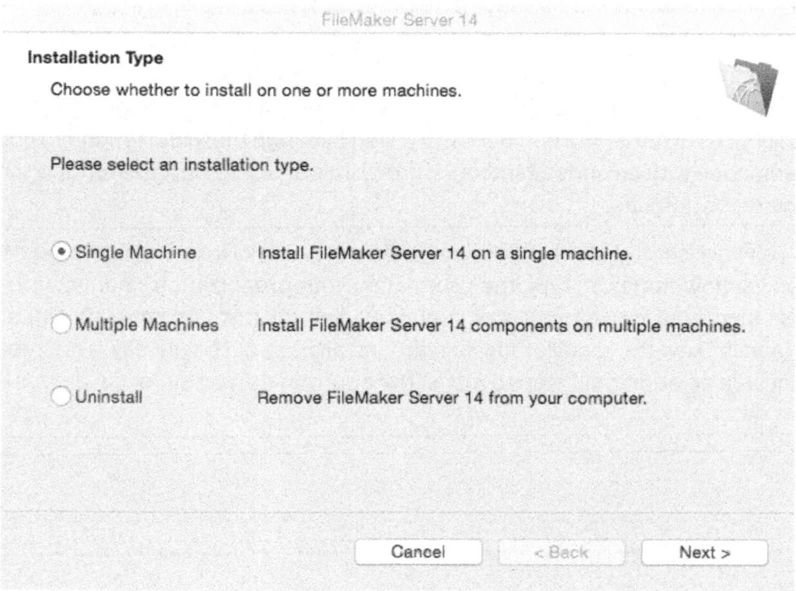

FIGURE 20-4

When you install FileMaker Server, the first question you have to answer is what type of installation you want. If you ever have to uninstall FileMaker Server, don't try to remove the bits and pieces manually. Use the Uninstall option instead. It removes the server, but leaves your databases and backup files intact, so it's not only easier, it's safer too.

After you choose an installation type, the User Account window appears (Figure 20-5). Here's where you type the operating system account information under which you'll run FileMaker Server. This is often the computer's admin account, but you can also let the installer use the default (fmserver) account.

FILEMAKER Server 14

FileMaker Server User Account

The FileMaker Server user account is the operating system account under which FileMaker Server is run.

Select either the default account (fmserver) or select User Name and specify a different account for FileMaker Server to run under.

◯ fmserver

◉ User Name:

Susan Prosser

Password:

•••••••••

Cancel   < Back   Next >

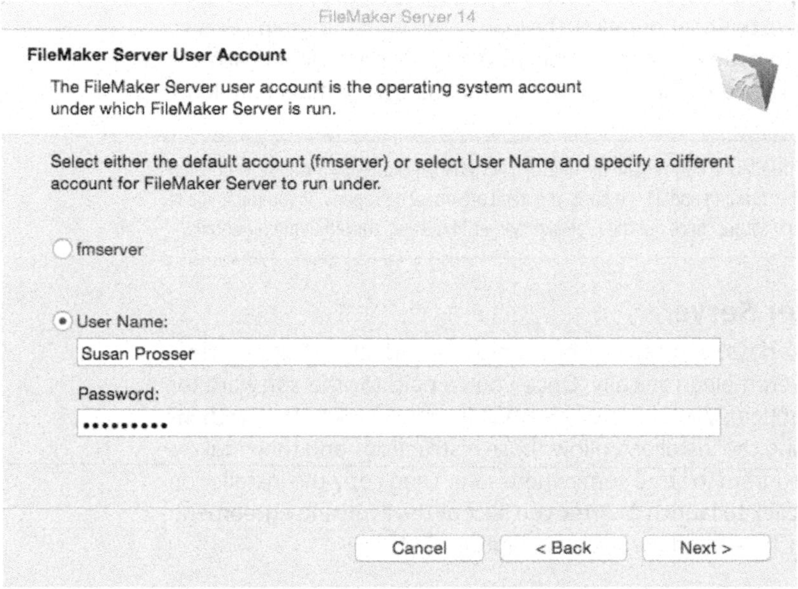

FIGURE 20-5

You can choose the default "fmserver" account, in which case the installer creates the account for you. Or you can use another account, usually the admin account for the computer.

After you click Next, you'll see the Ports for Web Connections window (Figure 20-6). The previous version of FileMaker Server took control of ports 80 and 443, even if you weren't serving web pages from FileMaker Pro. This new window lets you put those services on other ports, if necessary. Don't change these ports lightly, though. Only someone with an understanding of firewalls, ports, and port forwarding should change these defaults.

After you've accepted (or changed) your web ports, click Next. The Customer Information window appears. Type the user name, your organization's name, and your License Key (your download email contains a link for this information). Once you enter a valid key, the installer finishes the installation automatically. This process may include an additional step to install the appropriate version of Java.

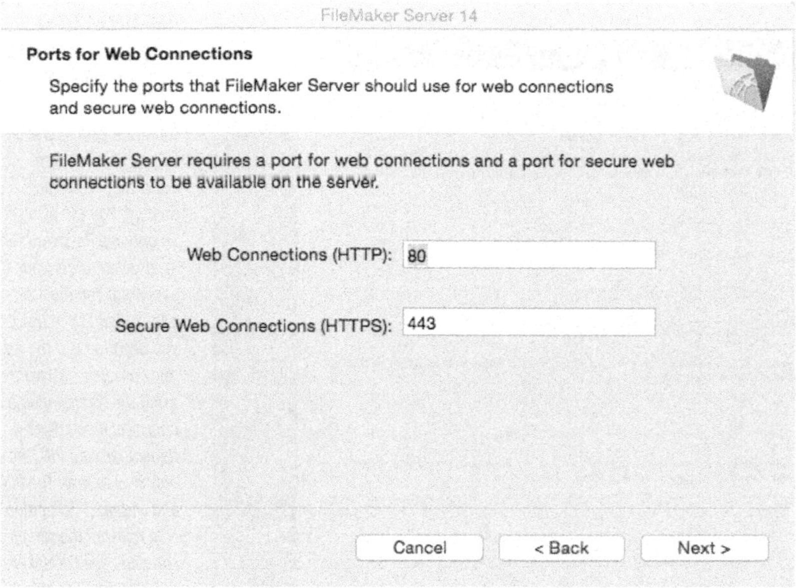

FIGURE 20-6

The default port for serving web pages is Port 80; Port 443 is the default if you're serving secure connections. You can change these defaults if they're being used by another application. However, unless you're an expert, or want to become one quickly, you should stick with the defaults.

Figure content:

FileMaker Server 14

Ports for Web Connections

Specify the ports that FileMaker Server should use for web connections and secure web connections.

FileMaker Server requires a port for web connections and a port for secure web connections to be available on the server.

Web Connections (HTTP): 80

Secure Web Connections (HTTPS): 443

[Cancel]   [< Back]   [Next >]

■ CONFIGURING YOUR SERVER

When the Installer is finished, you'll see a message telling you that the installation was successful and asking if you want to deploy FileMaker Server 14. You do. If you don't run the assistant, the software sits dormant on your computer until you configure and start it manually. Click Continue. The first screen of the Deployment Assistant appears (Figure 20-7), but it might take several seconds while FileMaker Server is being launched. The assistant walks you through the settings you need to make in a series of pages. A progress bar at the top lets you see the steps. Back, Next, and Cancel buttons let you move through the steps. The Finish button stays grayed out until the last step.

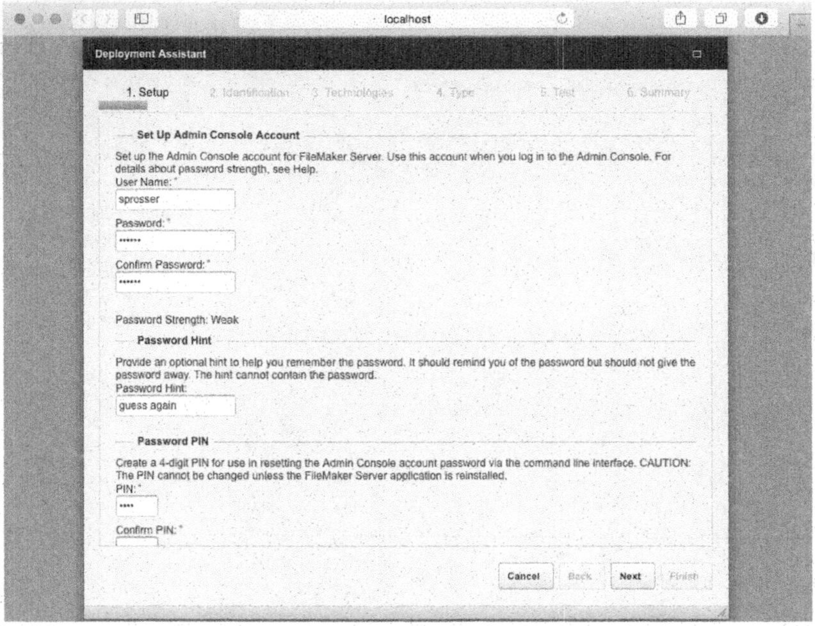

FIGURE 20-7

The Deployment Assistant walks you through the steps you need to take to configure your FileMaker Server. The first step is creating an admin account. You can also set an optional Password Hint in case you forget your password. You must set a four-digit PIN to use if you need to reset the Admin Console's password using the command line interface. If you don't remember your PIN, the only way to reset the PIN and account information is to reinstall the server software. See FileMaker Server's User Guide for more information on using the command line interface to control FileMaker Server.

NOTE   If you see a security alert about an application called "FMS14-YourServerName" trying to access your computer, don't panic. The FileMaker Admin tool is triggering your computer's third-party software authentication feature. You can click to accept, or look on the warning dialog box for a link or a button to display more detail. You'll see that the digital signature is from FileMaker, Inc., and has been verified, and you should allow this access.

In the first screen, you'll set up an Admin Console account, which is a secure account that lets you use the Admin Console to tweak the server's configuration settings, install new databases, perform backups, and more. You can open the Admin Console from any computer on the network, as long as you know the account information. Just enter the user name and password you want to use. You have to type the password twice so FileMaker can be sure you didn't mistype it. Then click Next.

The Identification window lets you fill in a little information about your server (Figure 20-8). The Server Name is required, but the description is optional.

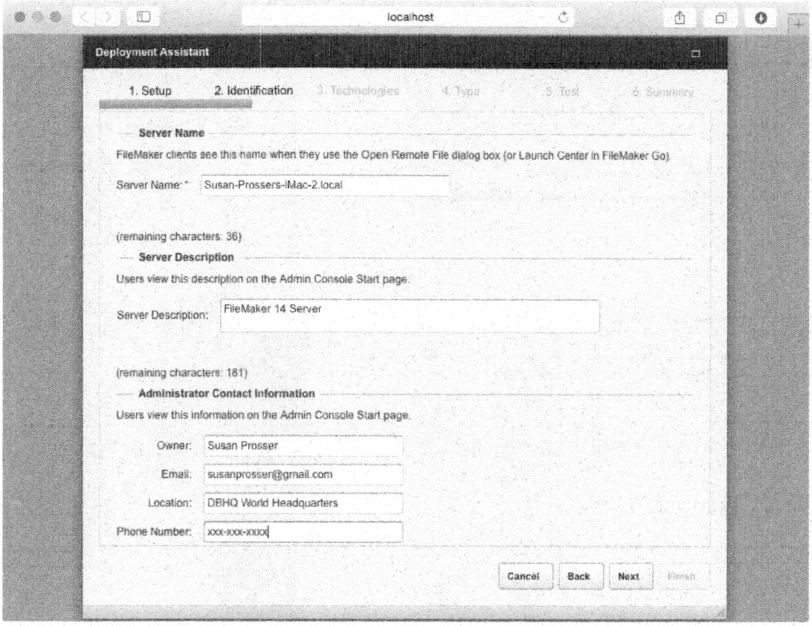

FIGURE 20-8

On the Identification page, you give your FileMaker Server a name, which people see in the Open Remote dialog box. You can also add a short description, which shows up on the Admin Console page. You can use this description to remind you (or your administrators) where the server computer is, what it's used for, or anything else useful.

The next page lets you decide if you'll use other sharing methods beyond FileMaker Server. Here's where you can select ODBC/JDBC and Web Publishing.

The ODBC/JDBC option controls whether *other* programs can talk to FileMaker using Open Database Connectivity (ODBC) or Java Database Connectivity (JDBC). They're application programming interfaces that impose standards on how databases talk to each other. If you don't need this ability, then leave this option turned off. (You can always turn it on later.)

If this is just a plain-vanilla FileMaker Server for FileMaker users only, turn the Web Publishing option off. But if you'll share any database by using a browser, turn it on and choose the web technologies you want to enable. Your choices are FileMaker WebDirect, XML, and PHP (Figure 20-9).

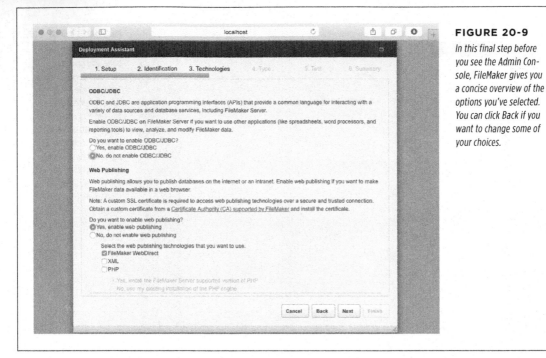

FIGURE 20-9

In this final step before you see the Admin Console, FileMaker gives you a concise overview of the options you've selected. You can click Back if you want to change some of your choices.

If you turn on PHP, you'll have to choose between the FileMaker Server-supported version of PHP or an existing version you may already have on your computer. Unless you have already installed a customized, FileMaker Server-compatible version of PHP, you should always choose the "Yes, install the FileMaker Server supported version of PHP" option. Click Next.

The next screen (Type) asks whether you want to deploy the server components on a single machine or multiple machines. The default choice is Single Machine, but if you chose a multiple machine installation, you'll have to tell the server where you put each component. Click Next. The Deployment Assistant's Test page appears, which should tell you that the web server test was successful. If it was, the Deployment Assistant has found and turned on your operating system's web server software.

NOTE If the assistant tells you that the web test wasn't successful, you may need to cancel the assistant and figure out what's wrong with the OS or the web server. Consult your usual source of OS wisdom and lore if this happens.

If the tests were successful, click Next. Now that you've made all the choices needed to get the server running, FileMaker shows you a summary of the settings you chose. Use the Back button if anything looks incorrect.

When you have the server set up the way you want, click Next. The assistant shows a Deployment Results window as it configures all the parts of your server. You see the changes in the window as they occur. This process can take a few minutes. When it's done, the Please Wait button changes to Finish. You can scroll through the installation and configuration log or click Finish to see the Admin Console.

Administering FileMaker Server

Once you have a server installed and deployed, you can configure settings, see who's connected to which database, and perform other administrative tasks using the Admin Console (Figure 20-10). The Admin Console opens automatically after you've finished the Deployment Assistant. But if you want to open the console on a server that's already been installed, you need to open the server's Start Page. Open your browser and type your server's address, followed by a colon and a specific port number into the URL box. It'll look something like this:

```
https:myserver:16001/
```

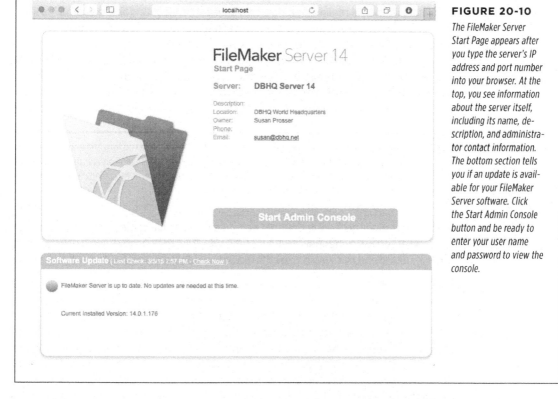

FIGURE 20-10

The FileMaker Server Start Page appears after you type the server's IP address and port number into your browser. At the top, you see information about the server itself, including its name, description, and administrator contact information. The bottom section tells you if an update is available for your FileMaker Server software. Click the Start Admin Console button and be ready to enter your user name and password to view the console.

The exact details may differ depending on where you're opening the console from. Use the format above if you're opening the console from the server itself. But you can run the console remotely, so long as your computer has network access to the server computer. In that case, you'll need to address port 16000 instead. The URL will look like this:

```
https:myserver:16000
```

You can type a domain name, as shown earlier, or one of three alternatives:

- The server's real IP address (it'll be something like 192.168.0.24). Use the actual IP address if your server doesn't have a domain name. Both a domain name and an IP address will work through a browser from any computer on your server's network.

- Its "home" address (127.0.0.1 works for every computer). This only works in a browser that's installed on the server itself. You can't use 127.0.0.1 to open the Admin Console from your desk.

- The name *localhost*. As with the home address, this only works on the server.

The "https" part of the address means that your connection to the server is secure; your browser will show the lock symbol, confirming a secure connection. Because you're using a secure connection protocol, your browser may expect to find a security certificate (a special registration that provides authentication for a domain). It's likely that your server doesn't have a custom certificate, and if you aren't opening your server up to the world outside your network, you don't need one. So you may see a warning the first time you try to connect. Don't worry: You can choose the option that says something like "I understand the risks" and create an exception for your server's address. Then the next time you log onto your server, your browser won't bug you. Create a bookmark and you won't have to bother typing the whole address next time.

NOTE FileMaker Server includes a security certificate, which is used when you turn on Secure Socket Layer (SSL) encryption. But that's not the same thing as a custom certificate, which your organization may need if you're serving secure pages to the general public. If you don't get a custom certificate, then each user will have to understand the risks and make an exception for your server.

If you're opening the Admin Console because you've just deployed your server, you won't be asked for credentials. But next time you start the console, you'll have to enter the user name and password you entered at the beginning of the deployment setup.

When you start the Admin Console, the Status pane is selected (Figure 20-11). Your administrator name appears in the Welcome message on the toolbar, which also shows the Server and Help menus and a Log Out button. Use the Server menu to edit your deployment, to save and load the schedules and group settings file, and to open the Start Page and Test Page. However, after reading this section, you will be able to do all those things manually as well. Use the Help menu to view FileMaker Server Help, find product documentation, check for updates, and register your copy of FileMaker Server. The Log Out button closes the Admin Console, but doesn't close any databases or stop the server. Some people leave their Admin Console open on the server 24/7 for convenience sake. But if security is a factor, you should always log out when you're done with your admin tasks. Even if security isn't on your list of worries, you can free up a few resources by not leaving the browser running all the time.

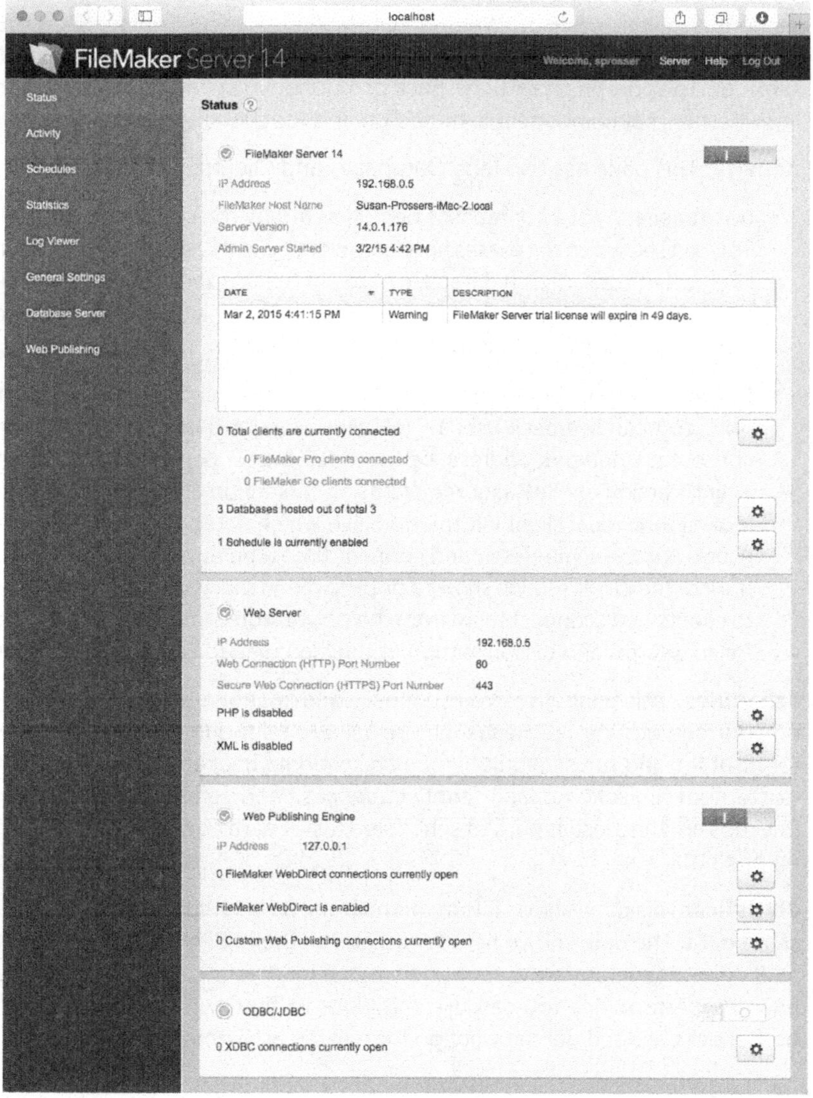

FIGURE 20-11

At the top of the FileMaker Server Admin Console, you see information about the server itself, including its name, description, software version, and date the server was started. There's a menu bar at the top right, and links for other panels down the left side. The blue slider button lets you start and stop the server, but always remember to close your databases before you stop the server. A little further down is connection information, and sections for each technology that's running. For each technology section, you'll see feedback on the components and their current status. A green checkmark means the component is turned on and functioning properly. A red exclamation point means the component is selected, but not functioning. A yellow question mark means the component is running, but hasn't been configured. A gray circle means the component is not running and must be started for FileMaker Server to use it.

The sidebar in the Admin Console contains links to panes that organize everything you need to administer FileMaker Server. Here's how the panels are organized:

- **Status.** This pane displays real-time information (updated every few seconds) about the status of each component of your deployment. It is divided into four sections: FileMaker Server, Web Server, Web Publishing Engine, and ODBC/JDBC. Each component section of the Status pane contains buttons providing shortcuts to appropriate settings. Each component displays an indicator, showing whether that component is turned on and functioning normally.

- **Activity.** This pane has two tabs: Databases and Clients.

  - **Databases.** A list of databases being hosted by the server (Figure 20-12). You can see which databases have connected clients and the type of sharing each client uses. Click a database name in the top section to see details in the bottom section. It shows the computer name, account name, type of connection, and the IP address of each connection.

  - **Clients.** A list of people connected to your server, and the type of connection. You can see each user's FileMaker account name, connection type, computer's network address, opened databases, connect time, and even which version of FileMaker they're using. A section at the bottom lets you look at individual client information, like which databases they have open, group name, privilege set, and connect time. The envelope icon at the top right of the Client section shows a pop-up menu that lets you send messages to clients or disconnect them from the server. You can select specific clients for messages and disconnection or you can manage them all at one time.

- **Schedules.** This pane gives you summary information about scheduled tasks on your server. Pop-up menus let you create, edit, duplicate, delete, enable (or disable), and run schedules. You can schedule backups, messages, scripts (system-level, FileMaker, and script sequences), and verify database integrity. Backups are the most important scheduled task. Learn how to create a schedule on page 812.

- **Statistics.** This pane shows information about your server and clients as users share data. The data shown here (or if you call them, FileMaker's tech support staff) give you information about how much load your server encounters and how it's performing. You can use this data to find out where performance bottlenecks are and get information for making adjustments.

  - **Log Viewer.** You tell FileMaker Server *what* to log in the Database Server pane on the Logging tab, but you'll view the logs on this panel. Click the Modules button to open a window that lets you choose logs from Server Events, Server Access, and Web Publishing Core. Set start and end dates to filter the log's events to a specific time period.

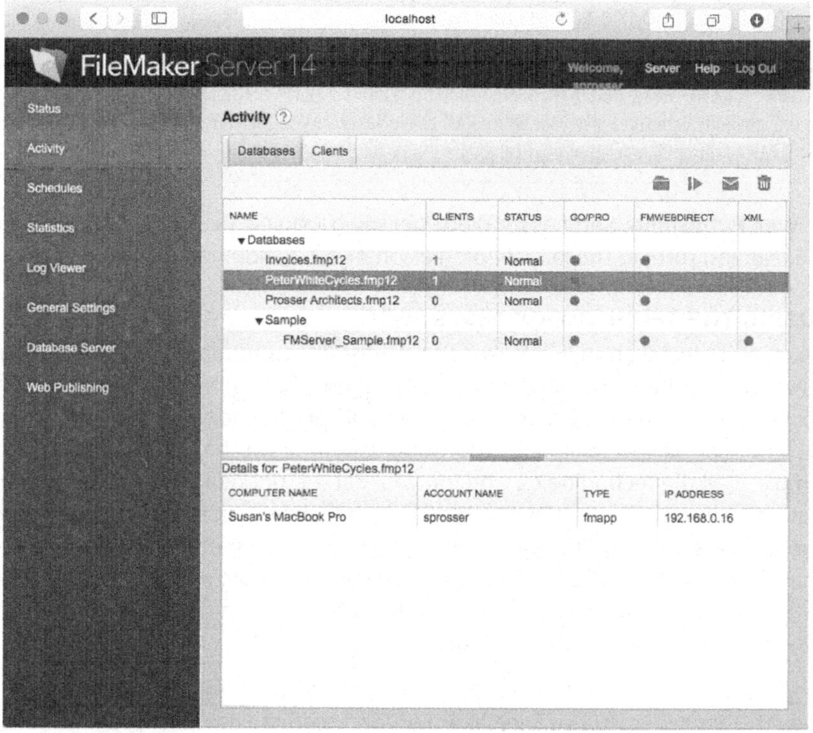

FIGURE 20-12

The Admin Console's Activity pane shows an overview of your server and its components. At the top of the Databases tab, you'll see a list of all open databases and a count of clients connected to each one. Use the Folder icon to Open, Close, Verify, or Download databases. The Arrow button lets you pause the databases, in case you want to make changes to the server, but not disconnect all your clients. Use the Envelope button to send messages to connected clients. The Trash icon removes a database from the server.

- **General Settings.** This panel includes all the configuration options you set when you set up your server, plus some additional options. You can rename your server (in the Server Information tab), tell the server to email you important information periodically (in the Email Notifications tab), change the administrator password (in the Admin Console tab), decide if the server should start automatically when the computer boots (in the Auto Start tab), enable FileMaker files to accept Open Database Connectivity (ODBC) and Java Database Connectivity (JDBC) queries (in the ODBC/JBBC tab), and log warning when you reach 80 percent of the connections limit (in the Connections tab). The Administrator Groups tab lets you delegate some administrative tasks. If your server hosts databases for the Sharks and the Jets, you can set up an Administrator Group for each of them so that each can manage its own databases without getting administrative access to the other's.

- **Database Server.** Shows configuration options specific to the database server portion of FileMaker Server. You can set limits on the number of connections the server allows or on the number of database files to host. You can tell the server what kind of security accounts to use and specify folders for storing additional databases and backup files. You also get to tell FileMaker Server how often to collect data and how much of that data to save in a log file. You can enable server plug-ins and set directory service information to help FileMaker Pro clients find the server on a network.

NOTE You can reserve part of the server computer's RAM cache for FileMaker Server on the Databases tab. But there are limits; you can't give your entire RAM to FileMaker Server. The console lets you use the smaller of physical RAM—1 GB *or* 90 percent of physical RAM.

- **Web Publishing.** Settings for Web Publishing logging, PHP, XML, and WebDirect, including turning those technologies on or off, reside here.

■ USING THE TECHNOLOGY TESTS PAGE

As part of its installation, FileMaker Server installs a sample database (called *FM-Server_Sample.fmp12*) and, if you've turned on PHP web technology, a sample website that you can use to test your system. It's a good idea to test each technology, because the tests will help you troubleshoot if you have problems later. For example, if all the technologies work on your server, but one of the client machines is having issues, that means the trouble is with the client computer or the network between the server and the client. To test, in the menu bar at the top right of the Admin Console, choose Server→Open Test Page. If your browser is set to block pop-up windows, you'll see an error message to that effect. You must turn that feature off to view the Technology tests page.

The test page opens in a new window, with links to tests for the technologies you selected when you installed FileMaker Server. The Test FileMaker Pro link launches FileMaker Pro (if you installed it on your server) and opens the sample database. If you've enabled WebDirect and PHP Custom Web Publishing, the Technologies pages will include links for testing each of them, too.

Uploading a Database to FileMaker Server

Although the server is ready to go, the sample database is the only one running on your server after the initial deployment. To share one of your custom databases, you must upload it to the server. But first, think about what version of software your users have. FileMaker Server 14 can run any file with the .fmp12 file extension and it can handle FileMaker Pro, FileMaker Pro Advanced, and FileMaker Go connections from version 12 on up. However, someone connecting to your server using FileMaker Pro 12 won't see newer features, like slide controls or popovers. Popover buttons are invisible to FileMaker Pro 12, so if you've used popovers to power new record creation or finds, version 12 users are out of luck. Upgrading all your software to the same version is the surefire, if costly, way to solve the problem.

SETTING A MINIMUM VERSION

If buying upgrades of FileMaker Pro isn't feasible, don't worry. It's not always necessary. For example, you might have some departments running databases that don't use any version 14 features. You can still move those older files to your new FileMaker Server 14 machine. You just don't want anyone with FileMaker Pro 12 trying to work in the shiny new databases without access to the new controls you've built. Protect your new files before you upload them to your server by setting a minimum version. In FileMaker Pro (or Advanced) 14, open the database and choose File→File Options. From the "Minimum version allowed to open this file" pop-up menu, choose 14.0. Even without adding security options, you can be assured that users can't open files protected this way until you've upgraded their software.

UPLOADING A DATABASE FROM FILEMAKER PRO

The easiest way to upload a file to your server is from inside FileMaker Pro, since it handles all the file preparation and moves the file into the proper folder for you (Figure 20-13). You'll need the administrator name and password you use to log into the Admin Console.

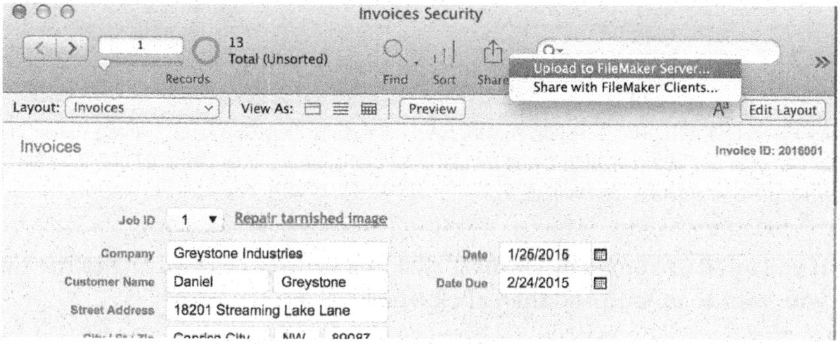

FIGURE 20-13

If the Share button isn't visible, widen your database window so it can show more tools. If that doesn't do it, you may need to restore your default Toolbar (Choose View→Customize Status Toolbar).

1. **Choose File→Sharing→Upload to FileMaker Server. Or click the Share button in the Status toolbar.**

   FileMaker Pro warns you that the file must be closed before it's uploaded.

2. **Click OK in the warning dialog box.**

   The file closes and the first panel of the Upload to FileMaker Server dialog box opens (Figure 20-14).

3. **Select your server from the list (even if it's the only choice) and then enter the account name and password into the appropriate fields. Click Next.**

   The dialog box changes panels to show the server IP address and destination folder. Your file is listed for upload and it's selected.

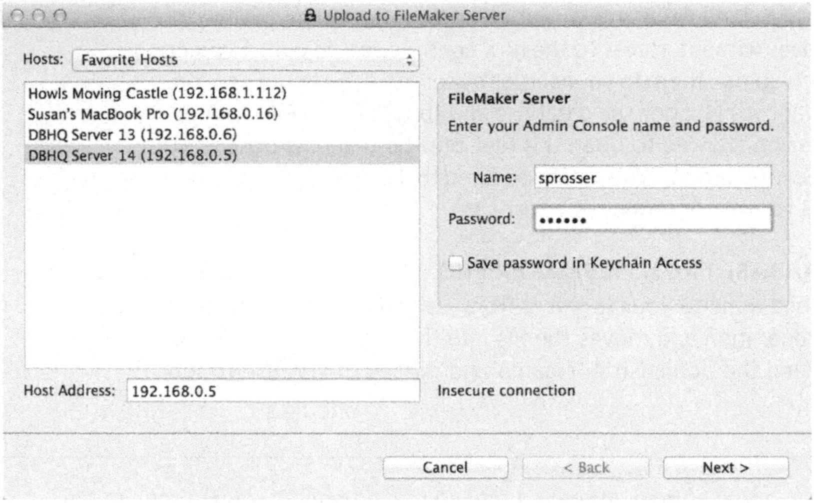

FIGURE 20-14

The "Upload to FileMaker Server" dialog box makes it easy to install databases on your FileMaker server. Choose the server and then enter its Admin Console user name and password. If the Next button isn't available, make sure to select the server name, even if it's the only one in the Hosts list.

WARNING Don't turn on "Save password in Credential Manager (Keychain Access)" unless you're sure that no one else can access your computer. If your computer isn't safe, black hat hackers could upload databases to your server while you're away from your desk.

4. **If you need to upload other files, click the Browse button, locate the file(s) you want to upload and then click Open.**

   Your file is added to the list, with a checkmark next to the file name. The Status means the file is ready to be uploaded. If you've uploaded a previous version of the file, the Status will read: "File already exists on the server." The "Automatically open databases (on server) after upload" option is turned on by default. If you're uploading a single file, leave it turned on. But if your solution contains multiple files, you should use Open→Remote to test your opening script's routine instead.

5. **After you've added all the files you need, click Upload. When the upload is completed, click Done.**

   The Status column changes to a progress bar and the file opens if you left the automatic open option selected. If not, choose Open→Remote, select the host, and then select the file you want to open.

When you use FileMaker Pro's upload command, you don't have to worry about setting network access privileges, as you do when you configure the file to be shared using FileMaker Network Sharing. But the process isn't as granular as you may like:

All your privilege sets get the "fmapp" extended privileges. If some of your users will use other means of connecting, like WebDirect or custom web publishing, you'll need to go set those privileges manually.

> **NOTE** If you try to open the local copy of your database after you've uploaded it to the server, FileMaker warns you and then gives you a choice to open the local or the server version of the file.

UPLOADING A DATABASE MANUALLY

If you're the hands-on type, or if you're used to the old ways, you can still prepare and move files to the server manually. Make sure the accounts and privilege sets of all clients who'll access the database through FileMaker Pro have the appropriate extended privileges (Chapter 19). If you need to limit the number of client's connected, select the option to "Disconnect user from FileMaker Server when idle." Turn off network sharing for the database (File→Sharing→Share with FileMaker Clients) and then close the file. Use your favorite method of moving the file to the server into the appropriate folder:

- Windows: *[drive]:\Program Files\FileMaker\FileMaker Server\Data\Databases*

- OS X: */Library/FileMaker Server/Data/Databases/*

If you're running a Mac server, check the file's privileges and ownership to make sure they match the sample file that's already on your server. For more information on these permissions see the FileMaker Server 14 Help file (Hosting Databases→Uploading Database Files→Uploading database file manually).

CLOSING DATABASE FILES

FileMaker Servers can run for years without stopping or crashing. But there are times when you need to close the database and stop the server; for example, when you need to upgrade your operating system or FileMaker Server itself. Sometimes you may need to close the files briefly to make changes. Before you can make any of these updates, you need to understand the proper sequence for closing your databases and stopping the server. Before you learned about FileMaker Server, you learned not to make copies of open databases because FileMaker performs maintenance tasks on your file every time you close a database. The reason for closing files and stopping the server is similar, except that FileMaker Server handles the routine maintenance. If you restart your computer without closing the databases inside FileMaker Server, for example, those tasks are not performed, and tiny bits of corruption start to creep into your file.

If you routinely abuse the file in this way, the chances of corruption go up. And because it takes its job seriously, FileMaker Server scans each file when opening it. If the program finds too much corruption, it simply won't open the database. When this rare occurrence happens, repairing the file can be costly and time-consuming. So the best strategy is to practice good server hygiene and follow recommended procedures. Here's what to do when you close your database files:

1. **Launch the Admin Console and click the Activity pane.**

   A list of open databases and connected clients appear.

2. **In the Folder pop-up menu, choose Close All.**

   The "Send Message to All" window appears.

3. **Type a short, informative message that lets users know that you're about to shut down the files, set a delay time (the time before the shutdown begins), and then click OK.**

   It's helpful to include a likely time at which users can expect to get back into the database. Users will see a message like the one in Figure 20-15, asking them to close their databases. When they click the Close Now button, their databases will be automatically closed for them. You should see users disappearing from the connected clients column. As all users disconnect from a file, the server closes it. You'll see the Status column update as files are closed.

4. **When all files are closed, click the Status pane. Click the blue On/Off button near the upper right of the pane.**

   The Stop Database Server window appears, so that you can send a message and set a delay. However, since you already waited for users to disconnect, you don't need to send another message.

5. **Click OK.**

   The Server is stopped.

If you try to view other panes, you'll see a message telling you that the database server is not available. All you can see is the Server Status and Log Viewer panes. You can log out of the Admin Console and close your browser. It's now safe to perform your updates. When you're done, reopen the Admin Console and click the blue button (that really ought to have a label) to turn the server on again. The databases will be opened automatically and users will be free to connect to the server again.

Any other type of server stoppage is less safe than the process described in this section, and you should assume that some database corruption might have occurred. That is, if a power failure shuts down your server, or if you try to perform an upgrade without closing the database and stopping the server properly, you should not use the affected files. Instead, restore your last good backup and consign yourself to either re-entering the data manually or importing it from the suspect files into a copy that you know is good.

Understanding Backups

FileMaker Server is smart about the way it handles database backups. It can manage backups without users even noticing that it's happening because it backs up all the parts of the database that nobody is using (all the unlocked records). When that's done, it briefly pauses the databases so it can save those locked records.

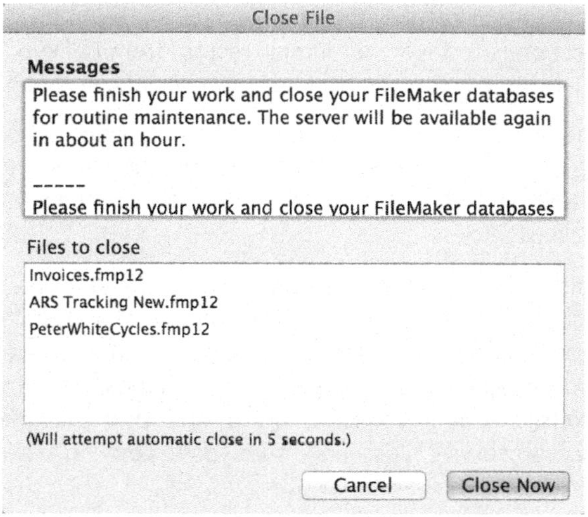

Close File

Messages

Please finish your work and close your FileMaker databases
for routine maintenance. The server will be available again
in about an hour.

Please finish your work and close your FileMaker databases

Files to close

Invoices.fmp12

ARS Tracking New.fmp12

PeterWhiteCycles.fmp12

(Will attempt automatic close in 5 seconds.)

Cancel   Close Now

FIGURE 20-15

*The "Close File" dialog box lets users close their databases
without activating each one and closing its windows. However, they can click Cancel instead and continue working for a
short while before the server disconnects them. If a user has
left his desk, the server will automatically disconnect him
after 30 seconds of inactivity. Since this disconnection can be
frustrating for users, make sure to schedule maintenance in
advance, whenever possible.*

Additionally, FileMaker Server makes a full copy of all your databases the first time
it backs them up. Then if they haven't changed, it makes a *hard link* to the database
instead. Hard links are a little like file aliases, in that you can get access to a file
without knowing its location if you can find the file's alias. But unlike an alias, which
is just a pointer to the real file, hard links really are the file itself. This distinction is
important for two reasons:

- **Backups are faster and more space efficient.** Instead of copying a database
  that hasn't changed, FileMaker Server can just make a hard link to the file. Most
  databases change frequently between backups, but some hold relatively static
  data may only change a few times a week (like product files or archives). And
  if you're using managed containers to store data externally (page 270), those
  files probably change infrequently, so most of their backups can be hard-linked
  and not copied.

- **Backup files must be copied before you can use them.** Because each hard
  link really is the original file itself, if you change any hard-link backup, you're
  changing every version of the backup also. That means you have lost the ability
  to restore any other backup except the one you just modified—because now
  they're all the same.

But if you have to grab a database backup—for example, you're restoring it after
a server crash—*don't* move the file from the backup folder. Copy and paste the
file to its new location instead. That gives you a copy of the file, which you can
safely edit without changing the hard-linked versions. To be safe, make the copy
outside the FileMaker Server folder structure.

■ SCHEDULING A BACKUP

One of FileMaker Server's primary advantages is the ability to perform automatic backups of databases without disruption to the users. You can't overestimate the importance of this step. Someday your server will crash, perhaps because a hard drive fails, the janitor pulls the server cord, or the power goes out. When this happens, your best course of action is to take your lumps, restore from backup, and re-enter any missing data. The more often you back up, the less difficult that'll be.

If you want, you can configure FileMaker Server to back up to a location different from the main hard drive on your server computer. It makes good sense, for example, to back up on a second hard drive. Then if the main hard drive fails, you don't lose your database *and* your backup.

But you should also make offline backups that are stored in a remote location. This protects against natural disaster scenarios where all the computers and drives in your office are lost. FileMaker's automated backup gets the files cleanly copied to a drive of your choice, but you'll need another process for copying those backups to CD, the cloud, or any other offsite location you choose. You can copy the file manually, or use a third-party backup service. Just make sure you're copying backups and not your live databases.

To configure the backup location, in the Admin Console sidebar, choose Database Server. Then switch to the Folders tab. In the middle of this window, you see the backup folder location (Figure 20-16).

In the Path box, type the full path to the folder where you want backups stored. The path has to start with *filewin: (Windows)* or *filemac: (Mac)*, and end with a slash. When you're done typing, click Validate, and FileMaker tells you if your path is valid.

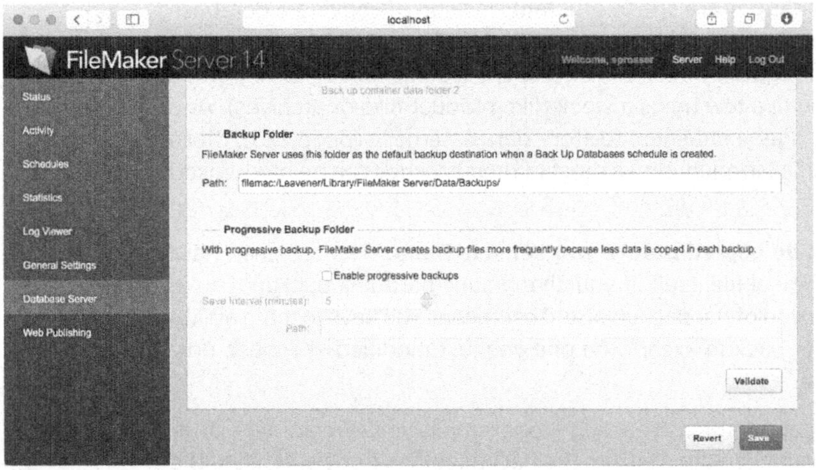

FIGURE 20-16

On the Folders tab, you tell FileMaker where to store your backup files. By default, FileMaker Server has auto-entered a path to a folder within the FileMaker Server folder. You can enter any valid path on your computer or network. Use the Validate button to check your syntax. Ideally, you'll create backups on a different hard drive than your live databases, in case of hardware failure.

Once you've set the backup location, you're ready to schedule the backup. Like many things in FileMaker, you can do it the easy way if your needs are basic, or you can peek under the hood and make numerous configuration choices to get exactly what you want. A backup schedule runs periodically (you control how often), and backs up certain files (you control which ones). Each time FileMaker makes a backup, it puts the files in a folder with the date and time in its name so you can easily tell how old the backup file is. You also configure the schedule to keep a certain number of copies. For instance, if you choose to keep three copies, then FileMaker automatically keeps three complete backups. When the schedule runs again, it deletes the oldest and makes one more new one.

FileMaker Server includes three handy built-in schedules. If you want the most basic backup (every file, every night, keeping a week's worth of copies), then you don't have to do anything. FileMaker Server comes preconfigured to run just such a backup automatically. (You can see it in the Admin Console's Schedules section, labeled Daily.)

If you want more frequent backups, turn off Daily, and turn on Hourly instead (you turn on a schedule using the checkbox by its name). This version keeps eight copies of your database, one for each hour from 8:00 a.m. to 5:00 p.m. Alternately, you can turn on Weekly if you just want backups every week (in this configuration, it keeps four copies).

It often makes sense to turn all these schedules on. That way, you get hourly backups for the current day, daily backups for the past week, and weekly backups for a month, which is a nice balance of frequent recent copies and a few old copies in case of catastrophe (imagine, for instance, you accidentally delete hundreds of older records, and don't notice for three weeks).

If you want to modify any of the built-in backups, in the left-side bar, click Schedules, select the schedule you want to change, and then choose "Edit a Schedule" from the Actions pop-up menu (identified by the calendar icon). FileMaker walks you through a step-by-step configuration. You can, for instance, switch the hourly backups to run starting at 7:00 a.m. instead of 8:00 a.m., or tell the weekly backup to keep eight copies instead of four.

■ CREATING A BACKUP SCHEDULE

If you need a more advanced setup (maybe you want to do a special backup that your offsite backup system picks up every Friday at midnight), then you can make as many new schedules as you want:

1. **On the Schedules panel, choose "Create a Schedule" from the Calendar pop-up menu.**

   The Schedule Assistant window appears.

2. **Select "Back up databases" and then click Next.**

   The Schedule Assistant asks which databases you want to back up. You can choose "All databases," "Databases in a folder," or "Select a dataset."

NOTE   Note: If you need to back up a specific collection of databases, you can put them into a folder in your database folder on the server computer. If that isn't an option (maybe they're already in different folders for other schedules), then you need to make a schedule for each one.

3. **Leave All Databases turned on and then click Next.**

   The screen shows Backup Options (Figure 20-17).

4. **In the Backup folder, enter the full path to the folder on your server where you want the backup stored.**

   In this hypothetical example, you might have your offsite backup system configured to copy every file from a certain folder every Friday at midnight, so you would send the backup to that folder.

5. **In the "Maximum number of backups to keep" box, enter 1.**

   You want to keep only one weekly copy of the database in this example, since the files will be copied by your offsite backup system.

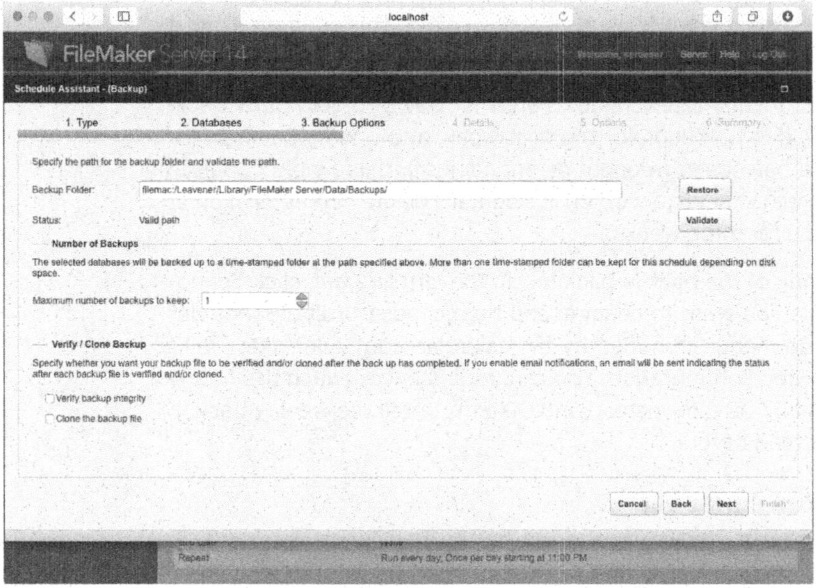

FIGURE 20-17

This step in the Schedule Assistant lets you choose where to store the backup, how many copies FileMaker Server should keep, and whether or not the backup file should be verified. By "verified," FileMaker means it checks the structure of the database file to be sure it has a clean bill of health. Cloning the backup file saves a record-less copy of each file it just backed up. Clones come in handy if you find yourself piecing together a corrupt database.

6. **Click Next.**

   The assistant asks you when the backup should run (Figure 20-18).

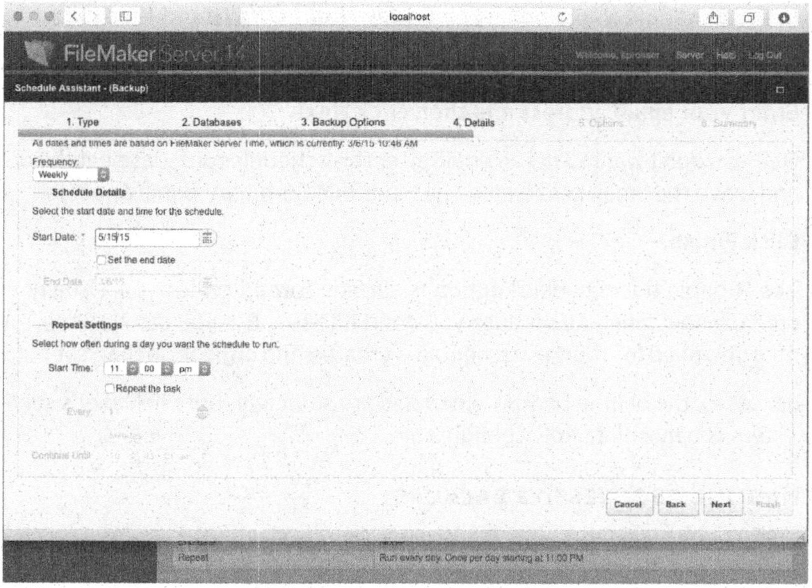

FIGURE 20-18

Finally, you get to tell FileMaker Server when to back up your files. First, from the Frequency pop-up menu, make a selection (your choices are Daily, "Every__days," Once Only, and Weekly). When you change the frequency of a backup, the options in the Schedule Detail section of the panel change too. In this case, Weekly is chosen, and you can choose which days of the week, and how often, the schedule will run.

7. **From the Frequency pop-up menu, choose Weekly.**

   You may have to scroll down to see the whole pane. The Start Date and Start Time show the current date and time. You can set a Start Date and End Date to have the backup run only during a selected time frame. To set a recurring schedule, it is only necessary to have a Start Date.

8. **Select a start date that matches the day of the week when you want the schedule to run.**

   The Start Date 5/15/15 falls on Friday, so the schedule will run weekly on Fridays. If the schedule is just a temporary measure, you can also set an End Date.

9. **In the Repeat Settings section, change the Start Time to *11:00 PM*.**

   This setting tells FileMaker Server to back up the file at 11:00 p.m. That way, the backup is finished in time for the offsite backup script at midnight. (For most databases, the backup takes just a few seconds, but this time can stretch if your database is very large or your server is very busy. You should test your backups to see how long they take, and leave a little extra time just in case.) Options are provided to "Repeat the task" for situations where you want more than one backup during the course of the day. You can set the interval between backups and set an ending time.

10. **Click Next.**

    The assistant asks you to name your schedule. This step helps you identify it in a long list of schedules you've created.

11. **In the Schedule Name box, type *Friday Night Offsite* and then click Next.**

    The Enable Email Notifications panel appears.

12. **Enter your email address and then click Next.**

    Or if you don't want to get an email after this schedule runs, deselect the option and leave the email field blank. The Schedule Summary panel appears.

13. **Click Finish.**

    The "Enable this schedule" option is already turned on for you. Usually you'll create a new schedule because you need it to run. But you can turn this option off if you need to. Your new schedule is created and appears in the Schedule list.

In most cases, the built-in backup schedules are sufficient, but FileMaker's scheduling system is almost infinitely configurable.

■ ENABLING PROGRESSIVE BACKUPS

Progressive backups save changes to your database in log files, which are then saved to one of a pair of backup files at an interval you choose. Because only a few changes are written to the file at each interval, you can save progressive backups every minute if you want to. That means that the oldest backup of your database will be no more than 60 seconds old. If the worst happens and you have to use your progressive backup after a catastrophic event, like a power outage, you'll have lost only a minute's worth of data entry. But this shorter interval also means that a problem you don't notice right away can be saved in your progressive backups. For instance, if you find out that your database has been corrupted, it's likely that the progressive backup, being only a minute old, also has the same corruption in it. In that case, you'll find the most recent scheduled backup file that hasn't been corrupted and use that instead. So you should use both progressive and scheduled backups because together they form a backup system that lets you choose the best file to restore based on the problem you're having.

Progressive backups need a folder to live in, so you'll create a folder on your server or on a remote volume before you can turn on the backup feature. This folder should be outside the FileMaker Server folder structure and can even be on a remote volume on your network. Backups will fail if the folder you enter isn't valid, so FileMaker Server gives you a Validate button to test the folder you entered. If you have problems specifying a valid path, search for "Tips for valid folders" in the FileMaker Server Help document. Once you have a folder created, turn on progressive backups on the Database Server panel of the FileMaker Server Admin Console (Figure 20-19).

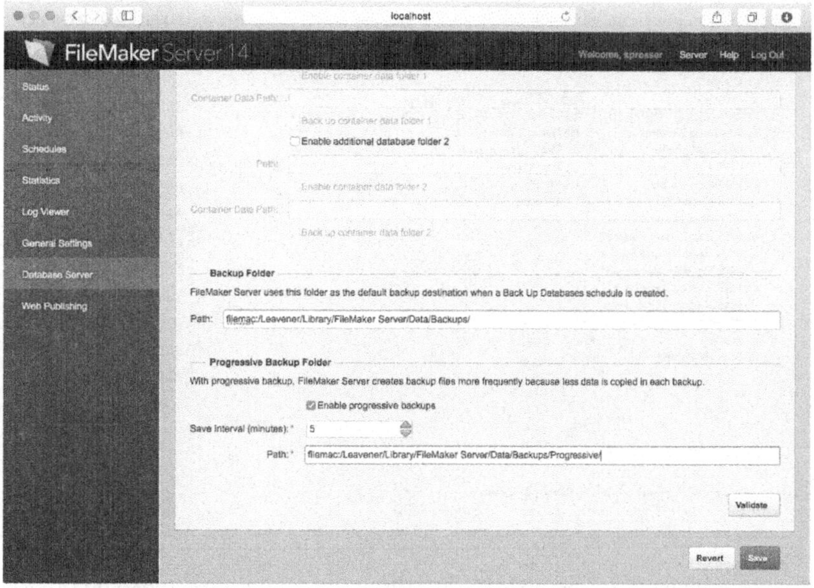

FIGURE 20-19

Click "Enable progressive backups" and set a Save interval. Then enter a path for FileMaker Server to save your backups in.

When you select the "Enable progressive backups" option, FileMaker Server shows a message that tells you the initial setup could take a while and may slow performance for your users. But after that first go-round, you'll never notice it. If you have a busy server with lots of users, you can make it easy on everybody by enabling progressive backups after hours, or while everybody is away at lunch. Set the save interval and enter the backup path. Once the path is validated and you click Save, your first progressive backup will start. If you decide to wait until a later time to start the progressive backups, be sure to click Revert.

WARNING   After you select "Enable progressive backups," if you close (or navigate away from) the Admin Console without clicking Save or Revert, you will have to restart FileMaker server to regain access to the Database Server pane.

▦ RESTORING FROM A BACKUP

Now that you have three different types of backup files, it's time to learn how to use them. If your server crashed, or the databases weren't closed properly before the server was stopped, you need to restore your last good backup. If the server is running, simply close your active files, then move the appropriate backups into your database folder, and then open the new files. But since you may have used FileMaker Pro to upload your files, you may not know where they're stored. See Figure 20-20 to see where to find the Backups folder.

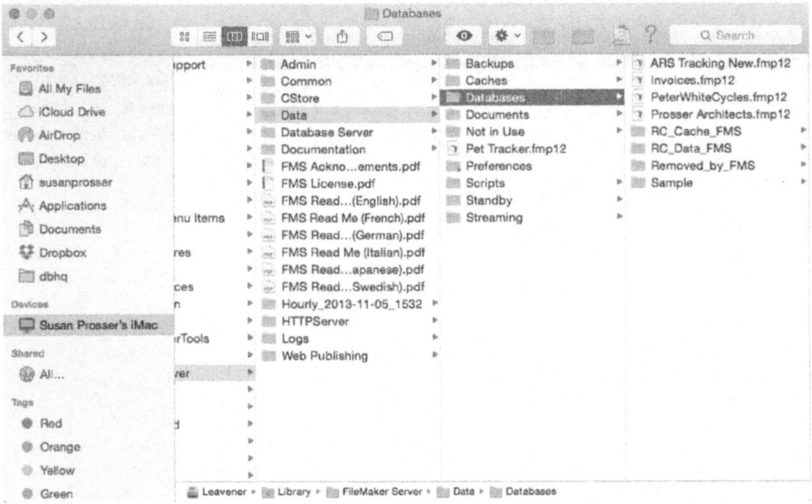

FIGURE 20-20

When the server is started, FileMaker Server automatically opens all files in the Database folder. Your backups are all stored in the Backups folder, which is at the same level as the Database folder. When you open Backups, you'll see one folder with a date and time for each backup made by any active schedule.

To restore a backup, you'll need to find the most recent one, make a copy of the databases you need, and then move them into the Databases folder. If you've created or edited lots of records since the last backup was made, you may need to find these records and import them into the backup (page 880). So it's a good idea to save copies of the live files, even if you think they might be corrupted. You can do the import after you've copied your backups and moved the copies into the live Database folder. Once that's done, you can return to the server's Admin Console and reopen all your files.

Understanding the Standby Server

Backups help you recover after you've lost data or had a server crash, but sometimes your data is so critical to your business that you can't even wait long enough to retrieve the backup. In that case, you should consider setting up a standby server. A standby server is an identical installation of FileMaker Server, ideally on an identical piece of hardware that can detect trouble on the primary server and automatically take over when the primary server can't function.

NOTE Some variance in processor speed and RAM are allowed between your two servers. However, they must use the same operating system (no mixing a Mac and a PC), and preferably the exact same versions of the OS.

You can use a single license of FileMaker Server to install the software on both your primary and standby machines. After installation, you'll configure each copy of the server software, making sure they match and that the same databases are installed on each server. Then you'll run a file synchronization process that ensures that the most recent copy of the files are deployed if the standby server has to take over from the primary server. During normal operations, users connect to the primary server only. The standby server does not accept client connections unless the primary server fails. (If you choose to go for this high-end option, the FileMaker Server User Guide has all the detail on setting it up.)

■ Server Hardware

If you have lots of users or lots of data (or both), your database server needs all the power you can give it. After all, FileMaker Server performs finds, edits records, sorts, imports, exports, and otherwise constantly busies itself with the work of *every user*. FileMaker Server is *multithreaded*, which means that it can handle several requests at once. This means that if one of the server's processors is busy doing a search for Don, Peggy doesn't have to wait until Don's work is done. FileMaker Server routes Peggy's request to an open processor, and both operations can be handled at one time. And FileMaker Server 14 is 64-bit compatible, which means it's even faster than before. But you'll need a 64-bit computer and operating system to take advantage of this speed increase.

The most important thing you can do to make FileMaker Server faster is give it faster access to the data on the disk. This means you should *never* store the files on a file server. They should always be on a hard drive on the host computer. If performance still isn't as fast as you need it to be, your best upgrade may be a faster system that isn't a disk at all. Solid State Drives, or SSDs, replace mechanical drives with memory chips that retain their contents even when switched off. SSDs are orders of magnitude faster than hard drives and very appealing for FileMaker Servers. On the other hand, SSDs cost considerably more per gigabyte and don't have hard drives' long track record, so be sure to keep your backups current.

In addition to a fast disk system, you should consider adding plenty of RAM to the host computer. The least important component is the CPU speed itself (but that's not to say it doesn't matter; don't expect a fast server with a 500 MHz processor).

If you find all this terribly confusing, be comforted by the fact that most major computer companies sell specially configured server computers. Let them know you're setting up a database server, and you can probably buy a fantastic host computer with SSDs, lots of RAM, and a fast CPU—all in one box. For all but the most basic multiuser purposes, you absolutely should consider a dedicated computer designed by the manufacturer to be used as a server. It may *seem* like one of their desktop computers has the same specs as the servers for less money, but appearances can be deceiving. Server computers may have the same processors, amount of memory, and hard drive space, but they generally use upgraded versions of key components.

Everything from the hard drive to the fan that keeps things cool is designed for much more intensive use than a normal desktop computer. Consider the cost of a good server computer part of your FileMaker installation, or you'll regret it down the road when you experience poor performance, poor reliability, or (worst of all) loss of data.

Finally, no matter how reliable your server computer is, if the power goes out, it will crash. And a crashed server can lead to database corruption and a lot of lost time. To protect against this, consider purchasing an *uninterruptible power supply,* or *UPS.* You plug one of these battery backup devices into the wall and then plug the computer into it. If the power goes out, an alarm sounds and the battery automatically kicks in to keep the server running for a few minutes, so that you can close the server's files and stop the server gracefully. Higher-quality UPS devices can even signal the computer to safely shut down when the power is out and the battery runs low, eliminating the possibility of a crash.

Sharing Data with WebDirect and FileMaker Go

As you learned in Chapter 20, FileMaker Network Sharing is the easiest way to share your database. Folks simply open the file and use it, much like a file stored on their local hard drive. They need a copy of FileMaker Pro on whatever computer they're using to connect. But with the rise of mobile devices, many people with jobs that require them to move around all day, like warehouse workers or field installers, need to access the company database on their phone or tablet. There's no computer—or copy of FileMaker Pro—in sight. Fortunately, you have lots of ways to share your database with people on the move. Your choices break down into two basic categories:

- **FileMaker Go** uses a free app, available in the Apple App Store. There are versions for iPad and iPhone (including iPod Touch). FileMaker Go users require licensed connections.

- **Internet sharing** shares your database through a browser. There are three flavors of Internet sharing:

  - **FileMaker WebDirect** uses FileMaker Server to publish layouts, and their data, on the Web. Database users need no additional software, but the same licensing fees for FileMaker Go apply.

  - **Custom Web Publishing** lets you write all the code needed to connect users to your database through a browser.

  - **Static Publishing** also uses a web browser, but your users aren't connected to a live database. They see the database information in the form of HTML pages. As the name suggests, this type of sharing is good for information that doesn't change frequently.

You can even mix and match the methods to fit the tasks your various users are doing. For instance, you might have salespeople on a showroom floor using a full-color, feature-rich catalog on an iPad. But the installers in the field might have a mix of iPhones and Android phones, so they'll use a web browser to connect to the database to clock in at a property and select their materials for a job.

In this chapter, you'll learn how to decide which method is the best one for your users, how to set up and use the method you've chosen, and some design considerations you should keep in mind.

> **NOTE** You can use any FileMaker database as a sample file for this chapter.

■ Understanding WebDirect

WebDirect is a feature of FileMaker Server that transforms layouts and their data so web browsers can interact with your database without FileMaker Pro. It works along with FileMaker Server and the web server software on the server computer to create everything you'll need to share databases beyond regular network sharing. WebDirect is best suited for light use by folks who need limited access to specific records—field technicians, vendors, customers, or other third-party users. It can also be useful where installation of FileMaker Pro is restricted by IT regulations.

WebDirect uses layouts you've designed specifically for folks who don't have a copy of FileMaker Pro. But even without FileMaker, users work with data in ways that look and feel very FileMaker-like. They can browse, find, and edit records; switch layouts; and run your carefully crafted scripts. As with FileMaker Network Sharing (page 785), each user must have an account with the fmwebdirect extended privilege (page 771), and they need to know your server's IP address or domain name. With all that in place, they can open and work on the database anywhere they have Internet access.

WebDirect sharing through a browser requires FileMaker Server, which starts out giving you a single connection without additional licensing fees. See the box on "Concurrent Connections" to learn how to figure out how many licenses you need to buy for simultaneous connections.

For non-Apple mobile devices, like Android, Blackberry, or Windows Phone, you must connect with the browser on those devices. Not all browsers are compatible, though. Here's the list of browsers that FileMaker supports:

Desktop
Safari 9.x; Internet Explorer 10.x and 11.x; Chrome 38 or later

Mobile Browsers
Mobile Safari 8.x on iOS 8.1; Chrome 38 or later for Android 4.4x

Browsers not listed above may still work—they just need to be able to handle CSS and JavaScript. If your love for your favorite unsupported browser outweighs compatibility concerns, then go ahead and test it out. But if you need to be sure all your database's features will work, stick with a browser on the list.

> **NOTE** The network you're using to connect to your FileMaker database has a big impact on performance. The best performance will be on a WiFi network within your company's LAN. Second best is WiFi over a WAN. But if you're on a cellular network, stick to LTE or 4G connections for all but the very lightest uses. Plus, larger files, especially those that transmit photos or PDFs, may well burn through your cellular plan limits, so take that into account, too.

UP TO SPEED

Concurrent Connections

FileMaker Go and WebDirect share data with your remote users, but FileMaker Server requires licenses for each simultaneous connection beyond the one included with your purchase of Server. These licensed connections are called *concurrent connections,* and they only relate to sharing with FileMaker Go or through the browser. FileMaker Pro connections are not included in the concurrent connection count, and neither are Custom Web Publishing or xDBC connections, which are covered by FileMaker Server's regular licensing fees.

Since most WebDirect use should be light and brief—as when users need to view or edit data quickly and then go about their non-computer work—you aren't likely to need an individual connection for every remote user. Figure out the largest number of users who'll need to connect to your database at one time and then buy just that many licenses. For example, if you have salespeople across the country who all need to view the database first thing in the morning to get their daily assignments, they'll have staggered start times, due to time zones, so this will decrease the number of concurrent connections you'll need. Remember, though, that one user can use up *more* than one concurrent connection. For example, if one person connects to your database using an iPhone, an iPad, and two web browser tabs, she's hogging four connections.

If you don't license enough concurrent connections, some users will be locked out until a connection becomes available. However, it's easy to buy another pack of connections once you know you need more.

Understanding WebDirect Compatibility

Although your database *looks* the same whether you view it in FileMaker Pro, FileMaker Go, or in a web browser through WebDirect, not all of FileMaker's features work in FileMaker Go or WebDirect. The biggest limitation is that you can't create new databases, and you can't edit much of anything but the data in your existing ones. So think of FileMaker Pro as the place where you do all your database development tasks, and FM Go and WebDirect as where you and your remote clients work with your data. Neither FileMaker Go nor WebDirect can create or modify:

- Tables
- Fields
- Relationships
- Layouts

- Scripts

- Value lists

- Custom menus

- Accounts

- Privileges

- Data sources

Other features behave differently, depending on whether your database is shared with FileMaker Go or WebDirect. Some differences are covered in Table 21-1.

TABLE 21-1 *Some FileMaker features work in FileMaker Go but not in WebDirect, and vice versa. This table covers the major differences.*

	FILEMAKER GO	WEBDIRECT (BROWSER)
Spell checking	Not available.	Uses the browser's spell checker.
Importing	Can only import records from one FileMaker database to another.	Can import from FileMaker Pro, tab-separated text, comma-separated text, DBF, merge, or Excel files.
Exporting	Exports to tab-separated text, comma-separated text, DBF, merge, HTML table, and Microsoft Excel XLSX (UTF-16) format.	Exports to tab-separated text, comma-separated text, DBF, merge, and HTML table formats.
Printing	Supports print, but print options set in FileMaker Pro have no effect.	Relies on the browser's Print features.
Text styles	Doesn't support highlight, superscript, and subscript conditional formatting options. Word underline appears as underline. Also doesn't support strike-through, condense, extend, or small caps.	Highlight, superscript, and subscript conditional formatting options. Word underline appears as underline.
Snapshot Link file (page 849)	Displayed in Browse mode, even when the link is created in Preview mode.	Displayed in Browse mode, even when the link is created in Preview mode.
External functions and plug-ins	Doesn't support external functions or plug-ins.	WebDirect limits plug-ins to those designed for the Web Publishing Engine (WPE). See FileMaker Server Help for more information on WPE compatible plug-ins.
Kiosk mode	Although you can design a Kiosk database (page 581) to run in FileMaker Go, you can't navigate through records by swiping with two fingers.	Doesn't support Runtime or Kiosk databases.

Script steps are a special case. FileMaker Go and WebDirect don't recognize all script steps. Some that work in Go don't work in a browser and vice versa. Fortunately the Edit Script dialog box is ready to help. The Compatibility pop-up menu lets you see the scripts that won't work or need special treatment. See Figure 21-1.

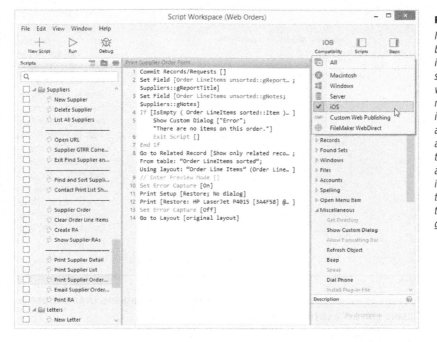

FIGURE 21-1

In the Edit Script dialog box, use the Compat-ibility pop-up menu to see whether a script step will work in the sharing method you're develop-ing. Here iOS is selected, and some script steps are grayed out, showing that they're unavail-able. If you've added incompatible steps in the script you're editing, those steps will also be grayed out.

NOTE For more Information on how each script step works, see the development guides for WebDirect and FileMaker Go. Choose Help→Product Documentation→More Documentation for links to download the FileMaker Go and WebDirect guides.

Enabling WebDirect in a Database

As with FileMaker Network Sharing, you get to decide which files are shared by WebDirect, and which privilege sets have web access. FileMaker provides an easy way to set these privileges for the entire file.

1. **In FileMaker Pro, open the database files.**

   You can open multiple files and configure them all at the same time.

2. **Choose File→Sharing→Configure for FileMaker WebDirect.**

   The WebDirect Settings dialog box opens (see Figure 21-2).

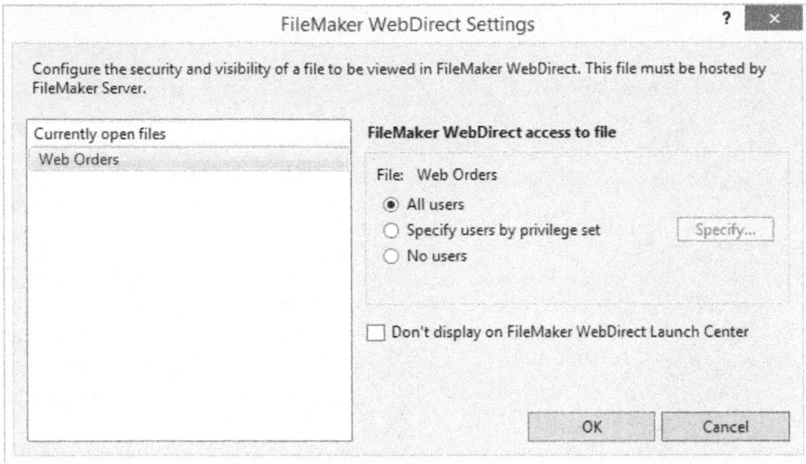

FIGURE 21-2

Use the FileMaker Web-Direct Settings dialog box to configure files, either individually or as a group. If you have multiple files open, you can choose them all to configure them all at once, but in that case the options for setting extended privileges are limited to "All users" and "No users." If your database uses multiple files, but you don't want them all to show up on the WebDirect home page, select "Don't display in Launch Center" for those files.

3. **From the list of open files, select the one(s) you need and then choose which users can access the file.**

   You have three options:

   - "All users" provides access to anyone who has the IP address or domain name of the server hosting the database.

   - "Specify users by privilege set" lets only selected users access the database through WebDirect. You may also require users to provide an account name and password.

   - "No users" prevents anyone from accessing the file through WebDirect.

4. **Repeat step 3 for each file you need to configure. When you're finished with all of your files, click OK.**

   The files are now ready to be uploaded to FileMaker Server (page 793).

WARNING If you're using files that you created in FileMaker 12 and shared with Instant Web Publishing (IWP), you must turn off the "fmiwp" extended privilege or the files won't be available in WebDirect.

Setting Up WebDirect on FileMaker Server

FileMaker Server is made up of three parts: a database server, a web server, and the Web Publishing Engine (WPE). The database server handles the sharing and distribution of data for all connections using FileMaker Pro. The web server is part of the server computer's operating system, and as such it handles HTTP or HTTPS requests from users on the Web. The Web Publishing Engine (WPE) handles WebDirect and Custom Web Publishing (page 841) services for your databases.

If you're starting from scratch and installing FileMaker Server for the first time, it's easy to turn on its web server components. Just select those options in the Deployment Assistant. But if you didn't do that up front, you can still turn on WebDirect after you've been sharing the database with network sharing only.

1. **Log in to the FileMaker Server Admin Console.**

   Use the account name and password you created when you installed FileMaker Server. After you log in, the Admin Console's Status panel appears.

2. **At the left side of the console, click the Web Publishing link.**

   The Web Publishing pane appears. It has four tabs: General Settings, PHP, XML, and FileMaker WebDirect.

NOTE   If the Web Publishing link doesn't appear, choose Server→Edit Deployment, and use the Deployment Assistant (page 797) to turn on Web Publishing and WebDirect.

---

3. **Click the FileMaker WebDirect tab.**

   The WebDirect settings appear.

4. **Click the Enable FileMaker WebDirect option.**

   Optionally, you can change the default session timeout setting of 15 minutes and change the Status Area Language. If you reduce the timeout setting to release connections more quickly, that can help manage a limited number of concurrent connection licenses.

5. **Click Save.**

   A warning box appears to let you know that you must restart the WPE to apply your changes. You have the option to revert the changes or save them. If you're starting WebDirect for the first time, you won't have any connected users. But, in the future, each time you change these settings, you have to restart the WPE, which could interrupt work for connected users. So you may want to only make changes at low-use times of the day.

You're ready to test WebDirect. You can use the Technology Tests page or manually open your database from FileMaker Go or from a browser. Read on to find out how.

Opening a Database in FileMaker Go

You can connect to hosted databases using FileMaker Go through a mobile device, such as an iPad, iPhone, or iPod Touch. First, go to the App Store and download the right software for your device.

> **NOTE** If you're using an Android, Samsung, or any other non-Apple mobile device, you can connect to a FileMaker database through a browser only.

You open a database in FileMaker Go much like you do in FileMaker Pro: Find your server, select the file, open it and then enter your account name and password. But since your mobile device's screen is much smaller and has a different aspect ratio, the process looks a little different. Figure 21-3 shows the iPad version of Go.

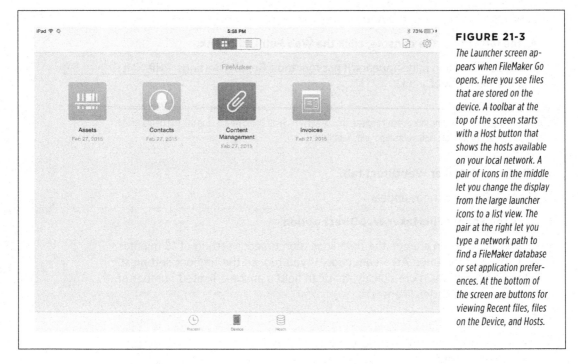

FIGURE 21-3

The Launcher screen appears when FileMaker Go opens. Here you see files that are stored on the device. A toolbar at the top of the screen starts with a Host button that shows the hosts available on your local network. A pair of icons in the middle let you change the display from the large launcher icons to a list view. The pair at the right let you type a network path to find a FileMaker database or set application preferences. At the bottom of the screen are buttons for viewing Recent files, files on the Device, and Hosts.

Your recent files list will be blank until you've opened your first database; the list will grow as you work with more files. Use this button in place of the Open Recent command in FileMaker Pro. If your files are shared on a server, click Hosts to let FileMaker Go see a list of your recently visited servers and to tell FileMaker how to find new servers Figure 21-4).

> **TIP** If you typically work in several databases, open them all in the File Browser window the first time you launch FileMaker Go. That seeds your Recent files list and makes it easier to find the file you need next time.

The iPhone and iPod Touch have the same features, but since these devices have less screen space, they arrange them a little differently (Figure 21-5).

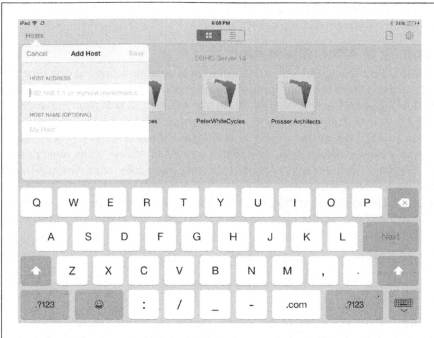

FIGURE 21-4

In the Host menu, you can choose from an existing host, or click the + button to add a new host. Add a Host the same way as in FileMaker Pro: Put the domain name or IP address in the Host Address field, and add an optional name to help you keep your servers straight. The iPad's keyboard appears automatically to help you enter your data.

FIGURE 21-5

The iPhone's Launch Center is smaller, and arranged differently than the iPad. Buttons along the bottom let you switch between the Recent, Device, and Hosts screens. The Device screen, show here, shows the FileMaker files that have been loaded onto your phone. The first two buttons on the top switch between icon and list view. The Check button lets you selects favorites, delete files, or share them with others via AirDrop, Messages, Mail, or other sharing apps. The Settings icon lets you manage your phone's Keychain, get help, register FileMaker Go, or take a Welcome Tour of the app.

Once you've opened a database, using it on a mobile device is much like working with it on your desktop. You can browse through records, perform finds, switch layouts, and click buttons to run scripts. As described in Chapter 3, you can do anything in FileMaker Go that's allowed by the privilege set attached to the account and password you used to log in with.

Logging In After Hibernation

The iPad, iPod Touch, and iPhone let you have several apps open at one time, but those apps don't act like open applications on your desktop or laptop. For example, the desktop version of FileMaker Pro stays connected to its host machine while you switch over to your email program or word processor. But if you tap the Home button on your iOS device, the device exits FileMaker Go and starts a process called *hibernation* immediately. When you switch screens or answer an incoming phone call, FileMaker Go stores any changes you've made and goes into a hibernate mode until you activate the app again. Because hibernation disconnects you from a hosted database after a default period of 10 minutes, you may need to log in when you return to FileMaker Go. But there are some situations in which you won't be required to log in again:

- If you are logged in using the file's Guest account

- If you are logged in with the account that's set in the File Options automatic login settings

- If the file has a custom extended privilege (page 774) with the keyword fmrauthenticate, and you're logged into an account that has this privilege enabled

WARNING The convenience of automatic re-login carries a security risk. If you leave your iPad, iPod Touch, or iPhone unattended and it's unprotected by a security passcode, unauthorized people can reactivate FileMaker Go and view or edit your data. Get in the habit of hitting the Home button to exit FileMaker Go before you turn off your mobile device or let it hibernate. It's also a good idea to set a security passcode on the device itself.

■ CUSTOMING REAUTHENTICATION PERIODS

Automatic restoration of a login can be a security risk. But in lower-risk situations, you can extend the reauthorization period with another extended privilege, called "fmreauthenticatexx," where the "xx" can be replaced by a time period you specify. By default, each database gets two versions of this extended privilege: one for 10 minutes and one for zero minutes. The zero-minute version is for pessimistic types who won't risk their data even for a short period of hibernation—after all, someone could steal an iPad and be away with your data in seconds. The 10-minute version is the one that's in effect if you don't specify any "fmreauthenticate" extended privileges. It's created for you so that you can assign different reauthentication periods to different privilege sets. Create a new version with the time period of your choice.

Connecting with a Web Browser

As you've learned, FileMaker uses JavaScript, Cascading Style Sheets (CSS3), and HTML 5 to convert your layouts into code a browser can understand. Most modern browsers let you disable JavaScript, so make sure your browser has it switched on. The setting is usually found in the Tools (Windows) or Preferences (Mac) command.

To connect to the database from a web browser, you need to know the IP address (or URL) for the FileMaker Server computer it's hosted on. In your browser's Location box, type *[IP address]/fmi/webd* (without the brackets). The WebDirect Home page looks like the one in Figure 21-6.

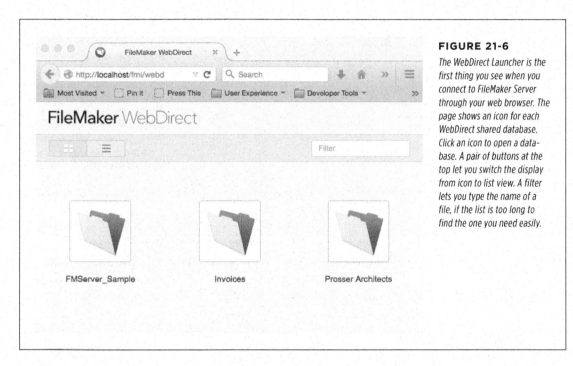

FIGURE 21-6

The WebDirect Launcher is the first thing you see when you connect to FileMaker Server through your web browser. The page shows an icon for each WebDirect shared database. Click an icon to open a database. A pair of buttons at the top let you switch the display from icon to list view. A filter lets you type the name of a file, if the list is too long to find the one you need easily.

When you click a database link on the web page, you'll need to log in, just as you would if you were using FileMaker Pro or FileMaker Go. Enter an account name and password that uses a privilege set with the WebDirect sharing privilege. After you log in, you see what probably looks a *lot* like your real database displayed right inside the web page (Figure 21-7).

Disconnecting from WebDirect

When they're finished their database tasks, users must log out to release their connection. If someone just closes her browser or goes to a different website, FileMaker doesn't know she's left your site. To keep people from tying up concurrent connections forever, FileMaker automatically disconnects anyone who hasn't requested a page, changed data, or otherwise made a request to FileMaker Server for a while. You get to decide how long "a while" is—you set that limit in the FileMaker Server

Admin Console (page 803). This setting, called Session Timeout, is in the FileMaker WebDirect tab of the Web Publishing pane. A short timeout (say, 15 minutes) ensures that people don't tie up connections for long if they forget to log out. But in that case, if someone spends more than 15 minutes looking at a single record (reading a long Notes field, for instance), then she could be disconnected even though she's still using the database. If you have situations like this one, then set the Session Timeout to a longer duration—the maximum is 60 minutes.

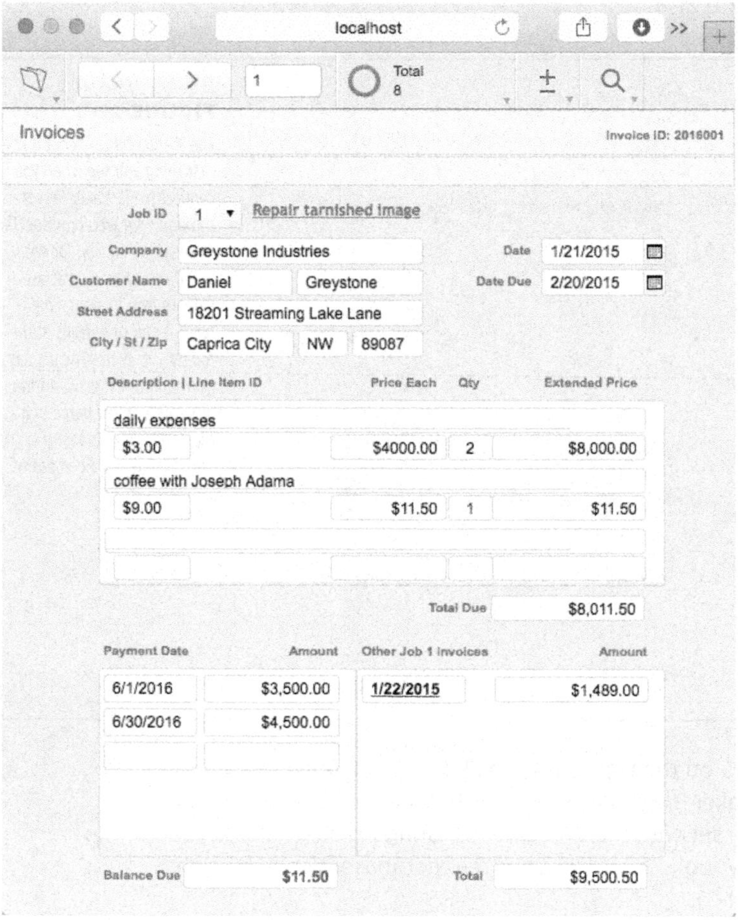

FIGURE 21-7

Here is the Invoices database you worked with in previous chapters as it appears in Safari. This file was not optimized for use in WebDirect, so all the fields, buttons, and so on appear exactly the same as they do when you access the file in FileMaker Pro. The most obvious difference is the appearance of the menu bar. Later in this chapter, you'll learn how to optimize your layouts for sharing on iOS and WebDirect.

Web users are returned to the WebDirect Home page when they log out or the session times out.

■ Designing for WebDirect and FileMaker Go

Sharing your FileMaker Pro databases through FileMaker Go and WebDirect is easy, but you shouldn't stop your design planning at changing a few options in the file. There are a number of ways that WebDirect connections differ from FileMaker Pro connections, and you should keep each of them in mind as you develop for those tracks. FileMaker Go uses the iPad or iPhone, which means they have a limited viewing area, and it changes when the device is rotated. WebDirect users see the database through a web browser, which can only load one layout at a time.

Also, performance should always be a consideration. An Internet connection will almost always be slower, and often considerably slower, than a network connection. The browser has to communicate with FileMaker Server every time the layout changes, records are opened or changed, calculations are evaluated, scripts are performed, or script triggers are activated, so your data is making round trips to the server many times during a session. These round trips take time, and even if they're fast by mobile standards, you know how slowly an extra second passes when you're waiting to do your work. So to optimize your users' experience, you'll need to design sets of layouts that respect the smaller screen size *and* that include only the elements your users absolutely need.

Reducing Overhead

Every time a browser requests a layout and its data, FileMaker Server's Web Publishing Engine has to translate that layout into HTML and generate the CSS and JavaScript coding for it. FileMaker Go doesn't require this conversion process, but your users will frequently use a cellular data plan to connect to the database, so you should reduce its overhead as much as possible. Layouts that are filled with a lot of styles, text formatting, graphics, and other features bog down data transfer, which in turn increases layout loading times. Bandwidth, computer processing speed, and the quality of the network connection can all contribute to the slowdown. The more complex your database is, the more you have to think about the extra load your data transfer carries.

Here's a list of things to consider for best performance. Individually, each item gives a slight performance boost, but the more of these bullet points you incorporate into your FileMaker Go or browser layout designs, the greater the benefit your users will reap:

- **Minimize the number of objects on the screen.** If necessary, break up busy layouts into multiple, smaller layouts.

- **Stick with simple themes.** Avoid gradients or image slices.

- **Use a custom theme with shared styles.** If every field on your layout has one style to rule them all, it takes only one snippet of CSS code to define them all.

  The same applies to text elements (like labels) and buttons. Use styles as much as possible in place of individual formatting.

- **Avoid the Format Painter (like you'd avoid the plague).** The Format Painter doesn't use styles, so any objects it generates have unique definitions, which bloats the CSS code.

- **Tab controls, slide controls, and popovers aren't your friends.** While these features may be handy for your desktop users, they require the server to send their data to the client just in case they're needed. So if you're used to piling lots of portals onto multiple tab controls on the desktop, you're creating layouts that have a heavy payload—whether the user actually asks to view them or not.

- **Field controls aren't too fond of you, either.** Radio buttons, checkbox sets, and pop-up calendars need to check with the server before you commit data in them. Use plain edit boxes whenever possible.

- **Minimize the use of images.** Use FileMaker's tools to create simple buttons. Avoid pasted icons or other frills.

- Use **script triggers, tooltips, and conditional formatting** sparingly, since they too must communicate with the server to make sure they function dynamically.

These tips just scratch the surface of ways to optimize your database for FileMaker Go and the Web. The FileMaker Pro Starter Solutions (page 113) provide some examples of layouts designed for WebDirect. Another free FileMaker template that addresses WebDirect optimization can be found at *www.fmstartingpoint.com*. For the most recent versions of the development guides, choose Help→Product Documentation→More Documentation.

Creating a Good User Experience

Consider the ways most people use their mobile devices—they're often on the move as they stare at their screens. So a layout that looks clean and uncluttered on a 1920 x 1200 monitor becomes tiny and hard to control on the iPhone's 640 x 960 screen. (And that's the dimensions for the newest iPhone. If your users are on pre–iPhone 6 models, they've got even fewer pixels to focus on.) The carefully scripted 16 × 16 pixels email button that you placed beside the Email field is perfectly adequate for a user with a mouse. But try to tap that button with a fingertip as you're rushing down the hallway frantically trying to send an email on the way to a meeting. Because a finger is not a precise pointing device, it's hard to hit the button instead of activating the field. If folks can't hit buttons to run scripts properly, it's more than a bad user experience. You could have users running the wrong scripts at the wrong time, which is an opportunity for all kinds of failure.

When users are on the go, they often have very specialized database needs. For instance, since salespeople are making contacts with customers, they may just need a list of customers and a way to review contact notes before a meeting. Warehouse workers don't need customer histories when they're filling orders; they just need to see a list of items to grab. Or stock personnel may need a very simple interface that lets them scan a product's bar code to find an item on a purchase order and mark the item as received.

Give users what they need to do their jobs, but nothing extra. When possible, break a task into several steps, each with its own layout, so you can send the smallest amount of data possible. For example, if users need to document their daily work on a desktop computer, you could create a single layout with one portal for entering their hours and a second where they can create a list of materials they've used. But on a mobile device or the Web, you should break those two tasks into separate layouts so that each one will load faster. Plus, the choices users have to make on each layout become more prominent, so the process is easier, even though it has two steps instead of one.

In addition to reducing layout clutter, use object styles (page 333) religiously. Remember that objects on the layout are rendered using CSS. When you format an object with a style instead of ad hoc formatting, you reduce the under-the-hood code that has to travel with your data. And as much as possible, limit the number of styles you use. That is, make all your field labels the same style, and use one style for all your fields as well. Of course, there are exceptions—fields that use pop-ups must use a different style than regular text fields, for example. But if you remember this rule, you'll be less tempted to make formatting changes without a very good reason.

Choosing Layouts for WebDirect and FileMaker Go

You control which set of layouts users see by writing a script that runs when the database opens. That way, no matter who opens the file, which platform they're viewing it on, or which device they're using to open your database, the script runs some tests and then sends each user to the proper opening layout for that device. Then you create navigation scripts that stay within the proper set of layouts.

For example, the Contacts template that comes with FileMaker Pro has four different Contact detail layouts: one each for desktop computers, iPhone/iPod Touch, iPad, and web browsers. Within each set of layouts, the navigation always stays within the set. So you check the user's platform at login, and there's no need to test again. Here are the two main functions you need to test:

- Get(SystemPlatform) returns a *3* on iOS, and a *4* if running in WebDirect. For desktop computers, the function returns *1* (Intel-based Macs), or *–2* (Windows).

- Get(ApplicationVersion) returns *Go x.x.x* for the iPhone or iPod touch and returns *Go iPad* for the iPad.

If your users only access your database from one of two platforms (either an iPad or a desktop computer, for example), then your opening script needs a test like this one:

```
If ( Get ( SystemPlatform ) = 3 )
    Go to Layout ( "Contacts | iPad" )
Else
    Go to Layout ( "Contacts | Desktop" )
End If
```

Throw iPhone and WebDirect users into the mix, and your script needs to be a bit more thorough:

```
If ( Get ( SystemPlatform ) < 3 )
     Go to Layout ( "Contacts | Desktop" )
Else If ( Get ( SystemPlatform ) = 4 )
     Go to Layout ( "Contacts | Web" )
Else If ( Get ( ApplicationVersion ) = "iPad" )
     Go to Layout ( "Contacts | iPad" )
Else
     Go to Layout ( "Contacts | iPhone" ))
End If
```

It's also a good idea to have your opening script Enter Browse Mode. WebDirect doesn't support Table view, so you might want to include a View As[] script step for web browser users. Check the opening scripts in the Starter Solutions for more FileMaker Go ideas, like hiding and locking toolbars or setting zoom levels.

■ Designing for Go

As you've learned, because of the unsupported features, behavioral differences, and smaller screens, you should create special layouts for FileMaker Go. Think about the tasks mobile users perform, and then design a set of layouts that give users what they need—and no more. To get an idea of what well-designed mobile layouts look like, take a look at the Starter Solutions. Figure 21-8 shows the Contact database's iPhone Layout. It's meant to help mobile users view their contacts, filter the list, see a specific contact's detail, and add a new contact. All these tasks are done on two lightweight layouts with minimal interfaces and limited features. See the box on page 838 for a way to avoid connecting to the server until the mobile user is back in your office.

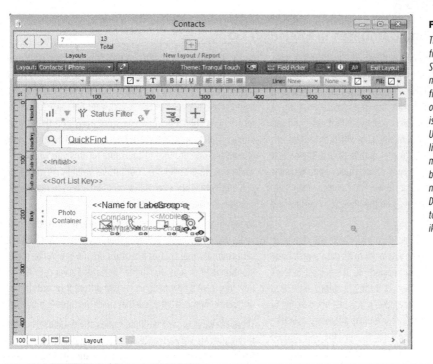

FIGURE 21-8

*This is the iPhone layout
from the Contacts Starter
Solution, shown in Layout
mode. It uses merge
fields to display data: The
only place a user can type
is in a Quick Find field.
Users can filter a long
list by using the pop-up
menu in the header. The +
button lets users enter a
new contact on a Contact
Detail page that's created
to be scrolled on a tiny
iPhone screen.*

■ Designing for WebDirect

The same basic rule of thumb you learned for FileMaker Go applies to designing for
the Web: Think about the tasks web users perform and then design a set of layouts
that give users exactly what they need. However, there are two more limitations on
the Web that you need to take into account.

Web browsers can only view one layout at a time (no multiple windows allowed).
You may need to rework any techniques you've employed that require users to view
or work with more than one window at a time. And the menus and available commands are limited in WebDirect. The next section explains.

Using Standalone Databases in FileMaker Go

If you're sharing a database with others, it's best to access the database only from FileMaker Server. However, there are times when you must have your company data on your own device—like when you're traveling in a remote area where Internet or cellphone service is sketchy. In that case, you can transfer the file, or more commonly, a file with reduced features and a small set of records, to your mobile device. The easiest way to transfer a file is to copy it into iTunes and then sync your device with that copy of iTunes. You can also email a file to yourself and open the email on the iPad. See FileMaker Go Help for more information.

Remember, though, that when you transfer a file you're making a *copy* of it, so any changes you make to its data aren't automatically transferred to your hosted file. It's easiest to work with local files on mobile devices if they're meant to be used only for viewing data; for example, if you just need a copy of your Contacts database so you can look up addresses as you're traveling. But if you expect to enter data in a file that's stored on a mobile device, you'll have to figure out how to sync that data with the copy of the database back in your office. In a simplest-case scenario, you can just move your mobile copy up to your server and throw away the file that stayed home.

But this situation is rare, since while you're away updating your notes on all those meetings you had, the office staff was busily updating records in the database on your FileMaker Server. Now you have two databases, each of which has some records that have been updated and some that have not. You might think that you can just search your database for all the records you changed while you were away and then do an Import Update into the shared database. But what if some else edited one or more of the *same* records you worked on while you were traveling? Your import would overwrite that person's data entry, even if it was edited after you made your changes in your local copy of the file.

Sometimes it's safest to import only the new records you create while you're traveling. But even that has pitfalls, because the serial number that creates a record's unique key will be incrementing in your copy *and* in the FileMaker Server copy of file. Now you have a new headache—two different records in two different copies of a database that share the same "unique" id.

There are ways to sync multiple copies of a database, but the techniques are very advanced and go beyond the scope of this book. So if this is an issue for you, there are some third-party syncing solutions you should investigate. Do a Web search for "FileMaker mobile sync" to learn about the commercial solutions that might make your mobile life easier.

Understanding the WebDirect Toolbar

FileMaker's toolbar is mimicked in your browser. The tools that carry over look very much like their FileMaker counterparts. The Share button is missing, and Show All has been moved to a popover found under the found count display (Figure 21-9).

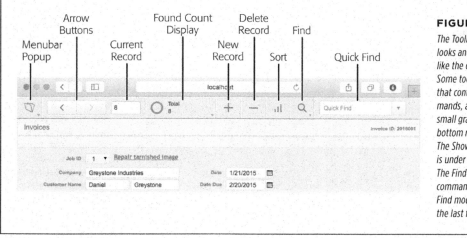

FIGURE 21-9

The Toolbar in a browser looks and acts very much like the one in FileMaker. Some tools have popovers that contain extra commands, as indicated by a small gray triangle at the bottom right of the tool. The Show All command is under the found count. The Find popover has commands for entering Find mode and repeating the last find.

Understanding WebDirect Menus

While it's up to you to optimize your layouts for better performance in WebDirect, the WPE takes the first step by simplifying the menus. Custom menus don't work in WebDirect, so you'll need to come up with a different solution, like providing more buttons with scripted actions on each layout. Plus, the Menu bar is reduced to eight menus (Figure 21-10), most of which are pared down significantly from what you're used to seeing in FileMaker:

- The **File menu** is limited to three commands: Import Records, Export Record, and Save→Snapshot Link.

- The **Edit menu** has two commands: Clear and Export Field Contents. Both commands act only on the currently active field.

- The **View menu** lets you switch between Browse and Find modes; View as Form or List; Show/Hide the Status Toolbar; and View Image Full Size.

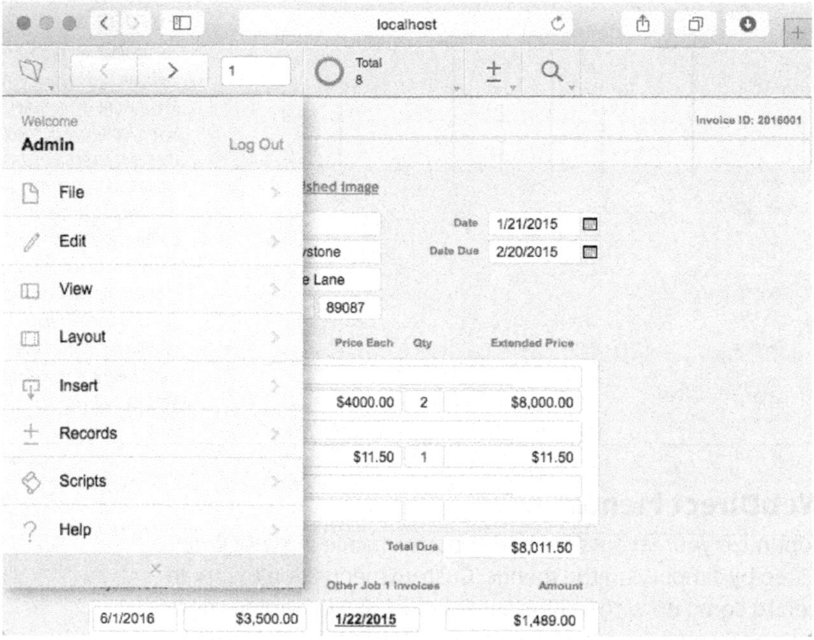

FIGURE 21-10

FileMaker's menus are all found under the folder icon at the left of the toolbar. Instead of typical hierarchical menus, these commands switch within the same popover space. To view a menu's commands, click the light gray arrow at the right of any item. That menu's commands open up in the same popover space, along with a Back button that takes you up one level of commands.

- The **Layout menu** acts like the Layout popup menu in FileMaker—layouts that are included in the menus are included here. If you inactivate all layouts, the Layout menu still appears, but has no choices. See Figure 21-11 for an organized set of layouts for each platform the file is accessed from.

- The **Insert menu** has four choices: Current Date, Current Time, Current User Name, and Insert Into Container. All commands are grayed out unless a field is active.

- The **Records menu** is almost the same as its FileMaker counterpart. The only options removed for WebDirect are Saved Finds and Replace Field Contents.

- The **Scripts menu** does not have a Modify Scripts command, but otherwise functions as it does in FileMaker. Scripts you mark as available are shown in the menu—if the user has permission to run them.

- The **Help menu** gives you links to FileMaker WebDirect Help and Provide FileMaker Feedback.

- The **Admin menu** lets users Log Out or Change Password (if their privileges allow this feature). Encourage your web users to log out at the end of their sessions to free up concurrent connections.

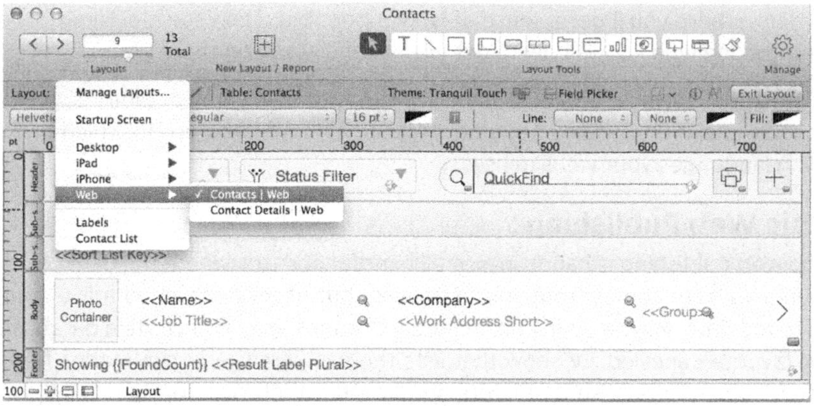

FIGURE 21-11

Here's the Contact detail page shown in Layout mode, as designed for a browser. As in the iPhone version, no fields are editable, and a minimal amount of data is shown. You can also see the Layout pop-up menu showing how the different versions of each layout are organized. Create navigation scripts that put users into the right set of layouts on login, and then keeps them there throughout their session.

The menus in this list are what your users get to see when they access a FileMaker database through a browser. You can still give them buttons to perform actions that aren't included in the menu. But make sure that all of your script steps are compatible with WebDirect, and take care to keep users off layouts that aren't designed for their platform. You'll probably use a mix of special navigation scripts, access privileges to restrict access to non-platform layouts, and enabling or disabling layouts in the pop-up menu.

■ Sharing Databases on the Internet without WebDirect

WebDirect lets you share FileMaker databases without learning the HTML, PHP, or XML code that most websites depend on. But if you need to do more than the light-weight uses that are most suited to WebDirect, or if you just want more control over the design and features of your FileMaker-driven website, you have other choices. You can write everything from scratch using Custom Web Publishing (CWP) or you can publish static web pages from exported data.

Custom Web Publishing

Custom Web Publishing requires you to roll your own solution from scratch. That is, you'll write HTML web pages that include custom code that interacts with your FileMaker database. Using XML/XSLT or PHP for the code, you can build incredibly powerful web-based databases. With add-on software, you can even use other web technologies like Ruby on Rails (*www.sixfriedrice.com/wp/products/rfm*) or Lasso (*www.lassosoft.com*). But all these custom coding languages have steep learning curves and are beyond the scope of this book. Get your feet wet with FileMaker Server 14's Help, where you'll get a sense of what's possible. Then start learning code, or hire someone who knows how to get FileMaker singing on the Web.

To configure FileMaker Server to share custom web publishing databases, you need to enable the Web Server and either PHP or XML, depending on which of those coding languages your website uses.

Static Web Publishing

Static web publishing is handy in a small handful of cases where the data you need to run a website comes from your database, but users don't need a live connection to the data. Maybe your website rarely changes—say you wrote a database for your favorite canceled TV show that lists the cast, crew, and summaries for each episode. You can publish that information on the Web by exporting HTML tables from FileMaker (page 863). Pretty up the HTML code to match your website and then upload your pages to your web server.

If your FileMaker Server machine is hosting your website, move the pages the root folder of the web server:

- Windows: *[drive]:\Program Files\FileMaker\FileMaker Server\HTTPServer\Conf*

- OS X: */Library/FileMaker Server/HTTPServer/htdocs*

Sharing Data with Other Systems

Sometimes you need to move data to other systems—when you're creating reports, for example, as described in Chapter 16. For example, perhaps you want to dump data into a spreadsheet for analysis by staff who don't use FileMaker. Or maybe that same person will have data she needs to send back to you, but you don't want to enter hundreds of records manually.

If you have data in almost any kind of program—spreadsheets full of figures, lists of names and phone numbers, electronic orders in XML, folders full of pictures or text documents—FileMaker can *import* it directly into your database. If your data is already in FileMaker, then you can *export* it to lists, other databases, XML, or most common formats. FileMaker takes a wonderfully flexible approach: It lets you handle simple imports and exports with just a click or two and provides the features to tackle the most complex cases as well—if you (or some hired help) are willing to do the necessary work.

If your company uses one of the vast corporate databases—Oracle, Microsoft SQL Server, or MySQL—FileMaker can integrate directly with them, bringing its powerful (and easy) developer tools to bear on their complex-yet-oh-so-speedy data. You can put your corporate SQL data right on the FileMaker layout, perform FileMaker finds, write scripts, and even add calculation fields, all without writing a single line of SQL code.

■ Sharing Your Data with Others

Most database systems don't live in a vacuum. Chances are, your information is important to someone else, or you need to see it in another program. You may want to transfer job information to your Accounting software, or send the sales report to your associate across town. Luckily, FileMaker provides options for getting the data out of your database in all kinds of forms.

Save/Send Records As

If your data is destined for a person (rather than some other computer program), then you want a format that's easy to look at and to work with on almost any computer. FileMaker lets you save your data in two common formats: an Excel spreadsheet and a PDF document, plus the unique Snapshot Link. Choose Excel if you want to be able to work with the data (perform analysis, combine it with other data, create graphs, and so forth). If you want the output to look just like it looks in FileMaker, and you don't need it to be editable, then a PDF is the perfect choice. Snapshot directly links other FileMaker users to a particular set of records in your database.

■ SAVING AS MICROSOFT EXCEL

If people need to work with the data you send them, but they aren't lucky enough to have FileMaker, you can create an Excel file for them. (And presumably, if they're working with data, they have either Excel or a program that can open Excel spreadsheets.) Usually you perform a find to get a found set of the records you need exported. Then choose File→Save/Send Records As→Excel. When you do, FileMaker shows the window in Figure 22-1.

The Save pop-up menu lets you choose whether you want to save all the "Records being browsed" (that is, the found set) or just the "Current record." Turn on "Automatically open file" if you want to see the spreadsheet as soon as FileMaker finishes saving it. When you do, FileMaker automatically launches Excel and shows you the spreadsheet. You also have the option to "Create email with file as attachment," so it's easy to check your work and create a quick email with the data your boss just asked you to email her. Once you save, FileMaker creates a new email message in your email program, attaches the spreadsheet, and opens the message so you can add recipients, a subject, and any message you want.

If you click Options, you can set up some basic details for your new Excel file. For example, you can choose whether you want your FileMaker field names to appear in the first row of the spreadsheet. You can also type a worksheet name and a title, subject, and author (each of which appears in the spreadsheet in the appropriate places). The dialog box doesn't let you control which fields are exported; all the fields on the current layout are included. Control which fields are exported by navigating to a layout that contains just the fields you want to export. If you need to export the fields in a specific order, switch to Table view, and rearrange the columns as you need them to appear in Excel.

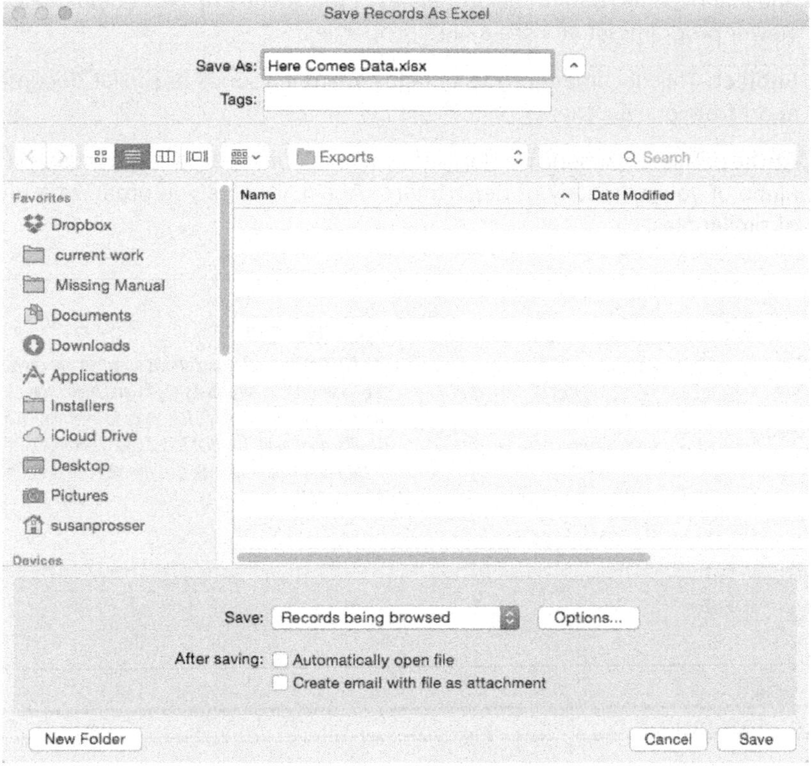

FIGURE 22-1

The Save Records As Excel window lets you tell FileMaker where to save the spreadsheet file. It also gives you the option of automatically opening the file you're creating, so you don't have to go rummaging around your hard drive looking for it. Most useful, though, is the option to create an email with the exported file as an attachment.

■ SAVING AS PORTABLE DOCUMENT FORMAT (PDF)

Just about anybody with a computer, smart phone, or tablet can view PDF files. With PDF, you get to choose exactly how the data looks, since this format preserves the styles applied on your layouts. With FileMaker's layout tools and the "Save/Send Record as PDF" command, you can use email to distribute invoices, product catalogs, sales brochures, or annual reports. You can even send vision-impaired people a file their software can read aloud. Even if all you need to do is send people data they can see but can't change, then a PDF file is just what the software engineer ordered.

TIP The most common PDF viewer, Adobe Reader, is a free download from adobe.com. Mac OS X also comes preloaded with its own PDF viewer, called Preview.

You can send just the current record, the whole found set, or one blank record set. As with Save As Excel, you have the option to have the file open automatically or to attach it to an email. But behind the Options button you find a much richer set of choices that are specific to PDF files. There are three tabs—Document, Security, and Initial View. Starting with the Document tab (Figure 22-2), you can set the following:

- **Title.** This title isn't the name you give the file in the dialog box. It's an additional title that becomes part of the properties of the document. Most, but not all, PDF viewer programs let you see a file's properties.

- **Subject.** This document property helps you tell a series of similar documents apart from one another.

- **Author.** This document property is usually your name but may also be the name of your company or department. Again, it helps you organize a bunch of similar files.

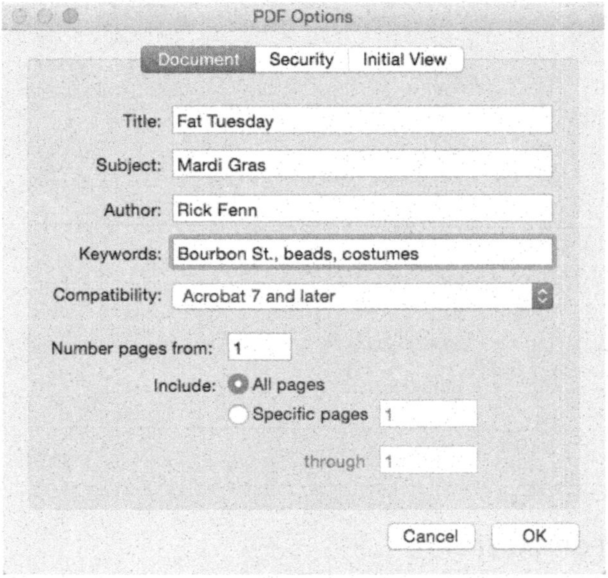

FIGURE 22-2

The PDF Options dialog box shows up when you choose File→Save/Send Records As→PDF and then click Options. The Document tab lets you add information to the PDF document. The first four options become part of the document's properties, as described in the note on page 847.

- **Keywords.** Some file management programs can search these keywords to locate documents.

- **Compatibility.** Choose from Acrobat 5, 6, or 7 and later. If you think your recipient might not have the latest and greatest PDF viewer, pick a lower number.

- **Number pages from.** You can make a different numbering system than the one you have in FileMaker. Keep in mind, though, if your layout displays page numbers in FileMaker, this setting won't change them. You could create a document where the page number in the PDF viewer is 3 but the number displayed on the page is 1, because that's where the main text begins.

- **Include.** You can set a limited page-number range with these options, so that only a part of the found set is included in the PDF file. You may have to go to Preview mode in FileMaker first, though, to help you set the page range properly.

> **NOTE**   You can see the PDF file's Title, Subject, and Author in Adobe Acrobat's PDF viewer's Document Properties window. In Mac OS X's Preview program, choose Tools→Inspector, instead.

In the Security tab (Figure 22-3), you can decide how much access you give your recipients when they receive your file.

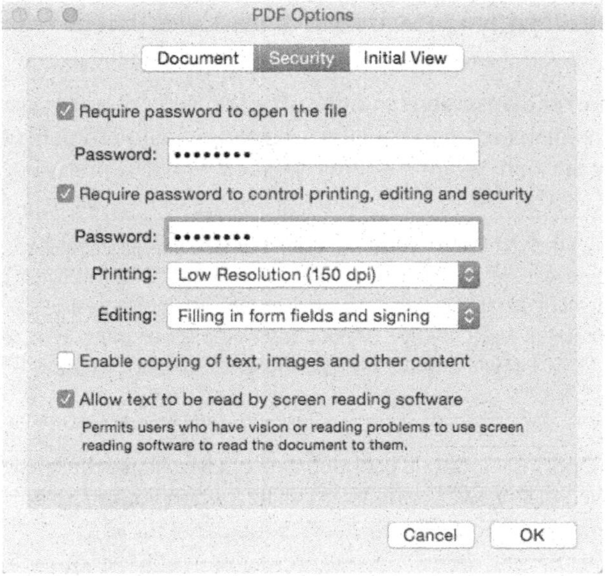

FIGURE 22-3

The Security tab lets you lock down your PDF file if you need to prevent inappropriate use. Some older PDF reading programs may not recognize all these options. If someone's PDF reader doesn't have security features, it can't open the PDF file at all, so your data is still safe.

You can choose:

- **Require password to open the file.** Click the checkbox to turn this option on and then enter a password. This checkbox is useful if you're selling a catalog and provide passwords only to people who've paid to receive it. Then, of course, there's the standard use; you just don't want every Malcolm, Reese, and Dewey poking around in your PDF files.

- **Require password to control printing, editing and security.** Click the checkbox to turn this option on and enter a password. You might want your PDF freely distributed but not so freely used. If so, don't require a password to open the file, but lock it down so nobody can use the material without your permission and a password. With this option checked, a whole raft of new options becomes available. You can set the following:

- **Printing.** Choose from Not Permitted, Low Resolution (150 dpi), or High Resolution. These options would protect photographic or other artwork images that you want to send in a catalog but don't want people to reprint freely. You also may want someone to *see* your document onscreen, but not print it and risk having it fall into the wrong hands.

- **Editing.** Although PDF files are generally considered view-only, with the right software, they can actually be edited. If you don't want to allow this (or want to restrict what can be done), choose options from the Editing pop-up menu. For example, if you're sending a contract for review, and you want to be sure no new clauses are snuck in while it's away, you can choose "Not permitted."

- **Enable copying of text, images and other content.** With this option turned on, recipients can copy and paste material from your PDF file.

- **Allow text to be read by screen reading software.** This option lets people with vision or reading problems have their screen-reading programs read your document out loud. Seems like turning this off would be pretty uncool.

> **NOTE** Looking for absolute, ironclad control of your information? Handwrite it on paper and store it in a secret vault. Vast amounts of money and time have been spent trying to secure digital information from unauthorized access and reuse. Ask the record companies how that worked out for them. The old chestnut about the lock only keeping the honest man honest applies here, too. PDF security settings are deterrents to unwanted use of your intellectual property, but they're all surmountable. When you use these tools, you're managing risk, not eliminating it.

The final tab in the PDF Options window is probably the one you'll use the least. But if you like to control which PDF viewer options are visible when your recipient first opens your PDF file, then Initial View (Figure 22-4) is the panel for you:

- **Show.** Your choices include Page Only (just the FileMaker layout, with no extra tools or panels), Bookmarks Panel and Page, or Pages Panel and Page, to offer viewers some navigation options.

- **Page Layout.** Control the way the PDF viewer displays multipage documents. If you choose *Default,* your recipients' preferred view remains in force. But you can also specify Single Page, Continuous, Facing, or Continuous-Facing.

- **Magnification.** Here you can define an automatic magnification as either a fixed percentage of the document's native size or automatically adjusted to fit the window.

> **WARNING** These Initial View options may or may not actually take effect, depending on what program and what version of that program the PDF is opened with.

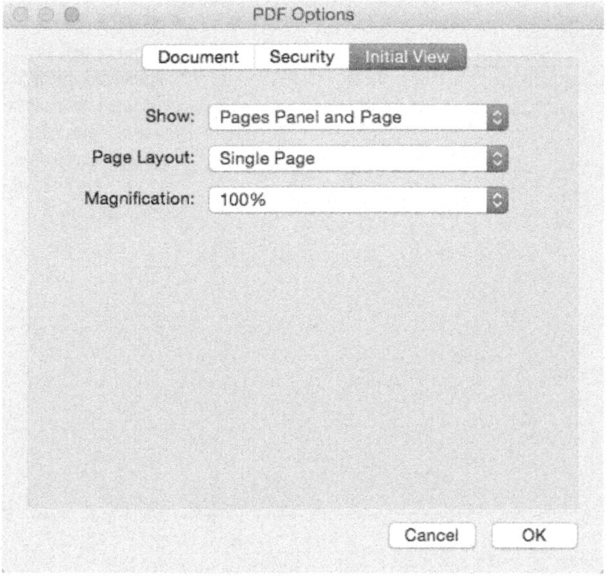

FIGURE 22-4

You get to decide what the user sees when she first opens the PDF containing your database info. Once again, not all these options work in older versions of PDF software, so consider your settings here a suggestion.

Snapshot Link

At times, collaborating with other users of the same database can get complicated. You may answer a question by saying "go to the monthly report layout, find the records for last May, and then sort by region," and be met with a vacant stare. But if your colleague knows how to click, Snapshot Links can help lead the way.

A Snapshot Link is a little package of instructions saved as a small file. Send that file to your less-savvy colleague, and with a double-click, the database opens to the layout and found set of records you chose.

Setting up the Snapshot Link is easy. Switch to the layout you want to share, find and sort the records, and then select File→Save/Send Records As→Snapshot Link. The Save Records As Snapshot Link dialog box appears (Figure 22-5), looking much like a Save dialog box. Choose where you want to save it, whether to include the current record or the whole found set, and if you want FileMaker to attach it to a new, outgoing email message for you. With that, FileMaker saves a Snapshot Link file, with an .fmpsl file name extension.

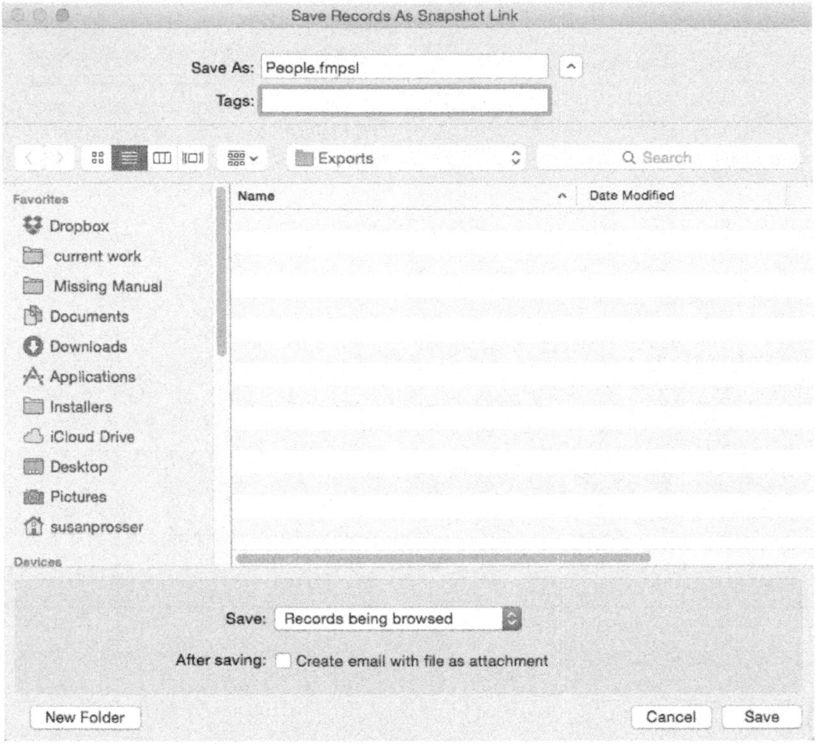

FIGURE 22-5

The Save Records As Snapshot Link dialog box looks suspiciously similar to any old Save dialog box. And it does indeed save a file, just one without any actual data.

Snapshot Links are XML files that contain eight pieces of information about your database that FileMaker uses to recreate the state of the database at the time the snapshot was taken.

- **The paths to the database.** Yes, that's plural. The snapshot records your database's location on your hard drive, as well as any potential network paths to the file. So long as the database is available through FileMaker Network sharing, Snapshot Link users on your network can access it.

- **The found set of records,** listed by their internal record IDs.

- **The current layout.** The Snapshot Link records the layout's internal ID number, not its name. You can rename that layout all day, but unless you delete it outright, the Snapshot Link is going to find it.

- **View state.** Whether you're looking at the layout as a form, a list, or a table, the link's recipient will, too.

- **Current record.** If you want to draw attention to a particular record in the found set, make sure that record is active when you create the link. That record will be active when your colleague opens the link.

- **Toolbar state.** Either showing or not.

- **Mode.** Create the Snapshot Link in Preview mode and you guessed it—that's what the user will see. Create it while in Browse or Layout mode, and the user will get Browse mode. You can't create Snapshot Links in Find mode.

- **Sort Order.** However you last sorted the current found set is retained.

Snapshot Links are slick, but it's important to understand what they don't include.

- **Your last find.** The Snapshot Link contains a list of record IDs. That list may be the result of a find for every customer who bought a pogo stick, but it's current only at the time the Snapshot was created. If you open that snapshot in six weeks, new pogo stick customers won't be on the list, and any deleted customers won't be magically restored.

- **Data.** Snapshot Links are instructions for FileMaker, not unlike a script. They tell FileMaker something like "Go to this layout; show me records 1, 3, and 5; and sort them by date." They don't possess any record data at all. When using a Snapshot Link, you always see the *most current* data.

- **Privileges.** Just because *you* can see a given layout doesn't mean others can. If the recipient of your Snapshot Link lacks the database permissions to see the layout or records specified in the link, FileMaker won't allow it.

■ External SQL Sources

If you don't know MySQL from MySpace, and have no interest in taking your File-Maker skills to the hard-core level of IT professionals, then feel free to skip right past this section. But if you have to cross between these worlds or need to bring the power and capability of industrial-grade database servers into your systems, then FileMaker's *External SQL Sources* (or ESS) feature will seem like magic.

In a nutshell, you point your FileMaker database in the general direction of an Oracle, Microsoft SQL Server, or MySQL database (hereafter referred to as a SQL database). FileMaker then takes in information about that database, learning all it needs to know to make those normally complicated systems almost as easy to use as FileMaker. You can create table occurrences in your Relationships graph that are actually references to the tables in the SQL database. You can draw relationship lines between SQL tables, and even between your FileMaker tables and the SQL tables. You can create a layout based on a SQL table, drop a few fields on the layout and then jump to Find mode, where FileMaker searches the real honest-to-goodness SQL data and shows you a found set of records.

Behind the Data

Snapshot Links are simply XML files.

XML, or *eXtensible Markup Language*, is a computer language designed to give different computer systems and programs a flexible way to share information among one another. XML can be very complex, but it's also fantastically flexible. You can muck about in a Snapshot Link's XML code if you wish. Just use a text editor or XML authoring program to open an .fmpsl file and you see something like this example. Even if you don't know XML, you can probably see that you can change the Snapshot Link's view by changing `<view type="form"></view>` to `<view type="list"></view>`.

While changing Snapshot Link XML code can't cause any harm to your database, it can very easily render the Snapshot Link itself unusable. That's OK, because you're working on a backup copy, *right?*

```
<?xml version="1.0" encoding="UTF-8"?>
<fpsl>
<uistate>
  <universalpathlist>
  filemac:/Macintosh HD/Users/Charts.fmp12
  </universalpathlist>
  <rows type="nativeIDList" rowcount="66"
  basetableid="130">
    &#10;<![CDATA[1-66]]>&#10;
</rows>
<layout id="6"></layout>
<view type="form"></view>
<selectedrow type="nativeID" id="1">
</selectedrow>
<statustoolbar visible="True">
</statustoolbar>
<mode value="browseMode"></mode>
<sortlist Maintain="True" value="True">
  <sort type="Ascending">
    <primaryfield>
      <field tableid="1065090"
      table="Attendance" id="2"
      name="Facility">
      </field>
    </primaryfield>
  </sort>
</sortlist>
</uistate>
</fpsl>
```

With few exceptions, a SQL table works just like any other FileMaker table. But instead of storing the data on your hard drive, the SQL database stores and manages the data. You don't need to know a lick of SQL programming to work with it. When you add a record by using the Records→New Record command, FileMaker sends the right secret code that adds the record to the SQL database. Just type in a field and then press Enter, and FileMaker updates the SQL database. It just doesn't get more seamless than this.

But before you get to the promised land of seamless data exchange, you have some setup to do. The process can be divided into three main tasks: setting up a data source, connecting FileMaker to the source, and then telling FileMaker how to use the connected data. The next sections teach you how to do each task.

Setting Up a Data Source

Before you can take advantage of ESS, you need to set up a few things. This business of getting things installed and configured is the hardest part—and it's not FileMaker's fault.

■ THE SQL DATABASE SERVER

First of all, you need an approved database. FileMaker needs to know exactly which database you're using:

- Microsoft SQL Server 2012

- Microsoft SQL Server 2008

- Oracle 11g

- MySQL 56 Community Edition

NOTE Supported version information was still in flux at the time of this writing. Check FileMaker Help (page 35) or the FileMaker Knowledge Base (*http://help.filemaker.com*) for up-to-date information.

If your SQL database isn't on the supported list, you have to upgrade or migrate to one that is. Trying to make a different type of database work is futile—just ask someone who's tried. Luckily, this list represents recent versions of three very common database systems. If you don't have a SQL database, but you want to get one, you need to research which is best for you. But if you just want to experiment, start with MySQL. For most purposes (including real commercial use), it's completely free. To get MySQL for Mac OS X or Windows, visit *www.mysql.com* and look for the MySQL Community Server link.

The rest of this section assumes you have a working SQL database server and that you have access to at least one database on that server.

■ INSTALLING THE ODBC DRIVER

In order for FileMaker to communicate with the SQL database, you need an ODBC driver. This software acts as the bridge between programs on your computer and the SQL database server software. The driver is specific to your database server. If you're using Oracle, you need an Oracle ODBC driver, for instance. If you use Microsoft Windows, this step is usually a breeze. Each of the supported SQL databases has an ODBC driver provided by the manufacturer. Just visit their website and find out how to get the driver you need.

NOTE If you're not sure what you need, try searching the Web for *microsoft sql server ODBC driver download*. The first site listed is probably the download page you need. (Substitute *oracle* or *mysql* for Microsoft SQL Server, as appropriate.)

Mac OS X users aren't so lucky. The big database developers don't provide free ODBC drivers for the Mac. Instead, head over to *www.actualtech.com* and then purchase the right driver (they're cheap and work beautifully). FileMaker, Inc., worked directly with Actual to ensure maximum compatibility, and they provide the drivers of choice. (For MySQL, choose the driver called "ODBC driver for Open Source Databases.")

Once you've acquired the correct driver, install it on your computer. After you've installed the driver, you have to configure it.

Your computer's operating system has the ODBC system built in. You use a special program on your computer to tell it which SQL databases you want to work with. The configuration process is entirely different on Mac OS X and Windows, so go directly to the section that applies to you.

■ CONFIGURING THE DATA SOURCE IN WINDOWS

You configure your Windows machine for ODBC in the Control Panel (Start→Control Panel). Open the System and Security category and then click Administrative Tools. If you don't have "System and Security," then look for Administrative Tools right in the Control Panel window and open it there.

Assuming you've found the Administrative Tools window, look inside it and then open Data Sources (ODBC). You should see a window that looks like Figure 22-6, although drivers vary.

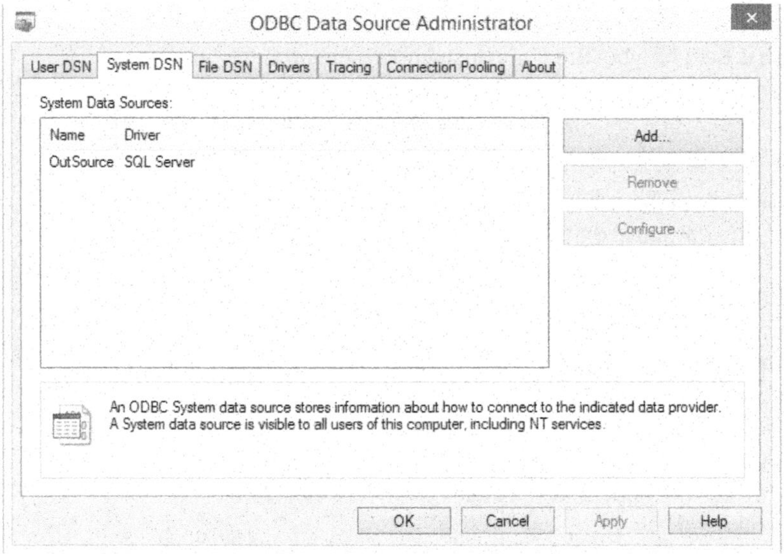

FIGURE 22-6

The ODBC Data Source Administrator in Windows lets you configure the SQL databases your computer has access to. The acronym DSN stands for Data Source Name, since you name each data source you define here and then refer to it by name in FileMaker.

In this window, you add a *DSN (data source name)* for each SQL database you want FileMaker to work with. A DSN can be one of two flavors: A *system* DSN is available to everyone who uses your computer, and a *user* DSN is available only to the person who created it. FileMaker works only with the System DSN variety, so to get started, switch to the System DSN tab. Unfortunately, you may not have permission to define these computer-wide data sources on your work computer. If Windows doesn't let you add a system DSN, then contact your system administrator.

Once you're on the System DSN tab, click Add. Windows shows you a list of available ODBC drivers. Select the appropriate one and then click Finish. (Don't get too excited by the label on this button; you're nowhere near finished.)

NOTE You may get a little confused by the list of available drivers in Windows. First, you may see many drivers whose names are apparently in a foreign language. Just scroll right past them. Also, you may be tempted to select the driver called SQL Server, but this driver is specifically for *Microsoft* SQL Server. The currently recommended drive is called "SQL Server Native Client 11.0."

From this point forward, configuration works a lot like Mac OS X. Skip ahead to "Finishing ODBC data source configuration.".

■ CONFIGURING DATA SOURCES ON MAC OS X

On Mac OS X, you configure ODBC data sources by using a program called ODBC Manager. If it's not already in your Applications→Utilities folder, download a free copy at *www.odbcmanager.net*. When you launch the program, you see the window in Figure 22-7.

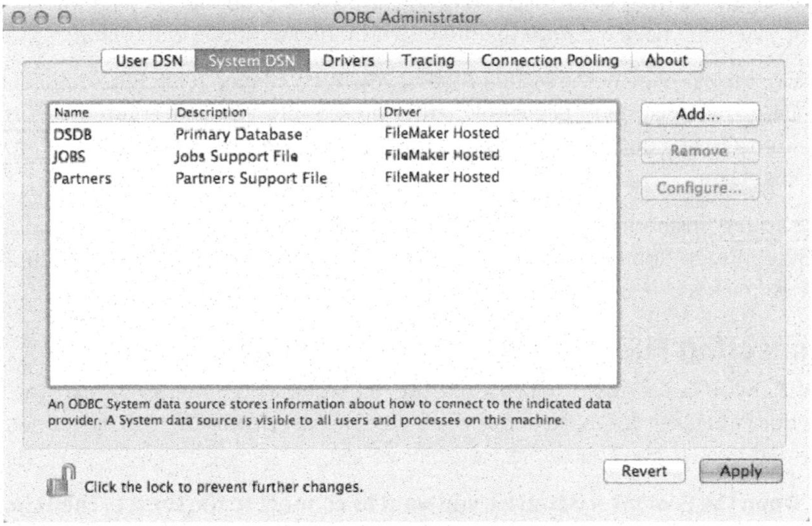

FIGURE 22-7

The ODBC Manager on Mac OS X lets you create ODBC data sources. You need to log in to your computer as an administrator to create the kind of data source FileMaker needs. You may also need to click the padlock icon in the bottom-left corner of this window before you can make changes.

When you open ODBC Manager, first click the padlock icon in the bottom-left corner to unlock it. Then click the System DSN tab. (FileMaker works only with system-wide data sources.) Next, click Add. A sheet slides down, showing a list of ODBC drivers installed on your computer. Select the one you want and then click OK.

At this point, the exact configuration will vary based on the driver you're using. If you aren't sure what settings to choose, work with the other system's database administrator.

■ FINISHING ODBC DATA SOURCE CONFIGURATION

The exact setup procedure varies with each ODBC driver, but a few things remain constant:

- On Mac OS X, even though you're in the System DSN tab, you have the option of creating either a *user* or a *system* DSN. Make sure you choose *system.*

- Give the data source any name you like. You'll use this name later when you connect FileMaker to the database. But bear in mind if you *change* a name here, you'll have to update every FileMaker database that uses it or the connections will break.

- The description isn't important. Leave it blank, or leave a note for yourself.

- You need to know the address (IP address or host name) of the database server, as well as a user name and password. You also need to know the name of the database you're connecting to (not Oracle or MySQL, but the name of the actual database on the server, like Products or Financial).

- Your driver may ask lots of questions, but you can usually accept the pre-entered answers for most of them. If you're not sure, talk to your database administrator. If you don't have a database administrator, make friends with one.

- On the last page of the setup process, you get a chance to test the data source. Click this button—it tells you whether all the info you just entered is correct. Better to find out now than try to unravel ODBC error messages passed through FileMaker.

Once you're finished, you see your data source listed in the System DSN tab of your ODBC configuration program. Go ahead and close the window. Your configuration work is finished.

Connecting FileMaker to a SQL Data Source

Now that you've set up the data source, the hardest part is done. Your next step is to tell your FileMaker database about the SQL database. You'll do that by connecting your database to the source file. Here's how:

1. **Open the FileMaker database you want to connect to the source. Then choose File→Manage→External Data Sources.**

   Here's where you tell your database about other places it can find data. You used this same window to connect one FileMaker database to another. This time, though, you're going to connect to a non-FileMaker database.

2. **Click New.**

   FileMaker shows you the Edit Data Source window.

Advanced ODBC Data Source Options

At the bottom of the Edit Data Source window, you see a section labeled "Filter tables" (Figure 22-8). These settings are entirely optional but may prove very useful if you're connecting to a complex database system. These settings tell FileMaker which tables you consider important, and which ones it can safely ignore. Doing so means you don't have to look at very long lists as you build your database, and it helps FileMaker keep things running as quickly as possible.

Database terminology is inconsistent from one system to another. The "Filter tables" section gives you three empty boxes to fill in, some with mysterious names. Here's how it shakes out:

- If you use Oracle, the Catalog box is irrelevant: Leave it empty. In the Schema box, you can enter a user name. When you do, FileMaker will look at only tables owned by that user.

- If you use Microsoft SQL Server, you can put the name of a particular database in the Catalog box to limit FileMaker to only tables in that database. If you use schemas, or collections of tables and views, you can also restrict FileMaker to just one schema.

- If you use MySQL, the Catalog box has no bearing on things, so you can leave it empty. If you want to see only tables for a particular user, enter the user name in the Schema box.

- Whatever your database, if you care only about one particular table, enter its name in the Table name box.

FileMaker will then show that table alone.

To the right of these three boxes, FileMaker offers three check-boxes. In the world of SQL databases, two or three *different* things act like tables.

- Tables are real honest-to-goodness tables, a lot like their FileMaker counterparts.

- Views are sort of like smart folders in iTunes or your mail program: They show portions of one or more tables based on criteria defined on the database server. If you're accessing a complex database and you need read-only access to a specific portion, you might consider asking your database administrator to create a view that includes just the data you need. This will make things simpler for you down the road.

- System tables are tables the database system creates itself for various purposes. (MySQL doesn't have this kind of table, so don't fret about it if you're a MySQL user.)

Your job is to turn on the checkbox for each type you want FileMaker to show. You can also turn off all three checkboxes, and FileMaker will show everything it can.

If you don't know what any of this means, try leaving every box blank, and turning on Tables and Views. If FileMaker takes a long time showing tables to pick from, If the table you want isn't in the list, or if you feel like you're seeing loads of tables you don't want to see, consult your SQL database administrator for help.

3. **In the Name box, type *Web Leads*.**

You can name the data source anything you want. This name appears when you're choosing tables to add to the Relationships graph, so make it descriptive.

4. **Click the ODBC radio button below the Name box.**

FileMaker revamps the dialog box so it looks like the one in Figure 22-8.

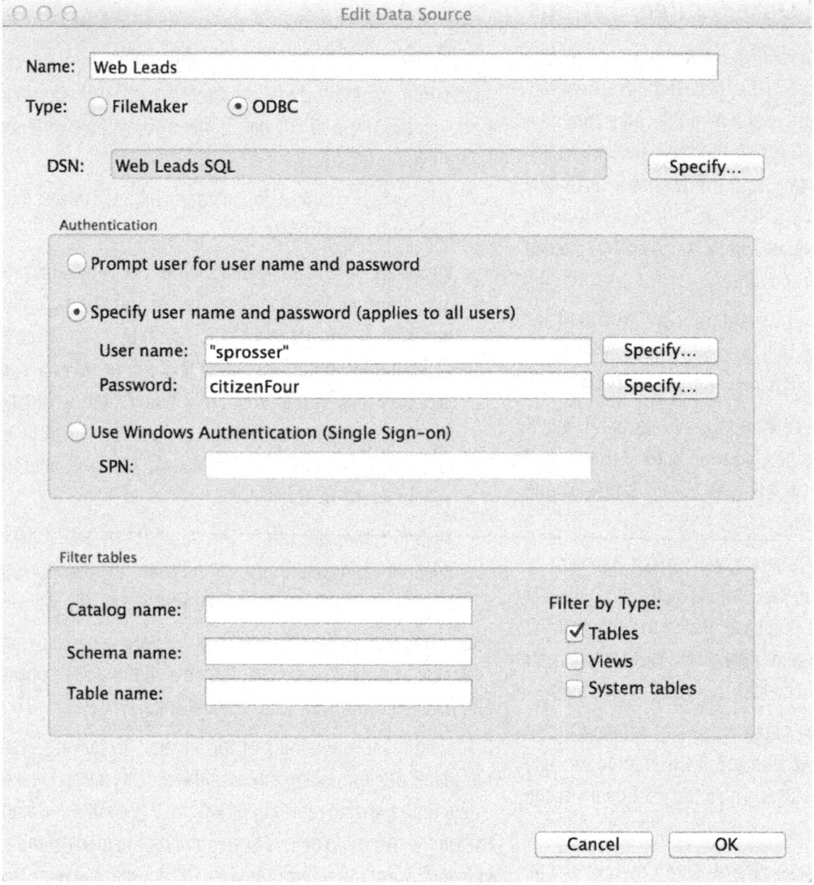

FIGURE 22-8

When you select ODBC as the type for your new data source, the Edit Data Source window takes on a whole new look. Instead of just the path to a FileMaker database, you tell FileMaker which ODBC data source to connect to, the user name and password to use, and which SQL objects you want to see. Don't worry if these terms don't make sense yet. You'll learn about them later in this chapter, and many of them don't matter much anyway.

5. **Click Specify.**

   You see a list of all the system ODBC data sources defined on your computer.

6. **Choose the data source you want to connect to and then click OK.**

   FileMaker puts the data source name in the box next to DSN.

At this point you have a decision to make. When someone opens this database, how does it log in to the remote database? You have three options here:

- Turn on **Prompt user for user name and password** if you want people to enter the login information when FileMaker makes the connection. This option means everyone has to log in to the SQL database every time they open the FileMaker database (in addition to any password they need to open the FileMaker file).

- Turn on **Specify username and password (applies to all users)** if you want FileMaker to automatically log in to the SQL database on everyone's behalf. When you do, you can enter a calculation to determine either value, so you can hard-code a text value, automatically use the current user's FileMaker account name (with the Get(AccountName) function), or any other mechanism you need.

- If you're using Microsoft Windows and Microsoft SQL Server, you can turn on **Use Windows Authentication (Single Sign-on).** This option lets FileMaker automatically connect to the SQL database by using the Windows user name and password. Your database administrator has to configure the Windows accounts properly for this setup to work (you can find details in the FileMaker help by searching for "ODBC Single Sign-on"). Also, you have to get the service principal name (SPN) from your database administrator.

> **NOTE** You may be wondering why you have to enter a user name and password here at all, since you already typed them in when you created the ODBC data source. The ODBC system uses that information only to test your data source. It doesn't actually *use* that login info when you open the database.

In this case, turn on "Specify user name and password (applies to all users)," and type the user name and password for your SQL database. Click OK to tell FileMaker you're done. Click OK again in the Manage External Data Sources window to get back to your main database window.

Adding SQL Tables to a FileMaker Database

Your database now has a pipeline to the tables in a SQL data source. But you haven't told it what to do with those tables yet. Your next stop is the Relationships tab of the Manage Database window, where you can add table occurrences from the SQL database tables to the relationships graph.

Choose File→Manage→Database, and switch to the Relationships tab. Then click the Add Table button, just as though you were adding a normal FileMaker table occurrence. But this time, when the Specify Table window pops up (Figure 22-9), click the Data Source pop-up menu and then choose the name of your SQL data source.

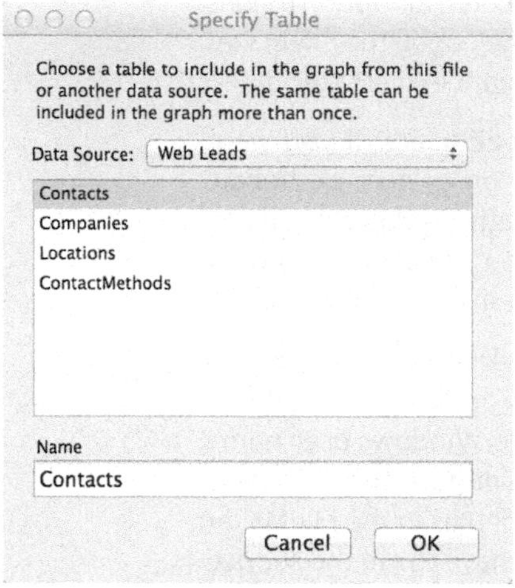

FIGURE 22-9

Once you've configured the data source, adding tables from a SQL database to your FileMaker Relationships graph works exactly the way you'd expect: simply. Here's the Specify Table dialog box from a SQL-based Web Leads database. Four tables are listed, and you can choose the one you need for a new TO on your graph.

The list below the pop-up menu changes to show all the available tables in the SQL database. Choose the table you're interested in, adjust the table name as necessary (in the Name box at the bottom of the window), and then click OK.

▇ CREATING RELATIONSHIPS

When you're viewing a record from the Web Lead's Contacts table, you might want FileMaker to show you if that person is already in your Customers table. To make this possible, you need some kind of connection between Customers and Contacts. When you add a table from an external data source, FileMaker puts a table occurrence right on the Relationship graph, so making the connection is easy. The table occurrence looks and functions just like a FileMaker table. Because they're coming from different sources, the two tables aren't likely to have appropriate primary key fields you can use to hook up the relationships. So you may need to use another field to create a relationship. In this case, you might consider using an Email Address or other field as a key field.

You're free to relate tables in any combination you want: Connect a FileMaker table to a SQL table, or connect two SQL tables together. Connect a SQL table to a FileMaker table, which then connects to another SQL table. You can even connect tables from two *different* SQL databases.

▇ SHADOW TABLES

If you switch to the Tables tab in the Manage Database window, you may see something unexpected. FileMaker includes every SQL table you've added to your graph in the Tables list (in stark contrast to tables from other FileMaker databases, which never show in the Tables tab).

The italicized entry in the Tables tab is called a *shadow table.* In other words, it isn't the table. Rather, it's a representation of the real table. It reflects information about the real table and even lets you add a little FileMaker magic to an otherwise bare bit of computer science.

If you double-click the table (or switch to the Fields tab and then select the table from the Table pop-up menu), you'll see the fields (sometimes called *columns* by non-FileMaker database folks) from the SQL table listed in italic as well. You can do certain things to these italicized fields:

- You can add a field comment if you want.

- You can click Options and set auto-enter and validation options for the field. Remember, though, that the rules you set here apply only when you add or edit records *in FileMaker.* Other systems that interact with the database are restricted only by settings in the SQL database.

- You can delete a field. You're not actually deleting the field from the SQL table. Rather, deleting a field tells FileMaker you simply don't want to see that field in FileMaker anymore. (You can always get it back later by clicking the Sync button, as explained below.)

However, you can't rename a field or change its type. The SQL database retains control of those edits. If you must change a field name, work with the SQL database administrator to get what you need.

SQL databases tend to be more restrictive about acceptable values than FileMaker itself. For instance, a text field in a SQL database usually has a maximum size that's relatively small, compared with FileMaker's 2 GB field limit. If you select a field, click the Options button and then visit the Validation tab, where you might see that the "Maximum number of characters" option is turned on, and you can't turn it off. Right by the checkbox, FileMaker also shows how many characters the field can hold.

Perhaps most important, you can *add new fields* to the shadow table. Specifically, you can add unstored or global calculation fields and summary fields. Neither of these field types works with SQL databases, but both are super important to FileMaker developers. By adding them to the shadow table, you can treat the SQL tables a little more like normal FileMaker tables. For example, you can add summary fields so you can do complex reporting on the SQL data, or add a calculation field to show a subtotal on a FileMaker layout.

Finally, if the underlying SQL table changes in some way (perhaps the database administrator added a new column you're particularly interested in seeing), click Sync at the top of the window. This button tells FileMaker to go back to the SQL database and find out if any columns have been added, removed, or adjusted.

Syncing has nothing to do with the *data* in the database, though. FileMaker always interacts with the SQL database directly to show up-to-the-moment data as you perform searches or make changes. The Sync button synchronizes only the field definitions from the SQL table.

Using SQL Tables

There's no secret to using a SQL table—it works just like any other FileMaker table. You can create a new layout to show records from the SQL table. You can view those records in List view, Form view, or Table view. You can write scripts that loop through SQL records, or use the "Go to Related Record" script step to find the records associated with a particular customer.

Everything you know about FileMaker still applies. But keep a few points in mind as you develop your database around SQL tables:

- You can configure access to a SQL table by using privilege sets just like any other FileMaker table. But a privilege set can't overrule the underlying SQL database. If the user name and password you're using to connect to the SQL database don't provide permission to delete records, FileMaker won't be able to delete them. FileMaker does its best to give meaningful error messages in such situations.

- Speaking of error messages, since SQL databases are more restrictive than FileMaker, you may see error messages in places you wouldn't normally expect. For example, a Name field might be limited to 30 characters. If you try to enter more than that, FileMaker lets you, but you can't then commit the record. It's up to you to go back and delete enough to make it happy.

- FileMaker does some powerful computing magic to make these SQL tables work. So if you have a large amount of data in your SQL table, FileMaker can take a long time to show you data.

- FileMaker may have trouble performing some finds efficiently. If you include only fields from one table in your find request, then it should move quickly. But if you search in related fields, and there are thousands of matches in the related table, FileMaker can take a very long time to sort things out. If you find that SQL tables aren't performing well, and you can't simplify your find requests, consider enlisting the help of a SQL expert (or learning it yourself). You may be able to offload some of the heavy lifting to the SQL database server, where ready access to the data makes things faster. For example, a complex find in FileMaker could be converted to a SQL view that's super snappy. This same advice applies to large summary reports. If you're dealing with lots of records, it may be faster to let the SQL database server calculate the subtotals and averages for FileMaker.

You can use ESS to get direct access to enterprise data, interact with the back end of your website, or even replace chunks of FileMaker data with a set of tables that's more open to other programs. This powerful feature may need a little setup and some new expertise, but if you have big needs, it can be an incredibly powerful option.

Exporting Data

The Save/Send Records As options (page 843) make sense when you just want to send FileMaker data to an associate. But sometimes your recipient is a computer. You may send your customer information to a mailing house to be printed on postcards, or you may need to load it into QuickBooks. In cases like this, you *export* the data.

When you export data, FileMaker needs to know *what* data to export. You tell it with the "Specify Field Order for Export" dialog box (Figure 22-10). The Table pop-up menu shows you the *current layout*—in this case, People Detail. Below it, the field list shows every field in that current layout. But click the pop-up menu and you can choose Current Table, which shows you all the fields in the current table, instead of just the fields on the layout. Or you can choose other tables from the pop-up menu and see their fields. If you choose fields from other tables, you're still export-ing invoice records, though. So when you need to export data from two fields, it's more common to export from the child table instead of the parent. For instance, if you need to export several Invoices, along with their items, do the export from a layout with the context of the Line Item table. Find the proper items, sort them into order (probably by Invoice Number), and then choose the fields you need from the Invoice table.

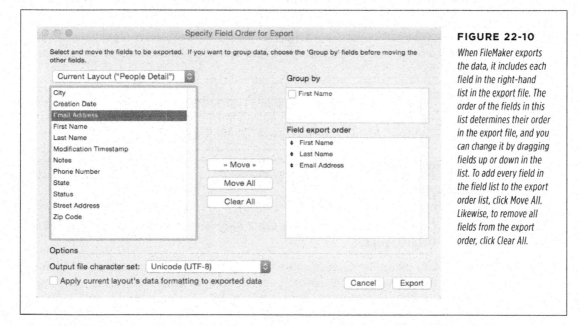

FIGURE 22-10

When FileMaker exports the data, it includes each field in the right-hand list in the export file. The order of the fields in this list determines their order in the export file, and you can change it by dragging fields up or down in the list. To add every field in the field list to the export order list, click Move All. Likewise, to remove all fields from the export order, click Clear All.

To choose a field for export, select it and then click Move (or double-click it). File-Maker adds the field to the "Field export order" list, but doesn't actually move it there. It just stays in the list of available fields. If you accidentally try to add a field to the Export order list more than once, FileMaker will see that it's already there and silently decline to add it again.

NOTE If a field isn't on the current layout, it doesn't show up in the list of available fields on the left side, so if you're wasting time scrolling through fields that you don't need, you can cancel and then switch to a simpler layout from the same table. But if you can't find a field that you *know* is in the table, use the pop-up menu to choose Current Table. That way, you'll get a list of all the fields in the table, regardless of which ones are on the current layout.

At the bottom of the window, the "Output file character set" pop-up menu lets you tell FileMaker how to *encode* characters in the export file so the receiving computer can read them properly. For instance, if you're using Mac OS X and you know the person receiving the export file is using Windows, it probably makes sense to choose the Windows (ANSI) choice. Unfortunately, the conversion from Macintosh to Windows or Windows to Mac is imperfect, so some less-common characters may be switched out for others in the output file. Unicode is the best choice, assuming your recipient can accept it, because it can handle *all* the characters you may have in your database (even foreign language characters like Chinese and Korean).

Finally, the checkbox called "Apply current layout's data formatting to exported data" might be confusing. It has nothing to do with font, size, style, or color. Rather, when you turn this option on, FileMaker formats numbers, dates, times, and timestamps according to the formatting options for each field on the layout: number of decimal places, date formats, and so forth. If you leave this option off, FileMaker exports the data exactly as it was originally entered.

NOTE The "Group by" list lets you summarize data as you export it. You'll learn how this feature works on page 865.

The following steps take you through a typical database export. You need to send an email blast to your customers, but you don't want to hand enter all that data on their website. Usually, plain text is fine, so that's what this example uses.

NOTE Download this chapter's sample database from this book's Missing CD page at *www.missingmanuals. com/cds/fmp14mm*.

1. **Open the sample database *CH22 People.fmp12* and switch to the People Detail layout.**

   Like many FileMaker features, the Export command is layout-based—that is, it decides which table to export (and from which table occurrence to find related data) by looking at the current layout. To export customer records, you need to be on a layout associated with the Customers table.

2. **Choose Records→Show All Records.**

   If this command is grayed out, then all records are already showing. Otherwise, take this step to ensure that you export *every* customer.

3. **Choose File→Export Records. If the command isn't available, you're prob-ably in Find mode, so switch to Browse mode.**

You can also export from Layout and Preview modes, too, should the need arise. The "Export Records to File" dialog box appears. It looks a lot like a normal Save dialog box, except that it has a pop-up menu at the bottom called Type.

4. **Name the file *MailChimp* and then choose any location you want.**

When FileMaker exports data, it creates a new file and puts the data in it. You use this window to tell FileMaker what to call the file and where to put it.

5. **From the Type pop-up menu, choose Comma-Separated Text and then click Save.**

The "Specify Field Order for Export" window appears (Figure 22-10). You'll learn what each of these types means in the next section.

6. **If fields appear in the Field Export Order list, click Clear All to remove them. Press Ctrl (⌘), and then select these fields in the field list: First Name, Last Name, and Email Address. Then click Move.**

The pressed key lets you select fields that aren't next to each other in the list. FileMaker adds the highlighted fields to the Field export order list.

TIP If you want to export most of your fields, but not quite all of them, it may be faster to click the Move All button and then clear the few you don't want from the Field export order list.

---

7. **Click Export.**

FileMaker creates the file and returns you to your database.

So what just happened? If you open the file you just created, you see names and email addresses from your customers file. Dig a little deeper and you notice:

- Each *record* is on its own line. If the program you're viewing the file in wraps lines, it might look like a record goes across two or more lines, but there's a return character at the *end* of each record, and nowhere else.

- Each field value is in quotes, and there are commas between them.

These factors are important because this file conforms to a standard. Other pro-grams—including the program used by the card printing company—that recognize the comma-separated text format can read this file and grab the data.

Grouped Exports

You may have noticed the "Group by" list in the "Specify Field Order for Export" dialog box. Under normal circumstances, you see "(Unsorted)" in this list. But if you sort the records in the found set *before* choosing the Export Records command, you see instead a list of the fields in your sort order, each with a checkbox by its name. You can see this in action in Figure 22-11.

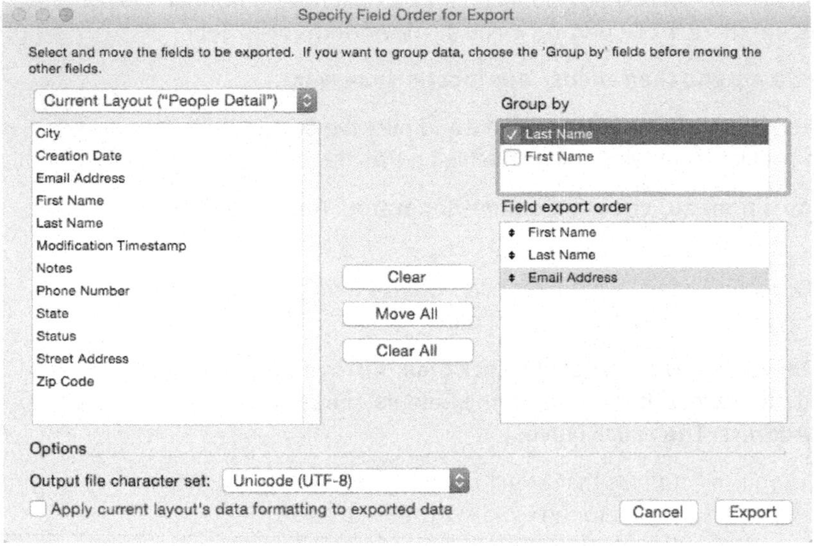

FIGURE 22-11

When your data is sorted, FileMaker shows the sort fields in the "Group by" list. By turning on one or more of these checkboxes, you tell FileMaker you want to group the data in the export file.

If you want to group the data, you'll get one record in the export file for each *unique* value in the "group by" field. For example, if you export 300 people records, grouped by state, you get one record for each state. That's not so helpful if you're interested in individual people's names, but it's perfect for summarized data. If you include *summary* fields in your Export order list, FileMaker summarizes all the records represented by each group. You can get a count, for example, of how many people you have in each state.

You're free to select as many fields as you want in the "group by" list. If you select more than one, you get a hierarchical list of records, similar to a Subsummary report (Chapter 16). For example, if you sort first by state, then by city, and turn on the checkbox next to both fields in the "group by" list, you get a list of states, and below each state, you see one record for each city in that state. Again, summary fields included in your export show proper totals for both the state as a whole and each city.

■ EXPORT FORMATS

When exporting data, you always create a file, but you get to decide what *format* the file should be in. In the previous example, you exported your data to a comma-separated text file. This example is one of the many file formats FileMaker can produce when it exports. Most formats exist simply because computer software has put forth a lot of standards in the last 50 years, and FileMaker wants to be as flexible as possible. Some formats do have unique advantages, though.

The first question you need to ask is, "Where's the data going?" Your export format choice almost always depends on what the person you're sending it to needs. Each is explained below:

- **Tab-separated text** and **comma-separated text** are very common formats for database data. They put each record on its own line. With tab-separated text, you get a tab between each field value, while comma-separated text has quotes around field values and commas between them. Almost every program that can import data supports one of these formats. If you're not sure, try tab-separated text first—it's the most common.

NOTE Sometimes the comma-separated text format is called *comma-separated values* in other programs. They're the same thing. Indeed you may have noticed that you get a .csv file type when FileMaker exports comma-separated text.

- **DBF** is a file format most commonly found in older database systems. It imposes significant restrictions on the content and length of field names as well as the amount of data that can be exported from a given field. The specific limitations are detailed in FileMaker's help system. Usually, the only reason you'd choose DBF is because the system that will be receiving your data requires it.

- The **Merge** format is just like comma-separated text format, with one difference: The first line of the file shows individual field names. The advantage is that when you import this file in another program, you can see what each field is called, making it easier to get the right data. Unfortunately, most programs don't expect this extra line and treat it as another record. People most often use this format for mail merge in word-processing programs.

NOTE If your destination program refuses to recognize a FileMaker-generated Merge file, try changing its file name extension from .mer to .csv.

- If you want to put the data on a web page, use **HTML Table.** The resulting file isn't suitable for importing into another program, but it can be displayed nicely in a web browser. You can also open the file, copy the HTML table from inside it and then paste it into another web page.

- The **FileMaker Pro** format is your best choice if your data is destined to go back into FileMaker someday, or if you just want to view and work with the exported data directly. When you choose this format, FileMaker creates a brand-new database with just one table and only the fields you choose to export. This format is the only one that preserves font, style, size, and color in field data (see the box next) and one of the few that supports repeating fields.

Where's My Style?

Most of FileMaker's export formats are *text based*. In other words, what gets produced is just a normal, plain text file. The structure of this file determines which format it is, but you can open them all in Notepad or TextEdit and read them directly. A side effect of this reality is that none of them support *styles*. In other words, if you go to great lengths to change the first names in all your records so the font matches the customer's personality, you can kiss your hard work goodbye when you export.

In addition to the font, you lose the size, style, and color of the text. The notable exception to this rule is the FileMaker Pro format. Since this export format creates another FileMaker Pro database, all the formatting you painstakingly put in place is preserved.

If you *must* have text styles in your exported data, there is an option, but it ain't pretty. FileMaker has two calculation functions designed to aid this process: GetAsCSS() and GetAsSVG().

Each function takes a single text parameter and returns a snippet of ordinary text with style information embedded using special *tags*. GetAsCSS() produces text that can be put on a web page. When viewed in a web browser, the text takes on its original fonts, sizes, styles, and colors. GetAsSVG() works the same way but uses a different tagging scheme: the one used in the SVG, or Scalable Vector Graphics format.

To take advantage of these functions, you need to create a calculation field with a formula something like this:

```
GetAsCSS ( First Name )
```

You then export *this* field instead of the First Name field. If you do this with the HTML Table export format, you get properly formatted text on your web page. More realistically, you'd use these along with the XML format and a special XSLT style sheet that produces a web page or an SVG image. You'll learn more about this option at the end of this chapter.

NOTE   Usually, if you just want to export records from one FileMaker file to another, you don't have to export them first. Just go to the database where you want the data to end up and then import it directly (described next). Of course, if one database is in South Africa and the other is in Tibet, then by all means export them first.

- For the ultimate in flexibility, choose **XML**—the un-format. When you export XML, you get to apply something called an XSLT style sheet. An XSLT style sheet is a document written in a programming language all its own that tells FileMaker exactly how the exported data looks. If you need to produce an export format that FileMaker doesn't support directly, XSLT is the way to do it. But be forewarned: XSLT is *not* in the same league as FileMaker itself, ease-of-use-wise. You may need some hired help. (XSLT is introduced briefly on page 883.)

NOTE   Although it applies to one *field value* and not a set of records, don't forget about the Export Field Contents command. This command lets you export the data in the current field to a file. It exports text, number, date, time, and timestamp fields to a plain text file. Container fields create a file whose type is appropriate for the data in the field.

- Last but not least, you can choose one of the **Excel** options to create a bona fide spreadsheet. The .xlsx option is generally your best bet, since even people using older versions of Excel can download free converters from Microsoft to work with this format. When you choose either format, FileMaker opens an extra dialog box, which lets you put FileMaker's field names in the first row of your new spreadsheet. You can even give your Excel file a worksheet Name, document Title, Subject, and Author if you so desire.

> **WARNING** Users of Mac OS X 10.7 and later *must* use the .xlsx option when exporting to Excel. The older .xls export code doesn't run in the newer operating system. There's no danger to your database should you choose the incompatible option, though; you'll just get an error message at the very end of the process.

Regardless of which format you choose, the "Export Records to File" dialog box has two options that let you determine what happens to the file after FileMaker creates it. Choose "Automatically open file" to avoid hunting down the file on your hard drive and then launching it yourself. And "Create email with file as attachment" does just what it promises: opens your email program and creates a new message with your fresh new document attached. To share your data, you just need to supply the email address, add a subject line and then click Send.

■ Importing Data

Sometimes, the data you need is already somewhere else, and you need to get it into FileMaker. Instead of spending hours doing data entry, consider doing an *import*. Chances are FileMaker can load the data directly into its tables with just a little help from you to tell it where things go.

FileMaker can handle the most common data types—and some lesser-known ones—by a straightforward process. You tell FileMaker which file contains your incoming data and then show it how you want to match the incoming data (the source) with the fields in your file (the target). This procedure is called *field mapping,* and it's the fiddly part of an import. See Figure 22-12 for a preview of the Import Field Mapping dialog box.

This window lists all the fields in the source file on the left, and the fields in your table on the right. The fields from the Source field list on the left move into the fields in the Target field list on the right. Most of the time, you'll import data from a system that doesn't use the same names you've used, so you use this dialog box to tell FileMaker how to match incoming data with your fields. Sometimes you can't make a good match by the field names alone. In that case, you may have to scan the data to figure it out. That's what the arrows below the target list are for: You can click through the data to see what's in each field.

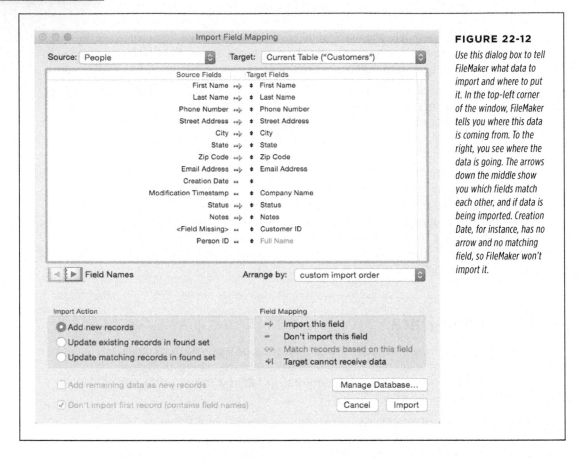

FIGURE 22-12

Use this dialog box to tell FileMaker what data to import and where to put it. In the top-left corner of the window, FileMaker tells you where this data is coming from. To the right, you see where the data is going. The arrows down the middle show you which fields match each other, and if data is being imported. Creation Date, for instance, has no arrow and no matching field, so FileMaker won't import it.

The concept of mapping your fields is simple, but the procedure can be a real drag. First of all, you can't rearrange the fields in the Source Fields list at all. They match the order in which they appear in the file you're importing. Your job is to move the target fields up or down so they line up next to the appropriate source fields. (You move them just like you do fields and tables in the Manage Database window—by dragging the little arrows.)

Making It Fit

A lot of FileMaker's Export formats use special characters for important things. For instance, the tab-separated text format uses a return character to separate records. What happens if I have a return character in my field?

Good question! Special characters are one of those problems with no ideal solution. But FileMaker does the best it can within the limitations of each export file type. For a file to be called tab-separated text, for example, you can't have return characters inside records. It's just against the rules. In this particular case, FileMaker turns the return character into something else, called a *vertical tab,* which is a standard but rarely used character left over from when computers had green screens. Presumably, you don't have any of these in your fields (you can't type them, so it's a pretty safe bet you don't), so it's easy enough to turn vertical tab characters back into return characters when you open the file in another program. In fact, that's exactly what happens when you *import* a tab-separated text file into FileMaker.

Another character of concern is the quote mark. If you have these in your fields, and you export a comma-separated text file, FIleMaker has to do something with them so they don't interfere with the quotes around field values. In this case, FileMaker turns your quote mark into two quote marks together.

That doesn't sound like a solution, but it is. If you assume any quote mark that's immediately followed by a second one is really just data, and not the end quote mark for a field value, you can figure out which is which in the export file. Most programs that support comma-separated text understand this convention. (You might think commas would also be a problem with comma-separated text, but they're not. Since every field value is in quotes, commas are OK. Only the commas between quoted values are considered field separators.)

The HTML and XML formats have all kinds of special characters, but each has a special *entity* form that's used if they're supposed to be treated as ordinary data. FileMaker converts any such characters appropriately, and every program that processes these formats understands the conventions.

Finally, FileMaker has a data-structure concept that most formats simply don't understand: repeating fields. The idea that one field could hold several values is foreign to most database programs. When you export repeating fields, File-Maker pulls another freaky character out of its hat: the Group Separator, which is used to separate each value. Thankfully, this action is almost never a problem because you generally don't export repeating field data to a file that needs to be read by a program that doesn't understand repeating fields. One last note: The FileMaker Pro export format *does* directly support repeating fields.

If you don't have many fields, this process is quick and painless. If you have lots of fields, it can be tough for a few reasons:

- Since the whole point of this operation is to put the target field list in a very particular order, you can't simply sort the list by name whenever you're having trouble finding a field. If you're looking for First Name in a long list, there's no way to find it short of looking through the list field by field. If this process proves overwhelming, here's a trick: Click Manage Database (bottom right), and in the Manage Database window, rename the field with a whole lot of X's at the end of its name. When you close the Manage Database window, the field in question will stand out from the list.

Mapping Out Your Options

FileMaker is smart, but when it comes to something as picayune as deciding which field to put where, there's no substitute for human input. Back in Figure 22-12, the Import Field Mapping dialog box looks a trifle crowded, but every tool, button, and gizmo has saved a life (or a career, anyway).

For example, your input data source may or may not include field names. If it doesn't, the Source Fields list shows you the first record in the import file instead. Or, even if your data already has named fields, you may *want* to see some of the data being imported so you can see what's really in that field called Q1GPFnw. Either way, FileMaker lets you check as many records as you wish before you import by providing arrow buttons below the list. As you click, FileMaker replaces items in the source field list with data from the next (right) or previous (left) record. When field names are included, you see them as the *first* record. Occasionally, the format you're importing doesn't accommodate field names, but the import file has them anyway, as the first record. When this happens, turn on "Don't import first record" so FileMaker doesn't treat that record as data.

The "Arrange by" pop-up menu lets you bulk-reorder the target fields in the list. Most choices are obvious (alphabetical by field name and by field type), but others aren't so clear. If you choose "matching names," FileMaker tries to match fields up by matching their names. If your input file has the same field names as your database, this option sets the right order for you. The "last order" choice restores the field order you used the last time you imported data. Choose "creation order" to see the fields in the order in which you created them. Finally, if you manually drag the fields in the list, FileMaker switches to the "custom import order" choice. If you decide to try one of the other arrangements, you can get back to the order you were working on by choosing "custom import order" yourself.

- As you drag fields up and down, if you have to drag beyond the visible list (because your destination has scrolled past the top or bottom), FileMaker sometimes scrolls the list by so quickly while you drag that you easily overshoot your destination, repeatedly. To avoid this runaround, don't drag. Instead, click the field you want to move to select it. Then hold down the Control key, and use the up or down arrow keys to move the field. As long as you hold the appropriate modifier key down, you can move the field up or down as far as you want by repeatedly pressing the arrow keys. The list scrolls as your field moves. This more controlled method is slower, but it's more accurate.

- Finally, if you accidentally drop a field in the wrong spot, the field you're moving changes places with the one you dropped it on top of. If the one you replaced was already in the right spot, it's now far away, and you have to reposition it once you correctly place the first field. In other words, an accidental drop leaves *two* fields in the wrong place. So be careful where you drop your fields. You can reduce frustration factor by starting at the top and working your way down. Jumping around almost always results in dumping fields where they don't belong.

Sometimes you don't care about some of the fields in your source file (maybe it includes a Fax Number for each customer, and you don't need that particular value). Between each source and destination field, you see one of two symbols: an arrow or a line. The arrow means FileMaker plans to import the data on the left side into the field on the right. A line tells FileMaker to ignore this particular piece of data in the import file. Click an arrow to change it to a line, or vice versa. Just make sure there's a line next to the field or fields you don't want to import. (You sometimes see *other* symbols between fields, but they show up only when you change the Import Action setting. You'll learn about that on page 878.)

> **NOTE** If you forget what the importing icons mean, never fear. The Import Field Mapping window has a legend at the bottom right.

For the sake of illustration, here's the simple rundown on how importing works:

1. **Go to a layout in your file that contains fields from the table you want to import data into.**

   The target table is based on the table used for the active layout. FileMaker is rather unwilling to let you choose a different table as a target, although it will let you import records into a new table.

2. **Choose File→Import Records→File.**

   FileMaker can import data from all kinds of sources. In this case, you're telling it you want to import records from a *file.* When you choose this command, the standard Open File dialog box appears.

3. **Choose the file you want to import and then click Open.**

   The Import Field Mapping dialog box pops up.

4. **Drag the fields in the target field list on the right so they line up properly with the input data on the left.**

   As you drag, you can ignore the field mapping arrows completely. You can fix them once you've got the fields in the right order.

> **TIP** If your data source has a field that doesn't match any existing field in your target table, and you decide you want to import that field anyway, just click the Manage Database button to create a new field and then return to your field mapping. See page 879 for how to handle an entire *table* that's missing.

5. **Click the arrows or lines between fields until each matching field has an arrow and each remaining field has a line.**

   This part is the most time-consuming. Just take it slow and be glad you don't have to type all this data.

6. **Make sure the "Add new records" radio button (in the Import Action area) is turned on.**

   This action tells FileMaker you want a new record created in the Customers table for each record in the import file. (The Import Field Mapping dialog box has more features, but you don't need them right now. See page 883 for the full details.)

7. **Click Import. When the Import Options dialog box appears (Figure 22-13), turn on "Perform auto-enter options while importing."**

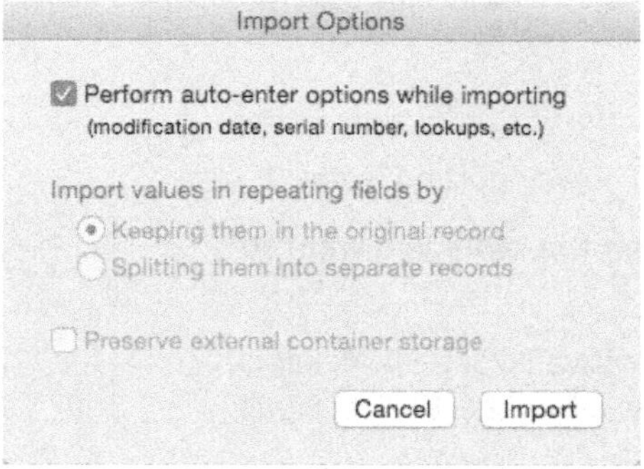

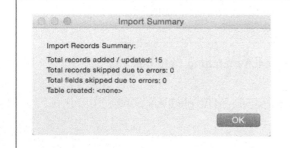

FIGURE 22-13

If you have any auto-enter fields in your target table, or if you're importing repeating fields, you see this window after clicking Import. Turn off "Perform auto-enter options while importing" if you don't want FileMaker to auto-enter data in your records as they're created. When importing repeating fields, you usually want to choose "Keeping them in the original record." If you don't, FileMaker makes a new record for each repetition that has data in it.

You want to make sure the new customers have valid customer IDs, and those come from auto-enter serial numbers.

Click Import one last time.

After a very short delay, the Import Summary dialog box appears (Figure 22-14). Click OK to make it go away.

> **NOTE** If you import into a field that has auto-enter options set, and you tell FileMaker to perform auto-enter options when importing, you might wonder *which* value will wind up in the field: the auto-entered data or the imported data. In almost every case, the imported data wins. There are two exceptions: lookups and auto-enter calculations will override important data.

Import Summary

Import Records Summary:

Total records added / updated: 15
Total records skipped due to errors: 0
Total fields skipped due to errors: 0
Table created: <none>

OK

FIGURE 22-14

This window appears after FileMaker completes the import. It tells you about your import, including how many records were imported. Sometimes problems can happen during import (for instance, some data in the import file may violate your field validation settings). When this happens, FileMaker may skip certain fields or whole records. This window tells you when that happens (although it doesn't tell you which fields or records were skipped).

After the import is complete, FileMaker shows you a found set of just the records it imported. But don't reach for the Show All Records command yet: The fact that it's a found set is your safety net. If something goes wrong with your import (the wrong records came through, field mapping doesn't look right, or whatever), just delete the found set and then start over. You can scan through the data and make sure you got what you wanted and that the data went into the fields you intended. You can also take this opportunity to perform other actions (like use the Replace Field Contents command) on every imported record.

Recurring Import

When you import records into FileMaker (File→Import Records→File), the Open File dialog box has an inconspicuous little checkbox labeled "Set up as automatic recurring import" (Figure 22-15). If you find yourself importing updated versions of the same spreadsheet over and over again, a recurring import can make that process almost automatic. See the box on page 877 to learn about when recurring import might not work for you.

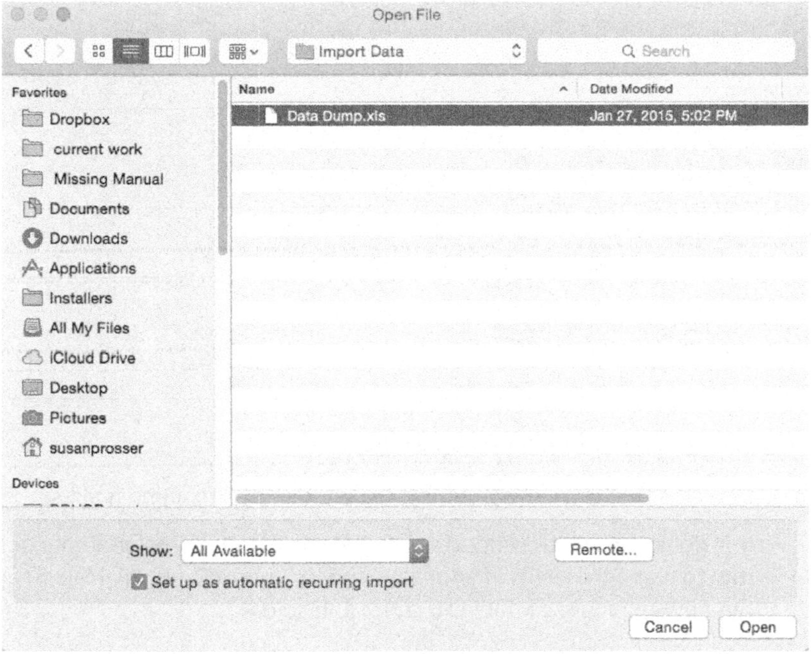

FIGURE 22-15

If you're about to do an import that you expect to do again and again, turn on the "Set up as automatic recurring import" checkbox before you click Open.

The Recurring Import Setup dialog box asks you questions about what you want FileMaker to do with the imported data. The result is a new table with the data you imported, a new layout to display it, a new script to rerun the import, and a script trigger that updates the data each time you switch to the new layout. These are all things you can program for yourself, but not in the 2 seconds it takes FileMaker to pull it off. Here's how to get your own recurring import:

1. **Choose File→Import Records→File and then select a file to import.**

   Make sure the "Set up as automatic recurring import" checkbox is turned on, of course. The Recurring Import Setup dialog box opens. As shown in Figure 22-16, it displays the path of the file you just chose.

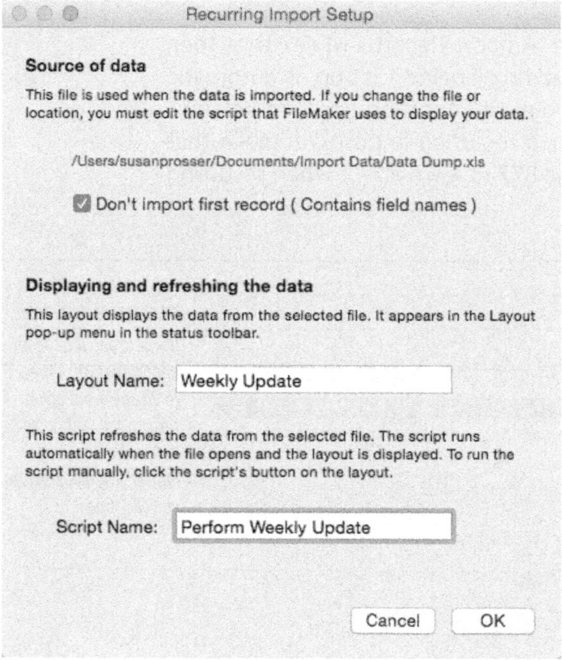

FIGURE 22-16

The Recurring Import Setup dialog box has only three settings to configure. "Don't import first record" is the only one of the three that affects the execution of a recurring import. Layout Name and Script Name can be anything you like.

2. **Answer the dialog box's three questions:**

   • Does the first row of your import file contain field/column names?

     If it does, turn on the checkbox, and FileMaker uses the contents of that row to name the fields. If you leave the box unchecked, FileMaker names the fields of your new table f1, f2, f3, and so on.

   • What do you want to name the new layout?

   • What do you want to name the script?

   For simplicity, FileMaker suggests using the same name as the file you selected. You can name it something different, but there's no compelling reason to.

UP TO SPEED

What a Recurring Import Is Not

Now that you know what a recurring import is, be sure you understand what it is *not*:

- It's not synchronization. Once it's in FileMaker, the data loses all association with the source file. It's strictly one, way.

- It's not a merge. When you switch to a recurring import layout, or push its button, the import script *deletes every record* in the table and imports them all over again. It doesn't update existing records or merge the current source file with the changes you made. It just obliterates the data and brings it in again.

- It's not your mom. Every time you trigger a recurring import, FileMaker looks for the source file in the exact same place with the exact same name. If you rename it, move it, or even change the name of the folder that it was in, FileMaker won't look all over your hard drive to find it for you.

- It's not a mind reader. FileMaker expects the same file, with the same columns, in the same order, every time. If you're presented with a new version of the source file with, say, a few new and reordered columns, FileMaker doesn't have a way to sense that and adjust. It merrily imports the records again, without displaying an error, even if phone numbers are going into the email address field. And those new columns you added? Ignored. If the structure of the source file changes, scrap your old recurring import and then set up a new one.

3. **Click OK.**

   Moments later you have it: a new table, a new field for every column in the source file, a new script to rerun the import, and a set of freshly imported records on a new layout (Figure 22-17).

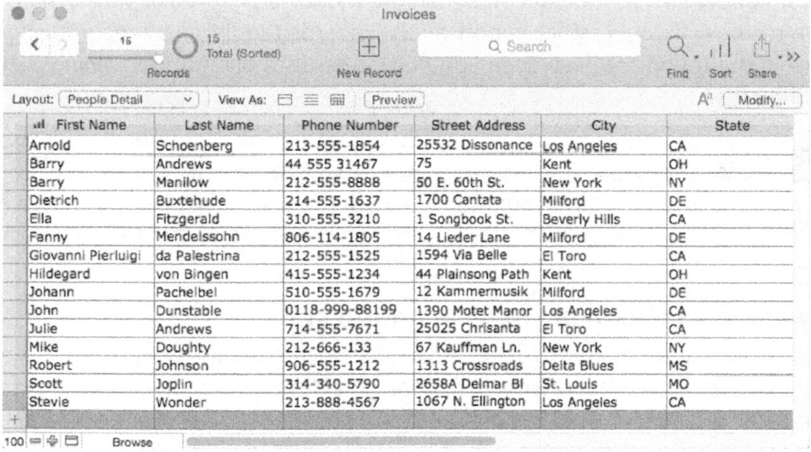

FIGURE 22-17

Your new table full of data is presented to you in Table view. You certainly don't have to leave it that way. You can switch among Form, List, and Table views to get what you need.

And now, here's the big payoff: Anytime you need to refresh that data, just switch to the new layout or, if you're already there, click the button furnished up in the header. FileMaker goes back to the source file, grabs the new information, and updates the database according to the choices you made in the Recurring Import Setup dialog box.

Importing over Existing Data

When you import data into a file that already has some records in it, the Import Action section of the Import Field Mapping dialog box (Figure 22-12) gives you three ways to specify how you want to deal with that existing data. Normally, it starts out with the "Add new records" setting turned on, meaning that FileMaker simply adds imported records to your database. Sometimes, though, you want to update existing records instead. For example, suppose your database holds shipping rates for every state you ship to. When your freight company updates its rates, it sends you a new file with one record for each state, and the new rates in a Rate field. If you add these records to your database, you end up with *two* records for each state, which is probably not what you want. But you shouldn't delete all those records and then reimport them to fix the problem. FileMaker gives you two choices that let you update records *as* you import.

■ UPDATE EXISTING RECORDS IN FOUND SET

To avoid creating duplicate records as in the shipping rates example, you can turn on "Update existing records in found set" and then map just the Rate field to the appropriate field in your table. When you import, FileMaker takes the rate from the first record in the import file and puts it in the first record in the found set. It then copies the second rate into the second record. This process continues until it has imported every rate.

If your import file has more records than the found set, FileMaker simply skips the extra records. If you'd rather import *all* the records (adding new records once all those in the found set have been updated), then turn on "Add remaining data as new records."

> **WARNING**   This import action is useful *only* if you're certain the records in the import file are in the *same order* as those in the export file. If they're not, FileMaker updates the wrong records, leaving you with incorrect data. If you aren't positive the records are in the right order, use "Update matching records in found set" instead.

■ UPDATE MATCHING RECORDS IN FOUND SET

"Update matching records in found set" works much the same way, except it's more targeted. When you import with this option, FileMaker looks for a matching record to update. You specify one or more *matching fields*, that FileMaker uses to get the right record before moving the data into your table (Figure 22-18).

WARNING Pay special attention to this command's name: "Update matching records in *found set*." When looking for matches, it looks only at the records *in the found set*. If you have a customer with a matching ID field, but that customer isn't in the found set, FileMaker will either skip that record or add a new duplicate, depending on your settings in the "Add remaining data as new records" setting.

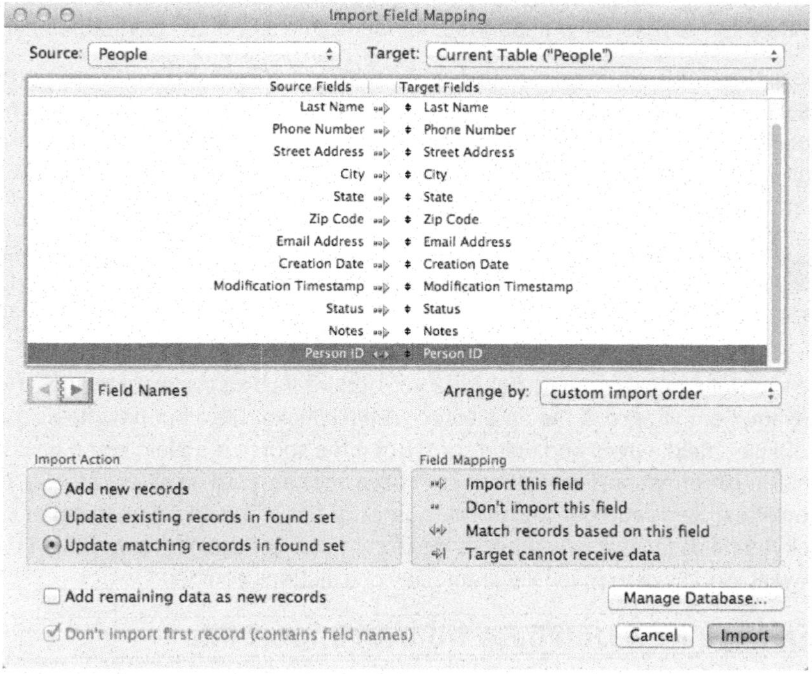

FIGURE 22-18

When you turn on "Update matching records in found set," FileMaker shows a new symbol between source and target fields. The <-> symbol between the Person ID fields at the bottom of the list tells FileMaker to match records using this ID. In other words, when it imports the first record, it finds a record in the found set with the same ID. FileMaker then updates that record's data based on the import file. If FileMaker doesn't find a match, it skips the import record. It's safest to use a key field for import matching.

To get the new symbol in the field mapping list, just click the spot between fields. FileMaker now toggles between the three possible symbols: "Import," "Don't import," and "Match." (If you forget what each symbol means, the Field Mapping area shows a legend.) Again, if you'd rather have FileMaker import every record in the import file, adding new records when no match is found, turn on "Add remaining data as new records."

Creating Tables on Import

All the importing you've learned about so far assumes that your tables and fields are already created. In other words, your target table is already in place when you choose your source file. But when you're doing a big conversion job (say, upgrading from 15 overextended Excel spreadsheets to a smooth-running FileMaker dream system), it'll take you quite some time to create all those tables and fields. And even though you have access to the Manage Database dialog box while you're importing, this process isn't quick or easy when you've got hundreds of fields coming in from dozens of files. FileMaker has already thought of that, and it offers to handle the tedious work of table and field creation for you.

Choose File→Import Records→File and then select a data source. In the Import Field Mapping window, there's a handy pop-up menu called Target. Click it, and you see the current table (remember that it's based on the layout that was active when you chose the Import command), all your other tables (grayed out so that you can't choose them), and a very useful command, New Table (Data Source). The stuff in parentheses is the name of your data source and the name FileMaker gives the new table it creates for you. (If you already have a table with the same name as your data source, FileMaker appends a number to the end of the new table's name.)

Choose New Table and then click Import. FileMaker creates a table and an appropriate set of fields for you and then populates the new fields with data. You also get a simple form layout for your new table and a table occurrence on your Relationships graph. You can treat this table just like one you created yourself. For example, you can start creating relationships to hook it up to other table occurrences.

TIP See page 540 to see how FileMaker Pro Advanced lets you import tables and fields *without* the data that normally comes with them.

When you let FileMaker create fields for you, it does its best to create the field types you want. For instance, if the data source is a FileMaker file, your new fields match the old file's field names and field types. But if the source is a plain text file with no formatting information, FileMaker doesn't have any names to go by, so the new fields become text fields and get the prosaic names of f1, f2, f3, and so on. In either case, check the fields in your new table to make sure you get the names and field types you want. You have to manually create any calculations you need.

Creating a New Database from an Import File

If you have a file full of data, and you want to build a brand new database around it, FileMaker has an even simpler option than creating a database and then importing the data. Just choose File→Open and then select the file you want to convert. You can also use drag and drop: In Windows, drag the file to the open FileMaker Pro window. FileMaker promptly converts it to a database for you. On the Mac, drag a file onto the FileMaker icon.

If FileMaker finds data with a first row that looks like field names, it asks whether you want to use those when FileMaker creates fields. If it can't find anything that looks like field names, you get those old standbys, f1, f2, f3. In addition to a single table and the appropriate number of fields (complete with data, of course), you get two very plain layouts. One is a generic form layout, showing one record at a time, and the other is a simple columnar list.

■ Import Data Sources

You've learned about the most common importing task—when your data is coming in from a single file. But you have other needs, and FileMaker has other choices. File→Import Records is an entire submenu, with commands to suit even the most demanding database manager. From there, you get to pick where the data should come from (the data source), and you get several choices.

NOTE If you can't see the file you want in the Open dialog box, or it's grayed out, change the option in the "Files of Type" (Windows) or "Show" (Mac) pop-up menu. If your file is one of the formats FileMaker supports, you can select it once you identify its type.

File

The File→Import Records→File command shows an Open File dialog box. Select any file that matches one of the export formats explained earlier in this chapter. You see your old friend, the Import Field Mapping dialog box (Figure 22-12). Match your source to your target, and away you go.

You can also use a similar command when you have to move data from one table to another within the same file. Go to your target layout and choose File→Import Records→File. In the dialog box, choose the database you're in, and you see the Import Field Mapping dialog box. Select the table that's your data source from the Source pop-up menu, and you're ready to go.

Folder

Using this command, you can pick any folder, and FileMaker imports the contents of each appropriate file in that folder. It creates *one* record for each file it imports and puts the file into the field you specify. In other words, if you have a folder full of letters you've written, you can import them into a Communications database using this command. The complete text of each letter would go in a field, with one record per letter. (Remember, though, that FileMaker only supports pictures, movies, and plain text files when importing. If your letters are in Microsoft Word format, for example, you're out of luck.)

Choosing File→Import Records→Folder summons the "Folder of Files Import Options" dialog box shown in Figure 22-19.

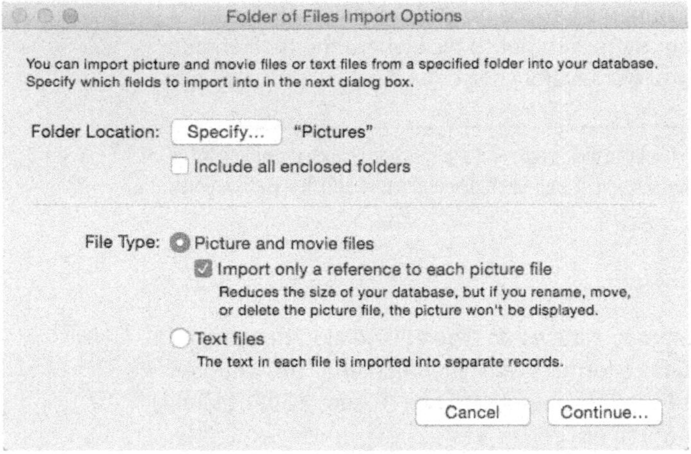

FIGURE 22-19

This window is what you see when you choose the File→Import→Folder command. In the top part of the "Folder of Files Import Options" window, you get to choose which folder to import (click Specify). In the bottom half, you decide what kind of files you're interested in. You'll see a warning if none of the files in the selected folder match the file type you chose.

Normally, FileMaker finds only files directly inside the folder you pick; it ignores any other folders contained inside. You have to turn on "Include all enclosed folders" to make FileMaker look inside those folders, too. With this option turned on, it digs as deep as necessary to find every file.

Once you've picked a folder, you get to decide what kind of files to import. You have only two choices: "Picture and movie files" and "Text files." In the first case, FileMaker ignores every file that isn't a supported picture or movie type. You choose whether the files themselves are inserted in the container field or just references to them. If you choose the "Text files" option instead, it seeks out only plain text files.

■ IMPORTING A FOLDER OF PICTURES OR MOVIES

When you choose the "Pictures and movie files" option and then click Continue, you see the now-familiar Import Field Mapping dialog box. But the list of source fields looks entirely unfamiliar—in a good way.

As outlined in Figure 22-20, FileMaker translates the file information into logical field types, perfect for database use. In the example shown, a new table has been assigned to accept the incoming data, which automatically creates fields matching the field types of the source data.

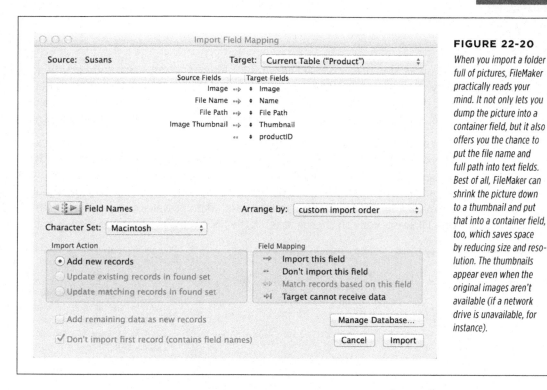

FIGURE 22-20

When you import a folder full of pictures, FileMaker practically reads your mind. It not only lets you dump the picture into a container field, but it also offers you the chance to put the file name and full path into text fields. Best of all, FileMaker can shrink the picture down to a thumbnail and put that into a container field, too, which saves space by reducing size and resolution. The thumbnails appear even when the original images aren't available (if a network drive is unavailable, for instance).

When you accept the field mapping and click Import, you may be in for a bit of a wait. Depending on the number of files FileMaker has to look through, you may see a progress dialog box for as long as several minutes.

■ IMPORTING A FOLDER OF TEXT FILES

When you choose to import text files, you still get an Import Field Mapping dialog box. This time, the source field list includes Text Content, File Name, and File Path. Each expects to be imported into a text field.

XML Data Source

Because there are so many programs and data formats, the World Wide Web Consortium (W3C) created the XML format to make data exchange more predictable. FileMaker uses a special subset of XML's code, called FMPXMLRESULT, to facilitate import. If your data source was created by another FileMaker Pro database, it already uses FMPXMLRESULT, and you can import that data straight up, no chaser. But if the XML document doesn't use FileMaker's Document Type Definition (DTD), you'll need an Extensible Stylesheet Language (XSLT) document to tell FileMaker how to make the XML file work with FileMaker. In fact, with the help of XSLT style sheets, FileMaker can import *any* XML file in any form. An XSLT style sheet converts the XML you're importing into FMPXMLRESULT.

NOTE You can learn to write your own XSLT style sheets, and thereby turn FileMaker's XML into just about anything, from specialized XML your accounting software uses, to an HTML web page, to a standard RSS news feed. XML and XSLT are complex languages, and this book can't cover them in full. If you're ready for a challenge, check out the book *Learning XSLT* by Michael Fitzgerald (O'Reilly). You can also find dozens of premade style sheets on FileMaker's website at *www.filemaker.com.*

To import XML data, choose File→Import Records→XML Data Source. When you do, you'll see the window in Figure 22-21. Here, you tell FileMaker where to get the XML data, and optionally what XSLT style sheet to apply. (If you don't apply a style sheet, FileMaker assumes the data is already in its special FMPXMLRESULT format.)

Unlike the typical import command, when you import XML data, you don't actually have to have a *file* to import from. This window also lets you specify an "HTTP request," which is just a fancy way of saying "web page." Type the URL of a web page here, and FileMaker goes out over the Internet, grabs the page, and pulls it down for you. Believe it or not, a lot of XML data is available hot off the Web like this. Likewise, you can choose to fetch the XSLT template from the Web as well.

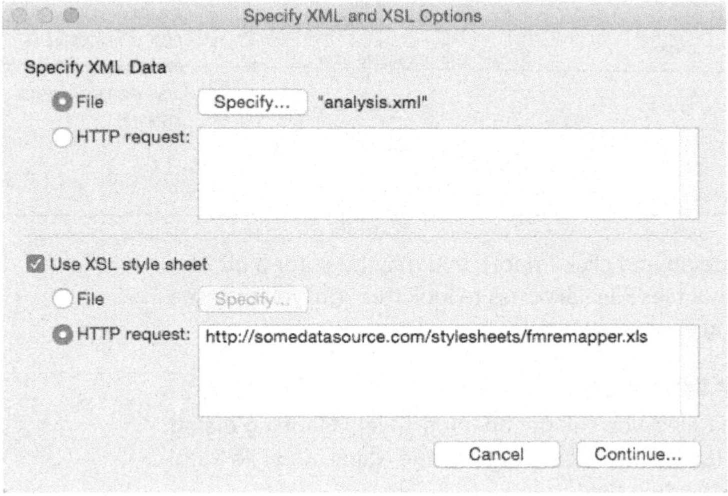

FIGURE 22-21

When you import from an XML data source, FileMaker first asks you where to get the data from and how to process it. You can instruct FileMaker to look in any XML file on your computer, or to fetch the XML data from a web server (see the box on page 885).

When you're finished choosing XML and XSL options, click Continue. FileMaker processes the XML and XSLT (which may take a few minutes) and then shows you the Import Field Mapping dialog box. From there, you can proceed like any import, as described earlier in this chapter.

XML and HTTP

Sometimes the XML data you want to import is in a file on your computer. But a big part of the XML data source feature's power is that FileMaker can also get XML data from other computers using *HTTP* (Hypertext Transport Protocol) or HTTPS (HyperText Transport Protocol over SSL). You probably recognize these acronyms because they often sit in front of web addresses (as in *http://www.missingmanuals.com*). HTTP is the way web browsers talk to websites, but it's used for a lot more than that. Often, companies make important information available on HTTP servers in XML format. It's this kind of information that FileMaker wants to let you tap into.

Many news-oriented websites make headlines and article excerpts available in XML formats called *RSS* or *Atom*. Using the XML Data Source feature in FileMaker, you could import news directly into your FileMaker database.

You can grab current or historical exchange rates from various sources to perform accurate currency conversions in FileMaker.

Some shippers let you track packages by downloading XML data. You can build package tracking right into FileMaker Pro.

When your database is talking to a server on the web, it may need to request data and then submit information back to the server. FileMaker supports this two-way communication, using a GET request to receive and a POST request to send information. There are other request methods, but FileMaker doesn't support them. So if the service you want to talk to requires other request methods, you'll need to find another way.

Web services that allow this kind of communication require specific information in a specific format. And they may have restrictions of what kind of data you can send or receive. So you'll need to do some research on the web service's website to find out how to meet their requirements before you start writing FileMaker code.

■ XML EXPORT

When you export to XML, FileMaker exports the data in the FMPXMLRESULT format and then applies the style sheet. You create the style sheet to translate this XML into the appropriate format for your intended recipient. You have slightly more flexibility when exporting than when importing: XSLT can translate only XML documents, but it can *produce* any text-based format. So although you can import only XML files, you can export just about anything.

■ BENTO DATA

Bento, a less powerful, but beloved, database in the FileMaker family was discontinued in 2013. If you still store data in Bento, it's time to start thinking about moving on. It's just a matter of time before an OS X update means that you can't even run Bento anymore. Rather than risk losing your data, move it into FileMaker using the Bento 4 to FileMaker Migration Tool. Download the tool by searching FileMaker's Knowledge Base at *http://help.filemaker.com*.

ODBC Data Sources

The last import data source is called ODBC. This data source is a popular standard to let programs access information stored in database systems. For instance, if your company has an Oracle, Sybase, or Microsoft SQL Server database to manage orders, you can extract data directly from that database and import it into your FileMaker Pro database (perhaps you want to make your own reports with FileMaker).

> **NOTE** Although you can *import* data from other big database systems, FileMaker also offers a much more powerful means to interact with some of them: External SQL Sources, or ESS (page 851), which lets you work directly with data from Oracle, Microsoft SQL Server, and MySQL in FileMaker. ESS is often a simpler and more powerful choice unless you're just after a one-shot copy of the data.

ODBC is the most complex import data source to set up. It's a two-step process:

- First, you need to install an ODBC driver for the kind of database you're connecting to. For example, if your corporate database is in Oracle, you need an ODBC driver for Oracle. These drivers are platform specific, and most vendors supply only drivers for Microsoft Windows. If you're using Mac OS X, you can buy high-quality FileMaker-compatible drivers from Actual Technologies at *www.actualtech.com/filemaker.php*. (When you visit its site, make sure you get the version that's appropriate for the number of simultaneous users you'll have.)

- Next, you need to set up an ODBC data source. FileMaker doesn't connect to the database directly. Rather, it uses a data source that's been specified in the ODBC system on your computer. So you have to set up that data source first. In Microsoft Windows, you do this setting up in the ODBC control panel. In Mac OS X, you use the ODBC Manager program in your Utilities folder.

Once you have a driver installed and a data source set up, you can use the File→Import Records→ODBC Data Source command. When you do, you see the Select ODBC Data Source window (Figure 22-22).

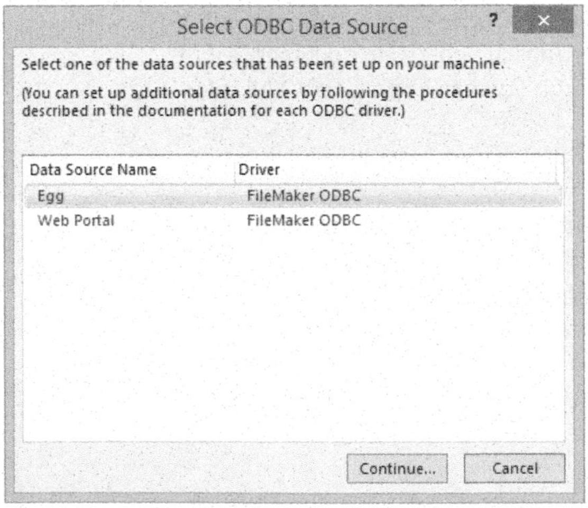

FIGURE 22-22

When you ask FileMaker to import from an ODBC data source, you choose which source to use. This window shows every data source you've created in your ODBC system. You just highlight the one you want and then click Continue.

When you click Continue in this window, you'll need to enter a user name and password for the database you're connecting to. You need to get this information from the database administrator, unless you created it in the ODBC software yourself.

Next, FileMaker shows the SQL Query Builder dialog box (Figure 22-23).

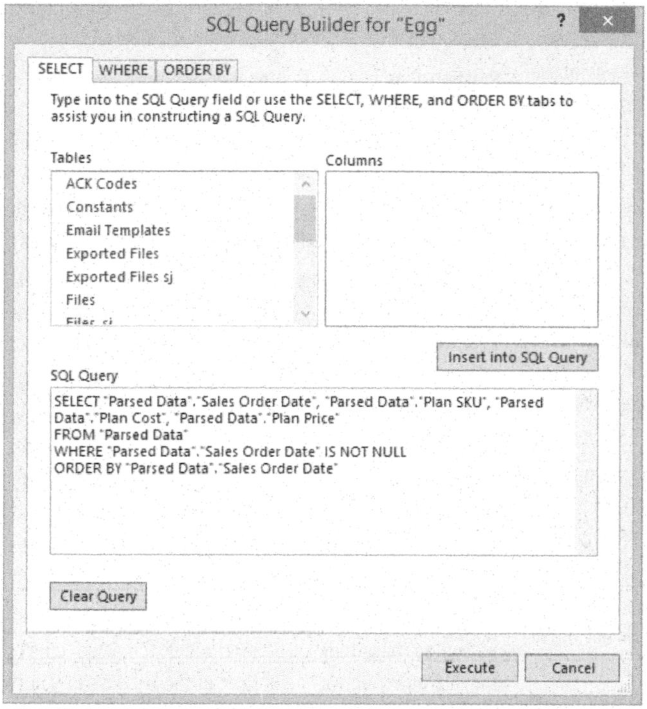

FIGURE 22-23

In the SQL Query Builder dialog box's SELECT tab, the Tables list shows every table available from the database you're connecting to. When you select a table, FileMaker lists all its fields (called columns in most database systems) in the Columns list. Select a field and then click "Insert into SQL Query" to include that field in the data you're importing. If you're a SQL pro, you can simply type in the SQL Query box instead.

When you extract data from *most* databases (FileMaker being the notable exception), you have to use a special programming language called Structured Query Language, or SQL (often pronounced *sequel*). Writing a SQL *query* (or program) is a complicated affair. Luckily, in most cases, FileMaker can do it for you—you just make the right choices. (For more detail, see the box on page 888.)

When you're all finished building your query, click Execute. FileMaker performs the query, gathers the data from the data source, and shows the same Import Field Mapping dialog box you always see when importing data. If you find yourself doing a lot of ODBC imports, you may be well served by a good book on SQL.

Although the query builder supports only a small part of SQL's power, you can use any SQL commands supported by your database server if you type the query directly. See the box on page 888 to learn some SQL query basics.

SQL Queries

To make use of FileMaker's query builder, you need to know just a little bit about SQL. A SQL query is made up of *clauses,* each of which influences the results you receive from the database server. Although SQL understands several clauses, the query builder window supports just three of them: SELECT, WHERE, and ORDER BY. The window has a tab for each of these.

The SELECT clause is where you tell the database what *fields* you want to import. You can include fields from more than one table if necessary. A SELECT clause alone imports every record in the table. If you include fields from more than one table, you get a result that may surprise you: Every record from each file is mixed in every possible combination. In other words, you import lots of records (multiply the record counts from each table to figure out how many).

The WHERE clause's job is to control which *records* get imported and how the tables are related. To specify certain records, you build find criteria into the WHERE clause. First, select a table and column from the pop-up menus. Then select something from the Operator pop-up menu. You can match this field with a value you type yourself (turn on the Value radio button) or with another field (turn on the Column radio button). Either way, enter or select the correct value. Finally, select either the And radio button or the Or radio button and then turn on Not if you want to *omit* the matching records. When you're finished defining the criteria, click "Insert into SQL Query."

Relationships in SQL are probably the most confusing. SQL databases don't have a Relationships graph like FileMaker, so the database doesn't know how things relate to one another at all. Each time you build a query, it's your job to tell it how to relate records from one table to those in another. You do this job by matching field values in each table in the WHERE clause.

For instance, you might pick the Customer ID field from the Customers table, the = operator, and the Customer ID field from the Orders table. When you add criteria like this to your WHERE clause, you've told the database how Order and Customer records relate. You can add as many criteria in this way as you need.

The last tab is called ORDER BY. This clause lets you specify a sort order for your data. It works just like FileMaker's normal Sort dialog box: Just add the fields to the Order By list, selecting Ascending or Descending as appropriate. When you've given it the order you want, click "Insert into SQL Query" again.

As you do these things, FileMaker builds the actual query in the SQL Query box at the bottom of the window so you can see how it comes together. If you feel adventurous, you can manually change this query at any time.

▇ Importing and Exporting in a Script

Like almost everything else in FileMaker, you can completely control the import and export process from a script. You use the Import Records and Export Records scripts, which you can find in the Records section of the script steps list. You also find script steps for "Save Records as Excel" and "Save Records as PDF," with similar options.

Save Records Script Steps

To automate the creation of Excel spreadsheets, use the "Save Records as Excel" script step. Not surprisingly, there's a "Save Records as PDF" script step as well. Each of these lets you specify all the options the standard menu commands offer, so you can completely automate the process.

As an added bonus, the "Save Records as PDF" script step includes one option you don't get when you run the command manually: an "Append to existing PDF" checkbox. When you turn this option on, if the file you're saving already exists, then FileMaker adds the new pages to the end of the existing file. This scheme makes it possible to lump together several reports, or data from several different layouts, into one complete PDF package for printing or distribution.

The Import Records Script Step

This script step has three options. First, you get to specify the data source to import from. Your choices match those in the File→Import Records menu: File, Folder, XML Data, and ODBC Data. Whichever option you choose, FileMaker asks you for more information (*which* file to import, or *which* ODBC data source to use, for instance). When specifying a file, you get the standard path list dialog box. In other words, you can specify several paths if you want; FileMaker imports the first one it finds. (If you don't specify a source, your users have to do it as they run the script, in a potentially confusing series of dialog boxes. Since you're presumably providing a script to make things easier for people, it's best to store source files in a safe place and have the script escort your users to them.)

Once you've specified the source, you can turn on "Specify import order" to record the import field mapping and other import options. Finally, you can turn on "Perform without dialog" if you want FileMaker to import the data directly, with no input from your users. If you leave this option off, FileMaker displays the Import Field Mapping dialog box when the script runs, so folks can make changes to any field mapping you specified.

The Export Records Script Step

The Export Records script step offers similar options. You can specify the output file and export order, and you can choose "Perform without dialog" if you don't want your users to see the export dialog box.

When you specify the output file, you may be surprised to see an Output File Path list. In other words, FileMaker lets you specify *more than one file*. This choice doesn't mean FileMaker exports more than one file, though. Instead, it exports to the first file path that's *valid*. If the first path in the list includes a folder name that doesn't exist, for example, FileMaker skips it and then tries the next one.

Appendixes

Getting Help

This book provides a solid foundation in FileMaker and takes you well into power user territory, but it doesn't cover *everything* there is to know about this vastly versatile program. (You wouldn't be able to lift it if it did.) This appendix is a guide to the many resources available to help you plumb the depths of FileMaker database design and development.

Some of these resources are accessible in more than one way. For example, you can get to FileMaker's online Knowledge Base by going to *www.filemaker.com,* clicking the Support menu, and then choosing Knowledge Base. But there are also quick links in the help files to specific Knowledge Base articles. Read on to see some of the ways to get to the bountiful resources provided by FileMaker and third parties.

▉ Getting Help from FileMaker Pro

Like most commercial software packages, FileMaker has a Help menu. Choose Help→FileMaker Pro Help to launch the Help file. The main screen (Figure A-1) lets you choose from a variety of ways to find help on the topic you're interested in. Major topics are listed on the left side of the screen, and some featured topics are listed on the top right.

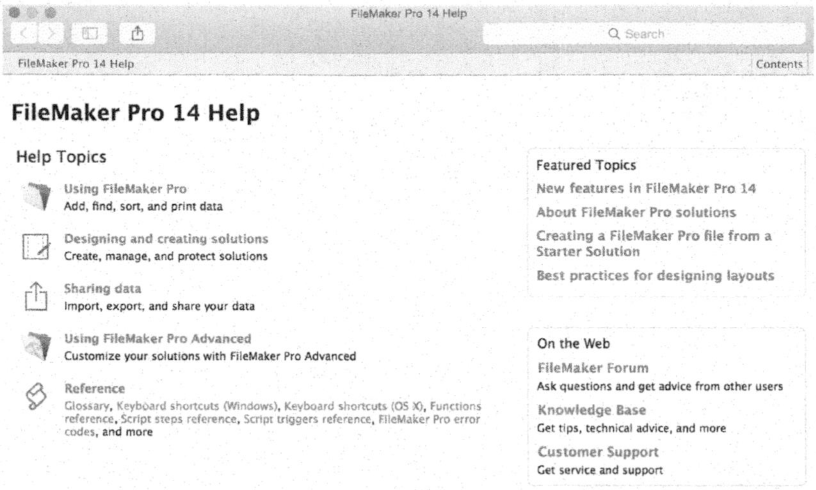

FIGURE A-1

You can click a link to see a topic you want, but it may be faster to type a question in the search box at the upper right. Type a few words to identify your subject and then press the Return key. You'll see a list of topics that relate to your search term. Click the item that best relates to your question. If it's not quite right, scroll to the bottom of the screen, where you'll usually find a "Related Topics" or "Topics in this section" area with similar links.

The Help file is organized by main topics, as listed on the main screen. Click a topic and you'll get a list of clickable subtopics. Use this method if you're searching for general information or aren't in a particular hurry. For example, to find information on creating a calculation field, you have to click through five lists to get to the "Defining calculation fields" detail page. Sometimes that's very helpful because the information goes from general to more specific and you're bound to learn something on the way. Sometimes you see an interesting related topic on your journey. But when you're in a hurry, just use the search box.

FileMaker gives context-sensitive help, but the methods vary by operating system. In Windows 7 and 8, most FileMaker windows have a question mark button in the upper right, near the Close box. Click the ? button and then click the window, and Help will launch directly to the topic that addresses that window (Figure A-2).

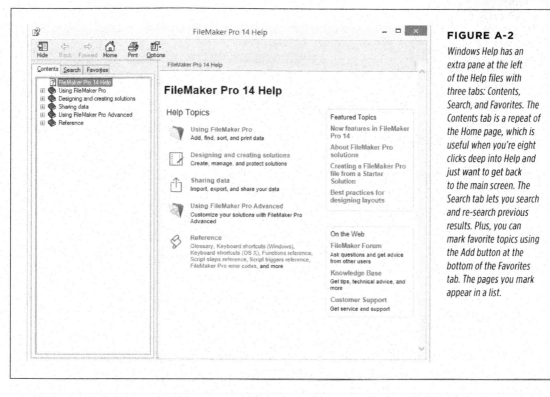

FIGURE A-2

Windows Help has an extra pane at the left of the Help files with three tabs: Contents, Search, and Favorites. The Contents tab is a repeat of the Home page, which is useful when you're eight clicks deep into Help and just want to get back to the main screen. The Search tab lets you search and re-search previous results. Plus, you can mark favorite topics using the Add button at the bottom of the Favorites tab. The pages you mark appear in a list.

On the Mac, the Help menu contains a search box. Type your term, and FileMaker gives you two lists of results. One lists menu commands that pertain to your search term, and the second lists Help topic pages (Figure A-3), one above the other in the menu. If your Help menu doesn't contain the normal Help commands, delete the search term in the box, and the menu returns to normal display.

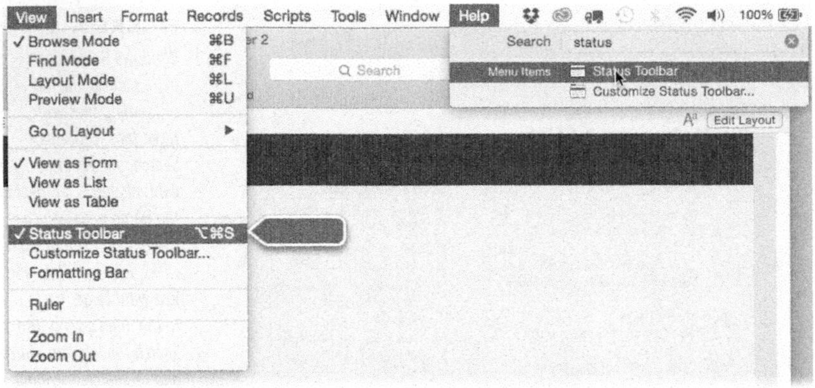

FIGURE A-3

The Mac Help menu gives you help two ways. If it can find a menu command or commands that match your search terms, it puts those results at the top of the Help menu in a section called Menu Items. If you select one of those items, the menu unfurls and a big blue dancing arrow (you can't miss it) points to the command you selected. That's very helpful when you know there's a command that does what you need, but you can't find it.

TIP If you type a layout name (like *Customers Refund Form*) into the search box (Mac only), one of the Menu Items will be "Go to Layout"→Customers Refund Form. That's incredibly helpful when you have hundreds of layouts and can't remember which folder you filed it away in or if it's near the bottom of your lengthy list and takes too long to scroll all the way down there.

A comprehensive list of FileMaker's functions is one of the Help file's most useful parts. The easiest way to find it is from a link on the Help home page's Reference section (it's called Functions reference).

The bottom right of the Help file's main screen also provides links so you can venture beyond the Help files:

- The **FileMaker Pro Forum** link goes to a forum created by FileMaker, Inc., to help you get in contact with other FileMaker Pro users and developers. Questions range from basic topics to detailed discussions on the best practice for designing layouts for FileMaker Go. Follow normal forum etiquette when you first visit. That is, you should scan or search the topics list to see if your question has been addressed. If it hasn't been covered, or if the thread you find doesn't answer your particular situation, then post a new question. You have to register to post a question or to answer somebody else's post, but registration is free and quick. The forum is moderated by FileMaker staff. It has an English language section (the busiest), and also French, German, Italian, Spanish, and Japanese areas.

- The **Knowledge Base** link takes you to a section of the FileMaker website where technical issues are addressed. New issues or alerts are posted on this page. You can search the knowledge base with keywords or skim through a list of recent documents to see what's new. If you're logged in (the same account you set up to use the forum), you can mark pertinent documents and get email sent to you if the document is updated.

- The **Customer Support** link goes to the main Support page, which shows links for common topics, like hot topics from the Knowledge Base, Updaters & Documentation, and News.

All these outside links, plus links to Downloads, Training, and Consultants are also found in the Support menu on FileMaker's website. This and other help available from FileMaker, Inc., is detailed later on in this appendix.

FileMaker's Installed Extras

The installation package for FileMaker Pro and FileMaker Pro Advanced includes a suite of ways to get extra help for FileMaker. In Windows, you can find these helpers at Program Files→FileMaker→FileMaker Pro 14→English Extras. And on the Mac, look in Applications→FileMaker Pro 14→English Extras.

NOTE The installer program *always* installs online help, but the other items are optional. In the Install panel of the installation wizard, choose Custom Install to pick which of the optional files you want installed. When you choose the Easy Install option, you get *everything*. If FileMaker is installed on your computer, but the helpers listed here are missing, you can then perform a Custom Install and choose the helper files you need without having to uninstall and reinstall FileMaker. (These files are also available in the Downloads section at *www.filemaker.com*.)

- **Electronic Documentation.** This folder includes the Installation and New Features Guide for FileMaker Pro 14 and FileMaker Pro 14 Advanced in PDF format.

- *FMP14 Getting Started.fmp12.* A guided tour to FileMaker Pro's key features.

- **Templates.** Sixteen template files you can customize. These are the templates the Starter Solutions use (see next section), so always make a copy of the file before you make any modifications. Any changes you make to the templates will affect files created through the Starter Solutions in the future.

Starter Solutions

You got a glimpse of these starter solutions in the box on page 113. When you select File→New From Starter Solution, you see a window that shows thumbnails of each solution, like Figure A-4 (on a Mac); Windows offers you a list of solutions with thumbnails. Pick the one you want, and FileMaker creates a new copy of the file for you. You can add data, create and edit scripts, or delete objects you don't need without affecting the original template.

NOTE If you prefer, you can navigate to the Templates folder and then launch the solution you want just like any other file. When you launch a solution file directly, though, you're opening the original template file, and any changes you make to the template are reflected in any new copies you make when you choose File→New Database.

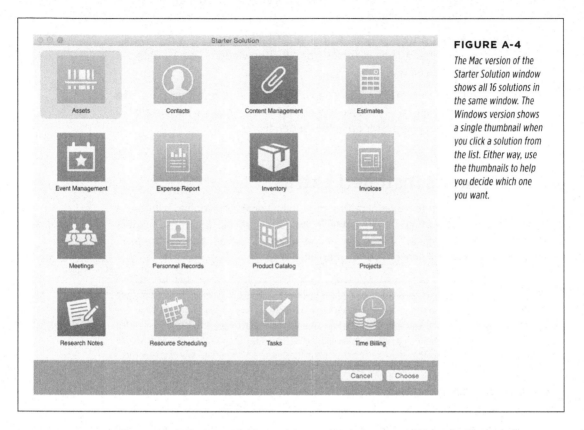

FIGURE A-4

The Mac version of the Starter Solution window shows all 16 solutions in the same window. The Windows version shows a single thumbnail when you click a solution from the list. Either way, use the thumbnails to help you decide which one you want.

Starter Solutions can help you get up and running with basic data management tasks if you don't have time to figure out how things work in FileMaker's universe. But these templates also serve another purpose—as an introduction to FileMaker Pro 14's new layout design tools. You'll see a variety of styles and techniques that you can adapt for your own databases—even if you aren't interested in the task the file was meant to perform.

Each template stores different kinds of data, so it's helpful to explore several templates to get ideas for arranging and grouping your data effectively. In general, you usually see an easy-to-read name near the top of the layout, which serves to orient people to the task at hand. Also near the top of each layout, you'll find a couple of rows of navigation tools and buttons grouped together by function. The largest portion of the layout is dedicated to a logical arrangement of data fields.

Finally, FileMaker's templates contain ideas you can use for creating relationships, buttons, and scripts to make your own databases more powerful. For instance, the

Contacts template contains four sets of layouts: one each for desktop, iPad, iPhone, and Web. When you open a template's first window, a login script figures out which device you're using and shows you the proper layouts for your device.

Getting Help from FileMaker, Inc.

FileMaker's website has the usual marketing materials you'd expect from a great software company. But there's lots of substance there, too. In its main navigation menu, go to Support→Contact Support, where you find free and fee-based help.

The Resource Center

After the Help files, your next best stop for FileMaker assistance is the FileMaker Resource Center. Just choose Help→Resource Center. FileMaker takes you to a special website covering many FileMaker topics. When you click a general topic, you see several related links. Not all these links are alike, though. Some are similar to the help topics FileMaker installs on your computer, but the Resource Center also has downloadable PDFs and short video demonstrations with tutorial databases. The Resource Center doesn't have everything there is to know about FileMaker, but the topics it covers are covered in depth.

Updates and Downloads

As with most programs, you can find FileMaker's latest software versions on the company's website. You'll find software updates and support files, like localized language packs, at *www.filemaker.com/support/downloads*. Updates for recent versions of FileMaker products are listed at the top of the page. A link to a page for previous versions appears just below the current updates.

> **NOTE** You get updates for FileMaker Go (iPad and iPhone) from the App Store. In the App Store app, click the Updates button. If your version of FileMaker Go isn't *au courant*, the new version will appear in the Updates list.

The Product Documentation section links to FileMaker's user guides and reference material for FileMaker Pro 14, FileMaker Pro 14 Advanced, FileMaker Server 14, and FileMaker Go 14. A search link to the product documentation archive helps you find product documentation for previous versions.

The Technical Resources Section includes web publishing resources, XML example files, and information on converting databases from earlier versions of FileMaker.

The Trial Software section lets you access 30-day trial versions of FileMaker Pro 14 and FileMaker Server 14.

The Regulatory Information section is useful if you need to make your database work with Windows screen-reading software or are looking for information on making your database comply with HIPAA regulations. You'll also find a list of PDFs with information about FileMaker Pro and Accessibility.

The Open Source Files section has direct download links to several open source tools, like tools for downloading files by using a GET command through a web viewer or CORBA tools. (If you don't know what those terms mean, you probably won't need to use these features.)

FileMaker Training

FileMaker, Inc., offers tutorials in video and book format that you can work through at your own pace.

▉ FILEMAKER TRAINING SERIES

This self-paced series is FileMaker's official training curriculum. Its 12 training modules cover the essentials of FileMaker solution development and are targeted at inter-mediate to advanced developers. FileMaker, Inc., recommends the training series as a preparation for taking the FileMaker Certification Exam. The advanced training series materials (book and CD) cost $39.99 and are also available in downloadable format ($19.99). The Basics training module is a free download.

▉ WEBINARS

FileMaker periodically presents live web seminars conducted by FileMaker staff or by recognized FileMaker trainers and developers. Invitations are usually sent by email to members of the FileMaker Community site (page 901), but you can view the webinars even if you're not a member. You can find the recordings at *www.file-maker.com/learning/webinars* a few days after the live event. Topics are grouped by New, Current, and Advanced, and range from getting started with FileMaker to beginning scripting; from virtualizing a server to using external SQL data sources.

▉ VIDEO AND TUTORIALS

These free online videos (*www.filemaker.com/products/demos*) are hosted by re-nowned FileMaker developers. They're divided into demos on the FileMaker product line and tutorials for FileMaker Pro and FileMaker Server. A screenshot tour is also available on the same page.

▉ THIRD-PARTY TRAINING MATERIALS

A selection of training manuals, books, and online videos are offered by FileMaker Business Alliance members.

Technical Support

FileMaker supports the current version of its software and one version prior. In ad-dition to the resources listed above, you can speak with a human to get help with specific issues. The phone number for free and fee-based tech support, as well as customer service to help you decide which products you need, is 1-800-325-2747. Phone tech support is available from 7:00 a.m. to 5:00 p.m. Pacific Time weekdays (except holidays).

Technical Support deals with technical problems, like when a feature isn't working as advertised and you need help figuring out why. Technical support doesn't cover teaching you how to create databases, or writing your calculations and scripts for you.

NOTE If your question isn't tech support, or your files are in an older version for which FileMaker, Inc., no longer offers support, then you need to get help from a third party, usually a consultant, trainer, or user group. See page 903 for info on finding those animals.

■ FREE SUPPORT

You can't start making databases until FileMaker has been bought and installed, so everybody who purchases FileMaker gets unlimited tech support phone calls regarding purchasing, installation, and configuration. You can submit nontechnical questions to FileMaker via an email link on the Contact Support web page or by phone at 1-800-325-2747.

■ PAID SUPPORT

If your question falls into the technical realm, get out your credit card when you call and then decide how you want to pay:

- **Priority Support.** For a $45 flat fee, tech support will solve a single issue for you.

- **Annual Support Contract.** For $899 per year, you can nominate one person from your company who can call a special toll-free number as many times as needed for 12 months. Add $699 for each additional person who needs the same access. If you have a volume license agreement (VLA), the rate goes down to $719 for the primary member and $559 for each additional member. Download the order form at *www.filemaker.com/support/docs/prof_support_form.pdf.*

TIP The Volume License Agreement gives you special incentives and discount pricing when you license five or more copies of FileMaker Pro. You can add seats whenever you need them and upgrades are free as long as your agreement is in effect.

Developer Programs

FileMaker runs two programs to help developers keep in touch with one another, and with FileMaker, Inc., itself.

■ FILEMAKER COMMUNITY

The FileMaker Community Site (*http://community.filemaker.com*) is free to join, but you have to create an account (Figure A-5). Membership gets you access to discussion boards crawling with FileMaker experts swapping ideas and helping one another. You also get access to exclusive technical white papers and how-to articles on important FileMaker topics. Best of all, if you're a member you get early review of unreleased software, a download copy of the FileMaker Training Series, and a development license for FileMaker Server Advanced for $99 per year. The development license is limited to three connections and is not meant to be used for production databases, but it's still a bargain, since the retail version costs over a thousand dollars!

FIGURE A-5

The FileMaker Community site used to be called TechNet, but it's just a rebranding. All the benefits, resources, and discussions that were part of TechNet are still present in the new site. And a basic membership is still free—the best deal you're going to find.

■ FILEMAKER BUSINESS ALLIANCE (FBA)

If you're a professional FileMaker developer (meaning you build FileMaker databases for other companies for pay), you may qualify to join the FileMaker Business Alliance (FBA) as well. In addition to online discussions, technical info, and free software, FBA members get outstanding software perks. You can purchase FileMaker products for your own use (or your company's use) at deep discounts. You can also get discount pricing on FileMaker products, which you can then resell to your customers. FBA members (along with their products and services) are listed on FileMaker's website and in the Resource Guide. Membership requires approval and costs $499 per year. Find out more at *www.filemaker.com/fba.*

DevCon

For total FileMaker immersion, the annual Developer's Conference (DevCon) is the way to go. Each day you can attend as many as five sessions on about 30 different topics, ranging from running a FileMaker consulting firm to web publishing, so you're sure to come away from the 3-day conference with a brainpan full of new ideas. For details, see *www.filemaker.com/learning/devcon/index.html.*

◼ Getting Help from the Community

Even outside the members-only programs, the FileMaker developer community is a congenial bunch. You'll find lots of resources on the Internet, including free news-groups and websites. Many independent consultants' sites have free or low-cost resources, too, like lists of custom functions free for the taking or sample files that show specific techniques.

Local User Groups

The most hands-on way to stay abreast of what's new with FileMaker is to join a local user group. There you'll meet other power users and developers. Meetings usually consist of a presentation and a Q&A session. Presenters can be FileMaker staff or out-of-town developers. Some groups also sponsor daylong programming camps. Check out *www.fmpug.com/chapters.php* to get the current list of local groups.

Internet Resources

The Internet is awash in FileMaker resources just waiting for you come try. Facebook and LinkedIn each has a variety of public discussion groups you can join. You can find dozens of active discussions and extensive archives at fmforums.com. Type *FileMaker Blog* into your favorite search engine and you're sure to get at least half a million hits (your humble coauthor's FileMaker Function of the Week blog among them).

Training/Consultants

FileMaker's website lists trainers and consultants who are members of the FBA. And the FileMaker Resource Guide also lists the FBA group, plus it takes paid advertise-ments. Your favorite search engine will yield hundreds of results. FileMaker has a certification program, so look for the FileMaker Certified Developer logo or ask the consultant if she's been certified as part of your selection process.

Layout Badges

FileMaker Pro offers so many ways to format and customize layout objects, even the most experienced users can have a hard time remembering which options have been applied to every object on every layout. As complexity has grown, FileMaker has added layout *object badges,* small icons that appear on layout objects in Layout mode. Each indicates the formatting or behavior applied to the object. Get to know these badges, and you can tell at a glance which items slide when printing, have script triggers, or display conditional formatting.

FileMaker Pro 14 brings a welcome enhancement to layout badges. Place your cursor over a badge (without clicking the mouse button), and you'll see details about that badge in a tooltip. Some tips are as simple as "Object slides left when printing" while others, like the example in Figure B-1, offer much more insight.

FIGURE B-1

This field has Conditional Formatting applied, earning it the red and blue diamond badge. When you hover over the badge, FileMaker reveals the conditions the field evaluates when deciding which formatting to apply. To modify these settings, right-click and select Conditional Formatting.

You may find that you don't want to see *every* badge all the time, and you don't have to. Suppose you're not a fan of FileMaker's Quick Find (page 22) and you disable it in all your databases. Having those green and yellow magnifying glasses littering your

layouts is going to be a distraction. You can just switch off that badge type by entering Layout mode and selecting View→Show→Conditional Formatting (Figure B-2).

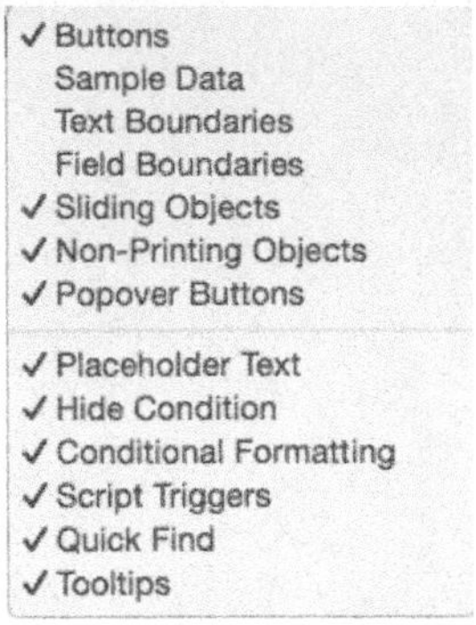

✓ Buttons
   Sample Data
   Text Boundaries
   Field Boundaries
✓ Sliding Objects
✓ Non-Printing Objects
✓ Popover Buttons

✓ Placeholder Text
✓ Hide Condition
✓ Conditional Formatting
✓ Script Triggers
✓ Quick Find
✓ Tooltips

FIGURE B-2

*In Layout mode, selecting View→Show will reveal this submenu. Here
you can toggle every layout object badge type. The three items on this
list that lack checkmarks are not badge types.*

Table B-1 displays all of FileMaker 14's layout object badges, which View→Show
menu option toggles them, and where you can learn more about the feature in this
very book.

BADGE	TOGGLE BY SELECTING VIEW→SHOW	LEARN MORE ON PAGE
▭	Buttons	365
◆	Conditional Formatting	648
🖶	Non-Printing Objects	365
▭	Placeholder Text	302
◀▭	Popover Buttons	372
 👁	Hide Condition	306
🔍 or 🔍	Quick Find	22
 ✺ or ✳	Script Triggers	469
← or ↑	Sliding Objects	360
 T	Tooltips	354

Using the Insert Commands with Container Fields

With FileMaker Pro 14's enhanced container fields, figuring out which of the many Insert commands to use is a little more confusing than it used to be—and a lot more important. This table will help you figure out which command works best for the situation at hand. Take into account the type of file you're inserting and the options you need to set as the file is inserted.

COMMAND	FIELD OPTIMIZATION	FORMATS	OPTIONS	RESULTS
Picture	Images or Interactive content	Encasulated Postscript (.eps), FlashPix (.fpx), GIF (.gif), JPEG/JFIF (.jpg), JPEG 2000 (.jp2), MacPaint (.mac), PDF (.pdf), PhotoShop (.psd), PNG (.png), QuickTime Image File (.qif), SGI (.sgi), Targa (.tga), TIFF (.tif), Windows bitmap (.bmp), Windows Metafile/Enhanced Metafile (.wmf/.emf)	Store only a reference to the file.	The file's content is displayed.

COMMAND	FIELD OPTIMIZATION	FORMATS	OPTIONS	RESULTS
Audio/ Video	Interactive content	AIFF Audio file (.aif, .aiff), AVI movie (.avi), MP3 Audio file (.mp3), MPEG-4 Audio file (.m4a), MPEG-4 movie (.mp4), MPEG movie (.mpg, .mpeg), MPEG-4 video file (.m4v), QuickTime Movie (.mov, .qt) (See notes below), Sun Audio file (.au), WAVE Audio File (.wav), Windows Media Audio (.wma), Windows Media Videos (.wmv) (See notes below)	Video, Audio, Store only a reference to the file.	The file can be streamed with the Autoplay option.
PDF	Interactive content	PDF	Store only a reference to the file.	PDF controls allow scrolling through the document, zooming and copying of text.
File	Images or Interactive content	All file formats	Compress, Store only a reference to the file.	A file icon and the file name is displayed.

▓ NOTES

- The Insert→QuickTime option from previous versions has been removed from FileMaker 14. However, all the same media formats are still supported. Just use Insert→Picture or Insert→Audio/Video.

- Some QuickTime Movie (.mov, .qt) formats, such as QuickTime VR, aren't supported.

- OS X: For Windows Media Videos (.wmv) format; requires Flip4Mac to be installed.

- When you insert a very large file into a container field, a dialog box appears showing you the progress.

FileMaker Error Codes

The following table lists the error codes that may pop up when FileMaker detects something out of whack in your database, especially when you're writing or running a script. You'll run into error codes when you're testing a script with the Script Debugger in FileMaker Pro Advanced or if you use a Get(LastError) calculation. Like many things written by and for computer programmers, these descriptions may not make much sense in English, but they may provide a little more guidance than the error number alone.

Error codes marked with an asterisk (*) apply only to web-published databases.

ERROR NUMBER	DESCRIPTION
-1	Unknown error
0	No error
1	User-canceled action
2	Memory error
3	Command is unavailable (for example, wrong operating system, wrong mode, and so on)
4	Command is unknown
5	Command is invalid (for example, a Set Field script step does not have a calculation specified)
6	File is read-only
7	Running out of memory

ERROR NUMBER	DESCRIPTION
8	Empty result
9	Insufficient privileges
10	Requested data is missing
11	Name is not valid
12	Name already exists
13	File or object is in use
14	Out of range
15	Can't divide by zero
16	Operation failed, request retry (for example, a user query)
17	Attempt to convert foreign character set to UTF-16 failed
18	Client must provide account information to proceed
19	String contains characters other than A-Z, a-z, 0-9 (ASCII)
20	Command/operation canceled by triggered script
21	Map Win32 error of "ERROR_NOT_Supported." Microsoft documentation is "the request is not supported."
26	The file path specified is not a valid file path
100	File is missing
101	Record is missing
102	Field is missing
103	Relationship is missing
104	Script is missing
105	Layout is missing
106	Table is missing
107	Index is missing
108	Value list is missing
109	Privilege set is missing
110	Related tables are missing
111	Field repetition is invalid
112	Window is missing
113	Function is missing
114	File reference is missing
115	Specified menu set is missing

ERROR NUMBER	DESCRIPTION
116	Specified layout object is missing
117	Specified data source is missing
130	Files are damaged or missing and must be reinstalled
131	Language pack files are missing (such as template files)
200	Record access is denied
201	Field cannot be modified
202	Field access is denied
203	No records in file to print, or password doesn't allow print access
204	No access to field(s) in sort order
205	User does not have access privileges to create new records; import will overwrite existing data
206	User does not have password change privileges, or file is not modifiable
207	User does not have sufficient privileges to change database schema, or file is not modifiable
208	Password does not contain enough characters
209	New password must be different from existing one
210	User account is inactive
211	Password has expired
212	Invalid user account and/or password. Please try again
213	User account and/or password does not exist
214	Too many login attempts
215	Administrator privileges cannot be duplicated
216	Guest account cannot be duplicated
217	User does not have sufficient privileges to modify administrator account
218	Password and verify password do not match (iPhone)
300	File is locked or in use
301	Record is in use by another user
302	Table is in use by another user
303	Database schema is in use by another user
304	Layout is in use by another user
306	Record modification ID does not match
307	Lost connection to the host and the transaction could not relock

ERROR NUMBER	DESCRIPTION
308	Theme is locked by another user
309	Object is checked out by another user
400	Find criteria are empty
401	No records match the request
402	Selected field is not a match field for a lookup
403	Exceeding maximum record limit for trial version of FileMaker Pro
404	Sort order is invalid
405	Number of records specified exceeds number of records that can be omitted
406	Replace/Reserialize criteria are invalid
407	One or both match fields are missing (invalid relationship)
408	Specified field has inappropriate data type for this operation
409	Import order is invalid
410	Export order is invalid
412	Wrong version of FileMaker Pro used to recover file
413	Specified field has inappropriate field type
414	Layout cannot display the result
415	One or more required related records are not available
416	Primary key required from data source table
417	Database is not supported for ESS operations
418	Internal failure in insert into field operation
500	Date value does not meet validation entry options
501	Time value does not meet validation entry options
502	Number value does not meet validation entry options
503	Value in field is not within the range specified in validation entry options
504	Value in field is not unique as required in validation entry options
505	Value in field is not an existing value in the database file as required in validation entry options
506	Value in field is not listed on the value list specified in validation entry option
507	Value in field failed calculation test of validation entry option
508	Invalid value entered in Find mode
509	Field requires a valid value
510	Related value is empty or unavailable

ERROR NUMBER	DESCRIPTION
511	Value in field exceeds maximum field size
512	Record was already modified by another user
513	No validation was specified, but data can't fit into the field (extended with DBFieldError)
600	Print error has occurred
601	Combined header and footer exceed one page
602	Body doesn't fit on a page for current column setup
603	Print connection lost
700	File is of the wrong file type for import
706	EPSF file has no preview image
707	Graphic translator cannot be found
708	Can't import the file or need color monitor support to import file
709	QuickTime movie import failed
710	Unable to update QuickTime reference because the database file is read-only
711	Import translator cannot be found
714	Password privileges do not allow the operation
715	Specified Excel worksheet or named range is missing
716	A SQL query using DELETE, INSERT, or UPDATE is not allowed for ODBC import
717	There is not enough XML/XSL information to proceed with the import or export
718	Error in parsing XML file (from Xerces)
719	Error in transforming XML using XSL (from Xalan)
720	Error when exporting; intended format does not support repeating fields
721	Unknown error occurred in the parser or the transformer
722	Cannot import data into a file that has no fields
723	You do not have permission to add records to or modify records in the target table
724	You do not have permission to add records to the target table
725	You do not have permission to modify records in the target table
726	There are more records in the import file than in the target table; not all records were imported
727	There are more records in the target table than in the import file; not all records were updated
729	Errors occurred during import. Records could not be imported

ERROR NUMBER	DESCRIPTION
730	Unsupported Excel version (convert file to Excel 7.0 (Excel 95), Excel 97, 2000 or XP format and try again)
731	File you are importing from contains no data
732	This file cannot be inserted because it contains other files
733	A table cannot be imported into itself
734	This file type cannot be displayed as a picture
735	This file type cannot be displayed as a picture; it will be inserted and displayed as a file
736	Too much data to export to this format; it will be truncated
738	A theme with the selected name already exists
800	Unable to create file on disk
801	Unable to create temporary file on System disk
802	Unable to open file
803	File is single user or host cannot be found
804	File cannot be opened as read-only in its current state
805	File is damaged; use Recover command
806	File cannot be opened with this version of FileMaker Pro
807	File is not a FileMaker Pro file or is severely damaged
808	Cannot open file because access privileges are damaged
809	Disk/volume is full
810	Disk/volume is locked
811	Temporary file cannot be opened as FileMaker Pro file
813	Record Synchronization error on network
814	File(s) cannot be opened because maximum number is open
815	Couldn't open lookup file
816	Unable to convert file
817	Unable to open file because it does not belong to this solution
819	Cannot save a local copy of a remote file
820	File is in the process of being closed
821	Host forced a disconnect
822	FMI files not found; reinstall missing files
823	Cannot set file to single-user, guests are connected

ERROR NUMBER	DESCRIPTION
824	File is damaged or not a FileMaker file
825	File is not authorized to reference the protected file
826	The file path specified is not a valid file path
827	File was not created because the source contained no data or is a reference [NEW in FMP 14.0]
850	Path is not valid (for the platform it represents)
851	The external file cannot be deleted from disk. Do you want to delete the reference to the file anyway?
852	Cannot write file to the external storage
853	One or more containers failed to transfer
900	General spelling engine error
901	Main spelling dictionary not installed
902	Could not launch the Help system
903	Command cannot be used in a shared file
905	No active field selected; command can only be used if there is an active field
906	Current file must be shared in order to use this command
920	Can't initialize the spelling engine
921	User dictionary cannot be loaded for editing
922	User dictionary cannot be found
923	User dictionary is read-only
951	An unexpected error occurred (*)
954	Unsupported XML grammar (*)
955	No database name (*)
956	Maximum number of database sessions exceeded (*)
957	Conflicting commands (*)
958	Parameter missing (*)
1200	Generic calculation error
1201	Too few parameters in the function
1202	Too many parameters in the function
1203	Unexpected end of calculation
1204	Number, text constant, field name or "(" expected
1205	Comment is not terminated with "*/"

ERROR NUMBER	DESCRIPTION
1206	Text constant must end with a quotation mark
1207	Unbalanced parenthesis
1208	Operator missing, function not found or "(" not expected
1209	Name (such as field name or layout name) is missing
1210	Plug-in function has already been registered
1211	List usage is not allowed in this function
1212	An operator (for example, +, -, *) is expected here
1213	This variable has already been defined in the Let function
1214	AVERAGE, COUNT, EXTEND, GETREPETITION, MAX, MIN, NPV, STDEV, SUM, and GETSUMMARY: expression found where a field alone is needed
1215	This parameter is an invalid Get function parameter
1216	Only Summary fields allowed as first argument in GETSUMMARY
1217	Break field is invalid
1218	Cannot evaluate the number
1219	A field cannot be used in its own formula
1220	Field type must be normal or calculated
1221	Data type must be number, date, time, or timestamp
1222	Calculation cannot be stored
1223	The function is not implemented
1224	The function is not defined
1225	The function is not supported in this context
1300	The specified name can't be used
1301	One of the parameters of the function being imported/pasted has the same name as a function already in the file.
1400	ODBC driver initialization failed; make sure the ODBC drivers are properly installed
1401	Failed to allocate environment (ODBC)
1402	Failed to free environment (ODBC)
1403	Failed to disconnect (ODBC)
1404	Failed to allocate connection (ODBC)
1405	Failed to free connection (ODBC)
1406	Failed check for SQL API (ODBC)
1407	Failed to allocate statement (ODBC)

ERROR NUMBER	DESCRIPTION
1408	Extended error (ODBC)
1409	Error (ODBC)
1413	Failed communication link (ODBC)
1414	ODBC/SQL statement is too long
1450	Action requires PHP privilege extension (*)
1451	Action requires that current file be remote
1501	The authentication failed
1502	The connection was refused by the SMTP server
1503	There was an error with SSL
1504	The server required the connection to be encrypted
1505	The specified authentication is not supported by SMTP server
1506	Email(s) could not be sent successfully
1507	Unable to log into the SMTP server
1550	The file isn't a plug-in, or can't load for some reason
1551	Can't delete an existing plug-in, can't write to the folder, can't put on disk for some reason
1626	The protocol is not supported
1627	The authentication failed
1628	There was an error with SSL
1629	The connection timed out
1630	The URL format is incorrect
1631	The connection failed
1632	The Certificate cannot be authenticated by a supported CA [NEW in FMP 14.0]
1633	The Certificate is valid, but still wrong (e.g. hostname doesn't match, or expired). [NEW in FMP 14.0]
2021	plug-ins configuration disallowed
2046	This command or action cannot be performed because that functionality is no longer supported
2047	Bento 2 (or later) is not presented on the system
2048	The selected workbook is not Excel 2007/2008 format
2056	This script step cannot be performed because this window is in a modal state
3000	Action never occurred because script was triggered

ERROR NUMBER	DESCRIPTION
3001	Set when a script returns but is not really finished (probably due to having to switch threads and keep engine thread running)
3002	The external file cannot be deleted from disk. Do you want to delete the reference to the file anyway?
3003	Cannot write file to the external storage
3004	Directory can't edit
3005	Directory can't delete
3100	Theme is in use
3219	Convert Global To Remote warning
3220	Directory Not Accessible warning
3316	Warning before clearing out existing find requests
3317	Warning before attempting to restore files from hibernation
3318	Warning undoing past the last saved point
3319	Warning: SSL certificate is invalid. Do you want to continue? [NEW in FMP 14.0]
3320	Warning: SSL certificate could not be verified. Do you want to continue? [NEW in FMP 14.0]
3427	Button cannot contain a tab control
3428	When a panel is deleted, all the objects on that panel will be deleted.
3429	One or more of the panels you've selected contain locked objects. Do you want to delete those panel(s) even though they contain locked object(s)?
3431	File reference syntax error
3437	Action requires that current file be local
3852	Preview was interrupted
3956	The total size of all base directory paths cannot exceed ^1 bytes.
3957	At least one filter must remain
3958	Please select at least one bar code type
3959	At least one window orientation must be enabled. [NEW in FMP 14.0]
4103	File path is invalid or cannot be resolved during file transfer
4104	File i/o issue during file tranfer
4106	The target base directory is not valid
4107	The target base directory could not be created
4603	Spell export complete
4708	File could not be closed for upload

ERROR NUMBER	DESCRIPTION
4709	Unsupported SVG, cannot be imported [NEW in FMP 14.0]
7100	Data deferred
8404	An installed OnTimer script could not be found or could not be run with current access privileges
8213	Too many temporary objects created, can't create any more
8310	There is an error in the syntax of the query
8498	Stale import order to be updated
8499	Import match may be invalid
8500	Host file closed
8501	Host file verifying
8502	Host file transferring
8503	Host file redirect
8504	Host file version incompatible
8505	Host flle read only
8506	Host file damaged
8507	Host file not FMP
8508	Host file unsupported language
8509	Host file too many files
8510	Host file out of resources
8511	Host files permission issue
8512	Host file encrypted
8513	Host file extended privilege off
8514	Host version not allowed
20413	Too many files
20600	Can't initialize networking stack
20602	Can't create a connection
20603	Lost communications with host/guest
20604	Single user install code conflict
20605	No network connection is available
20606	Fail to resolve network address
20650	Page doesn't have enough footer size for encryption

Index

FileMaker Pro 14

THE MISSING CD

There's no
CD with this book;
you just saved $5.00.

Instead, every single Web address, practice file, and
piece of downloadable software mentioned in this
book is available at *missingmanuals.com*
(click the Missing CD icon).
There you'll find a tidy list of links,
organized by chapter.

Don't miss a thing!
Sign up for the free Missing
Manual email announcement
list at missingmanuals.com.
We'll let you know when we
release new titles, make
free sample chapters available,
and update the features and
articles on the Missing Manual
website.

CPSIA information can be obtained at www.ICGtesting.com
Printed in the USA
BVOW09s1803220815

414575BV00001B/1/P